The
C++
Programming
Language

Third Edition

Bjarne Stroustrup

AT&T Labs
Murray Hill, New Jersey

Addison-Wesley
An Imprint of Addison Wesley Longman, Inc.

Reading, Massachusetts · Harlow, England · Menlo Park, California
Berkeley, California · Don Mills, Ontario · Sydney
Bonn · Amsterdam · Tokyo · Mexico City

The publisher offers discounts on this book when ordered in quantity for special sales. For more information please contact:

Corporate & Professional Publishing Group
Addison-Wesley Publishing Company
One Jacob Way
Reading, Massachusetts 01867

Library of Congress Cataloging-in-Publication Data

Stroustrup, Bjarne
    The C++ Programming Language / Bjarne Stroustrup. — 3rd. ed.
       p.   cm.
    Includes index.
    ISBN 0-201-88954-4
    1. C++ (Computer Programming Language) I. Title
QA76.73.C153S77   1997   97-20239
005.13'3—dc21   CIP

Text printed on recycled and acid-free paper.

ISBN 0201889544

13 1415161718 CRS 03 02 01 00

13th Printing   August 2000

Contents

Preface   **v**

Preface to Second Edition   **vii**

Preface to First Edition   **ix**

Introductory Material   **1**

   1   Notes to the Reader 3
   2   A Tour of C++ 21
   3   A Tour of the Standard Library 45

Part I: Basic Facilities   **67**

   4   Types and Declarations 69
   5   Pointers, Arrays, and Structures 87
   6   Expressions and Statements 107
   7   Functions 143
   8   Namespaces and Exceptions 165
   9   Source Files and Programs 197

Part II: Abstraction Mechanisms   221

10   Classes 223
11   Operator Overloading 261
12   Derived Classes 301
13   Templates 327
14   Exception Handling 355
15   Class Hierarchies 389

Part III: The Standard Library   427

16   Library Organization and Containers 429
17   Standard Containers 461
18   Algorithms and Function Objects 507
19   Iterators and Allocators 549
20   Strings 579
21   Streams 605
22   Numerics 657

Part IV: Design Using C++   689

23   Development and Design 691
24   Design and Programming 723
25   Roles of Classes 765

Appendices   791

A   The C++ Grammar 793
B   Compatibility 815
C   Technicalities 827
D   Locales 869
E   Standard Library Exception Safety 935

Index   969

Preface

Programming is understanding.
– Kristen Nygaard

I find using C++ more enjoyable than ever. C++'s support for design and programming has improved dramatically over the years, and lots of new helpful techniques have been developed for its use. However, C++ is not *just* fun. Ordinary practical programmers have achieved significant improvements in productivity, maintainability, flexibility, and quality in projects of just about any kind and scale. By now, C++ has fulfilled most of the hopes I originally had for it, and also succeeded at tasks I hadn't even dreamt of.

This book introduces standard C++† and the key programming and design techniques supported by C++. Standard C++ is a far more powerful and polished language than the version of C++ introduced by the first edition of this book. New language features such as namespaces, exceptions, templates, and run-time type identification allow many techniques to be applied more directly than was possible before, and the standard library allows the programmer to start from a much higher level than the bare language.

About a third of the information in the second edition of this book came from the first. This third edition is the result of a rewrite of even larger magnitude. It offers something to even the most experienced C++ programmer; at the same time, this book is easier for the novice to approach than its predecessors were. The explosion of C++ use and the massive amount of experience accumulated as a result makes this possible.

The definition of an extensive standard library makes a difference to the way C++ concepts can be presented. As before, this book presents C++ independently of any particular implementation, and as before, the tutorial chapters present language constructs and concepts in a "bottom up" order so that a construct is used only after it has been defined. However, it is much easier to use a well-designed library than it is to understand the details of its implementation. Therefore, the standard library can be used to provide realistic and interesting examples well before a reader can be assumed to understand its inner workings. The standard library itself is also a fertile source of programming examples and design techniques.

---

† ISO/IEC 14882, Standard for the C++ Programming Language.

This book presents every major C++ language feature and the standard library. It is organized around language and library facilities. However, features are presented in the context of their use. That is, the focus is on the language as the tool for design and programming rather than on the language in itself. This book demonstrates key techniques that make C++ effective and teaches the fundamental concepts necessary for mastery. Except where illustrating technicalities, examples are taken from the domain of systems software. A companion, *The Annotated C++ Language Standard*, presents the complete language definition together with annotations to make it more comprehensible.

The primary aim of this book is to help the reader understand how the facilities offered by C++ support key programming techniques. The aim is to take the reader far beyond the point where he or she gets code running primarily by copying examples and emulating programming styles from other languages. Only a good understanding of the ideas behind the language facilities leads to mastery. Supplemented by implementation documentation, the information provided is sufficient for completing significant real-world projects. The hope is that this book will help the reader gain new insights and become a better programmer and designer.

Acknowledgments

In addition to the people mentioned in the acknowledgement sections of the first and second editions, I would like to thank Matt Austern, Hans Boehm, Don Caldwell, Lawrence Crowl, Alan Feuer, Andrew Forrest, David Gay, Tim Griffin, Peter Juhl, Brian Kernighan, Andrew Koenig, Mike Mowbray, Rob Murray, Lee Nackman, Joseph Newcomer, Alex Stepanov, David Vandevoorde, Peter Weinberger, and Chris Van Wyk for commenting on draft chapters of this third edition. Without their help and suggestions, this book would have been harder to understand, contained more errors, been slightly less complete, and probably been a little bit shorter.

I would also like to thank the volunteers on the C++ standards committees who did an immense amount of constructive work to make C++ what it is today. It is slightly unfair to single out individuals, but it would be even more unfair not to mention anyone, so I'd like to especially mention Mike Ball, Dag Brück, Sean Corfield, Ted Goldstein, Kim Knuttila, Andrew Koenig, José Lajoie, Dmitry Lenkov, Nathan Myers, Martin O'Riordan, Tom Plum, Jonathan Shopiro, John Spicer, Jerry Schwarz, Alex Stepanov, and Mike Vilot, as people who each directly cooperated with me over some part of C++ and its standard library.

After the initial printing of this book, many dozens of people have mailed me corrections and suggestions for improvements. I have been able to accommodate many of their suggestions within the framework of the book so that later printings benefitted significantly. Translators of this book into many languages have also provided many clarifications. In response to requests from readers, I have added appendices D and E. Let me take this opportunity to thank a few of those who helped: Dave Abrahams, Matt Austern, Jan Bielawski, Janina Mincer Daszkiewicz, Andrew Koenig, Dietmar Kühl, Nicolai Josuttis, Nathan Myers, Paul E. Sevinç, Andy Tenne-Sens, Shoichi Uchida, Ping-Fai (Mike) Yang, and Dennis Yelle.

Murray Hill, New Jersey   *Bjarne Stroustrup*

Preface to the Second Edition

The road goes ever on and on.
– Bilbo Baggins

As promised in the first edition of this book, C++ has been evolving to meet the needs of its users. This evolution has been guided by the experience of users of widely varying backgrounds working in a great range of application areas. The C++ user-community has grown a hundredfold during the six years since the first edition of this book; many lessons have been learned, and many techniques have been discovered and/or validated by experience. Some of these experiences are reflected here.

The primary aim of the language extensions made in the last six years has been to enhance C++ as a language for data abstraction and object-oriented programming in general and to enhance it as a tool for writing high-quality libraries of user-defined types in particular. A "high-quality library," is a library that provides a concept to a user in the form of one or more classes that are convenient, safe, and efficient to use. In this context, *safe* means that a class provides a specific type-safe interface between the users of the library and its providers; *efficient* means that use of the class does not impose significant overheads in run-time or space on the user compared with hand-written C code.

This book presents the complete C++ language. Chapters 1 through 10 give a tutorial introduction; Chapters 11 through 13 provide a discussion of design and software development issues; and, finally, the complete C++ reference manual is included. Naturally, the features added and resolutions made since the original edition are integral parts of the presentation. They include refined overloading resolution, memory management facilities, and access control mechanisms, type-safe linkage, *const* and *static* member functions, abstract classes, multiple inheritance, templates, and exception handling.

C++ is a general-purpose programming language; its core application domain is systems programming in the broadest sense. In addition, C++ is successfully used in many application areas that are not covered by this label. Implementations of C++ exist from some of the most modest microcomputers to the largest supercomputers and for almost all operating systems. Consequently, this book describes the C++ language itself without trying to explain a particular implementation, programming environment, or library.

This book presents many examples of classes that, though useful, should be classified as "toys." This style of exposition allows general principles and useful techniques to stand out more clearly than they would in a fully elaborated program, where they would be buried in details. Most of the useful classes presented here, such as linked lists, arrays, character strings, matrices, graphics classes, associative arrays, etc., are available in ''bulletproof'' and/or ''goldplated'' versions from a wide variety of commercial and non-commercial sources. Many of these ''industrial strength'' classes and libraries are actually direct and indirect descendants of the toy versions found here.

This edition provides a greater emphasis on tutorial aspects than did the first edition of this book. However, the presentation is still aimed squarely at experienced programmers and endeavors not to insult their intelligence or experience. The discussion of design issues has been greatly expanded to reflect the demand for information beyond the description of language features and their immediate use. Technical detail and precision have also been increased. The reference manual, in particular, represents many years of work in this direction. The intent has been to provide a book with a depth sufficient to make more than one reading rewarding to most programmers. In other words, this book presents the C++ language, its fundamental principles, and the key techniques needed to apply it. Enjoy!

Acknowledgments

In addition to the people mentioned in the acknowledgements section in the preface to the first edition, I would like to thank Al Aho, Steve Buroff, Jim Coplien, Ted Goldstein, Tony Hansen, Lorraine Juhl, Peter Juhl, Brian Kernighan, Andrew Koenig, Bill Leggett, Warren Montgomery, Mike Mowbray, Rob Murray, Jonathan Shopiro, Mike Vilot, and Peter Weinberger for commenting on draft chapters of this second edition. Many people influenced the development of C++ from 1985 to 1991. I can mention only a few: Andrew Koenig, Brian Kernighan, Doug McIlroy, and Jonathan Shopiro. Also thanks to the many participants of the ''external reviews'' of the reference manual drafts and to the people who suffered through the first year of X3J16.

Murray Hill, New Jersey   *Bjarne Stroustrup*

Preface to the First Edition

Language shapes the way we think,
and determines what we can think about.
– B.L.Whorf

C++ is a general purpose programming language designed to make programming more enjoyable for the serious programmer. Except for minor details, C++ is a superset of the C programming language. In addition to the facilities provided by C, C++ provides flexible and efficient facilities for defining new types. A programmer can partition an application into manageable pieces by defining new types that closely match the concepts of the application. This technique for program construction is often called *data abstraction.* Objects of some user-defined types contain type information. Such objects can be used conveniently and safely in contexts in which their type cannot be determined at compile time. Programs using objects of such types are often called *object based.* When used well, these techniques result in shorter, easier to understand, and easier to maintain programs.

The key concept in C++ is *class.* A class is a user-defined type. Classes provide data hiding, guaranteed initialization of data, implicit type conversion for user-defined types, dynamic typing, user-controlled memory management, and mechanisms for overloading operators. C++ provides much better facilities for type checking and for expressing modularity than C does. It also contains improvements that are not directly related to classes, including symbolic constants, inline substitution of functions, default function arguments, overloaded function names, free store management operators, and a reference type. C++ retains C's ability to deal efficiently with the fundamental objects of the hardware (bits, bytes, words, addresses, etc.). This allows the user-defined types to be implemented with a pleasing degree of efficiency.

C++ and its standard libraries are designed for portability. The current implementation will run on most systems that support C. C libraries can be used from a C++ program, and most tools that support programming in C can be used with C++.

This book is primarily intended to help serious programmers learn the language and use it for nontrivial projects. It provides a complete description of C++, many complete examples, and many more program fragments.

Acknowledgments

C++ could never have matured without the constant use, suggestions, and constructive criticism of many friends and colleagues. In particular, Tom Cargill, Jim Coplien, Stu Feldman, Sandy Fraser, Steve Johnson, Brian Kernighan, Bart Locanthi, Doug McIlroy, Dennis Ritchie, Larry Rosler, Jerry Schwarz, and Jon Shopiro provided important ideas for development of the language. Dave Presotto wrote the current implementation of the stream I/O library.

In addition, hundreds of people contributed to the development of C++ and its compiler by sending me suggestions for improvements, descriptions of problems they had encountered, and compiler errors. I can mention only a few: Gary Bishop, Andrew Hume, Tom Karzes, Victor Milenkovic, Rob Murray, Leonie Rose, Brian Schmult, and Gary Walker.

Many people have also helped with the production of this book, in particular, Jon Bentley, Laura Eaves, Brian Kernighan, Ted Kowalski, Steve Mahaney, Jon Shopiro, and the participants in the C++ course held at Bell Labs, Columbus, Ohio, June 26-27, 1985.

Murray Hill, New Jersey   *Bjarne Stroustrup*

Introduction

This introduction gives an overview of the major concepts and features of the C++ programming language and its standard library. It also provides an overview of this book and explains the approach taken to the description of the language facilities and their use. In addition, the introductory chapters present some background information about C++, the design of C++, and the use of C++.

Chapters

1   Notes to the Reader
2   A Tour of C++
3   A Tour of the Standard Library

"... and you, Marcus, you have given me many things; now I shall give you this good advice. Be many people. Give up the game of being always Marcus Cocoza. You have worried too much about Marcus Cocoza, so that you have been really his slave and prisoner. You have not done anything without first considering how it would affect Marcus Cocoza's happiness and prestige. You were always much afraid that Marcus might do a stupid thing, or be bored. What would it really have mattered? All over the world people are doing stupid things ... I should like you to be easy, your little heart to be light again. You must from now, be more than one, many people, as many as you can think of ..."

    – Karen Blixen
        ("The Dreamers" from "Seven Gothic Tales"
        written under the pseudonym Isak Dinesen,
        Random House, Inc.
        Copyright, Isak Dinesen, 1934 renewed 1961)

1

Notes to the Reader

"The time has come," the Walrus said,
"to talk of many things."
– L. Carroll

Structure of this book — how to learn C++ — the design of C++ — efficiency and structure — philosophical note — historical note — what C++ is used for — C and C++ — suggestions for C programmers — suggestions for C++ programmers — thoughts about programming in C++ — advice — references.

1.1 The Structure of This Book

This book consists of six parts:

Introduction: Chapters 1 through 3 give an overview of the C++ language, the key programming styles it supports, and the C++ standard library.

Part I: Chapters 4 through 9 provide a tutorial introduction to C++'s built-in types and the basic facilities for constructing programs out of them.

Part II: Chapters 10 through 15 are a tutorial introduction to object-oriented and generic programming using C++.

Part III: Chapters 16 through 22 present the C++ standard library.

Part IV: Chapters 23 through 25 discuss design and software development issues.

Appendices: Appendices A through E provide language-technical details.

Chapter 1 provides an overview of this book, some hints about how to use it, and some background information about C++ and its use. You are encouraged to skim through it, read what appears interesting, and return to it after reading other parts of the book.

Chapters 2 and 3 provide an overview of the major concepts and features of the C++ programming language and its standard library. Their purpose is to motivate you to spend time on fundamental concepts and basic language features by showing what can be expressed using the complete

C++ language. If nothing else, these chapters should convince you that C++ isn't (just) C and that C++ has come a long way since the first and second editions of this book. Chapter 2 gives a high-level acquaintance with C++. The discussion focuses on the language features supporting data abstraction, object-oriented programming, and generic programming. Chapter 3 introduces the basic principles and major facilities of the standard library. This allows me to use standard library facilities in the following chapters. It also allows you to use library facilities in exercises rather than relying directly on lower-level, built-in features.

The introductory chapters provide an example of a general technique that is applied throughout this book: to enable a more direct and realistic discussion of some technique or feature, I occasionally present a concept briefly at first and then discuss it in depth later. This approach allows me to present concrete examples before a more general treatment of a topic. Thus, the organization of this book reflects the observation that we usually learn best by progressing from the concrete to the abstract – even where the abstract seems simple and obvious in retrospect.

Part I describes the subset of C++ that supports the styles of programming traditionally done in C or Pascal. It covers fundamental types, expressions, and control structures for C++ programs. Modularity – as supported by namespaces, source files, and exception handling – is also discussed. I assume that you are familiar with the fundamental programming concepts used in Part I. For example, I explain C++'s facilities for expressing recursion and iteration, but I do not spend much time explaining how these concepts are useful.

Part II describes C++'s facilities for defining and using new types. Concrete and abstract classes (interfaces) are presented here (Chapter 10, Chapter 12), together with operator overloading (Chapter 11), polymorphism, and the use of class hierarchies (Chapter 12, Chapter 15). Chapter 13 presents templates, that is, C++'s facilities for defining families of types and functions. It demonstrates the basic techniques used to provide containers, such as lists, and to support generic programming. Chapter 14 presents exception handling, discusses techniques for error handling, and presents strategies for fault tolerance. I assume that you either aren't well acquainted with object-oriented programming and generic programming or could benefit from an explanation of how the main abstraction techniques are supported by C++. Thus, I don't just present the language features supporting the abstraction techniques; I also explain the techniques themselves. Part IV goes further in this direction.

Part III presents the C++ standard library. The aim is to provide an understanding of how to use the library, to demonstrate general design and programming techniques, and to show how to extend the library. The library provides containers (such as *list*, *vector*, and *map*; Chapter 16, Chapter 17), standard algorithms (such as *sort*, *find*, and *merge*; Chapter 18, Chapter 19), strings (Chapter 20), Input/Output (Chapter 21), and support for numerical computation (Chapter 22).

Part IV discusses issues that arise when C++ is used in the design and implementation of large software systems. Chapter 23 concentrates on design and management issues. Chapter 24 discusses the relation between the C++ programming language and design issues. Chapter 25 presents some ways of using classes in design.

Appendix A is C++'s grammar, with a few annotations. Appendix B discusses the relation between C and C++ and between Standard C++ (also called ISO C++ and ANSI C++) and the versions of C++ that preceded it. Appendix C presents some language-technical examples. Appendix D explains the standard library's facilities supporting internationalization. Appendix E discusses the exception-safety guarantees and requirements of the standard library.

1.1.1 Examples and References

This book emphasizes program organization rather than the writing of algorithms. Consequently, I avoid clever or harder-to-understand algorithms. A trivial algorithm is typically better suited to illustrate an aspect of the language definition or a point about program structure. For example, I use a Shell sort where, in real code, a quicksort would be better. Often, reimplementation with a more suitable algorithm is an exercise. In real code, a call of a library function is typically more appropriate than the code used here for illustration of language features.

Textbook examples necessarily give a warped view of software development. By clarifying and simplifying the examples, the complexities that arise from scale disappear. I see no substitute for writing realistically-sized programs for getting an impression of what programming and a programming language are really like. This book concentrates on the language features, the basic techniques from which every program is composed, and the rules for composition.

The selection of examples reflects my background in compilers, foundation libraries, and simulations. Examples are simplified versions of what is found in real code. The simplification is necessary to keep programming language and design points from getting lost in details. There are no "cute" examples without counterparts in real code. Wherever possible, I relegated to Appendix C language-technical examples of the sort that use variables named x and y, types called A and B, and functions called $f()$ and $g()$.

In code examples, a proportional-width font is used for identifiers. For example:

```
#include<iostream>

int main()
{
    std::cout << "Hello, new world!\n";
}
```

At first glance, this presentation style will seem "unnatural" to programmers accustomed to seeing code in constant-width fonts. However, proportional-width fonts are generally regarded as better than constant-width fonts for presentation of text. Using a proportional-width font also allows me to present code with fewer illogical line breaks. Furthermore, my experiments show that most people find the new style more readable after a short while.

Where possible, the C++ language and library features are presented in the context of their use rather than in the dry manner of a manual. The language features presented and the detail in which they are described reflect my view of what is needed for effective use of C++. A companion, *The Annotated C++ Language Standard*, authored by Andrew Koenig and myself, is the complete definition of the language together with comments aimed at making it more accessible. Logically, there ought to be another companion, *The Annotated C++ Standard Library*. However, since both time and my capacity for writing are limited, I cannot promise to produce that.

References to parts of this book are of the form §2.3.4 (Chapter 2, section 3, subsection 4), §B.5.6 (Appendix B, subsection 5.6), and §6.6[10] (Chapter 6, exercise 10). Italics are used sparingly for emphasis (e.g., "a string literal is *not* acceptable"), for first occurrences of important concepts (e.g., *polymorphism*), for nonterminals of the C++ grammar (e.g., *for-statement*), and for comments in code examples. Semi-bold italics are used to refer to identifiers, keywords, and numeric values from code examples (e.g., *class*, *counter*, and *1712*).

1.1.2 Exercises

Exercises are found at the ends of chapters. The exercises are mainly of the write-a-program variety. Always write enough code for a solution to be compiled and run with at least a few test cases. The exercises vary considerably in difficulty, so they are marked with an estimate of their difficulty. The scale is exponential so that if a (∗1) exercise takes you ten minutes, a (∗2) might take an hour, and a (∗3) might take a day. The time needed to write and test a program depends more on your experience than on the exercise itself. A (∗1) exercise might take a day if you first have to get acquainted with a new computer system in order to run it. On the other hand, a (∗5) exercise might be done in an hour by someone who happens to have the right collection of programs handy.

Any book on programming in C can be used as a source of extra exercises for Part I. Any book on data structures and algorithms can be used as a source of exercises for Parts II and III.

1.1.3 Implementation Note

The language used in this book is ''pure C++'' as defined in the C++ standard [C++,1998]. Therefore, the examples ought to run on every C++ implementation. The major program fragments in this book were tried using several C++ implementations. Examples using features only recently adopted into C++ didn't compile on every implementation. However, I see no point in mentioning which implementations failed to compile which examples. Such information would soon be out of date because implementers are working hard to ensure that their implementations correctly accept every C++ feature. See Appendix B for suggestions on how to cope with older C++ compilers and with code written for C compilers.

1.2 Learning C++

The most important thing to do when learning C++ is to focus on concepts and not get lost in language-technical details. The purpose of learning a programming language is to become a better programmer; that is, to become more effective at designing and implementing new systems and at maintaining old ones. For this, an appreciation of programming and design techniques is far more important than an understanding of details; that understanding comes with time and practice.

C++ supports a variety of programming styles. All are based on strong static type checking, and most aim at achieving a high level of abstraction and a direct representation of the programmer's ideas. Each style can achieve its aims effectively while maintaining run-time and space efficiency. A programmer coming from a different language (say C, Fortran, Smalltalk, Lisp, ML, Ada, Eiffel, Pascal, or Modula-2) should realize that to gain the benefits of C++, they must spend time learning and internalizing programming styles and techniques suitable to C++. The same applies to programmers used to an earlier and less expressive version of C++.

Thoughtlessly applying techniques effective in one language to another typically leads to awkward, poorly performing, and hard-to-maintain code. Such code is also most frustrating to write because every line of code and every compiler error message reminds the programmer that the language used differs from ''the old language.'' You can write in the style of Fortran, C, Smalltalk, etc., in any language, but doing so is neither pleasant nor economical in a language with a different philosophy. Every language can be a fertile source of ideas of how to write C++ programs.

However, ideas must be transformed into something that fits with the general structure and type system of C++ in order to be effective in the different context. Over the basic type system of a language, only Pyrrhic victories are possible.

C++ supports a gradual approach to learning. How you approach learning a new programming language depends on what you already know and what you aim to learn. There is no one approach that suits everyone. My assumption is that you are learning C++ to become a better programmer and designer. That is, I assume that your purpose in learning C++ is not simply to learn a new syntax for doing things the way you used to, but to learn new and better ways of building systems. This has to be done gradually because acquiring any significant new skill takes time and requires practice. Consider how long it would take to learn a new natural language well or to learn to play a new musical instrument well. Becoming a better system designer is easier and faster, but not as much easier and faster as most people would like it to be.

It follows that you will be using C++ – often for building real systems – before understanding every language feature and technique. By supporting several programming paradigms (Chapter 2), C++ supports productive programming at several levels of expertise. Each new style of programming adds another tool to your toolbox, but each is effective on its own and each adds to your effectiveness as a programmer. C++ is organized so that you can learn its concepts in a roughly linear order and gain practical benefits along the way. This is important because it allows you to gain benefits roughly in proportion to the effort expended.

In the continuing debate on whether one needs to learn C before C++, I am firmly convinced that it is best to go directly to C++. C++ is safer, more expressive, and reduces the need to focus on low-level techniques. It is easier for you to learn the trickier parts of C that are needed to compensate for its lack of higher-level facilities after you have been exposed to the common subset of C and C++ and to some of the higher-level techniques supported directly in C++. Appendix B is a guide for programmers going from C++ to C, say, to deal with legacy code.

Several independently developed and distributed implementations of C++ exist. A wealth of tools, libraries, and software development environments are also available. A mass of textbooks, manuals, journals, newsletters, electronic bulletin boards, mailing lists, conferences, and courses are available to inform you about the latest developments in C++, its use, tools, libraries, implementations, etc. If you plan to use C++ seriously, I strongly suggest that you gain access to such sources. Each has its own emphasis and bias, so use at least two. For example, see [Barton,1994], [Booch,1994], [Henricson,1997], [Koenig,1997], [Martin,1995].

1.3 The Design of C++

Simplicity was an important design criterion: where there was a choice between simplifying the language definition and simplifying the compiler, the former was chosen. However, great importance was attached to retaining a high degree of compatibility with C [Koenig,1989] [Stroustrup,1994] (Appendix B); this precluded cleaning up the C syntax.

C++ has no built-in high-level data types and no high-level primitive operations. For example, the C++ language does not provide a matrix type with an inversion operator or a string type with a concatenation operator. If a user wants such a type, it can be defined in the language itself. In fact, defining a new general-purpose or application-specific type is the most fundamental programming activity in C++. A well-designed user-defined type differs from a built-in type only in the way it is defined, not in the way it is used. The C++ standard library described in Part III provides many examples of such types and their uses. From a user's point of view, there is little difference between a built-in type and a type provided by the standard library.

Features that would incur run-time or memory overheads even when not used were avoided in the design of C++. For example, constructs that would make it necessary to store "housekeeping information" in every object were rejected, so if a user declares a structure consisting of two 16-bit quantities, that structure will fit into a 32-bit register.

C++ was designed to be used in a traditional compilation and run-time environment, that is, the C programming environment on the UNIX system. Fortunately, C++ was never restricted to UNIX; it simply used UNIX and C as a model for the relationships between language, libraries, compilers, linkers, execution environments, etc. That minimal model helped C++ to be successful on essentially every computing platform. There are, however, good reasons for using C++ in environments that provide significantly more support. Facilities such as dynamic loading, incremental compilation, and a database of type definitions can be put to good use without affecting the language.

C++ type-checking and data-hiding features rely on compile-time analysis of programs to prevent accidental corruption of data. They do not provide secrecy or protection against someone who is deliberately breaking the rules. They can, however, be used freely without incurring run-time or space overheads. The idea is that to be useful, a language feature must not only be elegant; it must also be affordable in the context of a real program.

For a systematic and detailed description of the design of C++, see [Stroustrup,1994].

1.3.1 Efficiency and Structure

C++ was developed from the C programming language and, with few exceptions, retains C as a subset. The base language, the C subset of C++, is designed to ensure a very close correspondence between its types, operators, and statements and the objects that computers deal with directly: numbers, characters, and addresses. Except for the *new*, *delete*, *typeid*, *dynamic_cast*, and *throw* operators and the *try-block*, individual C++ expressions and statements need no run-time support.

C++ can use the same function call and return sequences as C – or more efficient ones. When even such relatively efficient mechanisms are too expensive, a C++ function can be substituted inline, so that we can enjoy the notational convenience of functions without run-time overhead.

One of the original aims for C was to replace assembly coding for the most demanding systems programming tasks. When C++ was designed, care was taken not to compromise the gains in this area. The difference between C and C++ is primarily in the degree of emphasis on types and structure. C is expressive and permissive. C++ is even more expressive. However, to gain that increase in expressiveness, you must pay more attention to the types of objects. Knowing the types of objects, the compiler can deal correctly with expressions when you would otherwise have had to specify operations in painful detail. Knowing the types of objects also enables the compiler to detect errors that would otherwise persist until testing – or even later. Note that using the type system to check function arguments, to protect data from accidental corruption, to provide new types, to provide new operators, etc., does not increase run-time or space overheads in C++.

The emphasis on structure in C++ reflects the increase in the scale of programs written since C was designed. You can make a small program (say, 1,000 lines) work through brute force even when breaking every rule of good style. For a larger program, this is simply not so. If the structure of a 100,000-line program is bad, you will find that new errors are introduced as fast as old ones are removed. C++ was designed to enable larger programs to be structured in a rational way so that it would be reasonable for a single person to cope with far larger amounts of code. In addition, the aim was to have an average line of C++ code express much more than the average line of C or Pascal code. C++ has by now been shown to over-fulfill these goals.

Not every piece of code can be well-structured, hardware-independent, easy-to-read, etc. C++ possesses features that are intended for manipulating hardware facilities in a direct and efficient way without regard for safety or ease of comprehension. It also possesses facilities for hiding such code behind elegant and safe interfaces.

Naturally, the use of C++ for larger programs leads to the use of C++ by groups of programmers. C++'s emphasis on modularity, strongly typed interfaces, and flexibility pays off here. C++ has as good a balance of facilities for writing large programs as any language has. However, as programs get larger, the problems associated with their development and maintenance shift from being language problems to more global problems of tools and management. Part IV explores some of these issues.

This book emphasizes techniques for providing general-purpose facilities, generally useful types, libraries, etc. These techniques will serve programmers of small programs as well as programmers of large ones. Furthermore, because all nontrivial programs consist of many semi-independent parts, the techniques for writing such parts serve programmers of all applications.

You might suspect that specifying a program by using a more detailed type structure would lead to a larger program source text. With C++, this is not so. A C++ program declaring function argument types, using classes, etc., is typically a bit shorter than the equivalent C program not using these facilities. Where libraries are used, a C++ program will appear much shorter than its C equivalent, assuming, of course, that a functioning C equivalent could have been built.

1.3.2 Philosophical Note

A programming language serves two related purposes: it provides a vehicle for the programmer to specify actions to be executed, and it provides a set of concepts for the programmer to use when thinking about what can be done. The first purpose ideally requires a language that is ''close to the machine'' so that all important aspects of a machine are handled simply and efficiently in a way that is reasonably obvious to the programmer. The C language was primarily designed with this in mind. The second purpose ideally requires a language that is ''close to the problem to be solved'' so that the concepts of a solution can be expressed directly and concisely. The facilities added to C to create C++ were primarily designed with this in mind.

The connection between the language in which we think/program and the problems and solutions we can imagine is very close. For this reason, restricting language features with the intent of eliminating programmer errors is at best dangerous. As with natural languages, there are great benefits from being at least bilingual. A language provides a programmer with a set of conceptual tools; if these are inadequate for a task, they will simply be ignored. Good design and the absence of errors cannot be guaranteed merely by the presence or the absence of specific language features.

The type system should be especially helpful for nontrivial tasks. The C++ class concept has, in fact, proven itself to be a powerful conceptual tool.

1.4 Historical Note

I invented C++, wrote its early definitions, and produced its first implementation. I chose and formulated the design criteria for C++, designed all its major facilities, and was responsible for the processing of extension proposals in the C++ standards committee.

Clearly, C++ owes much to C [Kernighan,1978]. Except for closing a few serious loopholes in the type system (see Appendix B), C is retained as a subset. I also retained C's emphasis on facilities that are low-level enough to cope with the most demanding systems programming tasks. C in turn owes much to its predecessor BCPL [Richards,1980]; in fact, BCPL's // comment convention was (re)introduced in C++. The other main source of inspiration for C++ was Simula67 [Dahl,1970] [Dahl,1972]; the class concept (with derived classes and virtual functions) was borrowed from it. C++'s facility for overloading operators and the freedom to place a declaration wherever a statement can occur resembles Algol68 [Woodward,1974].

Since the original edition of this book, the language has been extensively reviewed and refined. The major areas for revision were overload resolution, linking, and memory management facilities. In addition, several minor changes were made to increase C compatibility. Several generalizations and a few major extensions were added: these included multiple inheritance, *static* member functions, *const* member functions, *protected* members, templates, exception handling, run-time type identification, and namespaces. The overall theme of these extensions and revisions was to make C++ a better language for writing and using libraries. The evolution of C++ is described in [Stroustrup,1994].

The template facility was primarily designed to support statically typed containers (such as lists, vectors, and maps) and to support elegant and efficient use of such containers (generic programming). A key aim was to reduce the use of macros and casts (explicit type conversion). Templates were partly inspired by Ada's generics (both their strengths and their weaknesses) and partly by Clu's parameterized modules. Similarly, the C++ exception-handling mechanism was inspired partly by Ada [Ichbiah,1979], Clu [Liskov,1979], and ML [Wikström,1987]. Other developments in the 1985 to 1995 time span – such as multiple inheritance, pure virtual functions, and namespaces – were primarily generalizations driven by experience with the use of C++ rather than ideas imported from other languages.

Earlier versions of the language, collectively known as "C with Classes" [Stroustrup,1994], have been in use since 1980. The language was originally invented because I wanted to write some event-driven simulations for which Simula67 would have been ideal, except for efficiency considerations. "C with Classes" was used for major projects in which the facilities for writing programs that use minimal time and space were severely tested. It lacked operator overloading, references, virtual functions, templates, exceptions, and many details. The first use of C++ outside a research organization started in July 1983.

The name C++ (pronounced "see plus plus") was coined by Rick Mascitti in the summer of 1983. The name signifies the evolutionary nature of the changes from C; "++" is the C increment operator. The slightly shorter name "C+" is a syntax error; it has also been used as the name of an unrelated language. Connoisseurs of C semantics find C++ inferior to ++C. The language is not called D, because it is an extension of C, and it does not attempt to remedy problems by removing features. For yet another interpretation of the name C++, see the appendix of [Orwell,1949].

C++ was designed primarily so that my friends and I would not have to program in assembler,

C, or various modern high-level languages. Its main purpose was to make writing good programs easier and more pleasant for the individual programmer. In the early years, there was no C++ paper design; design, documentation, and implementation went on simultaneously. There was no ''C++ project'' either, or a ''C++ design committee.'' Throughout, C++ evolved to cope with problems encountered by users and as a result of discussions between my friends, my colleagues, and me.

Later, the explosive growth of C++ use caused some changes. Sometime during 1987, it became clear that formal standardization of C++ was inevitable and that we needed to start preparing the ground for a standardization effort [Stroustrup,1994]. The result was a conscious effort to maintain contact between implementers of C++ compilers and major users through paper and electronic mail and through face-to-face meetings at C++ conferences and elsewhere.

AT&T Bell Laboratories made a major contribution to this by allowing me to share drafts of revised versions of the C++ reference manual with implementers and users. Because many of these people work for companies that could be seen as competing with AT&T, the significance of this contribution should not be underestimated. A less enlightened company could have caused major problems of language fragmentation simply by doing nothing. As it happened, about a hundred individuals from dozens of organizations read and commented on what became the generally accepted reference manual and the base document for the ANSI C++ standardization effort. Their names can be found in *The Annotated C++ Reference Manual* [Ellis,1989]. Finally, the X3J16 committee of ANSI was convened in December 1989 at the initiative of Hewlett-Packard. In June 1991, this ANSI (American national) standardization of C++ became part of an ISO (international) standardization effort for C++. From 1990, these joint C++ standards committees have been the main forum for the evolution of C++ and the refinement of its definition. I served on these committees throughout. In particular, as the chairman of the working group for extensions, I was directly responsible for the handling of proposals for major changes to C++ and the addition of new language features. An initial draft standard for public review was produced in April 1995. The ISO C++ standard (ISO/IEC 14882) was ratified in 1998.

C++ evolved hand-in-hand with some of the key classes presented in this book. For example, I designed complex, vector, and stack classes together with the operator overloading mechanisms. String and list classes were developed by Jonathan Shopiro and me as part of the same effort. Jonathan's string and list classes were the first to see extensive use as part of a library. The string class from the standard C++ library has its roots in these early efforts. The task library described in [Stroustrup,1987] and in §12.7[11] was part of the first ''C with Classes'' program ever written. I wrote it and its associated classes to support Simula-style simulations. The task library has been revised and reimplemented, notably by Jonathan Shopiro, and is still in extensive use. The stream library as described in the first edition of this book was designed and implemented by me. Jerry Schwarz transformed it into the iostreams library (Chapter 21) using Andrew Koenig's manipulator technique (§21.4.6) and other ideas. The iostreams library was further refined during standardization, when the bulk of the work was done by Jerry Schwarz, Nathan Myers, and Norihiro Kumagai. The development of the template facility was influenced by the *vector*, *map*, *list*, and *sort* templates devised by Andrew Koenig, Alex Stepanov, me, and others. In turn, Alex Stepanov's work on generic programming using templates led to the containers and algorithms parts of the standard C++ library (§16.3, Chapter 17, Chapter 18, §19.2). The *valarray* library for numerical computation (Chapter 22) is primarily the work of Kent Budge.

1.5 Use of C++

C++ is used by hundreds of thousands of programmers in essentially every application domain. This use is supported by about a dozen independent implementations, hundreds of libraries, hundreds of textbooks, several technical journals, many conferences, and innumerable consultants. Training and education at a variety of levels are widely available.

Early applications tended to have a strong systems programming flavor. For example, several major operating systems have been written in C++ [Campbell,1987] [Rozier,1988] [Hamilton,1993] [Berg,1995] [Parrington,1995] and many more have key parts done in C++. I considered uncompromising low-level efficiency essential for C++. This allows us to use C++ to write device drivers and other software that rely on direct manipulation of hardware under real-time constraints. In such code, predictability of performance is at least as important as raw speed. Often, so is compactness of the resulting system. C++ was designed so that every language feature is usable in code under severe time and space constraints [Stroustrup,1994,§4.5].

Most applications have sections of code that are critical for acceptable performance. However, the largest amount of code is not in such sections. For most code, maintainability, ease of extension, and ease of testing is key. C++'s support for these concerns has led to its widespread use where reliability is a must and in areas where requirements change significantly over time. Examples are banking, trading, insurance, telecommunications, and military applications. For years, the central control of the U.S. long-distance telephone system has relied on C++ and every 800 call (that is, a call paid for by the called party) has been routed by a C++ program [Kamath,1993]. Many such applications are large and long-lived. As a result, stability, compatibility, and scalability have been constant concerns in the development of C++. Million-line C++ programs are not uncommon.

Like C, C++ wasn't specifically designed with numerical computation in mind. However, much numerical, scientific, and engineering computation is done in C++. A major reason for this is that traditional numerical work must often be combined with graphics and with computations relying on data structures that don't fit into the traditional Fortran mold [Budge,1992] [Barton,1994]. Graphics and user interfaces are areas in which C++ is heavily used. Anyone who has used either an Apple Macintosh or a PC running Windows has indirectly used C++ because the primary user interfaces of these systems are C++ programs. In addition, some of the most popular libraries supporting X for UNIX are written in C++. Thus, C++ is a common choice for the vast number of applications in which the user interface is a major part.

All of this points to what may be C++'s greatest strength: its ability to be used effectively for applications that require work in a variety of application areas. It is quite common to find an application that involves local and wide-area networking, numerics, graphics, user interaction, and database access. Traditionally, such application areas have been considered distinct, and they have most often been served by distinct technical communities using a variety of programming languages. However, C++ has been widely used in all of those areas. Furthermore, it is able to coexist with code fragments and programs written in other languages.

C++ is widely used for teaching and research. This has surprised some who − correctly − point out that C++ isn't the smallest or cleanest language ever designed. It is, however

- clean enough for successful teaching of basic concepts,
- realistic, efficient, and flexible enough for demanding projects,

- available enough for organizations and collaborations relying on diverse development and execution environments,
- comprehensive enough to be a vehicle for teaching advanced concepts and techniques, and
- commercial enough to be a vehicle for putting what is learned into non-academic use.

C++ is a language that you can grow with.

1.6 C and C++

C was chosen as the base language for C++ because it

[1] is versatile, terse, and relatively low-level;

[2] is adequate for most systems programming tasks;

[3] runs everywhere and on everything; and

[4] fits into the UNIX programming environment.

C has its problems, but a language designed from scratch would have some too, and we know C's problems. Importantly, working with C enabled "C with Classes" to be a useful (if awkward) tool within months of the first thought of adding Simula-like classes to C.

As C++ became more widely used, and as the facilities it provided over and above those of C became more significant, the question of whether to retain compatibility was raised again and again. Clearly some problems could be avoided if some of the C heritage was rejected (see, e.g., [Sethi,1981]). This was not done because

[1] there are millions of lines of C code that might benefit from C++, provided that a complete rewrite from C to C++ were unnecessary;

[2] there are millions of lines of library functions and utility software code written in C that could be used from/on C++ programs provided C++ were link-compatible with and syntactically very similar to C;

[3] there are hundreds of thousands of programmers who know C and therefore need only learn to use the new features of C++ and not relearn the basics; and

[4] C++ and C will be used on the same systems by the same people for years, so the differences should be either very large or very small so as to minimize mistakes and confusion.

The definition of C++ has been revised to ensure that a construct that is both legal C and legal C++ has the same meaning in both languages (§B.2).

The C language has itself evolved, partly under the influence of the development of C++ [Rosler,1984]. The ANSI C standard [C,1990] contains a function declaration syntax borrowed from "C with Classes." Borrowing works both ways. For example, the *void** pointer type was invented for ANSI C and first implemented in C++. As promised in the first edition of this book, the definition of C++ has been reviewed to remove gratuitous incompatibilities; C++ is now more compatible with C than it was originally. The ideal was for C++ to be as close to ANSI C as possible – but no closer [Koenig,1989]. One hundred percent compatibility was never a goal because that would compromise type safety and the smooth integration of user-defined and built-in types.

Knowing C is not a prerequisite for learning C++. Programming in C encourages many techniques and tricks that are rendered unnecessary by C++ language features. For example, explicit type conversion (casting) is less frequently needed in C++ than it is in C (§1.6.1). However, *good* C programs tend to be C++ programs. For example, every program in Kernighan and Ritchie, *The*

C Programming Language (2nd Edition) [Kernighan,1988], is a C++ program. Experience with any statically typed language will be a help when learning C++.

1.6.1 Suggestions for C Programmers

The better one knows C, the harder it seems to be to avoid writing C++ in C style, thereby losing some of the potential benefits of C++. Please take a look at Appendix B, which describes the differences between C and C++. Here are a few pointers to the areas in which C++ has better ways of doing something than C has:

[1] Macros are almost never necessary in C++. Use *const* (§5.4) or *enum* (§4.8) to define manifest constants, *inline* (§7.1.1) to avoid function-calling overhead, *templates* (Chapter 13) to specify families of functions and types, and *namespaces* (§8.2) to avoid name clashes.

[2] Don't declare a variable before you need it so that you can initialize it immediately. A declaration can occur anywhere a statement can (§6.3.1), in *for-statement* initializers (§6.3.3), and in conditions (§6.3.2.1).

[3] Don't use *malloc( )*. The *new* operator (§6.2.6) does the same job better, and instead of *realloc( )*, try a *vector* (§3.8).

[4] Try to avoid *void**, pointer arithmetic, unions, and casts, except deep within the implementation of some function or class. In most cases, a cast is an indication of a design error. If you must use an explicit type conversion, try using one of the ''new casts'' (§6.2.7) for a more precise statement of what you are trying to do.

[5] Minimize the use of arrays and C-style strings. The C++ standard library *string* (§3.5) and *vector* (§3.7.1) classes can often be used to simplify programming compared to traditional C style. In general, try not to build yourself what has already been provided by the standard library.

To obey C linkage conventions, a C++ function must be declared to have C linkage (§9.2.4).

Most important, try thinking of a program as a set of interacting concepts represented as classes and objects, instead of as a bunch of data structures with functions twiddling their bits.

1.6.2 Suggestions for C++ Programmers

By now, many people have been using C++ for a decade. Many more are using C++ in a single environment and have learned to live with the restrictions imposed by early compilers and first-generation libraries. Often, what an experienced C++ programmer has failed to notice over the years is not the introduction of new features as such, but rather the changes in relationships between features that make fundamental new programming techniques feasible. In other words, what you didn't think of when first learning C++ or found impractical just might be a superior approach today. You find out only by re-examining the basics.

Read through the chapters in order. If you already know the contents of a chapter, you can be through in minutes. If you don't already know the contents, you'll have learned something unexpected. I learned a fair bit writing this book, and I suspect that hardly any C++ programmer knows every feature and technique presented. Furthermore, to use the language well, you need a perspective that brings order to the set of features and techniques. Through its organization and examples, this book offers such a perspective.

1.7   Thinking about Programming in C++

Ideally, you approach the task of designing a program in three stages. First, you gain a clear under-standing of the problem (analysis), then you identify the key concepts involved in a solution (design), and finally you express that solution in a program (programming). However, the details of the problem and the concepts of the solution often become clearly understood only through the effort to express them in a program and trying to get it to run acceptably. This is where the choice of programming language matters.

In most applications, there are concepts that are not easily represented as one of the fundamental types or as a function without associated data. Given such a concept, declare a class to represent it in the program. A C++ class is a type. That is, it specifies how objects of its class behave: how they are created, how they can be manipulated, and how they are destroyed. A class may also specify how objects are represented, although in the early stages of the design of a program that should not be the major concern. The key to writing good programs is to design classes so that each cleanly represents a single concept. Often, this means that you must focus on questions such as: How are objects of this class created? Can objects of this class be copied and/or destroyed? What opera-tions can be applied to such objects? If there are no good answers to such questions, the concept probably wasn't ''clean'' in the first place. It might then be a good idea to think more about the problem and its proposed solution instead of immediately starting to ''code around'' the problems.

The concepts that are easiest to deal with are the ones that have a traditional mathematical for-malism: numbers of all sorts, sets, geometric shapes, etc. Text-oriented I/O, strings, basic contain-ers, the fundamental algorithms on such containers, and some mathematical classes are part of the standard C++ library (Chapter 3, §16.1.2). In addition, a bewildering variety of libraries supporting general and domain-specific concepts are available.

A concept does not exist in a vacuum; there are always clusters of related concepts. Organizing the relationship between classes in a program − that is, determining the exact relationship between the different concepts involved in a solution − is often harder than laying out the individual classes in the first place. The result had better not be a muddle in which every class (concept) depends on every other. Consider two classes, A and B. Relationships such as ''A calls functions from B,'' ''A creates Bs,'' and ''A has a B member'' seldom cause major problems, while relationships such as ''A uses data from B'' can typically be eliminated.

One of the most powerful intellectual tools for managing complexity is hierarchical ordering, that is, organizing related concepts into a tree structure with the most general concept as the root. In C++, derived classes represent such structures. A program can often be organized as a set of trees or directed acyclic graphs of classes. That is, the programmer specifies a number of base classes, each with its own set of derived classes. Virtual functions (§2.5.5, §12.2.6) can often be used to define operations for the most general version of a concept (a base class). When necessary, the interpretation of these operations can be refined for particular special cases (derived classes).

Sometimes even a directed acyclic graph seems insufficient for organizing the concepts of a program; some concepts seem to be inherently mutually dependent. In that case, we try to localize cyclic dependencies so that they do not affect the overall structure of the program. If you cannot eliminate or localize such mutual dependencies, then you are most likely in a predicament that no programming language can help you out of. Unless you can conceive of some easily stated rela-tionships between the basic concepts, the program is likely to become unmanageable.

One of the best tools for untangling dependency graphs is the clean separation of interface and implementation. Abstract classes (§2.5.4, §12.3) are C++'s primary tool for doing that.

Another form of commonality can be expressed through templates (§2.7, Chapter 13). A class template specifies a family of classes. For example, a list template specifies ''list of T,'' where ''T'' can be any type. Thus, a template is a mechanism for specifying how one type is generated given another type as an argument. The most common templates are container classes such as lists, arrays, and associative arrays and the fundamental algorithms using such containers. It is usually a mistake to express parameterization of a class and its associated functions with a type using inheritance. It is best done using templates.

Remember that much programming can be simply and clearly done using only primitive types, data structures, plain functions, and a few library classes. The whole apparatus involved in defining new types should not be used except when there is a real need.

The question ''How does one write good programs in C++?'' is very similar to the question ''How does one write good English prose?'' There are two answers: ''Know what you want to say'' and ''Practice. Imitate good writing.'' Both appear to be as appropriate for C++ as they are for English − and as hard to follow.

1.8 Advice

Here is a set of ''rules'' you might consider while learning C++. As you get more proficient you can evolve them into something suitable for your kind of applications and your style of programming. They are deliberately very simple, so they lack detail. Don't take them too literally. To write a good program takes intelligence, taste, and patience. You are not going to get it right the first time. Experiment!

[1] When you program, you create a concrete representation of the ideas in your solution to some problem. Let the structure of the program reflect those ideas as directly as possible:
  [a] If you can think of ''it'' as a separate idea, make it a class.
  [b] If you can think of ''it'' as a separate entity, make it an object of some class.
  [c] If two classes have a common interface, make that interface an abstract class.
  [d] If the implementations of two classes have something significant in common, make that commonality a base class.
  [e] If a class is a container of objects, make it a template.
  [f] If a function implements an algorithm for a container, make it a template function implementing the algorithm for a family of containers.
  [g] If a set of classes, templates, etc., are logically related, place them in a common namespace.

[2] When you define either a class that does not implement a mathematical entity like a matrix or a complex number or a low-level type such as a linked list:
  [a] Don't use global data (use members).
  [b] Don't use global functions.
  [c] Don't use public data members.
  [d] Don't use friends, except to avoid [a] or [c].
  [e] Don't put a ''type field'' in a class; use virtual functions.
  [f] Don't use inline functions, except as a significant optimization.

More specific or detailed rules of thumb can be found in the "Advice" section of each chapter. Remember, this advice is only rough rules of thumb, not immutable laws. A piece of advice should be applied only "where reasonable." There is no substitute for intelligence, experience, common sense, and good taste.

I find rules of the form "never do this" unhelpful. Consequently, most advice is phrased as suggestions of what to do, while negative suggestions tend not to be phrased as absolute prohibitions. I know of no major feature of C++ that I have not seen put to good use. The "Advice" sections do not contain explanations. Instead, each piece of advice is accompanied by a reference to the appropriate section of the book. Where negative advice is given, that section usually provides a suggested alternative.

1.8.1 References

There are few direct references in the text, but here is a short list of books and papers that are mentioned directly or indirectly.

[Barton,1994] John J. Barton and Lee R. Nackman: *Scientific and Engineering C++.* Addison-Wesley. Reading, Mass. 1994. ISBN 1-201-53393-6.

[Berg,1995] William Berg, Marshall Cline, and Mike Girou: *Lessons Learned from the OS/400 OO Project.* CACM. Vol. 38 No. 10. October 1995.

[Booch,1994] Grady Booch: *Object-Oriented Analysis and Design.* Benjamin/Cummings. Menlo Park, Calif. 1994. ISBN 0-8053-5340-2.

[Budge,1992] Kent Budge, J. S. Perry, and A. C. Robinson: *High-Performance Scientific Computation using C++.* Proc. USENIX C++ Conference. Portland, Oregon. August 1992.

[C,1990] X3 Secretariat: *Standard – The C Language.* X3J11/90-013. ISO Standard ISO/IEC 9899. Computer and Business Equipment Manufacturers Association. Washington, DC, USA.

[C++,1998] X3 Secretariat: *International Standard – The C++ Language.* X3J16-14882. Information Technology Council (NSITC). Washington, DC, USA.

[Campbell,1987] Roy Campbell, et al.: *The Design of a Multiprocessor Operating System.* Proc. USENIX C++ Conference. Santa Fe, New Mexico. November 1987.

[Coplien,1995] James O. Coplien and Douglas C. Schmidt (editors): *Pattern Languages of Program Design.* Addison-Wesley. Reading, Mass. 1995. ISBN 1-201-60734-4.

[Dahl,1970] O-J. Dahl, B. Myrhaug, and K. Nygaard: *SIMULA Common Base Language.* Norwegian Computing Center S-22. Oslo, Norway. 1970.

[Dahl,1972] O-J. Dahl and C. A. R. Hoare: *Hierarchical Program Construction* in *Structured Programming.* Academic Press, New York. 1972.

[Ellis,1989] Margaret A. Ellis and Bjarne Stroustrup: *The Annotated C++ Reference Manual.* Addison-Wesley. Reading, Mass. 1990. ISBN 0-201-51459-1.

[Gamma,1995] Erich Gamma, et al.: *Design Patterns.* Addison-Wesley. Reading, Mass. 1995. ISBN 0-201-63361-2.

[Goldberg,1983] A. Goldberg and D. Robson: *SMALLTALK-80 – The Language and Its Implementation.* Addison-Wesley. Reading, Mass. 1983.

[Griswold,1970]   R. E. Griswold, et al.: *The Snobol4 Programming Language*. Prentice-Hall. Englewood Cliffs, New Jersey. 1970.

[Griswold,1983]   R. E. Griswold and M. T. Griswold: *The ICON Programming Language*. Prentice-Hall. Englewood Cliffs, New Jersey. 1983.

[Hamilton,1993]   G. Hamilton and P. Kougiouris: *The Spring Nucleus: A Microkernel for Objects*. Proc. 1993 Summer USENIX Conference. USENIX.

[Henricson,1997]   Mats Henricson and Erik Nyquist: *Industrial Strength C++: Rules and Recommendations*. Prentice-Hall. Englewood Cliffs, New Jersey. 1997. ISBN 0-13-120965-5.

[Ichbiah,1979]   Jean D. Ichbiah, et al.: *Rationale for the Design of the ADA Programming Language*. SIGPLAN Notices. Vol. 14 No. 6. June 1979.

[Kamath,1993]   Yogeesh H. Kamath, Ruth E. Smilan, and Jean G. Smith: *Reaping Benefits with Object-Oriented Technology*. AT&T Technical Journal. Vol. 72 No. 5. September/October 1993.

[Kernighan,1978]   Brian W. Kernighan and Dennis M. Ritchie: *The C Programming Language*. Prentice-Hall. Englewood Cliffs, New Jersey. 1978.

[Kernighan,1988]   Brian W. Kernighan and Dennis M. Ritchie: *The C Programming Language (Second Edition)*. Prentice-Hall. Englewood Cliffs, New Jersey. 1988. ISBN 0-13-110362-8.

[Koenig,1989]   Andrew Koenig and Bjarne Stroustrup: *C++: As close to C as possible – but no closer*. The C++ Report. Vol. 1 No. 7. July 1989.

[Koenig,1997]   Andrew Koenig and Barbara Moo: *Ruminations on C++*. Addison Wesley Longman. Reading, Mass. 1997. ISBN 1-201-42339-1.

[Knuth,1968]   Donald Knuth: *The Art of Computer Programming*. Addison-Wesley. Reading, Mass.

[Liskov,1979]   Barbara Liskov et al.: *Clu Reference Manual*. MIT/LCS/TR-225. MIT Cambridge. Mass. 1979.

[Martin,1995]   Robert C. Martin: *Designing Object-Oriented C++ Applications Using the Booch Method*. Prentice-Hall. Englewood Cliffs, New Jersey. 1995. ISBN 0-13-203837-4.

[Orwell,1949]   George Orwell: *1984*. Secker and Warburg. London. 1949.

[Parrington,1995] Graham Parrington et al.: *The Design and Implementation of Arjuna*. Computer Systems. Vol. 8 No. 3. Summer 1995.

[Richards,1980]   Martin Richards and Colin Whitby-Strevens: *BCPL – The Language and Its Compiler*. Cambridge University Press, Cambridge. England. 1980. ISBN 0-521-21965-5.

[Rosler,1984]   L. Rosler: *The Evolution of C – Past and Future*. AT&T Bell Laboratories Technical Journal. Vol. 63 No. 8. Part 2. October 1984.

[Rozier,1988]   M. Rozier, et al.: *CHORUS Distributed Operating Systems*. Computing Systems. Vol. 1 No. 4. Fall 1988.

[Sethi,1981]   Ravi Sethi: *Uniform Syntax for Type Expressions and Declarations*. Software Practice & Experience. Vol. 11. 1981.

[Stepanov,1994]   Alexander Stepanov and Meng Lee: *The Standard Template Library*. HP Labs Technical Report HPL-94-34 (R. 1). August, 1994.

[Stroustrup,1986] Bjarne Stroustrup: *The C++ Programming Language.* Addison-Wesley. Reading, Mass. 1986. ISBN 0-201-12078-X.

[Stroustrup,1987] Bjarne Stroustrup and Jonathan Shopiro: *A Set of C Classes for Co-Routine Style Programming.* Proc. USENIX C++ Conference. Santa Fe, New Mexico. November 1987.

[Stroustrup,1991] Bjarne Stroustrup: *The C++ Programming Language (Second Edition).* Addison-Wesley. Reading, Mass. 1991. ISBN 0-201-53992-6.

[Stroustrup,1994] Bjarne Stroustrup: *The Design and Evolution of C++.* Addison-Wesley. Reading, Mass. 1994. ISBN 0-201-54330-3.

[Tarjan,1983] Robert E. Tarjan: *Data Structures and Network Algorithms.* Society for Industrial and Applied Mathematics. Philadelphia, Penn. 1983. ISBN 0-898-71187-8.

[Unicode,1996] The Unicode Consortium: *The Unicode Standard, Version 2.0.* Addison-Wesley Developers Press. Reading, Mass. 1996. ISBN 0-201-48345-9.

[UNIX,1985] *UNIX Time-Sharing System: Programmer's Manual. Research Version, Tenth Edition.* AT&T Bell Laboratories, Murray Hill, New Jersey. February 1985.

[Wilson,1996] Gregory V. Wilson and Paul Lu (editors): *Parallel Programming Using C++.* The MIT Press. Cambridge. Mass. 1996. ISBN 0-262-73118-5.

[Wikström,1987] Åke Wikström: *Functional Programming Using ML.* Prentice-Hall. Englewood Cliffs, New Jersey. 1987.

[Woodward,1974] P. M. Woodward and S. G. Bond: *Algol 68-R Users Guide.* Her Majesty's Stationery Office. London. England. 1974.

References to books relating to design and larger software development issues can be found at the end of Chapter 23.

2

A Tour of C++

The first thing we do, let´s
kill all the language lawyers.
– Henry VI, part II

What is C++? — programming paradigms — procedural programming — modularity — separate compilation — exception handling — data abstraction — user-defined types — concrete types — abstract types — virtual functions — object-oriented programming — generic programming — containers — algorithms — language and programming — advice.

2.1 What is C++?

C++ is a general-purpose programming language with a bias towards systems programming that
- is a better C,
- supports data abstraction,
- supports object-oriented programming, and
- supports generic programming.

This chapter explains what this means without going into the finer details of the language definition. Its purpose is to give you a general overview of C++ and the key techniques for using it, *not* to provide you with the detailed information necessary to start programming in C++.

If you find some parts of this chapter rough going, just ignore those parts and plow on. All will be explained in detail in later chapters. However, if you do skip part of this chapter, do yourself a favor by returning to it later.

Detailed understanding of language features – even of *all* features of a language – cannot compensate for lack of an overall view of the language and the fundamental techniques for using it.

2.2 Programming Paradigms

Object-oriented programming is a technique for programming − a paradigm for writing "good" programs for a set of problems. If the term "object-oriented programming language" means anything, it must mean a programming language that provides mechanisms that support the object-oriented style of programming well.

There is an important distinction here. A language is said to *support* a style of programming if it provides facilities that make it convenient (reasonably easy, safe, and efficient) to use that style. A language does not support a technique if it takes exceptional effort or skill to write such programs; it merely *enables* the technique to be used. For example, you can write structured programs in Fortran77 and object-oriented programs in C, but it is unnecessarily hard to do so because these languages do not directly support those techniques.

Support for a paradigm comes not only in the obvious form of language facilities that allow direct use of the paradigm, but also in the more subtle form of compile-time and/or run-time checks against unintentional deviation from the paradigm. Type checking is the most obvious example of this; ambiguity detection and run-time checks are also used to extend linguistic support for paradigms. Extra-linguistic facilities such as libraries and programming environments can provide further support for paradigms.

One language is not necessarily better than another because it possesses a feature the other does not. There are many examples to the contrary. The important issue is not so much what features a language possesses, but that the features it does possess are sufficient to support the desired programming styles in the desired application areas:

[1] All features must be cleanly and elegantly integrated into the language.

[2] It must be possible to use features in combination to achieve solutions that would otherwise require extra, separate features.

[3] There should be as few spurious and "special-purpose" features as possible.

[4] A feature's implementation should not impose significant overheads on programs that do not require it.

[5] A user should need to know only about the subset of the language explicitly used to write a program.

The first principle is an appeal to aesthetics and logic. The next two are expressions of the ideal of minimalism. The last two can be summarized as "what you don't know won't hurt you."

C++ was designed to support data abstraction, object-oriented programming, and generic programming in addition to traditional C programming techniques under these constraints. It was *not* meant to force one particular programming style upon all users.

The following sections consider some programming styles and the key language mechanisms supporting them. The presentation progresses through a series of techniques starting with procedural programming and leading up to the use of class hierarchies in object-oriented programming and generic programming using templates. Each paradigm builds on its predecessors, each adds something new to the C++ programmer's toolbox, and each reflects a proven design approach.

The presentation of language features is not exhaustive. The emphasis is on design approaches and ways of organizing programs rather than on language details. At this stage, it is far more important to gain an idea of what can be done using C++ than to understand exactly how it can be achieved.

2.3 Procedural Programming

The original programming paradigm is:

> *Decide which procedures you want;*
> *use the best algorithms you can find.*

The focus is on the processing − the algorithm needed to perform the desired computation. Languages support this paradigm by providing facilities for passing arguments to functions and returning values from functions. The literature related to this way of thinking is filled with discussion of ways to pass arguments, ways to distinguish different kinds of arguments, different kinds of functions (e.g., procedures, routines, and macros), etc.

A typical example of ''good style'' is a square-root function. Given a double-precision floating-point argument, it produces a result. To do this, it performs a well-understood mathematical computation:

```
double sqrt (double arg)
{
    // code for calculating a square root
}

void f()
{
    double root2 = sqrt (2);
    // ...
}
```

Curly braces, { }, express grouping in C++. Here, they indicate the start and end of the function bodies. The double slash, //, begins a comment that extends to the end of the line. The keyword *void* indicates that a function does not return a value.

From the point of view of program organization, functions are used to create order in a maze of algorithms. The algorithms themselves are written using function calls and other language facilities. The following subsections present a thumb-nail sketch of C++'s most basic facilities for expressing computation.

2.3.1 Variables and Arithmetic

Every name and every expression has a type that determines the operations that may be performed on it. For example, the declaration

```
int inch;
```

specifies that *inch* is of type *int*; that is, *inch* is an integer variable.

A *declaration* is a statement that introduces a name into the program. It specifies a type for that name. A *type* defines the proper use of a name or an expression.

C++ offers a variety of fundamental types, which correspond directly to hardware facilities. For example:

```
bool        // Boolean, possible values are true and false
char        // character, for example, 'a', 'z', and '9'
int         // integer, for example, 1, 42, and 1216
double      // double-precision floating-point number, for example, 3.14 and 299793.0
```

A *char* variable is of the natural size to hold a character on a given machine (typically a byte), and an *int* variable is of the natural size for integer arithmetic on a given machine (typically a word).

The arithmetic operators can be used for any combination of these types:

```
+           // plus, both unary and binary
−           // minus, both unary and binary
*           // multiply
/           // divide
%           // remainder
```

So can the comparison operators:

```
==          // equal
! =         // not equal
<           // less than
>           // greater than
<=          // less than or equal
>=          // greater than or equal
```

In assignments and in arithmetic operations, C++ performs all meaningful conversions between the basic types so that they can be mixed freely:

```
void  some_function ()      // function that doesn't return a value
{
     double  d = 2.2;       // initialize floating-point number
     int  i = 7;            // initialize integer
     d = d+i;               // assign sum to d
     i = d*i;               // assign product to i
}
```

As in C, = is the assignment operator and == tests equality.

2.3.2 Tests and Loops

C++ provides a conventional set of statements for expressing selection and looping. For example, here is a simple function that prompts the user and returns a Boolean indicating the response:

```
bool  accept ()
{
     cout << "Do you want to proceed (y or n)?\n";      // write question

     char  answer = 0;
     cin >> answer;                                     // read answer

     if (answer == 'y') return  true;
     return  false;
}
```

The << operator (''put to'') is used as an output operator; *cout* is the standard output stream. The
>> operator (''get from'') is used as an input operator; *cin* is the standard input stream. The type of
the right-hand operand of >> determines what input is accepted and is the target of the input operation. The \n character at the end of the output string represents a newline.

The example could be slightly improved by taking an 'n' answer into account:

```
bool  accept2()
{
      cout << "Do you want to proceed (y or n)?\n";      // write question

      char answer = 0;
      cin >> answer;                                       // read answer

      switch (answer) {
      case 'y':
           return true;
      case 'n':
           return false;
      default:
           cout << "I'll take that for a no.\n";
           return false;
      }
}
```

A *switch-statement* tests a value against a set of constants. The case constants must be distinct, and
if the value tested does not match any of them, the *default* is chosen. The programmer need not
provide a *default*.

Few programs are written without loops. In this case, we might like to give the user a few tries:

```
bool  accept3()
{
      int tries = 1;
      while (tries < 4) {
           cout << "Do you want to proceed (y or n)?\n";      // write question
           char answer = 0;
           cin >> answer;                                       // read answer

           switch (answer) {
           case 'y':
                return true;
           case 'n':
                return false;
           default:
                cout << "Sorry, I don't understand that.\n";
                tries = tries + 1;
           }
      }
      cout << "I'll take that for a no.\n";
      return false;
}
```

The *while-statement* executes until its condition becomes *false*.

2.3.3 Pointers and Arrays

An array can be declared like this:

    char v[10];   // array of 10 characters

Similarly, a pointer can be declared like this:

    char* p;   // pointer to character

In declarations, [ ] means "array of" and * means "pointer to." All arrays have *0* as their lower bound, so *v* has ten elements, *v[0]...v[9]*. A pointer variable can hold the address of an object of the appropriate type:

    p = &v[3];   // p points to v's fourth element

Unary & is the address-of operator.

Consider copying ten elements from one array to another:

    void another_function()
    {
        int v1[10];
        int v2[10];
        // ...
        for (int i=0; i<10; ++i) v1[i]=v2[i];
    }

This *for-statement* can be read as "set *i* to zero, while *i* is less than *10*, copy the *i*th element and increment *i*." When applied to an integer variable, the increment operator ++ simply adds *1*.

2.4 Modular Programming

Over the years, the emphasis in the design of programs has shifted from the design of procedures and toward the organization of data. Among other things, this reflects an increase in program size. A set of related procedures with the data they manipulate is often called a *module*. The programming paradigm becomes:

> *Decide which modules you want;*
> *partition the program so that data is hidden within modules.*

This paradigm is also known as the *data-hiding principle*. Where there is no grouping of procedures with related data, the procedural programming style suffices. Also, the techniques for designing "good procedures" are now applied for each procedure in a module. The most common example of a module is the definition of a stack. The main problems that have to be solved are:

[1] Provide a user interface for the stack (e.g., functions *push*() and *pop*()).

[2] Ensure that the representation of the stack (e.g., an array of elements) can be accessed only through this user interface.

[3] Ensure that the stack is initialized before its first use.

C++ provides a mechanism for grouping related data, functions, etc., into separate namespaces. For example, the user interface of a *Stack* module could be declared and used like this:

```
namespace Stack {          // interface
     void push(char);
     char pop();
}

void f()
{
     Stack::push('c');
     if (Stack::pop() != 'c') error("impossible");
}
```

The *Stack*:: qualification indicates that the *push* () and *pop* () are those from the *Stack* namespace. Other uses of those names will not interfere or cause confusion.

The definition of the *Stack* could be provided in a separately-compiled part of the program:

```
namespace Stack {          // implementation
     const int max_size = 200;
     char v[max_size];
     int top = 0;

     void push(char c) { /* check for overflow and push c */ }
     char pop() { /* check for underflow and pop */ }
}
```

The key point about this *Stack* module is that the user code is insulated from the data representation of *Stack* by the code implementing *Stack*::*push* () and *Stack*::*pop* (). The user doesn't need to know that the *Stack* is implemented using an array, and the implementation can be changed without affecting user code. The / * starts a comment that extends to the following * /.

Because data is only one of the things one might want to "hide," the notion of data hiding is trivially extended to the notion of *information hiding*; that is, the names of functions, types, etc., can also be made local to a module. Consequently, C++ allows any declaration to be placed in a namespace (§8.2).

This *Stack* module is one way of representing a stack. The following sections use a variety of stacks to illustrate different programming styles.

2.4.1 Separate Compilation

C++ supports C's notion of separate compilation. This can be used to organize a program into a set of semi-independent fragments.

Typically, we place the declarations that specify the interface to a module in a file with a name indicating its intended use. Thus,

```
namespace Stack {               // interface
     void push(char);
     char pop();
}
```

would be placed in a file *stack.h*, and users will *include* that file, called a *header file*, like this:

```
#include "stack.h"              // get the interface

void f()
{
    Stack::push('c');
    if (Stack::pop() != 'c') error("impossible");
}
```

To help the compiler ensure consistency, the file providing the implementation of the *Stack* module will also include the interface:

```
#include "stack.h"              // get the interface

namespace Stack {               // representation
    const int max_size = 200;
    char v[max_size];
    int top = 0;
}

void Stack::push(char c) { /* check for overflow and push c */ }

char Stack::pop() { /* check for underflow and pop */ }
```

The user code goes in a third file, say *user.c*. The code in *user.c* and *stack.c* shares the stack interface information presented in *stack.h*, but the two files are otherwise independent and can be separately compiled. Graphically, the program fragments can be represented like this:

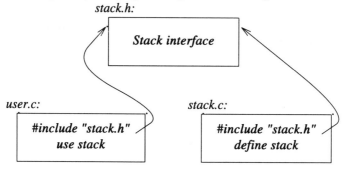

Separate compilation is an issue in all real programs. It is not simply a concern in programs that present facilities, such as a *Stack*, as modules. Strictly speaking, using separate compilation isn't a language issue; it is an issue of how best to take advantage of a particular language implementation. However, it is of great practical importance. The best approach is to maximize modularity, represent that modularity logically through language features, and then exploit the modularity physically through files for effective separate compilation (Chapter 8, Chapter 9).

2.4.2 Exception Handling

When a program is designed as a set of modules, error handling must be considered in light of these modules. Which module is responsible for handling what errors? Often, the module that detects an error doesn't know what action to take. The recovery action depends on the module that invoked the operation rather than on the module that found the error while trying to perform the operation. As programs grow, and especially when libraries are used extensively, standards for handling errors (or, more generally, "exceptional circumstances") become important.

Consider again the *Stack* example. What *ought* to be done when we try to *push*() one too many characters? The writer of the *Stack* module doesn't know what the user would like to be done in this case, and the user cannot consistently detect the problem (if the user could, the overflow wouldn't happen in the first place). The solution is for the *Stack* implementer to detect the overflow and then tell the (unknown) user. The user can then take appropriate action. For example:

```
namespace Stack {           // interface
    void push(char);
    char pop();

    class Overflow { };   // type representing overflow exceptions
}
```

When detecting an overflow, *Stack::push*() can invoke the exception-handling code; that is, "throw an *Overflow* exception:"

```
void Stack::push(char c)
{
    if (top == max_size) throw Overflow();
    // push c
}
```

The *throw* transfers control to a handler for exceptions of type *Stack::Overflow* in some function that directly or indirectly called *Stack::push*(). To do that, the implementation will unwind the function call stack as needed to get back to the context of that caller. Thus, the *throw* acts as a multilevel *return*. For example:

```
void f()
{
    // ...
    try { // exceptions here are handled by the handler defined below

        while (true) Stack::push('c');
    }
    catch (Stack::Overflow) {
        // oops: stack overflow; take appropriate action
    }
    // ...
}
```

The *while* loop will try to loop forever. Therefore, the *catch*-clause providing a handler for *Stack::Overflow* will be entered after some call of *Stack::push*() causes a *throw*.

Use of the exception-handling mechanisms can make error handling more regular and readable. See §8.3, Chapter 14, and Appendix E for further discussion, details, and examples.

2.5 Data Abstraction

Modularity is a fundamental aspect of all successful large programs. It remains a focus of all design discussions throughout this book. However, modules in the form described previously are not sufficient to express complex systems cleanly. Here, I first present a way of using modules to provide a form of user-defined types and then show how to overcome some problems with that approach by defining user-defined types directly.

2.5.1 Modules Defining Types

Programming with modules leads to the centralization of all data of a type under the control of a type manager module. For example, if we wanted many stacks − rather than the single one provided by the *Stack* module above − we could define a stack manager with an interface like this:

```
namespace Stack {
        struct Rep;                     // definition of stack layout is elsewhere
        typedef Rep& stack;

        stack create();                 // make a new stack
        void destroy(stack s);          // delete s

        void push(stack s, char c);     // push c onto s
        char pop(stack s);              // pop s
}
```

The declaration

```
    struct Rep;
```

says that *Rep* is the name of a type, but it leaves the type to be defined later (§5.7). The declaration

```
    typedef Rep& stack;
```

gives the name *stack* to a ''reference to *Rep*'' (details in §5.5). The idea is that a stack is identified by its *Stack::stack* and that further details are hidden from users.

A *Stack::stack* acts much like a variable of a built-in type:

```
struct Bad_pop { };

void f()
{
        Stack::stack s1 = Stack::create();    // make a new stack
        Stack::stack s2 = Stack::create();    // make another new stack

        Stack::push(s1, 'c');
        Stack::push(s2, 'k');

        if (Stack::pop(s1) != 'c') throw Bad_pop();
        if (Stack::pop(s2) != 'k') throw Bad_pop();

        Stack::destroy(s1);
        Stack::destroy(s2);
}
```

We could implement this *Stack* in several ways. It is important that a user doesn't need to know how we do it. As long as we keep the interface unchanged, a user will not be affected if we decide to re-implement *Stack*.

An implementation might preallocate a few stack representations and let *Stack::create*() hand out a reference to an unused one. *Stack::destroy*() could then mark a representation "unused" so that *Stack::create*() can recycle it:

```
namespace Stack {              // representation
    const int max_size = 200;
    struct Rep {
        char v[max_size];
        int top;
    };

    const int max = 16;   // maximum number of stacks

    Rep stacks[max];        // preallocated stack representations
    bool used[max];         // used[i] is true if stacks[i] is in use

    typedef Rep& stack;
}
void Stack::push(stack s, char c) { /* check s for overflow and push c */ }

char Stack::pop(stack s) { /* check s for underflow and pop */ }

Stack::stack Stack::create()
{
    // pick an unused Rep, mark it used, initialize it, and return a reference to it
}
void Stack::destroy(stack s) { /* mark s unused */ }
```

What we have done is to wrap a set of interface functions around the representation type. How the resulting "stack type" behaves depends partly on how we defined these interface functions, partly on how we presented the representation type to the users of *Stack*s, and partly on the design of the representation type itself.

This is often less than ideal. A significant problem is that the presentation of such "fake types" to the users can vary greatly depending on the details of the representation type – and users ought to be insulated from knowledge of the representation type. For example, had we chosen to use a more elaborate data structure to identify a stack, the rules for assignment and initialization of *Stack::stack*s would have changed dramatically. This may indeed be desirable at times. However, it shows that we have simply moved the problem of providing convenient stacks from the *Stack* module to the *Stack::stack* representation type.

More fundamentally, user-defined types implemented through a module providing access to an implementation type don't behave like built-in types and receive less and different support than do built-in types. For example, the time that a *Stack::Rep* can be used is controlled through *Stack::create*() and *Stack::destroy*() rather than by the usual language rules.

2.5.2 User-Defined Types

C++ attacks this problem by allowing a user to directly define types that behave in (nearly) the same way as built-in types. Such a type is often called an *abstract data type*. I prefer the term *user-defined type*. A more reasonable definition of *abstract data type* would require a mathematical "abstract" specification. Given such a specification, what are called *types* here would be concrete examples of such truly abstract entities. The programming paradigm becomes:

> *Decide which types you want;*
> *provide a full set of operations for each type.*

Where there is no need for more than one object of a type, the data-hiding programming style using modules suffices.

Arithmetic types such as rational and complex numbers are common examples of user-defined types. Consider:

```
class complex {
        double re, im;
public:
        complex(double r, double i) { re=r; im=i; }      // construct complex from two scalars
        complex(double r) { re=r; im=0; }                // construct complex from one scalar
        complex() { re = im = 0; }                       // default complex: (0,0)

        friend complex operator+(complex, complex);
        friend complex operator-(complex, complex);      // binary
        friend complex operator-(complex);               // unary
        friend complex operator*(complex, complex);
        friend complex operator/(complex, complex);

        friend bool operator==(complex, complex);        // equal
        friend bool operator!=(complex, complex);        // not equal
        // ...
};
```

The declaration of class (that is, user-defined type) *complex* specifies the representation of a complex number and the set of operations on a complex number. The representation is *private*; that is, *re* and *im* are accessible only to the functions specified in the declaration of class *complex*. Such functions can be defined like this:

```
complex operator+(complex a1, complex a2)
{
        return complex(a1.re+a2.re,a1.im+a2.im);
}
```

A member function with the same name as its class is called a *constructor*. A constructor defines a way to initialize an object of its class. Class *complex* provides three constructors. One makes a *complex* from a *double*, another takes a pair of *double*s, and the third makes a *complex* with a default value.

Class *complex* can be used like this:

```
void f(complex z)
{
    complex a = 2.3;
    complex b = 1/a;
    complex c = a+b*complex(1,2.3);
    // ...
    if (c != b) c = -(b/a)+2*b;
}
```

The compiler converts operators involving *complex* numbers into appropriate function calls. For example, *c!=b* means *operator!=(c,b)* and *1/a* means *operator/(complex(1),a)*.

Most, but not all, modules are better expressed as user-defined types.

2.5.3 Concrete Types

User-defined types can be designed to meet a wide variety of needs. Consider a user-defined *Stack* type along the lines of the *complex* type. To make the example a bit more realistic, this *Stack* type is defined to take its number of elements as an argument:

```
class Stack {
    char* v;
    int top;
    int max_size;
public:
    class Underflow { };        // used as exception
    class Overflow { };         // used as exception
    class Bad_size { };         // used as exception

    Stack(int s);               // constructor
    ~Stack();                   // destructor

    void push(char c);
    char pop();
};
```

The constructor *Stack(int)* will be called whenever an object of the class is created. This takes care of initialization. If any cleanup is needed when an object of the class goes out of scope, a complement to the constructor – called the *destructor* – can be declared:

```
Stack::Stack(int s)             // constructor
{
    top = 0;
    if (s<0 || 10000<s) throw Bad_size();    // "||" means "or"
    max_size = s;
    v = new char[s];            // allocate elements on the free store (heap, dynamic store)
}

Stack::~Stack()                 // destructor
{
    delete[] v;                 // free the elements for possible reuse of their space (§6.2.6)
}
```

The constructor initializes a new *Stack* variable. To do so, it allocates some memory on the free store (also called the *heap* or *dynamic store*) using the *new* operator. The destructor cleans up by freeing that memory. This is all done without intervention by users of *Stack*s. The users simply create and use *Stack*s much as they would variables of built-in types. For example:

```
Stack s_var1(10);              // global stack with 10 elements

void f(Stack& s_ref, int i)    // reference to Stack
{
    Stack s_var2(i);           // local stack with i elements
    Stack* s_ptr = new Stack(20);  // pointer to Stack allocated on free store

    s_var1.push('a');
    s_var2.push('b');
    s_ref.push('c');
    s_ptr->push('d');
    // ...
}
```

This *Stack* type obeys the same rules for naming, scope, allocation, lifetime, copying, etc., as does a built-in type such as *int* and *char*.

Naturally, the *push()* and *pop()* member functions must also be defined somewhere:

```
void Stack::push(char c)
{
    if (top == max_size) throw Overflow();
    v[top] = c;
    top = top + 1;
}

char Stack::pop()
{
    if (top == 0) throw Underflow();
    top = top - 1;
    return v[top];
}
```

Types such as *complex* and *Stack* are called *concrete types*, in contrast to *abstract types*, where the interface more completely insulates a user from implementation details.

2.5.4 Abstract Types

One property was lost in the transition from *Stack* as a "fake type" implemented by a module (§2.5.1) to a proper type (§2.5.3). The representation is not decoupled from the user interface; rather, it is a part of what would be included in a program fragment using *Stack*s. The representation is private, and therefore accessible only through the member functions, but it is present. If it changes in any significant way, a user must recompile. This is the price to pay for having concrete types behave exactly like built-in types. In particular, we cannot have genuine local variables of a type without knowing the size of the type's representation.

For types that don't change often, and where local variables provide much-needed clarity and efficiency, this is acceptable and often ideal. However, if we want to completely isolate users of a stack from changes to its implementation, this last *Stack* is insufficient. Then, the solution is to decouple the interface from the representation and give up genuine local variables.

First, we define the interface:

```
class Stack {
public :
        class Underflow { } ;        // used as exception
        class Overflow { } ;         // used as exception

        virtual void push (char c) = 0;
        virtual char pop () = 0;
} ;
```

The word *virtual* means "may be redefined later in a class derived from this one" in Simula and C++. A class derived from *Stack* provides an implementation for the *Stack* interface. The curious *=0* syntax says that some class derived from *Stack must* define the function. Thus, this *Stack* can serve as the interface to any class that implements its *push* ( ) and *pop* ( ) functions.

This *Stack* could be used like this:

```
void f(Stack& s_ref)
{
    s_ref.push ('c');
    if (s_ref.pop () != 'c') throw Bad_pop ();
}
```

Note how *f*( ) uses the *Stack* interface in complete ignorance of implementation details. A class that provides the interface to a variety of other classes is often called a *polymorphic type*.

Not surprisingly, the implementation could consist of everything from the concrete class *Stack* that we left out of the interface *Stack*:

```
class Array_stack : public Stack {      // Array_stack implements Stack
        char* p;
        int max_size;
        int top;
public :
        Array_stack (int s);
        ~Array_stack ();

        void push (char c);
        char pop ();
} ;
```

The " :*public*" can be read as "is derived from," "implements," and "is a subtype of."

For a function like *f*( ) to use a *Stack* in complete ignorance of implementation details, some other function will have to make an object on which it can operate. For example:

```
void g ()
{
    Array_stack as (200);
    f (as);
}
```

Since $f()$ doesn't know about *Array_stack*s but only knows the *Stack* interface, it will work just as well for a different implementation of a *Stack*. For example:

```
class List_stack : public Stack {          // List_stack implements Stack
     list<char> lc;                        // (standard library) list of characters (§3.7.3)
public:
     List_stack() { }

     void push(char c) { lc.push_front(c); }
     char pop();
};

char List_stack::pop()
{
     char x = lc.front();                  // get first element
     lc.pop_front();                       // remove first element
     return x;
}
```

Here, the representation is a list of characters. The $lc.push\_front(c)$ adds c as the first element of lc, the call $lc.pop\_front()$ removes the first element, and $lc.front()$ denotes lc's first element.

A function can create a *List_stack* and have $f()$ use it:

```
void h()
{
     List_stack ls;
     f(ls);
}
```

2.5.5 Virtual Functions

How is the call $s\_ref.pop()$ in $f()$ resolved to the right function definition? When $f()$ is called from $h()$, $List\_stack::pop()$ must be called. When $f()$ is called from $g()$, $Array\_stack::pop()$ must be called. To achieve this resolution, a *Stack* object must contain information to indicate the function to be called at run-time. A common implementation technique is for the compiler to convert the name of a *virtual* function into an index into a table of pointers to functions. That table is usually called "a virtual function table" or simply, a *vtbl*. Each class with virtual functions has its own *vtbl* identifying its virtual functions. This can be represented graphically like this:

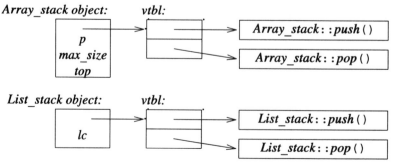

The functions in the *vtbl* allow the object to be used correctly even when the size of the object and the layout of its data are unknown to the caller. All the caller needs to know is the location of the *vtbl* in a *Stack* and the index used for each virtual function. This virtual call mechanism can be made essentially as efficient as the "normal function call" mechanism. Its space overhead is one pointer in each object of a class with virtual functions plus one *vtbl* for each such class.

2.6 Object-Oriented Programming

Data abstraction is fundamental to good design and will remain a focus of design throughout this book. However, user-defined types by themselves are not flexible enough to serve our needs. This section first demonstrates a problem with simple user-defined data types and then shows how to overcome that problem by using class hierarchies.

2.6.1 Problems with Concrete Types

A concrete type, like a "fake type" defined through a module, defines a sort of black box. Once the black box has been defined, it does not really interact with the rest of the program. There is no way of adapting it to new uses except by modifying its definition. This situation can be ideal, but it can also lead to severe inflexibility. Consider defining a type *Shape* for use in a graphics system. Assume for the moment that the system has to support circles, triangles, and squares. Assume also that we have

```
class Point{ /* ... */ };
class Color{ /* ... */ };
```

The /* and */ specify the beginning and end, respectively, of a comment. This comment notation can be used for multi-line comments and comments that end before the end of a line.
    We might define a shape like this:

```
enum Kind { circle, triangle, square };     // enumeration (§4.8)

class Shape {
        Kind k;          // type field
        Point center;
        Color col;
        // ...

public:
        void draw();
        void rotate(int);
        // ...
};
```

The "type field" *k* is necessary to allow operations such as *draw*() and *rotate*() to determine what kind of shape they are dealing with (in a Pascal-like language, one might use a variant record with tag *k*). The function *draw*() might be defined like this:

```
void  Shape :: draw ()
{
     switch (k) {
     case  circle :
               // draw a circle
               break ;
     case  triangle :
               // draw a triangle
               break ;
     case  square :
               // draw a square
               break ;
     }
}
```

This is a mess. Functions such as *draw* () must "know about" all the kinds of shapes there are. Therefore, the code for any such function grows each time a new shape is added to the system. If we define a new shape, every operation on a shape must be examined and (possibly) modified. We are not able to add a new shape to a system unless we have access to the source code for every operation. Because adding a new shape involves "touching" the code of every important operation on shapes, doing so requires great skill and potentially introduces bugs into the code that handles other (older) shapes. The choice of representation of particular shapes can get severely cramped by the requirement that (at least some of) their representation must fit into the typically fixed-sized framework presented by the definition of the general type *Shape*.

2.6.2 Class Hierarchies

The problem is that there is no distinction between the general properties of every shape (that is, a shape has a color, it can be drawn, etc.) and the properties of a specific kind of shape (a circle is a shape that has a radius, is drawn by a circle-drawing function, etc.). Expressing this distinction and taking advantage of it defines object-oriented programming. Languages with constructs that allow this distinction to be expressed and used support object-oriented programming. Other languages don't.

The inheritance mechanism (borrowed for C++ from Simula) provides a solution. First, we specify a class that defines the general properties of all shapes:

```
class  Shape {
     Point  center ;
     Color  col ;
     // ...
public :
     Point  where () { return  center ; }
     void  move (Point  to) { center = to ; /* ... */ draw () ; }

     virtual  void  draw () = 0 ;
     virtual  void  rotate (int  angle) = 0 ;
     // ...
} ;
```

As in the abstract type *Stack* in §2.5.4, the functions for which the calling interface can be defined – but where the implementation cannot be defined yet – are *virtual*. In particular, the functions *draw*() and *rotate*() can be defined only for specific shapes, so they are declared *virtual*.

Given this definition, we can write general functions manipulating vectors of pointers to shapes:

```
void rotate_all(vector<Shape*>& v, int angle) // rotate v's elements angle degrees
{
    for (int i = 0; i<v.size(); ++i) v[i]->rotate(angle);
}
```

To define a particular shape, we must say that it is a shape and specify its particular properties (including the virtual functions):

```
class Circle : public Shape {
    int radius;
public:
    void draw() { /* ... */ }
    void rotate(int) {}   // yes, the null function
};
```

In C++, class *Circle* is said to be *derived* from class *Shape*, and class *Shape* is said to be a *base* of class *Circle*. An alternative terminology calls *Circle* and *Shape* subclass and superclass, respectively. The derived class is said to inherit members from its base class, so the use of base and derived classes is commonly referred to as *inheritance*.

The programming paradigm is:

> *Decide which classes you want;*
> *provide a full set of operations for each class;*
> *make commonality explicit by using inheritance.*

Where there is no such commonality, data abstraction suffices. The amount of commonality between types that can be exploited by using inheritance and virtual functions is the litmus test of the applicability of object-oriented programming to a problem. In some areas, such as interactive graphics, there is clearly enormous scope for object-oriented programming. In other areas, such as classical arithmetic types and computations based on them, there appears to be hardly any scope for more than data abstraction, and the facilities needed for the support of object-oriented programming seem unnecessary.

Finding commonality among types in a system is not a trivial process. The amount of commonality to be exploited is affected by the way the system is designed. When a system is designed – and even when the requirements for the system are written – commonality must be actively sought. Classes can be designed specifically as building blocks for other types, and existing classes can be examined to see if they exhibit similarities that can be exploited in a common base class.

For attempts to explain what object-oriented programming is without recourse to specific programming language constructs, see [Kerr,1987] and [Booch,1994] in §23.6.

Class hierarchies and abstract classes (§2.5.4) complement each other instead of being mutually exclusive (§12.5). In general, the paradigms listed here tend to be complementary and often mutually supportive. For example, classes and modules contain functions, while modules contain classes and functions. The experienced designer applies a variety of paradigms as need dictates.

2.7 Generic Programming

Someone who wants a stack is unlikely always to want a stack of characters. A stack is a general concept, independent of the notion of a character. Consequently, it ought to be represented independently.

More generally, if an algorithm can be expressed independently of representation details and if it can be done so affordably and without logical contortions, it ought to be done so.

The programming paradigm is:

> *Decide which algorithms you want;*
> *parameterize them so that they work for*
> *a variety of suitable types and data structures.*

2.7.1 Containers

We can generalize a stack-of-characters type to a stack-of-anything type by making it a *template* and replacing the specific type *char* with a template parameter. For example:

```
template<class T> class Stack {
    T* v;
    int max_size;
    int top;
public:
    class Underflow { };
    class Overflow { };

    Stack(int s);    // constructor
    ~Stack();        // destructor

    void push(T);
    T pop();
};
```

The *template<class T>* prefix makes *T* a parameter of the declaration it prefixes.

The member functions might be defined similarly:

```
template<class T> void Stack<T>::push(T c)
{
    if (top == max_size) throw Overflow();
    v[top] = c;
    top = top + 1;
}
```

```
template<class T> T Stack<T>::pop()
{
    if (top == 0) throw Underflow();
    top = top - 1;
    return v[top];
}
```

Given these definitions, we can use stacks like this:

```
Stack<char> sc(200);            // stack of 200 characters
Stack<complex> scplx(30);       // stack of 30 complex numbers
Stack< list<int> > sli(45);     // stack of 45 lists of integers

void f()
{
    sc.push('c');
    if (sc.pop() != 'c') throw Bad_pop();

    scplx.push(complex(1,2));
    if (scplx.pop() != complex(1,2)) throw Bad_pop();
}
```

Similarly, we can define lists, vectors, maps (that is, associative arrays), etc., as templates. A class holding a collection of elements of some type is commonly called a *container class*, or simply a *container*.

Templates are a compile-time mechanism so that their use incurs no run-time overhead compared to "hand-written code."

2.7.2 Generic Algorithms

The C++ standard library provides a variety of containers, and users can write their own (Chapter 3, Chapter 17, Chapter 18). Thus, we find that we can apply the generic programming paradigm once more to parameterize algorithms by containers. For example, we want to sort, copy, and search *vectors*, *lists*, and arrays without having to write *sort*(), *copy*(), and *search*() functions for each container. We also don't want to convert to a specific data structure accepted by a single sort function. Therefore, we must find a generalized way of defining our containers that allows us to manipulate one without knowing exactly which kind of container it is.

One approach, the approach taken for the containers and non-numerical algorithms in the C++ standard library (§3.8, Chapter 18) is to focus on the notion of a sequence and manipulate sequences through iterators.

Here is a graphical representation of the notion of a sequence:

A sequence has a beginning and an end. An iterator refers to an element, and provides an operation that makes the iterator refer to the next element of the sequence. The end of a sequence is an iterator that refers one beyond the last element of the sequence. The physical representation of "the end" may be a sentinel element, but it doesn't have to be. In fact, the point is that this notion of sequences covers a wide variety of representations, including lists and arrays.

We need some standard notation for operations such as "access an element through an iterator" and "make the iterator refer to the next element." The obvious choices (once you get the idea) are to use the dereference operator * to mean "access an element through an iterator" and the increment operator ++ to mean "make the iterator refer to the next element."

Given that, we can write code like this:

```
template<class In, class Out> void copy (In from, In too_far, Out to)
{
    while (from != too_far) {
        *to = *from;      // copy element pointed to
        ++to;             // next output
        ++from;           // next input
    }
}
```

This copies any container for which we can define iterators with the right syntax and semantics.

C++'s built-in, low-level array and pointer types have the right operations for that, so we can write

```
char vc1 [200]; // array of 200 characters
char vc2 [500]; // array of 500 characters

void f()
{
    copy (&vc1 [0], &vc1 [200], &vc2 [0]);
}
```

This copies *vc1* from its first element until its last into *vc2* starting at *vc2*'s first element.

All standard library containers (§16.3, Chapter 17) support this notion of iterators and sequences.

Two template parameters *In* and *Out* are used to indicate the types of the source and the target instead of a single argument. This was done because we often want to copy from one kind of container into another. For example:

```
complex ac [200];

void g (vector<complex>& vc, list<complex>& lc)
{
    copy (&ac [0], &ac [200], lc.begin());
    copy (lc.begin(), lc.end(), vc.begin());
}
```

This copies the array to the *list* and the *list* to the *vector*. For a standard container, *begin*() is an iterator pointing to the first element.

2.8 Postscript

No programming language is perfect. Fortunately, a programming language does not have to be perfect to be a good tool for building great systems. In fact, a general-purpose programming language cannot be perfect for all of the many tasks to which it is put. What is perfect for one task is often seriously flawed for another because perfection in one area implies specialization. Thus, C++ was designed to be a good tool for building a wide variety of systems and to allow a wide variety of ideas to be expressed directly.

Not everything can be expressed directly using the built-in features of a language. In fact, that isn't even the ideal. Language features exist to support a variety of programming styles and techniques. Consequently, the task of learning a language should focus on mastering the native and natural styles for that language − not on the understanding of every little detail of all the language features.

In practical programming, there is little advantage in knowing the most obscure language features or for using the largest number of features. A single language feature in isolation is of little interest. Only in the context provided by techniques and by other features does the feature acquire meaning and interest. Thus, when reading the following chapters, please remember that the real purpose of examining the details of C++ is to be able to use them in concert to support good programming style in the context of sound designs.

2.9 Advice

[1] Don't panic! All will become clear in time; §2.1.
[2] You don't have to know every detail of C++ to write good programs; §1.7.
[3] Focus on programming techniques, not on language features; §2.1.

3

A Tour of the Standard Library

Why waste time learning
when ignorance is instantaneous?
– Hobbes

Standard libraries — output — strings — input — vectors — range checking — lists — maps — container overview — algorithms — iterators — I/O iterators — traversals and predicates — algorithms using member functions — algorithm overview — complex numbers — vector arithmetic— standard library overview — advice.

3.1 Introduction

No significant program is written in just a bare programming language. First, a set of supporting libraries are developed. These then form the basis for further work.

Continuing Chapter 2, this chapter gives a quick tour of key library facilities to give you an idea what can be done using C++ and its standard library. Useful library types, such as *string*, *vector*, *list*, and *map*, are presented as well as the most common ways of using them. Doing this allows me to give better examples and to set better exercises in the following chapters. As in Chapter 2, you are strongly encouraged not to be distracted or discouraged by an incomplete understanding of details. The purpose of this chapter is to give you a taste of what is to come and to convey an understanding of the simplest uses of the most useful library facilities. A more detailed introduction to the standard library is given in §16.1.2.

The standard library facilities described in this book are part of every complete C++ implementation. In addition to the standard C++ library, most implementations offer "graphical user interface" systems, often referred to as GUIs or window systems, for interaction between a user and a program. Similarly, most application development environments provide "foundation libraries" that support corporate or industrial "standard" development and/or execution environments. I do not describe such systems and libraries. The intent is to provide a self-contained description of C++

as defined by the standard and to keep the examples portable, except where specifically noted. Naturally, a programmer is encouraged to explore the more extensive facilities available on most systems, but that is left to exercises.

3.2 Hello, world!

The minimal C++ program is

```
int main() { }
```

It defines a function called *main*, which takes no arguments and does nothing.

Every C++ program must have a function named *main*(). The program starts by executing that function. The *int* value returned by *main*(), if any, is the program's return value to "the system." If no value is returned, the system will receive a value indicating successful completion. A nonzero value from *main*() indicates failure.

Typically, a program produces some output. Here is a program that writes out *Hello, world*!:

```
#include <iostream>

int main()
{
    std::cout << "Hello, world!\n";
}
```

The line *#include <iostream>* instructs the compiler to *include* the declarations of the standard stream I/O facilities as found in *iostream*. Without these declarations, the expression

```
std::cout << "Hello, world!\n"
```

would make no sense. The operator << ("put to") writes its second argument onto its first. In this case, the string literal "*Hello, world*!\n" is written onto the standard output stream *std::cout*. A string literal is a sequence of characters surrounded by double quotes. In a string literal, the backslash character \ followed by another character denotes a single special character. In this case, \n is the newline character, so that the characters written are *Hello, world*! followed by a newline.

3.3 The Standard Library Namespace

The standard library is defined in a namespace (§2.4, §8.2) called *std*. That is why I wrote *std::cout* rather than plain *cout*. I was being explicit about using the *standard cout*, rather than some other *cout*.

Every standard library facility is provided through some standard header similar to *<iostream>*. For example:

```
#include<string>
#include<list>
```

This makes the standard *string* and *list* available. To use them, the *std::* prefix can be used:

```
std::string s = "Four legs Good; two legs Baaad!";
std::list<std::string> slogans;
```

For simplicity, I will rarely use the *std::* prefix explicitly in examples. Neither will I always *#include* the necessary headers explicitly. To compile and run the program fragments here, you must *#include* the appropriate headers (as listed in §3.7.5, §3.8.6, and Chapter 16). In addition, you must either use the *std::* prefix or make every name from *std* global (§8.2.3). For example:

```
#include<string>            // make the standard string facilities accessible
using namespace std;        // make std names available without std:: prefix

string s = "Ignorance is bliss!";   // ok: string is std::string
```

It is generally in poor taste to dump every name from a namespace into the global namespace. However, to keep short the program fragments used to illustrate language and library features, I omit repetitive *#include*s and *std::* qualifications. In this book, I use the standard library almost exclusively, so if a name from the standard library is used, it either is a use of what the standard offers or part of an explanation of how the standard facility might be defined.

3.4 Output

The iostream library defines output for every built-in type. Further, it is easy to define output of a user-defined type. By default, values output to *cout* are converted to a sequence of characters. For example,

```
void f()
{
    cout << 10;
}
```

will place the character *1* followed by the character *0* on the standard output stream. So will

```
void g()
{
    int i = 10;
    cout << i;
}
```

Output of different types can be combined in the obvious way:

```
void h(int i)
{
    cout << "the value of i is ";
    cout << i;
    cout << '\n';
}
```

If *i* has the value *10*, the output will be

```
the value of i is 10
```

A character constant is a character enclosed in single quotes. Note that a character constant is output as a character rather than as a numerical value. For example,

```
void k()
{
    cout << 'a';
    cout << 'b';
    cout << 'c';
}
```

will output *abc*.

People soon tire of repeating the name of the output stream when outputting several related items. Fortunately, the result of an output expression can itself be used for further output. For example:

```
void h2(int i)
{
    cout << "the value of i is " << i << '\n';
}
```

This is equivalent to *h( )*. Streams are explained in more detail in Chapter 21.

3.5 Strings

The standard library provides a *string* type to complement the string literals used earlier. The *string* type provides a variety of useful string operations, such as concatenation. For example:

```
string s1 = "Hello";
string s2 = "world";

void m1()
{
    string s3 = s1 + ", " + s2 + "!\n";

    cout << s3;
}
```

Here, *s3* is initialized to the character sequence

Hello, world!

followed by a newline. Addition of strings means concatenation. You can add strings, string literals, and characters to a string.

In many applications, the most common form of concatenation is adding something to the end of a string. This is directly supported by the += operation. For example:

```
void m2(string& s1, string& s2)
{
    s1 = s1 + '\n';  // append newline
    s2 += '\n';      // append newline
}
```

The two ways of adding to the end of a string are semantically equivalent, but I prefer the latter because it is more concise and likely to be more efficiently implemented.

Naturally, *string*s can be compared against each other and against string literals. For example:

```
string incantation;

void respond(const string& answer)
{
    if (answer == incantation) {
        // perform magic
    }
    else if (answer == "yes") {
        // ...
    }
    // ...
}
```

The standard library string class is described in Chapter 20. Among other useful features, it provides the ability to manipulate substrings. For example:

```
string name = "Niels Stroustrup";

void m3()
{
    string s = name.substr(6,10);          // s = "Stroustrup"
    name.replace(0,5,"Nicholas");          // name becomes "Nicholas Stroustrup"
}
```

The *substr*() operation returns a string that is a copy of the substring indicated by its arguments. The first argument is an index into the string (a position), and the second argument is the length of the desired substring. Since indexing starts from *0*, *s* gets the value *Stroustrup*.

The *replace*() operation replaces a substring with a value. In this case, the substring starting at *0* with length *5* is *Niels*; it is replaced by *Nicholas*. Thus, the final value of *name* is *Nicholas Stroustrup*. Note that the replacement string need not be the same size as the substring that it is replacing.

3.5.1 C-Style Strings

A C-style string is a zero-terminated array of characters (§5.2.2). As shown, we can easily enter a C-style string into a *string*. To call functions that take C-style strings, we need to be able to extract the value of a *string* in the form of a C-style string. The *c_str*() function does that (§20.3.7). For example, we can print the *name* using the C output function *printf*() (§21.8) like this:

```
void f()
{
    printf("name: %s\n", name.c_str());
}
```

3.6 Input

The standard library offers *istream*s for input. Like *ostream*s, *istream*s deal with character string representations of built-in types and can easily be extended to cope with user-defined types.

The operator >> (''get from'') is used as an input operator; *cin* is the standard input stream. The type of the right-hand operand of >> determines what input is accepted and what is the target of the input operation. For example,

```
void f()
{
    int i;
    cin >> i;   // read an integer into i

    double d;
    cin >> d;   // read a double-precision, floating-point number into d
}
```

reads a number, such as *1234*, from the standard input into the integer variable *i* and a floating-point number, such as *12.34e5*, into the double-precision, floating-point variable *d*.

Here is an example that performs inch-to-centimeter and centimeter-to-inch conversions. You input a number followed by a character indicating the unit: centimeters or inches. The program then outputs the corresponding value in the other unit:

```
int main()
{
    const float factor = 2.54;  // 1 inch equals 2.54 cm
    float x, in, cm;
    char ch = 0;

    cout << "enter length: ";

    cin >> x;           // read a floating-point number
    cin >> ch;          // read a suffix

    switch (ch) {
    case 'i':           // inch
        in = x;
        cm = x*factor;
        break;
    case 'c':           // cm
        in = x/factor;
        cm = x;
        break;
    default:
        in = cm = 0;
        break;
    }

    cout << in << " in = " << cm << " cm\n";
}
```

The *switch-statement* tests a value against a set of constants. The *break-statement*s are used to exit the *switch-statement*. The case constants must be distinct. If the value tested does not match any of them, the *default* is chosen. The programmer need not provide a *default*.

Often, we want to read a sequence of characters. A convenient way of doing that is to read into a *string*. For example:

```
int main()
{
    string str;

    cout << "Please enter your name\n";
    cin >> str;
    cout << "Hello, " << str << "!\n";
}
```

If you type in

Eric

the response is

Hello, Eric!

By default, a whitespace character (§5.2.2) such as a space terminates the read, so if you enter

Eric Bloodaxe

pretending to be the ill-fated king of York, the response is still

Hello, Eric!

You can read a whole line using the *getline*() function. For example:

```
int main()
{
    string str;

    cout << "Please enter your name\n";
    getline(cin, str);
    cout << "Hello, " << str << "!\n";
}
```

With this program, the input

Eric Bloodaxe

yields the desired output:

Hello, Eric Bloodaxe!

The standard strings have the nice property of expanding to hold what you put in them, so if you enter a couple of megabytes of semicolons, the program will echo pages of semicolons back at you — unless your machine or operating system runs out of some critical resource first.

3.7 Containers

Much computing involves creating collections of various forms of objects and then manipulating such collections. Reading characters into a string and printing out the string is a simple example. A class with the main purpose of holding objects is commonly called a *container*. Providing suitable containers for a given task and supporting them with useful fundamental operations are important steps in the construction of any program.

To illustrate the standard library's most useful containers, consider a simple program for keeping names and telephone numbers. This is the kind of program for which different approaches appear "simple and obvious" to people of different backgrounds.

3.7.1 Vector

For many C programmers, a built-in array of (name,number) pairs would seem to be a suitable starting point:

```
struct Entry {
    string name;
    int number;
};

Entry phone_book[1000];

void print_entry(int i)      // simple use
{
    cout << phone_book[i].name << ' ' << phone_book[i].number << '\n';
}
```

However, a built-in array has a fixed size. If we choose a large size, we waste space; if we choose a smaller size, the array will overflow. In either case, we will have to write low-level memory-management code. The standard library provides a *vector* (§16.3) that takes care of that:

```
vector<Entry> phone_book(1000);

void print_entry(int i)      // simple use, exactly as for array
{
    cout << phone_book[i].name << ' ' << phone_book[i].number << '\n';
}

void add_entries(int n) // increase size by n
{
    phone_book.resize(phone_book.size()+n);
}
```

The *vector* member function *size*() gives the number of elements.

Note the use of parentheses in the definition of *phone_book*. We made a single object of type *vector<Entry>* and supplied its initial size as an initializer. This is very different from declaring a built-in array:

```
vector<Entry> book(1000);      // vector of 1000 elements
vector<Entry> books[1000];     // 1000 empty vectors
```

Should you make the mistake of using [ ] where you meant ( ) when declaring a *vector*, your compiler will almost certainly catch the mistake and issue an error message when you try to use the *vector*.

A *vector* is a single object that can be assigned. For example:

```
void f(vector<Entry>& v)
{
        vector<Entry> v2 = phone_book;
        v = v2;
        // ...
}
```

Assigning a *vector* involves copying its elements. Thus, after the initialization and assignment in *f*( ), *v* and *v2* each holds a separate copy of every *Entry* in the phone book. When a *vector* holds many elements, such innocent-looking assignments and initializations can be prohibitively expensive. Where copying is undesirable, references or pointers should be used.

3.7.2 Range Checking

The standard library *vector* does not provide range checking by default (§16.3.3). For example:

```
void f()
{
        int i = phone_book[1001].number;   // 1001 is out of range
        // ...
}
```

The initialization is likely to place some random value in *i* rather than giving an error. This is undesirable, so I will use a simple range-checking adaptation of *vector*, called *Vec*, in the following chapters. A *Vec* is like a *vector*, except that it throws an exception of type *out_of_range* if a subscript is out of range.

Techniques for implementing types such as *Vec* and for using exceptions effectively are discussed in §11.12, §8.3, and Chapter 14. However, the definition here is sufficient for the examples in this book:

```
template<class T> class Vec : public vector<T> {
public:
        Vec() : vector<T>() { }
        Vec(int s) : vector<T>(s) { }

        T& operator[](int i) { return at(i); }              // range-checked
        const T& operator[](int i) const { return at(i); }  // range-checked
};
```

The *at*( ) operation is a *vector* subscript operation that throws an exception of type *out_of_range* if its argument is out of the *vector*'s range (§16.3.3).

Returning to the problem of keeping names and telephone numbers, we can now use a *Vec* to ensure that out-of-range accesses are caught. For example:

```
Vec<Entry> phone_book(1000);
```

```
void print_entry(int i)      // simple use, exactly as for vector
{
    cout << phone_book[i].name << ´ ´ << phone_book[i].number << ´\n´;
}
```

An out-of-range access will throw an exception that the user can catch. For example:

```
void f()
{
    try {
        for (int i = 0; i<10000; i++) print_entry(i);
    }
    catch (out_of_range) {
        cout << "range error\n";
    }
}
```

The exception will be thrown, and then caught, when *phone_book*[*i*] is tried with *i==1000*.
If the user doesn't catch this kind of exception, the program will terminate in a well-defined manner
rather than proceeding or failing in an undefined manner. One way to minimize surprises from
exceptions is to use a *main*() with a *try-block* as its body:

```
int main()
try {
    // your code
}
catch (out_of_range) {
    cerr << "range error\n";
}
catch (...) {
    cerr << "unknown exception thrown\n";
}
```

This provides default exception handlers so that if we fail to catch some exception, an error message is printed on the standard error-diagnostic output stream *cerr* (§21.2.1).

3.7.3 List

Insertion and deletion of phone book entries could be common. Therefore, a list could be more
appropriate than a vector for representing a simple phone book. For example:

```
list<Entry> phone_book;
```

When we use a list, we tend not to access elements using subscripting the way we commonly do for
vectors. Instead, we might search the list looking for an element with a given value. To do this, we
take advantage of the fact that a *list* is a sequence as described in §3.8:

```
void print_entry(const string& s)
{
    typedef list<Entry>::const_iterator LI;
```

```
for (LI  i = phone_book.begin(); i != phone_book.end(); ++i) {
    const Entry& e = *i;  // reference used as shorthand
    if (s == e.name) {
        cout << e.name << ' ' << e.number << '\n';
        return;
    }
}
```

The search for *s* starts at the beginning of the list and proceeds until either *s* is found or the end is reached. Every standard library container provides the functions *begin* ( ) and *end* ( ), which return an iterator to the first and to one-past-the-last element, respectively (§16.3.2). Given an iterator *i*, the next element is *++i*. Given an iterator *i*, the element it refers to is **i*.

A user need not know the exact type of the iterator for a standard container. That iterator type is part of the definition of the container and can be referred to by name. When we don't need to modify an element of the container, *const_iterator* is the type we want. Otherwise, we use the plain *iterator* type (§16.3.1).

Adding elements to a *list* and removing elements from a *list* is easy:

```
void f(const Entry& e, list<Entry>::iterator i, list<Entry>::iterator p)
{
    phone_book.push_front(e);    // add at beginning
    phone_book.push_back(e);     // add at end
    phone_book.insert(i,e);      // add before the element referred to by 'i'

    phone_book.erase(p);         // remove the element referred to by 'p'
}
```

For a more complete description of *insert* ( ) and *erase* ( ), see §16.3.6.

3.7.4 Map

Writing code to look up a name in a list of (name,number) pairs is really quite tedious. In addition, a linear search is quite inefficient for all but the shortest lists. Other data structures directly support insertion, deletion, and searching based on values. In particular, the standard library provides the *map* type (§17.4.1). A *map* is a container of pairs of values. For example:

```
map<string, int> phone_book;
```

In other contexts, a *map* is known as an associative array or a dictionary.

When indexed by a value of its first type (called the *key*) a *map* returns the corresponding value of the second type (called the *value* or the *mapped type*). For example:

```
void print_entry(const string& s)
{
    if (int i = phone_book[s]) cout << s << ' ' << i << '\n';
}
```

If no match was found for the key *s*, a default value is returned from the *phone_book*. The default value for an integer type in a *map* is *0*. Here, I assume that *0* isn't a valid telephone number.

3.7.5 Standard Containers

A *map*, a *list*, and a *vector* can each be used to represent a phone book. However, each has strengths and weaknesses. For example, subscripting a *vector* is cheap and easy. On the other hand, inserting an element between two elements tends to be expensive. A *list* has exactly the opposite properties. A *map* resembles a *list* of (key,value) pairs except that it is optimized for finding values based on keys.

The standard library provides some of the most general and useful container types to allow the programmer to select a container that best serves the needs of an application:

Standard Container Summary	
vector<T>	A variable-sized vector (§16.3)
list<T>	A doubly-linked list (§17.2.2)
queue<T>	A queue (§17.3.2)
stack<T>	A stack (§17.3.1)
deque<T>	A double-ended queue (§17.2.3)
priority_queue<T>	A queue sorted by value (§17.3.3)
set<T>	A set (§17.4.3)
multiset<T>	A set in which a value can occur many times (§17.4.4)
map<key,val>	An associative array (§17.4.1)
multimap<key,val>	A map in which a key can occur many times (§17.4.2)

The standard containers are presented in §16.2, §16.3, and Chapter 17. The containers are defined in namespace *std* and presented in headers *<vector>*, *<list>*, *<map>*, etc. (§16.2).

The standard containers and their basic operations are designed to be similar from a notational point of view. Furthermore, the meanings of the operations are equivalent for the various containers. In general, basic operations apply to every kind of container. For example, *push_back*() can be used (reasonably efficiently) to add elements to the end of a *vector* as well as for a *list*, and every container has a *size*() member function that returns its number of elements.

This notational and semantic uniformity enables programmers to provide new container types that can be used in a very similar manner to the standard ones. The range-checked vector, *Vec* (§3.7.2), is an example of that. Chapter 17 demonstrates how a *hash_map* can be added to the framework. The uniformity of container interfaces also allows us to specify algorithms independently of individual container types.

3.8 Algorithms

A data structure, such as a list or a vector, is not very useful on its own. To use one, we need operations for basic access such as adding and removing elements. Furthermore, we rarely just store objects in a container. We sort them, print them, extract subsets, remove elements, search for objects, etc. Consequently, the standard library provides the most common algorithms for containers in addition to providing the most common container types. For example, the following sorts a *vector* and places a copy of each unique *vector* element on a *list*:

```
void f(vector<Entry>& ve, list<Entry>& le)
{
    sort(ve.begin(),ve.end());
    unique_copy(ve.begin(),ve.end(),le.begin());
}
```

The standard algorithms are described in Chapter 18. They are expressed in terms of sequences of elements (§2.7.2). A sequence is represented by a pair of iterators specifying the first element and the one-beyond-the-last element. In the example, *sort*() sorts the sequence from *ve.begin*() to *ve.end*() – which just happens to be all the elements of a *vector*. For writing, you need only to specify the first element to be written. If more than one element is written, the elements following that initial element will be overwritten.

If we wanted to add the new elements to the end of a container, we could have written:

```
void f(vector<Entry>& ve, list<Entry>& le)
{
    sort(ve.begin(),ve.end());
    unique_copy(ve.begin(),ve.end(),back_inserter(le));    // append to le
}
```

A *back_inserter*() adds elements at the end of a container, extending the container to make room for them (§19.2.4). Thus, the standard containers plus *back_inserter*()s eliminate the need to use error-prone, explicit C-style memory management using *realloc*() (§16.3.5). Forgetting to use a *back_inserter*() when appending can lead to errors. For example:

```
void f(vector<Entry>& ve, list<Entry>& le)
{
    copy(ve.begin(),ve.end(),le);            // error: le not an iterator
    copy(ve.begin(),ve.end(),le.end());      // bad: writes beyond the end
    copy(ve.begin(),ve.end(),le.begin());    // overwrite elements
}
```

3.8.1 Use of Iterators

When you first encounter a container, a few iterators referring to useful elements can be obtained; *begin*() and *end*() are the best examples of this. In addition, many algorithms return iterators. For example, the standard algorithm *find* looks for a value in a sequence and returns an iterator to the element found. Using *find*, we can count the number of occurrences of a character in a *string*:

```
int count(const string& s, char c)    // count occurrences of c in s
{
    int n = 0;
    string::const_iterator i = find(s.begin(),s.end(),c);
    while (i != s.end()) {
        ++n;
        i = find(i+1,s.end(),c);
    }
    return n;
}
```

The *find* algorithm returns an iterator to the first occurrence of a value in a sequence or the one-past-the-end iterator. Consider what happens for a simple call of *count*:

```
void f()
{
    string m = "Mary had a little lamb";
    int a_count = count(m, 'a');
}
```

The first call to *find*() finds the *'a'* in *Mary*. Thus, the iterator points to that character and not to *s.end*(), so we enter the loop. In the loop, we start the search at *i+1*; that is, we start one past where we found the *'a'*. We then loop finding the other three *'a'*s. That done, *find*() reaches the end and returns *s.end*() so that the condition *i!=s.end*() fails and we exit the loop.

That call of *count*() could be graphically represented like this:

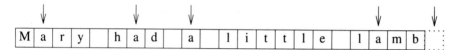

The arrows indicate the initial, intermediate, and final values of the iterator *i*.

Naturally, the *find* algorithm will work equivalently on every standard container. Consequently, we could generalize the *count*() function in the same way:

```
template<class C, class T> int count(const C& v, T val)
{
    typename C::const_iterator i = find(v.begin(), v.end(), val);  // "typename;" see §C.13.5
    int n = 0;
    while (i != v.end()) {
        ++n;
        ++i; // skip past the element we just found
        i = find(i, v.end(), val);
    }
    return n;
}
```

This works, so we can say:

```
void f(list<complex>& lc, vector<string>& vs, string s)
{
    int i1 = count(lc, complex(1,3));
    int i2 = count(vs, "Diogenes");
    int i3 = count(s, 'x');
}
```

However, we don't have to define a *count* template. Counting occurrences of an element is so generally useful that the standard library provides that algorithm. To be fully general, the standard library *count* takes a sequence as its argument, rather than a container, so we would say:

```
void f(list<complex>& lc, vector<string>& vs, string s)
{
    int i1 = count(lc.begin(),lc.end(),complex(1,3));
    int i2 = count(vs.begin(),vs.end(),"Diogenes");
    int i3 = count(s.begin(),s.end(),'x');
}
```

The use of a sequence allows us to use *count* for a built-in array and also to count parts of a container. For example:

```
void g(char cs[], int sz)
{
    int i1 = count(&cs[0],&cs[sz],'z');      // 'z's in array
    int i2 = count(&cs[0],&cs[sz/2],'z');    // 'z's in first half of array
}
```

3.8.2 Iterator Types

What are iterators really? Any particular iterator is an object of some type. There are, however, many different iterator types because an iterator needs to hold the information necessary for doing its job for a particular container type. These iterator types can be as different as the containers and the specialized needs they serve. For example, a *vector*'s iterator is most likely an ordinary pointer because a pointer is quite a reasonable way of referring to an element of a *vector*:

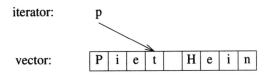

Alternatively, a *vector* iterator could be implemented as a pointer to the *vector* plus an index:

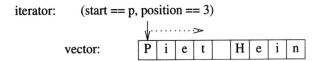

Using such an iterator would allow range checking (§19.3).

   A list iterator must be something more complicated than a simple pointer to an element because an element of a list in general does not know where the next element of that list is. Thus, a list iterator might be a pointer to a link:

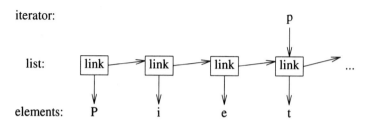

What is common for all iterators is their semantics and the naming of their operations. For example, applying ++ to any iterator yields an iterator that refers to the next element. Similarly, * yields the element to which the iterator refers. In fact, any object that obeys a few simple rules like these is an iterator (§19.2.1). Furthermore, users rarely need to know the type of a specific iterator; each container "knows" its iterator types and makes them available under the conventional names *iterator* and *const_iterator*. For example, *list<Entry>::iterator* is the general iterator type for *list<Entry>*. I rarely have to worry about the details of how that type is defined.

3.8.3 Iterators and I/O

Iterators are a general and useful concept for dealing with sequences of elements in containers. However, containers are not the only place where we find sequences of elements. For example, an input stream produces a sequence of values and we write a sequence of values to an output stream. Consequently, the notion of iterators can be usefully applied to input and output.

   To make an *ostream_iterator*, we need to specify which stream will be used and the type of objects written to it. For example, we can define an iterator that refers to the standard output stream, *cout*:

```
ostream_iterator<string> oo (cout);
```

The effect of assigning to **oo* is to write the assigned value to *cout*. For example:

```
int main ()
{
    *oo = "Hello, ";     // meaning cout << "Hello, "
    ++oo;
    *oo = "world!\n";    // meaning cout << "world!\n"
}
```

This is yet another way of writing the canonical message to standard output. The *++oo* is done to mimic writing into an array through a pointer. This way wouldn't be my first choice for that simple task, but the utility of treating output as a write-only container will soon be obvious – if it isn't already.

   Similarly, an *istream_iterator* is something that allows us to treat an input stream as a read-only container. Again, we must specify the stream to be used and the type of values expected:

```
istream_iterator<string> ii (cin);
```

Because input iterators invariably appear in pairs representing a sequence, we must provide an *istream_iterator* to indicate the end of input. This is the default *istream_iterator*:

```
istream_iterator<string> eos;
```

We could now read *Hello, world*! from input and write it out again like this:

```
int main()
{
    string s1 = *ii;
    ++ii;
    string s2 = *ii;

    cout << s1 << ' ' << s2 << '\n';
}
```

Actually, *istream_iterator*s and *ostream_iterator*s are not meant to be used directly. Instead, they are typically provided as arguments to algorithms. For example, we can write a simple program to read a file, sort the words read, eliminate duplicates, and write the result to another file:

```
int main()
{
    string from, to;
    cin >> from >> to;                          // get source and target file names

    ifstream is (from.c_str());                 // input stream (c_str(); see §3.5.1 and §20.3.7)
    istream_iterator<string> ii (is);           // input iterator for stream
    istream_iterator<string> eos;               // input sentinel

    vector<string> b (ii, eos);                 // b is a vector initialized from input
    sort (b.begin(), b.end());                  // sort the buffer

    ofstream os (to.c_str());                   // output stream
    ostream_iterator<string> oo (os, "\n");     // output iterator for stream

    unique_copy (b.begin(), b.end(), oo);       // copy buffer to output,
                                                // discard replicated values

    return !is.eof() || !os;                    // return error state (§3.2, §21.3.3)
}
```

An *ifstream* is an *istream* that can be attached to a file, and an *ofstream* is an *ostream* that can be attached to a file. The *ostream_iterator*'s second argument is used to delimit output values.

3.8.4 Traversals and Predicates

Iterators allow us to write loops to iterate through a sequence. However, writing loops can be tedious, so the standard library provides ways for a function to be called for each element of a sequence.

Consider writing a program that reads words from input and records the frequency of their occurrence. The obvious representation of the strings and their associated frequencies is a *map*:

```
map<string, int> histogram;
```

The obvious action to be taken for each string to record its frequency is:

```
void  record (const  string& s)
{
     histogram [s] ++ ;        // record frequency of "s"
}
```

Once the input has been read, we would like to output the data we have gathered. The *map* consists
of a sequence of (string,int) pairs. Consequently, we would like to call

```
void  print (const  pair<const  string , int>& r)
{
     cout << r.first << ' ' << r.second << '\n' ;
}
```

for each element in the map (the first element of a *pair* is called *first*, and the second element is
called *second*). The first element of the *pair* is a *const string* rather than a plain *string* because all
map keys are constants.

Thus, the main program becomes:

```
int  main ( )
{
     istream_iterator<string> ii (cin) ;
     istream_iterator<string> eos ;

     for_each (ii , eos , record) ;
     for_each (histogram.begin ( ) , histogram.end ( ) , print) ;
}
```

Note that we don't need to sort the *map* to get the output in order. A *map* keeps its elements
ordered so that an iteration traverses the *map* in (increasing) order.

Many programming tasks involve looking for something in a container rather than simply doing
something to every element. For example, the *find* algorithm (§18.5.2) provides a convenient way
of looking for a specific value. A more general variant of this idea looks for an element that fulfills
a specific requirement. For example, we might want to search a *map* for the first value larger than
42. A *map* is a sequence of (key,value) pairs, so we search that list for a *pair<const string , int>*
where the *int* is greater than *42*:

```
bool  gt_42 (const  pair<const  string , int>& r)
{
     return  r.second>42 ;
}

void  f (map<string , int>& m)
{
     typedef  map<string , int> :: const_iterator  MI ;
     MI  i = find_if (m.begin ( ) , m.end ( ) , gt_42) ;
     // ...
}
```

Alternatively, we could count the number of words with a frequency higher than 42:

```
void g(const map<string,int>& m)
{
    int c42 = count_if(m.begin(),m.end(),gt_42);
    // ...
}
```

A function, such as *gt_42*(), that is used to control the algorithm is called a *predicate*. A predicate is called for each element and returns a Boolean value, which the algorithm uses to perform its intended action. For example, *find_if*() searches until its predicate returns *true* to indicate that an element of interest has been found. Similarly, *count_if*() counts the number of times its predicate is *true*.

The standard library provides a few useful predicates and some templates that are useful for creating more (§18.4.2).

3.8.5 Algorithms Using Member Functions

Many algorithms apply a function to elements of a sequence. For example, in §3.8.4

```
for_each(ii,eos,record);
```

calls *record*() for each string read from input.

Often, we deal with containers of pointers and we really would like to call a member function of the object pointed to, rather than a global function on the pointer. For example, we might want to call the member function *Shape*::*draw*() for each element of a *list<Shape*>*. To handle this specific example, we simply write a nonmember function that invokes the member function. For example:

```
void draw(Shape* p)
{
    p->draw();
}

void f(list<Shape*>& sh)
{
    for_each(sh.begin(),sh.end(),draw);
}
```

By generalizing this technique, we can write the example like this:

```
void g(list<Shape*>& sh)
{
    for_each(sh.begin(),sh.end(),mem_fun(&Shape::draw));
}
```

The standard library *mem_fun*() template (§18.4.4.2) takes a pointer to a member function (§15.5) as its argument and produces something that can be called for a pointer to the member's class. The result of *mem_fun*(&*Shape*::*draw*) takes a *Shape** argument and returns whatever *Shape*::*draw*() returns.

The *mem_fun*() mechanism is important because it allows the standard algorithms to be used for containers of polymorphic objects.

3.8.6 Standard Library Algorithms

What is an algorithm? A general definition of an algorithm is ''a finite set of rules which gives a sequence of operations for solving a specific set of problems [and] has five important features: Finiteness ... Definiteness ... Input ... Output ... Effectiveness'' [Knuth,1968,§1.1]. In the context of the C++ standard library, an algorithm is a set of templates operating on sequences of elements.

The standard library provides dozens of algorithms. The algorithms are defined in namespace *std* and presented in the *<algorithm>* header. Here are a few I have found particularly useful:

Selected Standard Algorithms	
for_each()	Invoke function for each element (§18.5.1)
find()	Find first occurrence of arguments (§18.5.2)
find_if()	Find first match of predicate (§18.5.2)
count()	Count occurrences of element (§18.5.3)
count_if()	Count matches of predicate (§18.5.3)
replace()	Replace element with new value (§18.6.4)
replace_if()	Replace element that matches predicate with new value (§18.6.4)
copy()	Copy elements (§18.6.1)
unique_copy()	Copy elements that are not duplicates (§18.6.1)
sort()	Sort elements (§18.7.1)
equal_range()	Find all elements with equivalent values (§18.7.2)
merge()	Merge sorted sequences (§18.7.3)

These algorithms, and many more (see Chapter 18), can be applied to elements of containers, *strings*, and built-in arrays.

3.9 Math

Like C, C++ wasn't designed primarily with numerical computation in mind. However, a lot of numerical work is done in C++, and the standard library reflects that.

3.9.1 Complex Numbers

The standard library supports a family of complex number types along the lines of the *complex* class described in §2.5.2. To support complex numbers where the scalars are single-precision, floating-point numbers (*floats*), double precision numbers (*doubles*), etc., the standard library *complex* is a template:

```
template<class scalar> class complex {
public:
    complex(scalar re, scalar im);
    // ...
};
```

The usual arithmetic operations and the most common mathematical functions are supported for complex numbers. For example:

```
// standard exponentiation function from <complex>:
template<class  C> complex<C> pow (const  complex<C>&, int);

void f(complex<float> fl, complex<double> db)
{
     complex<long  double> ld = fl+sqrt (db);
     db += fl*3;
     fl = pow (1/fl, 2);
     // ...
}
```

For more details, see §22.5.

3.9.2 Vector Arithmetic

The *vector* described in §3.7.1 was designed to be a general mechanism for holding values, to be flexible, and to fit into the architecture of containers, iterators, and algorithms. However, it does not support mathematical vector operations. Adding such operations to *vector* would be easy, but its generality and flexibility precludes optimizations that are often considered essential for serious numerical work. Consequently, the standard library provides a vector, called *valarray*, that is less general and more amenable to optimization for numerical computation:

```
template<class  T> class  valarray {
     // ...
     T& operator[] (size_t);
     // ...
};
```

The type *size_t* is the unsigned integer type that the implementation uses for array indices.

The usual arithmetic operations and the most common mathematical functions are supported for *valarray*s. For example:

```
// standard absolute value function from <valarray>:
template<class  T> valarray<T> abs (const  valarray<T>&);

void f(valarray<double>& a1, valarray<double>& a2)
{
     valarray<double> a = a1*3.14+a2/a1;
     a2 += a1*3.14;
     a = abs (a);
     double  d = a2[7];
     // ...
}
```

For more details, see §22.4.

3.9.3 Basic Numeric Support

Naturally, the standard library contains the most common mathematical functions – such as *log* (), *pow* (), and *cos* () – for floating-point types; see §22.3. In addition, classes that describe the properties of built-in types – such as the maximum exponent of a *float* – are provided; see §22.2.

3.10 Standard Library Facilities

The facilities provided by the standard library can be classified like this:

[1] Basic run-time language support (e.g., for allocation and run-time type information); see §16.1.3.

[2] The C standard library (with very minor modifications to minimize violations of the type system); see §16.1.2.

[3] Strings and I/O streams (with support for international character sets and localization); see Chapter 20 and Chapter 21.

[4] A framework of containers (such as *vector*, *list*, and *map*) and algorithms using containers (such as general traversals, sorts, and merges); see Chapter 16, Chapter 17, Chapter 18, and Chapter 19.

[5] Support for numerical computation (complex numbers plus vectors with arithmetic operations, BLAS-like and generalized slices, and semantics designed to ease optimization); see Chapter 22.

The main criterion for including a class in the library was that it would somehow be used by almost every C++ programmer (both novices and experts), that it could be provided in a general form that did not add significant overhead compared to a simpler version of the same facility, and that simple uses should be easy to learn. Essentially, the C++ standard library provides the most common fundamental data structures together with the fundamental algorithms used on them.

Every algorithm works with every container without the use of conversions. This framework, conventionally called the STL [Stepanov,1994], is extensible in the sense that users can easily provide containers and algorithms in addition to the ones provided as part of the standard and have these work directly with the standard containers and algorithms.

3.11 Advice

[1] Don't reinvent the wheel; use libraries.

[2] Don't believe in magic; understand what your libraries do, how they do it, and at what cost they do it.

[3] When you have a choice, prefer the standard library to other libraries.

[4] Do not think that the standard library is ideal for everything.

[5] Remember to #*include* the headers for the facilities you use; §3.3.

[6] Remember that standard library facilities are defined in namespace *std*; §3.3.

[7] Use *string* rather than *char**; §3.5, §3.6.

[8] If in doubt use a range-checked vector (such as *Vec*); §3.7.2.

[9] Prefer *vector<T>*, *list<T>*, and *map<key, value>* to *T*[ ]; §3.7.1, §3.7.3, §3.7.4.

[10] When adding elements to a container, use *push_back* ( ) or *back_inserter* ( ) ; §3.7.3, §3.8.

[11] Use *push_back* ( ) on a *vector* rather than *realloc* ( ) on an array; §3.8.

[12] Catch common exceptions in *main* ( ) ; §3.7.2.

Part I

Basic Facilities

This part describes C++'s built-in types and the basic facilities for constructing programs out of them. The C subset of C++ is presented together with C++'s additional support for traditional styles of programming. It also discusses the basic facilities for composing a C++ program out of logical and physical parts.

Chapters

4   Types and Declarations
5   Pointers, Arrays, and Structures
6   Expressions and Statements
7   Functions
8   Namespaces and Exceptions
9   Source Files and Programs

4

Types and Declarations

Accept nothing short of perfection!
– anon

Perfection is achieved
only on the point of collapse.
– C. N. Parkinson

Types — fundamental types — Booleans — characters — character literals — integers — integer literals — floating-point types — floating-point literals — sizes — *void* — enumerations — declarations — names — scope — initialization — objects — *typedef*s — advice — exercises.

4.1 Types

Consider

```
x = y+f(2);
```

For this to make sense in a C++ program, the names *x*, *y*, and *f* must be suitably declared. That is, the programmer must specify that entities named *x*, *y*, and *f* exist and that they are of types for which = (assignment), + (addition), and ( ) (function call), respectively, are meaningful.

Every name (identifier) in a C++ program has a type associated with it. This type determines what operations can be applied to the name (that is, to the entity referred to by the name) and how such operations are interpreted. For example, the declarations

```
float x;          // x is a floating-point variable
int y = 7;        // y is an integer variable with the initial value 7
float f(int);     // f is a function taking an argument of type int and returning a floating-point number
```

would make the example meaningful. Because *y* is declared to be an *int*, it can be assigned to, used in arithmetic expressions, etc. On the other hand, *f* is declared to be a function that takes an *int* as its argument, so it can be called given a suitable argument.

This chapter presents fundamental types (§4.1.1) and declarations (§4.9). Its examples just demonstrate language features; they are not intended to do anything useful. More extensive and realistic examples are saved for later chapters after more of C++ has been described. This chapter simply provides the most basic elements from which C++ programs are constructed. You must know these elements, plus the terminology and simple syntax that goes with them, in order to complete a real project in C++ and especially to read code written by others. However, a thorough understanding of every detail mentioned in this chapter is not a requirement for understanding the following chapters. Consequently, you may prefer to skim through this chapter, observing the major concepts, and return later as the need for understanding of more details arises.

4.1.1 Fundamental Types

C++ has a set of fundamental types corresponding to the most common basic storage units of a computer and the most common ways of using them to hold data:

   §4.2   A Boolean type (*bool*)
   §4.3   Character types (such as *char*)
   §4.4   Integer types (such as *int*)
   §4.5   Floating-point types (such as *double*)

In addition, a user can define

   §4.8   Enumeration types for representing specific sets of values (*enum*)

There also is

   §4.7   A type, *void*, used to signify the absence of information

From these types, we can construct other types:

   §5.1   Pointer types (such as *int**)
   §5.2   Array types (such as *char* [ ])
   §5.5   Reference types (such as *double*&)
   §5.7   Data structures and classes (Chapter 10)

The Boolean, character, and integer types are collectively called *integral types*. The integral and floating-point types are collectively called *arithmetic types*. Enumerations and classes (Chapter 10) are called *user-defined types* because they must be defined by users rather than being available for use without previous declaration, the way fundamental types are. In contrast, other types are called *built-in types*.

The integral and floating-point types are provided in a variety of sizes to give the programmer a choice of the amount of storage consumed, the precision, and the range available for computations (§4.6). The assumption is that a computer provides bytes for holding characters, words for holding and computing integer values, some entity most suitable for floating-point computation, and addresses for referring to those entities. The C++ fundamental types together with pointers and arrays present these machine-level notions to the programmer in a reasonably implementation-independent manner.

For most applications, one could simply use *bool* for logical values, *char* for characters, *int* for integer values, and *double* for floating-point values. The remaining fundamental types are variations for optimizations and special needs that are best ignored until such needs arise. They must be known, however, to read old C and C++ code.

4.2 Booleans

A Boolean, *bool*, can have one of the two values *true* or *false*. A Boolean is used to express the results of logical operations. For example:

```
void f(int a, int b)
{
    bool b1 = a==b;      // = is assignment, == is equality
    // ...
}
```

If *a* and *b* have the same value, *b1* becomes *true*; otherwise, *b1* becomes *false*.

A common use of *bool* is as the type of the result of a function that tests some condition (a predicate). For example:

```
bool is_open(File*);

bool greater(int a, int b) { return a>b; }
```

By definition, *true* has the value *1* when converted to an integer and *false* has the value *0*. Conversely, integers can be implicitly converted to *bool* values: nonzero integers convert to *true* and *0* converts to *false*. For example:

```
bool b = 7;        // bool(7) is true, so b becomes true
int i = true;      // int(true) is 1, so i becomes 1
```

In arithmetic and logical expressions, *bool*s are converted to *int*s; integer arithmetic and logical operations are performed on the converted values. If the result is converted back to *bool*, a *0* is converted to *false* and a nonzero value is converted to *true*.

```
void g()
{
    bool a = true;
    bool b = true;

    bool x = a+b;    // a+b is 2, so x becomes true
    bool y = a|b;    // a|b is 1, so y becomes true
}
```

A pointer can be implicitly converted to a *bool* (§C.6.2.5). A nonzero pointer converts to *true*; zero-valued pointers convert to *false*.

4.3 Character Types

A variable of type *char* can hold a character of the implementation's character set. For example:

```
char ch = 'a';
```

Almost universally, a *char* has 8 bits so that it can hold one of 256 different values. Typically, the character set is a variant of ISO-646, for example ASCII, thus providing the characters appearing on your keyboard. Many problems arise from the fact that this set of characters is only partially standardized (§C.3).

Serious variations occur between character sets supporting different natural languages and also between different character sets supporting the same natural language in different ways. However, here we are interested only in how such differences affect the rules of C++. The larger and more interesting issue of how to program in a multi-lingual, multi-character-set environment is beyond the scope of this book, although it is alluded to in several places (§20.2, §21.7, §C.3.3).

It is safe to assume that the implementation character set includes the decimal digits, the 26 alphabetic characters of English, and some of the basic punctuation characters. It is not safe to assume that there are no more than 127 characters in an 8-bit character set (e.g., some sets provide 255 characters), that there are no more alphabetic characters than English provides (most European languages provide more), that the alphabetic characters are contiguous (EBCDIC leaves a gap between ´*i*´ and ´*j*´), or that every character used to write C++ is available (e.g., some national character sets do not provide { } [ ] | \; §C.3.1). Whenever possible, we should avoid making assumptions about the representation of objects. This general rule applies even to characters.

Each character constant has an integer value. For example, the value of ´*b*´ is *98* in the ASCII character set. Here is a small program that will tell you the integer value of any character you care to input:

```
#include <iostream>

int main()
{
    char c;
    std::cin >> c;
    std::cout << "the value of ´" << c << "´ is " << int(c) << '\n';
}
```

The notation *int (c)* gives the integer value for a character *c*. The possibility of converting a *char* to an integer raises the question: is a *char* signed or unsigned? The 256 values represented by an 8-bit byte can be interpreted as the values *0* to *255* or as the values *–127* to *127*. Unfortunately, which choice is made for a plain *char* is implementation-defined (§C.1, §C.3.4). C++ provides two types for which the answer is definite; *signed char*, which can hold at least the values *–127* to *127*, and *unsigned char*, which can hold at least the values *0* to *255*. Fortunately, the difference matters only for values outside the *0* to *127* range, and the most common characters are within that range.

Values outside that range stored in a plain *char* can lead to subtle portability problems. See §C.3.4 if you need to use more than one type of *char* or if you store integers in *char* variables.

A type *wchar_t* is provided to hold characters of a larger character set such as Unicode. It is a distinct type. The size of *wchar_t* is implementation-defined and large enough to hold the largest character set supported by the implementation's locale (see §21.7, §C.3.3). The strange name is a leftover from C. In C, *wchar_t* is a *typedef* (§4.9.7) rather than a built-in type. The suffix _*t* was added to distinguish standard *typedef*s.

Note that the character types are integral types (§4.1.1) so that arithmetic and logical operations (§6.2) apply.

4.3.1 Character Literals

A character literal, often called a character constant, is a character enclosed in single quotes, for example, *´a´* and *´0´*. The type of a character literal is *char*. Such character literals are really symbolic constants for the integer value of the characters in the character set of the machine on which the C++ program is to run. For example, if you are running on a machine using the ASCII character set, the value of *´0´* is *48*. The use of character literals rather than decimal notation makes programs more portable. A few characters also have standard names that use the backslash \ as an escape character. For example, *\n* is a newline and *\t* is a horizontal tab. See §C.3.2 for details about escape characters.

Wide character literals are of the form *L´ab´*, where the number of characters between the quotes and their meanings is implementation-defined to match the *wchar_t* type. A wide character literal has type *wchar_t*.

4.4 Integer Types

Like *char*, each integer type comes in three forms: "plain" *int*, *signed int*, and *unsigned int*. In addition, integers come in three sizes: *short int*, "plain" *int*, and *long int*. A *long int* can be referred to as plain *long*. Similarly, *short* is a synonym for *short int*, *unsigned* for *unsigned int*, and *signed* for *signed int*.

The *unsigned* integer types are ideal for uses that treat storage as a bit array. Using an *unsigned* instead of an *int* to gain one more bit to represent positive integers is almost never a good idea. Attempts to ensure that some values are positive by declaring variables *unsigned* will typically be defeated by the implicit conversion rules (§C.6.1, §C.6.2.1).

Unlike plain *char*s, plain *int*s are always signed. The signed *int* types are simply more explicit synonyms for their plain *int* counterparts.

4.4.1 Integer Literals

Integer literals come in four guises: decimal, octal, hexadecimal, and character literals (§A.3). Decimal literals are the most commonly used and look as you would expect them to:

> *7   1234   976   12345678901234567890*

The compiler ought to warn about literals that are too long to represent.

A literal starting with zero followed by *x* (*0x*) is a hexadecimal (base 16) number. A literal starting with zero but not followed by *x* is an octal (base 8) number. For example:

decimal:		*2*	*63*	*83*
octal:	*0*	*02*	*077*	*0123*
hexadecimal:	*0x0*	*0x2*	*0x3f*	*0x53*

The letters *a*, *b*, *c*, *d*, *e*, and *f*, or their uppercase equivalents, are used to represent *10, 11, 12, 13, 14*, and *15*, respectively. Octal and hexadecimal notations are most useful for expressing bit patterns. Using these notations to express genuine numbers can lead to surprises. For example, on a machine on which an *int* is represented as a two's complement 16-bit integer, *0xffff* is the negative decimal number *−1*. Had more bits been used to represent an integer, it would have been *65535*.

The suffix *U* can be used to write explicitly ***unsigned*** literals. Similarly, the suffix *L* can be used to write explicitly ***long*** literals. For example, *3* is an ***int***, 3U is an ***unsigned int***, and *3L* is a ***long int***. If no suffix is provided, the compiler gives an integer literal a suitable type based on its value and the implementation's integer sizes (§C.4).

It is a good idea to limit the use of nonobvious constants to a few well-commented ***const*** (§5.4) or enumerator (§4.8) initializers.

4.5 Floating-Point Types

The floating-point types represent floating-point numbers. Like integers, floating-point types come in three sizes: *float* (single-precision), ***double*** (double-precision), and *long double* (extended-precision).

The exact meaning of single-, double-, and extended-precision is implementation-defined. Choosing the right precision for a problem where the choice matters requires significant understanding of floating-point computation. If you don't have that understanding, get advice, take the time to learn, or use *double* and hope for the best.

4.5.1 Floating-Point Literals

By default, a floating-point literal is of type *double*. Again, a compiler ought to warn about floating-point literals that are too large to be represented. Here are some floating-point literals:

> *1.23   .23   0.23   1.   1.0   1.2e10   1.23e-15*

Note that a space cannot occur in the middle of a floating-point literal. For example, *65.43 e-21* is not a floating-point literal but rather four separate lexical tokens (causing a syntax error):

> *65.43   e   -   21*

If you want a floating-point literal of type *float*, you can define one using the suffix *f* or *F*:

> *3.14159265f   2.0f   2.997925F   2.9e-3f*

If you want a floating-point literal of type *long double*, you can define one using the suffix *l* or *L*:

> *3.14159265L   2.0L   2.997925L   2.9e-3L*

4.6 Sizes

Some of the aspects of C++'s fundamental types, such as the size of an *int*, are implementation-defined (§C.2). I point out these dependencies and often recommend avoiding them or taking steps to minimize their impact. Why should you bother? People who program on a variety of systems or use a variety of compilers care a lot because if they don't, they are forced to waste time finding and fixing obscure bugs. People who claim they don't care about portability usually do so because they use only a single system and feel they can afford the attitude that "the language is what my compiler implements." This is a narrow and shortsighted view. If your program is a success, it is likely to be ported, so someone will have to find and fix problems related to implementation-dependent features. In addition, programs often need to be compiled with other compilers for the same system, and even a future release of your favorite compiler may do some things differently from the current one. It is far easier to know and limit the impact of implementation dependencies when a program is written than to try to untangle the mess afterwards.

It is relatively easy to limit the impact of implementation-dependent language features. Limiting the impact of system-dependent library facilities is far harder. Using standard library facilities wherever feasible is one approach.

The reason for providing more than one integer type, more than one unsigned type, and more than one floating-point type is to allow the programmer to take advantage of hardware characteristics. On many machines, there are significant differences in memory requirements, memory access times, and computation speed between the different varieties of fundamental types. If you know a machine, it is usually easy to choose, for example, the appropriate integer type for a particular variable. Writing truly portable low-level code is harder.

Sizes of C++ objects are expressed in terms of multiples of the size of a *char*, so by definition the size of a *char* is *1*. The size of an object or type can be obtained using the *sizeof* operator (§6.2). This is what is guaranteed about sizes of fundamental types:

$1 \equiv sizeof(char) \leq sizeof(short) \leq sizeof(int) \leq sizeof(long)$

$1 \leq sizeof(bool) \leq sizeof(long)$

$sizeof(char) \leq sizeof(wchar\_t) \leq sizeof(long)$

$sizeof(float) \leq sizeof(double) \leq sizeof(long\ double)$

$sizeof(N) \equiv sizeof(signed\ N) \equiv sizeof(unsigned\ N)$

where *N* can be *char*, *short int*, *int*, or *long int*. In addition, it is guaranteed that a *char* has at least 8 bits, a *short* at least 16 bits, and a *long* at least 32 bits. A *char* can hold a character of the machine's character set.

Here is a graphical representation of a plausible set of fundamental types and a sample string:

char:	`'a'`
bool:	`1`
short:	`756`
int:	`100000000`
int*:	`&c1`
double:	`1234567e34`
char[14]:	`Hello, world!\0`

On the same scale (.2 inch to a byte), a megabyte of memory would stretch about three miles (five km) to the right.

The *char* type is supposed to be chosen by the implementation to be the most suitable type for holding and manipulating characters on a given computer; it is typically an 8-bit byte. Similarly, the *int* type is supposed to be chosen to be the most suitable for holding and manipulating integers on a given computer; it is typically a 4-byte (32-bit) word. It is unwise to assume more. For example, there are machines with 32 bit *char*s.

Implementation-defined aspects of fundamental types can be found in *<limits>*. For example:

```
#include <limits>      // §22.2
#include <iostream>

int main()
{
    std::cout << "largest float == " << std::numeric_limits<float>::max()
        << ", char is signed == " << std::numeric_limits<char>::is_signed << '\n';
}
```

The fundamental types can be mixed freely in assignments and expressions. Wherever possible, values are converted so as not to lose information (§C.6).

If a value *v* can be represented exactly in a variable of type *T*, a conversion of *v* to *T* is value-preserving and no problem. Conversions that are not value-preserving are best avoided (§C.6.2.6).

You need to understand implicit conversion in some detail in order to complete a major project and especially to understand real code written by others. However, such understanding is not required to read the following chapters.

4.7 Void

The type *void* is syntactically a fundamental type. It can, however, be used only as part of a more complicated type; there are no objects of type *void*. It is used either to specify that a function does not return a value or as the base type for pointers to objects of unknown type. For example:

```
void x;          // error: there are no void objects
void& r;         // error: there are no references to void
void f();        // function f does not return a value (§7.3)
void* pv;        // pointer to object of unknown type (§5.6)
```

When declaring a function, you must specify the type of the value returned. Logically, you would expect to be able to indicate that a function didn't return a value by omitting the return type. However, that would make the grammar (Appendix A) less regular and clash with C usage. Consequently, *void* is used as a "pseudo return type" to indicate that a function doesn't return a value.

4.8 Enumerations

An *enumeration* is a type that can hold a set of values specified by the user. Once defined, an enumeration is used very much like an integer type.

Named integer constants can be defined as members of an enumeration. For example,

```
enum { ASM, AUTO, BREAK };
```

defines three integer constants, called enumerators, and assigns values to them. By default, enumerator values are assigned increasing from *0*, so *ASM==0*, *AUTO==1*, and *BREAK==2*. An enumeration can be named. For example:

```
enum keyword { ASM, AUTO, BREAK };
```

Each enumeration is a distinct type. The type of an enumerator is its enumeration. For example, *AUTO* is of type *keyword*.

Declaring a variable *keyword* instead of plain *int* can give both the user and the compiler a hint as to the intended use. For example:

```
void f(keyword key)
{
    switch (key) {
    case ASM:
        // do something
        break;
    case BREAK:
        // do something
        break;
    }
}
```

A compiler can issue a warning because only two out of three *keyword* values are handled.

An enumerator can be initialized by a *constant-expression* (§C.5) of integral type (§4.1.1). The range of an enumeration holds all the enumeration's enumerator values rounded up to the nearest larger binary power minus *1*. The range goes down to *0* if the smallest enumerator is non-negative and to the nearest lesser negative binary power if the smallest enumerator is negative. This defines the smallest bit-field capable of holding the enumerator values. For example:

```
enum e1 { dark, light };                    // range 0:1
enum e2 { a = 3, b = 9 };                    // range 0:15
enum e3 { min = -10, max = 1000000 };        // range -1048576:1048575
```

A value of integral type may be explicitly converted to an enumeration type. The result of such a conversion is undefined unless the value is within the range of the enumeration. For example:

```
enum flag { x=1, y=2, z=4, e=8 };   // range 0:15

flag f1 = 5;          // type error: 5 is not of type flag
flag f2 = flag(5);    // ok: flag(5) is of type flag and within the range of flag

flag f3 = flag(z|e);  // ok: flag(12) is of type flag and within the range of flag
flag f4 = flag(99);   // undefined: 99 is not within the range of flag
```

The last assignment shows why there is no implicit conversion from an integer to an enumeration; most integer values do not have a representation in a particular enumeration.

The notion of a range of values for an enumeration differs from the enumeration notion in the Pascal family of languages. However, bit-manipulation examples that require values outside the set of enumerators to be well-defined have a long history in C and C++.

The *sizeof* an enumeration is the *sizeof* some integral type that can hold its range and not larger than *sizeof*(*int*), unless an enumerator cannot be represented as an *int* or as an *unsigned int*. For example, *sizeof*(*e1*) could be *1* or maybe *4* but not *8* on a machine where *sizeof*(*int*)==*4*.

By default, enumerations are converted to integers for arithmetic operations (§6.2). An enumeration is a user-defined type, so users can define their own operations, such as ++ and << for an enumeration (§11.2.3).

4.9 Declarations

Before a name (identifier) can be used in a C++ program, it must be declared. That is, its type must be specified to inform the compiler to what kind of entity the name refers. Here are some examples illustrating the diversity of declarations:

```
char  ch;
string  s;
int  count = 1;
const  double  pi = 3.1415926535897932385;
extern  int  error_number;

const  char* name = "Njal";
const  char* season[] = { "spring", "summer", "fall", "winter" };

struct Date { int d, m, y; };
int  day(Date* p) { return p->d; }
double  sqrt(double);
template<class T> T  abs(T  a) { return a<0 ? -a : a; }

typedef complex<short> Point;
struct User;
enum Beer { Carlsberg, Tuborg, Thor };
namespace NS { int a; }
```

As can be seen from these examples, a declaration can do more than simply associate a type with a name. Most of these *declarations* are also *definitions*; that is, they also define an entity for the name to which they refer. For *ch*, that entity is the appropriate amount of memory to be used as a variable – that memory will be allocated. For *day*, it is the specified function. For the constant *pi*, it is the value *3.1415926535897932385*. For *Date*, that entity is a new type. For *Point*, it is the type *complex<short>* so that *Point* becomes a synonym for *complex<short>*. Of the declarations above, only

```
double  sqrt(double);
extern  int  error_number;
struct User;
```

are not also definitions; that is, the entity they refer to must be defined elsewhere. The code (body) for the function *sqrt* must be specified by some other declaration, the memory for the *int* variable *error_number* must be allocated by some other declaration of *error_number*, and some other declaration of the type *User* must define what that type looks like. For example:

```
double sqrt(double d) { /* ... */ }
int error_number = 1;

struct User { /* ... */ };
```

There must always be exactly one definition for each name in a C++ program (for the effects of
#*include*, see §9.2.3). However, there can be many declarations. All declarations of an entity must
agree on the type of the entity referred to. So, this fragment has two errors:

```
int count;
int count; // error: redefinition

extern int error_number;
extern short error_number;        // error: type mismatch
```

and this has none (for the use of *extern* see §9.2):

```
extern int error_number;
extern int error_number;
```

Some definitions specify a ''value'' for the entities they define. For example:

```
struct Date { int d, m, y; };
typedef complex<short> Point;
int day(Date* p) { return p->d; }
const double pi = 3.1415926535897932385;
```

For types, templates, functions, and constants, the ''value'' is permanent. For nonconstant data
types, the initial value may be changed later. For example:

```
void f()
{
    int count = 1;
    const char* name = "Bjarne";   // name is a variable that points to a constant (§5.4.1)
    // ...
    count = 2;
    name = "Marian";
}
```

Of the definitions, only

```
char ch;
string s;
```

do not specify values. See §4.9.5 and §10.4.2 for explanations of how and when a variable is
assigned a default value. Any declaration that specifies a value is a definition.

4.9.1 The Structure of a Declaration

A declaration consists of four parts: an optional ''specifier,'' a base type, a declarator, and an
optional initializer. Except for function and namespace definitions, a declaration is terminated by a
semicolon. For example:

```
char* kings[] = { "Antigonus", "Seleucus", "Ptolemy" };
```

Here, the base type is *char*, the declarator is **kings*[], and the initializer is = { . . . }.

A specifier is an initial keyword, such as *virtual* (§2.5.5, §12.2.6) and *extern* (§9.2), that specifies some non-type attribute of what is being declared.

A declarator is composed of a name and optionally some declarator operators. The most common declarator operators are (§A.7.1):

*	*pointer*	*prefix*
*const	*constant pointer*	*prefix*
&	*reference*	*prefix*
[]	*array*	*postfix*
()	*function*	*postfix*

Their use would be simple if they were all either prefix or postfix. However, *, [], and () were designed to mirror their use in expressions (§6.2). Thus, * is prefix and [] and () are postfix. The postfix declarator operators bind tighter than the prefix ones. Consequently, **kings*[] is a vector of pointers to something, and we have to use parentheses to express types such as ''pointer to function;'' see examples in §5.1. For full details, see the grammar in Appendix A.

Note that the type cannot be left out of a declaration. For example:

```
const c = 7;    // error: no type
gt(int a, int b) { return (a>b) ? a : b; } // error: no return type

unsigned ui;    // ok: 'unsigned' is the type 'unsigned int'
long li;        // ok: 'long' is the type 'long int'
```

In this, standard C++ differs from earlier versions of C and C++ that allowed the first two examples by considering *int* to be the type when none were specified (§B.2). This ''implicit *int*'' rule was a source of subtle errors and confusion.

4.9.2 Declaring Multiple Names

It is possible to declare several names in a single declaration. The declaration simply contains a list of comma-separated declarators. For example, we can declare two integers like this:

```
int x, y;    // int x; int y;
```

Note that operators apply to individual names only -- and not to any subsequent names in the same declaration. For example:

```
int* p, y;          // int* p;  int y; NOT int* y;
int x, *q;          // int x;    int* q;
int v[10], *pv;     // int v[10];    int* pv;
```

Such constructs make a program less readable and should be avoided.

4.9.3 Names

A name (identifier) consists of a sequence of letters and digits. The first character must be a letter. The underscore character _ is considered a letter. C++ imposes no limit on the number of characters in a name. However, some parts of an implementation are not under the control of the compiler writer (in particular, the linker), and those parts, unfortunately, sometimes do impose limits. Some run-time environments also make it necessary to extend or restrict the set of characters accepted in an identifier. Extensions (e.g., allowing the character $ in a name) yield nonportable programs. A C++ keyword (Appendix A), such as *new* and *int*, cannot be used as a name of a user-defined entity. Examples of names are:

hello	*this_is_a_most_unusually_long_name*			
DEFINED	*foO*	*bAr*	*u_name*	*HorseSense*
var0	*var1*	*CLASS*	*_class*	___

Examples of character sequences that cannot be used as identifiers are:

012	*a fool*	*$sys*	*class*	*3var*
pay.due	*foo~bar*	*.name*	*if*	

Names starting with an underscore are reserved for special facilities in the implementation and the run-time environment, so such names should not be used in application programs.

When reading a program, the compiler always looks for the longest string of characters that could make up a name. Hence, *var10* is a single name, not the name *var* followed by the number *10*. Also, *elseif* is a single name, not the keyword *else* followed by the keyword *if*.

Uppercase and lowercase letters are distinct, so *Count* and *count* are different names, but it is unwise to choose names that differ only by capitalization. In general, it is best to avoid names that differ only in subtle ways. For example, the uppercase o (*O*) and zero (*0*) can be hard to tell apart, as can the lowercase L (*l*) and one (*1*). Consequently, *l0, lO, l1,* and *ll* are poor choices for identifier names.

Names from a large scope ought to have relatively long and reasonably obvious names, such as *vector, Window_with_border,* and *Department_number*. However, code is clearer if names used only in a small scope have short, conventional names such as *x, i,* and *p*. Classes (Chapter 10) and namespaces (§8.2) can be used to keep scopes small. It is often useful to keep frequently used names relatively short and reserve really long names for infrequently used entities. Choose names to reflect the meaning of an entity rather than its implementation. For example, *phone_book* is better than *number_list* even if the phone numbers happen to be stored in a *list* (§3.7). Choosing good names is an art.

Try to maintain a consistent naming style. For example, capitalize nonstandard library user-defined types and start nontypes with a lowercase letter (for example, *Shape* and *current_token*). Also, use all capitals for macros (if you must use macros; for example, *HACK*) and use underscores to separate words in an identifier. However, consistency is hard to achieve because programs are typically composed of fragments from different sources and several different reasonable styles are in use. Be consistent in your use of abbreviations and acronyms.

4.9.4 Scope

A declaration introduces a name into a scope; that is, a name can be used only in a specific part of the program text. For a name declared in a function (often called a *local name*), that scope extends from its point of declaration to the end of the block in which its declaration occurs. A *block* is a section of code delimited by a { } pair.

A name is called *global* if it is defined outside any function, class (Chapter 10), or namespace (§8.2). The scope of a global name extends from the point of declaration to the end of the file in which its declaration occurs. A declaration of a name in a block can hide a declaration in an enclosing block or a global name. That is, a name can be redefined to refer to a different entity within a block. After exit from the block, the name resumes its previous meaning. For example:

```
int x;              // global x

void f()
{
     int x;         // local x hides global x
     x = 1;         // assign to local x

     {
          int x;    // hides first local x
          x = 2;    // assign to second local x
     }

     x = 3;         // assign to first local x
}

int* p = &x;        // take address of global x
```

Hiding names is unavoidable when writing large programs. However, a human reader can easily fail to notice that a name has been hidden. Because such errors are relatively rare, they can be very difficult to find. Consequently, name hiding should be minimized. Using names such as *i* and *x* for global variables or for local variables in a large function is asking for trouble.

A hidden global name can be referred to using the scope resolution operator :: . For example:

```
int x;

void f2()
{
     int x = 1;  // hide global x
     ::x = 2;    // assign to global x
     x = 2;      // assign to local x
     // ...
}
```

There is no way to use a hidden local name.

The scope of a name starts at its point of declaration; that is, after the complete declarator and before the initializer. This implies that a name can be used even to specify its own initial value. For example:

```
int x;
```

```
void f3 ( )
{
    int x = x;  // perverse: initialize x with its own (uninitialized) value
}
```

This is not illegal, just silly. A good compiler will warn if a variable is used before it has been set (see also §5.9[9]).

It is possible to use a single name to refer to two different objects in a block without using the :: operator. For example:

```
int x = 11;

void f4 ( )                // perverse:
{
    int y = x;             // use global x: y = 11
    int x = 22;
    y = x;                 // use local x: y = 22
}
```

Function argument names are considered declared in the outermost block of a function, so

```
void f5 (int x)
{
    int x;     // error
}
```

is an error because *x* is defined twice in the same scope. Having this be an error allows a not uncommon, subtle mistake to be caught.

4.9.5 Initialization

If an initializer is specified for an object, that initializer determines the initial value of an object. If no initializer is specified, a global (§4.9.4), namespace (§8.2), or local static object (§7.1.2, §10.2.4) (collectively called *static objects*) is initialized to *0* of the appropriate type. For example:

```
int a;        // means "int a = 0;"
double d;     // means "double d = 0.0;"
```

Local variables (sometimes called *automatic objects*) and objects created on the free store (sometimes called *dynamic objects* or *heap objects*) are not initialized by default. For example:

```
void f( )
{
    int x;     // x does not have a well-defined value
    // ...
}
```

Members of arrays and structures are default initialized or not depending on whether the array or structure is static. User-defined types may have default initialization defined (§10.4.2).

More complicated objects require more than one value as an initializer. This is handled by initializer lists delimited by { and } for C-style initialization of arrays (§5.2.1) and structures (§5.7). For user-defined types with constructors, function-style argument lists are used (§2.5.2, §10.2.3).

Note that an empty pair of parentheses ( ) in a declaration always means "function" (§7.1). For example:

```
int a[] = { 1, 2 };       // array initializer
Point z(1,2);             // function-style initializer (initialization by constructor)
int f();                  // function declaration
```

4.9.6 Objects and Lvalues

We can allocate and use "variables" that do not have names, and it is possible to assign to strange-looking expressions (e.g., *p[a+10]=7). Consequently, there is a need for a name for "something in memory." This is the simplest and most fundamental notion of an object. That is, an *object* is a contiguous region of storage; an *lvalue* is an expression that refers to an object. The word *lvalue* was originally coined to mean "something that can be on the left-hand side of an assignment." However, not every lvalue may be used on the left-hand side of an assignment; an lvalue can refer to a constant (§5.5). An lvalue that has not been declared *const* is often called a *modifiable lvalue*. This simple and low-level notion of an object should not be confused with the notions of class object and object of polymorphic type (§15.4.3).

Unless the programmer specifies otherwise (§7.1.2, §10.4.8), an object declared in a function is created when its definition is encountered and destroyed when its name goes out of scope (§10.4.4). Such objects are called automatic objects. Objects declared in global or namespace scope and *statics* declared in functions or classes are created and initialized once (only) and "live" until the program terminates (§10.4.9). Such objects are called static objects. Array elements and nonstatic structure or class members have their lifetimes determined by the object of which they are part.

Using the *new* and *delete* operators, you can create objects whose lifetimes are controlled directly (§6.2.6).

4.9.7 Typedef

A declaration prefixed by the keyword *typedef* declares a new name for the type rather than a new variable of the given type. For example:

```
typedef char* Pchar;
Pchar p1, p2;       // p1 and p2 are char*s
char* p3 = p1;
```

A name defined like this, usually called a "*typedef*," can be a convenient shorthand for a type with an unwieldy name. For example, *unsigned char* is too long for really frequent use, so we could define a synonym, *uchar*:

```
typedef unsigned char uchar;
```

Another use of a *typedef* is to limit the direct reference to a type to one place. For example:

```
typedef int int32;
typedef short int16;
```

If we now use *int32* wherever we need a potentially large integer, we can port our program to a machine on which *sizeof*(*int*) is 2 by redefining the single occurrence of *int32* in our code to:

typedef long int32;

For good and bad, *typedefs* are synonyms for other types rather than distinct types. Consequently, *typedefs* mix freely with the types for which they are synonyms. People who would like to have distinct types with identical semantics or identical representation should look at enumerations (§4.8) or classes (Chapter 10).

4.10 Advice

[1]   Keep scopes small; §4.9.4.
[2]   Don't use the same name in both a scope and an enclosing scope; §4.9.4.
[3]   Declare one name (only) per declaration; §4.9.2.
[4]   Keep common and local names short, and keep uncommon and nonlocal names longer; §4.9.3.
[5]   Avoid similar-looking names; §4.9.3.
[6]   Maintain a consistent naming style; §4.9.3.
[7]   Choose names carefully to reflect meaning rather than implementation; §4.9.3.
[8]   Use a *typedef* to define a meaningful name for a built-in type in cases in which the built-in type used to represent a value might change; §4.9.7.
[9]   Use *typedefs* to define synonyms for types; use enumerations and classes to define new types; §4.9.7.
[10] Remember that every declaration must specify a type (there is no ''implicit *int*''); §4.9.1.
[11] Avoid unnecessary assumptions about the numeric value of characters; §4.3.1, §C.6.2.1.
[12] Avoid unnecessary assumptions about the size of integers; §4.6.
[13] Avoid unnecessary assumptions about the range of floating-point types; §4.6.
[14] Prefer a plain *int* over a *short int* or a *long int*; §4.6.
[15] Prefer a *double* over a *float* or a *long double*; §4.5.
[16] Prefer plain *char* over *signed char* and *unsigned char*; §C.3.4.
[17] Avoid making unnecessary assumptions about the sizes of objects; §4.6.
[18] Avoid unsigned arithmetic; §4.4.
[19] View *signed* to *unsigned* and *unsigned* to *signed* conversions with suspicion; §C.6.2.6.
[20] View floating-point to integer conversions with suspicion; §C.6.2.6.
[21] View conversions to a smaller type, such as *int* to *char*, with suspicion; §C.6.2.6.

4.11 Exercises

1. (*2) Get the ''Hello, world!'' program (§3.2) to run. If that program doesn't compile as written, look at §B.3.1.
2. (*1) For each declaration in §4.9, do the following: If the declaration is not a definition, write a definition for it. If the declaration is a definition, write a declaration for it that is not also a definition.
3. (*1.5) Write a program that prints the sizes of the fundamental types, a few pointer types, and a few enumerations of your choice. Use the *sizeof* operator.

4. (∗1.5) Write a program that prints out the letters ´*a*´ .. ´*z*´ and the digits ´*0*´ .. ´*9*´ and their integer values. Do the same for other printable characters. Do the same again but use hexa-decimal notation.
5. (∗2) What, on your system, are the largest and the smallest values of the following types: *char*, *short*, *int*, *long*, *float*, *double*, *long double*, and *unsigned*.
6. (∗1) What is the longest local name you can use in a C++ program on your system? What is the longest external name you can use in a C++ program on your system? Are there any restrictions on the characters you can use in a name?
7. (∗2) Draw a graph of the integer and fundamental types where a type points to another type if all values of the first can be represented as values of the second on every standards-conforming implementation. Draw the same graph for the types on your favorite implementation.

5

Pointers, Arrays, and Structures

The sublime and the ridiculous
are often so nearly related that
it is difficult to class them separately.
– Tom Paine

Pointers — zero — arrays — string literals — pointers into arrays — constants — pointers and constants — references — *void*★ — data structures — advice — exercises.

5.1 Pointers

For a type *T*, *T*★ is the type "pointer to *T*." That is, a variable of type *T*★ can hold the address of an object of type *T*. For example:

```
char  c = ´a´ ;
char* p = &c ;          // p holds the address of c
```

or graphically:

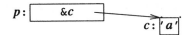

Unfortunately, pointers to arrays and pointers to functions need a more complicated notation:

```
int* pi ;               // pointer to int
char** ppc ;            // pointer to pointer to char
int* ap [15] ;          // array of 15 pointers to ints
int (*fp) (char*) ;     // pointer to function taking a char* argument; returns an int
int* f (char*) ;        // function taking a char* argument; returns a pointer to int
```

See §4.9.1 for an explanation of the declaration syntax and Appendix A for the complete grammar.

The fundamental operation on a pointer is *dereferencing*, that is, referring to the object pointed to by the pointer. This operation is also called *indirection*. The dereferencing operator is (prefix) unary *. For example:

```
char  c = 'a';
char* p = &c;    // p holds the address of c
char  c2 = *p;   // c2 == 'a'
```

The variable pointed to by *p* is *c*, and the value stored in *c* is ´*a*´, so the value of **p* assigned to *c2* is ´*a*´.

It is possible to perform some arithmetic operations on pointers to array elements (§5.3). Pointers to functions can be extremely useful; they are discussed in §7.7.

The implementation of pointers is intended to map directly to the addressing mechanisms of the machine on which the program runs. Most machines can address a byte. Those that can't tend to have hardware to extract bytes from words. On the other hand, few machines can directly address an individual bit. Consequently, the smallest object that can be independently allocated and pointed to using a built-in pointer type is a *char*. Note that a *bool* occupies at least as much space as a *char* (§4.6). To store smaller values more compactly, you can use logical operations (§6.2.4) or bit fields in structures (§C.8.1).

5.1.1 Zero

Zero (*0*) is an *int*. Because of standard conversions (§C.6.2.3), *0* can be used as a constant of any integral (§4.1.1), floating-point, pointer, or pointer-to-member type. The type of zero will be determined by context. Zero will typically (but not necessarily) be represented by the bit pattern *all-zeros* of the appropriate size.

No object is allocated with the address *0*. Consequently, *0* acts as a pointer literal, indicating that a pointer doesn't refer to an object.

In C, it has been popular to define a macro *NULL* to represent the zero pointer. Because of C++'s tighter type checking, the use of plain *0*, rather than any suggested *NULL* macro, leads to fewer problems. If you feel you must define *NULL*, use

```
const  int  NULL = 0;
```

The *const* qualifier (§5.4) prevents accidental redefinition of *NULL* and ensures that *NULL* can be used where a constant is required.

5.2 Arrays

For a type *T*, *T*[*size*] is the type "array of *size* elements of type *T*." The elements are indexed from *0* to *size-1*. For example:

```
float  v[3];      // an array of three floats: v[0], v[1], v[2]
char*  a[32];     // an array of 32 pointers to char: a[0] .. a[31]
```

The number of elements of the array, the array bound, must be a constant expression (§C.5). If you need variable bounds, use a *vector* (§3.7.1, §16.3). For example:

```
void f(int i)
{
    int v1[i];          // error: array size not a constant expression
    vector<int> v2(i);  // ok
}
```

Multidimensional arrays are represented as arrays of arrays. For example:

```
int d2[10][20];  // d2 is an array of 10 arrays of 20 integers
```

Using comma notation as used for array bounds in some other languages gives compile-time errors because comma (,) is a sequencing operator (§6.2.2) and is not allowed in constant expressions (§C.5). For example, try this:

```
int bad[5,2];         // error: comma not allowed in a constant expression
```

Multidimensional arrays are described in §C.7. They are best avoided outside low-level code.

5.2.1 Array Initializers

An array can be initialized by a list of values. For example:

```
int v1[] = { 1, 2, 3, 4 };
char v2[] = { 'a', 'b', 'c', 0 };
```

When an array is declared without a specific size, but with an initializer list, the size is calculated by counting the elements of the initializer list. Consequently, *v1* and *v2* are of type *int*[4] and *char*[4], respectively. If a size is explicitly specified, it is an error to give surplus elements in an initializer list. For example:

```
char v3[2] = { 'a', 'b', 0 };    // error: too many initializers
char v4[3] = { 'a', 'b', 0 };    // ok
```

If the initializer supplies too few elements, *0* is assumed for the remaining array elements. For example:

```
int v5[8] = { 1, 2, 3, 4 };
```

is equivalent to

```
int v5[] = { 1, 2, 3, 4, 0, 0, 0, 0 };
```

Note that there is no array assignment to match the initialization:

```
void f()
{
    v4 = { 'c', 'd', 0 }; // error: no array assignment
}
```

When you need such assignments, use a *vector* (§16.3) or a *valarray* (§22.4) instead.

An array of characters can be conveniently initialized by a string literal (§5.2.2).

5.2.2 String Literals

A *string literal* is a character sequence enclosed within double quotes:

> *"this is a string"*

A string literal contains one more character than it appears to have; it is terminated by the null character ´\0´, with the value *0*. For example:

> *sizeof("Bohr") ==5*

The type of a string literal is ''array of the appropriate number of *const* characters,'' so *"Bohr"* is of type *const char[5]*.

   A string literal can be assigned to a *char**. This is allowed because in previous definitions of C and C++ , the type of a string literal was *char**. Allowing the assignment of a string literal to a *char** ensures that millions of lines of C and C++ remain valid. It is, however, an error to try to modify a string literal through such a pointer:

```
void f()
{
    char* p = "Plato";
    p[4] = 'e';            // error: assignment to const; result is undefined
}
```

This kind of error cannot in general be caught until run-time, and implementations differ in their enforcement of this rule. See also §B.2.3. Having string literals constant not only is obvious, but also allows implementations to do significant optimizations in the way string literals are stored and accessed.

   If we want a string that we are guaranteed to be able to modify, we must copy the characters into an array:

```
void f()
{
    char p[] = "Zeno";     // p is an array of 5 char
    p[0] = 'R';            // ok
}
```

A string literal is statically allocated so that it is safe to return one from a function. For example:

```
const char* error_message(int i)
{
    // ...
    return "range error";
}
```

The memory holding *"range error"* will not go away after a call of *error_message()*.

   Whether two identical string literals are allocated as one is implementation-defined (§C.1). For example:

```
const char* p = "Heraclitus";
const char* q = "Heraclitus";
```

```
void g()
{
    if (p == q) cout << "one!\n";    // result is implementation-defined
    // ...
}
```

Note that == compares addresses (pointer values) when applied to pointers, and not the values pointed to.

The empty string is written as a pair of adjacent double quotes, " ", (and has the type *const char[1]*).

The backslash convention for representing nongraphic characters (§C.3.2) can also be used within a string. This makes it possible to represent the double quote (") and the escape character backslash (\ ) within a string. The most common such character by far is the newline character, ´\n´. For example:

```
cout<<"beep at end of message\a\n";
```

The escape character ´\a´ is the ASCII character *BEL* (also known as *alert*), which causes some kind of sound to be emitted.

It is not possible to have a ''real'' newline in a string:

```
"this is not a string
but a syntax error"
```

Long strings can be broken by whitespace to make the program text neater. For example:

```
char alpha[] = "abcdefghijklmnopqrstuvwxyz"
               "ABCDEFGHIJKLMNOPQRSTUVWXYZ";
```

The compiler will concatenate adjacent strings, so *alpha* could equivalently have been initialized by the single string:

```
"abcdefghijklmnopqrstuvwxyzABCDEFGHIJKLMNOPQRSTUVWXYZ";
```

It is possible to have the null character in a string, but most programs will not suspect that there are characters after it. For example, the string *"Jens\000Munk"* will be treated as *"Jens"* by standard library functions such as *strcpy()* and *strlen()*; see §20.4.1.

A string with the prefix *L*, such as *L"angst"*, is a string of wide characters (§4.3, §C.3.3). Its type is *const wchar_t[]*.

5.3 Pointers into Arrays

In C++, pointers and arrays are closely related. The name of an array can be used as a pointer to its initial element. For example:

```
int v[] = { 1, 2, 3, 4 };
int* p1 = v;            // pointer to initial element (implicit conversion)
int* p2 = &v[0];        // pointer to initial element
int* p3 = &v[4];        // pointer to one beyond last element
```

or graphically:

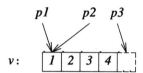

Taking a pointer to the element one beyond the end of an array is guaranteed to work. This is important for many algorithms (§2.7.2, §18.3). However, since such a pointer does not in fact point to an element of the array, it may not be used for reading or writing. The result of taking the address of the element before the initial element is undefined and should be avoided. On some machine architectures, arrays are often allocated on machine addressing boundaries, so "one before the initial element" simply doesn't make sense.

The implicit conversion of an array name to a pointer to the initial element of the array is extensively used in function calls in C-style code. For example:

```
extern "C" int strlen(const char*); // from <string.h>

void f()
{
    char v[] = "Annemarie";
    char* p = v;       // implicit conversion of char[] to char*
    strlen(p);
    strlen(v);         // implicit conversion of char[] to char*
    v = p;             // error: cannot assign to array
}
```

The same value is passed to the standard library function *strlen*() in both calls. The snag is that it is impossible to avoid the implicit conversion. In other words, there is no way of declaring a function so that the array *v* is copied when the function is called. Fortunately, there is no implicit or explicit conversion from a pointer to an array.

The implicit conversion of the array argument to a pointer means that the size of the array is lost to the called function. However, the called function must somehow determine the size to perform a meaningful operation. Like other C standard library functions taking pointers to characters, *strlen*() relies on zero to indicate end-of-string; *strlen*(*p*) returns the number of characters up to and not including the terminating *0*. This is all pretty low-level. The standard library *vector* (§16.3) and *string* (Chapter 20) don't suffer from this problem.

5.3.1 Navigating Arrays

Efficient and elegant access to arrays (and similar data structures) is the key to many algorithms (see §3.8, Chapter 18). Access can be achieved either through a pointer to an array plus an index or through a pointer to an element. For example, traversing a character string using an index,

```
void fi(char v[])
{
    for (int i = 0; v[i] !=0; i++) use(v[i]);
}
```

is equivalent to a traversal using a pointer:

```
void fp (char v[])
{
    for (char* p = v; *p!=0; p++) use(*p);
}
```

The prefix * operator dereferences a pointer so that *p is the character pointed to by p, and ++ increments the pointer so that it refers to the next element of the array.

There is no inherent reason why one version should be faster than the other. With modern compilers, identical code should be generated for both examples (see §5.9[8]). Programmers can choose between the versions on logical and aesthetic grounds.

The result of applying the arithmetic operators +, −, ++, or −− to pointers depends on the type of the object pointed to. When an arithmetic operator is applied to a pointer p of type $T*$, p is assumed to point to an element of an array of objects of type T; $p+1$ points to the next element of that array, and $p-1$ points to the previous element. This implies that the integer value of $p+1$ will be $sizeof(T)$ larger than the integer value of p. For example, executing

```
#include <iostream>

int main ()
{
    int vi[10];
    short vs[10];

    std::cout << &vi[0] << ' ' << &vi[1] << '\n';
    std::cout << &vs[0] << ' ' << &vs[1] << '\n';
}
```

produced

```
0x7fffaef0 0x7fffaef4
0x7fffaedc 0x7fffaede
```

using a default hexadecimal notation for pointer values. This shows that on my implementation, $sizeof(short)$ is 2 and $sizeof(int)$ is 4.

Subtraction of pointers is defined only when both pointers point to elements of the same array (although the language has no fast way of ensuring that is the case). When subtracting one pointer from another, the result is the number of array elements between the two pointers (an integer). One can add an integer to a pointer or subtract an integer from a pointer; in both cases, the result is a pointer value. If that value does not point to an element of the same array as the original pointer or one beyond, the result of using that value is undefined. For example:

```
void f()
{
    int v1[10];
    int v2[10];

    int i1 = &v1[5]-&v1[3];  // i1 = 2
    int i2 = &v1[5]-&v2[3];  // result undefined
```

```
        int* p1 = v2+2;            // p1 = &v2[2]
        int* p2 = v2-2;            // *p2 undefined
    }
```

Complicated pointer arithmetic is usually unnecessary and often best avoided. Addition of pointers makes no sense and is not allowed.

Arrays are not self-describing because the number of elements of an array is not guaranteed to be stored with the array. This implies that to traverse an array that does not contain a terminator the way character strings do, we must somehow supply the number of elements. For example:

```
    void fp (char v[], unsigned int size)
    {
        for (int i=0; i<size; i++) use(v[i]);

        const int N = 7;
        char v2[N];
        for (int i=0; i<N; i++) use(v2[i]);

    }
```

Note that most C++ implementations offer no range checking for arrays. This array concept is inherently low-level. A more advanced notion of arrays can be provided through the use of classes; see §3.7.1.

5.4 Constants

C++ offers the concept of a user-defined constant, a *const*, to express the notion that a value doesn't change directly. This is useful in several contexts. For example, many objects don't actually have their values changed after initialization, symbolic constants lead to more maintainable code than do literals embedded directly in code, pointers are often read through but never written through, and most function parameters are read but not written to.

The keyword *const* can be added to the declaration of an object to make the object declared a constant. Because it cannot be assigned to, a constant must be initialized. For example:

```
    const int model = 90;          // model is a const
    const int v[] = { 1, 2, 3, 4 };  // v[i] is a const
    const int x;                   // error: no initializer
```

Declaring something *const* ensures that its value will not change within its scope:

```
    void f()
    {
        model = 200;   // error
        v[2]++;        // error
    }
```

Note that *const* modifies a type; that is, it restricts the ways in which an object can be used, rather than specifying how the constant is to be allocated. For example:

```
void g(const X* p)
{
    // can't modify *p here
}

void h()
{
    X val;      // val can be modified
    g(&val);
    // ...
}
```

Depending on how smart it is, a compiler can take advantage of an object being a constant in several ways. For example, the initializer for a constant is often (but not always) a constant expression (§C.5); if it is, it can be evaluated at compile time. Further, if the compiler knows every use of the *const*, it need not allocate space to hold it. For example:

```
const int c1 = 1;
const int c2 = 2;
const int c3 = my_f(3);    // don't know the value of c3 at compile time
extern const int c4;       // don't know the value of c4 at compile time
const int* p = &c2;        // need to allocate space for c2
```

Given this, the compiler knows the values of $c1$ and $c2$ so that they can be used in constant expressions. Because the values of $c3$ and $c4$ are not known at compile time (using only the information available in this compilation unit; see §9.1), storage must be allocated for $c3$ and $c4$. Because the address of $c2$ is taken (and presumably used somewhere), storage must be allocated for $c2$. The simple and common case is the one in which the value of the constant is known at compile time and no storage needs to be allocated; $c1$ is an example of that. The keyword *extern* indicates that $c4$ is defined elsewhere (§9.2).

It is typically necessary to allocate store for an array of constants because the compiler cannot, in general, figure out which elements of the array are referred to in expressions. On many machines, however, efficiency improvements can be achieved even in this case by placing arrays of constants in read-only storage.

Common uses for *const*s are as array bounds and case labels. For example:

```
const int a = 42;
const int b = 99;
const int max = 128;

int v[max];

void f(int i)
{
    switch (i) {
    case a:
        // ...
```

```
        case b:
            // ...
        }
    }
```

Enumerators (§4.8) are often an alternative to *const*s in such cases.

The way *const* can be used with class member functions is discussed in §10.2.6 and §10.2.7.

Symbolic constants should be used systematically to avoid "magic numbers" in code. If a numeric constant, such as an array bound, is repeated in code, it becomes hard to revise that code because every occurrence of that constant must be changed to make a correct update. Using a symbolic constant instead localizes information. Usually, a numeric constant represents an assumption about the program. For example, *4* may represent the number of bytes in an integer, *128* the number of characters needed to buffer input, and *6.24* the exchange factor between Danish kroner and U.S. dollars. Left as numeric constants in the code, these values are hard for a maintainer to spot and understand. Often, such numeric values go unnoticed and become errors when a program is ported or when some other change violates the assumptions they represent. Representing assumptions as well-commented symbolic constants minimizes such maintenance problems.

5.4.1 Pointers and Constants

When using a pointer, two objects are involved: the pointer itself and the object pointed to. "Prefixing" a declaration of a pointer with *const* makes the object, but not the pointer, a constant. To declare a pointer itself, rather than the object pointed to, to be a constant, we use the declarator operator **const* instead of plain ***. For example:

```
    void f1(char* p)
    {
        char s[] = "Gorm";

        const char* pc = s;              // pointer to constant
        pc[3] = 'g';                     // error: pc points to constant
        pc = p;                          // ok

        char *const cp = s;              // constant pointer
        cp[3] = 'a';                     // ok
        cp = p;                          // error: cp is constant

        const char *const cpc = s;       // const pointer to const
        cpc[3] = 'a';                    // error: cpc points to constant
        cpc = p;                         // error: cpc is constant
    }
```

The declarator operator that makes a pointer constant is **const*. There is no *const** declarator operator, so a *const* appearing before the *** is taken to be part of the base type. For example:

```
    char *const cp;        // const pointer to char
    char const* pc;        // pointer to const char
    const char* pc2;       // pointer to const char
```

Some people find it helpful to read such declarations right-to-left. For example, "*cp* is a *const* pointer to a *char*" and "*pc2* is a pointer to a *char const*."

An object that is a constant when accessed through one pointer may be variable when accessed in other ways. This is particularly useful for function arguments. By declaring a pointer argument *const*, the function is prohibited from modifying the object pointed to. For example:

```
char* strcpy(char* p, const char* q); // cannot modify *q
```

You can assign the address of a variable to a pointer to constant because no harm can come from that. However, the address of a constant cannot be assigned to an unrestricted pointer because this would allow the object's value to be changed. For example:

```
void f4()
{
    int  a = 1;
    const int  c = 2;
    const int* p1 = &c;     // ok
    const int* p2 = &a;     // ok
    int* p3 = &c;           // error: initialization of int* with const int*
    *p3 = 7;                // try to change the value of c
}
```

It is possible to explicitly remove the restrictions on a pointer to *const* by explicit type conversion (§10.2.7.1 and §15.4.2.1).

5.5 References

A *reference* is an alternative name for an object. The main use of references is for specifying arguments and return values for functions in general and for overloaded operators (Chapter 11) in particular. The notation *X&* means *reference to X*. For example:

```
void f()
{
    int  i = 1;
    int& r = i;         // r and i now refer to the same int
    int  x = r;         // x = 1

    r = 2;              // i = 2
}
```

To ensure that a reference is a name for something (that is, bound to an object), we must initialize the reference. For example:

```
int  i = 1;
int& r1 = i;        // ok: r1 initialized
int& r2;            // error: initializer missing
extern  int& r3;    // ok: r3 initialized elsewhere
```

Initialization of a reference is something quite different from assignment to it. Despite appearances, no operator operates on a reference. For example:

```
void g ( )
{
    int  ii = 0;
    int& rr = ii;
    rr++;                // ii is incremented to 1
    int* pp = &rr;       // pp points to ii
}
```

This is legal, but *rr++* does not increment the reference *rr*; rather, ++ is applied to an *int* that happens to be *ii*. Consequently, the value of a reference cannot be changed after initialization; it always refers to the object it was initialized to denote. To get a pointer to the object denoted by a reference *rr*, we can write &*rr*.

The obvious implementation of a reference is as a (constant) pointer that is dereferenced each time it is used. It doesn't do much harm thinking about references that way, as long as one remembers that a reference isn't an object that can be manipulated the way a pointer is:

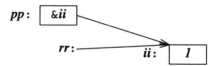

In some cases, the compiler can optimize away a reference so that there is no object representing that reference at run-time.

Initialization of a reference is trivial when the initializer is an lvalue (an object whose address you can take; see §4.9.6). The initializer for a "plain" *T&* must be an lvalue of type *T*.

The initializer for a *const T&* need not be an lvalue or even of type *T*. In such cases,

[1]   first, implicit type conversion to *T* is applied if necessary (see §C.6);
[2]   then, the resulting value is placed in a temporary variable of type *T*; and
[3]   finally, this temporary variable is used as the value of the initializer.
Consider:

```
double& dr = 1;          // error: lvalue needed
const  double& cdr = 1;  // ok
```

The interpretation of this last initialization might be:

```
double  temp = double (1);  // first create a temporary with the right value
const  double& cdr = temp;  // then use the temporary as the initializer for cdr
```

A temporary created to hold a reference initializer persists until the end of its reference's scope.

References to variables and references to constants are distinguished because the introduction of a temporary in the case of the variable is highly error-prone; an assignment to the variable would become an assignment to the − soon to disappear − temporary. No such problem exists for references to constants, and references to constants are often important as function arguments (§11.6).

A reference can be used to specify a function argument so that the function can change the value of an object passed to it. For example:

```
void increment(int& aa) { aa++; }

void f()
{
    int x = 1;
    increment(x);        // x = 2
}
```

The semantics of argument passing are defined to be those of initialization, so when called, *increment*'s argument *aa* became another name for *x*. To keep a program readable, it is often best to avoid functions that modify their arguments. Instead, you can return a value from the function explicitly or require a pointer argument:

```
int next(int p) { return p+1; }

void incr(int* p) { (*p)++; }

void g()
{
    int x = 1;
    increment(x);        // x = 2
    x = next(x);         // x = 3
    incr(&x);            // x = 4
}
```

The *increment*(x) notation doesn't give a clue to the reader that *x*'s value is being modified, the way *x=next*(x) and *incr*(&x) does. Consequently "plain" reference arguments should be used only where the name of the function gives a strong hint that the reference argument is modified.

References can also be used to define functions that can be used on both the left-hand and right-hand sides of an assignment. Again, many of the most interesting uses of this are found in the design of nontrivial user-defined types. As an example, let us define a simple associative array. First, we define struct *Pair* like this:

```
struct Pair {
    string name;
    double val;
};
```

The basic idea is that a *string* has a floating-point value associated with it. It is easy to define a function, *value*(), that maintains a data structure consisting of one *Pair* for each different string that has been presented to it. To shorten the presentation, a very simple (and inefficient) implementation is used:

```
vector<Pair> pairs;

double& value(const string& s)
/*
    maintain a set of Pairs:
    search for s, return its value if found; otherwise make a new Pair and return the default value 0
*/
{
```

```
    for (int i = 0; i < pairs.size(); i++)
        if (s == pairs[i].name) return pairs[i].val;

    Pair p = { s, 0 };
    pairs.push_back(p);  // add Pair at end (§3.7.3)

    return pairs[pairs.size()-1].val;
}
```

This function can be understood as an array of floating-point values indexed by character strings. For a given argument string, *value*() finds the corresponding floating-point object (*not* the value of the corresponding floating-point object); it then returns a reference to it. For example:

```
int main()  // count the number of occurrences of each word on input
{
    string buf;

    while (cin>>buf) value(buf)++;

    for (vector<Pair>::const_iterator p = pairs.begin(); p!=pairs.end(); ++p)
        cout << p->name << ": " << p->val << '\n';
}
```

Each time around, the *while*-loop reads one word from the standard input stream *cin* into the string *buf* (§3.6) and then updates the counter associated with it. Finally, the resulting table of different words in the input, each with its number of occurrences, is printed. For example, given the input

>   *aa bb bb aa aa bb aa aa*

this program will produce:

>   *aa*: 5
>   *bb*: 3

It is easy to refine this into a proper associative array type by using a template class with the subscript operator [] overloaded (§11.8). It is even easier just to use the standard library *map* (§17.4.1).

5.6 Pointer to Void

A pointer to any type of object can be assigned to a variable of type *void**, a *void** can be assigned to another *void**, *void**s can be compared for equality and inequality, and a *void** can be explicitly converted to another type. Other operations would be unsafe because the compiler cannot know what kind of object is really pointed to. Consequently, other operations result in compile-time errors. To use a *void**, we must explicitly convert it to a pointer to a specific type. For example:

```
void f(int* pi)
{
    void* pv = pi;   // ok: implicit conversion of int* to void*
    *pv;             // error: can't dereference void*
    pv++;            // error: can't increment void* (the size of the object pointed to is unknown)
```

```
        int* pi2 = static_cast<int*>(pv);          // explicit conversion back to int*

        double* pd1 = pv;                          // error
        double* pd2 = pi;                          // error
        double* pd3 = static_cast<double*>(pv);    // unsafe
    }
```

In general, it is not safe to use a pointer that has been converted ("cast") to a type that differs from the type the object pointed to. For example, a machine may assume that every *double* is allocated on an 8-byte boundary. If so, strange behavior could arise if *pi* pointed to an *int* that wasn't allocated that way. This form of explicit type conversion is inherently unsafe and ugly. Consequently, the notation used, *static_cast*, was designed to be ugly.

The primary use for *void** is for passing pointers to functions that are not allowed to make assumptions about the type of the object and for returning untyped objects from functions. To use such an object, we must use explicit type conversion.

Functions using *void** pointers typically exist at the very lowest level of the system, where real hardware resources are manipulated. For example:

```
    void* my_alloc(size_t n);  // allocate n bytes from my special heap
```

Occurrences of *void**s at higher levels of the system should be viewed with suspicion because they are likely indicators of design errors. Where used for optimization, *void** can be hidden behind a type-safe interface (§13.5, §24.4.2).

Pointers to functions (§7.7) and pointers to members (§15.5) cannot be assigned to *void**s.

5.7 Structures

An array is an aggregate of elements of the same type. A *struct* is an aggregate of elements of (nearly) arbitrary types. For example:

```
    struct address {
        char* name;          // "Jim Dandy"
        long int number;     // 61
        char* street;        // "South St"
        char* town;          // "New Providence"
        char state[2];       // 'N' 'J'
        long zip;            // 7974
    };
```

This defines a new type called *address* consisting of the items you need in order to send mail to someone. Note the semicolon at the end. This is one of very few places in C++ where it is necessary to have a semicolon after a curly brace, so people are prone to forget it.

Variables of type *address* can be declared exactly as other variables, and the individual *members* can be accessed using the . (dot) operator. For example:

```
void f()
{
    address jd;
    jd.name = "Jim Dandy";
    jd.number = 61;
}
```

The notation used for initializing arrays can also be used for initializing variables of structure types. For example:

```
address jd = {
    "Jim Dandy",
    61, "South St",
    "New Providence", {'N','J'}, 7974
};
```

Using a constructor (§10.2.3) is usually better, however. Note that *jd.state* could not be initialized by the string *"NJ"*. Strings are terminated by the character *'\0'*. Hence, *"NJ"* has three characters − one more than will fit into *jd.state*.

Structure objects are often accessed through pointers using the -> (structure pointer dereference) operator. For example:

```
void print_addr(address* p)
{
    cout << p->name << '\n'
         << p->number << ' ' << p->street << '\n'
         << p->town << '\n'
         << p->state[0] << p->state[1] << ' ' << p->zip << '\n';
}
```

When *p* is a pointer, *p->m* is equivalent to *(*p).m*.

Objects of structure types can be assigned, passed as function arguments, and returned as the result from a function. For example:

```
address current;

address set_current(address next)
{
    address prev = current;
    current = next;
    return prev;
}
```

Other plausible operations, such as comparison (== and !=), are not defined. However, the user can define such operators (Chapter 11).

The size of an object of a structure type is not necessarily the sum of the sizes of its members. This is because many machines require objects of certain types to be allocated on architecture-dependent boundaries or handle such objects much more efficiently if they are. For example, integers are often allocated on word boundaries. On such machines, objects are said to have to be *aligned* properly. This leads to "holes" in the structures. For example, on many machines, *sizeof* (*address*) is *24*, and not *22* as might be expected. You can minimize wasted space by simply ordering members by size (largest member first). However, it is usually best to order members for readability and sort them by size only if there is a demonstrated need to optimize.

The name of a type becomes available for use immediately after it has been encountered and not just after the complete declaration has been seen. For example:

```
struct Link {
    Link* previous;
    Link* successor;
};
```

It is not possible to declare new objects of a structure type until the complete declaration has been seen. For example:

```
struct No_good {
    No_good member;     // error: recursive definition
};
```

This is an error because the compiler is not able to determine the size of *No_good*. To allow two (or more) structure types to refer to each other, we can declare a name to be the name of a structure type. For example:

```
struct List;        // to be defined later

struct Link {
    Link* pre;
    Link* suc;
    List* member_of;
};

struct List {
    Link* head;
};
```

Without the first declaration of *List*, use of *List* in the declaration of *Link* would have caused a syntax error.

The name of a structure type can be used before the type is defined as long as that use does not require the name of a member or the size of the structure to be known. For example:

```
class S;    // 'S' is the name of some type

extern S a;
S f();
void g(S);
S* h(S*);
```

However, many such declarations cannot be used unless the type *S* is defined:

```
void k(S* p)
{
    S a;                // error: S not defined; size needed to allocate
```

```
f();               // error: S not defined; size needed to return value
g(a);              // error: S not defined; size needed to pass argument
p->m = 7;          // error: S not defined; member name not known

S* q = h(p);       // ok: pointers can be allocated and passed
q->m = 7;          // error: S not defined; member name not known
}
```

A *struct* is a simple form of a *class* (Chapter 10).

For reasons that reach into the pre-history of C, it is possible to declare a *struct* and a non-structure with the same name in the same scope. For example:

```
struct stat { /* ... */ };
int stat(char* name, struct stat* buf);
```

In that case, the plain name (*stat*) is the name of the non-structure, and the structure must be referred to with the prefix *struct*. Similarly, the keywords *class*, *union* (§C.8.2), and *enum* (§4.8) can be used as prefixes for disambiguation. However, it is best not to overload names to make that necessary.

5.7.1 Type Equivalence

Two structures are different types even when they have the same members. For example,

```
struct S1 { int a; };
struct S2 { int a; };
```

are two different types, so

```
S1 x;
S2 y = x;  // error: type mismatch
```

Structure types are also different from fundamental types, so

```
S1 x;
int i = x;  // error: type mismatch
```

Every *struct* must have a unique definition in a program (§9.2.3).

5.8 Advice

[1] Avoid nontrivial pointer arithmetic; §5.3.

[2] Take care not to write beyond the bounds of an array; §5.3.1.

[3] Use *0* rather than *NULL*; §5.1.1.

[4] Use *vector* and *valarray* rather than built-in (C-style) arrays; §5.3.1.

[5] Use *string* rather than zero-terminated arrays of *char*; §5.3.

[6] Minimize use of plain reference arguments; §5.5.

[7] Avoid *void** except in low-level code; §5.6.

[8] Avoid nontrivial literals (''magic numbers'') in code. Instead, define and use symbolic constants; §4.8, §5.4.

5.9 Exercises

1. (∗1) Write declarations for the following: a pointer to a character, an array of 10 integers, a reference to an array of 10 integers, a pointer to an array of character strings, a pointer to a pointer to a character, a constant integer, a pointer to a constant integer, and a constant pointer to an integer. Initialize each one.

2. (∗1.5) What, on your system, are the restrictions on the pointer types *char**, *int**, and *void**? For example, may an *int** have an odd value? Hint: alignment.

3. (∗1) Use *typedef* to define the types *unsigned char*, *const unsigned char*, pointer to integer, pointer to pointer to *char*, pointer to array of *char*, array of 7 pointers to *int*, pointer to an array of 7 pointers to *int*, and array of 8 arrays of 7 pointers to *int*.

4. (∗1) Write a function that swaps (exchanges the values of) two integers. Use *int** as the argument type. Write another swap function using *int&* as the argument type.

5. (∗1.5) What is the size of the array *str* in the following example:

   ```
   char str[] = "a short string";
   ```

   What is the length of the string *"a short string"*?

6. (∗1) Define functions *f(char)*, *g(char&)*, and *h(const char&)*. Call them with the arguments ´*a*´, *49*, *3300*, *c*, *uc*, and *sc*, where *c* is a *char*, *uc* is an *unsigned char*, and *sc* is a *signed char*. Which calls are legal? Which calls cause the compiler to introduce a temporary variable?

7. (∗1.5) Define a table of the names of months of the year and the number of days in each month. Write out that table. Do this twice; once using an array of *char* for the names and an array for the number of days and once using an array of structures, with each structure holding the name of a month and the number of days in it.

8. (∗2) Run some tests to see if your compiler really generates equivalent code for iteration using pointers and iteration using indexing (§5.3.1). If different degrees of optimization can be requested, see if and how that affects the quality of the generated code.

9. (∗1.5) Find an example where it would make sense to use a name in its own initializer.

10. (∗1) Define an array of strings in which the strings contain the names of the months. Print those strings. Pass the array to a function that prints those strings.

11. (∗2) Read a sequence of words from input. Use *Quit* as a word that terminates the input. Print the words in the order they were entered. Don't print a word twice. Modify the program to sort the words before printing them.

12. (∗2) Write a function that counts the number of occurrences of a pair of letters in a *string* and another that does the same in a zero-terminated array of *char* (a C-style string). For example, the pair "ab" appears twice in "xabaacbaxabb".

13. (∗1.5) Define a *struct Date* to keep track of dates. Provide functions that read *Date*s from input, write *Date*s to output, and initialize a *Date* with a date.

6

Expressions and Statements

Premature optimization
is the root of all evil.
– D. Knuth

On the other hand,
we cannot ignore efficiency.
– Jon Bentley

Desk calculator example — input — command line arguments — expression summary — logical and relational operators — increment and decrement — free store — explicit type conversion — statement summary — declarations — selection statements — declarations in conditions — iteration statements — the infamous *goto* — comments and indentation — advice — exercises.

6.1 A Desk Calculator

Statements and expressions are introduced by presenting a desk calculator program that provides the four standard arithmetic operations as infix operators on floating-point numbers. The user can also define variables. For example, given the input

> *r = 2.5*
> *area = pi * r * r*

(pi is predefined) the calculator program will write

> *2.5*
> *19.635*

where *2.5* is the result of the first line of input and *19.635* is the result of the second.

The calculator consists of four main parts: a parser, an input function, a symbol table, and a driver. Actually, it is a miniature compiler in which the parser does the syntactic analysis, the input function handles input and lexical analysis, the symbol table holds permanent information, and the driver handles initialization, output, and errors. We could add many features to this calculator to make it more useful (§6.6[20]), but the code is long enough as it is, and most features would just add code without providing additional insight into the use of C++.

6.1.1 The Parser

Here is a grammar for the language accepted by the calculator:

program:
    END   // *END is end-of-input*
    expr_list END

expr_list:
    expression PRINT   // *PRINT is semicolon*
    expression PRINT expr_list

expression:
    expression + term
    expression − term
    term

term:
    term / primary
    *term * primary*
    primary

primary:
    NUMBER
    NAME
    NAME = expression
    − primary
    (expression)

In other words, a program is a sequence of expressions separated by semicolons. The basic units of an expression are numbers, names, and the operators *, /, +, − (both unary and binary), and =. Names need not be declared before use.

The style of syntax analysis used is usually called *recursive descent*; it is a popular and straightforward top-down technique. In a language such as C++, in which function calls are relatively cheap, it is also efficient. For each production in the grammar, there is a function that calls other functions. Terminal symbols (for example, *END, NUMBER*, +, and −) are recognized by the lexical analyzer, *get_token*(); and nonterminal symbols are recognized by the syntax analyzer functions, *expr*(), *term*(), and *prim*(). As soon as both operands of a (sub)expression are known, the expression is evaluated; in a real compiler, code could be generated at this point.

The parser uses a function *get_token*() to get input. The value of the most recent call of *get_token*() can be found in the global variable *curr_tok*. The type of *curr_tok* is the enumeration *Token_value*:

```
enum Token_value {
    NAME,          NUMBER,      END,
    PLUS='+',      MINUS='-',   MUL='*',    DIV='/',
    PRINT=';',     ASSIGN='=',  LP='(',     RP=')'
};

Token_value curr_tok = PRINT;
```

Representing each token by the integer value of its character is convenient and efficient and can be a help to people using debuggers. This works as long as no character used as input has a value used as an enumerator − and no current character set I know of has a printing character with a single-digit integer value. I chose *PRINT* as the initial value for *curr_tok* because that is the value it will have after the calculator has evaluated an expression and displayed its value. Thus, I ''start the system'' in a normal state to minimize the chance of errors and the need for special startup code.

Each parser function takes a *bool* (§4.2) argument indicating whether the function needs to call *get_token* ( ) to get the next token. Each parser function evaluates ''its'' expression and returns the value. The function *expr* ( ) handles addition and subtraction. It consists of a single loop that looks for terms to add or subtract:

```
double expr(bool get)        // add and subtract
{
    double left = term(get);

    for (;;)                  // "forever"
        switch (curr_tok) {
        case PLUS:
            left += term(true);
            break;
        case MINUS:
            left -= term(true);
            break;
        default:
            return left;
        }
}
```

This function really does not do much itself. In a manner typical of higher-level functions in a large program, it calls other functions to do the work.

The *switch-statement* tests the value of its condition, which is supplied in parentheses after the *switch* keyword, against a set of constants. The *break-statement*s are used to exit the *switch-statement*. The constants following the *case* labels must be distinct. If the value tested does not match any *case* label, the *default* is chosen. The programmer need not provide a *default*.

Note that an expression such as *2-3+4* is evaluated as *(2-3)+4*, as specified in the grammar.

The curious notation *for*(;;) is the standard way to specify an infinite loop; you could pronounce it ''forever.'' It is a degenerate form of a *for-statement* (§6.3.3); *while*(*true*) is an alternative. The *switch-statement* is executed repeatedly until something different from + and − is found, and then the *return-statement* in the default case is executed.

The operators += and −= are used to handle the addition and subtraction; *left=left+term*( ) and *left=left-term* ( ) could have been used without changing the meaning of the program. However, *left+=term* ( ) and *left-=term* ( ) not only are shorter but also express the intended operation directly. Each assignment operator is a separate lexical token, so *a + = 1;* is a syntax error because of the space between the + and the =.

Assignment operators are provided for the binary operators

$$+ \quad - \quad * \quad / \quad \% \quad \& \quad | \quad ^ \quad << \quad >>$$

so that the following assignment operators are possible

$$= \quad += \quad -= \quad *= \quad /= \quad \%= \quad \&= \quad |= \quad ^= \quad <<= \quad >>=$$

The % is the modulo, or remainder, operator; &, |, and ^ are the bitwise logical operators AND, OR, and exclusive OR; << and >> are the left shift and right shift operators; §6.2 summarizes the operators and their meanings. For a binary operator @ applied to operands of built-in types, an expression *x@=y* means *x=x@y*, except that *x* is evaluated once only.

Chapter 8 and Chapter 9 discuss how to organize a program as a set of modules. With one exception, the declarations for this calculator example can be ordered so that everything is declared exactly once and before it is used. The exception is *expr* ( ), which calls *term* ( ), which calls *prim* ( ), which in turn calls *expr* ( ). This loop must be broken somehow. A declaration

> *double expr(bool);*

before the definition of *prim* ( ) will do nicely.

Function *term* ( ) handles multiplication and division in the same way *expr* ( ) handles addition and subtraction:

```
double  term(bool  get)            // multiply and divide
{
      double  left = prim(get);

      for (;;)
            switch (curr_tok) {
            case MUL:
                  left *= prim(true);
                  break;
            case DIV:
                  if (double  d = prim(true)) {
                        left /= d;
                        break;
                  }
                  return  error("divide by 0");
            default:
                  return  left;
            }
}
```

The result of dividing by zero is undefined and usually disastrous. We therefore test for *0* before dividing and call *error* ( ) if we detect a zero divisor. The function *error* ( ) is described in §6.1.4.

The variable *d* is introduced into the program exactly where it is needed and initialized immediately. The scope of a name introduced in a condition is the statement controlled by that condition, and the resulting value is the value of the condition (§6.3.2.1). Consequently, the division and assignment *left*/=*d* is done if and only if *d* is nonzero.

The function *prim*() handling a *primary* is much like *expr*() and *term*(), except that because we are getting lower in the call hierarchy a bit of real work is being done and no loop is necessary:

```
double  number_value;
string  string_value;

double  prim(bool  get)              // handle primaries
{
     if (get) get_token();

     switch (curr_tok) {
     case  NUMBER:              // floating-point constant
     {    double  v = number_value;
          get_token();
          return  v;
     }
     case  NAME:
     {    double& v = table[string_value];
          if (get_token() == ASSIGN) v = expr(true);
          return  v;
     }
     case  MINUS:          // unary minus
          return -prim(true);
     case  LP:
     {    double  e = expr(true);
          if (curr_tok != RP) return  error("')' expected");
          get_token();           // eat ')'
          return  e;
     }
     default:
          return  error("primary expected");
     }
}
```

When a *NUMBER* (that is, an integer or floating-point literal) is seen, its value is returned. The input routine *get_token*() places the value in the global variable *number_value*. Use of a global variable in a program often indicates that the structure is not quite clean – that some sort of optimization has been applied. So it is here. Ideally, a lexical token consists of two parts: a value specifying the kind of token (a *Token_value* in this program) and (when needed) the value of the token. Here, there is only a single, simple variable, *curr_tok*, so the global variable *number_value* is needed to hold the value of the last *NUMBER* read. Eliminating this spurious global variable is left as an exercise (§6.6[21]). Saving the value of *number_value* in the local variable *v* before calling *get_token*() is not really necessary. For every legal input, the calculator always uses one number in the computation before reading another from input. However, saving the value and displaying it correctly after an error helps the user.

In the same way that the value of the last *NUMBER* is kept in *number_value*, the character string representation of the last *NAME* seen is kept in *string_value*. Before doing anything to a name, the calculator must first look ahead to see if it is being assigned to or simply read. In both cases, the symbol table is consulted. The symbol table is a *map* (§3.7.4, §17.4.1):

> *map<string, double> table;*

That is, when *table* is indexed by a *string*, the resulting value is the *double* corresponding to the *string*. For example, if the user enters

> *radius = 6378.388;*

the calculator will execute

> *double& v = table ["radius"] ;*
> *// ... expr() calculates the value to be assigned ...*
> *v = 6378.388;*

The reference *v* is used to hold on to the *double* associated with *radius* while *expr* ( ) calculates the value *6378.388* from the input characters.

6.1.2 The Input Function

Reading input is often the messiest part of a program. This is because a program must communicate with a person, it must cope with that person's whims, conventions, and seemingly random errors. Trying to force the person to behave in a manner more suitable for the machine is often (rightly) considered offensive. The task of a low-level input routine is to read characters and compose higher-level tokens from them. These tokens are then the units of input for higher-level routines. Here, low-level input is done by *get_token* ( ). Writing a low-level input routine need not be an everyday task. Many systems provide standard functions for this.

I build *get_token* ( ) in two stages. First, I provide a deceptively simple version that imposes a burden on the user. Next, I modify it into a slightly less elegant, but much easier to use, version.

The idea is to read a character, use that character to decide what kind of token needs to be composed, and then return the *Token_value* representing the token read.

The initial statements read the first non-whitespace character into *ch* and check that the read operation succeeded:

> *Token_value get_token* ( )
> *{*
> *   char ch = 0;*
> *   cin>>ch;*
>
> *   switch* (*ch*) {
> *   case 0:*
> *   return curr_tok=END;   // assign and return*

By default, operator >> skips whitespace (that is, spaces, tabs, newlines, etc.) and leaves the value of *ch* unchanged if the input operation failed. Consequently, *ch==0* indicates end of input.

Assignment is an operator, and the result of the assignment is the value of the variable assigned to. This allows me to assign the value *END* to *curr_tok* and return it in the same statement. Having a single statement rather than two is useful in maintenance. If the assignment and the return became separated in the code, a programmer might update the one and forget to update the other.

Let us look at some of the cases separately before considering the complete function. The expression terminator ´ ; ´, the parentheses, and the operators are handled simply by returning their values:

```
case ´ ; ´ :
case ´ * ´ :
case ´ / ´ :
case ´ + ´ :
case ´ - ´ :
case ´ ( ´ :
case ´ ) ´ :
case ´ = ´ :
        return  curr_tok=Token_value(ch);
```

Numbers are handled like this:

```
case ´0´ : case ´1´ : case ´2´ : case ´3´ : case ´4´ :
case ´5´ : case ´6´ : case ´7´ : case ´8´ : case ´9´ :
case ´ . ´ :
        cin.putback(ch);
        cin >> number_value;
        return  curr_tok=NUMBER;
```

Stacking *case* labels horizontally rather than vertically is generally not a good idea because this arrangement is harder to read. However, having one line for each digit is tedious. Because operator >> is already defined for reading floating-point constants into a *double*, the code is trivial. First the initial character (a digit or a dot) is put back into *cin*. Then the constant can be read into *number_value*.

A name is handled similarly:

```
default:                 // NAME, NAME =, or error
        if (isalpha(ch)) {
                cin.putback(ch);
                cin>>string_value;
                return  curr_tok=NAME;
        }
        error("bad token");
        return  curr_tok=PRINT;
```

The standard library function *isalpha* ( ) (§20.4.2) is used to avoid listing every character as a separate *case* label. Operator >> applied to a string (in this case, *string_value*) reads until it hits whitespace. Consequently, a user must terminate a name by a space before an operator using the name as an operand. This is less than ideal, so we will return to this problem in §6.1.3.

Here, finally, is the complete input function:

```
Token_value  get_token()
{
        char ch = 0;
        cin>>ch;
```

```
switch (ch) {
case 0:
        return curr_tok=END;

case ';':
case '*':
case '/':
case '+':
case '-':
case '(':
case ')':
case '=':
        return curr_tok=Token_value(ch);

case '0': case '1': case '2': case '3': case '4':
case '5': case '6': case '7': case '8': case '9':
case '.':
        cin.putback(ch);
        cin >> number_value;
        return curr_tok=NUMBER;

default:                                // NAME, NAME =, or error
        if (isalpha(ch)) {
                cin.putback(ch);
                cin>>string_value;
                return curr_tok=NAME;
        }
        error("bad token");
        return curr_tok=PRINT;
    }
}
```

The conversion of an operator to its token value is trivial because the *Token_value* of an operator was defined as the integer value of the operator (§4.8).

6.1.3 Low-level Input

Using the calculator as defined so far reveals a few inconveniences. It is tedious to remember to add a semicolon after an expression in order to get its value printed, and having a name terminated by whitespace only is a real nuisance. For example, $x=7$ is an identifier – rather than the identifier x followed by the operator = and the number 7. Both problems are solved by replacing the type-oriented default input operations in *get_token*() with code that reads individual characters.

First, we'll make a newline equivalent to the semicolon used to mark the end of expression:

```
Token_value get_token()
{
    char ch;

    do { // skip whitespace except '\n'
            if(!cin.get(ch)) return curr_tok = END;
    } while (ch!='\n' && isspace(ch));
```

```
switch (ch) {
case ';':
case '\n':
        return curr_tok=PRINT;
```

A *do-statement* is used; it is equivalent to a *while-statement* except that the controlled statement is always executed at least once. The call *cin.get(ch)* reads a single character from the standard input stream into *ch*. By default, *get()* does not skip whitespace the way *operator* >> does. The test *if (!cin.get(ch))* succeeds if no character can be read from *cin*; in this case, *END* is returned to terminate the calculator session. The operator ! (NOT) is used because *get()* returns *true* in case of success.

The standard library function *isspace()* provides the standard test for whitespace (§20.4.2); *isspace(c)* returns a nonzero value if *c* is a whitespace character and zero otherwise. The test is implemented as a table lookup, so using *isspace()* is much faster than testing for the individual whitespace characters. Similar functions test if a character is a digit – *isdigit()* – a letter – *isalpha()* – or a digit or letter – *isalnum()*.

After whitespace has been skipped, the next character is used to determine what kind of lexical token is coming.

The problem caused by >> reading into a string until whitespace is encountered is solved by reading one character at a time until a character that is not a letter or a digit is found:

```
default:                 // NAME, NAME=, or error
    if (isalpha(ch)) {
        string_value = ch;
        while (cin.get(ch) && isalnum(ch)) string_value.push_back(ch);
        cin.putback(ch);
        return curr_tok=NAME;
    }
    error("bad token");
    return curr_tok=PRINT;
```

Fortunately, these two improvements could both be implemented by modifying a single local section of code. Constructing programs so that improvements can be implemented through local modifications only is an important design aim.

6.1.4 Error Handling

Because the program is so simple, error handling is not a major concern. The error function simply counts the errors, writes out an error message, and returns:

```
int no_of_errors;

double error(const string& s)
{
    no_of_errors++;
    cerr << "error: " << s << '\n';
    return 1;
}
```

The stream *cerr* is an unbuffered output stream usually used to report errors (§21.2.1).

The reason for returning a value is that errors typically occur in the middle of the evaluation of an expression, so we should either abort that evaluation entirely or return a value that is unlikely to cause subsequent errors. The latter is adequate for this simple calculator. Had *get_token* ( ) kept track of the line numbers, *error* ( ) could have informed the user approximately where the error occurred. This would be useful when the calculator is used noninteractively (§6.6[19]).

Often, a program must be terminated after an error has occurred because no sensible way of continuing has been devised. This can be done by calling *exit* ( ), which first cleans up things like output streams and then terminates the program with its argument as the return value (§9.4.1.1).

More stylized error-handling mechanisms can be implemented using exceptions (see §8.3, Chapter 14), but what we have here is quite suitable for a 150-line calculator.

6.1.5 The Driver

With all the pieces of the program in place, we need only a driver to start things. In this simple example, *main* ( ) can do that:

```
int main ( )  .
{
        table [ "pi" ] = 3.1415926535897932385;      // insert predefined names
        table [ "e" ] = 2.7182818284590452354;

        while (cin) {
             get_token ( );
             if (curr_tok == END) break;
             if (curr_tok == PRINT) continue;
             cout << expr (false) << '\n';
        }

        return no_of_errors;
}
```

Conventionally, *main* ( ) should return zero if the program terminates normally and nonzero otherwise (§3.2). Returning the number of errors accomplishes this nicely. As it happens, the only initialization needed is to insert the predefined names into the symbol table.

The primary task of the main loop is to read expressions and write out the answer. This is achieved by the line:

```
        cout << expr (false) << '\n';
```

The argument *false* tells *expr* ( ) that it does not need to call *get_token* ( ) to get a current token on which to work.

Testing *cin* each time around the loop ensures that the program terminates if something goes wrong with the input stream, and testing for *END* ensures that the loop is correctly exited when *get_token* ( ) encounters end-of-file. A *break-statement* exits its nearest enclosing *switch-statement* or loop (that is, a *for-statement*, *while-statement*, or *do-statement*). Testing for *PRINT* (that is, for '\n' and '; ') relieves *expr* ( ) of the responsibility for handling empty expressions. A *continue-statement* is equivalent to going to the very end of a loop, so in this case

```
while (cin) {
      // ...
      if (curr_tok == PRINT) continue;
      cout << expr(false) << '\n';
}
```

is equivalent to

```
while (cin) {
      // ...
      if (curr_tok != PRINT)
            cout << expr(false) << '\n';
}
```

6.1.6 Headers

The calculator uses standard library facilities. Therefore, appropriate headers must be #*included* to complete the program:

```
#include<iostream>    // I/O
#include<string>      // strings
#include<map>         // map
#include<cctype>      // isalpha(), etc.
```

All of these headers provide facilities in the *std* namespace, so to use the names they provide we must either use explicit qualification with *std*:: or bring the names into the global namespace by

```
using namespace std;
```

To avoid confusing the discussion of expressions with modularity issues, I did the latter. Chapter 8 and Chapter 9 discuss ways of organizing this calculator into modules using namespaces and how to organize it into source files. On many systems, standard headers have equivalents with a .*h* suffix that declare the classes, functions, etc., and place them in the global namespace (§9.2.1, §9.2.4, §B.3.1).

6.1.7 Command-Line Arguments

After the program was written and tested, I found it a bother to first start the program, then type the expressions, and finally quit. My most common use was to evaluate a single expression. If that expression could be presented as a command-line argument, a few keystrokes could be avoided.

A program starts by calling *main*() (§3.2, §9.4). When this is done, *main*() is given two arguments specifying the number of arguments, usually called *argc*, and an array of arguments, usually called *argv*. The arguments are character strings, so the type of *argv* is *char** [*argc*+1]. The name of the program (as it occurs on the command line) is passed as *argv*[0], so *argc* is always at least 1. The list of arguments is zero-terminated; that is, *argv*[*argc*]==0. For example, for the command

```
dc 150/1.1934
```

the arguments have these values:

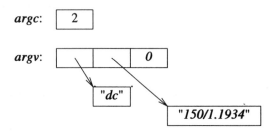

Because the conventions for calling *main* ( ) are shared with C, C-style arrays and strings are used.

It is not difficult to get hold of a command-line argument. The problem is how to use it with minimal reprogramming. The idea is to read from the command string in the same way that we read from the input stream. A stream that reads from a string is unsurprisingly called an *istringstream*. Unfortunately, there is no elegant way of making *cin* refer to an *istringstream*. Therefore, we must find a way of getting the calculator input functions to refer to an *istringstream*. Furthermore, we must find a way of getting the calculator input functions to refer to an *istringstream* or to *cin* depending on what kind of command-line argument we supply.

A simple solution is to introduce a global pointer *input* that points to the input stream to be used and have every input routine use that:

```
istream* input;  // pointer to input stream

int main (int argc, char* argv [ ] )
{
    switch (argc) {
    case 1:                                      // read from standard input
        input = &cin;
        break;
    case 2:                                      // read argument string
        input = new  istringstream (argv [1] );
        break;
    default:
        error ("too  many  arguments");
        return 1;
    }

    table ["pi"] = 3.1415926535897932385;        // insert predefined names
    table ["e"] = 2.7182818284590452354;

    while (*input) {
        get_token ();
        if (curr_tok == END) break;
        if (curr_tok == PRINT) continue;
        cout << expr (false) << '\n';
    }

    if (input != &cin) delete input;
    return no_of_errors;
}
```

An *istringstream* is a kind of *istream* that reads from its character string argument (§21.5.3). Upon reaching the end of its string, an *istringstream* fails exactly like other streams do when they hit the end of input (§3.6, §21.3.3). To use an *istringstream*, you must include <*sstream*>.

It would be easy to modify *main* () to accept several command-line arguments, but this does not appear to be necessary, especially as several expressions can be passed as a single argument:

> dc "rate=1.1934;150/rate;19.75/rate;217/rate"

I use quotes because ; is the command separator on my UNIX systems. Other systems have different conventions for supplying arguments to a program on startup.

It was inelegant to modify all of the input routines to use *input rather than *cin* to gain the flexibility to use alternative sources of input. The change could have been avoided had I shown foresight by introducing something like *input* from the start. A more general and useful view is to note that the source of input really should be the parameter of a calculator module. That is, the fundamental problem with this calculator example is that what I refer to as "the calculator" is only a collection of functions and data. There is no module (§2.4) or object (§2.5.2) that explicitly represents the calculator. Had I set out to design a calculator module or a calculator type, I would naturally have considered what its parameters should be (§8.5[3], §10.6[16]).

6.1.8 A Note on Style

To programmers unacquainted with associative arrays, the use of the standard library *map* as the symbol table seems almost like cheating. It is not. The standard library and other libraries are meant to be used. Often, a library has received more care in its design and implementation than a programmer could afford for a handcrafted piece of code to be used in just one program.

Looking at the code for the calculator, especially at the first version, we can see that there isn't much traditional C-style, low-level code presented. Many of the traditional tricky details have been replaced by uses of standard library classes such as *ostream*, *string*, and *map* (§3.4, §3.5, §3.7.4, Chapter 17).

Note the relative scarcity of arithmetic, loops, and even assignments. This is the way things ought to be in code that doesn't manipulate hardware directly or implement low-level abstractions.

6.2 Operator Summary

This section presents a summary of expressions and some examples. Each operator is followed by one or more names commonly used for it and an example of its use. In these tables, a *class_name* is the name of a class, a *member* is a member name, an *object* is an expression yielding a class object, a *pointer* is an expression yielding a pointer, an *expr* is an expression, and an *lvalue* is an expression denoting a nonconstant object. A *type* can be a fully general type name (with *, (), etc.) only when it appears in parentheses; elsewhere, there are restrictions (§A.5).

The syntax of expressions is independent of operand types. The meanings presented here apply when the operands are of built-in types (§4.1.1). In addition, you can define meanings for operators applied to operands of user-defined types (§2.5.2, Chapter 11).

Operator Summary	
scope resolution	*class_name* : : *member*
scope resolution	*namespace_name* : : *member*
global	: : *name*
global	: : *qualified-name*
member selection	*object . member*
member selection	*pointer –> member*
subscripting	*pointer* [*expr*]
function call	*expr* (*expr_list*)
value construction	*type* (*expr_list*)
post increment	*lvalue ++*
post decrement	*lvalue – –*
type identification	**typeid** (*type*)
run-time type identification	**typeid** (*expr*)
run-time checked conversion	**dynamic_cast** < *type* > (*expr*)
compile-time checked conversion	**static_cast** < *type* > (*expr*)
unchecked conversion	**reinterpret_cast** < *type* > (*expr*)
const conversion	**const_cast** < *type* > (*expr*)
size of object	**sizeof** *expr*
size of type	**sizeof** (*type*)
pre increment	*++ lvalue*
pre decrement	*– – lvalue*
complement	*˜ expr*
not	*! expr*
unary minus	*– expr*
unary plus	*+ expr*
address of	*& lvalue*
dereference	** expr*
create (allocate)	**new** *type*
create (allocate and initialize)	**new** *type* (*expr-list*)
create (place)	**new** (*expr-list*) *type*
create (place and initialize)	**new** (*expr-list*) *type* (*expr-list*)
destroy (deallocate)	**delete** *pointer*
destroy array	**delete** [ ] *pointer*
cast (type conversion)	(*type*) *expr*
member selection	*object . * pointer-to-member*
member selection	*pointer –>* pointer-to-member*
multiply	*expr * expr*
divide	*expr / expr*
modulo (remainder)	*expr % expr*

Operator Summary (continued)	
add (plus)	*expr + expr*
subtract (minus)	*expr − expr*
shift left	*expr << expr*
shift right	*expr >> expr*
less than	*expr < expr*
less than or equal	*expr <= expr*
greater than	*expr > expr*
greater than or equal	*expr >= expr*
equal	*expr == expr*
not equal	*expr ! = expr*
bitwise AND	*expr & expr*
bitwise exclusive OR	*expr ^ expr*
bitwise inclusive OR	*expr | expr*
logical AND	*expr && expr*
logical inclusive OR	*expr || expr*
conditional expression	*expr ? expr : expr*
simple assignment	*lvalue = expr*
multiply and assign	*lvalue *= expr*
divide and assign	*lvalue / = expr*
modulo and assign	*lvalue %= expr*
add and assign	*lvalue += expr*
subtract and assign	*lvalue − = expr*
shift left and assign	*lvalue <<= expr*
shift right and assign	*lvalue >>= expr*
AND and assign	*lvalue &= expr*
inclusive OR and assign	*lvalue | = expr*
exclusive OR and assign	*lvalue ^= expr*
throw exception	*throw expr*
comma (sequencing)	*expr , expr*

Each box holds operators with the same precedence. Operators in higher boxes have higher precedence than operators in lower boxes. For example: $a+b*c$ means $a+(b*c)$ rather than $(a+b)*c$ because $*$ has higher precedence than $+$. Similarly, $*p++$ means $*(p++)$, *not* $(*p)++$.

Unary operators and assignment operators are right-associative; all others are left-associative. For example, $a=b=c$ means $a=(b=c)$, $a+b+c$ means $(a+b)+c$.

A few grammar rules cannot be expressed in terms of precedence (also known as binding strength) and associativity. For example, $a=b<c?d=e:f=g$ means $a=((b<c)?(d=e):(f=g))$, but you need to look at the grammar (§A.5) to determine that.

6.2.1 Results

The result types of arithmetic operators are determined by a set of rules known as "the usual arithmetic conversions" (§C.6.3). The overall aim is to produce a result of the "largest" operand type. For example, if a binary operator has a floating-point operand, the computation is done using floating-point arithmetic and the result is a floating-point value. If it has a *long* operand, the computation is done using long integer arithmetic, and the result is a *long*. Operands that are smaller than an *int* (such as *bool* and *char*) are converted to *int* before the operator is applied.

The relational operators, ==, <=, etc., produce Boolean results. The meaning and result type of user-defined operators are determined by their declarations (§11.2).

Where logically feasible, the result of an operator that takes an lvalue operand is an lvalue denoting that lvalue operand. For example:

```
void f(int x, int y)
{
    int j = x = y;          // the value of x=y is the value of x after the assignment
    int* p = &++x;          // p points to x
    int* q = &(x++);        // error: x++ is not an lvalue (it is not the value stored in x)
    int* pp = &(x>y?x:y);   // address of the int with the larger value
}
```

If both the second and third operands of ? : are lvalues and have the same type, the result is of that type and is an lvalue. Preserving lvalues in this way allows greater flexibility in using operators. This is particularly useful when writing code that needs to work uniformly and efficiently with both built-in and user-defined types (e.g., when writing templates or programs that generate C++ code).

The result of *sizeof* is of an unsigned integral type called *size_t* defined in *<cstddef>*. The result of pointer subtraction is of a signed integral type called *ptrdiff_t* defined in *<cstddef>*.

Implementations do not have to check for arithmetic overflow and hardly any do. For example:

```
void f()
{
    int i = 1;
    while (0 < i) i++;
    cout << "i has become negative!" << i << '\n';
}
```

This will (eventually) try to increase *i* past the largest integer. What happens then is undefined, but typically the value "wraps around" to a negative number (on my machine -*2147483648*). Similarly, the effect of dividing by zero is undefined, but doing so usually causes abrupt termination of the program. In particular, underflow, overflow, and division by zero do not throw standard exceptions (§14.10).

6.2.2 Evaluation Order

The order of evaluation of subexpressions within an expression is undefined. In particular, you cannot assume that the expression is evaluated left to right. For example:

```
int x = f(2)+g(3);   // undefined whether f() or g() is called first
```

Better code can be generated in the absence of restrictions on expression evaluation order. However, the absence of restrictions on evaluation order can lead to undefined results. For example,

```
int i = 1;
v[i] = i++;      // undefined result
```

may be evaluated as either $v[1]=1$ or $v[2]=1$ or may cause some even stranger behavior. Compilers can warn about such ambiguities. Unfortunately, most do not.

The operators , (comma), && (logical and), and || (logical or) guarantee that their left-hand operand is evaluated before their right-hand operand. For example, $b=(a=2,a+1)$ assigns *3* to *b*. Examples of the use of || and && can be found in §6.2.3. For built-in types, the second operand of && is evaluated only if its first operand is *true*, and the second operand of || is evaluated only if its first operand is *false*; this is sometimes called *short-circuit evaluation*. Note that the sequencing operator , (comma) is logically different from the comma used to separate arguments in a function call. Consider:

```
f1(v[i],i++);      // two arguments
f2( (v[i],i++) );  // one argument
```

The call of *f1* has two arguments, $v[i]$ and $i++$, and the order of evaluation of the argument expressions is undefined. Order dependence of argument expressions is very poor style and has undefined behavior. The call of *f2* has one argument, the comma expression $(v[i],i++)$, which is equivalent to $i++$.

Parentheses can be used to force grouping. For example, $a*b/c$ means $(a*b)/c$ so parentheses must be used to get $a*(b/c)$; $a*(b/c)$ may be evaluated as $(a*b)/c$ only if the user cannot tell the difference. In particular, for many floating-point computations $a*(b/c)$ and $(a*b)/c$ are significantly different, so a compiler will evaluate such expressions exactly as written.

6.2.3 Operator Precedence

Precedence levels and associativity rules reflect the most common usage. For example,

```
if (i<=0 || max<i) // ...
```

means "if *i* is less than or equal to *0* or if *max* is less than *i*." That is, it is equivalent to

```
if ( (i<=0) || (max<i) ) // ...
```

and not the legal but nonsensical

```
if (i <= (0||max) < i) // ...
```

However, parentheses should be used whenever a programmer is in doubt about those rules. Use of parentheses becomes more common as the subexpressions become more complicated, but complicated subexpressions are a source of errors. Therefore, if you start feeling the need for parentheses, you might consider breaking up the expression by using an extra variable.

There are cases when the operator precedence does not result in the "obvious" interpretation. For example:

```
if (i&mask == 0)      // oops! == expression as operand for &
```

This does not apply a mask to *i* and then test if the result is zero. Because == has higher precedence than &, the expression is interpreted as *i*&(*mask==0*). Fortunately, it is easy enough for a compiler to warn about most such mistakes. In this case, parentheses are important:

> *if* ((*i&mask*) == *0*) // ...

It is worth noting that the following does not work the way a mathematician might expect:

> *if* (*0* <= *x* <= *99*) // ...

This is legal, but it is interpreted as (*0<=x*) <=*99*, where the result of the first comparison is either *true* or *false*. This Boolean value is then implicitly converted to *1* or *0*, which is then compared to *99*, yielding *true*. To test whether *x* is in the range *0..99*, we might use:

> *if* (*0<=x* && *x<=99*) // ...

A common mistake for novices is to use = (assignment) instead of == (equals) in a condition:

> *if* (*a* = *7*) // *oops! constant assignment in condition*

This is natural because = means ''equals'' in many languages. Again, it is easy for a compiler to warn about most such mistakes – and many do.

6.2.4 Bitwise Logical Operators

The bitwise logical operators &, |, ^, ~, >>, and << are applied to objects of integral types and enumerations – that is, *bool*, *char*, *short*, *int*, *long*, their *unsigned* counterparts, and *enum*s. The usual arithmetic conversions (§C.6.3) are performed to determine the type of the result.

A typical use of bitwise logical operators is to implement the notion of a small set (a bit vector). In this case, each bit of an unsigned integer represents one member of the set, and the number of bits limits the number of members. The binary operator & is interpreted as intersection, | as union, ^ as symmetric difference, and ~ as complement. An enumeration can be used to name the members of such a set. Here is a small example borrowed from an implementation of *ostream*:

> *enum ios_base*::*iostate* {
>   *goodbit=0, eofbit=1, failbit=2, badbit=4*
> };

The implementation of a stream can set and test its state like this:

> *state = goodbit;*
> // ...
> *if* (*state*&(*badbit*|*failbit*)) // *stream no good*

The extra parentheses are necessary because & has higher precedence than |.

A function that reaches the end of input might report it like this:

> *state* |= *eofbit;*

The |= operator is used to add to the state. A simple assignment, *state=eofbit*, would have cleared all other bits.

These stream state flags are observable from outside the stream implementation. For example, we could see how the states of two streams differ like this:

int diff = cin . rdstate ( ) ^cout . rdstate ( ) ;   // rdstate() returns the state

Computing differences of stream states is not very common. For other similar types, computing differences is essential. For example, consider comparing a bit vector that represents the set of interrupts being handled with another that represents the set of interrupts waiting to be handled.

Please note that this bit fiddling is taken from the implementation of iostreams rather than from the user interface. Convenient bit manipulation can be very important, but for reliability, maintainability, portability, etc., it should be kept at low levels of a system. For more general notions of a set, see the standard library *set* (§17.4.3), *bitset* (§17.5.3), and *vector<bool>* (§16.3.11).

Using fields (§C.8.1) is really a convenient shorthand for shifting and masking to extract bit fields from a word. This can, of course, also be done using the bitwise logical operators. For example, one could extract the middle 16 bits of a 32-bit *long* like this:

unsigned short middle (long a) { return (a>>8) &0xffff; }

Do not confuse the bitwise logical operators with the logical operators: &&, | |, and ! . The latter return either *true* or *false*, and they are primarily useful for writing the test in an *if*, *while*, or *for* statement (§6.3.2, §6.3.3). For example, *!0* (not zero) is the value *true*, whereas *~0* (complement of zero) is the bit pattern all-ones, which in two's complement representation is the value *-1*.

6.2.5 Increment and Decrement

The ++ operator is used to express incrementing directly, rather than expressing it indirectly using a combination of an addition and an assignment. By definition, *++lvalue* means *lvalue+=1*, which again means *lvalue=lvalue+1* provided *lvalue* has no side effects. The expression denoting the object to be incremented is evaluated once (only). Decrementing is similarly expressed by the -- operator. The operators ++ and -- can be used as both prefix and postfix operators. The value of *++x* is the new (that is, incremented) value of *x*. For example, *y=++x* is equivalent to *y= (x+=1)* . The value of *x++*, however, is the old value of *x*. For example, *y=x++* is equivalent to *y= (t=x , x+=1 , t)* , where *t* is a variable of the same type as *x*.

Like addition and subtraction of pointers, ++ and -- on pointers operate in terms of elements of the array into which the pointer points; *p++* makes *p* point to the next element (§5.3.1).

The increment operators are particularly useful for incrementing and decrementing variables in loops. For example, one can copy a zero-terminated string like this:

```
void cpy (char* p, const char* q)
{
    while (*p++ = *q++) ;
}
```

Like C, C++ is both loved and hated for enabling such terse, expression-oriented coding. Because

```
while (*p++ = *q++) ;
```

is more than a little obscure to non-C programmers and because the style of coding is not uncommon in C and C++, it is worth examining more closely.

Consider first a more traditional way of copying an array of characters:

```
int  length = strlen (q);
for (int  i = 0; i<=length; i++) p[i] = q[i];
```

This is wasteful. The length of a zero-terminated string is found by reading the string looking for the terminating zero. Thus, we read the string twice: once to find its length and once to copy it. So we try this instead:

```
int  i;
for (i = 0; q[i]!=0 ; i++) p[i] = q[i];
p[i] = 0;  // terminating zero
```

The variable *i* used for indexing can be eliminated because *p* and *q* are pointers:

```
while (*q != 0) {
    *p = *q;
    p++;        // point to next character
    q++;        // point to next character
}
*p = 0;         // terminating zero
```

Because the post-increment operation allows us first to use the value and then to increment it, we can rewrite the loop like this:

```
while (*q != 0) {
    *p++ = *q++;
}
*p = 0; // terminating zero
```

The value of $*p++ = *q++$ is $*q$. We can therefore rewrite the example like this:

```
while ((*p++ = *q++) != 0) { }
```

In this case, we don't notice that $*q$ is zero until we already have copied it into $*p$ and incremented *p*. Consequently, we can eliminate the final assignment of the terminating zero. Finally, we can reduce the example further by observing that we don't need the empty block and that the ''! = 0'' is redundant because the result of a pointer or integral condition is always compared to zero anyway. Thus, we get the version we set out to discover:

```
while (*p++ = *q++) ;
```

Is this version less readable than the previous versions? Not to an experienced C or C++ programmer. Is this version more efficient in time or space than the previous versions? Except for the first version that called *strlen* (), not really. Which version is the most efficient will vary among machine architectures and among compilers.

The most efficient way of copying a zero-terminated character string for your particular machine ought to be the standard string copy function:

```
char* strcpy (char*, const char*);   // from <string.h>
```

For more general copying, the standard *copy* algorithm (§2.7.2, §18.6.1) can be used. Whenever possible, use standard library facilities in preference to fiddling with pointers and bytes. Standard library functions may be inlined (§7.1.1) or even implemented using specialized machine instructions. Therefore, you should measure carefully before believing that some piece of hand-crafted code outperforms library functions.

6.2.6 Free Store

A named object has its lifetime determined by its scope (§4.9.4). However, it is often useful to create an object that exists independently of the scope in which it was created. In particular, it is common to create objects that can be used after returning from the function in which they were created. The operator *new* creates such objects, and the operator *delete* can be used to destroy them. Objects allocated by *new* are said to be ''on the free store'' (also, to be ''heap objects,'' or ''allocated in dynamic memory'').

Consider how we might write a compiler in the style used for the desk calculator (§6.1). The syntax analysis functions might build a tree of the expressions for use by the code generator:

```
struct Enode {
    Token_value oper;
    Enode* left;
    Enode* right;
    // ...
};

Enode* expr(bool get)
{
    Enode* left = term(get);

    for (;;)
        switch(curr_tok) {
        case PLUS:
        case MINUS:
            {   Enode* n = new Enode;      // create an Enode on free store
                n->oper = curr_tok;
                n->left = left;
                n->right = term(true);
                left = n;
                break;
            }
        default:
            return left;                   // return node
        }
}
```

A code generator would then use the resulting nodes and delete them:

```
void generate(Enode* n)
{
    switch (n->oper) {
    case PLUS:
        // ...
        delete n;  // delete an Enode from the free store
    }
}
```

An object created by *new* exists until it is explicitly destroyed by *delete*. Then, the space it occupied can be reused by *new*. A C++ implementation does not guarantee the presence of a "garbage collector" that looks out for unreferenced objects and makes them available to *new* for reuse. Consequently, I will assume that objects created by *new* are manually freed using *delete*. If a garbage collector is present, the *delete*s can be omitted in most cases (§C.9.1).

The *delete* operator may be applied only to a pointer returned by *new* or to zero. Applying *delete* to zero has no effect.

More specialized versions of operator *new* can also be defined (§15.6).

6.2.6.1 Arrays

Arrays of objects can also be created using *new*. For example:

```
char* save_string (const char* p)
{
    char* s = new char[strlen (p) +1];
    strcpy (s,p);          // copy from p to s
    return s;
}

int main (int argc, char* argv[])
{
    if (argc < 2) exit (1);
    char* p = save_string (argv[1]);
    // ...
    delete[] p;
}
```

The "plain" operator *delete* is used to delete individual objects; *delete* [ ] is used to delete arrays.

To deallocate space allocated by *new*, *delete* and *delete* [ ] must be able to determine the size of the object allocated. This implies that an object allocated using the standard implementation of *new* will occupy slightly more space than a static object. Typically, one word is used to hold the object's size.

Note that a *vector* (§3.7.1, §16.3) is a proper object and can therefore be allocated and deallocated using plain *new* and *delete*. For example:

```
void f(int n)
{
    vector<int>* p = new vector<int> (n);      // individual object
    int* q = new int[n];                        // array
    // ...
    delete p;
    delete[] q;
}
```

The *delete* [ ] operator may be applied only to a pointer to an array returned by *new* or to zero. Applying *delete* [ ] to zero has no effect.

6.2.6.2 Memory Exhaustion

The free store operators *new*, *delete*, *new* [ ], and *delete* [ ] are implemented using functions presented in the *<new>* header (§19.4.5):

```
void* operator new(size_t);      // space for individual object
void  operator delete(void*);
void* operator new[](size_t);    // space for array
void  operator delete[](void*);
```

When operator *new* needs to allocate space for an object, it calls *operator new* ( ) to allocate a suitable number of bytes. Similarly, when operator *new* needs to allocate space for an array, it calls *operator new* [ ] ( ).

The standard implementations of *operator new* ( ) and *operator new* [ ] ( ) do not initialize the memory returned.

What happens when *new* can find no store to allocate? By default, the allocator throws a *bad_alloc* exception (for an alternative, see §19.4.5). For example:

```
void f()
{
    try {
        for(;;) new char[10000];
    }
    catch(bad_alloc) {
        cerr << "Memory exhausted!\n";
    }
}
```

However much memory we have available, this will eventually invoke the *bad_alloc* handler.

We can specify what *new* should do upon memory exhaustion. When *new* fails, it first calls a function specified by a call to *set_new_handler* ( ) declared in *<new>*, if any. For example:

```
void out_of_store()
{
    cerr << "operator new failed: out of store\n";
    throw bad_alloc();
}

int main()
{
    set_new_handler(out_of_store); // make out_of_store the new_handler
    for (;;) new char[10000];
    cout << "done\n";
}
```

This will never get to write *done*. Instead, it will write

```
operator new failed: out of store
```

See §14.4.5 for a plausible implementation of an *operator new* ( ) that checks to see if there is a new handler to call and that throws *bad_alloc* if not. A *new_handler* might do something more clever than simply terminating the program. If you know how *new* and *delete* work – for example, because you provided your own *operator new*() and *operator delete*() – the handler might attempt to find some memory for *new* to return. In other words, a user might provide a garbage collector, thus rendering the use of *delete* optional. Doing this is most definitely not a task for a beginner, though. For almost everybody who needs an automatic garbage collector, the right thing to do is to acquire one that has already been written and tested (§C.9.1).

By providing a *new_handler*, we take care of the check for memory exhaustion for every ordinary use of *new* in the program. Two alternative ways of controlling memory allocation exist. We can either provide nonstandard allocation and deallocation functions (§15.6) for the standard uses of *new* or rely on additional allocation information provided by the user (§10.4.11, §19.4.5).

6.2.7 Explicit Type Conversion

Sometimes, we have to deal with"raw memory;" that is, memory that holds or will hold objects of a type not known to the compiler. For example, a memory allocator may return a *void** pointing to newly allocated memory or we might want to state that a given integer value is to be treated as the address of an I/O device:

```
void* malloc (size_t) ;

void f()
{
    int* p = static_cast<int*> (malloc ( 100 ) ) ;              // new allocation used as ints
    IO_device* d1 = reinterpret_cast<IO_device*> (0Xff00) ;    // device at 0Xff00
    // ...
}
```

A compiler does not know the type of the object pointed to by the *void**. Nor can it know whether the integer *0Xff00* is a valid address. Consequently, the correctness of the conversions are completely in the hands of the programmer. Explicit type conversion, often called *casting*, is occasionally essential. However, traditionally it is seriously overused and a major source of errors.

The *static_cast* operator converts between related types such as one pointer type to another in the same class hierarchy, an enumeration to an integral type, or a floating-point type to an integral type. The *reinterpret_cast* handles conversions between unrelated types such as an integer to a pointer or a pointer to an unrelated pointer type. This distinction allows the compiler to apply some minimal type checking for *static_cast* and makes it easier for a programmer to find the more dangerous conversions represented as *reinterpret_casts*. Some *static_casts* are portable, but few *reinterpret_casts* are. Hardly any guarantees are made for *reinterpret_cast*, but generally it produces a value of a new type that has the same bit pattern as its argument. If the target has at least as many bits as the original value, we can *reinterpret_cast* the result back to its original type and use it. The result of a *reinterpret_cast* is guaranteed to be usable only if its result type is the exact type used to define the value involved.

If you feel tempted to use an explicit type conversion, take the time to consider if it is *really* necessary. In C++, explicit type conversion is unnecessary in most cases when C needs it (§1.6) and also in many cases in which earlier versions of C++ needed it (§1.6.2, §B.2.3). In many programs, explicit type conversion can be completely avoided; in others, its use can be localized to a few routines. In this book, explicit type conversion is used in realistic situations in §6.2.7, §7.7, §13.5, §13.6, §17.6.2.3, §15.4, §25.4.1, and §E.3.1, only.

A form of run-time checked conversion, *dynamic_cast* (§15.4.1), and a cast for removing *const* qualifiers, *const_cast* (§15.4.2.1), are also provided.

From C, C++ inherited the notation $(T)e$, which performs any conversion that can be expressed as a combination of *static_cast*s, *reinterpret_cast*s, and *const_cast*s to make a value of type *T* from the expression *e* (§B.2.3). This C-style cast is far more dangerous than the named conversion operators because the notation is harder to spot in a large program and the kind of conversion intended by the programmer is not explicit. That is, $(T)e$ might be doing a portable conversion between related types, a nonportable conversion between unrelated types, or removing the *const* modifier from a pointer type. Without knowing the exact types of *T* and *e*, you cannot tell.

6.2.8 Constructors

The construction of a value of type *T* from a value *e* can be expressed by the functional notation $T(e)$. For example:

```
void f(double d)
{
    int  i = int (d);           // truncate d
    complex  z = complex (d);   // make a complex from d
    // ...
}
```

The $T(e)$ construct is sometimes referred to as a *function-style cast*. Unfortunately, for a built-in type *T*, $T(e)$ is equivalent to $(T)e$ (§6.2.7). This implies that for many built-in types $T(e)$ is not safe. For example, values of arithmetic types can be truncated. Even explicit conversion of a longer integer type to a shorter (such as *long* to *char*) can result in nonportable implementation-defined behavior. I try to use the notation exclusively where the construction of a value is well-defined; that is, for narrowing arithmetic conversions (§C.6), for integer to enumeration conversions (§4.8), and for construction of objects of user-defined types (§2.5.2, §10.2.3).

Conversions to pointer types cannot be expressed directly using the $T(e)$ notation. For example, *char* (2) is a syntax error. Unfortunately, the protection that the constructor notation provides against such dangerous conversions can be circumvented by using *typedef* names (§4.9.7) for pointer types.

The constructor notation $T()$ is used to express the default value of type *T*. For example:

```
void f(double d)
{
    int  j = int ();            // default int value
    complex  z = complex ();    // default complex value
    // ...
}
```

The value of an explicit use of the constructor for a built-in type is *0* converted to that type (§4.9.5). Thus, *int*() is another way of writing *0*. For a user-defined type *T*, $T()$ is defined by the default constructor (§10.4.2), if any.

The use of the constructor notation for built-in types is particularly important when writing templates. Then, the programmer does not know whether a template parameter will refer to a built-in type or a user-defined type (§16.3.4, §17.4.1.2).

6.3 Statement Summary

Here are a summary and some examples of C++ statements:

Statement Syntax
statement:
declaration
{ *statement-list$_{opt}$* }
try { *statement-list$_{opt}$* } *handler-list*
expression$_{opt}$;
if (*condition*) *statement*
if (*condition*) *statement else statement*
switch (*condition*) *statement*
while (*condition*) *statement*
do statement while (*expression*) ;
for (*for-init-statement condition$_{opt}$* ; *expression$_{opt}$*) *statement*
case constant-expression : *statement*
default : *statement*
break ;
continue ;
return expression$_{opt}$;
goto identifier ;
identifier : *statement*
statement-list:
statement statement-list$_{opt}$
condition:
expression
type-specifier declarator = *expression*
handler-list:
catch (*exception-declaration*) { *statement-list$_{opt}$* }
handler-list handler-list$_{opt}$

Note that a declaration is a statement and that there is no assignment statement or procedure call statement; assignments and function calls are expressions. The statements for handling exceptions, *try-block*s, are described in §8.3.1.

6.3.1 Declarations as Statements

A declaration is a statement. Unless a variable is declared *static*, its initializer is executed whenever the thread of control passes through the declaration (see also §10.4.8). The reason for allowing declarations wherever a statement can be used (and a few other places; §6.3.2.1, §6.3.3.1) is to enable the programmer to minimize the errors caused by uninitialized variables and to allow better locality in code. There is rarely a reason to introduce a variable before there is a value for it to hold. For example:

```
void f(vector<string>& v, int i, const char* p)
{
    if (p==0) return;
    if (i<0 || v.size() <=i) error("bad index");
    string s = v[i];
    if (s == p) {
        // ...
    }
    // ...
}
```

The ability to place declarations after executable code is essential for many constants and for single-assignment styles of programming where a value of an object is not changed after initialization. For user-defined types, postponing the definition of a variable until a suitable initializer is available can also lead to better performance. For example,

```
string s; /* ... */ s = "The best is the enemy of the good.";
```

can easily be much slower than

```
string s = "Voltaire";
```

The most common reason to declare a variable without an initializer is that it requires a statement to initialize it. Examples are input variables and arrays.

6.3.2 Selection Statements

A value can be tested by either an *if* statement or a *switch* statement:

```
if ( condition ) statement
if ( condition ) statement else statement
switch ( condition ) statement
```

The comparison operators

```
==    !=    <    <=    >    >=
```

return the *bool true* if the comparison is true and *false* otherwise.

In an *if* statement, the first (or only) statement is executed if the expression is nonzero and the second statement (if it is specified) is executed otherwise. This implies that any arithmetic or pointer expression can be used as a condition. For example, if *x* is an integer, then

```
if (x) // ...
```

means

> *if* (*x* != *0*) // ...

For a pointer *p*,

> *if* (*p*) // ...

is a direct statement of the test "does *p* point to a valid object," whereas

> *if* (*p* != *0*) // ...

states the same question indirectly by comparing to a value known not to point to an object. Note that the representation of the pointer *0* is not all-zeros on all machines (§5.1.1). Every compiler I have checked generated the same code for both forms of the test.

The logical operators

> && || !

are most commonly used in conditions. The operators && and || will not evaluate their second argument unless doing so is necessary. For example,

> *if* (*p* && *1*<*p*->*count*) // ...

first tests that *p* is nonzero. It tests *1*<*p*->*count* only if *p* is nonzero.

Some *if-statement*s can conveniently be replaced by *conditional-expression*s. For example,

> *if* (*a* <= *b*)
>   *max* = *b*;
> *else*
>   *max* = *a*;

is better expressed like this:

> *max* = (*a*<=*b*) ? *b* : *a*;

The parentheses around the condition are not necessary, but I find the code easier to read when they are used.

A *switch-statement* can alternatively be written as a set of *if-statement*s. For example,

> *switch* (*val*) {
> *case 1*:
>   *f*();
>   *break*;
> *case 2*:
>   *g*();
>   *break*;
> *default*:
>   *h*();
>   *break*;
> }

could alternatively be expressed as

```
if (val == 1)
    f();
else if (val == 2)
    g();
else
    h();
```

The meaning is the same, but the first (*switch*) version is preferred because the nature of the operation (testing a value against a set of constants) is explicit. This makes the *switch* statement easier to read for nontrivial examples. It can also lead to the generation of better code.

Beware that a case of a switch must be terminated somehow unless you want to carry on executing the next case. Consider:

```
switch (val) {                 // beware
case 1:
    cout << "case 1\n";
case 2:
    cout << "case 2\n";
default:
    cout << "default: case not found\n";
}
```

Invoked with *val==1*, this prints

```
case 1
case 2
default: case not found
```

to the great surprise of the uninitiated. It is a good idea to comment the (rare) cases in which a fall-through is intentional so that an uncommented fall-through can be assumed to be an error. A *break* is the most common way of terminating a case, but a *return* is often useful (§6.1.1).

6.3.2.1 Declarations in Conditions

To avoid accidental misuse of a variable, it is usually a good idea to introduce the variable into the smallest scope possible. In particular, it is usually best to delay the definition of a local variable until one can give it an initial value. That way, one cannot get into trouble by using the variable before its initial value is assigned.

One of the most elegant applications of these two principles is to declare a variable in a condition. Consider:

```
if (double d = prim(true)) {
    left /= d;
    break;
}
```

Here, *d* is declared and initialized and the value of *d* after initialization is tested as the value of the condition. The scope of *d* extends from its point of declaration to the end of the statement that the condition controls. For example, had there been an *else*-branch to the *if-statement*, *d* would be in scope on both branches.

The obvious and traditional alternative is to declare *d* before the condition. However, this opens the scope (literally) for the use of *d* before its initialization or after its intended useful life:

```
double d;
// ...

d2 = d;    // oops!
// ...

if (d = prim(true)) {
    left /= d;
    break;
}
// ...

d = 2.0; // two unrelated uses of d
```

In addition to the logical benefits of declaring variables in conditions, doing so also yields the most compact source code.

A declaration in a condition must declare and initialize a single variable or *const*.

6.3.3 Iteration Statements

A loop can be expressed as a *for*, *while*, or *do* statement:

```
while ( condition ) statement
do statement while ( expression ) ;
for ( for-init-statement condition_opt ; expression_opt ) statement
```

Each of these statements executes a statement (called the *controlled* statement or the *body of the loop*) repeatedly until the condition becomes false or the programmer breaks out of the loop some other way.

The *for-statement* is intended for expressing fairly regular loops. The loop variable, the termination condition, and the expression that updates the loop variable can be presented ''up front'' on a single line. This can greatly increase readability and thereby decrease the frequency of errors. If no initialization is needed, the initializing statement can be empty. If the *condition* is omitted, the *for-statement* will loop forever unless the user explicitly exits it by a **break**, **return**, **goto**, **throw**, or some less obvious way such as a call of *exit()* (§9.4.1.1). If the *expression* is omitted, we must update some form of loop variable in the body of the loop. If the loop isn't of the simple ''introduce a loop variable, test the condition, update the loop variable'' variety, it is often better expressed as a *while-statement*. A *for-statement* is also useful for expressing a loop without an explicit termination condition:

```
for(;;) { // "forever"
    // ...
}
```

A *while-statement* simply executes its controlled statement until its condition becomes *false*. I tend to prefer *while-statements* over *for-statements* when there isn't an obvious loop variable or where the update of a loop variable naturally comes in the middle of the loop body. An input loop is an example of a loop where there is no obvious loop variable:

```
while (cin>>ch) // ...
```

In my experience, the *do-statement* is a source of errors and confusion. The reason is that its body is always executed once before the condition is evaluated. However, for the body to work correctly, something very much like the condition must hold even the first time through. More often than I would have guessed, I have found that condition not to hold as expected either when the program was first written and tested or later after the code preceding it has been modified. I also prefer the condition ''up front where I can see it.'' Consequently, I tend to avoid *do-statements*.

6.3.3.1 Declarations in For-Statements

A variable can be declared in the initializer part of a *for-statement*. If that initializer is a declaration, the variable (or variables) it introduces is in scope until the end of the *for-statement*. For example:

```
void f(int v[], int max)
{
    for (int i = 0; i<max; i++) v[i] = i*i;
}
```

If the final value of an index needs to be known after exit from a *for*-loop, the index variable must be declared outside the *for*-loop (e.g., §6.3.4).

6.3.4 Goto

C++ possesses the infamous *goto*:

```
goto identifier ;
identifier : statement
```

The *goto* has few uses in general high-level programming, but it can be very useful when C++ code is generated by a program rather than written directly by a person; for example, *goto*s can be used in a parser generated from a grammar by a parser generator. The *goto* can also be important in the rare cases in which optimal efficiency is essential, for example, in the inner loop of some real-time application.

The scope of a label is the function it is in. This implies that you can use *goto* to jump both into and out of blocks. The only restriction is that you cannot jump past an initializer or into an exception handler (§8.3.1).

One of the few sensible uses of *goto* in ordinary code is to break out from a nested loop or *switch-statement* (a **break** breaks out of only the innermost enclosing loop or *switch-statement*). For example:

```
void f()
{
    int i;
    int j;
```

```
    for (i = 0; i<n; i++)
         for (j = 0; j<m; j++) if (nm[i][j] == a) goto found;
    // not found
    // ...
found:
    // nm[i][j] == a
}
```

There is also a *continue* statement that, in effect, goes to the end of a loop statement, as explained in §6.1.5.

6.4 Comments and Indentation

Judicious use of comments and consistent use of indentation can make the task of reading and understanding a program much more pleasant. Several different consistent styles of indentation are in use. I see no fundamental reason to prefer one over another (although, like most programmers, I have my preferences, and this book reflects them). The same applies to styles of comments.

Comments can be misused in ways that seriously affect the readability of a program. The compiler does not understand the contents of a comment, so it has no way of ensuring that a comment

[1]   is meaningful,
[2]   describes the program, and
[3]   is up to date.

Most programs contain comments that are incomprehensible, ambiguous, and just plain wrong. Bad comments can be worse than no comments.

If something can be stated *in the language itself*, it should be, and not just mentioned in a comment. This remark is aimed at comments such as these:

    // variable "v" must be initialized

    // variable "v" must be used only by function "f()"

    // call function "init()" before calling any other function in this file

    // call function "cleanup()" at the end of your program

    // don't use function "weird()"

    // function "f()" takes two arguments

Such comments can often be rendered unnecessary by proper use of C++. For example, one might utilize the linkage rules (§9.2) and the visibility, initialization, and cleanup rules for classes (see §10.4.1) to make the preceding examples redundant.

Once something has been stated clearly in the language, it should not be mentioned a second time in a comment. For example:

    a = b+c;   // a becomes b+c
    count++;   // increment the counter

Such comments are worse than simply redundant. They increase the amount of text the reader has to look at, they often obscure the structure of the program, and they may be wrong. Note, however, that such comments are used extensively for teaching purposes in programming language textbooks such as this. This is one of the many ways a program in a textbook differs from a real program.

My preference is for:

[1] A comment for each source file stating what the declarations in it have in common, references to manuals, general hints for maintenance, etc.

[2] A comment for each class, template, and namespace

[3] A comment for each nontrivial function stating its purpose, the algorithm used (unless it is obvious), and maybe something about the assumptions it makes about its environment

[4] A comment for each global and namespace variable and constant

[5] A few comments where the code is nonobvious and/or nonportable

[6] Very little else

For example:

```
//    tbl.c: Implementation of the symbol table.

/*
      Gaussian elimination with partial pivoting.
      See Ralston: "A first course ..." pg 411.
*/

//    swap() assumes the stack layout of an SGI R6000.

/*********************************

      Copyright (c) 1997 AT&T, Inc.
      All rights reserved

*********************************/
```

A well-chosen and well-written set of comments is an essential part of a good program. Writing good comments can be as difficult as writing the program itself. It is an art well worth cultivating.

Note also that if `//` comments are used exclusively in a function, then any part of that function can be commented out using `/* */` style comments, and vice versa.

6.5 Advice

[1] Prefer the standard library to other libraries and to ''handcrafted code;'' §6.1.8.

[2] Avoid complicated expressions; §6.2.3.

[3] If in doubt about operator precedence, parenthesize; §6.2.3.

[4] Avoid explicit type conversion (casts); §6.2.7.

[5] When explicit type conversion is necessary, prefer the more specific cast operators to the C-style cast; §6.2.7.

[6] Use the $T(e)$ notation exclusively for well-defined construction; §6.2.8.

[7] Avoid expressions with undefined order of evaluation; §6.2.2.

[8] Avoid *goto*; §6.3.4.

[9] Avoid *do-statements*; §6.3.3.

[10] Don't declare a variable until you have a value to initialize it with; §6.3.1, §6.3.2.1, §6.3.3.1.

[11] Keep comments crisp; §6.4.

[12] Maintain a consistent indentation style; §6.4.

[13] Prefer defining a member *operator new* ( ) (§15.6) to replacing the global *operator new* ( ) ; §6.2.6.2.

[14] When reading input, always consider ill-formed input; §6.1.3.

6.6 Exercises

1. (*1) Rewrite the following *for* statement as an equivalent *while* statement:

   for (*i=0*; *i<max_length*; *i++*) *if* (*input_line* [*i*] == ´?´) *quest_count++*;

   Rewrite it to use a pointer as the controlled variable, that is, so that the test is of the form **p==´?´* .

2. (*1) Fully parenthesize the following expressions:

   a = b + c * d << 2 & 8
   a & 077 != 3
   a == b || a == c && c < 5
   c = x != 0
   0 <= i < 7
   f(1,2) +3
   a = - 1 + + b -- - 5
   a = b == c ++
   a = b = c = 0
   a[4] [2] *= * b ? c : * d * 2
   a-b,c=d

3. (*2) Read a sequence of possibly whitespace-separated (name,value) pairs, where the name is a single whitespace-separated word and the value is an integer or a floating-point value. Compute and print the sum and mean for each name and the sum and mean for all names. Hint: §6.1.8.

4. (*1) Write a table of values for the bitwise logical operations (§6.2.4) for all possible combinations of *0* and *1* operands.

5. (*1.5) Find 5 different C++ constructs for which the meaning is undefined (§C.2). (*1.5) Find 5 different C++ constructs for which the meaning is implementation-defined (§C.2).

6. (*1) Find 10 different examples of nonportable C++ code.

7. (*2) Write 5 expressions for which the order of evaluation is undefined. Execute them to see what one or – preferably – more implementations do with them.

8. (*1.5) What happens if you divide by zero on your system? What happens in case of overflow and underflow?

9. (*1) Fully parenthesize the following expressions:

```
*p++
*--p
++a--
(int*)p->m
*p.m
*a[i]
```

10. (*2) Write these functions: *strlen* ( ), which returns the length of a C-style string; *strcpy* ( ), which copies a C-style string into another; and *strcmp* ( ), which compares two C-style strings. Consider what the argument types and return types ought to be. Then compare your functions with the standard library versions as declared in *<cstring>* (*<string.h>*) and as specified in §20.4.1.

11. (*1) See how your compiler reacts to these errors:

```
void f(int a, int b)
{
        if (a = 3) // ...
        if (a&077 == 0) // ...
        a := b+1;
}
```

Devise more simple errors and see how the compiler reacts.

12. (*2) Modify the program from §6.6[3] to also compute the median.

13. (*2) Write a function *cat* ( ) that takes two C-style string arguments and returns a string that is the concatenation of the arguments. Use *new* to find store for the result.

14. (*2) Write a function *rev* ( ) that takes a C-style string argument and reverses the characters in it. That is, after *rev* (*p*) the last character of *p* will be the first, etc.

15. (*1.5) What does the following example do?

```
void send(int* to, int* from, int count)
        // Duff's device. Helpful comment deliberately deleted.
{
        int n = (count+7)/8;
        switch (count%8) {
        case 0:    do { *to++ = *from++;
        case 7:         *to++ = *from++;
        case 6:         *to++ = *from++;
        case 5:         *to++ = *from++;
        case 4:         *to++ = *from++;
        case 3:         *to++ = *from++;
        case 2:         *to++ = *from++;
        case 1:         *to++ = *from++;
                } while (--n>0);
        }
}
```

Why would anyone write something like that?

16. (*2) Write a function *atoi* (*const char*) that takes a C-style string containing digits and returns the corresponding *int*. For example, *atoi* ("*123*") is *123*. Modify *atoi* ( ) to handle

C++ octal and hexadecimal notation in addition to plain decimal numbers. Modify *atoi* () to handle the C++ character constant notation.

17. (*2) Write a function *itoa* (*int i*, *char b* [ ]) that creates a string representation of *i* in *b* and returns *b*.

18. (*2) Type in the calculator example and get it to work. Do not "save time" by using an already entered text. You'll learn most from finding and correcting "little silly errors."

19. (*2) Modify the calculator to report line numbers for errors.

20. (*3) Allow a user to define functions in the calculator. Hint: Define a function as a sequence of operations just as a user would have typed them. Such a sequence can be stored either as a character string or as a list of tokens. Then read and execute those operations when the function is called. If you want a user-defined function to take arguments, you will have to invent a notation for that.

21. (*1.5) Convert the desk calculator to use a *symbol* structure instead of using the static variables *number_value* and *string_value*.

22. (*2.5) Write a program that strips comments out of a C++ program. That is, read from *cin*, remove both // comments and / * * / comments, and write the result to *cout*. Do not worry about making the layout of the output look nice (that would be another, and much harder, exercise). Do not worry about incorrect programs. Beware of //, / *, and * / in comments, strings, and character constants.

23. (*2) Look at some programs to get an idea of the variety of indentation, naming, and commenting styles actually used.

7

Functions

To iterate is human,
to recurse divine.
− L. Peter Deutsch

Function declarations and definitions — argument passing — return values — function overloading — ambiguity resolution — default arguments — *stdargs* — pointers to functions — macros — advice — exercises.

7.1 Function Declarations

The typical way of getting something done in a C++ program is to call a function to do it. Defining a function is the way you specify how an operation is to be done. A function cannot be called unless it has been previously declared.

A function declaration gives the name of the function, the type of the value returned (if any) by the function, and the number and types of the arguments that must be supplied in a call of the function. For example:

```
Elem* next_elem();
char* strcpy(char* to, const char* from);
void exit(int);
```

The semantics of argument passing are identical to the semantics of initialization. Argument types are checked and implicit argument type conversion takes place when necessary. For example:

```
double sqrt(double);

double sr2 = sqrt(2);          // call sqrt() with the argument double(2)
double sq3 = sqrt("three");    // error: sqrt() requires an argument of type double
```

The value of such checking and type conversion should not be underestimated.

A function declaration may contain argument names. This can be a help to the reader of a program, but the compiler simply ignores such names. As mentioned in §4.7, *void* as a return type means that the function does not return a value.

7.1.1 Function Definitions

Every function that is called in a program must be defined somewhere (once only). A function definition is a function declaration in which the body of the function is presented. For example:

```
extern void swap(int*, int*);    // a declaration

void swap(int* p, int* q)        // a definition
{
    int t = *p;
    *p = *q;
    *q = t;
}
```

The type of the definition and all declarations for a function must specify the same type. The argument names, however, are not part of the type and need not be identical.

It is not uncommon to have function definitions with unused arguments:

```
void search(table* t, const char* key, const char*)
{
    // no use of the third argument
}
```

As shown, the fact that an argument is unused can be indicated by not naming it. Typically, unnamed arguments arise from the simplification of code or from planning ahead for extensions. In both cases, leaving the argument in place, although unused, ensures that callers are not affected by the change.

A function can be defined to be *inline*. For example:

```
inline int fac(int n)
{
    return (n<2) ? 1 : n*fac(n-1);
}
```

The *inline* specifier is a hint to the compiler that it should attempt to generate code for a call of *fac*() inline rather than laying down the code for the function once and then calling through the usual function call mechanism. A clever compiler can generate the constant *720* for a call *fac*(*6*). The possibility of mutually recursive inline functions, inline functions that recurse or not depending on input, etc., makes it impossible to guarantee that every call of an *inline* function is actually inlined. The degree of cleverness of a compiler cannot be legislated, so one compiler might generate *720*, another *6*fac*(*5*), and yet another an un-inlined call *fac*(*6*).

To make inlining possible in the absence of unusually clever compilation and linking facilities, the definition – and not just the declaration – of an inline function must be in scope (§9.2). An *inline* specifier does not affect the semantics of a function. In particular, an inline function still has a unique address and so do *static* variables (§7.1.2) of an inline function.

7.1.2 Static Variables

A local variable is initialized when the thread of execution reaches its definition. By default, this happens in every call of the function and each invocation of the function has its own copy of the variable. If a local variable is declared *static*, a single, statically allocated object (§C.9) will be used to represent that variable in all calls of the function. It will be initialized only the first time the thread of execution reaches its definition. For example:

```
void f(int a)
{
    while (a--) {
        static int n = 0;          // initialized once
        int x = 0;                 // initialized 'a' times in each call of f()

        cout << "n == " << n++ << ", x == " << x++ << '\n';
    }
}

int main()
{
    f(3);
}
```

This prints:

```
n == 0, x == 0
n == 1, x == 0
n == 2, x == 0
```

A static variable provides a function with "a memory" without introducing a global variable that might be accessed and corrupted by other functions (see also §10.2.4).

7.2 Argument Passing

When a function is called, store is set aside for its formal arguments and each formal argument is initialized by its corresponding actual argument. The semantics of argument passing are identical to the semantics of initialization. In particular, the type of an actual argument is checked against the type of the corresponding formal argument, and all standard and user-defined type conversions are performed. There are special rules for passing arrays (§7.2.1), a facility for passing unchecked arguments (§7.6), and a facility for specifying default arguments (§7.5). Consider:

```
void f(int val, int& ref)
{
    val++;
    ref++;
}
```

When $f()$ is called, *val++* increments a local copy of the first actual argument, whereas *ref++* increments the second actual argument. For example,

```
void g()
{
    int i = 1;
    int j = 1;
    f(i,j);
}
```

will increment *j* but not *i*. The first argument, *i*, is passed *by value*, the second argument, *j*, is passed *by reference*. As mentioned in §5.5, functions that modify call-by-reference arguments can make programs hard to read and should most often be avoided (but see §21.3.2). It can, however, be noticeably more efficient to pass a large object by reference than to pass it by value. In that case, the argument might be declared *const* to indicate that the reference is used for efficiency reasons only and not to enable the called function to change the value of the object:

```
void f(const Large& arg)
{
    // the value of "arg" cannot be changed without explicit use of type conversion
}
```

The absence of *const* in the declaration of a reference argument is taken as a statement of intent to modify the variable:

```
void g(Large& arg);  // assume that g() modifies arg
```

Similarly, declaring a pointer argument *const* tells readers that the value of an object pointed to by that argument is not changed by the function. For example:

```
int strlen(const char*);                    // number of characters in a C-style string
char* strcpy(char* to, const char* from);   // copy a C-style string
int strcmp(const char*, const char*);       // compare C-style strings
```

The importance of using *const* arguments increases with the size of a program.

Note that the semantics of argument passing are different from the semantics of assignment. This is important for *const* arguments, reference arguments, and arguments of some user-defined types (§10.4.4.1).

A literal, a constant, and an argument that requires conversion can be passed as a *const&* argument, but not as a non-*const&* argument. Allowing conversions for a *const T&* argument ensures that such an argument can be given exactly the same set of values as a *T* argument by passing the value in a temporary, if necessary. For example:

```
float fsqrt(const float&);  // Fortran-style sqrt taking a reference argument

void g(double d)
{
    float r = fsqrt(2.0f);  // pass ref to temp holding 2.0f
    r = fsqrt(r);           // pass ref to r
    r = fsqrt(d);           // pass ref to temp holding float(d)
}
```

Disallowing conversions for non-*const* reference arguments (§5.5) avoids the possibility of silly mistakes arising from the introduction of temporaries. For example:

```
void update (float& i);

void g (double d, float r)
{
    update (2.0f);    // error: const argument
    update (r);       // pass ref to r
    update (d);       // error: type conversion required
}
```

Had these calls been allowed, *update*() would quietly have updated temporaries that immediately were deleted. Usually, that would come as an unpleasant surprise to the programmer.

7.2.1 Array Arguments

If an array is used as a function argument, a pointer to its initial element is passed. For example:

```
int strlen (const char*);

void f()
{
    char v[] = "an array";
    int i = strlen (v);
    int j = strlen ("Nicholas");
}
```

That is, an argument of type $T[]$ will be converted to a $T*$ when passed as an argument. This implies that an assignment to an element of an array argument changes the value of an element of the argument array. In other words, arrays differ from other types in that an array is not (and cannot be) passed by value.

The size of an array is not available to the called function. This can be a nuisance, but there are several ways of circumventing this problem. C-style strings are zero-terminated, so their size can be computed easily. For other arrays, a second argument specifying the size can be passed. For example:

```
void compute1 (int* vec_ptr, int vec_size);      // one way

struct Vec {
    int* ptr;
    int size;
};

void compute2 (const Vec& v);        // another way
```

Alternatively, a type such as *vector* (§3.7.1, §16.3) can be used instead of an array.

Multidimensional arrays are trickier (see §C.7), but often arrays of pointers can be used instead, and they need no special treatment. For example:

```
char* day[] = {
    "mon", "tue", "wed", "thu", "fri", "sat", "sun"
};
```

Again, *vector* and similar types are alternatives to the built-in, low-level arrays and pointers.

7.3 Value Return

A value must be returned from a function that is not declared *void* (however, *main* ( ) is special; §3.2). Conversely, a value cannot be returned from a *void* function. For example:

```
int f1() { }              // error: no value returned
void f2() { }             // ok

int f3() { return 1; }    // ok
void f4() { return 1; }   // error: return value in void function

int f5() { return; }      // error: return value missing
void f6() { return; }     // ok
```

A return value is specified by a return statement. For example:

```
int fac(int n) { return (n>1) ? n*fac(n-1) : 1; }
```

A function that calls itself is said to be *recursive*.

There can be more than one return statement in a function:

```
int fac2(int n)
{
    if (n > 1) return n*fac2(n-1);
    return 1;
}
```

Like the semantics of argument passing, the semantics of function value return are identical to the semantics of initialization. A return statement is considered to initialize an unnamed variable of the returned type. The type of a return expression is checked against the type of the returned type, and all standard and user-defined type conversions are performed. For example:

```
double f() { return 1; }   // 1 is implicitly converted to double(1)
```

Each time a function is called, a new copy of its arguments and local (automatic) variables is created. The store is reused after the function returns, so a pointer to a local variable should never be returned. The contents of the location pointed to will change unpredictably:

```
int* fp() { int local = 1; /* ... */ return &local; }   // bad
```

This error is less common than the equivalent error using references:

```
int& fr() { int local = 1; /* ... */ return local; }     // bad
```

Fortunately, a compiler can easily warn about returning references to local variables.

A *void* function cannot return a value. However, a call of a *void* function doesn't yield a value, so a *void* function can use a call of a *void* function as the expression in a *return* statement. For example:

```
void g(int* p);

void h(int* p) { /* ... */ return g(p); }   // ok: return of "no value"
```

This form of return is important when writing template functions where the return type is a template parameter (see §18.4.4.2).

7.4 Overloaded Function Names

Most often, it is a good idea to give different functions different names, but when some functions conceptually perform the same task on objects of different types, it can be more convenient to give them the same name. Using the same name for operations on different types is called *overloading*. The technique is already used for the basic operations in C++. That is, there is only one name for addition, +, yet it can be used to add values of integer, floating-point, and pointer types. This idea is easily extended to functions defined by the programmer. For example:

```
void  print(int);           // print an int
void  print(const char*);   // print a C-style character string
```

As far as the compiler is concerned, the only thing functions of the same name have in common is that name. Presumably, the functions are in some sense similar, but the language does not constrain or aid the programmer. Thus overloaded function names are primarily a notational convenience. This convenience is significant for functions with conventional names such as *sqrt*, *print*, and *open*. When a name is semantically significant, this convenience becomes essential. This happens, for example, with operators such as +, *, and <<, in the case of constructors (§11.7), and in generic programming (§2.7.2, Chapter 18). When a function *f* is called, the compiler must figure out which of the functions with the name *f* is to be invoked. This is done by comparing the types of the actual arguments with the types of the formal arguments of all functions called *f*. The idea is to invoke the function that is the best match on the arguments and give a compile-time error if no function is the best match. For example:

```
void  print(double);
void  print(long);

void  f()
{
    print(1L);         // print(long)
    print(1.0);        // print(double)
    print(1);          // error, ambiguous: print(long(1)) or print(double(1))?
}
```

Finding the right version to call from a set of overloaded functions is done by looking for a best match between the type of the argument expression and the parameters (formal arguments) of the functions. To approximate our notions of what is reasonable, a series of criteria are tried in order:

[1] Exact match; that is, match using no or only trivial conversions (for example, array name to pointer, function name to pointer to function, and *T* to const *T*)

[2] Match using promotions; that is, integral promotions (*bool* to *int*, *char* to *int*, *short* to *int*, and their *unsigned* counterparts; §C.6.1) and *float* to *double*

[3] Match using standard conversions (for example, *int* to *double*, *double* to *int*, *double* to *long double*, *Derived** to *Base** (§12.2), *T** to *void** (§5.6), *int* to *unsigned int*; §C.6)

[4] Match using user-defined conversions (§11.4)

[5] Match using the ellipsis . . . in a function declaration (§7.6)

If two matches are found at the highest level where a match is found, the call is rejected as ambiguous. The resolution rules are this elaborate primarily to take into account the elaborate C and C++ rules for built-in numeric types (§C.6). For example:

```
void print(int);
void print(const char*);
void print(double);
void print(long);
void print(char);

void h(char c, int i, short s, float f)
{
    print(c);          // exact match: invoke print(char)
    print(i);          // exact match: invoke print(int)
    print(s);          // integral promotion: invoke print(int)
    print(f);          // float to double promotion: print(double)

    print('a');        // exact match: invoke print(char)
    print(49);         // exact match: invoke print(int)
    print(0);          // exact match: invoke print(int)
    print("a");        // exact match: invoke print(const char*)
}
```

The call *print*(*0*) invokes *print*(*int*) because *0* is an *int*. The call *print*('*a*') invokes *print*(*char*) because '*a*' is a *char* (§4.3.1). The reason to distinguish between conversions and promotions is that we want to prefer safe promotions, such as *char* to *int*, over unsafe conversions, such as *int* to *char*.

The overloading resolution is independent of the order of declaration of the functions considered.

Overloading relies on a relatively complicated set of rules, and occasionally a programmer will be surprised which function is called. So, why bother? Consider the alternative to overloading. Often, we need similar operations performed on objects of several types. Without overloading, we must define several functions with different names:

```
void print_int(int);
void print_char(char);
void print_string(const char*); // C-style string

void g(int i, char c, const char* p, double d)
{
    print_int(i);          // ok
    print_char(c);         // ok
    print_string(p);       // ok

    print_int(c);          // ok? calls print_int(int(c))
    print_char(i);         // ok? calls print_char(char(i))
    print_string(i);       // error
    print_int(d);          // ok? calls print_int(int(d))
}
```

Compared to the overloaded *print*(), we have to remember several names and remember to use those correctly. This can be tedious, defeats attempts to do generic programming (§2.7.2), and generally encourages the programmer to focus on relatively low-level type issues. Because there is no overloading, all standard conversions apply to arguments to these functions. It can also lead to errors. In the previous example, this implies that only one of the four calls with a ''wrong'' argument is caught by the compiler. Thus, overloading can increase the chances that an unsuitable argument will be rejected by the compiler.

7.4.1 Overloading and Return Type

Return types are not considered in overload resolution. The reason is to keep resolution for an individual operator (§11.2.1, §11.2.4) or function call context-independent. Consider:

```
float  sqrt (float);
double  sqrt (double);

void f (double da, float fla)
{
    float  fl = sqrt (da);   // call sqrt(double)
    double  d = sqrt (da);  // call sqrt(double)
    fl = sqrt (fla);         // call sqrt(float)
    d = sqrt (fla);          // call sqrt(float)
}
```

If the return type were taken into account, it would no longer be possible to look at a call of *sqrt* ( ) in isolation and determine which function was called.

7.4.2 Overloading and Scopes

Functions declared in different non-namespace scopes do not overload. For example:

```
void  f (int);

void  g ()
{
    void  f (double);
    f (1);             // call f(double)
}
```

Clearly, *f* (*int*) would have been the best match for *f* (*1*), but only *f* (*double*) is in scope. In such cases, local declarations can be added or subtracted to get the desired behavior. As always, intentional hiding can be a useful technique, but unintentional hiding is a source of surprises. When overloading across class scopes (§15.2.2) or namespace scopes (§8.2.9.2) is wanted, *using-declarations* or *using-directives* can be used (§8.2.2). See also §8.2.6.

7.4.3 Manual Ambiguity Resolution

Declaring too few (or too many) overloaded versions of a function can lead to ambiguities. For example:

```
void  f1 (char);
void  f1 (long);

void  f2 (char*);
void  f2 (int*);
```

```
void k(int i)
{
    f1(i);      // ambiguous: f1(char) or f1(long)
    f2(0);      // ambiguous: f2(char*) or f2(int*)
}
```

Where possible, the thing to do in such cases is to consider the set of overloaded versions of a function as a whole and see if it makes sense according to the semantics of the function. Often the problem can be solved by adding a version that resolves ambiguities. For example, adding

```
inline void f1(int n) { f1(long(n)); }
```

would resolve all ambiguities similar to *f1*(*i*) in favor of the larger type *long int*.

One can also add an explicit type conversion to resolve a specific call. For example:

```
f2(static_cast<int*>(0));
```

However, this is most often simply an ugly stopgap. Soon another similar call will be made and have to be dealt with.

Some C++ novices get irritated by the ambiguity errors reported by the compiler. More experienced programmers appreciate these error messages as useful indicators of design errors.

7.4.4 Resolution for Multiple Arguments

Given the overload resolution rules, one can ensure that the simplest algorithm (function) will be used when the efficiency or precision of computations differs significantly for the types involved. For example:

```
int pow(int, int);
double pow(double, double);

complex pow(double, complex);
complex pow(complex, int);
complex pow(complex, double);
complex pow(complex, complex);

void k(complex z)
{
    int i = pow(2,2);           // invoke pow(int,int)
    double d = pow(2.0,2.0);    // invoke pow(double,double)
    complex z2 = pow(2,z);      // invoke pow(double,complex)
    complex z3 = pow(z,2);      // invoke pow(complex,int)
    complex z4 = pow(z,z);      // invoke pow(complex,complex)
}
```

In the process of choosing among overloaded functions with two or more arguments, a best match is found for each argument using the rules from §7.4. A function that is the best match for one argument and a better than or equal match for all other arguments is called. If no such function exists, the call is rejected as ambiguous. For example:

```
void g()
{
    double d = pow(2.0,2);   // error: pow(int(2.0),2) or pow(2.0,double(2))?
}
```

The call is ambiguous because *2.0* is the best match for the first argument of *pow(double, double)* and *2* is the best match for the second argument of *pow(int, int)*.

7.5 Default Arguments

A general function often needs more arguments than are necessary to handle simple cases. In particular, functions that construct objects (§10.2.3) often provide several options for flexibility. Consider a function for printing an integer. Giving the user an option of what base to print it in seems reasonable, but in most programs integers will be printed as decimal integer values. For example:

```
void print(int value, int base =10);  // default base is 10

void f()
{
    print(31);
    print(31,10);
    print(31,16);
    print(31,2);
}
```

might produce this output:

```
31  31  1f  11111
```

The effect of a default argument can alternatively be achieved by overloading:

```
void print(int value, int base);
inline void print(int value) { print(value,10); }
```

However, overloading makes it less obvious to the reader that the intent is to have a single print function plus a shorthand.

A default argument is type checked at the time of the function declaration and evaluated at the time of the call. Default arguments may be provided for trailing arguments only. For example:

```
int f(int, int =0, char* =0);    // ok
int g(int =0, int =0, char*);    // error
int h(int =0, int, char* =0);    // error
```

Note that the space between the * and the = is significant (*= is an assignment operator; §6.2):

```
int nasty(char*=0);              // syntax error
```

A default argument cannot be repeated or changed in a subsequent declaration in the same scope. For example:

```
void f(int x = 7);
void f(int = 7);          // error: cannot repeat default argument
void f(int = 8);          // error: different default arguments

void g()
{
    void f(int x = 9);    // ok: this declaration hides the outer one
    // ...
}
```

Declaring a name in a nested scope so that the name hides a declaration of the same name in an outer scope is error prone.

7.6 Unspecified Number of Arguments

For some functions, it is not possible to specify the number and type of all arguments expected in a call. Such a function is declared by terminating the list of argument declarations with the ellipsis (. . .), which means ''and maybe some more arguments.'' For example:

```
int printf(const char* ...);
```

This specifies that a call of the C standard library function *printf*() (§21.8) must have at least one argument, a *char**, but may or may not have others. For example:

```
printf("Hello, world!\n");
printf("My name is %s %s\n", first_name, second_name);
printf("%d + %d = %d\n", 2, 3, 5);
```

Such a function must rely on information not available to the compiler when interpreting its argument list. In the case of *printf*(), the first argument is a format string containing special character sequences that allow *printf*() to handle other arguments correctly; *%s* means ''expect a *char** argument'' and *%d* means ''expect an *int* argument.'' However, the compiler cannot in general know that, so it cannot ensure that the expected arguments are really there or that an argument is of the proper type. For example,

```
#include <stdio.h>

int main()
{
    printf("My name is %s %s\n", 2);
}
```

will compile and (at best) cause some strange-looking output (try it!).

Clearly, if an argument has not been declared, the compiler does not have the information needed to perform the standard type checking and type conversion for it. In that case, a *char* or a *short* is passed as an *int* and a *float* is passed as a *double*. This is not necessarily what the programmer expects.

A well-designed program needs at most a few functions for which the argument types are not completely specified. Overloaded functions and functions using default arguments can be used to take care of type checking in most cases when one would otherwise consider leaving argument types unspecified. Only when both the number of arguments *and* the type of arguments vary is the ellipsis necessary. The most common use of the ellipsis is to specify an interface to C library functions that were defined before C++ provided alternatives:

```
int fprintf(FILE*, const char* ...);      // from <cstdio>
int execl(const char* ...);               // from UNIX header
```

A standard set of macros for accessing the unspecified arguments in such functions can be found in <cstdarg>. Consider writing an error function that takes one integer argument indicating the severity of the error followed by an arbitrary number of strings. The idea is to compose the error message by passing each word as a separate string argument. The list of string arguments should be terminated by a null pointer to *char*:

```
extern void error(int ...);
extern char* itoa(int, char[]);        // see §6.6[17]

const char* Null_cp = 0;

int main(int argc, char* argv[])
{
    switch (argc) {
    case 1:
        error(0,argv[0],Null_cp);
        break;

    case 2:
        error(0,argv[0],argv[1],Null_cp);
        break;

    default:
        char buffer[8];
        error(1,argv[0], "with", itoa(argc-1,buffer), "arguments", Null_cp);
    }
    // ...
}
```

The function *itoa* ( ) returns the character string representing its integer argument.

Note that using the integer *0* as the terminator would not have been portable: on some implementations, the integer zero and the null pointer do not have the same representation. This illustrates the subtleties and extra work that face the programmer once type checking has been suppressed using the ellipsis.

The error function could be defined like this:

```
void error(int severity ...)  // "severity" followed by a zero-terminated list of char*s
{
    va_list ap;
    va_start(ap,severity);       // arg startup
```

```
for (;;) {
      char* p = va_arg (ap, char*);
      if (p == 0) break;
      cerr << p << ' ';
}

va_end (ap);                      // arg cleanup

cerr << '\n';
if (severity) exit (severity);
}
```

First, a *va_list* is defined and initialized by a call of *va_start*(). The macro *va_start* takes the name of the *va_list* and the name of the last formal argument as arguments. The macro *va_arg*() is used to pick the unnamed arguments in order. In each call, the programmer must supply a type; *va_arg*() assumes that an actual argument of that type has been passed, but it typically has no way of ensuring that. Before returning from a function in which *va_start*() has been used, *va_end*() must be called. The reason is that *va_start*() may modify the stack in such a way that a return cannot successfully be done; *va_end*() undoes any such modifications.

7.7 Pointer to Function

There are only two things one can do to a function: call it and take its address. The pointer obtained by taking the address of a function can then be used to call the function. For example:

```
void error (string s) { /* ... */ }

void (*efct) (string);          // pointer to function

void f()
{
      efct = &error;            // efct points to error
      efct("error");            // call error through efct
}
```

The compiler will discover that *efct* is a pointer and call the function pointed to. That is, dereferencing of a pointer to function using * is optional. Similarly, using & to get the address of a function is optional:

```
void (*f1) (string) = &error;    // ok
void (*f2) (string) = error;     // also ok; same meaning as &error

void g()
{
      f1("Vasa");               // ok
      (*f1)("Mary Rose");       // also ok
}
```

Pointers to functions have argument types declared just like the functions themselves. In pointer assignments, the complete function type must match exactly. For example:

```
void (*pf) (string);    // pointer to void(string)
void f1 (string);       // void(string)
int f2 (string);        // int(string)
void f3 (int*);         // void(int*)

void f()
{
    pf = &f1;           // ok
    pf = &f2;           // error: bad return type
    pf = &f3;           // error: bad argument type

    pf("Hera");         // ok
    pf(1);              // error: bad argument type

    int i = pf("Zeus"); // error: void assigned to int
}
```

The rules for argument passing are the same for calls directly to a function and for calls to a function through a pointer.

It is often convenient to define a name for a pointer-to-function type to avoid using the somewhat nonobvious declaration syntax all the time. Here is an example from a UNIX system header:

```
typedef void (*SIG_TYP) (int);       // from <signal.h>
typedef void (*SIG_ARG_TYP) (int);
SIG_TYP signal(int, SIG_ARG_TYP);
```

An array of pointers to functions is often useful. For example, the menu system for my mouse-based editor is implemented using arrays of pointers to functions to represent operations. The system cannot be described in detail here, but this is the general idea:

```
typedef void (*PF) ();

PF edit_ops[] = {            // edit operations
    &cut, &paste, &copy, &search
};

PF file_ops[] = {            // file management
    &open, &append, &close, &write
};
```

We can then define and initialize the pointers that control actions selected from a menu associated with the mouse buttons:

```
PF* button2 = edit_ops;
PF* button3 = file_ops;
```

In a complete implementation, more information is needed to define each menu item. For example, a string specifying the text to be displayed must be stored somewhere. As the system is used, the meaning of mouse buttons changes frequently with the context. Such changes are performed (partly) by changing the value of the button pointers. When a user selects a menu item, such as item 3 for button 2, the associated operation is executed:

```
button2[2] ();  // call button2's 3rd function
```

One way to gain appreciation of the expressive power of pointers to functions is to try to write such code without them − and without using their better-behaved cousins, the virtual functions (§12.2.6). A menu can be modified at run-time by inserting new functions into the operator table. It is also easy to construct new menus at run-time.

Pointers to functions can be used to provide a simple form of polymorphic routines, that is, routines that can be applied to objects of many different types:

```
typedef int (*CFT)(const void*, const void*);

void ssort(void* base, size_t n, size_t sz, CFT cmp)
/*
    Sort the "n" elements of vector "base" into increasing order
    using the comparison function pointed to by "cmp".
    The elements are of size "sz".

    Shell sort (Knuth, Vol3, pg84)
*/
{
    for (int gap=n/2; 0<gap; gap/=2)
        for (int i=gap; i<n; i++)
            for (int j=i-gap; 0<=j; j-=gap) {
                char* b = static_cast<char*>(base);   // necessary cast
                char* pj = b+j*sz;                     // &base[j]
                char* pjg = b+(j+gap)*sz;              // &base[j+gap]

                if (cmp(pjg,pj)<0) {                   // swap base[j] and base[j+gap]:
                    for (int k=0; k<sz; k++) {
                        char temp = pj[k];
                        pj[k] = pjg[k];
                        pjg[k] = temp;
                    }
                }
            }
}
```

The *ssort*() routine does not know the type of the objects it sorts, only the number of elements (the array size), the size of each element, and the function to call to perform a comparison. The type of *ssort*() was chosen to be the same as the type of the standard C library sort routine, *qsort*(). Real programs use *qsort*(), the C++ standard library algorithm *sort* (§18.7.1), or a specialized sort routine. This style of code is common in C, but it is not the most elegant way of expressing this algorithm in C++ (see §13.3, §13.5.2).

Such a sort function could be used to sort a table such as this:

```
struct User {
    char* name;
    char* id;
    int dept;
};
```

```
User heads[] = {
    "Ritchie D.M.",      "dmr",    11271,
    "Sethi R.",          "ravi",   11272,
    "Szymanski T.G.",    "tgs",    11273,
    "Schryer N.L.",      "nls",    11274,
    "Schryer N.L.",      "nls",    11275,
    "Kernighan B.W.", "bwk",    11276
};

void print_id(User* v, int n)
{
    for (int i=0; i<n; i++)
        cout << v[i].name << '\t' << v[i].id << '\t' << v[i].dept << '\n';
}
```

To be able to sort, we must first define appropriate comparison functions. A comparison function must return a negative value if its first argument is less than the second, zero if the arguments are equal, and a positive number otherwise:

```
int cmp1(const void* p, const void* q)    // Compare name strings
{
    return strcmp(static_cast<const User*>(p)->name, static_cast<const User*>(q)->name);
}

int cmp2(const void* p, const void* q)    // Compare dept numbers
{
    return static_cast<const User*>(p)->dept - static_cast<const User*>(q)->dept;
}
```

This program sorts and prints:

```
int main()
{
    cout << "Heads in alphabetical order:\n";
    ssort(heads,6,sizeof(User),cmp1);
    print_id(heads,6);
    cout << '\n';

    cout << "Heads in order of department number:\n";
    ssort(heads,6,sizeof(User),cmp2);
    print_id(heads,6);
}
```

You can take the address of an overloaded function by assigning to or initializing a pointer to function. In that case, the type of the target is used to select from the set of overloaded functions. For example:

```
void f(int);
int f(char);

void (*pf1)(int) = &f;    // void f(int)
int (*pf2)(char) = &f;    // int f(char)
void (*pf3)(char) = &f;   // error: no void f(char)
```

A function must be called through a pointer to function with exactly the right argument and return types. There is no implicit conversion of argument or return types when pointers to functions are assigned or initialized. This means that

> *int cmp3 (const mytype*, const mytype*);*

is not a suitable argument for *ssort ()*. The reason is that accepting *cmp3* as an argument to *ssort ()* would violate the guarantee that *cmp3* will be called with arguments of type *mytype** (see also §9.2.5).

7.8 Macros

Macros are very important in C but have far fewer uses in C++. The first rule about macros is: Don't use them unless you have to. Almost every macro demonstrates a flaw in the programming language, in the program, or in the programmer. Because they rearrange the program text before the compiler proper sees it, macros are also a major problem for many programming tools. So when you use macros, you should expect inferior service from tools such as debuggers, cross-reference tools, and profilers. If you must use macros, please read the reference manual for your own implementation of the C++ preprocessor carefully and try not to be too clever. Also to warn readers, follow the convention to name macros using lots of capital letters. The syntax of macros is presented in §A.11.

A simple macro is defined like this:

> *#define NAME rest of line*

Where *NAME* is encountered as a token, it is replaced by *rest of line*. For example,

> *named = NAME*

will expand into

> *named = rest of line*

A macro can also be defined to take arguments. For example:

> *#define MAC (x, y) argument1 : x argument2 : y*

When *MAC* is used, two argument strings must be presented. They will replace *x* and *y* when *MAC ()* is expanded. For example,

> *expanded = MAC (foo bar, yuk yuk)*

will be expanded into

> *expanded = argument1 : foo bar argument2 : yuk yuk*

Macro names cannot be overloaded, and the macro preprocessor cannot handle recursive calls:

```
#define PRINT (a, b) cout<< (a) << (b)
#define PRINT (a, b, c) cout<< (a) << (b) << (c)  /* trouble?: redefines, does not overload */

#define FAC (n) (n>1) ?n*FAC (n-1) :1          /* trouble: recursive macro */
```

Macros manipulate character strings and know little about C++ syntax and nothing about C++ types or scope rules. Only the expanded form of a macro is seen by the compiler, so an error in a macro will be reported when the macro is expanded, not when it is defined. This leads to very obscure error messages.

Here are some plausible macros:

```
#define CASE break; case
#define FOREVER for(;;)
```

Here are some completely unnecessary macros:

```
#define PI 3.141593
#define BEGIN {
#define END }
```

Here are some dangerous macros:

```
#define SQUARE(a) a*a
#define INCR_xx (xx)++
```

To see why they are dangerous, try expanding this:

```
int xx = 0;        // global counter

void f()
{
    int xx = 0;              // local variable
    int y = SQUARE(xx+2);    // y=xx+2*xx+2; that is y=xx+(2*xx)+2
    INCR_xx;                 // increments local xx
}
```

If you must use a macro, use the scope resolution operator :: when referring to global names (§4.9.4) and enclose occurrences of a macro argument name in parentheses whenever possible. For example:

```
#define MIN(a,b) (((a)<(b))?(a):(b))
```

If you must write macros complicated enough to require comments, it is wise to use /* */ comments because C preprocessors that do not know about // comments are sometimes used as part of C++ tools. For example:

```
#define M2(a) something(a)    /* thoughtful comment */
```

Using macros, you can design your own private language. Even if you prefer this ''enhanced language'' to plain C++, it will be incomprehensible to most C++ programmers. Furthermore, the C preprocessor is a very simple macro processor. When you try to do something nontrivial, you are likely to find it either impossible or unnecessarily hard to do. The *const*, *inline*, *template*, *enum*, and *namespace* mechanisms are intended as alternatives to many traditional uses of preprocessor constructs. For example:

```
const int answer = 42;
template<class T> inline T min(T a, T b) { return (a<b)?a:b; }
```

When writing a macro, it is not unusual to need a new name for something. A string can be created by concatenating two strings using the ## macro operator. For example,

> *#define NAME2 (a, b) a##b*
>
> *int NAME2 (hack, cah) ();*

will produce

> *int hackcah ();*

for the compiler to read.
The directive

> *#undef X*

ensures that no macro called *X* is defined − whether or not one was before the directive. This affords some protection against undesired macros. However, it is not always easy to know what the effects of *X* on a piece of code were supposed to be.

7.8.1 Conditional Compilation

One use of macros is almost impossible to avoid. The directive *#ifdef identifier* conditionally causes all input to be ignored until a *#endif* directive is seen. For example,

> *int f(int a*
> *#ifdef arg_two*
> *, int b*
> *#endif*
> *);*

produces

> *int f(int a*
> *);*

for the compiler to see unless a macro called *arg_two* has been *#define*d. This example confuses tools that assume sane behavior from the programmer.
Most uses of *#ifdef* are less bizarre, and when used with restraint, *#ifdef* does little harm. See also §9.3.3.
Names of the macros used to control *#ifdef* should be chosen carefully so that they don't clash with ordinary identifiers. For example:

> *struct Call_info {*
> *   Node* arg_one;*
> *   Node* arg_two;*
> *   // ...*
> *};*

This innocent-looking source text will cause some confusion should someone write:

> *#define arg_two x*

Unfortunately, common and unavoidable headers contain many dangerous and unnecessary macros.

7.9 Advice

[1] Be suspicious of non-*const* reference arguments; if you want the function to modify its arguments, use pointers and value return instead; §5.5.

[2] Use *const* reference arguments when you need to minimize copying of arguments; §5.5.

[3] Use *const* extensively and consistently; §7.2.

[4] Avoid macros; §7.8.

[5] Avoid unspecified numbers of arguments; §7.6.

[6] Don't return pointers or references to local variables; §7.3.

[7] Use overloading when functions perform conceptually the same task on different types; §7.4.

[8] When overloading on integers, provide functions to eliminate common ambiguities; §7.4.3.

[9] When considering the use of a pointer to function, consider whether a virtual function (§2.5.5) or a template (§2.7.2) would be a better alternative; §7.7.

[10] If you must use macros, use ugly names with lots of capital letters; §7.8.

7.10 Exercises

1. (∗1) Write declarations for the following: a function taking arguments of type pointer to character and reference to integer and returning no value; a pointer to such a function; a function taking such a pointer as an argument; and a function returning such a pointer. Write the definition of a function that takes such a pointer as an argument and returns its argument as the return value. Hint: Use *typedef*.

2. (∗1) What does the following mean? What would it be good for?

> *typedef int (&rifii) (int, int);*

3. (∗1.5) Write a program like "Hello, world!" that takes a name as a command-line argument and writes "Hello, *name* !". Modify this program to take any number of names as arguments and to say hello to each.

4. (∗1.5) Write a program that reads an arbitrary number of files whose names are given as command-line arguments and writes them one after another on *cout*. Because this program concatenates its arguments to produce its output, you might call it *cat*.

5. (∗2) Convert a small C program to C++. Modify the header files to declare all functions called and to declare the type of every argument. Where possible, replace #*define*s with *enum, const*, or *inline*. Remove *extern* declarations from *.c* files and if necessary convert all function definitions to C++ function definition syntax. Replace calls of *malloc* ( ) and *free* ( ) with *new* and *delete*. Remove unnecessary casts.

6. (∗2) Implement *ssort* ( ) (§7.7) using a more efficient sorting algorithm. Hint: *qsort* ( ).

7. (∗2.5) Consider:

```
struct Tnode {
    string word;
    int count;
    Tnode* left;
    Tnode* right;
};
```

Write a function for entering new words into a tree of *Tnode*s. Write a function to write out a tree of *Tnode*s. Write a function to write out a tree of *Tnode*s with the words in alphabetical order. Modify *Tnode* so that it stores (only) a pointer to an arbitrarily long word stored as an array of characters on free store using *new*. Modify the functions to use the new definition of *Tnode*.

8. (∗2.5) Write a function to invert a two-dimensional array. Hint: §C.7.

9. (∗2) Write an encryption program that reads from *cin* and writes the encoded characters to *cout*. You might use this simple encryption scheme: the encrypted form of a character *c* is *c^key*[*i*], where *key* is a string passed as a command-line argument. The program uses the characters in *key* in a cyclic manner until all the input has been read. Re-encrypting encoded text with the same key produces the original text. If no key (or a null string) is passed, then no encryption is done.

10. (∗3.5) Write a program to help decipher messages encrypted with the method described in §7.10[9] without knowing the key. Hint: See David Kahn: *The Codebreakers*, Macmillan, 1967, New York, pp. 207-213.

11. (∗3) Write an *error* function that takes a *printf*-style format string containing %*s*, %*c*, and %*d* directives and an arbitrary number of arguments. Don't use *printf*(). Look at §21.8 if you don't know the meaning of %*s*, %*c*, and %*d*. Use <*cstdarg*>.

12. (∗1) How would you choose names for pointer to function types defined using *typedef*?

13. (∗2) Look at some programs to get an idea of the diversity of styles of names actually used. How are uppercase letters used? How is the underscore used? When are short names such as *i* and *x* used?

14. (∗1) What is wrong with these macro definitions?

```
#define  PI = 3.141593;
#define  MAX(a,b)  a>b?a:b
#define  fac(a)  (a)*fac((a)-1)
```

15. (∗3) Write a macro processor that defines and expands simple macros (like the C preprocessor does). Read from *cin* and write to *cout*. At first, don't try to handle macros with arguments. Hint: The desk calculator (§6.1) contains a symbol table and a lexical analyzer that you could modify.

16. (∗2) Implement *print*() from §7.5.

17. (∗2) Add functions such as *sqrt*(), *log*(), and *sin*() to the desk calculator from §6.1. Hint: Predefine the names and call the functions through an array of pointers to functions. Don't forget to check the arguments in a function call.

18. (∗1) Write a factorial function that does not use recursion. See also §11.14[6].

19. (∗2) Write functions to add one day, one month, and one year to a *Date* as defined in §5.9[13]. Write a function that gives the day of the week for a given *Date*. Write a function that gives the *Date* of the first Monday following a given *Date*.

8

Namespaces and Exceptions

The year is 787!
A.D.?
− Monty Python

No rule is so general,
which admits not some exception.
− Robert Burton

Modularity, interfaces, and exceptions — namespaces — *using* — *using namespace* — avoiding name clashes — name lookup — namespace composition — namespace aliases — namespaces and C code — exceptions — *throw* and *catch* — exceptions and program structure — advice — exercises.

8.1 Modularization and Interfaces

Any realistic program consists of a number of separate parts. For example, even the simple "Hello, world!" program involves at least two parts: the user code requests *Hello, world!* to be printed, and the I/O system does the printing.

Consider the desk calculator example from §6.1. It can be viewed as being composed of five parts:

[1] The parser, doing syntax analysis
[2] The lexer, composing tokens out of characters
[3] The symbol table, holding (string,value) pairs
[4] The driver, *main* ( )
[5] The error handler

This can be represented graphically:

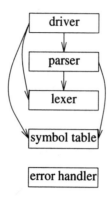

where an arrow means "using." To simplify the picture, I have not represented the fact that every part relies on error handling. In fact, the calculator was conceived as three parts, with the driver and error handler added for completeness.

When one module uses another, it doesn't need to know everything about the module used. Ideally, most of the details of a module are unknown to its users. Consequently, we make a distinction between a module and its interface. For example, the parser directly relies on the lexer's interface (only), rather than on the complete lexer. The lexer simply implements the services advertised in its interface. This can be presented graphically like this:

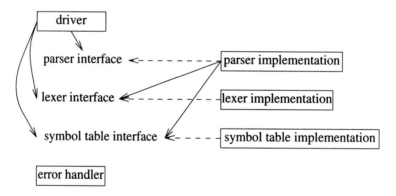

Dashed lines means "implements." I consider this to be the real structure of the program, and our job as programmers is to represent this faithfully in code. That done, the code will be simple, efficient, comprehensible, maintainable, etc., because it will directly reflect our fundamental design.

The following sections show how the logical structure of the desk calculator program can be made clear, and §9.3 shows how the program source text can be physically organized to take advantage of it. The calculator is a tiny program, so in "real life" I wouldn't bother using namespaces and separate compilation (§2.4.1, §9.1) to the extent I do here. It is simply used to present techniques useful for larger programs without our drowning in code. In real programs, each "module" represented by a separate namespace will often have hundreds of functions, classes, templates, etc.

To demonstrate a variety of techniques and language features, I develop the modularization of the calculator in stages. In "real life," a program is unlikely to grow through all of these stages. An experienced programmer might pick a design that is "about right" from the start. However, as a program evolves over the years, dramatic structural changes are not uncommon.

Error handling permeates the structure of a program. When breaking up a program into modules or (conversely) when composing a program out of modules, we must take care to minimize dependencies between modules caused by error handling. C++ provides exceptions to decouple the detection and reporting of errors from the handling of errors. Therefore, the discussion of how to represent modules as namespaces (§8.2) is followed by a demonstration of how we can use exceptions to further improve modularity (§8.3).

There are many more notions of modularity than the ones discussed in this chapter and the next. For example, we might use concurrently executing and communicating processes to represent important aspects of modularity. Similarly, the use of separate address spaces and the communication of information between address spaces are important topics not discussed here. I consider these notions of modularity largely independent and orthogonal. Interestingly, in each case, separating a system into modules is easy. The hard problem is to provide safe, convenient, and efficient communication across module boundaries.

8.2 Namespaces

A namespace is a mechanism for expressing logical grouping. That is, if some declarations logically belong together according to some criteria, they can be put in a common namespace to express that fact. For example, the declarations of the parser from the desk calculator (§6.1.1) may be placed in a namespace *Parser*:

```
namespace Parser {
    double expr(bool);
    double prim(bool get) { /* ... */ }
    double term(bool get) { /* ... */ }
    double expr(bool get) { /* ... */ }
}
```

The function *expr()* must be declared first and then later defined to break the dependency loop described in §6.1.1.

The input part of the desk calculator could be also placed in its own namespace:

```
namespace Lexer {
    enum Token_value {
        NAME,          NUMBER,          END,
        PLUS='+',      MINUS='-',       MUL='*',      DIV='/',
        PRINT=';',     ASSIGN='=',      LP='(',       RP=')'
    };

    Token_value curr_tok;
    double number_value;
    string string_value;

    Token_value get_token() { /* ... */ }
}
```

This use of namespaces makes it reasonably obvious what the lexer and the parser provide to a user. However, had I included the source code for the functions, this structure would have been obscured. If function bodies are included in the declaration of a realistically-sized namespace, you typically have to wade through pages or screenfuls of information to find what services are offered, that is, to find the interface.

An alternative to relying on separately specified interfaces is to provide a tool that extracts an interface from a module that includes implementation details. I don't consider that a good solution. Specifying interfaces is a fundamental design activity (see §23.4.3.4), a module can provide different interfaces to different users, and often an interface is designed long before the implementation details are made concrete.

Here is a version of the *Parser* with the interface separated from the implementation:

```
namespace Parser {
    double prim(bool);
    double term(bool);
    double expr(bool);
}

double Parser::prim(bool get) { /* ... */ }
double Parser::term(bool get) { /* ... */ }
double Parser::expr(bool get) { /* ... */ }
```

Note that as a result of separating the implementation from the interface, each function now has exactly one declaration and one definition. Users will see only the interface containing declarations. The implementation – in this case, the function bodies – will be placed "somewhere else" where a user need not look.

As shown, a member can be declared within a namespace definition and defined later using the *namespace-name::member-name* notation.

Members of a namespace must be introduced using this notation:

```
namespace namespace-name {
    // declaration and definitions
}
```

We cannot declare a new member of a namespace outside a namespace definition using the qualifier syntax. For example:

```
void Parser::logical(bool);     // error: no logical() in Parser
```

The idea is to make it reasonably easy to find all names in a namespace declaration and also to catch errors such as misspellings and type mismatches. For example:

```
double Parser::trem(bool);      // error: no trem() in Parser
double Parser::prim(int);       // error: Parser::prim() takes a bool argument
```

A namespace is a scope. Thus, "namespace" is a very fundamental and relatively simple concept. The larger a program is, the more useful namespaces are to express logical separations of its parts. Ordinary local scopes, global scopes, and classes are namespaces (§C.10.3).

Ideally, every entity in a program belongs to some recognizable logical unit ("module"). Therefore, every declaration in a nontrivial program should ideally be in some namespace named to

indicate its logical role in the program. The exception is *main*(), which must be global in order
for the run-time environment to recognize it as special (§8.3.3).

8.2.1 Qualified Names

A namespace is a scope. The usual scope rules hold for namespaces, so if a name is previously
declared in the namespace or in an enclosing scope, it can be used without further fuss. A name
from another namespace can be used when qualified by the name of its namespace. For example:

```
double Parser::term(bool get)           // note Parser:: qualification
{
    double left = prim(get);            // no qualification needed

    for (;;)
        switch (Lexer::curr_tok) {      // note Lexer:: qualification
        case Lexer::MUL:                // note Lexer:: qualification
            left *= prim(true);         // no qualification needed
        // ...
        }
    // ...
}
```

The *Parser* qualifier is necessary to state that this *term*() is the one declared in *Parser* and not
some unrelated global function. Because *term*() is a member of *Parser*, it need not use a qualifier
for *prim*(). However, had the *Lexer* qualifier not been present, *curr_tok* would have been considered undeclared because the members of namespace *Lexer* are not in scope from within the *Parser*
namespace.

8.2.2 Using Declarations

When a name is frequently used outside its namespace, it can be a bother to repeatedly qualify it
with its namespace name. Consider:

```
double Parser::prim(bool get)       // handle primaries
{
    if (get) Lexer::get_token();

    switch (Lexer::curr_tok) {
    case Lexer::NUMBER:             // floating-point constant
        Lexer::get_token();
        return Lexer::number_value;

    case Lexer::NAME:
    {   double& v = table[Lexer::string_value];
        if (Lexer::get_token() == Lexer::ASSIGN) v = expr(true);
        return v;
    }

    case Lexer::MINUS:              // unary minus
        return -prim(true);
```

```
        case Lexer::LP:
        {    double e = expr(true);
             if (Lexer::curr_tok != Lexer::RP) return Error::error(") expected");
             Lexer::get_token();         // eat ')'
             return e;
        }
        case Lexer::END:
             return 1;
        default:
             return Error::error("primary expected");
        }
    }
```

The repeated qualification *Lexer* is tedious and distracting. This redundancy can be eliminated by a *using-declaration* to state in one place that the *get_token* used in this scope is *Lexer*'s *get_token*. For example:

```
    double Parser::prim(bool get)         // handle primaries
    {
        using Lexer::get_token;    // use Lexer's get_token
        using Lexer::curr_tok;     // use Lexer's curr_tok
        using Error::error;        // use Error's error

        if (get) get_token();

        switch (curr_tok) {
        case Lexer::NUMBER:                 // floating-point constant
             get_token();
             return Lexer::number_value;
        case Lexer::NAME:
        {    double& v = table[Lexer::string_value];
             if (get_token() == Lexer::ASSIGN) v = expr(true);
             return v;
        }
        case Lexer::MINUS:                  // unary minus
             return -prim(true);
        case Lexer::LP:
        {    double e = expr(true);
             if (curr_tok != Lexer::RP) return error(") expected");
             get_token();                   // eat ')'
             return e;
        }
        case Lexer::END:
             return 1;
        default:
             return error("primary expected");
        }
    }
```

A *using-declaration* introduces a local synonym.

It is often a good idea to keep local synonyms as local as possible to avoid confusion.

However, all parser functions use similar sets of names from other modules. We can therefore place the *using-declarations* in the *Parser*'s namespace definition:

```
namespace Parser {
    double prim(bool);
    double term(bool);
    double expr(bool);

    using Lexer::get_token;   // use Lexer's get_token
    using Lexer::curr_tok;    // use Lexer's curr_tok
    using Error::error;       // use Error's error
}
```

This allows us to simplify the *Parser* functions almost to our original version (§6.1.1):

```
double Parser::term(bool get)        // multiply and divide
{
    double left = prim(get);

    for (;;)
        switch (curr_tok) {
        case Lexer::MUL:
            left *= prim(true);
            break;
        case Lexer::DIV:
            if (double d = prim(true)) {
                left /= d;
                break;
            }
            return error("divide by 0");
        default:
            return left;
        }
}
```

I could have introduced the token names into the *Parser*'s namespace. However, I left them explicitly qualified as a reminder of *Parser*'s dependency on *Lexer*.

8.2.3 Using Directives

What if our aim were to simplify the *Parser* functions to be *exactly* our original versions? This would be a reasonable aim for a large program that was being converted to using namespaces from a previous version with less explicit modularity.

A *using-directive* makes names from a namespace available almost as if they had been declared outside their namespace (§8.2.8). For example:

```
namespace Parser {
    double prim(bool);
    double term(bool);
    double expr(bool);
```

```
    using  namespace  Lexer;     // make all names from Lexer available
    using  namespace  Error;     // make all names from Error available
}
```

This allows us to write *Parser*'s functions exactly as we originally did (§6.1.1):

```
double  Parser::term(bool  get)          // multiply and divide
{
    double  left = prim(get);

    for (;;)
            switch (curr_tok) {                  // Lexer's curr_tok
            case MUL:                            // Lexer's MUL
                left *= prim(true);
                break;
            case DIV:                            // Lexer's DIV
                if (double  d = prim(true)) {
                    left /= d;
                    break;
                }
                return  error("divide by 0");   // Error's error
            default:
                return  left;
            }
}
```

Global *using-directive*s are a tool for transition (§8.2.9) and are otherwise best avoided. In a namespace, a *using-directive* is a tool for namespace composition (§8.2.8). In a function (only), a *using-directive* can be safely used as a notational convenience (§8.3.3.1).

8.2.4 Multiple Interfaces

It should be clear that the namespace definition we evolved for *Parser* is not the interface that the *Parser* presents to its users. Instead, it is the set of declarations that is needed to write the individual parser functions conveniently. The *Parser*'s interface to its users should be far simpler:

```
namespace  Parser {
    double  expr(bool);
}
```

Fortunately, the two *namespace-definition*s for *Parser* can coexist so that each can be used where it is most appropriate. We see the namespace *Parser* used to provide two things:

[1] The common environment for the functions implementing the parser

[2] The external interface offered by the parser to its users

Thus, the driver code, *main*(), should see only:

```
namespace  Parser {              // interface for users
    double  expr(bool);
}
```

The functions implementing the parser should see whichever interface we decided on as the best for expressing those functions' shared environment. That is:

```
namespace Parser {              // interface for implementers
    double prim(bool);
    double term(bool);
    double expr(bool);

    using Lexer::get_token;     // use Lexer's get_token
    using Lexer::curr_tok;      // use Lexer's curr_tok
    using Error::error;         // use Error's error
}
```

or graphically:

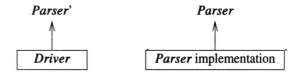

The arrows represent "relies on the interface provided by" relations.

Parser´ is the small interface offered to users. The name *Parser´* (Parser prime) is not a C++ identifier. It was chosen deliberately to indicate that this interface doesn't have a separate name in the program. The lack of a separate name need not lead to confusion because programmers naturally invent different and obvious names for the different interfaces and because the physical layout of the program (see §9.3.2) naturally provides separate (file) names.

The interface offered to implementers is larger than the interface offered to users. Had this interface been for a realistically-sized module in a real system, it would change more often than the interface seen by users. It is important that the users of a module (in this case, *main*() using *Parser*) are insulated from such changes.

We don't need to use two separate namespaces to express the two different interfaces, but if we wanted to, we could. Designing interfaces is one of the most fundamental design activities and one in which major benefits can be gained and lost. Consequently, it is worthwhile to consider what we are really trying to achieve and to discuss a number of alternatives.

Please keep in mind that the solution presented is the simplest of those we consider, and often the best. Its main weaknesses are that the two interfaces don't have separate names and that the compiler doesn't necessarily have sufficient information to check the consistency of the two definitions of the namespace. However, even though the compiler doesn't always get the opportunity to check the consistency, it usually does. Furthermore, the linker catches most errors missed by the compiler.

The solution presented here is the one I use for the discussion of physical modularity (§9.3) and the one I recommend in the absence of further logical constraints (see also §8.2.7).

8.2.4.1 Interface Design Alternatives

The purpose of interfaces is to minimize dependencies between different parts of a program. Minimal interfaces lead to systems that are easier to understand, have better data hiding properties, are easier to modify, and compile faster.

When dependencies are considered, it is important to remember that compilers and programmers tend to take a somewhat simple-minded approach to them: "If a definition is in scope at point X, then anything written at point X depends on anything stated in that definition." Typically, things are not really that bad because most definitions are irrelevant to most code. Given the definitions we have used, consider:

```
namespace Parser {          // interface for implementers
    // ...
    double  expr (bool) ;
    // ...
}

int  main ( )
{
    // ...
    Parser:: expr (false) ;
    // ...
}
```

The function *main* ( ) depends on *Parser* : : *expr* ( ) only, but it takes time, brain power, computation, etc., to figure that out. Consequently, for realistically-sized programs people and compilation systems often play it safe and assume that where there might be a dependency, there is one. This is typically a perfectly reasonable approach.

Thus, our aim is to express our program so that the set of potential dependencies is reduced to the set of actual dependencies.

First, we try the obvious: define a user interface to the parser in terms of the implementer interface we already have:

```
namespace Parser {              // interface for implementers
    // ...
    double  expr (bool) ;
    // ...
}

namespace Parser_interface {         // interface for users
    using  Parser:: expr;
}
```

Clearly, users of *Parser_interface* depend only, and indirectly, on *Parser* : : *expr* ( ) . However, a crude look at the dependency graph gives us this:

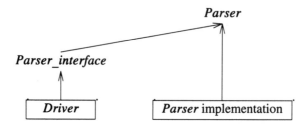

Now the *Driver* appears vulnerable to any change in the *Parser* interface from which it was supposed to be insulated. Even this appearance of a dependency is undesirable, so we explicitly restrict *Parser_interface*'s dependency on *Parser* by having only the relevant part of the implementer interface to parser (that was called *Parser′* earlier) in scope where we define *Parser_interface*:

```
namespace  Parser {          // interface for users
     double  expr (bool) ;
}
namespace  Parser_interface {    // separately named interface for users
     using  Parser :: expr ;
}
```

or graphically:

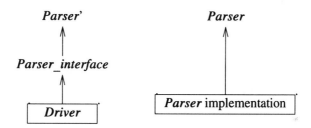

To ensure the consistency of *Parser* and *Parser′*, we again rely on the compilation system as a whole, rather than on just the compiler working on a single compilation unit. This solution differs from the one in §8.2.4 only by the extra namespace *Parser_interface*. If we wanted to, we could give *Parser_interface* a concrete representation by giving it its own *expr* () function:

```
namespace  Parser_interface {
     double  expr (bool) ;
}
```

Now *Parser* need not be in scope in order to define *Parser_interface*. It needs to be in scope only where *Parser_interface* :: *expr* () is defined:

```
double  Parser_interface :: expr (bool  get)
{
     return  Parser :: expr (get) ;
}
```

This last variant can be represented graphically like this:

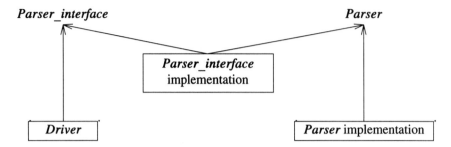

Now all dependencies are minimized. Everything is concrete and properly named. However, for most problems I face, this solution is also massive overkill.

8.2.5 Avoiding Name Clashes

Namespaces are intended to express logical structure. The simplest such structure is the distinction between code written by one person vs. code written by someone else. This simple distinction can be of great practical importance.

When we use only a single global scope, it is unnecessarily difficult to compose a program out of separate parts. The problem is that the supposedly-separate parts each define the same names. When combined into the same program, these names clash. Consider:

```
// my.h:
    char f(char);
    int f(int);
    class String { /* ... */ };

// your.h:
    char f(char);
    double f(double);
    class String { /* ... */ };
```

Given these definitions, a third party cannot easily use both *my.h* and *your.h*. The obvious solution is to wrap each set of declarations in its own namespace:

```
namespace My {
    char f(char);
    int f(int);
    class String { /* ... */ };
}

namespace Your {
    char f(char);
    double f(double);
    class String { /* ... */ };
}
```

Now we can use declarations from *My* and *Your* through explicit qualification (§8.2.1), *using-declarations* (§8.2.2), or *using-directives* (§8.2.3).

8.2.5.1 Unnamed Namespaces

It is often useful to wrap a set of declarations in a namespace simply to protect against the possibility of name clashes. That is, the aim is to preserve locality of code rather than to present an interface to users. For example:

```
#include "header.h"
namespace Mine {
    int a;
    void f() { /* ... */ }
    int g() { /* ... */ }
}
```

Since we don't want the name *Mine* to be known outside a local context, it simply becomes a bother to invent a redundant global name that might accidentally clash with someone else's names. In that case, we can simply leave the namespace without a name:

```
#include "header.h"
namespace {
    int a;
    void f() { /* ... */ }
    int g() { /* ... */ }
}
```

Clearly, there has to be some way of accessing members of an unnamed namespace from the outside. Consequently, an unnamed namespace has an implied *using-directive*. The previous declaration is equivalent to

```
namespace $$$ {
    int a;
    void f() { /* ... */ }
    int g() { /* ... */ }
}
using namespace $$$;
```

where $$$ is some name unique to the scope in which the namespace is defined. In particular, unnamed namespaces in different translation units are different. As desired, there is no way of naming a member of an unnamed namespace from another translation unit.

8.2.6 Name Lookup

A function taking an argument of type T is more often than not defined in the same namespace as T. Consequently, if a function isn't found in the context of its use, we look in the namespaces of its arguments. For example:

```
namespace Chrono {
    class Date { /* ... */ };

    bool operator==(const Date&, const std::string&);
```

```
        std::string format(const Date&);       // make string representation
        // ...
    }

    void f(Chrono::Date d, int i)
    {
        std::string s = format(d);        // Chrono::format()
        std::string t = format(i);        // error: no format() in scope
    }
```

This lookup rule saves the programmer a lot of typing compared to using explicit qualification, yet it doesn't pollute the namespace the way a *using-directive* (§8.2.3) can. It is especially useful for operator operands (§11.2.4) and template arguments (§C.13.8.4), where explicit qualification can be quite cumbersome.

Note that the namespace itself needs to be in scope and the function must be declared before it can be found and used.

Naturally, a function can take arguments from more than one namespace. For example:

```
    void f(Chrono::Date d, std::string s)
    {
        if (d == s) {
            // ...
        }
        else if (d == "August 4, 1914") {
            // ...
        }
    }
```

In such cases, we look for the function in the scope of the call (as ever) and in the namespaces of every argument (including each argument's class and base classes) and do the usual overload resolution (§7.4) of all functions we find. In particular, for the call *d==s*, we look for *operator==* in the scope surrounding *f()*, in the *std* namespace (where == is defined for *string*), and in the *Chrono* namespace. There is a *std::operator==()*, but it doesn't take a *Date* argument, so we use *Chrono::operator==()*, which does. See also §11.2.4.

When a class member invokes a named function, other members of the same class and its base classes are preferred over functions potentially found based on the argument types; operators differ (§11.2.1, §11.2.4).

8.2.7 Namespace Aliases

If users give their namespaces short names, the names of different namespaces will clash:

```
    namespace A {  // short name, will clash (eventually)
        // ...
    }

    A::String s1 = "Grieg";
    A::String s2 = "Nielsen";
```

However, long namespace names can be impractical in real code:

```
namespace American_Telephone_and_Telegraph {        // too long
    // ...
}

American_Telephone_and_Telegraph::String  s3 = "Grieg";
American_Telephone_and_Telegraph::String  s4 = "Nielsen";
```

This dilemma can be resolved by providing a short alias for a longer namespace name:

```
// use namespace alias to shorten names:

namespace ATT = American_Telephone_and_Telegraph;

ATT::String  s3 = "Grieg";
ATT::String  s4 = "Nielsen";
```

Namespace aliases also allow a user to refer to ''the library'' and have a single declaration defining what library that really is. For example:

```
namespace Lib = Foundation_library_v2r11;

// ...

Lib::set  s;
Lib::String  s5 = "Sibelius";
```

This can immensely simplify the task of replacing one version of a library with another. By using *Lib* rather than *Foundation_library_v2r11* directly, you can update to version ''v3r02'' by changing the initialization of the alias *Lib* and recompiling. The recompile will catch source level incompatibilities. On the other hand, overuse of aliases (of any kind) can lead to confusion.

8.2.8 Namespace Composition

Often, we want to compose an interface out of existing interfaces. For example:

```
namespace His_string {
    class String { /* ... */ };
    String operator+(const String&, const String&);
    String operator+(const String&, const char*);
    void fill(char);
    // ...
}

namespace Her_vector {
    template<class T> class Vector { /* ... */ };
    // ...
}

namespace My_lib {
    using namespace His_string;
    using namespace Her_vector;
    void my_fct(String&);
}
```

Given this, we can now write the program in terms of *My_lib*:

```
void f( )
{
    My_lib::String s = "Byron";      // finds My_lib::His_string::String
    // ...
}

using namespace My_lib;

void g(Vector<String>& vs)
{
    // ...
    my_fct(vs[5]);
    // ...
}
```

If an explicitly qualified name (such as *My_lib::String*) isn't declared in the namespace mentioned, the compiler looks in namespaces mentioned in *using-directives* (such as *His_string*).

Only if we need to define something, do we need to know the real namespace of an entity:

```
void My_lib::fill(char c)         // error: no fill() declared in My_lib
{
    // ...
}

void His_string::fill(char c)     // ok: fill() declared in His_string
{
    // ...
}

void My_lib::my_fct(String& v)    // ok; String is My_lib::String meaning His_string::String
{
    // ...
}
```

Ideally, a namespace should
   [1] express a logically coherent set of features,
   [2] not give users access to unrelated features, and
   [3] not impose a significant notational burden on users.
The composition techniques presented here and in the following subsections – together with the
#include mechanism (§9.2.1) – provide strong support for this.

8.2.8.1 Selection

Occasionally, we want access to only a few names from a namespace. We could do that by writing
a namespace declaration containing only those names we want. For example, we could declare a
version of *His_string* that provided the *String* itself and the concatenation operator only:

```
namespace His_string {                    // part of His_string only
    class String { /* ... */ };
    String operator+(const String&, const String&);
    String operator+(const String&, const char*);
}
```

However, unless I am the designer or maintainer of *His_string*, this can easily get messy. A change to the "real" definition of *His_string* will not be reflected in this declaration. Selection of features from a namespace is more explicitly made with *using-declaration*s:

```
namespace My_string {
    using His_string::String;
    using His_string::operator+;      // use any + from His_string
}
```

A *using-declaration* brings every declaration with a given name into scope. In particular, a single *using-declaration* can bring in every variant of an overloaded function.

In this way, if the maintainer of *His_string* adds a member function to *String* or an overloaded version of the concatenation operator, that change will automatically become available to users of *My_string*. Conversely, if a feature is removed from *His_string* or has its interface changed, affected uses of *My_string* will be detected by the compiler (see also §15.2.2).

8.2.8.2 Composition and Selection

Combining composition (by *using-directive*s) with selection (by *using-declaration*s) yields the flexibility needed for most real-world examples. With these mechanisms, we can provide access to a variety of facilities in such a way that we resolve name clashes and ambiguities arising from their composition. For example:

```
namespace His_lib {
    class String { /* ... */ };
    template<class T> class Vector { /* ... */ };
    // ...
}

namespace Her_lib {
    template<class T> class Vector { /* ... */ };
    class String { /* ... */ };
    // ...
}

namespace My_lib {
    using namespace His_lib; // everything from His_lib
    using namespace Her_lib; // everything from Her_lib

    using His_lib::String;      // resolve potential clash in favor of His_lib
    using Her_lib::Vector;      // resolve potential clash in favor of Her_lib

    template<class T> class List { /* ... */ }; // additional stuff
    // ...
}
```

When looking into a namespace, names explicitly declared there (including names declared by *using-declarations*) take priority over names made accessible in another scope by a *using-directive* (see also §C.10.1). Consequently, a user of *My_lib* will see the name clashes for *String* and *Vector* resolved in favor of *His_lib*::*String* and *Her_lib*::*Vector*. Also, *My_lib*::*List* will be used by default independently of whether *His_lib* or *Her_lib* are providing a *List*.

Usually, I prefer to leave a name unchanged when including it into a new namespace. In that way, I don't have to remember two different names for the same entity. However, sometimes a new name is needed or simply nice to have. For example:

```
namespace Lib2 {
    using namespace His_lib;  // everything from His_lib
    using namespace Her_lib;  // everything from Her_lib

    using His_lib::String;      // resolve potential clash in favor of His_lib
    using Her_lib::Vector;      // resolve potential clash in favor of Her_lib

    typedef Her_lib::String Her_string;       // rename

    template<class T> class His_vec          // ''rename''
        : public His_lib::Vector<T> { /* ... */ };

    template<class T> class List { /* ... */ }; // additional stuff
    // ...
}
```

There is no specific language mechanism for renaming. Instead, the general mechanisms for defining new entities are used.

8.2.9 Namespaces and Old Code

Millions of lines of C and C++ code rely on global names and existing libraries. How can we use namespaces to alleviate problems in such code? Redesigning existing code isn't always a viable option. Fortunately, it is possible to use C libraries as if they were defined in a namespace. However, this cannot be done for libraries written in C++ (§9.2.4). On the other hand, namespaces are designed so that they can be introduced with minimal disruption into an older C++ program.

8.2.9.1 Namespaces and C

Consider the canonical first C program:

```
#include <stdio.h>

int main()
{
    printf("Hello, world!\n");
}
```

Breaking this program wouldn't be a good idea. Making standard libraries special cases isn't a good idea either. Consequently, the language rules for namespaces are designed to make it relatively easy to take a program written without namespaces and turn it into a more explicitly structured one using namespaces. In fact, the calculator program (§6.1) is an example of this.

The *using-directive* is the key to achieving this. For example, the declarations of the standard C I/O facilities from the C header *stdio.h* are wrapped in a namespace like this:

```
// stdio.h:

    namespace std {
        int printf(const char* ... );
        // ...
    }
    using namespace std;
```

This achieves backwards compatibility. Also, a new header file *cstdio* is defined for people who don't want the names implicitly available:

```
// cstdio:

    namespace std {
        int printf(const char* ... );
        // ...
    }
```

C++ standard library implementers who worry about replication of declarations will, of course, define *stdio.h* by including *cstdio*:

```
// stdio.h:

    #include<cstdio>
    using std::printf;
    // ...
```

I consider nonlocal *using-directive*s primarily a transition tool. Most code referring to names from other namespaces can be expressed more clearly with explicit qualification and *using-declaration*s.

The relationship between namespaces and linkage is described in §9.2.4.

8.2.9.2 Namespaces and Overloading

Overloading (§7.4) works across namespaces. This is essential to allow us to migrate existing libraries to use namespaces with minimal source code changes. For example:

```
// old A.h:

    void f(int);
    // ...

// old B.h:

    void f(char);
    // ...

// old user.c:

    #include "A.h"
    #include "B.h"
```

```
void g()
{
    f('a');    // calls the f() from B.h
}
```

This program can be upgraded to a version using namespaces without changing the actual code:

```
// new A.h:

namespace A {
    void f(int);
    // ...
}
```

```
// new B.h:

namespace B {
    void f(char);
    // ...
}
```

```
// new user.c:

#include "A.h"
#include "B.h"

using namespace A;
using namespace B;

void g()
{
    f('a');    // calls the f() from B.h
}
```

Had we wanted to keep *user.c* completely unchanged, we would have placed the *using-directive*s in the header files.

8.2.9.3 Namespaces Are Open

A namespace is open; that is, you can add names to it from several namespace declarations. For example:

```
namespace A {
    int f(); // now A has member f()
}

namespace A {
    int g(); // now A has two members, f() and g()
}
```

In this way, we can support large program fragments within a single namespace the way an older library or application lives within the single global namespace. To do this, we must distribute the namespace definition over several header and source code files. As shown by the calculator example (§8.2.4), the openness of namespaces allows us to present different interfaces to different kinds of users by presenting different parts of a namespace. This openness is also an aid to transition. For example,

```
// my header:
    void f(); // my function
    // ...
    #include<stdio.h>
    int g(); // my function
    // ...
```

can be rewritten without reordering of the declarations:

```
// my header:

    namespace Mine {
        void f(); // my function
        // ...
    }

    #include<stdio.h>

    namespace Mine {
        int g(); // my function
        // ...
    }
```

When writing new code, I prefer to use many smaller namespaces (see §8.2.8) rather than putting really major pieces of code into a single namespace. However, that is often impractical when converting major pieces of software to use namespaces.

When defining a previously declared member of a namespace, it is safer to use the *Mine*:: syntax than to re-open *Mine*. For example:

```
void Mine::ff()      // error: no ff() declared in Mine
{
    // ...
}
```

A compiler catches this error. However, because new functions can be defined within a namespace, a compiler cannot catch the equivalent error in a re-opened namespace:

```
namespace Mine { // re-opening Mine to define functions

    void ff()  // oops! no ff() declared in Mine; ff() is added to Mine by this definition
    {
        // ...
    }

    // ...
}
```

The compiler has no way of knowing that you didn't want that new *ff*().

A namespace alias (§8.2.7) can be used to qualify a name in a definition. However, a namespace alias cannot be used to re-open a namespace.

8.3 Exceptions

When a program is composed of separate modules, and especially when those modules come from separately developed libraries, error handling needs to be separated into two distinct parts:

[1] The reporting of error conditions that cannot be resolved locally

[2] The handling of errors detected elsewhere

The author of a library can detect run-time errors but does not in general have any idea what to do about them. The user of a library may know how to cope with such errors but cannot detect them – or else they would be handled in the user's code and not left for the library to find.

In the calculator example, we bypassed this problem by designing the program as a whole. By doing that, we could fit error handling into our overall framework. However, when we separate the logical parts of the calculator into separate namespaces, we see that every namespace depends on namespace *Error* (§8.2.2) and that the error handling in *Error* relies on every module behaving appropriately after an error. Let's assume that we don't have the freedom to design the calculator as a whole and don't want the tight coupling between *Error* and all other modules. Instead, assume that the parser, etc., are written without knowledge of how a driver might like to handle errors.

Even though *error* ( ) was very simple, it embodied a strategy for error handling:

```
namespace Error {
    int no_of_errors;

    double error(const char* s)
    {
        std::cerr << "error: " << s << '\n';
        no_of_errors++;
        return 1;
    }
}
```

The *error* ( ) function writes out an error message, supplies a default value that allows its caller to continue a computation, and keeps track of a simple error state. Importantly, every part of the program knows that *error* ( ) exists, how to call it, and what to expect from it. For a program composed of separately-developed libraries, that would be too much to assume.

Exceptions are C++'s means of separating error reporting from error handling. In this section, exceptions are briefly described in the context of their use in the calculator example. Chapter 14 provides a more extensive discussion of exceptions and their uses.

8.3.1 Throw and Catch

The notion of an *exception* is provided to help deal with error reporting. For example:

```
struct Range_error {
    int i;
    Range_error(int ii) { i = ii; }   // constructor (§2.5.2, §10.2.3)
};
```

```
char to_char(int i)
{
    if (i<numeric_limits<char>::min() || numeric_limits<char>::max()<i)    // see §22.2
        throw Range_error(i);
    return i;
}
```

The *to_char*() function either returns the *char* with the numeric value *i* or throws a *Range_error*. The fundamental idea is that a function that finds a problem it cannot cope with *throws* an exception, hoping that its (direct or indirect) caller can handle the problem. A function that wants to handle a problem can indicate that it is willing to *catch* exceptions of the type used to report the problem. For example, to call *to_char*() and catch the exception it might throw, we could write:

```
void g(int i)
{
    try {
        char c = to_char(i);
        // ...
    }
    catch (Range_error) {
        cerr << "oops\n";
    }
}
```

The construct

```
catch ( /* ... */ ) {
    // ...
}
```

is called an *exception handler*. It can be used only immediately after a block prefixed with the keyword *try* or immediately after another exception handler; *catch* is also a keyword. The parentheses contain a declaration that is used in a way similar to how a function argument declaration is used. That is, it specifies the type of the objects that can be caught by this handler and optionally names the object caught. For example, if we wanted to know the value of the *Range_error* thrown, we would provide a name for the argument to *catch* exactly the way we name function arguments. For example:

```
void h(int i)
{
    try {
        char c = to_char(i);
        // ...
    }
    catch (Range_error x) {
        cerr << "oops: to_char(" << x.i << ")\n";
    }
}
```

If any code in a *try-block* – or called from it – throws an exception, the try-block's handlers will be examined. If the exception thrown is of a type specified for a handler, that handler is executed. If not, the exception handlers are ignored and the *try-block* acts just like an ordinary block. If an exception is thrown and no *try-block* catches it, the program terminates (§14.7).

Basically, C++ exception handling is a way to transfer control to designated code in a calling function. Where needed, some information about the error can be passed along to the caller. C programmers can think of exception handling as a well-behaved mechanism replacing *setjmp/longjmp* (§16.1.2). The important interaction between exception handling and classes is described in Chapter 14.

8.3.2 Discrimination of Exceptions

Typically, a program will have several different possible run-time errors. Such errors can be mapped into exceptions with distinct names. I prefer to define types with no other purpose than exception handling. This minimizes confusion about their purpose. In particular, I never use a built-in type, such as *int*, as an exception. In a large program, I would have no effective way to find unrelated uses of *int* exceptions. Thus, I could never be sure that such other uses didn't interfere with my use.

Our calculator (§6.1) must handle two kinds of run-time errors: syntax errors and attempts to divide by zero. No values need to be passed to a handler from the code that detects an attempt to divide by zero, so zero divide can be represented by a simple empty type:

```
struct Zero_divide { } ;
```

On the other hand, a handler would most likely prefer to get an indication of what kind of syntax error occurred. Here, we pass a string along:

```
struct Syntax_error {
    const char* p;
    Syntax_error (const char* q) { p = q; }
} ;
```

For notational convenience, I added a constructor (§2.5.2, §10.2.3) to the *struct*.

A user of the parser can discriminate between the two exceptions by adding handlers for both to a *try* block. Where needed, the appropriate handler will be entered. If we ''fall through the bottom'' of a handler, the execution continues at the end of the list of handlers:

```
try {
    // ...
    expr (false);
    // we get here if and only if expr() didn't cause an exception
    // ...
}
catch (Syntax_error) {
    // handle syntax error
}
```

```
    catch (Zero_divide) {
            // handle divide by zero
    }
    // we get here if expr didn't cause an exception or if a Syntax_error
    // or Zero_divide exception was caught (and its handler didn't return,
    // throw an exception, or in some other way alter the flow of control).
```

A list of handlers looks a bit like a *switch* statement, but there is no need for *break* statements. The syntax of a list of handlers differs from the syntax of a list of cases partly for that reason and partly to indicate that each handler is a scope (§4.9.4).

A function need not catch all possible exceptions. For example, the previous *try-block* didn't try to catch exceptions potentially generated by the parser's input operations. Those exceptions simply "pass through," searching for a caller with an appropriate handler.

From the language's point of view, an exception is considered handled immediately upon entry into its handler so that any exceptions thrown while executing a handler must be dealt with by the callers of the *try-block*. For example, this does not cause an infinite loop:

```
class Input_overflow { /* ... */ };

void f()
{
    try {
        // ...
    }
    catch (Input_overflow) {
        // ...
        throw Input_overflow();
    }
}
```

Exception handlers can be nested. For example:

```
class XXII { /* ... */ };

void f()
{
    // ...
    try {
        // ...
    }
    catch (XXII) {
        try {
            // something complicated
        }
        catch (XXII) {
            // complicated handler code failed
        }
    }
    // ...
}
```

However, such nesting is rare in human-written code and is more often than not an indication of poor style.

8.3.3 Exceptions in the Calculator

Given the basic exception-handling mechanism, we can rework the calculator example from §6.1 to separate the handling of errors found at run-time from the main logic of the calculator. This will result in an organization of the program that more realistically matches what is found in programs built from separate, loosely connected parts.

First, *error* ( ) can be eliminated. Instead, the parser functions know only the types used to signal errors:

```
namespace Error {
    struct Zero_divide { } ;

    struct Syntax_error {
        const char* p ;
        Syntax_error (const char* q) { p = q; }
    } ;
}
```

The parser detects three syntax errors:

```
Lexer::Token_value Lexer::get_token ()
{
    using namespace std;        // to use input, isalpha(), etc. (§6.1.7)

        // ...

        default:                    // NAME, NAME =, or error
            if (isalpha (ch) ) {
                string_value = ch;
                while (input->get (ch) && isalnum (ch) ) string_value.push_back (ch);
                input->putback (ch);
                return curr_tok=NAME;
            }
            throw Error::Syntax_error ("bad token");
    }
}

double Parser::prim (bool get)        // handle primaries
{
    // ...

    case Lexer::LP:
    {   double e = expr (true);
        if (curr_tok != Lexer::RP) throw Error::Syntax_error (" ` ) ´ expected");
        get_token ();        // eat ')'
        return e;
    }
```

```
        case Lexer::END:
            return 1;
        default:
            throw Error::Syntax_error("primary expected");
    }
}
```

When a syntax error is detected, *throw* is used to transfer control to a handler defined in some (direct or indirect) caller. The *throw* operator also passes a value to the handler. For example,

```
    throw Syntax_error("primary expected");
```

passes a *Syntax_error* object containing a pointer to the string *primary expected* to the handler.

Reporting a divide-by-zero error doesn't require any data to be passed along:

```
    double Parser::term(bool get)        // multiply and divide
    {
        // ...
        case Lexer::DIV:
            if (double d = prim(true)) {
                left /= d;
                break;
            }
            throw Error::Zero_divide();

        // ...
    }
```

The driver can now be defined to handle *Zero_divide* and *Syntax_error* exceptions. For example:

```
    int main(int argc, char* argv[])
    {
        // ...
        while (*input) {
            try {
                Lexer::get_token();
                if (Lexer::curr_tok == Lexer::END) break;
                if (Lexer::curr_tok == Lexer::PRINT) continue;
                cout << Parser::expr(false) << '\n';
            }
            catch(Error::Zero_divide) {
                cerr << "attempt to divide by zero\n";
                if (Lexer::curr_tok != Lexer::PRINT) skip();
            }
            catch(Error::Syntax_error e) {
                cerr << "syntax error:" << e.p << "\n";
                if (Lexer::curr_tok != Lexer::PRINT) skip();
            }
        }

        if (input != &cin) delete input;
        return no_of_errors;
    }
```

Unless an error was caused at the end of an expression terminated by a *PRINT* token (that is, an end-of-line or a semicolon), *main* ( ) calls the recovery function *skip* ( ). The function *skip* ( ) tries to bring the parser into a well-defined state by discarding characters until it finds an end-of-line or a semicolon. The *skip* ( ) function, *no_of_errors*, and *input* are obvious candidates for a *Driver* namespace:

```
namespace Driver {
     int no_of_errors;
     std::istream* input;
     void skip();
}

void Driver::skip()
{
     no_of_errors++;

     while (*input) {       // discard characters until newline or semicolon
          char ch;
          input->get(ch);

          switch (ch) {
          case '\n':
          case ';':
               return;
          }
     }
}
```

The code for *skip* ( ) is deliberately written at a lower level of abstraction than the parser code so as to avoid being caught by exceptions from the parser while handling parser exceptions.

I retained the idea of counting the number of errors and reporting that number as the program's return value. It is often useful to know if a program encountered an error even if it was able to recover from it.

I did not put *main* ( ) in the *Driver* namespace. The global *main* ( ) is the initial function of a program (§3.2); a *main* ( ) in another namespace has no special meaning. In a realistically-sized program, most of the code from *main* ( ) would be moved to a separate function in *Driver*.

8.3.3.1 Alternative Error-Handling Strategies

The original error-handling code was shorter and more elegant than the version using exceptions. However, it achieved that elegance by tightly coupling all parts of the program. That approach doesn't scale well to programs composed of separately developed libraries.

We could consider eliminating the separate error-handling function *skip* ( ) by introducing a state variable in *main* ( ). For example:

```
int main(int argc, char* argv[])       // example of poor style
{
     // ...

     bool in_error = false;
```

```
    while (*Driver::input) {
        try {
            Lexer::get_token();
            if (Lexer::curr_tok == Lexer::END) break;
            if (Lexer::curr_tok == Lexer::PRINT) {
                in_error = false;
                continue;
            }
            if (in_error == false) cout << Parser::expr(false) << '\n';
        }
        catch(Error::Zero_divide) {
            cerr << "attempt to divide by zero\n";
            ++no_of_errors;
            in_error = true;
        }
        catch(Error::Syntax_error e) {
            cerr << "syntax error:" << e.p << "\n";
            ++no_of_errors;
            in_error = true;
        }
    }

    if (Driver::input != &std::cin) delete Driver::input;
    return Driver::no_of_errors;
}
```

I consider this a bad idea for several reasons:

[1] State variables are a common source of confusion and errors, especially if they are allowed to proliferate and affect larger sections of a program. In particular, I consider the version of *main*() using *in_error* less readable than the version using *skip*().

[2] It is generally a good strategy to keep error handling and ''normal'' code separate.

[3] Doing error handling using the same level of abstraction as the code that caused the error is hazardous; the error-handling code might repeat the same error that triggered the error handling in the first place. I leave it as an exercise to find how that can happen for the version of *main*() using *in_error* (§8.5[7]).

[4] It is more work to modify the ''normal'' code to add error-handling code than to add separate error-handling routines.

Exception handling is intended for dealing with nonlocal problems. If an error can be handled locally, it almost always should be. For example, there is no reason to use an exception to handle the too-many-arguments error:

```
int main(int argc, char* argv[])
{
    using namespace std;
    using namespace Driver;
    switch (argc) {
    case 1:                                    // read from standard input
        input = &cin;
        break;
```

```
    case 2:                              // read argument string
        input = new istringstream(argv[1]);
        break;
    default:
        cerr << "too many arguments\n";
        return 1;
    }

    // as before
}
```

Exceptions are discussed further in Chapter 14.

8.4 Advice

[1] Use namespaces to express logical structure; §8.2.

[2] Place every nonlocal name, except *main* ( ), in some namespace; §8.2.

[3] Design a namespace so that you can conveniently use it without accidentally gaining access to unrelated namespaces; §8.2.4.

[4] Avoid very short names for namespaces; §8.2.7.

[5] If necessary, use namespace aliases to abbreviate long namespace names; §8.2.7.

[6] Avoid placing heavy notational burdens on users of your namespaces; §8.2.2, §8.2.3.

[7] Use the *Namespace* :: *member* notation when defining namespace members; §8.2.8.

[8] Use *using namespace* only for transition or within a local scope; §8.2.9.

[9] Use exceptions to decouple the treatment of "errors" from the code dealing with the ordinary processing; §8.3.3.

[10] Use user-defined rather than built-in types as exceptions; §8.3.2.

[11] Don't use exceptions when local control structures are sufficient; §8.3.3.1.

8.5 Exercises

1. (*2.5) Write a doubly-linked list of *string* module in the style of the *Stack* module from §2.4. Exercise it by creating a list of names of programming languages. Provide a *sort* ( ) function for that list, and provide a function that reverses the order of the strings in it.

2. (*2) Take some not-too-large program that uses at least one library that does not use namespaces and modify it to use a namespace for that library. Hint: §8.2.9.

3. (*2) Modify the desk calculator program into a module in the style of §2.4 using namespaces. Don't use any global *using-directive*s. Keep a record of the mistakes you made. Suggest ways of avoiding such mistakes in the future.

4. (*1) Write a program that throws an exception in one function and catches it in another.

5. (*2) Write a program consisting of functions calling each other to a calling depth of 10. Give each function an argument that determines at which level an exception is thrown. Have *main* ( ) catch these exceptions and print out which exception is caught. Don't forget the case in which an exception is caught in the function that throws it.

6. (*2) Modify the program from §8.5[5] to measure if there is a difference in the cost of catching exceptions depending on where in a class stack the exception is thrown. Add a string object to each function and measure again.

7. (*1) Find the error in the first version of *main* () in §8.3.3.1.

8. (*2) Write a function that either returns a value or that throws that value based on an argument. Measure the difference in run-time between the two ways.

9. (*2) Modify the calculator version from §8.5[3] to use exceptions. Keep a record of the mistakes you make. Suggest ways of avoiding such mistakes in the future.

10. (*2.5) Write *plus* (), *minus* (), *multiply* (), and *divide* () functions that check for possible overflow and underflow and that throw exceptions if such errors happen.

11. (*2) Modify the calculator to use the functions from §8.5[10].

9

Source Files and Programs

Form must follow function.
– Le Corbusier

Separate compilation — linking — header files — standard library headers — the one-
definition rule — linkage to non-C++ code — linkage and pointers to functions — using
headers to express modularity — single-header organization — multiple-header organization — include guards — programs — advice — exercises.

9.1 Separate Compilation

A file is the traditional unit of storage (in a file system) and the traditional unit of compilation.
There are systems that do not store, compile, and present C++ programs to the programmer as sets
of files. However, the discussion here will concentrate on systems that employ the traditional use
of files.

Having a complete program in one file is usually impossible. In particular, the code for the
standard libraries and the operating system is typically not supplied in source form as part of a
user's program. For realistically-sized applications, even having all of the user's own code in a single file is both impractical and inconvenient. The way a program is organized into files can help
emphasize its logical structure, help a human reader understand the program, and help the compiler
to enforce that logical structure. Where the unit of compilation is a file, all of a file must be recompiled whenever a change (however small) has been made to it or to something on which it depends.
For even a moderately sized program, the amount of time spent recompiling can be significantly
reduced by partitioning the program into files of suitable size.

A user presents a *source file* to the compiler. The file is then preprocessed; that is, macro processing (§7.8) is done and #*include* directives bring in headers (§2.4.1, §9.2.1). The result of preprocessing is called a *translation unit*. This unit is what the compiler proper works on and what the
C++ language rules describe. In this book, I differentiate between source file and translation unit

only where necessary to distinguish what the programmer sees from what the compiler considers.

To enable separate compilation, the programmer must supply declarations providing the type information needed to analyze a translation unit in isolation from the rest of the program. The declarations in a program consisting of many separately compiled parts must be consistent in exactly the same way the declarations in a program consisting of a single source file must be. Your system will have tools to help ensure this. In particular, the linker can detect many kinds of inconsistencies. The *linker* is the program that binds together the separately compiled parts. A linker is sometimes (confusingly) called a *loader*. Linking can be done completely before a program starts to run. Alternatively, new code can be added to the program (''dynamically linked'') later.

The organization of a program into source files is commonly called the *physical structure* of a program. The physical separation of a program into separate files should be guided by the logical structure of the program. The same dependency concerns that guide the composition of programs out of namespaces guide its composition into source files. However, the logical and physical structure of a program need not be identical. For example, it can be useful to use several source files to store the functions from a single namespace, to store a collection of namespace definitions in a single file, and to scatter the definition of a namespace over several files (§8.2.4).

Here, we will first consider some technicalities relating to linking and then discuss two ways of breaking the desk calculator (§6.1, §8.2) into files.

9.2 Linkage

Names of functions, classes, templates, variables, namespaces, enumerations, and enumerators must be used consistently across all translation units unless they are explicitly specified to be local.

It is the programmer's task to ensure that every namespace, class, function, etc. is properly declared in every translation unit in which it appears and that all declarations referring to the same entity are consistent. For example, consider two files:

```
// file1.c:
    int x = 1;
    int f() { /* do something */ }

// file2.c:
    extern int x;
    int f();
    void g() { x = f(); }
```

The *x* and *f*() used by *g*() in *file2.c* are the ones defined in *file1.c*. The keyword *extern* indicates that the declaration of *x* in *file2.c* is (just) a declaration and not a definition (§4.9). Had *x* been initialized, *extern* would simply be ignored because a declaration with an initializer is always a definition. An object must be defined exactly once in a program. It may be declared many times, but the types must agree exactly. For example:

```
// file1.c:
    int x = 1;
    int b = 1;
    extern int c;
```

```
// file2.c:
    int x;                   // meaning int x = 0;
    extern double b;
    extern int c;
```

There are three errors here: *x* is defined twice, *b* is declared twice with different types, and *c* is declared twice but not defined. These kinds of errors (linkage errors) cannot be detected by a compiler that looks at only one file at a time. Most, however, are detectable by the linker. Note that a variable defined without an initializer in the global or a namespace scope is initialized by default. This is *not* the case for local variables (§4.9.5, §10.4.2) or objects created on the free store (§6.2.6). For example, the following program fragment contains two errors:

```
// file1.c:
    int x;
    int f() { return x; }
// file2.c:
    int x;
    int g() { return f(); }
```

The call of *f*( ) in *file2.c* is an error because *f*( ) has not been declared in *file2.c*. Also, the program will not link because *x* is defined twice. Note that the call of *f*( ) is not an error in C (§B.2.2).

A name that can be used in translation units different from the one in which it was defined is said to have *external linkage*. All the names in the previous examples have external linkage. A name that can be referred to only in the translation unit in which it is defined is said to have *internal linkage*.

An *inline* function (§7.1.1, §10.2.9) must be defined – by identical definitions (§9.2.3) – in every translation unit in which it is used. Consequently, the following example isn't just bad taste; it is illegal:

```
// file1.c:
    inline int f(int i) { return i; }
// file2.c:
    inline int f(int i) { return i+1; }
```

Unfortunately, this error is hard for an implementation to catch, and the following – otherwise perfectly logical – combination of external linkage and inlining is banned to make life simpler for compiler writers:

```
// file1.c:
    extern inline int g(int i);
    int h(int i) { return g(i); }    // error: g() undefined in this translation unit
// file2.c:
    extern inline int g(int i) { return i+1; }
```

By default, *const*s (§5.4) and *typedef*s (§4.9.7) have internal linkage. Consequently, this example is legal (although potentially confusing):

```
// file1.c:
    typedef int  T;
    const int x = 7;
// file2.c:
    typedef void  T;
    const int x = 8;
```

Global variables that are local to a single compilation unit are a common source of confusion and are best avoided. To ensure consistency, you should usually place global *const*s and *inline*s in header files only (§9.2.1).

A *const* can be given external linkage by an explicit declaration:

```
// file1.c:
    extern const int  a = 77;
// file2.c:
    extern const int  a;

    void  g ( )
    {
        cout << a << ´\n´;
    }
```

Here, *g* ( ) will print *77*.

An unnamed namespace (§8.2.5) can be used to make names local to a compilation unit. The effect of an unnamed namespace is very similar to that of internal linkage. For example:

```
// file 1.c:
    namespace {
        class  X { /* ... */ };
        void f();
        int  i;
        // ...
    }
// file2.c:
    class  X { /* ... */ };
    void f();
    int  i;
    // ...
```

The function *f*( ) in *file1 . c* is not the same function as the *f*( ) in *file2 . c*. Having a name local to a translation unit and also using that same name elsewhere for an entity with external linkage is asking for trouble.

In C and older C++ programs, the keyword *static* is (confusingly) used to mean "use internal linkage" (§B.2.3). Don't use *static* except inside functions (§7.1.2) and classes (§10.2.4).

9.2.1 Header Files

The types in all declarations of the same object, function, class, etc., must be consistent. Consequently, the source code submitted to the compiler and later linked together must be consistent. One imperfect but simple method of achieving consistency for declarations in different translation units is to *#include header files* containing interface information in source files containing executable code and/or data definitions.

The *#include* mechanism is a text manipulation facility for gathering source program fragments together into a single unit (file) for compilation. The directive

    #include "to_be_included"

replaces the line in which the *#include* appears with the contents of the file *to_be_included*. The content should be C++ source text because the compiler will proceed to read it.

To include standard library headers, use the angle brackets < and > around the name instead of quotes. For example:

    #include <iostream>   *// from standard include directory*
    #include "myheader.h"   *// from current directory*

Unfortunately, spaces are significant within the < > or " " of an include directive:

    #include < iostream >   *// will not find <iostream>*

It may seem extravagant to recompile a file each time it is included somewhere, but the included files typically contain only declarations and not code needing extensive analysis by the compiler. Furthermore, most modern C++ implementations provide some form of precompiling of header files to minimize the work needed to handle repeated compilation of the same header.

As a rule of thumb, a header may contain:

Named namespaces	*namespace N { /* ... */ }*
Type definitions	*struct Point { int x, y; };*
Template declarations	*template<class T> class Z;*
Template definitions	*template<class T> class V { /* ... */ };*
Function declarations	*extern int strlen(const char*);*
Inline function definitions	*inline char get(char* p) { return *p++; }*
Data declarations	*extern int a;*
Constant definitions	*const float pi = 3.141593;*
Enumerations	*enum Light { red, yellow, green };*
Name declarations	*class Matrix;*
Include directives	*#include <algorithm>*
Macro definitions	*#define VERSION 12*
Conditional compilation directives	*#ifdef __cplusplus*
Comments	*/* check for end of file */*

This rule of thumb for what may be placed in a header is not a language requirement. It is simply a reasonable way of using the *#include* mechanism to express the physical structure of a program. Conversely, a header should never contain:

Ordinary function definitions	*char get (char* p) { return *p++; }*
Data definitions	*int a;*
Aggregate definitions	*short tbl* [ ] = { *1, 2, 3* };
Unnamed namespaces	*namespace { /* ... */ }*
Exported template definitions	*export template<class T> f(T t) { /* ... */ }*

Header files are conventionally suffixed by *.h*, and files containing function or data definitions are suffixed by *.c*. They are therefore often referred to as ''.h files'' and ''.c files,'' respectively. Other conventions, such as *.C*, *.cxx*, *.cpp*, and *.cc*, are also found. The manual for your compiler will be quite specific about this issue.

The reason for recommending that the definition of simple constants, but not the definition of aggregates, be placed in header files is that it is hard for implementations to avoid replication of aggregates presented in several translation units. Furthermore, the simple cases are far more common and therefore more important for generating good code.

It is wise not to be too clever about the use of *#include*. My recommendation is to *#include* only complete declarations and definitions and to do so only in the global scope, in linkage specification blocks, and in namespace definitions when converting old code (§9.2.2). As usual, it is wise to avoid macro magic. One of my least favorite activities is tracking down an error caused by a name being macro-substituted into something completely different by a macro defined in an indirectly *#include*d header that I have never even heard of.

9.2.2 Standard Library Headers

The facilities of the standard library are presented through a set of standard headers (§16.1.2). No suffix is needed for standard library headers; they are known to be headers because they are included using the *#include<...>* syntax rather than *#include"..."*. The absence of a *.h* suffix does not imply anything about how the header is stored. A header such as *<map>* may be stored as a text file called *map.h* in a standard directory. On the other hand, standard headers are not required to be stored in a conventional manner. An implementation is allowed to take advantage of knowledge of the standard library definition to optimize the standard library implementation and the way standard headers are handled. For example, an implementation might have knowledge of the standard math library (§22.3) built in and treat *#include<cmath>* as a switch that makes the standard math functions available without reading any file.

For each C standard-library header *<X.h>*, there is a corresponding standard C++ header *<cX>*. For example, *#include<cstdio>* provides what *#include<stdio.h>* does. A typical *stdio.h* will look something like this:

```
#ifdef __cplusplus      // for C++ compilers only (§9.2.4)
namespace std {         // the standard library is defined in namespace std (§8.2.9)

extern "C" {            // stdio functions have C linkage (§9.2.4)
#endif

    // ...
    int printf(const char* ...);
    // ...
```

```
#ifdef __cplusplus
    }
}
using namespace std;        // make stdio available in global namespace
#endif
```

That is, the actual declarations are (most likely) shared, but linkage and namespace issues must be addressed to allow C and C++ to share a header.

9.2.3 The One-Definition Rule

A given class, enumeration, and template, etc., must be defined exactly once in a program.

From a practical point of view, this means that there must be exactly one definition of, say, a class residing in a single file somewhere. Unfortunately, the language rule cannot be that simple. For example, the definition of a class may be composed through macro expansion (ugh!) and a definition of a class may be textually included in two source files by #*include* directives (§9.2.1). Worse, a ''file'' isn't a concept that is part of the C and C++ language definitions; there exist implementations that do not store programs in source files.

Consequently, the rule in the standard that says that there must be a unique definition of a class, template, etc., is phrased in a somewhat more complicated and subtle manner. This rule is commonly referred to as ''the one-definition rule,'' the ODR. That is, two definitions of a class, template, or inline function are accepted as examples of the same unique definition if and only if

[1] they appear in different translation units, and
[2] they are token-for-token identical, and
[3] the meanings of those tokens are the same in both translation units.

For example:

```
// file1.c:
    struct S { int a; char b; };
    void f(S*);

// file2.c:
    struct S { int a; char b; };
    void f(S* p) { /* ... */ }
```

The ODR says that this example is valid and that *S* refers to the same class in both source files. However, it is unwise to write out a definition twice like that. Someone maintaining *file2.c* will naturally assume that the definition of *S* in *file2.c* is the only definition of *S* and so feel free to change it. This could introduce a hard-to-detect error.

The intent of the ODR is to allow inclusion of a class definition in different translation units from a common source file. For example:

```
// file s.h:
    struct S { int a; char b; };
    void f(S*);
```

```
// file1.c:
    #include "s.h"
    // use f() here

// file2.c:
    #include "s.h"
    void f(S* p) { /* ... */ }
```

or graphically:

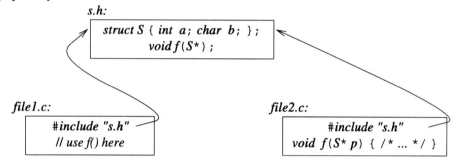

Here are examples of the three ways of violating the ODR:

```
// file1.c:
    struct S1 { int a; char b; };

    struct S1 { int a; char b; };   // error: double definition
```

This is an error because a *struct* may not be defined twice in a single translation unit.

```
// file1.c:
    struct S2 { int a; char b; };

// file2.c:
    struct S2 { int a; char bb; };  // error
```

This is an error because *S2* is used to name classes that differ in a member name.

```
// file1.c:
    typedef int X;
    struct S3 { X a; char b; };

// file2.c:
    typedef char X;
    struct S3 { X a; char b; };      // error
```

Here the two definitions of *S3* are token-for-token identical, but the example is an error because the meaning of the name *X* has sneakily been made to differ in the two files.

Checking against inconsistent class definitions in separate translation units is beyond the ability of most C++ implementations. Consequently, declarations that violate the ODR can be a source of subtle errors. Unfortunately, the technique of placing shared definitions in headers and *#including* them doesn't protect against this last form of ODR violation. Local typedefs and macros can change the meaning of *#included* declarations:

```
// file s.h:
    struct S { Point a; char b; };

// file1.c:
    #define Point int
    #include "s.h"
    // ...

// file2.c:
    class Point { /* ... */ };
    #include "s.h"
    // ...
```

The best defense against this kind of hackery is to make headers as self-contained as possible. For example, if class *Point* had been declared in the *s.h* header the error would have been detected.

A template definition can be #*include*d in several translation units as long as the ODR is adhered to. In addition, an exported template can be used given only a declaration:

```
// file1.c:
    export template<class T> T twice(T t) { return t+t; }

// file2.c:
    template<class T> T twice(T t);              // declaration
    int g(int i) { return twice(i); }
```

The keyword *export* means "accessible from another translation unit" (§13.7).

9.2.4 Linkage to Non-C++ Code

Typically, a C++ program contains parts written in other languages. Similarly, it is common for C++ code fragments to be used as parts of programs written mainly in some other language. Cooperation can be difficult between program fragments written in different languages and even between fragments written in the same language but compiled with different compilers. For example, different languages and different implementations of the same language may differ in their use of machine registers to hold arguments, the layout of arguments put on a stack, the layout of built-in types such as strings and integers, the form of names passed by the compiler to the linker, and the amount of type checking required from the linker. To help, one can specify a *linkage* convention to be used in an *extern* declaration. For example, this declares the C and C++ standard library function *strcpy()* and specifies that it should be linked according to the C linkage conventions:

```
    extern "C" char* strcpy(char*, const char*);
```

The effect of this declaration differs from the effect of the "plain" declaration

```
    extern char* strcpy(char*, const char*);
```

only in the linkage convention used for calling *strcpy()*.

The *extern "C"* directive is particularly useful because of the close relationship between C and C++. Note that the *C* in *extern "C"* names a linkage convention and not a language. Often, *extern "C"* is used to link to Fortran and assembler routines that happen to conform to the conventions of a C implementation.

An *extern "C"* directive specifies the linkage convention (only) and does not affect the semantics of calls to the function. In particular, a function declared *extern "C"* still obeys the C++ type checking and argument conversion rules and not the weaker C rules. For example:

```
extern "C" int f();

int g()
{
        return f(1);     // error: no argument expected
}
```

Adding *extern "C"* to a lot of declarations can be a nuisance. Consequently, there is a mechanism to specify linkage to a group of declarations. For example:

```
extern "C" {
        char* strcpy(char*, const char*);
        int strcmp(const char*, const char*);
        int strlen(const char*);
        // ...
}
```

This construct, commonly called a *linkage block*, can be used to enclose a complete C header to make a header suitable for C++ use. For example:

```
extern "C" {
#include <string.h>
}
```

This technique is commonly used to produce a C++ header from a C header. Alternatively, conditional compilation (§7.8.1) can be used to create a common C and C++ header:

```
#ifdef __cplusplus
extern "C" {
#endif

        char* strcpy(char*, const char*);
        int strcmp(const char*, const char*);
        int strlen(const char*);
        // ...

#ifdef __cplusplus
}
#endif
```

The predefined macro name *__cplusplus* is used to ensure that the C++ constructs are edited out when the file is used as a C header.

Any declaration can appear within a linkage block:

```
extern "C" {            // any declaration here, for example:
        int g1;         // definition
        extern int g2;  // declaration, not definition
}
```

In particular, the scope and storage class of variables are not affected, so *g1* is still a global variable

− and is still defined rather than just declared. To declare but not define a variable, you must apply the keyword *extern* directly in the declaration. For example:

```
extern "C" int g3;              // declaration, not definition
```

This looks odd at first glance. However, it is a simple consequence of keeping the meaning unchanged when adding *"C"* to an extern declaration and the meaning of a file unchanged when enclosing it in a linkage block.

A name with C linkage can be declared in a namespace. The namespace will affect the way the name is accessed in the C++ program, but not the way a linker sees it. The *printf()* from *std* is a typical example:

```
#include<cstdio>

void f()
{
    std::printf("Hello, ");     // ok
    printf("world!\n");         // error: no global printf()
}
```

Even when called *std::printf*, it is still the same old C *printf()* (§21.8).

Note that this allows us to include libraries with C linkage into a namespace of our choice rather than polluting the global namespace. Unfortunately, the same flexibility is not available to us for headers defining functions with C++ linkage in the global namespace. The reason is that linkage of C++ entities must take namespaces into account so that the object files generated will reflect the use or lack of use of namespaces.

9.2.5 Linkage and Pointers to Functions

When mixing C and C++ code fragments in one program, we sometimes want to pass pointers to functions defined in one language to functions defined in the other. If the two implementations of the two languages share linkage conventions and function-call mechanisms, such passing of pointers to functions is trivial. However, such commonality cannot in general be assumed, so care must be taken to ensure that a function is called the way it expects to be called.

When linkage is specified for a declaration, the specified linkage applies to all function types, function names, and variable names introduced by the declaration(s). This makes all kinds of strange − and occasionally essential − combinations of linkage possible. For example:

```
typedef int (*FT)(const void*, const void*);            // FT has C++ linkage

extern "C" {
    typedef int (*CFT)(const void*, const void*);       // CFT has C linkage
    void qsort(void* p, size_t n, size_t sz, CFT cmp);  // cmp has C linkage
}

void isort(void* p, size_t n, size_t sz, FT cmp);       // cmp has C++ linkage
void xsort(void* p, size_t n, size_t sz, CFT cmp);      // cmp has C linkage
extern "C" void ysort(void* p, size_t n, size_t sz, FT cmp);  // cmp has C++ linkage

int compare(const void*, const void*);                  // compare() has C++ linkage
extern "C" int ccmp(const void*, const void*);          // ccmp() has C linkage
```

```
void f(char* v, int sz)
{
    qsort(v,sz,1,&compare);  // error
    qsort(v,sz,1,&ccmp);     // ok

    isort(v,sz,1,&compare);  // ok
    isort(v,sz,1,&ccmp);     // error
}
```

An implementation in which C and C++ use the same calling conventions might accept the cases marked *error* as a language extension.

9.3 Using Header Files

To illustrate the use of headers, I present a few alternative ways of expressing the physical structure of the calculator program (§6.1, §8.2).

9.3.1 Single Header File

The simplest solution to the problem of partitioning a program into several files is to put the definitions in a suitable number of *.c* files and to declare the types needed for them to communicate in a single *.h* file that each *.c* file #*include*s. For the calculator program, we might use five *.c* files – *lexer.c*, *parser.c*, *table.c*, *error.c*, and *main.c* – to hold function and data definitions, plus the header *dc.h* to hold the declarations of every name used in more than one *.c* file.

The header *dc.h* would look like this:

```
// dc.h:

namespace Error {
    struct Zero_divide { };

    struct Syntax_error {
        const char* p;
        Syntax_error(const char* q) { p = q; }
    };
}

#include <string>

namespace Lexer {
    enum Token_value {
        NAME,        NUMBER,      END,
        PLUS='+',    MINUS='-',   MUL='*',    DIV='/',
        PRINT=';',   ASSIGN='=',  LP='(',     RP=')'
    };

    extern Token_value curr_tok;
    extern double number_value;
    extern std::string string_value;
```

```
        Token_value get_token();
}

namespace Parser {
        double prim(bool get);      // handle primaries
        double term(bool get);      // multiply and divide
        double expr(bool get);      // add and subtract

        using Lexer::get_token;
        using Lexer::curr_tok;
}

#include <map>

extern std::map<std::string, double> table;

namespace Driver {
        extern int no_of_errors;
        extern std::istream* input;
        void skip();
}
```

The keyword *extern* is used for every declaration of a variable to ensure that multiple definitions do not occur as we #*include dc.h* in the various .*c* files. The corresponding definitions are found in the appropriate .*c* files.

Leaving out the actual code, *lexer.c* will look something like this:

```
// lexer.c:

#include "dc.h"
#include <iostream>
#include <cctype>

Lexer::Token_value Lexer::curr_tok;
double Lexer::number_value;
std::string Lexer::string_value;

Lexer::Token_value Lexer::get_token() { /* ... */ }
```

Using headers in this manner ensures that every declaration in a header will at some point be included in the file containing its definition. For example, when compiling *lexer.c* the compiler will be presented with:

```
namespace Lexer {    // from dc.h
        // ...
        Token_value get_token();
}

// ...

Lexer::Token_value Lexer::get_token() { /* ... */ }
```

This ensures that the compiler will detect any inconsistencies in the types specified for a name. For example, had *get_token*() been declared to return a *Token_value*, but defined to return an *int*, the compilation of *lexer.c* would have failed with a type-mismatch error. If a definition is missing, the linker will catch the problem. If a declaration is missing, some . *c* file will fail to compile.

File *parser*. *c* will look like this:

```
// parser.c:

#include "dc.h"

double  Parser::prim(bool  get) { /* ... */ }
double  Parser::term(bool  get) { /* ... */ }
double  Parser::expr(bool  get) { /* ... */ }
```

File *table*. *c* will look like this:

```
// table.c:

#include "dc.h"

std::map<std::string, double> table;
```

The symbol table is simply a variable of the standard library *map* type. This defines *table* to be global. In a realistically-sized program, this kind of minor pollution of the global namespace builds up and eventually causes problems. I left this sloppiness here simply to get an opportunity to warn against it.

Finally, file *main*. *c* will look like this:

```
// main.c:

#include "dc.h"
#include <sstream>

int  Driver::no_of_errors = 0;
std::istream* Driver::input = 0;

void  Driver::skip() { /* ... */ }

int  main(int  argc, char* argv[]) { /* ... */ }
```

To be recognized as *the main*() of the program, *main*() must be a global function, so no namespace is used here.

The physical structure of the system can be presented like this:

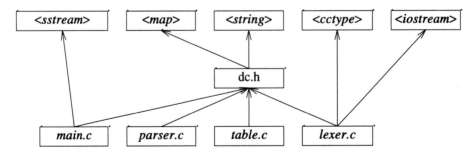

Note that the headers on the top are all headers for standard library facilities. For many forms of program analysis, these libraries can be ignored because they are well known and stable. For tiny programs, the structure can be simplified by moving all *#include* directives to the common header.

This single-header style of physical partitioning is most useful when the program is small and its parts are not intended to be used separately. Note that when namespaces are used, the logical structure of the program is still represented within *dc.h*. If namespaces are not used, the structure is obscured, although comments can be a help.

For larger programs, the single header file approach is unworkable in a conventional file-based development environment. A change to the common header forces recompilation of the whole program, and updates of that single header by several programmers are error-prone. Unless strong emphasis is placed on programming styles relying heavily on namespaces and classes, the logical structure deteriorates as the program grows.

9.3.2 Multiple Header Files

An alternative physical organization lets each logical module have its own header defining the facilities it provides. Each *.c* file then has a corresponding *.h* file specifying what it provides (its interface). Each *.c* file includes its own *.h* file and usually also other *.h* files that specify what it needs from other modules in order to implement the services advertised in the interface. This physical organization corresponds to the logical organization of a module. The interface for users is put into its *.h* file, the interface for implementers is put into a file suffixed *_impl.h*, and the module's definitions of functions, variables, etc. are placed in *.c* files. In this way, the parser is represented by three files. The parser's user interface is provided by *parser.h*:

```
// parser.h:

namespace Parser {          // interface for users
    double expr(bool get);
}
```

The shared environment for the functions implementing the parser is presented by *parser_impl.h*:

```
// parser_impl.h:

#include "parser.h"
#include "error.h"
#include "lexer.h"

namespace Parser {          // interface for implementers
    double prim(bool get);
    double term(bool get);
    double expr(bool get);

    using Lexer::get_token;
    using Lexer::curr_tok;
}
```

The user's header *parser.h* is *#include*d to give the compiler a chance to check consistency (§9.3.1).

The functions implementing the parser are stored in *parser.c* together with *#include* directives for the headers that the *Parser* functions need:

```
// parser.c:

#include "parser_impl.h"
#include "table.h"

double Parser::prim(bool get) { /* ... */ }
double Parser::term(bool get) { /* ... */ }
double Parser::expr(bool get) { /* ... */ }
```

Graphically, the parser and the driver's use of it look like this:

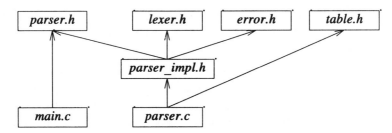

As intended, this is a rather close match to the logical structure described in §8.3.3. To simplify this structure, we could have #*included* *table . h* in *parser_impl . h* rather than in *parser . c*. However, *table . h* is an example of something that is not necessary to express the shared context of the parser functions; it is needed only by their implementation. In fact, it is used by just one function, *prim*(), so if we were really keen on minimizing dependencies we could place *prim*() in its own . c file and #*include table . h* there only:

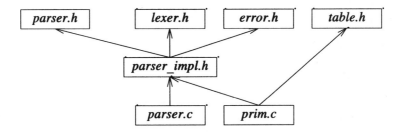

Such elaboration is not appropriate except for larger modules. For realistically-sized modules, it is common to #*include* extra files where needed for individual functions. Furthermore, it is not uncommon to have more than one _*impl . h*, since different subsets of the module's functions need different shared contexts.

Please note that the _*impl . h* notation is not a standard or even a common convention; it is simply the way I like to name things.

Why bother with this more complicated scheme of multiple header files? It clearly requires far less thought simply to throw every declaration into a single header, as was done for *dc . h*.

The multiple-header organization scales to modules several magnitudes larger than our toy parser and to programs several magnitudes larger than our calculator. The fundamental reason for using this type of organization is that it provides a better localization of concerns. When analyzing and modifying a large program, it is essential for a programmer to focus on a relatively small chunk of code. The multiple-header organization makes it easy to determine exactly what the parser code depends on and to ignore the rest of the program. The single-header approach forces us to look at every declaration used by any module and decide if it is relevant. The simple fact is that maintenance of code is invariably done with incomplete information and from a local perspective. The multiple-header organization allows us to work successfully "from the inside out" with only a local perspective. The single-header approach − like every other organization centered around a global repository of information − requires a top-down approach and will forever leave us wondering exactly what depends on what.

The better localization leads to less information needed to compile a module, and thus to faster compiles. The effect can be dramatic. I have seen compile times drop by a factor of ten as the result of a simple dependency analysis leading to a better use of headers.

9.3.2.1 Other Calculator Modules

The remaining calculator modules can be organized similarly to the parser. However, those modules are so small that they don't require their own _impl.h_ files. Such files are needed only where a logical module consists of many functions that need a shared context.

The error handler was reduced to the set of exception types so that no *error.c* was needed:

```
// error.h:

namespace Error {
    struct Zero_divide { } ;

    struct Syntax_error {
        const char* p;
        Syntax_error(const char* q) { p = q; }
    } ;
}
```

The lexer provides a rather large and messy interface:

```
// lexer.h:

#include <string>

namespace Lexer {
    enum Token_value {
        NAME,        NUMBER,      END,
        PLUS='+',    MINUS='-',   MUL='*',   DIV='/',
        PRINT=';',   ASSIGN='=',  LP='(',    RP=')'
    } ;

    extern Token_value curr_tok;
    extern double number_value;
    extern std::string string_value;

    Token_value get_token();
}
```

In addition to *lexer.h*, the implementation of the lexer depends on *error.h*, *<iostream>*, and the functions determining the kinds of characters declared in *<cctype>*:

```
// lexer.c:

#include "lexer.h"
#include "error.h"
#include <iostream>
#include <cctype>

Lexer::Token_value Lexer::curr_tok;
double Lexer::number_value;
std::string Lexer::string_value;

Lexer::Token_value Lexer::get_token() { /* ... */ }
```

We could have factored out the *#include* directive for *error.h* as the *Lexer*'s *_impl.h* file. However, I considered that excessive for this tiny program.

As usual, we *#include* the interface offered by the module – in this case, *lexer.h* – in the module's implementation to give the compiler a chance to check consistency.

The symbol table is essentially self-contained, although the standard library header *<map>* could drag in all kinds of interesting stuff to implement an efficient *map* template class:

```
// table.h:

#include <map>
#include <string>

extern std::map<std::string, double> table;
```

Because we assume that every header may be *#include*d in several *.c* files, we must separate the declaration of *table* from its definition, even though the difference between *table.c* and *table.h* is the single keyword *extern*:

```
// table.c:

#include "table.h"

std::map<std::string, double> table;
```

Basically, the driver depends on everything:

```
// main.c:

#include "parser.h"
#include "lexer.h"
#include "error.h"
#include "table.h"

namespace Driver {
    int no_of_errors;
    std::istream* input;
    void skip();
}
```

```
#include <sstream>

int main(int argc, char* argv[]) { /* ... */ }
```

Because the *Driver* namespace is used exclusively by *main()*, I placed it in *main.c*. Alternatively, I could have factored it out as *driver.h* and #*include*d it.

For a larger system, it is usually worthwhile organizing things so that the driver has fewer direct dependencies. Often, it is also worth minimizing what is done in *main()* by having *main()* call a driver function placed in a separate source file. This is particularly important for code intended to be used as a library. Then, we cannot rely on code in *main()* and must be prepared to be called from a variety of functions (§9.6[8]).

9.3.2.2 Use of Headers

The number of headers to use for a program is a function of many factors. Many of these factors have more to do with the way files are handled on your system than with C++. For example, if your editor does not have facilities for looking at several files at the same time, then using many headers becomes less attractive. Similarly, if opening and reading 20 files of 50 lines each is noticeably more time-consuming than reading a single file of 1000 lines, you might think twice before using the multiple-header style for a small project.

A word of caution: a dozen headers plus the standard headers for the program's execution environment (which can often be counted in the hundreds) are usually manageable. However, if you partition the declarations of a large program into the logically minimal-sized headers (putting each structure declaration in its own file, etc.), you can easily get an unmanageable mess of hundreds of files even for minor projects. I find that excessive.

For large projects, multiple headers are unavoidable. In such projects, hundreds of files (not counting standard headers) are the norm. The real confusion starts when they start to be counted in the thousands. At that scale, the basic techniques discussed here still apply, but their management becomes a Herculean task. Remember that for realistically-sized programs, the single-header style is not an option. Such programs will have multiple headers. The choice between the two styles of organization occurs (repeatedly) for the parts that make up the program.

The single-header style and the multiple-header style are not really alternatives to each other. They are complementary techniques that must be considered whenever a significant module is designed and must be reconsidered as a system evolves. It's crucial to remember that one interface doesn't serve all equally well. It is usually worthwhile to distinguish between the implementers' interface and the users' interface. In addition, many larger systems are structured so that providing a simple interface for the majority of users and a more extensive interface for expert users is a good idea. The expert users' interfaces ("complete interfaces") tend to #*include* many more features than the average user would ever want to know about. In fact, the average users' interface can often be identified by eliminating features that require the inclusion of headers that define facilities that would be unknown to the average user. The term "average user" is not derogatory. In the fields in which I don't *have* to be an expert, I strongly prefer to be an average user. In that way, I minimize hassles.

9.3.3 Include Guards

The idea of the multiple-header approach is to represent each logical module as a consistent, self-contained unit. Viewed from the program as a whole, many of the declarations needed to make each logical module complete are redundant. For larger programs, such redundancy can lead to errors, as a header containing class definitions or inline functions gets #*include*d twice in the same compilation unit (§9.2.3).

We have two choices. We can

[1] reorganize our program to remove the redundancy, or

[2] find a way to allow repeated inclusion of headers.

The first approach − which led to the final version of the calculator − is tedious and impractical for realistically-sized programs. We also need that redundancy to make the individual parts of the program comprehensible in isolation.

The benefits of an analysis of redundant #*include*s and the resulting simplifications of the program can be significant both from a logical point of view and by reducing compile times. However, it can rarely be complete, so some method of allowing redundant #*include*s must be applied. Preferably, it must be applied systematically, since there is no way of knowing how thorough an analysis a user will find worthwhile.

The traditional solution is to insert *include guards* in headers. For example:

```
// error.h:

#ifndef CALC_ERROR_H
#define CALC_ERROR_H

namespace Error {
    // ...
}

#endif     // CALC_ERROR_H
```

The contents of the file between the #*ifndef* and #*endif* are ignored by the compiler if *CALC_ERROR_H* is defined. Thus, the first time *error.h* is seen during a compilation, its contents are read and *CALC_ERROR_H* is given a value. Should the compiler be presented with *error.h* again during the compilation, the contents are ignored. This is a piece of macro hackery, but it works and it is pervasive in the C and C++ worlds. The standard headers all have include guards.

Header files are included in essentially arbitrary contexts, and there is no namespace protection against macro name clashes. Consequently, I choose rather long and ugly names as my include guards.

Once people get used to headers and include guards, they tend to include *lots* of headers directly and indirectly. Even with C++ implementations that optimize the processing of headers, this can be undesirable. It can cause unnecessarily long compile time, and it can bring *lots* of declarations and macros into scope. The latter might affect the meaning of the program in unpredictable and adverse ways. Headers should be included only when necessary.

9.4 Programs

A program is a collection of separately compiled units combined by a linker. Every function, object, type, etc., used in this collection must have a unique definition (§4.9, §9.2.3). The program must contain exactly one function called *main* () (§3.2). The main computation performed by the program starts with the invocation of *main* () and ends with a return from *main* (). The *int* returned by *main* () is passed to whatever system invoked *main* () as the result of the program.

This simple story must be elaborated on for programs that contain global variables (§10.4.9) or that throw an uncaught exception (§14.7).

9.4.1 Initialization of Nonlocal Variables

In principle, a variable defined outside any function (that is, global, namespace, and class *static* variables) is initialized before *main* () is invoked. Such nonlocal variables in a translation unit are initialized in their definition order (§10.4.9). If such a variable has no explicit initializer, it is by default initialized to the default for its type (§10.4.2). The default initializer value for built-in types and enumerations is *0*. For example:

```
double  x = 2;          // nonlocal variables
double  y;
double  sqx = sqrt (x+y);
```

Here, *x* and *y* are initialized before *sqx*, so *sqrt* (*2*) is called.

There is no guaranteed order of initialization of global variables in different translation units. Consequently, it is unwise to create order dependencies between initializers of global variables in different compilation units. In addition, it is not possible to catch an exception thrown by the initializer of a global variable (§14.7). It is generally best to minimize the use of global variables and in particular to limit the use of global variables requiring complicated initialization.

Several techniques exist for enforcing an order of initialization of global variables in different translation units. However, none are both portable and efficient. In particular, dynamically linked libraries do not coexist happily with global variables that have complicated dependencies.

Often, a function returning a reference is a good alternative to a global variable. For example:

```
int& use_count ()
{
     static  int  uc = 0;
     return  uc;
}
```

A call *use_count* () now acts as a global variable except that it is initialized at its first use (§5.5). For example:

```
void  f()
{
     cout << ++use_count ();     // read and increment
     // ...
}
```

The initialization of nonlocal static variables is controlled by whatever mechanism an implementation uses to start up a C++ program. This mechanism is guaranteed to work properly only if *main* ( ) is executed. Consequently, one should avoid nonlocal variables that require run-time initialization in C++ code intended for execution as a fragment of a non-C++ program.

Note that variables initialized by constant expressions (§C.5) cannot depend on the value of objects from other translation units and do not require run-time initialization. Such variables are therefore safe to use in all cases.

9.4.1.1 Program Termination

A program can terminate in several ways:
-   By returning from *main* ( )
-   By calling *exit* ( )
-   By calling *abort* ( )
-   By throwing an uncaught exception

In addition, there are a variety of ill-behaved and implementation-dependent ways of making a program crash.

If a program is terminated using the standard library function *exit* ( ), the destructors for constructed static objects are called (§10.4.9, §10.2.4). However, if the program is terminated using the standard library function *abort* ( ), they are not. Note that this implies that *exit* ( ) does not terminate a program immediately. Calling *exit* ( ) in a destructor may cause an infinite recursion. The type of *exit* ( ) is

```
void exit (int);
```

Like the return value of *main* ( ) (§3.2), *exit* ( )'s argument is returned to ''the system'' as the value of the program. Zero indicates successful completion.

Calling *exit* ( ) means that the local variables of the calling function and its callers will not have their destructors invoked. Throwing an exception and catching it ensures that local objects are properly destroyed (§14.4.7). Also, a call of *exit* ( ) terminates the program without giving the caller of the function that called *exit* ( ) a chance to deal with the problem. It is therefore often best to leave a context by throwing an exception and letting a handler decide what to do next.

The C (and C++) standard library function *atexit* ( ) offers the possibility to have code executed at program termination. For example:

```
void my_cleanup ( );

void somewhere ( )
{
    if (atexit (&my_cleanup) ==0) {
        // my_cleanup will be called at normal termination
    }
    else {
        // oops: too many atexit functions
    }
}
```

This strongly resembles the automatic invocation of destructors for global variables at program termination (§10.4.9, §10.2.4). Note that an argument to *atexit* ( ) cannot take arguments or return a result. Also, there is an implementation-defined limit to the number of atexit functions; *atexit* ( ) indicates when that limit is reached by returning a nonzero value. These limitations make *atexit* ( ) less useful than it appears at first glance.

The destructor of a constructed statically allocated object (a global, §10.4.9; function *static*, §7.1.2; or a class *static*, §10.2.4) created before a call of *atexit* (*f*) will be invoked after *f* is invoked. The destructor of such an an object created after a call of *atexit* (*f*) will be invoked before *f* is invoked.

The *exit* ( ), *abort* ( ), and *atexit* ( ) functions are declared in *<cstdlib>*.

9.5 Advice

[1] Use header files to represent interfaces and to emphasize logical structure; §9.1, §9.3.2.

[2] *#include* a header in the source file that implements its functions; §9.3.1.

[3] Don't define global entities with the same name and similar-but-different meanings in different translation units; §9.2.

[4] Avoid non-inline function definitions in headers; §9.2.1.

[5] Use #*include* only at global scope and in namespaces; §9.2.1.

[6] *#include* only complete declarations; §9.2.1.

[7] Use include guards; §9.3.3.

[8] *#include* C headers in namespaces to avoid global names; §8.2.9.1, §9.2.2.

[9] Make headers self-contained; §9.2.3.

[10] Distinguish between users' interfaces and implementers' interfaces; §9.3.2.

[11] Distinguish between average users' interfaces and expert users' interfaces; §9.3.2.

[12] Avoid nonlocal objects that require run-time initialization in code intended for use as part of non-C++ programs; §9.4.1.

9.6 Exercises

1. (∗2) Find where the standard library headers are kept on your system. List their names. Are any nonstandard headers kept together with the standard ones? Can any nonstandard headers be #*include*d using the <> notation?

2. (∗2) Where are the headers for nonstandard "foundation" libraries kept?

3. (∗2.5) Write a program that reads a source file and writes out the names of files #*include*d. Indent file names to show files #*include*d by included files. Try this program on some real source files (to get an idea of the amount of information included).

4. (∗3) Modify the program from the previous exercise to print the number of comment lines, the number of non-comment lines, and the number of non-comment, whitespace-separated words for each file #*include*d.

5. (∗2.5) An external include guard is a construct that tests outside the file it is guarding and *include*s only once per compilation. Define such a construct, devise a way of testing it, and discuss its advantages and disadvantages compared to the include guards described in §9.3.3. Is there any significant run-time advantage to external include guards on your system?

6. (*3) How is dynamic linking achieved on your system? What restrictions are placed on dynamically linked code? What requirements are placed on code for it to be dynamically linked?

7. (*3) Open and read 100 files containing 1500 characters each. Open and read one file containing 150,000 characters. Hint: See example in §21.5.1. Is there a performance difference? What is the highest number of files that can be simultaneously open on your system? Consider these questions in relation to the use of #*include* files.

8. (*2) Modify the desk calculator so that it can be invoked from *main* ( ) or from other functions as a simple function call.

9. (*2) Draw the ''module dependency diagrams'' (§9.3.2) for the version of the calculator that used *error* ( ) instead of exceptions (§8.2.2).

Part II

Abstraction Mechanisms

This part describes C++'s facilities for defining and using new types. Techniques commonly called object-oriented programming and generic programming are presented.

Chapters

10 Classes
11 Operator Overloading
12 Derived Classes
13 Templates
14 Exception Handling
15 Class Hierarchies

"... there is nothing more difficult to carry out, nor more doubtful of success, nor more dangerous to handle, than to initiate a new order of things. For the reformer makes enemies of all those who profit by the old order, and only lukewarm defenders in all those who would profit by the new order..."

— Niccolò Machiavelli ("The Prince" §vi)

10

Classes

Those types are not "abstract";
they are as real as int *and* float.
— Doug McIlroy

Concepts and classes — class members — access control — constructors — *static* members — default copy — *const* member functions — *this* — *struct*s — in-class function definition — concrete classes — member functions and helper functions — overloaded operators — use of concrete classes — destructors — default construction — local variables — user-defined copy — *new* and *delete* — member objects — arrays — static storage — temporary variables — unions — advice — exercises.

10.1 Introduction

The aim of the C++ class concept is to provide the programmer with a tool for creating new types that can be used as conveniently as the built-in types. In addition, derived classes (Chapter 12) and templates (Chapter 13) provide ways of organizing related classes that allow the programmer to take advantage of their relationships.

A type is a concrete representation of a concept. For example, the C++ built-in type *float* with its operations +, −, *, etc., provides a concrete approximation of the mathematical concept of a real number. A class is a user-defined type. We design a new type to provide a definition of a concept that has no direct counterpart among the built-in types. For example, we might provide a type *Trunk_line* in a program dealing with telephony, a type *Explosion* for a videogame, or a type *list<Paragraph>* for a text-processing program. A program that provides types that closely match the concepts of the application tends to be easier to understand and easier to modify than a program that does not. A well-chosen set of user-defined types makes a program more concise. In addition, it makes many sorts of code analysis feasible. In particular, it enables the compiler to detect illegal uses of objects that would otherwise remain undetected until the program is thoroughly tested.

The fundamental idea in defining a new type is to separate the incidental details of the implementation (e.g., the layout of the data used to store an object of the type) from the properties essential to the correct use of it (e.g., the complete list of functions that can access the data). Such a separation is best expressed by channeling all uses of the data structure and internal housekeeping routines through a specific interface.

This chapter focuses on relatively simple ''concrete'' user-defined types that logically don't differ much from built-in types. Ideally, such types should not differ from built-in types in the way they are used, only in the way they are created.

10.2   Classes

A *class* is a user-defined type. This section introduces the basic facilities for defining a class, creating objects of a class, and manipulating such objects.

10.2.1 Member Functions

Consider implementing the concept of a date using a *struct* to define the representation of a *Date* and a set of functions for manipulating variables of this type:

```
struct Date {          // representation
    int d, m, y;
};

void init_date(Date& d, int, int, int);    // initialize d
void add_year(Date& d, int n);             // add n years to d
void add_month(Date& d, int n);            // add n months to d
void add_day(Date& d, int n);              // add n days to d
```

There is no explicit connection between the data type and these functions. Such a connection can be established by declaring the functions as members:

```
struct Date {
    int d, m, y;

    void init(int dd, int mm, int yy);     // initialize
    void add_year(int n);                  // add n years
    void add_month(int n);                 // add n months
    void add_day(int n);                   // add n days
};
```

Functions declared within a class definition (a *struct* is a kind of class; §10.2.8) are called member functions and can be invoked only for a specific variable of the appropriate type using the standard syntax for structure member access. For example:

```
Date my_birthday;

void f()
{
    Date today;
```

```
        today.init(16,10,1996);
        my_birthday.init(30,12,1950);

        Date tomorrow = today;
        tomorrow.add_day(1);
        // ...
    }
```

Because different structures can have member functions with the same name, we must specify the structure name when defining a member function:

```
    void Date::init(int dd, int mm, int yy)
    {
        d = dd;
        m = mm;
        y = yy;
    }
```

In a member function, member names can be used without explicit reference to an object. In that case, the name refers to that member of the object for which the function was invoked. For example, when *Date::init()* is invoked for *today*, *m=mm* assigns to *today.m*. On the other hand, when *Date::init()* is invoked for *my_birthday*, *m=mm* assigns to *my_birthday.m*. A class member function always ''knows'' for which object it was invoked.

The construct

```
    class X { ... };
```

is called a *class definition* because it defines a new type. For historical reasons, a class definition is often referred to as a *class declaration*. Also, like declarations that are not definitions, a class definition can be replicated in different source files using #*include* without violating the one-definition rule (§9.2.3).

10.2.2 Access Control

The declaration of *Date* in the previous subsection provides a set of functions for manipulating a *Date*. However, it does not specify that those functions should be the only ones to depend directly on *Date*'s representation and the only ones to directly access objects of class *Date*. This restriction can be expressed by using a *class* instead of a *struct*:

```
    class Date {
        int d, m, y;
    public:
        void init(int dd, int mm, int yy);    // initialize

        void add_year(int n);                 // add n years
        void add_month(int n);                // add n months
        void add_day(int n);                  // add n days
    };
```

The *public* label separates the class body into two parts. The names in the first, *private*, part can be used only by member functions. The second, *public*, part constitutes the public interface to objects of the class. A *struct* is simply a *class* whose members are public by default (§10.2.8); member functions can be defined and used exactly as before. For example:

```
inline  void  Date::add_year(int  n)
{
    y += n;
}
```

However, nonmember functions are barred from using private members. For example:

```
void  timewarp(Date& d)
{
    d.y -= 200;      // error: Date::y is private
}
```

There are several benefits to be obtained from restricting access to a data structure to an explicitly declared list of functions. For example, any error causing a *Date* to take on an illegal value (for example, December 36, 1985) must be caused by code in a member function. This implies that the first stage of debugging – localization – is completed before the program is even run. This is a special case of the general observation that any change to the behavior of the type *Date* can and must be effected by changes to its members. In particular, if we change the representation of a class, we need only change the member functions to take advantage of the new representation. User code directly depends only on the public interface and need not be rewritten (although it may need to be recompiled). Another advantage is that a potential user need examine only the definition of the member functions in order to learn to use a class.

The protection of private data relies on restriction of the use of the class member names. It can therefore be circumvented by address manipulation and explicit type conversion. But this, of course, is cheating. C++ protects against accident rather than deliberate circumvention (fraud). Only hardware can protect against malicious use of a general-purpose language, and even that is hard to do in realistic systems.

The *init*() function was added partially because it is generally useful to have a function that sets the value of an object and partly because making the data private forces us to provide it.

10.2.3 Constructors

The use of functions such as *init*() to provide initialization for class objects is inelegant and error-prone. Because it is nowhere stated that an object must be initialized, a programmer can forget to do so – or do so twice (often with equally disastrous results). A better approach is to allow the programmer to declare a function with the explicit purpose of initializing objects. Because such a function constructs values of a given type, it is called a *constructor*. A constructor is recognized by having the same name as the class itself. For example:

```
class  Date {
    // ...
    Date(int, int, int);        // constructor
};
```

When a class has a constructor, all objects of that class will be initialized by a constructor call (§10.4.3). If the constructor requires arguments, these arguments must be supplied:

```
Date  today = Date (23,6,1983);
Date  xmas (25,12,1990);        // abbreviated form
Date  my_birthday;              // error: initializer missing
Date  release1_0(10,12);        // error: 3rd argument missing
```

It is often nice to provide several ways of initializing a class object. This can be done by providing several constructors. For example:

```
class  Date {
       int  d, m, y;
public:
       // ...
       Date (int, int, int);     // day, month, year
       Date (int, int);          // day, month, today's year
       Date (int);               // day, today's month and year
       Date ();                  // default Date: today
       Date (const char*);       // date in string representation
};
```

Constructors obey the same overloading rules as do other functions (§7.4). As long as the constructors differ sufficiently in their argument types, the compiler can select the correct one for each use:

```
Date  today (4);
Date  july4 ("July 4, 1983");
Date  guy ("5 Nov");
Date  now;                       // default initialized as today
```

The proliferation of constructors in the *Date* example is typical. When designing a class, a programmer is always tempted to add features just because somebody might want them. It takes more thought to carefully decide what features are really needed and to include only those. However, that extra thought typically leads to smaller and more comprehensible programs. One way of reducing the number of related functions is to use default arguments (§7.5). In the *Date*, each argument can be given a default value interpreted as "pick the default: *today*."

```
class  Date {
       int  d, m, y;
public:
       Date (int dd =0, int mm =0, int yy =0);
       // ...
};

Date :: Date (int dd, int mm, int yy)
{
       d = dd ? dd : today.d;
       m = mm ? mm : today.m;
       y = yy ? yy : today.y;

       // check that the Date is valid
}
```

When an argument value is used to indicate "pick the default," the value chosen must be outside the set of possible values for the argument. For *day* and *month*, this is clearly so, but for *year*, zero may not be an obvious choice. Fortunately, there is no year zero on the European calendar; 1AD (*year==1*) comes immediately after 1BC (*year==-1*).

10.2.4 Static Members

The convenience of a default value for *Date*s was bought at the cost of a significant hidden problem. Our *Date* class became dependent on the global variable *today*. This *Date* class can be used only in a context in which *today* is defined and correctly used by every piece of code. This is the kind of constraint that causes a class to be useless outside the context in which it was first written. Users get too many unpleasant surprises trying to use such context-dependent classes, and maintenance becomes messy. Maybe ''just one little global variable'' isn't too unmanageable, but that style leads to code that is useless except to its original programmer. It should be avoided.

Fortunately, we can get the convenience without the encumbrance of a publicly accessible global variable. A variable that is part of a class, yet is not part of an object of that class, is called a *static* member. There is exactly one copy of a *static* member instead of one copy per object, as for ordinary non-*static* members (§C.9). Similarly, a function that needs access to members of a class, yet doesn't need to be invoked for a particular object, is called a *static* member function.

Here is a redesign that preserves the semantics of default constructor values for *Date* without the problems stemming from reliance on a global:

```
class Date {
    int d, m, y;
    static Date default_date;
public:
    Date(int dd =0, int mm =0, int yy =0);
    // ...
    static void set_default(int dd, int mm, int yy);        // set default_date to Date(dd,mm,yy)
};
```

We can now define the *Date* constructor to use *default_date* like this:

```
Date::Date(int dd, int mm, int yy)
{
    d = dd ? dd : default_date.d;
    m = mm ? mm : default_date.m;
    y = yy ? yy : default_date.y;

    // check that the Date is valid
}
```

Using *set_default*(), we can change the default date when appropriate. A static member can be referred to like any other member. In addition, a static member can be referred to without mentioning an object. Instead, its name is qualified by the name of its class. For example:

```
void f()
{
    Date::set_default(4,5,1945);   // call Date's static member set_default()
}
```

Static members – both function and data members – must be defined somewhere. The keyword *static* is not be repeated in the definition of a *static* member. For example:

```
Date  Date::default_date(16,12,1770);        // definition of Date::default_date
void  Date::set_default(int d, int m, int y)   // definition of Date::set_default
{
    default_date = Date(d,m,y);    // assign new value to default_date
}
```

Now the default value is Beethoven's birth date – until someone decides otherwise.

Note that *Date*() serves as a notation for the value of *Date::default_date*. For example:

```
Date  copy_of_default_date = Date();
```

Consequently, we don't need a separate function for reading the default date.

10.2.5 Copying Class Objects

By default, objects can be copied. In particular, a class object can be initialized with a copy of an object of its class. This can be done even where constructors have been declared. For example:

```
Date  d = today;        // initialization by copy
```

By default, the copy of a class object is a copy of each member. If that default is not the behavior wanted for a class *X*, a more appropriate behavior can be provided by defining a copy constructor, *X::X(const X&)*. This is discussed further in §10.4.4.1.

Similarly, class objects can by default be copied by assignment. For example:

```
void  f(Date& d)
{
    d = today;
}
```

Again, the default semantics is memberwise copy. If that is not the right choice for a class *X*, the user can define an appropriate assignment operator (§10.4.4.1).

10.2.6 Constant Member Functions

The *Date* defined so far provides member functions for giving a *Date* a value and changing it. Unfortunately, we didn't provide a way of examining the value of a *Date*. This problem can easily be remedied by adding functions for reading the day, month, and year:

```
class  Date {
    int  d, m, y;
public:
    int  day() const { return d; }
    int  month() const { return m; }
    int  year() const;
    // ...
};
```

Note the *const* after the (empty) argument list in the function declarations. It indicates that these functions do not modify the state of a *Date*.

Naturally, the compiler will catch accidental attempts to violate this promise. For example:

```
inline int Date::year() const
{
    return y++;      // error: attempt to change member value in const function
}
```

When a *const* member function is defined outside its class, the *const* suffix is required:

```
inline int Date::year() const          // correct
{
    return y;
}

inline int Date::year()     // error: const missing in member function type
{
    return y;
}
```

In other words, the *const* is part of the type of *Date*::*day*() and *Date*::*year*().

A *const* member function can be invoked for both *const* and non-*const* objects, whereas a non-*const* member function can be invoked only for non-*const* objects. For example:

```
void f(Date& d, const Date& cd)
{
    int i = d.year();      // ok
    d.add_year(1);         // ok

    int j = cd.year();     // ok
    cd.add_year(1);        // error: cannot change value of const cd
}
```

10.2.7 Self-Reference

The state update functions *add_year*(), *add_month*(), and *add_day*() were defined not to return values. For such a set of related update functions, it is often useful to return a reference to the updated object so that the operations can be chained. For example, we would like to write

```
void f(Date& d)
{
    // ...
    d.add_day(1).add_month(1).add_year(1);
    // ...
}
```

to add a day, a month, and a year to *d*. To do this, each function must be declared to return a reference to a *Date*:

```
class Date {
    // ...
```

```
Date& add_year(int n);     // add n years
Date& add_month(int n);    // add n months
Date& add_day(int n);      // add n days
};
```

Each (nonstatic) member function knows what object it was invoked for and can explictly refer to it. For example:

```
Date& Date::add_year(int n)
{
    if (d==29 && m==2 && !leapyear(y+n)) {  // beware of February 29
        d = 1;
        m = 3;
    }
    y += n;
    return *this;
}
```

The expression *this refers to the object for which a member function is invoked. It is equivalent to Simula's *THIS* and Smalltalk's *self*.

In a nonstatic member function, the keyword *this* is a pointer to the object for which the function was invoked. In a non-*const* member function of class *X*, the type of *this* is *X**. However, *this* is not an ordinary variable; it is not possible to take the address of *this* or to assign to *this*. In a *const* member function of class *X*, the type of *this* is *const X** to prevent modification of the object itself (see also §5.4.1).

Most uses of *this* are implicit. In particular, every reference to a nonstatic member from within a class relies on an implicit use of *this* to get the member of the appropriate object. For example, the *add_year* function could equivalently, but tediously, have been defined like this:

```
Date& Date::add_year(int n)
{
    if (this->d==29 && this->m==2 && !leapyear(this->y+n)) {
        this->d = 1;
        this->m = 3;
    }
    this->y += n;
    return *this;
}
```

One common explicit use of *this* is in linked-list manipulation (e.g., §24.3.7.4).

10.2.7.1 Physical and Logical Constness

Occasionally, a member function is logically *const*, but it still needs to change the value of a member. To a user, the function appears not to change the state of its object. However, some detail that the user cannot directly observe is updated. This is often called *logical constness*. For example, the *Date* class might have a function returning a string representation that a user could use for output. Constructing this representation could be a relatively expensive operation. Therefore, it would make sense to keep a copy so that repeated requests would simply return the copy, unless the

Date's value had been changed. Caching values like that is more common for more complicated data structures, but let's see how it can be achieved for a *Date*:

```
class  Date {
      bool  cache_valid;
      string  cache;
      void  compute_cache_value();    // fill cache
      // ...
public:
      // ...
      string  string_rep() const;        // string representation
};
```

From a user's point of view, *string_rep* doesn't change the state of its *Date*, so it clearly should be a *const* member function. On the other hand, the cache needs to be filled before it can be used. This can be achieved through brute force:

```
string  Date::string_rep() const
{
      if (cache_valid == false) {
            Date* th = const_cast<Date*>(this);  // cast away const
            th->compute_cache_value();
            th->cache_valid = true;
      }
      return  cache;
}
```

That is, the *const_cast* operator (§15.4.2.1) is used to obtain a pointer of type *Date** to *this*. This is hardly elegant, and it is not guaranteed to work when applied to an object that was originally declared as a *const*. For example:

```
Date  d1;
const  Date  d2;
string  s1 = d1.string_rep();
string  s2 = d2.string_rep();      // undefined behavior
```

In the case of *d1*, *string_rep()* simply casts back to *d1*'s original type so that the call will work. However, *d2* was defined as a *const* and the implementation could have applied some form of memory protection to ensure that its value wasn't corrupted. Consequently, *d2.string_rep()* is not guaranteed to give a single predictable result on all implementations.

10.2.7.2 Mutable

The explicit type conversion "casting away *const*" and its consequent implementation-dependent behavior can be avoided by declaring the data involved in the cache management to be *mutable*:

```
class Date {
    mutable bool cache_valid;
    mutable string cache;
    void compute_cache_value() const;      // fill (mutable) cache
    // ...
public:
    // ...
    string string_rep() const;             // string representation
};
```

The storage specifier *mutable* specifies that a member should be stored in a way that allows updating – even when it is a member of a *const* object. In other words, *mutable* means "can never be *const*." This can be used to simplify the definition of *string_rep*():

```
string Date::string_rep() const
{
    if (!cache_valid) {
        compute_cache_value();
        cache_valid = true;
    }
    return cache;
}
```

and makes reasonable uses of *string_rep*() valid. For example:

```
Date d3;
const Date d4;
string s3 = d3.string_rep();
string s4 = d4.string_rep();      // ok!
```

Declaring members *mutable* is most appropriate when (only) part of a representation is allowed to change. If most of an object changes while the object remains logically *const*, it is often better to place the changing data in a separate object and access it indirectly. If that technique is used, the string-with-cache example becomes:

```
struct cache {
    bool valid;
    string rep;
};

class Date {
    cache* c;                              // initialize in constructor (§10.4.6)
    void compute_cache_value() const;      // fill what cache refers to
    // ...
public:
    // ...
    string string_rep() const;             // string representation
};
```

```
string Date::string_rep() const
{
    if (!c->valid) {
        compute_cache_value();
        c->valid = true;
    }
    return c->rep;
}
```

The programming techniques that support a cache generalize to various forms of lazy evaluation.

10.2.8 Structures and Classes

By definition, a *struct* is a class in which members are by default public; that is,

```
struct s { ...
```

is simply shorthand for

```
class s { public: ...
```

The access specifier *private*: can be used to say that the members following are private, just as *public*: says that the members following are public. Except for the different names, the following declarations are equivalent:

```
class Date1 {
    int d, m, y;
public:
    Date1(int dd, int mm, int yy);

    void add_year(int n);      // add n years
};
struct Date2 {
private:
    int d, m, y;
public:
    Date2(int dd, int mm, int yy);

    void add_year(int n);      // add n years
};
```

Which style you use depends on circumstances and taste. I usually prefer to use *struct* for classes that have all data public. I think of such classes as "not quite proper types, just data structures." Constructors and access functions can be quite useful even for such structures, but as a shorthand rather than guarantors of properties of the type (invariants, see §24.3.7.1).

It is not a requirement to declare data first in a class. In fact, it often makes sense to place data members last to emphasize the functions providing the public user interface. For example:

```
class Date3 {
public:
    Date3(int dd, int mm, int yy);
```

```
        void add_year(int n);      // add n years
private:
        int d, m, y;
};
```

In real code, where both the public interface and the implementation details typically are more extensive than in tutorial examples, I usually prefer the style used for *Date3*.

Access specifiers can be used many times in a single class declaration. For example:

```
class Date4 {
public:
        Date4(int dd, int mm, int yy);
private:
        int d, m, y;
public:
        void add_year(int n);      // add n years
};
```

Having more than one public section, as in *Date4*, tends to be messy. So does having more than one private section. However, allowing many access specifiers in a class is useful for machine-generated code.

10.2.9 In-Class Function Definitions

A member function defined within the class definition − rather than simply declared there − is taken to be an inline member function. That is, in-class definition of member functions is for small, frequently-used functions. Like the class definition it is part of, a member function defined in-class can be replicated in several translation units using #*include*. Like the class itself, its meaning must be the same wherever it is used (§9.2.3).

The style of placing the definition of data members last in a class can lead to a minor problem with public inline functions that refer to the representation. Consider:

```
class Date {     // potentially confusing
public:
        int day() const { return d; }    // return Date::d
        // ...
private:
        int d, m, y;
};
```

This is perfectly good C++ code because a member function declared within a class can refer to every member of the class as if the class were completely defined before the member function bodies were considered. However, this can confuse human readers.

Consequently, I usually either place the data first or define the inline member functions after the class itself. For example:

```
class Date {
public:
    int day() const;
    // ...
private:
    int d, m, y;
};

inline int Date::day() const { return d; }
```

10.3 Efficient User-Defined Types

The previous section discussed bits and pieces of the design of a *Date* class in the context of introducing the basic language features for defining classes. Here, I reverse the emphasis and discuss the design of a simple and efficient *Date* class and show how the language features support this design.

Small, heavily-used abstractions are common in many applications. Examples are Latin characters, Chinese characters, integers, floating-point numbers, complex numbers, points, pointers, coordinates, transforms, (*pointer,offset*) pairs, dates, times, ranges, links, associations, nodes, (*value,unit*) pairs, disk locations, source code locations, *BCD* characters, currencies, lines, rectangles, scaled fixed-point numbers, numbers with fractions, character strings, vectors, and arrays. Every application uses several of these. Often, a few of these simple concrete types are used heavily. A typical application uses a few directly and many more indirectly from libraries.

C++ and other programming languages directly support a few of these abstractions. However, most are not, and cannot be, supported directly because there are too many of them. Furthermore, the designer of a general-purpose programming language cannot foresee the detailed needs of every application. Consequently, mechanisms must be provided for the user to define small concrete types. Such types are called concrete types or concrete classes to distinguish them from abstract classes (§12.3) and classes in class hierarchies (§12.2.4, §12.4).

It was an explicit aim of C++ to support the definition and efficient use of such user-defined data types very well. They are a foundation of elegant programming. As usual, the simple and mundane is statistically far more significant than the complicated and sophisticated.

In this light, let us build a better date class:

```
class Date {
public:              // public interface:
    enum Month { jan=1, feb, mar, apr, may, jun, jul, aug, sep, oct, nov, dec };

    class Bad_date { };  // exception class

    Date(int dd =0, Month mm =Month(0), int yy =0);  // 0 means "pick a default"

// functions for examining the Date:
    int day() const;
    Month month() const;
    int year() const;
```

```
    string string_rep() const;          // string representation
    void char_rep(char s[]) const;       // C-style string representation

    static void set_default(int, Month, int);

// functions for changing the Date:
    Date& add_year(int n);               // add n years
    Date& add_month(int n);              // add n months
    Date& add_day(int n);                // add n days
private:
    int d, m, y;                         // representation
    static Date default_date;
};
```

This set of operations is fairly typical for a user-defined type:

    [1] A constructor specifying how objects/variables of the type are to be initialized.

    [2] A set of functions allowing a user to examine a *Date*. These functions are marked *const* to indicate that they don't modify the state of the object/variable for which they are called.

    [3] A set of functions allowing the user to manipulate *Date*s without actually having to know the details of the representation or fiddle with the intricacies of the semantics.

    [4] A set of implicitly defined operations to allow *Date*s to be freely copied.

    [5] A class, *Bad_date*, to be used for reporting errors as exceptions.

I defined a *Month* type to cope with the problem of remembering, for example, whether the 7th of June is written *Date(6,7)* (American style) or *Date(7,6)* (European style). I also added a mechanism for dealing with default arguments.

    I considered introducing separate types *Day* and *Year* to cope with possible confusion of *Date(1995,jul,27)* and *Date(27,jul,1995)*. However, these types would not be as useful as the *Month* type. Almost all such errors are caught at run-time anyway − the 26th of July year 27 is not a common date in my work. How to deal with historical dates before year 1800 or so is a tricky issue best left to expert historians. Furthermore, the day of the month can't be properly checked in isolation from its month and year. See §11.7.1 for a way of defining a convenient *Year* type.

    The default date must be defined as a valid *Date* somewhere. For example:

```
    Date Date::default_date(22,jan,1901);
```

I omitted the cache technique from §10.2.7.1 as unnecessary for a type this simple. If needed, it can be added as an implementation detail without affecting the user interface.

    Here is a small − and contrived − example of how *Date*s can be used:

```
    void f(Date& d)
    {
        Date lvb_day = Date(16,Date::dec,d.year());

        if (d.day()==29 && d.month()==Date::feb) {
            // ...
        }

        if (midnight()) d.add_day(1);

        cout << "day after:" << d+1 << '\n';
    }
```

This assumes that the output operator << and the addition operator + have been declared for *Date*s. I do that in §10.3.3.

Note the *Date*::*feb* notation. The function *f*( ) is not a member of *Date*, so it must specify that it is referring to *Date*'s *feb* and not to some other entity.

Why is it worthwhile to define a specific type for something as simple as a date? After all, we could define a structure:

```
struct Date {
    int day, month, year;
};
```

and let programmers decide what to do with it. If we did that, though, every user would either have to manipulate the components of *Date*s directly or provide separate functions for doing so. In effect, the notion of a date would be scattered throughout the system, which would make it hard to understand, document, or change. Inevitably, providing a concept as only a simple structure causes extra work for every user of the structure.

Also, even though the *Date* type seems simple, it takes some thought to get right. For example, incrementing a *Date* must deal with leap years, with the fact that months are of different lengths, and so on (note: §10.6[1]). Also, the day-month-and-year representation is rather poor for many applications. If we decided to change it, we would need to modify only a designated set of functions. For example, to represent a *Date* as the number of days before or after January 1, 1970, we would need to change only *Date*'s member functions (§10.6[2]).

10.3.1 Member Functions

Naturally, an implementation for each member function must be provided somewhere. For example, here is the definition of *Date*'s constructor:

```
Date::Date(int dd, Month mm, int yy)
{
    if (yy == 0) yy = default_date.year();
    if (mm == 0) mm = default_date.month();
    if (dd == 0) dd = default_date.day();

    int max;

    switch (mm) {
    case feb:
        max = 28+leapyear(yy);
        break;
    case apr: case jun: case sep: case nov:
        max = 30;
        break;
    case jan: case mar: case may: case jul: case aug: case oct: case dec:
        max = 31;
        break;
    default:
        throw Bad_date();    // someone cheated
    }
```

```
        if (dd<1 || max<dd) throw Bad_date();

        y = yy;
        m = mm;
        d = dd;
    }
```

The constructor checks that the data supplied denotes a valid *Date*. If not, say for *Date* (*30*, *Date* : : *feb*, *1994*), it throws an exception (§8.3, Chapter 14), which indicates that something went wrong in a way that cannot be ignored. If the data supplied is acceptable, the obvious initialization is done. Initialization is a relatively complicated operation because it involves data validation. This is fairly typical. On the other hand, once a *Date* has been created, it can be used and copied without further checking. In other words, the constructor establishes the invariant for the class (in this case, that it denotes a valid date). Other member functions can rely on that invariant and must maintain it. This design technique can simplify code immensely (see §24.3.7.1).

I'm using the value *Month* (*0*) − which doesn't represent a month − to represent "pick the default month." I could have defined an enumerator in *Month* specifically to represent that. But I decided that it was better to use an obviously anomalous value to represent "pick the default month" rather than give the appearance that there were 13 months in a year. Note that *0* can be used because it is within the range guaranteed for the enumeration *Month* (§4.8).

I considered factoring out the data validation in a separate function *is_date* (). However, I found the resulting user code more complicated and less robust than code relying on catching the exception. For example, assuming that >> is defined for *Date*:

```
    void fill (vector<Date>& aa)
    {
        while (cin) {
            Date d;
            try {
                cin >> d;
            }

            catch (Date::Bad_date) {
                // my error handling
                continue;
            }
            aa.push_back(d);    // see §3.7.3
        }
    }
```

As is common for such simple concrete types, the definitions of member functions vary between the trivial and the not-too-complicated. For example:

```
    inline int Date::day() const
    {
        return d;
    }
```

```
Date& Date::add_month(int n)
{
    if (n==0) return *this;

    if (n>0) {
        int delta_y = n/12;
        int mm = m+n%12;
        if (12 < mm) {  // note: int(dec)==12
            delta_y++;
            mm -= 12;
        }

        // handle the cases where Month(mm) doesn't have day d

        y += delta_y;
        m = Month(mm);
        return *this;
    }

    // handle negative n

    return *this;
}
```

10.3.2 Helper Functions

Typically, a class has a number of functions associated with it that need not be defined in the class itself because they don't need direct access to the representation. For example:

```
int diff(Date a, Date b);  // number of days in the range [a,b) or [b,a)
bool leapyear(int y);
Date next_weekday(Date d);
Date next_saturday(Date d);
```

Defining such functions in the class itself would complicate the class interface and increase the number of functions that would potentially need to be examined when a change to the representation was considered.

How are such functions "associated" with class *Date*? Traditionally, their declarations were simply placed in the same file as the declaration of class *Date*, and users who needed *Date*s would make them all available by including the file that defined the interface (§9.2.1). For example:

```
#include "Date.h"
```

In addition to using a specific *Date.h* header, or as an alternative, we can make the association explicit by enclosing the class and its helper functions in a namespace (§8.2):

```
namespace Chrono {       // facilities for dealing with time

    class Date { /* ... */ };
```

```
int diff(Date a, Date b);
bool leapyear(int y);
Date next_weekday(Date d);
Date next_saturday(Date d);
// ...
}
```

The *Chrono* namespace would naturally also contain related classes, such as *Time* and *Stopwatch*, and their helper functions. Using a namespace to hold a single class is usually an over-elaboration that leads to inconvenience.

10.3.3 Overloaded Operators

It is often useful to add functions to enable conventional notation. For example, the *operator==* function defines the equality operator == to work for *Date*s:

```
inline bool operator==(Date a, Date b)   // equality
{
    return a.day()==b.day() && a.month()==b.month() && a.year()==b.year();
}
```

Other obvious candidates are:

```
bool operator!=(Date, Date);             // inequality
bool operator<(Date, Date);              // less than
bool operator>(Date, Date);              // greater than
// ...

Date& operator++(Date& d);               // increase Date by one day
Date& operator--(Date& d);               // decrease Date by one day

Date& operator+=(Date& d, int n);        // add n days
Date& operator-=(Date& d, int n);        // subtract n days

Date operator+(Date d, int n);           // add n days
Date operator-(Date d, int n);           // subtract n days

ostream& operator<<(ostream&, Date d);   // output d
istream& operator>>(istream&, Date& d);  // read into d
```

For *Date*, these operators can be seen as mere conveniences. However, for many types – such as complex numbers (§11.3), vectors (§3.7.1), and function-like objects (§18.4) – the use of conventional operators is so firmly entrenched in people's minds that their definition is almost mandatory. Operator overloading is discussed in Chapter 11.

10.3.4 The Significance of Concrete Classes

I call simple user-defined types, such as *Date*, *concrete types* to distinguish them from abstract classes (§2.5.4) and class hierarchies (§12.3) and also to emphasize their similarity to built-in types such as *int* and *char*. They have also been called *value types*, and their use *value-oriented programming*. Their model of use and the "philosophy" behind their design are quite different from what is often advertised as object-oriented programming (§2.6.2).

The intent of a concrete type is to do a single, relatively small thing well and efficiently. It is not usually the aim to provide the user with facilities to modify the behavior of a concrete type. In particular, concrete types are not intended to display polymorphic behavior (see §2.5.5, §12.2.6).

If you don't like some detail of a concrete type, you build a new one with the desired behavior. If you want to ''reuse'' a concrete type, you use it in the implementation of your new type exactly as you would have used an *int*. For example:

```
class Date_and_time {
private :
        Date d;
        Time t;
public :
        Date_and_time (Date d, Time t);
        Date_and_time (int d, Date::Month m, int y, Time t);
        // ...
} ;
```

The derived class mechanism discussed in Chapter 12 can be used to define new types from a concrete class by describing the desired differences. The definition of *Vec* from *vector* (§3.7.2) is an example of this.

With a reasonably good compiler, a concrete class such as *Date* incurs no hidden overhead in time or space. The size of a concrete type is known at compile time so that objects can be allocated on the run-time stack (that is, without free-store operations). The layout of each object is known at compile time so that inlining of operations is trivially achieved. Similarly, layout compatibility with other languages, such as C and Fortran, comes without special effort.

A good set of such types can provide a foundation for applications. Lack of suitable ''small efficient types'' in an application can lead to gross run-time and space inefficiencies when overly general and expensive classes are used. Alternatively, lack of concrete types can lead to obscure programs and time wasted when each programmer writes code to directly manipulate ''simple and frequently used'' data structures.

10.4 Objects

Objects can be created in several ways. Some are local variables, some are global variables, some are members of classes, etc. This section discusses these alternatives, the rules that govern them, the constructors used to initialize objects, and the destructors used to clean up objects before they become unusable.

10.4.1 Destructors

A constructor initializes an object. In other words, it creates the environment in which the member functions operate. Sometimes, creating that environment involves acquiring a resource − such as a file, a lock, or some memory − that must be released after use (§14.4.7). Thus, some classes need a function that is guaranteed to be invoked when an object is destroyed in a manner similar to the way a constructor is guaranteed to be invoked when an object is created. Inevitably, such functions are called *destructors*. They typically clean up and release resources. Destructors are called implicitly when an automatic variable goes out of scope, an object on the free store is deleted, etc. Only in very unusual circumstances does the user need to call a destructor explicitly (§10.4.11).

The most common use of a destructor is to release memory acquired in a constructor. Consider a simple table of elements of some type *Name*. The constructor for *Table* must allocate memory to hold the elements. When the table is somehow deleted, we must ensure that this memory is reclaimed for further use elsewhere. We do this by providing a special function to complement the constructor:

```
class Name {
    const char* s;
    // ...
};

class Table {
    Name* p;
    size_t sz;
public:
    Table(size_t s = 15) { p = new Name[sz = s]; } // constructor

    ~Table() { delete[] p; }                        // destructor

    Name* lookup(const char *);
    bool insert(Name*);
};
```

The destructor notation *~Table*() uses the complement symbol ~ to hint at the destructor's relation to the *Table*() constructor.

A matching constructor/destructor pair is the usual mechanism for implementing the notion of a variably-sized object in C++. Standard library containers, such as *map*, use a variant of this technique for providing storage for their elements, so the following discussion illustrates techniques you rely on every time you use a standard container (including a standard *string*). The discussion applies to types without a destructor, also. Such types are seen simply as having a destructor that does nothing.

10.4.2 Default Constructors

Similarly, most types can be considered to have a default constructor. A default constructor is a constructor that can be called without supplying an argument. Because of the default argument *15*, *Table*::*Table*(*size_t*) is a default constructor. If a user has declared a default constructor, that one will be used; otherwise, the compiler will try to generate one if needed and if the user hasn't declared other constructors. A compiler-generated default constructor implicitly calls the default constructors for a class' members of class type and bases (§12.2.2). For example:

```
struct Tables {
    int i;
    int vi[10];
    Table t1;
    Table vt[10];
};
```

Tables tt;

Here, *tt* will be initialized using a generated default constructor that calls *Table* (*15*) for *tt . t1* and each element of *tt . vt*. On the other hand, *tt . i* and the elements of *tt . vi* are not initialized because those objects are not of a class type. The reasons for the dissimilar treatment of classes and built-in types are C compatibility and fear of run-time overhead.

   Because *const*s and references must be initialized (§5.5, §5.4), a class containing *const* or reference members cannot be default-constructed unless the programmer explicitly supplies a constructor (§10.4.6.1). For example:

```
struct  X {
      const  int  a;
      const  int& r;
};

X  x; // error: no default constructor for X
```

Default constructors can be invoked explicitly (§10.4.10). Built-in types also have default constructors (§6.2.8).

10.4.3 Construction and Destruction

Consider the different ways an object can be created and how it gets destroyed afterwards. An object can be created as:
   §10.4.4   A named automatic object, which is created each time its declaration is encountered in the execution of the program and destroyed each time the program exits the block in which it occurs
   §10.4.5   A free-store object, which is created using the *new* operator and destroyed using the *delete* operator
   §10.4.6   A nonstatic member object, which is created as a member of another class object and created and destroyed when the object of which it is a member is created and destroyed
   §10.4.7   An array element, which is created and destroyed when the array of which it is an element is created and destroyed
   §10.4.8   A local static object, which is created the first time its declaration is encountered in the execution of the program and destroyed once at the termination of the program
   §10.4.9   A global, namespace, or class static object, which is created once "at the start of the program" and destroyed once at the termination of the program
   §10.4.10 A temporary object, which is created as part of the evaluation of an expression and destroyed at the end of the full expression in which it occurs
   §10.4.11 An object placed in memory obtained from a user-supplied function guided by arguments supplied in the allocation operation
   §10.4.12 A *union* member, which may not have a constructor or a destructor
This list is roughly sorted in order of importance. The following subsections explain these various ways of creating objects and their uses.

10.4.4 Local Variables

The constructor for a local variable is executed each time the thread of control passes through the declaration of the local variable. The destructor for a local variable is executed each time the local variable's block is exited. Destructors for local variables are executed in reverse order of their construction. For example:

```
void f(int i)
{
    Table aa;
    Table bb;
    if (i>0) {
        Table cc;
        // ...
    }
    Table dd;
    // ...
}
```

Here, *aa*, *bb*, and *dd* are constructed (in that order) each time *f*( ) is called, and *dd*, *bb*, and *aa* are destroyed (in that order) each time we return from *f*( ). If *i>0* for a call, *cc* will be constructed after *bb* and destroyed before *dd* is constructed.

10.4.4.1 Copying Objects

If *t1* and *t2* are objects of a class *Table*, *t2=t1* by default means a memberwise copy of *t1* into *t2* (§10.2.5). Having assignment interpreted this way can cause a surprising (and usually undesired) effect when used on objects of a class with pointer members. Memberwise copy is usually the wrong semantics for copying objects containing resources managed by a constructor/destructor pair. For example:

```
void h()
{
    Table t1;
    Table t2 = t1;   // copy initialization: trouble
    Table t3;

    t3 = t2;          // copy assignment: trouble
}
```

Here, the *Table* default constructor is called twice: once each for *t1* and *t3*. It is not called for *t2* because that variable was initialized by copying *t1*. However, the *Table* destructor is called three times: once each for *t1*, *t2*, and *t3*! The default interpretation of assignment is memberwise copy, so *t1*, *t2*, and *t3* will, at the end of *h*( ), each contain a pointer to the array of names allocated on the free store when *t1* was created. No pointer to the array of names allocated when *t3* was created remains because it was overwritten by the *t3=t2* assignment. Thus, in the absence of automatic garbage collection (§10.4.5), its storage will be lost to the program forever. On the other hand, the array created for *t1* appears in *t1*, *t2*, and *t3*, so it will be deleted thrice. The result of that is undefined and probably disastrous.

Such anomalies can be avoided by defining what it means to copy a *Table*:

```
class Table {
    // ...
    Table(const Table&);                // copy constructor
    Table& operator=(const Table&);     // copy assignment
};
```

The programmer can define any suitable meaning for these copy operations, but the traditional one for this kind of container is to copy the contained elements (or at least to give the user of the container the appearance that a copy has been done; see §11.12). For example:

```
Table::Table(const Table& t)           // copy constructor
{
    p = new Name[sz=t.sz];
    for (int i = 0; i<sz; i++) p[i] = t.p[i];
}

Table& Table::operator=(const Table& t)        // assignment
{
    if (this != &t) {        // beware of self-assignment: t = t
        delete[] p;
        p = new Name[sz=t.sz];
        for (int i = 0; i<sz; i++) p[i] = t.p[i];
    }
    return *this;
}
```

As is almost always the case, the copy constructor and the copy assignment differ considerably. The fundamental reason is that a copy constructor initializes uninitialized memory, whereas the copy assignment operator must correctly deal with a well-constructed object.

Assignment can be optimized in some cases, but the general strategy for an assignment operator is simple: protect against self-assignment, delete old elements, initialize, and copy in new elements. Usually every nonstatic member must be copied (§10.4.6.3). Exceptions can be used to report failure to copy (Appendix E).

10.4.5 Free Store

An object created on the free store has its constructor invoked by the *new* operator and exists until the *delete* operator is applied to a pointer to it. Consider:

```
int main()
{
    Table* p = new Table;
    Table* q = new Table;

    delete p;
    delete p;   // probably causes run-time error
}
```

The constructor *Table::Table()* is called twice. So is the destructor *Table::~Table()*.

Unfortunately, the *new*s and the *delete*s in this example don't match, so the object pointed to by *p* is deleted twice and the object pointed to by *q* not at all. Not deleting an object is typically not an error as far as the language is concerned; it is only a waste of space. However, in a program that is meant to run for a long time, such a memory leak is a serious and hard-to-find error. There are tools available for detecting such leaks. Deleting *p* twice is a serious error; the behavior is undefined and most likely disastrous.

Some C++ implementations automatically recycle the storage occupied by unreachable objects (garbage collecting implementations), but their behavior is not standardized. Even when a garbage collector is running, *delete* will invoke a destructor if one is defined, so it is still a serious error to delete an object twice. In many cases, that is only a minor inconvenience. In particular, where a garbage collector is known to exist, destructors that do memory management only can be eliminated. This simplification comes at the cost of portability and for some programs, a possible increase in run time and a loss of predictability of run-time behavior (§C.9.1).

After *delete* has been applied to an object, it is an error to access that object in any way. Unfortunately, implementations cannot reliably detect such errors.

The user can specify how *new* does allocation and how *delete* does deallocation (see §6.2.6.2 and §15.6). It is also possible to specify the way an allocation, initialization (construction), and exceptions interact (see §14.4.5 and §19.4.5). Arrays on the free store are discussed in §10.4.7.

10.4.6 Class Objects as Members

Consider a class that might be used to hold information for a small organization:

```
class Club {
    string name;
    Table members;
    Table officers;
    Date founded;
    // ...
    Club(const string& n, Date fd);
};
```

The *Club*'s constructor takes the name of the club and its founding date as arguments. Arguments for a member's constructor are specified in a member initializer list in the definition of the constructor of the containing class. For example:

```
Club::Club(const string& n, Date fd)
    : name(n), members(), officers(), founded(fd)
{
    // ...
}
```

The member initializers are preceded by a colon and separated by commas.

The members' constructors are called before the body of the containing class' own constructor is executed. The constructors are called in the order in which the members are declared in the class rather than the order in which the members appear in the initializer list. To avoid confusion, it is best to specify the initializers in the member declaration order. The member destructors are called in the reverse order of construction after the body of the class' own destructor has been executed.

If a member constructor needs no arguments, the member need not be mentioned in the member initializer list, so

```
Club :: Club (const string& n, Date fd)
    : name (n), founded (fd)
{
    // ...
}
```

is equivalent to the previous version. In each case, *Club* :: *officers* is constructed by *Table* :: *Table* with the default argument *15*.

When a class object containing class objects is destroyed, the body of that object's own destructor (if one is specified) is executed first and then the members' destructors are executed in reverse order of declaration. A constructor assembles the execution environment for the member functions for a class from the bottom up (members first). The destructor disassembles it from the top down (members last).

10.4.6.1 Necessary Member Initialization

Member initializers are essential for types for which initialization differs from assignment – that is, for member objects of classes without default constructors, for *const* members, and for reference members. For example:

```
class X {
    const int i;
    Club c;
    Club& pc;
    // ...
    X (int ii, const string& n, Date d, Club& c) : i (ii), c (n, d), pc (c) { }
};
```

There isn't any other way to initialize such members, and it is an error not to initialize objects of those types. For most types, however, the programmer has a choice between using an initializer and using an assignment. In that case, I usually prefer to use the member initializer syntax, thus making explicit the fact that initialization is being done. Often, there also is an efficiency advantage to using the initializer syntax (compared to using an assignment). For example:

```
class Person {
    string name;
    string address;
    // ...
    Person (const Person&);
    Person (const string& n, const string& a);
};

Person :: Person (const string& n, const string& a)
    : name (n)
{
    address = a;
}
```

Here *name* is initialized with a copy of *n*. On the other hand, *address* is first initialized to the empty string and then a copy of *a* is assigned.

10.4.6.2 Member Constants

It is also possible to initialize a static integral constant member by adding a *constant-expression* initializer to its member declaration. For example:

```
class Curious {
public:
    static const int c1 = 7;        // ok, but remember definition
    static int c2 = 11;             // error: not const
    const int c3 = 13;              // error: not static
    static const int c4 = f(17);    // error: in-class initializer not constant
    static const float c5 = 7.0;    // error: in-class not integral
    // ...
};
```

If (and only if) you use an initialized member in a way that requires it to be stored as an object in memory, the member must be (uniquely) defined somewhere. The initializer may not be repeated:

```
const int Curious::c1;          // necessary, but don't repeat initializer here

const int* p = &Curious::c1;    // ok: Curious::c1 has been defined
```

Alternatively, you can use an enumerator (§4.8, §14.4.6, §15.3) as a symbolic constant within a class declaration. For example:

```
class X {
    enum { c1 = 7, c2 = 11, c3 = 13, c4 = 17 };
    // ...
};
```

In that way, you are not tempted to initialize variables, floating-point numbers, etc. within a class.

10.4.6.3 Copying Members

A default copy constructor or default copy assignment (§10.4.4.1) copies all elements of a class. If this copy cannot be done, it is an error to try to copy an object of such a class. For example:

```
class Unique_handle {
private:          // copy operations are private to prevent copying (§11.2.2)
    Unique_handle(const Unique_handle&);
    Unique_handle& operator=(const Unique_handle&);
public:
    // ...
};

struct Y {
    // ...
    Unique_handle a;     // requires explicit initialization
};
```

```
Y  y1;
Y  y2 = y1;        // error: cannot copy Y::a
```

In addition, a default assignment cannot be generated if a nonstatic member is a reference, a *const*, or a user-defined type without a copy assignment.

Note that the default copy constructor leaves a reference member referring to the same object in both the original and the copied object. This can be a problem if the object referred to is supposed to be deleted.

When writing a copy constructor, we must take care to copy every element that needs to be copied. By default, elements are default-initialized, but that is often not what is desired in a copy constructor. For example:

```
Person::Person(const Person& a) : name(a.name) { }    // beware!
```

Here, I forgot to copy the *address*, so *address* is initialized to the empty string by default. When adding a new member to a class, always check if there are user-defined constructors that need to be updated in order to initialize and copy the new member.

10.4.7 Arrays

If an object of a class can be constructed without supplying an explicit initializer, then arrays of that class can be defined. For example:

```
Table  tbl[10];
```

This will create an array of *10 Table*s and initialize each *Table* by a call of *Table::Table*() with the default argument *15*.

Except by using an initializer list (§5.2.1, §18.6.7), there is no way to specify explicit arguments for a constructor in an array declaration. If you absolutely must initialize members of an array with different values, you can write a default constructor that generates the desired values. For example:

```
class  Ibuffer {
      string  buf;
public:
      Ibuffer() { cin>>buf; }
      // ...
};

void  f()
{
      Ibuffer  words[100]; // each word initialized from cin
      // ...
}
```

It is usually best to avoid such subtleties.

The destructor for each constructed element of an array is invoked when that array is destroyed. This is done implicitly for arrays that are not allocated using *new*. Like C, C++ doesn't distinguish between a pointer to an individual object and a pointer to the initial element of an array (§5.3). Consequently, the programmer must state whether an array or an individual object is being deleted. For example:

```
void f(int sz)
{
    Table* t1 = new Table;
    Table* t2 = new Table[sz];
    Table* t3 = new Table;
    Table* t4 = new Table[sz];

    delete t1;          // right
    delete[] t2;        // right
    delete[] t3;        // wrong: trouble
    delete t4;          // wrong: trouble
}
```

Exactly how arrays and individual objects are allocated is implementation-dependent. Therefore, different implementations will react differently to incorrect uses of the *delete* and *delete*[] operators. In simple and uninteresting cases like the previous one, a compiler can detect the problem, but generally something nasty will happen at run time.

The special destruction operator for arrays, *delete*[], isn't logically necessary. However, suppose the implementation of the free store had been required to hold sufficient information for every object to tell if it was an individual or an array. The user could have been relieved of a burden, but that obligation would have imposed significant time and space overheads on some C++ implementations.

As always, if you find C-style arrays too cumbersome, use a class such as *vector* (§3.7.1, §16.3) instead. For example:

```
void g()
{
    vector<Table>* p1 = new vector<Table>(10);
    Table* p2 = new Table;

    delete p1;
    delete p2;
}
```

10.4.8 Local Static Store

The constructor for a local static object (§7.1.2) is called the first time the thread of control passes through the object's definition. Consider this:

```
void f(int i)
{
    static Table tbl;
    // ...
    if (i) {
        static Table tbl2;
        // ...
    }
}
```

```
int main()
{
    f(0);
    f(1);
    f(2);
    // ...
}
```

Here, the constructor is called for *tbl* once the first time *f*() is called. Because *tbl* is declared *static*, it does not get destroyed on return from *f*() and it does not get constructed a second time when *f*() is called again. Because the block containing the declaration of *tbl2* doesn't get executed for the call *f(0)*, *tbl2* doesn't get constructed until the call *f(1)*. It does not get constructed again when its block is entered a second time.

The destructors for local static objects are invoked in the reverse order of their construction when the program terminates (§9.4.1.1). Exactly when is unspecified.

10.4.9 Nonlocal Store

A variable defined outside any function (that is, global, namespace, and class *static* variables; §C.9) is initialized (constructed) before *main*() is invoked, and any such variable that has been constructed will have its destructor invoked after exit from *main*(). Dynamic linking complicates this picture slightly by delaying the initialization until the code is linked into the running program.

Constructors for nonlocal objects in a translation unit are executed in the order their definitions occur. Consider:

```
class X {
    // ...
    static Table memtbl;
};

Table tbl;

Table X::memtbl;

namespace Z {
    Table tbl2;
}
```

The order of construction is *tbl*, then *X::memtbl*, and then *Z::tbl2*. Note that a declaration (as opposed to a definition), such as the declaration of *memtbl* in *X*, doesn't affect the order of construction. The destructors are called in the reverse order of construction: *Z::tbl2*, then *X::memtbl*, and then *tbl*.

No implementation-independent guarantees are made about the order of construction of nonlocal objects in different compilation units. For example:

```
// file1.c:
    Table tbl1;

// file2.c:
    Table tbl2;
```

Whether *tbl1* is constructed before *tbl2* or vice versa is implementation-dependent. The order isn't even guaranteed to be fixed in every particular implementation. Dynamic linking, or even a small change in the compilation process, can alter the sequence. The order of destruction is similarly implementation-dependent.

Sometimes when you design a library, it is necessary, or simply convenient, to invent a type with a constructor and a destructor with the sole purpose of initialization and cleanup. Such a type would be used once only: to allocate a static object so that the constructor and the destructor are called. For example:

```
class Zlib_init {
    Zlib_init();      // get Zlib ready for use
    ~Zlib_init();     // clean up after Zlib
};

class Zlib {
    static Zlib_init x;
    // ...
};
```

Unfortunately, it is not guaranteed that such an object is initialized before its first use and destroyed after its last use in a program consisting of separately compiled units. A particular C++ implementation may provide such a guarantee, but most don't. A programmer may ensure proper initialization by implementing the strategy that the implementations usually employ for local static objects: a first-time switch. For example:

```
class Zlib {
    static bool initialized;
    static void initialize() { /* initialize */ initialized = true; }
public:
    // no constructor

    void f()
    {
        if (initialized == false) initialize();
        // ...
    }
    // ...
};
```

If there are many functions that need to test the first-time switch, this can be tedious, but it is often manageable. This technique relies on the fact that statically allocated objects without constructors are initialized to *0*. The really difficult case is the one in which the first operation may be time-critical so that the overhead of testing and possible initialization can be serious. In that case, further trickery is required (§21.5.2).

An alternative approach for a simple object is to present it as a function (§9.4.1):

```
int& obj() { static int x = 0; return x; }   // initialized upon first use
```

First-time switches do not handle every conceivable situation. For example, it is possible to create objects that refer to each other during construction. Such examples are best avoided. If such objects are necessary, they must be constructed carefully in stages. Also, there is no similarly simple last-time switch construct. Instead, see §9.4.1.1 and §21.5.2.

10.4.10 Temporary Objects

Temporary objects most often are the result of arithmetic expressions. For example, at some point in the evaluation of $x*y+z$ the partial result $x*y$ must exist somewhere. Except when performance is the issue (§11.6), temporary objects rarely become the concern of the programmer. However, it happens (§11.6, §22.4.7).

Unless bound to a reference or used to initialize a named object, a temporary object is destroyed at the end of the full expression in which it was created. A *full expression* is an expression that is not a subexpression of some other expression.

The standard *string* class has a member function *c_str*() that returns a C-style, zero-terminated array of characters (§3.5.1, §20.4.1). Also, the operator + is defined to mean string concatenation. These are very useful facilities for *strings*. However, in combination they can cause obscure problems. For example:

```
void f(string& s1, string& s2, string& s3)
{
    const char* cs = (s1+s2).c_str();
    cout << cs;

    if (strlen(cs=(s2+s3).c_str())<8 && cs[0]=='a') {
        // cs used here
    }
}
```

Probably, your first reaction is "but don't do that," and I agree. However, such code does get written, so it is worth knowing how it is interpreted.

A temporary object of class *string* is created to hold *s1+s2*. Next, a pointer to a C-style string is extracted from that object. Then – at the end of the expression – the temporary object is deleted. Now, where was the C-style string returned by *c_str*() allocated? Probably as part of the temporary object holding *s1+s2*, and that storage is not guaranteed to exist after that temporary is destroyed. Consequently, *cs* points to deallocated storage. The output operation *cout<<cs* might work as expected, but that would be sheer luck. A compiler can detect and warn against many variants of this problem.

The example with the *if-statement* is a bit more subtle. The condition will work as expected because the full expression in which the temporary holding *s2+s3* is created is the condition itself. However, that temporary is destroyed before the controlled statement is entered, so any use of *cs* there is not guaranteed to work.

Please note that in this case, as in many others, the problems with temporaries arose from using a high-level data type in a low-level way. A cleaner programming style would have not only yielded a more understandable program fragment, but also avoided the problems with temporaries completely. For example:

```
void f(string& s1, string& s2, string& s3)
{
    cout << s1+s2;
    string  s = s2+s3;
    if (s.length() <8 && s[0] == 'a') {
        // use s here
    }
}
```

A temporary can be used as an initializer for a *const* reference or a named object. For example:

```
void g(const string&, const string&);

void h(string& s1, string& s2)
{
    const string& s = s1+s2;
    string  ss = s1+s2;

    g(s,ss);   // we can use s and ss here
}
```

This is fine. The temporary is destroyed when ''its'' reference or named object goes out of scope. Remember that returning a reference to a local variable is an error (§7.3) and that a temporary object cannot be bound to a non-*const* reference (§5.5).

A temporary object can also be created by explicitly invoking a constructor. For example:

```
void f(Shape& s, int x, int y)
{
    s.move(Point(x,y));        // construct Point to pass to Shape::move()
    // ...
}
```

Such temporaries are destroyed in exactly the same way as the implicitly generated temporaries.

10.4.11 Placement of Objects

Operator *new* creates its object on the free store by default. What if we wanted the object allocated elsewhere? Consider a simple class:

```
class X {
public:
    X(int);
    // ...
};
```

We can place objects anywhere by providing an allocator function with extra arguments and then supplying such extra arguments when using *new*:

```
void* operator new(size_t, void* p) { return p; }     // explicit placement operator

void* buf = reinterpret_cast<void*>(0xF00F);  // significant address
X* p2 = new(buf)X;  // construct an X at 'buf;' invokes: operator new(sizeof(X),buf)
```

Because of this usage, the *new* (*buf*) *X* syntax for supplying extra arguments to *operator new* ( ) is known as the *placement syntax*. Note that every *operator new* ( ) takes a size as its first argument and that the size of the object allocated is implicitly supplied (§15.6). The *operator new* ( ) used by the *new* operator is chosen by the usual argument matching rules (§7.4); every *operator new* ( ) has a *size_t* as its first argument.

The "placement" *operator new* ( ) is the simplest such allocator. It is defined in the standard header *<new>*.

The *reinterpret_cast* is the crudest and potentially nastiest of the type conversion operators (§6.2.7). In most cases, it simply yields a value with the same bit pattern as its argument with the type required. Thus, it can be used for the inherently implementation-dependent, dangerous, and occasionally absolutely necessary activity of converting integer values to pointers and vice versa.

The placement *new* construct can also be used to allocate memory from a specific arena:

```
class Arena {
public :
      virtual  void* alloc (size_t) =0;
      virtual  void free (void*) =0;
      // ...
} ;

void* operator new (size_t sz, Arena* a)
{
      return  a->alloc (sz) ;
}
```

Now objects of arbitrary types can be allocated from different *Arena*s as needed. For example:

```
extern Arena* Persistent;
extern Arena* Shared;

void  g (int  i)
{
      X* p = new (Persistent) X (i) ;      // X in persistent storage
      X* q = new (Shared) X (i) ;          // X in shared memory
      // ...
}
```

Placing an object in an area that is not (directly) controlled by the standard free-store manager implies that some care is required when destroying the object. The basic mechanism for that is an explicit call of a destructor:

```
void  destroy (X* p, Arena* a)
{
      p->~X ( ) ;       // call destructor
      a->free (p) ;     // free memory
}
```

Note that explicit calls of destructors, like the use of special-purpose *global* allocators, should be avoided wherever possible. Occasionally, they are essential. For example, it would be hard to implement an efficient general container along the lines of the standard library *vector* (§3.7.1, §16.3.8) without using explicit destructor calls. However, a novice should think thrice before calling a destructor explicitly and also should ask a more experienced colleague before doing so.

See §14.4.4 for an explanation of how placement new interacts with exception handling.

There is no special syntax for placement of arrays. Nor need there be, since arbitrary types can be allocated by placement new. However, a special *operator delete* ( ) can be defined for arrays (§19.4.5).

10.4.12 Unions

A named union is defined as a *struct*, where every member has the same address (see §C.8.2). A union can have member functions but not static members.

In general, a compiler cannot know what member of a union is used; that is, the type of the object stored in a union is unknown. Consequently, a union may not have members with constructors or destructors. It wouldn't be possible to protect that object against corruption or to guarantee that the right destructor is called when the union goes out of scope.

Unions are best used in low-level code, or as part of the implementation of classes that keep track of what is stored in the union (see §10.6[20]).

10.5 Advice

[1] Represent concepts as classes; §10.1.

[2] Use public data (*struct*s) only when it really is just data and no invariant is meaningful for the data members; §10.2.8.

[3] A concrete type is the simplest kind of class. Where applicable, prefer a concrete type over more complicated classes and over plain data structures; §10.3.

[4] Make a function a member only if it needs direct access to the representation of a class; §10.3.2.

[5] Use a namespace to make the association between a class and its helper functions explicit; §10.3.2.

[6] Make a member function that doesn't modify the value of its object a *const* member function; §10.2.6.

[7] Make a function that needs access to the representation of a class but needn't be called for a specific object a *static* member function; §10.2.4.

[8] Use a constructor to establish an invariant for a class; §10.3.1.

[9] If a constructor acquires a resource, its class needs a destructor to release the resource; §10.4.1.

[10] If a class has a pointer member, it needs copy operations (copy constructor and copy assignment); §10.4.4.1.

[11] If a class has a reference member, it probably needs copy operations (copy constructor and copy assignment); §10.4.6.3.

[12] If a class needs a copy operation or a destructor, it probably needs a constructor, a destructor, a copy assignment, and a copy constructor; §10.4.4.1.

[13] Check for self-assignment in copy assignments; §10.4.4.1.

[14] When writing a copy constructor, be careful to copy every element that needs to be copied (beware of default initializers); §10.4.4.1.

[15] When adding a new member to a class, always check to see if there are user-defined constructors that need to be updated to initialize the member; §10.4.6.3.

[16] Use enumerators when you need to define integer constants in class declarations; §10.4.6.2 Avoid order dependencies when constructing global and namespace objects; §10.4.9.

[18] Use first-time switches to minimize order dependencies; §10.4.9.

[19] Remember that temporary objects are destroyed at the end of the full expression in which they are created; §10.4.10.

10.6   Exercises

1. (∗1) Find the error in *Date*::*add_year*() in §10.2.2. Then find two additional errors in the version in §10.2.7.

2. (∗2.5) Complete and test *Date*. Reimplement it with ''number of days after 1/1/1970'' representation.

3. (∗2) Find a *Date* class that is in commercial use. Critique the facilities it offers. If possible, then discuss that *Date* with a real user.

4. (∗1) How do you access *set_default* from class *Date* from namespace *Chrono* (§10.3.2)? Give at least three different ways.

5. (∗2) Define a class *Histogram* that keeps count of numbers in some intervals specified as arguments to *Histogram*'s constructor. Provide functions to print out the histogram. Handle out-of-range values.

6. (∗2) Define some classes for providing random numbers of certain distributions (for example, uniform and exponential). Each class has a constructor specifying parameters for the distribution and a function *draw* that returns the next value.

7. (∗2.5) Complete class *Table* to hold (name,value) pairs. Then modify the desk calculator program from §6.1 to use class *Table* instead of *map*. Compare and contrast the two versions.

8. (∗2) Rewrite *Tnode* from §7.10[7] as a class with constructors, destructors, etc. Define a tree of *Tnode*s as a class with constructors, destructors, etc.

9. (∗3) Define, implement, and test a set of integers, class *Intset*. Provide union, intersection, and symmetric difference operations.

10. (∗1.5) Modify class *Intset* into a set of nodes, where *Node* is a structure you define.

11. (∗3) Define a class for analyzing, storing, evaluating, and printing simple arithmetic expressions consisting of integer constants and the operators +, −, ∗, and /. The public interface should look like this:

```
class Expr {
    // ...
public:
    Expr(const char*);
    int eval();
    void print();
};
```

The string argument for the constructor *Expr*::*Expr*() is the expression. The function *Expr*::*eval*() returns the value of the expression, and *Expr*::*print*() prints a representation of the expression on *cout*. A program might look like this:

```
Expr x("123/4+123*4-3");
cout << "x = " << x.eval() << "\n";
x.print();
```

Define class *Expr* twice: once using a linked list of nodes as the representation and once using a character string as the representation. Experiment with different ways of printing the expression: fully parenthesized, postfix notation, assembly code, etc.

12. (*2) Define a class *Char_queue* so that the public interface does not depend on the representation. Implement *Char_queue* (a) as a linked list and (b) as a vector. Do not worry about concurrency.

13. (*3) Design a symbol table class and a symbol table entry class for some language. Have a look at a compiler for that language to see what the symbol table really looks like.

14. (*2) Modify the expression class from §10.6[11] to handle variables and the assignment operator =. Use the symbol table class from §10.6[13].

15. (*1) Given this program:

```
#include <iostream>

int main()
{
        std::cout << "Hello, world!\n";
}
```

modify it to produce this output:

```
Initialize
Hello, world!
Clean up
```

Do not change *main()* in any way.

16. (*2) Define a *Calculator* class for which the calculator functions from §6.1 provide most of the implementation. Create *Calculator*s and invoke them for input from *cin*, from command-line arguments, and for strings in the program. Allow output to be delivered to a variety of targets similar to the way input can be obtained from a variety of sources.

17. (*2) Define two classes, each with a *static* member, so that the construction of each *static* member involves a reference to the other. Where might such constructs appear in real code? How can these classes be modified to eliminate the order dependence in the constructors?

18. (*2.5) Compare class *Date* (§10.3) with your solution to §5.9[13] and §7.10[19]. Discuss errors found and likely differences in maintenance of the two solutions.

19. (*3) Write a function that, given an *istream* and a *vector<string>*, produces a *map<string, vector<int>>* holding each string and the numbers of the lines on which the string appears. Run the program on a text-file with no fewer than 1,000 lines looking for no fewer than 10 words.

20. (*2) Take class *Entry* from §C.8.2 and modify it so that each union member is always used according to its type.

11

Operator Overloading

*When **I** use a word it means just what*
I choose it to mean − neither more nor less.
− Humpty Dumpty

Notation — operator functions — binary and unary operators — predefined meanings for operators — user-defined meanings for operators — operators and namespaces — a complex type — member and nonmember operators — mixed-mode arithmetic — initialization — copying — conversions — literals — helper functions — conversion operators — ambiguity resolution — friends — members and friends — large objects — assignment and initialization — subscripting — function call — dereferencing — increment and decrement — a string class — advice — exercises.

11.1 Introduction

Every technical field − and most nontechnical fields − have developed conventional shorthand notation to make convenient the presentation and discussion involving frequently-used concepts. For example, because of long acquaintance

   x+y*z

is clearer to us than

   multiply y by z and add the result to x

It is hard to overestimate the importance of concise notation for common operations.

   Like most languages, C++ supports a set of operators for its built-in types. However, most concepts for which operators are conventionally used are not built-in types in C++, so they must be represented as user-defined types. For example, if you need complex arithmetic, matrix algebra, logic signals, or character strings in C++, you use classes to represent these notions. Defining operators for such classes sometimes allows a programmer to provide a more conventional and convenient notation for manipulating objects than could be achieved using only the basic functional notation. For example,

```
class complex {               // very simplified complex
     double re, im;
public:
     complex(double r, double i) : re(r), im(i) { }
     complex operator+(complex);
     complex operator*(complex);
};
```

defines a simple implementation of the concept of complex numbers. A *complex* is represented by a pair of double-precision floating-point numbers manipulated by the operators + and *. The programmer defines *complex::operator+()* and *complex::operator*()* to provide meanings for + and *, respectively. For example, if *b* and *c* are of type *complex*, *b+c* means *b.operator+(c)*. We can now approximate the conventional interpretation of *complex* expressions:

```
void f()
{
     complex a = complex(1, 3.1);
     complex b = complex(1.2, 2);
     complex c = b;

     a = b+c;
     b = b+c*a;
     c = a*b+complex(1,2);
}
```

The usual precedence rules hold, so the second statement means *b=b+(c*a)*, not *b=(b+c)*a*.

Many of the most obvious uses of operator overloading are for concrete types (§10.3). However, the usefulness of user-defined operators is not restricted to concrete types. For example, the design of general and abstract interfaces often leads to the use of operators such as ->, [], and ().

11.2 Operator Functions

Functions defining meanings for the following operators (§6.2) can be declared:

+	–	*	/	%	^	&
|	~	!	=	<	>	+=
-=	*=	/=	%=	^=	&=	|=
<<	>>	>>=	<<=	==	!=	<=
>=	&&	||	++	--	->*	,
->	[]	()	*new*	*new*[]	*delete*	*delete*[]

The following operators cannot be defined by a user:

  :: (scope resolution; §4.9.4, §10.2.4),

  . (member selection; §5.7), and

  .* (member selection through pointer to member; §15.5).

They take a name, rather than a value, as their second operand and provide the primary means of referring to members. Allowing them to be overloaded would lead to subtleties [Stroustrup,1994]. The ternary conditional expression operator, ?: (§6.3.2) cannot be overloaded. Neither can the named operators *sizeof* (§4.6) and *typeid* (§15.4.4).

It is not possible to define new operator tokens, but you can use the function-call notation when this set of operators is not adequate. For example, use *pow* (), not **. These restrictions may seem Draconian, but more flexible rules can easily lead to ambiguities. For example, defining an operator ** to mean exponentiation may seem an obvious and easy task at first glance, but think again. Should ** bind to the left (as in Fortran) or to the right (as in Algol)? Should the expression *a***p be interpreted as *a** (*p) or as (*a*) ** (*p*)?

The name of an operator function is the keyword *operator* followed by the operator itself; for example, *operator*<<. An operator function is declared and can be called like any other function. A use of the operator is only a shorthand for an explicit call of the operator function. For example:

```
void f(complex a, complex b)
{
    complex c = a + b;          // shorthand
    complex d = a.operator+(b);  // explicit call
}
```

Given the previous definition of *complex*, the two initializers are synonymous.

11.2.1 Binary and Unary Operators

A binary operator can be defined by either a nonstatic member function taking one argument or a nonmember function taking two arguments. For any binary operator @, *aa*@*bb* can be interpreted as either *aa*.*operator*@(*bb*) or *operator*@(*aa*,*bb*). If both are defined, overload resolution (§7.4) determines which, if any, interpretation is used. For example:

```
class X {
public:
    void operator+(int);
    X(int);
};

void operator+(X,X);
void operator+(X,double);

void f(X a)
{
    a+1;      // a.operator+(1)
    1+a;      // ::operator+(X(1),a)
    a+1.0;    // ::operator+(a,1.0)
}
```

A unary operator, whether prefix or postfix, can be defined by either a nonstatic member function taking no arguments or a nonmember function taking one argument. For any prefix unary operator @, @*aa* can be interpreted as either *aa*.*operator*@() or *operator*@(*aa*). If both are defined, overload resolution (§7.4) determines which, if any, interpretation is used. For any postfix unary operator @, *aa@* can be interpreted as either *aa . operator@* (*int*) or *operator@* (*aa , int*). This is explained further in §11.11. If both are defined, overload resolution (§7.4) determines which, if any, interpretation is used. An operator can be declared only for the syntax defined for it in the grammar (§A.5). For example, a user cannot define a unary % or a ternary +. Consider:

```
class  X {
        // members (with implicit 'this' pointer):

        X* operator& ();        // prefix unary & (address of)
        X operator& (X);        // binary & (and)
        X operator++ (int);     // postfix increment (see §11.11)
        X operator& (X, X);     // error: ternary
        X operator/ ();         // error: unary /
};

// nonmember functions :

X operator- (X);           // prefix unary minus
X operator- (X, X);        // binary minus
X operator-- (X&, int);    // postfix decrement
X operator- ();            // error: no operand
X operator- (X, X, X);     // error: ternary
X operator% (X);           // error: unary %
```

Operator [ ] is described in §11.8, operator ( ) in §11.9, operator –> in §11.10, operators ++ and –– in §11.11, and the allocation and deallocation operators in §6.2.6.2, §10.4.11, and §15.6.

11.2.2 Predefined Meanings for Operators

Only a few assumptions are made about the meaning of a user-defined operator. In particular, *operator=*, *operator*[ ], *operator*( ), and *operator*–> must be nonstatic member functions; this ensures that their first operands will be lvalues (§4.9.6).

The meanings of some built-in operators are defined to be equivalent to some combination of other operators on the same arguments. For example, if *a* is an int, *++a* means *a+=1*, which in turn means *a=a+1*. Such relations do not hold for user-defined operators unless the user happens to define them that way. For example, a compiler will not generate a definition of *Z* :: *operator+=* ( ) from the definitions of *Z* :: *operator+* ( ) and *Z* :: *operator=* ( ).

Because of historical accident, the operators = (assignment), & (address-of), and , (sequencing; §6.2.2) have predefined meanings when applied to class objects. These predefined meanings can be made inaccessible to general users by making them private:

```
class  X {
private :
        void operator= (const  X&);
        void operator& ();
        void operator, (const  X&);
        // ...
};
```

```
void f(X a, X b)
{
    a = b;       // error: operator= private
    &a;          // error: operator& private
    a,b;         // error: operator, private
}
```

Alternatively, they can be given new meanings by suitable definitions.

11.2.3 Operators and User-Defined Types

An operator function must either be a member or take at least one argument of a user-defined type (functions redefining the *new* and *delete* operators need not). This rule ensures that a user cannot change the meaning of an expression unless the expression contains an object of a user-defined type. In particular, it is not possible to define an operator function that operates exclusively on pointers. This ensures that C++ is extensible but not mutable (with the exception of operators =, &, and , for class objects).

An operator function intended to accept a basic type as its first operand cannot be a member function. For example, consider adding a complex variable *aa* to the integer *2*: *aa+2* can, with a suitably declared member function, be interpreted as *aa.operator+(2)*, but *2+aa* cannot because there is no class *int* for which to define + to mean *2.operator+(aa)*. Even if there were, two different member functions would be needed to cope with *2+aa* and *aa+2*. Because the compiler does not know the meaning of a user-defined +, it cannot assume that it is commutative and so interpret *2+aa* as *aa+2*. This example is trivially handled using nonmember functions (§11.3.2, §11.5).

Enumerations are user-defined types so that we can define operators for them. For example:

```
enum Day { sun, mon, tue, wed, thu, fri, sat };

Day& operator++(Day& d)
{
    return d = (sat==d) ? sun : Day(d+1);
}
```

Every expression is checked for ambiguities. Where a user-defined operator provides a possible interpretation, the expression is checked according to the rules in §7.4.

11.2.4 Operators in Namespaces

An operator is either a member of a class or defined in some namespace (possibly the global namespace). Consider this simplified version of string I/O from the standard library:

```
namespace std {            // simplified std

    class ostream {
        // ...
        ostream& operator<<(const char*);
    };

    extern ostream cout;
```

```
class string {
    // ...
};
ostream& operator<<(ostream&, const string&);
}

int main()
{
    char* p = "Hello";
    std::string s = "world";
    std::cout << p << ", " << s << "!\n";
}
```

Naturally, this writes out *Hello, world*! But why? Note that I didn't make everything from *std* accessible by writing:

```
using namespace std;
```

Instead, I used the *std::* prefix for *string* and *cout*. In other words, I was at my best behavior and didn't pollute the global namespace or in other ways introduce unnecessary dependencies.

The output operator for C-style strings (*char**) is a member of *std::ostream*, so by definition

```
std::cout << p
```

means

```
std::cout.operator<<(p)
```

However, *std::ostream* doesn't have a member function to output a *std::string*, so

```
std::cout << s
```

means

```
operator<<(std::cout, s)
```

Operators defined in namespaces can be found based on their operand types just like functions can be found based on their argument types (§8.2.6). In particular, *cout* is in namespace *std*, so *std* is considered when looking for a suitable definition of <<. In that way, the compiler finds and uses:

```
std::operator<<(std::ostream&, const std::string&)
```

Consider a binary operator @. If *x* is of type *X* and *y* is of type *Y*, *x@y* is resolved like this:
  – If *X* is a class, look for *operator@* as a member of *X* or as a member of a base of *X*; and
  – look for declarations of *operator@* in the context surrounding *x@y*; and
  – if *X* is defined in namespace *N*, look for declarations of *operator@* in *N*; and
  – if *Y* is defined in namespace *M*, look for declarations of *operator@* in *M*.
Declarations for several *operator@*s may be found and overload resolution rules (§7.4) are used to find the best match, if any. This lookup mechanism is applied only if the operator has at least one operand of a user-defined type. Therefore, user-defined conversions (§11.3.2, §11.4) will be considered. Note that a *typedef* name is just a synonym and not a user-defined type (§4.9.7).

Unary operators are resolved analogously.

Note that in operator lookup no preference is given to members over non-members. This differs from lookup of named functions (§8.2.6). The lack of hiding of operators ensures that built-in operators are never inaccessible and that users can supply new meanings for an operator without modifying existing class declarations. For example, the standard iostream library defines << member functions to output built-in types. A user can define << to output user-defined types without modifying class *ostream* (§21.2.1).

11.3 A Complex Number Type

The implementation of complex numbers presented in the introduction is too restrictive to please anyone. For example, from looking at a math textbook we would expect this to work:

```
void f()
{
    complex a = complex(1,2);
    complex b = 3;
    complex c = a+2.3;
    complex d = 2+b;
    complex e = -b-c;
    b = c*2*c;
}
```

In addition, we would expect to be provided with a few additional operators, such as == for comparison and << for output, and a suitable set of mathematical functions, such as *sin*() and *sqrt*().

Class *complex* is a concrete type, so its design follows the guidelines from §10.3. In addition, users of complex arithmetic rely so heavily on operators that the definition of *complex* brings into play most of the basic rules for operator overloading.

11.3.1 Member and Nonmember Operators

I prefer to minimize the number of functions that directly manipulate the representation of an object. This can be achieved by defining only operators that inherently modify the value of their first argument, such as +=, in the class itself. Operators that simply produce a new value based on the values of its arguments, such as +, are then defined outside the class and use the essential operators in their implementation:

```
class complex {
    double re, im;
public:
    complex& operator+=(complex a);    // needs access to representation
    // ...
};

complex operator+(complex a, complex b)
{
    complex r = a;
    return r += b;    // access representation through +=
}
```

Given these declarations, we can write:

```
void f(complex x, complex y, complex z)
{
    complex r1 = x+y+z;  // r1 = operator+(operator+(x,y),z)
    complex r2 = x;      // r2 = x
    r2 += y;             // r2.operator+=(y)
    r2 += z;             // r2.operator+=(z)
}
```

Except for possible efficiency differences, the computations of *r1* and *r2* are equivalent.

Composite assignment operators such as += and *= tend to be simpler to define than their "simple" counterparts + and *. This surprises most people at first, but it follows from the fact that three objects are involved in a + operation (the two operands and the result), whereas only two objects are involved in a += operation. In the latter case, run-time efficiency is improved by eliminating the need for temporary variables. For example:

```
inline complex& complex::operator+=(complex a)
{
    re += a.re;
    im += a.im;
    return *this;
}
```

does not require a temporary variable to hold the result of the addition and is simple for a compiler to inline perfectly.

A good optimizer will generate close to optimal code for uses of the plain + operator also. However, we don't always have a good optimizer and not all types are as simple as *complex*, so §11.5 discusses ways of defining operators with direct access to the representation of classes.

11.3.2 Mixed-Mode Arithmetic

To cope with

```
complex d = 2+b;
```

we need to define operator + to accept operands of different types. In Fortran terminology, we need *mixed-mode arithmetic*. We can achieve that simply by adding appropriate versions of the operators:

```
class complex {
    double re, im;
public:
    complex& operator+=(complex a) {
        re += a.re;
        im += a.im;
        return *this;
    }
```

```
        complex& operator+= (double a) {
            re += a;
            return *this;
        }
        // ...
    };

    complex operator+ (complex a, complex b)
    {
        complex r = a;
        return r += b;   // calls complex::operator+=(complex)
    }

    complex operator+ (complex a, double b)
    {
        complex r = a;
        return r += b;   // calls complex::operator+=(double)
    }

    complex operator+ (double a, complex b)
    {
        complex r = b;
        return r += a;   // calls complex::operator+=(double)
    }
```

Adding a *double* to a complex number is a simpler operation than adding a *complex*. This is reflected in these definitions. The operations taking *double* operands do not touch the imaginary part of a complex number and thus will be more efficient.

Given these declarations, we can write:

```
    void f(complex x, complex y)
    {
        complex r1 = x+y;   // calls operator+(complex,complex)
        complex r2 = x+2;   // calls operator+(complex,double)
        complex r3 = 2+x;   // calls operator+(double,complex)
    }
```

11.3.3 Initialization

To cope with assignments and initialization of *complex* variables with scalars, we need a conversion of a scalar (integer or floating-point number) to a *complex*. For example:

```
    complex b = 3;   // should mean b.re=3, b.im=0
```

A constructor taking a single argument specifies a conversion from its argument type to the constructor's type. For example:

```
class complex {
      double re, im;
public:
      complex(double r) : re(r), im(0) { }
      // ...
};
```

The constructor specifies the traditional embedding of the real line in the complex plane.

A constructor is a prescription for creating a value of a given type. The constructor is used when a value of a type is expected and when such a value can be created by a constructor from the value supplied as an initializer or assigned value. Thus, a constructor requiring a single argument need not be called explicitly. For example,

```
complex b = 3;
```

means

```
complex b = complex(3);
```

A user-defined conversion is implicitly applied only if it is unique (§7.4). See §11.7.1 for a way of specifying constructors that can only be explicitly invoked.

Naturally, we still need the constructor that takes two *double*s, and a default constructor initializing a *complex* to $(0,0)$ is also useful:

```
class complex {
      double re, im;
public:
      complex() : re(0), im(0) { }
      complex(double r) : re(r), im(0) { }
      complex(double r, double i) : re(r), im(i) { }
      // ...
};
```

Using default arguments, we can abbreviate:

```
class complex {
      double re, im;
public:
      complex(double r =0, double i =0) : re(r), im(i) { }
      // ...
};
```

When a constructor is explicitly declared for a type, it is not possible to use an initializer list (§5.7, §4.9.5) as the initializer. For example:

```
complex z1 = { 3 };       // error: complex has a constructor
complex z2 = { 3, 4 };    // error: complex has a constructor
```

11.3.4 Copying

In addition to the explicitly declared constructors, *complex* by default gets a copy constructor defined (§10.2.5). A default copy constructor simply copies all members. To be explicit, we could equivalently have written:

```
class complex {
    double re, im;
public:
    complex(const complex& c) : re(c.re), im(c.im) { }
    // ...
};
```

However, for types where the default copy constructor has the right semantics, I prefer to rely on that default. It is less verbose than anything I can write, and people should understand the default. Also, compilers know about the default and its possible optimization opportunities. Furthermore, writing out the memberwise copy by hand is tedious and error-prone for classes with many data members (§10.4.6.3).

I use a reference argument for the copy constructor because I must. The copy constructor defines what copying means – including what copying an argument means – so writing

```
complex::complex(complex c) : re(c.re), im(c.im) { }  // error
```

is an error because any call would have involved an infinite recursion.

For other functions taking *complex* arguments, I use value arguments rather than reference arguments. Here, the designer has a choice. From a user's point of view, there is little difference between a function that takes a *complex* argument and one that takes a *const complex*& argument. This issue is discussed further in §11.6.

In principle, copy constructors are used in simple initializations such as

```
complex  x = 2;                    // create complex(2); then initialize x with it
complex  y = complex(2,0);         // create complex(2,0); then initialize y with it
```

However, the calls to the copy constructor are trivially optimized away. We could equivalently have written:

```
complex  x(2);        // initialize x with 2
complex  y(2,0);      // initialize y with (2,0)
```

For arithmetic types, such as *complex*, I like the look of the version using = better. It is possible to restrict the set of values accepted by the = style of initialization compared to the ( ) style by making the copy constructor private (§11.2.2) or by declaring a constructor *explicit* (§11.7.1).

Similar to initialization, assignment of two objects of the same class is by default defined as memberwise assignment (§10.2.5). We could explicitly define *complex::operator=* to do that. However, for a simple type like *complex* there is no reason to do so. The default is just right.

The copy constructor – whether user-defined or compiler-generated – is used not only for the initialization of variables, but also for argument passing, value return, and exception handling (see §11.7). The semantics of these operations is defined to be the semantics of initialization (§7.1, §7.3, §14.2.1).

11.3.5 Constructors and Conversions

We defined three versions of each of the four standard arithmetic operators:

```
complex operator+ (complex, complex);
complex operator+ (complex, double);
complex operator+ (double, complex);
// ...
```

This can get tedious, and what is tedious easily becomes error-prone. What if we had three alternatives for the type of each argument for each function? We would need three versions of each single-argument function, nine versions of each two-argument function, twenty-seven versions of each three-argument function, etc. Often these variants are very similar. In fact, almost all variants involve a simple conversion of arguments to a common type followed by a standard algorithm.

The alternative to providing different versions of a function for each combination of arguments is to rely on conversions. For example, our *complex* class provides a constructor that converts a *double* to a *complex*. Consequently, we could simply declare only one version of the equality operator for *complex*:

```
bool operator== (complex, complex);

void f(complex x, complex y)
{
    x==y;       // means operator==(x,y)
    x==3;       // means operator==(x,complex(3))
    3==y;       // means operator==(complex(3),y)
}
```

There can be reasons for preferring to define separate functions. For example, in some cases the conversion can impose overheads, and in other cases, a simpler algorithm can be used for specific argument types. Where such issues are not significant, relying on conversions and providing only the most general variant of a function – plus possibly a few critical variants – contains the combinatorial explosion of variants that can arise from mixed-mode arithmetic.

Where several variants of a function or an operator exist, the compiler must pick ''the right'' variant based on the argument types and the available (standard and user-defined) conversions. Unless a best match exists, an expression is ambiguous and is an error (see §7.4).

An object constructed by explicit or implicit use of a constructor in an expression is automatic and will be destroyed at the first opportunity (see §10.4.10).

No implicit user-defined conversions are applied to the left-hand side of a . (or a ->). This is the case even when the . is implicit. For example:

```
void g (complex z)
{
    3+z;                    // ok: complex(3)+z
    3.operator+= (z);       // error: 3 is not a class object
    3+=z;                   // error: 3 is not a class object
}
```

Thus, you can express the notion that an operator requires an lvalue as its left-hand operand by making that operator a member.

11.3.6 Literals

It is not possible to define literals of a class type in the sense that *1.2* and *12e3* are literals of type *double*. However, literals of the basic types can often be used instead if class member functions are used to provide an interpretation for them. Constructors taking a single argument provide a general mechanism for this. When constructors are simple and inline, it is quite reasonable to think of constructor invocations with literal arguments as literals. For example, I think of *complex(3)* as a literal of type *complex*, even though technically it isn't.

11.3.7 Additional Member Functions

So far, we have provided class *complex* with constructors and arithmetic operators only. That is not quite sufficient for real use. In particular, we often need to be able to examine the value of the real and imaginary parts:

```
class complex {
        double re, im;
public:
        double real() const { return re; }
        double imag() const { return im; }
        // ...
};
```

Unlike the other members of *complex*, *real()* and *imag()* do not modify the value of a *complex*, so they can be declared *const*.

Given *real()* and *imag()*, we can define all kinds of useful operations without granting them direct access to the representation of *complex*. For example:

```
inline bool operator==(complex a, complex b)
{
        return a.real()==b.real() && a.imag()==b.imag();
}
```

Note that we need only to be able to read the real and imaginary parts; writing them is less often needed. If we must do a "partial update," we can:

```
void f(complex& z, double d)
{
        // ...
        z = complex(z.real(),d);  // assign d to z.im
}
```

A good optimizer generates a single assignment for that statement.

11.3.8 Helper Functions

If we put all the bits and pieces together, the *complex* class becomes:

```
class complex {
    double re, im;
public:
    complex(double r =0, double i =0) : re(r), im(i) { }

    double real() const { return re; }
    double imag() const { return im; }

    complex& operator+=(complex);
    complex& operator+=(double);
    // −=, *=, and /=
};
```

In addition, we must provide a number of helper functions:

```
complex operator+(complex, complex);
complex operator+(complex, double);
complex operator+(double, complex);

// −, *, and /

complex operator−(complex);    // unary minus
complex operator+(complex);    // unary plus

bool operator==(complex, complex);
bool operator!=(complex, complex);

istream& operator>>(istream&, complex&); // input
ostream& operator<<(ostream&, complex); // output
```

Note that the members *real*() and *imag*() are essential for defining the comparisons. The definition of most of the following helper functions similarly relies on *real*() and *imag*().

We might provide functions to allow users to think in terms of polar coordinates:

```
complex polar(double rho, double theta);
complex conj(complex);

double abs(complex);
double arg(complex);
double norm(complex);

double real(complex);    // for notational convenience
double imag(complex);    // for notational convenience
```

Finally, we must provide an appropriate set of standard mathematical functions:

```
complex acos(complex);
complex asin(complex);
complex atan(complex);
// ...
```

From a user's point of view, the complex type presented here is almost identical to the *complex<double>* found in *<complex>* in the standard library (§22.5).

11.4 Conversion Operators

Using a constructor to specify type conversion is convenient but has implications that can be undesirable. A constructor cannot specify

[1]   an implicit conversion from a user-defined type to a basic type (because the basic types are not classes), or

[2]   a conversion from a new class to a previously defined class (without modifying the declaration for the old class).

These problems can be handled by defining a *conversion operator* for the source type. A member function $X::operator\ T()$, where T is a type name, defines a conversion from X to T. For example, one could define a 6-bit non-negative integer, *Tiny*, that can mix freely with integers in arithmetic operations:

```
class Tiny {
    char v;
    void assign(int i) { if (i&~077) throw Bad_range(); v=i; }
public:
    class Bad_range { };

    Tiny(int i) { assign(i); }
    Tiny& operator=(int i) { assign(i); return *this; }

    operator int() const { return v; }     // conversion to int function
};
```

The range is checked whenever a *Tiny* is initialized by an *int* and whenever an *int* is assigned to one. No range check is needed when we copy a *Tiny*, so the default copy constructor and assignment are just right.

To enable the usual integer operations on *Tiny* variables, we define the implicit conversion from *Tiny* to *int*, $Tiny::operator\ int()$. Note that the type being converted to is part of the name of the operator and cannot be repeated as the return value of the conversion function:

```
Tiny::operator int() const { return v; }         // right
int Tiny::operator int() const { return v; }     // error
```

In this respect also, a conversion operator resembles a constructor.

Whenever a *Tiny* appears where an *int* is needed, the appropriate *int* is used. For example:

```
int main()
{
    Tiny c1 = 2;
    Tiny c2 = 62;
    Tiny c3 = c2-c1;     // c3 = 60
    Tiny c4 = c3;        // no range check (not necessary)
    int i = c1+c2;       // i = 64

    c1 = c1+c2;          // range error: c1 can't be 64
    i = c3-64;           // i = -4
    c2 = c3-64;          // range error: c2 can't be -4
    c3 = c4;             // no range check (not necessary)
}
```

Conversion functions appear to be particularly useful for handling data structures when reading (implemented by a conversion operator) is trivial, while assignment and initialization are distinctly less trivial.

The *istream* and *ostream* types rely on a conversion function to enable statements such as

> *while* (*cin>>x*) *cout<<x*;

The input operation *cin>>x* returns an *istream&*. That value is implicitly converted to a value indicating the state of *cin*. This value can then be tested by the *while* (see §21.3.3). However, it is typically *not* a good idea to define an implicit conversion from one type to another in such a way that information is lost in the conversion.

In general, it is wise to be sparing in the introduction of conversion operators. When used in excess, they lead to ambiguities. Such ambiguities are caught by the compiler, but they can be a nuisance to resolve. Probably the best idea is initially to do conversions by named functions, such as *X*::*make_int*(). If such a function becomes popular enough to make explicit use inelegant, it can be replaced by a conversion operator *X*::*operator int*().

If both user-defined conversions and user-defined operators are defined, it is possible to get ambiguities between the user-defined operators and the built-in operators. For example:

```
int operator+(Tiny, Tiny);

void f(Tiny t, int i)
{
    t+i;  // error, ambiguous: operator+(t,Tiny(i)) or int(t)+i ?
}
```

It is therefore often best to rely on user-defined conversions or user-defined operators for a given type, but not both.

11.4.1 Ambiguities

An assignment of a value of type *V* to an object of class *X* is legal if there is an assignment operator *X*::*operator*=(*Z*) so that *V* is *Z* or there is a unique conversion of *V* to *Z*. Initialization is treated equivalently.

In some cases, a value of the desired type can be constructed by repeated use of constructors or conversion operators. This must be handled by explicit conversions; only one level of user-defined implicit conversion is legal. In some cases, a value of the desired type can be constructed in more than one way; such cases are illegal. For example:

```
class X { /* ... */ X(int); X(char*); };
class Y { /* ... */ Y(int); };
class Z { /* ... */ Z(X); };

X f(X);
Y f(Y);

Z g(Z);
```

```
void  k1 ( )
{
    f(1);               // error: ambiguous f(X(1)) or f(Y(1))?
    f(X(1));            // ok
    f(Y(1));            // ok

    g("Mack");          // error: two user-defined conversions needed; g(Z(X("Mack"))) not tried
    g(X("Doc"));        // ok: g(Z(X("Doc")))
    g(Z("Suzy"));       // ok: g(Z(X("Suzy")))
}
```

User-defined conversions are considered only if they are necessary to resolve a call. For example:

```
class  XX { /* ... */ XX(int); };

void  h(double);
void  h(XX);

void  k2()
{
    h(1);       // h(double(1)) or h(XX(1))? h(double(1))!
}
```

The call *h(1)* means *h(double(1))* because that alternative uses only a standard conversion rather than a user-defined conversion (§7.4).

The rules for conversion are neither the simplest to implement, the simplest to document, nor the most general that could be devised. They are, however, considerably safer, and the resulting resolutions are less surprising. It is far easier to manually resolve an ambiguity than to find an error caused by an unsuspected conversion.

The insistence on strict bottom-up analysis implies that the return type is not used in overloading resolution. For example:

```
class  Quad {
public:
    Quad(double);
    // ...
};

Quad  operator+(Quad, Quad);

void  f(double a1, double a2)
{
    Quad  r1 = a1+a2;        // double-precision add
    Quad  r2 = Quad(a1)+a2;  // force quad arithmetic
}
```

The reason for this design choice is partly that strict bottom-up analysis is more comprehensible and partly that it is not considered the compiler's job to decide which precision the programmer might want for the addition.

Once the types of both sides of an initialization or assignment have been determined, both types are used to resolve the initialization or assignment. For example:

```
class Real {
public:
    operator double();
    operator int();
    // ...
};

void g(Real a)
{
    double d = a;   // d = a.double();
    int i = a;      // i = a.int();

    d = a;          // d = a.double();
    i = a;          // i = a.int();
}
```

In these cases, the type analysis is still bottom-up, with only a single operator and its argument types considered at any one time.

11.5 Friends

An ordinary member function declaration specifies three logically distinct things:

  [1] The function can access the private part of the class declaration, and

  [2] the function is in the scope of the class, and

  [3] the function must be invoked on an object (has a *this* pointer).

By declaring a member function *static* (§10.2.4), we can give it the first two properties only. By declaring a function a *friend*, we can give it the first property only.

For example, we could define an operator that multiplies a *Matrix* by a *Vector*. Naturally, *Vector* and *Matrix* each hide their representation and provide a complete set of operations for manipulating objects of their type. However, our multiplication routine cannot be a member of both. Also, we don't really want to provide low-level access functions to allow every user to both read and write the complete representation of both *Matrix* and *Vector*. To avoid this, we declare the *operator** a friend of both:

```
class Matrix;

class Vector {
    float v[4];
    // ...
    friend Vector operator*(const Matrix&, const Vector&);
};

class Matrix {
    Vector v[4];
    // ...
    friend Vector operator*(const Matrix&, const Vector&);
};
```

```
Vector operator* (const Matrix& m, const Vector& v)
{
    Vector r;
    for (int i = 0; i<4; i++) {        // r[i] = m[i] * v;
        r.v[i] = 0;
        for (int j = 0; j<4; j++) r.v[i] += m.v[i].v[j] * v.v[j];
    }
    return r;
}
```

A *friend* declaration can be placed in either the private or the public part of a class declaration; it does not matter where. Like a member function, a friend function is explicitly declared in the declaration of the class of which it is a friend. It is therefore as much a part of that interface as is a member function.

A member function of one class can be the friend of another. For example:

```
class List_iterator {
    // ...
    int* next();
};

class List {
    friend int* List_iterator::next();
    // ...
};
```

It is not unusual for all functions of one class to be friends of another. There is a shorthand for this:

```
class List {
    friend class List_iterator;
    // ...
};
```

This friend declaration makes all of *List_iterator*'s member functions friends of *List*.

Clearly, *friend* classes should be used only to express closely connected concepts. Often, there is a choice between making a class a member (a nested class) or a nonmember friend (§24.4).

11.5.1 Finding Friends

Like a member declaration, a *friend* declaration does not introduce a name into an enclosing scope. For example:

```
class Matrix {
    friend class Xform;
    friend Matrix invert(const Matrix&);
    // ...
};

Xform x;                              // error: no Xform in scope
Matrix (*p)(const Matrix&) = &invert; // error: no invert() in scope
```

For large programs and large classes, it is nice that a class doesn't "quietly" add names to its enclosing scope. For a template class that can be instantiated in many different contexts (Chapter 13), this is very important.

A friend class must be previously declared in an enclosing scope or defined in the non-class scope immediately enclosing the class that is declaring it a friend. Scopes outside the innermost enclosing namespace scope are not considered. For example:

```
class AE { /* ... */ };          // not a friend of Y

namespace N {
    class X { /* ... */ };       // Y's friend

    class Y {
        friend class X;
        friend class Z;
        friend class AE;
    };
    class Z { /* ... */ };       // Y's friend
}
```

A friend function can be explicitly declared just like friend classes, or it can be found through its arguments (§8.2.6) even if it was not declared in the immediately enclosing scope. For example:

```
void f(Matrix& m)
{
    invert(m);       // Matrix's friend invert()
}
```

It follows that a friend function should either be explicitly declared in an enclosing scope or take an argument of its class. If not, the friend cannot be called. For example:

```
// no f() in this scope

class X {
    friend void f();            // useless
    friend void h(const X&); // can be found through its argument
};

void g(const X& x)
{
    f();         // no f() in scope
    h(x);        // X's friend h()
}
```

11.5.2 Friends and Members

When should we use a friend function, and when is a member function the better choice for specifying an operation? First, we try to minimize the number of functions that access the representation of a class and try to make the set of access functions as appropriate as possible. Therefore, the first question is not, "Should it be a member, a static member, or a friend?" but rather, "Does it really need access?" Typically, the set of functions that need access is smaller than we are willing to believe at first. Some operations must be members – for example, constructors, destructors, and virtual functions (§12.2.6) – but typically there is a choice. Because member names are local to the class, a function that requires direct access to the representation should be a member unless there is a specific reason for it to be a nonmember.

Consider a class *X* supplying alternative ways of presenting an operation:

```
class X {
    // ...
    X(int);

    int m1();
    int m2() const;

    friend int f1(X&);
    friend int f2(const X&);
    friend int f3(X);
};
```

Member functions can be invoked for objects of their class only; no user-defined conversions are applied to leftmost operand of a . or -> (but see §11.10). For example:

```
void g()
{
    99.m1();  // error: X(99).m1() not tried
    99.m2();  // error: X(99).m2() not tried
}
```

The global function *f1* () has a similar property because implicit conversions are not used for non-*const* reference arguments (§5.5, §11.3.5). However, conversions may be applied to the arguments of *f2* () and *f3* ():

```
void h()
{
    f1(99);    // error: f1(X(99)) not tried
    f2(99);    // ok: f2(X(99));
    f3(99);    // ok: f3(X(99));
}
```

An operation modifying the state of a class object should therefore be a member or a global function taking a non-*const* reference argument (or a non-*const* pointer argument). Operators that require lvalue operands for the fundamental types (=, *=, ++, etc.) are most naturally defined as members for user-defined types.

Conversely, if implicit type conversion is desired for all operands of an operation, the function implementing it must be a nonmember function taking a *const* reference argument or a non-reference argument. This is often the case for the functions implementing operators that do not require lvalue operands when applied to fundamental types (+, -, | |, etc.). Such operators often need access to the representations of their operand class. Consequently, binary operators are the most common source of *friend* functions.

If no type conversions are defined, there appears to be no compelling reason to choose a member over a friend taking a reference argument, or vice versa. In some cases, the programmer may have a preference for one call syntax over another. For example, most people seem to prefer the notation *inv* (*m*) for inverting a *Matrix m* to the alternative *m* . *inv* ( ). Naturally, if *inv* ( ) really does invert *m* itself, rather than return a new *Matrix* that is the inverse of *m*, it should be a member.

All other things considered equal, choose a member. It is not possible to know if someone someday will define a conversion operator. It is not always possible to predict if a future change may require changes to the state of the object involved. The member function call syntax makes it clear to the user that the object may be modified; a reference argument is far less obvious. Furthermore, expressions in the body of a member can be noticeably shorter than the equivalent expressions in a global function; a nonmember function must use an explicit argument, whereas the member can use *this* implicitly. Also, because member names are local to the class they tend to be shorter than the names of nonmember functions.

11.6 Large Objects

We defined the *complex* operators to take arguments of type *complex*. This implies that for each use of a *complex* operator, each operand is copied. The overhead of copying two *double*s can be noticeable but often less than what a pair of pointers impose (access through a pointer can be relatively expensive). Unfortunately, not all classes have a conveniently small representation. To avoid excessive copying, one can declare functions to take reference arguments. For example:

```
class Matrix {
        double m[4] [4];
public:
        Matrix ( );
        friend Matrix operator+ (const Matrix&, const Matrix&);
        friend Matrix operator* (const Matrix&, const Matrix&);
} ;
```

References allow the use of expressions involving the usual arithmetic operators for large objects without excessive copying. Pointers cannot be used because it is not possible to redefine the meaning of an operator applied to a pointer. Addition could be defined like this:

```
Matrix operator+ (const Matrix& arg1, const Matrix& arg2)
{
        Matrix sum;
        for (int i=0; i<4; i++)
                for (int j=0; j<4; j++)
                        sum.m[i] [j] = arg1.m[i] [j] + arg2.m[i] [j];
        return sum;
}
```

This *operator+* ( ) accesses the operands of + through references but returns an object value. Returning a reference would appear to be more efficient:

```
class Matrix {
        // ...
        friend Matrix& operator+ (const Matrix&, const Matrix&);
        friend Matrix& operator* (const Matrix&, const Matrix&);
} ;
```

This is legal, but it causes a memory allocation problem. Because a reference to the result will be passed out of the function as a reference to the return value, the return value cannot be an automatic variable (§7.3). Since an operator is often used more than once in an expression, the result cannot be a *static* local variable. The result would typically be allocated on the free store. Copying the return value is often cheaper (in execution time, code space, and data space) than allocating and (eventually) deallocating an object on the free store. It is also much simpler to program.

There are techniques you can use to avoid copying the result. The simplest is to use a buffer of static objects. For example:

```
const int max_matrix_temp = 7;

Matrix& get_matrix_temp()
{
    static int nbuf = 0;
    static Matrix buf[max_matrix_temp];

    if (nbuf == max_matrix_temp) nbuf = 0;
    return buf[nbuf++];
}

Matrix& operator+(const Matrix& arg1, const Matrix& arg2)
{
    Matrix& res = get_matrix_temp();
    // ...
    return res;
}
```

Now a *Matrix* is copied only when the result of an expression is assigned. However, heaven help you if you write an expression that involves more than *max_matrix_temp* temporaries!

A less error-prone technique involves defining the matrix type as a handle (§25.7) to a representation type that really holds the data. In that way, the matrix handles can manage the representation objects in such a way that allocation and copying are minimized (see §11.12 and §11.14[18]). However, that strategy relies on operators returning objects rather than references or pointers. Another technique is to define ternary operations and have them automatically invoked for expressions such as $a=b+c$ and $a+b*i$ (§21.4.6.3, §22.4.7).

11.7 Essential Operators

In general, for a type X, the copy constructor $X(const\ X\&)$ takes care of initialization by an object of the same type X. It cannot be overemphasized that *assignment and initialization are different operations* (§10.4.4.1). This is especially important when a destructor is declared. If a class X has a destructor that performs a nontrivial task, such as free-store deallocation, the class is likely to need the full complement of functions that control construction, destruction, and copying:

```
class X {
    // ...
    X (Sometype);               // constructor: create objects
    X (const X&);               // copy constructor
    X& operator= (const X&);    // copy assignment: cleanup and copy
    ~X ();                      // destructor: cleanup
};
```

There are three more cases in which an object is copied: as a function argument, as a function return value, and as an exception. When an argument is passed, a hitherto uninitialized variable – the formal parameter – is initialized. The semantics are identical to those of other initializations. The same is the case for function return values and exceptions, although that is less obvious. In such cases, the copy constructor will be applied. For example:

```
string g (string arg)           // string passed by value (using copy constructor)
{
    return arg;                 // string returned (using copy constructor)
}

int main ()
{
    string s = "Newton";        // string initialized (using copy constructor)
    s = g (s);
}
```

Clearly, the value of *s* ought to be *"Newton"* after the call of *g* (). Getting a copy of the value of *s* into the argument *arg* is not difficult; a call of *string*'s copy constructor does that. Getting a copy of that value out of *g* () takes another call of *string* (*const string*&); this time, the variable initialized is a temporary one (§10.4.10), which is then assigned to *s*. Often one, but not both, of these copy operations can be optimized away.

For a class for which the copy assignment and the copy constructor are not explicitly declared by the programmer, the missing operation or operations will be generated by the compiler (§10.2.5). This implies that copy operations are not inherited (§12.2.3).

11.7.1 Explicit Constructors

By default, a single argument constructor also defines an implicit conversion. For some types, that is ideal. For example, a *complex* can be initialized with an *int*:

```
complex z = 2;  // initialize z with complex(2)
```

In other cases, the implicit conversion is undesirable and error-prone. For example, if we could initialize a *string* with an *int* size someone would write:

```
string s = 'a';  // make s a string with int('a') elements
```

It is quite unlikely that this was what the person defining *s* meant.

Implicit conversion can be suppressed by declaring a constructor *explicit*. That is, an *explicit* constructor will be invoked only explicitly. In particular, where a copy constructor is in principle needed (§11.3.4), an *explicit* constructor will not be implicitly invoked. For example:

```
class String {
    // ...
    explicit String (int n);        // preallocate n bytes
    String (const char* p);         // initial value is the C-style string p
};

String s1 = 'a';                    // error: no implicit char->String conversion
String s2 (10);                     // ok: String with space for 10 characters
String s3 = String (10);           // ok: String with space for 10 characters
String s4 = "Brian";               // ok: s4 = String("Brian")
String s5 ("Fawlty");

void f (String);

String g ()
{
    f (10);             // error: no implicit int->String conversion
    f (String (10));
    f ("Arthur");       // ok: f(String("Arthur"))
    f (s1);

    String* p1 = new String ("Eric");
    String* p2 = new String (10);

    return 10;          // error: no implicit int->String conversion
}
```

The distinction between

```
String s1 = 'a';                   // error: no implicit char->String conversion
```

and

```
String s2 (10);                    // ok: string with space for 10 characters
```

may seem subtle, but it is less so in real code than in contrived examples.

In *Date*, we used a plain *int* to represent a year (§10.3). Had *Date* been critical in our design, we might have introduced a *Year* type to allow stronger compile-time checking. For example:

```
class Year {
    int y;
public:
    explicit Year (int i) : y(i) { }    // construct Year from int
    operator int () const { return y; } // conversion: Year to int
};

class Date {
public:
    Date (int d, Month m, Year y);
    // ...
};

Date d3 (1978, feb, 21);        // error: 21 is not a Year
Date d4 (21, feb, Year (1978)); // ok
```

The *Year* class is a simple "wrapper" around an *int*. Thanks to the *operator int*(), a *Year* is implicitly converted into an *int* wherever needed. By declaring the constructor *explicit*, we make sure that the *int* to *Year* happens only when we ask for it and that "accidental" assignments are caught at compile time. Because *Year*'s member functions are easily inlined, no run-time or space costs are added.

A similar technique can be used to define range types (§25.6.1).

11.8 Subscripting

An *operator*[] function can be used to give subscripts a meaning for class objects. The second argument (the subscript) of an *operator*[] function may be of any type. This makes it possible to define *vector*s, associative arrays, etc.

As an example, let us recode the example from §5.5 in which an associative array is used to write a small program for counting the number of occurrences of words in a file. There, a function is used. Here, an associative array type is defined:

```
class Assoc {
    struct Pair {
        string name;
        double val;
        Pair(string n ="", double v =0) :name(n), val(v) { }
    };
    vector<Pair> vec;

    Assoc(const Assoc&);              // private to prevent copying
    Assoc& operator=(const Assoc&);   // private to prevent copying
public:
    Assoc() {}
    const double& operator[](const string&);
    double& operator[](string&);
    void print_all() const;
};
```

An *Assoc* keeps a vector of *Pair*s. The implementation uses the same trivial and inefficient search method as in §5.5:

```
double& Assoc::operator[](string& s)
    // search for s; return its value if found; otherwise, make a new Pair and return the default value 0
{
    for (vector<Pair>::const_iterator p = vec.begin(); p!=vec.end(); ++p)
        if (s == p->name) return p->val;

    vec.push_back(Pair(s,0));     // initial value: 0

    return vec.back().val;        // return last element (§16.3.3)
}
```

Because the representation of an *Assoc* is hidden, we need a way of printing it:

```
void Assoc::print_all() const
{
    for (vector<Pair>::const_iterator p = vec.begin(); p!=vec.end(); ++p)
        cout << p->name << ": " << p->val << '\n';
}
```

Finally, we can write the trivial main program:

```
int main()         // count the occurrences of each word on input
{
    string buf;
    Assoc vec;
    while (cin>>buf) vec[buf]++;
    vec.print_all();
}
```

A further development of the idea of an associative array can be found in §17.4.1.

An *operator*[]() must be a member function.

11.9 Function Call

Function call, that is, the notation *expression(expression-list),* can be interpreted as a binary operation with the *expression* as the left-hand operand and the *expression-list* as the right-hand operand.
The call operator () can be overloaded in the same way as other operators can. An argument list
for an *operator*()() is evaluated and checked according to the usual argument-passing rules.
Overloading function call seems to be useful primarily for defining types that have only a single
operation and for types for which one operation is predominant. The call operator is also known as
the application operator.

The most obvious, and probably also the most important, use of the () operator is to provide
the usual function call syntax for objects that in some way behave like functions. An object that
acts like a function is often called a *function-like object* or simply a *function object* (§18.4). Such
function objects are important because they allow us to write code that takes nontrivial operations
as parameters. For example, the standard library provides many algorithms that invoke a function
for each element of a container. Consider:

```
void negate(complex& c) { c = -c; }
void f(vector<complex>& aa, list<complex>& ll)
{
    for_each(aa.begin(), aa.end(), negate);   // negate all vector elements
    for_each(ll.begin(), ll.end(), negate);   // negate all list elements
}
```

This negates every element in the vector and the list.

What if we wanted to add *complex*(*2*, *3*) to every element? That is easily done like this:

```
void add23 (complex& c)
{
    c += complex (2,3);
}

void g (vector<complex>& aa, list<complex>& ll)
{
    for_each (aa.begin(), aa.end(), add23);
    for_each (ll.begin(), ll.end(), add23);
}
```

How would we write a function to repeatedly add an arbitrary complex value? We need something to which we can pass that arbitrary value and which can then use that value each time it is called. That does not come naturally for functions. Typically, we end up ''passing'' the arbitrary value by leaving it in the function's surrounding context. That's messy. However, we can write a class that behaves in the desired way:

```
class Add {
    complex val;
public:
    Add (complex c) { val = c; }                        // save value
    Add (double r, double i) { val = complex(r,i); }

    void operator() (complex& c) const { c += val; }    // add value to argument
};
```

An object of class *Add* is initialized with a complex number, and when invoked using ( ), it adds that number to its argument. For example:

```
void h (vector<complex>& aa, list<complex>& ll, complex z)
{
    for_each (aa.begin(), aa.end(), Add(2,3));
    for_each (ll.begin(), ll.end(), Add(z));
}
```

This will add *complex* (2, 3) to every element of the array and z to every element on the list. Note that *Add* (z) constructs an object that is used repeatedly by *for_each* ( ). It is not simply a function that is called once or even called repeatedly. The function that is called repeatedly is *Add* (z) 's *operator* ( ) ( ) .

This all works because *for_each* is a template that applies ( ) to its third argument without caring exactly what that third argument really is:

```
template<class Iter, class Fct> Fct for_each (Iter b, Iter e, Fct f)
{
    while (b != e) f(*b++);
    return f;
}
```

At first glance, this technique may look esoteric, but it is simple, efficient, and extremely useful (see §3.8.5, §18.4).

Other popular uses of *operator* ( ) ( ) are as a substring operator and as a subscripting operator for multidimensional arrays (§22.4.5).

An *operator* ( ) ( ) must be a member function.

11.10 Dereferencing

The dereferencing operator -> can be defined as a unary postfix operator. That is, given a class

```
class Ptr {
    // ...
    X* operator->();
};
```

objects of class *Ptr* can be used to access members of class *X* in a very similar manner to the way pointers are used. For example:

```
void f(Ptr p)
{
    p->m = 7;      // (p.operator->())->m = 7
}
```

The transformation of the object *p* into the pointer *p . operator->* ( ) does not depend on the member *m* pointed to. That is the sense in which *operator->* ( ) is a unary postfix operator. However, there is no new syntax introduced, so a member name is still required after the ->. For example:

```
void g (Ptr p)
{
    X* q1 = p->;              // syntax error
    X* q2 = p.operator->();   // ok
}
```

Overloading -> is primarily useful for creating "smart pointers," that is, objects that act like pointers and in addition perform some action whenever an object is accessed through them. For example, one could define a class *Rec_ptr* for accessing objects of class *Rec* stored on disk. *Rec_ptr*'s constructor takes a name that can be used to find the object on disk, *Rec_ptr :: operator->* ( ) brings the object into main memory when accessed through its *Rec_ptr*, and *Rec_ptr*'s destructor eventually writes the updated object back out to disk:

```
class Rec_ptr {
    const char* identifier;
    Rec* in_core_address;
    // ...
public :
    Rec_ptr (const char* p) : identifier (p), in_core_address (0) { }
    ~Rec_ptr () { write_to_disk (in_core_address, identifier); }
    Rec* operator->();
};
```

```
Rec* Rec_ptr::operator->()
{
    if (in_core_address == 0) in_core_address = read_from_disk(identifier);
    return in_core_address;
}
```

Rec_ptr might be used like this:

```
struct Rec {        // the Rec that a Rec_ptr points to
    string name;
    // ...
};

void update(const char* s)
{
    Rec_ptr p(s);                // get Rec_ptr for s

    p->name = "Roscoe";          // update s; if necessary, first retrieve from disk
    // ...
}
```

Naturally, a real *Rec_ptr* would be a template so that the *Rec* type is a parameter. Also, a realistic program would contain error-handling code and use a less naive way of interacting with the disk.

For ordinary pointers, use of -> is synonymous with some uses of unary * and []. Given

```
Y* p;
```

it holds that

$$p\text{->}m == (*p).m == p[0].m$$

As usual, no such guarantee is provided for user-defined operators. The equivalence can be provided where desired:

```
class Ptr_to_Y {
    Y* p;
public:
    Y* operator->() { return p; }
    Y& operator*() { return *p; }
    Y& operator[](int i) { return p[i]; }
};
```

If you provide more than one of these operators, it might be wise to provide the equivalence, just as it is wise to ensure that ++x and x+=1 have the same effect as x=x+1 for a simple variable x of some class if ++, +=, =, and + are provided.

The overloading of -> is important to a class of interesting programs and not just a minor curiosity. The reason is that *indirection* is a key concept and that overloading -> provides a clean, direct, and efficient way of representing indirection in a program. Iterators (Chapter 19) provide an important example of this. Another way of looking at operator -> is to consider it as a way of providing C++ with a limited, but useful, form of *delegation* (§24.3.6).

Operator -> must be a member function. If used, its return type must be a pointer or an object of a class to which you can apply ->. When declared for a template class, *operator->()* is frequently unused, so it makes sense to postpone checking the constraint on the return type until actual use.

11.11 Increment and Decrement

Once people invent "smart pointers," they often decide to provide the increment operator ++ and the decrement operator – – to mirror these operators' use for built-in types. This is especially obvious and necessary where the aim is to replace an ordinary pointer type with a "smart pointer" type that has the same semantics, except that it adds a bit of run-time error checking. For example, consider a troublesome traditional program:

```
void f1 (T  a)          // traditional use
{
    T  v[200];
    T* p = &v[0];
    p--;
    *p = a;      // Oops: 'p' out of range, uncaught
    ++p;
    *p = a;      // ok
}
```

We might want to replace the pointer *p* with an object of a class *Ptr_to_T* that can be dereferenced only provided it actually points to an object. We would also like to ensure that *p* can be incremented and decremented, only provided it points to an object within an array and the increment and decrement operations yield an object within the array. That is we would like something like this:

```
class  Ptr_to_T {
    // ...
};

void f2 (T  a)          // checked
{
    T  v[200];
    Ptr_to_T  p (&v[0], v, 200);
    p--;
    *p = a;      // run-time error: 'p' out of range
    ++p;
    *p = a;      // ok
}
```

The increment and decrement operators are unique among C++ operators in that they can be used as both prefix and postfix operators. Consequently, we must define prefix and postfix increment and decrement *Ptr_to_T*. For example:

```
class Ptr_to_T {
    T* p;
    T* array;
    int size;
public:
    Ptr_to_T(T* p, T* v, int s);    // bind to array v of size s, initial value p
    Ptr_to_T(T* p);                 // bind to single object, initial value p

    Ptr_to_T& operator++();         // prefix
    Ptr_to_T operator++(int);       // postfix

    Ptr_to_T& operator--();         // prefix
    Ptr_to_T operator--(int);       // postfix

    T& operator*();       // prefix
};
```

The *int* argument is used to indicate that the function is to be invoked for postfix application of ++. This *int* is never used; the argument is simply a dummy used to distinguish between prefix and postfix application. The way to remember which version of an *operator++* is prefix is to note that the version without the dummy argument is prefix, exactly like all the other unary arithmetic and logical operators. The dummy argument is used only for the "odd" postfix ++ and --.

Using *Ptr_to_T*, the example is equivalent to:

```
void f3(T a)          // checked
{
    T v[200];
    Ptr_to_T p(&v[0], v, 200);
    p.operator--(0);
    p.operator*() = a;   // run-time error: 'p' out of range
    p.operator++();
    p.operator*() = a;   // ok
}
```

Completing class *Ptr_to_T* is left as an exercise (§11.14[19]). Its elaboration into a template using exceptions to report the run-time errors is another exercise (§14.12[2]). An example of operators ++ and -- for iteration can be found in §19.3. A pointer template that behaves correctly with respect to inheritance is presented in §13.6.3.

11.12 A String Class

Here is a more realistic version of class *String*. I designed it as the minimal string that served my needs. This string provides value semantics, character read and write operations, checked and unchecked access, stream I/O, literal strings as literals, and equality and concatenation operators. It represents strings as C-style, zero-terminated arrays of characters and uses reference counts to minimize copying. Writing a better string class and/or one that provides more facilities is a good exercise (§11.14[7-12]). That done, we can throw away our exercises and use the standard library string (Chapter 20).

My almost-real *String* employs three auxiliary classes: *Srep*, to allow an actual representation to be shared between several *String*s with the same value; *Range*, to be thrown in case of range errors, and *Cref*, to help implement a subscript operator that distinguishes between reading and writing:

```
class String {
      struct Srep;                    // representation
      Srep *rep;
public:
      class Cref;                     // reference to char

      class Range { };                // for exceptions

      // ...
};
```

Like other members, a *member class* (often called a *nested class*) can be declared in the class itself and defined later:

```
struct String::Srep {
      char* s;            // pointer to elements
      int sz;             // number of characters
      int n;              // reference count

      Srep(int nsz, const char* p)
      {
            n = 1;
            sz = nsz;
            s = new char[sz+1];  // add space for terminator
            strcpy(s,p);
      }

      ~Srep() { delete[] s; }

      Srep* get_own_copy()         // clone if necessary
      {
            if (n==1) return this;
            n--;
            return new Srep(sz,s);
      }

      void assign(int nsz, const char* p)
      {
            if (sz != nsz) {
                  delete[] s;
                  sz = nsz;
                  s = new char[sz+1];
            }
            strcpy(s,p);
      }
```

```
private:                    // prevent copying:
    Srep(const Srep&);
    Srep& operator=(const Srep&);
};
```

Class *String* provides the usual set of constructors, destructor, and assignment operations:

```
class String {
    // ...

    String();                  // x = ""
    String(const char*);       // x = "abc"
    String(const String&);     // x = other_string
    String& operator=(const char *);
    String& operator=(const String&);
    ~String();

    // ...
};
```

This *String* has value semantics. That is, after an assignment *s1=s2*, the two strings *s1* and *s2* are fully distinct and subsequent changes to the one have no effect on the other. The alternative would be to give *String* pointer semantics. That would be to let changes to *s2* after *s1=s2* also affect the value of *s1*. For types with conventional arithmetic operations, such as complex, vector, matrix, and string, I prefer value semantics. However, for the value semantics to be affordable, a *String* is implemented as a handle to its representation and the representation is copied only when necessary:

```
String::String()            // the empty string is the default value
{
    rep = new Srep(0,"");
}

String::String(const String& x) // copy constructor
{
    x.rep->n++;
    rep = x.rep;     // share representation
}

String::~String()
{
    if (--rep->n == 0) delete rep;
}

String& String::operator=(const String& x)       // copy assignment
{
    x.rep->n++;                        // protects against "st = st"
    if (--rep->n == 0) delete rep;
    rep = x.rep;                       // share representation
    return *this;
}
```

Pseudo-copy operations taking *const char* arguments are provided to allow string literals:

```
String::String (const char* s)
{
    rep = new Srep (strlen (s), s);
}

String& String::operator= (const char* s)
{
    if (rep->n == 1)                    // recycle Srep
        rep->assign (strlen (s), s);
    else {                              // use new Srep
        rep->n--;
        rep = new Srep (strlen (s), s);
    }
    return *this;
}
```

The design of access operators for a string is a difficult topic because ideally access is by conventional notation (that is, using [ ]), maximally efficient, and range checked. Unfortunately, you cannot have all of these properties simultaneously. My choice here has been to provide efficient unchecked operations with a slightly inconvenient notation plus slightly less efficient checked operators with the conventional notation:

```
class String {
    // ...
    void check (int i) const { if (i<0 || rep->sz<=i) throw Range (); }

    char read (int i) const { return rep->s [i]; }
    void write (int i, char c) { rep=rep->get_own_copy (); rep->s [i] =c; }

    Cref operator[] (int i) { check (i); return Cref (*this, i); }
    char operator[] (int i) const { check (i); return rep->s [i]; }

    int size () const { return rep->sz; }

    // ...
};
```

The idea is to use [ ] to get checked access for ordinary use, but to allow the user to optimize by checking the range once for a set of accesses. For example:

```
int hash (const String& s)
{
    int h = s.read (0);
    const int max = s.size ();
    for (int i = 1; i<max; i++) h ^= s.read (i) >>1; // unchecked access to s
    return h;
}
```

Defining an operator, such as [ ], to be used for both reading and writing is difficult where it is not acceptable simply to return a reference and let the user decide what to do with it. Here, that is not a reasonable alternative because I have defined *String* so that the representation is shared between *String*s that have been assigned, passed as value arguments, etc., until someone actually writes to a

String. Then, and only then, is the representation copied. This technique is usually called *copy-on-write*. The actual copy is done by *String*::*Srep*::*get_own_copy*().

To get these access functions inlined, their definitions must be placed so that the definition of *Srep* is in scope. This implies that either *Srep* is defined within *String* or the access functions are defined *inline* outside *String* and after *String*::*Srep* (§11.14[2]).

To distinguish between a read and a write, *String*::*operator*[]() returns a *Cref* when called for a non-*const* object. A *Cref* behaves like a *char&*, except that it calls *String*::*Srep*::*get_own_copy*() when written to:

```
class String::Cref {          // reference to s[i]
friend class String;
     String& s;
     int i;
     Cref(String& ss, int ii) : s(ss), i(ii) { }
public:
     operator char() const { return s.read(i); }       // yield value
     void operator=(char c) { s.write(i,c); }           // change value
};
```

For example:

```
void f(String s, const String& r)
{
     char c1 = s[1];          // c1 = s.operator[](1).operator char()
     s[1] = 'c';              // s.operator[](1).operator=('c')

     char c2 = r[1];          // c2 = r.operator[](1)
     r[1] = 'd';              // error: assignment to char, r.operator[](1) = 'd'
}
```

Note that for a non-*const* object *s*.*operator*[]*(1)* is *Cref(s,1)*.

To complete class *String*, I provide a set of useful functions:

```
class String {
     // ...

     String& operator+=(const String&);
     String& operator+=(const char*);

     friend ostream& operator<<(ostream&, const String&);
     friend istream& operator>>(istream&, String&);

     friend bool operator==(const String& x, const char* s)
          { return strcmp(x.rep->s, s) == 0; }

     friend bool operator==(const String& x, const String& y)
          { return strcmp(x.rep->s, y.rep->s) == 0; }

     friend bool operator!=(const String& x, const char* s)
          { return strcmp(x.rep->s, s) != 0; }
```

```
        friend bool operator!=(const String& x, const String& y)
            { return strcmp(x.rep->s, y.rep->s) !=0; }
};

String operator+(const String&, const String&);
String operator+(const String&, const char*);
```

To save space, I have left the I/O and concatenation operations as exercises.

The main program simply exercises the *String* operators a bit:

```
String f(String a, String b)
{
    a[2] = 'x';
    char c = b[3];
    cout << "in f: " << a << ' ' << b << ' ' << c << '\n';
    return b;
}

int main()
{
    String x, y;
    cout << "Please enter two strings\n";
    cin >> x >> y;
    cout << "input: " << x << ' ' << y << '\n';
    String z = x;
    y = f(x,y);
    if (x != z) cout << "x corrupted!\n";
    x[0] = '!';
    if (x == z) cout << "write failed!\n";
    cout << "exit: " << x << ' ' << y << ' ' << z << '\n';
}
```

This *String* lacks many features that you might consider important or even essential. For example, it offers no operation of producing a C-string representation of its value (§11.14[10], Chapter 20).

11.13 Advice

[1]   Define operators primarily to mimic conventional usage; §11.1.

[2]   For large operands, use *const* reference argument types; §11.6.

[3]   For large results, consider optimizing the return; §11.6.

[4]   Prefer the default copy operations if appropriate for a class; §11.3.4.

[5]   Redefine or prohibit copying if the default is not appropriate for a type; §11.2.2.

[6]   Prefer member functions over nonmembers for operations that need access to the representation; §11.5.2.

[7]   Prefer nonmember functions over members for operations that do not need access to the representation; §11.5.2.

[8]   Use namespaces to associate helper functions with "their" class; §11.2.4.

[9]   Use nonmember functions for symmetric operators; §11.3.2.

[10] Use () for subscripting multidimensional arrays; §11.9.

[11] Make constructors that take a single "size argument" *explicit*; §11.7.1.

[12] For non-specialized uses, prefer the standard *string* (Chapter 20) to the result of your own exercises; §11.12.

[13] Be cautious about introducing implicit conversions; §11.4.

[14] Use member functions to express operators that require an lvalue as its left-hand operand; §11.3.5.

11.14 Exercises

1. (∗2) In the following program, which conversions are used in each expression?

```
struct X {
      int i;
      X(int);
      X operator+(int);
};

struct Y {
      int i;
      Y(X);
      Y operator+(X);
      operator int();
};

extern X operator*(X, Y);
extern int f(X);

X x = 1;
Y y = x;
int i = 2;

int main()
{
      i + 10;      y + 10;      y + 10 * y;
      x + y + i;   x * x + i;   f(7);
      f(y);        y + y;       106 + y;
}
```

Modify the program so that it will run and print the values of each legal expression.

2. (∗2) Complete and test class *String* from §11.12.

3. (∗2) Define a class *INT* that behaves exactly like an *int*. Hint: Define *INT::operator int()*.

4. (∗1) Define a class *RINT* that behaves like an *int* except that the only operations allowed are + (unary and binary), – (unary and binary), ∗, /, and %. Hint: Do not define *RINT::operator int()*.

5. (∗3) Define a class *LINT* that behaves like a *RINT*, except that it has at least 64 bits of precision.

6. (∗4) Define a class implementing arbitrary precision arithmetic. Test it by calculating the factorial of *1000*. Hint: You will need to manage storage in a way similar to what was done for class *String*.

7. (∗2) Define an external iterator for class *String*:

```
class  String_iter {
        // refer to string and string element
public:
        String_iter(String& s);          // iterator for s
        char& next();                    // reference to next element

        // more operations of your choice
};
```

Compare this in utility, programming style, and efficiency to having an internal iterator for *String* (that is, a notion of a current element for the *String* and operations relating to that element).

8. (∗1.5) Provide a substring operator for a string class by overloading (). What other operations would you like to be able to do on a string?

9. (∗3) Design class *String* so that the substring operator can be used on the left-hand side of an assignment. First, write a version in which a string can be assigned to a substring of the same length. Then, write a version in which the lengths may differ.

10. (∗2) Define an operation for *String* that produces a C-string representation of its value. Discuss the pros and cons of having that operation as a conversion operator. Discuss alternatives for allocating the memory for that C-string representation.

11. (∗2.5) Define and implement a simple regular expression pattern match facility for class *String*.

12. (∗1.5) Modify the pattern match facility from §11.14[11] to work on the standard library *string*. Note that you cannot modify the definition of *string*.

13. (∗2) Write a program that has been rendered unreadable through use of operator overloading and macros. An idea: Define + to mean − and vice versa for *INT*s. Then, use a macro to define *int* to mean *INT*. Redefine popular functions using reference type arguments. Writing a few misleading comments can also create great confusion.

14. (∗3) Swap the result of §11.14[13] with a friend. Without running it, figure out what your friend's program does. When you have completed this exercise, you'll know what to avoid.

15. (∗2) Define a type *Vec4* as a vector of four *float*s. Define *operator*[] for *Vec4*. Define operators +, −, ∗, /, =, +=, −=, ∗=, and /= for combinations of vectors and floating-point numbers.

16. (∗3) Define a class *Mat4* as a vector of four *Vec4*s. Define *operator*[] to return a *Vec4* for *Mat4*. Define the usual matrix operations for this type. Define a function doing Gaussian elimination for a *Mat4*.

17. (∗2) Define a class *Vector* similar to *Vec4* but with the size given as an argument to the constructor *Vector::Vector(int)*.

18. (∗3) Define a class *Matrix* similar to *Mat4* but with the dimensions given as arguments to the constructor *Matrix::Matrix(int, int)*.

19. (∗2) Complete class *Ptr_to_T* from §11.11 and test it. To be complete, *Ptr_to_T* must have at least the operators ∗, −>, =, ++, and −− defined. Do not cause a run-time error until a wild pointer is actually dereferenced.

20. (∗1) Given two structures:

> *struct S { int x, y; } ;*
> *struct T { char* p; char* q; } ;*

write a class *C* that allows the use of *x* and *p* from some *S* and *T*, much as if *x* and *p* had been members of *C*.

21. (∗1.5) Define a class *Index* to hold the index for an exponentiation function *mypow* (*double* , *Index*) . Find a way to have *2**I* call *mypow* (*2* , *I*) .

22. (∗2) Define a class *Imaginary* to represent imaginary numbers. Define class *Complex* based on that. Implement the fundamental arithmetic operators.

12

Derived Classes

Do not multiply objects without necessity.
– W. Occam

Concepts and classes — derived classes — member functions — construction and destruction — class hierarchies — type fields — virtual functions — abstract classes — traditional class hierarchies — abstract classes as interfaces — localizing object creation — abstract classes and class hierarchies — advice — exercises.

12.1 Introduction

From Simula, C++ borrowed the concept of a class as a user-defined type and the concept of class hierarchies. In addition, it borrowed the idea for system design that classes should be used to model concepts in the programmer's and the application's world. C++ provides language constructs that directly support these design notions. Conversely, using the language features in support of design concepts distinguishes effective use of C++. Using language constructs only as notational props for more traditional types of programming is to miss key strengths of C++.

A concept does not exist in isolation. It coexists with related concepts and derives much of its power from relationships with related concepts. For example, try to explain what a car is. Soon you'll have introduced the notions of wheels, engines, drivers, pedestrians, trucks, ambulances, roads, oil, speeding tickets, motels, etc. Since we use classes to represent concepts, the issue becomes how to represent relationships between concepts. However, we can't express arbitrary relationships directly in a programming language. Even if we could, we wouldn't want to. Our classes should be more narrowly defined than our everyday concepts – and more precise. The notion of a derived class and its associated language mechanisms are provided to express hierarchical relationships, that is, to express commonality between classes. For example, the concepts of a circle and a triangle are related in that they are both shapes; that is, they have the concept of a shape in common. Thus, we must explicitly define class *Circle* and class *Triangle* to have class *Shape* in common. Representing a circle and a triangle in a program without involving the notion of a shape would be to lose something essential. This chapter is an exploration of the implications of this simple idea, which is the basis for what is commonly called object-oriented programming.

The presentation of language features and techniques progress from the simple and concrete to the more sophisticated and abstract. For many programmers, this will also be a progression from the familiar towards the less well known. This is not a simple journey from ''bad old techniques'' towards ''the one right way.'' When I point out limitations of one technique as a motivation for another, I do so in the context of specific problems; for different problems or in other contexts, the first technique may indeed be the better choice. Useful software has been constructed using all of the techniques presented here. The aim is to help you attain sufficient understanding of the techniques to be able to make intelligent and balanced choices among them for real problems.

In this chapter, I first introduce the basic language features supporting object-oriented programming. Next, the use of those features to develop well-structured programs is discussed in the context of a larger example. Further facilities supporting object-oriented programming, such as multiple inheritance and run-time type identification, are discussed in Chapter 15.

12.2 Derived Classes

Consider building a program dealing with people employed by a firm. Such a program might have a data structure like this:

```
struct Employee {
    string first_name, family_name;
    char middle_initial;
    Date hiring_date;
    short department;
    // ...
};
```

Next, we might try to define a manager:

```
struct Manager {
    Employee emp;             // manager's employee record
    list<Employee*> group;    // people managed
    short level;
    // ...
};
```

A manager is also an employee; the *Employee* data is stored in the *emp* member of a *Manager* object. This may be obvious to a human reader – especially a careful reader – but there is nothing that tells the compiler and other tools that *Manager* is also an *Employee*. A *Manager** is not an *Employee**, so one cannot simply use one where the other is required. In particular, one cannot put a *Manager* onto a list of *Employee*s without writing special code. We could either use explicit type conversion on a *Manager** or put the address of the *emp* member onto a list of *employee*s. However, both solutions are inelegant and can be quite obscure. The correct approach is to explicitly state that a *Manager* is an *Employee*, with a few pieces of information added:

```
struct Manager : public Employee {
    list<Employee*> group;
    short level;
    // ...
};
```

The *Manager* is *derived* from *Employee*, and conversely, *Employee* is a *base class* for *Manager*.
The class *Manager* has the members of class *Employee* (*first_name*, *department*, etc.) in addition
to its own members (*group*, *level*, etc.).

Derivation is often represented graphically by a pointer from the derived class to its base class
indicating that the derived class refers to its base (rather than the other way around):

Employee

Manager

A derived class is often said to inherit properties from its base, so the relationship is also called
inheritance. A base class is sometimes called a *superclass* and a derived class a *subclass*. This terminology, however, is confusing to people who observe that the data in a derived class object is a
superset of the data of an object of its base class. A derived class is larger than its base class in the
sense that it holds more data and provides more functions.

A popular and efficient implementation of the notion of derived classes has an object of the
derived class represented as an object of the base class, with the information belonging specifically
to the derived class added at the end. For example:

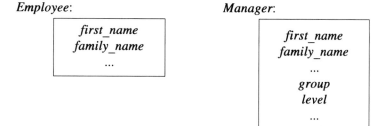

Deriving *Manager* from *Employee* in this way makes *Manager* a subtype of *Employee* so that a
Manager can be used wherever an *Employee* is acceptable. For example, we can now create a list
of *Employee*s, some of whom are *Manager*s:

```
void f(Manager m1, Employee e1)
{
    list<Employee*> elist;

    elist.push_front(&m1);
    elist.push_front(&e1);
    // ...
}
```

A *Manager* is (also) an *Employee*, so a *Manager** can be used as an *Employee**. However, an *Employee* is not necessarily a *Manager*, so an *Employee** cannot be used as a *Manager**. In general, if a class *Derived* has a public base class (§15.3) *Base*, then a *Derived** can be assigned to a variable of type *Base** without the use of explicit type conversion. The opposite conversion, from *Base** to *Derived**, must be explicit. For example:

```
void g (Manager mm, Employee ee)
{
    Employee* pe = &mm;          // ok: every Manager is an Employee
    Manager* pm = &ee;           // error: not every Employee is a Manager

    pm->level = 2;               // disaster: ee doesn't have a 'level'

    pm = static_cast<Manager*>(pe);     // brute force: works because pe points
                                        // to the Manager mm

    pm->level = 2;               // fine: pm points to the Manager mm that has a 'level'
}
```

In other words, an object of a derived class can be treated as an object of its base class when manipulated through pointers and references. The opposite is not true. The use of *static_cast* and *dynamic_cast* is discussed in §15.4.2.

Using a class as a base is equivalent to declaring an (unnamed) object of that class. Consequently, a class must be defined in order to be used as a base (§5.7):

```
class Employee;          // declaration only, no definition

class Manager : public Employee {    // error: Employee not defined
    // ...
};
```

12.2.1 Member Functions

Simple data structures, such as *Employee* and *Manager*, are really not that interesting and often not particularly useful. We need to give the information as a proper type that provides a suitable set of operations that present the concept, and we need to do this without tying us to the details of a particular representation. For example:

```
class Employee {
    string first_name, family_name;
    char middle_initial;
    // ...
public:
    void print() const;
    string full_name() const
        { return first_name + ' ' + middle_initial + ' ' + family_name; }
    // ...
};
```

```
class Manager : public Employee {
    // ...
public:
    void print() const;
    // ...
};
```

A member of a derived class can use the public − and protected (see §15.3) − members of its base class as if they were declared in the derived class itself. For example:

```
void Manager::print() const
{
    cout << "name is " << full_name() << '\n';
    // ...
}
```

However, a derived class cannot use a base class' private names:

```
void Manager::print() const
{
    cout << " name is " << family_name << '\n';    // error!
    // ...
}
```

This second version of *Manager*::*print*() will not compile. A member of a derived class has no special permission to access private members of its base class, so *family_name* is not accessible to *Manager*::*print*().

This comes as a surprise to some, but consider the alternative: that a member function of a derived class could access the private members of its base class. The concept of a private member would be rendered meaningless by allowing a programmer to gain access to the private part of a class simply by deriving a new class from it. Furthermore, one could no longer find all uses of a private name by looking at the functions declared as members and friends of that class. One would have to examine every source file of the complete program for derived classes, then examine every function of those classes, then find every class derived from those classes, etc. This is, at best, tedious and often impractical. Where it is acceptable, *protected* − rather than *private* − members can be used. A protected member is like a public member to a member of a derived class, yet it is like a private member to other functions (see §15.3).

Typically, the cleanest solution is for the derived class to use only the public members of its base class. For example:

```
void Manager::print() const
{
    Employee::print();    // print Employee information

    cout << level;        // print Manager-specific information
    // ...
}
```

Note that :: must be used because *print*() has been redefined in *Manager*. Such reuse of names is typical. The unwary might write this:

```
void  Manager::print() const
{
    print();    // oops!

    // print Manager-specific information
}
```

and find the program involved in an unexpected sequence of recursive calls.

12.2.2 Constructors and Destructors

Some derived classes need constructors. If a base class has constructors, then a constructor must be invoked. Default constructors can be invoked implicitly. However, if all constructors for a base require arguments, then a constructor for that base must be explicitly called. Consider:

```
class  Employee {
    string  first_name, family_name;
    short  department;
    // ...
public:
    Employee(const  string& n, int  d);
    // ...
};

class  Manager : public  Employee {
    list<Employee*> group;    // people managed
    short  level;
    // ...
public:
    Manager(const  string& n, int  d, int  lvl);
    // ...
};
```

Arguments for the base class' constructor are specified in the definition of a derived class' constructor. In this respect, the base class acts exactly like a member of the derived class (§10.4.6). For example:

```
Employee::Employee(const  string& n, int  d)
    : family_name(n), department(d)           // initialize members
{
    // ...
}

Manager::Manager(const  string& n, int  d, int  lvl)
    : Employee(n,d),         // initialize base
      level(lvl)             // initialize members
{
    // ...
}
```

A derived class constructor can specify initializers for its own members and immediate bases only; it cannot directly initialize members of a base. For example:

```
Manager::Manager(const string& n, int d, int lvl)
    : family_name(n),      // error: family_name not declared in manager
      department(d),       // error: department not declared in manager
      level(lvl)
{
    // ...
}
```

This definition contains three errors: it fails to invoke *Employee*'s constructor, and twice it attempts to initialize members of *Employee* directly.

Class objects are constructed from the bottom up: first the base, then the members, and then the derived class itself. They are destroyed in the opposite order: first the derived class itself, then the members, and then the base. Members and bases are constructed in order of declaration in the class and destroyed in the reverse order. See also §10.4.6 and §15.2.4.1.

12.2.3 Copying

Copying of class objects is defined by the copy constructor and assignments (§10.4.4.1). Consider:

```
class Employee {
    // ...
    Employee& operator=(const Employee&);
    Employee(const Employee&);
};

void f(const Manager& m)
{
    Employee e = m;     // construct e from Employee part of m
    e = m;              // assign Employee part of m to e
}
```

Because the *Employee* copy functions do not know anything about *Manager*s, only the *Employee* part of a *Manager* is copied. This is commonly referred to as *slicing* and can be a source of surprises and errors. One reason to pass pointers and references to objects of classes in a hierarchy is to avoid slicing. Other reasons are to preserve polymorphic behavior (§2.5.4, §12.2.6) and to gain efficiency.

Note that if you don't define a copy assignment operator, the compiler will generate one (§11.7). This implies that assignment operators are not inherited. Constructors are never inherited.

12.2.4 Class Hierarchies

A derived class can itself be a base class. For example:

```
class Employee { /* ... */ };
class Manager : public Employee { /* ... */ };
class Director : public Manager { /* ... */ };
```

Such a set of related classes is traditionally called a *class hierarchy*. Such a hierarchy is most often a tree, but it can also be a more general graph structure. For example:

```
class Temporary { /* ... */ };
class Secretary : public Employee { /* ... */ };
class Tsec : public Temporary, public Secretary { /* ... */ };
class Consultant : public Temporary, public Manager { /* ... */ };
```

Or graphically:

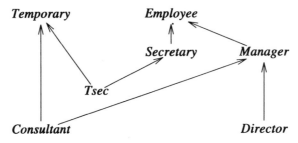

Thus, as is explained in detail in §15.2, C++ can express a directed acyclic graph of classes.

12.2.5 Type Fields

To use derived classes as more than a convenient shorthand in declarations, we must solve the following problem: Given a pointer of type *Base**, to which derived type does the object pointed to really belong? There are four fundamental solutions to the problem:

[1]   Ensure that only objects of a single type are pointed to (§2.7, Chapter 13).
[2]   Place a type field in the base class for the functions to inspect.
[3]   Use *dynamic_cast* (§15.4.2, §15.4.5).
[4]   Use virtual functions (§2.5.5, §12.2.6).

Pointers to base classes are commonly used in the design of *container classes* such as set, vector, and list. In this case, solution 1 yields homogeneous lists, that is, lists of objects of the same type. Solutions 2, 3, and 4 can be used to build heterogeneous lists, that is, lists of (pointers to) objects of several different types. Solution 3 is a language-supported variant of solution 2. Solution 4 is a special type-safe variation of solution 2. Combinations of solutions 1 and 4 are particularly interesting and powerful; in almost all situations, they yield cleaner code than do solutions 2 and 3.

Let us first examine the simple type-field solution to see why it is most often best avoided. The manager/employee example could be redefined like this:

```
struct Employee {
    enum Empl_type { M, E };
    Empl_type type;

    Employee() : type(E) { }

    string first_name, family_name;
    char middle_initial;

    Date hiring_date;
    short department;
    // ...
};
```

```
struct Manager : public Employee {
    Manager() { type = M; }
    list<Employee*> group;     // people managed
    short level;
    // ...
};
```

Given this, we can now write a function that prints information about each *Employee*:

```
void print_employee(const Employee* e)
{
    switch (e->type) {
    case Employee::E:
        cout << e->family_name << '\t' << e->department << '\n';
        // ...
        break;
    case Employee::M:
    {   cout << e->family_name << '\t' << e->department << '\n';
        // ...
        const Manager* p = static_cast<const Manager*>(e);
        cout << " level " << p->level << '\n';
        // ...
        break;
    }
    }
}
```

and use it to print a list of *Employee*s, like this:

```
void print_list(const list<Employee*>& elist)
{
    for (list<Employee*>::const_iterator p = elist.begin(); p!=elist.end(); ++p)
        print_employee(*p);
}
```

This works fine, especially in a small program maintained by a single person. However, it has the fundamental weakness in that it depends on the programmer manipulating types in a way that cannot be checked by the compiler. This problem is usually made worse because functions such as *print_employee*() are organized to take advantage of the commonality of the classes involved:

```
void print_employee(const Employee* e)
{
    cout << e->family_name << '\t' << e->department << '\n';
    // ...
    if (e->type == Employee::M) {
        const Manager* p = static_cast<const Manager*>(e);
        cout << " level " << p->level << '\n';
        // ...
    }
}
```

Finding all such tests on the type field buried in a large function that handles many derived classes can be difficult. Even when they have been found, understanding what is going on can be difficult. Furthermore, any addition of a new kind of *Employee* involves a change to all the key functions in the system − the ones containing the tests on the type field. The programmer must consider every function that could conceivably need a test on the type field after a change. This implies the need to access critical source code and the resulting necessary overhead of testing the affected code. The use of an explicit type conversion is a strong hint that improvement is possible.

In other words, use of a type field is an error-prone technique that leads to maintenance problems. The problems increase in severity as the size of the program increases because the use of a type field causes a violation of the ideals of modularity and data hiding. Each function using a type field must know about the representation and other details of the implementation of every class derived from the one containing the type field.

It also seems that the existence of any common data accessible from every derived class, such as a type field, tempts people to add more such data. The common base thus becomes the repository of all kinds of "useful information." This, in turn, gets the implementation of the base and derived classes intertwined in ways that are most undesirable. For clean design and simpler maintenance, we want to keep separate issues separate and avoid mutual dependencies.

12.2.6 Virtual Functions

Virtual functions overcome the problems with the type-field solution by allowing the programmer to declare functions in a base class that can be redefined in each derived class. The compiler and loader will guarantee the correct correspondence between objects and the functions applied to them. For example:

```
class Employee {
      string first_name, family_name;
      short department;
      // ...
public:
      Employee(const string& name, int dept);
      virtual void print() const;
      // ...
};
```

The keyword *virtual* indicates that *print*() can act as an interface to the *print*() function defined in this class and the *print*() functions defined in classes derived from it. Where such *print*() functions are defined in derived classes, the compiler ensures that the right *print*() for the given *Employee* object is invoked in each case.

To allow a virtual function declaration to act as an interface to functions defined in derived classes, the argument types specified for a function in a derived class cannot differ from the argument types declared in the base, and only very slight changes are allowed for the return type (§15.6.2). A virtual member function is sometimes called a *method*.

A virtual function *must* be defined for the class in which it is first declared (unless it is declared to be a pure virtual function; see §12.3). For example:

```
void Employee::print() const
{
    cout << family_name << '\t' << department << '\n';
    // ...
}
```

A virtual function can be used even if no class is derived from its class, and a derived class that does not need its own version of a virtual function need not provide one. When deriving a class, simply provide an appropriate function, if it is needed. For example:

```
class Manager : public Employee {
    list<Employee*> group;
    short level;
    // ...
public:
    Manager(const string& name, int dept, int lvl);
    void print() const;
    // ...
};

void Manager::print() const
{
    Employee::print();
    cout << "\tlevel " << level << '\n';
    // ...
}
```

A function from a derived class with the same name and the same set of argument types as a virtual function in a base is said to *override* the base class version of the virtual function. Except where we explicitly say which version of a virtual function is called (as in the call *Employee::print()*), the overriding function is chosen as the most appropriate for the object for which it is called.

The global function *print_employee()* (§12.2.5) is now unnecessary because the *print()* member functions have taken its place. A list of *Employee*s can be printed like this:

```
void print_list(const list<Employee*>& s)
{
    for (list<Employee*>::const_iterator p = s.begin(); p!=s.end(); ++p)   // see §2.7.2
        (*p)->print();
}
```

or even

```
void print_list(const list<Employee*>& s)
{
    for_each(s.begin(),s.end(),mem_fun(&Employee::print));   // see §3.8.5
}
```

Each *Employee* will be written out according to its type. For example:

```
int main()
{
    Employee e("Brown",1234);
    Manager m("Smith",1234,2);
    list<Employee*> empl;
    empl.push_front(&e);       // see §2.5.4
    empl.push_front(&m);
    print_list(empl);
}
```

produced:

```
Smith  1234
      level  2
Brown  1234
```

Note that this will work even if *print_list*() was written and compiled before the specific derived class *Manager* was even conceived of! This is a key aspect of classes. When used properly, it becomes the cornerstone of object-oriented designs and provides a degree of stability to an evolving program.

Getting ''the right'' behavior from *Employee*'s functions independently of exactly what kind of *Employee* is actually used is called *polymorphism*. A type with virtual functions is called a *polymorphic type*. To get polymorphic behavior in C++, the member functions called must be *virtual* and objects must be manipulated through pointers or references. When manipulating an object directly (rather than through a pointer or reference), its exact type is known by the compiler so that run-time polymorphism is not needed.

Clearly, to implement polymorphism, the compiler must store some kind of type information in each object of class *Employee* and use it to call the right version of the virtual function *print*(). In a typical implementation, the space taken is just enough to hold a pointer (§2.5.5). This space is taken only in objects of a class with virtual functions – not in every object, or even in every object of a derived class. You pay this overhead only for classes for which you declare virtual functions. Had you chosen to use the alternative type-field solution, a comparable amount of space would have been needed for the type field.

Calling a function using the scope resolution operator :: as is done in *Manager::print*() ensures that the virtual mechanism is not used. Otherwise, *Manager::print*() would suffer an infinite recursion. The use of a qualified name has another desirable effect. That is, if a *virtual* function is also *inline* (as is not uncommon), then inline substitution can be used for calls specified using ::. This provides the programmer with an efficient way to handle some important special cases in which one virtual function calls another for the same object. The *Manager::print*() function is an example of this. Because the type of the object is determined in the call of *Manager::print*(), it need not be dynamically determined again for the resulting call of *Employee::print*().

It is worth remembering that the traditional and obvious implementation of a virtual function call is simply an indirect function call (§2.5.5), so efficiency concerns should not deter anyone from using a virtual function where an ordinary function call would be acceptably efficient.

12.3 Abstract Classes

Many classes resemble class *Employee* in that they are useful both as themselves and also as bases for derived classes. For such classes, the techniques described in the previous section suffice. However, not all classes follow that pattern. Some classes, such as class *Shape*, represent abstract concepts for which objects cannot exist. A *Shape* makes sense only as the base of some class derived from it. This can be seen from the fact that it is not possible to provide sensible definitions for its virtual functions:

```
class Shape {
public:
    virtual void rotate(int) { error("Shape::rotate"); } // inelegant
    virtual void draw() { error("Shape::draw"); }
    // ...
};
```

Trying to make a shape of this unspecified kind is silly but legal:

```
Shape s;  // silly: "shapeless shape"
```

It is silly because every operation on *s* will result in an error.

A better alternative is to declare the virtual functions of class *Shape* to be *pure virtual functions*. A virtual function is "made pure" by the initializer = *0*:

```
class Shape {           // abstract class
public:
    virtual void rotate(int) = 0;     // pure virtual function
    virtual void draw() = 0;          // pure virtual function
    virtual bool is_closed() = 0;     // pure virtual function
    // ...
};
```

A class with one or more pure virtual functions is an *abstract class*, and no objects of that abstract class can be created:

```
Shape s;  // error: variable of abstract class Shape
```

An abstract class can be used only as an interface and as a base for other classes. For example:

```
class Point { /* ... */ };

class Circle : public Shape {
public:
    void rotate(int) { }              // override Shape::rotate
    void draw();                      // override Shape::draw
    bool is_closed() { return true; } // override Shape::is_closed

    Circle(Point p, int r);
private:
    Point center;
    int radius;
};
```

A pure virtual function that is not defined in a derived class remains a pure virtual function, so the derived class is also an abstract class. This allows us to build implementations in stages:

```
class Polygon : public Shape {              // abstract class
public:
        bool is_closed() { return true; }       // override Shape::is_closed
        // ... draw and rotate not overridden ...
};

Polygon b;        // error: declaration of object of abstract class Polygon

class Irregular_polygon : public Polygon {
        list<Point> lp;
public:
        void draw();                            // override Shape::draw
        void rotate(int);                       // override Shape::rotate
        // ...
};

Irregular_polygon poly(some_points);        // fine (assume suitable constructor)
```

An important use of abstract classes is to provide an interface without exposing any implementation details. For example, an operating system might hide the details of its device drivers behind an abstract class:

```
class Character_device {
public:
        virtual int open(int opt) = 0;
        virtual int close(int opt) = 0;
        virtual int read(char* p, int n) = 0;
        virtual int write(const char* p, int n) = 0;
        virtual int ioctl(int ...) = 0;
        virtual ~Character_device() { }         // virtual destructor
};
```

We can then specify drivers as classes derived from *Character_device*, and manipulate a variety of drivers through that interface. The importance of virtual destructors is explained in §12.4.2.

With the introduction of abstract classes, we have the basic facilities for writing a complete program in a modular fashion using classes as building blocks.

12.4 Design of Class Hierarchies

Consider a simple design problem: provide a way for a program to get an integer value from a user interface. This can be done in a bewildering number of ways. To insulate our program from this variety, and also to get a chance to explore the possible design choices, let us start by defining our program's model of this simple input operation. We will leave until later the details of implementing it using a real user-interface system.

The idea is to have a class *Ival_box* that knows what range of input values it will accept. A program can ask an *Ival_box* for its value and ask it to prompt the user if necessary. In addition, a program can ask an *Ival_box* if a user changed the value since the program last looked at it.

Because there are many ways of implementing this basic idea, we must assume that there will be many different kinds of *Ival_box*es, such as sliders, plain boxes in which a user can type a number, dials, and voice interaction.

The general approach is to build a "virtual user-interface system" for the application to use. This system provides some of the services provided by existing user-interface systems. It can be implemented on a wide variety of systems to ensure the portability of application code. Naturally, there are other ways of insulating an application from a user-interface system. I chose this approach because it is general, because it allows me to demonstrate a variety of techniques and design tradeoffs, because those techniques are also the ones used to build "real" user-interface systems, and – most important – because these techniques are applicable to problems far beyond the narrow domain of interface systems.

12.4.1 A Traditional Class Hierarchy

Our first solution is a traditional class hierarchy as is commonly found in Simula, Smalltalk, and older C++ programs.

Class *Ival_box* defines the basic interface to all *Ival_box*es and specifies a default implementation that more specific kinds of *Ival_box*es can override with their own versions. In addition, we declare the data needed to implement the basic notion:

```
class Ival_box {
protected:
    int val;
    int low, high;
    bool changed;  // changed by user using set_value()
public:
    Ival_box(int ll, int hh) { changed = false; val = low = ll; high = hh; }

    virtual int get_value() { changed = false; return val; }
    virtual void set_value(int i) { changed = true; val = i; }        // for user
    virtual void reset_value(int i) { changed = false; val = i; }     // for application
    virtual void prompt() { }
    virtual bool was_changed() const { return changed; }
};
```

The default implementation of the functions is pretty sloppy and is provided here primarily to illustrate the intended semantics. A realistic class would, for example, provide some range checking.

A programmer might use these "*ival* classes" like this:

```
void interact(Ival_box* pb)
{
    pb->prompt(); // alert user
    // ...
    int i = pb->get_value();
    if (pb->was_changed()) {
        // new value; do something
    }
```

```
        else {
                // old value was fine; do something else
        }
        // ...
}

void some_fct()
{
        Ival_box* p1 = new Ival_slider(0, 5);          // Ival_slider derived from Ival_box
        interact(p1);

        Ival_box* p2 = new Ival_dial(1, 12);
        interact(p2);
}
```

Most application code is written in terms of (pointers to) plain *Ival_box*es the way *interact*() is. That way, the application doesn't have to know about the potentially large number of variants of the *Ival_box* concept. The knowledge of such specialized classes is isolated in the relatively few functions that create such objects. This isolates users from changes in the implementations of the derived classes. Most code can be oblivious to the fact that there are different kinds of *Ival_box*es.

To simplify the discussion, I do not address issues of how a program waits for input. Maybe the program really does wait for the user in *get_value*(), maybe the program associates the *Ival_box* with an event and prepares to respond to a callback, or maybe the program spawns a thread for the *Ival_box* and later inquires about the state of that thread. Such decisions are crucial in the design of user-interface systems. However, discussing them here in any realistic detail would simply distract from the presentation of programming techniques and language facilities. The design techniques described here and the language facilities that support them are not specific to user interfaces. They apply to a far greater range of problems.

The different kinds of *Ival_box*es are defined as classes derived from *Ival_box*. For example:

```
class Ival_slider : public Ival_box {
        // graphics stuff to define what the slider looks like, etc.
public:
        Ival_slider(int, int);

        int get_value();
        void prompt();
};
```

The data members of *Ival_box* were declared *protected* to allow access from derived classes. Thus, *Ival_slider*::*get_value*() can deposit a value in *Ival_box*::*val*. A *protected* member is accessible from a class' own members and from members of derived classes, but not to general users (see §15.3).

In addition to *Ival_slider*, we would define other variants of the *Ival_box* concept. These could include *Ival_dial*, which lets you select a value by turning a knob; *Flashing_ival_slider*, which flashes when you ask it to *prompt*(); and *Popup_ival_slider*, which responds to *prompt*() by appearing in some prominent place, thus making it hard for the user to ignore.

From where would we get the graphics stuff? Most user-interface systems provide a class defining the basic properties of being an entity on the screen. So, if we use the system from "Big

Bucks Inc.,'' we would have to make each of our *Ival_slider*, *Ival_dial*, etc., classes a kind of *BBwindow*. This would most simply be achieved by rewriting our *Ival_box* so that it derives from *BBwindow*. In that way, all our classes inherit all the properties of a *BBwindow*. For example, every *Ival_box* can be placed on the screen, obey the graphical style rules, be resized, be dragged around, etc., according to the standard set by the *BBwindow* system. Our class hierarchy would look like this:

```
class Ival_box : public BBwindow { / * ... * / }; // rewritten to use BBwindow
class Ival_slider : public Ival_box { / * ... * / };
class Ival_dial : public Ival_box { / * ... * / };
class Flashing_ival_slider : public Ival_slider { / * ... * / };
class Popup_ival_slider : public Ival_slider { / * ... * / };
```

or graphically:

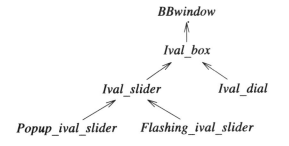

12.4.1.1 Critique

This design works well in many ways, and for many problems this kind of hierarchy is a good solution. However, there are some awkward details that could lead us to look for alternative designs.

We retrofitted *BBwindow* as the base of *Ival_box*. This is not quite right. The use of *BBwindow* isn't part of our basic notion of an *Ival_box*; it is an implementation detail. Deriving *Ival_box* from *BBwindow* elevated an implementation detail to a first-level design decision. That can be right. For example, using the environment defined by ''Big Bucks Inc.'' may be a key decision of how our organization conducts its business. However, what if we also wanted to have implementations of our *Ival_box*es for systems from ''Imperial Bananas,'' ''Liberated Software,'' and ''Compiler Whizzes?'' We would have to maintain four distinct versions of our program:

```
class Ival_box : public BBwindow { / * ... * / };     // BB version
class Ival_box : public CWwindow { / * ... * / };     // CW version
class Ival_box : public IBwindow { / * ... * / };     // IB version
class Ival_box : public LSwindow { / * ... * / };     // LS version
```

Having many versions could result in a version-control nightmare.

Another problem is that every derived class shares the basic data declared in *Ival_box*. That data is, of course, an implementation detail that also crept into our *Ival_box* interface. From a practical point of view, it is also the wrong data in many cases. For example, an *Ival_slider* doesn't need the value stored specifically. It can easily be calculated from the position of the slider when someone executes *get_value* ( ). In general, keeping two related, but different, sets of data is asking for trouble. Sooner or later someone will get them out of sync. Also, experience shows that novice programmers tend to mess with protected data in ways that are unnecessary and that cause maintenance problems. Data members are better kept private so that writers of derived classes cannot mess with them. Better still, data should be in the derived classes, where it can be defined to match requirements exactly and cannot complicate the life of unrelated derived classes. In almost all cases, a protected interface should contain only functions, types, and constants.

Deriving from *BBwindow* gives the benefit of making the facilities provided by *BBwindow* available to users of *Ival_box*. Unfortunately, it also means that changes to class *BBwindow* may force users to recompile or even rewrite their code to recover from such changes. In particular, the way most C++ implementations work implies that a change in the size of a base class requires a recompilation of all derived classes.

Finally, our program may have to run in a mixed environment in which windows of different user-interface systems coexist. This could happen either because two systems somehow share a screen or because our program needs to communicate with users on different systems. Having our user-interface systems ''wired in'' as the one and only base of our one and only *Ival_box* interface just isn't flexible enough to handle those situations.

12.4.2 Abstract Classes

So, let's start again and build a new class hierarchy that solves the problems presented in the critique of the traditional hierarchy:

[1] The user-interface system should be an implementation detail that is hidden from users who don't want to know about it.

[2] The *Ival_box* class should contain no data.

[3] No recompilation of code using the *Ival_box* family of classes should be required after a change of the user-interface system.

[4] *Ival_box*es for different interface systems should be able to coexist in our program.

Several alternative approaches can be taken to achieve this. Here, I present one that maps cleanly into the C++ language.

First, I specify class *Ival_box* as a pure interface:

```
class Ival_box {
public:
    virtual int get_value() = 0;
    virtual void set_value(int i) = 0;
    virtual void reset_value(int i) = 0;
    virtual void prompt() = 0;
    virtual bool was_changed() const = 0;
    virtual ~Ival_box() { }
};
```

This is much cleaner than the original declaration of *Ival_box*. The data is gone and so are the simplistic implementations of the member functions. Gone, too, is the constructor, since there is no data for it to initialize. Instead, I added a virtual destructor to ensure proper cleanup of the data that will be defined in the derived classes.

The definition of *Ival_slider* might look like this:

```
class Ival_slider : public Ival_box, protected BBwindow {
public:
     Ival_slider(int, int);
     ~Ival_slider();

     int get_value();
     void set_value(int i);
     // ...
protected:
     // functions overriding BBwindow virtual functions
     // e.g. BBwindow::draw(), BBwindow::mouse1hit()
private:
     // data needed for slider
};
```

The derived class *Ival_slider* inherits from an abstract class (*Ival_box*) that requires it to implement the base class' pure virtual functions. It also inherits from *BBwindow* that provides it with the means of doing so. Since *Ival_box* provides the interface for the derived class, it is derived using *public*. Since *BBwindow* is only an implementation aid, it is derived using *protected* (§15.3.2). This implies that a programmer using *Ival_slider* cannot directly use facilities defined by *BBwindow*. The interface provided by *Ival_slider* is the one inherited from *Ival_box*, plus what *Ival_slider* explicitly declares. I used *protected* derivation instead of the more restrictive (and usually safer) *private* derivation to make *BBwindow* available to classes derived from *Ival_slider*.

Deriving directly from more than one class is usually called *multiple inheritance* (§15.2). Note that *Ival_slider* must override functions from both *Ival_box* and *BBwindow*. Therefore, it must be derived directly or indirectly from both. As shown in §12.4.1.1, deriving *Ival_slider* indirectly from *BBwindow* by making *BBwindow* a base of *Ival_box* is possible, but doing so has undesirable side effects. Similarly, making the "implementation class" *BBwindow* a member of *Ival_box* is not a solution because a class cannot override virtual functions of its members (§24.3.4). Representing the window by a *BBwindow** member in *Ival_box* leads to a completely different design with a separate set of tradeoffs (§12.7[14], §25.7).

Interestingly, this declaration of *Ival_slider* allows application code to be written exactly as before. All we have done is to restructure the implementation details in a more logical way.

Many classes require some form of cleanup for an object before it goes away. Since the abstract class *Ival_box* cannot know if a derived class requires such cleanup, it must assume that it does require some. We ensure proper cleanup by defining a virtual destructor *Ival_box::~Ival_box()* in the base and overriding it suitably in derived classes. For example:

```
void f(Ival_box* p)
{
     // ...
     delete p;
}
```

The *delete* operator explicitly destroys the object pointed to by *p*. We have no way of knowing exactly to which class the object pointed to by *p* belongs, but thanks to *Ival_box*'s virtual destructor, proper cleanup as (optionally) defined by that class' destructor will be called.

The *Ival_box* hierarchy can now be defined like this:

```
class  Ival_box { / * ... * / } ;
class  Ival_slider : public Ival_box, protected BBwindow { / * ... * / } ;
class  Ival_dial : public Ival_box, protected BBwindow { / * ... * / } ;
class  Flashing_ival_slider : public Ival_slider { / * ... * / } ;
class  Popup_ival_slider : public Ival_slider { / * ... * / } ;
```

or graphically using obvious abbreviations:

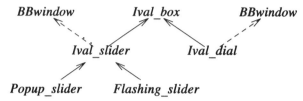

I used a dashed line to represent protected inheritance. As far as general users are concerned, doing that is simply an implementation detail.

12.4.3 Alternative Implementations

This design is cleaner and more easily maintainable than the traditional one − and no less efficient. However, it still fails to solve the version control problem:

```
class  Ival_box { / * ... * / } ;       // common
class  Ival_slider : public Ival_box, protected BBwindow { / * ... * / } ; // for BB
class  Ival_slider : public Ival_box, protected CWwindow { / * ... * / } ; // for CW
// ...
```

In addition, there is no way of having an *Ival_slider* for *BBwindow*s coexist with an *Ival_slider* for *CWwindow*s, even if the two user-interface systems could themselves coexist.

   The obvious solution is to define several different *Ival_slider* classes with separate names:

```
class  Ival_box { / * ... * / } ;
class  BB_ival_slider : public Ival_box, protected BBwindow { / * ... * / } ;
class  CW_ival_slider : public Ival_box, protected CWwindow { / * ... * / } ;
// ...
```

or graphically:

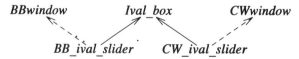

To further insulate our application-oriented *Ival_box* classes from implementation details, we can derive an abstract *Ival_slider* class from *Ival_box* and then derive the system-specific *Ival_sliders* from that:

```
class  Ival_box { / * ... * / } ;
class  Ival_slider : public Ival_box { / * ... * / } ;
```

```
class BB_ival_slider : public Ival_slider, protected BBwindow { /* ... */ };
class CW_ival_slider : public Ival_slider, protected CWwindow { /* ... */ };
// ...
```

or graphically:

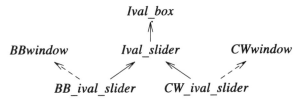

Usually, we can do better yet by utilizing more-specific classes in the implementation hierarchy. For example, if the "Big Bucks Inc." system has a slider class, we can derive our *Ival_slider* directly from the *BBslider*:

```
class BB_ival_slider : public Ival_slider, protected BBslider { /* ... */ };
class CW_ival_slider : public Ival_slider, protected CWslider { /* ... */ };
```

or graphically:

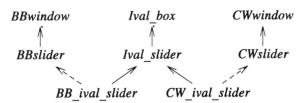

This improvement becomes significant where − as is not uncommon − our abstractions are not too different from the ones provided by the system used for implementation. In that case, programming is reduced to mapping between similar concepts. Derivation from general base classes, such as *BBwindow*, is then done only rarely.

The complete hierarchy will consist of our original application-oriented conceptual hierarchy of interfaces expressed as derived classes:

```
class Ival_box { /* ... */ };
class Ival_slider : public Ival_box { /* ... */ };
class Ival_dial : public Ival_box { /* ... */ };
class Flashing_ival_slider : public Ival_slider { /* ... */ };
class Popup_ival_slider : public Ival_slider { /* ... */ };
```

followed by the implementations of this hierarchy for various graphical user-interface systems, expressed as derived classes:

```
class BB_ival_slider : public Ival_slider, protected BBslider { /* ... */ };
class BB_flashing_ival_slider : public Flashing_ival_slider,
        protected BBwindow_with_bells_and_whistles { /* ... */ };
class BB_popup_ival_slider : public Popup_ival_slider, protected BBslider { /* ... */ };
class CW_ival_slider : public Ival_slider, protected CWslider { /* ... */ };
// ...
```

Using obvious abbreviations, this hierarchy can be represented graphically like this:

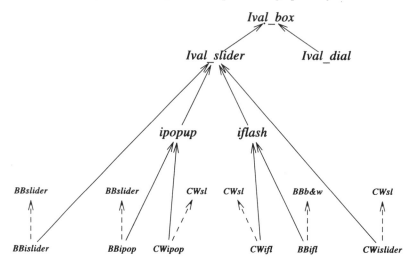

The original *Ival_box* class hierarchy appears unchanged surrounded by implementation classes.

12.4.3.1 Critique

The abstract class design is flexible and almost as simple to deal with as the equivalent design that relies on a common base defining the user-interface system. In the latter design, the windows class is the root of a tree. In the former, the original application class hierarchy appears unchanged as the root of classes that supply its implementations. From the application's point of view, these designs are equivalent in the strong sense that almost all code works unchanged and in the same way in the two cases. In either case, you can look at the *Ival_box* family of classes without bothering with the window-related implementation details most of the time. For example, we would not need to rewrite *interact*( ) from §12.4.1 if we switched from the one class hierarchy to the other.

In either case, the implementation of each *Ival_box* class must be rewritten when the public interface of the user-interface system changes. However, in the abstract class design, almost all user code is protected against changes to the implementation hierarchy and requires no recompilation after such a change. This is especially important when the supplier of the implementation hierarchy issues a new "almost compatible" release. In addition, users of the abstract class hierarchy are in less danger of being locked into a proprietary implementation than are users of a classical hierarchy. Users of the *Ival_box* abstract class application hierarchy cannot accidentally use facilities from the implementation because only facilities explicitly specified in the *Ival_box* hierarchy are accessible; nothing is implicitly inherited from an implementation-specific base class.

12.4.4 Localizing Object Creation

Most of an application can be written using the *Ival_box* interface. Further, should the derived interfaces evolve to provide more facilities than plain *Ival_box*, then most of an application can be written using the *Ival_box*, *Ival_slider*, etc., interfaces. However, the creation of objects must be done using implementation-specific names such as *CW_ival_dial* and *BB_flashing_ival_slider*. We would like to minimize the number of places where such specific names occur, and object creation is hard to localize unless it is done systematically.

As usual, the solution is to introduce an indirection. This can be done in many ways. A simple one is to introduce an abstract class to represent the set of creation operations:

```
class Ival_maker {
public:
    virtual Ival_dial* dial(int, int) =0;                // make dial
    virtual Popup_ival_slider* popup_slider(int, int) =0; // make popup slider
    // ...
};
```

For each interface from the *Ival_box* family of classes that a user should know about, class *Ival_maker* provides a function that makes an object. Such a class is sometimes called a *factory*, and its functions are (somewhat misleadingly) sometimes called *virtual constructors* (§15.6.2).

We now represent each user-interface system by a class derived from *Ival_maker*:

```
class BB_maker : public Ival_maker {         // make BB versions
public:
    Ival_dial* dial(int, int);
    Popup_ival_slider* popup_slider(int, int);
    // ...
};

class LS_maker : public Ival_maker {         // make LS versions
public:
    Ival_dial* dial(int, int);
    Popup_ival_slider* popup_slider(int, int);
    // ...
};
```

Each function creates an object of the desired interface and implementation type. For example:

```
Ival_dial* BB_maker::dial(int a, int b)
{
    return new BB_ival_dial(a,b);
}

Ival_dial* LS_maker::dial(int a, int b)
{
    return new LS_ival_dial(a,b);
}
```

Given a pointer to an *Ival_maker*, a user can now create objects without having to know exactly which user-interface system is used. For example:

```
void user(Ival_maker* pim)
{
    Ival_box* pb = pim->dial(0,99);       // create appropriate dial
    // ...
}
```

```
BB_maker  BB_impl;  // for BB users
LS_maker  LS_impl;   // for LS users

void  driver()
{
    user(&BB_impl);      // use BB
    user(&LS_impl);      // use LS
}
```

12.5   Class Hierarchies and Abstract Classes

An abstract class is an interface. A class hierarchy is a means of building classes incrementally. Naturally, every class provides an interface to users and some abstract classes provide significant functionality to build from, but "interface" and "building block" are the primary roles of abstract classes and class hierarchies.

A classical hierarchy is a hierarchy in which the individual classes both provide useful functionality for users and act as building blocks for the implementation of more advanced or specialized classes. Such hierarchies are ideal for supporting programming by incremental refinement. They provide the maximum support for the implementation of new classes as long as the new class relates strongly to the existing hierarchy.

Classical hierarchies do tend to couple implementation concerns rather strongly with the interfaces provided to users. Abstract classes can help here. Hierarchies of abstract classes provide a clean and powerful way of expressing concepts without encumbering them with implementation concerns or significant run-time overheads. After all, a virtual function call is cheap and independent of the kind of abstraction barrier it crosses. It costs no more to call a member of an abstract class than to call any other *virtual* function.

The logical conclusion of this line of thought is a system represented to users as a hierarchy of abstract classes and implemented by a classical hierarchy.

12.6   Advice

[1] Avoid type fields; §12.2.5.
[2] Use pointers and references to avoid slicing; §12.2.3.
[3] Use abstract classes to focus design on the provision of clean interfaces; §12.3.
[4] Use abstract classes to minimize interfaces; §12.4.2.
[5] Use abstract classes to keep implementation details out of interfaces; §12.4.2.
[6] Use virtual functions to allow new implementations to be added without affecting user code; §12.4.1.
[7] Use abstract classes to minimize recompilation of user code; §12.4.2.
[8] Use abstract classes to allow alternative implementations to coexist; §12.4.3.
[9] A class with a virtual function should have a virtual destructor; §12.4.2.
[10] An abstract class typically doesn't need a constructor; §12.4.2.
[11] Keep the representations of distinct concepts distinct; §12.4.1.1.

12.7 Exercises

1. (*1) Define

   ```
   class Base {
   public :
       virtual void iam ( ) { cout << "Base\n" ; }
   };
   ```

   Derive two classes from *Base*, and for each define *iam* ( ) to write out the name of the class. Create objects of these classes and call *iam* ( ) for them. Assign pointers to objects of the derived classes to *Base* ✶ pointers and call *iam* ( ) through those pointers.

2. (*3.5) Implement a simple graphics system using whatever graphics facilities are available on your system (if you don't have a good graphics system or have no experience with one, you might consider a simple "huge bit ASCII implementation" where a point is a character position and you write by placing a suitable character, such as ✶ in a position): *Window* (*n*, *m*) creates an area of size *n* times *m* on the screen. Points on the screen are addressed using (x,y) coordinates (Cartesian). A *Window w* has a current position *w* . *current* ( ) . Initially, *current* is *Point* (*0*, *0*) . The current position can be set by *w* . *current* (*p*) where *p* is a *Point*. A *Point* is specified by a coordinate pair: *Point* (*x*, *y*) . A *Line* is specified by a pair of *Point*s: *Line* (*w* . *current* ( ) , *p2*) ; class *Shape* is the common interface to *Dot*s, *Line*s, *Rectangle*s, *Circle*s, etc. A *Point* is not a *Shape*. A *Dot*, *Dot* (*p*) can be used to represent a *Point p* on the screen. A *Shape* is invisible unless *draw* ( ) n. For example: *w* . *draw* (*Circle* (*w* . *current* ( ) , *10*)) . Every *Shape* has 9 contact points: *e* (east), *w* (west), *n* (north), *s* (south), *ne*, *nw*, *se*, *sw*, and *c* (center). For example, *Line* (*x* . *c* ( ) , *y* . *nw* ( )) creates a line from *x*'s center to *y*'s top left corner. After *draw* ( ) ing a *Shape* the current position is the *Shape*'s *se* ( ) . A *Rectangle* is specified by its bottom left and top right corner: *Rectangle* (*w* . *current* ( ) , *Point* (*10*, *10*)) . As a simple test, display a simple "child's drawing of a house" with a roof, two windows, and a door.

3. (*2) Important aspects of a *Shape* appear on the screen as a set of line segments. Implement operations to vary the appearance of these segments: *s* . *thickness* (*n*) sets the line thickness to *0*, *1*, *2*, or *3*, where *2* is the default and *0* means invisible. In addition, a line segment can be *solid*, *dashed*, or *dotted*. This is set by the function *Shape* : : *outline* ( ) .

4. (*2.5) Provide a function *Line* : : *arrowhead* ( ) that adds arrow heads to an end of a line. A line has two ends and an arrowhead can point in two directions relative to the line, so the argument or arguments to *arrowhead* ( ) must be able to express at least four alternatives.

5. (*3.5) Make sure that points and line segments that fall outside the *Window* do not appear on the screen. This is often called "clipping." As an exercise only, do not rely on the implementation graphics system for this.

6. (*2.5) Add a *Text* type to the graphics system. A *Text* is a rectangular *Shape* displaying characters. By default, a character takes up one coordinate unit along each coordinate axis.

7. (*2) Define a function that draws a line connecting two shapes by finding the two closest "contact points" and connecting them.

8. (*3) Add a notion of color to the simple graphics system. Three things can be colored: the background, the inside of a closed shape, and the outlines of shapes.

9. (*2) Consider:

```
class Char_vec {
    int sz;
    char element[1];
public:
    static Char_vec* new_char_vec(int s);
    char& operator[](int i) { return element[i]; }
    // ...
};
```

Define *new_char_vec*() to allocate contiguous memory for a *Char_vec* object so that the elements can be indexed through *element* as shown. Under what circumstances does this trick cause serious problems?

10. (*2.5) Given classes *Circle*, *Square*, and *Triangle* derived from a class *Shape*, define a function *intersect*() that takes two *Shape** arguments and calls suitable functions to determine if the two shapes overlap. It will be necessary to add suitable (virtual) functions to the classes to achieve this. Don't bother to write the code that checks for overlap; just make sure the right functions are called. This is commonly referred to as *double dispatch* or a *multi-method*.

11. (*5) Design and implement a library for writing event-driven simulations. Hint: *<task.h>*. However, that is an old program, and you can do better. There should be a class *task*. An object of class *task* should be able to save its state and to have that state restored (you might define *task::save*() and *task::restore*()) so that it can operate as a coroutine. Specific tasks can be defined as objects of classes derived from class *task*. The program to be executed by a task might be specified as a virtual function. It should be possible to pass arguments to a new task as arguments to its constructor(s). There should be a scheduler implementing a concept of virtual time. Provide a function *task::delay*(*long*) that ''consumes'' virtual time. Whether the scheduler is part of class *task* or separate will be one of the major design decisions. The tasks will need to communicate. Design a class *queue* for that. Devise a way for a task to wait for input from several queues. Handle run-time errors in a uniform way. How would you debug programs written using such a library?

12. (*2) Define interfaces for *Warrior*, *Monster*, and *Object* (that is a thing you can pick up, drop, use, etc.) classes for an adventure-style game.

13. (*1.5) Why is there both a *Point* and a *Dot* class in §12.7[2]? Under which circumstances would it be a good idea to augment the *Shape* classes with concrete versions of key classes such as *Line*?

14. (*3) Outline a different implementation strategy for the *Ival_box* example (§12.4) based on the idea that every class seen by an application is an interface containing a single pointer to the implementation. Thus, each "interface class" will be a handle to an "implementation class," and there will be an interface hierarchy and an implementation hierarchy. Write code fragments that are detailed enough to illustrate possible problems with type conversion. Consider ease of use, ease of programming, ease of reusing implementations and interfaces when adding a new concept to the hierarchy, ease of making changes to interfaces and implementations, and need for recompilation after change in the implementation.

13

Templates

Your quote here.
– B. Stroustrup

Templates — a string template — instantiation — template parameters — type checking — function templates — template argument deduction — specifying template arguments — function template overloading — policy as template arguments — default template arguments — specialization — derivation and templates — member templates — conversions — source code organization — advice — exercises.

13.1 Introduction

Independent concepts should be independently represented and should be combined only when needed. Where this principle is violated, you either bundle unrelated concepts together or create unnecessary dependencies. Either way, you get a less flexible set of components out of which to compose systems. Templates provide a simple way to represent a wide range of general concepts and simple ways to combine them. The resulting classes and functions can match hand-written, more-specialized code in run-time and space efficiency.

Templates provide direct support for generic programming (§2.7), that is, programming using types as parameters. The C++ template mechanism allows a type to be a parameter in the definition of a class or a function. A template depends only on the properties that it actually uses from its parameter types and does not require different types used as arguments to be explicitly related. In particular, the argument types used for a template need not be from a single inheritance hierarchy.

Here, templates are introduced with the primary focus on techniques needed for the design, implementation, and use of the standard library. The standard library requires a greater degree of generality, flexibility, and efficiency than does most software. Consequently, techniques that can be used in the design and implementation of the standard library are effective and efficient in the design of solutions to a wide variety of problems. These techniques enable an implementer to hide sophisticated implementations behind simple interfaces and to expose complexity to the user only when the user has a specific need for it. For example, *sort* (*v*) can be the interface to a variety of sort algorithms for elements of a variety of types held in a variety of containers. The sort function that is most appropriate for the particular *v* will be automatically chosen.

Every major standard library abstraction is represented as a template (for example, *string*, *ostream*, *complex*, *list*, and *map*) and so are the key operations (for example, *string* compare, the output operator <<, *complex* addition, getting the next element from a *list*, and *sort* ( )). This makes the library chapters (Part III) of this book a rich source of examples of templates and programming techniques relying on them. Consequently, this chapter concentrates on smaller examples illustrating technical aspects of templates and fundamental techniques for using them:

§13.2: The basic mechanisms for defining and using class templates

§13.3: Function templates, function overloading, and type deduction

§13.4: Template parameters used to specify policies for generic algorithms

§13.5: Multiple definitions providing alternative implementations for a template

§13.6: Derivation and templates (run-time and compile-time polymorphism)

§13.7: Source code organization

Templates were introduced in §2.7.1 and §3.8. Detailed rules for template name resolution, template syntax, etc., can be found in §C.13.

13.2 A Simple String Template

Consider a string of characters. A string is a class that holds characters and provides operations such as subscripting, concatenation, and comparison that we usually associate with the notion of a "string." We would like to provide that behavior for many different kinds of characters. For example, strings of signed characters, of unsigned characters, of Chinese characters, of Greek characters, etc., are useful in various contexts. Thus, we want to represent the notion of "string" with minimal dependence on a specific kind of character. The definition of a string relies on the fact that a character can be copied, and little else. Thus, we can make a more general string type by taking the string of *char* from §11.12 and making the character type a parameter:

```
template<class C> class String {
    struct Srep;
    Srep *rep;
public:
    String();
    String(const C*);
    String(const String&);

    C read(int i) const;
    // ...
};
```

The *template* *<class C>* prefix specifies that a template is being declared and that a type argument *C* will be used in the declaration. After its introduction, *C* is used exactly like other type names. The scope of *C* extends to the end of the declaration prefixed by *template* *<class C>*. Note that *template<class C>* says that *C* is a *type* name; it need not be the name of a *class*.

The name of a class template followed by a type bracketed by < > is the name of a class (as defined by the template) and can be used exactly like other class names. For example:

```
String<char> cs;
String<unsigned char> us;
String<wchar_t> ws;

class Jchar {
        // Japanese character
};

String<Jchar> js;
```

Except for the special syntax of its name, *String<char>* works exactly as if it had been defined using the definition of class *String* in §11.12. Making *String* a template allows us to provide the facilities we had for *String* of *char* for *String*s of any kind of character. For example, if we use the standard library *map* and the *String* template, the word-counting example from §11.8 becomes:

```
int main()        // count the occurrences of each word on input
{
        String<char> buf;
        map<String<char>, int> m;
        while (cin>>buf) m[buf]++;
        // write out result
}
```

The version for our Japanese-character type *Jchar* would be:

```
int main()        // count the occurrences of each word on input
{
        String<Jchar> buf;
        map<String<Jchar>, int> m;
        while (cin>>buf) m[buf]++;
        // write out result
}
```

The standard library provides the template class *basic_string* that is similar to the templatized *String* (§11.12, §20.3). In the standard library, *string* is defined as a synonym for *basic_string<char>*:

```
typedef basic_string<char> string;
```

This allows us to write the word-counting program like this:

```
int main()        // count the occurrences of each word on input
{
        string buf;
        map<string, int> m;
        while (cin>>buf) m[buf]++;
        // write out result
}
```

In general, *typedef*s are useful for shortening the long names of classes generated from templates.

Also, we often prefer not to know the details of how a type is defined, and a *typedef* allows us to hide the fact that a type is generated from a template.

13.2.1 Defining a Template

A class generated from a class template is a perfectly ordinary class. Thus, use of a template does not imply any run-time mechanisms beyond what is used for an equivalent "hand-written" class. Nor does it necessarily imply any reduction in the amount of code generated.

It is usually a good idea to debug a particular class, such as *String*, before turning it into a template such as *String<C>*. By doing so, we handle many design problems and most of the code errors in the context of a concrete example. This kind of debugging is familiar to all programmers, and most people cope better with a concrete example than with an abstract concept. Later, we can deal with any problems that might arise from generalization without being distracted by more conventional errors. Similarly, when trying to understand a template, it is often useful to imagine its behavior for a particular type argument such as *char* before trying to comprehend the template in its full generality.

Members of a template class are declared and defined exactly as they would have been for a non-template class. A template member need not be defined within the template class itself. In that case, its definition must be provided somewhere else, as for non-template class members (§C.13.7). Members of a template class are themselves templates parameterized by the parameters of their template class. When such a member is defined outside its class, it must explicitly be declared a template. For example:

```
template<class C> struct String<C>::Srep {
    C* s;           // pointer to elements
    int sz;         // number of elements
    int n;          // reference count
    // ...
};

template<class C> C String<C>::read(int i) const { return rep->s[i]; }

template<class C> String<C>::String()
{
    rep = new Srep(0,C());
}
```

Template parameters, such as *C*, are parameters rather than names of types defined externally to the template. However, that doesn't affect the way we write the template code using them. Within the scope of *String<C>*, qualification with *<C>* is redundant for the name of the template itself, so *String<C>::String* is the name for the constructor. If you prefer, you can be explicit:

```
template<class C> String<C>::String<C>()
{
    rep = new Srep(0,C());
}
```

Just as there can be only one function defining a class member function in a program, there can be only one function template defining a class template member function in a program. However, overloading is a possibility for functions only (§13.3.2), while specialization (§13.5) enables us to provide alternative implementations for a template.

It is not possible to overload a class template name, so if a class template is declared in a scope, no other entity can be declared there with the same name (see also §13.5). For example:

> *template<class T> class String { /* ... */ };*
>
> *class String { /* ... */ }; // error: double definition*

A type used as a template argument must provide the interface expected by the template. For example, a type used as an argument to *String* must provide the usual copy operations (§10.4.4.1, §20.2.1). Note that there is no requirement that different arguments for the same template parameter should be related by inheritance.

13.2.2 Template Instantiation

The process of generating a class declaration from a template class and a template argument is often called *template instantiation* (§C.13.7). Similarly, a function is generated (''instantiated'') from a template function plus a template argument. A version of a template for a particular template argument is called a *specialization*.

In general, it is the implementation's job – *not* the programmer's – to ensure that versions of a template function are generated for each set of template arguments used (§C.13.7). For example:

> *String<char> cs;*
>
> *void f()*
> *{*
> > *String<Jchar> js;*
> >
> > *cs = "It´s the implementation´s job to figure out what code needs to be generated";*
> *}*

For this, the implementation generates declarations for *String<char>* and *String<Jchar>*, for their corresponding *Srep* types, for their destructors and default constructors, and for the assignment *String<char>::operator=(char*)*. Other member functions are not used and should not be generated. The generated classes are perfectly ordinary classes that obey all the usual rules for classes. Similarly, generated functions are ordinary functions that obey all the usual rules for functions.

Obviously, templates provide a powerful way of generating code from relatively short definitions. Consequently, a certain amount of caution is in order to avoid flooding memory with almost identical function definitions (§13.5).

13.2.3 Template Parameters

A template can take type parameters, parameters of ordinary types such as *int*s, and template parameters (§C.13.3). Naturally, a template can take several parameters. For example:

> *template<class T, T def_val> class Cont { /* ... */ };*

As shown, a template parameter can be used in the definition of subsequent template parameters.

Integer arguments come in handy for supplying sizes and limits. For example:

```
template<class T, int i> class Buffer {
    T v[i];
    int sz;
public:
    Buffer() : sz(i) {}
    // ...
};

Buffer<char, 127> cbuf;
Buffer<Record, 8> rbuf;
```

Simple and constrained containers such as *Buffer* can be important where run-time efficiency and compactness are paramount (thus preventing the use of a more general *string* or *vector*). Passing a size as a template argument allows *Buffer*'s implementer to avoid free store use. Another example is the *Range* type in §25.6.1.

A template argument can be a constant expression (§C.5), the address of an object or function with external linkage (§9.2), or a non-overloaded pointer to member (§15.5). A pointer used as a template argument must be of the form &*of*, where *of* is the name of an object or a function, or of the form *f*, where *f* is the name of a function. A pointer to member must be of the form &*X::of*, where *of* is the name of a member. In particular, a string literal is *not* acceptable as a template argument.

An integer template argument must be a constant:

```
void f(int i)
{
    Buffer<int, i> bx;      // error: constant expression expected
}
```

Conversely, a non-type template parameter is a constant within the template so that an attempt to change the value of a parameter is an error.

13.2.4 Type Equivalence

Given a template, we can generate types by supplying template arguments. For example:

```
String<char> s1;
String<unsigned char> s2;
String<int> s3;

typedef unsigned char Uchar;
String<Uchar> s4;
String<char> s5;

Buffer<String<char>, 10> b1;
Buffer<char, 10> b2;
Buffer<char, 20-10> b3;
```

When using the same set of template arguments for a template, we always refer to the same generated type. However, what does "the same" mean in this context? As usual, *typedef*s do not introduce new types, so *String<Uchar>* is the same type as *String<unsigned char>*. Conversely, because *char* and *unsigned char* are different types (§4.3), *String<char>* and *String<unsigned char>* are different types.

The compiler can evaluate constant expressions (§C.5), so *Buffer<char, 20-10>* is recognized to be the same type as *Buffer<char, 10>*.

13.2.5 Type Checking

A template is defined and then later used in combination with a set of template arguments. When the template is defined, the definition is checked for syntax errors and possibly also for other errors that can be detected in isolation from a particular set of template arguments. For example:

```
template<class T> class List {
        struct Link {
                Link* pre;
                Link* suc;
                T val;
                Link(Link* p, Link* s, const T& v) :pre(p), suc(s), val(v) { }
        }               // syntax error: missing semicolon
        Link* head;
public:
        List() : head(7) { }        // error: pointer initialized with int
        List(const T& t) : head(new Link(0,o,t)) { }       // error: undefined identifier 'o'
        // ...
        void print_all() const { for (Link* p = head; p; p=p->suc) cout << p->val << '\n'; }
};
```

A compiler can catch simple semantic errors at the point of definition or later at the point of use. Users generally prefer early detection, but not all "simple" errors are easy to detect. Here, I made three "mistakes." Independently of what the template parameter is, a pointer *Link** cannot be initialized by the integer *7*. Similarly, the identifier *o* (a mistyped *0*, of course) cannot be an argument to *List<T>::Link*'s constructor because there is no such name in scope.

A name used in a template definition must either be in scope or in some reasonably obvious way depend on a template parameter (§C.13.8.1). The most common and obvious way of depending on a template parameter *T* is to use a member of a *T* or to take an argument of type *T*. In *List<T>::print_all()*, *cout<<p->val* is a slightly more subtle example.

Errors that relate to the use of template parameters cannot be detected until the template is used. For example:

```
class Rec { /* ... */ };

void f(const List<int>& li, const List<Rec>& lr)
{
        li.print_all();
        lr.print_all();
}
```

The *li.print_all()* checks out fine, but *lr.print_all()* gives a type error because there is no << output operator defined for *Rec*. The earliest that errors relating to a template parameter can be detected is at the first point of use of the template for a particular template argument. That point is usually called the *first point of instantiation*, or simply the *point of instantiation* (see §C.13.7). The implementation is allowed to postpone this checking until the program is linked. If we had only a declaration of *print_all* ( ) available in this translation unit, rather than its definition, the implementation might have had to delay type checking (see §13.7). Independently of when checking is done, the same set of rules is checked. Again, users prefer early checking. It is possible to express constraints on template arguments in terms of member functions (see §13.9[16]).

13.3 Function Templates

For most people, the first and most obvious use of templates is to define and use container classes such as *basic_string* (§20.3), *vector* (§16.3), *list* (§17.2.2), and *map* (§17.4.1). Soon after, the need for template functions arises. Sorting an array is a simple example:

```
template<class T> void sort(vector<T>&);        // declaration

void f(vector<int>& vi, vector<string>& vs)
{
    sort(vi);   // sort(vector<int>&);
    sort(vs);   // sort(vector<string>&);
}
```

When a template function is called, the types of the function arguments determine which version of the template is used; that is, the template arguments are deduced from the function arguments (§13.3.1).

Naturally, the template function must be defined somewhere (§C.13.7):

```
template<class T> void sort(vector<T>& v)       // definition
        // Shell sort (Knuth, Vol. 3, pg. 84).
{
    const size_t n = v.size();

    for (int gap=n/2; 0<gap; gap/=2)
        for (int i=gap; i<n; i++)
            for (int j=i-gap; 0<=j; j-=gap)
                if (v[j+gap]<v[j]) {        // swap v[j] and v[j+gap]
                    T temp = v[j];
                    v[j] = v[j+gap];
                    v[j+gap] = temp;
                }
}
```

Please compare this definition to the *sort* ( ) defined in §7.7. This templatized version is cleaner and shorter because it can rely on more information about the type of the elements it sorts. Most likely, it is also faster because it doesn't rely on a pointer to function for the comparison. This implies that no indirect function calls are needed and that inlining of a simple < is easy.

A further simplification is to use the standard library template *swap* ( ) (§18.6.8) to reduce the action to its natural form:

```
if (v[j+gap]<v[j]) swap(v[j],v[j+gap]);
```

This does not introduce any new overheads.

In this example, operator < is used for comparison. However, not every type has a < operator. This limits the use of this version of *sort* ( ) , but the limitation is easily avoided (see §13.4).

13.3.1 Function Template Arguments

Function templates are essential for writing generic algorithms to be applied to a wide variety of container types (§2.7.2, §3.8, Chapter 18). The ability to deduce the template arguments for a call from the function arguments is crucial.

A compiler can deduce type and non-type arguments from a call, provided the function argument list uniquely identifies the set of template arguments (§C.13.4). For example:

```
template<class T, int i> T& lookup (Buffer<T,i>& b, const char* p);

class Record {
    const char[12];
    // ...
};

Record& f(Buffer<Record,128>& buf, const char* p)
{
    return lookup (buf,p); // use the lookup() where T is Record and i is 128
}
```

Here, *T* is deduced to be *Record* and *i* is deduced to be *128*.

Note that class template parameters are never deduced. The reason is that the flexibility provided by several constructors for a class would make such deduction impossible in many cases and obscure in many more. Specialization provides a mechanism for implicitly choosing between different implementations of a class (§13.5). If we need to create an object of a deduced type, we can often do that by calling a function to do the creation; see *make_pair* ( ) in §17.4.1.2.

If a template argument cannot be deduced from the template function arguments (§C.13.4), we must specify it explicitly. This is done in the same way template arguments are explicitly specified for a template class. For example:

```
template<class T> class vector { / * ... * / };
template<class T> T* create (); // make a T and return a pointer to it

void f()
{
    vector<int> v;              // class, template argument 'int'
    int* p = create<int> ();    // function, template argument 'int'
}
```

One common use of explicit specification is to provide a return type for a template function:

```
template<class T, class U> T implicit_cast (U u) { return u; }

void g (int i)
{
    implicit_cast (i);          // error: can't deduce T
    implicit_cast<double> (i);  // T is double; U is int
```

```
        implicit_cast<char,double>(i);  // T is char; U is double
        implicit_cast<char*,int>(i);     // T is char*; U is int; error: cannot convert int to char*
}
```

As with default function arguments (§7.5), only trailing arguments can be left out of a list of explicit template arguments.

Explicit specification of template arguments allows the definition of families of conversion functions and object creation functions (§13.3.2, §C.13.1, §C.13.5). An explicit version of the implicit conversions (§C.6), such as *implicit_cast*(), is frequently useful. The syntax for *dynamic_cast*, *static_cast*, etc., (§6.2.7, §15.4.1) matches the explicitly qualified template function syntax. However, the built-in type conversion operators supply operations that cannot be expressed by other language features.

13.3.2 Function Template Overloading

One can declare several function templates with the same name and even declare a combination of function templates and ordinary functions with the same name. When an overloaded function is called, overload resolution is necessary to find the right function or template function to invoke. For example:

```
template<class T> T sqrt(T);
template<class T> complex<T> sqrt(complex<T>);
double sqrt(double);

void f(complex<double> z)
{
    sqrt(2);        // sqrt<int>(int)
    sqrt(2.0);      // sqrt(double)
    sqrt(z);        // sqrt<double>(complex<double>)
}
```

In the same way that a template function is a generalization of the notion of a function, the rules for resolution in the presence of function templates are generalizations of the function overload resolution rules. Basically, for each template we find the specialization that is best for the set of function arguments. Then, we apply the usual function overload resolution rules to these specializations and all ordinary functions:

[1] Find the set of function template specializations (§13.2.2) that will take part in overload resolution. Do this by considering each function template and deciding which template arguments, if any, would be used if no other function templates or functions of the same name were in scope. For the call *sqrt*(z), this makes *sqrt<double>*(*complex<double>*) and *sqrt< complex<double> >*(*complex<double>*) candidates.

[2] If two template functions can be called and one is more specialized than the other (§13.5.1), consider only the most specialized template function in the following steps. For the call *sqrt*(z), this means that *sqrt<double>*(*complex<double>*) is preferred over *sqrt< complex<double> >*(*complex<double>*): any call that matches *sqrt<T>*(*complex<T>*) also matches *sqrt<T>*(*T*).

[3] Do overload resolution for this set of functions, plus any ordinary functions as for ordinary functions (§7.4). If a template function argument has been determined by template argument deduction (§13.3.1), that argument cannot also have promotions, standard conversions, or user-defined conversions applied. For *sqrt(2)*, *sqrt<int>(int)* is an exact match, so it is preferred over *sqrt(double)*.

[4] If a function and a specialization are equally good matches, the function is preferred. Consequently, *sqrt(double)* is preferred over *sqrt<double>(double)* for *sqrt(2.0)*.

[5] If no match is found, the call is an error. If we end up with two or more equally good matches, the call is ambiguous and is an error.

For example:

```
template<class T> T max(T,T);

const int s = 7;

void k()
{
    max(1,2);           // max<int>(1,2)
    max('a','b');       // max<char>('a','b')
    max(2.7,4.9);       // max<double>(2.7,4.9)
    max(s,7);           // max<int>(int(s),7) (trivial conversion used)

    max('a',1);         // error: ambiguous (no standard conversion)
    max(2.7,4);         // error: ambiguous (no standard conversion)
}
```

We could resolve the two ambiguities either by explicit qualification:

```
void f()
{
    max<int>('a',1);        // max<int>(int('a'),1)
    max<double>(2.7,4);     // max<double>(2.7,double(4))
}
```

or by adding suitable declarations:

```
inline int max(int i, int j) { return max<int>(i,j); }
inline double max(int i, double d) { return max<double>(i,d); }
inline double max(double d, int i) { return max<double>(d,i); }
inline double max(double d1, double d2) { return max<double>(d1,d2); }

void g()
{
    max('a',1);   // max(int('a'),1)
    max(2.7,4);   // max(2.7,double(4))
}
```

For ordinary functions, ordinary overloading rules (§7.4) apply, and the use of *inline* ensures that no extra overhead is imposed.

The definition of *max()* is trivial, so we could have written it explicitly. However, using a specialization of the template is an easy and general way of defining such resolution functions.

The overload resolution rules ensure that template functions interact properly with inheritance:

```
template<class T> class B { /* ... */ };
template<class T> class D : public B<T> { /* ... */ };

template<class T> void f(B<T>*);

void g(B<int>* pb, D<int>* pd)
{
    f(pb);      // f<int>(pb)
    f(pd);      // f<int>(static_cast<B<int>*>(pd)); standard conversion D<int>* to B<int>* used
}
```

In this example, the template function *f()* accepts a *B<T>** for any type *T*. We have an argument of type *D<int>**, so the compiler easily deduces that by choosing *T* to be *int*, the call can be uniquely resolved to a call of *f(B<int>*)*.

A function argument that is not involved in the deduction of a template parameter is treated exactly as an argument of a non-template function. In particular, the usual conversion rules hold. Consider:

```
template<class T, class C> T get_nth(C& p, int n); // get n-th element
```

This function presumably returns the value of the n-th element of a container of type *C*. Because *C* has to be deduced from an actual argument of *get_nth()* in a call, conversions are not applicable to the first argument. However, the second argument is perfectly ordinary, so the full range of possible conversions is considered. For example:

```
class Index {
public:
    operator int();
    // ...
};

void f(vector<int>& v, short s, Index i)
{
    int i1 = get_nth<int>(v, 2);     // exact match
    int i2 = get_nth<int>(v, s);     // standard conversion: short to int
    int i3 = get_nth<int>(v, i);     // user-defined conversion: Index to int
}
```

13.4 Using Template Arguments to Specify Policy

Consider how to sort strings. Three concepts are involved: the string, the element type, and the criteria used by the sort algorithm for comparing string elements.

We can't hardwire the sorting criteria into the container because the container can't (in general) impose its needs on the element types. We can't hardwire the sorting criteria into the element type because there are many different ways of sorting elements.

Consequently, the sorting criteria are built neither into the container nor into the element type. Instead, the criteria must be supplied when a specific operation needs to be performed. For example, if I have strings of characters representing names of Swedes, what collating criteria would I like to use for a comparison? Two different collating sequences (numerical orderings of the characters) are commonly used for sorting Swedish names. Naturally, neither a general string type nor a general sort algorithm should know about the conventions for sorting names in Sweden. Therefore, any general solution requires that the sorting algorithm be expressed in general terms that can be defined not just for a specific type but also for a specific use of a specific type. For example, let us generalize the standard C library function *strcmp* ( ) for *String*s of any type *T* (§13.2):

```
template<class T, class C>
int compare(const String<T>& str1, const String<T>& str2)
{
    for(int i=0; i<str1.length() && i< str2.length(); i++)
        if (!C::eq(str1[i],str2[i])) return C::lt(str1[i],str2[i]) ? -1 : 1;
    return str1.length()-str2.length();
}
```

If someone wants *compare* ( ) to ignore case, to reflect locale, etc., that can be done by defining suitable *C::eq* ( ) and *C::lt* ( ). This allows any (comparison, sorting, etc.) algorithm that can be described in terms of the operations supplied by the ''*C*-operations'' and the container to be expressed. For example:

```
template<class T> class Cmp {  // normal, default compare
public:
    static int eq(T a, T b) { return a==b; }
    static int lt(T a, T b) { return a<b; }
};

class Literate {  // compare Swedish names according to literary conventions
public:
    static int eq(char a, char b) { return a==b; }
    static int lt(char,char);  // a table lookup based on character value (§13.9[14])
};
```

We can now choose the rules for comparison by explicit specification of the template arguments:

```
void f(String<char> swede1, String<char> swede2)
{
    compare< char,Cmp<char> >(swede1,swede2);
    compare< char,Literate >(swede1,swede2);
}
```

Passing the comparison operations as a template parameter has two significant benefits compared to alternatives such as passing pointers to functions. Several operations can be passed as a single argument with no run-time cost. In addition, the comparison operators *eq* ( ) and *lt* ( ) are trivial to inline, whereas inlining a call through a pointer to function requires exceptional attention from a compiler.

Naturally, comparison operations can be provided for user-defined types as well as built-in types. This is essential to allow general algorithms to be applied to types with nontrivial comparison criteria (see §18.4).

Each class generated from a class template gets a copy of each *static* member of the class template (see §C.13.1).

13.4.1 Default Template Parameters

Explicitly specifying the comparison criteria for each call is tedious. Fortunately, it is easy to pick a default so that only uncommon comparison criteria have to be explicitly specified. This can be implemented through overloading:

```
template<class T, class C>
int compare(const String<T>& str1, const String<T>& str2); // compare using C

template<class T>
int compare(const String<T>& str1, const String<T>& str2); // compare using Cmp<T>
```

Alternatively, we can supply the normal convention as a default template argument:

```
template<class T, class C = Cmp<T> >
int compare(const String<T>& str1, const String<T>& str2)
{
    for(int i=0; i<str1.length() && i< str2.length(); i++)
        if (!C::eq(str1[i],str2[i])) return C::lt(str1[i],str2[i]) ? -1 : 1;
    return str1.length()-str2.length();
}
```

Given that, we can write:

```
void f(String<char> swede1, String<char> swede2)
{
    compare(swede1,swede2);                     // use Cmp<char>
    compare<char,Literate>(swede1,swede2);      // use Literate
}
```

A less esoteric example (for non-Swedes) is comparing with and without taking case into account:

```
class No_case { /* ... */ };

void f(String<char> s1, String<char> s2)
{
    compare(s1,s2);                     // case sensitive
    compare<char,No_case>(s1,s2);       // not sensitive to case
}
```

The technique of supplying a policy through a template argument and then defaulting that argument to supply the most common policy is widely used in the standard library (e.g., §18.4). Curiously enough, it is not used for *basic_string* (§13.2, Chapter 20) comparisons. Template parameters used to express policies are often called "traits." For example, the standard library string relies on *char_traits* (§20.2.1), the standard algorithms on iterator traits (§19.2.2), and the standard library containers on *allocators* (§19.4).

The semantic checking of a default argument for a template parameter is done if and (only) when that default argument is actually used. In particular, as long as we refrain from using the default template argument *Cmp<T>* we can *compare*() strings of a type *X* for which *Cmp<X>* wouldn't compile (say, because < wasn't defined for an *X*). This point is crucial in the design of the standard containers, which rely on a template argument to specify default values (§16.3.4).

13.5 Specialization

By default, a template gives a single definition to be used for every template argument (or combination of template arguments) that a user can think of. This doesn't always make sense for someone writing a template. I might want to say, "if the template argument is a pointer, use this implementation; if it is not, use that implementation" or "give an error unless the template argument is a pointer derived from class *My_base*." Many such design concerns can be addressed by providing alternative definitions of the template and having the compiler choose between them based on the template arguments provided where they are used. Such alternative definitions of a template are called *user-defined specializations*, or simply, *user specializations*.

Consider likely uses of a *Vector* template:

```
template<class T> class Vector {        // general vector type
    T* v;
    int sz;
public:
    Vector();
    explicit Vector(int);

    T& elem(int i) { return v[i]; }
    T& operator[](int i);

    void swap(Vector&);
    // ...
};

Vector<int> vi;
Vector<Shape*> vps;
Vector<string> vs;
Vector<char*> vpc;
Vector<Node*> vpn;
```

Most *Vector*s will be *Vector*s of some pointer type. There are several reasons for this, but the primary reason is that to preserve run-time polymorphic behavior, we must use pointers (§2.5.4, §12.2.6). That is, anyone who practices object-oriented programming and also uses type-safe containers (such as the standard library containers) will end up with a lot of containers of pointers.

The default behavior of most C++ implementations is to replicate the code for template functions. This is good for run-time performance, but unless care is taken it leads to code bloat in critical cases such as the *Vector* example.

Fortunately, there is an obvious solution. Containers of pointers can share a single implementation. This can be expressed through specialization. First, we define a version (a specialization) of *Vector* for pointers to *void*:

```
template<> class Vector<void*> {
    void** p;
    // ...
    void*& operator[](int i);
};
```

This specialization can then be used as the common implementation for all *Vector*s of pointers.

The *template<>* prefix says that this is a specialization that can be specified without a template parameter. The template arguments for which the specialization is to be used are specified in *<>* brackets after the name. That is, the *<void*>* says that this definition is to be used as the implementation of every *Vector* for which *T* is void* .

The *Vector<void*>* is a complete specialization. That is, there is no template parameter to specify or deduce when we use the specialization; *Vector<void*>* is used for *Vector*s declared like this:

```
Vector<void*> vpv;
```

To define a specialization that is used for every *Vector* of pointers and only for *Vector*s of pointers, we need a *partial specialization*:

```
template<class T> class Vector<T*> : private Vector<void*> {
public:
    typedef Vector<void*> Base;

    Vector() : Base() {}
    explicit Vector(int i) : Base(i) {}

    T*& elem(int i) { return static_cast<T*&>(Base::elem(i)); }
    T*& operator[](int i) { return static_cast<T*&>(Base::operator[](i)); }

    // ...
};
```

The specialization pattern *<T*>* after the name says that this specialization is to be used for every pointer type; that is, this definition is to be used for every *Vector* with a template argument that can be expressed as *T**. For example:

```
Vector<Shape*> vps;    // <T*> is <Shape*> so T is Shape
Vector<int**> vppi;    // <T*> is <int**> so T is int*
```

Note that when a partial specialization is used, a template parameter is deduced from the specialization pattern; the template parameter is not simply the actual template argument. In particular, for *Vector<Shape*>*, *T* is *Shape* and not *Shape**.

Given this partial specialization of *Vector*, we have a shared implementation for all *Vector*s of pointers. The *Vector<T*>* class is simply an interface to *Vector<void*>* implemented exclusively through derivation and inline expansion.

It is important that this refinement of the implementation of *Vector* is achieved without affecting the interface presented to users. Specialization is a way of specifying alternative implementations for different uses of a common interface. Naturally, we could have given the general *Vector* and the *Vector* of pointers different names. However, when I tried that, many people who should have known better forgot to use the pointer classes and found their code much larger than expected. In this case, it is much better to hide the crucial implementation details behind a common interface.

This technique proved successful in curbing code bloat in real use. People who do not use a technique like this (in C++ or in other languages with similar facilities for type parameterization) have found that replicated code can cost megabytes of code space even in moderately-sized programs. By eliminating the time needed to compile those additional versions of the vector operations, this technique can also cut compile and link times dramatically. Using a single specialization to implement all lists of pointers is an example of the general technique of minimizing code bloat by maximizing the amount of shared code.

The general template must be declared before any specialization. For example:

template<class T> class List<T*> { /* ... */ };

template<class T> class List { /* ... */ }; // error: general template after specialization

The critical information supplied by the general template is the set of template parameters that the user must supply to use it or any of its specializations. Consequently, a declaration of the general case is sufficient to allow the declaration or definition of a specialization:

template<class T> class List;

template<class T> class List<T*> { /* ... */ };

If used, the general template needs to be defined somewhere (§13.7).

If a user specializes a template somewhere, that specialization must be in scope for every use of the template with the type for which it was specialized. For example:

template<class T> class List { /* ... */ };

List<int*> li;

template<class T> class List<T*> { /* ... */ }; // error

Here, *List* was specialized for *int** after *List<int*>* had been used.

All specializations of a template must be declared in the same namespace as the template itself. If used, a specialization that is explicitly declared (as opposed to generated from a more general template) must also be explicitly defined somewhere (§13.7). In other words, explicitly specializing a template implies that no definition is generated for that specialization.

13.5.1 Order of Specializations

One specialization is *more specialized* than another if every argument list that matches its specialization pattern also matches the other, but not vice versa. For example:

```
template<class T> class Vector;          // general
template<class T> class Vector<T*>;      // specialized for any pointer
template<> class Vector<void*>;          // specialized for void*
```

Every type can be used as a template argument for the most general *Vector*, but only pointers can be used for *Vector<T*>* and only *void**s can be used for *Vector<void*>*.

The most specialized version will be preferred over the others in declarations of objects, pointers, etc., (§13.5) and in overload resolution (§13.3.2).

A specialization pattern can be specified in terms of types composed using the constructs allowed for template parameter deduction (§13.3.1, §C.13.4).

13.5.2 Template Function Specialization

Naturally, specialization is also useful for template functions. Consider the Shell sort from §7.7 and §13.3. It compares elements using < and swaps elements using detailed code. A better definition would be:

```
template<class T> bool less(T a, T b) { return a<b; }

template<class T> void sort(Vector<T>& v)
{
    const size_t n = v.size();

    for (int gap=n/2; 0<gap; gap/=2)
        for (int i=gap; i<n; i++)
            for (int j=i-gap; 0<=j; j-=gap)
                if (less(v[j+gap],v[j])) swap(v[j],v[j+gap]);
}
```

This does not improve the algorithm itself, but it allows improvements to its implementation. As written, *sort*() will not sort a *Vector<char*>* correctly because < will compare the two *char**s. That is, it will compare the addresses of the first *char* in each string. Instead, we would like it to compare the characters pointed to. A simple specialization of *less*() for *const char** will take care of that:

```
template<> bool less<const char*>(const char* a, const char* b)
{
    return strcmp(a,b)<0;
}
```

As for classes (§13.5), the *template<>* prefix says that this is a specialization that can be specified without a template parameter. The *<const char*>* after the template function name means that this specialization is to be used in cases where the template argument is *const char**. Because the template argument can be deduced from the function argument list, we need not specify it explicitly. So, we could simplify the definition of the specialization:

```
template<> bool less<>(const char* a, const char* b)
{
    return strcmp(a,b)<0;
}
```

Given the *template<>* prefix, the second empty *<>* is redundant, so we would typically simply write:

```
template<> bool less(const char* a, const char* b)
{
    return strcmp(a,b)<0;
}
```

I prefer this shorter form of declaration.

Consider the obvious definition of *swap*():

```
template<class T> void swap (T& x, T& y)
{
    T t = x;          // copy x to temporary
    x = y;            // copy y to x
    y = t;            // copy temporary to y
}
```

This is rather inefficient when invoked for *Vector*s of *Vector*s; it swaps *Vector*s by copying all elements. This problem can also be solved by appropriate specialization. A *Vector* object will itself hold only sufficient data to give indirect access to the elements (like *String*; §11.12, §13.2). Thus, a swap can be done by swapping those representations. To be able to manipulate that representation, I provided *Vector* with a member function *swap* ( ) (§13.5):

```
template<class T> void Vector<T>::swap (Vector & a)      // swap representations
{
    swap (v, a.v);
    swap (sz, a.sz);

}
```

This member *swap* ( ) can now be used to define a specialization of the general *swap* ( ):

```
template<class T> void swap (Vector<T>& a, Vector<T>& b)
{
    a.swap (b);
}
```

These specializations of *less* ( ) and *swap* ( ) are used in the standard library (§16.3.9, §20.3.16). In addition, they are examples of widely applicable techniques. Specialization is useful when there is a more efficient alternative to a general algorithm for a set of template arguments (here, *swap* ( )). In addition, specialization comes in handy when an irregularity of an argument type causes the general algorithm to give an undesired result (here, *less* ( )). These ''irregular types'' are often the built-in pointer and array types.

13.6 Derivation and Templates

Templates and derivation are mechanisms for building new types out of existing ones, and generally for writing useful code that exploits various forms of commonality. As shown in §3.7.1, §3.8.5, and §13.5, combinations of the two mechanisms are the basis for many useful techniques.

Deriving a template class from a non-template class is a way of providing a common implementation for a set of templates. The vector from §13.5 is a good example of this:

```
template<class T> class Vector<T*> : private Vector<void*> { /* ... */ };
```

Another way of looking at such examples is that a template is used to provide an elegant and type-safe interface to an otherwise unsafe and inconvenient-to-use facility.

Naturally, it is often useful to derive one template class from another. One use of a base class is as a building block in the implementation of further classes. If members of a base class depend on a template parameter of a derived class, the base itself must be parameterized; *Vec* from §3.7.2 is an example of this:

```
template<class T> class vector { /* ... */ };
template<class T> class Vec : public vector<T> { /* ... */ };
```

The overload resolution rules for template functions ensure that functions work ''correctly'' for such derived types (§13.3.2).

Having the same template parameter for the base and derived class is the most common case, but it is not a requirement. Interesting, although less frequently used, techniques rely on passing the derived type itself to the base class. For example:

```
template <class C> class Basic_ops { // basic operators on containers
public:
    bool operator==(const C&) const;    // compare all elements
    bool operator!=(const C&) const;
    // ...
    // give access to C's operations:
    const C& derived() const { return static_cast<const C&>(*this); }
};

template<class T> class Math_container : public Basic_ops< Math_container<T> > {
public:
    size_t size() const;
    T& operator[] (size_t);
    const T& operator[] (size_t) const;
    // ...
};
```

This allows the definition of the basic operations on containers to be separate from the definition of the containers themselves and defined once only. However, the definition of operations such as == and != must be expressed in terms of both the container and its elements, so the base class needs to be passed to the container template.

Assuming that a *Math_container* is similar to a traditional vector, the definitions of a *Basic_ops* member would look something like this:

```
template <class C> bool Basic_ops<C>::operator==(const C& a) const
{
    if (derived().size() != a.size()) return false;
    for (int i = 0; i<derived().size(); ++i)
        if (derived()[i] != a[i]) return false;
    return true;
}
```

An alternative technique for keeping the containers and operations separate would be to combine them from template arguments rather than use derivation:

```
template<class T, class C> class Mcontainer {
    C elements;
```

```
public:
    T& operator[](size_t i) { return elements[i]; }

    friend bool operator==<>(const Mcontainer&, const Mcontainer&); // compare elements
    friend bool operator!=<>(const Mcontainer&, const Mcontainer&);
    // ...
};

template<class T> class My_array { /* ... */ };

Mcontainer<double, My_array<double> > mc;
```

A class generated from a class template is a perfectly ordinary class. Consequently, it can have *friend* functions (§C.13.2). In this case, I used *friend*s to achieve the conventional symmetric argument style for == and != (§11.3.2). One might also consider passing a template rather than a container as the *C* argument in such cases (§C.13.3).

13.6.1 Parameterization and Inheritance

A template parameterizes the definition of a type or a function with another type. Source code implementing the template is identical for all parameter types, as is most code using the template. Where added flexibility is needed, specialization can be used. An abstract class defines an interface. Much code for different implementations of the abstract class can be shared in class hierarchies, and most code using the abstract class doesn't depend on its implementation. From a design perspective, the two approaches are so close that they deserve a common name. Since both allow an algorithm to be expressed once and applied to a variety of types, people sometimes refer to both as *polymorphic*. To distinguish them, what virtual functions provide is called *run-time polymorphism*, and what templates offer is called *compile-time polymorphism* or *parametric polymorphism*.

So when do we choose to use a template and when do we rely on an abstract class? In either case, we manipulate objects that share a common set of operations. If no hierarchical relationship is required between these objects, they are best used as template arguments. If the actual types of these objects cannot be known at compile-time, they are best represented as classes derived from a common abstract class. If run-time efficiency is at a premium, that is, if inlining of operations is essential, a template should be used. This issue is discussed in greater detail in §24.4.1.

13.6.2 Member Templates

A class or a class template can have members that are themselves templates. For example:

```
template<class Scalar> class complex {
    Scalar re, im;
public:
    template<class T> complex(const complex<T>& c) : re(c.real()), im(c.imag()) { }
    // ...
};

complex<float> cf(0,0);
complex<double> cd = cf;   // ok: uses float to double conversion
```

```
class  Quad {
      // no conversion to int
};

complex<Quad> cq;
complex<int> ci = cq;            // error: no Quad to int conversion
```

In other words, you can construct a *complex<T1>* from a *complex<T2>* if and only if you can initialize a *T1* by a *T2*. That seems reasonable.

Unfortunately, C++ accepts some unreasonable conversions between built-in types, such as from *double* to *int*. Truncation problems could be caught at run time using a checked conversion in the style of *implicit_cast* (§13.3.1) and *checked* (§C.6.2.6):

```
template<class Scalar> class complex {
      Scalar re, im;
public:
      complex() : re(0), im(0) { }
      complex(const complex<Scalar>& c) : re(c.real()), im(c.imag()) { }

      template<class T2> complex(const complex<T2>& c)
            : re(checked_cast<Scalar>(c.real())), im(checked_cast<Scalar>(c.imag())) { }
      // ...
};
```

For completeness, I added a default constructor and a copy constructor. Curiously enough, a template constructor is never used to generate a copy constructor, so without the explicitly declared copy constructor, a default copy constructor would have been generated. In that case, that generated copy constructor would have been identical to the one I explicitly specified. Similarly, copy assignment (§10.4.4.1, §11.7) must be defined as a non-template operator.

A member template cannot be *virtual*. For example:

```
class  Shape {
      // ...
      template<class T> virtual bool intersect(const T&) const =0; // error: virtual template
};
```

This must be illegal. If it were allowed, the traditional virtual function table technique for implementing virtual functions (§2.5.5) could not be used. The linker would have to add a new entry to the virtual table for class *Shape* each time someone called *intersect()* with a new argument type.

13.6.3 Inheritance Relationships

A class template is usefully understood as a specification of how particular types are to be created. In other words, the template implementation is a mechanism that generates types when needed based on the user's specification. Consequently, a class template is sometimes called a *type generator*.

As far as the C++ language rules are concerned, there is no relationship between two classes generated from a single class template. For example:

```
class Shape { / * ... * / } ;
class Circle : public Shape { / * ... * / } ;
```

Given these declarations, people sometimes try to treat a *set<Circle*>* as a *set<Shape*>*. This is a serious logical error based on a flawed argument: ''A *Circle* is a *Shape*, so a set of *Circle*s is also a set of *Shape*s; therefore, I should be able to use a set of *Circle*s as a set of *Shape*s.'' The ''therefore'' part of this argument doesn't hold. The reason is that a set of *Circle*s guarantees that the member of the set are *Circle*s; a set of *Shape*s does not provide that guarantee. For example:

```
class Triangle : public Shape { / * ... * / } ;

void f(set<Shape*>& s )
{
    // ...
    s . insert (new Triangle ( ) ) ;
    // ...
}

void g (set<Circle*>& s )
{
    f(s) ; // error, type mismatch: s is a set<Circle*>, not a set<Shape*>
}
```

This won't compile because there is no built-in conversion from *set<Circle*>*& to *set<Shape*>*&. Nor should there be. The guarantee that the members of a *set<Circle*>* are *Circle*s allows us to safely and efficiently apply *Circle*-specific operations, such as determining the radius, to members of the set. If we allowed a *set<Circle*>* to be treated as a *set<Shape*>*, we could no longer maintain that guarantee. For example, *f*() inserts a *Triangle** into its *set<Shape*>* argument. If the *set<Shape*>* could have been a *set<Circle*>*, the fundamental guarantee that a *set<Circle*>* contains *Circle**s only would have been violated.

13.6.3.1 Template Conversions

The example in the previous section demonstrates that there cannot be any *default* relationship between classes generated from the same templates. However, for some templates we would like to express such a relationship. For example, when we define a pointer template, we would like to reflect inheritance relationships among the objects pointed to. Member templates (§13.6.2) allow us to specify many such relationships where desired. Consider:

```
template<class T> class Ptr {    // pointer to T
    T* p ;
public :
    Ptr (T*) ;
    Ptr (const Ptr&) ;                        // copy constructor
    template<class T2> operator Ptr<T2> ( ) ; // convert Ptr<T> to Ptr<T2>
    // ...
} ;
```

We would like to define the conversion operators to provide the inheritance relationships we are accustomed to for built-in pointers for these user-defined *Ptr*s. For example:

```
void f (Ptr<Circle> pc)
{
    Ptr<Shape> ps = pc ;        // should work
    Ptr<Circle> pc2 = ps ;      // should give error
}
```

We want to allow the first initialization if and only if *Shape* really is a direct or indirect public base class of *Circle*. In general, we need to define the conversion operator so that the *Ptr<T>* to *Ptr<T2>* conversion is accepted if and only if a *T** can be assigned to a *T2**. That can be done like this:

```
template<class T>
    template<class T2>
        Ptr<T>::operator Ptr<T2> () { return Ptr<T2>(p); }
```

The return statement will compile if and only if *p* (which is a *T**) can be an argument to the *Ptr<T2>(T2*)* constructor. Therefore, if *T** can be implicitly converted into a *T2**, the *Ptr<T>* to *Ptr<T2>* conversion will work. For example

```
void f (Ptr<Circle> pc)
{
    Ptr<Shape> ps = pc ;        // ok: can convert Circle* to Shape*
    Ptr<Circle> pc2 = ps ;      // error: cannot convert Shape* to Circle*
}
```

Be careful to define logically meaningful conversions only.

Note that the template parameter lists of a template and its template member cannot be combined. For example:

```
template<class T, class T2>      // error
    Ptr<T>::operator Ptr<T2> () { return Ptr<T2>(p); }
```

13.7 Source Code Organization

There are two obvious ways of organizing code using templates:
[1] Include template definitions before their use in a translation unit.
[2] Include template declarations (only) before their use in a translation unit, and compile their definitions separately.
In addition, template functions are sometimes first declared, then used, and finally defined in a single translation unit.

To see the differences between the two main approaches, consider a simple template:

```
#include<iostream>

template<class T> void out (const T& t) { std::cerr << t; }
```

We could call this *out.c* and #*include* it wherever *out* () was needed. For example:

```
// user1.c:
    #include "out.c"
    // use out()

// user2.c:
    #include "out.c"
    // use out()
```

That is, the definition of *out* ( ) and all declarations it depends on are #*include*d in several different compilation units. It is up to the compiler to generate code when needed (only) and to optimize the process of reading redundant definitions. This strategy treats template functions the same way as inline functions.

One obvious problem with this is that everything on which the definition of *out* ( ) depends is added to each file using *out* ( ), thus increasing the amount of information that the compiler must process. Another problem is that users may accidentally come to depend on declarations included only for the benefit of the definition of *out* ( ). This danger can be minimized by using namespaces, by avoiding macros, and generally by reducing the amount of information included.

The separate compilation strategy is the logical conclusion of this line of thinking: if the template definition isn't included in the user code, none of its dependencies can affect that code. Thus we split the original *out* . *c* into two files:

```
// out.h:
    template<class  T> void  out(const  T& t);

// out.c:
    #include<iostream>
    #include "out.h"

    export  template<class  T> void  out(const  T& t)  { std::cerr << t;  }
```

The file *out* . *c* now holds all of the information needed to define *out* ( ), and *out* . *h* holds only what is needed to call it. A user #*include*s only the declaration (the interface):

```
// user1.c:
    #include "out.h"
    // use out()

// user2.c:
    #include "out.h"
    // use out()
```

This strategy treats template functions the same way it does non-inline functions. The definition (in *out* . *c*) is compiled separately, and it is up to the implementation to find the definition of *out* ( ) when needed. This strategy also puts a burden on the implementation. Instead of having to filter out redundant copies of a template definition, the implementation must find the unique definition when needed.

Note that to be accessible from other compilation units, a template definition must be explicitly declared *export* (§9.2.3). This can be done by adding *export* to the definition or to a preceding declaration. Otherwise, the definition must be in scope wherever the template is used.

Which strategy or combination of strategies is best depends on the compilation and linkage system used, the kind of application you are building, and the external constraints on the way you build systems. Generally, inline functions and small template functions that primarily call other template functions are candidates for inclusion into every compilation unit in which they are used. On an implementation with average support from the linker for template instantiation, doing this can speed up compilation and improve error messages.

Including a definition makes it vulnerable to having its meaning affected by macros and declarations in the context into which it is included. Consequently, larger template functions and template functions with nontrivial context dependencies are better compiled separately. Also, if the definition of a template requires a large number of declarations, these declarations can have undesirable side effects if they are included into the context in which the template is used.

I consider the approach of separately compiling template definitions and including declarations only in user code ideal. However, the application of ideals must be tempered by practical constraints, and separate compilation of templates is expensive on some implementations.

Whichever strategy is used, non-*inline static* members (§C.13.1) must have a unique definition in some compilation unit. This implies that such members are best not used for templates that are otherwise included in many translation units.

One ideal is for code to work the same whether it is compiled as a single unit or separated into several separately translated units. That ideal should be approached by restricting a template definition's dependency on its environment rather than by trying to carry as much as possible of its definition context with it into the instantiation process.

13.8 Advice

[1]   Use templates to express algorithms that apply to many argument types; §13.3.
[2]   Use templates to express containers; §13.2.
[3]   Provide specializations for containers of pointers to minimize code size; §13.5.
[4]   Always declare the general form of a template before specializations; §13.5.
[5]   Declare a specialization before its use; §13.5.
[6]   Minimize a template definition's dependence on its instantiation contexts; §13.2.5, §C.13.8.
[7]   Define every specialization you declare; §13.5.
[8]   Consider if a template needs specializations for C-style strings and arrays; §13.5.2.
[9]   Parameterize with a policy object; §13.4.
[10] Use specialization and overloading to provide a single interface to implementations of the same concept for different types; §13.5.
[11] Provide a simple interface for simple cases and use overloading and default arguments to express less common cases; §13.5, §13.4.
[12] Debug concrete examples before generalizing to a template; §13.2.1.
[13] Remember to *export* template definitions that need to be accessible from other translation units; §13.7.
[14] Separately compile large templates and templates with nontrivial context dependencies; §13.7.
[15] Use templates to express conversions but define those conversions very carefully; §13.6.3.1.
[16] Where necessary, constrain template arguments using a *constraint*() member function; §13.9[16], §C.13.10.

[17] Use explicit instantiation to minimize compile time and link time; §C.13.10.

[18] Prefer a template over derived classes when run-time efficiency is at a premium; §13.6.1.

[19] Prefer derived classes over a template if adding new variants without recompilation is important; §13.6.1.

[20] Prefer a template over derived classes when no common base can be defined; §13.6.1.

[21] Prefer a template over derived classes when built-in types and structures with compatibility constraints are important; §13.6.1.

13.9 Exercises

1. (*2) Fix the errors in the definition of *List* from §13.2.5 and write out C++ code equivalent to what the compiler must generate for the definition of *List* and the function $f()$. Run a small test case using your hand-generated code and the code generated by the compiler from the template version. If possible on your system given your knowledge, compare the generated code.

2. (*3) Write a singly-linked list class template that accepts elements of any type derived from a class *Link* that holds the information necessary to link elements. This is called an *intrusive list*. Using this list, write a singly-linked list that accepts elements of any type (a non-intrusive list). Compare the performance of the two list classes and discuss the tradeoffs between them.

3. (*2.5) Write intrusive and non-intrusive doubly-linked lists. What operations should be provided in addition to the ones you found necessary to supply for a singly-linked list?

4. (*2) Complete the *String* template from §13.2 based on the *String* class from §11.12.

5. (*2) Define a *sort*() that takes its comparison criterion as a template argument. Define a class *Record* with two data members *count* and *price*. Sort a *vector<Record>* on each data member.

6. (*2) Implement a *qsort*() template.

7. (*2) Write a program that reads (*key*, *value*) pairs and prints out the sum of the *value*s corresponding to each distinct *key*. Specify what is required for a type to be a *key* and a *value*.

8. (*2.5) Implement a simple *Map* class based on the *Assoc* class from §11.8. Make sure *Map* works correctly using both C-style strings and *string*s as keys. Make sure *Map* works correctly for types with and without default constructors. Provide a way of iterating over the elements of a *Map*.

9. (*3) Compare the performance of the word count program from §11.8 against a program not using an associative array. Use the same style of I/O in both cases.

10. (*3) Re-implement *Map* from §13.9[8] using a more suitable data structure (e.g., a red-black tree or a Splay tree).

11. (*2.5) Use *Map* to implement a topological sort function. Topological sort is described in [Knuth,1968] vol. 1 (second edition), pg 262.

12. (*1.5) Make the sum program from §13.9[7] work correctly for names containing spaces; for example, "thumb tack."

13. (*2) Write *readline*() templates for different kinds of lines. For example (item,count,price).

14. (*2) Use the technique outlined for *Literate* in §13.4 to sort strings in reverse lexicographical order. Make sure the technique works both for C++ implementations where *char* is *signed* and for C++ implementations where it is *unsigned*. Use a variant of that technique to provide a sort that is not case-sensitive.

15. (∗1.5) Construct an example that demonstrates at least three differences between a function template and a macro (not counting the differences in definition syntax).
16. (∗2) Devise a scheme that ensures that the compiler tests general constraints on the template arguments for every template for which an object is constructed. It is not sufficient just to test constraints of the form ''the argument *T* must be a class derived from *My_base*.''

14

Exception Handling

*Don't interrupt me
while I'm interrupting.
– Winston S. Churchill*

Error handling — grouping of exceptions — catching exceptions — catch all — re-throw — resource management — *auto_ptr* — exceptions and *new* — resource exhaustion — exceptions in constructors — exceptions in destructors — exceptions that are not errors — exception specifications — unexpected exceptions — uncaught exceptions — exceptions and efficiency — error-handling alternatives — standard exceptions — advice — exercises.

14.1 Error Handling

As pointed out in §8.3, the author of a library can detect run-time errors but does not in general have any idea what to do about them. The user of a library may know how to cope with such errors but cannot detect them – or else they would have been handled in the user's code and not left for the library to find. The notion of an *exception* is provided to help deal with such problems. The fundamental idea is that a function that finds a problem it cannot cope with *throws* an exception, hoping that its (direct or indirect) caller can handle the problem. A function that wants to handle that kind of problem can indicate that it is willing to *catch* that exception (§2.4.2, §8.3).

This style of error handling compares favorably with more traditional techniques. Consider the alternatives. Upon detecting a problem that cannot be handled locally, a function could:

[1] terminate the program,
[2] return a value representing ''error,''
[3] return a legal value and leave the program in an illegal state, or
[4] call a function supplied to be called in case of ''error.''

Case [1], "terminate the program," is what happens by default when an exception isn't caught. For most errors, we can and must do better. In particular, a library that doesn't know about the purpose and general strategy of the program in which it is embedded cannot simply *exit*() or *abort*(). A library that unconditionally terminates cannot be used in a program that cannot afford to crash. One way of viewing exceptions is as a way of giving control to a caller when no meaningful action can be taken locally.

Case [2], "return an error value," isn't always feasible because there is often no acceptable "error value." For example, if a function returns an *int*, *every int* might be a plausible result. Even where this approach is feasible, it is often inconvenient because every call must be checked for the error value. This can easily double the size of a program (§14.8). Consequently, this approach is rarely used systematically enough to detect all errors.

Case [3], "return a legal value and leave the program in an illegal state," has the problem that the calling function may not notice that the program has been put in an illegal state. For example, many standard C library functions set the global variable *errno* to indicate an error (§20.4.1, §22.3). However, programs typically fail to test *errno* consistently enough to avoid consequential errors caused by values returned from failed calls. Furthermore, the use of global variables for recording error conditions doesn't work well in the presence of concurrency.

Exception handling is not meant to handle problems for which case [4], "call an error-handler function," is relevant. However, in the absence of exceptions, an error-handler function has exactly the three other cases as alternatives for how *it* handles the error. For a further discussion of error-handling functions and exceptions, see §14.4.5.

The exception-handling mechanism provides an alternative to the traditional techniques when they are insufficient, inelegant, and error-prone. It provides a way of explicitly separating error-handling code from "ordinary" code, thus making the program more readable and more amenable to tools. The exception-handling mechanism provides a more regular style of error handling, thus simplifying cooperation between separately written program fragments.

One aspect of the exception-handling scheme that will appear novel to C and Pascal programmers is that the default response to an error (especially to an error in a library) is to terminate the program. The traditional response has been to muddle through and hope for the best. Thus, exception handling makes programs more "brittle" in the sense that more care and effort must be taken to get a program to run acceptably. This seems preferable, though, to getting wrong results later in the development process − or after the development process is considered complete and the program is handed over to innocent users. Where termination is unacceptable, we can catch all exceptions (§14.3.2) or catch all exceptions of a specific kind (§14.6.2). Thus, an exception terminates a program only if a programmer allows it to terminate. This is preferable to the unconditional termination that happens when a traditional incomplete recovery leads to a catastrophic error.

Sometimes people have tried to alleviate the unattractive aspects of "muddling through" by writing out error messages, putting up dialog boxes asking the user for help, etc. Such approaches are primarily useful in debugging situations in which the user is a programmer familiar with the structure of the program. In the hands of nondevelopers, a library that asks the (possibly absent) user/operator for help is unacceptable. Also, in many cases error messages have no place to go (say, if the program runs in an environment in which *cerr* doesn't connect to anything a user notices); they would be incomprehensible to an end user anyway. At a minimum, the error message might be in the wrong natural language (say, in Finnish to a English user). Worse, the error message would typically refer to library concepts completely unknown to a user (say, "bad argument to atan2," caused by bad input to a graphics system). A good library doesn't "blabber" in this way. Exceptions provide a way for code that detects a problem from which it cannot recover to pass the problem on to some part of the system that might be able to recover. Only a part of the system that has some idea of the context in which the program runs has any chance of composing a meaningful error message.

The exception-handling mechanism can be seen as a run-time analog to the compile-time type checking and ambiguity control mechanisms. It makes the design process more important and can increase the work needed to get an initial and buggy version of a program running. However, the result is code that has a much better chance to run as expected, to run as an acceptable part of a larger program, to be comprehensible to other programmers, and to be amenable to manipulation by tools. Similarly, exception handling provides specific language features to support "good style" in the same way other C++ features support "good style" that can be practiced only informally and incompletely in languages such as C and Pascal.

It should be recognized that error handling will remain a difficult task and that the exception-handling mechanism − although more formalized than the techniques it replaces − is still relatively unstructured compared with language features involving only local control flow. The C++ exception-handling mechanism provides the programmer with a way of handling errors where they are most naturally handled, given the structure of a system. Exceptions make the complexity of error handling visible. However, exceptions are not the cause of that complexity. Be careful not to blame the messenger for bad news.

This may be a good time to review §8.3, where the basic syntax, semantics, and style-of-use aspects of exception handling are presented.

14.1.1 Alternative Views on Exceptions

"Exception" is one of those words that means different things to different people. The C++ exception-handling mechanism is designed to support handling of errors and other exceptional conditions (hence the name). In particular, it is intended to support error handling in programs composed of independently developed components.

The mechanism is designed to handle only synchronous exceptions, such as array range checks and I/O errors. Asynchronous events, such as keyboard interrupts and certain arithmetic errors, are not necessarily exceptional and are not handled directly by this mechanism. Asynchronous events require mechanisms fundamentally different from exceptions (as defined here) to handle them cleanly and efficiently. Many systems offer mechanisms, such as signals, to deal with asynchrony, but because these tend to be system-dependent, they are not described here.

The exception-handling mechanism is a nonlocal control structure based on stack unwinding (§14.4) that can be seen as an alternative return mechanism. There are therefore legitimate uses of exceptions that have nothing to do with errors (§14.5). However, the primary aim of the exception-handling mechanism and the focus of this chapter is error handling and the support of fault tolerance.

Standard C++ doesn't have the notion of a thread or a process. Consequently, exceptional circumstances relating to concurrency are not discussed here. The concurrency facilities available on your system are described in its documentation. Here, I'll just note that the C++ exception-handling mechanism was designed to be effective in a concurrent program as long as the programmer (or system) enforces basic concurrency rules, such as properly locking a shared data structure while using it.

The C++ exception-handling mechanisms are provided to report and handle errors and exceptional events. However, the programmer must decide what it means to be exceptional in a given program. This is not always easy (§14.5). Can an event that happens most times a program is run be considered exceptional? Can an event that is planned for and handled be considered an error? The answer to both questions is yes. "Exceptional" does not mean "almost never happens" or "disastrous." It is better to think of an exception as meaning "some part of the system couldn't do what it was asked to do." Usually, we can then try something else. Exception *throws* should be infrequent compared to function calls or the structure of the system has been obscured. However, we should expect most large programs to *throw* and *catch* at least some exceptions in the course of a normal and successful run.

14.2 Grouping of Exceptions

An exception is an object of some class representing an exceptional occurrence. Code that detects an error (often a library) *throws* an object (§8.3). A piece of code expresses desire to handle an exception by a *catch* clause. The effect of a *throw* is to unwind the stack until a suitable *catch* is found (in a function that directly or indirectly invoked the function that threw the exception).

Often, exceptions fall naturally into families. This implies that inheritance can be useful to structure exceptions and to help exception handling. For example, the exceptions for a mathematical library might be organized like this:

```
class  Matherr { };
class  Overflow: public  Matherr { };
class  Underflow: public  Matherr { };
class  Zerodivide: public  Matherr { };
// ...
```

This allows us to handle any *Matherr* without caring precisely which kind it is. For example:

```
void f()
{
    try {
        // ...
    }
    catch (Overflow) {
        // handle Overflow or anything derived from Overflow
    }
    catch (Matherr) {
        // handle any Matherr that is not Overflow
    }
}
```

Here, an *Overflow* is handled specifically. All other *Matherr* exceptions will be handled by the general case.

Organizing exceptions into hierarchies can be important for robustness of code. For example, consider how you would handle all exceptions from a library of mathematical functions without such a grouping mechanism. This would have to be done by exhaustively listing the exceptions:

```
void g()
{
    try {
        // ...
    }
    catch (Overflow) { /* ... */ }
    catch (Underflow) { /* ... */ }
    catch (Zerodivide) { /* ... */ }
}
```

This is not only tedious, but a programmer can easily forget to add an exception to the list. Consider what would be needed if we didn't group math exceptions. When we added a new exception to the math library, every piece of code that tried to handle every math exception would have to be modified. In general, such universal update is not feasible after the initial release of the library. Often, there is no way of finding every relevant piece of code. Even when there is, we cannot in general assume that every piece of source code is available or that we would be willing to make changes if it were. These recompilation and maintenance problems would lead to a policy that no new exceptions can be added to a library after its first release; *that* would be unacceptable for almost all libraries. This reasoning leads exceptions to be defined as per-library or per-subsystem class hierarchies (§14.6.2).

Please note that neither the built-in mathematical operations nor the basic math library (shared with C) reports arithmetic errors as exceptions. One reason for this is that detection of some arithmetic errors, such as divide-by-zero, are asynchronous on many pipelined machine architectures. The *Matherr* hierarchy described here is only an illustration. The standard library exceptions are described in §14.10.

14.2.1 Derived Exceptions

The use of class hierarchies for exception handling naturally leads to handlers that are interested only in a subset of the information carried by exceptions. In other words, an exception is typically caught by a handler for its base class rather than by a handler for its exact class. The semantics for catching and naming an exception are identical to those of a function accepting an argument. That is, the formal argument is initialized with the argument value (§7.2). This implies that the exception thrown is "sliced" to the exception caught (§12.2.3). For example:

```
class Matherr {
    // ...
    virtual void debug_print() const { cerr << "Math error"; }
};

class Int_overflow: public Matherr {
    const char* op;
    int a1, a2;
```

```
public:
    Int_overflow(const char* p, int a, int b) { op = p; a1 = a; a2 = b; }
    virtual void debug_print() const { cerr << op << '(' << a1 << ',' << a2 << ')'; }
    // ...
};

void f()
{
    try {
        g();
    }
    catch (Matherr m) {
        // ...
    }
}
```

When the *Matherr* handler is entered, *m* is a *Matherr* object − even if the call to *g*() threw *Int_overflow*. This implies that the extra information found in an *Int_overflow* is inaccessible.

As always, pointers or references can be used to avoid losing information permanently. For example, we might write:

```
int add(int x, int y)
{
    if ( (x>0 && y>0 && x>INT_MAX-y) || (x<0 && y<0 && x<INT_MIN-y) )
        throw Int_overflow("+",x,y);

    return x+y;      // x+y will not overflow
}

void f()
{
    try {
        int i1 = add(1,2);
        int i2 = add(INT_MAX,-2);
        int i3 = add(INT_MAX,2);      // here we go!
    }
    catch (Matherr& m) {
        // ...
        m.debug_print();
    }
}
```

The last call of *add*() triggers an exception that causes *Int_overflow*::*debug_print*() to be invoked. Had the exception been caught by value rather than by reference, *Matherr*::*debug_print*() would have been invoked instead.

14.2.2 Composite Exceptions

Not every grouping of exceptions is a tree structure. Often, an exception belongs to two groups. For example:

```
class Netfile_err : public Network_err, public File_system_err { /* ... */ };
```

Such a *Netfile_err* can be caught by functions dealing with network exceptions:

```
void f()
{
    try {
        // something
    }
    catch(Network_err& e) {
        // ...
    }
}
```

and also by functions dealing with file system exceptions:

```
void g()
{
    try {
        // something else
    }
    catch(File_system_err& e) {
        // ...
    }
}
```

This nonhierarchical organization of error handling is important where services, such as networking, are transparent to users. In this case, the writer of *g*() might not even be aware that a network is involved (see also §14.6).

14.3 Catching Exceptions

Consider:

```
void f()
{
    try {
        throw E();
    }
    catch(H) {
        // when do we get here?
    }
}
```

The handler is invoked:

[1] If *H* is the same type as *E*.

[2] If *H* is an unambiguous public base of *E*.

[3] If *H* and *E* are pointer types and [1] or [2] holds for the types to which they refer.

[4] If *H* is a reference and [1] or [2] holds for the type to which *H* refers.

In addition, we can add *const* to the type used to catch an exception in the same way that we can add it to a function parameter. This doesn't change the set of exceptions we can catch; it only restricts us from modifying the exception caught.

In principle, an exception is copied when it is thrown, so the handler gets hold of a copy of the original exception. In fact, an exception may be copied several times before it is caught. Consequently, we cannot throw an exception that cannot be copied. The implementation may apply a wide variety of strategies for storing and transmitting exceptions. It is guaranteed, however, that there is sufficient memory to allow *new* to throw the standard out-of-memory exception, *bad_alloc* (§14.4.5).

14.3.1 Re-Throw

Having caught an exception, it is common for a handler to decide that it can't completely handle the error. In that case, the handler typically does what can be done locally and then throws the exception again. Thus, an error can be handled where it is most appropriate. This is the case even when the information needed to best handle the error is not available in a single place, so that the recovery action is best distributed over several handlers. For example:

```
void h ( )
{
    try {
            // code that might throw Math errors
    }
    catch (Matherr) {
        if (can_handle_it_completely) {
                // handle the Matherr

                return;
        }
        else {
                // do what can be done here

                throw;     // re-throw the exception
        }
    }
}
```

A re-throw is indicated by a *throw* without an operand. If a re-throw is attempted when there is no exception to re-throw, *terminate* ( ) (§14.7) will be called. A compiler can detect and warn about some, but not all, such cases.

The exception re-thrown is the original exception caught and not just the part of it that was accessible as a *Matherr*. In other words, had an *Int_overflow* been thrown, a caller of *h* ( ) could still catch an *Int_overflow* that *h* ( ) had caught as a *Matherr* and decided to re-throw.

14.3.2 Catch Every Exception

A degenerate version of this catch-and-rethrow technique can be important. As for functions, the ellipsis . . . indicates "any argument" (§7.6), so *catch* (. . .) means "catch any exception." For example:

```
void m()
{
    try {
        // something
    }
    catch (...) {          // handle every exception
        // cleanup
        throw;
    }
}
```

That is, if any exception occurs as the result of executing the main part of *m*(), the cleanup action in the handler is invoked. Once the local cleanup is done, the exception that caused the cleanup is re-thrown to trigger further error handling. See §14.6.3.2 for a technique to gain information about an exception caught by a ... handler.

One important aspect of error handling in general and exception handling in particular is to maintain invariants assumed by the program (§24.3.7.1). For example, if *m*() is supposed to leave certain pointers in the state in which it found them, then we can write code in the handler to give them acceptable values. Thus, a ''catch every exception'' handler can be used to maintain arbitrary invariants. However, for many important cases such a handler is not the most elegant solution to this problem (see §14.4).

14.3.2.1 Order of Handlers

Because a derived exception can be caught by handlers for more than one exception type, the order in which the handlers are written in a *try* statement is significant. The handlers are tried in order. For example:

```
void f()
{
    try {
        // ...
    }
    catch (std::ios_base::failure) {
        // handle any stream io error (§14.10)
    }
    catch (std::exception& e) {
        // handle any standard library exception (§14.10)
    }
    catch (...) {
        // handle any other exception (§14.3.2)
    }
}
```

Because the compiler knows the class hierarchy, it can catch many logical mistakes. For example:

```
void g ( )
{
    try {
        // ...
    }
    catch ( . . . ) {
        // handle every exception (§14.3.2)
    }
    catch (std::exception& e) {
        // handle any standard library exception (§14.10)
    }
    catch (std::bad_cast) {
        // handle dynamic_cast failure (§15.4.2)
    }
}
```

Here, the *exception* will never be considered. Even if we removed the ''catch-all'' handler, *bad_cast* wouldn't be considered because it is derived from *exception*.

14.4 Resource Management

When a function acquires a resource – that is, it opens a file, allocates some memory from the free store, sets an access control lock, etc., – it is often essential for the future running of the system that the resource be properly released. Often that ''proper release'' is achieved by having the function that acquired it release it before returning to its caller. For example:

```
void use_file (const char* fn)
{
    FILE* f = fopen (fn, "r");

    // use f

    fclose (f);
}
```

This looks plausible until you realize that if something goes wrong after the call of *fopen* ( ) and before the call of *fclose* ( ), an exception may cause *use_file* ( ) to be exited without *fclose* ( ) being called. Exactly the same problem can occur in languages that do not support exception handling. For example, the standard C library function *longjmp* ( ) can cause the same problem. Even an ordinary *return*-statement could exit *use_file* without closing *f*.

A first attempt to make *use_file* ( ) to be fault-tolerant looks like this:

```
void use_file (const char* fn)
{
    FILE* f = fopen (fn, "r");
    try {
        // use f
    }
```

```
        catch ( ... ) {
            fclose (f);
            throw;
        }
        fclose (f);
    }
```

The code using the file is enclosed in a *try* block that catches every exception, closes the file, and re-throws the exception.

The problem with this solution is that it is verbose, tedious, and potentially expensive. Furthermore, any verbose and tedious solution is error-prone because programmers get bored. Fortunately, there is a more elegant solution. The general form of the problem looks like this:

```
    void acquire ()
    {
        // acquire resource 1
        // ...
        // acquire resource n

        // use resources

        // release resource n
        // ...
        // release resource 1
    }
```

It is typically important that resources are released in the reverse order of their acquisition. This strongly resembles the behavior of local objects created by constructors and destroyed by destructors. Thus, we can handle such resource acquisition and release problems by a suitable use of objects of classes with constructors and destructors. For example, we can define a class *File_ptr* that acts like a *FILE**:

```
    class File_ptr {
        FILE* p;
    public:
        File_ptr (const char* n, const char* a) { p = fopen (n, a); }
        File_ptr (FILE* pp) { p = pp; }
        // suitable copy operations
        ~File_ptr () { if (p) fclose (p); }

        operator FILE* () { return p; }
    };
```

We can construct a *File_ptr* given either a *FILE** or the arguments required for *fopen* ( ). In either case, a *File_ptr* will be destroyed at the end of its scope and its destructor will close the file. Our function now shrinks to this minimum:

```
    void use_file (const char* fn)
    {
        File_ptr f(fn, "r");
        // use f
    }
```

The destructor will be called independently of whether the function is exited normally or exited because an exception is thrown. That is, the exception-handling mechanisms enable us to remove the error-handling code from the main algorithm. The resulting code is simpler and less error-prone than its traditional counterpart.

The process of searching ''up through the stack'' to find a handler for an exception is commonly called ''stack unwinding.'' As the call stack is unwound, the destructors for constructed local objects are invoked.

14.4.1 Using Constructors and Destructors

The technique for managing resources using local objects is usually referred to as ''resource acquisition is initialization.'' This is a general technique that relies on the properties of constructors and destructors and their interaction with exception handling.

An object is not considered constructed until its constructor has completed. Then and only then will stack unwinding call the destructor for the object. An object composed of sub-objects is constructed to the extent that its sub-objects have been constructed. An array is constructed to the extent that its elements have been constructed (and only fully constructed elements are destroyed during unwinding).

A constructor tries to ensure that its object is completely and correctly constructed. When that cannot be achieved, a well-written constructor restores – as far as possible – the state of the system to what it was before creation. Ideally, naively written constructors always achieve one of these alternatives and don't leave their objects in some ''half-constructed'' state. This can be achieved by applying the ''resource acquisition is initialization'' technique to the members.

Consider a class X for which a constructor needs to acquire two resources: a file x and a lock y. This acquisition might fail and throw an exception. Class X's constructor must never return having acquired the file but not the lock. Furthermore, this should be achieved without imposing a burden of complexity on the programmer. We use objects of two classes, *File_ptr* and *Lock_ptr*, to represent the acquired resources. The acquisition of a resource is represented by the initialization of the local object that represents the resource:

```
class X {
    File_ptr aa;
    Lock_ptr bb;
public:
    X(const char* x, const char* y)
        : aa(x, "rw"), // acquire 'x'
          bb(y)        // acquire 'y'
    {}
    // ...
};
```

Now, as in the local object case, the implementation can take care of all of the bookkeeping. The user doesn't have to keep track at all. For example, if an exception occurs after *aa* has been constructed but before *bb* has been, then the destructor for *aa* but not for *bb* will be invoked.

This implies that where this simple model for acquisition of resources is adhered to, the author of the constructor need not write explicit exception-handling code.

The most common resource acquired in an ad-hoc manner is memory. For example:

```
class Y {
    int* p;
    void init();
public:
    Y(int s) { p = new int[s]; init(); }
    ~Y() { delete[] p; }
    // ...
};
```

This practice is common and can lead to "memory leaks." If an exception is thrown by *init*(),
then the store acquired will not be freed; the destructor will not be called because the object wasn't
completely constructed. A safe variant is:

```
class Z {
    vector<int> p;
    void init();
public:
    Z(int s) : p(s) { init(); }
    // ...
};
```

The memory used by *p* is now managed by *vector*. If *init*() throws an exception, the memory
acquired will be freed when the destructor for *p* is (implicitly) invoked.

14.4.2 Auto_ptr

The standard library provides the template class *auto_ptr*, which supports the "resource acquisition
is initialization" technique. Basically, an *auto_ptr* is initialized by a pointer and can be dereferenced in the way that a pointer can. Also, the object pointed to will be implicitly deleted at the end
of the *auto_ptr*'s scope. For example:

```
void f(Point p1, Point p2, auto_ptr<Circle> pc, Shape* pb) // remember to delete pb on exit
{
    auto_ptr<Shape> p(new Rectangle(p1,p2));     // p points to a rectangle
    auto_ptr<Shape> pbox(pb);

    p->rotate(45); // use auto_ptr<Shape> exactly as a Shape*
    // ...
    if (in_a_mess) throw Mess();
    // ...
}
```

Here the *Rectangle*, the *Shape* pointed to by *pb*, and the *Circle* pointed to by *pc* are deleted
whether or not an exception is thrown.

To achieve this *ownership semantics* (also called *destructive copy semantics*), *auto_ptr*s have a
copy semantics that differs radically from that of ordinary pointers: When one *auto_ptr* is copied
into another, the source no longer points to anything. Because copying an *auto_ptr* modifies it, a
const auto_ptr cannot be copied.

The *auto_ptr* template is declared in *<memory>*. It can be described by an implementation:

```
template<class X> class std::auto_ptr {
    template <class Y> struct auto_ptr_ref { /* ... */ };   // helper class
    X* ptr;
public:
    typedef X element_type;

    explicit auto_ptr(X* p =0) throw() { ptr=p; } // throw() means "throws nothing;" see §14.6
    ~auto_ptr() throw() { delete ptr; }

    // note copy constructors and assignments take non-const arguments:
    auto_ptr(auto_ptr& a) throw();                              // copy, then a.ptr=0
    template<class Y> auto_ptr(auto_ptr<Y>& a) throw();         // copy, then a.ptr=0
    auto_ptr& operator=(auto_ptr& a) throw();                   // copy, then a.ptr=0
    template<class Y> auto_ptr& operator=(auto_ptr<Y>& a) throw();   // copy, then a.ptr=0

    X& operator*() const throw() { return *ptr; }
    X* operator->() const throw() { return ptr; }
    X* get() const throw() { return ptr; }                     // extract pointer
    X* release() throw() { X* t = ptr; ptr=0; return t; }      // relinquish ownership
    void reset(X* p =0) throw() { if (p!=ptr) { delete ptr; ptr=p; } }

    auto_ptr(auto_ptr_ref<X>) throw();                         // copy from auto_ptr_ref
    template<class Y> operator auto_ptr_ref<Y>() throw();      // copy to auto_ptr_ref
    template<class Y> operator auto_ptr<Y>() throw();          // destructive copy from auto_ptr
};
```

The purpose of *auto_ptr_ref* is to implement the destructive copy semantics for ordinary *auto_ptr*s while making it impossible to copy a *const auto_ptr*. If a *D** can be converted to a *B** then the template constructor and template assignment can (explicitly or implicitly) convert an *auto_ptr<D>* to an *auto_ptr<B>*. For example:

```
void g(Circle* pc)
{
    auto_ptr<Circle> p2(pc);   // now p2 is responsible for deletion
    auto_ptr<Circle> p3(p2);   // now p3 is responsible for deletion (and p2 isn't)
    p2->m = 7;                 // programmer error: p2.get()==0
    Shape* ps = p3.get();      // extract the pointer from an auto_ptr
    auto_ptr<Shape> aps(p3);   // transfer of ownership and convert type
    auto_ptr<Circle> p4(pc);   // programmer error: now p4 is also responsible for deletion
}
```

The effect of having more than one *auto_ptr* own an object is undefined; most likely, the object will be deleted twice (with bad effects).

Note that *auto_ptr*'s destructive copy semantics means that it does not meet the requirements for elements of a standard container or for standard algorithms such as *sort()*. For example:

```
vector< auto_ptr<Shape> >& v;   // dangerous: use of auto_ptr in container
// ...
sort(v.begin(),v.end());        // Don't do this: The sort will probably mess up v
```

Clearly, *auto_ptr* isn't a general smart pointer. However, it provides the service for which it was designed – exception safety for automatic pointers – with essentially no overhead.

14.4.3 Caveat

Not all programs need to be resilient against all forms of failure, and not all resources are critical enough to warrant the effort to protect them using "resource acquisition is initialization," *auto_ptr*, and *catch* (. . .). For example, for many programs that simply read an input and run to completion, the most suitable response to a serious run-time error is to abort the process (after producing a suitable diagnostic). That is, let the system release all acquired resources and let the user re-run the program with a more suitable input. The strategy discussed here is intended for applications for which such a simplistic response to a run-time error is unacceptable. In particular, a library designer usually cannot make assumptions about the fault tolerance requirements of a program using the library and is thus forced to avoid all unconditional run-time failures and to release all resources before a library function returns to the calling program. The "resource acquisition is initialization" strategy, together with the use of exceptions to signal failure, is suitable for many such libraries.

14.4.4 Exceptions and New

Consider:

```
void f(Arena& a, X* buffer)
{
    X* p1 = new X;
    X* p2 = new X[10];

    X* p3 = new(buffer[10]) X;           // place X in buffer (no deallocation needed)
    X* p4 = new(buffer[11]) X[10];

    X* p5 = new(a) X;                    // allocation from Arena a (deallocate from a)
    X* p6 = new(a) X[10];
}
```

What happens if *X´s* constructor throws an exception? Is the memory allocated by the *operator new* ( ) freed? For the ordinary case, the answer is yes, so the initializations of *p1* and *p2* don't cause memory leaks.

When the placement syntax (§10.4.11) is used, the answer cannot be that simple. Some uses of that syntax allocate memory, which then ought to be released; however, some don't. Furthermore, the point of using the placement syntax is to achieve nonstandard allocation, so nonstandard freeing is typically required. Consequently, the action taken depends on the allocator used. If an allocator *Z::operator new* ( ) is used, *Z::operator delete* ( ) is invoked if it exists; otherwise, no deallocation is attempted. Arrays are handled equivalently (§15.6.1). This strategy correctly handles the standard library placement *new* operator (§10.4.11), as well as any case in which the programmer has provided a matching pair of allocation and deallocation functions.

14.4.5 Resource Exhaustion

A recurring programming problem is what to do when an attempt to acquire a resource fails. For example, previously we blithely opened files (using *fopen* ( )) and requested memory from the free store (using operator *new*) without worrying about what happened if the file wasn't there or if we had run out of free store. When confronted with such problems, programmers come up with two styles of solutions:

Resumption: Ask some caller to fix the problem and carry on.

Termination: Abandon the computation and return to some caller.

In the former case, a caller must be prepared to help out with resource acquisition problems in unknown pieces of code. In the latter, a caller must be prepared to cope with failure of the attempt to acquire the resource. The latter is in most cases far simpler and allows a system to maintain a better separation of levels of abstraction. Note that it is not the program that terminates when one uses the termination strategy; only an individual computation terminates. ''Termination'' is the traditional term for a strategy that returns from a ''failed'' computation to an error handler associated with a caller (which may re-try the failed computation), rather than trying to repair a bad situation and resume from the point at which the problem was detected.

In C++, the resumption model is supported by the function-call mechanism and the termination model is supported by the exception-handling mechanism. Both can be illustrated by a simple implementation and use of the standard library *operator new* ( ) :

```
void* operator new (size_t size)
{
    for ( ; ; ) {
        if (void* p = malloc (size) ) return p;        // try to find memory
        if ( _new_handler == 0) throw bad_alloc ();    // no handler: give up
        _new_handler ();                               // ask for help
    }
}
```

Here, I use the standard C library *malloc* ( ) to do the real search for memory; other implementations of *operator new* ( ) may choose other ways. If memory is found, *operator new* ( ) can return a pointer to it. Otherwise, *operator new* ( ) calls the *_new_handler*. If the *_new_handler* can find more memory for *malloc* ( ) to allocate, all is fine. If it can't, the handler cannot return to *operator new* ( ) without causing an infinite loop. The *_new_handler* ( ) might then choose to throw an exception, thus leaving the mess for some caller to handle:

```
void my_new_handler ()
{
    int no_of_bytes_found = find_some_memory ();
    if (no_of_bytes_found < min_allocation) throw bad_alloc ();    // give up
}
```

Somewhere, there ought to be a *try_block* with a suitable handler:

```
try {
    // ...
}
catch (bad_alloc) {
    // somehow respond to memory exhaustion
}
```

The *_new_handler* used in the implementation of *operator new* ( ) is a pointer to a function maintained by the standard function *set_new_handler* ( ). If I want *my_new_handler* ( ) to be used as the _new_handler_, I say:

```
set_new_handler(&my_new_handler);
```

If I also want to catch *bad_alloc*, I might say:

```
void f()
{
    void(*oldnh)() = set_new_handler(&my_new_handler);

    try {
        // ...
    }
    catch (bad_alloc) {
        // ...
    }
    catch ( ... ) {
        set_new_handler(oldnh);   // re-set handler
        throw;      // re-throw
    }

    set_new_handler(oldnh);         // re-set handler
}
```

Even better, avoid the *catch*(...) handler by applying the "resource acquisition is initialization" technique described in §14.4 to the _new_handler_ (§14.12[1]).

With the _new_handler_, no extra information is passed along from where the error is detected to the helper function. It is easy to pass more information. However, the more information that is passed between the code detecting a run-time error and a function helping correct that error, the more the two pieces of code become dependent on each other. This implies that changes to the one piece of code require understanding of and maybe even changes to the other. To keep separate pieces of software separate, it is usually a good idea to minimize such dependencies. The exception-handling mechanism supports such separation better than do function calls to helper routines provided by a caller.

In general, it is wise to organize resource allocation in layers (levels of abstraction) and avoid having one layer depend on help from the layer that called it. Experience with larger systems shows that successful systems evolve in this direction.

Throwing an exception requires an object to throw. A C++ implementation is required to have enough spare memory to be able to throw *bad_alloc* in case of memory exhaustion. However, it is possible that throwing some other exception will cause memory exhaustion.

14.4.6 Exceptions in Constructors

Exceptions provide a solution to the problem of how to report errors from a constructor. Because a constructor does not return a separate value for a caller to test, the traditional (that is, non-exception-handling) alternatives are:

[1] Return an object in a bad state, and trust the user to test the state.

[2] Set a nonlocal variable (e.g., *errno*) to indicate that the creation failed, and trust the user to test that variable.

[3] Don't do any initialization in the constructor, and rely on the user to call an initialization function before the first use (§E.3.5).

[4] Mark the object "uninitialized" and have the first member function called for the object do the real initialization, and that function can then report an error if initialization fails.

Exception handling allows the information that a construction failed to be transmitted out of the constructor. For example, a simple *Vector* class might protect itself from excessive demands on memory like this:

```
class Vector {
public:
    class Size { } ;

    enum { max = 32000 } ;

    Vector(int sz)
    {
        if (sz<0 || max<sz) throw Size();
        // ...
    }

    // ...
} ;
```

Code creating *Vector*s can now catch *Vector::Size* errors, and we can try to do something sensible with them:

```
Vector* f(int i)
{
    try {
        Vector* p = new Vector(i);
        // ...
        return p;
    }
    catch (Vector::Size) {
        // deal with size error
    }
}
```

As always, the error handler itself can use the standard set of fundamental techniques for error reporting and recovery. Each time an exception is passed along to a caller, the view of what went wrong changes. If suitable information is passed along in the exception, the amount of information available to deal with the problem could increase. In other words, the fundamental aim of the error-handling techniques is to pass information about an error from the original point of detection to a point where there is sufficient information available to recover from the problem, and to do so reliably and conveniently.

The "resource acquisition is initialization" technique is the safest and most elegant way of handling constructors that acquire more than one resource (§14.4). In essence, the technique reduces the problem of handling many resources to repeated application of the (simple) technique for handling one resource.

14.4.6.1 Exceptions and Member Initialization

What happens if a member initializer (directly or indirectly) throws an exception? By default, the exception is passed on to whatever invoked the constructor for the member's class. However, the constructor itself can catch such exceptions by enclosing the complete function body – including the member initializer list – in a *try-block*. For example:

```
class X {
    Vector v;
    // ...
public:
    X(int);
    // ...
};

X::X(int s)
try
    :v(s)       // initialize v by s
{
    // ...
}
catch (Vector::Size) { // exceptions thrown for v are caught here
    // ...
}
```

14.4.6.2 Exceptions and Copying

Like other constructors, a copy constructor can signal a failure by throwing an exception. In that case, no object is constructed. For example, *vector*'s copy constructor often need to allocate memory and copy elements (§16.3.4, §E.3.2) and that can cause exceptions to be thrown. Before throwing an exception, a copy constructor need to release any resources that it acquired. See §E.2 and §E.3 for a detailed discussion of exception handling and resource management for containers.

A copy assignment resembles a copy constructor in that it may have to acquire resources and may have to exit by throwing an exception. Before throwing an exception, an assignment must ensure that both of its operands are left in valid states. Otherwise, standard library requirements may be violated and undefined behavior might result (§E.2, §E.3.3).

14.4.7 Exceptions in Destructors

From the point of view of exception handling, a destructor can be called in one of two ways:

[1] *Normal call*: As the result of a normal exit from a scope (§10.4.3), a *delete* (§10.4.5), etc.
[2] *Call during exception handling*: During stack unwinding (§14.4), the exception-handling mechanism exits a scope containing an object with a destructor.

In the latter case, an exception may not escape from the destructor itself. If it does, it is considered a failure of the exception-handling mechanism and *std::terminate()* (§14.7) is called. After all, there is no general way for the exception-handling mechanism or the destructor to determine whether it is acceptable to ignore one of the exceptions in favor of handling the other. Exiting from a destructor by throwing an exception is also a violation of the standard library requirements (§E.2).

If a destructor calls functions that may throw exceptions, it can protect itself. For example:

```
X::~X()
try {
    f(); // might throw
}
catch (...) {
    // do something
}
```

The standard library function *uncaught_exception*() returns *true* if an exception has been thrown but hasn't yet been caught. This allows the programmer to specify different actions in a destructor depending on whether an object is destroyed normally or as part of stack unwinding.

14.5 Exceptions That Are Not Errors

If an exception is expected and caught so that it has no bad effects on the behavior of the program, then how can it be an error? Only because the programmer thinks of it as an error and of the exception-handling mechanisms as tools for handling errors. Alternatively, one might think of the exception-handling mechanisms as simply another control structure. For example:

```
void f(Queue<X>& q)
try {
    for (;;) {
        X m = q.get();        // throws 'Empty' if queue is empty
        // ...
    }
}
catch (Queue<X>::Empty) {
    return;
}
```

This actually has some charm, so it is a case in which it is not entirely clear what should be considered an error and what should not.

Exception handling is a less structured mechanism than local control structures such as *if* and *for* and is often less efficient when an exception is actually thrown. Therefore, exceptions should be used only where the more traditional control structures are inelegant or impossible to use. Note that the standard library offers a *queue* of arbitrary elements without using exceptions (§17.3.2).

Using exceptions as alternate returns can be an elegant technique for terminating search functions – especially highly recursive search functions such as a lookup in a tree. For example:

```
void fnd(Tree* p, const string& s)
{
    if (s == p->str) throw p;        // found s
    if (p->left) fnd(p->left, s);
    if (p->right) fnd(p->right, s);
}
```

```
Tree* find (Tree* p, const string& s)
{
    try {
        fnd (p,s);
    }
    catch (Tree* q) {      // q->str==s
        return q;
    }
    return 0;
}
```

However, such use of exceptions can easily be overused and lead to obscure code. Whenever reasonable, one should stick to the "exception handling is error handling" view. When this is done, code is clearly separated into two categories: ordinary code and error-handling code. This makes code more comprehensible. Unfortunately, the real world isn't so clear cut. Program organization will (and to some extent should) reflect that.

Error handling is inherently difficult. Anything that helps preserve a clear model of what is an error and how it is handled should be treasured.

14.6 Exception Specifications

Throwing or catching an exception affects the way a function relates to other functions. It can therefore be worthwhile to specify the set of exceptions that might be thrown as part of the function declaration. For example:

```
void f(int a) throw (x2, x3);
```

This specifies that f() may throw only exceptions x2, x3, and exceptions derived from these types, but no others. When a function specifies what exceptions it might throw, it effectively offers a guarantee to its callers. If during execution that function does something that tries to abrogate the guarantee, the attempt will be transformed into a call of std::unexpected(). The default meaning of unexpected() is std::terminate(), which in turn normally calls abort(); see §9.4.1.1 for details.

In effect,

```
void f() throw (x2, x3)
{
    // stuff
}
```

is equivalent to:

```
void f()
try
{
    // stuff
}
```

```
catch (x2) { throw; }       // re-throw
catch (x3) { throw; }       // re-throw
catch (...) {
    std::unexpected();    // unexpected() will not return
}
```

The most important advantage is that the function *declaration* belongs to an interface that is visible to its callers. Function *definitions*, on the other hand, are not universally available. Even when we do have access to the source code of all our libraries, we strongly prefer not to have to look at it very often. In addition, a function with an *exception-specification* is shorter and clearer than the equivalent hand-written version.

A function declared without an *exception-specification* is assumed to throw every exception. For example:

```
int f();          // can throw any exception
```

A function that will throw no exceptions can be declared with an empty list:

```
int g() throw ();     // no exception thrown
```

One might think that the default should be that a function throws no exceptions. However, that would require exception specifications for essentially every function, would be a significant cause for recompilation, and would inhibit cooperation with software written in other languages. This would encourage programmers to subvert the exception-handling mechanisms and to write spurious code to suppress exceptions. It would provide a false sense of security to people who failed to notice the subversion.

14.6.1 Checking Exception Specifications

It is not possible to catch every violation of an interface specification at compile time. However, much compile-time checking is done. The way to think about *exception-specification*s is to assume that a function *will* throw any exception it can. The rules for compile-time checking *exception-specification*s outlaw easily detected absurdities.

If any declaration of a function has an *exception-specification*, every declaration of that function (including the definition) must have an *exception-specification* with exactly the same set of exception types. For example:

```
int f() throw (std::bad_alloc);

int f()      // error: exception-specification missing
{
    // ...
}
```

Importantly, *exception-specification*s are not required to be checked exactly across compilation-unit boundaries. Naturally, an implementation can check. However, for many large and long-lived systems, it is important that the implementation does not − or, if it does, that it carefully gives hard errors only where violations will not be caught at run time.

The point is to ensure that adding an exception somewhere doesn't force a complete update of related exception specifications and a recompilation of all potentially affected code. A system can then function in a partially updated state relying on the dynamic (run-time) detection of unexpected exceptions. This is essential for the maintenance of large systems in which major updates are expensive and not all source code is accessible.

A virtual function may be overridden only by a function that has an *exception-specification* at least as restrictive as its own (explicit or implicit) *exception-specification*. For example:

```
class B {
public:
    virtual void f();              // can throw anything
    virtual void g() throw(X,Y);
    virtual void h() throw(X);
};

class D : public B {
public:
    void f() throw(X);             // ok
    void g() throw(X);             // ok: D::g() is more restrictive than B::g()
    void h() throw(X,Y);           // error: D::h() is less restrictive than B::h()
};
```

This rule is really only common sense. If a derived class threw an exception that the original function didn't advertise, a caller couldn't be expected to catch it. On the other hand, an overriding function that throws fewer exceptions clearly obeys the rule set out by the overridden function's *exception-specification*.

Similarly, you can assign a pointer to function that has a more restrictive *exception-specification* to a pointer to function that has a less restrictive *exception-specification*, but not vice versa. For example:

```
void f() throw(X);
void (*pf1)() throw(X,Y) = &f;    // ok
void (*pf2)() throw() = &f;       // error: f() is less restrictive than pf2
```

In particular, you cannot assign a pointer to a function without an *exception-specification* to a pointer to function that has one:

```
void g(); // might throw anything

void (*pf3)() throw(X) = &g;      // error: g() less restrictive than pf3
```

An *exception-specification* is not part of the type of a function and a *typedef* may not contain one. For example:

```
typedef void (*PF)() throw(X);    // error
```

14.6.2 Unexpected Exceptions

An *exception-specification* can lead to calls to **unexpected()**. Such calls are typically undesirable except during testing. Such calls can be avoided through careful organization of exceptions and specification of interfaces. Alternatively, calls to **unexpected()** can be intercepted and rendered harmless.

A well-defined subsystem Y will often have all its exceptions derived from a class *Yerr*. For example, given

> *class Some_Yerr : public Yerr { / * ... * / } ;*

a function declared

> *void f ( ) throw (Xerr, Yerr, exception) ;*

will pass any *Yerr* on to its caller. In particular, *f* ( ) would handle a *Some_Yerr* by passing it on to its caller. Thus, no *Yerr* in *f* ( ) will trigger *unexpected* ( ).

All exceptions thrown by the standard library are derived from class *exception* (§14.10).

14.6.3 Mapping Exceptions

Occasionally, the policy of terminating a program upon encountering an unexpected exception is too Draconian. In such cases, the behavior of *unexpected* ( ) must be modified into something acceptable.

The simplest way of achieving that is to add the standard library exception *std* :: *bad_exception* to an *exception-specification*. In that case, *unexpected* ( ) will simply throw *bad_exception* instead of invoking a function to try to cope. For example:

```
class  X { } ;
class  Y { } ;
void  f ( )  throw (X , std :: bad_exception)
{
    // ...
    throw  Y ( );      // throw "bad" exception
}
```

The *exception-specification* will catch the unacceptable exception *Y* and throw an exception of type *bad_exception* instead.

There is actually nothing particularly bad about *bad_exception*; it simply provides a mechanism that is less drastic than calling *terminate* ( ). However, it is still rather crude. In particular, information about which exception caused the problem is lost.

14.6.3.1 User Mapping of Exceptions

Consider a function *g* ( ) written for a non-networked environment. Assume further that *g* ( ) has been declared with an *exception-specification* so that it will throw only exceptions related to its "subsystem Y:"

> *void g ( ) throw (Yerr) ;*

Now assume that we need to call *g* ( ) in a networked environment.

Naturally, *g* ( ) will not know about network exceptions and will invoke *unexpected* ( ) when it encounters one. To use *g* ( ) in a distributed environment, we must either provide code that handles network exceptions or rewrite *g* ( ). Assuming a rewrite is infeasible or undesirable, we can handle the problem by redefining the meaning of *unexpected* ( ).

Memory exhaustion is dealt with by the _new_handler_ determined by *set_new_handler*(). Similarly, the response to an unexpected exception is determined by an _unexpected_handler_ set by *std*::*set_unexpected*() from *<exception>*:

```
typedef void(*unexpected_handler)();
unexpected_handler set_unexpected(unexpected_handler);
```

To handle unexpected exceptions well, we first define a class to allow us to use the ''resource acquisition is initialization'' technique for *unexpected*() functions:

```
class STC {      // store and reset class
    unexpected_handler old;
public:
    STC(unexpected_handler f) { old = set_unexpected(f); }
    ~STC() { set_unexpected(old); }
};
```

Then, we define a function with the meaning we want for *unexpected*() in this case:

```
class Yunexpected : public Yerr { };

void throwY() throw(Yunexpected) { throw Yunexpected(); }
```

Used as an *unexpected*() function, *throwY*() maps any unexpected exception into *Yunexpected*.
   Finally, we provide a version of *g*() to be used in the networked environment:

```
void networked_g() throw(Yerr)
{
    STC xx(&throwY);    // now unexpected() throws Yunexpected
    g();
}
```

Because *Yunexpected* is derived from *Yerr*, the *exception-specification* is not violated. Had *throwY*() thrown an exception that did violate the *exception-specification*, *terminate*() would have been called.
   By saving and restoring the _unexpected_handler_, we make it possible for several subsystems to control the handling of unexpected exceptions without interfering with each other. Basically, this technique for mapping an unexpected exception into an expected one is a more flexible variant of what the system offers in the form of *bad_exception*.

14.6.3.2 Recovering the Type of an Exception

Mapping unexpected exceptions to *Yunexpected* would allow a user of *networked_g*() to know that an unexpected exception had been mapped into *Yunexpected*. However, such a user wouldn't know which exception had been mapped. That information was lost in *throwY*(). A simple technique allows that information to be recorded and passed on. For example, we might collect information about *Network_exception*s like this:

```
class Yunexpected : public Yerr {
public:
    Network_exception* pe;
    Yunexpected(Network_exception* p) :pe(p?p->clone():0) { }
    ~Yunexpected() { delete pe; }
};

void throwY() throw(Yunexpected)
try {
    throw; // re-throw to be caught immediately!
}
catch(Network_exception& p) {
    throw Yunexpected(&p);   // throw mapped exception
}
catch(...) {
        throw Yunexpected(0);
}
```

Re-throwing an exception and catching it allows us to get a handle on any exception of a type we can name. The *throwY*() function is called from *unexpected*(), which is conceptually called from a *catch*(...) handler. There therefore is definitely an exception to re-throw. It is not possible for an *unexpected*() function to ignore the exception and return. If it tries to, *unexpected*() itself will throw a *bad_exception* (§14.6.3).

The *clone*() function is used to allocate a copy of an exception on free store. This copy will survive the exception handler's cleanup of local variables.

14.7 Uncaught Exceptions

If an exception is thrown but not caught, the function *std::terminate*() will be called. The *terminate*() function will also be called when the exception-handling mechanism finds the stack corrupted and when a destructor called during stack unwinding caused by an exception tries to exit using an exception.

An unexpected exception is dealt with by the *_unexpected_handler* determined by *set_unexpected*(). Similarly, the response to an uncaught exception is determined by an *_uncaught_handler* set by *std::set_terminate*() from *<exception>*:

```
typedef void (*terminate_handler)();
terminate_handler set_terminate(terminate_handler);
```

The return value is the previous function given to *set_terminate*().

The reason for *terminate*() is that exception handling must occasionally be abandoned for less subtle error-handling techniques. For example, *terminate*() could be used to abort a process or maybe to re-initialize a system. The intent is for *terminate*() to be a drastic measure to be applied when the error-recovery strategy implemented by the exception-handling mechanism has failed and it is time to go to another level of a fault tolerance strategy.

By default, *terminate*() will call *abort*() (§9.4.1.1). This default is the correct choice for most users – especially during debugging.

An *_uncaught_handler* is assumed not to return to its caller. If it tries to, *terminate* ( ) will call *abort* ( ) .

Note that *abort* ( ) indicates abnormal exit from the program. The function *exit* ( ) can be used to exit a program with a return value that indicates to the surrounding system whether the exit is normal or abnormal (§9.4.1.1).

It is implementation-defined whether destructors are invoked when a program is terminated because of an uncaught exception. On some systems, it is essential that the destructors are not called so that the program can be resumed from the debugger. On other systems, it is architecturally close to impossible *not* to invoke the destructors while searching for a handler.

If you want to ensure cleanup when an uncaught exception happens, you can add a catch-all handler (§14.3.2) to *main* ( ) in addition to handlers for exceptions you really care about. For example:

```
int main()
try {
    // ...
}
catch (std::range_error)
{
    cerr << "range error: Not again!\n";
}
catch (std::bad_alloc)
{
    cerr << "new ran out of memory\n";
}
catch (...) {
    // ...
}
```

This will catch every exception, except those thrown by construction and destruction of global variables. There is no way of catching exceptions thrown during initialization of global variables. The only way of gaining control in case of *throw* from an initializer of a nonlocal static object is *set_unexpected* ( ) (§14.6.2). This is another reason to avoid global variables whenever possible.

When an exception is caught, the exact point where it was thrown is generally not known. This represents a loss of information compared to what a debugger might know about the state of a program. In some C++ development environments, for some programs, and for some people, it might therefore be preferable *not* to catch exceptions from which the program isn't designed to recover.

14.8 Exceptions and Efficiency

In principle, exception handling can be implemented so that there is no run-time overhead when no exception is thrown. In addition, this can be done so that throwing an exception isn't all that expensive compared to calling a function. Doing so without adding significant memory overhead while maintaining compatibility with C calling sequences, debugger conventions, etc., is possible, but hard. However, please remember that the alternatives to exceptions are not free either. It is not unusual to find traditional systems in which half of the code is devoted to error handling.

Consider a simple function *f* ( ) that appears to have nothing to do with exception handling:

```
void g (int);

void f ()
{
    string s;
    // ...
    g (1);
    g (2);
}
```

However, *g* ( ) may throw an exception, so *f* ( ) must contain code ensuring that *s* is destroyed correctly in case of an exception. However, had *g* ( ) not thrown an exception it would have had to report its error some other way. Consequently, the comparable code using ordinary code to handle errors instead of exceptions isn't the plain code above, but something like:

```
bool g (int);

bool f ()
{
    string s;
    // ...
    if (g (1))
            if (g (2))
                    return true;
            else
                    return false;
    else
            return false;
}
```

People don't usually handle errors this systematically, though, and it is not always critical to do so. However, when careful and systematic handling of errors is necessary, such housekeeping is best left to a computer, that is, to the exception-handling mechanisms.

Exception-specifications (§14.6) can be most helpful in improving generated code. Had we stated that *g* ( ) didn't throw an exception:

```
void g (int) throw ();
```

the code generation for *f* ( ) could have been improved. It is worth observing that no traditional C function throws an exception, so in most programs every C function can be declared with the empty throw specification *throw* ( ). In particular, an implementation knows that only a few standard C library functions (such as *atexit* ( ) and *qsort* ( )) can throw exceptions, and it can take advantage of that fact to generate better code.

Before giving a ''C function'' an empty *exception-specification, throw* ( ), take a minute to consider if it could possibly throw an exception. For example, it might have been converted to use the C++ operator *new*, which can throw *bad_alloc*, or it might call a C++ library that throws an exception.

14.9 Error-Handling Alternatives

The purpose of the exception-handling mechanisms is to provide a means for one part of a program to inform another part of a program that an ''exceptional circumstance'' has been detected. The assumption is that the two parts of the program are written independently and that the part of the program that handles the exception often can do something sensible about the error.

To use handlers effectively in a program, we need an overall strategy. That is, the various parts of the program must agree on how exceptions are used and where errors are dealt with. The exception-handling mechanisms are inherently nonlocal, so adherence to an overall strategy is essential. This implies that the error-handling strategy is best considered in the earliest phases of a design. It also implies that the strategy must be simple (relative to the complexity of the total program) and explicit. Something complicated would not be consistently adhered to in an area as inherently tricky as error recovery.

First of all, the idea that a single mechanism or technique can handle all errors must be dispelled; it would lead to complexity. Successful fault-tolerant systems are multilevel. Each level copes with as many errors as it can without getting too contorted and leaves the rest to higher levels. The notion of *terminate*() is intended to support this view by providing an escape if the exception-handling mechanism itself is corrupted or if it has been incompletely used, thus leaving exceptions uncaught. Similarly, the notion of *unexpected*() is intended to provide an escape when the strategy using *exception-specifications* to provide firewalls fails.

Not every function should be a firewall. In most systems, it is not feasible to write every function to do sufficient checking to ensure that it either completes successfully or fails in a well-defined manner. The reasons that this will not work varies from program to program and from programmer to programmer. However, for larger programs:

[1] The amount of work needed to ensure this notion of ''reliability'' is too great to be done consistently.

[2] The overheads in time and space are too great for the system to run acceptably (there will be a tendency to check for the same errors, such as invalid arguments, over and over again).

[3] Functions written in other languages won't obey the rules.

[4] This purely local notion of ''reliability'' leads to complexities that actually become a burden to overall system reliability.

However, separating the program into distinct subsystems that either complete successfully or fail in well-defined ways is essential, feasible, and economical. Thus, a major library, subsystem, or key function should be designed in this way. Exception specifications are intended for interfaces to such libraries and subsystems.

Usually, we don't have the luxury of designing all of the code of a system from scratch. Therefore, to impose a general error-handling strategy on all parts of a program, we must take into account program fragments implemented using strategies different from ours. To do this we must address a variety of concerns relating to the way a program fragment manages resources and the state in which it leaves the system after an error. The aim is to have the program fragment appear to follow the general error-handling strategy even if it internally follows a different strategy.

Occasionally, it is necessary to convert from one style of error reporting to another. For example, we might check *errno* and possibly throw an exception after a call to a C library or, conversely, catch an exception and set *errno* before returning to a C program from a C++ library:

```
void  callC ( )  throw ( C_blewit)
{
     errno = 0;
     c_function ( );
     if (errno) {
          // cleanup, if possible and necessary
          throw  C_blewit (errno);
     }
}

extern "C" void  call_from_C ( )  throw ( )
{
     try {
          c_plus_plus_function ( );
     }
     catch ( . . . ) {
          // cleanup, if possible and necessary
          errno = E_CPLPLFCTBLEWIT;
     }
}
```

In such cases, it is important to be systematic enough to ensure that the conversion of error reporting styles is complete.

Error handling should be – as far as possible – hierarchical. If a function detects a run-time
error, it should not ask its caller for help with recovery or resource acquisition. Such requests set
up cycles in the system dependencies. That in turn makes the program hard to understand and
introduces the possibility of infinite loops in the error-handling and recovery code.

Simplifying techniques such as ''resource acquisition is initialization'' and simplifying assumptions such as ''exceptions represent errors'' should be used to make the error-handling code more
regular. See also §24.3.7.1 for ideas about how to use invariants and assertions to make the triggering of exceptions more regular.

14.10 Standard Exceptions

Here is a table of standard exceptions and the functions, operators, and general facilities that throw
them:

Standard Exceptions (thrown by the language)			
Name	Thrown by	Reference	Header
bad_alloc	new	§6.2.6.2, §19.4.5	<new>
bad_cast	dynamic_cast	§15.4.1.1	<typeinfo>
bad_typeid	typeid	§15.4.4	<typeinfo>
bad_exception	exception specification	§14.6.3	<exception>

Standard Exceptions (thrown by the standard library)			
Name	Thrown by	Reference	Header
out_of_range	*at()*	§3.7.2, §16.3.3, §20.3.3	<stdexcept>
	bitset<>::operator[]()	§17.5.3	<stdexcept>
invalid_argument	*bitset constructor*	§17.5.3.1	<stdexcept>
overflow_error	*bitset<>::to_ulong()*	§17.5.3.3	<stdexcept>
ios_base::failure	*ios_base::clear()*	§21.3.6	<ios>

The library exceptions are part of a class hierarchy rooted in the standard library exception class *exception* presented in *<exception>*:

```
class exception {
public:
    exception() throw();
    exception(const exception&) throw();
    exception& operator=(const exception&) throw();
    virtual ~exception() throw();

    virtual const char* what() const throw();
private:
    // ...
};
```

The hierarchy looks like this:

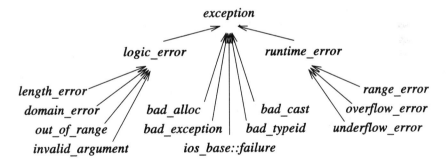

This seems rather elaborate for organizing the eight standard exceptions. This hierarchy attempts to provide a framework for exceptions beyond the ones defined by the standard library. Logic errors are errors that in principle could be caught either before the program starts executing or by tests of arguments to functions and constructors. Run-time errors are all other errors. Some people view this as a useful framework for all errors and exceptions; I don't.

The standard library exception classes don't add functions to the set provided by *exception*; they simply define the required virtual functions appropriately. Thus, we can write:

```
void f()
try {
    // use standard library
}
```

```
catch (exception& e) {
    cout << "standard library exception " << e.what() << '\n';      // well, maybe
    // ...
}
catch (...) {
    cout << "other exception\n";
    // ...
}
```

The standard exceptions are derived from *exception*. However, not every exception is, so it would be a mistake to try to catch every exception by catching *exception*. Similarly, it would be a mistake to assume that every exception derived from *exception* is a standard library exception: programmers can add their own exceptions to the *exception* hierarchy .

Note that *exception* operations do not themselves throw exceptions. In particular, this implies that throwing a standard library exception doesn't cause a *bad_alloc* exception. The exception-handling mechanism keeps a bit of memory to itself for holding exceptions (possibly on the stack). Naturally, it is possible to write code that eventually consumes all memory in the system, thus forcing a failure. For example, here is a function that – if called – tests whether the function call or the exception-handling mechanism runs out of memory first:

```
void perverted()
{
    try {
        throw exception();   // recursive exception throw
    }
    catch (exception& e) {
        perverted();              // recursive function call
        cout << e.what();
    }
}
```

The purpose of the output statement is simply to prevent the compiler from re-using the memory occupied by the exception named *e*.

14.11 Advice

[1] Use exceptions for error handling; §14.1, §14.5, §14.9.
[2] Don't use exceptions where more local control structures will suffice; §14.1.
[3] Use the ''resource allocation is initialization'' technique to manage resources; §14.4.
[4] Not every program needs to be exception safe; §14.4.3.
[5] Use ''resource acquisition is initialization'' and exception handlers to maintain invariants; §14.3.2.
[6] Minimize the use of *try-block*s. Use ''resource acquisition is initialization'' instead of explicit handler code; §14.4.
[7] Not every function needs to handle every possible error; §14.9.
[8] Throw an exception to indicate failure in a constructor; §14.4.6.

[9]   Leave operands in valid states before throwing an exception from an assignment; §14.4.6.2.

[10] Avoid throwing exceptions from destructors; §14.4.7.

[11] Have *main* ( ) catch and report all exceptions; §14.7.

[12] Keep ordinary code and error-handling code separate; §14.4.5, §14.5.

[13] Be sure that every resource acquired in a constructor is released when throwing an exception in that constructor; §14.4.

[14] Keep resource management hierarchical; §14.4.

[15] Use *exception-specification*s for major interfaces; §14.9.

[16] Beware of memory leaks caused by memory allocated by *new* not being released in case of an exception; §14.4.1, §14.4.2, §14.4.4.

[17] Assume that every exception that can be thrown by a function will be thrown; §14.6.

[18] Don't assume that every exception is derived from class *exception*; §14.10.

[19] A library shouldn't unilaterally terminate a program. Instead, throw an exception and let a caller decide; §14.1.

[20] A library shouldn't produce diagnostic output aimed at an end user. Instead, throw an exception and let a caller decide; §14.1.

[21] Develop an error-handling strategy early in a design; §14.9.

14.12 Exercises

1. (∗2) Generalize the *STC* class (§14.6.3.1) to a template that can use the "resource acquisition is initialization" technique to store and reset functions of a variety of types.

2. (∗3) Complete the *Ptr_to_T* class from §11.11 as a template that uses exceptions to signal run-time errors.

3. (∗3) Write a function that searches a binary tree of nodes based on a *char∗* field for a match. If a node containing *hello* is found, *find* ("*hello*") will return a pointer to that node. Use an exception to indicate "not found."

4. (∗3) Define a class *Int* that acts exactly like the built-in type *int*, except that it throws exceptions rather than overflowing or underflowing.

5. (∗2.5) Take the basic operations for opening, closing, reading, and writing from the C interface to your operating system and provide equivalent C++ functions that call the C functions but throw exceptions in case of errors.

6. (∗2.5) Write a complete *Vector* template with *Range* and *Size* exceptions.

7. (∗1) Write a loop that computes the sum of a *Vector* as defined in §14.12[6] without examining the size of the *Vector*. Why is this a bad idea?

8. (∗2.5) Consider using a class *Exception* as the base of all classes used as exceptions. What should it look like? How should it be used? What good might it do? What disadvantages might result from a requirement to use such a class?

9. (∗1) Given a

> *int main* ( ) { / ∗ ... ∗ / }

change it so that it catches all exceptions, turns them into error messages, and *abort* ( ) s. Hint: *call_from_C* ( ) in §14.9 doesn't quite handle all cases.

10. (*2) Write a class or template suitable for implementing callbacks.
11. (*2.5) Write a *Lock* class for some system supporting concurrency.

15

Class Hierarchies

Abstraction is selective ignorance.
– Andrew Koenig

Multiple inheritance — ambiguity resolution — inheritance and *using-declarations* — replicated base classes — virtual base classes — uses of multiple inheritance — access control — protected — access to base classes — run-time type information — *dynamic_cast* — static and dynamic casts — casting from virtual bases — *typeid* — extended type information — uses and misuses of run-time type information — pointers to members — free store — virtual constructors — advice — exercises.

15.1 Introduction and Overview

This chapter discusses how derived classes and virtual functions interact with other language facilities such as access control, name lookup, free store management, constructors, pointers, and type conversions. It has five main parts:

§15.2 Multiple Inheritance
§15.3 Access Control
§15.4 Run-time Type Identification
§15.5 Pointers to Members
§15.6 Free Store Use

In general, a class is constructed from a lattice of base classes. Because most such lattices historically have been trees, a *class lattice* is often called a *class hierarchy*. We try to design classes so that users need not be unduly concerned about the way a class is composed out of other classes. In particular, the virtual call mechanism ensures that when we call a function $f()$ on an object, the same function is called whichever class in the hierarchy provided the declaration of $f()$ used for the call. This chapter focuses on ways to compose class lattices and to control access to parts of classes and on facilities for navigating class lattices at compile time and run time.

15.2 Multiple Inheritance

As shown in §2.5.4 and §12.3, a class can have more than one direct base class, that is, more than one class specified after the : in the class declaration. Consider a simulation in which concurrent activities are represented by a class *Task* and data gathering and display is achieved through a class *Displayed*. We can then define a class of simulated entities, class *Satellite*:

```
class Satellite : public Task, public Displayed {
    // ...
};
```

The use of more than one immediate base class is usually called *multiple inheritance*. In contrast, having just one direct base class is called *single inheritance*.

In addition to whatever operations are defined specifically for a *Satellite*, the union of operations on *Task*s and *Displayed*s can be applied. For example:

```
void f(Satellite& s)
{
    s.draw();        // Displayed::draw()
    s.delay(10);     // Task::delay()
    s.transmit();    // Satellite::transmit()
}
```

Similarly, a *Satellite* can be passed to functions that expect a *Task* or a *Displayed*. For example:

```
void highlight(Displayed*);
void suspend(Task*);

void g(Satellite* p)
{
    highlight(p);    // pass a pointer to the Displayed part of the Satellite
    suspend(p);      // pass a pointer to the Task part of the Satellite
}
```

The implementation of this clearly involves some (simple) compiler technique to ensure that functions expecting a *Task* see a different part of a *Satellite* than do functions expecting a *Displayed*. Virtual functions work as usual. For example:

```
class Task {
    // ...
    virtual void pending() = 0;
};

class Displayed {
    // ...
    virtual void draw() = 0;
};
```

```
class Satellite : public Task, public Displayed {
    // ...
    void pending();        // override Task::pending()
    void draw();           // override Displayed::draw()
};
```

This ensures that *Satellite::draw()* and *Satellite::pending()* will be called for a *Satellite* treated as a *Displayed* and a *Task*, respectively.

Note that with single inheritance (only), the programmer's choices for implementing the classes *Displayed*, *Task*, and *Satellite* would be limited. A *Satellite* could be a *Task* or a *Displayed*, but not both (unless *Task* was derived from *Displayed* or vice versa). Either alternative involves a loss of flexibility.

Why would anyone want a class *Satellite*? Contrary to some people's conjectures, the *Satellite* example is real. There really was − and maybe there still is − a program constructed along the lines used to describe multiple inheritance here. It was used to study the design of communication systems involving satellites, ground stations, etc. Given such a simulation, we can answer questions about traffic flow, determine proper responses to a ground station that is being blocked by a rainstorm, consider tradeoffs between satellite connections and Earth-bound connections, etc. Such simulations do involve a variety of display and debugging operations. Also, we do need to store the state of objects such as *Satellite*s and their subcomponents for analysis, debugging, and error recovery.

15.2.1 Ambiguity Resolution

Two base classes may have member functions with the same name. For example:

```
class Task {
    // ...
    virtual debug_info* get_debug();
};
class Displayed {
    // ...
    virtual debug_info* get_debug();
};
```

When a *Satellite* is used, these functions must be disambiguated:

```
void f(Satellite* sp)
{
    debug_info* dip = sp->get_debug();      // error: ambiguous
    dip = sp->Task::get_debug();            // ok
    dip = sp->Displayed::get_debug();       // ok
}
```

However, explicit disambiguation is messy, so it is usually best to resolve such problems by defining a new function in the derived class:

```
class Satellite : public Task, public Displayed {
    // ...
    debug_info* get_debug()   // override Task::get_debug() and Displayed::get_debug()
    {
        debug_info* dip1 = Task::get_debug();
        debug_info* dip2 = Displayed::get_debug();
        return dip1->merge(dip2);
    }
};
```

This localizes the information about *Satellite*'s base classes. Because *Satellite::get_debug()* overrides the *get_debug()* functions from both of its base classes, *Satellite::get_debug()* is called wherever *get_debug()* is called for a *Satellite* object.

A qualified name *Telstar::draw* can refer to a *draw* declared either in *Telstar* or in one of its base classes. For example:

```
class Telstar : public Satellite {
    // ...
    void draw()
    {
        draw();                        // oops!: recursive call
        Satellite::draw();             // finds Displayed::draw
        Displayed::draw();
        Satellite::Displayed::draw();  // redundant double qualification
    }
};
```

In other words, if a *Satellite::draw* doesn't resolve to a *draw* declared in *Satellite*, the compiler recursively looks in its base classes; that is, it looks for *Task::draw* and *Displayed::draw*. If exactly one match is found, that name will be used. Otherwise, *Satellite::draw* is either not found or is ambiguous.

15.2.2 Inheritance and Using-Declarations

Overload resolution is not applied across different class scopes (§7.4). In particular, ambiguities between functions from different base classes are not resolved based on argument types.

When combining essentially unrelated classes, such as *Task* and *Displayed* in the *Satellite* example, similarity in naming typically does not indicate a common purpose. When such name clashes occur, they often come as quite a surprise to the programmer. For example:

```
class Task {
    // ...
    void debug(double p);    // print info only if priority is lower than p
};
```

```
class Displayed {
    // ...
    void debug(int v);   // the higher the 'v,' the more debug information is printed
};

class Satellite : public Task, public Displayed {
    // ...
};

void g(Satellite* p)
{
    p->debug(1);           // error: ambiguous. Displayed::debug(int) or Task::debug(double) ?
    p->Task::debug(1);      // ok
    p->Displayed::debug(1); // ok
}
```

What if the use of the same name in different base classes was the result of a deliberate design decision and the user wanted selection based on the argument types? In that case, a *using-declaration* (§8.2.2) can bring the functions into a common scope. For example:

```
class A {
public:
    int f(int);
    char f(char);
    // ...
};

class B {
public:
    double f(double);
    // ...
};

class AB: public A, public B {
public:
    using A::f;
    using B::f;
    char f(char);   // hides A::f(char)
    AB f(AB);
};

void g(AB& ab)
{
    ab.f(1);       // A::f(int)
    ab.f('a');     // AB::f(char)
    ab.f(2.0);     // B::f(double)
    ab.f(ab);      // AB::f(AB)
}
```

Using-declarations allow a programmer to compose a set of overloaded functions from base classes and the derived class. Functions declared in the derived class hide functions that would otherwise be available from a base. Virtual functions from bases can be overridden as ever (§15.2.3.1).

A *using-declaration* (§8.2.2) in a class definition must refer to members of a base class. A *using-declaration* may not be used for a member of a class from outside that class, its derived classes, and their member functions. A *using-directive* (§8.2.3) may not appear in a class definition and may not be used for a class.

A *using-declaration* cannot be used to gain access to additional information. It is simply a mechanism for making accessible information more convenient to use (§15.3.2.2).

15.2.3 Replicated Base Classes

With the ability of specifying more than one base class comes the possibility of having a class as a base twice. For example, had *Task* and *Displayed* each been derived from a *Link* class, a *Satellite* would have two *Link*s:

```
struct Link {
    Link* next;
};

class Task : public Link {
    // the Link is used to maintain a list of all Tasks (the scheduler list)
    // ...
};

class Displayed : public Link {
    // the Link is used to maintain a list of all Displayed objects (the display list)
    // ...
};
```

This causes no problems. Two separate *Link* objects are used to represent the links, and the two lists do not interfere with each other. Naturally, one cannot refer to members of the *Link* class without risking an ambiguity (§15.2.3.1). A *Satellite* object could be drawn like this:

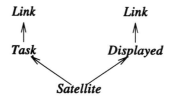

Examples of where the common base class shouldn't be represented by two separate objects can be handled using a virtual base class (§15.2.4).

Usually, a base class that is replicated the way *Link* is here is an implementation detail that shouldn't be used from outside its immediate derived class. If such a base must be referred to from a point where more than one copy of the base is visible, the reference must be explicitly qualified to resolve the ambiguity. For example:

```
void mess_with_links(Satellite* p)
{
    p->next = 0;                    // error: ambiguous (which Link?)
    p->Link::next = 0;             // error: ambiguous (which Link?)
```

```
        p->Task::next = 0;          // ok
        p->Displayed::next = 0;     // ok

        // ...
    }
```

This is exactly the mechanism used to resolve ambiguous references to members (§15.2.1).

15.2.3.1 Overriding

A virtual function of a replicated base class can be overridden by a (single) function in a derived class. For example, one might represent the ability of an object to read itself from a file and write itself back to a file like this:

```
    class Storable {
    public:
        virtual const char* get_file() = 0;
        virtual void read() = 0;
        virtual void write() = 0;
        virtual ~Storable() { }
    };
```

Naturally, several programmers might rely on this to develop classes that can be used independently or in combination to build more elaborate classes. For example, one way of stopping and restarting a simulation is to store components of a simulation and then restore them later. That idea might be implemented like this:

```
    class Transmitter : public Storable {
    public:
        void write();
        // ...
    };
    class Receiver : public Storable {
    public:
        void write();
        // ...
    };
    class Radio : public Transmitter, public Receiver {
    public:
        const char* get_file();
        void read();
        void write();
        // ...
    };
```

Typically, an overriding function calls its base class versions and then does the work specific to the derived class:

```
void  Radio::write()
{
      Transmitter::write();
      Receiver::write();
      // write radio-specific information
}
```

Casting from a replicated base class to a derived class is discussed in §15.4.2. For a technique for overriding each of the *write* () functions with separate functions from derived classes, see §25.6.

15.2.4 Virtual Base Classes

The *Radio* example in the previous subsection works because class *Storable* can be safely, conveniently, and efficiently replicated. Often, that is not the case for the kind of class that makes a good building block for other classes. For example, we might define *Storable* to hold the name of the file to be used for storing the object:

```
class  Storable {
public:
      Storable(const  char* s);
      virtual  void  read() = 0;
      virtual  void  write() = 0;
      virtual  ~Storable();
private:
      const  char* store;

      Storable(const  Storable&);
      Storable& operator=(const  Storable&);
};
```

Given this apparently minor change to *Storable*, we must change the design of *Radio*. All parts of an object must share a single copy of *Storable*; otherwise, it becomes unnecessarily hard to avoid storing multiple copies of the object. One mechanism for specifying such sharing is a virtual base class. Every *virtual* base of a derived class is represented by the same (shared) object. For example:

```
class  Transmitter : public  virtual  Storable {
public:
      void  write();
      // ...
};

class  Receiver : public  virtual  Storable {
public:
      void  write();
      // ...
};
```

```
class Radio : public Transmitter, public Receiver {
public:
    void write();
    // ...
};
```

Or graphically:

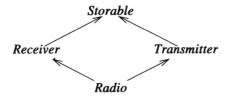

Compare this diagram with the drawing of the *Satellite* object in §15.2.3 to see the difference between ordinary inheritance and virtual inheritance. In an inheritance graph, every base class of a given name that is specified to be virtual will be represented by a single object of that class. On the other hand, each base class not specified *virtual* will have its own sub-object representing it.

15.2.4.1 Programming Virtual Bases

When defining the functions for a class with a virtual base, the programmer in general cannot know whether the base will be shared with other derived classes. This can be a problem when implementing a service that requires a base class function to be called exactly once. For example, the language ensures that a constructor of a virtual base is called exactly once. The constructor of a virtual base is invoked (implicitly or explicitly) from the constructor for the complete object (the constructor for the most derived class). For example:

```
class A {  // no constructor
    // ...
};

class B {
public:
    B(); // default constructor
    // ...
};

class C {
public:
    C(int);    // no default constructor
};

class D : virtual public A, virtual public B, virtual public C
{
    D() { /* ... */ }                // error: no default constructor for C
    D(int i) : C(i) { /* ... */ };   // ok
    // ...
};
```

The constructor for a virtual base is called before the constructors for its derived classes.

Where needed, the programmer can simulate this scheme by calling a virtual base class function only from the most derived class. For example, assume we have a basic *Window* class that knows how to draw its contents:

```
class Window {
    // basic stuff
    virtual void draw();
};
```

In addition, we have various ways of decorating a window and adding facilities:

```
class Window_with_border : public virtual Window {
    // border stuff
    void own_draw();    // display the border
    void draw();
};

class Window_with_menu : public virtual Window {
    // menu stuff
    void own_draw();    // display the menu
    void draw();
};
```

The *own_draw*() functions need not be virtual because they are meant to be called from within a virtual *draw*() function that "knows" the type of the object for which it was called.

From this, we can compose a plausible *Clock* class:

```
class Clock : public Window_with_border, public Window_with_menu {
    // clock stuff
    void own_draw();    // display the clock face and hands
    void draw();
};
```

Or graphically:

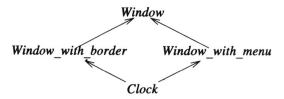

The *draw*() functions can now be written using the *own_draw*() functions so that a caller of any *draw*() gets *Window*::*draw*() invoked exactly once. This is done independently of the kind of *Window* for which *draw*() is invoked:

```
void Window_with_border::draw()
{
    Window::draw();
    own_draw();    // display the border
}
void Window_with_menu::draw()
{
    Window::draw();
    own_draw();    // display the menu
}
void Clock::draw()
{
    Window::draw();
    Window_with_border::own_draw();
    Window_with_menu::own_draw();
    own_draw();    // display the clock face and hands
}
```

Casting from a *virtual* base class to a derived class is discussed in §15.4.2.

15.2.5 Using Multiple Inheritance

The simplest and most obvious use of multiple inheritance is to "glue" two otherwise unrelated classes together as part of the implementation of a third class. The *Satellite* class built out of the *Task* and *Displayed* classes in §15.2 is an example of this. This use of multiple inheritance is crude, effective, and important, but not very interesting. Basically, it saves the programmer from writing a lot of forwarding functions. This technique does not affect the overall design of a program significantly and can occasionally clash with the wish to keep implementation details hidden. However, a technique doesn't have to be clever to be useful.

Using multiple inheritance to provide implementations for abstract classes is more fundamental in that it affects the way a program is designed. Class *BB_ival_slider* (§12.4.3) is an example:

```
class BB_ival_slider
    : public Ival_slider  // interface
    , protected BBslider  // implementation
{
    // implementation of functions required by 'Ival_slider' and 'BBslider'
    // using the facilities provided by 'BBslider'
};
```

In this example, the two base classes play logically distinct roles. One base is a public abstract class providing the interface and the other is a protected concrete class providing implementation "details." These roles are reflected in both the style of the classes and in the access control provided. The use of multiple inheritance is close to essential here because the derived class needs to override virtual functions from both the interface and the implementation.

Multiple inheritance allows sibling classes to share information without introducing a dependence on a unique common base class in a program. This is the case in which the so-called *diamond-shaped inheritance* occurs (for example, the *Radio* (§15.2.4) and *Clock* (§15.2.4.1)). A virtual base class, as opposed to an ordinary base class, is needed if the base class cannot be replicated.

I find that a diamond-shaped inheritance lattice is most manageable if either the virtual base class or the classes directly derived from it are abstract classes. For example, consider again the *Ival_box* classes from §12.4. In the end, I made all the *Ival_box* classes abstract to reflect their role as pure interfaces. Doing that allowed me to place all implementation details in specific implementation classes. Also, all sharing of implementation details was done in the classical hierarchy of the windows system used for the implementation.

It would make sense for the class implementing a *Popup_ival_slider* to share most of the implementation of the class implementing a plain *Ival_slider*. After all, these implementation classes would share everything except the handling of prompts. However, it would then seem natural to avoid replication of *Ival_slider* objects within the resulting slider implementation objects. Therefore, we could make *Ival_slider* a virtual base:

```
class BB_ival_slider : public virtual Ival_slider, protected BBslider { /* ... */ };
class Popup_ival_slider : public virtual Ival_slider { /* ... */ };
class BB_popup_ival_slider
    : public virtual Popup_ival_slider, protected BB_ival_slider { /* ... */ };
```

or graphically:

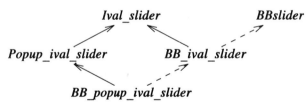

It is easy to imagine further interfaces derived from *Popup_ival_slider* and further implementation classes derived from such classes and *BB_popup_ival_slider*.

If we take this idea to its logical conclusion, all of the derivations from the abstract classes that constitute our application's interfaces would become virtual. This does indeed seem to be the most logical, general, and flexible approach. The reason I didn't do that was partly historical and partly because the most obvious and common techniques for implementing virtual bases impose time and space overhead that make their extensive use within a class unattractive. Should this overhead become an issue for an otherwise attractive design, note that an object representing an *Ival_slider* usually holds only a virtual table pointer. As noted in §15.2.4, such an abstract class holding no variable data can be replicated without ill effects. Thus, we can eliminate the virtual base in favor of ordinary ones:

```
class BB_ival_slider : public Ival_slider, protected BBslider { /* ... */ };
class Popup_ival_slider : public Ival_slider { /* ... */ };
class BB_popup_ival_slider
    : public Popup_ival_slider, protected BB_ival_slider { /* ... */ };
```

or graphically:

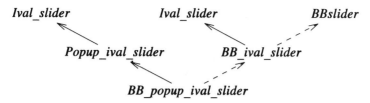

This is most likely a viable optimization to the admittedly cleaner alternative presented previously.

15.2.5.1 Overriding Virtual Base Functions

A derived class can override a virtual function of its direct or indirect virtual base class. In particular, two different classes might override different virtual functions from the virtual base. In that way, several derived classes can contribute implementations to the interface presented by a virtual base class. For example, the *Window* class might have functions *set_color*() and *prompt*(). In that case, *Window_with_border* might override *set_color*() as part of controlling the color scheme and *Window_with_menu* might override *prompt*() as part of its control of user interactions:

```
class Window {
    // ...
    virtual void set_color(Color) = 0;    // set background color
    virtual void prompt() = 0;
};

class Window_with_border : public virtual Window {
    // ...
    void set_color(Color);     // control background color
};

class Window_with_menu : public virtual Window {
    // ...
    void prompt(); // control user interactions
};

class My_window : public Window_with_menu, public Window_with_border {
    // ...
};
```

What if different derived classes override the same function? This is allowed if and only if some overriding class is derived from every other class that overrides the function. That is, one function must override all others. For example, *My_window* could override *prompt*() to improve on what *Window_with_menu* provides:

```
class My_window : public Window_with_menu, public Window_with_border {
    // ...
    void prompt(); // don't leave user interactions to base
};
```

or graphically:

Window { *set_color*() , *prompt*() }

Window_with_border { *set_color*() }   *Window_with_menu* { *prompt*() }

My_window { *prompt*() }

If two classes override a base class function, but neither overrides the other, the class hierarchy is an error. No virtual function table can be constructed because a call to that function on the complete object would have been ambiguous. For example, had *Radio* in §15.2.4 not declared *write*(), the declarations of *write*() in *Receiver* and *Transmitter* would have caused an error when defining *Radio*. As with *Radio*, such a conflict is resolved by adding an overriding function to the most derived class.

A class that provides some – but not all – of the implementation for a virtual base class is often called a ''mixin.''

15.3 Access Control

A member of a class can be *private*, *protected*, or *public*:
- If it is *private*, its name can be used only by member functions and friends of the class in which it is declared.
- If it is *protected*, its name can be used only by member functions and friends of the class in which it is declared and by member functions and friends of classes derived from this class (see §11.5).
- If it is *public*, its name can be used by any function.

This reflects the view that there are three kinds of functions accessing a class: functions implementing the class (its friends and members), functions implementing a derived class (the derived class' friends and members), and other functions. This can be presented graphically:

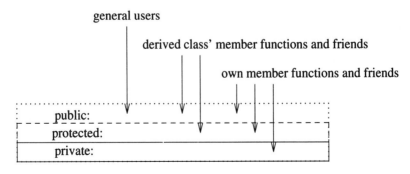

The access control is applied uniformly to names. What a name refers to does not affect the control of its use. This means that we can have private member functions, types, constants, etc., as well as private data members. For example, an efficient non-intrusive (§16.2.1) list class often requires data structures to keep track of elements. Such information is best kept private:

```
template<class T> class List {
private:
      struct Link { T val; Link* next; };
      struct Chunk {
            enum { chunk_size = 15 };
            Link v[chunk_size];
            Chunk* next;
      };
      Chunk* allocated;
      Link* free;
      Link* get_free();
      Link* head;
public:
      class Underflow { }; // exception class

      void insert(T);
      T get();
      // ...
};

template<class T> void List<T>::insert(T val)
{
      Link* lnk = get_free();
      lnk->val = val;
      lnk->next = head;
      head = lnk;
}

template<class T> List<T>::Link* List<T>::get_free()
{
      if (free == 0) {
            // allocate a new chunk and place its Links on the free list
      }
      Link* p = free;
      free = free->next;
      return p;
}

template<class T> T List<T>::get()
{
      if (head == 0) throw Underflow();

      Link* p= head;
      head = p->next;
      p->next = free;
      free = p;
      return p->val;
}
```

The *List<T>* scope is entered by saying *List<T>*:: in a member function definition. Because the return type of *get_free*() is mentioned before the name *List<T>*::*get_free*() is mentioned, the full name *List<T>*::*Link* must be used instead of the abbreviation *Link*.

Nonmember functions (except friends) do not have such access:

```
void would_be_meddler(List<T>* p)
{
        List<T>::Link* q = 0;                    // error: List<T>::Link is private
        q = p->free;                             // error: List<T>::free is private
        // ...
        if (List<T>::Chunk::chunk_size > 31) {   // error: List<T>::Chunk::chunk_size is private
                // ...
        }
}
```

In a *class*, a member is by default private; in a *struct*, a member is by default public (§10.2.8).

15.3.1 Protected Members

Consider the *Window* example from §15.2.4.1. The *own_draw*() functions were designed as building blocks for use by derived classes and are not safe for general use. The *draw*() operations, on the other hand, were designed for general use. This distinction can be expressed by separating the interface of the *Window* classes in two, the *protected* interface and the *public* interface:

```
class Window_with_border {
public:
        virtual void draw();
        // ...
protected:
        void own_draw();
        // other tool-building stuff
private:
        // representation, etc.
};
```

A derived class can access a base class' protected members only for objects of its own type:

```
class Buffer {
protected:
        char a[128];
        // ...
};

class Linked_buffer : public Buffer { /* ... */ };

class Cyclic_buffer : public Buffer {
        // ...
        void f(Linked_buffer* p) {
                a[0] = 0;        // ok: access to cyclic_buffer's own protected member
                p->a[0] = 0;     // error: access to protected member of different type
        }
};
```

This prevents subtle errors that would otherwise occur when one derived class corrupts data belonging to other derived classes.

15.3.1.1 Use of Protected Members

The simple private/public model of data hiding serves the notion of concrete types (§10.3) well. However, when derived classes are used, there are two kinds of users of a class: derived classes and "the general public." The members and friends that implement the operations on the class operate on the class objects on behalf of these users. The private/public model allows the programmer to distinguish clearly between the implementers and the general public, but it does not provide a way of catering specifically to derived classes.

Members declared *protected* are far more open to abuse than members declared *private*. In particular, declaring data members protected is usually a design error. Placing significant amounts of data in a common class for all derived classes to use leaves that data open to corruption. Worse, protected data, like public data, cannot easily be restructured because there is no good way of finding every use. Thus, protected data becomes a software maintenance problem.

Fortunately, you don't have to use protected data; *private* is the default in classes and is usually the better choice. In my experience, there have always been alternatives to placing significant amounts of information in a common base class for derived classes to use directly.

Note that none of these objections are significant for protected member *functions*; *protected* is a fine way of specifying operations for use in derived classes. The *Ival_slider* in §12.4.2 is an example of this. Had the implementation class been *private* in this example, further derivation would have been infeasible.

Technical examples illustrating access to members can be found in §C.11.1.

15.3.2 Access to Base Classes

Like a member, a base class can be declared *private*, *protected*, or *public*. For example:

```
class X : public B { /* ... */ } ;
class Y : protected B { /* ... */ } ;
class Z : private B { /* ... */ } ;
```

Public derivation makes the derived class a subtype of its base; this is the most common form of derivation. Protected and private derivation are used to represent implementation details. Protected bases are useful in class hierarchies in which further derivation is the norm; the *Ival_slider* from §12.4.2 is a good example of that. Private bases are most useful when defining a class by restricting the interface to a base so that stronger guarantees can be provided. For example, the *Vector* of pointers template adds type checking to its *Vector<void*>* base (§13.5). Also, if we wanted to make sure that every access to a *Vec* (§3.7.2) was checked, we would declare *Vec*'s base class private (to prevent conversion of a *Vec* to its unchecked *vector* base):

```
template<class T> class Vec : private vector<T> { /* ... */ } ;   // range-checked vector
```

The access specifier for a base class can be left out. In that case, the base defaults to a private base for a *class* and a public base for a *struct*. For example:

```
class XX : B { /* ... */ } ;       // B is a private base
struct YY : B { /* ... */ } ;      // B is a public base
```

For readability, it is best always to use an explicit access specifier.

The access specifier for a base class controls the access to members of the base class and the conversion of pointers and references from the derived class type to the base class type. Consider a class *D* derived from a base class *B*:

- If *B* is a *private* base, its public and protected members can be used only by member functions and friends of *D*. Only friends and members of *D* can convert a *D** to a *B**.
- If *B* is a *protected* base, its public and protected members can be used only by member functions and friends of *D* and by member functions and friends of classes derived from *D*. Only friends and members of *D* and friends and members of classes derived from *D* can convert a *D** to a *B**.
- If *B* is a *public* base, its public members can be used by any function. In addition, its protected members can be used by members and friends of *D* and members and friends of classes derived from *D*. Any function can convert a *D** to a *B**.

This basically restates the rules for member access (§15.3). We choose access for bases in the same way as for members. For example, I chose to make *BBwindow* a *protected* base of *Ival_slider* (§12.4.2) because *BBwindow* was part of the implementation of *Ival_slider* rather than part of its interface. However, I couldn't completely hide *BBwindow* by making it a private base because I wanted to be able to derive further classes from *Ival_slider*, and those derived classes would need access to the implementation.

Technical examples illustrating access to bases can be found in §C.11.2.

15.3.2.1 Multiple Inheritance and Access Control

If a name or a base class can be reached through multiple paths in a multiple inheritance lattice, it is accessible if it is accessible through any path. For example:

```
struct B {
    int m;
    static int sm;
    // ...
};

class D1 : public virtual B { /* ... */ } ;
class D2 : public virtual B { /* ... */ } ;
class DD : public D1, private D2 { /* ... */ };

DD* pd = new DD;
B* pb = pd;             // ok: accessible through D1
int i1 = pd->m;         // ok: accessible through D1
```

If a single entity is reachable through several paths, we can still refer to it without ambiguity. For example:

```
class X1 : public B { /* ... */ } ;
class X2 : public B { /* ... */ } ;
class XX : public X1, public X2 { /* ... */ };

XX* pxx = new XX;
int i1 = pxx->m;        // error, ambiguous: XX::X1::B::m or XX::X2::B::m
int i2 = pxx->sm;       // ok: there is only one B::sm in an XX
```

15.3.2.2 Using-Declarations and Access Control

A *using-declaration* cannot be used to gain access to additional information. It is simply a mechanism for making accessible information more convenient to use. On the other hand, once access is available, it can be granted to other users. For example:

```
class B {
private :
      int a;
protected :
      int b;
public :
      int c;
};

class D : public B {
public :
      using B::a;      // error: B::a is private
      using B::b;      // make B::b publicly available through D
};
```

When a *using-declaration* is combined with private or protected derivation, it can be used to specify interfaces to some, but not all, of the facilities usually offered by a class. For example:

```
class BB : private B {      // give access to B::b and B::c, but not B::a
public :
      using B::b;
      using B::c;
};
```

See also §15.2.2.

15.4 Run-Time Type Information

A plausible use of the *Ival_box*es defined in §12.4 would be to hand them to a system that controlled a screen and have that system hand objects back to the application program whenever some activity had occurred. This is how many user-interfaces work. However, a user-interface system will not know about our *Ival_box*es. The system's interfaces will be specified in terms of the system's own classes and objects rather than our application's classes. This is necessary and proper. However, it does have the unpleasant effect that we lose information about the type of objects passed to the system and later returned to us.

Recovering the "lost" type of an object requires us to somehow ask the object to reveal its type. Any operation on an object requires us to have a pointer or reference of a suitable type for the object. Consequently, the most obvious and useful operation for inspecting the type of an object at run time is a type conversion operation that returns a valid pointer if the object is of the expected type and a null pointer if it isn't. The *dynamic_cast* operator does exactly that. For example, assume that "the system" invokes *my_event_handler*() with a pointer to a *BBwindow*, where an activity has occurred. I then might invoke my application code using *Ival_box*'s *do_something*():

```
void my_event_handler (BBwindow* pw)
{
    if (Ival_box* pb = dynamic_cast<Ival_box*> (pw))      // does pw point to an Ival_box?
        pb->do_something ();
    else {
        // Oops! unexpected event
    }
}
```

One way of explaining what is going on is that *dynamic_cast* translates from the implementation-oriented language of the user-interface system to the language of the application. It is important to note what is *not* mentioned in this example: the actual type of the object. The object will be a particular kind of *Ival_box*, say an *Ival_slider*, implemented by a particular kind of *BBwindow*, say a *BBslider*. It is neither necessary nor desirable to make the actual type of the object explicit in this interaction between ''the system'' and the application. An interface exists to represent the essentials of an interaction. In particular, a well-designed interface hides inessential details.

Graphically, the action of

> *pb = dynamic_cast<Ival_box*> (pw)*

can be represented like this:

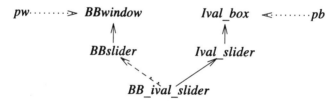

The arrows from *pw* and *pb* represent the pointers into the object passed, whereas the rest of the arrows represent the inheritance relationships between the different parts of the object passed.

The use of type information at run time is conventionally referred to as ''run-time type information'' and often abbreviated to RTTI.

Casting from a base class to a derived class is often called a *downcast* because of the convention of drawing inheritance trees growing from the root down. Similarly, a cast from a derived class to a base is called an *upcast*. A cast that goes from a base to a sibling class, like the cast from *BBwindow* to *Ival_box*, is called a *crosscast*.

15.4.1 Dynamic_cast

The *dynamic_cast* operator takes two operands, a type bracketed by < and >, and a pointer or reference bracketed by (and).

Consider first the pointer case:

> *dynamic_cast<T*> (p)*

If *p* is of type *T** or an accessible base class of *T*, the result is exactly as if we had simply assigned *p* to a *T**. For example:

```
class BB_ival_slider : public Ival_slider, protected BBslider {
    // ...
};

void f(BB_ival_slider* p)
{
    Ival_slider* pi1 = p;        // ok
    Ival_slider* pi2 = dynamic_cast<Ival_slider*>(p);         // ok

    BBslider* pbb1 = p;          // error: BBslider is a protected base
    BBslider* pbb2 = dynamic_cast<BBslider*>(p);         // ok: pbb2 becomes 0
}
```

That is the uninteresting case. However, it is reassuring to know that *dynamic_cast* doesn't allow accidental violation of the protection of private and protected base classes.

The purpose of *dynamic_cast* is to deal with the case in which the correctness of the conversion cannot be determined by the compiler. In that case,

```
dynamic_cast<T*>(p)
```

looks at the object pointed to by *p* (if any). If that object is of class *T* or has a unique base class of type *T*, then *dynamic_cast* returns a pointer of type *T** to that object; otherwise, *0* is returned. If the value of *p* is *0*, *dynamic_cast<T*>(p)* returns *0*. Note the requirement that the conversion must be to a uniquely identified object. It is possible to construct examples where the conversion fails and *0* is returned because the object pointed to by *p* has more than one sub-object representing bases of type *T* (see §15.4.2).

A *dynamic_cast* requires a pointer or a reference to a polymorphic type in order to do a down-cast or a crosscast. For example:

```
class My_slider: public Ival_slider {  // polymorphic base (Ival_slider has virtual functions)
    // ...
};

class My_date : public Date {   // base not polymorphic (Date has no virtual functions)
    // ...
};

void g(Ival_box* pb, Date* pd)
{
    My_slider* pd1 = dynamic_cast<My_slider*>(pb);    // ok
    My_date* pd2 = dynamic_cast<My_date*>(pd);        // error: Date not polymorphic
}
```

Requiring the pointer's type to be polymorphic simplifies the implementation of *dynamic_cast* because it makes it easy to find a place to hold the necessary information about the object's type. A typical implementation will attach a "type information object" to an object by placing a pointer to the type information in the object's virtual function table (§2.5.5). For example:

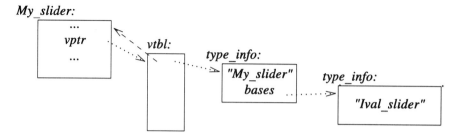

The dashed arrow represents an offset that allows the start of the complete object to be found given only a pointer to a polymorphic sub-object. It is clear that *dynamic_cast* can be efficiently implemented. All that is involved are a few comparisons of *type_info* objects representing base classes; no expensive lookups or string comparisons are needed.

Restricting *dynamic_cast* to polymorphic types also makes sense from a logical point of view. This is, if an object has no virtual functions, it cannot safely be manipulated without knowledge of its exact type. Consequently, care should be taken not to get such an object into a context in which its type isn't known. If its type *is* known, we don't need to use *dynamic_cast*.

The target type of *dynamic_cast* need not be polymorphic. This allows us to wrap a concrete type in a polymorphic type, say for transmission through an object I/O system (see §25.4.1), and then "unwrap" the concrete type later. For example:

```
class Io_obj {                 // base class for object I/O system
    virtual Io_obj* clone() = 0;
};

class Io_date : public Date, public Io_obj { };

void f(Io_obj* pio)
{
    Date* pd = dynamic_cast<Date*>(pio);
    // ...
}
```

A *dynamic_cast* to *void** can be used to determine the address of the beginning of an object of polymorphic type. For example:

```
void g(Ival_box* pb, Date* pd)
{
    void* pd1 = dynamic_cast<void*>(pb);     // ok
    void* pd2 = dynamic_cast<void*>(pd);     // error: Date not polymorphic
}
```

This is only useful for interaction with very low-level functions.

15.4.1.1 Dynamic_cast of References

To get polymorphic behavior, an object must be manipulated through a pointer or a reference. When a *dynamic_cast* is used for a pointer type, a *0* indicates failure. That is neither feasible nor desirable for references.

Given a pointer result, we must consider the possibility that the result is *0*; that is, that the pointer doesn't point to an object. Consequently, the result of a *dynamic_cast* of a pointer should always be explicitly tested. For a pointer *p*, *dynamic_cast<T*>* (*p*) can be seen as the question, "Is the object pointed to by *p* of type *T*?"

On the other hand, we may legitimately assume that a reference refers to an object. Consequently, *dynamic_cast<T&>* (*r*) of a reference *r* is not a question but an assertion: "The object referred to by *r* is of type *T*." The result of a *dynamic_cast* for a reference is implicitly tested by the implementation of *dynamic_cast* itself. If the operand of a *dynamic_cast* to a reference isn't of the expected type, a *bad_cast* exception is thrown. For example:

```
void f(Ival_box* p, Ival_box& r)
{
    if (Ival_slider* is = dynamic_cast<Ival_slider*>(p)) {      // does p point to an Ival_slider?
        // use 'is'
    }
    else {
        // *p not a slider
    }

    Ival_slider& is = dynamic_cast<Ival_slider&>(r);            // r references an Ival_slider!
    // use 'is'
}
```

The difference in results of a failed dynamic pointer cast and a failed dynamic reference cast reflects a fundamental difference between references and pointers. If a user wants to protect against bad casts to references, a suitable handler must be provided. For example:

```
void g()
{
    try {
        f(new BB_ival_slider, *new BB_ival_slider);      // arguments passed as Ival_boxs
        f(new BBdial, *new BBdial);                      // arguments passed as Ival_boxs
    }
    catch (bad_cast) {    // §14.10
        // ...
    }
}
```

The first call to *f*() will return normally, while the second will cause a *bad_cast* exception that will be caught by *g*().

Explicit tests against *0* can be – and therefore occasionally will be – accidentally omitted. If that worries you, you can write a conversion function that throws an exception instead of returning *0* (§15.8[1]) in case of failure.

15.4.2 Navigating Class Hierarchies

When only single inheritance is used, a class and its base classes constitute a tree rooted in a single base class. This is simple but often constraining. When multiple inheritance is used, there is no single root. This in itself doesn't complicate matters much. However, if a class appears more than once in a hierarchy, we must be a bit careful when we refer to the object or objects that represent that class.

Naturally, we try to keep hierarchies as simple as our application allows (and no simpler). However, once a nontrivial hierarchy has been made we soon need to navigate it to find an appropriate class to use as an interface. This need occurs in two variants. That is, sometimes, we want to explicitly name an object of a base class or a member of a base class; §15.2.3 and §15.2.4.1 are examples of this. At other times, we want to get a pointer to the object representing a base or derived class of an object given a pointer to a complete object or some sub-object; §15.4 and §15.4.1 are examples of this.

Here, we consider how to navigate a class hierarchy using type conversions (casts) to gain a pointer of the desired type. To illustrate the mechanisms available and the rules that guide them, consider a lattice containing both a replicated base and a virtual base:

```
class Component : public virtual Storable { /* ... */ };
class Receiver : public Component { /* ... */ };
class Transmitter : public Component { /* ... */ };
class Radio : public Receiver, public Transmitter { /* ... */ };
```

Or graphically:

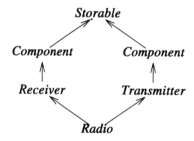

Here, a *Radio* object has two sub-objects of class *Component*. Consequently, a *dynamic_cast* from *Storable* to *Component* within a *Radio* will be ambiguous and return a *0*. There is simply no way of knowing which *Component* the programmer wanted:

```
void h1 (Radio& r)
{
    Storable* ps = &r;
    // ...
    Component* pc = dynamic_cast<Component*> (ps); // pc = 0
}
```

This ambiguity is not in general detectable at compile time:

```
void h2 (Storable* ps)        // ps might or might not point to a Component
{
    Component* pc = dynamic_cast<Component*> (ps);
    // ...
}
```

This kind of run-time ambiguity detection is needed only for virtual bases. For ordinary bases, there is always a unique sub-object of a given cast (or none) when downcasting (that is, towards a derived class; §15.4). The equivalent ambiguity occurs when upcasting (that is, towards a base; §15.4) and such ambiguities are caught at compile time.

15.4.2.1 Static and Dynamic Casts

A *dynamic_cast* can cast from a polymorphic virtual base class to a derived class or a sibling class (§15.4.1). A *static_cast* (§6.2.7) does not examine the object it casts from, so it cannot:

```
void g(Radio& r)
{
    Receiver* prec = &r;                       // Receiver is ordinary base of Radio
    Radio* pr = static_cast<Radio*>(prec);     // ok, unchecked
    pr = dynamic_cast<Radio*>(prec);           // ok, run-time checked

    Storable* ps = &r;                         // Storable is virtual base of Radio
    pr = static_cast<Radio*>(ps);              // error: cannot cast from virtual base
    pr = dynamic_cast<Radio*>(ps);             // ok, run-time checked
}
```

The *dynamic_cast* requires a polymorphic operand because there is no information stored in a non-polymorphic object that can be used to find the objects for which it represents a base. In particular, an object of a type with layout constraints determined by some other language – such as Fortran or C – may be used as a virtual base class. For objects of such types, only static type information will be available. However, the information needed to provide run-time type identification includes the information needed to implement the *dynamic_cast*.

Why would anyone want to use a *static_cast* for class hierarchy navigation? There is a small run-time cost associated with the use of a *dynamic_cast* (§15.4.1). More significantly, there are millions of lines of code that were written before *dynamic_cast* became available. This code relies on alternative ways of making sure that a cast is valid, so the checking done by *dynamic_cast* is seen as redundant. However, such code is typically written using the C-style cast (§6.2.7); often obscure errors remain. Where possible, use the safer *dynamic_cast*.

The compiler cannot assume anything about the memory pointed to by a *void**. This implies that *dynamic_cast* – which must look into an object to determine its type – cannot cast from a *void**. For that, a *static_cast* is needed. For example:

```
Radio* f(void* p)
{
    Storable* ps = static_cast<Storable*>(p);  // trust the programmer
    return dynamic_cast<Radio*>(ps);
}
```

Both *dynamic_cast* and *static_cast* respect *const* and access controls. For example:

```
class Users : private set<Person> { /* ... */ };
```

```
void f(Users* pu, const Receiver* pcr)
{
        static_cast<set<Person>*>(pu);          // error: access violation
        dynamic_cast<set<Person>*>(pu);         // error: access violation

        static_cast<Receiver*>(pcr);            // error: can't cast away const
        dynamic_cast<Receiver*>(pcr);           // error: can't cast away const

        Receiver* pr = const_cast<Receiver*>(pcr);      // ok
        // ...
}
```

It is not possible to cast to a private base class, and "casting away *const*" requires a *const_cast* (§6.2.7). Even then, using the result is safe only provided the object wasn't originally declared *const* (§10.2.7.1).

15.4.3 Class Object Construction and Destruction

A class object is more than simply a region of memory (§4.9.6). A class object is built from "raw memory" by its constructors and it reverts to "raw memory" as its destructors are executed. Construction is bottom up, destruction is top down, and a class object is an object to the extent that it has been constructed or destroyed. This is reflected in the rules for RTTI, exception handling (§14.4.7), and virtual functions.

It is extremely unwise to rely on details of the order of construction and destruction, but that order can be observed by calling virtual functions, *dynamic_cast*, or *typeid* (§15.4.4) at a point where the object isn't complete. For example, if the constructor for *Component* in the hierarchy from §15.4.2 calls a virtual function, it will invoke a version defined for *Storable* or *Component*, but not one from *Receiver*, *Transmitter*, or *Radio*. At that point of construction, the object isn't yet a *Radio*; it is merely a partially constructed object. It is best to avoid calling virtual functions during construction and destruction.

15.4.4 Typeid and Extended Type Information

The *dynamic_cast* operator serves most needs for information about the type of an object at run time. Importantly, it ensures that code written using it works correctly with classes derived from those explicitly mentioned by the programmer. Thus, *dynamic_cast* preserves flexibility and extensibility in a manner similar to virtual functions.

However, it is occasionally essential to know the exact type of an object. For example, we might like to know the name of the object's class or its layout. The *typeid* operator serves this purpose by yielding an object representing the type of its operand. Had *typeid*() been a function, its declaration would have looked something like this:

```
class type_info;
const type_info& typeid(type_name) throw();             // pseudo declaration
const type_info& typeid(expression) throw(bad_typeid);  // pseudo declaration
```

That is, *typeid*() returns a reference to a standard library type called *type_info* defined in *<typeinfo>*. Given a *type-name* as its operand, *typeid*() returns a reference to a *type_info* that represents the *type-name*. Given an *expression* as its operand, *typeid*() returns a reference to a *type_info* that represents the type of the object denoted by the *expression*. A *typeid*() is most commonly used to find the type of an object referred to by a reference or a pointer:

```
void f(Shape& r, Shape* p)
{
    typeid(r);          // type of object referred to by r
    typeid(*p);         // type of object pointed to by p
    typeid(p);          // type of pointer, that is, Shape* (uncommon, except as a mistake)
}
```

If the value of a pointer or a reference operand is *0*, *typeid*() throws a *bad_typeid* exception.

The implementation-independent part of *type_info* looks like this:

```
class type_info {
public:
    virtual ~type_info();                       // is polymorphic

    bool operator==(const type_info&) const;   // can be compared
    bool operator!=(const type_info&) const;
    bool before(const type_info&) const;       // ordering

    const char* name() const;                  // name of type
private:
    type_info(const type_info&);               // prevent copying
    type_info& operator=(const type_info&);    // prevent copying
    // ...
};
```

The *before*() function allows *type_info*s to be sorted. There is no relation between the relationships defined by *before* and inheritance relationships.

It is *not* guaranteed that there is only one *type_info* object for each type in the system. In fact, where dynamically linked libraries are used it can be hard for an implementation to avoid duplicate *type_info* objects. Consequently, we should use == on *type_info* objects to test equality, rather than == on pointers to such objects.

We sometimes want to know the exact type of an object so as to perform some standard service on the whole object (and not just on some base of the object). Ideally, such services are presented as virtual functions so that the exact type needn't be known. In some cases, no common interface can be assumed for every object manipulated, so the detour through the exact type becomes necessary (§15.4.4.1). Another, much simpler, use has been to obtain the name of a class for diagnostic output:

```
#include<typeinfo>

void g(Component* p)
{
    cout << typeid(*p).name();
}
```

The character representation of a class' name is implementation-defined. This C-style string resides in memory owned by the system, so the programmer should not attempt to *delete*[] it.

15.4.4.1 Extended Type Information

Typically, finding the exact type of an object is simply the first step to acquiring and using more-detailed information about that type.

Consider how an implementation or a tool could make information about types available to users at run time. Suppose I have a tool that generates descriptions of object layouts for each class used. I can put these descriptors into a *map* to allow user code to find the layout information:

```
map<const char*, Layout> layout_table;

void f(B* p)
{
     Layout& x = layout_table[typeid(*p).name()];
     // use x
}
```

Someone else might provide a completely different kind of information:

```
struct TI_eq {
     bool operator()(const type_info* p, const type_info* q) { return *p==*q; }
};

struct TI_hash {
     int operator()(const type_info* p);   // compute hash value (§17.6.2.2)
};

hash_map<type_info*, Icon, hash_fct, TI_hash, TI_eq> icon_table;       // §17.6

void g(B* p)
{
     Icon& i = icon_table[&typeid(*p)];
     // use i
}
```

This way of associating *typeid*s with information allows several people or tools to associate different information with types totally independently of each other:

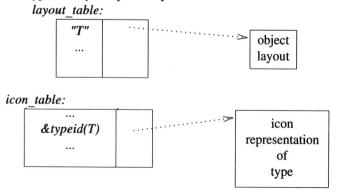

This is most important because the likelihood is zero that someone can come up with a single set of information that satisfies every user.

15.4.5 Uses and Misuses of RTTI

One should use explicit run-time type information only when necessary. Static (compile-time) checking is safer, implies less overhead, and – where applicable – leads to better-structured programs. For example, RTTI can be used to write thinly disguised *switch-statements*:

```
// misuse of run-time type information:

void rotate(const Shape& r)
{
    if (typeid(r) == typeid(Circle)) {
        // do nothing
    }
    else if (typeid(r) == typeid(Triangle)) {
        // rotate triangle
    }
    else if (typeid(r) == typeid(Square)) {
        // rotate square
    }
    // ...
}
```

Using *dynamic_cast* rather than *typeid* would improve this code only marginally.

Unfortunately, this is not a strawman example; such code really does get written. For many people trained in languages such as C, Pascal, Modula-2, and Ada, there is an almost irresistible urge to organize software as a set of *switch-statements*. This urge should usually be resisted. Use virtual functions (§2.5.5, §12.2.6) rather than RTTI to handle most cases when run-time discrimination based on type is needed.

Many examples of proper use of RTTI arise when some service code is expressed in terms of one class and a user wants to add functionality through derivation. The use of *Ival_box* in §15.4 is an example of this. If the user is willing and able to modify the definitions of the library classes, say *BBwindow*, then the use of RTTI can be avoided; otherwise, it is needed. Even if the user is willing to modify the base classes, such modification may cause its own problems. For example, it may be necessary to introduce dummy implementations of virtual functions in classes for which those functions are not needed or not meaningful. This problem is discussed in some detail in §24.4.3. A use of RTTI to implement a simple object I/O system can be found in §25.4.1.

For people with a background in languages that rely heavily on dynamic type checking, such as Smalltalk or Lisp, it is tempting to use RTTI in conjunction with overly general types. Consider:

```
// misuse of run-time type information:

class Object { /* ... */ }; // polymorphic

class Container : public Object {
public:
    void put(Object*);
    Object* get();
    // ...
};
```

```
class Ship : public Object { /* ... */ } ;

Ship* f(Ship* ps, Container* c)
{
    c->put(ps);
    // ...
    Object* p = c->get();
    if (Ship* q = dynamic_cast<Ship*>(p)) { // run-time check
        return q;
    }
    else {
        // do something else (typically, error handling)
    }
}
```

Here, class *Object* is an unnecessary implementation artifact. It is overly general because it does not correspond to an abstraction in the application domain and forces the application programmer to use an implementation-level abstraction. Problems of this kind are often better solved by using container templates that hold only a single kind of pointer:

```
Ship* f(Ship* ps, list<Ship*>& c)
{
    c.push_front(ps);
    // ...
    return c.pop_front();
}
```

Combined with the use of virtual functions, this technique handles most cases.

15.5 Pointers to Members

Many classes provide simple, very general interfaces intended to be invoked in several different ways. For example, many ''object-oriented'' user-interfaces define a set of requests to which every object represented on the screen should be prepared to respond. In addition, such requests can be presented directly or indirectly from programs. Consider a simple variant of this idea:

```
class Std_interface {
public:
        virtual void start() = 0;
        virtual void suspend() = 0;
        virtual void resume() = 0;
        virtual void quit() = 0;
        virtual void full_size() = 0;
        virtual void small() = 0;

        virtual ~Std_interface() {}
};
```

The exact meaning of each operation is defined by the object on which it is invoked. Often, there is a layer of software between the person or program issuing the request and the object receiving it.

Ideally, such intermediate layers of software should not have to know anything about the individual operations such as *resume*() and *full_size*(). If they did, the intermediate layers would have to be updated each time the set of operations changed. Consequently, such intermediate layers simply transmit some data representing the operation to be invoked from the source of the request to its recipient.

One simple way of doing that is to send a *string* representing the operation to be invoked. For example, to invoke *suspend*() we could send the string *"suspend"*. However, someone has to create that string and someone has to decode it to determine to which operation it corresponds – if any. Often, that seems indirect and tedious. Instead, we might simply send an integer representing the operation. For example, *2* might be used to mean *suspend*(). However, while an integer may be convenient for machines to deal with, it can get pretty obscure for people. We still have to write code to determine that *2* means *suspend*() and to invoke *suspend*().

C++ offers a facility for indirectly referring to a member of a class. A pointer to a member is a value that identifies a member of a class. You can think of it as the position of the member in an object of the class, but of course an implementation takes into account the differences between data members, virtual functions, non-virtual functions, etc.

Consider *Std_interface*. If I want to invoke *suspend*() for some object without mentioning *suspend*() directly, I need a pointer to member referring to *Std_interface*::*suspend*(). I also need a pointer or reference to the object I want to suspend. Consider a trivial example:

```
typedef void (Std_interface::* Pstd_mem)();     // pointer to member type

void f(Std_interface* p)
{
        Pstd_mem  s = &Std_interface::suspend;

        p->suspend();           // direct call

        (p->*s)();              // call through pointer to member
}
```

A *pointer to member* can be obtained by applying the address-of operator & to a fully qualified class member name, for example, &*Std_interface*::*suspend*. A variable of type ''pointer to member of class *X*'' is declared using a declarator of the form *X*::*.

The use of *typedef* to compensate for the lack of readability of the C declarator syntax is typical. However, please note how the *X*::* declarator matches the traditional * declarator exactly.

A pointer to member *m* can be used in combination with an object. The operators ->* and .* allow the programmer to express such combinations. For example, *p*->**m* binds *m* to the object pointed to by *p*, and *obj*.**m* binds *m* to the object *obj*. The result can be used in accordance with *m*'s type. It is not possible to store the result of a ->* or a .* operation for later use.

Naturally, if we knew which member we wanted to call we would invoke it directly rather than mess with pointers to members. Just like ordinary pointers to functions, pointers to member functions are used when we need to refer to a function without having to know its name. However, a pointer to member isn't a pointer to a piece of memory the way a pointer to a variable or a pointer to a function is. It is more like an offset into a structure or an index into an array. When a pointer to member is combined with a pointer to an object of the right type, it yields something that identifies a particular member of a particular object.

This can be represented graphically like this:

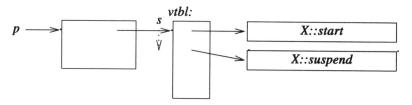

Because a pointer to a virtual member (*s* in this example) is a kind of offset, it does not depend on an object's location in memory. A pointer to a virtual member can therefore safely be passed between different address spaces as long as the same object layout is used in both. Like pointers to ordinary functions, pointers to non-virtual member functions cannot be exchanged between address spaces.

Note that the function invoked through the pointer to function can be *virtual*. For example, when we call *suspend*() through a pointer to function, we get the right *suspend*() for the object to which the pointer to function is applied. This is an essential aspect of pointers to functions.

An interpreter might use pointers to members to invoke functions presented as strings:

```
map<string, Std_interface*> variable;
map<string, Pstd_mem> operation;

void call_member(string var, string oper)
{
        (variable[var]->*operation[oper])();    // var.oper()
}
```

A critical use of pointers to member functions is found in *mem_fun*() (§3.8.5, §18.4).

A static member isn't associated with a particular object, so a pointer to a static member is simply an ordinary pointer. For example:

```
class Task {
        // ...
        static void schedule();
};

void (*p)() = &Task::schedule;              // ok
void (Task::* pm)() = &Task::schedule;   // error: ordinary pointer assigned
                                          // to pointer to member
```

Pointers to data members are described in §C.12.

15.5.1 Base and Derived Classes

A derived class has at least the members that it inherits from its base classes. Often it has more. This implies that we can safely assign a pointer to a member of a base class to a pointer to a member of a derived class, but not the other way around. This property is often called *contravariance*. For example:

```
class text : public Std_interface {
public:
    void start();
    void suspend();
    // ...
    virtual void print();
private:
    vector s;
};

void (Std_interface::* pmi)() = &text::print;     // error
void (text::*pmt)() = &Std_interface::start;      // ok
```

This contravariance rule appears to be the opposite of the rule that says we can assign a pointer to a derived class to a pointer to its base class. In fact, both rules exist to preserve the fundamental guarantee that a pointer may never point to an object that doesn't at least have the properties that the pointer promises. In this case, *Std_interface* :: * can be applied to any *Std_interface*, and most such objects presumably are not of type *text*. Consequently, they do not have the member *text* :: *print* with which we tried to initialize *pmi*. By refusing the initialization, the compiler saves us from a run-time error.

15.6 Free Store

It is possible to take over memory management for a class by defining *operator new* () and *operator delete* () (§6.2.6.2). However, replacing the global *operator new* () and *operator delete* () is not for the fainthearted. After all, someone else might rely on some aspect of the default behavior or might even have supplied other versions of these functions.

A more selective, and often better, approach is to supply these operations for a specific class. This class might be the base for many derived classes. For example, we might like to have the *Employee* class from §12.2.6 provide a specialized allocator and deallocator for itself and all of its derived classes:

```
class Employee {
    // ...
public:
    // ...
    void* operator new(size_t);
    void operator delete(void*, size_t);
};
```

Member *operator new* ()s and *operator delete* ()s are implicitly *static* members. Consequently, they don't have a *this* pointer and do not modify an object. They provide storage that a constructor can initialize and a destructor can clean up.

```
void* Employee::operator new(size_t s)
{
    // allocate 's' bytes of memory and return a pointer to it
}
```

```
void  Employee::operator  delete(void*  p,  size_t  s)
{
        // assume 'p' points to 's' bytes of memory allocated by Employee::operator new()
        // and free that memory for reuse
}
```

The use of the hitherto mysterious *size_t* argument now becomes obvious. It is the size of the object actually deleted. Deleting a ''plain'' **Employee** gives an argument value of *sizeof*(*Employee*); deleting a **Manager** gives an argument value of *sizeof*(*Manager*). This allows a class-specific allocator to avoid storing size information with each allocation. Naturally, a class-specific allocator can store such information (like a general-purpose allocator must) and ignore the *size_t* argument to *operator delete*(). However, that makes it harder to improve significantly on the speed and memory consumption of a general-purpose allocator.

How does a compiler know how to supply the right size to *operator delete*()? As long as the type specified in the *delete* operation matches the actual type of the object, this is easy. However, that is not always the case:

```
class  Manager : public  Employee {
        int  level;
        // ...
};

void  f()
{
        Employee*  p = new  Manager;    // trouble (the exact type is lost)
        delete  p;
}
```

In this case, the compiler will not get the size right. As when an array is deleted, the user must help. This is done by adding a virtual destructor to the base class, *Employee*:

```
class  Employee {
public:
        void*  operator  new(size_t);
        void  operator  delete(void*, size_t);
        virtual  ~Employee();
        // ...
};
```

Even an empty destructor will do:

```
Employee::~Employee() { }
```

In principle, deallocation is then done from within the destructor (which knows the size). Furthermore, the presence of a destructor in *Employee* ensures that every class derived from it will be supplied with a destructor (thus getting the size right), even if the derived class doesn't have a user-defined destructor. For example:

```
void f()
{
    Employee* p = new Manager;
    delete p;          // now fine (Employee is polymorphic)
}
```

Allocation is done by a (compiler-generated) call:

$$Employee::operator\ new\,(sizeof(Manager)\,)$$

and deallocation by a (compiler-generated) call:

$$Employee::operator\ delete\,(p,sizeof(Manager)\,)$$

In other words, if you want to supply an allocator/deallocator pair that works correctly for derived classes, you must either supply a virtual destructor in the base class or refrain from using the *size_t* argument in the deallocator. Naturally, the language could have been designed to save you from such concerns. However, that can be done only by also "saving" you from the benefits of the optimizations possible in the less safe system.

15.6.1 Array Allocation

The *operator new()* and *operator delete()* functions allow a user to take over allocation and deallocation of individual objects; *operator new[]()* and *operator delete[]()* serve exactly the same role for the allocation and deallocation of arrays. For example:

```
class Employee {
public:
    void* operator new[](size_t);
    void operator delete[](void*);
    // ...
};

void f(int s)
{
    Employee* p = new Employee[s];
    // ...
    delete[] p;
}
```

Here, the memory needed will be obtained by a call,

$$Employee::operator\ new[]\,(sizeof(Employee)*s+delta)$$

where *delta* is some minimal implementation-defined overhead, and released by a call:

$$Employee::operator\ delete[]\,(p);\ //\ release\ s*sizeof(Employee)+delta\ bytes$$

The number of elements, *s* and the delta are "remembered" by the system. Had the two-argument form of *delete[]()* been declared instead of the one-argument form, it would have been called with $s*sizeof(Employee)+delta$ as its second argument.

15.6.2 "Virtual Constructors"

After hearing about virtual destructors, the obvious question is, "Can constructors be virtual?" The short answer is no; a slightly longer one is, no, but you can easily get the effect you are looking for.

To construct an object, a constructor needs the exact type of the object it is to create. Consequently, a constructor cannot be virtual. Furthermore, a constructor is not quite an ordinary function. In particular, it interacts with memory management routines in ways ordinary member functions don't. Consequently, you cannot have a pointer to a constructor.

Both of these restrictions can be circumvented by defining a function that calls a constructor and returns a constructed object. This is fortunate because creating a new object without knowing its exact type is often useful. The *Ival_box_maker* (§12.4.4) is an example of a class designed specifically to do that. Here, I present a different variant of that idea, where objects of a class can provide users with a clone (copy) of themselves or a new object of their type. Consider:

```
class Expr {
public:
    Expr();                 // default constructor
    Expr(const Expr&);      // copy constructor

    virtual Expr* new_expr() { return new Expr(); }
    virtual Expr* clone() { return new Expr(*this); }
    // ...
};
```

Because functions such as *new_expr()* and *clone()* are virtual and they (indirectly) construct objects, they are often called "virtual constructors" – by a strange misuse of the English language. Each simply uses a constructor to create a suitable object.

A derived class can override *new_expr()* and/or *clone()* to return an object of its own type:

```
class Cond : public Expr {
public:
    Cond();
    Cond(const Cond&);

    Cond* new_expr() { return new Cond(); }
    Cond* clone() { return new Cond(*this); }
    // ...
};
```

This means that given an object of class *Expr*, a user can create a new object of "just the same type." For example:

```
void user(Expr* p)
{
    Expr* p2 = p->new_expr();
    // ...
}
```

The pointer assigned to *p2* is of an appropriate, but unknown, type.

The return type of *Cond::new_expr()* and *Cond::clone()* was *Cond** rather than *Expr**.

This allows a *Cond* to be cloned without loss of type information. For example:

```
void user2(Cond* pc, Expr* pe)
{
    Cond* p2 = pc->clone();
    Cond* p3 = pe->clone();  // error
    // ...
}
```

The type of an overriding function must be the same as the type of the virtual function it overrides, except that the return type may be relaxed. That is, if the original return type was *B**, then the return type of the overriding function may be *D**, provided *B* is a public base of *D*. Similarly, a return type of *B&* may be relaxed to *D&*.

Note that a similar relaxation of the rules for argument types would lead to type violations (see §15.8 [12]).

15.7 Advice

[1] Use ordinary multiple inheritance to express a union of features; §15.2, §15.2.5.
[2] Use multiple inheritance to separate implementation details from an interface; §15.2.5.
[3] Use a *virtual* base to represent something common to some, but not all, classes in a hierarchy; §15.2.5.
[4] Avoid explicit type conversion (casts); §15.4.5.
[5] Use *dynamic_cast* where class hierarchy navigation is unavoidable; §15.4.1.
[6] Prefer *dynamic_cast* over *typeid*; §15.4.4.
[7] Prefer *private* to *protected*; §15.3.1.1.
[8] Don't declare data members *protected*; §15.3.1.1.
[9] If a class defines *operator delete*( ), it should have a virtual destructor; §15.6.
[10] Don't call virtual functions during construction or destruction; §15.4.3.
[11] Use explicit qualification for resolution of member names sparingly and preferably use it in overriding functions; §15.2.1

15.8 Exercises

1. (*1) Write a template *ptr_cast* that works like *dynamic_cast*, except that it throws *bad_cast* rather than returning *0*.
2. (*2) Write a program that illustrates the sequence of constructor calls at the state of an object relative to RTTI during construction. Similarly illustrate destruction.
3. (*3.5) Implement a version of a Reversi/Othello board game. Each player can be either a human or the computer. Focus on getting the program correct and (then) getting the computer player ''smart'' enough to be worth playing against.
4. (*3) Improve the user interface of the game from §15.8[3].
5. (*3) Define a graphical object class with a plausible set of operations to serve as a common base class for a library of graphical objects; look at a graphics library to see what operations were

supplied there. Define a database object class with a plausible set of operations to serve as a common base class for objects stored as sequences of fields in a database; look at a database library to see what operations were supplied there. Define a graphical database object with and without the use of multiple inheritance and discuss the relative merits of the two solutions.

6. (*2) Write a version of the *clone* ( ) operation from §15.6.2 that can place its cloned object in an *Arena* (see §10.4.11) passed as an argument. Implement a simple *Arena* as a class derived from *Arena*.

7. (*2) Without looking in the book, write down as many C++ keywords as you can.

8. (*2) Write a standards-conforming C++ program containing a sequence of at least ten different consecutive keywords not separated by identifiers, operators, punctuation characters, etc.

9. (*2.5) Draw a plausible memory layout for a *Radio* as defined in §15.2.3.1. Explain how a virtual function call could be implemented.

10. (*2) Draw a plausible memory layout for a *Radio* as defined in §15.2.4. Explain how a virtual function call could be implemented.

11. (*3) Consider how *dynamic_cast* might be implemented. Define and implement a *dcast* template that behaves like *dynamic_cast* but relies on functions and data you define only. Make sure that you can add new classes to the system without having to change the definitions of *dcast* or previously-written classes.

12. (*2) Assume that the type-checking rules for arguments were relaxed in a way similar to the relaxation for return types so that a function taking a *Derived** could override a function taking a *Base**. Then write a program that would corrupt an object of class *Derived* without using a cast. Describe a safe relaxation of the overriding rules for argument types.

Part III

The Standard Library

This part describes the C++ standard library. It presents the design of the library and key techniques used in its implementation. The aim is to provide understanding of how to use the library, to demonstrate generally useful design and programming techniques, and to show how to extend the library in the ways in which it was intended to be extended.

Chapters

16 Library Organization and Containers
17 Standard Containers
18 Algorithms and Function Objects
19 Iterators and Allocators
20 Strings
21 Streams
22 Numerics

Library Organization and Containers

It was new. It was singular.
It was simple. It must succeed!
– H. Nelson

Design criteria for the standard library — library organization — standard headers — language support — container design — iterators — based containers — STL containers — *vector* — iterators — element access — constructors — modifiers — list operations — size and capacity — *vector<bool>*— advice — exercises.

16.1 Standard Library Design

What ought to be in the standard C++ library? One ideal is for a programmer to be able to find every interesting, significant, and reasonably general class, function, template, etc., in a library. However, the question here is not, "What ought to be in *some* library?" but "What ought to be in the *standard* library?" The answer "Everything!" is a reasonable first approximation to an answer to the former question but not to the latter. A standard library is something that every implementer must supply so that every programmer can rely on it.

The C++ standard library:

[1] Provides support for language features, such as memory management (§6.2.6) and run-time type information (§15.4).

[2] Supplies information about implementation-defined aspects of the language, such as the largest *float* value (§22.2).

[3] Supplies functions that cannot be implemented optimally in the language itself for every system, such as *sqrt()* (§22.3) and *memmove()* (§19.4.6).

[4] Supplies nonprimitive facilities that a programmer can rely on for portability, such as lists (§17.2.2), maps (§17.4.1), sort functions (§18.7.1), and I/O streams (Chapter 21).

[5] Provides a framework for extending the facilities it provides, such as conventions and

support facilities that allow a user to provide I/O of a user-defined type in the style of I/O for built-in types.

[6]   Provides the common foundation for other libraries.

In addition, a few facilities − such as random-number generators (§22.7) − are provided by the standard library simply because it is conventional and useful to do so.

The design of the library is primarily determined by the last three roles. These roles are closely related. For example, portability is commonly an important design criterion for a specialized library, and common container types such as lists and maps are essential for convenient communication between separately developed libraries.

The last role is especially important from a design perspective because it helps limit the scope of the standard library and places constraints on its facilities. For example, string and list facilities are provided in the standard library. If they were not, separately developed libraries could communicate only by using built-in types. However, pattern matching and graphics facilities are not provided. Such facilities are obviously widely useful, but they are rarely directly involved in communication between separately developed libraries.

Unless a facility is somehow needed to support these roles, it can be left to some library outside the standard. For good and bad, leaving something out of the standard library opens the opportunity for different libraries to offer competing realizations of an idea.

16.1.1 Design Constraints

The roles of a standard library impose several constraints on its design. The facilities offered by the C++ standard library are designed to be:

[1]   Invaluable and affordable to essentially every student and professional programmer, including the builders of other libraries.

[2]   Used directly or indirectly by every programmer for everything within the scope of the library.

[3]   Efficient enough to provide genuine alternatives to hand-coded functions, classes, and templates in the implementation of further libraries.

[4]   Either policy-free or give the user the option to supply policies as arguments.

[5]   Primitive in the mathematical sense. That is, a component that serves two weakly related roles will almost certainly suffer overheads compared to individual components designed to perform only a single role.

[6]   Convenient, efficient, and reasonably safe for common uses.

[7]   Complete at what they do. The standard library may leave major functions to other libraries, but if it takes on a task, it must provide enough functionality so that individual users or implementers need not replace it to get the basic job done.

[8]   Blend well with and augment built-in types and operations.

[9]   Type safe by default.

[10] Supportive of commonly accepted programming styles.

[11] Extensible to deal with user-defined types in ways similar to the way built-in types and standard-library types are handled.

For example, building the comparison criteria into a sort function is unacceptable because the same data can be sorted according to different criteria. This is why the C standard library *qsort* ( ) takes a comparison function as an argument rather than relying on something fixed, say, the < operator (§7.7). On the other hand, the overhead imposed by a function call for each comparison compromises *qsort*() as a building block for further library building. For almost every data type, it is easy to do a comparison without imposing the overhead of a function call.

Is that overhead serious? In most cases, probably not. However, the function call overhead can dominate the execution time for some algorithms and cause users to seek alternatives. The technique of supplying comparison criteria through a template argument described in §13.4 solves that problem. The example illustrates the tension between efficiency and generality. A standard library is not just required to perform its tasks. It must also perform them efficiently enough not to tempt users to supply their own mechanisms. Otherwise, implementers of more advanced features are forced to bypass the standard library in order to remain competitive. This would add a burden to the library developer and seriously complicate the lives of users wanting to stay platform-independent or to use several separately developed libraries.

The requirements of ''primitiveness'' and ''convenience of common uses'' appear to conflict. The former requirement precludes exclusively optimizing the standard library for common cases. However, components serving common, but nonprimitive, needs can be included in the standard library in addition to the primitive facilities, rather than as replacements. The cult of orthogonality must not prevent us from making life convenient for the novice and the casual user. Nor should it cause us to leave the default behavior of a component obscure or dangerous.

16.1.2 Standard Library Organization

The facilities of the standard library are defined in the *std* namespace and presented as a set of headers. The headers identify the major parts of the library. Thus, listing them gives an overview of the library and provides a guide to the description of the library in this and subsequent chapters.

The rest of this subsection is a list of headers grouped by function, accompanied by brief explanations and annotated by references to where they are discussed. The grouping is chosen to match the organization of the standard. A reference to the standard (such as §s.18.1) means that the facility is not discussed here.

A standard header with a name starting with the letter *c* is equivalent to a header in the C standard library. For every header *<X.h>* defining part of the C standard library in the global namespace, there is a header *<cX>* defining the same names in the *std* namespace (see §9.2.2).

Containers		
<vector>	*one-dimensional array of T*	§16.3
<list>	*doubly-linked list of T*	§17.2.2
<deque>	*double-ended queue of T*	§17.2.3
<queue>	*queue of T*	§17.3.2
<stack>	*stack of T*	§17.3.1
<map>	*associative array of T*	§17.4.1
<set>	*set of T*	§17.4.3
<bitset>	*array of booleans*	§17.5.3

The associative containers *multimap* and *multiset* can be found in *<map>* and *<set>*, respectively. The *priority_queue* is declared in *<queue>*.

General Utilities		
<utility>	*operators and pairs*	§17.1.4, §17.4.1.2
<functional>	*function objects*	§18.4
<memory>	*allocators for containers*	§19.4.4
<ctime>	*C-style date and time*	§s.20.5

The *<memory>* header also contains the ***auto_ptr*** template that is primarily used to smooth the interaction between pointers and exceptions (§14.4.2).

Iterators	
<iterator>	*iterators and iterator support* Chapter 19

Iterators provide the mechanism to make standard algorithms generic over the standard containers and similar types (§2.7.2, §19.2.1).

Algorithms		
<algorithm>	*general algorithms*	Chapter 18
<cstdlib>	*bsearch*() *qsort*()	§18.11

A typical general algorithm can be applied to any sequence (§3.8, §18.3) of any type of elements. The C standard library functions *bsearch*() and *qsort*() apply to built-in arrays with elements of types without user-defined copy constructors and destructors only (§7.7).

Diagnostics		
<exception>	*exception class*	§14.10
<stdexcept>	*standard exceptions*	§14.10
<cassert>	*assert macro*	§24.3.7.2
<cerrno>	*C-style error handling*	§20.4.1

Assertions relying on exceptions are described in §24.3.7.1.

Strings		
<string>	*string of T*	Chapter 20
<cctype>	*character classification*	§20.4.2
<cwctype>	*wide-character classification*	§20.4.2
<cstring>	*C-style string functions*	§20.4.1
<cwchar>	*C-style wide-character string functions*	§20.4
<cstdlib>	*C-style string functions*	§20.4.1

The *<cstring>* header declares the *strlen*(), *strcpy*(), etc., family of functions. The *<cstdlib>* declares *atof*() and *atoi*() that convert C-style strings to numeric values.

Input/Output		
<iosfwd>	*forward declarations of I/O facilities*	§21.1
<iostream>	*standard iostream objects and operations*	§21.2.1
<ios>	*iostream bases*	§21.2.1
<streambuf>	*stream buffers*	§21.6
<istream>	*input stream template*	§21.3.1
<ostream>	*output stream template*	§21.2.1
<iomanip>	*manipulators*	§21.4.6.2
<sstream>	*streams to/from strings*	§21.5.3
<cstdlib>	*character classification functions*	§20.4.2
<fstream>	*streams to/from files*	§21.5.1
<cstdio>	*printf( ) family of I/O*	§21.8
<cwchar>	*printf( )-style I/O of wide characters*	§21.8

Manipulators are objects used to manipulate the state of a stream (e.g., changing the format of floating-point output) by applying them to the stream (§21.4.6).

Localization		
<locale>	*represent cultural differences*	§21.7
<clocale>	*represent cultural differences C-style*	§21.7

A *locale* localizes differences such as the output format for dates, the symbol used to represent currency, and string collation criteria that vary among different natural languages and cultures.

Language Support		
<limits>	*numeric limits*	§22.2
<climits>	*C-style numeric scalar-limit macros*	§22.2.1
<cfloat>	*C-style numeric floating-point limit macros*	§22.2.1
<new>	*dynamic memory management*	§16.1.3
<typeinfo>	*run-time type identification support*	§15.4.1
<exception>	*exception-handling support*	§14.10
<cstddef>	*C library language support*	§6.2.1
<cstdarg>	*variable-length function argument lists*	§7.6
<csetjmp>	*C-style stack unwinding*	§s.18.7
<cstdlib>	*program termination*	§9.4.1.1
<ctime>	*system clock*	§D.4.4.1
<csignal>	*C-style signal handling*	§s.18.7

The *<cstddef>* header defines the type of values returned by *sizeof( )*, *size_t*, the type of the result of pointer subtraction and of array subscripts, *ptrdiff_t* (§6.2.1), and the infamous *NULL* macro (§5.1.1).

    The C-style stack unwinding (using *setjmp* and *longjmp* from *<csetjmp>*) is incompatible with exception handling (§8.3, Chapter 14, Appendix E) and is best avoided.

Numerics		
<complex>	*complex numbers and operations*	§22.5
<valarray>	*numeric vectors and operations*	§22.4
<numeric>	*generalized numeric operations*	§22.6
<cmath>	*standard mathematical functions*	§22.3
<cstdlib>	*C-style random numbers*	§22.7

For historical reasons, *abs* ( ), *fabs* ( ), and *div* ( ) are found in *<cstdlib>* rather than in *<cmath>* with the rest of the mathematical functions (§22.3).

A user or a library implementer is not allowed to add or subtract declarations from the standard headers. Nor is it acceptable to try to change the contents of headers by defining macros before they are included or to try to change the meaning of the declarations in the headers by declarations in their context (§9.2.3). Any program or implementation that plays such games does not conform to the standard, and programs that rely on such tricks are not portable. Even if they work today, the next release of any part of an implementation may break them. Avoid such trickery.

For a standard library facility to be used its header must be included. Writing out the relevant declarations yourself is *not* a standards-conforming alternative. The reason is that some implementations optimize compilation based on standard header inclusion and others provide optimized implementations of standard library facilities triggered by the headers. In general, implementers use standard headers in ways programmers cannot predict and shouldn't have to know about.

A programmer can, however, specialize utility templates, such as *swap* ( ) (§16.3.9), for nonstandard-library, user-defined types.

16.1.3 Language Support

A small part of the standard library is language support; that is, facilities that must be present for a program to run because language features depend on them.

The library functions supporting operators *new* and *delete* are discussed in §6.2.6, §10.4.11, §14.4.4, and §15.6; they are presented in *<new>*.

Run-time type identification relies on class *type_info*, which is described in §15.4.4 and presented in *<typeinfo>*.

The standard exception classes are discussed in §14.10 and presented in *<new>*, *<typeinfo>*, *<ios>*, *<exception>*, and *<stdexcept>*.

Program start and termination are discussed in §3.2, §9.4, and §10.4.9.

16.2 Container Design

A container is an object that holds other objects. Examples are lists, vectors, and associative arrays. In general, you can add objects to a container and remove objects from it.

Naturally, this idea can be presented to users in many different ways. The C++ standard library containers were designed to meet two criteria: to provide the maximum freedom in the design of an individual container, while at the same time allowing containers to present a common interface to users. This allows optimal efficiency in the implementation of containers and enables users to write code that is independent of the particular container used.

Container designs typically meet just one or the other of these two design criteria. The container and algorithms part of the standard library (often called the STL) can be seen as a solution to the problem of simultaneously providing generality and efficiency. The following sections present the strengths and weaknesses of two traditional styles of containers as a way of approaching the design of the standard containers.

16.2.1 Specialized Containers and Iterators

The obvious approach to providing a vector and a list is to define each in the way that makes the most sense for its intended use:

```
template<class T> class Vector {      // optimal
public:
    explicit Vector(size_t n);  // initialize to hold n objects with value T()

    T& operator[](size_t);      // subscripting
    // ...
};
template<class T> class List {   // optimal
public:
    class Link { /* ... */ };

    List();           // initially empty
    void put(T*);     // put before current element
    T* get();         // get current element

    // ...
};
```

Each class provides operations that are close to ideal for their use, and for each class we can choose a suitable representation without worrying about other kinds of containers. This allows the implementations of operations to be close to optimal. In particular, the most common operations such as *put*() for a *List* and *operator*[]() for a *Vector* are small and easily inlined.

A common use of most kinds of containers is to iterate through the container looking at the elements one after the other. This is typically done by defining an iterator class appropriate to the kind of container (see §11.5 and §11.14[7]).

However, a user iterating over a container often doesn't care whether data is stored in a *List* or a *Vector*. In that case, the code iterating should not depend on whether a *List* or a *Vector* was used. Ideally, the same piece of code should work in both cases.

A solution is to define an iterator class that provides a get-next-element operation that can be implemented for any container. For example:

```
template<class T> class Itor {   // common interface (abstract class §2.5.4, §12.3)
public:
    // return 0 to indicate no-more-elements

    virtual T* first() = 0;      // pointer to first element
    virtual T* next() = 0;       // pointer to next element
};
```

We can now provide implementations for *Vector*s and *List*s:

```
template<class T> class Vector_itor : public Itor<T> {      // Vector implementation
    Vector<T>& v;
    size_t index;      // index of current element
public:
    Vector_itor(Vector<T>& vv) :v(vv), index(0) { }
    T* first() { return (v.size()) ? &v[index=0] : 0; }
    T* next() { return (++index<v.size()) ? &v[index] : 0; }
};

template<class T> class List_itor : public Itor<T> {          // List implementation
    List<T>& lst;
    List<T>::Link p;      // points to current element
public:
    List_itor(List<T>&);
    T* first();
    T* next();
};
```

Or graphically, using dashed lines to represent "implemented using:"

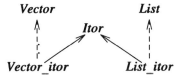

The internal structure of the two iterators is quite different, but that doesn't matter to users. We can now write code that iterates over anything for which we can implement an *Itor*. For example:

```
int count(Itor<char>& ii, char term)
{
    int c = 0;
    for (char* p = ii.first(); p; p=ii.next()) if (*p==term) c++;
    return c;
}
```

There is a snag, however. The operations on an *Itor* iterator are simple, yet they incur the overhead of a (virtual) function call. In many situations, this overhead is minor compared to what else is being done. However, iterating through a simple container is the critical operation in many high-performance systems and a function call is many times more expensive than the integer addition or pointer dereferencing that implements *next*() for a *Vector* and a *List*. Consequently, this model is unsuitable, or at least not ideal, for a standard library.

However, this container-and-iterator model has been successfully used in many systems. For years, it was my favorite for most applications. Its strengths and weaknesses can be summarized like this:

+   Individual containers are simple and efficient.

+   Little commonality is required of containers. Iterators and wrapper classes (§25.7.1) can be used to fit independently developed containers into a common framework.

+ Commonality of use is provided through iterators (rather than through a general container type; §16.2.2).
+ Different iterators can be defined to serve different needs for the same container.
+ Containers are by default type safe and homogeneous (that is, all elements in a container are of the same type). A heterogeneous container can be provided as a homogeneous container of pointers to a common base.
+ The containers are non-intrusive (that is, an object need not have a special base class or link field to be a member of a container). Non-intrusive containers work well with built-in types and with *struct*s with externally-imposed layouts.
− Each iterator access incurs the overhead of a virtual function call. The time overhead can be serious compared to simple inlined access functions.
− A hierarchy of iterator classes tends to get complicated.
− There is nothing in common for every container and nothing in common for every object in every container. This complicates the provision of universal services such as persistence and object I/O.

A + indicates an advantage and a − indicates a disadvantage.

I consider the flexibility provided by iterators especially important. A common interface, such as *Itor*, can be provided long after the design and implementation of containers (here, *Vector* and *List*). When we design, we typically first invent something fairly concrete. For example, we design an array and invent a list. Only later do we discover an abstraction that covers both arrays and lists in a given context.

As a matter of fact, we can do this ''late abstraction'' several times. Suppose we want to represent a set. A set is a very different abstraction from *Itor*, yet we can provide a *Set* interface to *Vector* and *List* in much the same way that I provided *Itor* as an interface to *Vector* and *List*:

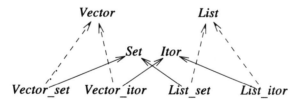

Thus, late abstraction using abstract classes allows us to provide different implementations of a concept even when there is no significant similarity between the implementations. For example, lists and vectors have some obvious commonality, but we could easily implement an *Itor* for an *istream*.

Logically, the last two points on the list are the main weaknesses of the approach. That is, even if the function call overhead for iterators and similar interfaces to containers were eliminated (as is possible in some contexts), this approach would not be ideal for a standard library.

Non-intrusive containers incur a small overhead in time and space for some containers compared with intrusive containers. I have not found this a problem. Should it become a problem, an iterator such as *Itor* can be provided for an intrusive container (§16.5[11]).

16.2.2 Based Containers

One can define an intrusive container without relying on templates or any other way of parameterizing a type declaration. For example:

```
struct Link {
    Link* pre;
    Link* suc;
    // ...
};

class List {
    Link* head;
    Link* curr;              // current element
public:
    Link* get();             // remove and return current element
    void put(Link*);         // insert before current element
    // ...
};
```

A *List* is now a list of *Link*s, and it can hold objects of any type derived from *Link*. For example:

```
class Ship : public Link { /* ... */ };

void f(List* lst)
{
    while (Link* po = lst->get()) {
        if (Ship* ps = dynamic_cast<Ship*>(po)) {        // Ship must be polymorphic (§15.4.1)
            // use ship
        }
        else {
            // Oops, do something else
        }
    }
}
```

Simula defined its standard containers in this style, so this approach can be considered the original for languages supporting object-oriented programming. These days, a common class for all objects is usually called *Object* or something similar. An *Object* class typically provides other common services in addition to serving as a link for containers.

Often, but not necessarily, this approach is extended to provide a common container type:

```
class Container : public Object {
public:
    virtual Object* get();                   // remove and return current element
    virtual void put(Object*);               // insert before current element
    virtual Object*& operator[](size_t);     // subscripting
    // ...
};
```

Note that the operations provided by *Container* are virtual so that individual containers can override them appropriately:

```
class List : public Container {
public:
    Object* get();
    void put(Object*);
    // ...
};

class Vector : public Container {
public:
    Object*& operator[](size_t);
    // ...
};
```

One problem arises immediately. What operations do we want *Container* to provide? We could provide only the operations that every container can support. However, the intersection of the sets of operations on all containers is a ridiculously narrow interface. In fact, in many interesting cases that intersection is empty. So, realistically, we must provide the union of essential operations on the variety of containers we intend to support. Such a union of interfaces to a set of concepts is called a *fat interface* (§24.4.3).

We can either provide default implementations of the functions in the fat interface or force every derived class to implement every function by making them pure virtual functions. In either case, we end up with a lot of functions that simply report a run-time error. For example:

```
class Container : public Object {
public:
    struct Bad_op { // exception class
        const char* p;
        Bad_op(const char* pp) :p(pp) { }
    };

    virtual void put(Object*) { throw Bad_op("put"); }
    virtual Object* get() { throw Bad_op("get"); }
    virtual Object*& operator[](int) { throw Bad_op("[]"); }
    // ...
};
```

If we want to protect against the possibility of a container that does not support *get()*, we must catch *Container::Bad_op* somewhere. We could now write the *Ship* example like this:

```
class Ship : public Object { /* ... */ };

void f1(Container* pc)
{
    try {
        while (Object* po = pc->get()) {
            if (Ship* ps = dynamic_cast<Ship*>(po)) {
                // use ship
            }
```

```
                        else {
                                // Oops, do something else
                        }
                }
        }
        catch (Container::Bad_op& bad) {
                // Oops, do something else
        }
}
```

This is tedious, so the checking for *Bad_op* will typically be elsewhere. By relying on exceptions caught elsewhere, we can reduce the example to:

```
void f2 (Container* pc)
{
        while (Object* po = pc->get()) {
                Ship& s = dynamic_cast<Ship&> (*po);
                // use ship
        }
}
```

However, I find unnecessary reliance on run-time checking distasteful and inefficient. In this kind of case, I prefer the statically-checked alternative:

```
void f3 (Itor<Ship>* i)
{
        while (Ship* ps = i->next()) {
                // use ship
        }
}
```

The strengths and weakness of the ''based object'' approach to container design can be summarized like this (see also §16.5[10]):
- – Operations on individual containers incur virtual function overhead.
- – All containers must be derived from *Container*. This implies the use of fat interfaces, requires a large degree of foresight, and relies on run-time type checking. Fitting an independently developed container into the common framework is awkward at best (see §16.5[12]).
- + The common base *Container* makes it easy to use containers that supply similar sets of operations interchangeably.
- – Containers are heterogeneous and not type safe by default (all we can rely on is that elements are of type *Object**). When desired, type-safe and homogeneous containers can be defined using templates.
- – The containers are intrusive (that is, every element must be of a type derived from *Object*). Objects of built-in types and structs with externally imposed layouts cannot be placed directly in containers.
- – An element retrieved from a container must be given a proper type using explicit type conversion before it can be used.
- + Class *Container* and class *Object* are handles for implementing services for every object or

every container. This greatly eases the provision of universal services such as persistence and object I/O.

As before (§16.2.1), + indicates an advantage and – indicates a disadvantage.

Compared to the approach using unrelated containers and iterators, the based-object approach unnecessarily pushes complexity onto the user, imposes significant run-time overheads, and restricts the kinds of objects that can be placed in a container. In addition, for many classes, to derive from *Object* is to expose an implementation detail. Thus, this approach is far from ideal for a standard library.

However, the generality and flexibility of this approach should not be underestimated. Like its alternatives, it has been used successfully in many applications. Its strengths lie in areas in which efficiency is less important than the simplicity afforded by a single *Container* interface and services such as object I/O.

16.2.3 STL Containers

The standard library containers and iterators (often called the STL framework, §3.10) can be understood as an approach to gain the best of the two traditional models described previously. That wasn't the way the STL was designed, though. The STL was the result of a single-minded search for uncompromisingly efficient and generic algorithms.

The aim of efficiency rules out hard-to-inline virtual functions for small, frequently-used access functions. Therefore, we cannot present a standard interface to containers or a standard iterator interface as an abstract class. Instead, each kind of container supports a standard set of basic operations. To avoid the problems of fat interfaces (§16.2.2, §24.4.3), operations that cannot be efficiently implemented for all containers are not included in the set of common operations. For example, subscripting is provided for *vector* but not for *list*. In addition, each kind of container provides its own iterators that support a standard set of iterator operations.

The standard containers are not derived from a common base. Instead, every container implements all of the standard container interface. Similarly, there is no common iterator base class. No explicit or implicit run-time type checking is involved in using the standard containers and iterators.

The important and difficult issue of providing common services for all containers is handled through "allocators" passed as template arguments (§19.4.3) rather than through a common base.

Before I go into details and code examples, the strengths and weaknesses of the STL approach can be summarized:

+ Individual containers are simple and efficient (not quite as simple as truly independent containers can be, but just as efficient).

+ Each container provides a set of standard operations with standard names and semantics. Additional operations are provided for a particular container type as needed. Furthermore, wrapper classes (§25.7.1) can be used to fit independently developed containers into a common framework (§16.5[14]).

+ Additional commonality of use is provided through standard iterators. Each container provides iterators that support a set of standard operations with standard names and semantics. An iterator type is defined for each particular container type so that these iterators are as simple and efficient as possible.

+ To serve different needs for containers, different iterators and other generalized interfaces can be defined in addition to the standard iterators.
+ Containers are by default type-safe and homogeneous (that is, all elements in a container are of the same type). A heterogeneous container can be provided as a homogeneous container of pointers to a common base.
+ The containers are non-intrusive (that is, an object need not have a special base class or link field to be a member of a container). Non-intrusive containers work well with built-in types and with *struct*s with externally imposed layouts.
+ Intrusive containers can be fitted into the general framework. Naturally, an intrusive container will impose constraints on its element types.
+ Each container takes an argument, called an *allocator*, which can be used as a handle for implementing services for every container. This greatly eases the provision of universal services such as persistence and object I/O (§19.4.3).
− There is no standard run-time representation of containers or iterators that can be passed as a function argument (although it is easy to define such representations for the standard containers and iterators where needed for a particular application; §19.3).

As before (§16.2.1), + indicates an advantage and − indicates a disadvantage.

In other words, containers and iterators do not have fixed standard representations. Instead, each container provides a standard interface in the form of a set of operations so that containers can be used interchangeably. Iterators are handled similarly. This implies minimal overheads in time and space while allowing users to exploit commonality both at the level of containers (as with the based-object approach) and at the level of iterators (as with the specialized container approach).

The STL approach relies heavily on templates. To avoid excessive code replication, partial specialization to provide shared implementations for containers of pointers is usually required (§13.5).

16.3 Vector

Here, *vector* is described as an example of a complete standard container. Unless otherwise stated, what is said about *vector* holds for every standard container. Chapter 17 describes features peculiar to *list*s, *set*s, *map*s, etc. The facilities offered by *vector* − and similar containers − are described in some detail. The aim is to give an understanding both of the possible uses of *vector* and of its role in the overall design of the standard library.

An overview of the standard containers and the facilities they offer can be found in §17.1. Below, *vector* is introduced in stages: member types, iterators, element access, constructors, stack operations, list operations, size and capacity, helper functions, and *vector<bool>*.

16.3.1 Types

The standard *vector* is a template defined in namespace *std* and presented in *<vector>*. It first defines a set of standard names of types:

```
template <class T, class A = allocator<T> > class std::vector {
public:
    // types:
```

```
    typedef T value_type;                               // type of element
    typedef A allocator_type;                           // type of memory manager
    typedef typename A::size_type size_type;
    typedef typename A::difference_type difference_type;

    typedef implementation_dependent1 iterator;         // T*
    typedef implementation_dependent2 const_iterator;   // const T*
    typedef std::reverse_iterator<iterator> reverse_iterator;
    typedef std::reverse_iterator<const_iterator> const_reverse_iterator;

    typedef typename A::pointer pointer;                // pointer to element
    typedef typename A::const_pointer const_pointer;
    typedef typename A::reference reference;            // reference to element
    typedef typename A::const_reference const_reference;
    // ...
};
```

Every standard container defines these typenames as members. Each defines them in the way most appropriate to its implementation.

The type of the container's elements is passed as the first template argument and is known as its *value_type*. The *allocator_type*, which is optionally supplied as the second template argument, defines how the *value_type* interacts with various memory management mechanisms. In particular, an allocator supplies the functions that a container uses to allocate and deallocate memory for its elements. Allocators are discussed in §19.4. In general, *size_type* specifies the type used for indexing into the container, and *difference_type* is the type of the result of subtracting two iterators for a container. For most containers, they correspond to *size_t* and *ptrdiff_t* (§6.2.1).

Appendix E discusses how *vector* behaves if allocators or element operations throw exceptions.

Iterators were introduced in §2.7.2 and are described in detail in Chapter 19. They can be thought of as pointers to elements of the container. Every container provides a type called *iterator* for pointing to elements. It also provides a *const_iterator* type for use when elements don't need to be modified. As with pointers, we use the safer *const* version unless there is a reason to do otherwise. The actual types of *vector*'s iterators are implementation-defined. The obvious definitions for a conventionally-defined *vector* would be *T** and *const T**, respectively.

The reverse iterator types for *vector* are constructed from the standard *reverse_iterator* templates (§19.2.5). They present a sequence in the reverse order.

As shown in §3.8.1, these member typenames allow a user to write code using a container without having to know about the actual types involved. In particular, they allow a user to write code that will work for any standard container. For example:

```
template<class C> typename C::value_type sum(const C& c)
{
    typename C::value_type s = 0;
    typename C::const_iterator p = c.begin();   // start at the beginning
    while (p!=c.end()) {                         // continue until the end
        s += *p;          // get value of element
        ++p;              // make p point to next element
    }
    return s;
}
```

Having to add *typename* before the names of member types of a template parameter is a nuisance. However, the compiler isn't psychic. There is no general way for it to know whether a member of a template argument type is a typename (§C.13.5).

As for pointers, prefix * means dereference the iterator (§2.7.2, §19.2.1) and ++ means increment the iterator.

16.3.2 Iterators

As shown in the previous subsection, iterators can be used to navigate containers without the programmer having to know the actual type used to identify elements. A few key member functions allow the programmer to get hold of the ends of the sequence of elements:

```
template <class T, class A = allocator<T> > class vector {
public:
        // ...
        // iterators:

        iterator begin();                       // points to first element
        const_iterator begin() const;
        iterator end();                         // points to one-past-last element
        const_iterator end() const;

        reverse_iterator rbegin();              // points to first element of reverse sequence
        const_reverse_iterator rbegin() const;
        reverse_iterator rend();                // points to one-past-last element of reverse sequence
        const_reverse_iterator rend() const;

        // ...
};
```

The *begin*() / *end*() pair gives the elements of the container in the ordinary element order. That is, element *0* is followed by element *1*, element *2*, etc. The *rbegin*() / *rend*() pair gives the elements in the reverse order. That is, element *n–1* is followed by element *n–2*, element *n–3*, etc. For example, a sequence seen like this using an *iterator*:

can be viewed like this using a *reverse_iterator* (§19.2.5):

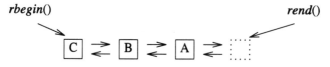

This allows us to use algorithms in a way that views a sequence in the reverse order. For example:

```
template<class C> typename C::iterator find_last(C& c, typename C::value_type v)
{
    typename C::reverse_iterator ri = find(c.rbegin(),c.rend(),v);
    if (ri == c.rend()) return c.end();  // use c.end() to indicate "not found"
    typename C::iterator i = ri.base();
    return --i;
}
```

For a *reverse_iterator*, *ri*.*base*() returns an *iterator* pointing one beyond the position pointed to by *ri* (§19.2.5). Without reverse iterators, we could have had to write an explicit loop:

```
template<class C> typename C::iterator find_last(C& c, typename C::value_type v)
{
    typename C::iterator p = c.end();  // search backwards from end
    while (p!=c.begin())
        if (*--p==v) return p;
    return c.end();                    // use c.end() to indicate "not found"
}
```

A reverse iterator is a perfectly ordinary iterator, so we could have written:

```
template<class C> typename C::iterator find_last(C& c, typename C::value_type v)
{
    typename C::reverse_iterator p = c.rbegin();  // view sequence in reverse order
    while (p!=c.rend()) {
        if (*p==v) {
            typename C::iterator i = p.base();
            return --i;
        }
        ++p;                // note: increment, not decrement (--)
    }
    return c.end();         // use c.end() to indicate "not found"
}
```

Note that *C::reverse_iterator* is not the same type as *C::iterator*.

16.3.3 Element Access

One important aspect of a *vector* compared with other containers is that one can easily and efficiently access individual elements in any order:

```
template <class T, class A = allocator<T> > class vector {
public:
    // ...
    // element access:

    reference operator[](size_type n);            // unchecked access
    const_reference operator[](size_type n) const;

    reference at(size_type n);                    // checked access
    const_reference at(size_type n) const;
```

```
    reference front ( );                        // first element
    const_reference front ( ) const;
    reference back ( );                          // last element
    const_reference back ( ) const;

    // ...
};
```

Indexing is done by *operator* [ ] ( ) and *at* ( ); *operator* [ ] ( ) provides unchecked access, whereas *at* ( ) does a range check and throws *out_of_range* if an index is out of range. For example:

```
void f(vector<int>& v, int i1, int i2)
try {
    for(int i = 0; i < v.size ( ); i++) {
        // range already checked: use unchecked v[i] here
    }

    v.at(i1) = v.at(i2); // check range on access

    // ...
}
catch (out_of_range) {
    // oops: out-of-range error
}
```

This illustrates one idea for use. That is, if the range has already been checked, the unchecked subscripting operator can be used safely; otherwise, it is wise to use the range-checked *at* ( ) function. This distinction is important when efficiency is at a premium. When that is not the case or when it is not perfectly obvious whether a range has been correctly checked, it is safer to use a vector with a checked [ ] operator (such as *Vec* from §3.7.2) or a checked iterator (§19.3).

The default access is unchecked to match arrays. Also, you can build a safe (checked) facility on top of a fast one but not a faster facility on top of a slower one.

The access operations return values of type *reference* or *const_reference* depending on whether or not they are applied to a *const* object. A reference is some suitable type for accessing elements. For the simple and obvious implementation of *vector<X>*, *reference* is simply *X&* and *const_reference* is simply *const X&*. The effect of trying to create an out-of-range reference is undefined. For example:

```
void f(vector<double>& v)
{
    double d = v[v.size ( )];    // undefined: bad index

    list<char> lst;
    char c = lst.front ( );       // undefined: list is empty
}
```

Of the standard sequences, only *vector* and *deque* (§17.2.3) support subscripting. The reason is the desire not to confuse users by providing fundamentally inefficient operations. For example, subscripting could have been provided for *list* (§17.2.2), but doing that would have been dangerously inefficient (that is, $O(n)$).

The members *front* ( ) and *back* ( ) return references to the first and last element, respectively.

They are most useful where these elements are known to exist and in code where these elements are of particular interest. A *vector* used as a *stack* (§16.3.5) is an obvious example. Note that *front* ( ) returns a reference to the element to which *begin* ( ) returns an iterator. I often think of *front* ( ) as the first element and *begin* ( ) as a pointer to the first element. The correspondence between *back* ( ) and *end* ( ) is less simple: *back* ( ) is the last element and *end* ( ) points to the last-plus-one element position.

16.3.4 Constructors

Naturally, *vector* provides a complete set (§11.7) of constructors, destructor, and copy operations:

```
template <class T, class A = allocator<T> > class vector {
public:
    // ...
    // constructors, etc.:

    explicit vector(const A& = A ( ) );
    explicit vector(size_type n, const T& val = T ( ), const A& = A ( ) );    // n copies of val
    template <class In>                              // In must be an input iterator (§19.2.1)
        vector(In first, In last, const A& = A ( ) ); // copy from [first:last[
    vector(const vector& x);

    ~vector ( );

    vector& operator= (const vector& x);

    template <class In>                              // In must be an input iterator (§19.2.1)
        void assign(In first, In last);              // copy from [first:last[
    void assign(size_type n, const T& val);          // n copies of val

    // ...
};
```

A *vector* provides fast access to arbitrary elements, but changing its size is relatively expensive. Consequently, we typically give an initial size when we create a *vector*. For example:

```
vector<Record> vr(10000);

void f(int s1, int s2)
{
    vector<int> vi(s1);
    vector<double>* p = new vector<double>(s2);
}
```

Elements of a vector allocated this way are initialized by the default constructor for the element type. That is, each of *vr*'s *10000* elements is initialized by *Record* ( ) and each of *vi*'s *s1* elements is initialized by *int* ( ). Note that the default constructor for a built-in type performs initialization to *0* of the appropriate type (§4.9.5, §10.4.2).

If a type does not have a default constructor, it is not possible to create a vector with elements of that type without explicitly providing the value of each element. For example:

```
class Num {      // infinite precision
public:
     Num (long);
     // no default constructor
     // ...
};

vector<Num> v1 (1000);                   // error: no default Num
vector<Num> v2 (1000, Num (0));          // ok
```

Since a *vector* cannot have a negative number of elements, its size must be non-negative. This is reflected in the requirement that *vector*'s *size_type* must be an **unsigned** type. This allows a greater range of vector sizes on some architectures. However, it can also lead to surprises:

```
void f(int i)
{
     vector<char> vc0 (-1);      // fairly easy for compiler to warn against
     vector<char> vc1 (i);
}

void g()
{
     f(-1);      // trick f() into accepting a large positive number!
}
```

In the call $f(-1)$, -1 is converted into a (rather large) positive integer (§C.6.3). If we are lucky, the compiler will find a way of complaining.

The size of a *vector* can also be provided implicitly by giving the initial set of elements. This is done by supplying the constructor with a sequence of values from which to construct the *vector*. For example:

```
void f(const list<X>& lst)
{
     vector<X> v1 (lst.begin(), lst.end());        // copy elements from list

     char p[] = "despair";
     vector<char> v2 (p, &p[sizeof(p) -1]);        // copy characters from C-style string
}
```

In each case, the *vector* constructor adjusts the size of the *vector* as it copies elements from its input sequence.

The *vector* constructors that can be invoked with a single argument are declared *explicit* to prevent accidental conversions (§11.7.1). For example:

```
vector<int> v1 (10);                     // ok: vector of 10 ints
vector<int> v2 = vector<int> (10);       // ok: vector of 10 ints
vector<int> v3 = v2;                     // ok: v3 is a copy of v2
vector<int> v4 = 10;                     // error: attempted implicit conversion of 10 to vector<int>
```

The copy constructor and the copy-assignment operators copy the elements of a *vector*. For a *vector* with many elements, that can be an expensive operation, so *vectors* are typically passed by reference. For example:

```
void f1 (vector<int>&);        // common style
void f2 (const vector<int>&);  // common style
void f3 (vector<int>);         // rare style

void h()
{
    vector<int> v (10000);

    // ...

    f1 (v);    // pass a reference
    f2 (v);    // pass a reference
    f3 (v);    // copy the 10000 elements into a new vector for f3() to use
}
```

The *assign* functions exist to provide counterparts to the multi-argument constructors. They are needed because = takes a single right-hand operand, so *assign* ( ) is used where a default argument value or a range of values is needed. For example:

```
class Book {
    // ...
};
void f(vector<Num>& vn, vector<char>& vc, vector<Book>& vb, list<Book>& lb)
{
    vn . assign (10, Num (0));             // assign vector of 10 copies of Num(0) to vn

    char s[] = "literal";
    vc . assign (s, &s [sizeof(s) -1]);    // assign "literal" to vc

    vb . assign (lb . begin (), lb . end ());  // assign list elements

    // ...
}
```

Thus, we can initialize a *vector* with any sequence of its element type and similarly assign any such sequence. Importantly, this is done without explicitly introducing a multitude of constructors and conversion functions. Note that assignment completely changes the elements of a vector. Conceptually, all old elements are erased and the new ones are inserted. After assignment, the size of a *vector* is the number of elements assigned. For example:

```
void f()
{
    vector<char> v (10, 'x');   // v.size()==10, each element has the value 'x'
    v . assign (5, 'a');        // v.size()==5, each element has the value 'a'
    // ...
}
```

Naturally, what *assign* ( ) does could be done indirectly by first creating a suitable *vector* and then assigning that. For example:

```
void f2 (vector<Book>& vh, list<Book>& lb)
{
        vector<Book> vt (lb.begin(), lb.end());
        vh = vt;
        // ...
}
```

However, this can be both ugly and inefficient.

Constructing a *vector* with two arguments of the same type can lead to an apparent ambiguity:

```
vector<int> v (10, 50);      // vector(size,value) or vector(iterator1,iterator2)? vector(size,value)!
```

However, an *int* isn't an iterator and the implementation must ensure that this actually invokes

```
vector (vector<int>::size_type, const int&, const vector<int>::allocator_type&);
```

rather than

```
vector (vector<int>::iterator, vector<int>::iterator, const vector<int>::allocator_type&);
```

The library achieves this by suitable overloading of the constructors and handles the equivalent ambiguities for *assign*() and *insert*() (§16.3.6) similarly.

16.3.5 Stack Operations

Most often, we think of a *vector* as a compact data structure that we can index to access elements. However, we can ignore this concrete notion and view *vector* as an example of the more abstract notion of a sequence. Looking at a *vector* this way, and observing common uses of arrays and *vector*s, it becomes obvious that stack operations make sense for a *vector*:

```
template <class T, class A = allocator<T> > class vector {
public:
        // ...
        // stack operations:

        void push_back (const T& x);    // add to end
        void pop_back();                // remove last element
        // ...
};
```

These functions treat a *vector* as a stack by manipulating its end. For example:

```
void f(vector<char>& s)
{
    s.push_back('a');
    s.push_back('b');
    s.push_back('c');
    s.pop_back();
    if (s[s.size()-1] != 'b') error("impossible!");
    s.pop_back();
    if (s.back() != 'a') error("should never happen!");
}
```

Each time *push_back*() is called, the *vector s* grows by one element and that element is added at the end. So *s*[*s.size*()−*1*], also known as *s.back*() (§16.3.3), is the element most recently pushed onto the *vector*.

Except for the word *vector* instead of *stack*, there is nothing unusual in this. The suffix _*back* is used to emphasize that elements are added to the end of the *vector* rather than to the beginning. Adding an element to the end of a *vector* could be an expensive operation because extra memory needs to be allocated to hold it. However, an implementation must ensure that repeated stack operations incur growth-related overhead only infrequently.

Note that *pop_back*() does not return a value. It just pops, and if we want to know what was on the top of the stack before the pop, we must look. This happens not to be my favorite style of stack (§2.5.3, §2.5.4), but it's arguably more efficient and it's the standard.

Why would one do stack-like operations on a *vector*? An obvious reason is to implement a *stack* (§17.3.1), but a more common reason is to construct a *vector* incrementally. For example, we might want to read a *vector* of points from input. However, we don't know how many points will be read, so we can't allocate a vector of the right size and then read into it. Instead, we might write:

```
vector<Point> cities;

void add_points(Point sentinel)
{
    Point buf;

    while (cin >> buf) {
        if (buf == sentinel) return;
        // check new point
        cities.push_back(buf);
    }
}
```

This ensures that the *vector* expands as needed. If all we needed to do with a new point were to put it into the *vector*, we might have initialized *cities* directly from input in a constructor (§16.3.4). However, it is common to do a bit of processing on input and expand a data structure gradually as a program progresses; *push_back*() supports that.

In C programs, this is one of the most common uses of the C standard library function *realloc*(). Thus, *vector* − and, in general, any standard container − provides a more general, more elegant, and no less efficient alternative to *realloc*().

The *size*() of a *vector* is implicitly increased by *push_back*() so the *vector* cannot overflow (as long as there is memory available to acquire; see §19.4.1). However, a *vector* can underflow:

```
void f()
{
    vector<int> v;
    v.pop_back();        // undefined effect: the state of v becomes undefined
    v.push_back(7);      // undefined effect (the state of v is undefined), probably bad
}
```

The effect of underflow is undefined, but the obvious implementation of *pop_back*() causes memory not owned by the *vector* to be overwritten. Like overflow, underflow must be avoided.

16.3.6 List Operations

The *push_back* ( ), *pop_back* ( ), and *back* ( ) operations (§16.3.5) allow a *vector* to be used effectively as a stack. However, it is sometimes also useful to add elements in the middle of a *vector* and to remove elements from a *vector*:

```
template <class T, class A = allocator<T> > class vector {
public :
        // ...
        // list operations:

        iterator insert(iterator pos, const T& x);          // add x before pos
        void insert(iterator pos, size_type n, const T& x); // add n copies of x before pos
        template <class In>                                 // In must be an input iterator (§19.2.1)
            void insert(iterator pos, In first, In last);   // insert elements from sequence

        iterator erase(iterator pos);                       // remove element at pos
        iterator erase(iterator first, iterator last);      // erase sequence
        void clear();                                       // erase all elements
        // ...
};
```

An iterator returned by *insert* ( ) points to the newly inserted element. An *iterator* returned by *erase* ( ) points to the element after the last element erased.

To see how these operations work, let's do some (nonsensical) manipulation of a *vector* of names of fruit. First, we define the *vector* and populate it with some names:

```
vector<string> fruit;

fruit.push_back("peach");
fruit.push_back("apple");
fruit.push_back("kiwifruit");
fruit.push_back("pear");
fruit.push_back("starfruit");
fruit.push_back("grape");
```

If I take a dislike to fruits whose names start with the letter *p*, I can remove those names like this:

```
sort(fruit.begin(),fruit.end());
vector<string>::iterator p1 = find_if(fruit.begin(),fruit.end(),initial('p'));
vector<string>::iterator p2 = find_if(p1,fruit.end(),initial_not('p'));
fruit.erase(p1,p2);
```

In other words, sort the *vector*, find the first and the last fruit with a name that starts with the letter *p*, and erase those elements from *fruit*. How to write predicate functions such as *initial* (*x*) (is the initial letter *x*?) and *initial_not* ( ) (is the initial letter different from *p*?) is explained in §18.4.2.

The *erase* (*p1* , *p2*) operation removes elements starting from *p1* up to and not including *p2*. This can be illustrated graphically:

The *erase* (*p1* , *p2*) removes *peach* and *pear*, yielding:

> *fruit* [ ] :
>
> > *apple   grape   kiwifruit   starfruit*

As usual, the sequence specified by the user is from the beginning to one-past-the-end of the sequence affected by the operation.

It would be tempting to write:

> *vector<string>* : : *iterator p1* = *find_if* (*fruit* . *begin* ( ) , *fruit* . *end* ( ) , *initial* (´ *p* ´)) ;
> *vector<string>* : : *reverse_iterator p2* = *find_if* (*fruit* . *rbegin* ( ) , *fruit* . *rend* ( ) , *initial* (´ *p* ´)) ;
> *fruit* . *erase* (*p1* , *p2+1*) ;   // *oops!: type error*

However, *vector<fruit>* : : *iterator* and *vector<fruit>* : : *reverse_iterator* need not be the same type, so we couldn't rely on the call of *erase* ( ) to compile. To be used with an *iterator*, a *reverse_iterator* must be explicitly converted:

> *fruit* . *erase* (*p1* , *p2* . *base* ( )) ;   // *extract iterator from reverse_iterator* (§19.2.5)

Erasing an element from a *vector* changes the size of the *vector*, and the elements after the erased elements are copied into the freed positions. In this example, *fruit* . *size* ( ) becomes *4* and the *star-fruit* that used to be *fruit* [*5*] is now *fruit* [*3*].

Naturally, it is also possible to *erase* ( ) a single element. In that case, only an iterator for that element is needed (rather than a pair of iterators). For example,

> *fruit* . *erase* (*find* (*fruit* . *begin* ( ) , *fruit* . *end* ( ) , "*starfruit*")) ;
> *fruit* . *erase* (*fruit* . *begin* ( ) +*1*) ;

gets rid of the *starfruit* and the *grape*, thus leaving *fruit* with two elements:

> *fruit* [ ] :
>
> > *apple   kiwifruit*

It is also possible to insert elements into a vector. For example:

> *fruit* . *insert* (*fruit* . *begin* ( ) +*1* , "*cherry*") ;
> *fruit* . *insert* (*fruit* . *end* ( ) , "*cranberry*") ;

The new element is inserted before the position mentioned, and the elements from there to the end are moved to make space. We get:

> *fruit* [ ] :
>
> > *apple   cherry   kiwifruit   cranberry*

Note that *f* . *insert* (*f* . *end* ( ) , *x*) is equivalent to *f* . *push_back* (*x*) .

We can also insert whole sequences:

> *fruit* . *insert* (*fruit* . *begin* ( ) +*2* , *citrus* . *begin* ( ) , *citrus* . *end* ( )) ;

If *citrus* is a container

>   *citrus* [ ] :
>   *lemon   grapefruit   orange   lime*

we get:

>   *fruit* [ ] :
>   *apple   cherry   lemon   grapefruit   orange   lime   kiwifruit   cranberry*

The elements of *citrus* are copied into *fruit* by *insert* ( ) . The value of *citrus* is unchanged.

Clearly, *insert* ( ) and *erase* ( ) are more general than are operations that affect only the tail end of a *vector* (§16.3.5). They can also be more expensive. For example, to make room for a new element, *insert* ( ) may have to reallocate every element to a new part of memory. If insertions into and deletions from a container are common, maybe that container should be a *list* rather than a *vector*. A *list* is optimized for *insert* ( ) and *erase* ( ) rather than for subscripting (§16.3.3).

Insertion into and erasure from a *vector* (but not a *list* or an associative container such as *map*) potentially move elements around. Consequently, an iterator pointing to an element of a *vector* may after an *insert* ( ) or *erase* ( ) point to another element or to no element at all. Never access an element through an invalid iterator; the effect is undefined and quite likely disastrous. In particular, beware of using the iterator that was used to indicate where an insertion took place; *insert* ( ) makes its first argument invalid. For example:

```
void  duplicate_elements (vector<string>& f)
{
    for(vector<string>::iterator  p = f.begin(); p!=f.end(); ++p) f.insert(p, *p); // No!
}
```

Just think of it (§16.5[15]). A *vector* implementation would move all elements – or at least all elements after *p* – to make room for the new element.

The operation *clear* ( ) erases all elements of a container. Thus, *c . clear* ( ) is a shorthand for *c . erase* (*c . begin* ( ) , *c . end* ( )) . After *c . clear* ( ) , *c . size* ( ) is *0*.

16.3.7 Addressing Elements

Most often, the target of an *erase* ( ) or *insert* ( ) is a well-known place (such as *begin* ( ) or *end* ( )), the result of a search operation (such as *find* ( )), or a location found during an iteration. In such cases, we have an iterator pointing to the relevant element. However, we often refer to elements of a *vector* by subscripting. How do we get an iterator suitable as an argument for *erase* ( ) or *insert* ( ) for the element with index *7* of a vector (or a *vector–like*) container *c*? Since that element is the 7th element after the beginning, *c . begin* ( ) +7 is a good answer. Other alternatives that may seem plausible by analogy to arrays should be avoided. Consider:

```
template<class  C> void  f(C& c)
{
    c . erase (c . begin ( ) +7) ;            // ok (if c's iterators support + (see §19.2.1))
    c . erase (&c [7] ) ;                      // not general
    c . erase (c+7) ;                          // error: adding 7 to a container makes no sense
```

```
        c.erase(c.back());        // error: c.back() is a reference, not an iterator
        c.erase(c.end()-2);       // ok (second to last element)
        c.erase(c.rbegin()+2);    // error: vector's reverse_iterator and iterator are different types
        c.erase((c.rbegin()+2).base());   // obscure, but ok (see §19.2.5)
    }
```

The most tempting alternative, &*c*[*7*], actually works with the obvious implementation of *vector*, where *c*[*7*] refers to an element and its address is a valid iterator. However, *c* might be a container where the iterator isn't a simple pointer to an element. For example, *map*'s subscripting operator (§17.4.1.3) returns a *mapped_type*& rather than a reference to an element (a *value_type*&).

Not all containers support + for their iterators. For example, a *list* does not support even *c.begin()+7*. If you really want to add *7* to a *list*::*iterator*, you'll have to use ++ repeatedly or use *advance()* (§19.2.1).

The alternatives *c+7* and *c.back()* are simple type errors. A container is not a numeric variable to which we can add *7*, and *c.back()* is an element with a value like *"pear"* that does not identify the pear's location in the container *c*.

16.3.8 Size and Capacity

So far, *vector* has been described with minimal reference to memory management. A *vector* grows as needed. Usually, that is all that matters. However, it is possible to ask directly about the way a *vector* uses memory, and occasionally it is worthwhile to affect it directly. The operations are:

```
template <class T, class A = allocator<T> > class vector {
public:
    // ...
    // capacity:

    size_type size() const;                      // number of elements
    bool empty() const { return size()==0; }
    size_type max_size() const;                  // size of the largest possible vector
    void resize(size_type sz, T val = T());      // added elements initialized by val

    size_type capacity() const;                  // size of the memory (in number of elements) allocated
    void reserve(size_type n);                   // make room for a total of n elements; don't initialize
                                                 // throw a length_error if n>max_size()
    // ...
};
```

At any given time, a *vector* holds a number of elements. This number can be obtained by calling *size()* and can be changed using *resize()*. Thus, a user can determine the size of a vector and change it if it seems insufficient or excessive. For example:

```
class Histogram {
    vector<int> count;
public:
    Histogram(int h) : count(max(h,8)) {}
    void record(int i);
    // ...
};
```

```
void  Histogram::record(int  i)
{
    if (i<0)  i = 0;
    if (count.size()<=i)  count.resize(i+i);      // make lots of room
    count[i]++;
}
```

Using *resize()* on a *vector* is very similar to using the C standard library function *realloc()* on a C array allocated on the free store.

When a *vector* is resized to accommodate more (or fewer) elements, all of its elements may be moved to new locations. Consequently, it is a bad idea to keep pointers to elements in a *vector* that might be resized; after *resize()*, such pointers could point to deallocated memory. Instead, we can keep indices. Note that *push_back()*, *insert()*, and *erase()* implicitly resize a *vector*.

In addition to the elements held, an application may keep some space for potential expansion. A programmer who knows that expansion is likely can tell the *vector* implementation to *reserve()* space for future expansion. For example:

```
struct  Link {
    Link* next;
    Link(Link* n =0)  : next(n) {}
    // ...
};

vector<Link> v;

void  chain(size_t  n)  // fill v with n Links so that each Link points to its predecessor
{
    v.reserve(n);
    v.push_back(Link(0));
    for (int  i = 1; i<n; i++) v.push_back(Link(&v[i-1]));
    // ...
}
```

A call *v.reserve(n)* ensures that no allocation will be needed when the size of *v* is increased until *v.size()* exceeds *n*.

Reserving space in advance has two advantages. First, even a simple-minded implementation can then allocate sufficient space in one operation rather than slowly acquiring enough memory along the way. However, in many cases there is a logical advantage that outweighs the potential efficiency gain. The elements of a container are potentially relocated when a *vector* grows. Thus, the links built between the elements of *v* in the previous example are guaranteed only because the call of *reserve()* ensures that there are no allocations while the vector is being built. That is, in some cases *reserve()* provides a guarantee of correctness in addition to whatever efficiency advantages it gives.

That same guarantee can be used to ensure that potential memory exhaustion and potentially expensive reallocation of elements take place at predictable times. For programs with stringent real-time constraints, this can be of great importance.

Note that *reserve()* doesn't change the size of a *vector*. Thus, it does not have to initialize any new elements. In both respects, it differs from *resize()*.

In the same way as *size* ( ) gives the current number of elements, *capacity* ( ) gives the current number of reserved memory slots; *c . capacity* ( ) *–c . size* ( ) is the number of elements that can be inserted without causing reallocation.

Decreasing the size of a *vector* doesn't decrease its capacity. It simply leaves room for the *vector* to grow into later. To give memory back to the system, a small trick is needed:

```
vector<int> tmp = v;    // copy of v with default capacity
v . swap (tmp);          // now v has the default capacity (see §16.3.9)
```

A *vector* gets the memory it needs for its elements by calling member functions of its allocator (supplied as a template parameter). The default allocator, called *allocator* (§19.4.1), uses *new* to obtain storage so that it will throw *bad_alloc* if no more storage is obtainable. Other allocators can use different strategies (see §19.4.2).

The *reserve* ( ) and *capacity* ( ) functions are unique to *vector* and similar compact containers. Containers such as *list* do not provide equivalents.

16.3.9 Other Member Functions

Many algorithms – including important sort algorithms – involve swapping elements. The obvious way of swapping (§13.5.2) simply copies elements. However, a *vector* is typically implemented with a structure that acts as a handle (§13.5, §17.1.3) to the elements. Thus, two *vector*s can be swapped much more efficiently by interchanging the handles; *vector::swap* ( ) does that. The time difference between this and the default *swap* ( ) is orders of magnitude in important cases:

```
template <class T, class A = allocator<T> > class vector {
public:
    // ...
    void swap (vector&);

    allocator_type get_allocator() const;
};
```

The *get_allocator* ( ) function gives the programmer a chance to get hold of a *vector*'s allocator (§16.3.1, §16.3.4). Typically, the reason for this is to ensure that data from an application that is related to a *vector* is allocated similarly to the *vector* itself (§19.4.1).

16.3.10 Helper Functions

Two *vector*s can be compared using == and <:

```
template <class T, class A>
bool std::operator==(const vector<T,A>& x, const vector<T,A>& y);

template <class T, class A>
bool std::operator<(const vector<T,A>& x, const vector<T,A>& y);
```

Two *vector*s *v1* and *v2* compare equal if *v1 . size* ( ) ==*v2 . size* ( ) and *v1* [*n*] ==*v2* [*n*] for every valid index *n*. Similarly, < is a lexicographical ordering. In other words, < for *vector*s could be defined like this:

```
template <class T, class A>
inline bool std::operator<(const vector<T,A>& x, const vector<T,A>& y)
{
    return lexicographical_compare(x.begin(),x.end(),y.begin(),y.end()); // see §18.9
}
```

This means that *x* is less than *y* if the first element *x*[*i*] that is not equal to the corresponding element *y*[*i*] is less than *y*[*i*], or *x.size*() <*y.size*() with every *x*[*i*] equal to its corresponding *y*[*i*].

The standard library also provides !=, <=, >, and >=, with definitions that correspond to those of == and <.

Because *swap*() is a member, it is called using the *v1.swap*(*v2*) syntax. However, not every type has a *swap*() member, so generic algorithms use the conventional *swap*(*a*,*b*) syntax. To make that work for *vectors* also, the standard library provides the specialization:

```
template <class T, class A> void std::swap(vector<T,A>& x, vector<T,A>& y)
{
    x.swap(y);
}
```

16.3.11 Vector<bool>

The specialization (§13.5) *vector<bool>* is provided as a compact *vector* of *bool*. A *bool* variable is addressable, so it takes up at least one byte. However, it is easy to implement *vector<bool>* so that each element takes up only a bit.

The usual *vector* operations work for *vector<bool>* and retain their usual meanings. In particular, subscripting and iteration work as expected. For example:

```
void f(vector<bool>& v)
{
    for (int i = 0; i<v.size(); ++i) cin >> v[i];            // iterate using subscripting

    typedef vector<bool>::const_iterator VI;
    for (VI p = v.begin(); p!=v.end(); ++p) cout<<*p;        // iterate using iterators
}
```

To achieve this, an implementation must simulate addressing of a single bit. Since a pointer cannot address a unit of memory smaller than a byte, *vector<bool>::iterator* cannot be a pointer. In particular, one cannot rely on *bool** as an iterator for a *vector<bool>*:

```
void f(vector<bool>& v)
{
    bool* p = v.begin(); // error: type mismatch
    // ...
}
```

A technique for addressing a single bit is outlined in §17.5.3.

The library also provides *bitset* as a set of Boolean values with Boolean set operations (§17.5.3).

16.4 Advice

[1] Use standard library facilities to maintain portability; §16.1.

[2] Don't try to redefine standard library facilities; §16.1.2.

[3] Don't believe that the standard library is best for everything.

[4] When building a new facility, consider whether it can be presented within the framework offered by the standard library; §16.3.

[5] Remember that standard library facilities are defined in namespace *std*; §16.1.2.

[6] Declare standard library facilities by including its header, not by explicit declaration; §16.1.2.

[7] Take advantage of late abstraction; §16.2.1.

[8] Avoid fat interfaces; §16.2.2.

[9] Prefer algorithms with reverse iterators over explicit loops dealing with reverse order; §16.3.2.

[10] Use *base* ( ) to extract an *iterator* from a *reverse_iterator*; §16.3.2.

[11] Pass containers by reference; §16.3.4.

[12] Use iterator types, such as *list<char>* :: *iterator*, rather than pointers to refer to elements of a container; §16.3.1.

[13] Use *const* iterators where you don't need to modify the elements of a container; §16.3.1.

[14] Use *at* ( ) , directly or indirectly, if you want range checking; §16.3.3.

[15] Use *push_back* ( ) or *resize* ( ) on a container rather than *realloc* ( ) on an array; §16.3.5.

[16] Don't use iterators into a resized *vector*; §16.3.8.

[17] Use *reserve* ( ) to avoid invalidating iterators; §16.3.8.

[18] When necessary, use *reserve* ( ) to make performance predictable; §16.3.8.

16.5 Exercises

The solutions to several exercises for this chapter can be found by looking at the source text of an implementation of the standard library. Do yourself a favor: try to find your own solutions before looking to see how your library implementer approached the problems.

1. (*1.5) Create a *vector<char>* containing the letters of the alphabet in order. Print the elements of that vector in order and in reverse order.

2. (*1.5) Create a *vector<string>* and read a list of names of fruits from *cin* into it. Sort the list and print it.

3. (*1.5) Using the *vector* from §16.5[2], write a loop to print the names of all fruits with the initial letter *a*.

4. (*1) Using the *vector* from §16.5[2], write a loop to delete all fruits with the initial letter *a*.

5. (*1) Using the *vector* from §16.5[2], write a loop to delete all citrus fruits.

6. (*1.5) Using the *vector* from §16.5[2], write a loop to delete all fruits that you don't like.

7. (*2) Complete the *Vector*, *List*, and *Itor* classes from §16.2.1.

8. (*2.5) Given an *Itor* class, consider how to provide iterators for forwards iteration, backwards iteration, iteration over a container that might change during an iteration, and iteration over an immutable container. Organize this set of containers so that a user can interchangeably use iterators that provide sufficient functionality for an algorithm. Minimize replication of effort in the implementation of the containers. What other kinds of iterators might a user need? List the strengths and weaknesses of your approach.

9. (∗2) Complete the *Container*, *Vector*, and *List* classes from §16.2.2.

10. (∗2.5) Generate 10,000 uniformly distributed random numbers in the range 0 to 1,023 and store them in (a) an standard library *vector*, (b) a *Vector* from §16.5[7], and (c) a *Vector* from §16.5[9]. In each case, calculate the arithmetic mean of the elements of the vector (as if you didn't know it already). Time the resulting loops. Estimate, measure, and compare the memory consumption for the three styles of vectors.

11. (∗1.5) Write an iterator to allow *Vector* from §16.2.2 to be used as a container in the style of §16.2.1.

12. (∗1.5) Write a class derived from *Container* to allow *Vector* from §16.2.1 to be used as a container in the style of §16.2.2.

13. (∗2) Write classes to allow *Vector* from §16.2.1 and *Vector* from §16.2.2 to be used as standard containers.

14. (∗2) Write a template that implements a container with the same member functions and member types as the standard *vector* for an existing (nonstandard, non-student-exercise) container type. Do not modify the (pre)existing container type. How would you deal with functionality offered by the nonstandard *vector* but not by the standard *vector*?

15. (∗1.5) Outline the possible behavior of *duplicate_elements*( ) from §16.3.6 for a *vector<string>* with the three elements *don't do this*.

17

Standard Containers

Now is a good time to put your work
on a firm theoretical foundation.
– Sam Morgan

Standard containers — container and operation summaries — efficiency — representation — element requirements — sequences — *vector* — *list* — *deque* — adapters —
stack — *queue* — *priority_queue* — associative containers — *map* — comparisons —
multimap — *set* — *multiset* — ''almost containers'' — *bitset* — arrays — hash tables
— implementing a *hash_map* — advice — exercises.

17.1 Standard Containers

The standard library defines two kinds of containers: sequences and associative containers. The
sequences are all much like *vector* (§16.3). Except where otherwise stated, the member types and
functions mentioned for *vector* can also be used for any other container and produce the same
effect. In addition, associative containers provide element access based on keys (§3.7.4).

Built-in arrays (§5.2), *strings* (Chapter 20), *valarrays* (§22.4), and *bitsets* (§17.5.3) hold elements and can therefore be considered containers. However, these types are not fully-developed
standard containers. If they were, that would interfere with their primary purpose. For example, a
built-in array cannot both hold its own size and remain layout-compatible with C arrays.

A key idea for the standard containers is that they should be logically interchangeable wherever
reasonable. The user can then choose between them based on efficiency concerns and the need for
specialized operations. For example, if lookup based on a key is common, a *map* (§17.4.1) can be
used. On the other hand, if general list operations dominate, a *list* (§17.2.2) can be used. If many
additions and removals of elements occur at the ends of the container, a *deque* (double-ended
queue, §17.2.3), a *stack* (§17.3.1), or a *queue* (§17.3.2) should be considered. In addition, a user
can design additional containers to fit into the framework provided by the standard containers

(§17.6). By default, a *vector* (§16.3) should be used; it will be implemented to perform well over a wide range of uses.

The idea of treating different kinds of containers – and more generally all kinds of information sources – in uniform ways leads to the notion of generic programming (§2.7.2, §3.8). The standard library provides many generic algorithms to support this idea (Chapter 18). Such algorithms can save the programmer from having to deal directly with details of individual containers.

17.1.1 Operations Summary

This section lists the common and almost common members of the standard containers. For more details, read your standard headers (*<vector>*, *<list>*, *<map>*, etc.; §16.1.2).

Member Types (§16.3.1)	
value_type	Type of element.
allocator_type	Type of memory manager.
size_type	Type of subscripts, element counts, etc.
difference_type	Type of difference between iterators.
iterator	Behaves like *value_type**.
const_iterator	Behaves like *const value_type**.
reverse_iterator	View container in reverse order; like *value_type**.
const_reverse_iterator	View container in reverse order; like *const value_type**.
reference	Behaves like *value_type*&.
const_reference	Behaves like *const value_type*&.
key_type	Type of key (for associative containers only).
mapped_type	Type of *mapped_value* (for associative containers only).
key_compare	Type of comparison criterion (for associative containers only).

A container can be viewed as a sequence either in the order defined by the container's *iterator* or in reverse order. For an associative container, the order is based on the container's comparison criterion (by default <):

Iterators (§16.3.2)	
begin()	Points to first element.
end()	Points to one-past-last element.
rbegin()	Points to first element of reverse sequence.
rend()	Points to one-past-last element of reverse sequence.

Some elements can be accessed directly:

Element Access (§16.3.3)	
front()	First element.
back()	Last element.
[]	Subscripting, unchecked access (not for list).
at()	Subscripting, checked access (for vector and deque only).

Vectors and deques provide efficient operations at the end (back) of their sequence of elements. In addition, lists and deques provide the equivalent operations on the start (front) of their sequences:

Stack and Queue Operations (§16.3.5, §17.2.2.2)	
push_back()	Add to end.
pop_back()	Remove last element.
push_front()	Add new first element (for list and deque only).
pop_front()	Remove first element (for list and deque only).

Containers provide list operations:

List Operations (§16.3.6)	
insert(p,x)	Add *x* before *p*.
insert(p,n,x)	Add *n* copies of *x* before *p*.
insert(p,first,last)	Add elements from [*first*:*last*[before *p*.
erase(p)	Remove element at *p*.
erase(first,last)	Erase [*first*:*last*[.
clear()	Erase all elements.

Appendix E discusses how containers behave if allocators or element operations throw exceptions.

All containers provide operations related to the number of elements and a few other operations:

Other Operations (§16.3.8, §16.3.9, §16.3.10)	
size()	Number of elements.
empty()	Is the container empty?
max_size()	Size of the largest possible container.
capacity()	Space allocated for *vector* (for vector only).
reserve()	Reserve space for future expansion (for vector only).
resize()	Change size of container (for vector, list, and deque only).
swap()	Swap elements of two containers.
get_allocator()	Get a copy of the container's allocator.
==	Is the content of two containers the same?
!=	Is the content of two containers different?
<	Is one container lexicographically before another?

Containers provide a variety of constructors and assignment operations:

Constructors, etc. (§16.3.4)	
container()	Empty container.
container(n)	*n* elements default value (not for associative containers).
container(n,x)	*n* copies of *x* (not for associative containers).
container(first,last)	Initial elements from [*first*:*last*[.
container(x)	Copy constructor; initial elements from container *x*.
~container()	Destroy the container and all of its elements.

Assignments (§16.3.4)	
operator=(x)	Copy assignment; elements from container *x*.
assign(n,x)	Assign *n* copies of *x* (not for associative containers).
assign(first,last)	Assign from [*first*:*last*[.

Associative containers provide lookup based on keys:

Associative Operations (§17.4.1)	
operator[ ](k)	Access the element with key *k* (for containers with unique keys).
find(k)	Find the element with key *k*.
lower_bound(k)	Find the first element with key *k*.
upper_bound(k)	Find the first element with key greater than *k*.
equal_range(k)	Find the *lower_bound* and *upper_bound* of elements with key *k*.
key_comp()	Copy of the key comparison object.
value_comp()	Copy of the *mapped_value* comparison object.

In addition to these common operations, most containers provide a few specialized operations.

17.1.2 Container Summary

The standard containers can be summarized like this:

Standard Container Operations					
	[]	List Operations	Front Operations	Back (Stack) Operations	Iterators
	§16.3.3 §17.4.1.3	§16.3.6 §20.3.9	§17.2.2.2 §20.3.9	§16.3.5 §20.3.12	§19.2.1
vector	const	O(n)+		const+	Ran
list		const	const	const	Bi
deque	const	O(n)	const	const	Ran
stack				const	
queue			const	const	
priority_queue			O(log(n))	O(log(n))	
map	O(log(n))	O(log(n))+			Bi
multimap		O(log(n))+			Bi
set		O(log(n))+			Bi
multiset		O(log(n))+			Bi
string	const	O(n)+	O(n)+	const+	Ran
array	const				Ran
valarray	const				Ran
bitset	const				

In the *iterators* column, **Ran** means random-access iterator and **Bi** means bidirectional iterator; the operations for a bidirectional operator are a subset of those of a random-access iterator (§19.2.1).

Other entries are measures of the efficiency of the operations. A *const* entry means the operation takes an amount of time that does not depend on the number of elements in the container; another conventional notation for *constant time* is $O(1)$. $O(n)$ means the operation takes time proportional to the number of elements involved. A + suffix indicates that occasionally a significant extra cost is incurred. For example, inserting an element into a *list* has a fixed cost (so it is listed as *const*), whereas the same operation on a *vector* involves moving the elements following the insertion point (so it is listed as $O(n)$). Occasionally, all elements must be relocated (so I added a +). The "big O" notation is conventional. I added the + for the benefit of programmers who care about predictability in addition to average performance. A conventional term for $O(n)+$ is *amortized linear time*.

Naturally, if a constant is large it can dwarf a small cost proportional to the number of elements. However, for large data structures *const* tends to mean "cheap," $O(n)$ to mean "expensive," and $O(log(n))$ to mean "fairly cheap." For even moderately large values of n, $O(log(n))$ is closer to constant time than to $O(n)$. People who care about cost must take a closer look. In particular, they must understand what elements are counted to get the n. No basic operation is "very expensive," that is, $O(n*n)$ or worse.

Except for *string*, the measures of costs listed here reflect requirements in the standard. The *string* estimates are my assumptions. The entries for *stack* and *queue* reflect the cost for the default implementation using a *deque* (§17.3.1, §17.3.2).

These measures of complexity and cost are upper bounds. The measures exist to give users some guidance as to what they can expect from implementations. Naturally, implementers will try to do better in important cases.

17.1.3 Representation

The standard doesn't prescribe a particular representation for each standard container. Instead, the standard specifies the container interfaces and some complexity requirements. Implementers will choose appropriate and often cleverly optimized implementations to meet the general requirements. A container will almost certainly be represented by a data structure holding the elements accessed through a handle holding size and capacity information. For a *vector*, the element data structure is most likely an array:

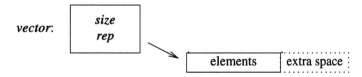

Similarly, a *list* is most likely represented by a set of links pointing to the elements:

A *map* is most likely implemented as a (balanced) tree of nodes pointing to (key,value) pairs:

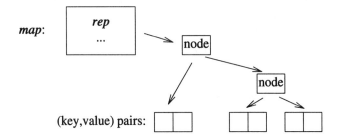

A *string* might be implemented as outlined in §11.12 or maybe as a sequence of arrays holding a few characters each:

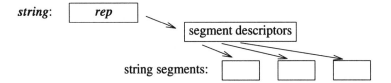

17.1.4 Element Requirements

Elements in a container are copies of the objects inserted. Thus, to be an element of a container, an object must be of a type that allows the container implementation to copy it. The container may copy elements using a copy constructor or an assignment; in either case, the result of the copy must be an equivalent object. This roughly means that any test for equality that you can devise on the value of the objects must deem the copy equal to the original. In other words, copying an element must work much like an ordinary copy of built-in types (including pointers). For example,

```
X& X::operator=(const X& a)    // proper assignment operator
{
        // copy all of a's members to *this
        return *this;
}
```

makes *X* acceptable as an element type for a standard container, but

```
void Y::operator=(const Y& a) // improper assignment operator
{
        // zero out all of a's members
}
```

renders *Y* unsuitable because *Y*'s assignment has neither the conventional return type nor the conventional semantics.

Some violations of the rules for standard containers can be detected by a compiler, but others cannot and might then cause unexpected behavior. For example, an assignment operation that throws an exception might leave a partially copied element behind. It could even leave an element in an invalid state that could cause trouble later. Such copy operations are themselves bad design (§14.4.6.1, Appendix E).

When copying elements isn't right, the alternative is to put pointers to objects into containers instead of the objects themselves. The most obvious example is polymorphic types (§2.5.4, §12.2.6). For example, we use *vector<Shape*>* rather than *vector<Shape>* to preserve polymorphic behavior.

17.1.4.1 Comparisons

Associative containers require that their elements can be ordered. So do many operations that can be applied to containers (for example *sort()*). By default, the < operator is used to define the order. If < is not suitable, the programmer must provide an alternative (§17.4.1.5, §18.4.2). The ordering criterion must define a *strict weak ordering*. Informally, this means that both less-than and equality must be transitive. That is, for an ordering criterion *cmp*:

[1] *cmp*(*x*, *x*) is *false*.

[2] If *cmp*(*x*, *y*) and *cmp*(*y*, *z*), then *cmp*(*x*, *z*).

[3] Define *equiv*(*x*, *y*) to be !(*cmp*(*x*, *y*) || *cmp*(*y*, *x*)). If *equiv*(*x*, *y*) and *equiv*(*y*, *z*), then *equiv*(*x*, *z*).

Consider:

```
template<class Ran> void sort(Ran first, Ran last);              // use < for comparison
template<class Ran, class Cmp> void sort(Ran first, Ran last, Cmp cmp);     // use cmp
```

The first version uses < and the second uses a user-supplied comparison *cmp*. For example, we might decide to sort *fruit* using a comparison that isn't case-sensitive. We do that by defining a function object (§11.9, §18.4) that does the comparison when invoked for a pair of *string*s:

```
class Nocase {          // case-insensitive string compare
public:
        bool operator()(const string&, const string&) const;
};

bool Nocase::operator()(const string& x, const string& y) const
        // return true if x is lexicographically less than y, not taking case into account
{
        string::const_iterator p = x.begin();
        string::const_iterator q = y.begin();

        while (p!=x.end() && q!=y.end() && toupper(*p)==toupper(*q)) {
                ++p;
                ++q;
        }
        if (p == x.end()) return q != y.end();
        if (q == y.end()) return false;
        return toupper(*p) < toupper(*q);
}
```

We can call *sort* ( ) using that comparison criterion. For example, given:

> *fruit* :
>> *apple   pear   Apple   Pear   lemon*

sorting using *sort* (*fruit* . *begin* ( ) , *fruit* . *end* ( ) , *Nocase* ( )) would yield something like:

> *fruit* :
>> *Apple   apple   lemon   Pear   pear*

whereas plain *sort* (*fruit* . *begin* ( ) , *fruit* . *end* ( )) would give:

> *fruit* :
>> *Apple   Pear   apple   lemon   pear*

assuming a character set in which uppercase letters precede lowercase letters.

Beware that < on C-style strings (that is, *char**) does not define lexicographical order (§13.5.2). Thus, associative containers will not work as most people would expect them to when C-style strings are used as keys. To make them work properly, a less-than operation that compares based on lexicographical order must be used. For example:

```
struct Cstring_less {
      bool operator ( ) (const char* p, const char* q) const { return strcmp (p, q) <0; }
} ;

map<char* , int, Cstring_less> m;        // map that uses strcmp() to compare const char* keys
```

17.1.4.2 Other Relational Operators

By default, containers and algorithms use < when they need to do a less-than comparison. When the default isn't right, a programmer can supply a comparison criterion. However, no mechanism is provided for also passing an equality test. Instead, when a programmer supplies a comparison *cmp*, equality is tested using two comparisons. For example:

> *if* (*x* == *y*) // not done where the user supplied a comparison

> *if* (! *cmp* (*x*, *y*) && ! *cmp* (*y*, *x*)) // done where the user supplied a comparison cmp

This saves us from having to add an equality parameter to every associative container and most algorithms. It may look expensive, but the library doesn't check for equality very often, and in 50% of the cases, only a single call of *cmp* ( ) is needed.

Using an equivalence relationship defined by less-than (by default <) rather than equality (by default ==) also has practical uses. For example, associative containers (§17.4) compare keys using an equivalence test ! (*cmp* (*x*, *y*) | | *cmp* (*y*, *x*)). This implies that equivalent keys need not be equal. For example, a *multimap* (§17.4.2) that uses case-insensitive comparison as its comparison criteria will consider the strings *Last*, *last*, *lAst*, *laSt*, and *lasT* equivalent, even though == for strings deems them different. This allows us to ignore differences we consider insignificant when sorting.

Given < and ==, we can easily construct the rest of the usual comparisons. The standard library defines them in the namespace *std* : : *rel_ops* and presents them in <*utility*>:

```
template<class T> bool rel_ops::operator!=(const T& x, const T& y) { return !(x==y); }
template<class T> bool rel_ops::operator>(const T& x, const T& y) { return y<x; }
template<class T> bool rel_ops::operator<=(const T& x, const T& y) { return !(y<x); }
template<class T> bool rel_ops::operator>=(const T& x, const T& y) { return !(x<y); }
```

Placing these operations in *rel_ops* ensures that they are easy to use when needed, yet they don't get created implicitly unless extracted from that namespace:

```
void f()
{
    using namespace std;
    // !=, >, etc., not generated by default
}

void g()
{
    using namespace std;
    using namespace std::rel_ops;
    // !=, >, etc., generated by default
}
```

The !=, etc., operations are not defined directly in *std* because they are not always needed and sometimes their definition would interfere with user code. For example, if I were writing a generalized math library, I would want *my* relational operators and not the standard library versions.

17.2 Sequences

Sequences follow the pattern described for *vector* (§16.3). The fundamental sequences provided by the standard library are:

> *vector*   *list*   *deque*

From these,

> *stack*   *queue*   *priority_queue*

are created by providing suitable interfaces. These sequences are called *container adapters*, *sequence adapters*, or simply *adapters* (§17.3).

17.2.1 Vector

The standard *vector* is described in detail in §16.3. The facilities for reserving space (§16.3.8) are unique to *vector*. By default, subscripting using [ ] is not range checked. If a check is needed, use *at*() (§16.3.3), a checked vector (§3.7.2), or a checked iterator (§19.3). A *vector* provides random-access iterators (§19.2.1).

17.2.2 List

A *list* is a sequence optimized for insertion and deletion of elements. Compared to *vector* (and *deque*; §17.2.3), subscripting would be painfully slow, so subscripting is not provided for *list*. Consequently, *list* provides bidirectional iterators (§19.2.1) rather than random-access iterators. This implies that a *list* will typically be implemented using some form of a doubly-linked list (see §17.8[16]).

A *list* provides all of the member types and operations offered by *vector* (§16.3), with the exceptions of subscripting, *capacity* ( ) , and *reserve* ( ) :

```
template <class T, class A = allocator<T> > class std::list {
public:
        // types and operations like vector's, except [], at(), capacity(), and reserve()
        // ...
};
```

17.2.2.1 Splice, Sort, and Merge

In addition to the general sequence operations, *list* provides several operations specially suited for list manipulation:

```
template <class T, class A = allocator<T> > class list {
public:
        // ...
        // list-specific operations:

        void splice (iterator pos, list& x);            // move all elements from x to before
                                                        // pos in this list without copying.
        void splice (iterator pos, list& x, iterator p);  // move *p from x to before
                                                        // pos in this list without copying.
        void splice (iterator pos, list& x, iterator first, iterator last);

        void merge (list&);            // merge sorted lists
        template <class Cmp> void merge (list&, Cmp);

        void sort ();
        template <class Cmp> void sort (Cmp);

        // ...
};
```

These *list* operations are all *stable*; that is, they preserve the relative order of elements that have equivalent values.

The *fruit* examples from §16.3.6 work with *fruit* defined to be a *list*. In addition, we can extract elements from one list and insert them into another by a single "splice" operation. Given:

```
fruit:
        apple   pear

citrus:
        orange   grapefruit   lemon
```

we can splice the *orange* from *citrus* into *fruit* like this:

```
list<string> :: iterator  p = find_if (fruit . begin ( ) , fruit . end ( ) , initial ( ´p´ ) );
fruit . splice (p , citrus , citrus . begin ( ) );
```

The effect is to remove the first element from *citrus* (*citrus . begin* ( )) and place it just before the first element of *fruit* with the initial letter *p*, thereby giving:

fruit :
>   apple   orange   pear

citrus :
>   grapefruit   lemon

Note that *splice* ( ) doesn't copy elements the way *insert* ( ) does (§16.3.6). It simply modifies the *list* data structures that refer to the element.

In addition to splicing individual elements and ranges, we can *splice* ( ) all elements of a *list*:

```
fruit . splice (fruit . begin ( ) , citrus );
```

This yields:

fruit :
>   grapefruit   lemon   apple   orange   pear

citrus :
>   <empty>

Each version of *splice* ( ) takes as its second argument the *list* from which elements are taken. This allows elements to be removed from their original *list*. An iterator alone wouldn't allow that because there is no general way to determine the container holding an element given only an iterator to that element (§18.6).

Naturally, an iterator argument must be a valid iterator for the *list* into which it is supposed to point. That is, it must point to an element of that *list* or be the *list*'s *end* ( ). If not, the result is undefined and possibly disastrous. For example:

```
list<string> :: iterator  p = find_if (fruit . begin ( ) , fruit . end ( ) , initial ( ´p´ ) );
fruit . splice (p , citrus , citrus . begin ( ) );        // ok
fruit . splice (p , citrus , fruit . begin ( ) );         // error: fruit.begin() doesn't point into citrus
citrus . splice (p , fruit , fruit . begin ( ) );         // error: p doesn't point into citrus
```

The first *splice* ( ) is ok even though *citrus* is empty.

A *merge* ( ) combines two sorted lists by removing the elements from one *list* and entering them into the other while preserving order. For example,

f1 :
>   apple   quince   pear

f2 :
>   lemon   grapefruit   orange   lime

can be sorted and merged like this:

f1.*sort*();
f2.*sort*();
f1.*merge*(*f2*);

This yields:

f1:

    apple   grapefruit   lemon   lime   orange   pear   quince

f2:

    <empty>

If one of the lists being merged is not sorted, *merge*() will still produce a list containing the union of elements of the two lists. However, there are no guarantees made about the order of the result.

Like *splice*(), *merge*() refrains from copying elements. Instead, it removes elements from the source list and splices them into the target list. After an *x*.*merge*(*y*), the *y* list is empty.

17.2.2.2 Front Operations

Operations that refer to the first element of a *list* are provided to complement the operations referring to the last element provided by every sequence (§16.3.6):

```
template <class T, class A = allocator<T> > class list {
public:
    // ...
    // element access:

    reference front();              // reference to first element
    const_reference front() const;

    void push_front(const T&);      // add new first element
    void pop_front();               // remove first element

    // ...
};
```

The first element of a container is called its *front*. For a *list*, front operations are as efficient and convenient as back operations (§16.3.5). When there is a choice, back operations should be preferred over front operations. Code written using back operations can be used for a *vector* as well as for a *list*. So if there is a chance that the code written using a *list* will ever evolve into a generic algorithm applicable to a variety of containers, it is best to prefer the more widely available back operations. This is a special case of the rule that to achieve maximal flexibility, it is usually wise to use the minimal set of operations to do a task (§17.1.4.1).

17.2.2.3 Other Operations

Insertion and removal of elements are particularly efficient for *list*s. This, of course, leads people to prefer *list*s when these operations are frequent. That, in turn, makes it worthwhile to support common ways of removing elements directly:

```
template <class  T,  class  A = allocator<T> >  class  list {
public:
    // ...

    void  remove (const  T& val);
    template <class  Pred> void  remove_if(Pred  p);

    void  unique ();                                // remove duplicates using ==
    template <class  BinPred> void  unique (BinPred  b);   // remove duplicates using b

    void  reverse ();                               // reverse order of elements
};
```

For example, given

fruit:
> apple   orange   grapefruit   lemon   orange   lime   pear   quince

we can remove all elements with the value "*orange*" like this:

> *fruit*. *remove* ("*orange*");

yielding:

fruit:
> apple   grapefruit   lemon   lime   pear   quince

Often, it is more interesting to remove all elements that meet some criterion rather than simply all elements with a given value. The *remove_if*() operation does that. For example,

> *fruit*. *remove_if*(*initial* ('*l*'));

removes every element with the initial '*l*' from *fruit* giving:

fruit:
> apple   grapefruit   pear   quince

A common reason for removing elements is to eliminate duplicates. The *unique* () operation is provided for that. For example:

> *fruit*. *sort* ();
> *fruit*. *unique* ();

The reason for sorting is that *unique* removes only duplicates that appear consecutively. For example, had fruit contained:

> apple   pear   apple   apple   pear

a simple *fruit*. *unique* () would have produced

> apple   pear   apple   pear

whereas sorting first gives:

> apple   pear

If only certain duplicates should be eliminated, we can provide a predicate to specify which duplicates we want to remove. For example, we might define a binary predicate (§18.4.2) *initial2* (*x*) to compare *string*s that have the initial *x* but yield *false* for every *string* that doesn't. Given:

>   *pear   pear   apple   apple*

we can remove consecutive duplicates of every *fruit* with the initial *p* by a call

>   *fruit . unique* (*initial2* (´*p*´)) ;

This would give

>   *pear   apple   apple*

As noted in §16.3.2, we sometimes want to view a container in reverse order. For a *list*, it is possible to reverse the elements so that the first becomes the last, etc., without copying the elements. The *reverse* ( ) operation is provided to do that. Given:

>   *fruit* :
>   *banana cherry   lime   strawberry*

fruit . reverse ( ) produces:

>   *fruit* :
>   *strawberry lime   cherry banana*

An element that is removed from a list is destroyed. However, note that destroying a pointer does not imply that the object it points to is *delete*d. If you want a container of pointers that *delete*s elements pointed to when the pointer is removed from the container or the container is destroyed, you must write one yourself (§17.8[13]).

17.2.3 Deque

A *deque* (it rhymes with check) is a double-ended queue. That is, a *deque* is a sequence optimized so that operations at both ends are about as efficient as for a *list*, whereas subscripting approaches the efficiency of a *vector*:

```
template <class T, class A = allocator<T> > class std::deque {
    // types and operations like vector (§16.3.3, §16.3.5, §16.3.6) except capacity() and reserve()
    // plus front operations (§17.2.2.2) like list
};
```

Insertion and deletion of elements "in the middle" have *vector*-like (in)efficiencies rather than *list*-like efficiencies. Consequently, a *deque* is used where additions and deletions take place "at the ends." For example, we might use a *deque* to model a section of a railroad or to represent a deck of cards in a game:

```
deque<car> siding_no_3;
deque<Card> bonus;
```

17.3 Sequence Adapters

The *vector*, *list*, and *deque* sequences cannot be built from each other without loss of efficiency. On the other hand, *stack*s and *queue*s can be elegantly and efficiently implemented using those three basic sequences. Therefore, *stack* and *queue* are defined not as separate containers, but as adaptors of basic containers.

A container adapter provides a restricted interface to a container. In particular, adapters do not provide iterators; they are intended to be used only through their specialized interfaces.

The techniques used to create a container adapter from a container are generally useful for non-intrusively adapting the interface of a class to the needs of its users.

17.3.1 Stack

The *stack* container adapter is defined in *<stack>*. It is so simple that the best way to describe it is to present an implementation:

```
template <class T, class C = deque<T> > class std::stack {
protected:
    C c;
public:
    typedef typename C::value_type value_type;
    typedef typename C::size_type size_type;
    typedef C container_type;

    explicit stack(const C& a = C()) : c(a) { }

    bool empty() const { return c.empty(); }
    size_type size() const { return c.size(); }

    value_type& top() { return c.back(); }
    const value_type& top() const { return c.back(); }

    void push(const value_type& x) { c.push_back(x); }
    void pop() { c.pop_back(); }
};
```

That is, a *stack* is simply an interface to a container of the type passed to it as a template argument. All *stack* does is to eliminate the non-stack operations on its container from the interface and give *back*(), *push_back*(), and *pop_back*() their conventional names: *top*(), *push*(), and *pop*().

By default, a *stack* makes a *deque* to hold its elements, but any sequence that provides *back*(), *push_back*(), and *pop_back*() can be used. For example:

```
stack<char> s1;                    // uses a deque<char> to store elements of type char
stack< int, vector<int> > s2;      // uses a vector<int> to store elements of type int
```

It is possible to supply an existing container to initialize a stack. For example:

```
void print_backwards (vector<int>& v)
{
    stack< int, vector<int> > state (v);        // initialize state from v
    while (state.size()) {
        cout << state.top();
        state.pop();
    }
}
```

However, the elements of a container argument are copied, so supplying an existing container can be expensive.

Elements are added to a *stack* using *push_back*() on the container that is used to store the elements. Consequently, a *stack* cannot overflow as long as there is memory available on the machine for the container to acquire (using its allocator; see §19.4).

On the other hand, a *stack* can underflow:

```
void f()
{
    stack<int> s;
    s.push (2);
    if (s.empty()) {                             // underflow is preventable
        // don't pop
    }
    else {                                       // but not impossible
        s.pop();   // fine: s.size() becomes 0
        s.pop();   // undefined effect, probably bad
    }
}
```

Note that one does not *pop*() an element to use it. Instead, the *top*() is accessed and then *pop*()'d when it is no longer needed. This is not too inconvenient, and it is more efficient when the *pop*() isn't necessary:

```
void f(stack<char>& s)
{
    if (s.top() == 'c') s.pop();    // remove optional initial 'c'
    // ...
}
```

Unlike fully developed containers, *stack* (like other container adapters) doesn't have an allocator template parameter. Instead, the *stack* and its users rely on the allocator from the container used to implement the *stack*.

17.3.2 Queue

Defined in *<queue>*, a *queue* is an interface to a container that allows the insertion of elements at the *back*() and the extraction of elements at the *front*():

```
template <class T, class C = deque<T> > class std::queue {
protected:
      C c;
public:
      typedef typename C::value_type value_type;
      typedef typename C::size_type size_type;
      typedef C container_type;

      explicit queue(const C& a = C()) : c(a) { }

      bool empty() const { return c.empty(); }
      size_type size() const { return c.size(); }

      value_type& front() { return c.front(); }
      const value_type& front() const { return c.front(); }

      value_type& back() { return c.back(); }
      const value_type& back() const { return c.back(); }

      void push(const value_type& x) { c.push_back(x); }
      void pop() { c.pop_front(); }
};
```

By default, a *queue* makes a *deque* to hold its elements, but any sequence that provides *front* ( ),
back ( ), *push_back* ( ), and *pop_front* ( ) can be used. Because a *vector* does not provide
pop_front ( ), a *vector* cannot be used as the underlying container for a queue.

Queues seem to pop up somewhere in every system. One might define a server for a simple
message-based system like this:

```
struct Message {
      // ...
};

void server(queue<Message>& q)
{
      while (!q.empty()) {
            Message& m = q.front();      // get hold of message
            m.service();                 // call function to serve request
            q.pop();                     // destroy message
      }
}
```

Messages would be put on the *queue* using *push* ( ).

If the requester and the server are running in different processes or threads, some form of syn-
chronization of the queue access would be necessary. For example:

```
void server2(queue<Message>& q, Lock& lck)
{
      while (!q.empty()) {
            Message m;
            {     LockPtr h(lck);          // hold lock only while extracting message (see §14.4.1)
                  if (q.empty()) return;   // somebody else got the message
```

```
                        m = q.front();
                        q.pop();
                    }
                    m.service();                          // call function to serve request
                }
            }
```

There is no standard definition of concurrency or locking in C++ or in the world in general. Have a look to see what your system has to offer and how to access it from C++ (§17.8[8]).

17.3.3 Priority Queue

A *priority_queue* is a queue in which each element is given a priority that controls the order in which the elements get to be *top*() :

```
    template <class T, class C = vector<T>, class Cmp = less<typename C::value_type> >
    class std::priority_queue {
    protected:
        C c;
        Cmp cmp;
    public:
        typedef typename C::value_type value_type;
        typedef typename C::size_type size_type;
        typedef C container_type;

        explicit priority_queue(const Cmp& a1 = Cmp(), const C& a2 = C())
            : c(a2), cmp(a1) { make_heap(c.begin(),c.end(),cmp); }   // see §18.8
        template <class In>
        priority_queue(In first, In last, const Cmp& = Cmp(), const C& = C());

        bool empty() const { return c.empty(); }
        size_type size() const { return c.size(); }

        const value_type& top() const { return c.front(); }

        void push(const value_type&);
        void pop();
    };
```

The declaration of *priority_queue* is found in *<queue>*.

By default, the *priority_queue* simply compares elements using the < operator and *top*() returns the largest element:

```
    struct Message {
        int priority;
        bool operator<(const Message& x) const { return priority < x.priority; }
        // ...
    };
```

```
void server(priority_queue<Message>& q, Lock& lck)
{
    while (!q.empty()) {
        Message m;
        {   LockPtr h(lck);              // hold lock only while extracting message (see §14.4.1)
            if (q.empty()) return;       // somebody else got the message
            m = q.top();
            q.pop();
        }
        m.service();     // call function to serve request
    }
}
```

This example differs from the *queue* example (§17.3.2) in that *messages* with higher priority will get served first. The order in which elements with equal priority come to the head of the queue is not defined. Two elements are considered of equal priority if neither has higher priority than the other (§17.4.1.5).

An alternative to < for comparison can be provided as a template argument. For example, we could sort strings in a case-insensitive manner by placing them in

```
priority_queue<string, vector<string>, Nocase> pq;     // use Nocase for comparisons (§17.1.4.1)
```

using *pq.push()* and then retrieving them using *pq.top()* and *pq.pop()*.

Objects defined by templates given different template arguments are of different types (§13.6.3.1). For example:

```
priority_queue<string>& pq1 = pq;      // error: type mismatch
```

We can supply a comparison criterion without affecting the type of a *priority_queue* by providing a comparison object of the appropriate type as a constructor argument. For example:

```
struct String_cmp {   // type used to express comparison criteria at run time
    String_cmp(int n = 0);     // use comparison criteria n
    // ...
};

typedef priority_queue<string, vector<string>, String_cmp> Pqueue;

void g(Pqueue& pq)  // pq uses String_cmp() for comparisons
{
    Pqueue pq2(String_cmp(nocase));
    pq = pq2;  // ok: pq and pq2 are of the same type, pq now also uses String_cmp(nocase)
}
```

Keeping elements in order isn't free, but it needn't be expensive either. One useful way of implementing a *priority_queue* is to use a tree structure to keep track of the relative positions of elements. This gives an $O(log(n))$ cost of both *push()* and *pop()*.

By default, a *priority_queue* makes a *vector* to hold its elements, but any sequence that provides *front()*, *push_back()*, *pop_back()*, and random iterators can be used. A *priority_queue* is most likely implemented using a *heap* (§18.8).

17.4   Associative Containers

An *associative array* is one of the most useful general, user-defined types. In fact, it is often a built-in type in languages primarily concerned with text processing and symbolic processing. An associative array, often called a *map* and sometimes called a *dictionary*, keeps pairs of values. Given one value, called the *key*, we can access the other, called the *mapped value*. An associative array can be thought of as an array for which the index need not be an integer:

```
template<class K, class V> class Assoc {
public:
    V& operator[] (const K&); // return a reference to the V corresponding to K
    // ...
};
```

Thus, a key of type *K* names a mapped value of type *V*.

Associative containers are a generalization of the notion of an associative array. The *map* is a traditional associative array, where a single value is associated with each unique key. A *multimap* is an associative array that allows duplicate elements for a given key, and *set* and *multiset* can be seen as degenerate associative arrays in which no value is associated with a key.

17.4.1   Map

A *map* is a sequence of (key,value) pairs that provides for fast retrieval based on the key. At most one value is held for each key; in other words, each key in a *map* is unique. A *map* provides bidirectional iterators (§19.2.1).

The *map* requires that a less-than operation exist for its key types (§17.1.4.1) and keeps its elements sorted so that iteration over a *map* occurs in order. For elements for which there is no obvious order or when there is no need to keep the container sorted, we might consider using a *hash_map* (§17.6).

17.4.1.1   Types

A *map* has the usual container member types (§16.3.1) plus a few relating to its specific function:

```
template <class Key, class T, class Cmp = less<Key>,
          class A = allocator< pair<const Key,T> > >
class std::map {
public:
    // types:

    typedef Key key_type;
    typedef T mapped_type;

    typedef pair<const Key, T> value_type;

    typedef Cmp key_compare;
    typedef A allocator_type;

    typedef typename A::reference reference;
    typedef typename A::const_reference const_reference;
```

```
        typedef implementation_defined1  iterator;
        typedef implementation_defined2  const_iterator;

        typedef typename A::size_type  size_type;
        typedef typename A::difference_type  difference_type;

        typedef std::reverse_iterator<iterator>  reverse_iterator;
        typedef std::reverse_iterator<const_iterator>  const_reverse_iterator;
        // ...
    };
```

Note that the *value_type* of a *map* is a (key,value) *pair*. The type of the mapped values is referred to as the *mapped_type*. Thus, a *map* is a sequence of *pair<const Key, mapped_type>* elements.

As usual, the actual iterator types are implementation-defined. Since a *map* most likely is implemented using some form of a tree, these iterators usually provide some form of tree traversal.

The reverse iterators are constructed from the standard *reverse_iterator* templates (§19.2.5).

17.4.1.2 Iterators and Pairs

A *map* provides the usual set of functions that return iterators (§16.3.2):

```
    template <class Key, class T, class Cmp = less<Key>,
             class A = allocator< pair<const Key, T> > > class map {
    public:
        // ...
        // iterators:

        iterator begin();
        const_iterator begin() const;

        iterator end();
        const_iterator end() const;

        reverse_iterator rbegin();
        const_reverse_iterator rbegin() const;

        reverse_iterator rend();
        const_reverse_iterator rend() const;

        // ...
    };
```

Iteration over a *map* is simply an iteration over a sequence of *pair<const Key, mapped_type>* elements. For example, we might print out the entries of a phone book like this:

```
    void f(map<string, number>& phone_book)
    {
        typedef map<string, number>::const_iterator CI;
        for (CI p = phone_book.begin(); p!=phone_book.end(); ++p)
            cout << p->first << '\t' << p->second << '\n';
    }
```

A *map* iterator presents the elements in ascending order of its keys (§17.4.1.5). Therefore, the *phone_book* entries will be output in lexicographical order.

We refer to the first element of any *pair* as *first* and the second as *second* independently of what types they actually are:

```
template <class T1, class T2> struct std::pair {
        typedef T1 first_type;
        typedef T2 second_type;

        T1 first;
        T2 second;

        pair() :first(T1()), second(T2()) { }
        pair(const T1& x, const T2& y) :first(x), second(y) { }
        template<class U, class V>
                pair(const pair<U, V>& p) :first(p.first), second(p.second) { }
};
```

The last constructor exists to allow conversion of *pair*s (§13.6.2). For example:

```
pair<int, double> f(char c, int i)
{
        pair<char, int> x(c,i);
        // ...
        return x;  // pair<char,int> to pair<int,double> conversion required
}
```

In a *map*, the key is the first element of the pair and the mapped value is the second.

The usefulness of *pair* is not limited to the implementation of *map*, so it is a standard library class in its own right. The definition of *pair* is found in *<utility>*. A function to make it convenient to create *pair*s is also provided:

```
template <class T1, class T2> pair<T1, T2> std::make_pair(const T1& t1, const T2& t2)
{
        return pair<T1, T2>(t1, t2);
}
```

A *pair* is by default initialized to the default values of its element types. In particular, this implies that elements of built-in types are initialized to *0* (§5.1.1) and *string*s are initialized to the empty string (§20.3.4). A type without a default constructor can be an element of a *pair* only provided the pair is explicitly initialized.

17.4.1.3 Subscripting

The characteristic *map* operation is the associative lookup provided by the subscript operator:

```
template <class Key, class T, class Cmp = less<Key>,
        class A = allocator< pair<const Key, T> > >
class map {
public:
        // ...
        mapped_type& operator[] (const key_type& k);   // access element with key k
        // ...
};
```

The subscript operator performs a lookup on the key given as an index and returns the corresponding value. If the key isn't found, an element with the key and the default value of the *mapped_type* is inserted into the *map*. For example:

```
void f()
{
    map<string, int> m;    // map starting out empty
    int x = m["Henry"];    // create new entry for "Henry", initialize to 0, return 0
    m["Harry"] = 7;        // create new entry for "Harry", initialize to 0, and assign 7
    int y = m["Henry"];    // return the value from "Henry"'s entry
    m["Harry"] = 9;        // change the value from "Harry"'s entry to 9
}
```

As a slightly more realistic example, consider a program that calculates sums of items presented as input in the form of (item-name,value) pairs such as

nail 100 hammer 2 saw 3 saw 4 hammer 7 nail 1000 nail 250

and also calculates the sum for each item. The main work can be done while reading the (item-name,value) pairs into a *map*:

```
void readitems(map<string, int>& m)
{
    string word;
    int val = 0;
    while (cin >> word >> val) m[word] += val;
}
```

The subscript operation *m[word]* identifies the appropriate *(string, int)* pair and returns a reference to its *int* part. This code takes advantage of the fact that a new element gets its *int* value set to *0* by default.

A *map* constructed by *readitems()* can then be output using a conventional loop:

```
int main()
{
    map<string, int> tbl;
    readitems(tbl);

    int total = 0;
    typedef map<string, int>::const_iterator CI;

    for (CI p = tbl.begin(); p!=tbl.end(); ++p) {
        total += p->second;
        cout << p->first << '\t' << p->second << '\n';
    }

    cout << "---------------\ntotal\t" << total << '\n';

    return !cin;
}
```

Given the input above, the output is:

```
hammer    9
nail      1350
saw       7
----------------
total     1366
```

Note that the items are printed in lexical order (§17.4.1, §17.4.1.5).

A subscripting operation must find the key in the *map*. This, of course, is not as cheap as subscripting an array with an integer. The cost is $O(log(size\_of\_map))$, which is acceptable for many applications. For applications for which this is too expensive, a hashed container is often the answer (§17.6).

Subscripting a *map* adds a default element when the key is not found. Therefore, there is no version of *operator*[]() for *const map*s. Furthermore, subscripting can be used only if the *mapped_type* (value type) has a default value. If the programmer simply wants to see if a key is present, the *find*() operation (§17.4.1.6) can be used to locate a *key* without modifying the *map*.

17.4.1.4 Constructors

A *map* provides the usual complement of constructors, etc. (§16.3.4) :

```
template <class Key, class T, class Cmp =less<Key>,
        class A =allocator<pair<const Key,T> > >
class map {
public:
    // ...
    // construct/copy/destroy:

    explicit map(const Cmp& = Cmp(), const A& = A());
    template <class In> map(In first, In last, const Cmp& = Cmp(), const A& = A());
    map(const map&);

    ~map();

    map& operator=(const map&);

    // ...
};
```

Copying a container implies allocating space for its elements and making copies of each element (§16.3.4). This can be very expensive and should be done only when necessary. Consequently, containers such as *map*s tend to be passed by reference.

The member template constructor takes a sequence of *pair<const Key, T>*s described by a pair of input iterators. It *insert*()s (§17.4.1.7) the elements from the sequence into the *map*.

17.4.1.5 Comparisons

To find an element in a *map* given a key, the *map* operations must compare keys. Also, iterators traverse a *map* in order of increasing key values, so insertion will typically also compare keys (to place an element into a tree structure representing the *map*).

By default, the comparison used for keys is < (less than), but an alternative can be provided as a template parameter or as a constructor argument (see §17.3.3). The comparison given is a comparison of keys, but the *value_type* of a *map* is a (key,value) pair. Consequently, *value_comp* ( ) is provided to compare such pairs using the key comparison function:

```
template <class Key, class T, class Cmp = less<Key>,
         class A = allocator< pair<const Key, T> > >
class map {
public :
    // ...

    typedef Cmp key_compare;

    class value_compare : public binary_function<value_type, value_type, bool> {
    friend class map;
    protected :
        Cmp cmp;
        value_compare (Cmp c) : cmp (c) { }
    public :
        bool operator( ) (const value_type& x, const value_type& y) const
            { return cmp (x.first, y.first); }
    };

    key_compare key_comp ( ) const;
    value_compare value_comp ( ) const;
    // ...
};
```

For example:

```
map<string, int> m1;
map<string, int, Nocase> m2;                              // specify comparison type (§17.1.4.1)
map<string, int, String_cmp> m3;                         // specify comparison type (§17.1.4.1)
map<string, int, String_cmp> m4 (String_cmp (literary));  // pass comparison object
```

The *key_comp* ( ) and *value_comp* ( ) member functions make it possible to query a *map* for the kind of comparisons used for keys and values. This is usually done to supply the same comparison criterion to some other container or algorithm. For example:

```
void f(map<string, int>& m)
{
    map<string, int> mm;                        // compare using < by default
    map<string, int> mmm (m.key_comp ( ));      // compare the way m does
    // ...
}
```

See §17.1.4.1 for an example of how to define a particular comparison and §18.4 for an explanation of function objects in general.

17.4.1.6 Map Operations

The crucial idea for *map*s and indeed for all associative containers is to gain information based on a key. Several specialized operations are provided for that:

```
template <class Key, class T, class Cmp = less<Key>,
         class A = allocator< pair<const Key,T> > >
class map {
public:
    // ...
    // map operations:

    iterator find(const key_type& k);              // find element with key k
    const_iterator find(const key_type& k) const;

    size_type count(const key_type& k) const;      // find number of elements with key k

    iterator lower_bound(const key_type& k);       // find first element with key k
    const_iterator lower_bound(const key_type& k) const;
    iterator upper_bound(const key_type& k);       // find first element with key greater than k
    const_iterator upper_bound(const key_type& k) const;

    pair<iterator,iterator> equal_range(const key_type& k);
    pair<const_iterator,const_iterator> equal_range(const key_type& k) const;

    // ...
};
```

A *m.find*(*k*) operation simply yields an iterator to an element with the key *k*. If there is no such element, the iterator returned is *m*.*end*(). For a container with unique keys, such as *map* and *set*, the resulting iterator will point to the unique element with the key *k*. For a container with non-unique keys, such as *multimap* and *multiset*, the resulting iterator will point to the first element that has that key. For example:

```
void f(map<string,int>& m)
{
    map<string,int>::iterator p = m.find("Gold");
    if (p!=m.end()) {                     // if "Gold" was found
        // ...
    }
    else if (m.find("Silver")!=m.end()) {  // look for "Silver"
        // ...
    }
    // ...
}
```

For a *multimap* (§17.4.2), finding the first match is rarely as useful as finding all matches; *m*.*lower_bound*(*k*) and *m*.*upper_bound*(*k*) give the beginning and the end of the subsequence of elements of *m* with the key *k*. As usual, the end of a sequence is an iterator to the one-past-the-last element of the sequence. For example:

```
void f(multimap<string,int>& m)
{
    multimap<string,int>::iterator lb = m.lower_bound("Gold");
    multimap<string,int>::iterator ub = m.upper_bound("Gold");
```

```
        for (multimap<string,int>::iterator p = lb; p!=ub; ++p) {
            // ...
        }
    }
```

Finding the upper bound and lower bound by two separate operations is neither elegant nor efficient. Consequently, the operation *equal_range*() is provided to deliver both. For example:

```
    void f(multimap<string,int>& m)
    {
        typedef multimap<string,int>::iterator MI;
        pair<MI,MI> g = m.equal_range("Gold");

        for (MI p = g.first; p!=g.second; ++p) {
            // ...
        }
    }
```

If *lower_bound*(*k*) doesn't find *k*, it returns an iterator to the first element that has a key greater than *k*, or *end*() if no such greater element exists. This way of reporting failure is also used by *upper_bound*() and *equal_range*().

17.4.1.7 List Operations

The conventional way of entering a value into an associative array is simply to assign to it using subscripting. For example:

```
    phone_book["Order department"] = 8226339;
```

This will make sure that the Order department has the desired entry in the *phone_book* independently of whether it had a prior entry. It is also possible to *insert*() entries directly and to remove entries using *erase*():

```
    template <class Key, class T, class Cmp = less<Key>,
              class A = allocator< pair<const Key,T> > >
    class map {
    public:
        // ...
        // list operations:

        pair<iterator, bool> insert(const value_type& val);    // insert (key,value) pair
        iterator insert(iterator pos, const value_type& val);  // pos is just a hint
        template <class In> void insert(In first, In last);    // insert elements from sequence

        void erase(iterator pos);                   // erase the element pointed to
        size_type erase(const key_type& k);         // erase element with key k (if present)
        void erase(iterator first, iterator last);  // erase range
        void clear();                               // Erase all elements

        // ...
    };
```

The operation *m.insert*(*val*) attempts to add a (*Key,T*) pair *val* to *m*. Since *map*s rely on unique keys, insertion takes place only if there is not already an element in the *m* with that key. The return value of *m.insert(val)* is a *pair<iterator, bool>*. The *bool* is *true* if *val* was actually inserted. The iterator refers to the element of *m* holding *val*'s key (*val.first*). For example:

```
void f(map<string, int>& m)
{
    pair<string, int> p99("Paul", 99);

    pair<map<string, int>::iterator, bool> p = m.insert(p99);
    if (p.second) {
        // "Paul" was inserted
    }
    else {
        // "Paul" was there already
    }
    map<string, int>::iterator i = p.first;      // points to m["Paul"]
    // ...
}
```

Usually, we do not care whether a key is newly inserted or was present in the *map* before the *insert()*. When we are interested, it is often because we want to register the fact that a value is in a *map* somewhere else (outside the *map*). The other two versions of *insert()* do not return an indication of whether a value was actually inserted.

Specifying a position, *insert(pos, val)*, is simply a hint to the implementation to start the search for the key *val* at *pos*. If the hint is good, significant performance improvements can result. If the hint is bad, you'd have done better without it both notationally and efficiency-wise. For example:

```
void f(map<string, int>& m)
{
    m["Dilbert"] = 3;    // neat, possibly less efficient
    m.insert(m.begin(), make_pair(const string("Dogbert"), 99));      // ugly
}
```

In fact, [] is little more than a convenient notation for *insert()*. The result of *m[k]* is equivalent to the result of *(*(m.insert(make_pair(k, V()))).first)).second*, where *V()* is the default value for the mapped type. When you understand that equivalence, you probably understand associative containers.

Because [] always uses *V()*, you cannot use subscripting on a *map* with a value type that does not have a default value. This is an unfortunate limitation of the standard associative containers. However, the requirement of a default value is not a fundamental property of associative containers (see §17.6.2).

You can erase elements specified by a key. For example:

```
void f(map<string, int>& m)
{
    int count = m.erase("Ratbert");
    // ...
}
```

The integer returned is the number of erased elements. In particular, *count* is *0* if there was no element with the key *"Ratbert"* to erase. For a *multimap* or *multiset*, the value can be larger than *1*.
Alternatively, one can erase an element given an iterator pointing to it or a range of elements given
a sequence. For example:

```
void  g (map<string, int>& m)
{
      m .erase (m .find ("Catbert") );
      m .erase (m .find ("Alice"), m .find ("Wally") );
}
```

Naturally, it is faster to erase an element for which you already have an iterator than to first find the
element given its key and then erase it. After *erase* (), the iterator cannot be used again because
the element to which it pointed is no longer there. Iterators to other *map* elements are not affected
and still valid. A call *m .erase (b, e)* where *e* is *m .end* () is harmless (provided *b* refers to an element of *m* or is *m .end* ()). However, a call *m .erase (p)* where *p* is *m .end* () is a serious error
that could corrupt the container.

17.4.1.8 Other Functions

Finally, a *map* provides the usual functions dealing with the number of elements and a *swap* ():

```
template <class  Key,  class  T,  class  Cmp = less<Key>,
          class  A = allocator< pair<const  Key, T> > >
class  map {
public :
      // ...
      // capacity:

      size_type  size () const;            // number of elements
      size_type  max_size () const;        // size of largest possible map
      bool  empty () const { return  size () ==0; }

      void  swap (map&);
};
```

As usual, a value returned by *size* () or *max_size* () is a number of elements.
    In addition, *map* provides ==, ! =, <, >, <=, >=, and *swap* () as nonmember functions:

```
template <class  Key,  class  T,  class  Cmp,  class  A>
bool  operator== (const  map<Key, T, Cmp, A>&,  const  map<Key, T, Cmp, A>&);

// similarly !=, <, >, <=, and >=

template <class  Key,  class  T,  class  Cmp,  class  A>
void  swap (map<Key, T, Cmp, A>&,  map<Key, T, Cmp, A>&);
```

Why would anyone want to compare two *map*s? When we specifically compare two *map*s, we usually want to know not just if the *map*s differ, but also how they differ if they do. In such cases, we
don't use == or ! =. However, by providing ==, <, and *swap* () for every container, we make it
possible to write algorithms that can be applied to every container. For example, these functions
allow us to *sort* () a *vector* of *map*s and to have a *set* of *map*s.

17.4.2 Multimap

A *multimap* is like a *map*, except that it allows duplicate keys:

```
template <class Key, class T, class Cmp = less<Key>,
        class A = allocator< pair<const Key,T> > >
class std::multimap {
public:
        // like map, except:

        iterator insert(const value_type&);    // returns iterator, not pair

        // no subscript operator []
};
```

For example (using *Cstring_less* from §17.1.4.1 to compare C-style strings):

```
void f(map<char*, int, Cstring_less>& m, multimap<char*, int, Cstring_less>& mm)
{
        m.insert(make_pair("x",4));
        m.insert(make_pair("x",5));  // no effect: there already is an entry for "x" (§17.4.1.7)
        // now m["x"] == 4

        mm.insert(make_pair("x",4));
        mm.insert(make_pair("x",5));
        // mm now holds both ("x",4) and ("x",5)
}
```

This implies that *multimap* cannot support subscripting by key values in the way *map* does. The *equal_range*(), *lower_bound*(), and *upper_bound*() operations (§17.4.1.6) are the primary means of accessing multiple values with the same key.

Naturally, where several values can exist for a single key, a *multimap* is preferred over a *map*. That happens far more often than people first think when they hear about *multimap*. In some ways, a *multimap* is even cleaner and more elegant than a *map*.

Because a person can easily have several phone numbers, a phone book is a good example of a *multimap*. I might print my phone numbers like this:

```
void print_numbers(const multimap<string,int>& phone_book)
{
        typedef multimap<string,int>::const_iterator I;
        pair<I,I> b = phone_book.equal_range("Stroustrup");
        for (I i = b.first; i != b.second; ++i) cout << i->second << '\n';
}
```

For a *multimap*, the argument to *insert*() is always inserted. Consequently, the *multimap*::*insert*() returns an iterator rather than a *pair<iterator, bool>* like *map* does. For uniformity, the library could have provided the general form of *insert*() for both *map* and *multimap* even though the *bool* would have been redundant for a *multimap*. Yet another design alternative would have been to provide a simple *insert*() that didn't return a *bool* in either case and then supply users of *map* with some other way of figuring out whether a key was newly inserted. This is a case in which different interface design ideas clash.

17.4.3 Set

A *set* can be seen as a *map* (§17.4.1), where the values are irrelevant, so we keep track of only the keys. This leads to only minor changes to the user interface:

```
template <class Key, class Cmp = less<Key>, class A = allocator<Key> >
class std::set {
public:
    // like map except:

    typedef Key value_type;          // the key itself is the value
    typedef Cmp value_compare;
    // no subscript operator []
};
```

Defining *value_type* as the *Key* type (*key_type*; §17.4.1.1) is a trick to allow code that uses *map*s and *set*s to be identical in many cases.

Note that *set* relies on a comparison operation (by default <) rather than equality (==). This implies that equivalence of elements is defined by inequality (§17.1.4.1) and that iteration through a *set* has a well-defined order.

Like *map*, *set* provides ==, !=, <, >, <=, >=, and *swap* ( ).

17.4.4 Multiset

A *multiset* is a *set* that allows duplicate keys:

```
template <class Key, class Cmp = less<Key>, class A = allocator<Key> >
class std::multiset {
public:
    // like set, except:
    iterator insert(const value_type&);    // returns iterator, not pair
};
```

The *equal_range* ( ), *lower_bound* ( ), and *upper_bound* ( ) operations (§17.4.1.6) are the primary means of accessing multiple occurrences of a key.

17.5 Almost Containers

Built-in arrays (§5.2), *string*s (Chapter 20), *valarray*s (§22.4), and *bitset*s (§17.5.3) hold elements and can therefore be considered containers for many purposes. However, each lacks some aspect or other of the standard container interface, so these ''almost containers'' are not completely interchangeable with fully developed containers such as *vector* and *list*.

17.5.1 String

A *basic_string* provides subscripting, random-access iterators, and most of the notational conveniences of a container (Chapter 20). However, *basic_string* does not provide as wide a selection of types as elements. It also is optimized for use as a string of characters and is typically used in ways that differ significantly from a container.

17.5.2 Valarray

A *valarray* (§22.4) is a vector for optimized numeric computation. Consequently, a *valarray* doesn't attempt to be a general container. A *valarray* provides many useful numeric operations. However, of the standard container operations (§17.1.1), it offers only *size* ( ) and a subscript operator (§22.4.2). A pointer to an element of a *valarray* is a random-access iterator (§19.2.1).

17.5.3 Bitset

Often, aspects of a system, such as the state of an input stream (§21.3.3), are represented as a set of flags indicating binary conditions such as good/bad, true/false, and on/off. C++ supports the notion of small sets of flags efficiently through bitwise operations on integers (§6.2.4). These operations include & (and), | (or), ^ (exclusive or), << (shift left), and >> (shift right). Class *bitset<N>* generalizes this notion and offers greater convenience by providing operations on a set of *N* bits indexed from *0* through *N–1*, where *N* is known at compile time. For sets of bits that don't fit into a *long int*, using a *bitset* is much more convenient than using integers directly. For smaller sets, there may be an efficiency tradeoff. If you want to name the bits, rather than numbering them, using a *set* (§17.4.3), an enumeration (§4.8), or a bitfield (§C.8.1) are alternatives.

A *bitset<N>* is an array of *N* bits. A *bitset* differs from a *vector<bool>* (§16.3.11) by being of fixed size, from *set* (§17.4.3) by having its bits indexed by integers rather than associatively by value, and from both *vector<bool>* and *set* by providing operations to manipulate the bits.

It is not possible to address a single bit directly using a built-in pointer (§5.1). Consequently, *bitset* provides a reference-to-bit type. This is actually a generally useful technique for addressing objects for which a built-in pointer for some reason is unsuitable:

```
template<size_t N> class std::bitset {
public:

        class reference {            // reference to a single bit:
                friend class bitset;
                reference();
        public:                                    // b[i] refers to the (i+1)'th bit:
                ~reference();
                reference& operator=(bool x);              // for b[i] = x;
                reference& operator=(const reference&);    // for b[i] = b[j];
                bool operator~() const;                    // return ~b[i]
                operator bool() const;                     // for x = b[i];
                reference& flip();                         // b[i].flip();
        };

        // ...
};
```

The *bitset* template is defined in namespace *std* and presented in *<bitset>*.

For historical reasons, *bitset* differs somewhat in style from other standard library classes. For example, if an index (also known as a *bit position*) is out of range, an *out_of_range* exception is thrown. No iterators are provided. Bit positions are numbered right to left in the same way bits often are in a word, so the value of *b* [*i*] is *pow* (*2*, *i*). Thus, a bitset can be thought of as an *N*-bit binary number:

```
position:       9  8  7  6  5  4  3  2  1  0
bitset<10>(989): | 1 | 1 | 1 | 1 | 0 | 1 | 1 | 1 | 0 | 1 |
```

17.5.3.1 Constructors

A *bitset* can be constructed with default values, from the bits in an *unsigned long int*, or from a *string*:

```
template<size_t N> class bitset {
public:
    // ...
    // constructors:

    bitset();                          // N zero-bits
    bitset(unsigned long val);         // bits from val

    template<class Ch, class Tr, class A>              // Tr is a character trait (§20.2)
    explicit bitset(const basic_string<Ch,Tr,A>& str,   // bits from string str
        typename basic_string<Ch,Tr,A>::size_type pos = 0,
        typename basic_string<Ch,Tr,A>::size_type n = basic_string<Ch,Tr,A>::npos);

    // ...
};
```

The default value of a bit is *0*. When an *unsigned long int* argument is supplied, each bit in the integer is used to initialize the corresponding bit in the bitset (if any). A *basic_string* (Chapter 20) argument does the same, except that the character ´0´ gives the bitvalue *0*, the character ´1´ gives the bitvalue *1*, and other characters cause an *invalid_argument* exception to be thrown. By default, a complete string is used for initialization. However, in the style of a *basic_string* constructor (§20.3.4), a user can specify that only the range of characters from *pos* to the end of the string or to *pos+n* are to be used. For example:

```
void f()
{
    bitset<10> b1;   // all 0

    bitset<16> b2 = 0xaaaa;                        // 1010101010101010
    bitset<32> b3 = 0xaaaa;                        // 00000000000000001010101010101010

    bitset<10> b4(string("1010101010"));          // 1010101010
    bitset<10> b5(string("10110111011110",4));    // 0111011110
    bitset<10> b6(string("10110111011110",2,8));  // 0011011101

    bitset<10> b7(string("n0g00d"));              // invalid_argument thrown
    bitset<10> b8 = string("n0g00d");             // error: no string to bitset conversion
}
```

A key idea in the design of *bitset* is that an optimized implementation can be provided for bitsets that fit in a single word. The interface reflects this assumption.

17.5.3.2 Bit Manipulation Operations

A *bitset* provides the operators for accessing individual bits and for manipulating all bits in the set:

```
template<size_t N> class std::bitset {
public:
        // ...
        // bitset operations:

        reference operator[](size_t pos);          // b[i]

        bitset& operator&=(const bitset& s);       // and
        bitset& operator|=(const bitset& s);       // or
        bitset& operator^=(const bitset& s);       // exclusive or

        bitset& operator<<=(size_t n);             // logical left shift (fill with zeros)
        bitset& operator>>=(size_t n);             // logical right shift (fill with zeros)

        bitset& set();                             // set every bit to 1
        bitset& set(size_t pos, int val = 1);      // b[pos]=val

        bitset& reset();                           // set every bit to 0
        bitset& reset(size_t pos);                 // b[pos]=0

        bitset& flip();                            // change the value of every bit
        bitset& flip(size_t pos);                  // change the value of b[pos]

        bitset operator~() const { return bitset<N>(*this).flip(); }     // make complement set
        bitset operator<<(size_t n) const { return bitset<N>(*this)<<=n; }  // make shifted set
        bitset operator>>(size_t n) const { return bitset<N>(*this)>>=n; }  // make shifted set

        // ...
};
```

The subscript operator throws *out_of_range* if the subscript is out of range. There is no unchecked subscript operation.

The *bitset&* returned by these operations is **this*. An operator returning a *bitset* (rather than a *bitset&*) makes a copy of **this*, applies its operation to that copy, and returns the result. In particular, >> and << really are shift operations rather than I/O operations. The output operator for a *bitset* is a << that takes an *ostream* and a *bitset* (§17.5.3.3).

When bits are shifted, a logical (rather than cyclic) shift is used. That implies that some bits "fall off the end" and that some positions get the default value 0. Note that because *size_t* is an unsigned type, it is not possible to shift by a negative number. It does, however, imply that $b<<-1$ shifts by a very large positive value, thus leaving every bit of the *bitset b* with the value *0*. Your compiler should warn against this.

17.5.3.3 Other Operations

A *bitset* also supports common operations such as *size*(), ==, I/O, etc.:

```
template<size_t N> class bitset {
public:
    // ...

    unsigned long to_ulong() const;

    template <class Ch, class Tr, class A> basic_string<Ch,Tr,A> to_string() const;

    size_t count() const;              // number of bits with value 1
    size_t size() const { return N; }  // number of bits

    bool operator==(const bitset& s) const;
    bool operator!=(const bitset& s) const;

    bool test(size_t pos) const;       // true if b[pos] is 1
    bool any() const;                  // true if any bit is 1
    bool none() const;                 // true if no bit is 1
};
```

The operations *to_ulong*() and *to_string*() provide the inverse operations to the constructors. To avoid nonobvious conversions, named operations were preferred over conversion operations. If the value of the *bitset* has so many significant bits that it cannot be represented as an *unsigned long*, *to_ulong*() throws *overflow_error*.

The *to_string*() operation produces a string of the desired type holding a sequence of ´0´ and ´1´ characters; *basic_string* is the template used to implement strings (Chapter 20). We could use *to_string* to write out the binary representation of an *int*:

```
void binary(int i)
{
    bitset<8*sizeof(int)> b = i;      // assume 8-bit byte (see also §22.2)
    cout << b.template to_string< char,char_traits<char>,allocator<char> >() << ´\n´;
}
```

Unfortunately, invoking an explicitly qualified member template requires a rather elaborate and rare syntax (§C.13.6).

In addition to the member functions, *bitset* provides binary & (and), | (or), ^ (exclusive or), and the usual I/O operators:

```
template<size_t N> bitset<N> std::operator&(const bitset<N>&, const bitset<N>&);
template<size_t N> bitset<N> std::operator|(const bitset<N>&, const bitset<N>&);
template<size_t N> bitset<N> std::operator^(const bitset<N>&, const bitset<N>&);

template <class charT, class Tr, size_t N>
basic_istream<charT,Tr>& std::operator>>(basic_istream<charT,Tr>&, bitset<N>&);
template <class charT, class Tr, size_t N>
basic_ostream<charT,Tr>& std::operator<<(basic_ostream<charT,Tr>&, const bitset<N>&);
```

We can therefore write out a bitset without first converting it to a string. For example:

```
void binary (int i)
{
    bitset<8*sizeof(int)> b = i;        // assume 8-bit byte (see also §22.2)
    cout << b << '\n';
}
```

This prints the bits represented as *1*s and *0*s left-to-right, with the most significant bit leftmost.

17.5.4 Built-In Arrays

A built-in array supplies subscripting and random-access iterators in the form of ordinary pointers (§2.7.2). However, an array doesn't know its own size, so users must keep track of that size. In general, an array doesn't provide the standard member operations and types.

It is possible, and sometimes useful, to provide an ordinary array in a guise that provides the notational convenience of a standard container without changing its low-level nature:

```
template<class T, int max> struct c_array {
    typedef T value_type;

    typedef T* iterator;
    typedef const T* const_iterator;

    typedef T& reference;
    typedef const T& const_reference;

    T v[max];
    operator T*() { return v; }

    reference operator[] (ptrdiff_t i) { return v[i]; }
    const_reference operator[] (ptrdiff_t i) const { return v[i]; }

    iterator begin() { return v; }
    const_iterator begin() const { return v; }

    iterator end() { return v+max; }
    const_iterator end() const { return v+max; }

    size_t size() const { return max; }
};
```

For compatibility with arrays, I use the signed *ptrdiff_t* (§16.1.2) rather than the unsigned *size_t* as the subscript type. Using *size_t* could lead to subtle ambiguities when using [ ] on a *c_array*.

The *c_array* template is not part of the standard library. It is presented here as a simple example of how to fit a "foreign" container into the standard container framework. It can be used with standard algorithms (Chapter 18) using *begin()*, *end()*, etc. It can be allocated on the stack without any indirect use of dynamic memory. Also, it can be passed to a C-style function that expects a pointer. For example:

```
void f(int* p, int sz);        // C-style

void g()
{
    c_array<int, 10> a;
```

```
    f(a,a.size());                                    // C-style use
    c_array<int,10>::iterator p = find(a.begin(),a.end(),777);  // C++/STL style use
    // ...
}
```

17.6 Defining a New Container

The standard containers provide a framework to which a user can add. Here, I show how to provide a container in such a way that it can be used interchangeably with the standard containers wherever reasonable. The implementation is meant to be realistic, but it is not optimal. The interface is chosen to be very close to that of existing, widely-available, and high-quality implementations of the notion of a *hash_map*. Use the *hash_map* provided here to study the general issues. Then, use a supported *hash_map* for production use.

17.6.1 Hash_map

A *map* is an associative container that accepts almost any type as its element type. It does that by relying only on a less-than operation for comparing elements (§17.4.1.5). However, if we know more about a key type we can often reduce the time needed to find an element by providing a hash function and implementing a container as a hash table.

A hash function is a function that quickly maps a value to an index in such a way that two distinct values rarely end up with the same index. Basically, a hash table is implemented by placing a value at its index, unless another value is already placed there, and ''nearby'' if one is. Finding an element placed at its index is fast, and finding one ''nearby'' is not slow, provided equality testing is reasonably fast. Consequently, it is not uncommon for a *hash_map* to provide five to ten times faster lookup than a *map* for larger containers, where the speed of lookup matters most. On the other hand, a *hash_map* with an ill-chosen hash function can be much slower than a *map*.

There are many ways of implementing a hash table. The interface of *hash_map* is designed to differ from that of the standard associative containers only where necessary to gain performance through hashing. The most fundamental difference between a *map* and a *hash_map* is that a *map* requires a < for its element type, while a *hash_map* requires an == and a hash function. Thus, a *hash_map* must differ from a *map* in the non-default ways of creating one. For example:

```
    map<string,int> m1;                    // compare strings using <
    map<string,int,Nocase> m2;             // compare strings using Nocase() (§17.1.4.1)

    hash_map<string,int> hm1;              // hash using Hash<string>() (§17.6.2.3), compare using ==
    hash_map<string,int,hfct> hm2;         // hash using hfct(), compare using ==
    hash_map<string,int,hfct,eql> hm3;     // hash using hfct(), compare using eql
```

A container using hashed lookup is implemented using one or more tables. In addition to holding its elements, the container needs to keep track of which values have been associated with each hashed value (''index'' in the prior explanation); this is done using a ''hash table.'' Most hash table implementations seriously degrade in performance if that table gets ''too full,'' say 75% full. Consequently, the *hash_map* defined next is automatically resized when it gets too full. However, resizing can be expensive, so it is useful to be able to specify an initial size.

Thus, a first approximation of a *hash_map* looks like this:

```
template<class Key, class T, class H = Hash<Key>,
         class EQ = equal_to<Key>, class A = allocator< pair<const Key,T> > >
class hash_map {
    // like map, except:

    typedef H Hasher;
    typedef EQ key_equal;

    hash_map(const T& dv =T(), size_type n =101, const H& hf =H(), const EQ& =EQ());
    template<class In> hash_map(In first, In last,
            const T& dv =T(), size_type n =101, const H& hf =H(), const EQ& =EQ());
};
```

Basically, this is the *map* interface (§17.4.1.4), with < replaced by == and a hash function.

The uses of a *map* in this book so far (§3.7.4, §6.1, §17.4.1) can be converted to use a *hash_map* simply by changing the name *map* to *hash_map*. Often, a change between a *map* and a *hash_map* can be eased by using *typedef*. For example:

```
typedef hash_map<string,record> Map;
Map dictionary;
```

The *typedef* is also useful to further hide the actual type of the dictionary from its users.

Though not strictly correct, I think of the tradeoff between a *map* and a *hash_map* as simply a space/time tradeoff. If efficiency isn't an issue, it isn't worth wasting time choosing between them: either will do well. For large and heavily used tables, *hash_map* has a definite speed advantage and should be used unless space is a premium. Even then, I might consider other ways of saving space before choosing a ''plain'' *map*. Actual measurement is essential to avoid optimizing the wrong code.

The key to efficient hashing is the quality of the hash function. If a good hash function isn't available, a *map* can easily outperform a *hash_map*. Hashing based on a C-style string, a *string*, or an integer is usually very effective. However, it is worth remembering that the effectiveness of a hash function critically depends on the actual values being hashed (§17.8[35]). A *hash_map* must be used where < is not defined or is unsuitable for the intended key. Conversely, a hash function does not define an ordering the way < does, so a *map* must be used when it is important to keep the elements sorted.

Like *map*, *hash_map* provides *find*() to allow a programmer to determine whether a key has been inserted.

17.6.2 Representation and Construction

Many different implementations of a *hash_map* are possible. Here, I use one that is reasonably fast and whose most important operations are fairly simple. The key operations are the constructors, the lookup (operator [ ]), the resize operation, and the operation removing an element (*erase*()).

The simple implementation chosen here relies on a hash table that is a *vector* of pointers to entries. Each *Entry* holds a *key*, a *value*, a pointer to the next *Entry* (if any) with the same hash value, and an *erased* bit :

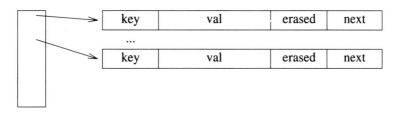

Expressed as declarations, it looks like this:

```
template<class Key, class T, class H = Hash<Key>,
        class EQ = equal_to<Key>, class A = allocator< pair<const Key, T> > >
class hash_map {
    // ...
private:                    // representation
    struct Entry {
        key_type key;
        mapped_type val;
        bool erased;
        Entry* next;        // hash overflow link
        Entry(key_type k, mapped_type v, Entry* n)
            : key(k), val(v), erased(false), next(n) { }
    };

    vector<Entry> v;        // the actual entries
    vector<Entry*> b;       // the hash table: pointers into v

    // ...
};
```

Note the *erased* bit. The way several values with the same hash value are handled here makes it hard to remove an element. So instead of actually removing an element when *erase*() is called, I simply mark the element *erased* and ignore it until the table is resized.

In addition to the main data structure, a *hash_map* needs a few pieces of administrative data. Naturally, each constructor needs to set up all of this. For example:

```
template<class Key, class T, class H = Hash<Key>,
        class EQ = equal_to<Key>, class A = allocator< pair<const Key, T> > >
class hash_map {
    // ...

    hash_map(const T& dv =T(), size_type n =101, const H& h =H(), const EQ& e =EQ())
        : default_value(dv), b(n), no_of_erased(0), hash(h), eq(e)
    {
        set_load();                         // defaults
        v.reserve(max_load*b.size());       // reserve space for growth
    }

    void set_load(float m = 0.7, float g = 1.6) { max_load = m; grow = g; }

    // ...
```

```
private:
     float max_load;           // keep v.size()<=b.size()*max_load
     float grow;               // when necessary, resize(bucket_count()*grow)
     size_type no_of_erased;   // number of entries in v occupied by erased elements
     Hasher hash;              // hash function
     key_equal eq;             // equality

     const T default_value;    // default value used by []
};
```

The standard associative containers require that a mapped type have a default value (§17.4.1.7). This restriction is not logically necessary and can be inconvenient. Making the default value an argument allows us to write:

```
hash_map<string,Number> phone_book1;                    // default: Number()
hash_map<string,Number> phone_book2(Number(411));       // default: Number(411)
```

17.6.2.1 Lookup

Finally, we can provide the crucial lookup operations:

```
template<class Key, class T, class H = Hash<Key>,
          class EQ = equal_to<Key>, class A = allocator< pair<const Key,T> > >
class hash_map {
     // ...
     mapped_type& operator[] (const key_type&);

     iterator find(const key_type&);
     const_iterator find(const key_type&) const;
     // ...
};
```

To find a *value*, *operator*[]() uses a hash function to find an index in the hash table for the *key*. It then searches through the entries until it finds a matching *key*. The *value* in that *Entry* is the one we are seeking. If it is not found, a default value is entered:

```
template<class Key, class T, class H = Hash<Key>,
          class EQ = equal_to<Key>, class A = allocator< pair<const Key,T> > >
hash_map<Key,T,H,EQ,A>::mapped_type&
     hash_map<Key,T,H,EQ,A>::operator[] (const key_type& k)
{
     size_type i = hash(k)%b.size();              // hash

     for(Entry* p = b[i]; p; p = p->next) // search among entries hashed to i
          if (eq(k,p->key)) {             // found
               if (p->erased) {           // re-insert
                    p->erased = false;
                    no_of_erased--;
                    return p->val = default_value;
               }
               return p->val;
          }
```

```
        // not found:
        if (size_type (b.size () *max_load) <= v.size ()) {        // if "too full"
            resize (b.size () *grow);              // grow
            return operator[] (k);                 // rehash
        }

        v.push_back (Entry (k, default_value, b[i]));    // add Entry
        b[i] = &v.back ();                               // point to new element

        return b[i]->val;
    }
```

Unlike *map*, *hash_map* doesn't rely on an equality test synthesized from a less-than operation (§17.1.4.1). This is because of the call of *eq*() in the loop that looks through elements with the same hash value. This loop is crucial to the performance of the lookup, and for common and obvious key types such as *string* and C-style strings, the overhead of an extra comparison could be significant.

I could have used a *set<Entry>* to represent the set of values that have the same hash value. However, if we have a good hash function (*hash*()) and an appropriately-sized hash table (*b*), most such sets will have exactly one element. Consequently, I linked the elements of that set together using the *next* field of *Entry* (§17.8[27]).

Note that *b* keeps pointers to elements of *v* and that elements are added to *v*. In general, *push_back*() can cause reallocation and thus invalidate pointers to elements (§16.3.5). However, in this case constructors (§17.6.2) and *resize*() carefully *reserve*() enough space so that no unexpected reallocation happens.

17.6.2.2 Erase and Resize

Hashed lookup becomes inefficient when the table gets too full. To lower the chance of that happening, the table is automatically *resize*()d by the subscript operator. The *set_load*() (§17.6.2) provides a way of controlling when and how resizing happens. Other functions are provided to allow a programmer to observe the state of a *hash_map*:

```
    template<class Key, class T, class H = Hash<Key>,
            class EQ = equal_to<Key>, class A = allocator< pair<const Key, T> > >
    class hash_map {
        // ...

        void resize (size_type n);                 // make the size of the hash table n

        void erase (iterator position);            // erase the element pointed to

        size_type size () const { return v.size () -no_of_erased; }   // number of elements

        size_type bucket_count () const { return b.size (); }    // size of hash table

        Hasher hash_fun () const { return hash; }         // hash function used
        key_equal key_eq () const { return eq; }          // equality used
```

```
        // ...
    };
```

The *resize*() operation is essential, reasonably simple, and potentially expensive:

```
    template<class Key, class T, class H = Hash<Key>,
            class EQ = equal_to<Key>, class A = allocator< pair<const Key,T> > >
    void hash_map<Key,T,H,EQ,A>::resize(size_type s)
    {
        size_type i = v.size();
        while (no_of_erased) {              // really remove erased elements
            if (v[--i].erased) {
                v.erase(&v[i]);
                --no_of_erased;
            }
        }

        if (s <= b.size()) return;
        b.resize(s);                        // add s-b.size() pointers
        fill(b.begin(),b.end(),0);          // zero out the entries (§18.6.6)
        v.reserve(s*max_load);              // if v needs to reallocate, let it happen now

        for (size_type i = 0; i<v.size(); i++) {          // rehash:
            size_type ii = hash(v[i].key)%b.size();       // hash
            v[i].next = b[ii];                            // link
            b[ii] = &v[i];
        }
    }
```

If necessary, a user can "manually" call *resize*() to ensure that the cost is incurred at a predictable time. I have found a *resize*() operation important in some applications, but it is not fundamental to the notion of hash tables. Some implementation strategies don't need it.

All of the real work is done elsewhere (and only if a **hash_map** is resized), so *erase*() is trivial:

```
    template<class Key, class T, class H = Hash<Key>,
            class EQ = equal_to<Key>, class A = allocator< pair<const Key,T> > >
    void hash_map<Key,T,H,EQ,A>::erase(iterator p)          // erase the element pointed to
    {
        if (p->erased == false) no_of_erased++;
        p->erased = true;
    }
```

17.6.2.3 Hashing

To complete *hash_map*::*operator*[](), we need to define *hash*() and *eq*(). For reasons that will become clear in §18.4, a hash function is best defined as *operator*()() for a function object:

```
    template <class T> struct Hash : unary_function<T, size_t> {
        size_t operator()(const T& key) const;
    };
```

A good hash function takes a key and returns an integer so that different keys yield different integers with high probability. Choosing a good hash function is an art. However, exclusive-or'ing the bits of the key's representation into an integer is often acceptable:

```
template <class T> size_t Hash<T>::operator()(const T& key) const
{
    size_t res = 0;

    size_t len = sizeof(T);
    const char* p = reinterpret_cast<const char*>(&key);  // access object as sequence of bytes

    while (len--) res = (res<<1)^*p++; // use bytes of key's representation
    return res;
}
```

The use of *reinterpret_cast* (§6.2.7) is a good indication that something unsavory is going on and that we can do better in cases when we know more about the object being hashed. In particular, if an object contains a pointer, if the object is large, or if the alignment requirements on members have left unused space ("holes") in the representation, we can usually do better (see §17.8[29]).

A C-style string is a pointer (to the characters), and a *string* contains a pointer. Consequently, specializations are in order:

```
typedef char* Pchar;

template<> size_t Hash<Pchar>::operator()(const Pchar& key) const
{
    size_t res = 0;
    Pchar p = key;
    while (*p) res = (res<<1)^*p++;      // use int value of characters
    return res;
}

template <class C>
size_t Hash< basic_string<C> >::operator()(const basic_string<C>& key) const
{
    size_t res = 0;

    typedef typename basic_string<C>::const_iterator CI;
    CI p = key.begin();
    CI end = key.end();

    while (p!=end) res = (res<<1)^*p++;      // use int value of characters
    return res;
}
```

An implementation of *hash_map* will include hash functions for at least integer and string keys. For more adventurous key types, the user may have to help out with suitable specializations. Experimentation supported by good measurement is essential when choosing a hash function. Intuition tends to work poorly in this area.

To complete the *hash_map*, we need to define the iterators and a minor host of trivial functions; this is left as an exercise (§17.8[34]).

17.6.3 Other Hashed Associative Containers

For consistency and completeness, the *hash_map* should have matching *hash_set*, *hash_multimap*, and *hash_multiset*. Their definitions are obvious from those of *hash_map*, *map*, *multimap*, *set*, and *multiset*, so I leave these as an exercise (§17.8[34]). Good public domain and commercial implementations of these hashed associative containers are available. For real programs, these should be preferred to locally concocted versions, such as mine.

17.7 Advice

[1] By default, use *vector* when you need a container; §17.1.

[2] Know the cost (complexity, big-O measure) of every operation you use frequently; §17.1.2.

[3] The interface, implementation, and representation of a container are distinct concepts. Don't confuse them; §17.1.3.

[4] You can sort and search according to a variety of criteria; §17.1.4.1.

[5] Do not use a C-style string as a key unless you supply a suitable comparison criterion; §17.1.4.1.

[6] You can define comparison criteria so that equivalent, yet different, key values map to the same key; §17.1.4.1.

[7] Prefer operations on the end of a sequence (*back*-operations) when inserting and deleting elements; §17.1.4.1.

[8] Use *list* when you need to do many insertions and deletions from the front or the middle of a container; §17.2.2.

[9] Use *map* or *multimap* when you primarily access elements by key; §17.4.1.

[10] Use the minimal set of operations to gain maximum flexibility; §17.1.1

[11] Prefer a *map* to a *hash_map* if the elements need to be kept in order; §17.6.1.

[12] Prefer a *hash_map* to a *map* when speed of lookup is essential; §17.6.1.

[13] Prefer a *hash_map* to a *map* if no less-than operation can be defined for the elements; §17.6.1.

[14] Use *find* ( ) when you need to check if a key is in an associative container; §17.4.1.6.

[15] Use *equal_range* ( ) to find all elements of a given key in an associative container; §17.4.1.6.

[16] Use *multimap* when several values need to be kept ordered for a single key; §17.4.2.

[17] Use *set* or *multiset* when the key itself is the only value you need to keep; §17.4.3.

17.8 Exercises

The solutions to several exercises for this chapter can be found by looking at the source text of an implementation of the standard library. Do yourself a favor: try to find your own solutions before looking to see how your library implementer approached the problems. Then, look at your implementation's version of the containers and their operations.

1. (*2.5) Understand the O ( ) notation (§17.1.2). Do some measurements of operations on standard containers to determine the constant factors involved.

2. (*2) Many phone numbers don't fit into a *long*. Write a *phone_number* type and a class that provides a set of useful operations on a container of *phone_numbers*.

3. (∗2) Write a program that lists the distinct words in a file in alphabetical order. Make two versions: one in which a word is simply a whitespace-separated sequence of characters and one in which a word is a sequence of letters separated by any sequence of non-letters.
4. (∗2.5) Implement a simple solitaire card game.
5. (∗1.5) Implement a simple test of whether a word is a palindrome (that is, if its representation is symmetric; examples are *ada*, *otto*, and *tut*). Implement a simple test of whether an integer is a palindrome. Implement a simple test of a whether sentence is a palindrome. Generalize.
6. (∗1.5) Define a queue using (only) two *stacks*.
7. (∗1.5) Define a stack similar to *stack* (§17.3.1), except that it doesn't copy its underlying container and that it allows iteration over its elements.
8. (∗3) Your computer will have support for concurrent activities through the concept of a thread, task, or process. Figure out how that is done. The concurrency mechanism will have a concept of locking to prevent two tasks accessing the same memory simultaneously. Use the machine's locking mechanism to implement a lock class.
9. (∗2.5) Read a sequence of dates such as *Dec85*, *Dec50*, *Jan76*, etc., from input and then output them so that later dates come first. The format of a date is a three-letter month followed by a two-digit year. Assume that all the years are from the same century.
10. (∗2.5) Generalize the input format for dates to allow dates such as *Dec1985*, *12/3/1990*, (*Dec*, *30*, *1950*), *3/6/2001*, etc. Modify exercise §17.8[9] to cope with the new formats.
11. (∗1.5) Use a *bitset* to print the binary values of some numbers, including *0*, *1*, *−1*, *18*, *−18*, and the largest positive *int*.
12. (∗1.5) Use *bitset* to represent which students in a class were present on a given day. Read the *bitset*s for a series of 12 days and determine who was present every day. Determine which students were present at least 8 days.
13. (∗1.5) Write a *List* of pointers that *delete*s the objects pointed to when it itself is destroyed or if the element is removed from the *List*.
14. (∗1.5) Given a *stack* object, print its elements in order (without changing the value of the stack).
15. (∗2.5) Complete *hash_map* (§17.6.1). This involves implementing *find*() and *equal_range*() and devising a way of testing the completed template. Test *hash_map* with at least one key type for which the default hash function would be unsuitable.
16. (∗2.5) Implement and test a list in the style of the standard *list*.
17. (∗2) Sometimes, the space overhead of a *list* can be a problem. Write and test a singly-linked list in the style of a standard container.
18. (∗2.5) Implement a list that is like a standard *list*, except that it supports subscripting. Compare the cost of subscripting for a variety of lists to the cost of subscripting a *vector* of the same length.
19. (∗2) Implement a template function that merges two containers.
20. (∗1.5) Given a C-style string, determine whether it is a palindrome. Determine whether an initial sequence of at least three words in the string is a palindrome.
21. (∗2) Read a sequence of (*name*, *value*) pairs and produce a sorted list of (*name*, *total*, *mean*, *median*) 4-tuples. Print that list.
22. (∗2.5) Determine the space overhead of each of the standard containers on your implementation.
23. (∗3.5) Consider what would be a reasonable implementation strategy for a *hash_map* that needed to use minimal space. Consider what would be a reasonable implementation strategy for

a *hash_map* that needed to use minimal lookup time. In each case, consider what operations you might omit so as to get closer to the ideal (no space overhead and no lookup overhead, respectively). Hint: There is an enormous literature on hash tables.

24. (*2) Devise a strategy for dealing with overflow in *hash_map* (different values hashing to the same hash value) that makes *equal_range* ( ) trivial to implement.

25. (*2.5) Estimate the space overhead of a *hash_map* and then measure it. Compare the estimate to the measurements. Compare the space overhead of your *hash_map* and your implementation's *map*.

26. (*2.5) Profile your *hash_map* to see where the time is spent. Do the same for your implementation's *map* and a widely-distributed *hash_map*.

27. (*2.5) Implement a *hash_map* based on a *vector<map<K, V>*>* so that each *map* holds all keys that have the same hash value.

28. (*3) Implement a *hash_map* using Splay trees (see D. Sleator and R. E. Tarjan: *Self-Adjusting Binary Search Trees*, JACM, Vol. 32. 1985).

29. (*2) Given a data structure describing a string-like entity:

```
struct St {
    int  size;
    char  type_indicator;
    char*  buf;          // point to size characters
    St (const  char*  p);   // allocate and fill buf
};
```

Create 1000 *St*s and use them as keys for a *hash_map*. Devise a program to measure the performance of the *hash_map*. Write a hash function (a *Hash*; §17.6.2.3) specifically for *St* keys.

30. (*2) Give at least four different ways of removing the *erased* elements from a *hash_map*. You should use a standard library algorithm (§3.8, Chapter 18) to avoid an explicit loop.

31. (*3) Implement a *hash_map* that erases elements immediately.

32. (*2) The hash function presented in §17.6.2.3 doesn't always consider all of the representation of a key. When will part of a representation be ignored? Write a hash function that always considers all of the representations of a key. Give an example of when it might be wise to ignore part of a key and write a hash function that computes its value based only on the part of a key considered relevant.

33. (*2.5) The code of hash functions tends to be similar: a loop gets more data and then hashes it. Define a *Hash* (§17.6.2.3) that gets its data by repeatedly calling a function that a user can define on a per-type basis. For example:

```
size_t  res = 0;
while (size_t  v = hash (key)) res = (res<<3) ^v;
```

Here, a user can define *hash* (*K*) for each type *K* that needs to be hashed.

34. (*3) Given some implementation of *hash_map*, implement *hash_multimap*, *hash_set*, and *hash_multiset*.

35. (*2.5) Write a hash function intended to map uniformly distributed *int* values into hash values intended for a table size of about 1024. Given that function, devise a set of 1024 key values, all of which map to the same value.

18

Algorithms and Function Objects

Form is liberating.
– engineers´ proverb

Introduction — overview of standard algorithms — sequences — function objects — predicates — arithmetic objects — binders — member function objects — *for_each* — finding elements — *count* — comparing sequences — searching — copying — *transform* — replacing and removing elements — filling a sequence — reordering — *swap* — sorted sequences — *binary_search* — *merge* — set operations — *min* and *max* — heaps — permutations — C-style algorithms — advice — exercises.

18.1 Introduction

A container by itself is really not that interesting. To be genuinely useful, a container must be supported by basic operations such as finding its size, iterating, copying, sorting, and searching for elements. Fortunately, the standard library provides algorithms to serve the most common and basic needs that users have of containers.

This chapter summarizes the standard algorithms and gives a few examples of their uses, a presentation of the key principles and techniques used to express the algorithms in C++, and a more detailed explanation of a few key algorithms.

Function objects provide a mechanism through which a user can customize the behavior of the standard algorithms. Function objects supply key information that an algorithm needs in order to operate on a user's data. Consequently, emphasis is placed on how function objects can be defined and used.

18.2 Overview of Standard Library Algorithms

At first glimpse, the standard library algorithms can appear overwhelming. However, there are just 60 of them. I have seen classes with more member functions. Furthermore, many algorithms share a common basic behavior and a common interface style that eases understanding. As with language features, a programmer should use the algorithms actually needed and understood − and only those. There are no awards for using the highest number of standard algorithms in a program. Nor are there awards for using standard algorithms in the most clever and obscure way. Remember, a primary aim of writing code is to make its meaning clear to the next person reading it − and that person just might be yourself a few years hence. On the other hand, when doing something with elements of a container, consider whether that action could be expressed as an algorithm in the style of the standard library. That algorithm might already exist. If you don't consider work in terms of general algorithms, you will reinvent the wheel.

Each algorithm is expressed as a template function (§13.3) or a set of template functions. In that way, an algorithm can operate on many kinds of sequences containing elements of a variety of types. Algorithms that return an iterator (§19.1) as a result generally use the end of an input sequence to indicate failure. For example:

```
void f(list<string>& ls)
{
    list<string>::const_iterator p = find(ls.begin(), ls.end(), "Fred");

    if (p == ls.end()) {
        // didn't find "Fred"
    }
    else {
        // here, p points to "Fred"
    }
}
```

The algorithms do not perform range checking on their input or output. Range errors must be prevented by other means (§18.3.1, §19.3). When an algorithm returns an iterator, that iterator is of the same type as one of its inputs. In particular, an algorithm's arguments control whether it returns a *const_iterator* or a non-*const iterator*. For example:

```
void f(list<int>& li, const list<string>& ls)
{
    list<int>::iterator p = find(li.begin(), li.end(), 42);
    list<string>::const_iterator q = find(ls.begin(), ls.end(), "Ring");
}
```

The algorithms in the standard library cover the most common general operations on containers such as traversals, sorting, searching, and inserting and removing elements. The standard algorithms are all in the *std* namespace and their declarations are found in *<algorithm>*. Interestingly, most of the really common algorithms are so simple that the template functions are typically inline. This implies that the loops expressed by the algorithms benefit from aggressive per-function optimization.

The standard function objects are also in namespace *std*, but their declarations are found in *<functional>*. The function objects are designed to be easy to inline.

Nonmodifying sequence operations are used to extract information from a sequence or to find the positions of elements in a sequence:

Nonmodifying Sequence Operations (§18.5) <algorithm>	
for_each()	Do operation for each element in a sequence.
find()	Find first occurrence of a value in a sequence.
find_if()	Find first match of a predicate in a sequence.
find_first_of()	Find a value from one sequence in another.
adjacent_find()	Find an adjacent pair of values.
count()	Count occurrences of a value in a sequence.
count_if()	Count matches of a predicate in a sequence.
mismatch()	Find the first elements for which two sequences differ.
equal()	True if the elements of two sequences are pairwise equal.
search()	Find the first occurrence of a sequence as a subsequence.
find_end()	Find the last occurrence of a sequence as a subsequence.
search_n()	Find the nth occurrence of a value in a sequence.

Most algorithms allow a user to specify the actual action performed for each element or pair of elements. This makes the algorithms much more general and useful than they appear at first glance. In particular, a user can supply the criteria used for equality and difference (§18.4.2). Where reasonable, the most common and useful action is provided as a default.

Modifying sequence operations have little in common beyond the obvious fact that they might change the values of elements of a sequence:

Modifying Sequence Operations (§18.6) <algorithm>	
transform()	Apply an operation to every element in a sequence.
copy()	Copy a sequence starting with its first element.
copy_backward()	Copy a sequence starting with its last element.
swap()	Swap two elements.
iter_swap()	Swap two elements pointed to by iterators.
swap_ranges()	Swap elements of two sequences.
replace()	Replace elements with a given value.
replace_if()	Replace elements matching a predicate.
replace_copy()	Copy sequence replacing elements with a given value.
replace_copy_if()	Copy sequence replacing elements matching a predicate.
fill()	Replace every element with a given value.
fill_n()	Replace first n elements with a given value.
generate()	Replace every element with the result of an operation.
generate_n()	Replace first n elements with the result of an operation.
remove()	Remove elements with a given value.
remove_if()	Remove elements matching a predicate.

Modifying Sequence Operations (continued) (§18.6) <algorithm>	
remove_copy()	Copy a sequence removing elements with a given value.
remove_copy_if()	Copy a sequence removing elements matching a predicate.
unique()	Remove equal adjacent elements.
unique_copy()	Copy a sequence removing equal adjacent elements.
reverse()	Reverse the order of elements.
reverse_copy()	Copy a sequence into reverse order.
rotate()	Rotate elements.
rotate_copy()	Copy a sequence into a rotated sequence.
random_shuffle()	Move elements into a uniform distribution.

Every good design shows traces of the personal traits and interests of its designer. The containers and algorithms in the standard library clearly reflect a strong concern for classical data structures and the design of algorithms. The standard library provides not only the bare minimum of containers and algorithms needed by essentially every programmer. It also includes many of the tools used to provide those algorithms and needed to extend the library beyond that minimum.

The emphasis here is not on the design of algorithms or even on the use of any but the simplest and most obvious algorithms. For information on the design and analysis of algorithms, you should look elsewhere (for example, [Knuth,1968] and [Tarjan,1983]). Instead, this chapter lists the algorithms offered by the standard library and explains how they are expressed in C++. This focus allows someone who understands algorithms to use the library well and to extend it in the spirit in which it was built.

The standard library provides a variety of operations for sorting, searching, and manipulating sequences based on an ordering:

Sorted Sequences (§18.7) <algorithm>	
sort()	Sort with good average efficiency.
stable_sort()	Sort maintaining order of equal elements.
partial_sort()	Get the first part of sequence into order.
partial_sort_copy()	Copy getting the first part of output into order.
nth_element()	Put the nth element in its proper place.
lower_bound()	Find the first occurrence of a value.
upper_bound()	Find the first element larger than a value.
equal_range()	Find a subsequence with a given value.
binary_search()	Is a given value in a sorted sequence?
merge()	Merge two sorted sequences.
inplace_merge()	Merge two consecutive sorted subsequences.
partition()	Place elements matching a predicate first.
stable_partition()	Place elements matching a predicate first, preserving relative order.

Set Algorithms (§18.7.5) <algorithm>	
includes()	True if a sequence is a subsequence of another.
set_union()	Construct a sorted union.
set_intersection()	Construct a sorted intersection.
set_difference()	Construct a sorted sequence of elements in the first but not the second sequence.
set_symmetric_difference()	Construct a sorted sequence of elements in one but not both sequences.

Heap operations keep a sequence in a state that makes it easy to sort when necessary:

Heap Operations (§18.8) <algorithm>	
make_heap()	Make sequence ready to be used as a heap.
push_heap()	Add element to heap.
pop_heap()	Remove element from heap.
sort_heap()	Sort the heap.

The library provides a few algorithms for selecting elements based on a comparison:

Minimum and Maximum (§18.9) <algorithm>	
min()	Smaller of two values.
max()	Larger of two values.
min_element()	Smallest value in sequence.
max_element()	Largest value in sequence.
lexicographical_compare()	Lexicographically first of two sequences.

Finally, the library provides ways of permuting a sequence:

Permutations (§18.10) <algorithm>	
next_permutation()	Next permutation in lexicographical order.
prev_permutation()	Previous permutation in lexicographical order.

In addition, a few generalized numerical algorithms are provided in *<numeric>* (§22.6).

In the description of algorithms, the template parameter names are significant. *In*, *Out*, *For*, *Bi*, and *Ran* mean input iterator, output iterator, forward iterator, bidirectional iterator, and random-access iterator, respectively (§19.2.1). *Pred* means unary predicate, *BinPred* means binary predicate (§18.4.2), *Cmp* means a comparison function (§17.1.4.1, §18.7.1), *Op* means unary operation, and *BinOp* means binary operation (§18.4). Conventionally, much longer names have been used for template parameters. However, I find that after only a brief acquaintance with the standard library, those long names decrease readability rather than enhancing it.

A random-access iterator can be used as a bidirectional iterator, a bidirectional iterator as a forward iterator, and a forward iterator as an input or an output iterator (§19.2.1). Passing a type that doesn't provide the required operations will cause template-instantiation-time errors (§C.13.7). Providing a type that has the right operations with the wrong semantics will cause unpredictable run-time behavior (§17.1.4).

18.3   Sequences and Containers

It is a good general principle that the most common use of something should also be the shortest, the easiest to express, and the safest. The standard library violates this principle in the name of generality. For a standard library, generality is essential. For example, we can find the first two occurrences of *42* in a list like this:

```
void f(list<int>& li)
{
        list<int>::iterator p = find(li.begin(),li.end(),42);        // first occurrence
        if (p != li.end()) {
                list<int>::iterator q = find(++p,li.end(),42);        // second occurrence
                // ...
        }
        // ...
}
```

Had *find* ( ) been expressed as an operation on a container, we would have needed some additional mechanism for finding the second occurrence. Importantly, generalizing such an "additional mechanism" for every container and every algorithm is hard. Instead, standard library algorithms work on sequences of elements. That is, the input of an algorithm is expressed as a pair of iterators that delineate a sequence. The first iterator refers to the first element of the sequence, and the second refers to a point one-beyond-the-last element (§3.8, §19.2). Such a sequence is called "half open" because it includes the first value mentioned and not the second. A half-open sequence allows many algorithms to be expressed without making the empty sequence a special case.

A sequence − especially a sequence in which random access is possible − is often called a *range*. Traditional mathematical notations for a half-open range are [*first*, *last*) and [*first*, *last*[. Importantly, a sequence can be the elements of a container or a subsequence of a container. Further, some sequences, such as I/O streams, are not containers. However, algorithms expressed in terms of sequences work just fine.

18.3.1 Input Sequences

Writing *x*.*begin* ( ), *x*.*end* ( ) to express "all the elements of *x*" is common, tedious, and can even be error-prone. For example, when several iterators are used, it is too easy to provide an algorithm with a pair of arguments that does not constitute a sequence:

```
void f(list<string>& fruit,  list<string>& citrus)
{
        typedef list<string>::const_iterator LI;

        LI p1 = find(fruit.begin(),citrus.end(),"apple");        // wrong! (different sequences)
        LI p2 = find(fruit.begin(),fruit.end(),"apple");        // ok
        LI p3 = find(citrus.begin(),citrus.end(),"pear");        // ok
        LI p4 = find(p2,p3,"peach");                              // wrong! (different sequences)
        // ...
}
```

In this example there are two errors. The first is obvious (once you suspect an error), but it isn't easily detected by a compiler. The second is hard to spot in real code even for an experienced programmer. Cutting down on the number of explicit iterators used alleviates this problem. Here, I outline an approach to dealing with this problem by making the notion of an input sequence explicit. However, to keep the discussion of standard algorithms strictly within the bounds of the standard library, I do not use explicit input sequences when presenting algorithms in this chapter.

The key idea is to be explicit about taking a sequence as input. For example:

```
template<class In, class T> In find(In first, In last, const T& v)      // standard
{
    while (first!=last && *first!=v) ++first;
    return first;
}

template<class In, class T> In find(Iseq<In> r, const T& v)             // extension
{
    return find(r.first,r.second,v);
}
```

In general, overloading (§13.3.2) allows the input-sequence version of an algorithm to be preferred when an *Iseq* argument is used.

Naturally, an input sequence is implemented as a pair (§17.4.1.2) of iterators:

```
template<class In> struct Iseq : public pair<In,In> {
    Iseq(In i1, In i2) : pair<In,In>(i1,i2) { }
};
```

We can explicitly make the *Iseq* needed to invoke the second version of *find*():

```
LI  p = find(Iseq<LI>(fruit.begin(),fruit.end()), "apple");
```

However, that is even more tedious than calling the original *find*() directly. Simple helper functions relieve the tedium. In particular, the *Iseq* of a container is the sequence of elements from its *begin*() to its *end*():

```
template<class C> Iseq<typename C::iterator> iseq(C& c)              // for container
{
    return Iseq<typename C::iterator>(c.begin(),c.end());
}
```

This allows us to express algorithms on containers compactly and without repetition. For example:

```
void f(list<string>& ls)
{
    list<string>::iterator p = find(ls.begin(),ls.end(), "standard");
    list<string>::iterator q = find(iseq(ls), "extension");
    // ..
}
```

It is easy to define versions of *iseq*() that produce *Iseq*s for arrays, input streams, etc. (§18.13[6]).

The key benefit of *Iseq* is that it makes the notion of an input sequence explicit. The immediate practical effect is that use of *iseq*() eliminates much of the tedious and error-prone repetition needed to express every input sequence as a pair of iterators.

The notion of an output sequence is also useful. However, it is less simple and less immediately useful than the notion of an input sequence (§18.13[7]; see also §19.2.4).

18.4 Function Objects

Many algorithms operate on sequences using iterators and values only. For example, we can *find* ( ) the first element with the value *7* in a sequence like this:

```
void f(list<int>& c)
{
    list<int>::iterator p = find(c.begin(),c.end(),7);
    // ...
}
```

To do more interesting things we want the algorithms to execute code that we supply (§3.8.4). For example, we can find the first element in a sequence with a value of less than *7* like this:

```
bool less_than_7(int v)
{
    return v<7;
}

void f(list<int>& c)
{
    list<int>::iterator p = find_if(c.begin(),c.end(),less_than_7);
    // ...
}
```

There are many obvious uses for functions passed as arguments: logical predicates, arithmetic operations, operations for extracting information from elements, etc. It is neither convenient nor efficient to write a separate function for each use. Nor is a function logically sufficient to express all that we would like to express. Often, the function called for each element needs to keep data between invocations and to return the result of many applications. A member function of a class serves such needs better than a free-standing function does because its object can hold data. In addition, the class can provide operations for initializing and extracting such data.

Consider how to write a function − or rather a function-like class − to calculate a sum:

```
template<class T> class Sum {
    T res;
public:
    Sum(T i = 0) : res(i) { }          // initialize
    void operator()(T x) { res += x; }  // accumulate
    T result() const { return res; }    // return sum
};
```

Clearly, *Sum* is designed for arithmetic types for which initialization by *0* and += are defined. For example:

```
void f(list<double>& ld)
{
    Sum<double> s;
    s = for_each(ld.begin(), ld.end(), s);          // invoke s() for each element of ld
    cout << "the sum is " << s.result() << '\n';
}
```

Here, *for_each*() (§18.5.1) invokes *Sum<double>*::*operator*() (*double*) for each element of *ld* and returns the object passed as its third argument.

The key reason this works is that *for_each*() doesn't actually assume its third argument to be a function. It simply assumes that its third argument is something that can be called with an appropriate argument. A suitably-defined object serves as well as – and often better than – a function. For example, it is easier to inline the application operator of a class than to inline a function passed as a pointer to function. Consequently, function objects often execute faster than do ordinary functions. An object of a class with an application operator (§11.9) is called a *function-like object*, a *functor*, or simply a *function object*.

18.4.1 Function Object Bases

The standard library provides many useful function objects. To aid the writing of function objects, in *<functional>* the library provides a couple of base classes:

```
template <class Arg, class Res> struct unary_function {
    typedef Arg argument_type;
    typedef Res result_type;
};

template <class Arg, class Arg2, class Res> struct binary_function {
    typedef Arg first_argument_type;
    typedef Arg2 second_argument_type;
    typedef Res result_type;
};
```

The purpose of these classes is to provide standard names for the argument and return types for use by users of classes derived from *unary_function* and *binary_function*. Using these bases consistently the way the standard library does will save the programmer from discovering the hard way why they are useful (§18.4.4.1).

18.4.2 Predicates

A predicate is a function object (or a function) that returns a *bool*. For example, *<functional>* defines:

```
template <class T> struct logical_not : public unary_function<T, bool> {
    bool operator()(const T& x) const { return !x; }
};

template <class T> struct less : public binary_function<T, T, bool> {
    bool operator()(const T& x, const T& y) const { return x<y; }
};
```

Unary and binary predicates are often useful in combination with algorithms. For example, we can compare two sequences, looking for the first element of one that is not less than its corresponding element in the other:

```
void f(vector<int>& vi, list<int>& li)
{
    typedef list<int>::iterator LI;
    typedef vector<int>::iterator VI;
    pair<VI,LI> p1 = mismatch(vi.begin(),vi.end(),li.begin(),less<int>());
    // ...
}
```

The *mismatch*() algorithm applies its binary predicate repeatedly to pairs of corresponding elements until it fails (§18.5.4). It then returns the iterators for the elements that failed the comparison. Because an object is needed rather than a type, *less<int>*() (with the parentheses) is used rather than the tempting *less<int>*.

Instead of finding the first element *not less* than its corresponding element in the other sequence, we might like to find the first element *less* than its corresponding element. We can do this by looking for the first pair that fails the complementary predicate *greater_equal*:

```
p1 = mismatch(vi.begin(),vi.end(),li.begin(),greater_equal<int>());
```

Alternatively, we could present the sequences in the opposite order and use *less_equal*:

```
pair<LI,VI> p2 = mismatch(li.begin(),li.end(),vi.begin(),less_equal<int>());
```

In §18.4.4.4, I show how to express the predicate ''not less.''

18.4.2.1 Overview of Predicates

In *<functional>*, the standard library supplies a few common predicates:

Predicates <functional>		
equal_to	Binary	arg1==arg2
not_equal_to	Binary	arg1!=arg2
greater	Binary	arg1>arg2
less	Binary	arg1<arg2
greater_equal	Binary	arg1>=arg2
less_equal	Binary	arg1<=arg2
logical_and	Binary	arg1&&arg2
logical_or	Binary	arg1||arg2
logical_not	Unary	!arg

The definitions of *less* and *logical_not* are presented in §18.4.2.

In addition to the library-provided predicates, users can write their own. Such user-supplied predicates are essential for simple and elegant use of the standard libraries and algorithms. The ability to define predicates is particularly important when we want to use algorithms for classes designed without thought of the standard library and its algorithms. For example, consider a variant of the *Club* class from §10.4.6:

```
class Person { /* ... */ };

struct Club {
    string name;
    list<Person*> members;
    list<Person*> officers;
    // ...

    Club(const string& n);
};
```

Looking for a *Club* with a given name in a *list<Club>* is clearly a reasonable thing to do. However, the standard library algorithm *find_if*() doesn't know about *Club*s. The library algorithms know how to test for equality, but we don't want to find a *Club* based on its complete value. Rather, we want to use *Club*::*name* as the key. So we write a predicate to reflect that:

```
class Club_eq : public unary_function<Club, bool> {
    string s;
public:
    explicit Club_eq(const string& ss) : s(ss) { }
    bool operator()(const Club& c) const { return c.name==s; }
};
```

Defining useful predicates is simple. Once suitable predicates have been defined for user-defined types, their use with the standard algorithms is as simple and efficient as examples involving containers of simple types. For example:

```
void f(list<Club>& lc)
{
    typedef list<Club>::iterator LCI;
    LCI p = find_if(lc.begin(), lc.end(), Club_eq("Dining Philosophers"));
    // ...
}
```

18.4.3 Arithmetic Function Objects

When dealing with numeric classes, it is sometimes useful to have the standard arithmetic functions available as function objects. Consequently, in *<functional>* the standard library provides:

Arithmetic Operations <functional>		
plus	Binary	arg1+arg2
minus	Binary	arg1−arg2
multiplies	Binary	arg1*arg2
divides	Binary	arg1/arg2
modulus	Binary	arg1%arg2
negate	Unary	−arg

We might use *multiplies* to multiply elements in two vectors, thereby producing a third:

```
void  discount(vector<double>& a,  vector<double>& b,  vector<double>& res)
{
      transform(a.begin(),a.end(),b.begin(),back_inserter(res),multiplies<double>());
}
```

The *back_inserter()* is described in §19.2.4. A few numerical algorithms can be found in §22.6.

18.4.4 Binders, Adapters, and Negaters

We can use predicates and arithmetic function objects we have written ourselves and rely on the ones provided by the standard library. However, when we need a new predicate we often find that the new predicate is a minor variation of an existing one. The standard library supports the composition of function objects:

§18.4.4.1   A *binder* allows a two-argument function object to be used as a single-argument function by binding one argument to a value.

§18.4.4.2   A *member function adapter* allows a member function to be used as an argument to algorithms.

§18.4.4.3   A *pointer to function adapter* allows a pointer to function to be used as an argument to algorithms.

§18.4.4.4   A *negater* allows us to express the opposite of a predicate.

Collectively, these function objects are referred to as *adapters*. These adapters all have a common structure relying on the function object bases *unary_function* and *binary_function* (§18.4.1). For each of these adapters, a helper function is provided to take a function object as an argument and return a suitable function object. When invoked by its *operator()()*, that function object will perform the desired action. That is, an adapter is a simple form of a higher-order function: it takes a function argument and produces a new function from it:

Binders, Adapters, and Negaters <functional>		
bind2nd(y)	*binder2nd*	Call binary function with y as 2nd argument.
bind1st(x)	*binder1st*	Call binary function with x as 1st argument.
mem_fun()	*mem_fun_t*	Call 0-arg member through pointer.
	mem_fun1_t	Call unary member through pointer.
	const_mem_fun_t	Call 0-arg const member through pointer.
	const_mem_fun1_t	Call unary const member through pointer.
mem_fun_ref()	*mem_fun_ref_t*	Call 0-arg member through reference.
	mem_fun1_ref_t	Call unary member through reference.
	const_mem_fun_ref_t	Call 0-arg const member through reference.
	const_mem_fun1_ref_t	Call unary const member through reference.
ptr_fun()	*pointer_to_unary_function*	Call unary pointer to function.
ptr_fun()	*pointer_to_binary_function*	Call binary pointer to function.
not1()	*unary_negate*	Negate unary predicate.
not2()	*binary_negate*	Negate binary predicate.

18.4.4.1 Binders

Binary predicates such as *less* (§18.4.2) are useful and flexible. However, we soon discover that the most useful kind of predicate is one that compares a fixed argument repeatedly against a container element. The *less_than_7*() function (§18.4) is a typical example. The *less* operation needs two arguments explicitly provided in each call, so it is not immediately useful. Instead, we might define:

```
template <class T> class less_than : public unary_function<T,bool> {
        T arg2;
public:
        explicit less_than(const T& x) : arg2(x) { }
        bool operator()(const T& x) const { return x<arg2; }
};
```

We can now write:

```
void f(list<int>& c)
{
        list<int>::const_iterator p = find_if(c.begin(),c.end(),less_than<int>(7));
        // ...
}
```

We must write *less_than<int>* (*7*) rather than *less_than* (*7*) because the template argument *<int>* cannot be deduced from the type of the constructor argument (*7*) (§13.3.1).

The *less_than* predicate is generally useful. Importantly, we defined it by fixing or binding the second argument of *less*. Such composition by binding an argument is so common, useful, and occasionally tedious that the standard library provides a standard class for doing it:

```
template <class BinOp>
class binder2nd
        : public unary_function<typename BinOp::first_argument_type,
                                  typename BinOp::result_type> {
protected:
        BinOp op;
        typename BinOp::second_argument_type arg2;
public:
        binder2nd(const BinOp& x, const typename BinOp::second_argument_type& v)
                : op(x), arg2(v) { }
        result_type operator()(const argument_type& x) const { return op(x,arg2); }
};

template <class BinOp, class T> binder2nd<BinOp> bind2nd(const BinOp& op, const T& v)
{
        return binder2nd<BinOp>(op,v);
}
```

For example, we can use *bind2nd*() to create the unary predicate "less than 7" from the binary predicate "less" and the value 7:

```
void f(list<int>& c)
{
    list<int>::const_iterator p = find_if(c.begin(),c.end(),bind2nd(less<int>(),7));
    // ...
}
```

Is this readable? Is this efficient? Given an average C++ implementation, this version is actually more efficient in time and space than is the original version using the function *less_than_7*() from §18.4! The comparison is easily inlined.

The notation is logical, but it does take some getting used to. Often, the definition of a named operation with a bound argument is worthwhile after all:

```
template <class T> struct less_than : public binder2nd< less<T> > {
    explicit less_than(const T& x) : binder2nd< less<T> >(less<T>(),x) { }
};

void f(list<int>& c)
{
    list<int>::const_iterator p = find_if(c.begin(),c.end(),less_than<int>(7));
    // ...
}
```

It is important to define *less_than* in terms of *less* rather than using < directly. That way, *less_than* benefits from any specializations that *less* might have (§13.5, §19.2.2).

In parallel to *bind2nd*() and *binder2nd*, *<functional>* provides *bind1st*() and *binder1st* for binding the first argument of a binary function.

By binding an argument, *bind1st*() and *bind2nd*() perform a service very similar to what is commonly referred to as *Currying*.

18.4.4.2 Member Function Adapters

Most algorithms invoke a standard or user-defined operation. Naturally, users often want to invoke a member function. For example (§3.8.5):

```
void draw_all(list<Shape*>& c)
{
    for_each(c.begin(),c.end(),&Shape::draw);   // oops! error
}
```

The problem is that a member function *mf*() needs to be invoked for an object: *p->mf*(). However, algorithms such as *for_each*() invoke their function operands by simple application: *f*(). Consequently, we need a convenient and efficient way of creating something that allows an algorithm to invoke a member function. The alternative would be to duplicate the set of algorithms: one version for member functions plus one for ordinary functions. Worse, we'd need additional versions of algorithms for containers of objects (rather than pointers to objects). As for the binders (§18.4.4.1), this problem is solved by a class plus a function. First, consider the common case in which we want to call a member function taking no arguments for the elements of a container of pointers:

```
template<class R, class T> class mem_fun_t : public unary_function<T*,R> {
    R (T::*pmf)();
public:
    explicit mem_fun_t(R (T::*p)()) :pmf(p) {}
    R operator()(T* p) const { return (p->*pmf)(); }    // call through pointer
};

template<class R, class T> mem_fun_t<R,T> mem_fun(R (T::*f)())
{
    return mem_fun_t<R,T>(f);
}
```

This handles the *Shape::draw()* example:

```
void draw_all(list<Shape*>& lsp)        // call 0-argument member through pointer to object
{
    for_each(lsp.begin(),lsp.end(),mem_fun(&Shape::draw));    // draw all shapes
}
```

In addition, we need a class and a *mem_fun()* function for handling a member function taking an argument. We also need versions to be called directly for an object rather than through a pointer; these are named *mem_fun_ref()*. Finally, we need versions for *const* member functions:

```
template<class R, class T> mem_fun_t<R,T> mem_fun(R (T::*f)());
// and versions for unary member, for const member, and const unary member (see table in §18.4.4)

template<class R, class T> mem_fun_ref_t<R,T> mem_fun_ref(R (T::*f)());
// and versions for unary member, for const member, and const unary member (see table in §18.4.4)
```

Given these member function adapters from *<functional>*, we can write:

```
void f(list<string>& ls)        // use member function that takes no argument for object
{
    typedef list<string>::iterator LSI;
    LSI p = find_if(ls.begin(),ls.end(),mem_fun_ref(&string::empty));        // find ""
}

void rotate_all(list<Shape*>& ls, int angle)
      // use member function that takes one argument through pointer to object
{
    for_each(ls.begin(),ls.end(),bind2nd(mem_fun(&Shape::rotate),angle));
}
```

The standard library need not deal with member functions taking more than one argument because no standard library algorithm takes a function with more than two arguments as operands.

18.4.4.3 Pointer to Function Adapters

An algorithm doesn't care whether a "function argument" is a function, a pointer to function, or a function object. However, a binder (§18.4.4.1) does care because it needs to store a copy for later use. Consequently, in *<functional>* the standard library supplies two adapters to allow pointers to functions to be used together with the standard algorithms. The definition and implementation closely follows that of the member function adapters (§18.4.4.2). Again, a pair of functions and a pair of classes are used:

```
template <class A, class R> pointer_to_unary_function<A,R> ptr_fun(R (*f)(A));

template <class A, class A2, class R>
    pointer_to_binary_function<A,A2,R> ptr_fun(R (*f)(A, A2));
```

Given these pointer to function adapters, we can use ordinary functions together with binders:

```
class Record { /* ... */ };

bool name_key_eq(const Record&, const char*);      // compare based on names
bool ssn_key_eq(const Record&, long);              // compare based on number

void f(list<Record>& lr)    // use pointer to function
{
    typedef list<Record>::iterator LI;
    LI p = find_if(lr.begin(), lr.end(), bind2nd(ptr_fun(name_key_eq), "John Brown"));
    LI q = find_if(lr.begin(), lr.end(), bind2nd(ptr_fun(ssn_key_eq), 1234567890));
    // ...
}
```

This looks for elements of the list *lr* that match the keys *John Brown* and *1234567890*.

18.4.4.4 Negaters

The predicate negaters are related to the binders in that they take an operation and produce a related operation from it. The definition and implementation of negaters follow the pattern of the member function adapters (§18.4.4.2). Their definitions are trivial, but their simplicity is obscured by the use of long standard names:

```
template <class Pred>
class unary_negate : public unary_function<typename Pred::argument_type,bool> {

    Pred op;
public:
    explicit unary_negate(const Pred& p) : op(p) { }
    bool operator()(const argument_type& x) const { return !op(x); }
};

template <class Pred>
class binary_negate : public binary_function<typename Pred::first_argument_type,
                                    typename Pred::second_argument_type, bool> {

    typedef first_argument_type Arg;
    typedef second_argument_type Arg2;

    Pred op;
public:
    explicit binary_negate(const Pred& p) : op(p) { }
    bool operator()(const Arg& x, const Arg2& y) const { return !op(x,y); }
};
```

```
template<class Pred> unary_negate<Pred> not1(const Pred& p);      // negate unary
template<class Pred> binary_negate<Pred> not2(const Pred& p);     // negate binary
```

These classes and functions are declared in *<functional>*. The names *first_argument_type*, *second_argument_type*, etc., come from the standard base classes *unary_function* and *binary_function*.

    Like the binders, the negaters are most conveniently used indirectly through their helper functions. For example, we can express the binary predicate "not less than" and use it to find the first corresponding pair of elements whose first element is less than its second:

```
void f(vector<int>& vi, list<int>& li)  // revised example from §18.4.2
{
    // ...
    p1 = mismatch(vi.begin(), vi.end(), li.begin(), not2(less<int>()));  // not not < means <
    // ...
}
```

That is, *p1* identifies the first pair of elements for which the predicate *not less than* failed.

    Predicates deal with Boolean conditions, so there are no equivalents to the bitwise operators |, &, ^, and ~.

    Naturally, binders, adapters, and negaters are useful in combination. For example:

```
extern "C" int strcmp(const char*, const char*);      // from <cstdlib>

void f(list<char*>& ls)      // use pointer to function
{
    typedef list<char*>::const_iterator LI;
    LI p = find_if(ls.begin(), ls.end(), not1(bind2nd(ptr_fun(strcmp), "funny")));
}
```

This finds an element of the list *ls* that contains the C-style string *"funny"*. The negater is needed because *strcmp()* returns *0* when strings compare equal.

18.5 Nonmodifying Sequence Algorithms

Nonmodifying sequence algorithms are the basic means for finding something in a sequence without writing a loop. In addition, they allow us to find out things about elements. These algorithms can take const-iterators (§19.2.1) and – with the exception of *for_each()* – should not be used to invoke operations that modify the elements of the sequence.

18.5.1 For_each

We use a library to benefit from the work of others. Using a library function, class, algorithm, etc., saves the work of inventing, designing, writing, debugging, and documenting something. Using the standard library also makes the resulting code easier to read for others who are familiar with that library, but who would have to spend time and effort understanding home-brewed code.

    A key benefit of the standard library algorithms is that they save the programmer from writing explicit loops. Loops can be tedious and error-prone. The *for_each()* algorithm is the simplest algorithm in the sense that it does nothing but eliminate an explicit loop. It simply calls its operator argument for a sequence:

```
template<class In, class Op> Op for_each(In first, In last, Op f)
{
        while (first != last) f(*first++);
        return f;
}
```

What functions would people want to call this way? If you want to accumulate information from the elements, consider *accumulate*() (§22.6). If you want to find something in a sequence, consider *find*() and *find_if*() (§18.5.2). If you change or remove elements, consider *replace*() (§18.6.4) or *remove*() (§18.6.5). In general, before using *for_each*(), consider if there is a more specialized algorithm that would do more for you.

The result of *for_each*() is the function or function object passed as its third argument. As shown in the *Sum* example (§18.4), this allows information to be passed back to a caller.

One common use of *for_each*() is to extract information from elements of a sequence. For example, consider collecting the names of any of a number of *Club*s:

```
void extract(const list<Club>& lc, list<Person*>& off) // place the officers from 'lc' on 'off'
{
        for_each(lc.begin(), lc.end(), Extract_officers(off));
}
```

In parallel to the examples from §18.4 and §18.4.2, we define a function class that extracts the desired information. In this case, the names to be extracted are found in *list<Person*>*s in our *list<Club>*. Consequently, *Extract_officers* needs to copy the officers from a *Club*'s *officers* list to our list:

```
class Extract_officers {
        list<Person*>& lst;
public:
        explicit Extract_officers(list<Person*>& x) : lst(x) { }

        void operator()(const Club& c) const
                { copy(c.officers.begin(), c.officers.end(), back_inserter(lst)); }
};
```

We can now print out the names, again using *for_each*():

```
void extract_and_print(const list<Club>& lc)
{
        list<Person*> off;
        extract(lc, off);
        for_each(off.begin(), off.end(), Print_name(cout));
}
```

Writing *Print_name* is left as an exercise (§18.13[4]).

The *for_each*() algorithm is classified as nonmodifying because it doesn't explicitly modify a sequence. However, if applied to a non-*const* sequence *for_each*()'s operation (its third argument) may change the elements of the sequence. For an example, see the use of *negate*() in §11.9.

18.5.2 The Find Family

The *find* ( ) algorithms look through a sequence or a pair of sequences to find a value or a match on a predicate. The simple versions of *find* ( ) look for a value or for a match with a predicate:

>   *template<class In, class T> In find (In first, In last, const T& val);*

>   *template<class In, class Pred> In find_if (In first, In last, Pred p);*

The algorithms *find* ( ) and *find_if* ( ) return an iterator to the first element that matches a value and a predicate, respectively. In fact, *find* ( ) can be understood as the version of *find_if* ( ) with the predicate ==. Why aren't they both called *find* ( )? The reason is that function overloading cannot always distinguish calls of two template functions with the same number of arguments. Consider:

```
bool pred (int);

void f (vector<bool (*f) (int)>& v1, vector<int>& v2)
{
        find (v1.begin (), v1.end (), pred);         // find 'pred'
        find_if (v2.begin (), v2.end (), pred);      // find int for which pred() returns true
}
```

If *find* ( ) and *find_if* ( ) had had the same name, surprising ambiguities would have resulted. In general, the *_if* suffix is used to indicate that an algorithm takes a predicate.

The *find_first_of* ( ) algorithm finds the first element of a sequence that has a match in a second sequence:

>   *template<class For, class For2>*
>   *For find_first_of (For first, For last, For2 first2, For2 last2);*

>   *template<class For, class For2, class BinPred>*
>   *For find_first_of (For first, For last, For2 first2, For2 last2, BinPred p);*

For example:

```
int x[] = { 1,3,4 };
int y[] = { 0,2,3,4,5};

void f ()
{
        int* p = find_first_of (x,x+3,y,y+5);        // p = &x[1]
        int* q = find_first_of (p+1,x+3,y,y+5);      // q = &x[2]
}
```

The pointer *p* will point to *x*[*1*] because *3* is the first element of *x* with a match in *y*. Similarly, *q* will point to *x*[*2*].

The *adjacent_find* ( ) algorithm finds a pair of adjacent matching values:

>   *template<class For> For adjacent_find (For first, For last);*

>   *template<class For, class BinPred> For adjacent_find (For first, For last, BinPred p);*

The return value is an iterator to the first matching element. For example:

```
void f(vector<string>& text)
{
    vector<string>::iterator p = adjacent_find(text.begin(),text.end());
    if (p!=text.end() && *p=="the") { // I duplicated "the" again!
        text.erase(p);
        // ...
    }
}
```

18.5.3 Count

The *count*() and *count_if*() algorithms count occurrences of a value in a sequence:

```
template<class In, class T>
    typename iterator_traits<In>::difference_type count(In first, In last, const T& val);

template<class In, class Pred>
    typename iterator_traits<In>::difference_type count_if(In first, In last, Pred p);
```

The return type of *count*() is interesting. Consider an obvious and somewhat simple-minded version of *count*():

```
template<class In, class T> int count(In first, In last, const T& val)
{
    int res = 0;
    while (first != last) if (*first++ == val) ++res;
    return res;
}
```

The problem is that an *int* might not be the right type for the result. On a machine with small *int*s, there might be too many elements in the sequence for *count*() to fit in an *int*. Conversely, a high-performance implementation on a specialized machine might prefer to keep the count in a *short*.

Clearly, the number of elements in the sequence cannot be larger than the maximum difference between its iterators (§19.2.1). Consequently, the first idea for a solution to this problem is to define the return type as

```
typename In::difference_type
```

However, a standard algorithm should be applicable to built-in arrays as well as to standard containers. For example:

```
void f(char* p, int size)
{
    int n = count(p,p+size,'e');   // count the number of occurrences of the letter 'e'
    // ...
}
```

Unfortunately, *char*::*difference_type* is not valid C++. This problem is solved by partial specialization of an *iterator_traits* (§19.2.2).

18.5.4 Equal and Mismatch

The *equal* ( ) and *mismatch* ( ) algorithms compare two sequences:

```
template<class In, class In2> bool equal(In first, In last, In2 first2);

template<class In, class In2, class BinPred>
    bool equal(In first, In last, In2 first2, BinPred p);

template<class In, class In2> pair<In, In2> mismatch(In first, In last, In2 first2);

template<class In, class In2, class BinPred>
    pair<In, In2> mismatch(In first, In last, In2 first2, BinPred p);
```

The *equal* ( ) algorithm simply tells whether all corresponding pairs of elements of two sequences compare equal; *mismatch* ( ) looks for the first pair of elements that compares unequal and returns iterators to those elements. No end is specified for the second sequence; that is, there is no *last2*. Instead, it is assumed that there are at least as many elements in the second sequence as in the first and *first2+(last–first)* is used as *last2*. This technique is used throughout the standard library, where pairs of sequences are used for operations on pairs of elements.

As shown in §18.5.1, these algorithms are even more useful than they appear at first glance because the user can supply predicates defining what it means to be equal and to match.

Note that the sequences need not be of the same type. For example:

```
void f(list<int>& li, vector<double>& vd)
{
    bool b = equal(li.begin(), li.end(), vd.begin());
}
```

All that is required is that the elements be acceptable as operands of the predicate.

The two versions of *mismatch* ( ) differ only in their use of predicates. In fact, we could implement them as one function with a default template argument:

```
template<class In, class In2, class BinPred>
pair<In, In2> mismatch(In first, In last, In2 first2,
                BinPred p = equal_to<typename In::value_type>())  // §18.4.2.1
{
    while (first != last && p(*first, *first2)) {
        ++first;
        ++first2;
    }
    return pair<In, In2>(first, first2);
}
```

The difference between having two functions and having one with a default argument can be observed by someone taking pointers to functions. However, thinking of many of the variants of the standard algorithms as simply "the version with the default predicate" roughly halves the number of template functions that need to be remembered.

18.5.5 Search

The *search*(), *search_n*(), and *find_end*() algorithms find one sequence as a subsequence in another:

```
template<class For, class For2>
    For search(For first, For last, For2 first2, For2 last2);

template<class For, class For2, class BinPred>
    For search(For first, For last, For2 first2, For2 last2, BinPred p);

template<class For, class For2>
    For find_end(For first, For last, For2 first2, For2 last2);

template<class For, class For2, class BinPred>
    For find_end(For first, For last, For2 first2, For2 last2, BinPred p);

template<class For, class Size, class T>
    For search_n(For first, For last, Size n, const T& val);

template<class For, class Size, class T, class BinPred>
    For search_n(For first, For last, Size n, const T& val, BinPred p);
```

The *search*() algorithm looks for its second sequence as a subsequence of its first. If that second sequence is found, an iterator for the first matching element in the first sequence is returned. The end of sequence (*last*) is returned to represent "not found." Thus, the return value is always in the [*first*, *last*] sequence. For example:

```
string quote("Why waste time learning, when ignorance is instantaneous?");

bool in_quote(const string& s)
{
    typedef string::const_iterator SCI;
    SCI p = search(quote.begin(),quote.end(),s.begin(),s.end());    // find s in quote
    return p!=quote.end();
}

void g()
{
    bool b1 = in_quote("learning");      // b1 = true
    bool b2 = in_quote("lemming");       // b2 = false
}
```

Thus, *search*() is an operation for finding a substring generalized to all sequences. This implies that *search*() is a very useful algorithm.

The *find_end*() algorithm looks for its second input sequence as a subsequence of its first input sequence. If that second sequence is found, *find_end*() returns an iterator pointing to the last match in its first input. In other words, *find_end*() is *search*() "backwards." It finds the last occurrence of its second input sequence in its first input sequence, rather than the first occurrence of its second sequence.

The *search_n*() algorithm finds a sequence of at least *n* matches for its *value* argument in the sequence. It returns an iterator to the first element of the sequence of *n* matches.

18.6 Modifying Sequence Algorithms

If you want to change a sequence, you can explicitly iterate through it. You can then modify values. Wherever possible, however, we prefer to avoid this kind of programming in favor of simpler and more systematic styles of programming. The alternative is algorithms that traverse sequences performing specific tasks. The nonmodifying algorithms (§18.5) serve this need when we just read from the sequence. The modifying sequence algorithms are provided to do the most common forms of updates. Some update a sequence, while others produce a new sequence based on information found during a traversal.

Standard algorithms work on data structures through iterators. This implies that inserting a new element into a container or deleting one is not easy. For example, given only an iterator, how can we find the container from which to remove the element pointed to? Unless special iterators are used (e.g., inserters, §3.8, §19.2.4), operations through iterators do not change the size of a container. Instead of inserting and deleting elements, the algorithms change the values of elements, swap elements, and copy elements. Even *remove* ( ) operates by overwriting the elements to be removed (§18.6.5). In general, the fundamental modifying operations produce outputs that are modified copies of their inputs. The algorithms that appear to modify a sequence are variants that copy within a sequence.

18.6.1 Copy

Copying is the simplest way to produce one sequence from another. The definitions of the basic copy operations are trivial:

```
template<class In, class Out> Out copy(In first, In last, Out res)
{
    while (first != last) *res++ = *first++;
    return res;
}

template<class Bi, class Bi2> Bi2 copy_backward(Bi first, Bi last, Bi2 res)
{
    while (first != last) *--res = *--last;
    return res;
}
```

The target of a copy algorithm need not be a container. Anything that can be described by an output iterator (§19.2.6) will do. For example:

```
void f(list<Club>& lc, ostream& os)
{
    copy(lc.begin(), lc.end(), ostream_iterator<Club>(os));
}
```

To read a sequence, we need a sequence describing where to begin and where to end. To write, we need only an iterator describing where to write to. However, we must take care not to write beyond the end of the target. One way to ensure that we don't do this is to use an inserter (§19.2.4) to grow the target as needed. For example:

```
void f(const vector<char>& vs, vector<char>& v)
{
    copy(vs.begin(),vs.end(),v.begin());          // might overwrite end of v
    copy(vs.begin(),vs.end(),back_inserter(v));   // add elements from vs to end of v
}
```

The input sequence and the output sequence may overlap. We use *copy*() when the sequences do not overlap or if the end of the output sequence is in the input sequence. We use *copy_backward*() when the beginning of the output sequence is in the input sequence. In that way, no element is overwritten until after it has been copied. See also §18.13[13].

Naturally, to copy something backwards we need a bidirectional iterator (§19.2.1) for both the input and the output sequences. For example:

```
void f(vector<char>& vc)
{
    copy_backward(vc.begin(),vc.end(),ostream_iterator<char>(cout));   // error

    vector<char> v(vc.size());
    copy_backward(vc.begin(),vc.end(),v.end());                        // ok
    copy(v.begin(),v.end(),ostream_iterator<char>(cout));             // ok

}
```

Often, we want to copy only elements that fulfill some criterion. Unfortunately, *copy_if*() was somehow dropped from the set of algorithms provided by the standard library (mea culpa). On the other hand, it is trivial to define:

```
template<class In, class Out, class Pred>
Out copy_if(In first, In last, Out res, Pred p)
{
    while (first != last) {
        if (p(*first)) *res++ = *first;
        ++first;
    }
    return res;
}
```

Now if we want to print elements with a value larger than *n*, we can do it like this:

```
void f(list<int>&ld, int n, ostream& os)
{
    copy_if(ld.begin(),ld.end(),ostream_iterator<int>(os),bind2nd(greater<int>(),n));
}
```

See also *remove_copy_if*() (§18.6.5).

18.6.2 Transform

Somewhat confusingly, *transform*() doesn't necessarily change its input. Instead, it produces an output that is a transformation of its input based on a user-supplied operation:

```
template<class In, class Out, class Op>
Out transform(In first, In last, Out res, Op op)
{
    while (first != last) *res++ = op(*first++);
    return res;
}
template<class In, class In2, class Out, class BinOp>
Out transform(In first, In last, In2 first2, Out res, BinOp op)
{
    while (first != last) *res++ = op(*first++, *first2++);
    return res;
}
```

The *transform()* that reads a single sequence to produce its output is rather similar to *copy()*. Instead of writing its element, it writes the result of its operation on that element. Thus, we could have defined *copy()* as *transform()* with an operation that returns its argument:

```
template<class T> T identity(const T& x) { return x; }
```

```
template<class In, class Out> Out ccopy(In first, In last, Out res)
{
    return transform(first, last, res, identity<typename iterator_traits<In>::value_type>);
}
```

The the explicit qualification of *identity* is needed to get a specific function from the function template. The *iterator_traits* template (§19.2.2) is used to get *In*'s element type.

Another way to view *transform()* is as a variant of *for_each* that explicitly produces output. For example, we can produce a list of name *string*s from a list of *Club*s using *transform()*:

```
string nameof(const Club& c) { return c.name; }    // extract name string

void f(list<Club>& lc)
{
    transform(lc.begin(), lc.end(), ostream_iterator<string>(cout, "\n"), nameof);
}
```

One reason *transform()* is called "transform" is that the result of the operation is often written back to where the argument came from. Consider deleting objects pointed to by a set of pointers:

```
struct Delete_ptr {    // use function object to get inlining
    template<class T> T* operator()(T* p) const { delete p; return 0; }
};
void purge(deque<Shape*>& s)
{
    transform(s.begin(), s.end(), s.begin(), Delete_ptr());
}
```

The *transform()* algorithm always produces an output sequence. Here, I directed the result back to the input sequence so that *Delete_ptr()(p)* has the effect *p=Delete_ptr()(p)*. This was why I chose to return 0 from *Delete_ptr::operator()()*.

The *transform* () algorithm that takes two sequences allows people to combine information from two sources. For example, an animation may have a routine that updates the position of a list of shapes by applying a translation:

```
Shape* move_shape(Shape* s, Point p)    // *s += p
{
    s->move_to(s->center()+p);
    return s;
}

void update_positions(list<Shape*>& ls, vector<Point>& oper)
{
    // invoke operation on corresponding object:
    transform(ls.begin(), ls.end(), oper.begin(), ls.begin(), move_shape);
}
```

I didn't really want to produce a return value from *move_shape* (). However, *transform* () insists on assigning the result of its operation, so I let *move_shape* () return its first operand so that I could write it back to where it came from.

Sometimes, we do not have the freedom to do that. For example, an operation that I didn't write and don't want to modify might not return a value. Sometimes, the input sequence is *const*. In such cases, we might define a two-sequence *for_each* () to match the two-sequence *transform* ():

```
template<class In, class In2, class BinOp>
BinOp for_each(In first, In last, In2 first2, BinOp op)
{
    while (first != last) op(*first++, *first2++);
    return op;
}

void update_positions(list<Shape*>& ls, vector<Point>& oper)
{
    for_each(ls.begin(), ls.end(), oper.begin(), move_shape);
}
```

At other times, it can be useful to have an output iterator that doesn't actually write anything (§19.6[2]).

There are no standard library algorithms that read three or more sequences. Such algorithms are easily written, though. Alternatively, you can use *transform* () repeatedly.

18.6.3 Unique

Whenever information is collected, duplication can occur. The *unique* () and *unique_copy* () algorithms eliminate adjacent duplicate values:

```
template<class For> For unique(For first, For last);
template<class For, class BinPred> For unique(For first, For last, BinPred p);

template<class In, class Out> Out unique_copy(In first, In last, Out res);
template<class In, class Out, class BinPred>
    Out unique_copy(In first, In last, Out res, BinPred p);
```

The *unique* ( ) algorithm eliminates adjacent duplicates from a sequence, *unique_copy* ( ) makes a copy without duplicates. For example:

```
void f(list<string>& ls, vector<string>& vs)
{
    ls.sort(); // list sort (§17.2.2.1)
    unique_copy(ls.begin(), ls.end(), back_inserter(vs));
}
```

This copies *ls* to *vs*, eliminating duplicates in the process. The *sort* ( ) is needed to get equal strings adjacent.

Like other standard algorithms, *unique* ( ) operates on iterators. It has no way of knowing the type of container these iterators point into, so it cannot modify that container. It can only modify the values of the elements. This implies that *unique* ( ) does not eliminate duplicates from its input sequence in the way we naively might expect. Rather, it moves unique elements towards the front (head) of a sequence and returns an iterator to the end of the subsequence of unique elements:

```
template <class For> For unique(For first, For last)
{
    first = adjacent_find(first, last);      // §18.5.2
    return unique_copy(first, last, first);
}
```

The elements after the unique subsequence are left unchanged. Therefore, this does not eliminate duplicates in a vector:

```
void f(vector<string>& vs)        // warning: bad code!
{
    sort(vs.begin(), vs.end());            // sort vector
    unique(vs.begin(), vs.end());          // eliminate duplicates (no it doesn't!)
}
```

In fact, by moving the last elements of a sequence forward to eliminate duplicates, *unique* ( ) can introduce new duplicates. For example:

```
int main()
{
    char v[] = "abbcccde";

    char* p = unique(v, v+strlen(v));
    cout << v << ' ' << p-v << '\n';
}
```

produced

> *abcdecde 5*

That is, *p* points to the second *c*.

Algorithms that might have removed elements (but can't) generally come in two forms: the "plain" version that reorders elements in a way similar to *unique* ( ) and a version that produces a new sequence in a way similar to *unique_copy* ( ). The *_copy* suffix is used to distinguish these two kinds of algorithms.

To eliminate duplicates from a container, we must explicitly shrink it:

```
template<class C> void eliminate_duplicates(C& c)
{
    sort(c.begin(),c.end());                                    // sort
    typename C::iterator p = unique(c.begin(),c.end());         // compact
    c.erase(p,c.end());                                         // shrink
}
```

Note that *eliminate_duplicates*() would make no sense for a built-in array, yet *unique*() can still be applied to arrays.

An example of *unique_copy*() can be found in §3.8.3.

18.6.3.1 Sorting Criteria

To eliminate all duplicates, the input sequences must be sorted (§18.7.1). Both *unique*() and *unique_copy*() use == as the default criterion for comparison and allow the user to supply alternative criteria. For instance, we might modify the example from §18.5.1 to eliminate duplicate names. After extracting the names of the *Club* officers, we were left with a *list<Person*>* called *off* (§18.5.1). We could eliminate duplicates like this:

```
eliminate_duplicates(off);
```

However, this relies on sorting pointers and assumes that each pointer uniquely identifies a person. In general, we would have to examine the *Person* records to determine whether we would consider them equal. We might write:

```
bool operator==(const Person& x, const Person& y)  // equality for object
{
    // compare x and y for equality
}
bool operator<(const Person& x, const Person& y)   // less than for object
{
    // compare x and y for order
}
bool Person_eq(const Person* x, const Person* y)   // equality through pointer
{
    return *x == *y;
}
bool Person_lt(const Person* x, const Person* y)   // less than through pointer
{
    return *x < *y;
}
```

```
void extract_and_print(const list<Club>& lc)
{
    list<Person*> off;
    extract(lc, off);
    off.sort(off, Person_lt);
    list<Club>::iterator p = unique(off.begin(), off.end(), Person_eq);
    for_each(off.begin(), p, Print_name(cout));
}
```

I use *list::sort()* (§17.2.2.1) because the standard *sort()* algorithm (§18.7.1) requires random access iterators and *list* offers only bidirectional iterators (§17.1.2).

It is wise to make sure that the criterion used to sort matches the one used to eliminate duplicates. The default meanings of < and == for pointers are rarely useful as comparison criteria for the objects pointed to.

18.6.4 Replace

The *replace()* algorithms traverse a sequence, replacing values by other values as specified. They follow the patterns outlined by *find/find_if* and *unique/unique_copy*, thus yielding four variants in all. Again, the code is simple enough to be illustrative:

```
template<class For, class T>
void replace(For first, For last, const T& val, const T& new_val)
{
    while (first != last) {
        if (*first == val) *first = new_val;
        ++first;
    }
}

template<class For, class Pred, class T>
void replace_if(For first, For last, Pred p, const T& new_val)
{
    while (first != last) {
        if (p(*first)) *first = new_val;
        ++first;
    }
}

template<class In, class Out, class T>
Out replace_copy(In first, In last, Out res, const T& val, const T& new_val)
{
    while (first != last) {
        *res++ = (*first == val) ? new_val : *first;
        ++first;
    }
    return res;
}
```

```
template<class In, class Out, class Pred, class T>
Out replace_copy_if(In first, In last, Out res, Pred p, const T& new_val)
{
      while (first != last) {
             *res++ = p(*first) ? new_val : *first;
             ++first;
      }
      return res;
}
```

We might want to go through a list of *string*s, replacing the usual English transliteration of the name of my home town Aarhus with its proper name Århus:

```
void f(list<string>& towns)
{
      replace(towns.begin(),towns.end(),"Aarhus","Århus");
}
```

This relies on an extended character set (§C.3.3).

18.6.5 Remove

The *remove*() algorithms remove elements from a sequence based on a value or a predicate:

```
template<class For, class T> For remove(For first, For last, const T& val);
```

```
template<class For, class Pred> For remove_if(For first, For last, Pred p);
```

```
template<class In, class Out, class T>
      Out remove_copy(In first, In last, Out res, const T& val);
```

```
template<class In, class Out, class Pred>
      Out remove_copy_if(In first, In last, Out res, Pred p);
```

Assuming that a *Club* has an address, we could produce a list of *Club*s located in Copenhagen:

```
class located_in : public unary_function<Club,bool> {
      string town;
public:
      located_in(const string& ss) :town(ss) { }
      bool operator()(const Club& c) const { return c.town == town; }
};

void f(list<Club>& lc)
{
      remove_copy_if(lc.begin(),lc.end(),
                     ostream_iterator<Club>(cout),not1(located_in("København")));
}
```

Thus, *remove_copy_if*() is *copy_if*() (§18.6.1) with the inverse condition. That is, an element is placed on the output by *remove_copy_if*() if the element does not match the predicate.

The "plain" *remove*() compacts non-matching elements at the beginning of the sequence and returns an iterator for the end of the compacted sequence (see also §18.6.3).

18.6.6 Fill and Generate

The *fill* ( ) and *generate* ( ) algorithms exist to systematically assign values to sequences:

```
template<class For, class T> void fill(For first, For last, const T& val);
template<class Out, class Size, class T> void fill_n(Out res, Size n, const T& val);

template<class For, class Gen> void generate(For first, For last, Gen g);
template<class Out, class Size, class Gen> void generate_n(Out res, Size n, Gen g);
```

The *fill* ( ) algorithm assigns a specified value; the *generate* ( ) algorithm assigns values obtained by calling its function argument repeatedly. Thus, *fill* ( ) is simply the special case of *generate* ( ) in which the generator function returns the same value repeatedly. The *_n* versions assign to the first *n* elements of the sequence.

For example, using the random-number generators *Randint* and *Urand* from §22.7:

```
int  v1[900];
int  v2[900];
vector  v3;

void  f()
{
     fill(v1, &v1[900], 99);              // set all elements of v1 to 99
     generate(v2, &v2[900], Randint());   // set to random values (§22.7)

     // output 200 random integers in the interval [0..99]:
     generate_n(ostream_iterator<int>(cout), 200, Urand(100));     // see §22.7

     fill_n(back_inserter(v3), 20, 99);        // add 20 elements with the value 99 to v3
}
```

The *generate* ( ) and *fill* ( ) functions assign rather than initialize. If you need to manipulate raw storage, say to turn a region of memory into objects of well-defined type and state, you must use an algorithm like *uninitialized_fill* ( ) from *<memory>* (§19.4.4) rather than algorithms from *<algorithm>*.

18.6.7 Reverse and Rotate

Occasionally, we need to reorder the elements of a sequence:

```
template<class Bi> void reverse(Bi first, Bi last);
template<class Bi, class Out> Out reverse_copy(Bi first, Bi last, Out res);

template<class For> void rotate(For first, For middle, For last);
template<class For, class Out> Out rotate_copy(For first, For middle, For last, Out res);

template<class Ran> void random_shuffle(Ran first, Ran last);
template<class Ran, class Gen> void random_shuffle(Ran first, Ran last, Gen& g);
```

The *reverse* ( ) algorithm reverses the order of the elements so that the first element becomes the last, etc. The *reverse_copy* ( ) algorithm produces a copy of its input in reverse order.

The *rotate* ( ) algorithm considers its [*first, last*[sequence a circle and rotates its elements until its former *middle* element is placed where its *first* element used to be. That is, the element in position *first+i* moves to position *first+* (*i+* (*last−middle*)) % (*last−first*). The % (modulo) is what makes the rotation cyclic rather than simply a shift to the left. For example:

```
void f()
{
    string v[] = { "Frog", "and", "Peach" };

    reverse(v,v+3);              // Peach and Frog
    rotate(v,v+1,v+3);           // and Frog Peach
}
```

The *rotate_copy*() algorithm produces a copy of its input in rotated order.

By default, *random_shuffle*() shuffles its sequence using a uniform distribution random-number generator. That is, it chooses a permutation of the elements of the sequence in such a way that each permutation has the same chance of being chosen. If you want a different distribution or simply a better random-number generator, you can supply one. For example, using the *Urand* generator from §22.7 we might shuffle a deck of cards like this:

```
void f(deque<Card>& dc)
{
    Urand r(52);
    random_shuffle(dc.begin(),dc.end(),r);
    // ...
}
```

The movement of elements done by *rotate*(), etc., is done using *swap*() (§18.6.8).

18.6.8 Swap

To do anything at all interesting with elements in a container, we need to move them around. Such movement is best expressed − that is, expressed most simply and most efficiently − as *swap*()s:

```
template<class T> void swap(T& a, T& b)
{
    T tmp = a;
    a = b;
    b = tmp;
}

template<class For, class For2> void iter_swap(For x, For2 y);

template<class For, class For2> For2 swap_ranges(For first, For last, For2 first2)
{
    while (first != last) iter_swap(first++, first2++);
    return first2;
}
```

To swap elements, you need a temporary. There are clever tricks to eliminate that need in specialized cases, but they are best avoided in favor of the simple and obvious. The *swap*() algorithm is specialized for important types for which it matters (§16.3.9, §13.5.2).

The *iter_swap*() algorithm swaps the elements pointed to by its iterator arguments.

The *swap_ranges* algorithm swaps elements in its two input ranges.

18.7 Sorted Sequences

Once we have collected some data, we often want to sort it. Once the sequence is sorted, our options for manipulating the data in a convenient manner increase significantly.

To sort a sequence, we need a way of comparing elements. This is done using a binary predicate (§18.4.2). The default comparison is *less* (§18.4.2), which in turn uses < by default.

18.7.1 Sorting

The *sort*() algorithms require random-access iterators (§19.2.1). That is, they work best for *vector*s (§16.3) and similar containers:

```
template<class Ran> void sort(Ran first, Ran last);
template<class Ran, class Cmp> void sort(Ran first, Ran last, Cmp cmp);

template<class Ran> void stable_sort(Ran first, Ran last);
template<class Ran, class Cmp> void stable_sort(Ran first, Ran last, Cmp cmp);
```

The standard *list* (§17.2.2) does not provide random-access iterators, so *list*s should be sorted using the specific *list* operations (§17.2.2.1).

The basic *sort*() is efficient – on average $N*log(N)$ – but its worst-case performance is poor – $O(N*N)$. Fortunately, the worst case is rare. If guaranteed worst-case behavior is important or a stable sort is required, *stable_sort*() should be used; that is, an $N*log(N)*log(N)$ algorithm that improves towards $N*log(N)$ when the system has sufficient extra memory. The relative order of elements that compare equal is preserved by *stable_sort*() but not by *sort*().

Sometimes, only the first elements of a sorted sequence are needed. In that case, it makes sense to sort the sequence only as far as is needed to get the first part in order. That is a partial sort:

```
template<class Ran> void partial_sort(Ran first, Ran middle, Ran last);
template<class Ran, class Cmp>
    void partial_sort(Ran first, Ran middle, Ran last, Cmp cmp);

template<class In, class Ran>
    Ran partial_sort_copy(In first, In last, Ran first2, Ran last2);
template<class In, class Ran, class Cmp>
    Ran partial_sort_copy(In first, In last, Ran first2, Ran last2, Cmp cmp);
```

The plain *partial_sort*() algorithms put the elements in the range *first* to *middle* in order. The *partial_sort_copy*() algorithms produce *N* elements, where *N* is the lower of the number of elements in the output sequence and the number of elements in the input sequence. We need to specify both the start and the end of the result sequence because that's what determines how many elements we need to sort. For example:

```
class Compare_copies_sold {
public:
    int operator()(const Book& b1, const Book& b2) const
        { return b1.copies_sold()>b2.copies_sold(); }        // sort in decreasing order
};
```

```
void f(const vector<Book>& sales)      // find the top ten books
{
    vector<Book> bestsellers(10);
    partial_sort_copy(sales.begin(), sales.end(),
                bestsellers.begin(), bestsellers.end(), Compare_copies_sold());
    copy(bestsellers.begin(), bestsellers.end(), ostream_iterator<Book>(cout, "\n"));
}
```

Because the target of *partial_sort_copy*() must be a random-access iterator, we cannot sort directly to *cout*.

Finally, algorithms are provided to sort only as far as is necessary to get the *N*th element to its proper place with no element comparing less than the *N*th element placed after it in the sequence:

```
template<class Ran> void nth_element(Ran first, Ran nth, Ran last);
template<class Ran, class Cmp> void nth_element(Ran first, Ran nth, Ran last, Cmp cmp);
```

This algorithm is particularly useful for people – such as economists, sociologists, and teachers – who need to look for medians, percentiles, etc.

18.7.2 Binary Search

A sequential search such as *find*() (§18.5.2) is terribly inefficient for large sequences, but it is about the best we can do without sorting or hashing (§17.6). Once a sequence is sorted, however, we can use a binary search to determine whether a value is in a sequence:

```
template<class For, class T> bool binary_search(For first, For last, const T& val);

template<class For, class T, class Cmp>
    bool binary_search(For first, For last, const T& value, Cmp cmp);
```

For example:

```
void f(list<int>& c)
{
    if (binary_search(c.begin(), c.end(), 7)) {      // is 7 in c?
        // ...
    }
    // ...
}
```

A *binary_search*() returns a *bool* indicating whether a value was present. As with *find*(), we often also want to know where the elements with that value are in that sequence. However, there can be many elements with a given value in a sequence, and we often need to find either the first or all such elements. Consequently, algorithms are provided for finding a range of equal elements, *equal_range*(), and algorithms for finding the *lower_bound*() and *upper_bound*() of that range:

```
template<class For, class T> For lower_bound(For first, For last, const T& val);
template<class For, class T, class Cmp>
    For lower_bound(For first, For last, const T& val, Cmp cmp);
```

```
template<class For, class T> For upper_bound(For first, For last, const T& val);
template<class For, class T, class Cmp>
    For upper_bound(For first, For last, const T& val, Cmp cmp);

template<class For, class T> pair<For, For> equal_range(For first, For last, const T& val);
template<class For, class T, class Cmp>
    pair<For, For> equal_range(For first, For last, const T& val, Cmp cmp);
```

These algorithms correspond to the operations on *multimap*s (§17.4.2). We can think of *lower_bound*() as a fast *find*() and *find_if*() for sorted sequences. For example:

```
void g(vector<int>& c)
{
    typedef vector<int>::iterator VI;

    VI p = find(c.begin(),c.end(),7);              // probably slow: O(N); c needn't be sorted
    VI q = lower_bound(c.begin(),c.end(),7);       // probably fast: O(log(N)); c must be sorted
    // ...
}
```

If *lower_bound*(*first*, *last*, *k*) doesn't find *k*, it returns an iterator to the first element with a key greater than *k*, or *last* if no such greater element exists. This way of reporting failure is also used by *upper_bound*() and *equal_range*(). This means that we can use these algorithms to determine where to insert a new element into a sorted sequence so that the sequence remains sorted.

18.7.3 Merge

Given two sorted sequences, we can merge them into a new sorted sequence using *merge*() or merge two parts of a sequence using *inplace_merge*():

```
template<class In, class In2, class Out>
    Out merge(In first, In last, In2 first2, In2 last2, Out res);
template<class In, class In2, class Out, class Cmp>
    Out merge(In first, In last, In2 first2, In2 last2, Out res, Cmp cmp);

template<class Bi> void inplace_merge(Bi first, Bi middle, Bi last);
template<class Bi, class Cmp> void inplace_merge(Bi first, Bi middle, Bi last, Cmp cmp);
```

Note that these merge algorithms differ from *list*'s merge (§17.2.2.1) by *not* removing elements from their input sequences. Instead, elements are copied.

For elements that compare equal, elements from the first range will always precede elements from the second.

The *inplace_merge*() algorithm is primarily useful when you have a sequence that can be sorted by more than one criterion. For example, you might have a *vector* of fish sorted by species (for example, cod, haddock, and herring). If the elements of each species are sorted by weight, you can get the whole vector sorted by weight by applying *inplace_merge*() to merge the information for the different species (§18.13[20]).

18.7.4 Partitions

To partition a sequence is to place every element that satisfies a predicate before every element that doesn't. The standard library provides a *stable_partition*(), which maintains relative order among the elements that do and do not satisfy the predicate. In addition, the library offers *partition*() which doesn't maintain relative order, but which runs a bit faster when memory is limited:

> *template<class Bi, class Pred> Bi partition(Bi first, Bi last, Pred p);*
> *template<class Bi, class Pred> Bi stable_partition(Bi first, Bi last, Pred p);*

You can think of a partition as a kind of sort with a very simple sorting criterion. For example:

> *void f(list<Club>& lc)*
> *{*
>   *list<Club>::iterator p = partition(lc.begin(), lc.end(), located_in("København"));*
>   *// ...*
> *}*

This ''sorts'' the *list* so that *Club*s in Copenhagen comes first. The return value (here *p*) points either to the first element that doesn't satisfy the predicate or to the end.

18.7.5 Set Operations on Sequences

A sequence can be considered a set. Looked upon that way, it makes sense to provide set operations such as union and intersection for sequences. However, such operations are horribly inefficient unless the sequences are sorted, so the standard library provides set operations for sorted sequences only. In particular, the set operations work well for *set*s (§17.4.3) and *multiset*s (§17.4.4), both of which are sorted anyway.

If these set algorithms are applied to sequences that are not sorted, the resulting sequences will not conform to the usual set-theoretical rules. These algorithms do not change their input sequences, and their output sequences are ordered.

The *includes*() algorithm tests whether every member of the second sequence, [*first2*:*last2*[, is also a member of the first, [*first*:*last*[:

> *template<class In, class In2>*
>   *bool includes(In first, In last, In2 first2, In2 last2);*
> *template<class In, class In2, class Cmp>*
>   *bool includes(In first, In last, In2 first2, In2 last2, Cmp cmp);*

The *set_union*() and *set_intersection*() produce their obvious outputs as sorted sequences:

> *template<class In, class In2, class Out>*
>   *Out set_union(In first, In last, In2 first2, In2 last2, Out res);*
> *template<class In, class In2, class Out, class Cmp>*
>   *Out set_union(In first, In last, In2 first2, In2 last2, Out res, Cmp cmp);*
>
> *template<class In, class In2, class Out>*
>   *Out set_intersection(In first, In last, In2 first2, In2 last2, Out res);*
> *template<class In, class In2, class Out, class Cmp>*
>   *Out set_intersection(In first, In last, In2 first2, In2 last2, Out res, Cmp cmp);*

The *set_difference*() algorithm produces a sequence of elements that are members of its first, but not its second, input sequence. The *set_symmetric_difference* ( ) algorithm produces a sequence of elements that are members of either, but not of both, of its input sequences:

```
template<class In, class In2, class Out>
    Out set_difference(In first, In last, In2 first2, In2 last2, Out res);
template<class In, class In2, class Out, class Cmp>
    Out set_difference(In first, In last, In2 first2, In2 last2, Out res, Cmp cmp);

template<class In, class In2, class Out>
    Out set_symmetric_difference(In first, In last, In2 first2, In2 last2, Out res);
template<class In, class In2, class Out, class Cmp>
    Out set_symmetric_difference(In first, In last, In2 first2, In2 last2, Out res, Cmp cmp);
```

For example:

```
char v1[] = "abcd";
char v2[] = "cdef";

void f(char v3[])
{
    set_difference(v1,v1+4,v2,v2+4,v3);              // v3 = "ab"
    set_symmetric_difference(v1,v1+4,v2,v2+4,v3);    // v3 = "abef"
}
```

18.8 Heaps

The word *heap* means different things in different contexts. When discussing algorithms, ''heap'' often refers to a way of organizing a sequence such that it has a first element that is the element with the highest value. Addition of an element (using *push_heap* ( )) and removal of an element (using *pop_heap* ( )) are reasonably fast, with a worst-case performance of $O(log(N))$, where N is the number of elements in the sequence. Sorting (using *sort_heap* ( )) has a worst-case performance of $O(N*log(N))$. A heap is implemented by this set of functions:

```
template<class Ran> void push_heap(Ran first, Ran last);
template<class Ran, class Cmp> void push_heap(Ran first, Ran last, Cmp cmp);

template<class Ran> void pop_heap(Ran first, Ran last);
template<class Ran, class Cmp> void pop_heap(Ran first, Ran last, Cmp cmp);

template<class Ran> void make_heap(Ran first, Ran last);       // turn sequence into heap
template<class Ran, class Cmp> void make_heap(Ran first, Ran last, Cmp cmp);

template<class Ran> void sort_heap(Ran first, Ran last);       // turn heap into sequence
template<class Ran, class Cmp> void sort_heap(Ran first, Ran last, Cmp cmp);
```

The style of the heap algorithms is odd. A more natural way of presenting their functionality would be to provide an adapter class with four operations. Doing that would yield something like a *priority_queue* (§17.3.3). In fact, a *priority_queue* is almost certainly implemented using a heap.

The value pushed by *push_heap* (*first*, *last*) is * (*last-1*). The assumption is that [*first*, *last-1* [is already a heap, so *push_heap* ( ) extends the sequence to [*first*, *last* [by including the next element. Thus, you can build a heap from an existing sequence by a series of *push_heap* ( ) operations. Conversely, *pop_heap* (*first* , *last*) removes the first element of the heap by swapping it with the last element (* (*last–1*)) and making [*first* , *last–1* [into a heap.

18.9 Min and Max

The algorithms described here select a value based on a comparison. It is obviously useful to be able to find the maximum and minimum of two values:

```
template<class T> const T& max (const T& a, const T& b)
{
    return (a<b) ? b : a;
}

template<class T, class Cmp> const T& max (const T& a, const T& b, Cmp cmp)
{
    return (cmp (a,b)) ? b : a;
}

template<class T> const T& min (const T& a, const T& b);

template<class T, class Cmp> const T& min (const T& a, const T& b, Cmp cmp);
```

The *max* ( ) and *min* ( ) operations can be generalized to apply to sequences in the obvious manner:

```
template<class For> For max_element (For first, For last);
template<class For, class Cmp> For max_element (For first, For last, Cmp cmp);

template<class For> For min_element (For first, For last);
template<class For, class Cmp> For min_element (For first, For last, Cmp cmp);
```

Finally, lexicographical ordering is easily generalized from strings of characters to sequences of values of a type with comparison:

```
template<class In, class In2>
bool lexicographical_compare (In first, In last, In2 first2, In2 last2);

template<class In, class In2, class Cmp>
bool lexicographical_compare (In first, In last, In2 first2, In2 last2, Cmp cmp)
{
    while (first != last && first2 != last2) {
        if (cmp (*first, *first2)) return true;
        if (cmp (*first2++, *first++)) return false;
    }
    return first == last && first2 != last2;
}
```

This is very similar to the function presented for general strings in §13.4.1. However, *lexicographical_compare* ( ) compares sequences in general and not just strings. It also returns a *bool* rather than the more useful *int*. The result is *true* (only) if the first sequence compares < the second. In particular, the result is *false* when the sequences compare equal.

C-style strings and *string*s are sequences, so *lexicographical_compare* ( ) can be used as a string compare function. For example:

```
char v1[] = "yes";
char v2[] = "no";
string s1 = "Yes";
string s2 = "No";

void f()
{
     bool b1 = lexicographical_compare(v1,v1+strlen(v1),v2,v2+strlen(v2));
     bool b2 = lexicographical_compare(s1.begin(),s1.end(),s2.begin(),s2.end());

     bool b3 = lexicographical_compare(v1,v1+strlen(v1),s1.begin(),s1.end());
     bool b4 = lexicographical_compare(s1.begin(),s1.end(),v1,v1+strlen(v1),Nocase());
}
```

The sequences need not be of the same type – all we need is to compare their elements – and the comparison criterion can be supplied. This makes *lexicographical_compare*() more general and potentially a bit slower than *string*'s compare. See also §20.3.8.

18.10 Permutations

Given a sequence of four elements, we can order them in 4*3*2 ways. Each of these orderings is called a *permutation*. For example, from the four characters *abcd* we can produce 24 permutations:

> abcd abdc acbd acdb adbc adcb bacd badc
> bcad bcda bdac bdca cabd cadb cbad cbda
> cdab cdba dabc dacb dbac dbca dcab dcba

The *next_permutation*() and *prev_permutation*() functions deliver such permutations of a sequence:

```
template<class Bi> bool next_permutation(Bi first, Bi last);
template<class Bi, class Cmp> bool next_permutation(Bi first, Bi last, Cmp cmp);

template<class Bi> bool prev_permutation(Bi first, Bi last);
template<class Bi, class Cmp> bool prev_permutation(Bi first, Bi last, Cmp cmp);
```

The permutations of *abcd* were produced like this:

```
int main()
{
     char v[] = "abcd";
     cout << v << '\t';
     while(next_permutation(v,v+4)) cout << v << '\t';
}
```

The permutations are produced in lexicographical order (§18.9). The return value of *next_permutation*() indicates whether a next permutation actually exists. If not, *false* is returned and the sequence is the permutation in which the elements are in lexicographical order. The return value of *prev_permutation*() indicates whether a previous permutation actually exists. If not, *false* is returned and the sequence is the permutation in which the elements are in reverse lexicographical order.

18.11 C-Style Algorithms

From the C standard library, the C++ standard library inherited a few algorithms dealing with C-style strings (§20.4.1), plus a quicksort and a binary search, both limited to arrays.

The *qsort*( ) and *bsearch*( ) functions are presented in *<cstdlib>* and *<stdlib . h>*. They each operate on an array of *n* elements of size *elem_size* using a less-than comparison function passed as a pointer to function. The elements must be of a type without a user-defined copy constructor, copy assignment, or destructor:

```
typedef int (*__cmp) (const void*, const void*);        // typedef for presentation only

void qsort (void* p, size_t n, size_t elem_size, __cmp);                     // sort p
void* bsearch (const void* key, void* p, size_t n, size_t elem_size, __cmp);   // find key in p
```

The use of *qsort*( ) is described in §7.7.

These algorithms are provided solely for C compatibility; *sort*( ) (§18.7.1) and *search*( ) (§18.5.5) are more general and should also be more efficient.

18.12 Advice

[1]   Prefer algorithms to loops; §18.5.1.
[2]   When writing a loop, consider whether it could be expressed as a general algorithm; §18.2.
[3]   Regularly review the set of algorithms to see if a new application has become obvious; §18.2.
[4]   Be sure that a pair of iterator arguments really do specify a sequence; §18.3.1.
[5]   Design so that the most frequently-used operations are simple and safe; §18.3, §18.3.1.
[6]   Express tests in a form that allows them to be used as predicates; §18.4.2.
[7]   Remember that predicates are functions and objects, not types; §18.4.2.
[8]   You can use binders to make unary predicates out of binary predicates; §18.4.4.1.
[9]   Use *mem_fun*( ) and *mem_fun_ref*( ) to apply algorithms on containers; §18.4.4.2.
[10] Use *ptr_fun*( ) when you need to bind an argument of a function; §18.4.4.3.
[11] Remember that *strcmp*( ) differs from == by returning *0* to indicate ''equal;'' §18.4.4.4.
[12] Use *for_each*( ) and *transform*( ) only when there is no more-specific algorithm for a task; §18.5.1.
[13] Use predicates to apply algorithms using a variety of comparison and equality criteria; §18.4.2.1, §18.6.3.1.
[14] Use predicates and other function objects so as to use standard algorithms with a wider range of meanings; §18.4.2.
[15] The default == and < on pointers are rarely adequate for standard algorithms; §18.6.3.1.
[16] Algorithms do not directly add or subtract elements from their argument sequences; §18.6.
[17] Be sure that the less-than and equality predicates used on a sequence match; §18.6.3.1.
[18] Sometimes, sorted sequences can be used to increase efficiency and elegance; §18.7.
[19] Use *qsort*( ) and *bsearch*( ) for compatibility only; §18.11.

18.13 Exercises

The solutions to several exercises for this chapter can be found by looking at the source text of an implementation of the standard library. Do yourself a favor: try to find your own solutions before looking to see how your library implementer approached the problems.

1. (*2) Learn $O()$ notation. Give a realistic example in which an $O(N*N)$ algorithm is faster than an $O(N)$ algorithm for some $N>10$.

2. (*2) Implement and test the four *mem_fun*() and *mem_fun_ref*() functions (§18.4.4.2).

3. (*1) Write an algorithm *match*() that is like *mismatch*(), except that it returns iterators to the first corresponding pair that matches the predicate.

4. (*1.5) Implement and test *Print_name* from §18.5.1.

5. (*1) Sort a *list* using only standard library algorithms.

6. (*2.5) Define versions of *iseq*() (§18.3.1) for built-in arrays, *istream*, and iterator pairs. Define a suitable set of overloads for the nonmodifying standard algorithms (§18.5) for *Iseq*s. Discuss how best to avoid ambiguities and an explosion in the number of template functions.

7. (*2) Define an *oseq*() to complement *iseq*(). The output sequence given as the argument to *oseq*() should be replaced by the output produced by an algorithm using it. Define a suitable set of overloads for at least three standard algorithms of your choice.

8. (*1.5) Produce a *vector* of squares of numbers 1 through 100. Print a table of squares. Take the square root of the elements of that *vector* and print the resulting vector.

9. (*2) Write a set of functional objects that do bitwise logical operations on their operands. Test these objects on vectors of *char*, *int*, and *bitset<67>*.

10. (*1) Write a *binder3*() that binds the second and third arguments of a three-argument function to produce a unary predicate. Give an example where *binder3*() is a useful function.

11. (*1.5) Write a small program that that removes adjacent repeated words from from a file file. Hint: The program should remove a *that*, a *from*, and a *file* from the previous statement.

12. (*2.5) Define a format for records of references to papers and books kept in a file. Write a program that can write out records from the file identified by year of publication, name of author, keyword in title, or name of publisher. The user should be able to request that the output be sorted according to similar criteria.

13. (*2) Implement a *move*() algorithm in the style of *copy*() in such a way that the input and output sequences can overlap. Be reasonably efficient when given random-access iterators as arguments.

14. (*1.5) Produce all anagrams of the word *food*. That is, all four-letter combinations of the letters *f*, *o*, *o*, and *d*. Generalize this program to take a word as input and produce anagrams of that word.

15. (*1.5) Write a program that produces anagrams of sentences; that is, a program that produces all permutations of the words in the sentences (rather than permutations of the letters in the words).

16. (*1.5) Implement *find_if*() (§18.5.2) and then implement *find*() using *find_if*(). Find a way of doing this so that the two functions do not need different names.

17. (*2) Implement *search*() (§18.5.5). Provide an optimized version for random-access iterators.

18. (*2) Take a sort algorithm (such as *sort*() from your standard library or the Shell sort from §13.5.2) and insert code so that it prints out the sequence being sorted after each swap of elements.

19. (∗2) There is no *sort* ( ) for bidirectional iterators. The conjecture is that copying to a vector and then sorting is faster than sorting a sequence using bidirectional iterators. Implement a general sort for bidirectional iterators and test the conjecture.

20. (∗2.5) Imagine that you keep records for a group of sports fishermen. For each catch, keep a record of species, length, weight, date of catch, name of fisherman, etc. Sort and print the records according to a variety of criteria. Hint: *inplace_merge* ( ).

21. (∗2) Create lists of students taking Math, English, French, and Biology. Pick about 20 names for each class out of a set of 40 names. List students who take both Math and English. List students who take French but not Biology or Math. List students who do not take a science course. List students who take French and Math but neither English nor Biology.

22. (∗1.5) Write a *remove* ( ) function that actually removes elements from a container.

19

Iterators and Allocators

The reason that data structures and algorithms
can work together seamlessly is ... that they
do not know anything about each other.
– Alex Stepanov

Iterators and sequences — operations on iterators — iterator traits — iterator categories — inserters — reverse iterators — stream iterators — checked iterators — exceptions and algorithms — allocators — the standard *allocator* — user-defined allocators — low-level memory functions — advice — exercises.

19.1 Introduction

Iterators are the glue that holds containers and algorithms together. They provide an abstract view of data so that the writer of an algorithm need not be concerned with concrete details of a myriad of data structures. Conversely, the standard model of data access provided by iterators relieves containers from having to provide a more extensive set of access operations. Similarly, allocators are used to insulate container implementations from details of access to memory.

Iterators support an abstract model of data as sequences of objects (§19.2). Allocators provide a mapping from a lower-level model of data as arrays of bytes into the higher-level object model (§19.4). The most common lower-level memory model is itself supported by a few standard functions (§19.4.4).

Iterators are a concept with which every programmer should be familiar. In contrast, allocators are a support mechanism that a programmer rarely needs to worry about and few programmers will ever need to write a new allocator.

19.2 Iterators and Sequences

An iterator is a pure abstraction. That is, anything that behaves like an iterator is an iterator (§3.8.2). An iterator is an abstraction of the notion of a pointer to an element of a sequence. Its key concepts are
   -   "the element currently pointed to" (dereferencing, represented by operators * and ->),
   -   "point to next element" (increment, represented by operator ++), and
   -   equality (represented by operator ==).

For example, the built-in type *int** is an iterator for an *int* [ ] and the class *list<int>* :: *iterator* is an iterator for a *list* class.

A sequence is an abstraction of the notion "something where we can get from the beginning to the end by using a next-element operation:"

Examples of such sequences are arrays (§5.2), vectors (§16.3), singly-linked lists (§17.8[17]), doubly-linked lists (§17.2.2), trees (§17.4.1), input (§21.3.1), and output (§21.2.1). Each has its own appropriate kind of iterator.

The iterator classes and functions are declared in namespace *std* and found in *<iterator>*.

An iterator is *not* a general pointer. Rather, it is an abstraction of the notion of a pointer into an array. There is no concept of a "null iterator." The test to determine whether an iterator points to an element or not is conventionally done by comparing it against the *end* of its sequence (rather than comparing it against a *null* element). This notion simplifies many algorithms by removing the need for a special end case and generalizes nicely to sequences of arbitrary types.

An iterator that points to an element is said to be *valid* and can be dereferenced (using *, [ ], or -> appropriately). An iterator can be invalid either because it hasn't been initialized, because it pointed into a container that was explicitly or implicitly resized (§16.3.6, §16.3.8), because the container into which it pointed was destroyed, or because it denotes the end of a sequence (§18.2). The end of a sequence can be thought of as an iterator pointing to a hypothetical element position one-past-the-last element of a sequence.

19.2.1 Iterator Operations

Not every kind of iterator supports exactly the same set of operations. For example, reading requires different operations from writing, and a *vector* allows convenient and efficient random access in a way that would be prohibitively expensive to provide for a *list* or an *istream*. Consequently, we classify iterators into five categories according to the operations they are capable of providing efficiently (that is, in constant time; §17.1):

Iterator Operations and Categories					
Category:	output	input	forward	bidirectional	random-access
Abbreviation:	*Out*	*In*	*For*	*Bi*	*Ran*
Read:		=*p	=*p	=*p	=*p
Access:		->	->	->	-> [ ]
Write:	*p=		*p=	*p=	*p=
Iteration:	++	++	++	++ --	++ -- + - += -=
Comparison:		== !=	== !=	== !=	== != < > >= <=

Both read and write are through the iterator dereferenced by *:

```
*p = x;     // write x through p
x = *p;     // read through p into x
```

To be an iterator type, a type must provide an appropriate set of operations. These operations must have their conventional meanings. That is, each operation must have the same effect it has on an ordinary pointer.

Independently of its category, an iterator can allow *const* or non-*const* access to the object it points to. You cannot write to an element using an iterator to *const* – whatever its category. An iterator provides a set of operators, but the type of the element pointed to is the final arbiter of what can be done to that element.

Reads and writes copy objects, so element types must have the conventional copy semantics (§17.1.4).

Only random-access iterators can have an integer added or subtracted for relative addressing. However, except for output iterators, the distance between two iterators can always be found by iterating through the elements, so a *distance*() function is provided:

```
template<class In> typename iterator_traits<In>::difference_type distance(In first, In last)
{
        typename iterator_traits<In>::difference_type d = 0;
        while (first++!=last) d++;
        return d;
}
```

An *iterator_traits<In>::difference_type* is defined for every iterator *In* to hold distances between elements (§19.2.2).

This function is called *distance*() rather than *operator-*() because it can be expensive and the operators provided for an iterator all operate in constant time (§17.1). Counting elements one by one is not the kind of operation I would like to invoke unwittingly for a large sequence. The library also provides a far more efficient implementation of *distance*() for a random-access iterator.

Similarly, *advance*() is provided as a potentially slow +=:

```
template <class In, class Dist> void advance(In& i, Dist n);    // i+=n
```

19.2.2 Iterator Traits

We use iterators to gain information about the objects they point to and the sequences they point into. For example, we can dereference an iterator and manipulate the resulting object and we can find the number of elements in a sequence, given the iterators that describe it. To express such operations, we must be able to refer to types related to an iterator such as "the type of the object referred to by an iterator" and "the type of the distance between two iterators." The related types of an iterator are described by a small set of declarations in an *iterator_traits* template class:

```
template<class Iter> struct iterator_traits {
    typedef typename Iter::iterator_category iterator_category;     // §19.2.3
    typedef typename Iter::value_type value_type;                   // type of element
    typedef typename Iter::difference_type difference_type;
    typedef typename Iter::pointer pointer;                         // return type of operator->()
    typedef typename Iter::reference reference;                     // return type of operator*()
};
```

The *difference_type* is the type used to represent the difference between two iterators, and the *iterator_category* is a type indicating what operations the iterator supports. For ordinary pointers, specializations (§13.5) for *<T*>* and *<const T*>* are provided. In particular:

```
template<class T> struct iterator_traits<T*> {        // specialization for pointers
    typedef random_access_iterator_tag iterator_category;
    typedef T value_type;
    typedef ptrdiff_t difference_type;
    typedef T* pointer;
    typedef T& reference;
};
```

That is, the difference between two pointers is represented by the standard library type *ptrdiff_t* from *<cstddef>* (§6.2.1) and a pointer provides random access (§19.2.3). Given *iterator_traits*, we can write code that depends on properties of an iterator parameter. The *count*() algorithm is the classical example:

```
template<class In, class T>
typename iterator_traits<In>::difference_type count(In first, In last, const T& val)
{
    typename iterator_traits<In>::difference_type res = 0;
    while (first != last) if (*first++ == val) ++res;
    return res;
}
```

The type of the result is expressed using *iterator_traits<In>*. The reason is that there is no language primitive for directly expressing an arbitrary type in terms combinations of other types. In particular, there is no way to directly express "the type of the result of subtracting two *Ins*."

Instead of using *iterator_traits*, we might have specialized *count*() for pointers:

```
template<class In, class T>
typename In::difference_type count(In first, In last, const T& val);

template<class In, class T> ptrdiff_t count<T*,T>(T* first, T* last, const T& val);
```

However, this would have solved the problem for *count* ( ) only. Had we used this technique for a dozen algorithms, the information about distance types would have been replicated a dozen times. In general, it is better to represent a design decision in one place (§23.4.2). In that way, the decision can − if necessary − be changed in one place.

Because *iterator_traits<Iterator>* is defined for every iterator, we implicitly define an *iterator_traits* whenever we design a new iterator type. If the default traits generated from the general *iterator_traits* template are not right for our new iterator type, we provide a specialization in a way similar to what the standard library does for pointer types. The *iterator_traits* that are implicitly generated assume that the iterator is a class with the member types *difference_type*, *value_type*, etc. In *<iterator>*, the library provides a base type that can be used to define those member types:

```
template<class Cat, class T, class Dist = ptrdiff_t, class Ptr = T*, class Ref = T&>
struct iterator {
        typedef Cat iterator_category;      // §19.2.3
        typedef T value_type;               // type of element
        typedef Dist difference_type;       // type of iterator difference
        typedef Ptr pointer;                // return type for ->
        typedef Ref reference;              // return type for *
};
```

Note that *reference* and *pointer* are not iterators. They are intended to be the return types of *operator* ( ) and *operator->* ( ), respectively, for some iterator.

The *iterator_traits* are the key to the simplicity of many interfaces that rely on iterators and to the efficient implementation of many algorithms.

19.2.3 Iterator Categories

The different kinds of iterators − usually referred to as iterator categories − fit into a hierarchical ordering:

```
        Input
            ╲
             ╲
              ╲→ Forward ⟵─ Bidirectional ⟵─Random access
             ╱
        Output ╱
```

This is not a class inheritance diagram. An iterator category is a classification of a type based on the operations it provides. Many otherwise unrelated types can belong to the same iterator category. For example, both ordinary pointers (§19.2.2) and *Checked_iters* (§19.3) are random-access iterators.

As noted in Chapter 18, different algorithms require different kinds of iterators as arguments. Also, the same algorithm can sometimes be implemented with different efficiencies for different kinds of iterators. To support overload resolution based on iterator categories, the standard library provides five classes representing the five iterator categories:

```
struct input_iterator_tag { } ;
struct output_iterator_tag { } ;
struct forward_iterator_tag : public input_iterator_tag { } ;
struct bidirectional_iterator_tag : public forward_iterator_tag { } ;
struct random_access_iterator_tag : public bidirectional_iterator_tag { } ;
```

Looking at the operations supported by input and forward iterators (§19.2.1), we would expect *forward_iterator_tag* to be derived from *output_iterator_tag* as well as from *input_iterator_tag*. The reasons that it is not are obscure and probably invalid. However, I have yet to see an example in which that derivation would have simplified real code.

The inheritance of tags is useful (only) to save us from defining separate versions of a function where several – but not all – kinds of iterators can use the same algorithms. Consider how to implement *distance*:

```
template<class In>
typename iterator_traits<In>::difference_type distance(In first, In last);
```

There are two obvious alternatives:

[1] If *In* is a random-access iterator, we can subtract *first* from *last*.

[2] Otherwise, we must increment an iterator from *first* to *last* and count the distance.

We can express these two alternatives as a pair of helper functions:

```
template<class In>
typename iterator_traits<In>::difference_type
dist_helper(In first, In last, input_iterator_tag)
{
    typename iterator_traits<In>::difference_type d = 0;
    while (first++!=last) d++;                          // use increment only
    return d;
}

template<class Ran>
typename iterator_traits<Ran>::difference_type
dist_helper(Ran first, Ran last, random_access_iterator_tag)
{
    return last-first;      // rely on random access
}
```

The iterator category tag arguments make it explicit what kind of iterator is expected. The iterator tag is used exclusively for overload resolution; the tag takes no part in the actual computation. It is a purely compile-time selection mechanism. In addition to automatic selection of a helper function, this technique provides immediate type checking (§13.2.5).

It is now trivial to define *distance*() by calling the appropriate helper function:

```
template<class In>
typename iterator_traits<In>::difference_type distance(In first, In last)
{
    return dist_helper(first, last, iterator_traits<In>::iterator_category());
}
```

For a *dist_helper* ( ) to be called, the *iterator_traits<In>* : : *iterator_category* used must be a *input_iterator_tag* or a *random_access_iterator_tag*. However, there is no need for separate versions of *dist_helper* ( ) for forward or bidirectional iterators. Thanks to tag inheritance, those cases are handled by the *dist_helper* ( ) which takes an *input_iterator_tag*. The absence of a version for *output_iterator_tag* reflects the fact that *distance* ( ) is not meaningful for output iterators:

```
void f(vector<int>& vi,
    list<double>& ld,
    istream_iterator<string>& is1, istream_iterator<string>& is2,
    ostream_iterator<char>& os1, ostream_iterator<char>& os2)
{
    distance(vi.begin(),vi.end());       // use subtraction algorithm
    distance(ld.begin(),ld.end());       // use increment algorithm
    distance(is1,is2);                   // use increment algorithm
    distance(os1,os2);   // error: wrong iterator category, dist_helper() argument type mismatch
}
```

Calling *distance* ( ) for an *istream_iterator* probably doesn't make much sense in a real program, though. The effect would be to read the input, throw it away, and return the number of values thrown away.

Using *iterator_traits<T>* : : *iterator_category* allows a programmer to provide alternative implementations so that a user who cares nothing about the implementation of algorithms automatically gets the most appropriate implementation for each data structure used. In other words, it allows us to hide an implementation detail behind a convenient interface. Inlining can be used to ensure that this elegance is not bought at the cost of run-time efficiency.

19.2.4 Inserters

Producing output through an iterator into a container implies that elements following the one pointed to by the iterator can be overwritten. This implies the possibility of overflow and consequent memory corruption. For example:

```
void f(vector<int>& vi)
{
    fill_n(vi.begin(),200,7);       // assign 7 to vi[0]..[199]
}
```

If *vi* has fewer than *200* elements, we are in trouble.

In *<iterator>*, the standard library provides three iterator template classes to deal with this problem, plus three functions to make it convenient to use those iterators:

```
template <class Cont> back_insert_iterator<Cont> back_inserter(Cont& c);
template <class Cont> front_insert_iterator<Cont> front_inserter(Cont& c);
template <class Cont, class Out> insert_iterator<Cont> inserter(Cont& c, Out p);
```

The *back_inserter* ( ) causes elements to be added to the end of the container, *front_inserter* ( ) causes elements to be added to the front, and ''plain'' *inserter* ( ) causes elements to be added before its iterator argument. For *inserter* (*c* , *p*) , *p* must be a valid iterator for *c*. Naturally, a container grows each time a value is written to it through an insert iterator.

When written to, an inserter inserts a new element into a sequence using *push_back* ( ) , *push_front* ( ) , or *insert* ( ) (§16.3.6) rather than overwriting an existing element. For example:

```
void  g (vector<int>& vi)
{
    fill_n (back_inserter (vi) , 200 , 7) ;      // add 200 7s to the end of vi
}
```

Inserters are as simple and efficient as they are useful. For example:

```
template <class  Cont>
class  insert_iterator : public  iterator<output_iterator_tag , void , void , void , void> {
protected :
    Cont& container ;                  // container to insert into
    typename  Cont :: iterator  iter ;   // points into the container
public :
    explicit  insert_iterator (Cont&  x , typename  Cont :: iterator  i)
        : container (x) , iter (i) { }

    insert_iterator& operator= (const  typename  Cont :: value_type& val)
    {
        iter = container . insert (iter , val) ;
        ++iter ;
        return *this ;
    }

    insert_iterator& operator* () { return *this ; }
    insert_iterator& operator++ () { return *this ; }       // prefix ++
    insert_iterator  operator++ (int) { return *this ; }    // postfix ++
} ;
```

Clearly, inserters are output iterators.

An *insert_iterator* is a special case of an output sequence. In parallel to the *iseq* from §18.3.1, we might define:

```
template<class  Cont>
insert_iterator<Cont>
oseq (Cont& c , typename  Cont :: iterator  first , typename  Cont :: iterator  last)
{
    return  insert_iterator<Cont> (c , c . erase (first , last) ) ; // erase is explained in §16.3.6
}
```

In other words, an output sequence removes its old elements and replaces them with the output. For example:

```
void  f (list<int>& li , vector<int>& vi)   // replace second half of vi by a copy of li
{
    copy (li . begin () , li . end () , oseq (vi , vi . begin () +vi . size () /2 , vi . end () ) ) ;
}
```

The container needs to be an argument to an *oseq* because it is not possible to decrease the size of a container, given only iterators into it (§18.6, §18.6.3).

19.2.5 Reverse Iterators

The standard containers provide *rbegin*() and *rend*() for iterating through elements in reverse order (§16.3.2). These member functions return *reverse_iterator*s:

```
template <class Iter>
class reverse_iterator : public iterator<typename iterator_traits<Iter>::iterator_category,
                                         typename iterator_traits<Iter>::value_type,
                                         typename iterator_traits<Iter>::difference_type,
                                         typename iterator_traits<Iter>::pointer,
                                         typename iterator_traits<Iter>::reference> {
protected:
        Iter current;      // current points to the element after the one *this refers to.
public:
        typedef Iter iterator_type;

        reverse_iterator() : current() { }
        explicit reverse_iterator(Iter x) : current(x) { }
        template<class U> reverse_iterator(const reverse_iterator<U>& x) : current(x.base()) { }

        Iter base() const { return current; } // current iterator value

        reference operator*() const { Iter tmp = current; return *--tmp; }
        pointer operator->() const;
        reference operator[](difference_type n) const;

        reverse_iterator& operator++() { --current; return *this; }       // note: not ++
        reverse_iterator operator++(int) { reverse_iterator t = current; --current;  return t; }
        reverse_iterator& operator--() { ++current; return *this; }       // note: not —
        reverse_iterator operator--(int) { reverse_iterator t = current; ++current;  return t; }

        reverse_iterator operator+(difference_type n) const;
        reverse_iterator& operator+=(difference_type n);
        reverse_iterator operator-(difference_type n) const;
        reverse_iterator& operator-=(difference_type n);
};
```

A *reverse_iterator* is implemented using an *iterator* called *current*. That *iterator* can (only) point to the elements of its sequence plus its one-past-the-end element. However, the *reverse_iterator*'s one-past-the-end element is the original sequence's (inaccessible) one-before-the-beginning element. Thus, to avoid access violations, *current* points to the element after the one the *reverse_iterator* refers to. This implies that * returns the value *(*current-1*) and that ++ is implemented using -- on *current*.

A *reverse_iterator* supports the operations that its initializer supports (only). For example:

```
void f(vector<int>& v, list<char>& lst)
{
        v.rbegin()[3] = 7;              // ok: random-access iterator
        lst.rbegin()[3] = '4';          // error: bidirectional iterator doesn't support []
        *(++++++lst.rbegin()) = '4';  // ok!
}
```

In addition, the library provides ==, !=, <, <=, >, >=, + and – for *reverse_iterator*s.

19.2.6 Stream Iterators

Ordinarily, I/O is done using the streams library (Chapter 21), a graphical user-interface system (not covered by the C++ standard), or the C I/O functions (§21.8). These I/O interfaces are primarily aimed at reading and writing individual values of a variety of types. The standard library provides four iterator types to fit stream I/O into the general framework of containers and algorithms:

- *ostream_iterator*: for writing to an *ostream* (§3.4, §21.2.1).
- *istream_iterator*: for reading from an *istream* (§3.6, §21.3.1).
- *ostreambuf_iterator*: for writing to a stream buffer (§21.6.1).
- *istreambuf_iterator*: for reading from a stream buffer (§21.6.2).

The idea is simply to present input and output of collections as sequences:

```
template <class T, class Ch = char, class Tr = char_traits<Ch> >
class ostream_iterator : public iterator<output_iterator_tag, void, void, void, void> {
public:
        typedef Ch char_type;
        typedef Tr traits_type;
        typedef basic_ostream<Ch, Tr> ostream_type;

        ostream_iterator(ostream_type& s);
        ostream_iterator(ostream_type& s, const Ch* delim);   // write delim after each output value
        ostream_iterator(const ostream_iterator&);
        ~ostream_iterator();

        ostream_iterator& operator=(const T& val);            // write val to output

        ostream_iterator& operator*();
        ostream_iterator& operator++();
        ostream_iterator& operator++(int);
};
```

This iterator accepts the usual write and increment operations of an output iterator and converts them into << output operations on an *ostream*. For example:

```
void f()
{
        ostream_iterator<int> os(cout);      // write ints to cout through os
        *os = 7;          // output 7 (using cout<<7)
        ++os;             // get ready for next output
        *os = 79;         // output 79
}
```

The ++ operation might trigger an actual output operation, or it might have no effect. Different implementations will use different implementation strategies. Consequently, for code to be portable a ++ must occur between every two assignments to an *ostream_iterator*. Naturally, every standard algorithm is written that way – or it would not work for a *vector*. This is why *ostream_iterator* is defined this way.

An implementation of *ostream_iterator* is trivial and is left as an exercise (§19.6[4]). The standard I/O supports different character types; *char_traits* (§20.2) describes the aspects of a character type that can be important for I/O and *string*s.

An input iterator for *istream*s is defined analogously:

```
template <class T, class Ch = char, class Tr = char_traits<Ch>, class Dist = ptrdiff_t>
class istream_iterator : public iterator<input_iterator_tag, T, Dist, const T*, const T&> {
public:
    typedef Ch char_type;
    typedef Tr traits_type;
    typedef basic_istream<Ch,Tr> istream_type;

    istream_iterator();                    // end of input
    istream_iterator(istream_type& s);
    istream_iterator(const istream_iterator&);
    ~istream_iterator();

    const T& operator*() const;
    const T* operator->() const;
    istream_iterator& operator++();
    istream_iterator operator++(int);
};
```

This iterator is specified so that what would be conventional use for a container triggers >> input from an *istream*. For example:

```
void f()
{
    istream_iterator<int> is(cin);       // read ints from cin through is
    int i1 = *is;           // read an int (using cin>>i1)
    ++is;                   // get ready for next input
    int i2 = *is;           // read an int
}
```

The default *istream_iterator* represents the end of input so that we can specify an input sequence:

```
void f(vector<int>& v)
{
    copy(istream_iterator<int>(cin), istream_iterator<int>(), back_inserter(v));
}
```

To make this work, the standard library supplies == and != for *istream_iterator*s.

An implementation of *istream_iterator* is less trivial than an *ostream_iterator* implementation, but it is still simple. Implementing an *istream_iterator* is also left as an exercise (§19.6[5]).

19.2.6.1 Stream Buffers

As described in §21.6, stream I/O is based on the idea of *ostream*s and *istream*s filling and emptying buffers from and to which the low-level physical I/O is done. It is possible to bypass the standard iostreams formatting and operate directly on the stream buffers (§21.6.4). That ability is also provided to algorithms through the notion of *istreambuf_iterator*s and *ostreambuf_iterator*s:

```
template<class Ch, class Tr = char_traits<Ch> >
class istreambuf_iterator
        : public iterator<input_iterator_tag, Ch, typename Tr::off_type, Ch*, Ch&> {
public:
        typedef Ch char_type;
        typedef Tr traits_type;
        typedef typename Tr::int_type int_type;
        typedef basic_streambuf<Ch, Tr> streambuf_type;
        typedef basic_istream<Ch, Tr> istream_type;

        class proxy;                                          // helper type

        istreambuf_iterator() throw();                        // end of buffer
        istreambuf_iterator(istream_type& is) throw();        // read from is's streambuf
        istreambuf_iterator(streambuf_type*) throw();
        istreambuf_iterator(const proxy& p) throw();          // read from p's streambuf

        Ch operator*() const;
        istreambuf_iterator& operator++();                    // prefix
        proxy operator++(int);                                // postfix

        bool equal(istreambuf_iterator&);                     // both or neither streambuf at eof
};
```

In addition, == and != are supplied.

Reading from a *streambuf* is a lower-level operation than reading from an *istream*. Consequently, the *istreambuf_iterator* interface is messier than the *istream_iterator* interface. However, once the *istreambuf_iterator* is properly initialized, *, ++, and = have their usual meanings when used in the usual way.

The *proxy* type is an implementation-defined helper type that allows the postfix ++ to be implemented without imposing constraints on the *streambuf* implementation. A *proxy* holds the result value while the iterator is incremented:

```
template<class Ch, class Tr = char_traits<Ch> >
class istreambuf_iterator<Ch, Tr>::proxy {
        Ch val;
        basic_streambuf<Ch, Tr>* buf;

        proxy(Ch v, basic_streambuf<Ch, Tr>* b) :val(v), buf(b) { }
public:
        Ch operator*() { return val; }
};
```

An *ostreambuf_iterator* is defined similarly:

```
template <class Ch, class Tr = char_traits<Ch> >
class ostreambuf_iterator : public iterator<output_iterator_tag, void, void, void, void>{
public:
        typedef Ch char_type;
        typedef Tr traits_type;
```

```
        typedef basic_streambuf<Ch, Tr> streambuf_type;
        typedef basic_ostream<Ch, Tr> ostream_type;

        ostreambuf_iterator(ostream_type& os) throw();        // write to os's streambuf
        ostreambuf_iterator(streambuf_type*) throw();
        ostreambuf_iterator& operator=(Ch);

        ostreambuf_iterator& operator*();
        ostreambuf_iterator& operator++();
        ostreambuf_iterator& operator++(int);

        bool failed() const throw();                          // true if Tr::eof() seen
    };
```

19.3   Checked Iterators

A programmer can provide iterators in addition to those provided by the standard library. This is often necessary when providing a new kind of container, and sometimes a new kind of iterator is a good way to support a different way of using existing containers. As an example, I here describe an iterator that range checks access to its container.

Using standard containers reduces the amount of explicit memory management. Using standard algorithms reduces the amount of explicit addressing of elements in containers. Using the standard library together with language facilities that maintain type safety dramatically reduces run-time errors compared to traditional C coding styles. However, the standard library still relies on the programmer to avoid access beyond the limits of a container. If by accident element $x[x.size()+7]$ of some container x is accessed, then unpredictable – and usually bad – things happen. Using a range-checked *vector*, such as *Vec* (§3.7.2), helps in some cases. More cases can be handled by checking every access through an iterator.

To achieve this degree of checking without placing a serious notational burden on the programmer, we need checked iterators and a convenient way of attaching them to containers. To make a *Checked_iter*, we need a container and an iterator into that container. As for binders (§18.4.4.1), inserters (§19.2.4), etc., I provide functions for making a *Checked_iter*:

```
    template<class Cont, class Iter> Checked_iter<Cont, Iter> make_checked(Cont& c, Iter i)
    {
        return Checked_iter<Cont, Iter>(c, i);
    }

    template<class Cont> Checked_iter<Cont, typename Cont::iterator> make_checked(Cont& c)
    {
        return Checked_iter<Cont, typename Cont::iterator>(c, c.begin());
    }
```

These functions offer the notational convenience of deducing the types from arguments rather than stating those types explicitly. For example:

```
void f(vector<int>& v, const vector<int>& vc)
{
    typedef Checked_iter<vector<int>, vector<int>::iterator> CI;
    CI p1 = make_checked(v, v.begin()+3);
    CI p2 = make_checked(v);                // by default: point to first element

    typedef Checked_iter<const vector<int>, vector<int>::const_iterator> CIC;
    CIC p3 = make_checked(vc, vc.begin()+3);
    CIC p4 = make_checked(vc);

    const vector<int>& vv = v;
    CIC p5 = make_checked(v, vv.begin());
}
```

By default, *const* containers have *const* iterators, so their *Checked_iter*s must also be constant iterators. The iterator *p5* shows one way of getting a *const* iterator for a non-*const* iterator.

This demonstrates why *Checked_iter* needs two template parameters: one for the container type and one to express the *const*/non-*const* distinction.

The names of these *Checked_iter* types become fairly long and unwieldy, but that doesn't matter when iterators are used as arguments to a generic algorithm. For example:

```
template<class Iter> void mysort(Iter first, Iter last);

void f(vector<int>& c)
{
    try {
        mysort(make_checked(c), make_checked(c, c.end()));
    }
    catch (out_of_bounds) {
        cerr<<"oops: bug in mysort()\n";
        abort();
    }
}
```

An early version of such an algorithm is exactly where I would most suspect a range error so that using checked iterators would make sense.

The representation of a *Checked_iter* is a pointer to a container plus an iterator pointing into that container:

```
template<class Cont, class Iter = typename Cont::iterator>
class Checked_iter : public iterator_traits<Iter> {
    Iter curr; // iterator for current position
    Cont* c;   // pointer to current container

    // ...
};
```

Deriving from *iterator_traits* is one technique for defining the desired *typedef*s. The obvious alternative – deriving from *iterator* – would be verbose in this case (as it was for *reverse_iterator*; §19.2.5). Just as there is no requirement that an iterator should be a class, there is no requirement that iterators that are classes should be derived from *iterator*.

The *Checked_iter* operations are all fairly trivial:

```
template<class Cont, class Iter = typename Cont::iterator>
class Checked_iter : public iterator_traits<Iter> {
    // ...
public:
    void valid(Iter p) const
    {
        if (c->end() == p) return;
        for (Iter pp = c->begin(); pp!=c->end(); ++pp) if (pp == p) return;
        throw out_of_bounds();
    }

    friend bool operator==(const Checked_iter& i, const Checked_iter& j)
    {
        return i.c==j.c && i.curr==j.curr;
    }

    // No default initializer.
    // Use default copy constructor and copy assignment.

    Checked_iter(Cont& x, Iter p) : c(&x), curr(p) { valid(p); }
    Checked_iter(Cont& x) : c(&x), curr(x.begin()) { }

    reference operator*() const
    {
        if (curr==c->end()) throw out_of_bounds();
        return *curr;
    }

    pointer operator->() const
    {
        if (curr==c->end()) throw out_of_bounds();
        return &*curr;
    }

    Checked_iter operator+(difference_type d) const      // for random-access iterators only
    {
        if (c->end()-curr<d || d<curr-c->begin()) throw out_of_bounds();
        return Checked_iter(c,curr+d);
    }

    reference operator[](difference_type d) const        // for random-access iterators only
    {
        if (c->end()-curr<=d || d<curr-c->begin()) throw out_of_bounds();
        return curr[d];
    }

    Checked_iter& operator++()                           // prefix ++
    {
        if (curr == c->end()) throw out_of_bounds();
        ++curr;
        return *this;
    }
}
```

```
        Checked_iter operator++(int)                           // postfix ++
        {
                Checked_iter tmp = *this;
                ++*this;                                        // checked by prefix ++
                return tmp;
        }
        Checked_iter& operator--()                             // prefix --
        {
                if (curr == c->begin()) throw out_of_bounds();
                --curr;
                return *this;
        }
        Checked_iter operator--(int)                           // postfix --
        {
                Checked_iter tmp = *this;
                --*this;                                        // checked by prefix --
                return tmp;
        }
        difference_type index() const { return curr-c.begin(); }  // random-access only

        Iter unchecked() const { return curr; }

        // +, -, <, etc. (§19.6[6])
};
```

A *Checked_iter* can be initialized only for a particular iterator pointing into a particular container. In a full-blown implementation, a more efficient version of *valid*() should be provided for random-access iterators (§19.6[6]). Once a *Checked_iter* is initialized, every operation that changes its position is checked to make sure the iterator still points into the container. An attempt to make the iterator point outside the container causes an *out_of_bounds* exception to be thrown. For example:

```
        void f(list<string>& ls)
        {
                int count = 0;
                try {
                        Checked_iter< list<string> > p(ls, ls.begin());
                        while (true) {
                                ++p;            // sooner or later this will reach the end
                                ++count;
                        }
                }
                catch (out_of_bounds) {
                        cout << "overrun after " << count << " tries\n";
                }
        }
```

A *Checked_iter* knows which container it is pointing into. This allows it to catch some, but not all, cases in which iterators into a container have been invalidated by an operation on it (§16.3.6,

§16.3.8). To protect against all such cases, a different and more expensive iterator design would be needed (see §19.6[7]).

Note that postincrement (postfix ++) involves a temporary and preincrement does not. For this reason, it is best to prefer *++p* over *p++* for iterators.

Because a *Checked_iter* keeps a pointer to a container, it cannot be used for a built-in array directly. When necessary, a *c_array* (§17.5.4) can be used.

To complete the notion of checked iterators, we must make them trivial to use. There are two basic approaches:

[1] Define a checked container type that behaves like other containers, except that it provides only a limited set of constructors and its *begin* ( ) , *end* ( ) , etc., supply *Checked_iter*s rather than ordinary iterators.

[2] Define a handle that can be initialized by an arbitrary container and that provides checked access functions to its container (§19.6[8]).

The following template attaches checked iterators to a container:

```
template<class C> class Checked : public C {
public:
    explicit Checked(size_t n) : C(n) { }
    Checked() : C() { }

    typedef Checked_iter<C> iterator;
    typedef Checked_iter<C, C::const_iterator> const_iterator;

    iterator begin() { return iterator(*this, C::begin()); }
    iterator end() { return iterator(*this, C::end()); }
    const_iterator begin() const { return const_iterator(*this, C::begin()); }
    const_iterator end() const { return const_iterator(*this, C::end()); }

    typename C::reference_type operator[] (typename C::size_type n)
        { return Checked_iter<C>(*this)[n]; }

    C& base() { return *this; }       // get hold of the base container
};
```

This allows us to write:

```
Checked< vector<int> > vec(10);
Checked< list<double> > lst;

void f()
{
    int i1 = vec[5];           // ok
    int i2 = vec[15];          // throws out_of_bounds
    // ...
    mysort(vec.begin(), vec.end());
    copy(vec.begin(), vec.end(), lst.begin());
}
```

The apparently redundant *base* ( ) function is provided to make *Checked* ( )'s interface similar to that of handles to containers. Container handles don't usually provide an implicit conversion to their containers.

If a container is resized, iterators – including *Checked_iter*s – into it may become invalid. In that case, the *Checked_iter* can be re-initialized:

```
void  g (vector<int>& vi)
{
     Checked_iter< vector<int> > p (vi);
     // ..
     int  i = p.index ();                        // get current position
     vi.resize (100);                            // p becomes invalid
     p = Checked_iter< vector<int> > (vi, vi.begin () +i);   // restore current position
}
```

The old – and invalid – current position is lost. I provided *index* ( ) as a means of extracting an index, so that a *Checked_iter* could be restored.

19.3.1 Exceptions, Containers, and Algorithms

You could argue that using both standard algorithms and checked iterators is like wearing both belt and suspenders: either should keep you safe. However, experience shows that for many people and for many applications a dose of paranoia is reasonable – especially during times when a program goes through frequent changes that involve several people.

One way of using run-time checks is to keep them in the code only while debugging. The checks are then removed before the program is shipped. This practice has been compared to wearing a life jacket while paddling around close to the shore and then removing it before setting out onto the open sea. However, some uses of run-time checks do impose significant time and space overheads, so insisting on such checks at all times is not realistic. In any case, it is unwise to optimize without measurements, so before removing checks, do an experiment to see if worthwhile improvements actually emerge from doing so. To do such an experiment, we must be able to remove run-time checks easily (see §24.3.7.1). Once measurements have been done, we could remove the run-time testing from the most run-time critical – and hopefully most thoroughly tested – code and leave the rest of the code checked as a relatively cheap form of insurance.

Using a *Checked_iter* allows us to detect many mistakes. It does not, however, make it easy to recover from these errors. People rarely write code that is 100% robust against every ++, --, *, [ ], ->, and = potentially throwing an exception. This leaves us with two obvious strategies:

   [1] Catch exceptions close to the point from which they are thrown so that the writer of the exception handler has a decent chance of knowing what went wrong and can take appropriate action.

   [2] Catch the exception at a high level of a program, abandon a significant portion of a computation, and consider all data structures written to during the failed computation suspect (maybe there are no such data structures or maybe they can be sanity checked).

It is irresponsible to catch an exception from some unknown part of a program and proceed under the assumption that no data structure is left in an undesirable state, unless there is a further level of error handling that will catch subsequent errors. A simple example of this is when a final check (by computer or human) is done before the results are accepted. In such cases, it can be simpler and cheaper to proceed blithely rather than to try to catch every error at a low level. This would be an example of a simplification made possible by a multilevel error recovery scheme (§14.9).

19.4 Allocators

An *allocator* is used to insulate implementers of algorithms and containers that must allocate memory from the details of physical memory. An allocator provides standard ways of allocating and deallocating memory and standard names of types used as pointers and references. Like an iterator, an allocator is a pure abstraction. Any type that behaves like an allocator is an allocator.

The standard library provides a standard allocator intended to serve most users of a given implementation well. In addition, users can provide allocators that represent alternative views of memory. For example, we can write allocators that use shared memory, garbage-collected memory, memory from preallocated pools of objects (§19.4.2), etc.

The standard containers and algorithms obtain and access memory through the facilities provided by an allocator. Thus, by providing a new allocator we provide the standard containers with a way of using a new and different kind of memory.

19.4.1 The Standard Allocator

The standard *allocator* template from *<memory>* allocates memory using *operator new* ( ) (§6.2.6) and is by default used by all standard containers:

```
template <class T> class std::allocator {
public:
        typedef T value_type;
        typedef size_t size_type;
        typedef ptrdiff_t difference_type;

        typedef T* pointer;
        typedef const T* const_pointer;

        typedef T& reference;
        typedef const T& const_reference;

        pointer address(reference r) const { return &r; }
        const_pointer address(const_reference r) const { return &r; }

        allocator() throw();
        template <class U> allocator(const allocator<U>&) throw();
        ~allocator() throw();

        pointer allocate(size_type n, allocator<void>::const_pointer hint = 0);  // space for n Ts
        void deallocate(pointer p, size_type n);    // deallocate n Ts, don't destroy

        void construct(pointer p, const T& val) { new(p) T(val); }      // initialize *p by val
        void destroy(pointer p) { p->~T(); }                 // destroy *p but don't deallocate

        size_type max_size() const throw();

        template <class U>
        struct rebind { typedef allocator<U> other; };    // in effect: typedef allocator<U> other
};

template<class T> bool operator==(const allocator<T>&, const allocator<T>&) throw();
template<class T> bool operator!=(const allocator<T>&, const allocator<T>&) throw();
```

An *allocate* (*n*) operation allocates space for *n* objects that can be deallocated by a corresponding call of *deallocate* (*p*, *n*) . Note that *deallocate* ( ) also takes a number-of-elements argument *n*. This allows for close-to-optimal allocators that maintain only minimal information about allocated memory. On the other hand, such allocators require that the user always provide the right *n* when they *deallocate* ( ) .

The default *allocator* uses *operator new* (*size_t*) to obtain memory and *operator delete* (*void**) to free it. This implies that the *new_handler* ( ) might be called and *std* : : *bad_alloc* might be thrown in case of memory exhaustion (§6.2.6.2).

Note that *allocate* ( ) is not obliged to call a lower-level allocator each time. Often, a better strategy is for the allocator to maintain a free list of space ready to hand out with minimal time overhead (§19.4.2).

The optional *hint* argument to *allocate* ( ) is completely implementation-dependent. However, it is intended as a help to allocators for systems where locality is important. For example, an allocator might try to allocate space for related objects on the same page in a paging system. The type of the *hint* argument is the *pointer* from the ultra-simplified specialization:

```
template <> class allocator<void> {
public :
    typedef void* pointer;
    typedef const void* const_pointer;
    // note: no reference
    typedef void value_type;
    template <class  U>
    struct  rebind { typedef allocator<U> other; } ; // in effect: typedef allocator<U> other
} ;
```

The *allocator<void>* : : *pointer* type acts as a universal pointer type and is *void** for all standard allocators.

Unless the documentation for an allocator says otherwise, the user has two reasonable choices when calling *allocate* ( ) :

[1] Don't give a hint.

[2] Use a pointer to an object that is frequently used together with the new object as the hint; for example, the previous element in a sequence.

Allocators are intended to save implementers of containers from having to deal with raw memory directly. As an example, consider how a *vector* implementation might use memory:

```
template <class  T, class  A = allocator<T> > class  vector {
public :
    typedef typename  A : : pointer  iterator;
    // ...
private :
    A  alloc;        // allocator object
    iterator  v;     // pointer to elements
    // ...
```

```
public:
    explicit vector(size_type n, const T& val = T(), const A& a = A())
        : alloc(a)
    {
        v = alloc.allocate(n);
        for(iterator p = v; p<v+n; ++p) alloc.construct(p,val);
        // ...
    }

    void reserve(size_type n)
    {
        if (n<=capacity()) return;

        iterator p = alloc.allocate(n);
        iterator q = v;

        while (q<v+size()) {                        // copy existing elements
            alloc.construct(p++,*q);
            alloc.destroy(q++);
        }
        alloc.deallocate(v,capacity());             // free old space
        v = p-size();
        // ...
    }

    // ...
};
```

The *allocator* operations are expressed in terms of *pointer* and *reference typedef*s to give the user a chance to supply alternative types for accessing memory. This is very hard to do in general. For example, it is not possible to define a perfect reference type within the C++ language. However, language and library implementers can use these *typedef*s to support types that couldn't be provided by an ordinary user. An example would be an allocator that provided access to a persistent store. Another example would be a "long" pointer type for accessing main memory beyond what a default pointer (usually 32 bits) could address.

The ordinary user can supply an unusual pointer type to an allocator for specific uses. The equivalent cannot be done for references, but that may be an acceptable constraint for an experiment or a specialized system.

An allocator is designed to make it easy to handle objects of the type specified by its template parameter. However, most container implementations require objects of additional types. For example, the implementer of a *list* will need to allocate *Link* objects. Usually, such *Link*s must be allocated using their *list*'s allocator.

The curious *rebind* type is provided to allow an allocator to allocate objects of arbitrary type. Consider:

```
    typedef typename A::template rebind<Link>::other Link_alloc;  // "template;" see §C.13.6
```

If *A* is an *allocator*, then *rebind<Link>::other* is *typedef*'d to mean *allocator<Link>*, so the previous *typedef* is an indirect way of saying:

```
    typedef allocator<Link> Link_alloc;
```

The indirection frees us from having to mention *allocator* directly. It expresses the *Link_alloc* type in terms of a template parameter *A*. For example:

```
template <class T, class A = allocator<T> > class list {
private:
        class Link { /* ... */ } ;

        typedef typename A::rebind<Link>::other Link_alloc;       // allocator<Link>

        Link_alloc a;    // link allocator
        A alloc;         // list allocator
        // ...
public:
        typedef typename A::pointer iterator;
        // ...

        iterator insert(iterator pos, const T& x )
        {
                Link_alloc::pointer p = a.allocate(1);       // get a Link
                // ...
        }
        // ...
};
```

Link is a member of *list*, so it too is parameterized by an allocator (§13.2.1). Consequently, *Link*s from *list*s with different allocators are of different types, just like the *list*s themselves (§17.3.3).

19.4.2 A User-Defined Allocator

Implementers of containers often *allocate*() and *deallocate*() objects one at a time. For a naive implementation of *allocate*(), this implies lots of calls of operator *new*, and not all implementations of operator *new* are efficient when used like that. As an example of a user-defined allocator, I present a scheme for using pools of fixed-sized pieces of memory from which the allocator can *allocate*() more efficiently than can a conventional and more general *operator new*().

I happen to have a pool allocator that does approximately the right thing, but it has the wrong interface (because it was designed years before allocators were invented). This *Pool* class implements the notion of a pool of fixed-sized elements from which a user can do fast allocations and deallocations. It is a low-level type that deals with memory directly and worries about alignment:

```
class Pool {
        struct Link { Link* next; } ;

        struct Chunk {
                enum { size = 8*1024-16 } ;       // slightly less than 8K so that a chunk will fit in 8K
                char mem[size];                   // allocation area first to get stringent alignment
                Chunk* next;
        } ;

        Chunk* chunks;
        const unsigned int esize;
        Link* head;
```

```
        Pool (Pool&);                  // copy protection
        void operator= (Pool&);        // copy protection
        void grow ();                  // make pool larger
public:
        Pool (unsigned int n);         // n is the size of elements
        ~Pool ();

        void* alloc ();                // allocate one element
        void free (void* b);           // put an element back into the pool
};

inline void* Pool::alloc ()
{
        if (head==0) grow ();
        Link* p = head;                // return first element
        head = p->next;
        return p;
}

inline void Pool::free (void* b)
{
        Link* p = static_cast<Link*> (b);
        p->next = head;                // put b back as first element
        head = p;
}

Pool::Pool (unsigned int sz)
        : esize (sz<sizeof(Link) ?sizeof(Link) :sz)
{
        head = 0;
        chunks = 0;
}

Pool::~Pool ()  // free all chunks
{
        Chunk* n = chunks;
        while (n) {
                Chunk* p = n;
                n = n->next;
                delete p;
        }
}

void Pool::grow ()    // allocate new 'chunk,' organize it as a linked list of elements of size 'esize'
{
        Chunk* n = new Chunk;
        n->next = chunks;
        chunks = n;

        const int nelem = Chunk::size/esize;
        char* start = n->mem;
        char* last = &start[ (nelem-1) *esize];
```

```
for (char* p = start; p<last; p+=esize)
    reinterpret_cast<Link*>(p)->next = reinterpret_cast<Link*>(p+esize);
reinterpret_cast<Link*>(last)->next = 0;
head = reinterpret_cast<Link*>(start);
}
```

To add a touch of realism, I'll use *Pool* unchanged as part of the implementation of my allocator, rather than rewrite it to give it the right interface. The pool allocator is intended for fast allocation and deallocation of single elements and that is what my *Pool* class supports. Extending this implementation to handle allocations of arbitrary numbers of objects and to objects of arbitrary size (as required by *rebind*) is left as an exercise (§19.6[9]).

Given *Pool*, the definition of *Pool_alloc* is trivial;

```
template <class T> class Pool_alloc {
private:
    static Pool mem;       // pool of elements of sizeof(T)
public:
    // like the standard allocator (§19.4.1)
};

template <class T> Pool Pool_alloc<T>::mem(sizeof(T));

template <class T> Pool_alloc<T>::Pool_alloc() { }

template <class T>
T* Pool_alloc<T>::allocate(size_type n, void* = 0)
{
    if (n == 1) return static_cast<T*>(mem.alloc());
    // ...
}

template <class T>
void Pool_alloc<T>::deallocate(pointer p, size_type n)
{
    if (n == 1) {
        mem.free(p);
        return;
    }
    // ...
}
```

This allocator can now be used in the obvious way:

```
vector< int, Pool_alloc<int> > v;
map<string, number, Pool_alloc< pair<const string, number> > > m;

// use exactly as usual

vector<int> v2 = v;    // error: different allocator parameters
```

I chose to make the *Pool* for a *Pool_alloc* static because of a restriction that the standard library imposes on allocators used by the standard containers: the implementation of a standard container is allowed to treat every object of its allocator type as equivalent. This can lead to significant performance advantages. For example, because of this restriction, memory need not be set aside for allocators in *Link* objects (which are typically parameterized by the allocator of the container for which they are *Link*s; §19.4.1), and operations that may access elements of two sequences (such as *swap*()) need not check whether the objects manipulated all have the same allocator. However, the restriction does imply that such allocators cannot use per-object data.

Before applying this kind of optimization, make sure that it is necessary. I expect that many default *allocator*s will implement exactly this kind of classic C++ optimization − thus saving you the bother.

19.4.3 Generalized Allocators

An *allocator* is a simplified and optimized variant of the idea of passing information to a container through a template parameter (§13.4.1, §16.2.3). For example, it makes sense to require that every element in a container is allocated by the container's allocator. However, if two *list*s of the same type were allowed to have different allocators, then *splice*() (§17.2.2.1) couldn't be implemented through relinking. Instead, *splice*() would have to be defined in terms of copying of elements to protect against the rare cases in which we want to splice elements from a *list* with one allocator into another with a different allocator of the same allocator type. Similarly, if allocators were allowed to be perfectly general, the *rebind* mechanism that allows an allocator to allocate elements of arbitrary types would have to be more elaborate. Consequently, a standard allocator is assumed to hold no per-object data and an implementation of a standard may take advantage of that.

Surprisingly, the apparently Draconian restriction against per-object information in allocators is not particularly serious. Most allocators do not need per-object data and can be made to run faster without such data. Allocators can still hold data on a per-allocator-type basis. If separate data is needed, separate allocator types can be used. For example:

```
template<class T, class D> class My_alloc {      // allocator for T implemented using D
    D d;        // data needed for My_alloc<T,D>
    // ...
};

typedef My_alloc<int, Persistent_info> Persistent;
typedef My_alloc<int, Shared_info> Shared;
typedef My_alloc<int, Default_info> Default;

list<int, Persistent> lst1;
list<int, Shared> lst2;
list<int, Default> lst3;
```

The lists *lst1*, *lst2*, and *lst3* are of different types. Therefore, we must use general algorithms (Chapter 18) when operating on two of these lists rather than specialized list operations (§17.2.2.1). This implies that copying rather than relinking is done, so having different allocators poses no problems.

The restriction against per-object data in allocators is imposed because of the stringent demands on the run-time and space efficiency of the standard library. For example, the space overhead of allocator data for a list probably wouldn't be significant. However, it could be serious if each link of a list suffered overhead.

Consider how the allocator technique could be used when the efficiency constraints of the standard library don't apply. This would be the case for a nonstandard library that wasn't meant to deliver high performance for essentially every data structure and every type in a program and for some special-purpose implementations of the standard library. In such cases, an allocator can be used to carry the kind of information that often inhabits universal base classes (§16.2.2). For example, an allocator could be designed to answer requests about where its objects are allocated, present data representing object layout, and answer questions such as ''is this element in this container?'' It could also provide controls for a container that acts as a cache for memory in permanent storage, provide association between the container and other objects, etc.

In this way, arbitrary services can be provided transparently to the ordinary container operations. However, it is best to distinguish between issues relating to storage of data and issues of the use of data. The latter do not belong in a generalized allocator, but they could be provided through a separate template argument.

19.4.4 Uninitialized Memory

In addition to the standard *allocator*, the *<memory>* header provides a few functions for dealing with uninitialized memory. They share the dangerous and occasionally essential property of using a type name *T* to refer to space sufficient to hold an object of type *T* rather than to a properly constructed object of type *T*.

The library provides three ways to copy values into uninitialized space:

```
template <class In, class For>
For uninitialized_copy(In first, In last, For res)      // copy into res
{
        typedef typename iterator_traits<For>::value_type V;

        while (first != last)
                new (static_cast<void*>(&*res++)) V(*first++);       // construct in res (§10.4.11)
        return res;
}
template <class For, class T>
void uninitialized_fill(For first, For last, const T& val)          // copy into [first,last)
{
        typedef typename iterator_traits<For>::value_type V;

        while (first != last) new (static_cast<void*>(&*first++)) V(val);       // construct in first
}
template <class For, class Size, class T>
void uninitialized_fill_n(For first, Size n, const T& val)          // copy into [first,first+n)
{
        typedef typename iterator_traits<For>::value_type V;

        while (n--) new (static_cast<void*>(&*first++)) V(val); // construct in first
}
```

These functions are intended primarily for implementers of containers and algorithms. For example, *reserve()* and *resize()* (§16.3.8) are most easily implemented using these functions

(§19.6[10]). It would clearly be most unfortunate if an uninitialized object escaped from the internals of a container into the hands of general users. See also §E.4.4.

Algorithms often require temporary space to perform acceptably. Often, such temporary space is best allocated in one operation but not initialized until a particular location is actually needed. Consequently, the library provides a pair of functions for allocating and deallocating uninitialized space:

```
template <class T> pair<T*, ptrdiff_t> get_temporary_buffer(ptrdiff_t); // allocate, don't initialize
template <class T> void return_temporary_buffer(T*);                    // deallocate, don't destroy
```

A *get_temporary_buffer<X>* (*n*) operation tries to allocate space for *n* or more objects of type *X*. If it succeeds in allocating some memory, it returns a pointer to the first uninitialized space and the number of objects of type *X* that will fit into that space; otherwise, the *second* value of the pair is zero. The idea is that a system may keep a number of fixed-sized buffers ready for fast allocation so that requesting space for *n* objects may yield space for more than *n*. It may also yield less, however, so one way of using *get_temporary_buffer* () is to optimistically ask for a lot and then use what happens to be available.

A buffer obtained by *get_temporary_buffer* () must be freed for other use by a call of *return_temporary_buffer* (). Just as *get_temporary_buffer* () allocates without constructing, *return_temporary_buffer* () frees without destroying. Because *get_temporary_buffer* () is low-level and likely to be optimized for managing temporary buffers, it should not be used as an alternative to *new* or *allocator* :: *allocate* () for obtaining longer-term storage.

The standard algorithms that write into a sequence assume that the elements of that sequence have been previously initialized. That is, the algorithms use assignment rather than copy construction for writing. Consequently, we cannot use uninitialized memory as the immediate target of an algorithm. This can be unfortunate because assignment can be significantly more expensive than initialization. Besides, we are not interested in the values we are about to overwrite anyway (or we wouldn't be overwriting them). The solution is to use a *raw_storage_iterator* from <*memory*> that initializes instead of assigns:

```
template <class Out, class T>
class raw_storage_iterator : public iterator<output_iterator_tag, void, void, void, void> {
    Out p;
public:
    explicit raw_storage_iterator(Out pp) : p(pp) { }
    raw_storage_iterator& operator*() { return *this; }
    raw_storage_iterator& operator=(const T& val) {
        T* pp = &*p;
        new(pp) T(val);      // place val in pp (§10.4.11)
        return *this;
    }
    raw_storage_iterator& operator++() {++p; return *this; }
    raw_storage_iterator operator++(int) {
        raw_storage_iterator t = *this;
        ++p;
        return t;
    }
};
```

For example, we might write a template that copies the contents of a *vector* into a buffer:

```
template<class T, class A> T* temporary_dup(vector<T,A>& v)
{
        pair<T*,ptrdiff_t> p = get_temporary_buffer<T>(v.size());
        if (p.second < v.size()) {        // check that enough memory was available
                if (p.first != 0) return_temporary_buffer(p.first);
                return 0;
        }
        copy(v.begin(),v.end(),raw_storage_iterator<T*,T>(p.first));
        return p.first;
}
```

Had *new* been used instead of *get_temporary_buffer*(), initialization would have been done. Once initialization is avoided, the *raw_storage_iterator* becomes necessary for dealing with the uninitialized space. In this example, the caller of *temporary_dup*() is responsible for calling *return_temporary_buffer*() for the pointer it received.

19.4.5 Dynamic Memory

The facilities used to implement the *new* and *delete* operators are declared in *<new>*:

```
class bad_alloc : public exception { /* ... */ };

struct nothrow_t {};
extern const nothrow_t nothrow;        // indicator for allocation that doesn't throw exceptions

typedef void (*new_handler)();
new_handler set_new_handler(new_handler new_p) throw();

void* operator new(size_t) throw(bad_alloc);
void operator delete(void*) throw();

void* operator new(size_t, const nothrow_t&) throw();
void operator delete(void*, const nothrow_t&) throw();

void* operator new[](size_t) throw(bad_alloc);
void operator delete[](void*) throw();

void* operator new[](size_t, const nothrow_t&) throw();
void operator delete[](void*, const nothrow_t&) throw();

void* operator new (size_t, void* p) throw() { return p; }      // placement (§10.4.11)
void operator delete (void* p, void*) throw() { }    // do nothing

void* operator new[](size_t, void* p) throw() { return p; }
void operator delete[](void* p, void*) throw() { } // do nothing
```

An *operator new*() or *operator new*[]() with an empty *exception-specification* (§14.6) cannot signal memory exhaustion by throwing *std::bad_alloc*. Instead, if allocation fails they return *0*. A *new-expression* (§6.2.6.2) tests the value returned by an allocator with an empty *exception-specification*; if the returned value is *0*, no constructor is invoked and the *new-expression* returns *0*. In particular, the *nothrow* allocators return *0* to indicate failure to allocate rather than throwing *bad_alloc*. For example:

```
void f()
{
    int* p = new int[100000]; // may throw bad_alloc

    if (int* q = new(nothrow) int[100000]) { // will not throw exception
        // allocation succeeded
    }
    else {
        // allocation failed
    }
}
```

This allows us to use pre-exception error-handling strategies for allocation.

19.4.6 C-Style Allocation

From C, C++ inherited a functional interface to dynamic memory. It can be found in *<cstdlib>*:

```
void* malloc(size_t s);          // allocate s bytes
void* calloc(size_t n, size_t s); // allocate n times s bytes initialized to 0
void free(void* p);              // free space allocated by malloc() or calloc()
void* realloc(void* p, size_t s); // change the size of the array pointed to by p to s;
                                  // if that cannot be done, allocate s bytes, copy
                                  // the array pointed to by p to it, and free p
```

These functions should be avoided in favor of *new*, *delete*, and standard containers. These functions deal with uninitialized memory. In particular, *free*() does not invoke destructors for the memory it frees. An implementation of *new* and *delete* may use these functions, but there is no guarantee that it does. For example, allocating an object using *new* and deleting it using *free*() is asking for trouble. If you feel the need to use *realloc*(), consider relying on a standard container instead; doing that is usually simpler and just as efficient (§16.3.5).

The library also provides a set of functions intended for efficient manipulation of bytes. Because C originally accessed untyped bytes through *char** pointers, these functions are found in *<cstring>*. The *void** pointers are treated as if they were *char** pointers within these functions:

```
void* memcpy(void* p, const void* q, size_t n);   // copy non-overlapping areas
void* memmove(void* p, const void* q, size_t n);  // copy potentially overlapping areas
```

Like *strcpy*() (§20.4.1), these functions copy *n* bytes from *q* to *p* and return *p*. The ranges copied by *memmove*() may overlap. However, *memcpy*() assumes that the ranges do not overlap and is usually optimized to take advantage of that assumption. Similarly:

```
void* memchr(const void* p, int b, size_t n); // like strchr() (§20.4.1): find b in p[0]..p[n-1]
int memcmp(const void* p, const void* q, size_t n); // like strcmp(): compare byte sequences
void* memset(void* p, int b, size_t n);       // set n bytes to b, return p
```

Many implementations provide highly optimized versions of these functions.

19.5 Advice

[1] When writing an algorithm, decide which kind of iterator is needed to provide acceptable effi-
     ciency and express the algorithm using the operators supported by that kind of iterator (only);
     §19.2.1.
[2] Use overloading to provide more-efficient implementations of an algorithm when given as
     arguments iterators that offer more than minimal support for the algorithm; §19.2.3.
[3] Use *iterator_traits* to express suitable algorithms for different iterator categories; §19.2.2.
[4] Remember to use ++ between accesses of *istream_iterator*s and *ostream_iterator*s; §19.2.6.
[5] Use inserters to avoid container overflow; §19.2.4.
[6] Use extra checking during debugging and remove checking later only where necessary;
     §19.3.1.
[7] Prefer *++p* to *p++*; §19.3.
[8] Use uninitialized memory to improve the performance of algorithms that expand data struc-
     tures; §19.4.4.
[9] Use temporary buffers to improve the performance of algorithms that require temporary data
     structures; §19.4.4.
[10] Think twice before writing your own allocator; §19.4.
[11] Avoid *malloc* ( ) , *free* ( ) , *realloc* ( ) , etc.; §19.4.6.
[12] You can simulate a *typedef* of a template by the technique used for *rebind*; §19.4.1.

19.6 Exercises

1. (∗1.5) Implement *reverse* ( ) from §18.6.7. Hint: See §19.2.3.
2. (∗1.5) Write an output iterator, *Sink*, that doesn't actually write anywhere. When can *Sink* be
    useful?
3. (∗2) Implement *reverse_iterator* (§19.2.5).
4. (∗1.5) Implement *ostream_iterator* (§19.2.6).
5. (∗2) Implement *istream_iterator* (§19.2.6).
6. (∗2.5) Complete *Checked_iter* (§19.3).
7. (∗2.5) Redesign *Checked_iter* to check for invalidated iterators.
8. (∗2) Design and implement a handle class that can act as a proxy for a container by providing a
    complete container interface to its users. Its implementation should consist of a pointer to a
    container plus implementations of container operations that do range checking.
9. (∗2.5) Complete or reimplement *Pool_alloc* (§19.4.2) so that it provides all of the facilities of
    the standard library *allocator* (§19.4.1). Compare the performance of *allocator* and
    Pool_alloc to see if there is any reason to use a *Pool_alloc* on your system.
10. (∗2.5) Implement *vector* using allocators rather than *new* and *delete*.

Strings

Prefer the standard to the offbeat.
− Strunk & White

Strings — characters — *char_traits* — *basic_string* — iterators — element access — constructors — error handling — assignment — conversions — comparisons — insertion — concatenation — find and replace — size and capacity — string I/O — C-style strings — character classification — C library functions — advice — exercises.

20.1 Introduction

A string is a sequence of characters. The standard library *string* provides string manipulation operations such as subscripting (§20.3.3), assignment (§20.3.6), comparison (§20.3.8), appending (§20.3.9), concatenation (§20.3.10), and searching for substrings (§20.3.11). No general substring facility is provided by the standard, so one is provided here as an example of standard string use (§20.3.11). A standard string can be a string of essentially any kind of character (§20.2).

Experience shows that it is impossible to design the perfect *string*. People's taste, expectations, and needs differ too much for that. So, the standard library *string* isn't ideal. I would have made some design decisions differently, and so would you. However, it serves many needs well, auxiliary functions to serve further needs are easily provided, and *std::string* is generally known and available. In most cases, these factors are more important than any minor improvement we could provide. Writing string classes has great educational value (§11.12, §13.2), but for code meant to be widely used, the standard library *string* is the one to use.

From C, C++ inherited the notion of strings as zero-terminated arrays of *char* and a set of functions for manipulating such C-style strings (§20.4.1).

20.2 Characters

''Character'' is itself an interesting concept. Consider the character *C*. The *C* that you see as a curved line on the page (or screen), I typed into my computer many months ago. There, it lives as the numeric value *67* in an 8-bit byte. It is the third letter in the Latin alphabet, the usual abbreviation for the sixth atom (Carbon), and, incidentally, the name of a programming language (§1.6). What matters in the context of programming with strings is that there is a correspondence between squiggles with conventional meaning, called characters, and numeric values. To complicate matters, the same character can have different numeric values in different character sets, not every character set has values for every character, and many different character sets are in common use. A character set is a mapping between a character (some conventional symbol) and an integer value.

C++ programmers usually assume that the standard American character set (ASCII) is available, but C++ makes allowances for the possibility that some characters may be missing in a programmer's environment. For example, in the absence of characters such as [and {, keywords and digraphs can be used (§C.3.1).

Character sets with characters not in ASCII offer a greater challenge. Languages such as Chinese, Danish, French, Icelandic, and Japanese cannot be written properly using ASCII only. Worse, the character sets used for these languages can be mutually incompatible. For example, the characters used for European languages using Latin alphabets *almost* fit into a 256-character character set. Unfortunately, different sets are still used for different languages and some different characters have ended up with the same integer value. For example, French (using Latin1) doesn't coexist well with Icelandic (which therefore requires Latin2). Ambitious attempts to present every character known to man in a single character set have helped a lot, but even 16-bit character sets – such as Unicode – are not enough to satisfy everyone. The 32-bit character sets that could – as far as I know – hold every character are not widely used.

Basically, the C++ approach is to allow a programmer to use any character set as the character type in strings. An extended character set or a portable numeric encoding can be used (§C.3.3).

20.2.1 Character Traits

As shown in §13.2, a string can, in principle, use any type with proper copy operations as its character type. However, efficiency can be improved and implementations can be simplified for types that don't have user-defined copy operations. Consequently, the standard *string* requires that a type used as its character type does not have user-defined copy operations. This also helps to make I/O of strings simple and efficient.

The properties of a character type are defined by its *char_traits*. A *char_traits* is a specialization of the template:

```
template<class Ch> struct char_traits { };
```

All *char_traits* are defined in *std*, and the standard ones are presented in *<string>*. The general *char_traits* itself has no properties; only *char_traits* specializations for a particular character type have. Consider *char_traits<char>*:

```
template<> struct char_traits<char> {        // char_traits operations should not throw exceptions
    typedef char char_type;          // type of character
```

```
        static void assign(char_type&, const char_type&);          // = for char_type

        // integer representation of characters:

        typedef int int_type;              // type of integer value of character

        static char_type to_char_type(const int_type&);          // int to char conversion
        static int_type to_int_type(const char_type&);           // char to int conversion
        static bool eq_int_type(const int_type&, const int_type&); // ==

        // char_type comparisons:

        static bool eq(const char_type&, const char_type&);       // ==
        static bool lt(const char_type&, const char_type&);       // <

        // operations on s[n] arrays:

        static char_type* move(char_type* s, const char_type* s2, size_t n);
        static char_type* copy(char_type* s, const char_type* s2, size_t n);
        static char_type* assign(char_type* s, size_t n, char_type a);

        static int compare(const char_type* s, const char_type* s2, size_t n);
        static size_t length(const char_type*);
        static const char_type* find(const char_type* s, int n, const char_type&);

        // I/O related:

        typedef streamoff off_type;       // offset in stream
        typedef streampos pos_type;       // position in stream
        typedef mbstate_t state_type;     // multi-byte stream state

        static int_type eof();                      // end-of-file
        static int_type not_eof(const int_type& i); // i unless i equals eof(); if not any value!=eof()
        static state_type get_state(pos_type p);    // multibyte conversion state of character in p
    };
```

The implementation of the standard string template, *basic_string* (§20.3), relies on these types and functions. A type used as a character type for *basic_string* must provide a *char_traits* specialization that supplies them all.

For a type to be a *char_type*, it must be possible to obtain an integer value corresponding to each character. The type of that integer is *int_type*, and the conversion between it and the *char_type* is done by *to_char_type*() and *to_int_type*(). For a *char*, this conversion is trivial.

Both *move*(*s*,*s2*,*n*) and *copy*(*s*,*s2*,*n*) copy *n* characters from *s2* to *s* using *assign*(*s*[*i*],*s2*[*i*]). The difference is that *move*() works correctly even if *s2* is in the [*s*,*s+n*[range. Thus, *copy*() can be faster. This mirrors the standard C library functions *memcpy*() and *memmove*() (§19.4.6). A call *assign*(*s*,*n*,*x*) assigns *n* copies of *x* into *s* using *assign*(*s*[*i*],*x*).

The *compare*() function uses *lt*() and *eq*() to compare characters. It returns an *int*, where *0* represents an exact match, a negative number means that its first argument comes lexicographically before the second, and a positive number means that its first argument comes after its second. This use of return values mirrors the standard C library function *strcmp*() (§20.4.1).

The I/O-related functions are used by the implementation of low-level I/O (§21.6.4).

A wide character − that is, an object of type *wchar_t* (§4.3) − is like a *char*, except that it takes up two or more bytes. The properties of a *wchar_t* are described by *char_traits<wchar_t>*:

```
template<> struct char_traits<wchar_t> {
    typedef wchar_t char_type;
    typedef wint_t int_type;
    typedef wstreamoff off_type;
    typedef wstreampos pos_type;

    // like char_traits<char>
};
```

A *wchar_t* is typically used to hold characters of a 16-bit character set such as Unicode.

20.3 Basic_string

The standard library string facilities are based on the template *basic_string* that provides member types and operations similar to those provided by standard containers (§16.3):

```
template<class Ch, class Tr = char_traits<Ch>, class A = allocator<Ch> >
class std::basic_string {
public:
    // ...
};
```

This template and its associated facilities are defined in namespace *std* and presented by *<string>*.

Two *typedef*s provide conventional names for common string types:

```
typedef basic_string<char> string;
typedef basic_string<wchar_t> wstring;
```

The *basic_string* is similar to *vector* (§16.3), except that *basic_string* provides some typical string operations, such as searching for substrings, instead of the complete set of operations offered by *vector*. A *string* is unlikely to be implemented by a simple array or *vector*. Many common uses of strings are better served by implementations that minimize copying, use no free store for short strings, allow for simple modification of longer strings, etc. (see §20.6[12]). The number of *string* functions reflects the importance of string manipulation and also the fact that some machines provide specialized hardware instructions for string manipulation. Such functions are most easily utilized by a library implementer if there is a standard library function with similar semantics.

Like other standard library types, a *basic_string<T>* is a concrete type (§2.5.3, §10.3) without virtual functions. It can be used as a member when designing more sophisticated text manipulation classes, but it is not intended to be a base for derived classes (§25.2.1; see also §20.6[10]).

20.3.1 Types

Like *vector*, *basic_string* makes its related types available through a set of member type names:

```
template<class Ch, class Tr = char_traits<Ch>, class A = allocator<Ch> >
class basic_string {
public:
    // types (much like vector, list, etc.: §16.3.1):
```

```
        typedef Tr traits_type;              // specific to basic_string

        typedef typename Tr::char_type value_type;
        typedef A allocator_type;
        typedef typename A::size_type size_type;
        typedef typename A::difference_type difference_type;

        typedef typename A::reference reference;
        typedef typename A::const_reference const_reference;
        typedef typename A::pointer pointer;
        typedef typename A::const_pointer const_pointer;

        typedef implementation_defined iterator;
        typedef implementation_defined const_iterator;

        typedef std::reverse_iterator<iterator> reverse_iterator;
        typedef std::reverse_iterator<const_iterator> const_reverse_iterator;

        // ...
};
```

The *basic_string* notion supports strings of many kinds of characters in addition to the simple *basic_string<char>* known as *string*. For example:

```
typedef basic_string<unsigned char> Ustring;

struct Jchar { /* ... */ };          // Japanese character type
typedef basic_string<Jchar> Jstring;
```

Strings of such characters can be used just like strings of *char* as far as the semantics of the characters allows. For example:

```
Ustring first_word(const Ustring& us)
{
        Ustring::size_type pos = us.find(' ');     // see §20.3.11
        return Ustring(us,0,pos);                  // see §20.3.4
}

Jstring first_word(const Jstring& js)
{
        Jstring::size_type pos = js.find(' ');     // see §20.3.11
        return Jstring(js,0,pos);                  // see §20.3.4
}
```

Naturally, templates that take string arguments can also be used:

```
template<class S> S first_word(const S& s)
{
        typename S::size_type pos = s.find(' '); // see §20.3.11
        return S(s,0,pos);                       // see §20.3.4
}
```

A *basic_string<Ch>* can contain any character of the set *Ch*. In particular, *string* can contain a *0* (zero). The "character type" *Ch* must behave like a character. In particular, it may not have a user-specified copy constructor, destructors, or copy assignments.

20.3.2 Iterators

Like other containers, a *string* provides iterators for ordinary and reverse iteration:

```
template<class Ch, class Tr = char_traits<Ch>, class A = allocator<Ch> >
class basic_string {
public:
        // ...
        // iterators (like vector, list, etc.: §16.3.2):

        iterator begin();
        const_iterator begin() const;
        iterator end();
        const_iterator end() const;

        reverse_iterator rbegin();
        const_reverse_iterator rbegin() const;
        reverse_iterator rend();
        const_reverse_iterator rend() const;

        // ...
};
```

Because *string* has the required member types and the functions for obtaining iterators, *string*s can be used together with the standard algorithms (Chapter 18). For example:

```
void f(string& s)
{
        string::iterator p = find(s.begin(),s.end(),'a');
        // ...
}
```

The most common operations on *string*s are supplied directly by *string*. Hopefully, these versions will be optimized for *string*s beyond what would be easy to do for general algorithms.

The standard algorithms (Chapter 18) are not as useful for strings as one might think. General algorithms tend to assume that the elements of a container are meaningful in isolation. This is typically not the case for a string. The meaning of a string is encoded in its exact sequence of characters. Thus, sorting a string (that is, sorting the characters in a string) destroys its meaning, whereas sorting a general container typically makes it more useful.

The *string* iterators are not range checked.

20.3.3 Element Access

Individual characters of a *string* can be accessed through subscripting:

```
template<class Ch, class Tr = char_traits<Ch>, class A = allocator<Ch> >
class basic_string {
public:
        // ...
        // element access (like vector: §16.3.3):
```

```
        const_reference operator[](size_type n) const;  // unchecked access
        reference operator[](size_type n);

        const_reference at(size_type n) const;                    // checked access
        reference at(size_type n);

        // ...
};
```

Out-of-range access causes *at()* to throw an *out_of_range*.

Compared to *vector*, *string* lacks *front()* and *back()*. To refer to the first and the last character of a *string*, we must say *s[0]* and *s[s.length()-1]*, respectively. The pointer/array equivalence (§5.3) doesn't hold for *strings*. If *s* is a *string*, &*s[0]* is not the same as *s*.

20.3.4 Constructors

The set of initialization and copy operations for a *string* differs from what is provided for other containers (§16.3.4) in many details:

```
template<class Ch, class Tr = char_traits<Ch>, class A = allocator<Ch> >
class basic_string {
public:
        // ...
        // constructors, etc. (a bit like vector and list: §16.3.4):

        explicit basic_string(const A& a = A());
        basic_string(const basic_string& s,
                    size_type pos = 0, size_type n = npos, const A& a = A());
        basic_string(const Ch* p, size_type n, const A& a = A());
        basic_string(const Ch* p, const A& a = A());
        basic_string(size_type n, Ch c, const A& a = A());
        template<class In> basic_string(In first, In last, const A& a = A());

        ~basic_string();

        static const size_type npos;       // "all characters" marker

        // ...
};
```

A *string* can be initialized by a C-style string, by another *string*, by part of a C-style string, by part of a *string*, or from a sequence of characters. However, a *string* cannot be initialized by a character or an integer:

```
void f(char* p, vector<char>&v)
{
        string s0;                         // the empty string
        string s00 = "";                   // also the empty string

        string s1 = 'a';                   // error: no conversion from char to string
        string s2 = 7;                     // error: no conversion from int to string
        string s3(7);                      // error: no constructor taking one int argument
```

```
    string  s4(7,'a');          // 7 copies of 'a'; that is "aaaaaaa"

    string  s5 = "Frodo";       // copy of "Frodo"
    string  s6 = s5;            // copy of s5

    string  s7(s5,3,2);         // s5[3] and s5[4]; that is "do"
    string  s8(p+7,3);          // p[7], p[8], and p[9]
    string  s9(p,7,3);          // string(string(p),7,3), possibly expensive

    string  s10(v.begin(),v.end());      // copy all characters from v
}
```

Characters are numbered starting at position *0* so that a string is a sequence of characters numbered *0* to *length* ( ) *–1*.

The *length* ( ) of a string is simply a synonym for its *size* ( ); both functions return the number of characters in the string. Note that they do not count a C-string-style, zero-terminator character (§20.4.1). An implementation of **basic_string** stores its length rather than relying on a terminator.

Substrings are expressed as a character position plus a number of characters. The default value **npos** is initialized to the largest possible value and used to mean ''all of the elements.''

There is no constructor that creates a string of *n* unspecified characters. The closest we come to that is the constructor that makes a string of *n* copies of a given character. The absence of a constructor that takes a single character only and of a constructor that takes a number of elements only allows the compiler to detect mistakes such as the definitions of *s2* and *s3* in the previous example.

The copy constructor is the constructor taking four arguments. Three of those arguments have defaults. For efficiency, that constructor could be implemented as two separate constructors. The user wouldn't be able to tell without actually looking at the generated code.

The constructor that is a template member is the most general. It allows a string to be initialized with values from an arbitrary sequence. In particular, it allows a string to be initialized with elements of a different character type as long as a conversion exists. For example:

```
    void f(string s)
    {
        wstring  ws(s.begin(),s.end());      // copy all characters from s
        // ...
    }
```

Each *wchar_t* in *ws* is initialized by its corresponding *char* from *s*.

20.3.5 Errors

Often, strings are simply read, written, printed, stored, compared, copied, etc. This causes no problems, or, at worst, performance problems. However, once we start manipulating individual substrings and characters to compose new string values from existing ones, we sooner or later make mistakes that could cause us to write beyond the end of a string.

For explicit access to individual characters, *at* ( ) checks and throws *out_of_range* ( ) if we try to access beyond the end of the string; [ ] does not.

Most string operations take a character position plus a number of characters. A position larger than the size of the string throws an *out_of_range* exception. A ''too large'' character count is simply taken to be equivalent to ''the rest'' of the characters. For example:

```
void f()
{
    string  s = "Snobol4";
    string  s2(s,100,2);  // character position beyond end of string: throw out_of_range()
    string  s3(s,2,100);  // character count too large: equivalent to s3(s,2,s.size()-2)
    string  s4(s,2,string::npos);    // the characters starting from s[2]
}
```

Thus, "too large" positions are to be avoided, but "too large" character counts are useful. In fact, *npos* is really just the largest possible value for *size_type*.

We could try to give a negative position or character count:

```
void  g(string& s)
{
    string  s5(s,-2,3);  // large position!: throw out_of_range()
    string  s6(s,3,-2);  // large character count!: ok
}
```

However, the *size_type* used to represent positions and counts is an *unsigned* type, so a negative number is simply a confusing way of specifying a large positive number (§16.3.4).

Note that the functions used to find substrings of a *string* (§20.3.11) return *npos* if they don't find anything. Thus, they don't throw exceptions. However, later using *npos* as a character position does.

A pair of iterators is another way of specifying a substring. The first iterator identifies a position, and the difference between two iterators is a character count. As usual, iterators are not range checked.

Where a C-style string is used, range checking is harder. When given a C-style string (a pointer to *char*) as an argument, *basic_string* functions assume the pointer is not *0*. When given character positions for C-style strings, they assume that the C-style string is long enough for the position to be valid. Be careful! In this case, being careful means being paranoid, except when using character literals.

All strings have *length*() <*npos*. In a few cases, such as inserting one string into another (§20.3.9), it is possible (although not likely) to construct a string that is too long to be represented. In that case, a *length_error* is thrown. For example:

```
    string  s(string::npos, 'a');     // throw length_error()
```

20.3.6 Assignment

Naturally, assignment is provided for strings:

```
template<class  Ch, class  Tr = char_traits<Ch>, class  A = allocator<Ch> >
class  basic_string {
public:
    // ...
    // assignment (a bit like vector and list: §16.3.4):
```

```
basic_string& operator=(const basic_string& s);
basic_string& operator=(const Ch* p);
basic_string& operator=(Ch c);

basic_string& assign(const basic_string&);
basic_string& assign(const basic_string& s, size_type pos, size_type n);
basic_string& assign(const Ch* p, size_type n);
basic_string& assign(const Ch* p);
basic_string& assign(size_type n, Ch c);
template<class In> basic_string& assign(In first, In last);

// ...
};
```

Like other standard containers, *string*s have value semantics. That is, when one string is assigned to another, the assigned string is copied and two separate strings with the same value exist after the assignment. For example:

```
void g()
{
    string s1 = "Knold";
    string s2 = "Tot";

    s1 = s2;         // two copies of "Tot"
    s2[1] = 'u';     // s2 is "Tut", s1 is still "Tot"
}
```

Assignment with a single character to a string is supported even though initialization by a single character isn't:

```
void f()
{
    string s = 'a'; // error: initialization by char
    s = 'a';        // ok: assignment
    s = "a";
    s = s;
}
```

Being able to assign a *char* to a *string* isn't much use and could even be considered error-prone. However, appending a *char* using += is at times essential (§20.3.9), and it would be odd to be able to say *s+='c'* but not *s='c'*.

The name *assign()* is used for the assignments, which are the counterparts to multiple argument constructors (§16.3.4, §20.3.4).

As mentioned in §11.12, it is possible to optimize a *string* so that copying doesn't actually take place until two copies of a *string* are needed. The design of the standard *string* encourages implementations that minimize actual copying. This makes read-only uses of strings and passing of strings as function arguments much cheaper than one could naively have assumed. However, it would be equally naive for programmers not to check their implementations before writing code that relied on *string* copy being optimized (§20.6[13]).

20.3.7 Conversion to C-Style Strings

As shown in §20.3.4, a *string* can be initialized by a C-style string and C-style strings can be assigned to *strings*. Conversely, it is possible to place a copy of the characters of a *string* into an array:

```
template<class Ch, class Tr = char_traits<Ch>, class A = allocator<Ch> >
class basic_string {
public:
    // ...
    // conversion to C-style string:

    const Ch* c_str() const;
    const Ch* data() const;
    size_type copy(Ch* p, size_type n, size_type pos = 0) const;

    // ...
};
```

The *data*() function writes the characters of the string into an array and returns a pointer to that array. The array is owned by the *string*, and the user should not try to delete it. The user also cannot rely on its value after a subsequent call on a non-*const* function on the string. The *c_str*() function is like *data*(), except that it adds a 0 (zero) at the end as a C-string-style terminator. For example:

```
void f()
{
    string s = "equinox";             // s.length()==7
    const char* p1 = s.data();        // p1 points to seven characters
    printf("p1 = %s\n",p1);           // bad: missing terminator
    p1[2] = 'a';                      // error: p1 points to a const array
    s[2] = 'a';
    char c = p1[1];                   // bad: access of s.data() after modification of s

    const char* p2 = s.c_str();       // p2 points to eight characters
    printf("p2 = %s\n",p2);           // ok: c_str() adds terminator
}
```

In other words, *data*() produces an array of characters, whereas *c_str*() produces a C-style string. These functions are primarily intended to allow simple use of functions that take C-style strings. Consequently, *c_str*() tends to be more useful than *data*(). For example:

```
void f(string s)
{
    int i = atoi(s.c_str());    // get int value of digits in string (§20.4.1)
    // ...
}
```

Typically, it is best to leave characters in a *string* until you need them. However, if you can't use the characters immediately, you can copy them into an array rather than leave them in the buffer allocated by *c_str*() or *data*(). The *copy*() function is provided for that. For example:

```
char* c_string(const string& s)
{
    char* p = new char[s.length()+1];  // note: +1
    s.copy(p,string::npos);
    p[s.length()] = 0;                 // note: add terminator
    return p;
}
```

A call *s.copy(p,n,m)* copies at most *n* characters to *p* starting with *s[m]*. If there are fewer than *n* characters in *s* to copy, *copy()* simply copies all the characters there are.

Note that a *string* can contain the *0* character. Functions manipulating C-style strings will interprete such a *0* as a terminator. Be careful to put *0*s into a string only if you don't apply C-style functions to it or if you put the *0* there exactly to be a terminator.

Conversion to a C-style string could have been provided by an *operator const char*()* rather than *c_str()*. This would have provided the convenience of an implicit conversion at the cost of surprises in cases in which such a conversion was unexpected.

If you find *c_str()* appearing in your program with great frequency, it is probably because you rely heavily on C-style interfaces. Often, an interface that relies on *string*s rather than C-style strings is available and can be used to eliminate the conversions. Alternatively, you can avoid most of the explicit calls of *c_str()* by providing additional definitions of the functions that caused you to write the *c_str()* calls:

```
extern "C" int atoi(const char*);

int atoi(const string& s)
{
    return atoi(s.c_str());
}
```

20.3.8 Comparisons

Strings can be compared to strings of their own type and to arrays of characters with the same character type:

```
template<class Ch, class Tr = char_traits<Ch>, class A = allocator<Ch> >
class basic_string {
public:
    // ...

    int compare(const basic_string& s) const;  // combined > and ==
    int compare(const Ch* p) const;

    int compare(size_type pos, size_type n, const basic_string& s) const;
    int compare(size_type pos, size_type n,
            const basic_string& s, size_type pos2, size_type n2) const;
    int compare(size_type pos, size_type n, const Ch* p, size_type n2 = npos) const;

    // ...
};
```

When a position and a size are supplied for a string in a *compare* ( ) , only the indicated substring is used. For example, *s . compare* (*pos* , *n* , *s2*) is equivalent to *string* (*s* , *pos* , *n*) *. compare* (*s2*). The comparison criterion is *char_traits<Ch>*'s *compare* ( ) (§20.2.1). Thus, *s . compare* (*s2*) returns *0* if the strings have the same value, a negative number if *s* is lexicographically before *s2*, and a positive number otherwise.

A user cannot supply a comparison criterion the way it was done in §13.4. When that degree of flexibility is needed, we can use *lexicographical_compare* ( ) (§18.9), define a function like the one in §13.4, or write an explicit loop. For example, the *toupper* ( ) function (§20.4.2) allows us to write case-insensitive comparisons:

```
int  cmp_nocase (const  string& s,  const  string& s2)
{
      string::const_iterator p = s.begin();
      string::const_iterator p2 = s2.begin();

      while (p!=s.end() && p2!=s2.end()) {
            if (toupper(*p)!=toupper(*p2)) return (toupper(*p)<toupper(*p2)) ? -1 : 1;
            ++p;
            ++p2;
      }

      return (s2.size()==s.size()) ? 0 : (s.size()<s2.size()) ? -1 : 1; // size is unsigned
}

void  f(const  string& s,  const  string& s2)
{
      if (s == s2) {                            // case sensitive compare of s and s2
            // ...
      }

      if (cmp_nocase(s,s2) == 0) {              // case insensitive compare of s and s2
            // ...
      }

      // ...
}
```

The usual comparison operators ==, ! =, >, <, >=, and <= are provided for *basic_string*s:

```
template<class  Ch,  class  Tr,  class  A>
bool  operator==(const  basic_string<Ch,Tr,A>&,  const  basic_string<Ch,Tr,A>&);

template<class  Ch,  class  Tr,  class  A>
bool  operator==(const  Ch*,  const  basic_string<Ch,Tr,A>&);

template<class  Ch,  class  Tr,  class  A>
bool  operator==(const  basic_string<Ch,Tr,A>&,  const  Ch*);

// similar declarations for !=, >, <, >=, and <=
```

Comparison operators are nonmember functions so that conversions can be applied in the same way to both operands (§11.2.3). The versions taking C-style strings are provided to optimize comparisons against string literals. For example:

```
void f(const string& name)
{
    if (name =="Obelix" || "Asterix"==name) {      // use optimized ==
        // ...
    }
}
```

20.3.9 Insert

Once created, a string can be manipulated in many ways. Of the operations that modify the value of a string, one of the most common is appending to it − that is, adding characters to the end. Insertion at other points of a string is rarer:

```
template<class Ch, class Tr = char_traits<Ch>, class A = allocator<Ch> >
class basic_string {
public:
    // ...
    // add characters after (*this)[length()−1]:

    basic_string& operator+=(const basic_string& s);
    basic_string& operator+=(const Ch* p);
    basic_string& operator+=(Ch c);
    void push_back(Ch c);

    basic_string& append(const basic_string& s);
    basic_string& append(const basic_string& s, size_type pos, size_type n);
    basic_string& append(const Ch* p, size_type n);
    basic_string& append(const Ch* p);
    basic_string& append(size_type n, Ch c);
    template<class In> basic_string& append(In first, In last);

    // insert characters before (*this)[pos]:

    basic_string& insert(size_type pos, const basic_string& s);
    basic_string& insert(size_type pos, const basic_string& s, size_type pos2, size_type n);
    basic_string& insert(size_type pos, const Ch* p, size_type n);
    basic_string& insert(size_type pos, const Ch* p);
    basic_string& insert(size_type pos, size_type n, Ch c);

    // insert characters before p:

    iterator insert(iterator p, Ch c);
    void insert(iterator p, size_type n, Ch c);
    template<class In> void insert(iterator p, In first, In last);

    // ...
};
```

Basically, the variety of operations provided for initializing a string and assigning to a string is also available for appending and for inserting characters before some character position.

The += operator is provided as the conventional notation for the most common forms of append. For example:

```
string complete_name(const string& first_name, const string& family_name)
{
     string s = first_name;
     s += ´ ´;
     s += family_name;
     return s;
}
```

Appending to the end can be noticeably more efficient than inserting into other positions. For example:

```
string complete_name2(const string& first_name, const string& family_name) // poor algorithm
{
     string s = family_name;
     s.insert(s.begin(), ´ ´);
     return s.insert(0, first_name);
}
```

Insertion usually forces the *string* implementation to do extra memory management and to move characters around.

Because *string* has a *push_back()* operation (§16.3.5), a *back_inserter* can be used for a *string* exactly as for general containers.

20.3.10 Concatenation

Appending is a special form of concatenation. *Concatenation* − constructing a string out of two strings by placing one after the other − is provided by the + operator:

```
template<class Ch, class Tr, class A>
basic_string<Ch,Tr,A>
operator+(const basic_string<Ch,Tr,A>&, const basic_string<Ch,Tr,A>&);

template<class Ch, class Tr, class A>
basic_string<Ch,Tr,A> operator+(const Ch*, const basic_string<Ch,Tr,A>&);

template<class Ch, class Tr, class A>
basic_string<Ch,Tr,A> operator+(Ch, const basic_string<Ch,Tr,A>&);

template<class Ch, class Tr, class A>
basic_string<Ch,Tr,A> operator+(const basic_string<Ch,Tr,A>&, const Ch*);

template<class Ch, class Tr, class A>
basic_string<Ch,Tr,A> operator+(const basic_string<Ch,Tr,A>&, Ch);
```

As usual, + is defined as a nonmember function. For templates with several template parameters, this implies a notational disadvantage, since the template parameters are mentioned repeatedly.

On the other hand, use of concatenation is obvious and convenient. For example:

```
string complete_name3(const string& first_name, const string& family_name)
{
     return first_name + ´ ´ + family_name;
}
```

This notational convenience may be bought at the cost of some run-time overhead compared to *complete_name* ( ) . One extra temporary (§11.3.2) is needed in *complete_name3* ( ) . In my experience, this is rarely important, but it is worth remembering when writing an inner loop of a program where performance matters. In that case, we might even consider avoiding a function call by making *complete_name* ( ) inline and composing the result string in place using lower-level operations (§20.6[14]).

20.3.11 Find

There is a bewildering variety of functions for finding substrings:

```
template<class Ch, class Tr = char_traits<Ch>, class A = allocator<Ch> >
class basic_string {
public:
    // ...
    // find subsequence (like search() §18.5.5):

    size_type find(const basic_string& s, size_type i = 0) const;
    size_type find(const Ch* p, size_type i, size_type n) const;
    size_type find(const Ch* p, size_type i = 0) const;
    size_type find(Ch c, size_type i = 0) const;

    // find subsequence searching backwards from the end (like find_end(), §18.5.5):

    size_type rfind(const basic_string& s, size_type i = npos) const;
    size_type rfind(const Ch* p, size_type i, size_type n) const;
    size_type rfind(const Ch* p, size_type i = npos) const;
    size_type rfind(Ch c, size_type i = npos) const;

    // find character (like find_first_of() in §18.5.2):

    size_type find_first_of(const basic_string& s, size_type i = 0) const;
    size_type find_first_of(const Ch* p, size_type i, size_type n) const;
    size_type find_first_of(const Ch* p, size_type i = 0) const;
    size_type find_first_of(Ch c, size_type i = 0) const;

    // find character from argument searching backwards from the end:

    size_type find_last_of(const basic_string& s, size_type i = npos) const;
    size_type find_last_of(const Ch* p, size_type i, size_type n) const;
    size_type find_last_of(const Ch* p, size_type i = npos) const;
    size_type find_last_of(Ch c, size_type i = npos) const;

    // find character not in argument:

    size_type find_first_not_of(const basic_string& s, size_type i = 0) const;
    size_type find_first_not_of(const Ch* p, size_type i, size_type n) const;
    size_type find_first_not_of(const Ch* p, size_type i = 0) const;
    size_type find_first_not_of(Ch c, size_type i = 0) const;

    // find character not in argument searching backwards from the end:
```

```
        size_type find_last_not_of(const basic_string& s, size_type i = npos) const;
        size_type find_last_not_of(const Ch* p, size_type i, size_type n) const;
        size_type find_last_not_of(const Ch* p, size_type i = npos) const;
        size_type find_last_not_of(Ch c, size_type i = npos) const;
        // ...
    };
```

These are all *const* members. That is, they exist to locate a substring for some use, but they do not change the value of the string to which they are applied.

The meaning of the *basic_string::find* functions can be understood from their general algorithm equivalents. Consider an example:

```
    void f()
    {
        string s = "accdcde";
        string::size_type i1 = s.find("cd");             // i1 = 2   s[2]=='c' && s[3]=='d'
        string::size_type i2 = s.rfind("cd");            // i2 = 4   s[4]=='c' && s[5]=='d'
        string::size_type i3 = s.find_first_of("cd");    // i3 = 1   s[1] == 'c'
        string::size_type i4 = s.find_last_of("cd");     // i4 = 5   s[5] == 'd'
        string::size_type i5 = s.find_first_not_of("cd");// i5 = 0   s[0]!='c' && s[0]!='d'
        string::size_type i6 = s.find_last_not_of("cd"); // i6 = 6   s[6]!='c' && s[6]!='d'
    }
```

If a *find()* function fails to find anything, it returns *npos*, which represents an illegal character position. If *npos* is used as a character position, *out_of_range* will be thrown (§20.3.5).

Note that result of a *find()* is an *unsigned* value.

20.3.12 Replace

Once a position in a string is identified, the value of individual character positions can be changed using subscripting or whole substrings can be replaced with new characters using *replace()*:

```
    template<class Ch, class Tr = char_traits<Ch>, class A = allocator<Ch> >
    class basic_string {
    public:
        // ...
        // replace [ (*this)[i], (*this)[i+n] [ with other characters:

        basic_string& replace(size_type i, size_type n, const basic_string& s);
        basic_string& replace(size_type i, size_type n,
                              const basic_string& s, size_type i2, size_type n2);
        basic_string& replace(size_type i, size_type n, const Ch* p, size_type n2);
        basic_string& replace(size_type i, size_type n, const Ch* p);
        basic_string& replace(size_type i, size_type n, size_type n2, Ch c);

        basic_string& replace(iterator i, iterator i2, const basic_string& s);
        basic_string& replace(iterator i, iterator i2, const Ch* p, size_type n);
        basic_string& replace(iterator i, iterator i2, const Ch* p);
        basic_string& replace(iterator i, iterator i2, size_type n, Ch c);
        template<class In> basic_string& replace(iterator i, iterator i2, In j, In j2);
```

```
// remove characters from string ("replace with nothing"):

basic_string& erase(size_type i = 0, size_type n = npos);
iterator erase(iterator i);
iterator erase(iterator first, iterator last);
void clear();   // erase all characters

// ...
};
```

Note that the number of new characters need not be the same as the number of characters previously in the string. The size of the string is changed to accommodate the new substring. In particular, *erase*() simply removes a substring and adjusts its size accordingly. For example:

```
void f()
{
    string s = "but I have heard it works even if you don't believe in it";
    s.erase(0,4);                          // erase initial "but "
    s.replace(s.find("even"),4,"only");
    s.replace(s.find("don't"),5,"");   // erase by replacing with ""
}
```

Like *clear*(), the simple call *erase*(), with no argument, makes the string into an empty string.

The variety of *replace*() functions matches that of assignment. After all, *replace*() is an assignment to a substring.

20.3.13 Substrings

The *substr*() function lets you specify a substring as a position plus a length:

```
template<class Ch, class Tr = char_traits<Ch>, class A = allocator<Ch> >
class basic_string {
public:
    // ...
    // address substring:
    basic_string substr(size_type i = 0, size_type n = npos) const;
    // ...
};
```

The *substr*() function is simply a way of reading a part of a string. On the other hand, *replace*() lets you write to a substring. Both rely on the low-level position plus number of characters notation. However, *find*() lets us find substrings by value. Together, they allow us to define a substring that can be used for both reading and writing:

```
template<class Ch> class Basic_substring {
public:
    typedef typename basic_string<Ch>::size_type size_type;

    Basic_substring(basic_string<Ch>& s, size_type i, size_type n);       // s[i]..s[i+n-1]
    Basic_substring(basic_string<Ch>& s, const basic_string<Ch>& s2);     // s2 in s
    Basic_substring(basic_string<Ch>& s, const Ch* p);                     // *p in s
```

```
        Basic_substring& operator=(const basic_string<Ch>&);          // write through to *ps
        Basic_substring& operator=(const Basic_substring<Ch>&);
        Basic_substring& operator=(const Ch*);
        Basic_substring& operator=(Ch);

        operator basic_string<Ch>() const;                            // read from *ps
        operator const Ch*() const;                                   // use c_str()
private:
        basic_string<Ch>* ps;
        size_type pos;
        size_type n;
};
```

The implementation is largely trivial. For example:

```
template<class Ch>
Basic_substring<Ch>::Basic_substring(basic_string<Ch>& s, const basic_string<Ch>& s2)
        :ps(&s), n(s2.length())
{
        pos = s.find(s2);
}

template<class Ch>
Basic_substring<Ch>& Basic_substring<Ch>::operator=(const basic_string<Ch>& s)
{
        ps->replace(pos,n,s);     // write through to *ps
        return *this;
}

template<class Ch> Basic_substring<Ch>::operator basic_string<Ch>() const
{
        return basic_string<Ch>(*ps,pos,n);       // copy from *ps
}
```

If *s2* isn't found in *s*, *pos* will be *npos*. Attempts to read or write it will throw *out_of_range* (§20.3.5).

This *Basic_substring* can be used like this:

```
typedef Basic_substring<char> Substring;

void f()
{
        string s = "Mary had a little lamb";
        Substring(s,"lamb") = "fun";
        Substring(s,"a little") = "no";
        string s2 = "Joe" + Substring(s,s.find(' '),string::npos);
}
```

Naturally, this would be much more interesting if *Substring* could do some pattern matching (§20.6[7]).

20.3.14 Size and Capacity

Memory-related issues are handled much as they are for *vector* (§16.3.8):

```
template<class Ch, class Tr = char_traits<Ch>, class A = allocator<Ch> >
class basic_string {
public:
        // ...
        // size, capacity, etc. (like §16.3.8):

        size_type size() const;                              // number of characters (§20.3.4)
        size_type max_size() const;                          // largest possible string
        size_type length() const { return size(); }
        bool empty() const { return size()==0; }

        void resize(size_type n, Ch c);
        void resize(size_type n) { resize(n, Ch()); }

        size_type capacity() const;                          // like vector: §16.3.8
        void reserve(size_type res_arg = 0);                 // like vector: §16.3.8

        allocator_type get_allocator() const;
};
```

A call *reserve(res_arg)* throws *length_error* if *res_arg>max_size()*.

20.3.15 I/O Operations

One of the main uses of *string*s is as the target of input and as the source of output. Input and output operators for *basic_string* are provided in *<string>* (not in *<iostream>*):

```
template<class Ch, class Tr, class A>
basic_istream<Ch,Tr>& operator>>(basic_istream<Ch,Tr>&, basic_string<Ch,Tr,A>&);

template<class Ch, class Tr, class A>
basic_ostream<Ch,Tr>& operator<<(basic_ostream<Ch,Tr>&, const basic_string<Ch,Tr,A>&);

template<class Ch, class Tr, class A>
basic_istream<Ch,Tr>& getline(basic_istream<Ch,Tr>&, basic_string<Ch,Tr,A>&, Ch eol);

template<class Ch, class Tr, class A>
basic_istream<Ch,Tr>& getline(basic_istream<Ch,Tr>&, basic_string<Ch,Tr,A>&);
```

The << operator writes a string to an *ostream* (§21.2.1). The >> operator reads a whitespace-terminated word (§3.6, §21.3.1) to its string, expanding the string as needed to hold the word. Initial whitespace is skipped, and the terminating whitespace character is not entered into the string.

The *getline()* function reads a line terminated by *eol* to its string, expanding the string as needed to hold the line (§3.6). If no *eol* argument is provided, a newline ´\n´ is used as the delimiter. The line terminator is removed from the stream but not entered into the string. Because a *string* expands to hold the input, there is no reason to leave the terminator in the stream or to provide a count of characters read in the way *get()* and *getline()* do for character arrays (§21.3.4).

20.3.16 Swap

As for *vectors* (§16.3.9), a *swap* ( ) function for strings can be much more efficient than the general algorithm, so a specific version is provided:

> *template<class Ch, class Tr, class A>*
> *void swap (basic_string<Ch, Tr, A>&, basic_string<Ch, Tr, A>&);*

20.4 The C Standard Library

The C++ standard library inherited the C-style string functions from the C standard library. This section lists some of the most useful C string functions. The description is not meant to be exhaustive; for further information, check your reference manual. Beware that implementers often add their own nonstandard functions to the standard header files, so it is easy to get confused about which functions are guaranteed to be available on every implementation.

The headers presenting the standard C library facilities are listed in §16.1.2. Memory management functions can be found in §19.4.6, C I/O functions in §21.8, and the C math library in §22.3. The functions concerned with startup and termination are described in §3.2 and §9.4.1.1, and the facilities for reading unspecified function arguments are presented in §7.6. C-style functions for wide character strings are found in *<cwchar>* and *<wchar.h>*.

20.4.1 C-Style Strings

Functions for manipulating C-style strings are found in *<string.h>* and *<cstring>*:

> *char* strcpy (char* p, const char* q);*   *// copy from q into p (incl. terminator)*
> *char* strcat (char* p, const char* q);*   *// append from q to p (incl. terminator)*
> *char* strncpy (char* p, const char* q, int n);*   *// copy n char from q into p*
> *char* strncat (char* p, const char* q, int n);*   *// append n char from q to p*
>
> *size_t strlen (const char* p);*   *// length of p (not counting the terminator)*
>
> *int strcmp (const char* p, const char* q);*   *// compare: p and q*
> *int strncmp (const char* p, const char* q, int n);*   *// compare first n char*
>
> *char* strchr (char* p, int c);*   *// find first c in p*
> *const char* strchr (const char* p, int c);*
> *char* strrchr (char* p, int c);*   *// find last c in p*
> *const char* strrchr (const char* p, int c);*
> *char* strstr (char* p, const char* q);*   *// find first q in p*
> *const char* strstr (const char* p, const char* q);*
>
> *char* strpbrk (char* p, const char* q);*   *// find first char from q in p*
> *const char* strpbrk (const char* p, const char* q);*
>
> *size_t strspn (const char* p, const char* q);*   *// number of char in p before any char in q*
> *size_t strcspn (const char* p, const char* q);*   *// number of char in p before a char not in q*

A pointer is assumed to be nonzero, and the array of *char* that it points to is assumed to be terminated by *0*. The *strn*-functions pad with *0* if there are not *n* characters to copy. String comparisons return *0* if the strings are equal, a negative number if the first argument is lexicographically before the second, and a positive number otherwise.

Naturally, C doesn't provide the pairs of overloaded functions. However, they are needed in C++ for *const* safety. For example:

```
void f(const char* pcc, char* pc)    // C++
{
    *strchr(pcc, 'a') = 'b';  // error: cannot assign to const char
    *strchr(pc, 'a') = 'b';   // ok, but sloppy: there might not be an 'a' in pc
}
```

The C++ *strchr* () does not allow you to write to a *const*. However, a C program may "take advantage" of the weaker type checking in the C *strchr* ( ) :

```
char* strchr(const char* p, int c);  /* C standard library function, not C++ */

void g(const char* pcc, char* pc)    /* C, will not compile in C++ */
{
    *strchr(pcc, 'a') = 'b';  /* converts const to non-const: ok in C, error in C++ */
    *strchr(pc, 'a') = 'b';   /* ok in C and C++ */
}
```

Whenever possible, C-style strings are best avoided in favor of *strings*. C-style strings and their associated standard functions can be used to produce very efficient code, but even experienced C and C++ programmers are prone to make uncaught "silly errors" when using them. However, no C++ programmer can avoid seeing some of these functions in old code. Here is a nonsense example illustrating the most common functions:

```
void f(char* p, char* q)
{
    if (p==q) return;           // pointers are equal
    if (strcmp(p, q) ==0) {     // string values are equal
        int i = strlen(p);      // number of characters (not counting the terminator)
        // ...
    }
    char buf[200];
    strcpy(buf, p);             // copy p into buf (including the terminator)
                                // sloppy: will overflow some day.
    strncpy(buf, p, 200);       // copy 200 char from p into buf
                                // sloppy: will fail to copy the terminator some day.
    // ...
}
```

Input and output of C-style strings are usually done using the *printf* family of functions (§21.8).

In *<stdlib.h>* and *<cstdlib>*, the standard library provides useful functions for converting strings representing numeric values into numeric values:

```
double atof(const char* p);   // convert p to double
int atoi(const char* p);      // convert p to int
long atol(const char* p);     // convert p to long
```

Leading whitespace is ignored. If the string doesn't represent a number, zero is returned. For example, the value of *atoi* ("*seven*") is *0*. If the string represents a number that cannot be represented in the intended result type, *errno* (§16.1.2, §22.3) is set to *ERANGE* and an appropriately huge or tiny value is returned.

20.4.2 Character Classification

In *<ctype . h>* and *<cctype>*, the standard library provides a set of useful functions for dealing with ASCII and similar character sets:

```
int  isalpha (int);      // letter: 'a'..'z' 'A'..'Z' in C locale (§20.2.1, §21.7)
int  isupper (int);      // upper case letter: 'A'..'Z' in C locale (§20.2.1, §21.7)
int  islower (int);      // lower case letter: 'a'..'z' in C locale (§20.2.1, §21.7)
int  isdigit (int);      // decimal digit: '0'..'9'
int  isxdigit (int);     // hexadecimal digit: '0'..'9' or 'a'..'f' or 'A'..'F'
int  isspace (int);      // ' ' '\t' '\v' return newline formfeed
int  iscntrl (int);      // control character (ASCII 0..31 and 127)
int  ispunct (int);      // punctuation: none of the above
int  isalnum (int);      // isalpha() | isdigit()
int  isprint (int);      // printable: ascii ' '..'~'
int  isgraph (int);      // isalpha() | isdigit() | ispunct()

int  toupper (int c);    // uppercase equivalent to c
int  tolower (int c);    // lowercase equivalent to c
```

All are usually implemented by a simple lookup, using the character as an index into a table of character attributes. This means that constructs such as:

```
if ( ( 'a' <=c && c<= 'z' )  ||  ( 'A' <=c && c<= 'Z' ) ) {      // alphabetic
    // ...
}
```

are inefficient in addition to being tedious to write and error-prone (on a machine with the EBCDIC character set, this will accept nonalphabetic characters).

These functions take *int* arguments, and the integer passed must be representable as an *unsigned char* or *EOF* (which is most often −*1*). This can be a problem on systems where *char* is signed (see §20.6[11]).

Equivalent functions for wide characters are found in *<cwctype>* and *<wctype . h>*.

20.5 Advice

[1] Prefer *string* operations to C-style string functions; §20.4.1.

[2] Use *strings* as variables and members, rather than as base classes; §20.3, §25.2.1.

[3] You can pass *strings* as value arguments and return them by value to let the system take care of memory management; §20.3.6.

[4] Use *at* ( ) rather than iterators or [ ] when you want range checking; §20.3.2, §20.3.5.

[5] Use iterators and [ ] rather than *at* ( ) when you want to optimize speed; §20.3.2, §20.3.5.

[6] Directly or indirectly, use *substr* ( ) to read substrings and *replace* ( ) to write substrings; §20.3.12, §20.3.13.

[7] Use the *find* ( ) operations to locate values in a *string* (rather than writing an explicit loop); §20.3.11.

[8] Append to a *string* when you need to add characters efficiently; §20.3.9.

[9] Use *string*s as targets of non-time-critical character input; §20.3.15.

[10] Use *string* : : *npos* to indicate ''the rest of the *string*;'' §20.3.5.

[11] If necessary, implement heavily-used *string*s using low-level operations (rather than using low-level data structures everywhere); §20.3.10.

[12] If you use *string*s, catch *length_error* and *out_of_range* somewhere; §20.3.5.

[13] Be careful not to pass a *char** with the value *0* to a string function; §20.3.7.

[14] Use *c_str* ( ) produce a C-style string representation of a *string* (only) when you have to; §20.3.7.

[15] Use *isalpha* ( ), *isdigit* ( ), etc., when you need to know the classification of a character rather that writing your own tests on character values; §20.4.2.

20.6 Exercises

The solutions to several exercises for this chapter can be found by looking at the source text of an implementation of the standard library. Do yourself a favor: try to find your own solutions before looking to see how your library implementer approached the problems.

1. (∗2) Write a function that takes two *string*s and returns a *string* that is the concatenation of the strings with a dot in the middle. For example, given *file* and *write*, the function returns *file . write*. Do the same exercise with C-style strings using only C facilities such as *malloc* ( ) and *strlen* ( ). Compare the two functions. What are reasonable criteria for a comparison?

2. (∗2) Make a list of differences between *vector* and *basic_string*. Which differences are important?

3. (∗2) The string facilities are not perfectly regular. For example, you can assign a *char* to a string, but you cannot initialize a *string* with a *char*. Make a list of such irregularities. Which could have been eliminated without complicating the use of strings? What other irregularities would this introduce?

4. (∗1.5) Class *basic_string* has a lot of members. Which could be made nonmember functions without loss of efficiency or notational convenience?

5. (∗1.5) Write a version of *back_inserter* ( ) (§19.2.4) that works for *basic_string*.

6. (∗2) Complete *Basic_substring* from §20.3.13 and integrate it with a *String* type that overloads ( ) to mean ''substring of'' and otherwise acts like *string*.

7. (∗2.5) Write a *find* ( ) function that finds the first match for a simple regular expression in a *string*. Use ? to mean ''any character,'' ∗ to mean any number of characters not matching the next part of the regular expression, and [*abc*] to mean any character from the set specified between the square braces (here *a*, *b*, and *c*). Other characters match themselves. For example, *find* (*s*, "*name* : ") returns a pointer to the first occurrence of *name* : in *s*; *find* (*s*, " [*nN*] *ame* : ") returns a pointer to the first occurrence of *name* : or *Name* : in *s*; and *find* (*s*, " [*nN*] *ame* (∗) ") returns a pointer to the first occurence of *Name* or *name* followed by a (possibly empty) parenthesized sequence of characters in *s*.

8. (∗2.5) What operations do you find missing from the simple regular expression function from

§20.6[7]? Specify and add them. Compare the expressiveness of your regular expression matcher to that of a widely distributed one. Compare the performance of your regular expression matcher to that of a widely distributed one.

9. (*2.5) Use a regular expression library to implement pattern-matching operations on a *String* class that has an associated *Substring* class.

10. (*2.5) Consider writing an ''ideal'' class for general text processing. Call it *Text*. What facilities should it have? What implementation constraints and overheads are imposed by your set of ''ideal'' facilities?

11. (*1.5) Define a set of overloaded versions for *isalpha* ( ), *isdigit* ( ), etc., so that these functions work correctly for *char*, *unsigned char*, and *signed char*.

12. (*2.5) Write a *String* class optimized for strings having no more than eight characters. Compare its performance to that of the *String* from §11.12 and your implementation's version of the standard library *string*. Is it possible to design a string that combines the advantages of a string optimized for very short strings with the advantages of a perfectly general string?

13. (*2) Measure the performance of copying of *strings*. Does your implementation's implementation of *string* adequately optimize copying?

14. (*2.5) Compare the performance of the three *complete_name* ( ) functions from §20.3.9 and §20.3.10. Try to write a version of *complete_name* ( ) that runs as fast as possible. Keep a record of mistakes found during its implementation and testing.

15. (*2.5) Imagine that reading medium-long strings (most are 5 to 25 characters long) from *cin* is the bottleneck in your system. Write an input function that reads such strings as fast as you can think of. You can choose the interface to that function to optimize for speed rather than for convenience. Compare the result to your implementation's >> for *strings*.

16. (*1.5) Write a function *itos* (*int*) that returns a *string* representing its *int* argument.

21

Streams

What you see is all you get.
– Brian Kernighan

Input and output — ostreams — output of built-in types — output of user-defined types
— virtual output functions — *istreams* — input of built-in types — unformatted input
— stream state — input of user-defined types — I/O exceptions — tying of streams —
sentries — formatting integer and floating-point output — fields and adjustments —
manipulators — standard manipulators — user-defined manipulators — file streams —
closing streams — string streams — stream buffers — locale — stream callbacks —
printf( ) — advice — exercises.

21.1 Introduction

Designing and implementing a general input/output facility for a programming language is notori-
ously difficult. Traditionally, I/O facilities have been designed exclusively to handle a few built-in
data types. However, a nontrivial C++ program uses many user-defined types, and the input and
output of values of those types must be handled. An I/O facility should be easy, convenient, and
safe to use; efficient and flexible; and, above all, complete. Nobody has come up with a solution
that pleases everyone. It should therefore be possible for a user to provide alternative I/O facilities
and to extend the standard I/O facilities to cope with special applications.

C++ was designed to enable a user to define new types that are as efficient and convenient to
use as built-in types. It is therefore a reasonable requirement that an I/O facility for C++ should be
provided in C++ using only facilities available to every programmer. The stream I/O facilities presented here are the result of an effort to meet this challenge:

§21.2 *Output:* What the application programmer thinks of as output is really the conversion of
objects of types, such as *int*, *char**, and *Employee_record*, into sequences of characters. The facilities for writing built-in and user-defined types to output are described.

§21.3 *Input:* The facilities for requesting input of characters, strings, and values of other built-in and user-defined types are presented.

§21.4 *Formatting:* There are often specific requirements for the layout of the output. For example, *int*s may have to be printed in decimal and pointers in hexadecimal or floating-point numbers must appear with exactly specified precision. Formatting controls and the programming techniques used to provide them are discussed.

§21.5 *Files and Streams:* By default, every C++ program can use standard streams, such as standard output (*cout*), standard input (*cin*), and error output (*cerr*). To use other devices or files, streams must be created and attached to those files or devices. The mechanisms for opening and closing files and for attaching streams to files and *string*s are described.

§21.6 *Buffering:* To make I/O efficient, we must use a buffering strategy that is suitable for both the data written (read) and the destination it is written to (read from). The basic techniques for buffering streams are presented.

§21.7 *Locale:* A *locale* is an object that specifies how numbers are printed, what characters are considered letters, etc. It encapsulates many cultural differences. Locales are implicitly used by the I/O system and are only briefly described here.

§21.8 *C I/O:* The *printf*( ) function from the C *<stdio.h>* library and the C library's relation to the C++ *<iostream>* library are discussed.

Knowledge of the techniques used to implement the stream library is not needed to use the library. Also, the techniques used for different implementations will differ. However, implementing I/O is a challenging task. An implementation contains examples of techniques that can be applied to many other programming and design tasks. Therefore, the techniques used to implement I/O are worthy of study.

This chapter discusses the stream I/O system to the point where you should be able to appreciate its structure, to use it for most common kinds of I/O, and to extend it to handle new user-defined types. If you need to implement the standard streams, provide a new kind of stream, or provide a new locale, you need a copy of the standard, a good systems manual, and/or examples of working code in addition to what is presented here.

The key components of the stream I/O systems can be represented graphically like this:

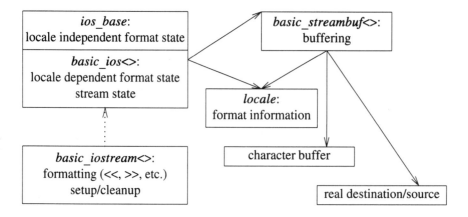

The dotted arrow from *basic_iostream<>* indicates that *basic_ios<>* is a virtual base class; the solid arrows represent pointers. The classes marked with <> are templates parameterized by a character type and containing a *locale*.

The streams concept and the general notation it provides can be applied to a large class of communication problems. Streams have been used for transmitting objects between machines (§25.4.1), for encrypting message streams (§21.10[22]), for data compression, for persistent storage of objects, and much more. However, the discussion here is restricted to simple character-oriented input and output.

Declarations of stream I/O classes and templates (sufficient to refer to them but not to apply operations to them) and standard *typedef*s are presented in *<iosfwd>*. This header is occasionally needed when you want to include some but not all of the I/O headers.

21.2 Output

Type-safe and uniform treatment of both built-in and user-defined types can be achieved by using a single overloaded function name for a set of output functions. For example:

```
put(cerr, "x = "); // cerr is the error output stream
put(cerr, x);
put(cerr, '\n');
```

The type of the argument determines which *put* function will be invoked for each argument. This solution is used in several languages. However, it is repetitive. Overloading the operator << to mean "put to" gives a better notation and lets the programmer output a sequence of objects in a single statement. For example:

```
cerr << "x = " << x << '\n';
```

If *x* is an *int* with the value *123*, this statement would print

```
x = 123
```

followed by a newline onto the standard error output stream, *cerr*. Similarly, if *x* is of type *complex* (§22.5) with the value (*1*,*2*.*4*), the statement will print

```
x = (1,2.4)
```

on *cerr*. This style can be used as long as *x* is of a type for which operator << is defined and a user can trivially define operator << for a new type.

An output operator is needed to avoid the verbosity that would have resulted from using an output function. But why <<? It is not possible to invent a new lexical token (§11.2). The assignment operator was a candidate for both input and output, but most people seemed to prefer to use different operators for input and output. Furthermore, = binds the wrong way; that is, *cout=a=b* means *cout=*(*a=b*) rather than (*cout=a*)*=b* (§6.2). I tried the operators < and >, but the meanings "less than" and "greater than" were so firmly implanted in people's minds that the new I/O statements were for all practical purposes unreadable.

The operators << and >> are not used frequently enough for built-in types to cause that problem. They are symmetric in a way that can be used to suggest "to" and "from." When they are used for I/O, I refer to << as *put to* and to >> as *get from*. People who prefer more technical-sounding names call them *inserters* and *extractors*, respectively. The precedence of << is low enough to allow arithmetic expressions as operands without using parentheses. For example:

>   *cout* << " *a*b+c=* " << *a*b+c* << '\n';

Parentheses must be used to write expressions containing operators with precedence lower than <<'s. For example:

>   *cout* << " *a^b|c=* " << (*a^b|c*) << '\n';

The left shift operator (§6.2.4) can be used in an output statement, but of course it, too, must appear within parentheses:

>   *cout* << " *a<<b=* " << (*a<<b*) << '\n';

21.2.1 Output Streams

An *ostream* is a mechanism for converting values of various types into sequences of characters. Usually, these characters are then output using lower-level output operations. There are many kinds of characters (§20.2) that can be characterized by *char_traits* (§20.2.1). Consequently, an *ostream* is a specialization for a particular kind of character of a general *basic_ostream* template:

```
template <class Ch, class Tr = char_traits<Ch> >
class std::basic_ostream : virtual public basic_ios<Ch,Tr> {
public:
        virtual ~basic_ostream();
        // ...
};
```

This template and its associated output operations are defined in namespace *std* and presented by *<ostream>*, which contains the output-related parts of *<iostream>*.

   The *basic_ostream* template parameters control the type of characters that is used by the implementation; they do not affect the types of values that can be output. Streams implemented using ordinary *char*s and streams implemented using wide characters are directly supported by every implementation:

```
typedef basic_ostream<char> ostream;
typedef basic_ostream<wchar_t> wostream;
```

On many systems, it is possible to optimize writing of wide characters through *wostream* to an extent that is hard to match for streams using bytes as the unit of output.

   It is possible to define streams for which the physical I/O is not done in terms of characters. However, such streams are beyond the scope of the C++ standard and beyond the scope of this book (§21.10[15]).

   The *basic_ios* base class is presented in *<ios>*. It controls formatting (§21.4), locale (§21.7), and access to buffers (§21.6). It also defines a few types for notational convenience:

```
template <class Ch, class Tr = char_traits<Ch> >
class std::basic_ios : public ios_base {
public:
    typedef Ch char_type;
    typedef Tr traits_type;
    typedef typename Tr::int_type int_type;    // type of integer value of character
    typedef typename Tr::pos_type pos_type;   // position in buffer
    typedef typename Tr::off_type off_type;    // offset in buffer

    // ... see also §21.3.3, §21.3.7, §21.4.4, §21.6.3, and §21.7.1 ...

    // copying prevented by private (and undefined) assignment and copy constructor (§11.2.2)
};
```

Class *basic_ios* prohibits copy construction and assignment (§11.2.2). This implies that *ostream*s and *istream*s cannot be copied. Therefore, if you need to change the target of a stream you must either change stream buffers (§21.6.4) or indirect through a pointer (§6.1.7).

Class *ios_base* contains information and operations that are independent of the character type used, such as the precision used for floating-point output. Thus, it doesn't need to be a template.

In addition to the *typedef*s in *basic_ios*, the stream I/O library uses a signed integral type *streamsize* to represent buffer sizes and the number of characters transferred in an I/O operation. Similarly, a *typedef* called *streamoff* is supplied for expressing offsets in streams and buffers.

Several standard streams are declared in *<iostream>*:

```
ostream cout;         // standard output stream of char
ostream cerr;         // standard unbuffered output stream for error messages
ostream clog;         // standard output stream for error messages

wostream wcout;       // wide stream corresponding to cout
wostream wcerr;       // wide stream corresponding to cerr
wostream wclog;       // wide stream corresponding to clog
```

The *cerr* and *clog* streams writes to the same destination; they simply differ in the buffering they provide. The *cout* writes to the same destination as *stdout* (§21.8), while *cerr* and *clog* write to the same destination as *stderr*. The programmer can create more streams as needed (see §21.5).

21.2.2 Output of Built-In Types

The class *ostream* is defined with the operator << ("put to") to handle output of the built-in types:

```
template <class Ch, class Tr = char_traits<Ch> >
class basic_ostream : virtual public basic_ios<Ch,Tr> {
public:
    // ...
    basic_ostream& operator<<(short n);
    basic_ostream& operator<<(int n);
    basic_ostream& operator<<(long n);

    basic_ostream& operator<<(unsigned short n);
    basic_ostream& operator<<(unsigned int n);
    basic_ostream& operator<<(unsigned long n);
```

```
            basic_ostream& operator<<(float f);
            basic_ostream& operator<<(double f);
            basic_ostream& operator<<(long double f);

            basic_ostream& operator<<(bool n);
            basic_ostream& operator<<(const void* p);          // write pointer value

            basic_ostream& put(Ch c);        // write c
            basic_ostream& write(const Ch* p, streamsize n);   // p[0]..p[n-1]

            // ...
    };
```

The *put*() and *write*() functions simply write characters. Consequently, the << for outputting characters need not be a member. The *operator*<<() functions that take a character operand can be implemented as nonmembers using *put*():

```
    template<class Ch, class Tr>
        basic_ostream<Ch,Tr>& operator<<(basic_ostream<Ch,Tr>&, Ch);
    template<class Ch, class Tr>
        basic_ostream<Ch,Tr>& operator<<(basic_ostream<Ch,Tr>&, char);
    template<class Tr>
        basic_ostream<char,Tr>& operator<<(basic_ostream<char,Tr>&, char);
    template<class Tr>
        basic_ostream<char,Tr>& operator<<(basic_ostream<char,Tr>&, signed char);
    template<class Tr>
        basic_ostream<char,Tr>& operator<<(basic_ostream<char,Tr>&, unsigned char);
```

Similarly, << is provided for writing out zero-terminated character arrays:

```
    template<class Ch, class Tr>
        basic_ostream<Ch,Tr>& operator<<(basic_ostream<Ch,Tr>&, const Ch*);
    template<class Ch, class Tr>
        basic_ostream<Ch,Tr>& operator<<(basic_ostream<Ch,Tr>&, const char*);
    template<class Tr>
        basic_ostream<char,Tr>& operator<<(basic_ostream<char,Tr>&, const char*);
    template<class Tr>
        basic_ostream<char,Tr>& operator<<(basic_ostream<char,Tr>&, const signed char*);
    template<class Tr>
        basic_ostream<char,Tr>& operator<<(basic_ostream<char,Tr>&, const unsigned char*);
```

The output operators for *string*s are presented in <*string*>; see §20.3.15.

An *operator*<<() returns a reference to the *ostream* for which it was called so that another *operator*<<() can be applied to it. For example,

```
    cerr << "x = " << x;
```

where *x* is an *int*, will be interpreted as:

```
    operator<<(cerr, "x = ").operator<<(x);
```

In particular, this implies that when several items are printed by a single output statement, they will be printed in the expected order: left to right. For example:

```
void val(char c)
{
    cout << "int('" << c << "') = " << int(c) << '\n';
}

int main()
{
    val('A');
    val('Z');
}
```

On an implementation using ASCII characters, this will print:

```
int('A') = 65
int('Z') = 90
```

Note that a character literal has type *char* (§4.3.1) so that *cout<< 'Z'* will print the letter *Z* and not the integer value *90*.

A *bool* value will be output as *0* or *1* by default. If you don't like that, you can set the formatting flag *boolalpha* from *<iomanip>* (§21.4.6.2) and get *true* or *false*. For example:

```
int main()
{
    cout << true << ' ' << false << '\n';
    cout << boolalpha;                          // use symbolic representation for true and false
    cout << true << ' ' << false << '\n';
}
```

This prints:

```
1 0
true false
```

More precisely, *boolalpha* ensures that we get a locale-dependent representation of *bool* values. By setting my locale (§21.7) just right, I can get:

```
1 0
sandt falsk
```

Formatting floating-point numbers, the base used for integers, etc., are discussed in §21.4.

The function *ostream::operator<<(const void*)* prints a pointer value in a form appropriate to the architecture of the machine used. For example,

```
int main()
{
    int* p = new int;
    cout << "local " << &p << ", free store " << p << '\n';
}
```

printed

```
local 0x7fffead0, free store 0x500c
```

on my machine. Other systems have different conventions for printing pointer values.

21.2.3 Output of User-Defined Types

Consider a user-defined type *complex* (§11.3):

```
class complex {
public:
      double real() const { return re; }
      double imag() const { return im; }
      // ...
};
```

Operator << can be defined for the new type *complex* like this:

```
ostream& operator<<(ostream&s, const complex& z)
{
      return s << '(' << z.real() << ',' << z.imag() << ')';
}
```

This << can then be used exactly like << for a built-in type. For example,

```
int main()
{
      complex x(1,2);
      cout << "x = " << x << '\n';
}
```

produces

```
x = (1,2)
```

Defining an output operation for a user-defined type does not require modification of the declaration of class *ostream*. This is fortunate because *ostream* is defined in *<ostream>*, which users cannot and should not modify. Not allowing additions to *ostream* also provides protection against accidental corruption of that data structure and makes it possible to change the implementation of an *ostream* without affecting user programs.

21.2.3.1 Virtual Output Functions

The *ostream* members are not *virtual*. The output operations that a programmer can add are not members, so they cannot be *virtual* either. One reason for this is to achieve close to optimal performance for simple operations such as putting a character into a buffer. This is a place where run-time efficiency is crucial and where inlining is a must. Virtual functions are used to achieve flexibility for the operations dealing with buffer overflow and underflow only (§21.6.4).

However, a programmer sometimes wants to output an object for which only a base class is known. Since the exact type isn't known, correct output cannot be achieved simply by defining a << for each new type. Instead, a virtual output function can be provided in the abstract base:

```
class My_base {
public:
    // ...

    virtual ostream& put(ostream& s) const = 0;      // write *this to s
};

ostream& operator<<(ostream& s, const My_base& r)
{
    return r.put(s);      // use the right put()
}
```

That is, *put*() is a virtual function that ensures that the right output operation is used in <<. Given that, we can write:

```
class Sometype : public My_base {
public:
    // ...

    ostream& put(ostream& s) const;      // the real output function: override My_base::put()
};

void f(const My_base& r, Sometype& s)      // use << which calls the right put()
{
    cout << r << s;
}
```

This integrates the virtual *put*() into the framework provided by *ostream* and <<. The technique is generally useful to provide operations that act like virtual functions, but with the run-time selection based on their second argument.

21.3 Input

Input is handled similarly to output. There is a class *istream* that provides an input operator >> (''get from'') for a small set of standard types. An *operator>>*() can then be defined for a user-defined type.

21.3.1 Input Streams

In parallel to *basic_ostream* (§21.2.1), *basic_istream* is defined in *<istream>*, which contains the input-related parts of *<iostream>*, like this:

```
template <class Ch, class Tr = char_traits<Ch> >
class std::basic_istream : virtual public basic_ios<Ch,Tr> {
public:
    virtual ~basic_istream();

    // ...
};
```

The base class *basic_ios* is described in §21.2.1.

Two standard input streams *cin* and *wcin* are provided in *<iostream>*:

```
typedef basic_istream<char> istream;
typedef basic_istream<wchar_t> wistream;

istream cin;      // standard input stream of char
wistream wcin;    // standard input stream of wchar_t
```

The *cin* stream reads from the same source as C's *stdin* (§21.8).

21.3.2 Input of Built-In Types

An *istream* provides operator >> for the built-in types:

```
template <class Ch, class Tr = char_traits<Ch> >
class basic_istream : virtual public basic_ios<Ch,Tr> {
public:
        // ...
        // formatted input:

        basic_istream& operator>>(short& n);           // read into n
        basic_istream& operator>>(int& n);
        basic_istream& operator>>(long& n);

        basic_istream& operator>>(unsigned short& u);  // read into u
        basic_istream& operator>>(unsigned int& u);
        basic_istream& operator>>(unsigned long& u);

        basic_istream& operator>>(float& f);           // read into f
        basic_istream& operator>>(double& f);
        basic_istream& operator>>(long double& f);

        basic_istream& operator>>(bool& b);            // read into b
        basic_istream& operator>>(void*& p);           // read pointer value into p

        // ...
};
```

The *operator>>*( ) input functions are defined in this style:

```
istream& istream::operator>>(T& tvar)      // T is a type for which istream::operator>> is declared
{
        // skip whitespace, then somehow read a T into 'tvar'
        return *this;
}
```

Because >> skips whitespace, you can read a sequence of whitespace-separated integers like this:

```
int read_ints(vector<int>& v)      // fill v, return number of ints read
{
        int i = 0;
        while (i<v.size() && cin>>v[i]) i++;
        return i;
}
```

A non-*int* on the input will cause the input operation to fail and thus terminate the input loop. For example, the input:

>   *1 2 3 4 5.6 7 8.*

will have *read_ints*() read in the five integers

>   *1 2 3 4 5*

and leave the dot as the next character to be read from input. Whitespace is defined as the standard C whitespace (blank, tab, newline, formfeed, and carriage return) by a call to *isspace*() as defined in *<cctype>* (§20.4.2).

By default, the >> operators skip whitespace. However, we can modify that behavior: *is.unsetf*(*ios_base*::*skipws*) will cause *is*'s >> operators to treat whitespace characters as ordinary characters (see §21.4.1, §21.4.6, and §21.4.6.2).

The most common mistake when using *istream*s is to fail to notice that input didn't happen as expected because the input wasn't of the expected format. One should either check the state of an input stream (§21.3.3) before relying on values supposedly read in or use exceptions (§21.3.6).

The format expected for input is specified by the current locale (§21.7). By default, the *bool* values *true* and *false* are represented by *1* and *0*, respectively. Integers must be decimal and floating-point numbers of the form used to write them in a C++ program. By setting *basefield* (§21.4.2), it is possible to read *0123* as an octal number with the decimal value *83* and *0xff* as a hexadecimal number with the decimal value *255*. The format used to read pointers is completely implementation-dependent (have a look to see what your implementation does).

Surprisingly, there is no member >> for reading a character. The reason is simply that >> for characters can be implemented using the *get*() character input operations (§21.3.4), so it doesn't need to be a member. From a stream, we can read a character into the stream's character type. If that character type is *char*, we can also read into a *signed char* and *unsigned char*:

```
template<class Ch, class Tr>
basic_istream<Ch,Tr>& operator>>(basic_istream<Ch,Tr>&, Ch&);

template<class Tr>
basic_istream<char,Tr>& operator>>(basic_istream<char,Tr>&, unsigned char&);

template<class Tr>
basic_istream<char,Tr>& operator>>(basic_istream<char,Tr>&, signed char&);
```

From a user's point of view, it does not matter whether a >> is a member.

Like the other >> operators, these functions first skip whitespace. For example:

```
void f()
{
    char c;
    cin >> c;
    // ...
}
```

This places the first non-whitespace character from *cin* into *c*.

In addition, we can read into an array of characters:

```
template<class Ch, class Tr>
    basic_istream<Ch,Tr>& operator>>(basic_istream<Ch,Tr>&, Ch*);
template<class Tr>
    basic_istream<char,Tr>& operator>>(basic_istream<char,Tr>&, unsigned char*);
template<class Tr>
    basic_istream<char,Tr>& operator>>(basic_istream<char,Tr>&, signed char*);
```

These operations first skip whitespace. Then they read into their array operand until they encounter a whitespace character or end-of-file. Finally, they terminate the string with a *0*. Clearly, this offers ample opportunity for overflow, so reading into a *string* (§20.3.15) is usually better. However, you can specify a maximum for the number of characters to be read by >>: *is.width(n)* specifies that the next >> on *is* will read at most *n-1* characters into an array. For example:

```
void g()
{
    char v[4];
    cin.width(4);
    cin >> v;
    cout << "v = " << v << endl;
}
```

This will read at most three characters into *v* and add a terminating *0*.

Setting *width()* for an *istream* affects only the immediately following >> into an array and does not affect reading into other types of variables.

21.3.3 Stream State

Every stream (*istream* or *ostream*) has a *state* associated with it. Errors and nonstandard conditions are handled by setting and testing this state appropriately.

The stream state is found in *basic_istream*'s base *basic_ios* from <*ios*>:

```
template <class Ch, class Tr = char_traits<Ch> >
class basic_ios : public ios_base {
public:
    // ...

    bool good() const;    // next operation might succeed
    bool eof() const;     // end of input seen
    bool fail() const;    // next operation will fail
    bool bad() const;     // stream is corrupted

    iostate rdstate() const;                      // get io state flags
    void clear(iostate f = goodbit);              // set io state flags
    void setstate(iostate f) { clear(rdstate()|f); } // add f to io state flags

    operator void*() const;                       // nonzero if !fail()
    bool operator!() const { return fail(); }

    // ...
};
```

If the state is *good()* the previous input operation succeeded. If the state is *good()*, the next input operation might succeed; otherwise, it will fail. Applying an input operation to a stream that is not in the *good* () state is a null operation as far as the variable being read into is concerned. If we try to read into a variable *v* and the operation fails, the value of *v* should be unchanged (it is unchanged if *v* is a variable of one of the types handled by *istream* or *ostream* member functions). The difference between the states *fail* () and *bad* () is subtle. When the state is *fail* () but not also *bad* (), it is assumed that the stream is uncorrupted and that no characters have been lost. When the state is *bad* (), all bets are off.

The state of a stream is represented as a set of flags. Like most constants used to express the behavior of streams, these flags are defined in *basic_ios*' base *ios_base*:

```
class ios_base {
public:
    // ...

    typedef implementation_defined2 iostate;
    static const iostate badbit,     // stream is corrupted
                         eofbit,     // end-of-file seen
                         failbit,    // next operation will fail
                         goodbit;    // goodbit==0

    // ...
};
```

The I/O state flags can be directly manipulated. For example:

```
void f()
{
    ios_base::iostate s = cin.rdstate();   // returns a set of iostate bits

    if (s & ios_base::badbit) {
        // cin characters possibly lost
    }
    // ...
    cin.setstate(ios_base::failbit);
    // ...
}
```

When a stream is used as a condition, the state of the stream is tested by *operator void** () or *operator!* (). The tests succeed only if the state is !*fail* () and *fail* (), respectively. For example, a general copy function can be written like this:

```
template<class T> void iocopy(istream& is, ostream& os)
{
    T buf;
    while (is>>buf) os << buf << '\n';
}
```

The *is>>buf* returns a reference to *is*, which is tested by a call of *is::operator void** (). For example:

```
void f(istream& i1, istream& i2, istream& i3, istream& i4)
{
      iocopy<complex>(i1,cout);        // copy complex numbers
      iocopy<double>(i2,cout);         // copy doubles
      iocopy<char>(i3,cout);           // copy chars
      iocopy<string>(i4,cout);         // copy whitespace-separated words
}
```

21.3.4 Input of Characters

The >> operator is intended for formatted input; that is, reading objects of an expected type and format. When we want to read characters without making assumptions about their meaning, we use the *unformatted input* functions:

```
template <class Ch, class Tr = char_traits<Ch> >
class basic_istream : virtual public basic_ios<Ch,Tr> {
public:
      // ...
      // unformatted input:

      streamsize gcount() const;       // number of char read by last get()

      int_type get();                  // read one Ch (or Tr::eof())

      basic_istream& get(Ch& c);       // read one Ch into c

      basic_istream& get(Ch* p, streamsize n);       // newline is terminator
      basic_istream& get(Ch* p, streamsize n, Ch term);

      basic_istream& getline(Ch* p, streamsize n);   // newline is terminator
      basic_istream& getline(Ch* p, streamsize n, Ch term);

      basic_istream& ignore(streamsize n = 1, int_type t = Tr::eof());
      basic_istream& read(Ch* p, streamsize n);      // read at most n char
      // ...
};
```

In addition, *<string>* offers *getline*() for standard *strings* (§20.3.15).

The unformatted input functions do not skip whitespace.

If a *get*() or *getline*() function doesn't read and remove at least one character from the stream, *setstate*(*failbit*) is called, so that subsequent reads from the stream will fail (or an exception is thrown (§21.3.6)).

The *get*(*char&*) function reads a single character into its argument. For example:

```
int main()
{
      char c;
      while(cin.get(c)) cout.put(c);       // character-by-character copy
}
```

The three-argument *s*.*get*(*p*,*n*,*term*) reads at most *n−1* characters into *p*[0]..*p*[*n−2*]. A call of *get*() will always place a *0* at the end of the characters (if any) it placed in *p*[], so *p* must point to an array of at least *n* characters. The third argument, *term*, specifies a terminator. A typical use of the three-argument *get*() is to read a "line" into a fixed-sized buffer for further analysis:

```
void f()
{
    char buf[100];
    cin >> buf;                  // suspect: will overflow some day
    cin.get(buf, 100, '\n');     // safe
    // ...
}
```

If the terminator is found, it is left as the first unread character on the stream. Never call *get*() twice without removing the terminator. For example:

```
void subtle_error()
{
    char buf[256];

    while (cin) {
        cin.get(buf, 256);    // read a line
        cout << buf;          // print a line
        // Oops: forgot to remove '\n' from cin - the next get() will fail
    }
}
```

This example is a good reason to prefer *getline*() over *get*(). A *getline*() behaves like its corresponding *get*(), except that it removes its terminator from the *istream*. For example:

```
void f()
{
    char word[MAX_WORD][MAX_LINE];    // MAX_WORD arrays of MAX_LINE char each
    int i = 0;
    while (cin.getline(word[i++], MAX_LINE, '\n') && i<MAX_WORD);
    // ...
}
```

When efficiency isn't paramount, it is better to read into a *string* (§3.6, §20.3.15). In that way, the most common allocation and overflow problems cannot occur. However, the *get*(), *getline*(), and *read*() functions are needed to implement such higher-level facilities. The relatively messy interface is the price we pay for speed, for not having to re-scan the input to figure out what terminated the input operation, for being able to reliably limit the number of characters read, etc.

A call *read*(*p*, *n*) reads at most *n* characters into *p*[*0*]..*p*[*n*−*1*]. The read function does not rely on a terminator, and it doesn't put a terminating *0* into its target. Consequently, it really can read *n* characters (rather than just *n*−*1*). In other words, it simply reads characters and doesn't try to make its target into a C-style string.

The *ignore*() function reads characters like *read*(), but it doesn't store them anywhere. Like *read*(), it really can read *n* characters (rather than *n*−*1*). The default number of characters read by *ignore*() is *1*, so a call of *ignore*() without an argument means "throw the next character away." Like *getline*(), it optionally takes a terminator and removes that terminator from the input stream if it gets to it. Note that *ignore*()'s default terminator is end-of-file.

For all of these functions, it is not immediately obvious what terminated the read – and it can be hard even to remember which function has what termination criterion. However, we can always inquire whether we reached end-of-file (§21.3.3). Also, *gcount* ( ) gives the number of characters read from the stream by the most recent, unformatted input function call. For example:

```
void read_a_line (int max)
{
    // ...
    if (cin.fail( )) {        // Oops: bad input format
        cin.clear( );                 // clear the input flags (§21.3.3)
        cin.ignore (max, ´ ; ´ );     // skip to semicolon

        if ( !cin) {
            // oops: we reached the end of the stream
        }
        else if (cin.gcount( ) ==max) {
            // oops: read max characters
        }
        else {
            // found and discarded the semicolon
        }
    }
}
```

Unfortunately, if the maximum number of characters are read there is no way of knowing whether the terminator was found (as the last character).

The *get* ( ) that doesn't take an argument is the *<iostream>* version of the *<cstdio>* getchar ( ) (§21.8). It simply reads a character and returns the character's numeric value. In that way, it avoids making assumptions about the character type used. If there is no input character to return, *get* ( ) returns a suitable "end-of-file" marker (that is, the stream's *traits_type* : : *eof* ( )) and sets the *istream* into *eof*-state (§21.3.3). For example:

```
void f(unsigned char* p)
{
    int i;
    while ( (i = cin.get( )) && i!=EOF) {
        *p++ = i;
        // ...
    }
}
```

EOF is the value of *eof* ( ) from the usual *char_traits* for *char*. *EOF* is presented in *<iostream>*. Thus, this loop could have been written *read* (p, *MAX_INT*), but presumably we wrote an explicit loop because we wanted to look at each character as it came in. It has been said that C's greatest strength is its ability to read a character and decide to do nothing with it – and to do this fast. It is indeed an important and underrated strength, and one that C++ aims to preserve.

The standard header *<cctype>* defines several functions that can be useful when processing input (§20.4.2). For example, an *eatwhite* ( ) function that reads whitespace characters from a stream could be defined like this:

```
istream& eatwhite(istream& is)
{
    char c;
    while (is.get(c)) {
        if (!isspace(c)) {     // is c a whitespace character?
            is.putback(c);  // put c back into the input buffer
            break;
        }
    }
    return is;
}
```

The call *is.putback(c)* makes *c* be the next character read from the stream *is* (§21.6.4).

21.3.5 Input of User-Defined Types

An input operation can be defined for a user-defined type exactly as an output operation was. However, for an input operation, it is essential that the second argument be of a non-*const* reference type. For example:

```
istream& operator>>(istream& s, complex& a)
/*
    input formats for a complex ("f" indicates a floating-point number):
        f
        (f)
        (f,f)
*/
{
    double re = 0, im = 0;
    char c = 0;

    s >> c;
    if (c == '(') {
        s >> re >> c;
        if (c == ',') s >> im >> c;
        if (c != ')') s.clear(ios_base::badbit);  // set state
    }
    else {
        s.putback(c);
        s >> re;
    }

    if (s) a = complex(re, im);
    return s;
}
```

Despite the scarcity of error-handling code, this will actually handle most kinds of errors. The local variable *c* is initialized to avoid having its value accidentally be ´ (´ after a failed first >> operation. The final check of the stream state ensures that the value of the argument *a* is changed only if everything went well.

The operation for setting a stream state is called *clear* ( ) because its most common use is to reset the state of a stream to *good* ( ) ; *ios_base* : : *goodbit* is the default argument value for *clear* ( ) (§21.3.3).

21.3.6 Exceptions

It is not convenient to test for errors after each I/O operation, so a common cause of error is failing to do so where it matters. In particular, output operations are typically unchecked, but they do occasionally fail.

The only function that directly changes the state of a stream is *clear* ( ). Thus, an obvious way of getting notified by a state change is to ask *clear* ( ) to throw an exception. The *basic_ios* member *exceptions* ( ) does just that:

```
template <class Ch, class Tr = char_traits<Ch> >
class basic_ios : public ios_base {
public :
        // ...

        class failure;    // exception class (see §14.10)

        iostate exceptions () const;             // get exception state
        void exceptions (iostate except);        // set exception state

        // ...
};
```

For example,

```
cout.exceptions (ios_base : : badbit | ios_base : : failbit | ios_base : : eofbit);
```

requests that *clear* ( ) should throw an *ios_base* : : *failure* exception if *cout* goes into states *bad*, *fail*, or *eof* – in other words, if any output operation on *cout* doesn't perform flawlessly. If necessary, we can examine *cout* to determine exactly what went wrong. Similarly,

```
cin.exceptions (ios_base : : badbit | ios_base : : failbit);
```

allows us to catch the not-too-uncommon case in which the input is not in the format we expected, so that an input operation wouldn't return a value from the stream.

A call of *exceptions* ( ) with no arguments returns the set of I/O state flags that triggers an exception. For example:

```
void print_exceptions (ios_base& ios)
{
        ios_base : : iostate s = ios.exceptions ();
        if (s&ios_base : : badbit) cout << "throws for bad";
        if (s&ios_base : : failbit) cout << "throws for fail";
        if (s&ios_base : : eofbit) cout << "throws for eof";
        if (s == 0) cout << "doesn't throw";
}
```

The primary use of I/O exceptions is to catch unlikely – and therefore often forgotten – errors. Another is to control I/O. For example:

```
void readints (vector<int>& s)            // not my favorite style!
{
      ios_base::iostate old_state = cin.exceptions();  // save exception state
      cin.exceptions(ios_base::eofbit);                // throw for eof

      for (;;)
            try {
                  int i;
                  cin>>i;
                  s.push_back(i);
            }
            catch(ios_base::failure) {
                  // ok: end of file reached
            }

      cin.exceptions(old_state);        // reset exception state
}
```

The question to ask about this use of exceptions is, "Is that an error?" or "Is that really exceptional?" (§14.5). Usually, I find that the answer to either question is no. Consequently, I prefer to deal with the stream state directly. What can be handled with local control structures within a function is rarely improved by the use of exceptions.

21.3.7 Tying of Streams

The *basic_ios* function *tie()* is used to set up and break connections between an *istream* and an *ostream*:

```
template <class Ch, class Tr = char_traits<Ch> >
class std::basic_ios : public ios_base {
      // ...
      basic_ostream<Ch,Tr>* tie() const;              // get pointer to tied stream
      basic_ostream<Ch,Tr>* tie(basic_ostream<Ch,Tr>* s);   // tie *this to s

      // ...
};
```

Consider:

```
string get_passwd()
{
      string s;
      cout << "Password: ";
      cin >> s;
      // ...
}
```

How can we be sure that *Password*: appears on the screen before the read operation is executed? The output on *cout* is buffered, so if *cin* and *cout* had been independent, *Password*: would not have appeared on the screen until the output buffer was full. The answer is that *cout* is tied to *cin* by the operation *cin.tie(&cout)*.

When an *ostream* is tied to an *istream*, the *ostream* is flushed whenever an input operation on the *istream* causes underflow; that is, whenever new characters are needed from the ultimate input source to complete the input operation. Thus,

```
cout << "Password: ";
cin >> s;
```

is equivalent to:

```
cout << "Password: ";
cout.flush();
cin >> s;
```

A stream can have at most one *ostream* at a time tied to it. A call *s.tie(0)* unties the stream *s* from the stream it was tied to, if any. Like most other stream functions that set a value, *tie(s)* returns the previous value; that is, it returns the previously tied stream or *0*. A call without an argument, *tie()*, returns the current value without changing it.

Of the standard streams, *cout* is tied to *cin* and *wcout* is tied to *wcin*. The *cerr* streams need not be tied because they are unbuffered, while the *clog* streams are not meant for user interaction.

21.3.8 Sentries

When I wrote operators << and >> for *complex*, I did not worry about tied streams (§21.3.7) or whether changing stream state would cause exceptions (§21.3.6). I assumed — correctly — that the library-provided functions would take care of that for me. But how? There are a couple of dozen such functions. If we had to write intricate code to handle tied streams, *locale*s (§21.7), exceptions, etc., in each, then the code could get rather messy.

The approach taken is to provide the common code through a *sentry* class. Code that needs to be executed first (the ''prefix code'') — such as flushing a tied stream — is provided as the *sentry*'s constructor. Code that needs to be executed last (the ''suffix code'') — such as throwing exceptions caused by state changes — is provided as the *sentry*'s destructor:

```
template <class Ch, class Tr = char_traits<Ch> >
class basic_ostream : virtual public basic_ios<Ch,Tr> {
    // ...
    class sentry;
    // ...
};

template <class Ch, class Tr = char_traits<Ch> >
class basic_ostream<Ch,Tr>::sentry {
public:
    explicit sentry(basic_ostream<Ch,Tr>& s);
    ~sentry();
    operator bool();

    // ...
};
```

Thus, common code is factored out and an individual function can be written like this:

```
template <class Ch, class Tr = char_traits<Ch> >
basic_ostream<Ch,Tr>& basic_ostream<Ch,Tr>::operator<<(int i)
{
    sentry s(*this);
    if (!s) {   // check whether all is well for output to start
        setstate(failbit);
        return *this;
    }

    // output the int
    return *this;
}
```

This technique of using constructors and destructors to provide common prefix and suffix code through a class is useful in many contexts.

Naturally, *basic_istream* has a similar *sentry* member class.

21.4 Formatting

The examples in §21.2 were all of what is commonly called *unformatted output*. That is, an object was turned into a sequence of characters according to default rules. Often, the programmer needs more detailed control. For example, we need to be able to control the amount of space used for an output operation and the format used for output of numbers. Similarly, some aspects of input can be explicitly controlled.

Control of I/O formatting resides in class *basic_ios* and its base *ios_base*. For example, class *basic_ios* holds the information about the base (octal, decimal, or hexadecimal) to be used when integers are written or read, the precision of floating-point numbers written or read, etc. It also holds the functions to set and examine these per-stream control variables.

Class *basic_ios* is a base of *basic_istream* and *basic_ostream*, so format control is on a per-stream basis.

21.4.1 Format State

Formatting of I/O is controlled by a set of flags and integer values in the stream's *ios_base*:

```
class ios_base {
public:
    // ...
    // names of format flags:

    typedef implementation_defined1 fmtflags;
    static const fmtflags
        skipws,             // skip whitespace on input

        left,               // field adjustment: pad after value
        right,              // pad before value
        internal,           // pad between sign and value
```

boolalpha,	// *use symbolic representation of true and false*
dec,	// *integer base: base 10 output (decimal)*
hex,	// *base 16 output (hexadecimal)*
oct,	// *base 8 output (octal)*
scientific,	// *floating-point notation: d.ddddddEdd*
fixed,	// *dddd.dd*
showbase,	// *on output prefix oct by 0 and hex by 0x*
showpoint,	// *print trailing zeros*
showpos,	// *explicit '+' for positive ints*
uppercase,	// *'E', 'X' rather than 'e', 'x'*
adjustfield,	// *flags related to field adjustment (§21.4.5)*
basefield,	// *flags related to integer base (§21.4.2)*
floatfield,	// *flags related to floating-point output (§21.4.3)*
unitbuf;	// *flush output after each output operation*

```
    fmtflags flags() const;          // read flags
    fmtflags flags(fmtflags f);      // set flags

    fmtflags setf(fmtflags f) { return flags(flags()|f); }          // add flag
    // clear and set flags in mask:
    fmtflags setf(fmtflags f, fmtflags mask) { return flags((flags()&~mask)|(f&mask)); }
    void unsetf(fmtflags mask) { flags(flags()&~mask); }            // clear flags

    // ...
};
```

The values of the flags are implementation-defined. Use the symbolic names exclusively, rather than numeric values, even if those values happen to be correct on your implementation today.

Defining an interface as a set of flags, and providing operations for setting and clearing those flags is a time-honored if somewhat old-fashioned technique. Its main virtue is that a user can compose a set of options. For example:

```
    const ios_base::fmtflags my_opt = ios_base::left|ios_base::oct|ios_base::fixed;
```

This allows us to pass options around and install them where needed. For example:

```
    void your_function(ios_base::fmtflags opt)
    {
        ios_base::fmtflags old_options = cout.flags(opt);    // save old_options and set new ones
        // ...
        cout.flags(old_options);    // reset options
    }

    void my_function()
    {
        your_function(my_opt);
        // ...
    }
```

The *flags*() function returns the old option set.

Being able to read and set all options allows us to set an individual flag. For example:

> *myostream . flags* (*myostream . flags* ( ) | *ios_base* : : *showpos*) ;

This makes *myostream* display an explicit + in front of positive numbers without affecting other options. The old options are read, and *showpos* is set by or-ing it into the set. The function *setf* ( ) does exactly that, so the example could equivalently have been written:

> *myostream . setf* (*ios_base* : : *showpos*) ;

Once set, a flag retains its value until it is unset.

Controlling I/O options by explicitly setting and clearing flags is crude and error-prone. For simple cases, manipulators (§21.4.6) provide a cleaner interface. Using flags to control stream state is a better study in implementation technique than in interface design.

21.4.1.1 Copying Format State

The complete format state of a stream can be copied by *copyfmt* ( ) :

```
template <class  Ch,  class  Tr = char_traits<Ch> >
class  basic_ios : public  ios_base {
public :
        // ...
        basic_ios& copyfmt (const  basic_ios& f) ;
        // ...
} ;
```

The stream's buffer (§21.6) and the state of that buffer isn't copied by *copyfmt* ( ). However, all of the rest of the state is, including the requested exceptions (§21.3.6) and any user-supplied additions to that state (§21.7.1).

21.4.2 Integer Output

The technique of or-ing in a new option with *flags* ( ) or *setf* ( ) works only when a single bit controls a feature. This is not the case for options such as the base used for printing integers and the style of floating-point output. For such options, the value that specifies a style is not necessarily represented by a single bit or as a set of independent single bits.

The solution adopted in *<iostream>* is to provide a version of *setf* ( ) that takes a second ''pseudo argument'' that indicates which kind of option we want to set in addition to the new value. For example,

```
cout . setf (ios_base : : oct , ios_base : : basefield) ;    // octal
cout . setf (ios_base : : dec , ios_base : : basefield) ;    // decimal
cout . setf (ios_base : : hex , ios_base : : basefield) ;    // hexadecimal
```

sets the base of integers without side effects on other parts of the stream state. Once set, a base is used until reset. For example,

```
cout << 1234 << ' ' << 1234 << ' ' ;              // default: decimal
```

```
cout.setf(ios_base::oct,ios_base::basefield);    // octal
cout << 1234 << ´ ´ << 1234 << ´ ´;

cout.setf(ios_base::hex,ios_base::basefield);    // hexadecimal
cout << 1234 << ´ ´ << 1234 << ´ ´;
```

produces *1234 1234 2322 2322 4d2 4d2*.

If we need to be able to tell which base was used for each number, we can set *showbase*. Thus, adding

```
cout.setf(ios_base::showbase);
```

before the previous operations, we get *1234 1234 02322 02322 0x4d2 0x4d2*. The standard manipulators (§21.4.6.2) provide a more elegant way of specifying the base of integer output.

21.4.3 Floating-Point Output

Floating-point output is controlled by a *format* and a *precision*:
- The *general* format lets the implementation choose a format that presents a value in the style that best preserves the value in the space available. The precision specifies the maximum number of digits. It corresponds to *printf()*'s %g (§21.8).
- The *scientific* format presents a value with one digit before a decimal point and an exponent. The precision specifies the maximum number of digits after the decimal point. It corresponds to *printf()*'s %e.
- The *fixed* format presents a value as an integer part followed by a decimal point and a fractional part. The precision specifies the maximum number of digits after the decimal point. It corresponds to *printf()*'s %f.

We control the floating-point output format through the state manipulation functions. In particular, we can set the notation used for printing floating-point values without side effects on other parts of the stream state. For example,

```
cout << "default:\t" << 1234.56789 << ´\n´;

cout.setf(ios_base::scientific,ios_base::floatfield);    // use scientific format
cout << "scientific:\t" << 1234.56789 << ´\n´;

cout.setf(ios_base::fixed,ios_base::floatfield);         // use fixed-point format
cout << "fixed:\t" << 1234.56789 << ´\n´;

cout.setf(ios_base::fmtflags(0),ios_base::floatfield);   // reset to default (that is, general format)
cout << "default:\t" << 1234.56789 << ´\n´;
```

produces

```
default:    1234.57
scientific: 1.234568e+03
fixed:      1234.567890
default:    1234.57
```

The default precision (for all formats) is *6*. The precision is controlled by an *ios_base* member function:

```
class ios_base {
public:
    // ...
    streamsize  precision() const;           // get precision
    streamsize  precision(streamsize  n);    // set precision (and get old precision)
    // ...
};
```

A call of *precision*() affects all floating-point I/O operations for a stream up until the next call of *precision*(). Thus,

```
cout.precision(8);
cout << 1234.56789 << ' ' << 1234.56789 << ' ' << 123456 << '\n';

cout.precision(4);
cout << 1234.56789 << ' ' << 1234.56789 << ' ' << 123456 << '\n';
```

produces

```
1234.5679  1234.5679  123456
1235  1235  123456
```

Note that floating-point values are rounded rather than just truncated and that *precision*() doesn't affect integer output.

The *uppercase* flag (§21.4.1) determines whether *e* or *E* is used to indicate the exponents in the scientific format.

Manipulators provide a more elegant way of specifying output format for floating-point output (§21.4.6.2).

21.4.4 Output Fields

Often, we want to fill a specific space on an output line with text. We want to use exactly *n* characters and not fewer (and more only if the text does not fit). To do this, we specify a field width and a character to be used if padding is needed:

```
class ios_base {
public:
    // ...
    streamsize  width() const;              // get field width
    streamsize  width(streamsize  wide);    // set field width
    // ...
};

template <class Ch, class Tr = char_traits<Ch> >
class basic_ios : public ios_base {
public:
    // ...
    Ch  fill() const;                       // get filler character
    Ch  fill(Ch  ch);                       // set filler character
    // ...
};
```

The *width* ( ) function specifies the minimum number of characters to be used for the next standard library << output operation of a numeric value, *bool*, C-style string, character, pointer (§21.2.1), *string* (§20.3.15), and *bitset* (§17.5.3.3). For example,

```
cout.width(4);
cout << 12;
```

will print *12* preceded by two spaces.

The ''padding'' or ''filler'' character can be specified by the *fill* ( ) function. For example,

```
cout.width(4);
cout.fill('#');
cout << "ab";
```

gives the output ##*ab*.

The default fill character is the space character and the default field size is *0*, meaning ''as many characters as needed.'' The field size can be reset to its default value like this:

```
cout.width(0); // ''as many characters as needed''
```

A call *width* (*n*) function sets the minimum number of characters to *n*. If more characters are provided, they will all be printed. For example,

```
cout.width(4);
cout << "abcdef";
```

produces *abcdef* rather than just *abcd*. It is usually better to get the right output looking ugly than to get the wrong output looking just fine (see also §21.10[21]).

A *width* (*n*) call affects only the immediately following << output operation:

```
cout.width(4);
cout.fill('#');
cout << 12 << ':' << 13;
```

This produces ##*12*:*13*, rather than ##*12*###:##*13*, as would have been the case had *width* (*4*) applied to subsequent operations. Had all subsequent output operations been affected by *width* ( ), we would have had to explicitly specify *width* ( ) for essentially all values.

The standard manipulators (§21.4.6.2) provide a more elegant way of specifying the width of an output field.

21.4.5 Field Adjustment

The adjustment of characters within a field can be controlled by *setf* ( ) calls:

```
cout.setf(ios_base::left, ios_base::adjustfield);      // left
cout.setf(ios_base::right, ios_base::adjustfield);     // right
cout.setf(ios_base::internal, ios_base::adjustfield);  // internal
```

This sets the adjustment of output within an output field defined by *ios_base* :: *width* ( ) without side effects on other parts of the stream state.

Adjustment can be specified like this:

```
cout.fill('#');

cout << '(';
cout.width(4);
cout << -12 << "),(";

cout.width(4);
cout.setf(ios_base::left, ios_base::adjustfield);
cout << -12 << "),(";

cout.width(4);
cout.setf(ios_base::internal, ios_base::adjustfield);
cout << -12 << ")";
```

This produces: `(#-12)`, `(-12#)`, `(-#12)`. Internal adjustment places fill characters between the sign and the value. As shown, right adjustment is the default. It is undefined what happens if more than one adjustment flag are simultaneously set.

21.4.6 Manipulators

To save the programmer from having to deal with the state of a stream in terms of flags, the standard library provides a set of functions for manipulating that state. The key idea is to insert an operation that modifies the state in between the objects being read or written. For example, we can explicitly request that an output buffer be flushed:

```
cout << x << flush << y << flush;
```

Here, `cout.flush()` is called at the appropriate times. This is done by a version of `<<` that takes a pointer to function argument and invokes it:

```
template <class Ch, class Tr = char_traits<Ch> >
class basic_ostream : virtual public basic_ios<Ch,Tr> {
public:
    // ...

    basic_ostream& operator<<(basic_ostream& (*f)(basic_ostream&)) { return f(*this); }
    basic_ostream& operator<<(ios_base& (*f)(ios_base&));
    basic_ostream& operator<<(basic_ios<Ch,Tr>& (*f)(basic_ios<Ch,Tr>&));

    // ...
};
```

For this to work, a function must be a nonmember or static-member function with the right type. In particular, `flush()` is defined like this:

```
template <class Ch, class Tr = char_traits<Ch> >
basic_ostream<Ch,Tr>& flush(basic_ostream<Ch,Tr>& s)
{
    return s.flush();     // call ostream's member flush()
}
```

These declarations ensure that

>   *cout* << *flush*;

is resolved as

>   *cout*.*operator*<< (*flush*);

which calls

>   *flush* (*cout*);

which then invokes

>   *cout*.*flush*();

The whole rigmarole is done (at compile time) to allow *basic_ostream*::*flush*() to be called using the *cout<<flush* notation.

There is a wide variety of operations we might like to perform just before or just after an input or output operation. For example:

```
cout << x;
cout.flush();
cout << y;

cin.unsetf(ios_base::skipws);    // don't skip whitespace (§21.4.1)
cin >> x;
```

When the operations are written as separate statements, the logical connections between the operations are not obvious. Once the logical connection is lost, the code gets harder to understand. The notion of manipulators allows operations such as *flush*() and *unsetf*(*ios_base*::*skipws*) to be inserted directly in the list of input or output operations. For example:

```
cout << x << flush << y << flush;
cin >> noskipws >> x;
```

Note that manipulators are in the *std* namespace so that they must be explicitly qualified where *std* isn't part of the current scope:

```
std::cout << endl;         // error: endl not in scope
std::cout << std::endl;    // ok
```

Naturally, class *basic_istream* provides >> operators for invoking manipulators in a way similar to class *basic_ostream*:

```
template <class Ch, class Tr = char_traits<Ch> >
class basic_istream : virtual public basic_ios<Ch,Tr> {
public:
    // ...
    basic_istream& operator>> (basic_istream& (*pf) (basic_istream&));
    basic_istream& operator>> (basic_ios<Ch,Tr>& (*pf) (basic_ios<Ch,Tr>&));
    basic_istream& operator>> (ios_base& (*pf) (ios_base&));
    // ...
};
```

21.4.6.1 Manipulators Taking Arguments

Manipulators that take arguments can also be useful. For example, we might want to write

> *cout << setprecision (4) << angle;*

to print the value of the floating-point variable *angle* with four digits.

To do this, *setprecision* must return an object that is initialized by *4* and that calls *cout.precision (4)* when invoked. Such a manipulator is a function object that is invoked by *<<* rather than by ( ). The exact type of that function object is implementation-defined, but it might be defined like this:

```
struct smanip {
    ios_base& (*f) (ios_base&, int);        // function to be called
    int i;

    smanip (ios_base& (*ff) (ios_base&, int), int ii) : f(ff), i(ii) { }
};

template<class Ch, class Tr>
ostream<Ch, Tr>& operator<< (ostream<Ch, Tr>& os, const smanip& m)
{
    return m.f(os, m.i);
}
```

The *smanip* constructor stores its arguments in *f* and *i*, and *operator<<* calls *f(i)*. We can now define *setprecision ( )* like this:

```
ios_base& set_precision (ios_base& s, int n)      // helper
{
    return s.precision (n);      // call the member function
}

inline smanip setprecision (int n)
{
    return smanip (set_precision, n);        // make the function object
}
```

We can now write:

> *cout << setprecision (4) << angle ;*

A programmer can define new manipulators in the style of *smanip* as needed (§21.10[22]). Doing this does not require modification of the definitions of standard library templates and classes such as *basic_istream, basic_ostream, basic_ios,* and *ios_base*.

21.4.6.2 Standard I/O Manipulators

The standard library provides manipulators corresponding to the various format states and state changes. The standard manipulators are defined in namespace *std*. Manipulators taking *ios_base* are presented in *<ios>*. Manipulators taking *istream* and *ostream* are presented in *<istream>* and *<ostream>*, respectively, and also in *<iostream>*. The rest of the standard manipulators are presented in *<iomanip>*.

```
ios_base& boolalpha(ios_base&);          // symbolic representation of true and false (input and output)
ios_base& noboolalpha(ios_base& s);      // s.unsetf(ios_base::boolalpha)

ios_base& showbase(ios_base&);           // on output prefix oct by 0 and hex by 0x
ios_base& noshowbase(ios_base& s);       // s.unsetf(ios_base::showbase)

ios_base& showpoint(ios_base&);
ios_base& noshowpoint(ios_base& s);      // s.unsetf(ios_base::showpoint)

ios_base& showpos(ios_base&);
ios_base& noshowpos(ios_base& s);        // s.unsetf(ios_base::showpos)

ios_base& skipws(ios_base&);             // skip whitespace
ios_base& noskipws(ios_base& s);         // s.unsetf(ios_base::skipws)

ios_base& uppercase(ios_base&);          // X and E rather than x and e
ios_base& nouppercase(ios_base&);        // x and e rather than X and E

ios_base& internal(ios_base&);           // adjust §21.4.5
ios_base& left(ios_base&);               // pad after value
ios_base& right(ios_base&);              // pad before value

ios_base& dec(ios_base&);                // integer base is 10 (§21.4.2)
ios_base& hex(ios_base&);                // integer base is 16
ios_base& oct(ios_base&);                // integer base is 8

ios_base& fixed(ios_base&);              // floating-point format dddd.dd (§21.4.3)
ios_base& scientific(ios_base&);         // scientific format d.ddddEdd

template <class Ch, class Tr>
    basic_ostream<Ch,Tr>& endl(basic_ostream<Ch,Tr>&);    // put '\n' and flush
template <class Ch, class Tr>
    basic_ostream<Ch,Tr>& ends(basic_ostream<Ch,Tr>&);    // put '\0'
template <class Ch, class Tr>
    basic_ostream<Ch,Tr>& flush(basic_ostream<Ch,Tr>&);   // flush stream

template <class Ch, class Tr>
    basic_istream<Ch,Tr>& ws(basic_istream<Ch,Tr>&);      // eat whitespace

smanip resetiosflags(ios_base::fmtflags f);     // clear flags (§21.4)
smanip setiosflags(ios_base::fmtflags f);       // set flags (§21.4)
smanip setbase(int b);                          // output integers in base b (§21.4.2)
smanip setfill(int c);                          // make c the fill character (§21.4.4)
smanip setprecision(int n);                     // n digits (§21.4.3, §21.4.6)
smanip setw(int n);                             // next field width is n char (§21.4.4)
```

For example,

```
cout << 1234 << ',' << hex << 1234 << ',' << oct << 1234 << endl;
```

produces *1234,4d2,2322* and

```
cout << '(' << setw(4) << setfill('#') << 12 << ") (" << 12 << ")\n";
```

produces (*##12*) (*12*).

When using manipulators that do not take arguments, *do not* add parentheses. When using standard manipulators that take arguments, remember to #*include <iomanip>*. For example:

```
#include <iostream>
using namespace std;

int main()
{
    cout << setprecision(4)          // error: setprecision undefined (forgot <iomanip>)
         << scientific()             // error: ostream<<ostream& (spurious parentheses)
         << 1.41421 << endl;
}
```

21.4.6.3 User-Defined Manipulators

A programmer can add manipulators in the style of the standard ones. Here, I present an additional style that I have found useful for formatting floating-point numbers.

The *precision* used persists for all output operations, but a *width*() operation applies to the next numeric output operation only. What I want is something that makes it simple to output a floating-point number in a predefined format without affecting future output operations on the stream. The basic idea is to define a class that represents formats, another that represents a format plus a value to be formatted, and then an operator << that outputs the value to an *ostream* according to the format. For example:

```
Form gen4(4);  // general format, precision is 4

void f(double d)
{
    Form sci8 = gen4;
    sci8.scientific().precision(8);  // scientific format, precision 8

    cout << d << ´ ´ << gen4(d) << ´ ´ << sci8(d) << ´ ´ << d << ´\n´;
}
```

A call *f(1234.56789)* writes

```
1234.57  1235  1.23456789e+03  1234.57
```

Note how the use of a *Form* doesn't affect the state of the stream so that the last output of *d* has the same default format as the first.

Here is a simplified implementation:

```
class Bound_form;      // Form plus value

class Form {
    friend ostream& operator<<(ostream&, const Bound_form&);

    int prc;      // precision
    int wdt;      // width, 0 means as wide as necessary
    int fmt;      // general, scientific, or fixed (§21.4.3)
    // ...
```

```
public:
    explicit Form(int p = 6) : prc(p)      // default precision is 6
    {
        fmt = 0;     // general format (§21.4.3)
        wdt = 0;     // as wide as necessary
    }

    Bound_form operator()(double d) const;  // make a Bound_form for *this and d

    Form& scientific() { fmt = ios_base::scientific; return *this; }
    Form& fixed() { fmt = ios_base::fixed; return *this; }
    Form& general() { fmt = 0; return *this; }

    Form& uppercase();
    Form& lowercase();
    Form& precision(int p) { prc = p; return *this; }

    Form& width(int w) { wdt = w; return *this; }          // applies to all types
    Form& fill(char);

    Form& plus(bool b = true);                             // explicit plus
    Form& trailing_zeros(bool b = true);                   // print trailing zeros
    // ...
};
```

The idea is that a *Form* holds all the information needed to format one data item. The default is chosen to be reasonable for many uses, and the various member functions can be used to reset individual aspects of formatting. The () operator is used to bind a value with the format to be used to output it. A *Bound_form* can then be output to a given stream by a suitable << function:

```
struct Bound_form {
    const Form& f;
    double val;

    Bound_form(const Form& ff, double v) : f(ff), val(v) { }
};

Bound_form Form::operator()(double d) const { return Bound_form(*this, d); }

ostream& operator<<(ostream& os, const Bound_form& bf)
{
    ostringstream s;           // string streams are described in §21.5.3
    s.precision(bf.f.prc);
    s.setf(bf.f.fmt, ios_base::floatfield);
    s << bf.val;               // compose string in s
    return os << s.str();      // output s to os
}
```

Writing a less simplistic implementation of << is left as an exercise (§21.10[21]). The *Form* and *Bound_form* classes are easily extended for formatting integers, strings, etc. (see §21.10[20]).

Note that these declarations make the combination of << and () into a ternary operator; *cout<<sci4(d)* collects the *ostream*, the format, and the value into a single function before doing any real computation.

21.5 File Streams and String Streams

When a C++ program starts, *cout*, *cerr*, *clog*, *cin*, and their wide-character equivalents (§21.2.1) are available for use. These streams are set up by default and their correspondence with I/O devices or files is determined by ''the system.'' In addition, you can create your own streams. In this case, you must specify to what the streams are attached. Attaching a stream to a file or to a *string* is common enough so as to be supported directly by the standard library. Here is the hierarchy of standard stream classes:

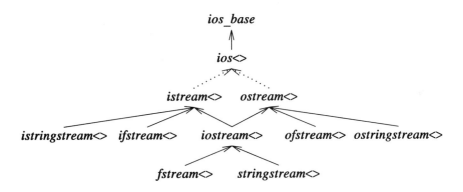

The classes suffixed by <> are templates parameterized on the character type, and their names have a *basic_* prefix. A dotted line indicates a virtual base class (§15.2.4).

Files and strings are examples of containers that you can both read from and write to. Consequently, you can have a stream that supports both << and >>. Such a stream is called an *iostream*, which is defined in namespace *std* and presented in *<iostream>*:

```
template <class Ch, class Tr = char_traits<Ch> >
class basic_iostream : public basic_istream<Ch,Tr>, public basic_ostream<Ch,Tr> {
public:
    explicit basic_iostream(basic_streambuf<Ch,Tr>* sb);
    virtual ~basic_iostream();
};

typedef basic_iostream<char> iostream;
typedef basic_iostream<wchar_t> wiostream;
```

Reading and writing from an *iostream* is controlled through the put-buffer and get-buffer operations on the *iostream*'s *streambuf* (§21.6.4).

21.5.1 File Streams

Here is a complete program that copies one file to another. The file names are taken as command-line arguments:

```
#include <fstream>
#include <cstdlib>
```

```
void error(const char* p, const char* p2 = " ")
{
    cerr << p << ' ' << p2 << '\n';
    std::exit(1);
}

int main(int argc, char* argv[])
{
    if (argc != 3) error("wrong number of arguments");

    std::ifstream from(argv[1]);                        // open input file stream
    if (!from) error("cannot open input file", argv[1]);

    std::ofstream to(argv[2]);                          // open output file stream
    if (!to) error("cannot open output file", argv[2]);

    char ch;
    while (from.get(ch)) to.put(ch);    // copy characters

    if (!from.eof() || !to) error("something strange happened");
}
```

A file is opened for input by creating an object of class *ifstream* (input file stream) with the file name as the argument. Similarly, a file is opened for output by creating an object of class *ofstream* (output file stream) with the file name as the argument. In both cases, we test the state of the created object to see if the file was successfully opened.

A *basic_ofstream* is declared like this in *<fstream>*:

```
template <class Ch, class Tr = char_traits<Ch> >
class basic_ofstream : public basic_ostream<Ch, Tr> {
public:
    basic_ofstream();
    explicit basic_ofstream(const char* p, openmode m = out);

    basic_filebuf<Ch, Tr>* rdbuf() const;        // get pointer to current file buffer (§21.6.4)

    bool is_open() const;
    void open(const char* p, openmode m = out);
    void close();
};
```

A *basic_ifstream* is like an *basic_ofstream*, except that it is derived from *basic_istream* and is by default opened for reading. In addition, the standard library offers *basic_fstream*, which is like *basic_ofstream*, except that it is derived from *basic_iostream* and by default can be both read from and written to.

As usual, *typedef*s are available for the most common types:

```
typedef basic_ifstream<char> ifstream;
typedef basic_ofstream<char> ofstream;
typedef basic_fstream<char> fstream;
typedef basic_ifstream<wchar_t> wifstream;
typedef basic_ofstream<wchar_t> wofstream;
typedef basic_fstream<wchar_t> wfstream;
```

File stream constructors take a second argument specifying alternative modes of opening:

```
class ios_base {
public:
    // ...

    typedef implementation_defined3 openmode;
    static openmode app,       // append
                ate,       // open and seek to end of file (pronounced "at end")
                binary,    // I/O to be done in binary mode (rather than text mode)
                in,        // open for reading
                out,       // open for writing
                trunc;     // truncate file to 0-length

    // ...
};
```

The actual values of *openmode*s and their meanings are implementation-defined. Please consult your systems and library manual for details − and do experiment. The comments should give some idea of the intended meaning of the modes. For example, we can open a file so that anything written to it is appended to the end:

```
ofstream mystream(name.c_str(),ios_base::app);
```

It is also possible to open a file for both input and output. For example:

```
fstream dictionary("concordance",ios_base::in|ios_base::out);
```

21.5.2 Closing of Streams

A file can be explicitly closed by calling *close*() on its stream:

```
void f(ostream& mystream)
{
    // ...

    mystream.close();
}
```

However, this is implicitly done by the stream's destructor. So an explicit call of *close*() is needed only if the file must be closed before reaching the end of the scope in which its stream was declared.

This raises the question of how an implementation can ensure that the predefined streams *cout*, *cin*, *cerr*, and *clog* are created before their first use and closed (only) after their last use. Naturally, different implementations of the *<iostream>* stream library can use different techniques to achieve this. After all, exactly how it is done is an implementation detail that should not be visible to the user. Here, I present just one technique that is general enough to be used to ensure proper order of construction and destruction of global objects of a variety of types. An implementation may be able to do better by taking advantage of special features of a compiler or linker.

The fundamental idea is to define a helper class that is a counter that keeps track of how many times *<iostream>* has been included in a separately compiled source file:

```
class ios_base::Init {
    static int count;
public:
    Init();
    ~Init();
};

namespace { ios_base::Init __ioinit; } // in <iostream>, one copy in each file #including <iostream>

int ios_base::Init::count = 0;         // in some .c file
```

Each translation unit (§9.1) declares its own object called __*ioinit*. The constructor for the __*ioinit* objects uses *ios_base*::*Init*::*count* as a first-time switch to ensure that actual initialization of the global objects of the stream I/O library is done exactly once:

```
ios_base::Init::Init() { if (count++ == 0) { /* initialize cout, cerr, cin, etc. */ } }
```

Conversely, the destructor for the __*ioinit* objects uses *ios_base*::*Init*::*count* as a last-time switch to ensure that the streams are closed:

```
ios_base::Init::~Init() { if (--count == 0) { /* clean up cout (flush, etc.), cerr, cin, etc. */ } }
```

This is a general technique for dealing with libraries that require initialization and cleanup of global objects. In a system in which all code resides in main memory during execution, the technique is almost free. When that is not the case, the overhead of bringing each object file into main memory to execute its initialization function can be noticeable. When possible, it is better to avoid global objects. For a class in which each operation performs significant work, it can be reasonable to test a first-time switch (like *ios_base*::*Init*::*count*) in each operation to ensure initialization. However, that approach would have been prohibitively expensive for streams. The overhead of a first-time switch in the functions that read and write single characters would have been quite noticeable.

21.5.3 String Streams

A stream can be attached to a *string*. That is, we can read from a *string* and write to a *string* using the formatting facilities provided by streams. Such streams are called *stringstream*s. They are defined in <*sstream*>:

```
template <class Ch, class Tr = char_traits<Ch>, class A = allocator<Ch> >
class basic_stringstream : public basic_iostream<Ch,Tr> {
public:
    explicit basic_stringstream(ios_base::openmode m = out|in);
    explicit basic_stringstream(const basic_string<Ch,Tr,A>& s, openmode m = out|in);

    basic_string<Ch,Tr,A> str() const;            // get copy of string
    void str(const basic_string<Ch,Tr,A>& s);     // set value to copy of s

    basic_stringbuf<Ch,Tr,A>* rdbuf() const;      // get pointer to current file buffer
};
```

A *basic_istringstream* is like a *basic_stringstream*, except that it is derived from *basic_istream* and is by default opened for reading. A *basic_ostringstream*, is like a *basic_stringstream*, except that it is derived from *basic_ostream* and is by default opened for writing.

As usual, typedefs are provided for the most common specializations:

```
typedef basic_istringstream<char> istringstream;
typedef basic_ostringstream<char> ostringstream;
typedef basic_stringstream<char> stringstream;
typedef basic_istringstream<wchar_t> wistringstream;
typedef basic_ostringstream<wchar_t> wostringstream;
typedef basic_stringstream<wchar_t> wstringstream;
```

For example, an *ostringstream* can be used to format message *strings*:

```
string compose(int n, const string& cs)
{
    extern const char* std_message[];
    ostringstream ost;
    ost << "error(" << n << ") " << std_message[n] << " (user comment: " << cs << ')';
    return ost.str();
}
```

There is no need to check for overflow because *ost* is expanded as needed. This technique can be most useful for coping with cases in which the formatting required is more complicated than what is common for a line-oriented output device.

An initial value for a string stream is treated analogously to the way a file stream treats its file:

```
string compose2(int n, const string& cs)    // equivalent to compose()
{
    extern const char* std_message[];
    ostringstream ost("error(", ios_base::ate); // start writing at end of initial string
    ost << n << ") " << std_message[n] << " (user comment: " << cs << ')';
    return ost.str();
}
```

An *istringstream* is an input stream that reads from its initial *string* value (exactly as a *ifilestream* reads from its file):

```
#include <sstream>

void word_per_line(const string& s)  // prints one word per line
{
    istringstream ist(s);
    string w;
    while (ist>>w) cout << w << '\n';
}

int main()
{
    word_per_line("If you think C++ is difficult, try English");
}
```

The initializer *string* is copied into the *istringstream*. The end of the string terminates input.

It is possible to define streams that directly read from and write to arrays of characters (§21.10[26]). This is often useful when dealing with older code, especially since the *ostrstream* and *istrstream* classes doing that were part of the original streams library.

21.6 Buffering

Conceptually, an output stream puts characters into a buffer. Some time later, the characters are then written to wherever they are supposed to go. Such a buffer is called a *streambuf* (§21.6.4). Its definition is found in *<streambuf>*. Different types of *streambuf*s implement different buffering strategies. Typically, the *streambuf* stores characters in an array until an overflow forces it to write the characters to their real destination. Thus, an *ostream* can be represented graphically like this:

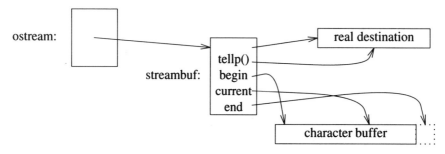

The set of template arguments for an *ostream* and its *streambuf* must be the same and determines the type of character used in the character buffer.

An *istream* is similar, except that the characters flow the other way.

Unbuffered I/O is simply I/O where the streambuf immediately transfers each character, rather than holding on to characters until enough have been gathered for efficient transfer.

21.6.1 Output Streams and Buffers

An *ostream* provides operations for converting values of various types into character sequences according to conventions (§21.2.1) and explicit formatting directives (§21.4). In addition, an *ostream* provides operations that deal directly with its *streambuf*:

```
template <class Ch, class Tr = char_traits<Ch> >
class basic_ostream : virtual public basic_ios<Ch,Tr> {
public:
    // ...
    explicit basic_ostream(basic_streambuf<Ch,Tr>* b);

    pos_type tellp();                              // get current position
    basic_ostream& seekp(pos_type);                // set current position
    basic_ostream& seekp(off_type, ios_base::seekdir);   // set current position

    basic_ostream& flush();          // empty buffer (to real destination)

    basic_ostream& operator<<(basic_streambuf<Ch,Tr>* b);  // write from b
};
```

An *ostream* is constructed with a *streambuf* argument, which determines how the characters written are handled and where they eventually go. For example, an *ostringstream* (§21.5.3) or an *ofstream* (§21.5.1) is created by initializing an *ostream* with a suitable *streambuf* (§21.6.4).

The *seekp*() functions are used to position an *ostream* for writing. The *p* suffix indicates that it is the position used for *putting* characters into the stream. These functions have no effect unless the stream is attached to something for which positioning is meaningful, such as a file. The *pos_type* represents a character position in a file, and the *off_type* represents an offset from a point indicated by an *ios_base* :: *seekdir*:

```
class ios_base {
    // ...
    typedef implementation_defined4 seekdir;
    static const seekdir beg,    // seek from beginning of current file
                         cur,    // seek from current position
                         end;    // seek backwards from end of current file
    // ...
};
```

Stream positions start at *0*, so we can think of a file as an array of *n* characters. For example:

```
int f(ofstream& fout) // fout refers to some file
{
    fout.seekp(10);
    fout << '#';                    // add character and move position (+1)
    fout.seekp(-2,ios_base::cur);
    fout << '*';
}
```

This places a # into *file* [*10*] and a * in *file* [*9*]. There is no similar way to do random access on elements of a plain *istream* or *ostream* (see §21.10[13]). Attempting to seek beyond the beginning or the end of a file puts the stream into the *bad* () state (§21.3.3).

The *flush* () operation allows the user to empty the buffer without waiting for an overflow.

It is possible to use << to write a *streambuf* directly into an *ostream*. This is primarily handy for implementers of I/O mechanisms.

21.6.2 Input Streams and Buffers

An *istream* provides operations for reading characters and converting them into values of various types (§21.3.1). In addition, an *istream* provides operations that deal directly with its *streambuf*:

```
template <class Ch, class Tr = char_traits<Ch> >
class basic_istream : virtual public basic_ios<Ch,Tr> {
public:
    // ...
    explicit basic_istream(basic_streambuf<Ch,Tr>* b);

    pos_type tellg();                                    // get current position
    basic_istream& seekg(pos_type);                      // set current position
    basic_istream& seekg(off_type, ios_base::seekdir);   // set current position

    basic_istream& putback(Ch c);  // put c back into the buffer
    basic_istream& unget();        // putback most recent char read
    int_type peek();               // look at next character to be read

    int sync();                    // clear buffer (flush)
```

```
        basic_istream& operator>>(basic_streambuf<Ch,Tr>* b);  // read into b
        basic_istream& get(basic_streambuf<Ch,Tr>& b, Ch t = Tr::newline());

        streamsize readsome(Ch* p, streamsize n);       // read at most n char
    };
```

The positioning functions work like their *ostream* counterparts (§21.6.1). The *g* suffix indicates
that it is the position used for *getting* characters from the stream. The *p* and *g* suffixes are needed
because we can create an *iostream* derived from both *istream* and *ostream* and such a stream needs
to keep track of both a get position and a put position.

The *putback*() function allows a program to put an unwanted character back to be read some
other time, as shown in §21.3.5. The *unget*() function puts the most recently read character back.
Unfortunately, backing up an input stream is not always possible. For example, trying to back up
past the first character read will set *ios_base*::*failbit*. What is guaranteed is that you can back up
one character after a successful read. The *peek*() reads the next character but leaves it in the
streambuf so that it can be read again. Thus, *c=peek*() is equivalent to (*c=get*(), *unget*(), *c*)
and to (*putback*(*c=get*()), *c*). Note that setting *failbit* might trigger an exception (§21.3.6).

Flushing an *istream* is done using *sync*(). This cannot always be done right. For some kinds
of streams, we would have to reread characters from the real source – and that is not always possible or desirable. Consequently, *sync*() returns *0* if it succeeded. If it failed, it sets
ios_base::*badbit* (§21.3.3) and returns −*1*. Again, setting *badbit* might trigger an exception
(§21.3.6). A *sync*() on a buffer attached to an *ostream* flushes the buffer to output.

The >> and *get*() operations that target a *streambuf* are primarily useful for implementers of
I/O facilities. Only such implementers should manipulate *streambuf*s directly.

The *readsome*() function is a low-level operation that allows a user to peek at a stream to see
if there are any characters available to read. This can be most useful when it is undesirable to wait
for input, say, from a keyboard. See also *in_avail*() (§21.6.4).

21.6.3 Streams and Buffers

The connection between a stream and its buffer is maintained in the stream's *basic_ios*:

```
    template <class Ch, class Tr = char_traits<Ch> >
    class basic_ios : public ios_base {
    public:
        // ...
        basic_streambuf<Ch,Tr>* rdbuf() const;                          // get buffer
        // set buffer, clear(), and return pointer to old buffer:
        basic_streambuf<Ch,Tr>* rdbuf(basic_streambuf<Ch,Tr>* b);

        locale imbue(const locale& loc);                    // set locale (and return old locale)

        char narrow(char_type c, char d) const;             // make char value from char_type c
        char_type widen(char c) const;                      // make char_type value from char c
        // ...
    protected:
        basic_ios();
        void init(basic_streambuf<Ch,Tr>* b);               // set initial buffer
    };
```

In addition to reading and setting the stream's *streambuf* (§21.6.4), *basic_ios* provides *imbue*() to read and re-set the stream's locale (§21.7) by calling *imbue*() on its *ios_base* (§21.7.1) and *pubimbue*() on its buffer (§21.6.4).

The *narrow*() and *widen*() functions are used to convert *chars* to and from a buffer's *char_type*. The second argument of *narrow*(*c*, *d*) is the *char* returned if there isn't a *char* corresponding to the *char_type* value *c*.

21.6.4 Stream Buffers

The I/O operations are specified without any mention of file types, but not all devices can be treated identically with respect to buffering strategies. For example, an *ostream* bound to a *string* (§21.5.3) needs a different kind of buffer than does an *ostream* bound to a file (§21.5.1). These problems are handled by providing different buffer types for different streams at the time of initialization. There is only one set of operations on these buffer types, so the *ostream* functions do not contain code distinguishing them. The different types of buffers are derived from class *streambuf*. Class *streambuf* provides virtual functions for operations where buffering strategies differ, such as the functions that handle overflow and underflow.

The *basic_streambuf* class provides two interfaces. The public interface is aimed primarily at implementers of stream classes such as *istream*, *ostream*, *fstream*, *stringstream*, etc. In addition, a protected interface is provided for implementers of new buffering strategies and of *streambufs* for new input sources and output destinations.

To understand a *streambuf*, it is useful first to consider the underlying model of a buffer area provided by the protected interface. Assume that the *streambuf* has a *put area* into which << writes, and a *get area* from which >> reads. Each area is described by a beginning pointer, current pointer, and one-past-the-end pointer. These pointers are made available through functions:

```
template <class Ch, class Tr = char_traits<Ch> >
class basic_streambuf {
protected:

        Ch* eback() const;          // start of get-buffer
        Ch* gptr() const;           // next filled character (next char read comes from here)
        Ch* egptr() const;          // one-past-end of get-buffer

        void gbump(int n);          // add n to gptr()
        void setg(Ch* begin, Ch* next, Ch* end); // set eback(), gptr(), and egptr()

        Ch* pbase() const;          // start of put-buffer
        Ch* pptr() const;           // next free char (next char written goes here)
        Ch* epptr() const;          // one-past-end of put-buffer
        void pbump(int n);          // add n to pptr()
        void setp(Ch* begin, Ch* end);      // set pbase() and pptr() to begin, and epptr() to end
        // ...
};
```

Given an array of characters, *setg*() and *setp*() can set up the pointers appropriately. An implementation might access its get area like this:

```
template <class Ch, class Tr = char_traits<Ch> >
basic_streambuf<Ch,Tr>::int_type basic_streambuf<Ch,Tr>::snextc()
// skip current character, then read next character
{
    if (1 < egptr()-gptr()) { // if there is at least two characters in the buffer
        gbump(1);                               // skip current character
        return Tr::to_int_type(*gptr());        // return the new current character
    }
    if (1 == egptr()-gptr()) {        // if there is exactly one character in the buffer
        gbump(1);        // skip current character
        return underflow();
    }
    // the buffer is empty (or there is no buffer), try to fill it:
    if (Tr::eq_int_type(uflow(),Tr::eof())) return Tr::eof();
    if(0 < egptr()-gptr()) return Tr::to_int_type(*gptr()); // return the new current character
    return underflow();
}
```

The buffer is accessed through *gptr* ( ) ; *egptr* ( ) marks the limit of the get area. Characters are read from the real source by *uflow* ( ) and *underflow* ( ). The calls to *traits_type* :: *to_int_type* ( ) ensure that this code is independent of the actual character type. This code allows for a variety of stream buffer types, and takes into account the possibility that the virtual functions *uflow* ( ) and *underflow* (·) may decide to introduce a new get area (using *setg* ( )).

The public interface of a *streambuf* looks like this:

```
template <class Ch, class Tr = char_traits<Ch> >
class basic_streambuf {
public:
    // usual typedefs (§21.2.1)

    virtual ~basic_streambuf();

    locale pubimbue(const locale &loc);             // set locale (and get old locale)
    locale getloc() const;                          // get locale

    basic_streambuf* pubsetbuf(Ch* p, streamsize n);    // set buffer space

    pos_type pubseekoff(off_type off, ios_base::seekdir way,      // position (§21.6.1)
                ios_base::openmode m = ios_base::in|ios_base::out);
    pos_type pubseekpos(pos_type p, ios_base::openmode m = ios_base::in|ios_base::out);

    int pubsync();                                  // sync(); see §21.6.2

    int_type snextc();              // skip current character, then get next character
    int_type sbumpc();              // advance gptr() by 1
    int_type sgetc();               // get current character
    streamsize sgetn(Ch* p, streamsize n);      // get into p[0]..p[n-1]

    int_type sputbackc(Ch c);       // put c back into buffer (§21.6.2)
    int_type sungetc();             // unget last character

    int_type sputc(Ch c);           // put c
    streamsize sputn(const Ch* p, streamsize n);  // put p[0]..p[n-1]
```

```
    streamsize  in_avail();                          // is input ready?
    // ...
};
```

The public interface contains functions for inserting characters into the buffer and extracting characters from the buffer. These functions are simple and easily inlined. This is crucial for efficiency.

Functions that implement parts of a specific buffering strategy invoke corresponding functions in the protected interface. For example, *pubsetbuf*() calls *setbuf*(), which is overridden by a derived class to implement that class' notion of getting memory for the buffered characters. Using two functions to implement an operation such as *setbuf*() allows an *iostream* implementer to do some "housekeeping" before and after the user's code. For example, an implementer might wrap a *try-block* around the call of the virtual function and catch exceptions thrown by the user code.

By default, *setbuf*(0,0) means "unbuffered" and *setbuf*(p,n) means use $p[0]..p[n-1]$ to hold buffered characters.

A call to *in_avail*() is used to see how many characters are available in the buffer. This can be used to avoid waiting for input. When reading from a stream connected to a keyboard, *cin*.*get*(c) might wait until the user comes back from lunch. On some systems and for some applications, it can be worthwhile taking that into account when reading. For example:

```
if (cin.rdbuf()->in_avail()) { // get() will not block
    cin.get(c);
    // do something
}
else {                          // get() might block
    // do something else
}
```

Note that on some systems, it can be hard to determine if input is available. Thus, *in_avail*() might be (poorly) implemented to return *0* in cases where an input operation would succeed.

In addition to the public interface used by *basic_istream* and *basic_ostream*, *basic_streambuf* offers a protected interface to implementers of *streambuf*s. This is where the virtual functions that determine policy are declared:

```
template <class  Ch,  class  Tr = char_traits<Ch> >
class  basic_streambuf {
protected:
    // ...

    basic_streambuf();

    virtual  void  imbue(const  locale &loc);                    // set locale

    virtual  basic_streambuf*  setbuf(Ch* p,  streamsize  n);

    virtual  pos_type  seekoff(off_type  off,  ios_base::seekdir  way,
                    ios_base::openmode  m = ios_base::in | ios_base::out);
    virtual  pos_type  seekpos(pos_type  p,
                    ios_base::openmode  m = ios_base::in | ios_base::out);

    virtual  int  sync();                                        // sync(); see §21.6.2
```

```
        virtual  int  showmanyc();
        virtual  streamsize  xsgetn(Ch* p,  streamsize  n);          // get n chars
        virtual  int_type  underflow(); // replentish get area; return character or eof
        virtual  int_type  uflow();      // replentish get area; return character or eof; increment gptr()

        virtual  int_type  pbackfail(int_type  c = Tr::eof());          // putback failed

        virtual  streamsize  xsputn(const  Ch* p,  streamsize  n);     // put n chars
        virtual  int_type  overflow(int_type  c = Tr::eof());          // put area full
    };
```

The *underflow*() and *uflow*() functions are called to get the next character from the real input
source when the buffer is empty. If no more input is available from that source, the stream is set
into *eof* state (§21.3.3), and if setting the state doesn't cause an exception, *traits_type::eof*() is
returned. The *gptr*() is incremented past the returned character by *uflow*() but not by *underflow*(). Remember that there typically are more buffers in your system than the ones introduced
by the *iostream* library, so you can suffer buffering delays even when using unbuffered stream I/O.

The *overflow*() function is called to transfer characters to the real output destination when the
buffer is full. A call *overflow*(*c*) outputs the contents of the buffer plus the character *c*. If no
more output can be written to that target, the stream is put into *eof* state (§21.3.3). If doing that
doesn't cause an exception, *traits_type::eof*() is returned.

The *showmanyc*() – ''show how many characters'' – function is an odd function intended to
allow a user to learn something about the state of a machine's input system. It returns an estimate
of how many characters can be read ''soon,'' say, by emptying the operating system's buffers
rather than waiting for a disc read. A call to *showmanyc*() returns -1 if it cannot promise that any
character can be read without encountering end-of-file. This is (necessarily) rather low-level and
highly implementation-dependent. Don't use *showmanyc*() without a careful reading of your system documentation and a few experiments.

By default, every stream gets the global locale (§21.7). A *pubimbue*(*loc*) or *imbue*(*loc*) call
makes a stream use *loc* as its locale.

A *streambuf* for a particular kind of stream is derived from *basic_streambuf*. It provides the
constructors and initialization functions that connect the *streambuf* to a real source of (target for)
characters and overrides the virtual functions that determine the buffering strategy. For example:

```
    template <class  Ch,  class  Tr = char_traits<Ch> >
    class  basic_filebuf : public  basic_streambuf<Ch,Tr> {
    public:
        basic_filebuf();
        virtual ~basic_filebuf();

        bool  is_open() const;
        basic_filebuf* open(const  char* p,  ios_base::openmode  mode);
        basic_filebuf* close();

    protected:
        virtual  int  showmanyc();
        virtual  int_type  underflow();
        virtual  int_type  uflow();
```

```
        virtual int_type pbackfail(int_type c = Tr::eof());
        virtual int_type overflow(int_type c = Tr::eof());

        virtual basic_streambuf<Ch,Tr>* setbuf(Ch* p, streamsize n);
        virtual pos_type seekoff(off_type off, ios_base::seekdir way,
                        ios_base::openmode m = ios_base::in|ios_base::out);
        virtual pos_type seekpos(pos_type p,
                        ios_base::openmode m = ios_base::in|ios_base::out);
        virtual int sync();
        virtual void imbue(const locale& loc);
    };
```

The functions for manipulating buffers, etc., are inherited unchanged from *basic_streambuf*. Only functions that affect initialization and buffering policy need to be separately provided.

As usual, the obvious *typedef*s and their wide stream counterparts are provided:

```
    typedef basic_streambuf<char> streambuf;
    typedef basic_stringbuf<char> stringbuf;
    typedef basic_filebuf<char> filebuf;

    typedef basic_streambuf<wchar_t> wstreambuf;
    typedef basic_stringbuf<wchar_t> wstringbuf;
    typedef basic_filebuf<wchar_t> wfilebuf;
```

21.7 Locale

A *locale* is an object that controls the classification of characters into letters, digits, etc.; the collation order of strings; and the appearance of numeric values on input and output. Most commonly a *locale* is used implicitly by the *iostream*s library to ensure that the usual conventions for some natural language or culture is adhered to. In such cases, a programmer never sees a *locale* object. However, by changing a *stream*'s *locale*, a programmer can change the way the stream behaves to suit a different set of conventions

A locale is an object of class *locale* defined in namespace *std* presented in *<locale>* (§D.2).

```
    class locale {          // complete declaration in §D.2
    public:
        // ...

        locale() throw();                               // copy of current global locale
        explicit locale(const char* name);             // construct locale using C locale name
        basic_string<char> name() const;               // give name of this locale

        locale(const locale&) throw();                          // copy locale
        const locale& operator=(const locale&) throw();   // copy locale

        static locale global(const locale&);           // set the global locale (get the previous locale)
        static const locale& classic();                // get the locale that C defines
    };
```

The simplest use of locales is to switch from one existing locale to another. For example:

```
void f( )
{
    std::locale  loc("POSIX");              // standard locale for POSIX

    cin.imbue(loc);                         // let cin use loc
    // ...
    cin.imbue(std::locale( ));              // reset cin to use the default (global) locale
}
```

The *imbue*( ) function is a member of *basic_ios* (§21.7.1).

As shown, some fairly standard locales have character string names. These tend to be shared with C.

It is possible to set the *locale* that is used by all newly constructed streams:

```
void  g(const locale& loc = locale( ))          // use current global locale by default
{
    locale  old_global = locale::global(loc);   // make loc the default locale
    // ...
}
```

Setting the global *locale* does not change the behavior of existing streams that are using the previous value of the global *locale*. In particular, *cin*, *cout*, etc., are not affected. If they should be changed, they must be explicitly *imbue*( )d.

Imbuing a stream with a *locale* changes facets of its behavior. It is possible to use members of a *locale* directly, to define new *locale*s, and to extend *locale*s with new facets. For example, a *locale* can also be used explicitly to control the appearance of monetary units, dates, etc., on input and output (§21.10[25]) and conversion between codesets. The locale concept, the *locale* and *facet* classes, and the standard locales and facets are described in Appendix D.

The C-style locale is presented in *<clocale>* and *<locale.h>*.

21.7.1 Stream Callbacks

Sometimes, people want to add to the state of a stream. For example, one might want a stream to "know" whether a *complex* should be output in polar or Cartesian coordinates. Class *ios_base* provides a function *xalloc*( ) to allocate space for such simple state information. The value returned by *xalloc*( ) identifies a pair of locations that can be accessed by *iword*( ) and *pword*( ):

```
class ios_base {
public:
    // ...

    ~ios_base( );

    locale  imbue(const locale& loc);    // set locale and return old locale; see §D.2.3
    locale  getloc( ) const;             // get locale

    static  int  xalloc( );        // get an integer and a pointer (both initialized to 0)
    long& iword(int i);            // access the integer iword(i)
    void*& pword(int i);           // access the pointer pword(i)
```

```
// callbacks:

enum event { erase_event, imbue_event, copyfmt_event } ;   // event type

typedef void (*event_callback) (event, ios_base&, int i);
void register_callback(event_callback f, int i);           // attach f to word(i)
} ;
```

Sometimes, an implementer or a user needs to be notified about a change in a stream's state. The *register_callback*() function "registers" a function to be called when its "event" occurs. Thus, a call of *imbue*(), *copyfmt*(), or *˜ios_base*() will call a function "registered" for an *imbue_event*, *copyfmt_event*, or *erase_event*, respectively. When the state changes, registered functions are called with the argument *i* supplied by their *register_callback*().

This storage and callback mechanism is fairly obscure. Use it only when you absolutely need to extend the low-level formatting facilities.

21.8 C Input/Output

Because C++ and C code are often intermixed, C++ stream I/O is sometimes mixed with the C *printf*() family of I/O functions. The C-style I/O functions are presented by *<cstdio>* and *<stdio.h>*. Also, because C functions can be called from C++ some programmers may prefer to use the more familiar C I/O functions. Even if you prefer stream I/O, you will undoubtedly encounter C-style I/O at some time.

C and C++ I/O can be mixed on a per-character basis. A call of *sync_with_stdio*() before the first stream I/O operation in the execution of a program guarantees that the C-style and C++-style I/O operations share buffers. A call of *sync_with_stdio*(*false*) before the first stream I/O operation prevents buffer sharing and can improve I/O performance on some implementations.

```
class ios_base {
    // ...
    static bool sync_with_stdio(bool sync = true);   // get and set
} ;
```

The general advantage of the stream output functions over the C standard library function *printf*() is that the stream functions are type safe and have a common style for specifying output of objects of built-in and user-defined types.

The general C output functions

```
int printf(const char* format ...);          // write to stdout
int fprintf(FILE*, const char* format ...);   // write to "file" (stdout, stderr)
int sprintf(char* p, const char* format ...);  // write to p[0] ...
```

produce formatted output of an arbitrary sequence of arguments under control of the format string *format*. The format string contains two types of objects: plain characters, which are simply copied to the output stream, and conversion specifications, each of which causes conversion and printing of the next argument. Each conversion specification is introduced by the character %. For example:

```
printf("there were %d members present.", no_of_members);
```

Here *%d* specifies that *no_of_members* is to be treated as an *int* and printed as the appropriate sequence of decimal digits. With *no_of_members==127*, the output is

> *there were 127 members present.*

The set of conversion specifications is quite large and provides a great degree of flexibility. Following the %, there may be:

- − an optional minus sign that specifies left-adjustment of the converted value in the field;
- + an optional plus sign that specifies that a value of a signed type will always begin with a + or − sign;
- 0 an optional zero that specifies that leading zeros are used for padding of a numeric value. If − or a pecision is specified this *0* is ignored;
- \# an optional # that specifies that floating-point values will be printed with a decimal point even if no nonzero digits follow, that trailing zeroes will be printed, that octal values will be printed with an initial *0*, and that hexadecimal values will be printed with an initial *0x* or *0X*;
- *d* an optional digit string specifying a field width; if the converted value has fewer characters than the field width, it will be blank-padded on the left (or right, if the left-adjustment indicator has been given) to make up the field width; if the field width begins with a zero, zero-padding will be done instead of blank-padding;
- . an optional period that serves to separate the field width from the next digit string;
- *d* an optional digit string specifying a precision that specifies the number of digits to appear after the decimal point, for e- and f-conversion, or the maximum number of characters to be printed from a string;
- * a field width or precision may be * instead of a digit string. In this case an integer argument supplies the field width or precision;
- h an optional character *h*, specifying that a following *d*, *o*, *x*, or *u* corresponds to a short integer argument;
- l an optional character *l*, specifying that a following *d*, *o*, *x*, or *u* corresponds to a long integer argument;
- % indicating that the character % is to be printed; no argument is used;
- *c* a character that indicates the type of conversion to be applied. The conversion characters and their meanings are:
  - d The integer argument is converted to decimal notation;
  - i The integer argument is converted to decimal notation;
  - o The integer argument is converted to octal notation;
  - x The integer argument is converted to hexadecimal notation with an initial *0x*;
  - X The integer argument is converted to hexadecimal notation with an initial *0X*;
  - f The *float* or *double* argument is converted to decimal notation in the style *[-]ddd.ddd*. The number of *d*'s after the decimal point is equal to the precision for the argument. If necessary, the number is rounded. If the precision is missing, six digits are given; if the precision is explicitly *0* and # isn't specified, no decimal point is printed;
  - e The *float* or *double* argument is converted to decimal notation in the scientific style *[-]d.ddde+dd* or *[-]d.ddde-dd*, where there is one digit before the decimal point and the number of digits after the decimal point is equal to the precision specification for

the argument. If necessary, the number is rounded. If the precision is missing, six digits are given; if the precision is explicitly *0* and # isn't specified, no digits and no decimal point are printed;

E   As *e*, but with an uppercase *E* used to identify the exponent;

g   The *float* or *double* argument is printed in style d, in style f, or in style e, whichever gives the greatest precision in minimum space;

G   As *g*, but with an uppercase *E* used to identify the exponent;

c   The character argument is printed. Null characters are ignored;

s   The argument is taken to be a string (character pointer), and characters from the string are printed until a null character or until the number of characters indicated by the precision specification is reached; however, if the precision is 0 or missing, all characters up to a null are printed;

p   The argument is taken to be a pointer. The representation printed is implementation-dependent;

u   The unsigned integer argument is converted to decimal notation;

n   The number of characters written so far by the call of *printf*( ), *fprintf*( ), or *sprintf*( ) is *written to* the *int* pointed to by the pointer to *int* argument.

In no case does a nonexistent or small field width cause truncation of a field; padding takes place only if the specified field width exceeds the actual width.

Here is a more elaborate example:

```
char* line_format = "#line %d \"%s\"\n";
int line = 13;
char* file_name = "C++/main.c";

printf("int a;\n");
printf(line_format, line, file_name);
printf("int b;\n");
```

which produces:

```
int a;
#line 13 "C++/main.c"
int b;
```

Using *printf*( ) is unsafe in the sense that type checking is not done. For example, here is a well-known way of getting unpredictable output, a core dump, or worse:

```
char x;
// ...
printf("bad input char: %s", x);          // %s should have been %c
```

The *printf*( ) does, however, provide great flexibility in a form that is familiar to C programmers.

Similarly, *getchar*( ) provides a familiar way of reading characters from input:

```
int i;
while ((i=getchar()) !=EOF) { /* use i */ }
```

Note that to be able to test for end-of-file against the *int* value *EOF*, the value of *getchar*( ) must be put into an *int* rather than into a *char*.

For further details of C I/O, see your C reference manual or Kernighan and Ritchie: *The C Programming Language* [Kernighan,1988].

21.9 Advice

[1] Define << and >> for user-defined types with values that have meaningful textual representations; §21.2.3, §21.3.5.

[2] Use parentheses when printing expressions containing operators of low precedence; §21.2.

[3] You don't need to modify *istream* or *ostream* to add new << and >> operators; §21.2.3.

[4] You can define a function so that it behaves as a *virtual* function based on its *second* (or subsequent) argument; §21.2.3.1.

[5] Remember that by default >> skips whitespace; §21.3.2.

[6] Use lower-level input functions such as *get* ( ) and *read* ( ) primarily in the implementation of higher-lever input functions; §21.3.4.

[7] Be careful with the termination criteria when using *get* ( ) , *getline* ( ) , and *read* ( ) ; §21.3.4.

[8] Prefer manipulators to state flags for controlling I/O; §21.3.3, §21.4, §21.4.6.

[9] Use exceptions to catch rare I/O errors (only); §21.3.6.

[10] Tie streams used for interactive I/O; §21.3.7.

[11] Use sentries to concentrate entry and exit code for many functions in one place; §21.3.8.

[12] Don't use parentheses after a no-argument manipulator; §21.4.6.2.

[13] Remember to #*include* <*iomanip*> when using standard manipulators; §21.4.6.2.

[14] You can achieve the effect (and efficiency) of a ternary operator by defining a simple function object; §21.4.6.3.

[15] Remember that *width* specifications apply to the following I/O operation only; §21.4.4.

[16] Remember that *precision* specifications apply to all following floating-point output operations; §21.4.3.

[17] Use string streams for in-memory formatting; §21.5.3.

[18] You can specify a mode for a file stream ; §21.5.1.

[19] Distinguish sharply between formatting (*iostream*s) and buffering (*streambuf*s) when extending the I/O system; §21.1, §21.6.

[20] Implement nonstandard ways of transmitting values as stream buffers; §21.6.4.

[21] Implement nonstandard ways of formatting values as stream operations; §21.2.3, §21.3.5.

[22] You can isolate and encapsulate calls of user-defined code by using a pair of functions; §21.6.4.

[23] You can use *in_avail* ( ) to determine whether an input operation will block before reading; §21.6.4.

[24] Distinguish between simple operations that need to be efficient and operations that implement policy (make the former *inline* and the latter *virtual*); §21.6.4.

[25] Use *locale* to localize ''cultural differences;'' §21.7.

[26] Use *sync_with_stdio* (*x*) to mix C-style and C++-style I/O and to disassociate C-style and C++-style I/O; §21.8.

[27] Beware of type errors in C-style I/O; §21.8.

21.10 Exercises

1. (*1.5) Read a file of floating-point numbers, make complex numbers out of pairs of numbers read, and write out the complex numbers.

2. (*1.5) Define a type *Name_and_address*. Define << and >> for it. Copy a stream of *Name_and_address* objects.

3. (*2.5) Copy a stream of *Name_and_address* objects in which you have inserted as many errors as you can think of (e.g., format errors and premature end of string). Handle these errors in a way that ensures that the copy function reads most of the correctly formatted *Name_and_address*es, even when the input is completely messed up.

4. (*2.5) Redefine the I/O format *Name_and_address* to make it more robust in the présence of format errors.

5. (*2.5) Design some functions for requesting and reading information of various types. Ideas: integer, floating-point number, file name, mail address, date, personal information, etc. Try to make them foolproof.

6. (*1.5) Write a program that prints (a) all lowercase letters, (b) all letters, (c) all letters and digits, (d) all characters that may appear in a C++ identifier on your system, (e) all punctuation characters, (f) the integer value of all control characters, (g) all whitespace characters, (h) the integer value of all whitespace characters, and finally (i) all printing characters.

7. (*2) Read a sequence of lines of text into a fixed-sized character buffer. Remove all whitespace characters and replace each alphanumeric character with the next character in the alphabet (replace *z* by *a* and *9* by *0*). Write out the resulting line.

8. (*3) Write a ''miniature'' stream I/O system that provides classes *istream*, *ostream*, *ifstream*, *ofstream* providing functions such as *operator<<* ( ) and *operator>>* ( ) for integers and operations such as *open* ( ) and *close* ( ) for files.

9. (*4) Implement the C standard I/O library (<*stdio.h*>) using the C++ standard I/O library (<*iostream*>).

10. (*4) Implement the C++ standard I/O library (<*iostream*>) using the C standard I/O library (<*stdio.h*>).

11. (*4) Implement the C and C++ libraries so that they can be used simultaneously.

12. (*2) Implement a class for which [ ] is overloaded to implement random reading of characters from a file.

13. (*3) Repeat §21.10[12] but make [ ] useful for both reading and writing. Hint: Make [ ] return an object of a ''descriptor type'' for which assignment means ''assign through descriptor to file'' and implicit conversion to *char* ''means read from file through descriptor.''

14. (*2) Repeat §21.10[13] but let [ ] index objects of arbitrary types, not just characters.

15. (*3.5) Implement versions of *istream* and *ostream* that read and write numbers in their binary form rather than converting them into a character representation. Discuss the advantages and disadvantages of this approach compared to the character-based approach.

16. (*3.5) Design and implement a pattern-matching input operation. Use *printf*-style format strings to specify a pattern. It should be possible to try out several patterns against some input to find the actual format. One might derive a pattern-matching input class from *istream*.

17. (*4) Invent (and implement) a much better kind of pattern for pattern matching. Be specific about what is better about it.

18. (*2) Define an output manipulator *based* that takes two arguments − a base and an *int* value − and outputs the integer in the representation specified by the base. For example, *based* (*2*, *9*) should print *1001*.

19. (*2) Write manipulators that turn character echoing on and off.

20. (*2) Implement *Bound_form* from §21.4.6.3 for the usual set of built-in types.

21. (*2) Re-implement *Bound_form* from §21.4.6.3 so that an output operation never overflows its *width* (). It should be possible for a programmer to ensure that output is never quietly truncated beyond its specified precision.

22. (*3) Implement an *encrypt* (*k*) manipulator that ensures that output on its *ostream* is encrypted using the key *k*. Provide a similar *decrypt* (*k*) manipulator for an *istream*. Provide the means for turning the encryption off for a stream so that further I/O is cleartext.

23. (*2) Trace a character's route through your system from the keyboard to the screen for a simple:

```
char c;
cin >> c;
cout << c << endl;
```

24. (*2) Modify *readints* () (§21.3.6) to handle all exceptions. Hint: Resource acquisition is initialization.

25. (*2.5) There is a standard way of reading, writing, and representing dates under control of a *locale*. Find it in the documentation of your implementation and write a small program that reads and writes dates using this mechanism. Hint: *struct tm*.

26. (*2.5) Define an *ostream* called *ostrstream* that can be attached to an array of characters (a C-style string) in a way similar to the way *ostringstream* is attached to a *string*. However, do not copy the array into or out of the *ostrstream*. The *ostrstream* should simply provide a way of writing to its array argument. It might be used for in-memory formatting like this:

```
char buf[message_size];
ostrstream ost(buf, message_size);
do_something(arguments, ost);      // output to buf through ost
cout << buf;                        // ost adds terminating 0
```

An operation such as *do_something* () can write to the stream *ost*, pass *ost* on to its suboperations, etc., using the standard output operations. There is no need to check for overflow because *ost* knows its size and will go into *fail* () state when it is full. Finally, a *display* () operation can write the message to a "real" output stream. This technique can be most useful for coping with cases in which the final display operation involves writing to something more complicated than a traditional line-oriented output device. For example, the text from *ost* could be placed in a fixed-sized area somewhere on a screen. Similarly, define class *istrstream* as an input string stream reading from a zero-terminated string of characters. Interpret the terminating zero character as end-of-file. These *strstream*s were part of the original streams library and can often be found in *<strstream.h>*.

27. (*2.5) Implement a manipulator *general* () that resets a stream to its original (general) format in the same way a *scientific* () (§21.4.6.2) sets a stream to use scientific format.

22

Numerics

The purpose of computing is insight, not numbers.
– R.W. Hamming

... but for the student,
numbers are often the best road to insight.
– A. Ralston

Introduction — numeric limits — mathematical functions — *valarray* — vector operations — slices — *slice_array* — elimination of temporaries — *gslice_array* — *mask_array* — *indirect_array* — *complex* — generalized algorithms — random numbers — advice — exercises.

22.1 Introduction

It is rare to write any real code without doing some calculation. However, most code requires little mathematics beyond simple arithmetic. This chapter presents the facilities the standard library offers to people who go beyond that.

Neither C nor C++ were designed primarily with numeric computation in mind. However, numeric computation typically occurs in the context of other work – such as database access, networking, instrument control, graphics, simulation, financial analysis, etc. – so C++ becomes an attractive vehicle for computations that are part of a larger system. Furthermore, numeric methods have come a long way from being simple loops over vectors of floating-point numbers. Where more complex data structures are needed as part of a computation, C++'s strengths become relevant. The net effect is that C++ is increasingly used for scientific and engineering computation involving sophisticated numerics. Consequently, facilities and techniques supporting such computation have emerged. This chapter describes the parts of the standard library that support numerics and presents a few techniques for dealing with issues that arise when people express numeric computations in C++. I make no attempt to teach numeric methods. Numeric computation is a fascinating topic in its own right. To understand it, you need a good course in numerical methods or at least a good textbook − not just a language manual and tutorial.

22.2 Numeric Limits

To do anything interesting with numbers, we typically need to know something about general properties of built-in numeric types that are implementation-defined rather than fixed by the rules of the language itself (§4.6). For example, what is the largest *int*? What is the smallest *float*? Is a *double* rounded or truncated when assigned to a *float*? How many bits are there in a *char*?

Answers to such questions are provided by the specializations of the *numeric_limits* template presented in *<limits>*. For example:

```
void f(double d, int i)
{
    if (numeric_limits<unsigned char>::digits != 8) {
        // unusual bytes (number of bits not 8)
    }

    if (i<numeric_limits<short>::min() || numeric_limits<short>::max()<i) {
        // i cannot be stored in a short without loss of precision
    }

    if (0<d && d<numeric_limits<double>::epsilon()) d = 0;

    if (numeric_limits<Quad>::is_specialized) {
        // limits information available for type Quad
    }
}
```

Each specialization provides the relevant information for its argument type. Thus, the general *numeric_limits* template is simply a notational handle for a set of constants and inline functions:

```
template<class T> class numeric_limits {
public:
    static const bool is_specialized = false;  // is information available for numeric_limits<T>?

    // uninteresting defaults
};
```

The real information is in the specializations. Each implementation of the standard library provides a specialization of *numeric_limits* for each fundamental type (the character types, the integer and floating-point types, and *bool*) but not for any other plausible candidates such as *void*, enumerations, or library types (such as *complex<double>*).

For an integral type such as *char*, only a few pieces of information are of interest. Here is *numeric_limits<char>* for an implementation in which a *char* has 8 bits and is signed:

```
class numeric_limits<char> {
public:
      static const bool is_specialized = true;        // yes, we have information

      static const int digits = 7;                     // number of bits ("binary digits") excluding sign

      static const bool is_signed = true;              // this implementation has char signed
      static const bool is_integer = true;             // char is an integral type

      static char min() throw() { return -128; }       // smallest value
      static char max() throw() { return 127; }        // largest value

      // lots of declarations not relevant to a char
};
```

Note that for a signed integer type *digits* is one less than the number of bits used to store the type.

Most members of *numeric_limits* are intended to describe floating-point numbers. For example, this describes one possible implementation of *float*:

```
class numeric_limits<float> {
public:
      static const bool is_specialized = true;

      static const int radix = 2;       // base of exponent (in this case, binary)
      static const int digits = 24;     // number radix digits in mantissa
      static const int digits10 = 6;    // number of base 10 digits in mantissa

      static const bool is_signed = true;
      static const bool is_integer = false;
      static const bool is_exact = false;

      static float min() throw() { return 1.17549435E-38F; }
      static float max() throw() { return 3.40282347E+38F; }

      static float epsilon() throw() { return 1.19209290E-07F; }
      static float round_error() throw() { return 0.5F; }

      static float infinity() throw() { return /* some value */; }
      static float quiet_NaN() throw() { return /* some value */; }
      static float signaling_NaN() throw() { return /* some value */; }
      static float denorm_min() throw() { return min(); }

      static const int min_exponent = -125;
      static const int min_exponent10 = -37;
      static const int max_exponent = +128;
      static const int max_exponent10 = +38;

      static const bool has_infinity = true;
      static const bool has_quiet_NaN = true;
      static const bool has_signaling_NaN = true;
      static const float_denorm_style has_denorm = denorm_absent;   // enum from <limits>
      static const bool has_denorm_loss = false;
```

```
           static  const  bool  is_iec559 = true ;      // conforms to IEC-559
           static  const  bool  is_bounded = true ;
           static  const  bool  is_modulo = false ;
           static  const  bool  traps = true ;
           static  const  bool  tinyness_before = true ;

           static  const  float_round_style  round_style = round_to_nearest ;     // enum from <limits>
     } ;
```

Note that *min* ( ) is the smallest *positive* normalized number and that *epsilon* is the smallest positive floating-point number such that *1+epsilon–1* is representable.

When defining a scalar type along the lines of the built-in ones, it is a good idea also to provide a suitable specialization of *numeric_limits*. For example, if I wrote a quadruple-precision type *Quad* or if a vendor provided an extended-precision integer *long long*, a user could reasonably expect *numeric_limits<Quad>* and *numeric_limits<long long>* to be supplied.

One can imagine specializations of *numeric_limits* describing properties of user-defined types that have little to do with floating-point numbers. In such cases, it is usually better to use the general technique for describing properties of a type than to specialize *numeric_limits* with properties not considered in the standard.

Floating-point values are represented as inline functions. Integral values in *numeric_limits*, however, must be represented in a form that allows them to be used in constant expressions. That implies that they must have in-class initializers (§10.4.6.2). If you use *static const* members rather than enumerators for that, remember to define the *static*s.

22.2.1 Limit Macros

From C, C++ inherited macros that describe properties of integers. These are found in *<climits>* and *<limits.h>* and have names such as *CHAR_BIT* and *INT_MAX*. Similarly, *<cfloat>* and *<float.h>* define macros describing properties of floating-point numbers. They have names such as *DBL_MIN_EXP*, *FLT_RADIX*, and *LDBL_MAX*.

As ever, macros are best avoided.

22.3 Standard Mathematical Functions

The headers *<cmath>* and *<math.h>* provide what is commonly referred to as ''the usual mathematical functions:''

```
     double  abs (double) ;              // absolute value; not in C, same as fabs()
     double  fabs (double) ;             // absolute value

     double  ceil (double  d) ;          // smallest integer not less than d
     double  floor (double  d) ;         // largest integer not greater than d

     double  sqrt (double  d) ;          // square root of d, d must be non-negative

     double  pow (double  d, double  e) ;     // d to the power of e,
                                         // error if d==0 and e<=0 or if d<0 and e isn't an integer.
     double  pow (double  d, int  i) ;   // d to the power of i; not in C
```

```
double cos(double);              // cosine
double sin(double);              // sine
double tan(double);              // tangent

double acos(double);             // arc cosine
double asin(double);             // arc sine
double atan(double);             // arc tangent
double atan2(double x, double y); // atan(x/y)

double sinh(double);             // hyperbolic sine
double cosh(double);             // hyperbolic cosine
double tanh(double);             // hyperbolic tangent

double exp(double);              // exponential, base e
double log(double d);            // natural (base e) logarithm, d must be > 0
double log10(double d);          // base 10 logarithm, d must be > 0

double modf(double d, double* p); // return fractional part of d, place integral part in *p
double frexp(double d, int* p);   // find x in [.5,1) and y so that d = x*pow(2,y),
                                  // return x and store y in *p
double fmod(double d, double m);  // floating-point remainder, same sign as d
double ldexp(double d, int i);    // d*pow(2,i)
```

In addition, *<cmath>* and *<math.h>* supply these functions for *float* and *long double* arguments.

Where several values are possible results − as with *asin*() − the one nearest to *0* is returned. The result of *acos*() is non-negative.

Errors are reported by setting *errno* from *<cerrno>* to *EDOM* for a domain error and to *ERANGE* for a range error. For example:

```
void f()
{
    errno = 0; // clear old error state
    sqrt(-1);
    if (errno==EDOM) cerr << "sqrt() not defined for negative argument";
    pow(numeric_limits<double>::max(),2);
    if (errno == ERANGE) cerr << "result of pow() too large to represent as a double";
}
```

For historical reasons, a few mathematical functions are found in the *<cstdlib>* header rather than in *<cmath>*:

```
int abs(int);            // absolute value
long abs(long);          // absolute value (not in C)
long labs(long);         // absolute value

struct div_t { implementation_defined quot, rem; };
struct ldiv_t { implementation_defined quot, rem; };

div_t div(int n, int d);               // divide n by d, return (quotient,remainder)
ldiv_t div(long int n, long int d);    // divide n by d, return (quotient,remainder) (not in C)
ldiv_t ldiv(long int n, long int d);   // divide n by d, return (quotient,remainder)
```

22.4 Vector Arithmetic

Much numeric work relies on relatively simple single-dimensional vectors of floating-point values. In particular, such vectors are well supported by high-performance machine architectures, libraries relying on such vectors are in wide use, and very aggressive optimization of code using such vectors is considered essential in many fields. Consequently, the standard library provides a vector – called *valarray* – designed specifically for speed of the usual numeric vector operations.

When looking at the *valarray* facilities, it is wise to remember that they are intended as a relatively low-level building block for high-performance computation. In particular, the primary design criterion wasn't ease of use, but rather effective use of high-performance computers when relying on aggressive optimization techniques. If your aim is flexibility and generality rather than efficiency, you are probably better off building on the standard containers from Chapter 16 and Chapter 17 than trying to fit into the simple, efficient, and deliberately traditional framework of *valarray*.

One could argue that *valarray* should have been called *vector* because it is a traditional mathematical vector and that *vector* (§16.3) should have been called *array*. However, this is not the way the terminology evolved. A *valarray* is a vector optimized for numeric computation, a *vector* is a flexible container designed for holding and manipulating objects of a wide variety of types, and an array is a low-level, built-in type.

The *valarray* type is supported by four auxiliary types for specifying subsets of a *valarray*:
- *slice_array* and *gslice_array* represent the notion of slices (§22.4.6, §22.4.8),
- *mask_array* specifies a subset by marking each element in or out (§22.4.9), and
- *indirect_array* lists the indices of the elements to be considered (§22.4.10).

22.4.1 Valarray Construction

The *valarray* type and its associated facilities are defined in namespace *std* and presented in *<valarray>*:

```
template<class T> class std::valarray {
        // representation
public:
        typedef T value_type;

        valarray();                                  // valarray with size()==0
        explicit valarray(size_t n);                 // n elements with value T()
        valarray(const T& val, size_t n);            // n elements with value val
        valarray(const T* p, size_t n);              // n elements with values p[0], p[1], ...
        valarray(const valarray& v);                 // copy of v

        valarray(const slice_array<T>&);             // see §22.4.6
        valarray(const gslice_array<T>&);            // see §22.4.8
        valarray(const mask_array<T>&);              // see §22.4.9
        valarray(const indirect_array<T>&);          // see §22.4.10

        ~valarray();

        // ...
};
```

This set of constructors allows us to initialize *valarray*s from the auxiliary numeric array types and from single values. For example:

```
valarray<double> v0;                 // placeholder, we can assign to v0 later
valarray<float> v1 (1000);           // 1000 elements with value float()==0.0F

valarray<int> v2 (-1 , 2000);        // 2000 elements with value -1
valarray<double> v3 (100 , 9.8064);  // bad mistake: floating-point valarray size

valarray<double> v4 = v3;            // v4 has v3.size() elements
```

In the two-argument constructors, the value comes before the number of elements. This differs from the convention for other standard containers (§16.3.4).

The number of elements of an argument *valarray* to a copy constructor determines the size of the resulting *valarray*.

Most programs need data from tables or input; this is supported by a constructor that copies elements from a built-in array. For example:

```
const double vd[] = { 0, 1, 2, 3, 4 };
const int vi[] = { 0, 1, 2, 3, 4 };

valarray<double> v3 (vd, 4);   // 4 elements: 0,1,2,3
valarray<double> v4 (vi, 4);   // type error: vi is not pointer to double
valarray<double> v5 (vd, 8);   // undefined: too few elements in initializer
```

This form of initialization is important because numeric software that produces data in the form of large arrays is common.

The *valarray* and its auxiliary facilities were designed for high-speed computing. This is reflected in a few constraints on users and by a few liberties granted to implementers. Basically, an implementer of *valarray* is allowed to use just about every optimization technique you can think of. For example, operations may be inlined and the *valarray* operations are assumed to be free of side effects (except on their explicit arguments of course). Also, *valarray*s are assumed to be alias free, and the introduction of auxiliary types and the elimination of temporaries is allowed as long as the basic semantics are maintained. Thus, the declarations in <*valarray*> may look somewhat different from what you find here (and in the standard), but they should provide the same operations with the same meaning for code that doesn't go out of the way to break the rules. In particular, the elements of a *valarray* should have the usual copy semantics (§17.1.4).

22.4.2 Valarray Subscripting and Assignment

For *valarray*s, subscripting is used both to access individual elements and to obtain subarrays:

```
template<class T> class valarray {
public:
    // ...
    valarray& operator= (const valarray& v);   // copy v
    valarray& operator= (const T& val);        // assign val to every element

    T operator[] (size_t) const;
    T& operator[] (size_t);
```

```
valarray operator[](slice) const;                      // see §22.4.6
slice_array<T> operator[](slice);

valarray operator[](const gslice&) const;              // see §22.4.8
gslice_array<T> operator[](const gslice&);

valarray operator[](const valarray<bool>&) const;      // see §22.4.9
mask_array<T> operator[](const valarray<bool>&);

valarray operator[](const valarray<size_t>&) const;    // see §22.4.10
indirect_array<T> operator[](const valarray<size_t>&);

valarray& operator=(const slice_array<T>&);            // see §22.4.6
valarray& operator=(const gslice_array<T>&);           // see §22.4.8
valarray& operator=(const mask_array<T>&);             // see §22.4.9
valarray& operator=(const indirect_array<T>&);         // see §22.4.10

// ...
};
```

A *valarray* can be assigned to another of the same size. As one would expect, *v1=v2* copies every element of *v2* into its corresponding position in *v1*. If *valarray*s have different sizes, the result of assignment is undefined. Because *valarray* is designed to be optimized for speed, it would be unwise to assume that assigning with a *valarray* of the wrong size would cause an easily comprehensible error (such as an exception) or other ''reasonable'' behavior.

In addition to this conventional assignment, it is possible to assign a scalar to a *valarray*. For example, *v=7* assigns *7* to every element of the *valarray v*. This may be surprising, and is best understood as an occasionally useful degenerate case of the operator assignment operations (§22.4.3).

Subscripting with an integer behaves conventionally and does not perform range checking.

In addition to the selection of individual elements, *valarray* subscripting provides four ways of extracting subarrays (§22.4.6). Conversely, assignment (and constructors §22.4.1) accepts such subarrays as operands. The set of assignments on *valarray* ensures that it is not necessary to convert an auxiliary array type, such as *slice_array*, to *valarray* before assigning it. An implementation may similarly replicate other vector operations, such as + and *, to assure efficiency. In addition, many powerful optimization techniques exist for vector operations involving *slice*s and the other auxiliary vector types.

22.4.3 Member Operations

The obvious, as well as a few less obvious, member functions are provided:

```
template<class T> class valarray {
public:
    // ...
    valarray& operator*=(const T& arg);       // v[i]*=arg for every element
    // similarly: /=, %=, +=, -=, ^=, &=, |=, <<=, and >>=

    T sum() const;                            // sum of elements, using += for addition
    T min() const;                            // smallest value, using < for comparison
    T max() const;                            // largest value, using < for comparison
```

```
        valarray  shift(int i) const;              // logical shift (left for 0<i, right for i<0)
        valarray  cshift(int i) const;             // cyclic shift (left for 0<i, right for i<0)

        valarray  apply(T f(T)) const;             // result[i] = f(v[i]) for every element
        valarray  apply(T f(const T&)) const;

        valarray  operator-() const;               // result[i] = –v[i] for every element
        // similarly: +, ˜, !

        size_t size() const;                       // number of elements
        void resize(size_t n, const T& val = T()); // n elements with value val
    };
```

If *size*() ==*0*, the value of *sum*(), *min*(), and *max*() are undefined.

For example, if *v* is a *valarray*, it can be scaled like this: $v*=.2$, and this: $v/=1.3$. That is, applying a scalar to a vector means applying the scalar to each element of the vector. As usual, it is easier to optimize uses of $*=$ than uses of a combination of $*$ and $=$ (§11.3.1).

Note that the non-assignment operations construct a new *valarray*. For example:

```
        double incr(double d) { return d+1; }

        void f(valarray<double>& v)
        {
                valarray<double> v2 = v.apply(incr);      // produce incremented valarray
        }
```

This does not change the value of *v*. Unfortunately, *apply*() does not accept a function object (§18.4) as an argument (§22.9[1]).

The logical and cyclic shift functions, *shift*() and *cshift*(), return a new *valarray* with the elements suitably shifted and leave the original one unchanged. For example, the cyclic shift $v2=v.cshift(n)$ produces a *valarray* so that $v2[i]==v[(i+n)\%v.size()]$. The logical shift $v3=v.shift(n)$ produces a *valarray* so that $v3[i]$ is $v[i+n]$ if $i+n$ is a valid index for v. Otherwise, the result is the default element value. This implies that both *shift*() and *cshift*() shift left when given a positive argument and right when given a negative argument. For example:

```
        void f()
        {
                int alpha[] = { 1, 2, 3, 4, 5 ,6, 7, 8 };
                valarray<int> v(alpha,8);          // 1, 2, 3, 4, 5, 6, 7, 8
                valarray<int> v2 = v.shift(2);     // 3, 4, 5, 6, 7, 8, 0, 0
                valarray<int> v3 = v<<2;           // 4, 8, 12, 16, 20, 24, 28, 32
                valarray<int> v4 = v.shift(-2);    // 0, 0, 1, 2, 3, 4, 5, 6
                valarray<int> v5 = v>>2;           // 0, 0, 0, 1, 1, 1, 1, 2
                valarray<int> v6 = v.cshift(2);    // 3, 4, 5, 6, 7, 8, 1, 2
                valarray<int> v7 = v.cshift(-2);   // 7, 8, 1, 2, 3, 4, 5, 6
        }
```

For *valarray*s, $>>$ and $<<$ are bit shift operators, rather than element shift operators or I/O operators (§22.4.4). Consequently, $<<=$ and $>>=$ can be used to shift bits within elements of an integral type. For example:

```
void f(valarray<int> vi, valarray<double> vd)
{
    vi <<= 2;  // vi[i]<<=2 for all elements of vi
    vd <<= 2;  // error: shift is not defined for floating-point values
}
```

It is possible to change the size of a *valarray*. However, *resize* ( ) is *not* an operation intended to
make *valarray* into a data structure that can grow dynamically the way a *vector* and a *string* can.
Instead, *resize* ( ) is a re-initialize operation that replaces the existing contents of a *valarray* by a
set of default values. The old values are lost.

Often, a resized *valarray* is one that we created as an empty vector. Consider how we might
initialize a *valarray* from input:

```
void f( )
{
    int n = 0;
    cin >> n;                              // read array size
    if (n<=0) error("bad array bound");

    valarray<double> v(n);                 // make an array of the right size
    int i = 0;
    while (i<n && cin>>v[i++]) ;           // fill array
    if (i!=n) error("too few elements on input");

    // ...
}
```

If we want to handle the input in a separate function, we might do it like this:

```
void initialize_from_input(valarray<double>& v)
{
    int n = 0;
    cin >> n;                              // read array size
    if (n<=0) error("bad array bound");

    v.resize(n);                           // make v the right size
    int i = 0;
    while (i<n && cin>>v[i++]) ;           // fill array
    if (i!=n) error("too few elements on input");
}

void g()
{
    valarray<double> v;                    // make a default array
    initialize_from_input(v);              // give v the right size and elements

    // ...
}
```

This avoids copying large amounts of data.

If we want a *valarray* holding valuable data to grow dynamically, we must use a temporary:

```
void grow (valarray<int>& v, size_t n)
{
    if (n<=v.size()) return;

    valarray<int> tmp (n);                      // n default elements

    copy (&v[0],&v[v.size()],&tmp[0]);          // copy algorithm from §18.6.1
    v.resize (n);
    copy (&tmp[0],&tmp[v.size()],&v[0]);
}
```

This is *not* the intended way to use *valarray*. A *valarray* is intended to have a fixed size after being given its initial value.

The elements of a *valarray* form a sequence; that is, $v[0]..v[n-1]$ are contiguous in memory. This implies that $T*$ is a random-access iterator (§19.2.1) for *valarray<T>* so that standard algorithms, such as *copy()*, can be used. However, it would be more in the spirit of *valarray* to express the copy in terms of assignment and subarrays:

```
void grow2 (valarray<int>& v, size_t n)
{
    if (n<=v.size()) return;

    valarray<int> tmp = v;
    slice s (0,v.size(),1);        // subarray of v.size() elements (see §22.4.5)

    v.resize (n);                  // resizing doesn't preserve element values
    v[s] = tmp;                    // copy elements back into the first part of v
}
```

If for some reason input data is organized so that you have to count the elements before knowing the size of vector needed to hold them, it is usually best to read the input into a *vector* (§16.3.5) and then copy the elements into a *valarray*.

22.4.4 Nonmember Operations

The usual binary operators and mathematical functions are provided:

```
template<class T> valarray<T> operator* (const valarray<T>&, const valarray<T>&);
template<class T> valarray<T> operator* (const valarray<T>&, const T&);
template<class T> valarray<T> operator* (const T&, const valarray<T>&);

// similarly: /, %, +, –, ^, &, |, <<, >>, &&, ||, ==, !=, <, >, <=, >=, atan2, and pow

template<class T> valarray<T> abs (const valarray<T>&);

// similarly: acos, asin, atan, cos, cosh, exp, log, log10, sin, sinh, sqrt, tan, and tanh
```

The binary operations are defined for *valarray*s and for combinations of a *valarray* and its scalar type. For example:

```
void f(valarray<double>& v, valarray<double>& v2, double d)
{
      valarray<double> v3 = v*v2;    // v3[i] = v[i]*v2[i] for all i
      valarray<double> v4 = v*d;     // v4[i] = v[i]*d for all i
      valarray<double> v5 = d*v2;    // v5[i] = d*v2[i] for all i

      valarray<double> v6 = cos(v);  // v6[i] = cos(v[i]) for all i
}
```

These vector operations all apply their operations to each element of their operand(s) in the way indicated by the * and *cos*() examples. Naturally, an operation can be used only if the corresponding operation is defined for the template argument type. Otherwise, the compiler will issue an error when trying to specialize the template (§13.5).

Where the result is a *valarray*, its length is the same as its *valarray* operand. If the lengths of the two arrays are not the same, the result of a binary operator on two *valarray*s is undefined.

Curiously enough, no I/O operations are provided for *valarray* (§22.4.3); << and >> are shift operations. However, I/O versions of >> and << for *valarray* are easily defined (§22.9[5]).

Note that these *valarray* operations return new *valarray*s rather than modifying their operands. This can be expensive, but it doesn't have to be when aggressive optimization techniques are applied (e.g., see §22.4.7).

All of the operators and mathematical functions on *valarray*s can also be applied to *slice_array*s (§22.4.6), *gslice_array*s (§22.4.8), *mask_array*s (§22.4.9), *indirect_array*s (§22.4.10), and combinations of these types. However, an implementation is allowed to convert an operand that is not a *valarray* to a *valarray* before performing a required operation.

22.4.5 Slices

A *slice* is an abstraction that allows us to manipulate a vector efficiently as a matrix of arbitrary dimension. It is the key notion of Fortran vectors and of the BLAS (Basic Linear Algebra Subprograms) library, which is the basis for much numeric computation. Basically, a slice is every *n*th element of some part of a *valarray*:

```
class std::slice {
      // starting index, a length, and a stride
public:
      slice();
      slice(size_t start, size_t size, size_t stride);

      size_t start() const;     // index of first element
      size_t size() const;      // number of elements
      size_t stride() const;    // element n is at start()+n*stride()
};
```

A *stride* is the distance (in number of elements) between two elements of the *slice*. Thus, a *slice* describes a sequence of integers. For example:

```
size_t slice_index(const slice& s, size_t i) // map i to its corresponding index
{
    return s.start()+i*s.stride();
}

void print_seq(const slice& s)    // print the elements of s
{
    for (size_t i = 0; i<s.size(); i++) cout << slice_index(s,i) << " ";
}

void f()
{
    print_seq(slice(0,3,4)); // row 0
    cout << ", ";
    print_seq(slice(1,3,4)); // row 1
    cout << ", ";
    print_seq(slice(0,4,1)); // column 0
    cout << ", ";
    print_seq(slice(4,4,1)); // column 1
}
```

prints *0 4 8 , 1 5 9 , 0 1 2 3 , 4 5 6 7*.

In other words, a *slice* describes a mapping of non-negative integers into indices. The number of elements (the *size()*) doesn't affect the mapping (addressing) but simply allows us to find the end of a sequence. This mapping can be used to simulate two-dimensional arrays within a one-dimensional array (such as *valarray*) in an efficient, general, and reasonably convenient way. Consider a 3-by-4 matrix the way we often think of it (§C.7):

00	01	02
10	11	12
20	21	22
30	31	32

Following Fortran conventions, we can lay it out in memory like this:

```
0           4           8
00 10 20 30 01 11 21 31 02 12 22 32
0  1  2  3
```

This is *not* the way arrays are laid out in C++ (see §C.7). However, we should be able to present a concept with a clean and logical interface and then choose a representation to suit the constraints of the problem. Here, I have chosen to use Fortran layout to ease the interaction with numeric software that follows that convention. I have not, however, gone so far as to start indexing from *1* rather than *0*; that is left as an exercise (§22.9[9]). Much numeric computation is done and will remain done in a mixture of languages and using a variety of libraries. Often the ability to manipulate data in a variety of formats determined by those libraries and language standards is essential.

Row x can be described by a *slice* $(x, 3, 4)$. That is, the first element of row x is the xth element of the vector, the next element of the row is the $(x+4)$ th, etc., and there are *3* elements in each row. In the figures, *slice* $(0, 3, 4)$ describes the row *00*, *01*, and *02*.

Column y can be described by *slice* $(4*y, 4, 1)$. That is, the first element of column y is the $4*y$th element of the vector, the next element of the column is the $(4*y+1)$ th, etc., and there are *4* elements in each column. In the figures, *slice* $(0, 4, 1)$ describes the column *00*, *10*, *20*, and *30*.

In addition to its use for simulating two-dimensional arrays, a *slice* can describe many other sequences. It is a fairly general way of specifying very simple sequences. This notion is explored further in §22.4.8.

One way of thinking of a slice is as an odd kind of iterator: a *slice* allows us to describe a sequence of indices for a *valarray*. We could build a real iterator based on that:

```
template<class T> class Slice_iter {
    valarray<T>* v;
    slice s;
    size_t curr;      // index of current element

    T& ref(size_t i) const { return (*v)[s.start()+i*s.stride()]; }
public:
    Slice_iter(valarray<T>* vv, slice ss) :v(vv), s(ss), curr(0) { }

    Slice_iter end() const
    {
        Slice_iter t = *this;
        t.curr = s.size();         // index of last-plus-one element
        return t;
    }

    Slice_iter& operator++() { curr++; return *this; }
    Slice_iter operator++(int) { Slice_iter t = *this; curr++; return t; }

    T& operator[](size_t i) { return ref(i); }      // C style subscript
    T& operator()(size_t i) { return ref(i); }      // Fortran-style subscript
    T& operator*() { return ref(curr); }            // current element

    friend bool operator==<>(const Slice_iter& p, const Slice_iter& q);
    friend bool operator!=<>(const Slice_iter& p, const Slice_iter& q);
    friend bool operator< <>(const Slice_iter& p, const Slice_iter& q);
};
```

Since a *slice* has a size, we could even provide range checking. Here, I have taken advantage of *slice*::*size*() to provide an *end*() operation to provide an iterator for the one-past-the-end element of the *valarray*.

Since a *slice* can describe either a row or a column, the *Slice_iter* allows us to traverse a *valarray* by row or by column.

The comparisons could be defined like this:

```
template<class T> bool operator==(const Slice_iter<T>& p, const Slice_iter<T>& q)
{
    return p.curr==q.curr && p.s.stride()==q.s.stride() && p.s.start()==q.s.start();
}
```

```
template<class T> bool operator!=(const Slice_iter<T>& p, const Slice_iter<T>& q)
{
    return !(p==q);
}

template<class T> bool operator<(const Slice_iter<T>& p, const Slice_iter<T>& q)
{
    return p.curr<q.curr && p.s.stride()==q.s.stride() && p.s.start()==q.s.start();
}
```

22.4.6 Slice_array

From a *valarray* and a *slice*, we can build something that looks and feels like a *valarray*, but which is really simply a way of referring to the subset of the array described by the slice. Such a *slice_array* is defined like this:

```
template <class T> class std::slice_array {
public:
    typedef T value_type;

    void operator=(const valarray<T>&);
    void operator=(const T& val);              // assign val to each element

    void operator*=(const valarray<T>& val);   // v[i]*=val[i] for each element
    // similarly: /=, %=, +=, -=, ^=, &=, |=, <<=, >>=

    ~slice_array();
private:
    slice_array();                             // prevent construction
    slice_array(const slice_array&);           // prevent copying
    slice_array& operator=(const slice_array&); // prevent copying

    valarray<T>* p;                            // implementation-defined representation
    slice s;
};
```

A user cannot directly create a *slice_array*. Instead, the user subscripts a *valarray* to create a *slice_array* for a given slice. Once the *slice_array* is initialized, all references to it indirectly go to the *valarray* for which it is created. For example, we can create something that represents every second element of an array like this:

```
void f(valarray<double>& d)
{
    slice_array<double>& v_even = d[slice(0,d.size()/2+d.size()%2,2)];
    slice_array<double>& v_odd = d[slice(1,d.size()/2,2)];

    v_even *= v_odd;    // multiply element pairs and store results in even elements
    v_odd = 0;          // assign 0 to every odd element of d
}
```

The ban on copying *slice_array*s is necessary so as to allow optimizations that rely on absence of aliases. It can be quite constraining. For example:

```
slice_array<double> row (valarray<double>& d, int i)
{
      slice_array<double> v = d[slice(0,2,d.size()/2)];   // error: attempt to copy

      return d[slice(i%2,i,d.size()/2)];                  // error: attempt to copy
}
```

Often copying a *slice* is a reasonable alternative to copying a *slice_array*.

Slices can be used to express a variety of subsets of an array. For example, we might use slices to manipulate contiguous subarrays like this:

```
inline slice sub_array(size_t first, size_t count)  // [first:first+count[
{
      return slice(first,count,1);
}

void f(valarray<double>& v)
{
      size_t sz = v.size();
      if (sz<2) return;
      size_t n = sz/2;
      size_t n2 = sz-n;

      valarray<double> half1(n);
      valarray<double> half2(n2);

      half1 = v[sub_array(0,n)];          // copy of first half of v
      half2 = v[sub_array(n,n2)];         // copy of second half of v

      // ...
}
```

The standard library does not provide a matrix class. Instead, the intent is for *valarray* and *slice* to provide the tools for building matrices optimized for a variety of needs. Consider how we might implement a simple two-dimensional matrix using a *valarray* and *slice_array*s:

```
class Matrix {
      valarray<double>* v;        // stores elements by column as described in §22.4.5
      size_t d1, d2;              // d1 == number of columns, d2 == number of rows
public:
      Matrix(size_t x, size_t y);               // note: no default constructor
      Matrix(const Matrix&);
      Matrix& operator=(const Matrix&);
      ~Matrix();

      size_t size() const { return d1*d2; }
      size_t dim1() const { return d1; }   // number of columns
      size_t dim2() const { return d2; }   // number of rows

      Slice_iter<double> row(size_t i);
      Cslice_iter<double> row(size_t i) const;
```

```
        Slice_iter<double> column(size_t i);
        Cslice_iter<double> column(size_t i) const;

        double& operator()(size_t x, size_t y);                    // Fortran-style subscripts
        double operator()(size_t x, size_t y) const;

        Slice_iter<double> operator()(size_t i) { return column(i); }
        Cslice_iter<double> operator()(size_t i) const { return column(i); }

        Slice_iter<double> operator[](size_t i) { return column(i); }   // C-style subscript
        Cslice_iter<double> operator[](size_t i) const { return column(i); }

        Matrix& operator*=(double);

        valarray<double>& array() { return *v; }
    };
```

The representation of a *Matrix* is a *valarray*. We impose dimensionality on that array through slicing. When necessary, we can view that representation as having one, two, three, etc., dimensions in the same way that we provide the default two-dimensional view through *row*() and *column*(). The *Slice_iters* are used to circumvent the ban on copying *slice_arrays*. I couldn't return a *slice_array*:

```
        slice_array<double> row(size_t i) { return (*v)(slice(i,d1,d2)); } // error
```

so I returned an iterator containing a pointer to the *valarray* and the *slice* itself instead of a *slice_array*.

We need an additional class "iterator for slice of constants," *Cslice_iter* to express the distinction between a slice of a *const Matrix* and a slice of a non-*const Matrix*:

```
    inline Slice_iter<double> Matrix::row(size_t i)
    {
        return Slice_iter<double>(v,slice(i,d1,d2));
    }

    inline Cslice_iter<double> Matrix::row(size_t i) const
    {
        return Cslice_iter<double>(v,slice(i,d1,d2));
    }

    inline Slice_iter<double> Matrix::column(size_t i)
    {
        return Slice_iter<double>(v,slice(i*d2,d2,1));
    }

    inline Cslice_iter<double> Matrix::column(size_t i) const
    {
        return Cslice_iter<double>(v,slice(i*d2,d2,1));
    }
```

The definition of *Cslice_iter* is identical to that of *Slice_iter*, except that it returns *const* references to elements of its slice.

The rest of the member operations are fairly trivial:

```
Matrix::Matrix(size_t x, size_t y)
{
      // check that x and y are sensible
      d1 = x;
      d2 = y;
      v = new valarray<double>(x*y);
}

double& Matrix::operator()(size_t x, size_t y)
{
      return column(x)[y];
}

double mul(const Cslice_iter<double>& v1, const valarray<double>& v2)
{
      double res = 0;
      for (size_t i = 0; i<v2.size(); i++) res+= v1[i]*v2[i];
      return res;
}

valarray<double> operator*(const Matrix& m, const valarray<double>& v)
{
      valarray<double> res(m.dim2());
      for (size_t i = 0; i<m.dim2(); i++) res[i] = mul(m.row(i),v);
      return res;
}

Matrix& Matrix::operator*=(double d)
{
      (*v) *= d;
      return *this;
}
```

I provided (i,j) to express *Matrix* subscripting because $()$ is a single operator and because that notation is the most familiar to many in the numeric community. The concept of a row provides the more familiar (in the C and C++ communities) $[i][j]$ notation:

```
void f(Matrix& m)
{
      m(1,2) = 5;              // Fortran-style subscripts
      m.row(1)(2) = 6;
      m.row(1)[2] = 7;
      m[1](2) = 8;             // undesirable mixed style (but it works)
      m[1][2] = 9;             // C++-style subscripts
}
```

The use of *slice_arrays* to express subscripting assumes a good optimizer.

Generalizing this to an *n*-dimensional matrix of arbitrary elements and with a reasonable set of operations is left as an exercise (§22.9[7]).

Maybe your first idea for a two-dimensional vector was something like this:

```
class Matrix {
    valarray< valarray<double> > v;
public:
    // ...
};
```

This would also work (§22.9[10]). However, it is not easy to match the efficiency and compatibility required by high-performance computations without dropping to the lower and more conventional level represented by *valarray* plus *slice*s.

22.4.7 Temporaries, Copying, and Loops

If you build a vector or a matrix class, you will soon find that three related problems have to be faced to satisfy performance-conscious users:

[1] The number of temporaries must be minimized.

[2] Copying of matrices must be minimized.

[3] Multiple loops over the same data in composite operations must be minimized.

These issues are not directly addressed by the standard library. However, I can outline a technique that can be used to produce highly optimized implementations.

Consider *U=M*V+W*, where *U*, *V*, and *W* are vectors and *M* is a matrix. A naive implementation introduces temporary vectors for *M*V* and *M*V+W* and copies the results of *M*V* and *M*V+W*. A smart implementation calls a function *mul_add_and_assign* (&*U*, &*M*, &*V*, &*W*) that introduces no temporaries, copies no vectors, and touches each element of the matrices the minimum number of times.

This degree of optimization is rarely necessary for more than a few kinds of expressions, so a simple solution to efficiency problems is to provide functions such as *mul_add_and_assign* ( ) and let the user call those where it matters. However, it is possible to design a *Matrix* so that such optimizations are applied automatically for expressions of the right form. That is, we can treat *U=M*V+W* as a use of a single operator with four operands. The basic technique was demonstrated for *ostream* manipulators (§21.4.6.3). In general, it can be used to make a combination of *n* binary operators act like an (*n+1*) -ary operator. Handling *U=M*V+W* requires the introduction of two auxiliary classes. However, the technique can result in impressive speedups (say, 30 times) on some systems by enabling more-powerful optimization techniques.

First, we define the result of multiplying a *Matrix* by a *Vector*:

```
struct MVmul {
    const Matrix& m;
    const Vector& v;

    MVmul(const Matrix& mm, const Vector &vv) :m(mm), v(vv) { }

    operator Vector();    // evaluate and return result
};

inline MVmul operator* (const Matrix& mm, const Vector& vv)
{
    return MVmul(mm,vv);
}
```

This "multiplication" does nothing except store references to its operands; the evaluation of *M*V* is deferred. The object produced by * is closely related to what is called a *closure* in many technical communities. Similarly, we can deal with what happens if we add a *Vector*:

```
struct MVmulVadd {
    const Matrix& m;
    const Vector& v;
    const Vector& v2;

    MVmulVadd(const MVmul& mv, const Vector& vv) :m(mv.m), v(mv.v), v2(vv) { }

    operator Vector();    // evaluate and return result
};

inline MVmulVadd operator+(const MVmul& mv, const Vector& vv)
{
    return MVmulVadd(mv,vv);
}
```

This defers the evaluation of *M*V+W*. We now have to ensure that it all gets evaluated using a good algorithm when it is assigned to a *Vector*:

```
class Vector {
    // ...
public:
    Vector(const MVmulVadd& m)                  // initialize by result of m
    {
        // allocate elements, etc.
        mul_add_and_assign(this, &m.m, &m.v, &m.v2);
    }

    Vector& operator=(const MVmulVadd& m)       // assign the result of m to *this
    {
        mul_add_and_assign(this, &m.m, &m.v, &m.v2);
        return *this;
    }
    // ...
};
```

Now *U=M*V+W* is automatically expanded to

```
    U.operator=(MVmulVadd(MVmul(M, V), W))
```

which because of inlining resolves to the desired simple call

```
    mul_add_and_assign(&U, &M, &V, &W);
```

Clearly, this eliminates the copying and the temporaries. In addition, we might write *mul_add_and_assign()* in an optimized fashion. However, if we just wrote it in a fairly simple and unoptimized fashion, it would still be in a form that offered great opportunities to an optimizer.

I introduced a new *Vector* (rather than using a *valarray*) because I needed to define assignment (and assignment must be a member function; §11.2.2). However, *valarray* is a strong candidate for the representation of that *Vector*.

The importance of this technique is that most really time-critical vector and matrix computations are done using a few relatively simple syntactic forms. Typically, there is no real gain in optimizing expressions of half-a-dozen operators this way; more conventional techniques (§11.6) suffice.

This technique is based on the idea of using compile-time analysis and closure objects to transfer evaluation of subexpression into an object representing a composite operation. It can be applied to a variety of problems with the common attribute that several pieces of information need to be gathered into one function before evaluation can take place. I refer to the objects generated to defer evaluation as *composition closure objects*, or simply *compositors*.

22.4.8 Generalized Slices

The *Matrix* example in §22.4.6 showed how two *slice*s could be used to describe rows and columns of a two-dimensional array. In general, a *slice* can describe any row or column of an *n*-dimensional array (§22.9[7]). However, sometimes we need to extract a subarray that is not a row or a column. For example, we might want to extract the 2-by-3 matrix from the top-left corner of a 3-by-4 matrix:

$$
\begin{array}{|c|c||c|}
\hline
00 & 01 & 02 \\
\hline
10 & 11 & 12 \\
\hline
20 & 21 & 22 \\
\hline
30 & 31 & 32 \\
\hline
\end{array}
$$

Unfortunately, these elements are not allocated in a way that can be described by a single slice:

$$
\begin{array}{ccccccccccccc}
0 & 1 & 2 \\
\hline
00 & 10 & 20 & 30 & 01 & 11 & 21 & 31 & 02 & 12 & 22 & 32 \\
\hline
 & & & & 4 & 5 & 6
\end{array}
$$

A *gslice* is a "generalized slice" that contains (almost) the information from *n* slices:

```
class std::gslice {
        // instead of 1 stride and one size like slice, gslice holds n strides and n sizes
public:
        gslice();
        gslice(size_t s, const valarray<size_t>& l, const valarray<size_t>& d);

        size_t start() const;                 // index of first element
        valarray<size_t> size() const;        // number of elements in dimension
        valarray<size_t> stride() const;      // stride for index[0], index[1], ...
};
```

The extra values allow a *gslice* to specify a mapping between *n* integers and an index to be used to address elements of an array. For example, we can describe the layout of the 2-by-3 matrix by a pair of (length,stride) pairs. As shown in §22.4.5, a length of *2* and a stride of *4* describes two elements of a row of the 3-by-4 matrix, when Fortran layout is used. Similarly, a length of *3* and a stride of *1* describes 3 elements of a column. Together, they describe every element of the 2-by-3 submatrix. To list the elements, we can write:

```
size_t gslice_index (const gslice& s, size_t i, size_t j)
{
    return s.start()+i*s.stride()[0]+j*s.stride()[1];
}

size_t len[] = { 2, 3 };        // (len[0],str[0]) describes a row
size_t str[] = { 4, 1 };        // (len[1],str[1]) describes a column

valarray<size_t> lengths (len, 2);
valarray<size_t> strides (str, 2);

void f()
{
    gslice s (0, lengths, strides);

    for (int i = 0 ; i<s.size()[0]; i++) cout << gslice_index(s,i,0) << " "; // row
    cout << ", ";
    for (int j = 0 ; j<s.size()[1]; j++) cout << gslice_index(s,0,j) << " "; // column
}
```

This prints *0 4 , 0 1 2*.

In this way, a *gslice* with two (length,stride) pairs describes a subarray of a 2-dimensional array, a *gslice* with three (length,stride) pairs describes a subarray of a 3-dimensional array, etc. Using a *gslice* as the index of a *valarray* yields a *gslice_array* consisting of the elements described by the *gslice*. For example:

```
void f(valarray<float>& v)
{
    gslice m (0, lengths, strides);
    v[m] = 0; // assign 0 to v[0],v[1],v[2],v[4],v[5],v[6]
}
```

The *gslice_array* offers the same set of members as *slice_array*. In particular, a *gslice_array* cannot be constructed directly by the user and cannot be copied (§22.4.6). Instead, a *gslice_array* is the result of using a *gslice* as the subscript of a *valarray* (§22.4.2).

22.4.9 Masks

A *mask_array* provides yet another way of specifying a subset of a *valarray* and making the result look like a *valarray*. In the context of *valarray*s, a mask is simply a *valarray<bool>*. When a mask is used as a subscript for a *valarray*, a *true* bit indicates that the corresponding element of the *valarray* is considered part of the result. This allows us to operate on a subset of a *valarray* even if there is no simple pattern (such as a *slice*) that describes that subset. For example:

```
void f(valarray<double>& v)
{
        bool b[] = { true , false, false, true, false, true };
        valarray<bool> mask(b,6);                  // elements 0, 3, and 5

        valarray<double> vv = cos(v[mask]);        // vv[0]==cos(v[0]), vv[1]==cos(v[3]),
                                                   // vv[2]==cos(v[5])
}
```

The *mask_array* offers the same set of members as *slice_array*. In particular, a *mask_array* cannot be constructed directly by the user and cannot be copied (§22.4.6). Instead, a *mask_array* is the result of using a *valarray<bool>* as the subscript of a *valarray* (§22.4.2). The number of elements of a *valarray* used as a mask must not be greater than the number of elements of the *valarray* for which it is used as a subscript.

22.4.10 Indirect Arrays

An *indirect_array* provides a way of arbitrarily subsetting and reordering a *valarray*. For example:

```
void f(valarray<double>& v)
{
        size_t i[] = { 3, 2, 1, 0 };               // first four elements in reverse order
        valarray<size_t> index(i,4);               // elements 3, 2, 1, 0 (in that order)

        valarray<double> vv = log(v[index]);       // vv[0]==log(v[3]), vv[1]==log(v[2]),
                                                   // vv[2]==log(v[1]), vv[3]==log(v[0])
}
```

If an index is specified twice, we have referred to an element of a *valarray* twice in the same operation. That's exactly the kind of aliasing that *valarray*s do not allow, so the behavior of an *indirect_array* is undefined if an index is repeated.

The *indirect_array* offers the same set of members as *slice_array*. In particular, an *indirect_array* cannot be constructed directly by the user and cannot be copied (§22.4.6). Instead, an *indirect_array* is the result of using a *valarray<size_t>* as the subscript of a *valarray* (§22.4.2). The number of elements of a *valarray* used as a subscript must not be greater than the number of elements of the *valarray* for which it is used as a subscript.

22.5 Complex Arithmetic

The standard library provides a *complex* template along the lines of the *complex* class described in §11.3. The library *complex* needs to be a template to serve the need for complex numbers based on different scalar types. In particular, specializations are provided for *complex* using *float*, *double*, and *long double* as its scalar type.

The *complex* template is defined in namespace *std* and presented in *<complex>*:

```
template<class T> class std::complex {
    T re, im;
public:
    typedef T value_type;

    complex(const T& r = T(), const T& i = T()) : re(r), im(i) { }
    template<class X> complex(const complex<X>& a) : re(a.real()), im(a.imag()) { }

    T real() const { return re; }
    T imag() const { return im; }

    complex<T>& operator=(const T& z); // assign complex(z,0)
    template<class X> complex<T>& operator=(const complex<X>&);
    // similarly: +=, -=, *=, /=
};
```

The representation and the inline functions are here for illustration. One could – barely – imagine a standard library *complex* that used a different representation. Note the use of member templates to ensure initialization and assignment of any *complex* type with any other (§13.6.2).

Throughout this book, I have used *complex* as a class rather than as a template. This is feasible because I assumed a bit of namespace magic to get the *complex* of *double* that I usually prefer:

```
typedef std::complex<double> complex;
```

The usual unary and binary operators are defined:

```
template<class T> complex<T> operator+(const complex<T>&, const complex<T>&);
template<class T> complex<T> operator+(const complex<T>&, const T&);
template<class T> complex<T> operator+(const T&, const complex<T>&);

// similarly: -, *, /, ==, and !=

template<class T> complex<T> operator+(const complex<T>&);
template<class T> complex<T> operator-(const complex<T>&);
```

The coordinate functions are provided:

```
template<class T> T real(const complex<T>&);
template<class T> T imag(const complex<T>&);

template<class T> complex<T> conj(const complex<T>&);

// construct from polar coordinates (abs(),arg()):
template<class T> complex<T> polar(const T& rho, const T& theta);


template<class T> T abs(const complex<T>&);      // sometimes called rho
template<class T> T arg(const complex<T>&);      // sometimes called theta

template<class T> T norm(const complex<T>&);     // square of abs()
```

The usual set of mathematical functions is provided:

```
template<class T> complex<T> sin (const complex<T>&);
//similarly: sinh, sqrt, tan, tanh, cos, cosh, exp, log, and log10

template<class T> complex<T> pow (const complex<T>&, int);
template<class T> complex<T> pow (const complex<T>&, const T&);
template<class T> complex<T> pow (const complex<T>&, const complex<T>&);
template<class T> complex<T> pow (const T&, const complex<T>&);
```

Finally, stream I/O is provided:

```
template<class T, class Ch, class Tr>
basic_istream<Ch,Tr>& operator>> (basic_istream<Ch,Tr>&, complex<T>&);
template<class T, class Ch, class Tr>
basic_ostream<Ch,Tr>& operator<< (basic_ostream<Ch,Tr>&, const complex<T>&);
```

A complex is written out in the format (x, y) and can be read in the formats x, (x), and (x, y) (§21.2.3, §21.3.5). The specializations *complex<float>*, *complex<double>*, and *complex<long double>* are provided to restrict conversions (§13.6.2) and to provide opportunities for optimized implementations. For example:

```
template<> class complex<double> {
    double re, im;
public:
    typedef double value_type;

    complex (double r = 0.0, double i = 0.0) : re (r), im (i) { }
    complex (const complex<float>& a) : re (a.real ()), im (a.imag ()) { }
    explicit complex (const complex<long double>& a) : re (a.real ()), im (a.imag ()) { }

    // ...
};
```

Now a *complex<float>* can be quietly converted to a *complex<double>*, while a *complex< long double>* can't. Similar specializations ensure that a *complex<float>* and a *complex<double>* can be quietly converted to a *complex< long double>* but that a *complex< long double>* cannot be implicitly converted to a *complex<double>* or to a *complex<float>* and a *complex<double>* cannot be implicitly converted to a *complex<float>*. Curiously, the assignments don't offer the same protection as the constructors. For example:

```
void f(complex<float> cf, complex<double> cd, complex<long double> cld, complex<int> ci)
{
    complex<double> c1 = cf;         // fine
    complex<double> c2 = cd;         // fine
    complex<double> c3 = cld;        // error: possible truncation
    complex<double> c4 (cld);        // ok: explicit conversion
    complex<double> c5 = ci;         // error: no conversion

    c1 = cld;                        // ok, but beware: possible truncation
    c1 = cf;                         // ok
    c1 = ci;                         // ok
}
```

22.6   Generalized Numeric Algorithms

In *<numeric>*, the standard library provides a few generalized numeric algorithms in the style of the non-numeric algorithms from *<algorithm>* (Chapter 18) :

Generalized Numeric Algorithms <numeric>	
accumulate()	Accumulate results of operation on a sequence
inner_product()	Accumulate results of operation on two sequences
partial_sum()	Generate sequence by operation on a sequence
adjacent_difference()	Generate sequence by operation on a sequence

These algorithms generalize common operations such as computing a sum by letting them apply to all kinds of sequences and by making the operation applied to elements on those sequences a parameter. For each algorithm, the general version is supplemented by a version applying the most common operator for that algorithm.

22.6.1 Accumulate

The *accumulate* ( ) algorithm can be understood as the generalization of a sum of the elements of a vector. The *accumulate* ( ) algorithm is defined in namespace *std* and presented in *<numeric>*:

```
template <class In, class T> T accumulate(In first, In last, T init)
{
    while (first != last) init = init + *first++;   // plus
    return init;
}

template <class In, class T, class BinOp> T accumulate(In first, In last, T init, BinOp op)
{
    while (first != last) init = op(init, *first++);     // general operation
    return init;
}
```

The simple version of *accumulate* ( ) adds elements of a sequence using their + operator. For example:

```
void f(vector<int>& price, list<float>& incr)
{
    int i = accumulate(price.begin(), price.end(), 0);   // accumulate in int
    double d = 0;
    d = accumulate(incr.begin(), incr.end(), d);         // accumulate in double
    // ...
}
```

Note how the type of the initial value passed determines the return type.

Not all items that we want to add are available as elements of a sequence. Where they are not, we can often supply an operation for *accumulate* ( ) to call in order to produce the items to be added. The most obvious kind of operation to pass is one that extracts a value from a data structure. For example:

```
struct Record {
    // ...
    int unit_price;
    int number_of_units;
};

long price(long val, const Record& r)
{
    return val + r.unit_price * r.number_of_units;
}

void f(const vector<Record>& v)
{
    cout << "Total value: " << accumulate(v.begin(),v.end(),0,price) << '\n';
}
```

Operations similar to *accumulate* are called *reduce* and *reduction* in some communities.

22.6.2 Inner_product

Accumulating from a sequence is very common, while accumulating from a pair of sequences is not uncommon. The *inner_product*() algorithm is defined in namespace *std* and presented in *<numeric>*:

```
template <class In, class In2, class T>
T inner_product(In first, In last, In2 first2, T init)
{
    while (first != last) init = init + *first++ * *first2++;
    return init;
}

template <class In, class In2, class T, class BinOp, class BinOp2>
T inner_product(In first, In last, In2 first2, T init, BinOp op, BinOp2 op2)
{
    while (first != last) init = op(init, op2(*first++, *first2++));
    return init;
}
```

As usual, only the beginning of the second input sequence is passed as an argument. The second input sequence is assumed to be at least as long as the first.

The key operation in multiplying a *Matrix* by a *valarray* is an *inner_product*:

```
valarray<double> operator*(const Matrix& m, valarray<double>& v)
{
    valarray<double> res(m.dim2());

    for (size_t i = 0; i<m.dim2(); i++) {
        const Cslice_iter<double>& ri = m.row(i);
        res[i] = inner_product(ri,ri.end(),&v[0],double(0));
    }
    return res;
}
```

```
valarray<double> operator* (valarray<double>& v, const Matrix& m)
{
     valarray<double> res (m.dim1 ());

     for (size_t i = 0; i<m.dim1 (); i++) {
          const Cslice_iter<double>& ci = m.column (i);
          res [i] = inner_product (ci, ci.end (), &v [0], double (0) );
     }
     return res;
}
```

Some forms of *inner_product* are often referred to as "dot product."

22.6.3 Incremental Change

The *partial_sum* ( ) and *adjacent_difference* ( ) algorithms are inverses of each other and deal with the notion of incremental change. They are defined in namespace *std* and presented in *<numeric>*:

```
template <class In, class Out> Out adjacent_difference (In first, In last, Out res);
```

```
template <class In, class Out, class BinOp>
     Out adjacent_difference (In first, In last, Out res, BinOp op);
```

Given a sequence *a, b, c, d*, etc., *adjacent_difference* ( ) produces *a, b−a, c−b, d−c*, etc.

Consider a vector of temperature readings. We could transform it into a vector of temperature changes like this:

```
vector<double> temps;

void f()
{
     adjacent_difference (temps.begin (), temps.end (), temps.begin () );
}
```

For example, *17, 19, 20, 20, 17* turns into *17, 2, 1, 0, −3*.

Conversely, *partial_sum* ( ) allows us to compute the end result of a set of incremental changes:

```
template <class In, class Out, class BinOp>
Out partial_sum (In first, In last, Out res, BinOp op)
{
     if (first==last) return res;
     *res = *first;
     T  val = *first;
     while (++first != last) {
          val = op (val, *first);
          *++res = val;
     }
     return ++res;
}
```

```
template <class In, class Out> Out partial_sum (In first, In last, Out res)
{
        return partial_sum (first, last, res, plus);     // §18.4.3
}
```

Given a sequence *a*, *b*, *c*, *d*, etc. , *partial_sum* ( ) produces *a*, *a+b*, *a+b+c*, *a+b+c+d*, etc. For example:

```
void f()
{
        partial_sum (temps.begin(), temps.end(), temps.begin());
}
```

Note the way *partial_sum* ( ) increments *res* before assigning a new value through it. This allows *res* to be the same sequence as its input; *adjacent_difference* ( ) behaves similarly. Thus,

```
partial_sum (v.begin(), v.end(), v.begin());
```

turns the sequence *a*, *b*, *c*, *d* into *a*, *a+b*, *a+b+c*, *a+b+c+d*, and

```
adjacent_difference (v.begin(), v.end(), v.begin());
```

turns it back into the original. In particular, *partial_sum* ( ) turns *17, 2, 1, 0, -3* back into *17, 19, 20, 20, 17*.

These operations are useful for analysing any series of changes. For example, analyzing variations in stock prices involves exactly the same two operations.

22.7 Random Numbers

Random numbers are essential to many simulations and games. In *<cstdlib>* and *<stdlib.h>*, the standard library provides a simple basis for the generation of random numbers:

```
#define RAND_MAX implementation_defined /* large positive integer */

int rand();                    // pseudo-random number between 0 and RAND_MAX
void srand(unsigned int i);    // seed random number generator by i
```

Producing a good random-number generator isn't easy, and unfortunately not all systems deliver a good *rand* ( ). In particular, the low-order bits of a random number are often suspect, so *rand* ( ) %*n* is not a good portable way of generating a random number between *0* and *n-1*. Often, *int* ((*double* (*rand* ( )) /*RAND_MAX*) **n*) gives acceptable results. However, to seriously use that formula, we must take care of the miniscule propability that the result will be *n*.

A call of *srand* ( ) starts a new sequence of random numbers from the *seed* given as argument. For debugging, it is often important that a sequence of random numbers from a given seed be repeatable. However, we often want to start each real run with a new seed. In fact, to make games unpredictable, it is often useful to pick a seed from the environment of a program. For such programs, some bits from a real-time clock often make a good seed.

If you must write your own random-number generator, be sure to test it carefully (§22.9[14]).

A random-number generator is often more useful if represented as a class. In that way, random-number generators for different distributions are easily built:

```
class Randint {        // uniform distribution, assuming 32-bit long
    unsigned long randx;
public:
    Randint(long s = 0) { randx=s; }
    void seed(long s) { randx=s; }

    // magic numbers chosen to use 31 bits of a 32-bit long:

    long abs(long x) { return x&0x7fffffff; }
    static double max() { return 2147483648.0; } // note: a double
    long draw() { return randx = randx*1103515245 + 12345; }

    double fdraw() { return abs(draw())/max(); }        // in the interval [0,1]

    long operator()() { return abs(draw()); }     // in the interval [0,pow(2,31)]
};

class Urand : public Randint { // uniform distribution in the interval [0:n[
    long n;
public:
    Urand(long nn) { n = nn; }

    long operator()() { long r = n*fdraw(); return (r==n) ? n-1 : r; }
};

class Erand : public Randint { // exponential distribution random number generator
    long mean;
public:
    Erand(long m) { mean=m; }
    long operator()() { return -mean * log( (max()-draw())/max() + .5); }
};
```

Here is a simple test:

```
int main()
{
    Urand draw(10);
    map<int,int> bucket;
    for (int i = 0; i< 1000000; i++) bucket[draw()]++;
    for(int j = 0; j<10; j++) cout << bucket[j] << '\n';
}
```

Unless each bucket has approximately the value 100,000, there is a bug somewhere.

These random-number generators are slightly edited versions of what I shipped with the very first C++ library (actually, the first ''C with Classes'' library; §1.4).

22.8 Advice

[1] Numerical problems are often subtle. If you are not 100% certain about the mathematical aspects of a numerical problem, either take expert advice or experiment; §22.1.
[2] Use *numeric_limits* to determine properties of built-in types; §22.2.
[3] Specialize *numeric_limits* for user-defined scalar types; §22.2.

[4] Use *valarray* for numeric computation when run-time efficiency is more important than flexibility with respect to operations and element types; §22.4.

[5] Express operations on part of an array in terms of slices rather than loops; §22.4.6.

[6] Use compositors to gain efficiency through elimination of temporaries and better algorithms; §22.4.7.

[7] Use *std::complex* for complex arithmetic; §22.5.

[8] You can convert old code that uses a *complex* class to use the *std::complex* template by using a *typedef*; §22.5.

[9] Consider *accumulate()*, *inner_product()*, *partial_sum()*, and *adjacent_difference()* before you write a loop to compute a value from a list; §22.6.

[10] Prefer a random-number class for a particular distribution over direct use of *rand()*; §22.7.

[11] Be careful that your random numbers are sufficiently random; §22.7.

22.9 Exercises

1. (∗1.5) Write a function that behaves like *apply()* from §22.4.3, except that it is a nonmember function and accepts function objects.

2. (∗1.5) Write a function that behaves like *apply()* from §22.4.3 , except that it is a nonmember function, accepts function objects, and modifies its *valarray* argument.

3. (∗2) Complete *Slice_iter* (§22.4.5). Take special care when defining the destructor.

4. (∗1.5) Rewrite the program from §17.4.1.3 using *accumulate()* .

5. (∗2) Implement I/O operators << and >> for *valarray*. Implement a *get_array()* function that creates a *valarray* of a size specified as part of the input itself.

6. (∗2.5) Define and implement a three-dimensional matrix with suitable operations.

7. (∗2.5) Define and implement an n–dimensional matrix with suitable operations.

8. (∗2.5) Implement a *valarray*-like class and implement + and ∗ for it. Compare its performance to the performance of your C++ implementation's *valarray*. Hint: Include $x=0.5(x+y)+z$ among your test cases and try it with a variety of sizes for the vectors x, y, and z.

9. (∗3) Implement a Fortran-style array *Fort_array* where indices start from 1 rather than 0.

10. (∗3) Implement *Matrix* using a *valarray* member as the representation of the elements (rather than a pointer or a reference to a *valarray*).

11. (∗2.5) Use compositors (§22.4.7) to implement efficient multidimensional subscripting using the [ ] notation. For example, $v1[x]$, $v2[x][y]$, $v2[x]$, $v3[x][y][z]$, $v3[x][y]$, and $v3[x]$ should all yield the appropriate elements and subarrays using a simple calculation of an index.

12. (∗2) Generalize the idea from the program in §22.7 into a function that, given a generator as an argument, prints a simple graphical representation of its distribution that can be used as a crude visual check of the generator's correctness.

13. (∗1) If n is an *int*, what is the distribution of $(double(rand())/RAND\_MAX)*n$?

14. (∗2.5) Plot points in a square output area. The coordinate pairs for the points should be generated by *Urand(N)*, where N is the number of pixels on a side of the output area. What does the output tell you about the distribution of numbers generated by *Urand*?

15. (∗2) Implement a Normal distribution generator, *Nrand*.

Part IV

Design Using C++

This part presents C++ and the techniques it supports in the larger picture of software development. The focus is on design and the effective realization of design in terms of language constructs.

Chapters

23 Development and Design
24 Design and Programming
25 Roles of Classes

''... I am just now beginning to discover the difficulty of expressing one's ideas on paper. As long as it consists solely of description it is pretty easy; but where reasoning comes into play, to make a proper connection, a clearness & a moderate fluency, is to me, as I have said, a difficulty of which I had no idea ...''

– Charles Darwin

23

Development and Design

> *There is no silver bullet.*
> *– F. Brooks*

Building software — aims and means — development process — development cycle — design aims — design steps — finding classes — specifying operations — specifying dependencies — specifying interfaces — reorganizing class hierarchies — models — experimentation and analysis — testing — software maintenance — efficiency — management — reuse — scale — the importance of individuals — hybrid design — bibliography — advice.

23.1 Overview

This chapter is the first of three that present the production of software in increasing detail, starting from a relatively high-level view of design and ending with C++ specific programming techniques and concepts directly supporting such design. After the introduction and a brief discussion of the aims and means of software development in §23.3, this chapter has two major parts:

§23.4 A view of the software development process

§23.5 Practical observations about the organization of software development

Chapter 24 discusses the relationship between design and programming language. Chapter 25 presents some roles that classes play in the organization of software from a design perspective. Taken as a whole, the three chapters of Part 4 aim to bridge the gap between would-be language-independent design and programming that is myopically focussed on details. Both ends of this spectrum have their place in a large project, but to avoid disaster and excessive cost, they must be part of a continuum of concerns and techniques.

23.2 Introduction

Constructing any nontrivial piece of software is a complex and often daunting task. Even for an individual programmer, the actual writing of program statements is only one part of the process. Typically, issues of problem analysis, overall program design, documentation, testing, and maintenance, as well as the management of all of this, dwarf the task of writing and debugging individual pieces of code. Naturally, one might simply label the totality of these activities "programming" and thereafter make a logically coherent claim that "I don't design, I just program;" but whatever one calls the activity, it is important sometimes to focus on its individual parts – just as it is important occasionally to consider the complete process. Neither the details nor the big picture must be permanently lost in the rush to get a system shipped – although often enough that is exactly what happens.

This chapter focusses on the parts of program development that do not involve writing and debugging individual pieces of code. The discussion is less precise and less detailed than the discussions of individual language features and specific programming techniques presented elsewhere in this book. This is necessary because there can be no cookbook method for creating good software. Detailed "how to" descriptions can exist for specific well-understood kinds of applications, but not for more general application areas. There is no substitute for intelligence, experience, and taste in programming. In consequence, this chapter offers only general advice, alternative approaches, and cautionary observations.

The discussion is hampered by the abstract nature of software and the fact that techniques that work for smaller projects (say, for one or two people writing 10,000 lines of code) do not necessarily scale to medium and large projects. For this reason, some discussions are formulated in terms of analogies from less abstract engineering disciplines rather than in terms of code examples. Please remember that "proof by analogy" is fraud, so analogy is used here for exposition only. Discussions of design issues phrased in C++ specific terms and with examples can be found in Chapter 24 and Chapter 25. The ideas expressed in this chapter are reflected in both the C++ language itself and in the presentation of the individual examples throughout this book.

Please also remember that because of the extraordinary diversity of application areas, people, and program-development environments, you cannot expect every observation made here to apply directly to your current problem. The observations are drawn from real-life projects and apply to a wide variety of situations, but they cannot be considered universal. Look at these observations with a healthy degree of skepticism.

C++ can be used simply as a better C. However, doing so leaves the most powerful techniques and language features unused so that only a small fraction of the potential benefits of using C++ will be gained. This chapter focusses on approaches to design that enable effective use of C++'s data abstraction and object-oriented programming facilities; such techniques are often called *object-oriented design*.

A few major themes run through this chapter:

- The most important single aspect of software development is to be clear about what you are trying to build.
- Successful software development is a long-term activity.
- The systems we construct tend to be at the limit of the complexity that we and our tools can handle.

- There are no "cookbook" methods that can replace intelligence, experience, and good taste in design and programming.
- Experimentation is essential for all nontrivial software development.
- Design and programming are iterative activities.
- The different phases of a software project, such as design, programming, and testing, cannot be strictly separated.
- Programming and design cannot be considered without also considering the management of these activities.

It is easy – and typically expensive – to underestimate any of these points. It is hard to transform the abstract ideas they embody into practice. The need for experience should be noted. Like boat building, bicycling, and programming, design is not a skill that can be mastered through theoretical study alone.

Too often, we forget the human aspects of system building and consider the software development process as simply "a series of well-defined steps, each performing specific actions on inputs according to predefined rules to produce the desired outputs." The very language used conceals the human involvement! Design and programming are human activities; forget that and all is lost.

This chapter is concerned with the design of systems that are ambitious relative to the experience and resources of the people building the system. It seems to be the nature of individuals and organizations to attempt projects that are at the limits of their ability. Projects that don't offer such challenges don't need a discussion of design. Such projects already have established frameworks that need not be upset. Only when something ambitious is attempted is there a need to adopt new and better tools and procedures. There is also a tendency to assign projects that "we know how to do" to relative novices who don't.

There is no "one right way" to design and build all systems. I would consider belief in "the one right way" a childhood disease, if experienced programmers and designers didn't succumb to it so often. Please remember that just because a technique worked for you last year and for one project, it does not follow that it will work unmodified for someone else or for a different project. It is most important to keep an open mind.

Clearly, much of the discussion here relates to larger-scale software development. Readers who are not involved in such development can sit back and enjoy a look at the horrors they have escaped. Alternatively, they can look for the subset of the discussion that relates to individual work. There is no lower limit to the size of programs for which it is sensible to design before starting to code. There is, however, a lower limit for which any particular approach to design and documentation is appropriate. See §23.5.2 for a discussion of issues of scale.

The most fundamental problem in software development is complexity. There is only one basic way of dealing with complexity: divide and conquer. A problem that can be separated into two sub-problems that can be handled separately is more than half solved by that separation. This simple principle can be applied in an amazing variety of ways. In particular, the use of a module or a class in the design of systems separates the program into two parts – the implementation and its users – connected only by an (ideally) well-defined interface. This is the fundamental approach to handling the inherent complexity of a program. Similarly, the process of designing a program can be broken into distinct activities with (ideally) well-defined interactions between the people involved. This is the basic approach to handling the inherent complexity of the development process and the people involved in it.

In both cases, the selection of the parts and the specification of the interfaces between the parts is where the most experience and taste is required. Such selection is not a simple mechanical process but typically requires insights that can be achieved only through a thorough understanding of a system at suitable levels of abstraction (see §23.4.2, §24.3.1, and §25.3). A myopic view of a program or of a software development process often leads to seriously flawed systems. Note also that for both people and programs, *separation* is easy. The hard part is to ensure effective *communication* between parties on different sides of a barrier without destroying the barrier or stifling the communication necessary to achieve cooperation.

This chapter presents an approach to design, not a complete design method. A complete formal design method is beyond the scope of this book. The approach presented here can be used with different degrees of formalization and as the basis for different formalizations. Similarly, this chapter is not a literature survey and does not attempt to touch every topic relevant to software development or to present every viewpoint. Again, that is beyond the scope of this book. A literature survey can be found in [Booch,1994]. Note that terms are used here in fairly general and conventional ways. Most ''interesting'' terms, such as *design*, *prototype*, and *programmer*, have several different and often conflicting definitions in the literature. Please be careful not to read something unintended into what is said here based on specialized or locally precise definitions of the terms.

23.3 Aims and Means

The purpose of professional programming is to deliver a product that satisfies its users. The primary means of doing so is to produce software with a clean internal structure and to grow a group of designers and programmers skilled enough and motivated enough to respond quickly and effectively to change and opportunities.

Why? The internal structure of the program and the process by which it was created are ideally of no concern to the end user. Stronger: if the end user has to worry about how the program was written, then there is something wrong with that program. Given that, what is the importance of the structure of a program and of the people who create the program?

A program needs a clean internal structure to ease:

- testing,
- porting,
- maintenance,
- extension,
- reorganization, and
- understanding.

The main point is that every successful major piece of software has an extended life in which it is worked on by a succession of programmers and designers, ported to new hardware, adapted to unanticipated uses, and repeatedly reorganized. Throughout the software's life, new versions of it must be produced with acceptable error rates and on time. Not planning for this is planning to fail.

Note that even though end users ideally don't have to know the internal structure of a system, they might actually want to. For example, a user might want to know the design of a system in detail to be able to assess its likely reliability and potential for revision and extension. If the software in question is not a complete system − rather, a set of libraries for building other software −

then the users will want to know more "details" to be able to better use the libraries and also to better benefit from them as sources of ideas.

A balance has to be struck between the lack of an overall design for a piece of software and overemphasis on structure. The former leads to endless cutting of corners ("we'll just ship this one and fix the problem in the next release"). The latter leads to overelaborate designs in which essentials are lost in formalism and to situations where implementation gets delayed by program reorganizations ("but this new structure is *much* better than the old one; people will want to wait for it"). It also often results in systems so demanding of resources that they are unaffordable to most potential users. Such balancing acts are the most difficult aspects of design and the area in which talent and experience show themselves. The choices are hard for the individual designer or programmer and harder for the larger projects in which more people with differing skills are involved.

A program needs to be produced and maintained by an organization that can do this despite changes of personnel, direction, and management structure. A popular approach to coping with this problem has been to try to reduce system development into a few relatively low-level tasks slotted into a rigid framework. That is, the idea is to create a class of easy-to-train (cheap) and interchangeable low-level programmers ("coders") and a class of somewhat less cheap but equally interchangeable (and therefore equally dispensable) designers. The coders are not supposed to make design decisions, while the designers are not supposed to concern themselves with the grubby details of coding. This approach often fails. Where it does work, it produces overly large systems with poor performance.

The problems with this approach are:

– insufficient communication between implementers and designers, which leads to missed opportunities, delays, inefficiencies, and repeated problems due to failure to learn from experience; and

– insufficient scope for initiative among implementers, which leads to lack of professional growth, lack of initiative, sloppiness, and high turnover.

Basically, such a system lacks feedback mechanisms to allow people to benefit from other people's experience. It is wasteful of scarce human talent. Creating a framework within which people can utilize diverse talents, develop new skills, contribute ideas, and enjoy themselves is not just the only decent thing to do but also makes practical and economic sense.

On the other hand, a system cannot be built, documented, and maintained indefinitely without some form of formal structure. Simply finding the best people and letting them attack the problem as they think best is often a good start for a project requiring innovation. However, as the project progresses, more scheduling, specialization, and formalized communication between the people involved in the project become necessary. By "formal" I don't mean a mathematical or mechanically verifiable notation (although that is nice, where available and applicable) but rather a set of guidelines for notation, naming, documentation, testing, etc. Again, a balance and a sense of appropriateness is necessary. A too-rigid system can prevent growth and stifle innovation. In this case, it is the manager's talent and experience that is tested. For the individual, the equivalent dilemma is to choose where to try to be clever and where to simply "do it by the book."

The recommendation is to plan not just for the next release of the current project but also for the longer term. Looking only to the next release is planning to fail. We must develop organizations and software development strategies aimed at producing and maintaining many releases of many projects; that is, we must plan for a series of successes.

The purpose of ''design'' is to create a clean and relatively simple internal structure, sometimes also called an *architecture*, for a program. In other words, we want to create a framework into which the individual pieces of code can fit and thereby guide the writing of those individual pieces of code.

A design is the end product of the design process (as far as there is an *end* product of an iterative process). It is the focus of the communication between the designer and the programmer and between programmers. It is important to have a sense of proportion here. If I − as an individual programmer − design a small program that I'm going to implement tomorrow, the appropriate level of precision and detail may be some scribbles on the back of an envelope. At the other extreme, the development of a system involving hundreds of designers and programmers may require books of specifications carefully written using formal or semi-formal notations. Determining a suitable level of detail, precision, and formality for a design is in itself a challenging technical and managerial task.

In this and the following chapters, I assume that the design of a system is expressed as a set of class declarations (typically with their private declarations omitted as spurious details) and their relationships. This is a simplification. Many more issues enter into a specific design; for example, concurrency, management of namespaces, uses of nonmember function and data, parameterization of classes and functions, organization of code to minimize recompilation, persistence, and use of multiple computers. However, simplification is necessary for a discussion at this level of detail, and classes are the proper focus of design in the context of C++. Some of these other issues are mentioned in passing in this chapter, and some that directly affect the design of C++ programs are discussed in Chapter 24 and Chapter 25. For a more detailed discussion and examples of a specific object-oriented design method, see [Booch,1994].

I leave the distinction between analysis and design vague because a discussion of this issue is beyond the scope of this book and is sensitive to variations in specific design methods. It is essential to pick an analysis method to match the design method and to pick a design method to match the programming style and language used.

23.4 The Development Process

Software development is an iterative and incremental process. Each stage of the process is revisited repeatedly during the development, and each visit refines the end products of that stage. In general, the process has no beginning and no end. When designing and implementing a system, you start from a base of other people's designs, libraries, and application software. When you finish, you leave a body of design and code for others to refine, revise, extend, and port. Naturally, a specific project can have a definite beginning and end, and it is important (though often surprisingly hard) to delimit the project cleanly and precisely in time and scope. However, pretending that you are starting from a clean slate can cause serious problems. Pretending that the world ends at the ''final delivery'' can cause equally serious problems for your successors (often yourself in a different role).

One implication of this is that the following sections could be read in any order because the aspects of design and implementation can be almost arbitrarily interleaved in a real project. That is, ''design'' is almost always redesign based on a previous design and some implementation experience. Furthermore, the design is constrained by schedules, the skills of the people involved, compatibility issues, etc. A major challenge to a designer/manager/programmer is to create order in this process without stifling innovation and destroying the feedback loops that are necessary for successful development.

The development process has three stages:

- Analysis: defining the scope of the problem to be solved
- Design: creating an overall structure for a system
- Implementation: writing and testing the code

Please remember the iterative nature of this process – it is significant that these stages are not numbered. Note that some major aspects of program development don't appear as separate stages because they ought to permeate the process:

- Experimentation
- Testing
- Analysis of the design and the implementation
- Documentation
- Management

Software "maintenance" is simply more iterations through this development process (§23.4.6).

It is most important that analysis, design, and implementation don't become too detached from each other and that the people involved share a culture so that they can communicate effectively. In larger projects, this is all too often not the case. Ideally, individuals move from one stage to another during a project; the best way to transfer subtle information is in a person's head. Unfortunately, organizations often establish barriers against such transfers, for example, by giving designers higher status and/or higher pay than "mere programmers." If it is not practical for people to move around to learn and teach, they should at least be encouraged to talk regularly with individuals involved in "the other" stages of the development.

For small-to-medium projects, there often is no distinction made between analysis and design; these two phases have been merged into one. Similarly, in small projects there often is no distinction made between design and programming. Naturally, this solves the communication problems. It is important to apply an appropriate degree of formality for a given project and to maintain an appropriate degree of separation between these phases (§23.5.2). There is no one right way to do this.

The model of software development described here differs radically from the traditional "waterfall model." In a waterfall model, the development progresses in an orderly and linear fashion through the development stages from analysis to testing. The waterfall model suffers from the fundamental problem that information tends to flow only one way. When problems are found "downstream," there is often strong methodological and organizational pressure to provide a local fix; that is, there is pressure to solve the problem without affecting the previous stages of the process. This lack of feedback leads to deficient designs, and the local fixes lead to contorted implementations. In the inevitable cases in which information does flow back toward the source and cause changes to the design, the result is a slow and cumbersome ripple effect through a system that is geared to prevent the need for such change and therefore unwilling and slow to respond. The argument for "no change" or for a "local fix" thus becomes an argument that one suborganization cannot impose large amounts of work on other suborganizations "for its own convenience." In particular, by the time a major flaw is found there has often been so much paperwork generated relating to the flawed decision that the effort involved in modifying the documentation dwarfs the effort needed to fix the code. In this way, paperwork can become the major problem of software development. Naturally, such problems can − and do − occur however one organizes the development of large systems. After all, *some* paperwork is essential. However, the pretense of a linear model of development (a waterfall) greatly increases the likelihood that this problem will get out of hand.

The problem with the waterfall model is insufficient feedback and the inability to respond to change. The danger of the iterative approach outlined here is a temptation to substitute a series of nonconverging changes for real thought and progress. Both problems are easier to diagnose than to solve, and however one organizes a task, it is easy and tempting to mistake activity for progress. Naturally, the emphasis on the different stages of the development process changes as a project progresses. Initially, the emphasis is on analysis and design, and programming issues receive less attention. As time passes, resources shift towards design and programming and then become more focussed on programming and testing. However, the key is never to focus on one part of the analysis/design/implementation spectrum to the exclusion of all other concerns.

Remember that no amount of attention to detail, no application of proper management technique, no amount of advanced technology can help you if you don't have a clear idea of what you are trying to achieve. More projects fail for lack of well-defined and realistic goals than for any other reason. Whatever you do and however you go about it, be clear about your aims, define tangible goals and milestones, and don't look for technological solutions to sociological problems. On the other hand, do use whatever *appropriate* technology is available − even if it involves an investment; people do work better with appropriate tools and in reasonable surroundings. Don't get fooled into believing that following this advice is easy.

23.4.1 The Development Cycle

Developing a system should be an iterative activity. The main loop consists of repeated trips through this sequence:

[0] Examine the problem.
[1] Create an overall design.
[2] Find standard components.
  − Customize the components for this design.
[3] Create new standard components.
  − Customize the components for this design.
[4] Assemble the design.

As an analogy, consider a car factory. For a project to start, there needs to be an overall design for a new type of car. This first cut will be based on some kind of analysis and specifies the car in general terms related mostly to its intended use rather than to details of how to achieve desired properties. Deciding which properties are desirable − or even better, providing a relatively simple guide to deciding which properties are desirable − is often the hardest part of a project. When done well, this is typically the work of a single insightful individual and is often called a *vision*. It is quite common for projects to lack such clear goals − and for projects to falter or fail for that reason.

Say we want to build a medium-sized car with four doors and a fairly powerful engine. The first stage in the design is most definitely not to start designing the car (and all of its subcomponents) from scratch. A software designer or programmer in a similar circumstance might unwisely try exactly that.

The first stage is to consider which components are available from the factory's own inventory and from reliable suppliers. The components thus found need not be exactly right for the new car. There will be ways of customizing the components. It might even be possible to affect the specification of the ''next release'' of such components to make them more suitable for our project. For example, there may be an engine available with the right properties except for a slight deficiency in delivered power. Either we or the engine supplier might be able to add a turbocharger to compensate without affecting the basic design. Note that making such a change ''without affecting the basic design'' is unlikely unless the original design anticipated at least some form of customization. Such customization will typically require cooperation between you and your engine supplier. A software designer or programmer has similar options. In particular, polymorphic classes and templates can often be used effectively for customization. However, don't expect to be able to effect arbitrary extensions without foresight by or cooperation with the provider of such a class.

Having run out of suitable standard components, the car designer doesn't rush to design optimal new components for the new car. That would simply be too expensive. Assume that there were no suitable air conditioning unit available and that there was a suitable L-shaped space available in the engine compartment. One solution would be to design an L-shaped air conditioning unit. However, the probability that this oddity could be used in other car types − even after extensive customization − is low. This implies that our car designer will not be able to share the cost of producing such units with the designers of other car types and that the useful life of the unit will be short. It will thus be worthwhile to design a unit that has a wider appeal; that is, design a unit that has a cleaner design and is more suited for customization than our hypothetical L-shaped oddity. This will probably involve more work than the L-shaped unit and might even involve a modification of the overall design of our car to accommodate the more general-purpose unit. Because the new unit was designed to be more widely useful than our L-shaped wonder, it will presumably need a bit of customization to fit our revised needs perfectly. Again, the software designer or programmer has a similar option. That is, rather than writing project-specific code the designer can design a new component of a generality that makes it a good candidate to become a standard in some universe.

Finally, when we have run out of potential standard components we assemble the ''final'' design. We use as few specially designed widgets as possible because next year we will have to go through a variant of this exercise again for the next new model and the specially designed widgets will be the ones we most likely will have to redo or throw away. Sadly, the experience with traditionally designed software is that few parts of a system can even be recognized as discrete components, and few of those are of use outside their original project.

I'm not saying that all car designers are as rational as I have outlined in this analogy or that all software designers make the mistakes mentioned. On the contrary, this model can be made to work with software. In particular, this chapter and the next present techniques for making it work with C++. I do claim, however, that the intangible nature of software makes those mistakes harder to avoid (§24.3.1, §24.3.4), and in §23.5.3 I argue that corporate culture often discourages people from using the model outlined here.

Note that this model of development really works well only when you consider the longer term. If your horizon extends only to the next release, the creation and maintenance of standard components makes no sense. It will simply be seen as spurious overhead. This model is suggested for an organization with a life that spans several projects and of a size that makes worthwhile the necessary extra investment in tools (for design, programming, and project management) and education (of designers, programmers, and managers). It is a sketch of a kind of software factory. Curiously enough, it differs only in scale from the practices of the best individual programmers, who over the years build up a stock of techniques, designs, tools, and libraries to enhance their personal effectiveness. It seems, in fact, that most organizations have failed to take advantage of the best personal practices due to both a lack of vision and an inability to manage such practices on more than a very small scale.

Note that it is unreasonable to expect "standard components" to be universally standard. There will exist a few international standard libraries. However, most components will be standard (only) within a country, an industry, a company, a product line, a department, an application area, etc. The world is simply too large for universal standards to be a realistic or indeed be a desirable aim for all components and tools.

Aiming for universality in an initial design is a prescription for a project that will never be completed. One reason that the development cycle is a cycle is that it is essential to have a working system from which to gain experience (§23.4.3.6).

23.4.2 Design Aims

What are the overall aims of a design? Simplicity is one, of course, but simplicity according to what criteria? We assume that a design will have to evolve. That is, the system will have to be extended, ported, tuned, and generally changed in a number of ways that cannot all be foreseen. Consequently, we must aim for a design and an implemented system that is simple under the constraint that it will be changed in many ways. In fact, it is realistic to assume that the requirements for the system will change several times between the time of the initial design and the first release of the system.

The implication is that the system must be designed to *remain* as simple as possible under a sequence of changes. We must design for change; that is, we must aim for

- flexibility,
- extensibility, and
- portability.

This is best done by trying to encapsulate the areas of a system that are likely to change and by providing non-intrusive ways for a later designer/programmer to modify the behavior of the code. This is done by identifying the key concepts of an application and giving each class the exclusive responsibility for the maintenance of all information relating to a single concept. In that case, a change can be effected by a modification of that class only. Ideally, a change to a single concept can be done by deriving a new class (§23.4.3.5) or by passing a different argument to a template. Naturally, this ideal is much easier to state than to follow.

Consider an example. In a simulation involving meteorological phenomena, we want to display a rain cloud. How do we do that? We cannot have a general routine to display the cloud because what a cloud looks like depends on the internal state of the cloud, and that state should be the sole responsibility of the cloud.

A first solution to this problem is to let the cloud display itself. This style of solution is acceptable in many limited contexts. However, it is not general because there are many ways to view a cloud: for example, as a detailed picture, as a rough outline, or as an icon on a map. In other words, what a cloud looks like depends on both the cloud and its environment.

A second solution to the problem is to make the cloud aware of its environment and then let the cloud display itself. This solution is acceptable in even more contexts. However, it is still not a general solution. Having the cloud know about such details of its environment violates the dictum that a class is responsible for one thing only and that every "thing" is the responsibility of some class. It may not be possible to come up with a coherent notion of "the cloud's environment" because in general what a cloud looks like depends on both the cloud and the viewer. Even in real life, what the cloud looks like to me depends rather strongly on how I look at it; for example, with my naked eyes, through a polarizing filter, or with a weather radar. In addition to the viewer and the cloud, some "general background" such as the relative position of the sun might have to be taken into account. Adding other objects, such as other clouds and airplanes, further complicates the matter. To make life really hard for the designer, add the possibility of having several simultaneous viewers.

A third solution is to have the cloud − and other objects such as airplanes and the sun − describe themselves to a viewer. This solution has sufficient generality to serve most purposes†. It may, however, impose a significant cost in both complexity and run-time overhead. For example, how do we arrange for a viewer to understand the descriptions produced by clouds and other objects?

Rain clouds are not particularly common in programs (but for an example, see §15.2), but objects that need to be involved in a variety of I/O operations are. This makes the cloud example relevant to programs in general and to the design of libraries in particular. C++ code for a logically similar example can be found in the manipulators used for formatted output in the stream I/O system (§21.4.6, §21.4.6.3). Note that the third solution is not "the right solution;" it is simply the most general solution. A designer must balance the various needs of a system to choose the level of generality and abstraction that is appropriate for a given problem in a given system. As a rule of thumb, the right level of abstraction for a long-lived program is the most general you can comprehend and afford, *not* the absolutely most general. Generalization beyond the scope of a given project and beyond the experience of the people involved can be harmful; that is, it can cause delays, unacceptable inefficiencies, unmanageable designs, and plain failure.

To make such techniques manageable and economical, we must also design and manage for reuse (§23.5.1) and not completely forget about efficiency (§23.4.7).

23.4.3 Design Steps

Consider designing a single class. Typically, this is *not* a good idea. Concepts do *not* exist in isolation; rather, a concept is defined in the context of other concepts. Similarly, a class does not exist in isolation but is defined together with logically related classes. Typically, one works on a set of related classes. Such a set is often called a *class library* or a *component*. Sometimes all classes in a component constitute a single class hierarchy, sometimes they are members of a single namespace, and sometimes they are a more ad-hoc collection of declarations (§24.4).

---

† Even this model is unlikely to be sufficient for extreme cases like high-quality graphics based on ray tracing. I suspect that achieving such detail requires the designer to move to a different level of abstraction.

The set of classes in a component is united by some logical criteria, often by a common style and often by a reliance on common services. A component is thus the unit of design, documentation, ownership, and often reuse. This does not mean that if you use one class from a component, you must understand and use all the classes from the component or maybe get the code for every class in the component loaded into your program. On the contrary, we typically strive to ensure that a class can be used with only minimal overhead in machine resources and human effort. However, to use any part of a component we need to understand the logical criteria that define the component (hopefully made abundantly clear in the documentation), the conventions and style embodied in the design of the component and its documentation, and the common services (if any).

So consider how one might approach the design of a component. Because this is often a challenging task, it is worthwhile breaking it into steps to help focus on the various subtasks in a logical and complete way. As usual, there is no one right way of doing this. However, here is a series of steps that have worked for some people:

[1] Find the concepts/classes and their most fundamental relationships.

[2] Refine the classes by specifying the sets of operations on them.
   - Classify these operations. In particular, consider the needs for construction, copying, and destruction.
   - Consider minimalism, completeness, and convenience.

[3] Refine the classes by specifying their dependencies.
   - Consider parameterization, inheritance, and use dependencies.

[4] Specify the interfaces.
   - Separate functions into public and protected operations.
   - Specify the exact type of the operations on the classes.

Note that these are steps in an iterative process. Typically, several loops through this sequence are needed to produce a design one can comfortably use for an initial implementation or a re-implementation. One advantage of well-done analysis and data abstraction as described here is that it becomes relatively easy to reshuffle class relationships even after code has been written. This is never a trivial task, though.

After that, we implement the classes and go back and review the design based on what was learned from implementing them. In the following subsections, I discuss these steps one by one.

23.4.3.1 Step 1: Find Classes

Find the concepts/classes and their most fundamental relationships. The key to a good design is to model some aspect of ''reality'' directly – that is, capture the concepts of an application as classes, represent the relationships between classes in well-defined ways such as inheritance, and do this repeatedly at different levels of abstraction. But how do we go about finding those concepts? What is a practical approach to deciding which classes we need?

The best place to start looking is in the application itself, as opposed to looking in the computer scientist's bag of abstractions and concepts. Listen to someone who will become an expert user of the system once it has been built and to someone who is a somewhat dissatisfied user of the system being replaced. Note the vocabulary they use.

It is often said that the nouns will correspond to the classes and objects needed in the program; often that is indeed the case. However, that is by no means the end of the story. Verbs may denote operations on objects, traditional (global) functions that produce new values based on the value of their arguments, or even classes. As examples of the latter, note the function objects (§18.4) and manipulators (§21.4.6). Verbs such as ''iterate'' or ''commit'' can be represented by an iterator object and an object representing a database commit operation, respectively. Even adjectives can often usefully be represented by classes. Consider the adjectives ''storable,'' ''concurrent,'' ''registered,'' and ''bounded.'' These may be classes intended to allow a designer or programmer to pick and choose among desirable attributes for later-designed classes by specifying virtual base classes (§15.2.4).

Not all classes correspond to application-level concepts. For example, some represent system resources and implementation-level abstractions (§24.3.1). It is also important to avoid modeling an old system too closely. For example, we don't want a system that is centered around a database to faithfully replicate aspects of a manual system that exist only to allow individuals to manage the physical shuffling of pieces of paper.

Inheritance is used to represent commonality among concepts. Most important, it is used to represent hierachical organization based on the behavior of classes representing individual concepts (§1.7, §12.2.6, §24.3.2). This is sometimes referred to as *classification* or even *taxonomy*. Commonality must be actively sought. Generalization and classification are high-level activities that require insight to give useful and lasting results. A common base should represent a more general concept rather than simply a similar concept that happens to require less data to represent.

Note that the classification should be of aspects of the concepts that we model in our system, rather than aspects that may be valid in other areas. For example, in mathematics a circle is a kind of an ellipse, but in most programs a circle should not be derived from an ellipse or an ellipse derived from a circle. The often-heard arguments ''because that's the way it is in mathematics'' and ''because the representation of a circle is a subset of that of an ellipse'' are not conclusive and most often wrong. This is because for most programs, the key property of a circle is that it has a center and a fixed distance to its perimeter. All behavior of a circle (all operations) must maintain this property (invariant; §24.3.7.1). On the other hand, an ellipse is characterized by two focal points that in many programs can be changed independently of each other. If those focal points coincide, the ellipse looks like a circle, but it is not a circle because its operations do not preserve the circle invariant. In most systems, this difference will be reflected by having a circle and an ellipse provide sets of operations that are not subsets of each other.

We don't just think up a set of classes and relationships between classes and use them for the final system. Instead, we create an initial set of classes and relationships. These are then refined repeatedly (§23.4.3.5) to reach a set of class relationships that are sufficiently general, flexible, and stable to be of real help in the further evolution of a system.

The best tool for finding initial key concepts/classes is a blackboard. The best method for their initial refinement is discussions with experts in the application domain and a couple of friends. Discussion is necessary to develop a viable initial vocabulary and conceptual framework. Few people can do that alone. One way to evolve a set of useful classes from an initial set of candidates is to simulate a system, with designers taking the roles of classes. This brings the inevitable absurdities of the initial ideas out into the open, stimulates discussion of alternatives, and creates a shared understanding of the evolving design. This activity can be supported by and documented by notes on index cards. Such cards are usually called CRC cards (''Class, Responsibility, and Collaborators''; [Wirfs-Brock,1990]) because of the information they record.

A *use case* is a description of a particular use of a system. Here is a simple example of a use case for a telephony system: take the phone off hook, dial a number, the phone at the other end rings, the phone at the other end is taken off hook. Developing a set of such use cases can be of immense value at all stages of development. Initially, finding use cases can help us understand what we are trying to build. During design, they can be used to trace a path through the system (for example, using CRC cards) to check that the relatively static description of the system in terms of classes and objects actually makes sense from a user's point of view. During programming and testing, the use cases become a source of test cases. In this way, use cases provide an orthogonal way of viewing the system and act as a reality check.

Use cases view the system as a (dynamic) working entity. They can therefore trap a designer into a functional view of a system and distract from the essential task of finding useful concepts that can be mapped into classes. Especially in the hands of someone with a background in structured analysis and weak experience with object-oriented programming/design, an emphasis on use cases can lead to a functional decomposition. A set of use cases is not a design. A focus on the use of the system must be matched by a complementary focus on the system's structure.

A team can become trapped into an inherently futile attempt to find and describe *all* of the use cases. This is a costly mistake. Much as when we look for candidate classes for a system, there comes a time when we must say, ''Enough is enough. The time has come to try out what we have and see what happens.'' Only by using a plausible set of classes and a plausible set of use cases in further development can we obtain the feedback that is essential to obtaining a good system. It is always hard to know when to stop a useful activity. It is especially hard to know when to stop when we know that we must return later to complete the task.

How many cases are enough? In general it is impossible to answer that question. However, in a given project, there comes a time when it is clear that most of the ordinary functioning of the system has been covered and a fair bit of the more unusual and error handling issues have been touched upon. Then it is time to get on with the next round of design and programming.

When you are trying to estimate the coverage of the system by a set of use cases, it can be useful to separate the cases into primary and secondary use cases. The primary ones describe the system's most common and ''normal'' actions, and the secondary describe the more unusual and error-handling scenarios. An example of a secondary use case would be a variant of the ''make a phone call'' case, in which the called phone is off hook, dialing its caller. It is often said that when 80% of the primary use cases and some of the secondary ones have been covered, it is time to proceed, but since we cannot know what constitutes ''all of the cases'' in advance, this is simply a rule of thumb. Experience and good sense matter here.

The concepts, operations, and relationships mentioned here are the ones that come naturally from our understanding of the application area or that arise from further work on the class structure. They represent our fundamental understanding of the application. Often, they are classifications of the fundamental concepts. For example, a hook-and-ladder is a fire engine, which is a truck, which is a vehicle. Sections §23.4.3.2 and §23.4.5 explain a few ways of looking at classes and class hierarchies with the view of making improvements.

Beware of viewgraph engineering! At some stage, you will be asked to present the design to someone and you will produce a set of diagrams explaining the structure of the system being built. This can be a very useful exercise because it helps focus your attention on what is important about the system and forces you to express your ideas in terms that others can understand. A presentation is an invaluable design tool. Preparing a presentation with the aim of conveying real understanding to people with the interest and ability to produce constructive criticism is an exercise in conceptualization and clean expression of ideas.

However, a formal presentation of a design is also a very dangerous activity because there is a strong temptation to present an ideal system – a system you wish you could build, a system your high management wish they had – rather than what you have and what you might possibly produce in a reasonable time. When different approaches compete and executives don't really understand or care about ''the details,'' presentations can become lying competitions, in which the team that presents the most grandiose system gets to keep its job. In such cases, clear expression of ideas is often replaced by heavy jargon and acronyms. If you are a listener to such a presentation – and especially if you are a decision maker and you control development resources – it is desperately important that you distinguish wishful thinking from realistic planning. High-quality presentation materials are no guarantee of quality of the system described. In fact, I have often found that organizations that focus on the real problems get caught short when it comes to presenting their results compared to organizations that are less concerned with the production of real systems.

When looking for concepts to represent as classes, note that there are important properties of a system that cannot be represented as classes. For example, reliability, performance, and testability are important measurable properties of a system. However, even the most thoroughly object-oriented system will not have its reliability localized in a reliability object. Pervasive properties of a system can be specified, designed for, and eventually verified through measurement. Concern for such properties must be applied across all classes and may be reflected in rules for the design and implementation of individual classes and components (§23.4.3).

23.4.3.2 Step 2: Specify Operations

Refine the classes by specifying the sets of operations on them. Naturally, it is not possible to separate finding the classes from figuring out what operations are needed on them. However, there is a practical difference in that finding the classes focusses on the key concepts and deliberately de-emphasizes the computational aspects of the classes, whereas specifying the operations focusses on finding a complete and usable set of operations. It is most often too hard to consider both at the same time, especially since related classes should be designed together. When it is time to consider both together, CRC cards (§23.4.3.1) are often helpful.

In considering what functions are to be provided, several philosophies are possible. I suggest the following strategy:

[1] Consider how an object of the class is to be constructed, copied (if at all), and destroyed.

[2] Define the *minimal* set of operations required by the concept the class is representing. Typically, these operations become the member functions (§10.3).

[3] Consider which operations could be added for notational convenience. Include only a few really important ones. Often, these operations become the nonmember ''helper functions'' (§10.3.2).

[4] Consider which operations are to be virtual, that is, operations for which the class can act as an interface for an implementation supplied by a derived class.

[5] Consider what commonality of naming and functionality can be achieved across all the classes of the component.

This is clearly a statement of minimalism. It is far easier to add every function that could conceivably be useful and to make all operations virtual. However, the more functions, the more likely they are to remain unused and the more likely they are to constrain the implementation and the further evolution of the system. In particular, functions that directly read or write part of the state of an object of a class often constrain the class to a single implementation strategy and severely limit the potential for redesign. Such functions lower the level of abstraction from a concept to one implementation of it. Adding functions also causes more work for the implementer − and for the designer in the next redesign. It is *much* easier to add a function once the need for it has been clearly established than to remove it once it has become a liability.

The reason for requiring that the decision to make a function virtual be explicit rather than a default or an implementation detail is that making a function virtual critically affects the use of its class and the relationships between that class and other classes. Objects of a class with even a single virtual function have a nontrivial layout compared to objects in languages such as C and Fortran. A class with even a single virtual function potentially acts as the interface to yet-to-be-defined classes, and a virtual function implies a dependency on yet-to-be-defined classes (§24.3.2.1).

Note that minimalism requires more work from the designer, rather than less.

When choosing operations, it is important to focus on what is to be done rather than how it is to be done. That is, we should focus more on desired behavior than on implementation issues.

It is sometimes useful to classify operations on a class in terms of their use of the internal state of objects:

- Foundation operators: constructors, destructors and copy operators
- Inspectors: operations that do not modify the state of an object
- Modifiers: operations that do modify the state of an object
- Conversions: operations that produce an object of another type based on the value (state) of the object to which they are applied
- Iterators: operations that allow access to or use of a sequence of contained objects

These categories are not orthogonal. For example, an iterator can be designed to be either an inspector or a modifier. These categories are simply a classification that has helped people approach the design of class interfaces. Naturally, other classifications are possible. Such classifications are especially useful for maintaining consistency across a set of classes within a component.

C++ provides support for the distinction between inspectors and modifiers in the form of *const* and non-*const* member functions. Similarly, the notions of constructors, destructors, copy operations, and conversion functions are directly supported.

23.4.3.3 Step 3: Specify Dependencies

Refine the classes by specifying their dependencies. The various dependencies are discussed in §24.3. The key ones to consider in the context of design are parameterization, *inheritance*, and *use* relationships. Each involves consideration of what it means for a class to be responsible for a single property of a system. To be responsible certainly doesn't mean that the class has to hold all the data itself or that its member functions have to perform all the necessary operations directly. On the contrary, each class having a single area of responsibility ensures that much of the work of a class is done by directing requests "elsewhere" for handling by some other class that has that particular subtask as its responsibility. However, be warned that overuse of this technique can lead to inefficient and incomprehensible designs by proliferating classes and objects to the point where no work is done except by a cascade of forwarded requests for service. What *can* be done here and now, should be.

The need to consider inheritance and use relationships at the design stage (and not just during implementation) follows directly from the use of classes to represent concepts. It also implies that the component (§23.4.3, §24.4), and not the individual class, is the unit of design.

Parameterization − often leading to the use of templates − is a way of making implicit dependencies explicit so that several alternatives can be represented without adding new concepts. Often, there is a choice between leaving something as a dependency on a context, representing it as a branch of an inheritance tree, or using a parameter (§24.4.1).

23.4.3.4 Step 4: Specify Interfaces

Specify the interfaces. Private functions don't usually need to be considered at the design stage. What implementation issues must be considered in the design stage are best dealt with as part of the consideration of dependencies in Step 2. Stronger: I use as a rule of thumb that unless at least two significantly different implementations of a class are possible, then there is probably something wrong with the class. That is, it is simply an implementation in disguise and not a representation of a proper concept. In many cases, considering if some form of lazy evaluation is feasible for a class is a good way of approaching the question, ''Is the interface to this class sufficiently implementation-independent?''

Note that public bases and friends are part of the public interface of a class; see also §11.5 and §24.4.2. Providing separate interfaces for inheriting and general clients by defining separate protected and public interfaces can be a rewarding exercise.

This is the step where the exact types of arguments are considered and specified. The ideal is to have as many interfaces as possible statically typed with application-level types; see §24.2.3 and §24.4.2.

When specifying the interfaces, look out for classes where the operations seem to support more than one level of abstraction. For example, some member functions of a class *File* may take arguments of type *File_descriptor* and others string arguments that are meant to be file names. The *File_descriptor* operations operate on a different level of abstraction than do the file name operations, so one must wonder whether they belong in the same class. Maybe it would be better to have two file classes, one supporting the notion of a file descriptor and another supporting the notion of a file name. Typically, all operations on a class should support the same level of abstraction. When they don't, a reorganization of the class and related classes should be considered.

23.4.3.5 Reorganization of Class Hierarchies

In Step 1 and again in Step 3, we examine the classes and class hierarchies to see if they adequately serve our needs. Typically they don't, and we have to reorganize to improve that structure or a design and/or an implementation.

The most common reorganizations of a class hierarchy are factoring the common part of two classes into a new class and splitting a class into two new ones. In both cases, the result is three classes: a base class and two derived classes. When should such reorganizations be done? What are common indicators that such a reorganization might be useful?

Unfortunately, there are no simple, general answers to such questions. This is not really surprising because what we are talking about are not minor implementation details, but changes to the basic concepts of a system. The fundamental – and nontrivial – operation is to look for commonality between classes and factor out the common part. The exact criteria for commonality are undefined but should reflect commonality in the concepts of the system, not just implementation conveniences. Clues that two or more classes have commonality that might be factored out into a common base class are common patterns of use, similarity of sets of operations, similarity of implementations, and simply that these classes often turn up together in design discussions. Conversely, a class might be a good candidate for splitting into two if subsets of the operations of that class have distinct usage patterns, if such subsets access separate subsets of the representation, and if the class turns up in apparently unrelated design discussions. Sometimes, making a set of related classes into a template is a way of providing necessary alternatives in a systematic manner (§24.4.1).

Because of the close relationship between classes and concepts, problems with the organization of a class hierarchy often surface as problems with the naming of classes and the use of class names in design discussions. If design discussion using class names and the classification implied by the class hierarchies sounds awkward, then there is probably an opportunity to improve the hierarchies. Note that I'm implying that two people are much better at analyzing a class hierarchy than is one. Should you happen to be without someone with whom to discuss a design, then writing a tutorial description of the design using the class names can be a useful alternative.

One of the most important aims of a design is to provide interfaces that can remain stable in the face of changes (§23.4.2). Often, this is best achieved by making a class on which many classes and functions depend into an abstract class presenting very general operations. Details are best relegated to more specialized derived classes on which fewer classes and functions directly depend. Stronger: the more classes that depend on a class, the more general that class should be and the fewer details it should reveal.

There is a strong temptation to add operations (and data) to a class used by many. This is often seen as a way of making that class more useful and less likely to need (further) change. The effect of such thinking is a class with a fat interface (§24.4.3) and with data members supporting several weakly related functions. This again implies that the class must be modified whenever there is a significant change to one of the many classes it supports. This, in turn, implies changes to apparently unrelated user classes and derived classes. Instead of complicating a class that is central to a design, we should usually keep it general and abstract. When necessary, specialized facilities should be presented as derived classes. See [Martin,1995] for examples.

This line of thought leads to hierarchies of abstract classes, with the classes near the roots being the most general and having the most other classes and functions dependent on them. The leaf classes are the most specialized and have only very few pieces of code depending directly on them. As an example, consider the final version of the *Ival_box* hierarchy (§12.4.3, §12.4.4).

23.4.3.6 Use of Models

When I write an article, I try to find a suitable model to follow. That is, rather than immediately starting to type I look for papers on a similar topic to see if I can find one that can be an initial pattern for my paper. If the model I choose is a paper I wrote myself on a related topic, I might even be able to leave parts of the text in place, modify other parts as needed, and add new information only where the logic of the information I'm trying to convey requires it. For example, this book is written that way based on its first and second editions. An extreme form of this writing technique is the form letter. In that case, I simply fill in a name and maybe add a few lines to "personalize" the letter. In essence, I'm writing such letters by specifying the differences from a basic model.

Such use of existing systems as models for new designs is the norm rather than the exception in all forms of creative endeavors. Whenever possible, design and programming should be based on previous work. This limits the degrees of freedom that the designer has to deal with and allows attention to be focussed on a few issues at a time. Starting a major project "completely from scratch" can be exhilarating. However, often a more accurate description is "intoxicating" and the result is a drunkard's walk through the design alternatives. Having a model is not constraining and does not require that the model should be slavishly followed; it simply frees the designer to consider one aspect of a design at a time.

Note that the use of models is inevitable because any design will be synthesized from the experiences of its designers. Having an explicit model makes the choice of a model a conscious decision, makes assumptions explicit, defines a common vocabulary, provides an initial framework for the design, and increases the likelihood that the designers have a common approach.

Naturally, the choice of an initial model is in itself an important design decision and often can be made only after a search for potential models and careful evaluation of alternatives. Furthermore, in many cases a model is suitable only with the understanding that major modification is necessary to adapt the ideas to a particular new application. Software design is hard, and we need all the help we can get. We should not reject the use of models out of misplaced disdain for "imitation." Imitation is the sincerest form of flattery, and the use of models and previous work as inspiration is − within the bounds of propriety and copyright law − acceptable technique for innovative work in all fields: what was good enough for Shakespeare is good enough for us. Some people refer to such use of models in design as "design reuse."

Documenting general elements that turn up in many designs together with some description of the design problem they solve and the conditions under which they can be used is an obvious idea − at least once you think of it. The word *pattern* is often used to describe such a general and useful design element, and a literature exists documenting patterns and their use (for example, [Gamma,1994] and [Coplien,1995]).

It is a good idea for a designer to be acquainted with popular patterns in a given application domain. As a programmer, I prefer patterns that have some code associated with them as concrete examples. Like most people, I understand a general idea (in this case, a pattern) best when I have a concrete example (in this case, a piece of code illustrating a use of the pattern) to help me. People who use patterns heavily have a specialized vocabulary to ease communication among themselves. Unfortunately, this can become a private language that effectively excludes outsiders from understanding. As always, it is essential to ensure proper communication among people involved in different parts of a project (§23.3) and also with the design and programming communities at large.

Every successful large system is a redesign of a somewhat smaller working system. I know of no exceptions to this rule. The closest I can think of are projects that failed, muddled on for years at great cost, and then eventually became successes years after their intended completion date. Such projects unintentionally − and often unacknowledged − simply first built a nonworking system, then transformed that into a working system, and finally redesigned that into a system that approximated the original aims. This implies that it is a folly to set out to build a large system from scratch exactly right according to the latest principles. The larger and the more ambitious a system we aim for, the more important it is to have a model from which to work. For a large system, the only really acceptable model is a somewhat smaller, related *working* system.

23.4.4 Experimentation and Analysis

At the start of an ambitious development project, we do not know the best way to structure the system. Often, we don't even know precisely what the system should do because particulars will become clear only through the effort of building, testing, and using the system. How − short of building the complete system − do we get the information necessary to understand what design decisions are significant and to estimate their ramifications?

We conduct experiments. Also, we analyze the design and implementation as soon as we have something to analyze. Most frequently and importantly, we discuss the design and implementation alternatives. In all but the rarest cases, design is a social activity in which designs are developed through presentations and discussions. Often, the most important design tool is a blackboard; without it, the embryonic concepts of a design cannot be developed and shared among designers and programmers.

The most popular form of experiment seems to be to build a prototype, that is, a scaled-down version of the system or a part of the system. A prototype doesn't have stringent performance criteria, machine and programming-environment resources are typically ample, and the designers and programmers tend to be uncommonly well educated, experienced, and motivated. The idea is to get a version running as fast as possible to enable exploration of design and implementation choices.

This approach can be very successful when done well. It can also be an excuse for sloppiness. The problem is that the emphasis of a prototype can easily shift from ''exploring design alternatives'' to ''getting some sort of system running as soon as possible.'' This easily leads to a disinterest in the internal structure of the prototype (''after all, it is only a prototype'') and a neglect of the design effort in favor of playing around with the prototype implementation. The snag is that such an implementation can degenerate into the worst kind of resource hog and maintenance nightmare while giving the illusion of an ''almost complete'' system. Almost by definition, a prototype does not have the internal structure, the efficiency, and the maintenance infrastructure that allows it to scale to real use. Consequently, a ''prototype'' that becomes an ''almost product'' soaks up time and energy that could have been better spent on the product. The temptation for both developers and managers is to make the prototype into a product and postpone ''performance engineering'' until the next release. Misused this way, prototyping is the negation of all that design stands for.

A related problem is that the prototype developers can fall in love with their tools. They can forget that the expense of their (necessary) convenience cannot always be afforded by a production system and that the freedom from constraints and formalities offered by their small research group cannot easily be maintained for a larger group working toward a set of interlocking deadlines.

On the other hand, prototypes can be invaluable. Consider designing a user interface. In this case, the internal structure of the part of the system that doesn't interact directly with the user often *is* irrelevant and there are no other feasible ways of getting experience with users' reactions to the look and feel of a system. Another example is a prototype designed strictly for studying the internal workings of a system. Here, the user interface can be rudimentary − possibly with simulated users instead of real ones.

Prototyping is a way of experimenting. The desired results from building a prototype are the insights that building it brings, not the prototype itself. Maybe the most important criterion for a prototype is that it has to be so incomplete that it is obviously an experimental vehicle and cannot be turned into a product without a major redesign and reimplementation. Having a prototype "incomplete" helps keep the focus on the experiment and minimizes the danger of having the prototype become a product. It also minimizes the temptation to try to base the design of the product too closely on the design of the prototype – thus forgetting or ignoring the inherent limitations of the prototype. After use, a prototype should be thrown away.

It should be remembered that in many cases, there are experimental techniques that can be used as alternatives to prototyping. Where those can be used, they are often preferable because of their greater rigor and lower demands on designer time and system resources. Examples are mathematical models and various forms of simulators. In fact, one can see a continuum from mathematical models, through more and more detailed simulations, through prototypes, through partial implementations, to a complete system.

This leads to the idea of growing a system from an initial design and implementation through repeated redesign and reimplementation. This is the ideal strategy, but it can be very demanding on design and implementation tools. Also, the approach suffers from the risk of getting burdened with so much code reflecting initial design decisions that a better design cannot be implemented. At least for now, this strategy seems limited to small-to-medium-scale projects, in which major changes to the overall design are unlikely, and for redesigns and reimplementations after the initial release of the system, where such a strategy is inevitable.

In addition to experiments designed to provide insights into design choices, analysis of a design and/or an implementation itself can be an important source of further insights. For example, studies of the various dependencies between classes (§24.3) can be most helpful, and traditional implementer's tools such as call graphs, performance measurements, etc., must not be ignored.

Note that specifications (the output of the analysis phase) and designs are as prone to errors as is the implementation. In fact, they may be more so because they are even less concrete, are often specified less precisely, are not executable, and typically are not supported by tools of a sophistication comparable to what is available for checking and analyzing the implementation. Increasing the formality of the language/notation used to express a design can go some way toward enabling the application of tools to help the designer. This must not be done at the cost of impoverishing the programming language used for implementation (§24.3.1). Also, a formal notation can itself be a source of complexity and problems. This happens when the formalism is ill suited to the practical problem to which it is applied, when the rigor of the formalism exceeds the mathematical background and maturity of the designers and programmers involved, and when the formal description of a system gets out of touch with the system it is supposedly describing.

Design is inherently error-prone and hard to support with effective tools. This makes experience and feedback essential. Consequently, it is fundamentally flawed to consider the software-development process a linear process starting with analysis and ending with testing. An emphasis on iterative design and implementation is needed to gain sufficient feedback from experience during the various stages of development.

23.4.5 Testing

A program that has not been tested does not work. The ideal of designing and/or verifying a program so that it works the first time is unattainable for all but the most trivial programs. We should strive toward that ideal, but we should not be fooled into thinking that testing is easy.

"How to test?" is a question that cannot be answered in general. "When to test?" however, does have a general answer: as early and as often as possible. Test strategies should be generated as part of the design and implementation efforts or at least should be developed in parallel with them. As soon as there is a running system, testing should begin. Postponing serious testing until "after the implementation is complete" is a prescription for slipped schedules and/or flawed releases.

Wherever possible, a system should be designed specifically so that it is relatively easy to test. In particular, mechanisms for testing can often be designed right into the system. Sometimes this is not done out of fear of causing expensive run-time testing or for fear that the redundancy necessary for consistency checks will unduly enlarge data structures. Such fear is usually misplaced because most actual testing code and redundancy can, if necessary, be stripped out of the code before the system is shipped. Assertions (§24.3.7.2) are sometimes useful here.

More important than specific tests is the idea that the structure of the system should be such that we have a reasonable chance of convincing ourselves and our users/customers that we can eliminate errors by a combination of static checking, static analysis, and testing. Where a strategy for fault tolerance is developed (§14.9), a testing strategy can usually be designed as a complementary and closely related aspect of the total design.

If testing issues are completely discounted in the design phase, then testing, delivery date, and maintenance problems will result. The class interfaces and the class dependencies (as described in §24.3 and §24.4.2) are usually a good place to start work on a testing strategy.

Determining how much testing is enough is usually hard. However, too little testing is a more common problem than too much. Exactly how many resources should be allocated to testing compared to design and implementation naturally depends on the nature of the system and the methods used to construct it. However, as a rule of thumb, I can suggest that more resources in time, effort, and talent should be spent testing a system than on constructing the initial implementation. Testing should focus on problems that would have disastrous consequences and on problems that would occur frequently.

23.4.6 Software Maintenance

"Software maintenance" is a misnomer. The word "maintenance" suggests a misleading analogy to hardware. Software doesn't need oiling, doesn't have moving parts that wear down, and doesn't have crevices in which water can collect and cause rust. Software can be replicated *exactly* and transported over long distances at minute costs. Software is not hardware.

The activities that go under the name of software maintenance are really redesign and reimplementation and thus belong under the usual program development cycle. When flexibility, extensibility, and portability are emphasized in the design, the traditional sources of maintenance problems are addressed directly.

Like testing, maintenance must not be an afterthought or an activity segregated from the mainstream of development. In particular, it is important to have some continuity in the group of people involved in a project. It is not easy to successfully transfer maintenance to a new (and typically less-experienced) group of people with no links to the original designers and implementers. When a major change of people is necessary, there must be an emphasis on transferring an understanding of the system's structure and of the system's aims to the new people. If a "maintenance crew" is left guessing about the architecture of the system or must deduce the purpose of system components from their implementation, the structure of a system can deteriorate rapidly under the impact of local patches. Documentation is typically much better at conveying details than in helping new people to understand key ideas and principles.

23.4.7 Efficiency

Donald Knuth observed that "premature optimization is the root of all evil." Some people have learned that lesson all too well and consider all concern for efficiency evil. On the contrary, efficiency must be kept in mind throughout the design and implementation effort. However, that does not mean the designer should be concerned with micro-efficiencies, but that first-order efficiency issues must be considered.

The best strategy for efficiency is to produce a clean and simple design. Only such a design can remain relatively stable over the lifetime of the project and serve as a base for performance tuning. Avoiding the gargantuanism that plagues large projects is essential. Far too often people add features "just in case" (§23.4.3.2, §23.5.3) and end up doubling and quadrupling the size and runtime of systems to support frills. Worse, such overelaborate systems are often unnecessarily hard to analyze so that it becomes difficult to distinguish the avoidable overheads from the unavoidable. Thus, even basic analysis and optimization is discouraged. Optimization should be the result of analysis and performance measurement, not random fiddling with the code. Especially in larger systems, a designer's or programmer's "intuition" is an unreliable guide in matters of efficiency.

It is important to avoid inherently inefficient constructs and constructs that will take much time and cleverness to optimize to an acceptable performance level. Similarly, it is important to minimize the use of inherently nonportable constructs and tools because using such tools and constructs condemns the project to run on older (less powerful and/or more expensive) computers.

23.5 Management

Provided it makes some minimum of sense, most people do what they are encouraged to do. In particular, if in the context of a software project you reward certain ways of operating and penalize others, only exceptional programmers and designers will risk their careers to do what they consider right in the face of management opposition, indifference, and red tape†. It follows that an organization should have a reward structure that matches its stated aims of design and programming. However, all too often this is not the case: a major change of programming style can be achieved only through a matching change of design style, and both typically require changes in management style to be effective. Mental and organizational inertia all too easily leads to a local change that is not

---

† An organization that treats its programmers as morons will soon have programmers that are willing and able to act like morons only.

supported by global changes required to ensure its success. A fairly typical example is a change to a language that supports object-oriented programming, such as C++, without a matching change in the design strategies to take advantage of its facilities (see also §24.2). Another is a change to "object-oriented design" without the introduction of a programming language to support it.

23.5.1 Reuse

Increased reuse of code and design is often cited as a major reason for adopting a new programming language or design strategy. However, most organizations reward individuals and groups that choose to re-invent the wheel. For example, a programmer may have his productivity measured in lines of code; will he produce small programs relying on standard libraries at the cost of income and, possibly, status? A manager may be paid somewhat proportionally to the number of people in her group; is she going to use software produced in another group when she can hire another couple of programmers for her own group instead? A company can be awarded a government contract, where the profit is a fixed percentage of the development cost; is that company going to minimize its profits by using the most effective development tools? Rewarding reuse is hard, but unless management finds ways to encourage and reward it, reuse will not happen.

Reuse is primarily a social phenomenon. I can use someone else's software provided that:

[1] It works: to be reusable, software must first be usable.

[2] It is comprehensible: program structure, comments, documentation, and tutorial material are important.

[3] It can coexist with software not specifically written to coexist with it.

[4] It is supported (or I'm willing to support it myself; typically, I'm not).

[5] It is economical (can I share the development and maintenance costs with other users?).

[6] I can find it.

To this, we may add that a component is not reusable until someone has "reused" it. The task of fitting a component into an environment typically leads to refinements in its operation, generalizations of its behavior, and improvements in its ability to coexist with other software. Until this exercise has been done at least once, even components that have been designed and implemented with the greatest care tend to have unintended and unexpected rough corners.

My experience is that the conditions necessary for reuse will exist only if someone makes it their business to make such sharing work. In a small group, this typically means that an individual, by design or by accident, becomes the keeper of common libraries and documentation. In a larger organization, this means that a group or department is chartered to gather, build, document, popularize, and maintain software for use by many groups.

The importance of such a "standard components" group cannot be overestimated. Note that as a first approximation, a system reflects the organization that produced it. If an organization has no mechanism for promoting and rewarding cooperation and sharing, cooperation and sharing will be rare. A standard components group must actively promote its components. This implies that good traditional documentation is essential but insufficient. In addition, the components group must provide tutorials and other information that allow a potential user to find a component and understand why it might be of help. This implies that activities that traditionally are associated with marketing and education must be undertaken by the components group.

Whenever possible, the members of this group should work in close cooperation with applications builders. Only then can they be sufficiently aware of the needs of users and alert to the opportunities for sharing components among different applications. This argues for there to be a consultancy role for such an organization and for the use of internships to transfer information into and out of the components group.

The success of a "components group" must be measured in terms of the success of its clients. If its success is measured simply in terms of the amount of tools and services it can convince development organizations to accept, such a group can become corrupted into a mere peddler of commercial software and a proponent of ever-changing fads.

Not all code needs to be reusable, and reusability is not a universal property. Saying that a component is "reusable" means that its reuse within a certain framework requires little or no work. In most cases, moving to a different framework will require significant work. In this respect, reuse strongly resembles portability. It is important to note that reuse is the result of design aimed at reuse, refinement of components based on experience, and deliberate effort to search out existing components to (re)use. Reuse does not magically arise from mindless use of specific language features or coding techniques. C++ features such as classes, virtual functions, and templates allow designs to be expressed so that reuse is made easier (and thus more likely), but in themselves such features do not ensure reusability.

23.5.2 Scale

It is easy for an individual or an organization to get excited about "doing things right." In an institutional setting, this often translates into "developing and strictly following proper procedures." In both cases, common sense can be the first victim of a genuine and often ardent desire to improve the way things are done. Unfortunately, once common sense is missing there is no limit to the damage that can unwittingly be done.

Consider the stages of the development process listed in §23.4 and the stages of the design steps listed in §23.4.3. It is relatively easy to elaborate these stages into a proper design method where each stage is more precisely defined and has well-defined inputs and outputs and a semiformal notation for expressing these inputs and outputs. Checklists can be developed to ensure that the design method is adhered to, and tools can be developed to enforce a large number of the procedural and notational conventions. Further, looking at the classification of dependencies presented in §24.3 one could decree that certain dependencies were good and others bad and provide analysis tools to ensure that these value judgements were applied uniformly across a project. To complete this "firming up" of the software-production process, one would define standards for documentation (including rules for spelling and grammar and typesetting conventions) and for the general look of the code (including specifications of which language features can and cannot be used, specifications of what kinds of libraries can and cannot be used, conventions for indentation and the naming of functions, variables, and types, etc.).

Much of this can be helpful for the success of a project. At least, it would be a folly to set out to design a system that will eventually contain ten million lines of code that will be developed by hundreds of people and maintained and supported by thousands more over a decade or more without a fairly well-defined and somewhat rigid framework along the lines described previously.

Fortunately, most systems do not fall into this category. However, once the idea is accepted that such a design method or adherence to such a set of coding and documentation standards is ''the right way,'' pressure builds to apply it universally and in every detail. This can lead to ludicrous constraints and overheads on small projects. In particular, it can lead to paper shuffling and forms filling replacing productive work as the measure of progress and success. If that happens, real designers and programmers will leave the project and be replaced with bureaucrats.

Once such a ridiculous misapplication of a (hopefully perfectly reasonable) design method has occurred in a community, its failure becomes the excuse for avoiding almost all formality in the development process. This in turn naturally leads to the kind of messes and failures that the design method was designed to prevent in the first place.

The real problem is to find an appropriate degree of formality for the development of a particular project. Don't expect to find an easy answer to this problem. Essentially every approach works for a small project. Worse, it seems that essentially every approach – however ill conceived and however cruel to the individuals involved – also works for a large project, provided you are willing to throw indecent amounts of time and money at the problem.

A key problem in every software project is how to maintain the integrity of the design. This problem increases more than linearly with scale. Only an individual or a small group of people can grasp and keep sight of the overall aims of a major project. Most people must spend so much of their time on subprojects, technical details, day-to-day administration, etc., that the overall design aims are easily forgotten or subordinated to more local and immediate goals. It also is a recipe for failure not to have an individual or group with the explicit task of maintaining the integrity of the design. It is a recipe for failure not to enable such an individual or group to have an effect on the project as a whole.

Lack of a consistent long-term aim is much more damaging to a project and an organization than the lack of any individual feature. It should be the job of some small number of individuals to formulate such an overall aim, to keep that aim in mind, to write the key overall design documents, to write the introductions to the key concepts, and generally to help others to keep the overall aim in mind.

23.5.3 Individuals

Use of design as described here places a premium on skillful designers and programmers. Thus, it makes the choice of designers and programmers critical to the success of an organization.

Managers often forget that organizations consist of individuals. A popular notion is that programmers are equal and interchangeable. This is a fallacy that can destroy an organization by driving out many of the most effective individuals and condemning the remaining people to work at levels well below their potential. Individuals are interchangeable only if they are not allowed to take advantage of skills that raise them above the absolute minimum required for the task in question. Thus, the fiction of interchangeability is inhumane and inherently wasteful.

Most programming performance measures encourage wasteful practices and fail to take critical individual contributions into account. The most obvious example is the relatively widespread practice of measuring progress in terms of number of lines of code produced, number of pages of documentation produced, number of tests passed, etc. Such figures look good on management charts but bear only the most tenuous relation to reality. For example, if productivity is measured in terms of number of lines of code produced, a successful application of reuse will appear to cause negative performance of programmers. A successful application of the best principles in the redesign of a major piece of software typically has the same effect.

Quality of work produced is far harder to measure than quantity of output, yet individuals and groups must be rewarded based on the quality of their output rather than by crude quantity measures. Unfortunately, the design of practical quality measures has − to the best of my knowledge − hardly begun. In addition, measures that incompletely describe the state of a project tend to warp development. People adapt to meet local deadlines and to optimize individual and group performance as defined by the measures. As a direct result, overall system integrity and performance suffer. For example, if a deadline is defined in terms of bugs removed or known bugs remaining, we may see that deadline met at the expense of run-time performance or hardware resources needed to run the system. Conversely, if only run-time performance is measured the error rate will surely rise when the developers struggle to optimize the system for benchmarks. The lack of good and comprehensive quality measures places great demands on the technical expertise of managers, but the alternative is a systematic tendency to reward random activity rather than progress. Don't forget that managers are also individuals. Managers need at least as much education on new techniques as do the people they manage.

As in other areas of software development, we must consider the longer term. It is essentially impossible to judge the performance of an individual on the basis of a single year's work. Most individuals do, however, have consistent long-term track records that can be reliable predictors of technical judgement and a useful help in evaluating immediate past performance. Disregard of such records − as is done when individuals are considered merely as interchangeable cogs in the wheels of an organization − leaves managers at the mercy of misleading quantity measurements.

One consequence of taking a long-term view and avoiding the ''interchangeable morons school of management'' is that individuals (both developers and managers) need longer to grow into the more demanding and interesting jobs. This discourages job hopping as well as job rotation for ''career development.'' A low turnover of both key technical people and key managers must be a goal. No manager can succeed without a rapport with key designers and programmers and some recent and relevant technical knowledge. Conversely, no group of designers and developers can succeed in the long run without support from competent managers and a minimum of understanding of the larger nontechnical context in which they work.

Where innovation is needed, senior technical people, analysts, designers, programmers, etc., have a critical and difficult role to play in the introduction of new techniques. These are the people who must learn new techniques and in many cases unlearn old habits. This is not easy. These individuals have typically made great personal investments in the old ways of doing things and rely on successes achieved using these ways of operating for their technical reputation. So do many technical managers.

Naturally, there is often a fear of change among such individuals. This can lead to an overestimation of the problems involved in a change and a reluctance to acknowledge problems with the old ways of doing things. Equally naturally, people arguing for change tend to overestimate the beneficial effects of new ways of doing things and to underestimate the problems involved in a change. These two groups of individuals *must* communicate, they *must* learn to talk the same language, they *must* help each other hammer out a model for transition. The alternative is organizational paralysis and the departure of the most capable individuals from both groups. Both groups should remember that the most successful "old timers" are often the "young turks" of yesteryear. Given a chance to learn without humiliation, more experienced programmers and designers can become the most successful and insightful proponents of change. Their healthy skepticism, knowledge of users, and acquaintance with the organizational hurdles can be invaluable. Proponents of immediate and radical change must realize that a transition, often involving a gradual adoption of new techniques, is more often than not necessary. Conversely, individuals who have no desire to change should search out areas in which no change is needed rather than fight vicious rear-guard battles in areas in which new demands have already significantly altered the conditions for success.

23.5.4 Hybrid Design

Introducing new ways of doing things into an organization can be painful. The disruption to the organization and the individuals in the organization can be significant. In particular, an abrupt change that overnight turns productive and proficient members of "the old school" into ineffective novices in "the new school" is typically unacceptable. However, it is rare to achieve major gains without changes, and significant changes typically involve risks.

C++ was designed to minimize such risks by allowing a gradual adoption of techniques. Although it is clear that the largest benefits from using C++ are achieved through data abstraction, object-oriented programming, and object-oriented design, it is not clear that the fastest way to achieve these gains is a radical break with the past. Occasionally, such a clean break is feasible. More often, the desire for improvement is − or should be − tempered by concerns about how to manage the transition. Consider:

 − Designers and programmers need time to acquire new skills.
 − New code needs to cooperate with old code.
 − Old code needs to be maintained (often indefinitely).
 − Work on existing designs and programs needs to be completed (on time).
 − Tools supporting the new techniques need to be introduced into the local environment.

These factors lead naturally to a hybrid style of design − even where that isn't the intention of some designers. It is easy to underestimate the first two points.

By supporting several programming paradigms, C++ supports the notion of a gradual introduction into an organization in several ways:

 − Programmers can remain productive while learning C++.
 − C++ can yield significant benefits in a tool-poor environment.
 − C++ program fragments can cooperate well with code written in C and other traditional languages.
 − C++ has a large C-compatible subset.

The idea is that programmers can make the move to C++ from a traditional language by first adopting C++ while retaining a traditional (procedural) style of programming. Then they use the data abstraction techniques. Finally − when the language and its associated tools have been mastered − they move on to object-oriented programming and generic programming. Note that a well-designed library is much easier to use than it was to design and implement, so a novice can benefit from the more advanced uses of abstraction even during the early stages of this progress.

The idea of learning object-oriented design, object-oriented programming, and C++ in stages is supported by facilities for mixing C++ code with code written in languages that do not support

C++'s notions of data abstraction and object-oriented programming (§24.2.1). Many interfaces can simply be left procedural because there will be no immediate benefits in doing anything more complicated. For many key libraries, this will already have been done by the library provider so that the C++ programmer can stay ignorant of the actual implementation language. Using libraries written in languages such as C is the first, and initially most important, form of reuse in C++.

The next stage – to be used only where a more elaborate technique is actually needed – is to present facilities written in languages such as C and Fortran as classes by encapsulating the data structures and functions in C++ interface classes. A simple example of lifting the semantics from the procedure plus data structure level to the data abstraction level is the string class from §11.12. There, encapsulation of the C character string representation and the standard C string functions is used to produce a string type that is much simpler to use.

A similar technique can be used to fit a built-in or stand-alone type into a class hierarchy (§23.5.1). This allows designs for C++ to evolve to use data abstraction and class hierarchies in the presence of code written in languages in which these concepts are missing and even under the constraint that the resulting code must be callable from procedural languages.

23.6 Annotated Bibliography

This chapter only scratches the surface of the issues of design and of the management of programming projects. For that reason, a short annotated bibliography is provided. An extensive annotated bibliography can be found in [Booch,1994].

[Anderson,1990]   Bruce Anderson and Sanjiv Gossain: *An Iterative Design Model for Reusable Object-Oriented Software*. Proc. OOPSLA'90. Ottawa, Canada. A description of an iterative design and redesign model with a specific example and a discussion of experience.

[Booch,1994]   Grady Booch: *Object-Oriented Analysis and Design with Applications*. Benjamin/Cummings. 1994. ISBN 0-8053-5340-2. Contains a detailed description of design, a specific design method with a graphical notation, and several large examples of designs expressed in C++. It is an excellent book to which this chapter owes much. It provides a more in-depth treatment of many of the issues in this chapter.

[Booch,1996]   Grady Booch: *Object Solutions*. Benjamin/Cummings. 1996. ISBN 0-8053-0594-7. Describes the development of object-oriented systems from a management perspective. Contains extensive C++ code examples.

[Brooks,1982]   Fred Brooks: *The Mythical Man Month*. Addison-Wesley. 1982. Everyone should read this book every couple of years. A warning against hubris. It is a bit dated on technical matters, but it is not at all dated in matters related to individuals, organizations, and scale. Republished with additions in 1997. ISBN 1-201-83595-9.

[Brooks,1987]   Fred Brooks: *No Silver Bullet*. IEEE Computer, Vol. 20, No. 4. April 1987. A summary of approaches to large-scale software development, with a much-needed warning against belief in miracle cures (''silver bullets'').

[Coplien,1995]   James O. Coplien and Douglas C. Schmidt (editors): *Pattern Languages of Program Design*. Addison-Wesley. 1995. ISBN 1-201-60734-4.

[DeMarco,1987]   T. DeMarco and T. Lister: *Peopleware*. Dorset House Publishing Co. 1987. One of the few books that focusses on the role of people in the production of software. A must for every manager. Smooth enough for bedside reading. An antidote for much silliness.

[Gamma,1994]   Eric Gamma, et. al.: *Design Patterns*. Addison-Wesley. 1994. ISBN 0-201-63361-2. A practical catalog of techniques for creating flexible and reusable software, with a nontrivial, well-explained example. Contains extensive C++ code examples.

[Jacobson,1992]   Ivar Jacobson et. al.: *Object-Oriented Software Engineering*. Addison-Wesley. 1992. ISBN 0-201-54435-0. A thorough and practical description of software development in an industrial setting with an emphasis on use cases (§23.4.3.1). Miscasts C++ by describing it as it was ten years ago.

[Kerr,1987]   Ron Kerr: *A Materialistic View of the Software "Engineering" Analogy*. In SIGPLAN Notices, March 1987. The use of analogy in this chapter and the next owes much to the observations in this paper and to the presentations by and discussions with Ron that preceded it.

[Liskov,1987]   Barbara Liskov: *Data Abstraction and Hierarchy*. Proc. OOPSLA'87 (Addendum). Orlando, Florida. A discussion of how the use of inheritance can compromise data abstraction. Note, C++ has specific language support to help avoid most of the problems mentioned (§24.3.4).

[Martin,1995]   Robert C. Martin: *Designing Object-Oriented C++ Applications Using the Booch Method*. Prentice-Hall. 1995. ISBN 0-13-203837-4. Shows how to go from a problem to C++ code in a fairly systematic way. Presents alternative designs and principles for choosing between them. More practical and more concrete than most books on design. Contains extensive C++ code examples.

[Meyer,1988]   Bertrand Meyer: *Object Oriented Software Construction*. Prentice Hall. 1988. Pages 1-64 and 323-334 give a good introduction to one view of object-oriented programming and design with many sound pieces of practical advice. The rest of the book describes the Eiffel language. Tends to confuse Eiffel with universal principles.

[Parkinson,1957]   C. N. Parkinson: *Parkinson's Law and other Studies in Administration*. Houghton Mifflin. Boston. 1957. One of the funniest and most cutting descriptions of disasters caused by administrative processes.

[Shlaer,1988]   S. Shlaer and S. J. Mellor: *Object-Oriented Systems Analysis* and *Object Lifecycles*. Yourdon Press. ISBN 0-13-629023-X and 0-13-629940-7. Presents a view of analysis, design, and programming that differs strongly from the one presented here and embodied in C++ and does so using a vocabulary that makes it sound rather similar.

[Snyder,1986]   Alan Snyder: *Encapsulation and Inheritance in Object-Oriented Programming Languages*. Proc. OOPSLA'86. Portland, Oregon. Probably the first good description of the interaction between encapsulation and inheritance. Also provides a nice discussion of some notions of multiple inheritance.

[Wirfs-Brock,1990] Rebecca Wirfs-Brock, Brian Wilkerson, and Lauren Wiener: *Designing Object-Oriented Software*. Prentice Hall. 1990. Describes an anthropomorphic design method based on role playing using CRC (Classes, Responsibilities, and Collaboration) cards. The text, if not the method itself, is biased toward Smalltalk.

23.7 Advice

[1] Know what you are trying to achieve; §23.3.
[2] Keep in mind that software development is a human activity; §23.2, §23.5.3.
[3] Proof by analogy is fraud; §23.2.
[4] Have specific and tangible aims; §23.4.
[5] Don't try technological fixes for sociological problems; §23.4.
[6] Consider the longer term in design and in the treatment of people; §23.4.1, §23.5.3.
[7] There is no lower limit to the size of programs for which it is sensible to design before starting to code; §23.2.
[8] Design processes to encourage feedback; §23.4.
[9] Don't confuse activity for progress; §23.3, §23.4.
[10] Don't generalize beyond what is needed, what you have direct experience with, and what can be tested; §23.4.1, §23.4.2.
[11] Represent concepts as classes; §23.4.2, §23.4.3.1.
[12] There are properties of a system that should not be represented as a class; §23.4.3.1.
[13] Represent hierarchical relationships between concepts as class hierarchies; §23.4.3.1.
[14] Actively search for commonality in the concepts of the application and implementation and represent the resulting more general concepts as base classes; §23.4.3.1, §23.4.3.5.
[15] Classifications in other domains are not necessarily useful classifications in an inheritance model for an application; §23.4.3.1.
[16] Design class hierarchies based on behavior and invariants; §23.4.3.1, §23.4.3.5, §24.3.7.1.
[17] Consider use cases; §23.4.3.1.
[18] Consider using CRC cards; §23.4.3.1.
[19] Use existing systems as models, as inspiration, and as starting points; §23.4.3.6.
[20] Beware of viewgraph engineering; §23.4.3.1.
[21] Throw a prototype away before it becomes a burden; §23.4.4
[22] Design for change, focusing on flexibility, extensibility, portability, and reuse; §23.4.2.
[23] Focus on component design; §23.4.3.
[24] Let each interface represent a concept at a single level of abstraction; §23.4.3.1.
[25] Design for stability in the face of change; §23.4.2.
[26] Make designs stable by making heavily-used interfaces minimal, general, and abstract; §23.4.3.2, §23.4.3.5.
[27] Keep it small. Don't add features "just in case;" §23.4.3.2.

[28] Always consider alternative representations for a class. If no alternative representation is plausible, the class is probably not representing a clean concept; §23.4.3.4.

[29] Repeatedly review and refine both the design and the implementation; §23.4, §23.4.3.

[30] Use the best tools available for testing and for analyzing the problem, the design, and the implementation; §23.3, §23.4.1, §23.4.4.

[31] Experiment, analyze, and test as early as possible and as often as possible; §23.4.4, §23.4.5.

[32] Don't forget about efficiency; §23.4.7.

[33] Keep the level of formality appropriate to the scale of the project; §23.5.2.

[34] Make sure that someone is in charge of the overall design; §23.5.2.

[35] Document, market, and support reusable components; §23.5.1.

[36] Document aims and principles as well as details; §23.4.6.

[37] Provide tutorials for new developers as part of the documentation; §23.4.6.

[38] Reward and encourage reuse of designs, libraries, and classes; §23.5.1.

24

Design and Programming

Keep it simple:
as simple as possible,
but no simpler.
– A. Einstein

Design and programming language — classes — inheritance — type checking — programming — what do classes represent? — class hierarchies — dependencies — containment — containment and inheritance — design tradeoffs — use relationships — programmed-in relationships — invariants — assertions — encapsulation — components — templates — interfaces and implementations — advice.

24.1 Overview

This chapter considers the ways programming languages in general and C++ in particular can support design:

§24.2 The fundamental role of classes, class hierarchies, type checking, and programming itself

§24.3 Uses of classes and class hierarchies, focussing on dependencies between different parts of a program

§24.4 The notion of a *component*, which is the basic unit of design, and some practical observations about how to express interfaces

More general design issues are found in Chapter 23, and the various uses of classes are discussed in more detail in Chapter 25.

24.2 Design and Programming Language

If I were to build a bridge, I would seriously consider what material to build it out of. Also, the design of the bridge would be heavily influenced by the choice of material and vice versa. Reasonable designs for stone bridges differ from reasonable designs for steel bridges, from reasonable designs for wooden bridges, etc. I would not expect to be able to select the proper material for a bridge without knowing a bit about the various materials and their uses. Naturally, you don't have to be an expert carpenter to design a wooden bridge, but you do have to know the fundamentals of wooden constructions to choose between wood and iron as the material for a bridge. Furthermore, even though you don't personally have to be an expert carpenter to design a wooden bridge, you do need quite a detailed knowledge of the properties of wood and the mores of carpenters.

The analogy is that to choose a language for some software, you need knowledge of several languages, and to design a piece of software successfully, you need a fairly detailed knowledge of the chosen implementation language – even if you never personally write a single line of that software. The good bridge designer respects the properties of materials and uses them to enhance the design. Similarly, the good software designer builds on the strengths of the implementation language and – as far as possible – avoids using it in ways that cause problems for implementers.

One might think that this sensitivity to language issues comes naturally when only a single designer/programmer is involved. However, even in such cases the programmer can be seduced into misusing the language due to inadequate experience or undue respect for styles of programming established for radically different languages. When the designer is different from the programmer – and especially if they do not share a common culture – the likelihood of introducing error, inelegance, and inefficiencies into the resulting system approaches certainty.

So what can a programming language do for a designer? It can provide features that allow the fundamental notions of the design to be represented directly in the programming language. This eases the implementation, makes it easier to maintain the correspondence between the design and the implementation, enables better communication between designers and implementers, and allows better tools to be built to support both designers and implementers.

For example, most design methods are concerned about dependencies between different parts of a program (usually to minimize them and to ensure that they are well defined and understood). A language that supports explicit interfaces between parts of a program can support such design notions. It can guarantee that only the expected dependencies actually exist. Because many dependencies are explicit in code written in such a language, tools that read a program to produce charts of dependencies can be provided. This eases the job of designers and others that need to understand the structure of a program. A programming language such as C++ can be used to decrease the gap between design and program and consequently reduce the scope for confusion and misunderstandings.

The key notion of C++ is that of a class. A C++ class is a type. Together with namespaces, classes are also a primary mechanism for information hiding. Programs can be specified in terms of user-defined types and hierarchies of such user-defined types. Both built-in and user-defined types obey statically checked type rules. Virtual functions provide a mechanism for run-time binding without breaking the static type rules. Templates support the design of parameterized types. Exceptions provide a way of making error handling more regular. These C++ features can be used without incurring overhead compared to C programs. These are the first-order properties of C++

that must be understood and considered by a designer. In addition, generally available major libraries – such as matrix libraries, database interfaces, graphical user interface libraries, and concurrency support libraries – can strongly affect design choices.

Fear of novelty sometimes leads to sub-optimal use of C++. So does misapplication of lessons from other languages, systems, and application areas. Poor design tools can also warp designs. Five ways designers fail to take advantage of language features and fail to respect limitations are worth mentioning:

[1] Ignore classes and express the design in a way that constrains implementers to use the C subset only.

[2] Ignore derived classes and virtual functions and use only the data abstraction subset.

[3] Ignore the static type checking and express the design in such a way that implementers are constrained to simulate dynamic type checking.

[4] Ignore programming and express systems in a way that aims to eliminate programmers.

[5] Ignore everything except class hierarchies.

These variants are typical for designers with

[1] a C, traditional CASE, or structured design background,

[2] an Ada83, Visual Basic, or data abstraction background,

[3] a Smalltalk or Lisp background,

[4] a nontechnical or very specialized background,

[5] a background with heavy emphasis on ''pure'' object-oriented programming,

respectively. In each case, one must wonder if the implementation language was well chosen, if the design method was well chosen, or if the designer had failed to adapt to the tool in hand.

There is nothing unusual or shameful in such a mismatch. It is simply a mismatch that delivers sub-optimal designs and imposes unnecessary burdens on programmers. It does the same to designers when the conceptual framework of the design method is noticeably poorer than C++'s conceptual framework. Therefore, we avoid such mismatches wherever possible.

The following discussion is phrased as answers to objections because that is the way it often occurs in real life.

24.2.1 Ignoring Classes

Consider design that ignores classes. The resulting C++ program will be roughly equivalent to the C program that would have resulted from the same design process – and this program would again be roughly equivalent to the COBOL program that would have resulted from the same design process. In essence, the design has been made ''programming language independent'' at the cost of forcing the programmer to code in the common subset of C and COBOL. This approach does have advantages. For example, the strict separation of data and code that results makes it easy to use traditional databases that are designed for such programs. Because a minimal programming language is used, it would appear that less skill – or at least different skills – would be required from programmers. For many applications – say, a traditional sequential database update program – this way of thinking is quite reasonable, and the traditional techniques developed over decades are adequate for the job.

However, suppose the application differs sufficiently from traditional sequential processing of records (or characters) or the complexity involved is higher – say, in an interactive CASE system.

The lack of language support for data abstraction implied by the decision to ignore classes will hurt. The inherent complexity will show up in the application somewhere, and if the system is implemented in an impoverished language, the code will not reflect the design directly. The program will have too many lines of source code, lack type checking, and will in general not be amenable to tools. This is the prescription for a maintenance nightmare.

A common band-aid for this problem is to build specific tools to support the notions of the design method. These tools then provide higher-level constructs and checking to compensate for deficiencies of the (deliberately impoverished) implementation language. Thus, the design method becomes a special-purpose and typically corporate-owned programming language. Such programming languages are in most contexts poor substitutes for a widely available, general-purpose programming language supported by suitable design tools.

The most common reason for ignoring classes in design is simple inertia. Traditional programming languages don't support the notion of a class, and traditional design techniques reflect this deficiency. The most common focus of design has been the decomposition of the problems into a set of procedures performing required actions. This notion, called procedural programming in Chapter 2, is in the context of design often called *functional decomposition*. A common question is, "Can we use C++ together with a design method based on functional decomposition?" You can, but you will most likely end up using C++ as simply a better C and will suffer the problems mentioned previously. This may be acceptable in a transition period, for already completed designs, and for subsystems in which classes do not appear to offer significant benefits (given the experience of the individuals involved at this time). For the longer term and in general, however, the policy against large-scale use of classes implied by functional decomposition is not compatible with effective use of C++ or any other language that has support for abstraction.

The procedure-oriented and object-oriented views of programming are fundamentally different and typically lead to radically different solutions to the same problem. This observation is as true for the design phase as it is for the implementation phase: you can focus the design on the actions taken or on the entities represented, but not simultaneously on both.

So why prefer "object-oriented design" over the traditional design methods based on functional decomposition? A first-order answer is that functional decomposition leads to insufficient data abstraction. From this, it follows that the resulting design is

- less resilient to change,
- less amenable to tools,
- less suited for parallel development, and
- less suited for concurrent execution.

The problem is that functional decomposition causes interesting data to become global because when a system is structured as a tree of functions, any data accessed by two functions must be global to both. This ensures that "interesting" data bubbles up toward the root of the tree as more and more functions require access to it (as ever in computing, trees grow from the root down). Exactly the same process can be seen in single-rooted class hierarchies, in which "interesting" data and functions tend to bubble up toward a root class (§24.4). Focussing on the specification of classes and the encapsulation of data addresses this problem by making the dependencies between different parts of a program explicit and tractable. More important, though, it reduces the number of dependencies in a system by improving locality of reference to data.

However, some problems are best solved by writing a set of procedures. The point of an "object-oriented" approach to design is not that there should never be any nonmember functions in a program or that no part of a system may be procedure-oriented. Rather, the key point is to decouple different parts of a program to better reflect the concepts of the application. Typically, that is best done when classes, not functions, are the primary focus of the design effort. The use of a procedural style should be a conscious decision and not simply a default. Both classes and procedures should be used appropriately relative to the application and not just as artifacts of an inflexible design method.

24.2.2 Avoiding Inheritance

Consider design that avoids inheritance. The resulting programs simply fail to take advantage of a key C++ feature, while still reaping many benefits of C++ compared to C, Pascal, Fortran, COBOL, etc. Common reasons for doing this – apart from inertia – are claims that "inheritance is an implementation detail," "inheritance violates information hiding," and "inheritance makes cooperation with other software harder."

Considering inheritance merely an implementation detail ignores the way that class hierarchies can directly model key relationships between concepts in the application domain. Such relationships should be explicit in the design to allow designers to reason about them.

A strong case can be made for excluding inheritance from the parts of a C++ program that must interface directly with code written in other languages. This is, however, *not* a sufficient reason for avoiding the use of inheritance throughout a system; it is simply a reason for carefully specifying and encapsulating a program's interface to "the outer world." Similarly, worries about compromising information hiding through the use of inheritance (§24.3.2.1) are a reason to be careful with the use of virtual functions and protected members (§15.3). They are not a reason for general avoidance.

In many cases, there is no real advantage to be gained from inheritance. However, in a large project a policy of "no inheritance" will result in a less comprehensible and less flexible system in which inheritance is "faked" using more traditional language and design constructs. Further, I suspect that despite such a policy, inheritance will eventually be used anyway because C++ programmers will find convincing arguments for inheritance-based designs in various parts of the system. Therefore, a "no inheritance" policy will ensure only that a coherent overall architecture will be missing and will restrict the use of class hierarchies to specific subsystems.

In other words, keep an open mind. Class hierarchies are not an essential part of every good program, but in many cases they can help in both the understanding of the application and the expression of a solution. The fact that inheritance can be misused and overused is a reason for caution; it is a not reason for prohibition.

24.2.3 Ignoring Static Type Checking

Consider design that ignores static type checking. Commonly stated reasons to ignore static type checking in the design phase are that "types are an artifact of the programming language," that "it is more natural to think about objects without bothering about types," and that "static type checking forces us to think about implementation issues too early." This attitude is fine as far as it goes and harmless up to a point. It is reasonable to ignore details of type checking in the design stage, and it is often safe to ignore type issues almost completely in the analysis stage and early design stages. However, classes and class hierarchies are very useful in the design. In particular, they allow us to be specific about concepts, allow us to be precise about their relationships, and help us reason about the concepts. As the design progresses, this precision takes the form of increasingly precise statements about classes and their interfaces.

It is important to realize that precisely-specified and strongly-typed interfaces are a fundamental design tool. C++ was designed with this in mind. A strongly-typed interface ensures (up to a point) that only compatible pieces of software can be compiled and linked together and thus allows these pieces of software to make relatively strong assumptions about each other. These assumptions are guaranteed by the type system. The effect of this is to minimize the use of run-time tests, thus promoting efficiency and causing significant reductions in the integration phase of multiperson projects. In fact, strong positive experience with integrating systems that provide strongly-typed interfaces is the reason integration isn't a major topic of this chapter.

Consider an analogy. In the physical world, we plug gadgets together all the time, and a seemingly infinite number of standards for plugs exists. The most obvious thing about these plugs is that they are specifically designed to make it impossible to plug two gadgets together unless the gadgets were designed to be plugged together, and then they can be connected only in the right way. You cannot plug an electric shaver into a high-power socket. Had you been able to, you would have ended up with a fried shaver or a fried shavee. Much ingenuity is expended on ensuring that incompatible pieces of hardware cannot be plugged together. The alternative to using many incompatible plugs is gadgets that protect themselves against undesirable behavior from gadgets plugged into their sockets. A surge protector is a good example of this. Because perfect compatibility cannot be guaranteed at the ''plug compatibility level,'' we occasionally need the more expensive protection of circuitry that dynamically adapts to and/or protects from a range of inputs.

The analogy is almost exact. Static type checking is equivalent to plug compatibility, and dynamic checking corresponds to protection/adaptation circuitry. If both checks fail – in either the physical world or the software world – serious damage can result. In large systems, both forms of checking are used. In the early stages of a design, it may be reasonable simply to say, ''These two gadgets should be plugged together.'' However, it soon becomes relevant exactly how they should be plugged together. What guarantees does the plug provide about behavior? What error conditions are possible? What are the first-order cost estimates?

The use of ''static typing'' is not limited to the physical world. The use of units (for example, meters, kilograms, and seconds) to prevent the mixing of incompatible entities is pervasive in physics and engineering.

In the description of the design steps in §23.4.3, type information enters the picture in Step 2 (presumably after being superficially considered in Step 1) and becomes a major issue in Step 4.

Statically-checked interfaces are the prime vehicle for ensuring cooperation between C++ software developed by different groups. The documentation of these interfaces (including the exact types involved) is the primary means of communication between separate groups of programmers. These interfaces are one of the most important outputs of the design process and a focus of communication between designers and programmers.

Ignoring type issues when considering interfaces leads to designs that obscure the structure of the program and postpone error detection until run time. For example, an interface can be specified in terms of self-identifying objects:

```
// Example assuming dynamic type checking instead of static checking:

Stack s; // Stack can hold pointers to objects of any type

void f()
{
    s.push(new Saab900);
    s.push(new Saab37B);

    s.pop()->takeoff();      // fine: a Saab 37B is a plane
    s.pop()->takeoff();      // run-time error: car cannot take off
}
```

This is a severe underspecification of the interface (of *Stack::push*()) that forces dynamic checking rather than static checking. The stack *s* is meant to hold *Plane*s, but that was left implicit in the code, so it becomes the user's obligation to make sure the requirement is upheld.

A more precise specification – a template plus virtual functions rather than unconstrained dynamic type checking – moves error detection from run time to compile time:

```
Stack<Plane*> s; // Stack can hold pointers to Planes

void f()
{
    s.push(new Saab900);     // error: a Saab900 is not a Plane
    s.push(new Saab37B);

    s.pop()->takeoff();      // fine: a Saab 37B is a plane
    s.pop()->takeoff();
}
```

A similar point is made in §16.2.2. The difference in run time between dynamic checking and static checking can be significant. The overhead of dynamic checking is usually a factor in the range of 3 to 10.

One should not go to the other extreme, though. It is not possible to catch all errors by static checking. For example, even the most thoroughly statically checked program is vulnerable to hardware failures. See also §25.4.1 for an example where complete static checking would be infeasible. However, the ideal is to have the vast majority of interfaces be statically typed with application-level types; see §24.4.2.

Another problem is that a design can be perfectly reasonable in the abstract but can cause serious trouble because it fails to take into account limitations of a basic tool, in this case C++. For example, a function *f*() that needs to perform an operation *turn_right*() on an argument can do so only provided all of its arguments are of a common type:

```
class Plane {
    // ...
    void turn_right();
};
```

```
class  Car {
    // ...
    void  turn_right ();
};

void f(X* p)    // what type should X be?
{
    p->turn_right ();
    // ...
}
```

Some languages (such as Smalltalk and CLOS) allow two types to be used interchangeably if they have the same operations by relating every type through a common base and postponing name resolution until run time. However, C++ (intentionally) supports this notion through templates and compile-time resolution only. A non-template function can accept arguments of two types only if the two types can be implicitly converted to a common type. Thus, in the previous example *X* must be a common base of *Plane* and *Car* (e.g., a *Vehicle* class).

Typically, examples inspired by notions alien to C++ *can* be mapped into C++ by expressing the assumptions explicitly. For example, given *Plane* and *Car* (without a common base), we can still create a class hierarchy that allows us to pass an object containing a *Car* or a *Plane* to f(X*) (§25.4.1). However, doing this often requires an undesirable amount of mechanism and cleverness. Templates are often a useful tool for such concept mappings. A mismatch between design notions and C++ typically leads to "unnatural-looking" and inefficient code. Maintenance programmers tend to dislike the non-idiomatic code that arises from such mismatches.

A mismatch between the design technique and the implementation language can be compared to word-for-word translation between natural languages. For example, English with German grammar is as awkward as German with English grammar, and both can be close to incomprehensible to someone fluent in only one of those languages.

Classes in a program are the concrete representation of the concepts of the design. Consequently, obscuring the relationships between the classes obscures the fundamental concepts of the design.

24.2.4 Avoiding Programming

Programming is costly and unpredictable compared to many other activities, and the resulting code is often less than 100% reliable. Programming is labor-intensive and − for a variety of reasons − most serious project delays manifest themselves by code not being ready to ship. So, why not eliminate programming as an activity altogether?

To many managers, getting rid of the arrogant, undisciplined, over-paid, technology-obsessed, improperly-dressed, etc. programmers† would appear to be a significant added benefit. To a programmer, this suggestion may sound absurd. However, important problem areas with realistic alternatives to traditional programming do exist. For specific areas, it is possible to generate code directly from a high-level specification. In other areas, code can be generated by manipulating shapes on a screen. For example, useful user interfaces can be constructed by direct manipulation

---

† Yes, I'm a programmer.

in a tiny fraction of the time it would take to construct the same interface by writing traditional code. Similarly, database layouts and the code for accessing data according to such layouts can be generated from specifications that are far simpler than the code needed to express those operations directly in C++ or in any other general-purpose programming language. State machines that are smaller, faster, and more correct than most programmers could produce can be generated from specifications or by a direct manipulation interface.

These techniques work well in specific areas where there is either a sound theoretical foundation (e.g., math, state machines, and relational databases) or where a general framework exists into which small application fragments can be embedded (e.g., graphical user interfaces, network simulations, and database schema). The obvious usefulness of these techniques in limited – and typically crucial – areas can tempt people to think that the elimination of traditional programming by these techniques is "just around the corner." It is not. The reason is that expanding specification techniques outside areas with sound theoretical frameworks implies that the complexity of a general-purpose programming language would be needed in the specification language. This defeats the purpose of a clean and well-founded specification language.

It is sometimes forgotten that the framework that allows elimination of traditional programming in an area is a system or library that has been designed, programmed, and tested in the traditional way. In fact, one popular use of C++ and the techniques described in this book is to design and build such systems.

A compromise that provides a small fraction of the expressiveness of a general-purpose language is the worst of both worlds when applied outside a restricted application domain. Designers who stick to a high-level modeling point of view are annoyed by the added complexity and produce specifications from which horrendous code is produced. Programmers who apply ordinary programming techniques are frustrated by the lack of language support and generate better code only by excessive effort and by abandoning high-level models.

I see no signs that programming as an activity can be successfully eliminated outside areas that either have well-founded theoretical bases or in which the basic programming is provided by a framework. In either case, there is a dramatic drop in the effectiveness of the techniques as one leaves the original framework and attempts more general-purpose work. Pretending otherwise is tempting and dangerous. Conversely, ignoring the high-level specification techniques and the direct-manipulation techniques in domains in which they are well-founded and reasonably mature would be a folly.

Designing tools, libraries, and frameworks is one of the highest forms of design and programming. Constructing a useful mathematically-based model of an application area is one of the highest forms of analysis. Thus, providing a tool, language, framework, etc., that makes the result of such work available to thousands is a way for programmers and designers to escape the trap of becoming craftsmen of one-of-a-kind artifacts.

It is most important that a specification system or a foundation library be able to interface effectively with a general-purpose programming language. Otherwise, the framework provided is inherently limiting. This implies that specification systems and direct-manipulation systems that generate code at a suitable high level into an accepted general-purpose programming language have a great advantage. A proprietary language is a long-term advantage to its provider only. If the code generated is so low-level that general code added must be written without the benefits of abstraction, then reliability, maintainability, and economy are lost. In essence, a generation system should be designed to combine the strengths of higher-level specifications and higher-level programming languages. To exclude one or the other is to sacrifice the interests of system builders to the interests of tool providers. Successful large systems are multilevel and modular and evolve over time. Consequently, successful efforts to produce such systems involve a variety of languages, libraries, tools, and techniques.

24.2.5 Using Class Hierarchies Exclusively

When we find that something new actually works, we often go a bit overboard and apply it indiscriminately. In other words, a great solution to some problems often appears to be *the* solution to almost all problems. Class hierarchies and operations that are polymorphic on their (one) object provide a great solution to many problems. However, not every concept is best represented as a part of a hierarchy and not every software component is best represented as a class hierarchy.

Why not? A class hierarchy expresses relationships between its classes and a class represents a concept. Now what is the common relationship between a smile, the driver for my CD-ROM reader, a recording of Richard Strauss' Don Juan, a line of text, a satellite, my medical records, and a real-time clock? Placing them all in a single hierarchy when their only shared property is that they are programming artifacts (they are all ''objects'') is of little fundamental value and can cause confusion (§15.4.5). Forcing everything into a single hierarchy can introduce artificial similarities and obscure real ones. A hierarchy should be used only if analysis reveals conceptual commonality or if design and programming discover useful commonality in the structures used to implement the concepts. In the latter case, we have to be very careful to distinguish genuine commonality (to be reflected as subtyping by public inheritance) and useful implementation simplifications (to be reflected as private inheritance; §24.3.2.1).

This line of thinking leads to a program that has several unrelated or weakly-related class hierarchies, each representing a set of closely related concepts. It also leads to the notion of a concrete class (§25.2) that is not part of a hierarchy because placing such a class in a hierarchy would compromise its performance and its independence of the rest of the system.

To be effective, most critical operations on a class that is part of a class hierarchy must be virtual functions. Furthermore, much of that class' data must be protected rather than private. This makes it vulnerable to modification from further derived classes and can seriously complicate testing. Where stricter encapsulation makes sense from a design point of view, non-virtual functions and private data should be used (§24.3.2.1).

Having one argument of an operation (the one designating ''the object'') special can lead to contorted designs. When several arguments are best treated equally, an operation is best represented as a nonmember function. This does not imply that such functions should be global. In fact, almost all such free-standing functions should be members of a namespace (§24.4).

24.3 Classes

The most fundamental notion of object-oriented design and programming is that the program is a model of some aspects of reality. The classes in the program represent the fundamental concepts of the application and, in particular, the fundamental concepts of the ''reality'' being modeled. Real-world objects and artifacts of the implementation are represented by objects of these classes.

The analysis of relationships between classes and within parts of a class is central to the design of a system:

§24.3.2 Inheritance relationships
§24.3.3 Containment relationships
§24.3.5 Use relationships
§24.3.6 Programmed-in relationships
§24.3.7 Relationships within a class

Because a C++ class is a type, classes and the relationships between classes receive significant support from compilers and are generally amenable to static analysis.

To be relevant in a design, a class doesn't just have to represent a useful concept; it must also provide a suitable interface. Basically, the ideal class has a minimal and well-defined dependence on the rest of the world and presents an interface that exposes the minimal amount of information necessary to the rest of the world (§24.4.2).

24.3.1 What Do Classes Represent?

There are essentially two kinds of classes in a system:

[1] Classes that directly reflect the concepts in the application domain; that is, concepts that are used by end-users to describe their problems and solutions

[2] Classes that are artifacts of the implementation; that is, concepts that are used by the designers and programmers to describe their implementation techniques.

Some of the classes that are artifacts of the implementation may also represent real-world entities. For example, the hardware and software resources of a system provide good candidates for classes in an application. This reflects the fact that a system can be viewed from several viewpoints. This implies that one person's implementation detail is another person's application. A well-designed system will contain classes supporting logically separate views of the system. For example:

[1] Classes representing user-level concepts (e.g., cars and trucks)
[2] Classes representing generalizations of the user-level concepts (e.g. vehicles)
[3] Classes representing hardware resources (e.g., a memory management class)
[4] Classes representing system resources (e.g., output streams)
[5] Classes used to implement other classes (e.g., lists, queues, locks)
[6] Built-in data types and control structures.

In larger systems, keeping logically separate types of classes separate and maintaining separation between several levels of abstraction becomes a challenge. A simple example can be considered to have three levels of abstraction:

[1+2] Provide an application level view of the system
[3+4] Represent the machine on which the model runs
[5+6] Represent a low-level (programming language) view of the implementation.

The larger the system, the more levels of abstraction are typically needed for the description of the system and the more difficult it becomes to define and maintain the levels. Note that such levels of abstraction have direct counterparts in nature and in other types of human constructions. For example, a house can be considered as consisting of

[1] atoms;
[2] molecules;

[3] lumber and bricks;

[4] floors, walls, and ceilings; and

[5] rooms.

As long as these levels of abstraction are kept separate, you can maintain a coherent view of the house. However, if you mix them, absurdities arise. For example, the statement, ''My house consists of several thousand pounds of carbon, some complex polymers, about 5,000 bricks, two bathrooms, and 13 ceilings,'' is silly. Given the abstract nature of software, the equivalent statement about a complex system is not always recognized for what it is.

The translation of a concept in the application area into a class in a design is not a simple mechanical operation. It often requires significant insights. Note that the concepts in an application area are themselves abstractions. For example, ''taxpayers,'' ''monks,'' and ''employees'' don't really exist in nature; such concepts are themselves labels put on individuals to classify them relative to some system. The real or even the imagined world (literature, especially science fiction) is sometimes simply a source of ideas for concepts that mutate radically in the transition into classes. For example, the screen of my PC doesn't really resemble my desktop despite its being designed to support the desktop metaphor†, and the windows on my screen bear only the slightest relation to the contraptions that let drafts into my office. The point about modeling reality is not to slavishly follow what we see but rather to use it as a starting point for design, a source of inspiration, and an anchor to hold on to when the intangible nature of software threatens to overcome our ability to understand our programs.

A word of caution: beginners often find it hard to ''find the classes,'' but that problem is usually soon overcome without long-term ill effects. Next, however, often follows a phase in which classes − and their inheritance relationships − seem to multiply uncontrollably. This can cause long-term problems with the complexity, comprehensibility, and efficiency of the resulting program. Not every minute detail needs to be represented by a distinct class, and not every relationship between classes needs to be represented as an inheritance relationship. Try to remember that the aim of a design is to model a system at an *appropriate* level of detail and at *appropriate* levels of abstraction. Finding a balance between simplicity and generality is not easy.

24.3.2 Class Hierarchies

Consider simulating the traffic flow of a city to determine the likely times needed for emergency vehicles to reach their destinations. Clearly, we need to represent cars, trucks, ambulances, fire engines of various sorts, police cars, busses, etc. Inheritance comes into play because a real-world concept does not exist in isolation; it exists with numerous relationships to other concepts. Without understanding these relationships, we cannot understand the concepts. Consequently, a model that does not represent such relationships does not adequately represent our concepts. That is, in our programs we need classes to represent concepts, but that is not enough. We also need ways of representing relationships between classes. Inheritance is one powerful way of representing hierarchical relationships directly. In our example, we would probably consider emergency vehicles special and want also to distinguish between car-like and truck-like vehicles. This would yield a class hierarchy along these lines:

---

† I wouldn't be able to tolerate such a mess on my screen, anyway.

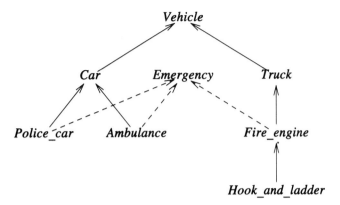

Here, *Emergency* represents the aspects of an emergency vehicle that are relevant to the simulation: it can violate some traffic rules, has priority in intersections when on an emergency call, it is under control of a dispatcher, etc.

Here is the C++ version:

```
class Vehicle { /* ... */ };
class Emergency { /* ... */ };
class Car : public Vehicle { /* ... */ };
class Truck : public Vehicle { /* ... */ };
class Police_car : public Car , protected Emergency { /* ... */ };
class Ambulance : public Car , protected Emergency { /* ... */ };
class Fire_engine : public Truck , protected Emergency { /* ... */ };
class Hook_and_ladder : public Fire_engine { /* ... */ };
```

Inheritance is the highest level relationship that can be represented directly in C++ and the one that figures largest in the early stages of a design. Often there is a choice between using inheritance to represent a relationship and using membership. Consider an alternative notion of what it means to be an emergency vehicle: a vehicle is an emergency vehicle if it displays a flashing light. This would allow a simplification of the class hierarchy by replacing the *Emergency* class by a member in class *Vehicle*:

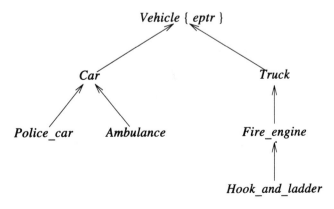

Class *Emergency* is now simply used as a member in classes that might need to act as emergency vehicles:

```
class  Emergency { /* ... */ };
class  Vehicle { protected: Emergency* eptr; /* ... */ };  // better: provide proper interface to eptr
class  Car : public  Vehicle { /* ... */ };
class  Truck : public  Vehicle { /* ... */ };
class  Police_car : public  Car { /* ... */ };
class  Ambulance : public  Car { /* ... */ };
class  Fire_engine : public  Truck { /* ... */ };
class  Hook_and_ladder : public  Fire_engine { /* ... */ };
```

Here, a vehicle is an emergency vehicle if *Vehicle*::*eptr* is nonzero. The "plain" cars and trucks are initialized with *Vehicle*::*eptr* zero; the others are initialized with *Vehicle*::*eptr* nonzero. For example:

```
Car::Car()      // Car constructor
{
     eptr = 0;
}

Police_car::Police_car()  // Police_car constructor
{
     eptr = new  Emergency;
}
```

Defining things this way enables a simple conversion of an emergency vehicle to an ordinary vehicle and vice versa:

```
void  f(Vehicle* p)
{
     delete  p->eptr;
     p->eptr = 0;                // no longer an emergency vehicle

     // ...

     p->eptr = new  Emergency;       // an emergency vehicle again
}
```

So, which variant of the class hierarchy is best? The general answer is, "The program that most directly models the aspects of the real world that we are interested in is the best." That is, in choosing between models we should aim for greater realism under the inevitable constraints of efficiency and simplicity. In this case, the easy conversion between ordinary vehicles and emergency vehicles seems unrealistic to me. Fire engines and ambulances are purpose-built vehicles manned by trained personnel and operated using dispatch procedures requiring specialized communication equipment. This view indicates that being an emergency vehicle should be a fundamental concept and represented directly in the program to improve type checking and other uses of tools. Had we been modeling a place where the roles of vehicles were less firmly defined − say, an area where private vehicles were routinely used to carry emergency personnel to accident sites and where communication was primarily based on portable radios − the other way of modeling the system might have been more appropriate.

For people who consider traffic simulations esoteric, it might be worth pointing out that such tradeoffs between inheritance and membership almost invariably occur in a design. The scrollbar example in §24.3.3 is an equivalent example.

24.3.2.1 Dependencies within a Class Hierarchy

Naturally, a derived class depends on its base classes. It is less often appreciated that the opposite can also be true†. If a class has a virtual function, the class depends on derived classes to implement part of its functionality whenever a derived class overrides that function. If a member of a base class itself calls one of the class' virtual functions, then the base class depends on its derived classes for its own implementation. Similarly, if a class uses a protected member, then it is again dependent on its derived classes for its own implementation. Consider:

```
class B {
    // ...
protected:
    int a;
public:
    virtual int f();
    int g() { int x = f(); return x-a; }
};
```

What does $g()$ do? The answer critically depends on the definition of $f()$ in some derived class. Here is a version that will ensure that $g()$ returns 1:

```
class D1 : public B {
    int f() { return a+1; }
};
```

and a version that makes $g()$ write *"Hello, world!"* and return 0:

```
class D2 : public B {
    int f() { cout<<"Hello, world!\n"; return a; }
};
```

This example illustrates one of the most important points about virtual functions. Why is it silly? Why wouldn't a programmer ever write something like that? The answer is that a virtual function is part of an interface to a base class, and that class can supposedly be used without knowledge of the classes derived from it. Consequently, it must be possible to describe the expected behavior of an object of the base class in such a way that programs can be written without knowledge of the derived classes. Every class that overrides the virtual function must implement a variant of that behavior. For example, the virtual function *rotate()* of a *Shape* class rotates a shape. The *rotate()* functions for derived classes such as *Circle* and *Triangle* must rotate objects of their respective type; otherwise, a fundamental assumption about class *Shape* is violated. No such assumption about behavior is made for class *B* or its derived classes *D1* and *D2*; thus, the example is nonsensical. Even the names *B, D1, D2, f,* and *g* were chosen to obscure any possible meanings.

---

† This observation has been summarized as: "Insanity is hereditary. You get it from your children."

The specification of the expected behavior of virtual functions is a *major* focus of class design. Choosing good names for classes and functions is important – and not always easy.

Is a dependency on unknown (possibly yet unwritten) derived classes good or bad? Naturally, that depends on the intent of the programmer. If the intent is to isolate a class from all external influences so that it can be proven to behave in a specific way, then protected members and virtual functions are best avoided. If, however, the intent is to provide a framework into which a later programmer (such as the same programmer a few weeks later) can add code, then virtual functions are often an elegant mechanism for achieving this; and protected member functions have proven convenient for supporting such use. This technique is used in the stream I/O library (§21.6) and was illustrated by the final version of the *Ival_box* hierarchy (§12.4.2).

If a *virtual* function is meant to be used only indirectly by a derived class, it can be left *private*. For example, consider a simple buffer template:

```
template<class T> class Buffer {
public:
        void put(T);      // call overflow(T) if buffer is full
        T get();          // call underflow() if buffer is empty
        // ...
private:
        virtual int overflow(T);
        virtual int underflow();
        // ...
};
```

The *put*() and *get*() functions call *virtual* functions *overflow*() and *underflow*(), respectively. A user can now implement a variety of buffer types to suit a variety of needs by overriding *overflow*() and *underflow*():

```
template<class T> class Circular_buffer : public Buffer<T> {
        int overflow(T);      // wrap around if full
        int underflow();
        // ...
};
```

```
template<class T> class Expanding_buffer : public Buffer<T> {
        int overflow(T);      // increase buffer size if full
        int underflow();
        // ...
};
```

Only if a derived class needed to call *overflow*() and *underflow*() directly would these functions need to be *protected* rather than *private*.

24.3.3 Containment Relationships

Where containment is used, there are two major alternatives for representing an object of a class X:

[1] Declare a member of type X.
[2] Declare a member of type $X\star$ or type $X\&$.

If the value of the pointer is never changed, these alternatives are equivalent, except for efficiency issues and the way you write constructors and destructors:

```
class X {
public:
    X(int);
    // ...
};

class C {
    X a;
    X* p;
    X& r;
public:
    C(int i, int j, int k) : a(i), p(new X(j)), r(*new X(k)) { }
    ~C() { delete p; delete &r; }
};
```

In such cases, membership of the object itself, as in the case of *C::a*, is usually preferable because it is the most efficient in time, space, and keystrokes. It is also less error-prone because the connection between the contained object and the containing object is covered by the rules of construction and destruction (§10.4.1, §12.2.2, §14.4.1). However, see also §24.4.2 and §25.7.

The pointer solution should be used when there is a need to change the pointer to the "contained" object during the life of the "containing" object. For example:

```
class C2 {
    X* p;
public:
    C2(int i) : p(new X(i)) { }
    ~C2() { delete p; }

    X* change(X* q)
    {
        X* t = p;
        p = q;
        return t;
    }
};
```

Another reason for using a pointer member is to allow the "contained" member to be supplied as an argument:

```
class C3 {
    X* p;
public:
    C3(X* q) : p(q) { }
    // ...
};
```

By having objects contain pointers to other objects, we create what are often called *object hierarchies*. This is an alternative and complementary technique to using class hierarchies. As shown in the emergency vehicle example in §24.3.2, it is often a tricky design issue to choose between representing a property of a class as a base class or representing it as a member. A need to override is an indication that the former is the better choice. Conversely, a need to be able to allow the property to be represented by a variety of types is an indication that the latter is the better choice. For example:

```
class XX : public X { / * ... * / } ;

class XXX : public X { / * ... * / } ;

void f()
{
    C3* p1 = new C3(new X);       // C3 "contains" an X
    C3* p2 = new C3(new XX);      // C3 "contains" an XX
    C3* p3 = new C3(new XXX);     // C3 "contains" an XXX
    // ...
}
```

This could not be modeled by a derivation of $C3$ from X or by $C3$ having a member of type X, because the exact type of a member needs to be used. This is important for classes with virtual functions, such as a shape class (§2.6.2) or an abstract set class (§25.3).

References can be used to simplify classes based on pointer membership when only one object is referred to during the life of the containing object. For example:

```
class C4 {
    X& r;
public :
    C4(X& q) : r(q) { }
    // ...
} ;
```

Pointer and reference members are also needed when an object needs to be shared:

```
X* p = new XX;
C4 obj1(*p);
C4 obj2(*p);  // obj1 and obj2 now share the new XX
```

Naturally, management of shared objects requires extra care – especially in concurrent systems.

24.3.4 Containment and Inheritance

Given the importance of inheritance relationships, it is not surprising that they are frequently overused and misunderstood. When a class D is publicly derived from another class B, it is often said that a D is a B:

```
class B { / * ... * / } ;
class D : public B { / * ... * / } ;     // D is a kind of B
```

Alternatively, this is expressed by saying that inheritance is an *is-a* relationship or – somewhat more precisely – that a D *is a kind of* B. In contrast, a class D that has a member of another class B is often said to *have* a B or *contain* a B. For example:

```
class  D {  // a D contains a B
public:
     B  b;
     // ...
};
```

Alternatively, this is expressed by saying that membership is a *has-a* relationship.

For given classes *B* and *D*, how do we choose between inheritance and membership? Consider an *Airplane* and an *Engine*. Novices often wonder if it might be a good idea to derive class *Airplane* from *Engine*. This is a bad idea, though, because an *Airplane is* not an *Engine*; it *has* an *Engine*. One way of seeing this is to consider if an *Airplane* might have two or more engines. Because that seems feasible (even if we are considering a program in which all of our *Airplanes* will be single-engine ones), we should use membership rather than inheritance. The question "can it have two?" is useful in many cases when there is doubt. As usual, it is the intangible nature of software that makes this discussion relevant. Had all classes been as easy to visualize as *Airplane* and *Engine*, trivial mistakes like deriving an *Airplane* from an *Engine* would be easily avoided. Such mistakes are, however, quite frequent – particularly among people who consider derivation as simply another mechanism for combining programming-language-level constructs. Despite the conveniences and shorthand notation that derivation provides, it should be used almost exclusively to express relationships that are well defined in a design. Consider:

```
class  B {
public:
     virtual void f();
     void g();
};

class  D1 {               // a D1 contains a B
public:
     B  b;
     void f();            // does not override b.f()
};

void  h1(D1* pd)
{
     B* pb = pd;          // error: no D1* to B* conversion
     pb = &pd->b;
     pb->g();             // calls B::g()
     pd->g();             // error: D1 doesn't have a member g()
     pd->b.g();
     pb->f();             // calls B::f (not overridden by D1::f())
     pd->f();             // calls D1::f()
}
```

Note that there is no implicit conversion from a class to one of its members and that a class containing a member of another class does not override the virtual functions of that member. This contrasts with the public derivation case:

```
class D2 : public B {        // a D2 is a B
public:
      void f();           // overrides B::f()
};

void h2 (D2* pd)
{
      B* pb = pd;          // ok: implicit D2* to B* conversion
      pb->g();             // calls B::g()
      pd->g();             // calls B::g()
      pb->f();             // virtual call: invokes D2::f()
      pd->f();             // invokes D2::f()
}
```

The notational convenience provided by the *D2* example compared to the *D1* example is a factor that can lead to overuse. It should be remembered, though, that there is a cost of increased dependency between *B* and *D2* to be paid for that notational convenience (see §24.3.2.1). In particular, it is easy to forget the implicit conversion from *D2* to *B*. Unless such conversions are an acceptable part of the semantics of your classes, *public* derivation is to be avoided. When a class is used to represent a concept and derivation is used to represent an *is-a* relationship, such conversions are most often exactly what is desired.

There are cases in which you would like inheritance but cannot afford to have the conversion happen. Consider writing a class *Cfield* (controlled field) that – in addition to whatever else it does – provides run-time access control for another class *Field*. At first glance, defining *Cfield* by deriving it from *Field* seems just right:

```
class Cfield : public Field { /* ... */ };
```

This expresses the notion that a *Cfield* really is a kind of *Field*, allows notational convenience when writing a *Cfield* function that uses a member of the *Field* part of the *Cfield*, and – most importantly – allows a *Cfield* to override *Field* virtual functions. The snag is that the *Cfield** to *Field** conversion implied in the declaration of *Cfield* defeats all attempts to control access to the *Field*:

```
void g (Cfield* p)
{
      *p = "asdf";      // access to Field controlled by Cfield's assignment operator:
                        // p->Cfield::operator=("asdf")

      Field* q = p;     // implicit Cfield* to Field* conversion
      *q = "asdf";      // OOPS! no control
}
```

A solution would be to define *Cfield* to have a *Field* as a member, but doing that precludes *Cfield* from overriding *Field* virtual functions. A better solution would be to use *private* derivation:

```
class Cfield : private Field { /* ... */ };
```

From a design perspective, private derivation is equivalent to containment, except for the (occasionally essential) issue of overriding. An important use of this is the technique of deriving a class publicly from an abstract base class that defines an interface and using private or protected derivation from a concrete class to provide an implementation (§2.5.4, §12.3, §25.3). Because the inheritance implied in *private* and *protected* derivation is an implementation detail that is not reflected in the type of the derived class, it is sometimes called *implementation inheritance* and contrasted to *public* derivation, whereby the interface of the base class is inherited and the implicit conversion to the base type is allowed. The latter is sometimes referred to as *subtyping*, or *interface inheritance*.

Another way of stating this is to point out that an object of a derived class should be usable wherever an object of its public base class is. This is sometimes called ''the Liskov Substitution Principle'' (§23.6[Liskov,1987]). The public/protected/private distinction supports this directly for polymorphic types manipulated through pointers and references.

24.3.4.1 Member/Hierarchy Tradeoffs

To further examine the design choices involving containment and inheritance, consider how to represent a scrollbar in an interactive graphics system and how to attach a scrollbar to a window. We need two kinds of scrollbars: horizontal and vertical. We can represent this either by two types – *Horizontal_scrollbar* and *Vertical_scrollbar* – or by a single *Scrollbar* type that takes an argument that says whether its layout is horizontal or vertical. The former choice implies the need for a third type, the plain *Scrollbar*, as the base class of the two specific scollbar types. The latter choice implies the need for an extra argument to the scrollbar type and the need to choose values to represent the two kinds of scrollbars. For example:

> **enum Orientation** { *horizontal*, *vertical* } ;

Once a choice is made, it determines the kind of change needed to extend the system. In the scrollbar example, we might want to introduce a third type of scrollbar. We may originally have thought that there could be only two kinds of scrollbars (''after all, a window has only two dimensions''). However, in this case – as in most – there are possible extensions that surface as redesign issues. For example, one might like to use a ''navigation button'' instead of two scrollbars. Such a button would cause scrolling in different directions depending on where a user pressed it. Pressing the middle of the top would cause ''scrolling up,'' pressing the middle left would cause ''scrolling left,'' while pressing the top-left corner would cause ''scrolling up and left.'' Such buttons are not uncommon. They can be seen as a refinement of the notion of a scrollbar that is particularly suited to applications in which the information scrolled over isn't plain text but rather more general sorts of pictures.

Adding a navigation button to a program with a three-scrollbar class hierarchy involves adding a new class, but it requires no changes to the old scrollbar code:

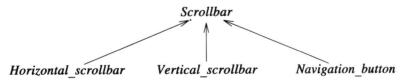

This is the nice aspect of the ''hierarchical'' solution.

Passing the orientation of the scrollbar as an argument implies the presence of type fields in the scrollbar objects and the use of switch statements in the code of the scrollbar member functions.

That is, we are facing a tradeoff between expressing this aspect of the structure of the system in terms of declarations or in terms of code. The former increases the degree of static checking and the amount of information on which tools have to work. The latter postpones decisions to run time and allows changes to be made by modifying individual functions without affecting the overall structure of the system as seen by the type checker and other tools. In most situations, I recommend using a class hierarchy to directly model hierarchical relationships of the concepts.

The single scrollbar type solution makes it easy to store and pass information specifying a kind of scrollbar:

```
void helper(Orientation oo)
{
    // ...
    p = new Scrollbar(oo);
    // ...
}

void me()
{
    helper(horizontal);
    // ...
}
```

This representation would also make it easy to re-orient a scrollbar at run time. This is unlikely to be of major importance in the case of scrollbars, but it can be important for equivalent examples. The point here is that there are always tradeoffs, and the tradeoffs are often nontrivial.

24.3.4.2 Containment/Hierarchy Tradeoffs

Now consider how to attach a scrollbar to a window. If we consider a *Window_with_scrollbar* as something that is both a *Window* and a *Scrollbar*, we get something like:

```
class Window_with_scrollbar : public Window, public Scrollbar {
    // ...
};
```

This allows any *Window_with_scrollbar* to act like a *Scrollbar* and like a *Window*, but it constrains us to using the single scrollbar-type solution.

On the other hand, if we consider a *Window_with_scrollbar* as a *Window* that has a *Scrollbar*, we get something like:

```
class Window_with_scrollbar : public Window {
    // ...
    Scrollbar* sb;
public:
    Window_with_scrollbar(Scrollbar* p, /* ... */) : Window(/* ...*/), sb(p) { /* ... */ }
    // ...
};
```

This allows us to use the scrollbar-hierarchy solution. Passing the scrollbar as an argument allows the window to be oblivious to the exact type of its scrollbar. We could even pass a *Scrollbar* around the way we passed an *Orientation* (§24.3.4.1). If we need to have *Window_with_scrollbar* act as a scrollbar, we can add a conversion operator:

```
Window_with_scrollbar::operator Scrollbar&()
{
    return *sb;
}
```

My preference is to have a window contain a scrollbar. I find it easier to think of a window *having* a scrollbar than of a window *being* a scrollbar in addition to being a window. In fact, my favorite design strategy involves a scrollbar being a special kind of window, which is then contained in a window that needs scrollbar services. This strategy forces the decision in favor of the containment solution. An alternative argument for the containment solution comes from the ''can it have two?'' rule of thumb (§24.3.4). Because there is no logical reason why a window shouldn't have two scrollbars (in fact, many windows do have both a horizontal and a vertical scrollbar), *Window_with_scrollbar* ought not be derived from *Scrollbar*.

Note that it is not possible to derive from an unknown class. The exact type of a base class must be known at compile time (§12.2). On the other hand, if an attribute of a class is passed as an argument to its constructor, then somewhere in the class there must be a member that represents it. However, if that member is a pointer or a reference we can pass an object of a class derived from the class specified for the member. For example, The *Scrollbar** member *sb* in the previous example can point to a *Scrollbar* of a type, such as *Navigation_button*, that is unknown to users of the *Scrollbar**.

24.3.5 Use Relationships

Knowledge of what other classes are used by a class and in which ways is often critical in order to express and understand a design. Such dependencies are supported only implicitly by C++. A class can use only names that have been declared (somewhere), but a list of names used is not provided in the C++ source. Tools (or in the absence of suitable tools, careful reading) are necessary for extracting such information. The ways a class *X* can use another class *Y* can be classified in several ways. Here is one way:
  - *X* uses the name *Y*.
  - *X* uses *Y*.
    - *X* calls a *Y* member function.
    - *X* reads a member of *Y*.
    - *X* writes a member of *Y*.
  - *X* creates a *Y*.
    - *X* allocates an *auto* or *static* variable of *Y*.
    - *X* creates a *Y* using *new*.
  - *X* takes the size of a *Y*.

Taking the size of an object is classified separately because doing so requires knowledge of the class declaration, but doesn't depend on the constructors. Naming *Y* is also classified as a separate dependency because just doing that − for example, in declaring a *Y** or mentioning *Y* in the declaration of an external function − doesn't require access to the declaration of *Y* at all (§5.7):

```
class Y;    // Y is the name of a class
Y* p;
extern Y f(const Y&);
```

It is often important to distinguish between the dependencies of a class' interface (the class declaration) and the dependencies of the class implementation (the class member definitions). In a well-designed system, the latter typically have many more dependencies, and those are far less interesting to a user than are the dependencies of the class declaration (§24.4.2). Typically, a design aims at minimizing the dependencies of an interface because they become dependencies of the class' users (§8.2.4.1, §9.3.2, §12.4.1.1, §24.4).

C++ doesn't require the implementer of a class to specify in detail what other classes are used and how. One reason for this is that most significant classes depend on so many other classes, that an abbreviation of the list of those classes, such as an #*include* directive, would be necessary for readability. Another is that the classification and granularity of such dependencies doesn't appear to be a programming language issue. Rather, exactly how *uses* dependencies are viewed depends on the purpose of the designer, programmer, or tool. Finally, which dependencies are interesting may also depend on details of the language implementation.

24.3.6 Programmed-In Relationships

A programming language cannot − and should not − directly support every concept from every design method. Similarly, a design language should not support every feature of every programming language. A design language should be richer and less concerned with details than a language suitable for systems programming must be. Conversely, a programming language must be able to support a variety of design philosophies, or it will fail for lack of adaptability.

When a programming language does not provide facilities for representing a concept from the design directly, a conventional mapping between the design construct and the programming language constructs should be used. For example, a design method may have a notion of delegation. That is, the design can specify that every operation not defined for a class *A* should be serviced by an object of a class *B* pointed to by a pointer *p*. C++ cannot express this directly. However, the expression of that idea in C++ is so stylized that one could easily imagine a program generating the code. Consider:

```
class B {
    // ...
    void f();
    void g();
    void h();
};

class A {
    B* p;
    // ...
    void f();
    void ff();
};
```

A specification that *A* delegated to *B* through *A*::*p* would result in code like this:

```
class A {
    B* p;        // delegation through p
    // ...
    void f();
    void ff();
    void g() { p->g(); }      // delegate g()
    void h() { p->h(); }      // delegate h()
};
```

It is fairly obvious to a programmer what is going on here, but simulating a design concept in code is clearly inferior to a one-to-one correspondence. Such "programmed-in" relationships are not as well "understood" by the programming language and are therefore less amenable to manipulation by tools. For example, standard tools would not recognize the "delegation" from A to B through $A::p$ as different from any other use of a $B*$.

A one-to-one mapping between the design concepts and the programming language concepts should be used wherever possible. A one-to-one mapping ensures simplicity and guarantees that the design really is reflected in the program so that programmers and tools can take advantage of it.

Conversion operators provide a language mechanism for expressing a class of programmed-in relationships. That is, a conversion operator $X::operator\ Y()$ specifies that wherever a Y is acceptable, an X can be used (§11.4.1). A constructor $Y::Y(X)$ expresses the same relationship. Note that a conversion operator (and a constructor) produces a new object rather than changing the type of an existing object. Declaring a conversion function to Y is simply a way of requesting *implicit* application of a function that returns a Y. Because the implicit application of conversions defined by constructors and conversion operators can be treacherous, it is sometimes useful to analyze them separately in a design.

It is important to ensure that the conversion graphs for a program do not contain cycles. If they do, the resulting ambiguity errors will render the types involved in the cycles unusable in combination. For example:

```
class Rational;

class Big_int {
public:
    friend Big_int operator+(Big_int, Big_int);
    operator Rational();
    // ...
};

class Rational {
public:
    friend Rational operator+(Rational, Rational);
    operator Big_int();
    // ...
};
```

The *Rational* and *Big_int* types will not interact as smoothly as one might have hoped:

```
void f(Rational r, Big_int i)
{
    g(r+i);                 // error, ambiguous: operator+(r,Rational(i)) or operator+(Big_int(r),i) ?
    g(r+Rational(i));       // one explicit resolution
    g(Big_int(r)+i);        // another explicit resolution
}
```

One can avoid such "mutual" conversions by making at least some of them explicit. For example, the *Big_int* to *Rational* conversion might have been defined as *make_Rational*() instead of as a conversion operator, and the addition would have been resolved to *g*(*Big_int*(*r*),*i*). Where "mutual" conversion operators cannot be avoided, one must resolve the resulting clashes either by explicit conversions as shown or by defining many separate versions of binary operators, such as +.

24.3.7 Relationships within a Class

A class can conceal just about any implementation detail and just about any amount of dirt – and sometimes it has to. However, the objects of most classes do themselves have a regular structure and are manipulated in ways that are fairly easy to describe. An object of a class is a collection of other sub-objects (often called members), and many of these are pointers and references to other objects. Thus, an object can be seen as the root of a tree of objects and the objects involved can be seen as constituting an "object hierarchy" that is complementary to the class hierarchy, as described in §24.3.2.1. For example, consider a very simple *String*:

```
class String {
    int sz;
    char* p;
public:
    String(const char* q);
    ~String();
    // ...
};
```

A *String* object can be represented graphically like this:

24.3.7.1 Invariants

The values of the members and the objects referred to by members are collectively called the *state* of the object (or simply, its *value*). A major concern of a class design is to get an object into a well-defined state (initialization/construction), to maintain a well-defined state as operations are performed, and finally to destroy the object gracefully. The property that makes the state of an object well-defined is called its *invariant*.

Thus, the purpose of initialization is to put an object into a state for which the invariant holds. Typically, this is done by a constructor. Each operation on a class can assume it will find the invariant true on entry and must leave the invariant true on exit. The destructor finally invalidates the invariant by destroying the object. For example, the constructor *String* : : *String* (*const char**) ensures that *p* points to an array of at least *sz+1* elements, where *sz* has a reasonable value and *p* [*sz*] ==*0*. Every string operation must leave that assertion true.

Much of the skill in class design involves making a class simple enough to make it possible to implement it so that it has a useful invariant that can be expressed simply. It is easy enough to state that every class needs an invariant. The hard part is to come up with a useful invariant that is easy to comprehend and that doesn't impose unacceptable constraints on the implementer or on the efficiency of the operations. Note that ''invariant'' here is used to denote a piece of code that can potentially be run to check the state of an object. A stricter and more mathematical notion is clearly possible and, in some contexts, more appropriate. An invariant, as discussed here, is a practical − and therefore typically economical and logically incomplete − check on an object's state.

The notion of invariants has its origins in the work of Floyd, Naur, and Hoare on preconditions and postconditions and is present in essentially all work on abstract data types and program verification done over the last 30 years or so. It is also a staple of C debugging.

Typically, the invariant is not maintained during the execution of a member function. Functions that may be called while the invariant is invalid should not be part of the public interface. Private and protected functions can serve that purpose.

How can we express the notion of an invariant in a C++ program? A simple way is to define an invariant-checking function and insert calls to it in the public operations. For example:

```
class  String {
        int  sz;
        char*  p;
public :
        class  Range { } ;                      // exception classes
        class  Invariant { } ;

        enum { TOO_LARGE = 16000 } ;            // length limit

        void  check ( ) ;                        // invariant check

        String (const  char*  q) ;
        String (const  String&) ;
        ~String ( ) ;

        char&  operator [ ] (int  i) ;
        int  size ( ) { return  sz; }

        // ...
} ;

void  String : : check ( )
{
        if (p==0 || sz<0 || TOO_LARGE<=sz || p [sz] )  throw  Invariant ( ) ;
}
```

```
char& String::operator[] (int i)
{
    check();                        // check on entry
    if (i<0 || sz<=i) throw Range();  // do work
    check();                        // check on exit
    return p[i];
}
```

This will work nicely and is hardly any work for the programmer. However, for a simple class like *String* the invariant checking will dominate the run time and maybe even the code size. Therefore, programmers often execute the invariant checks only during debugging:

```
inline void String::check()
{
#ifndef NDEBUG
    if (p==0 || sz<0 || TOO_LARGE<=sz || p[sz]) throw Invariant();
#endif
}
```

Here, the *NDEBUG* macro is used in a way similar to the way it is used in the standard C *assert()* macro. *NDEBUG* is conventionally set to indicate that debugging is *not* being done.

The simple act of defining invariants and using them during debugging is an invaluable help in getting the code right and − more importantly − in getting the concepts represented by the classes well defined and regular. The point is that when you are designing invariants, a class will be considered from an alternative viewpoint and the code will contain redundancy. Both increase the likelihood of spotting mistakes, inconsistencies, and oversights.

24.3.7.2 Assertions

An invariant is a special form of an assertion. An assertion is simply a statement that a given logical criterion must hold. The question is what to do when it doesn't.

The C standard library − and by implication the C++ standard library − provides the *assert()* macro in *<cassert>* or *<assert.h>*. An *assert()* evaluates its argument and calls *abort()* if the result is zero (*false*). For example:

```
void f(int* p)
{
    assert(p!=0);   // assert that p!=0; abort() if p is zero
    // ...
}
```

Before aborting, *assert()* outputs the name of its source file and the number of the line on which it appears. This makes *assert()* a useful debugging aid. *NDEBUG* is usually set by compiler options on a per-compilation-unit basis. This implies that *assert()* shouldn't be used in inline functions and template functions that are included in several translation units unless great care is taken that *NDEBUG* is set consistently (§9.2.3). Like all macro magic, this use of *NDEBUG* is too low-level, messy, and error-prone. Also, it is typically a good idea to leave at least some checks active in even the best-checked program, and *NDEBUG* isn't well suited for that. Furthermore, calling *abort()* is rarely acceptable in production code.

The alternative is to use an *Assert*() template that throws an exception rather than aborting so that assertions can be left in production code when that is desirable. Unfortunately, the standard library doesn't provide an *Assert*(). However, it is trivially defined:

```
template<class X, class A> inline void Assert(A assertion)
{
    if (!assertion) throw X();
}
```

Assert() throws the exception *X*() if the *assertion* is false. For example:

```
class Bad_arg { };

void f(int* p)
{
    Assert<Bad_arg>(p!=0);    // assert p!=0; throw Bad_arg unless p!=0
    // ...
}
```

This style of assertion has the condition explicit, so if we want to check only while debugging we must say so. For example:

```
void f2(int* p)
{
    Assert<Bad_arg>(NDEBUG || p!=0);      // either I'm not debugging or p!=0
    // ...
}
```

The use of || rather than && in the assertion may appear surprising. However, *Assert*<*E*>(*a*||*b*) tests !(*a*||*b*) which is !*a*&&!*b*.

Using *NDEBUG* in this way requires that we define *NDEBUG* with a suitable value whether or not we are debugging. A C++ implementation does not do this for us by default, so it is better to use a value. For example:

```
#ifdef NDEBUG
const bool ARG_CHECK = false;       // we are not debugging: disable checks
#else
const bool ARG_CHECK = true;        // we are debugging
#endif

void f3(int* p)
{
    Assert<Bad_arg>(!ARG_CHECK || p!=0);     // either I'm not debugging or p!=0
    // ...
}
```

If the exception associated with an assertion is not caught, a failed *Assert*() *terminate*()s the program much like an equivalent *assert*() would *abort*(). However, an exception handler may be able to take some less drastic action.

In any realistically-sized program, I find myself turning assertions on and off in groups to suit the need for testing. Using *NDEBUG* is simply the crudest form of that technique. Early on in development, most assertions are enabled, whereas only key sanity checks are left enabled in shipped code. This style of usage is most easily managed if the actual assertion is in two parts, with the first being an enabling condition (such as *ARG_CHECK*) and the second being the assertion proper.

If the enabling condition is a constant expression, the whole assertion will be compiled away when not enabled. However, the enabling condition can also be a variable so that it can be turned on and off at run time as debugging needs dictate. For example:

```
bool  string_check = true;

inline  void  String::check()
{
    Assert<Invariant> (!string_check || (p && 0<=sz && sz<TOO_LARGE && p[sz]==0));
}

void  f()
{
    String  s = "wonder";
    // strings are checked here
    string_check = false;
    // no checking of strings here
}
```

Naturally, code will be generated in such cases, so we must keep an eye out for code bloat if we use such assertions extensively.

Saying

```
Assert<E> (a);
```

is simply another way of saying

```
if (!a) throw E();
```

Then why bother with *Assert()*, rather than writing out the statement directly? Using *Assert()* makes the designer's intent explicit. It says that this is an assertion of something that is supposed to be always true. It is not an ordinary part of the program logic. This is valuable information to a reader of the program. A more practical advantage is that it is easy to search for *assert()* or *Assert()* whereas searching for conditional statements that throw exceptions is nontrival.

Assert() can be generalized to throw exceptions taking arguments and variable exceptions:

```
template<class A, class E> inline  void  Assert(A  assertion, E  except)
{
    if (!assertion) throw except;
}

struct  Bad_g_arg {
    int* p;
    Bad_g_arg(int* pp) :p(pp) { }
};

bool  g_check = true;
int  g_max = 100;
```

```
void g (int* p, exception e)
{
    Assert (!g_check || p!=0, e);                  // pointer is valid
    Assert (!g_check || (0<*p&&*p<=g_max), Bad_g_arg (p));    // value is plausible
    // ...
}
```

In many programs, it is crucial that no code is generated for an *Assert* ( ) where the assertion can be evaluated at compile time. Unfortunately, some compilers are unable to achieve this for the generalized *Assert* ( ). Consequently, the two-argument *Assert* ( ) should be used only when the exception is not of the form *E* ( ) and it is also acceptable for some code to be generated independently of the value of the assertion.

In §23.4.3.5, it was mentioned that the two most common forms of class hierarchy reorganizations were to split a class into two and to factor out the common part of two classes into a base class. In both cases, well-designed invariants can give a clue to the potential for reorganization. Comparing the invariant with the code of operations will show most of the invariant checking to be redundant in a class that is ripe for splitting. In such cases, subsets of the operations will access only subsets of the object state. Conversely, classes that are ripe for merging will have similar invariants even if their detailed implementations differ.

24.3.7.3 Preconditions and Postconditions

One popular use of assertions is to express preconditions and postconditions of a function. That is, checking that basic assumptions about input hold and verifying that the function leaves the world in the expected state upon exit. Unfortunately, the assertions we would like to make are often at a higher level than the programming language allows us to express conveniently and efficiently. For example:

```
template<class Ran> void sort (Ran first, Ran last)
{
    Assert<Bad_sequence> (" [first,last) is a valid sequence");     // pseudo code

    // ... sorting algorithm ...

    Assert<Failed_sort> (" [first,last) is in increasing order");     // pseudo code
}
```

This problem is fundamental. What we want to say *about* a program is best expressed in a mathematically-based higher language, rather than in the algorithmic programming language *in which* we write the program.

As for invariants, a certain amount of cleverness is needed to translate the ideal of what we would like to assert into something that is algorithmically feasible to check. For example:

```
template<class Ran> void sort (Ran first, Ran last)
{
    // [first,last) is a valid sequence: check plausibility:
    Assert<Bad_sequence> (NDEBUG || first<=last);

    // ... sorting algorithm ...
```

```
        // [first,last) is in increasing order: check a sample:
        Assert<Failed_sort>(NDEBUG ||
            (last-first<2 || (*first<=last[-1]
                && *first<=first[(last-first)/2] && first[(last-first)/2]<=last[-1]))));
    }
```

I often find writing ordinary code-checking arguments and results simpler than composing assertions. However, it is important to try to express the real (ideal) preconditions and postconditions −
and at least document them as comments − before reducing them to something less abstract that
can be effectively expressed in a programming language.

Precondition checking can easily degenerate into simple checking of argument values. As an
argument is often passed through several functions, this checking can be repetitive and expensive.
However, simply asserting that every pointer argument is nonzero in every function is not particularly helpful and can give a false sense of security − especially if the tests are done during debugging only to prevent overhead. This is a major reason why I recommend a focus on invariants.

24.3.7.4 Encapsulation

Note that in C++, the class − not the individual object − is the unit of encapsulation. For example:

```
class List {
    List* next;
public:
    bool on(List*);
    // ...
};

bool List::on(List* p)
{
    if (p == 0) return false;
    for(List* q = this; q; q=q->next) if (p == q) return true;
    return false;
}
```

The chasing of the private *List::next* pointer is accepted because *List::on*() has access to every
object of class *List* it can somehow reference. Where that is inconvenient, matters can be simplified by not taking advantage of the ability to access the representation of other objects from a member function. For example:

```
bool List::on(List* p)
{
    if (p == 0) return false;
    if (p == this) return true;
    if (next==0) return false;
    return next->on(p);
}
```

However, this turns iteration into recursion, and doing that can cause a major performance hit when
a compiler isn't able to optimize the recursion back into an iteration.

24.4 Components

The unit of design is a collection of classes, functions, etc., rather than an individual class. Such a collection, often called a *library* or a *framework* (§25.8), is also the unit of reuse (§23.5.1), maintenance, etc. C++ provides three mechanisms for expressing the notion of a set of facilities united by a logical criteria:

    [1] A class − containing a collection of data, function, template, and type members

    [2] A class hierarchy − containing a collection of classes

    [3] A namespace − containing a collection of data, function, template, and type members

A class provides many facilities to make it convenient to create objects of the type it defines. However, many significant components are not best described by a mechanism for creating objects of a single type. A class hierarchy expresses the notion of a set of related types. However, the individual members of a component are not always best expressed as classes and not all classes possess the basic similarity required to fit into a meaningful class hierarchy (§24.2.5). Therefore, a namespace is the most direct and the most general embodiment of the notion of a component in C++. A component is sometimes referred to as a "class category." However, not every element of a component is or should be a class.

Ideally, a component is described by the set of interfaces it uses for its implementation plus the set of interfaces it provides for its users. Everything else is "implementation detail" and hidden from the rest of the system. This may indeed be the designer's description of a component. To make it real, the programmer needs to map it into declarations. Classes and class hierarchies provide the interfaces, and namespaces allow the programmer to group the interfaces and to separate interfaces used from interfaces provided. Consider:

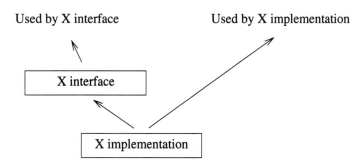

Using the techniques described in §8.2.4.1, this becomes:

```
namespace A {  // some facilities used by X's interface
    // ...
}

namespace X {  // interface of component X

    using namespace A;  // dependent on declarations from A
    // ...
    void f();
}
```

```
namespace X_impl {  // facilities needed by X's implementation
     using namespace X;
     // ...
}

void X::f()
{
     using namespace X_impl;  // dependent on declarations from X_impl
     // ...
}
```

The general interface *X* should not depend on the implementation interface *X_impl*.

A component can have many classes that are not intended for general use. Such classes should be "hidden" within implementation classes or namespaces:

```
namespace X_impl {  // component X implementation details

     class Widget {
          // ...
     };

     // ...
}
```

This ensures that *Widget* isn't used from other parts of the program. However, classes that represent coherent concepts are often candidates for reuse and should therefore be considered for inclusion into the interface of the component. Consider:

```
class Car {
     class Wheel {
          // ...
     };

     Wheel flw, frw, rlw, rrw;
     // ...
public:
     // ...
};
```

In most contexts, we need to have the actual wheels hidden to maintain the abstraction of a car (when you use a car you cannot operate the wheels independently). However, the *Wheel* class itself seems a good candidate for wider use, so moving it outside class *Car* might be better:

```
class Wheel {
     // ...
};

class Car {
     Wheel flw, frw, rlw, rrw;
     // ...
public:
     // ...
};
```

The decision to nest or not depends on the aims of the design and the generality of the concepts involved. Both nesting and "non-nesting" are widely applicable techniques for expressing a design. The default should be to make a class as local as possible until a need to make it more generally available is demonstrated.

There is a nasty tendency for "interesting" functions and data to "bubble up" to the global namespace, to widely-used namespaces, or to ultimate base classes in a hierarchy. This can easily lead to unintentional exposure of implementation details and to the problems associated with global data and global functions. This is most likely to happen in a single-rooted hierarchy, and in a program where only very few namespaces are used. Virtual base classes (§15.2.4) can be used to combat this phenomenon in the context of class hierarchies. Small "implementation" namespaces are the main tool for avoiding the problem in the context of namespaces.

Note that header files provide a powerful mechanism for supplying different views of a component to different users and for excluding classes that are considered part of the implementation from the user's view (§9.3.2).

24.4.1 Templates

From a design perspective, templates serve two, weakly-related needs:
- Generic programming
- Policy parameterization

Early in a design effort, operations are just operations. Later, when it is time to specify the type of operands templates become essential when using a statically-typed programming language, such as C++. Without templates, function definitions would have to be replicated or checking would have to be unnecessarily postponed to run time (§24.2.3). An operation that implements an algorithm for a variety of operand types is a candidate to be implemented as a template. If all operands fit into a single class hierarchy, and especially if there is a need to add new operand types at run time, the operand type is best represented as a class – often as an abstract class. If the operand types do not fit into a single hierarchy and especially if run-time performance is critical, the operation is best implemented as a template. The standard containers and their supporting algorithms are an example of when the need to take operands of a variety of unrelated types combined with a need for run-time performance lead to the use of templates (§16.2).

To make the template/hierarchy tradeoff more concrete, consider how to generalize a simple iteration:

```
void print_all (Iter_for_T x)
{
    for (T* p = x.first(); p; p = x.next()) cout << *p;
}
```

Here, the assumption is that *Iter_for_T* provides operations that yield *T**s.

We can make the iterator *Iter_for_T* a template parameter:

```
template<class Iter_for_T> void print_all (Iter_for_T x)
{
    for (T* p = x.first(); p; p = x.next()) cout << *p;
}
```

This allows us to use a variety of unrelated iterators as long as they all provide *first* ( ) and *next* ( ) with the right meanings and as long as we know the type of iterator for each call of *print_all* ( ) at compile time. The standard library containers and algorithms are based on this idea.

Alternatively, we can use the observation that *first* ( ) and *next* ( ) constitute an interface to iterators. We can then define a class to represent that interface:

```
class Iter {
public:
        virtual T* first ( ) const = 0;
        virtual T* next ( ) = 0;
} ;

void print_all2 (Iter& x)
{
        for (T* p = x.first ( ); p; p = x.next ( )) cout << *p;
}
```

We can now use every iterator derived from *Iter*. The actual code doesn't differ depending on whether we use templates or a class hierarchy to represent the parameterization – only the run-time, recompilation, etc., tradeoffs differ. In particular, class *Iter* is a candidate for use as an argument for the template:

```
void f (Iter& i)
{
        print_all (i);       // use the template
        print_all2 (i);
}
```

Consequently, the two approaches can be seen as complementary.

Often, a template needs to use functions and classes as part of its implementation. Many of those must themselves be templates so as to maintain generality and efficiency. In that way, algorithms become generic over a range of types. This style of template use is called *generic programming* (§2.7). When we call *std::sort* ( ) on a *vector*, the elements of the vector are the operands of the *sort* ( ) ; thus, *sort* ( ) is generic for the element types. In addition, the standard sort is generic for the container types because it is invoked on iterators for arbitrary, standard-conforming containers (§16.3.1).

The *sort* ( ) algorithm is also parameterized on the comparison criteria (§18.7.1). From a design perspective, this is different from taking an operation and making it generic on its operand type. Deciding to parameterize an algorithm on an object (or operation) in a way that controls the way the algorithm operates is a much higher-level design decision. It is a decision to give the designer/programmer control over some part of the policy governing the operation of the algorithm. From a programming language point of view, however, there is no difference.

24.4.2 Interfaces and Implementations

The ideal interface
- presents a complete and coherent set of concepts to a user,
- is consistent over all parts of a component,

  - does not reveal implementation details to a user,
  - can be implemented in several ways,
  - is statically typed,
  - is expressed using application-level types, and
  - depends in limited and well-defined ways on other interfaces.

Having noted the need for consistency across the classes that present the component's interface to the rest of the world (§24.4), we can simplify the discussion by looking at only a single class. Consider:

```
class Y { / * ... * / } ;        // needed by X

class Z { / * ... * / } ;        // needed by X

class X {  // example of poor interface style
      Y a;
      Z b;
public:
      void f(const char * ...);
      void g(int[], int);
      void set_a(Y&);
      Y& get_a();
};
```

This interface has several potential problems:
  - The interface uses the types *Y* and *Z* in a way that requires the declarations of *Y* and *Z* to be known to compile it.
  - The function *X::f()* takes an arbitrary number of arguments of unknown types (probably somehow controlled by a ''format string'' supplied as the first argument; §21.8).
  - The function *X::g()* takes an *int*[] argument. This may be acceptable, but typically it is a sign that the level of abstraction is too low. An array of integers is not self-describing, so it is not obvious how many elements it is supposed to have.
  - The *set_a()* and *get_a()* functions most likely expose the representation of objects of class *X* by allowing direct access to *X::a*.

These member functions provide an interface at a very low level of abstraction. Basically, classes with interfaces at this level belong among the implementation details of a larger component − if they belong anywhere at all. Ideally, an argument of an interface function carries enough information to make it self-describing. A rule of thumb is that it should be possible to transmit the request for service over a thin wire for service at a remote server.

   C++ allows the programmer to expose the representation of a class as part of the interface. This representation may be hidden (using *private* or *protected*), but it is available to the compiler to allow allocation of automatic variables, to allow inline substitution of functions, etc. The negative effect of this is that use of class types in the representation of a class may introduce undesirable dependencies. Whether the use of members of types *Y* and *Z* is a problem depends on what kind of types *Y* and *Z* actually are. If they are simple types, such as *list*, *complex*, and *string*, their use is most often quite appropriate. Such types can be considered stable, and the need to include their class declarations is an acceptable burden on the compiler. However, if *Y* and *Z* themselves had been interface classes of significant components, such as a graphics system or a bank account management system, it might be wise not to depend too directly on them. In such cases, using a pointer or a reference member is often a better choice:

```
class Y;
class Z;

class X {  // X accesses Y and Z through pointers and references only
    Y* a;
    Z& b;
    // ...
};
```

This decouples the definition of X from the definitions of Y and Z; that is, the definition of X depends on the names Y and Z only. The implementation of X will, of course, still depend on the definitions of Y and Z, but this will not adversely affect the users of X.

This illustrates an important point: an interface that hides significant amounts of information – as a useful interface ought to – will have far fewer dependencies than the implementation it hides. For example, the definition of class X can be compiled without access to the definitions of Y and Z. However, the definitions of X's member functions that manipulate the Y and Z objects will need access to the definitions of Y and Z. When dependencies are analyzed, the dependencies of the interface and the implementation must be considered separately. In both cases, the ideal is for the dependency graphs of a system to be directed acyclic graphs to ease understanding and testing of the system. However, this ideal is far more critical and far more often achievable for interfaces than for implementations.

Note that a class can define three interfaces:

```
class X {
private:
    // accessible to members and friends only
protected:
    // accessible to members and friends and
    // to members and friends of derived classes only
public:
    // accessible to the general public
};
```

In addition, a *friend* is part of the public interface (§11.5).

A member should be part of the most restrictive interface possible. That is, a member should be *private* unless there is a reason for it to be more accessible. If it needs to be more accessible, it should be *protected* unless there is a reason for it to be *public*. It is almost always a bad idea to make a data member *public* or *protected*. The functions and classes that constitute the public interface should present a view of the class that fits with its role as representing a concept.

Note that abstract classes can be used to provide a further level of representation hiding (§2.5.4, §12.3, §25.3).

24.4.3 Fat Interfaces

Ideally, an interface should offer only operations that make sense and that can be implemented well by every derived class implementing that interface. However, this is not always easy. Consider lists, arrays, associative arrays, trees, etc. As shown in §16.2.2, it is tempting and sometimes useful to provide a generalization of all of these types − usually called a *container* − that can be used as the interface to every one of these. This (apparently) relieves the user of having to deal with the details of all of these containers. However, defining the interface of a general container class is nontrivial. Assume that we want to define *Container* as an abstract type. What operations do we want *Container* to provide? We could provide only the operations that every container can support − the intersection of the sets of operations − but that is a ridiculously narrow interface. In fact, in many interesting cases that intersection is empty. Alternatively, we could provide the union of all the sets of operations and give a run-time error if a ''non-existent'' operation is applied to an object through this interface. An interface that is such a union of interfaces to a set of concepts is called a *fat interface*. Consider a ''general container'' of objects of type *T*:

```
class Container {
public :
        struct Bad_oper {        // exception class
                const char* p;
                Bad_oper(const char* pp) : p(pp) { }
        };

        virtual void put(const T*) { throw Bad_oper("Container::put"); }
        virtual T* get() { throw Bad_oper("Container::get"); }

        virtual T*& operator[](int) { throw Bad_oper("Container::[](int)"); }
        virtual T*& operator[](const char*) { throw Bad_oper("Container::[](char*)"); }
        // ...
};
```

*Container*s could then be declared like this:

```
class List_container : public Container, private list {
public :
        void put(const T*);
        T* get();
        // ... no operator[] ...
};

class Vector_container : public Container, private vector {
public :
        T*& operator[](int);
        T*& operator[](const char*);
        // ... no put() or get() ...
};
```

As long as one is careful, all is well:

```
void f()
{
    List_container sc;
    Vector_container vc;
    // ...
    user(sc, vc);
}

void user(Container& c1, Container& c2)
{
    T* p1 = c1.get();
    T* p2 = c2[3];
    // don't use c2.get() or c1[3]
    // ...
}
```

However, few data structures support both the subscripting and the list-style operations well. Consequently, it is probably not a good idea to specify an interface that requires both. Doing so leads to the use of run-time type-inquiry (§15.4) or exception handling (Chapter 14) to avoid run-time errors. For example:

```
void user2(Container& c1, Container& c2) // detection is easy, but recovery can be hard
{
    try {
        T* p1 = c1.get();
        T* p2 = c2[3];
        // ...
    }
    catch (Container::Bad_oper& bad) {
        // Oops!
        // Now what?
    }
}
```

or

```
void user3(Container& c1, Container& c2) // early detection is tedious; recovery can still be hard
{
    if (dynamic_cast<List_container*>(&c1) && dynamic_cast<Vector_container*>(&c2)) {
        T* p1 = c1.get();
        T* p2 = c2[3];
        // ...
    }
    else {
        // Oops!
        // Now what?
    }
}
```

In both cases, run-time performance can suffer and the generated code can be surprisingly large. As a result, people are tempted to ignore the potential errors and hope that they don't actually occur when the program is in the hands of users. The problem with this approach is that exhaustive testing is also hard and expensive.

Consequently, fat interfaces are best avoided where run-time performance is at a premium, where strong guarantees about the correctness of code are required, and in general wherever there is a good alternative. The use of fat interfaces weakens the correspondence between concepts and classes and thus opens the floodgates for the use of derivation as a mere implementation convenience.

24.5 Advice

[1] Evolve use towards data abstraction and object-oriented programming; §24.2.
[2] Use C++ features and techniques as needed (only); §24.2.
[3] Match design and programming styles; §24.2.1.
[4] Use classes/concepts as a primary focus for design rather than functions/processing; §24.2.1.
[5] Use classes to represent concepts; §24.2.1, §24.3.
[6] Use inheritance to represent hierarchical relationships between concepts (only); §24.2.2, §24.2.5, §24.3.2.
[7] Express strong guarantees about interfaces in terms of application-level static types; §24.2.3.
[8] Use program generators and direct-manipulation tools to ease well-defined tasks; §24.2.4.
[9] Avoid program generators and direct-manipulation tools that do not interface cleanly with a general-purpose programming language; §24.2.4.
[10] Keep distinct levels of abstraction distinct; §24.3.1.
[11] Focus on component design; §24.4.
[12] Make sure that a virtual function has a well-defined meaning and that every overriding function implements a version of that desired behavior; §24.3.4, §24.3.2.1.
[13] Use public inheritance to represent *is-a* relationships; §24.3.4.
[14] Use membership to represent *has-a* relationships; §24.3.4.
[15] Prefer direct membership over a pointer to a separately-allocated object for expressing simple containment; §24.3.3, §24.3.4.
[16] Make sure that the *uses* dependencies are understood, non-cyclic wherever possible, and minimal; §24.3.5.
[17] Define invariants for all classes; §24.3.7.1.
[18] Explicitly express preconditions, postconditions, and other assertions as assertions (possibly using *Assert* ( )); §24.3.7.2.
[19] Define interfaces to reveal the minimal amount of information needed; §24.4.
[20] Minimize an interface's dependencies on other interfaces; §24.4.2.
[21] Keep interfaces strongly typed; §24.4.2.
[22] Express interfaces in terms of application-level types; §24.4.2.
[23] Express an interface so that a request could be transmitted to a remote server; §24.4.2.
[24] Avoid fat interfaces; §24.4.3.
[25] Use *private* data and member functions wherever possible; §24.4.2.
[26] Use the *public*/*protected* distinction to distinguish between the needs of designers of derived classes and general users; §24.4.2.

[27] Use templates for generic programming; §24.4.1.
[28] Use templates to parameterize an algorithm by a policy; §24.4.1.
[29] Use templates where compile-time type resolution is needed; §24.4.1.
[30] Use class hierarchies where run-time type resolution is needed; §24.4.1.

25

Roles of Classes

Some things better change ...
but fundamental themes
should revel in persistence.
– Stephen J. Gould

Kinds of classes — concrete types — abstract types — nodes — changing interfaces — object I/O — actions — interface classes — handles — use counts — application frameworks — advice — exercises.

25.1 Kinds of Classes

The C++ class is a programming language construct that serves a variety of design needs. In fact, I find that the solution to most knotty design problems involves the introduction of a new class to represent some notion that had been left implicit in the previous draft design (and maybe the elimination of other classes). The great variety of roles that a class can play leads to a variety of kinds of classes that are specialized to serve a particular need well. In this chapter, a few archetypical kinds of classes are described, together with their inherent strengths and weaknesses:

§25.2 Concrete types
§25.3 Abstract types
§25.4 Nodes
§25.5 Operations
§25.6 Interfaces
§25.7 Handles
§25.8 Application frameworks

These ''kinds of classes'' are design notions and not language constructs. The unattained, and probably unattainable, ideal is to have a minimal set of simple and orthogonal kinds of classes from which all well-behaved and useful classes could be constructed. It is important to note that each of these kinds of classes has a place in design and none is inherently better than the others for all uses. Much confusion in discussions of design and programming comes from people trying to use only one or two kinds of classes exclusively. This is usually done in the name of simplicity, yet it leads to contorted and unnatural uses of the favored kinds of classes.

The description here emphasizes the pure forms of these kinds of classes. Naturally, hybrid forms can also be used. However, a hybrid ought to appear as the result of a design decision based on an evaluation of the engineering tradeoffs and not a result of some misguided attempt to avoid making decisions. ''Delaying decisions'' is too often a euphemism for ''avoiding thinking.'' Novice designers will usually do best by staying away from hybrids and also by following the style of an existing component with properties that resemble the desired properties for the new component. Only experienced programmers should attempt to write a general-purpose component or library, and every library designer should be ''condemned'' to use, document, and support his or her creation for some years. Also, please note §23.5.1.

25.2 Concrete Types

Classes such as *vector* (§16.3), *list* (§17.2.2), *Date* (§10.3), and *complex* (§11.3, §22.5) are *concrete* in the sense that each is the representation of a relatively simple concept with all the operations essential for the support of that concept. Also, each has a one-to-one correspondence between its interface and an implementation and none are intended as a base for derivation. Typically, concrete types are not fitted into a hierarchy of related classes. Each concrete type can be understood in isolation with minimal reference to other classes. If a concrete type is implemented well, programs using it are comparable in size and speed to programs a user would write using a hand-crafted and specialized version of the concept. Similarly, if the implementation changes significantly the interface is usually modified to reflect the change. In all of this, a concrete type resembles a built-in type. Naturally, the built-in types are all concrete. User-defined concrete types, such as complex numbers, matrices, error messages, and symbolic references, often provide fundamental types for some application domain.

The exact nature of a class' interface determines what implementation changes are significant in this context; more abstract interfaces leave more scope for implementation changes but can compromise run-time efficiency. Furthermore, a good implementation does not depend on other classes more than absolutely necessary so that the class can be used without compile-time or run-time overheads caused by the accommodation of other ''similar'' classes in a program.

To sum up, a class providing a concrete type aims:

[1] to be a close match to a particular concept and implementation strategy;

[2] to provide run-time and space efficiency comparable to ''hand-crafted'' code through the use of inlining and of operations taking full advantage of the properties of the concept and its implementation;

[3] to have only minimal dependency on other classes; and

[4] to be comprehensible and usable in isolation.

The result is a tight binding between user code and implementation code. If the implementation changes in any way, user code will have to be recompiled because user code almost always contains calls of inline functions or local variables of a concrete type.

The name ''concrete type'' was chosen to contrast with the common term ''abstract type.'' The relationship between concrete and abstract types is discussed in §25.3.

Concrete types cannot directly express commonality. For example, *list* and *vector* provide similar sets of operations and can be used interchangeably by some template functions. However, there is no relationship between the types *list<int>* and *vector<int>* or between *list<Shape*>* and *list<Circle*>* (§13.6.3), even though *we* can discern their similarities.

For naively designed concrete types, this implies that code using them in similar ways will look dissimilar. For example, iterating through a *List* using a *next* ( ) operation differs dramatically from iterating through a *Vector* using subscripting:

```
void my (List& sl)
{
    for (T* p = sl.first(); p; p = sl.next()) { // "natural" list iteration
        // my stuff
    }
    // ...
}

void your (Vector& v)
{
    for (int i = 0; i<v.size(); i++) {     // "natural" vector iteration
        // your stuff
    }
    // ...
}
```

The difference in iteration style is natural in the sense that a get-next-element operation is essential to the notion of a list (but not that common for a vector) and subscripting is essential to the notion of a vector (but not for a list). The availability of operations that are ''natural'' relative to a chosen implementation strategy is often crucial for efficiency and important for ease of writing the code.

The obvious snag is that the code for fundamentally similar operations, such as the previous two loops, can look dissimilar, and code that uses different concrete types for similar operations cannot be used interchangeably. In realistic examples, it takes significant thought to find similarities and significant redesign to provide ways of exploiting such similarities once found. The standard containers and algorithms are an example of a thorough rethinking that makes it possible to exploit similarities between concrete types without losing their efficiency and elegance benefits (§16.2).

To take a concrete type as an argument, a function must specify that exact concrete type as an argument type. There will be no inheritance relationships that can be used to make the argument declaration less specific. Consequently, an attempt to exploit similarities between concrete types will involve templates and generic programming as described in §3.8. When the standard library is used, iteration becomes:

```
template<class C> void ours (const C& c)
{
    for (C::const_iterator p = c.begin(); p!=c.end(); ++p) { // standard library iteration
        // ...
    }
}
```

The fundamental similarity between containers is exploited, and this in turn opens the possibility for further exploitation as done by the standard algorithms (Chapter 18).

To use a concrete type well, the user must understand its particular details. There are (typically) no general properties that hold for all concrete types in a library that can be relied on to save the user the bother of knowing the individual classes. This is the price of run-time compactness and efficiency. Sometimes that is a price well worth paying; sometimes it is not. It can also be the case that an individual concrete class is easier to understand and use than is a more general (abstract) class. This is often the case for classes that represent well-known data types such as arrays and lists.

Note, however, that the ideal is still to hide as much of the implementation as is feasible without seriously hurting performance. Inline functions can be a great win in this context. Exposing member variables by making them public or by providing set and get functions that allow the user to manipulate them directly is almost never a good idea (§24.4.2). Concrete types should still be types and not just bags of bits with a few functions added for convenience.

25.2.1 Reuse of Concrete Types

Concrete types are rarely useful as bases for further derivation. Each concrete type aims at providing a clean and efficient representation of a single concept. A class that does that well is rarely a good candidate for the creation of different but related classes through public derivation. Such classes are more often useful as members or private base classes. There, they can be used effectively without having their interfaces and implementations mixed up with and compromised by those of the new classes. Consider deriving a new class from *Date*:

```
class My_date : public Date {
        // ...
};
```

Is it ever valid for *My_date* to be used as a plain *Date*? Well, that depends on what *My_date* is, but in my experience it is rare to find a concrete type that makes a good base class without modification.

A concrete type is "reused" unmodified in the same way as built-in types such as *int* are (§10.3.4). For example:

```
class Date_and_time {
private:
        Date d;
        Time t;
public:
        // ...
};
```

This form of use (reuse?) is usually simple, effective, and efficient.

Maybe it was a mistake not to design *Date* to be easy to modify through derivation? It is sometimes asserted that *every* class should be open to modification by overriding and by access from derived class member functions. This view leads to a variant of *Date* along these lines:

```
class Date2 {
public:
        // public interface, consisting primarily of virtual functions
protected:
        // other implementation details (possibly including some representation)
private:
        // representation and other implementation details
};
```

To make writing overriding functions easy and efficient, the representation is declared *protected*. This achieves the objective of making *Date2* arbitrarily malleable by derivation, yet keeping its user interface unchanged. However, there are costs:

[1] *Less efficient basic operations.* A C++ virtual function call is a fraction slower than an ordinary function call, virtual functions cannot be inlined as often as non-virtual functions, and a class with virtual functions typically incurs a one-word space overhead.

[2] *The need to use free store.* The aim of *Date2* is to allow objects of different classes derived from *Date2* to be used interchangeably. Because the sizes of these derived classes differ, the obvious thing to do is to allocate them on the free store and access them through pointers or references. Thus, the use of genuine local variables dramatically decreases.

[3] *Inconvenience to users.* To benefit from the polymorphism provided by the virtual functions, accesses to *Date2*s must be through pointers or references.

[4] *Weaker encapsulation.* The virtual operations can be overridden and protected data can be manipulated from derived classes (§12.4.1.1).

Naturally, these costs are not always significant, and the behavior of a class defined in this way is often exactly what we want (§25.3, §25.4). However, for a simple concrete type, such as *Date2*, the costs are unnecessary and can be significant.

Finally, a well-designed concrete type is often the ideal representation for a more malleable type. For example:

```
class Date3 {
public:
        // public interface, consisting primarily of virtual functions
private:
        Date d;
};
```

This is the way to fit concrete types (including built-in types) into a class hierarchy when that is needed. See also §25.10[1].

25.3 Abstract Types

The simplest way of loosening the coupling between users of a class and its implementers and also between code that creates objects and code that uses such objects is to introduce an abstract class that represents the interface to a set of implementations of a common concept. Consider a naive *Set*:

```
template<class T> class Set {
public:
        virtual void insert(T*) = 0;
        virtual void remove(T*) = 0;

        virtual int is_member(T*) = 0;

        virtual T* first() = 0;
        virtual T* next() = 0;

        virtual ~Set() { }
};
```

This defines an interface to a set with a built-in notion of iteration over its elements. The absence of a constructor and the presence of a virtual destructor is typical (§12.4.2). Several implementations are possible (§16.2.1). For example:

```
template<class T> class List_set : public Set<T>, private list<T> {
        // ...
};

template<class T> class Vector_set : public Set<T>, private vector<T> {
        // ...
};
```

The abstract class provides the common interface to the implementations. This means we can use a *Set* without knowing which kind of implementation is used. For example:

```
void f(Set<Plane*>& s)
{
        for (Plane** p = s.first(); p; p = s.next()) {
                // my stuff
        }
        // ...
}

List_set<Plane*> sl;
Vector_set<Plane*> v(100);

void g()
{
        f(sl);
        f(v);
}
```

For concrete types, we required a redesign of the implementation classes to express commonality and used a template to exploit it. Here, we must design a common interface (in this case *Set*), but no commonality beyond the ability to implement the interface is required of the classes used for implementation.

Furthermore, users of *Set* need not know the declarations of *List_set* and *Vector_set*, so users need not depend on these declarations and need not be recompiled or in any way changed if *List_set* or *Vector_set* changes or even if a new implementation of *Set* − say *Tree_set* − is introduced. All dependencies are contained in functions that explicitly use a class derived from *Set*. In particular, assuming the conventional use of header files the programmer writing $f(Set\&)$ needs only include *Set.h* and not *List_set.h* or *Vector_set.h*. An "implementation header" is needed only where a *List_set* or a *Vector_set*, respectively, is created. An implementation can be further insulated from the actual classes by introducing an abstract class that handles requests to create objects ("a factory;" §12.4.4).

This separation of the interface from the implementations implies the absence of access to operations that are "natural" to a particular implementation but not general enough to be part of the interface. For example, because a *Set* doesn't have a notion of ordering we cannot support a subscripting operator in the *Set* interface even if we happen to be implementing a particular *Set* using an array. This implies a run-time cost due to missed hand optimizations. Furthermore, inlining typically becomes infeasible (except in a local context, when the compiler knows the real type), and all interesting operations on the interface become virtual function calls. As with concrete types, sometimes the cost of an abstract type is worth it; sometimes it is not. To sum up, an abstract type aims to:

[1] define a single concept in a way that allows several implementations of it to coexist in a program;

[2] provide reasonable run-time and space efficiency through the use of virtual functions;

[3] let each implementation have only minimal dependency on other classes; and

[4] be comprehensible in isolation.

Abstract types are not better than concrete types, just different. There are difficult and important tradeoffs for the user to make. The library provider can dodge the issue by providing both, thus leaving the choice to the user. The important thing is to be clear about to which world a class belongs. Limiting the generality of an abstract type in an attempt to compete in speed with a concrete type usually fails. It compromises the ability to use interchangeable implementations without significant recompilation after changes. Similarly, attempting to provide "generality" in concrete types to compete with the abstract type notion also usually fails. It compromises the efficiency and appropriateness of a simple class. The two notions can coexist − indeed, they *must* coexist because concrete classes provide the implementations for the abstract types − but they must not be muddled together.

Abstract types are often not intended to be bases for further derivation beyond their immediate implementation. Derivation is most often used just to supply implementation. However, a new interface can be constructed from an abstract class by deriving a more extensive abstract class from it. This new abstract class must then in turn be implemented through further derivation by a non-abstract class (§15.2.5).

Why didn't we derive *List* and *Vector* classes from *Set* in the first place to save the introduction of *List_set* and *Vector_set* classes? In other words, why have concrete types when we can have abstract types?

[1] *Efficiency*. We want to have concrete types such as *vector* and *list* without the overheads implied by decoupling the implementations from the interfaces (as implied by the abstract type style).

[2] *Reuse*. We need a mechanism to fit types designed "elsewhere" (such as *vector* and *list*) into a new library or application by giving them a new interface (rather than rewriting them).

[3] *Multiple interfaces.* Using a single common base for a variety of classes leads to fat interfaces (§24.4.3). Often, it is better to provide a new interface to a class used for new purposes (such as a *Set* interface for a *vector*) rather than modify its interface to serve multiple
purposes.

Naturally, these points are related. They are discussed in some detail for the *Ival_box* example
(§12.4.2, §15.2.5) and in the context of container design (§16.2). Using the *Set* base class would
have resulted in a based-container solution relying on node classes (§25.4).

Section §25.7 describes a more flexible iterator in that the binding of the iterator to the implementation yielding the objects can be specified at the point of initialization and changed at run
time.

25.4 Node Classes

A class hierarchy is built with a view of derivation different from the interface/implementer view
used for abstract types. Here, a class is viewed as a foundation on which to build. Even if it is an
abstract class, it usually has some representation and provides some services for its derived classes.
Examples of node classes are *Polygon* (§12.3), the initial *Ival_slider* (§12.4.1), and *Satellite*
(§15.2).

Typically, a class in a hierarchy represents a general concept of which its derived classes can be
seen as specializations. The typical class designed as an integral part of a hierarchy, a *node class*,
relies on services from base classes to provide its own services. That is, it calls base class member
functions. A typical node class provides not just an implementation of the interface specified by its
base class (the way an implementation class does for an abstract type). It also adds new functions
itself, thus providing a wider interface. Consider *Car* from the traffic-simulation example in
§24.3.2:

```
class Car : public Vehicle {
public:
    Car(int passengers, Size_category size, int weight, int fc)
        : Vehicle(passengers, size, weight), fuel_capacity(fc) { /* ... */ }

    // override relevant virtual functions from Vehicle:

    void turn(Direction);
    // ...

    // add Car-specific functions:

    virtual void add_fuel(int amount);    // a car needs fuel to run
    // ...
};
```

The important functions are the constructor through which the programmer specifies the basic properties that are relevant to the simulation and the (virtual) functions that allow the simulation routines to manipulate a *Car* without knowing its exact type. A *Car* might be created and used like
this:

```
void user()
{
    // ...
    Car* p = new Car(3, economy, 1500, 60);
    drive(p, bs_home, MH);    // enter into simulated traffic pattern
    // ...
}
```

A node class usually needs constructors and often a nontrivial constructor. In this, node classes differ from abstract types, which rarely have constructors.

The operations on *Car* will typically use operations from the base class *Vehicle* in their implementations. In addition, the user of a *Car* relies on services from its base classes. For example, *Vehicle* provides the basic functions dealing with weight and size so that *Car* doesn't have to:

```
bool Bridge::can_cross(const Vehicle& r)
{
    if (max_weight<r.weight()) return false;
    // ...
}
```

This allows programmers to create new classes such as *Car* and *Truck* from a node class *Vehicle* by specifying and implementing only what needs to differ from *Vehicle*. This is often referred to as "programming by difference" or "programming by extension."

Like many node classes, a *Car* is itself a good candidate for further derivation. For example, an *Ambulance* needs additional data and operations to deal with emergencies:

```
class Ambulance : public Car, public Emergency {
public:
    Ambulance();

    // override relevant Car virtual functions:

    void turn(Direction);
    // ...

    // override relevant Emergency virtual functions:

    virtual void dispatch_to(const Location&);
    // ...

    // add Ambulance-specific functions:

    virtual int patient_capacity();    // number of stretchers
    // ...
};
```

To sum up, a node class
   [1] relies on its base classes both for its implementation and for supplying services to its users;
   [2] provides a wider interface (that is, an interface with more public member functions) to its
       users than do its base classes;
   [3] relies primarily (but not necessarily exclusively) on virtual functions in its public interface;
   [4] depends on all of its (direct and indirect) base classes;

[5] can be understood only in the context of its base classes;

[6] can be used as a base for further derivation; and

[7] can be used to create objects.

Not every node class will conform to all of points 1, 2, 6, and 7, but most do. A class that does not conform to point 6 resembles a concrete type and could be called a *concrete node class*. For example, a concrete node class can be used to implement an abstract class (§12.4.2) and variables of such a class can be allocated statically and on the stack. Such a class is sometimes called a *leaf class*. However, any code operating on a pointer or reference to a class with virtual functions must take into account the possibility of a further derived class (or assume without language support that further derivation hasn't happened). A class that does not conform to point 7 resembles an abstract type and could be called an *abstract node class*. Because of unfortunate traditions, many node classes have at least some *protected* members to provide a less restricted interface for derived classes (§12.4.1.1).

Point 4 implies that to compile a node class, a programmer must include the declarations of all of its direct and indirect base classes and all of the declarations that they, in turn, depend on. In this, a node class again provides a contrast to an abstract type. A user of an abstract type does not depend on the classes used to implement it and need not include them to compile.

25.4.1 Changing Interfaces

By definition, a node class is part of a class hierarchy. Not every class in a hierarchy needs to offer the same interface. In particular, a derived class can provide more member functions, and a sibling class can provide a completely different set of functions. From a design perspective, *dynamic_cast* (§15.4) can be seen as a mechanism for asking an object if it provides a given interface.

As an example, consider a simple object I/O system. Users want to read objects from a stream, determine that they are of the expected types, and then use them. For example:

```
void user()
{
    // ... open file assumed to hold shapes, and attach ss as an istream for that file ...

    Io_obj* p = get_obj(ss);   // read object from stream

    if (Shape* sp = dynamic_cast<Shape*>(p)) {
        sp->draw();     // use the Shape
        // ...
    }
    else {
        // oops: non-shape in Shape file
    }
}
```

The function *user*() deals with shapes exclusively through the abstract class *Shape* and can therefore use every kind of shape. The use of *dynamic_cast* is essential because the object I/O system can deal with many other kinds of objects and the user may accidentally have opened a file containing perfectly good objects of classes that the user has never heard of.

This object I/O system assumes that every object read or written is of a class derived from *Io_obj*. Class *Io_obj* must be a polymorphic type to allow us to use *dynamic_cast*. For example:

```
class Io_obj {
public:
    virtual Io_obj* clone() const =0;        // polymorphic
    virtual ~Io_obj() {}
};
```

The critical function in the object I/O system is *get_obj*(), which reads data from an *istream* and creates class objects based on that data. Assume that the data representing an object on an input stream is prefixed by a string identifying the object's class. The job of *get_obj*() is to read that string prefix and call a function capable of creating and initializing an object of the right class. For example:

```
typedef Io_obj* (*PF)(istream&);        // pointer to function returning an Io_obj*

map<string, PF> io_map;                  // maps strings to creation functions

bool get_word(istream& is, string& s);   // read a word from is into s

Io_obj* get_obj(istream& s)
{
    string str;
    bool b = get_word(s, str);            // read initial word into str
    if (b == false) throw No_class();     // io format problem

    PF f = io_map[str];                   // lookup 'str' to get function
    if (f == 0) throw Unknown_class();    // no match for 'str'

    return f(s);                          // construct object from stream
}
```

The *map* called *io_map* holds pairs of name strings and functions that can construct objects of the class with that name.

We could define class *Shape* in the usual way, except for deriving it from *Io_obj* as required by *user*():

```
class Shape : public Io_obj {
    // ...
};
```

However, it would be more interesting (and in many cases more realistic) to use a defined *Shape* (§2.6.2) unchanged:

```
class Io_circle : public Circle, public Io_obj {
public:
    Io_circle* clone() const { return new Io_circle(*this); }  // using copy constructor
    Io_circle(istream&);  // initialize from input stream
    static Io_obj* new_circle(istream& s) { return new Io_circle(s); }
    // ...
};
```

This is an example of how a class can be fitted into a hierarchy using an abstract class with less foresight than would have been required to build it as a node class in the first place (§12.4.2, §25.3).

The *Io_circle* (*istream&*) constructor initializes an object with data from its *istream* argument. The *new_circle* ( ) function is the one put into the *io_map* to make the class known to the object I/O system. For example:

```
io_map["Io_circle"]=&Io_circle::new_circle;
```

Other shapes are constructed in the same way:

```
class Io_triangle : public Triangle, public Io_obj {
    // ...
};
```

If the provision of the object I/O scaffolding becomes tedious, a template might help:

```
template<class T> class Io : public T, public Io_obj {
public:
    Io* clone() const { return new Io(*this); }      // override Io_obj::clone()

    Io(istream&);                                    // initialize from input stream

    static Io* new_io(istream& s) { return new Io(s); }
    // ...
};
```

Given this, we can define *Io_circle*:

```
typedef Io<Circle> Io_circle;
```

We still need to define *Io<Circle>* :: *Io* (*istream&*) explicitly, though, because it needs to know about the details of *Circle*.

The *Io* template is an example of a way to fit concrete types into a class hierarchy by providing a handle that is a node in that hierarchy. It derives from its template parameter to allow casting from *Io_obj*. Unfortunately, this precludes using *Io* for a built-in type:

```
typedef Io<Date> Io_date;      // wrap concrete type
typedef Io<int> Io_int;        // error: cannot derive from built-in type
```

This problem can be handled by providing a separate template for built-in types or by using a class representing a built-in type (§25.10[1]).

This simple object I/O system may not do everything anyone ever wanted, but it almost fits on a single page and the key mechanisms have many uses. In general, these techniques can be used to invoke a function based on a string supplied by a user and to manipulate objects of unknown type through interfaces discovered through run-time type identification.

25.5 Actions

The simplest and most obvious way to specify an action in C++ is to write a function. However, if an action has to be delayed, has to be transmitted "elsewhere" before being performed, requires its own data, has to be combined with other actions (§25.10[18,19]), etc., then it often becomes attractive to provide the action in the form of a class that can execute the desired action and provide other services as well. A function object used with the standard algorithms is an obvious example

(§18.4), and so are the manipulators used with *iostream*s (§21.4.6). In the former case, the actual action is performed by the application operator, and in the latter case, by the << or >> operators. In the case of *Form* (§21.4.6.3) and *Matrix* (§22.4.7), compositor classes were used to delay execution until sufficient information had been gathered for efficient execution.

A common form of action class is a simple class containing just one virtual function (typically called something like "do_it"):

```
struct Action {
      virtual int do_it (int) = 0;
      virtual ~Action () { }
};
```

Given this, we can write code – say a menu – that can store actions for later execution without using pointers to functions, without knowing anything about the objects invoked, and without even knowing the name of the operation it invokes. For example:

```
class Write_file : public Action {
      File& f;
public:
      int do_it (int) { return f.write () .succeed (); }
};

class Error_response : public Action {
      string message;
public:
      Error_response (const string& s) : message (s) { }
      int do_it (int);
};

int Error_response :: do_it (int)
{
      Response_box db (message . c_str (), "continue", "cancel", "retry");

      switch (db . get_response ()) {
      case 0:
            return 0;
      case 1:
            abort ();
      case 2:
            current_operation . redo ();
            return 1;
      }
}

Action* actions [] = {
      new Write_file (f),
      new Error_response ("you blew it again"),
      // ...
};
```

A user of *Action* can be completely insulated from any knowledge of derived classes such as *Write_file* and *Error_response*.

This is a powerful technique that should be treated with some care by people with a background in functional decomposition. If too many classes start looking like *Action*, the overall design of the system may have deteriorated into something unduly functional.

Finally, a class can encode an operation for execution on a remote machine or for storage for future use (§25.10[18]).

25.6 Interface Classes

One of the most important kinds of classes is the humble and mostly overlooked interface class. An interface class doesn't do much − if it did, it wouldn't be an interface class. It simply adjusts the appearance of some service to local needs. Because it is impossible in principle to serve all needs equally well all the time, interface classes are essential to allow sharing without forcing all users into a common straitjacket.

The purest form of an interface doesn't even cause any code to be generated. Consider the *Vector* specialization from §13.5:

```
template<class T> class Vector<T*> : private Vector<void*> {
public:
    typedef Vector<void*> Base;

    Vector() : Base() {}
    Vector(int i) : Base(i) {}

    T*& operator[](int i) { return static_cast<T*&>(Base::operator[](i)); }

    // ...
};
```

This (partial) specialization turns the unsafe *Vector<void*>* into a much more useful family of type-safe vector classes. Inline functions are often essential for making interface classes affordable. In cases such as this, when an inline forwarding function does only type adjustment, there is no added overhead in time or space.

Naturally, an abstract base class representing an abstract type implemented by concrete types (§25.2) is a form of interface class, as are the handles from §25.7. However, here we will focus on classes that have no more specific function than adjusting an interface.

Consider the problem of merging two hierarchies using multiple inheritance. What can be done if there is a name clash, that is, two classes have used the same name for virtual functions performing completely different operations? For example, consider a Wild-West videogame in which user interactions are handled by a general window class:

```
class Window {
    // ...
    virtual void draw(); // display image
};

class Cowboy {
    // ...
    virtual void draw(); // pull gun from holster
};
```

```
class Cowboy_window : public Cowboy, public Window {
    // ...
};
```

A *Cowboy_window* represents the animation of a cowboy in the game and handles the user/player's interactions with the cowboy character. We would prefer to use multiple inheritance, rather than declaring either the *Window* or the *Cowboy* as members, because there will be many service functions defined for both *Window*s and *Cowboy*s. We would like to pass a *Cowboy_window* to such functions without special actions required by the programmer. However, this leads to a problem defining *Cowboy_window* versions of *Cowboy::draw()* and *Window::draw()*.

There can be only one function defined in *Cowboy_window* called *draw()*. Yet because service functions manipulate *Window*s and *Cowboy*s without knowledge of *Cowboy_window*s, *Cowboy_window* must override both *Cowboy*'s *draw()* and *Window*'s *draw()*. Overriding both functions by a single *draw()* function would be wrong because, despite the common name, the *draw()* functions are unrelated and cannot be redefined by a common function.

Finally, we would also like *Cowboy_window* to have distinct, unambiguous names for the inherited functions *Cowboy::draw()* and *Window::draw()*.

To solve this problem, we need to introduce an extra class for *Cowboy* and an extra class for *Window*. These classes introduce the two new names for the *draw()* functions and ensure that a call of the *draw()* functions in *Cowboy* and *Window* calls the functions with the new names:

```
class CCowboy : public Cowboy {          // interface to Cowboy renaming draw()
public:
    virtual int cow_draw() = 0;
    void draw() { cow_draw(); }          // override Cowboy::draw()
};
class WWindow : public Window {          // interface to Window renaming draw()
public:
    virtual int win_draw() = 0;
    void draw() { win_draw(); }          // override Window::draw()
};
```

We can now compose a *Cowboy_window* from the interface classes *CCowboy* and *WWindow* and override *cow_draw()* and *win_draw()* with the desired effect:

```
class Cowboy_window : public CCowboy, public WWindow {
    // ...
    void cow_draw();
    void win_draw();
};
```

Note that this problem was serious only because the two *draw()* functions have the same argument type. If they have different argument types, the usual overloading resolution rules will ensure that no problem manifests itself despite the unrelated functions having the same name.

For each use of an interface class, one could imagine a special-purpose language extension that could perform the desired adjustment a little bit more efficiently or a little more elegantly. However, each use of an interface class is infrequent and supporting them all with specialized language constructs would impose a prohibitive burden of complexity. In particular, name clashes arising from the merging of class hierarchies are not common (compared with how often a programmer will write a class) and tend to arise from the merging of hierarchies generated from dissimilar cultures – such as games and window systems. Merging such dissimilar hierarchies is not easy, and resolving name clashes will more often than not be the least of the programmer's problems. Other problems include dissimilar error handling, dissimilar initialization, and dissimilar memory-management strategies. The resolution of name clashes is discussed here because the technique of introducing an interface class with a forwarding function has many other applications. It can be used not only to change names, but also to change argument and return types, to introduce run-time checking, etc.

Because the forwarding functions *CCowboy::draw()* and *WWindow::draw()* are virtual functions, they cannot be optimized away by simple inlining. It is, however, possible for a compiler to recognize them as simple forwarding functions and then optimize them out of the call chains that go through them.

25.6.1 Adjusting Interfaces

A major use of interface functions is to adjust an interface to match users' expectations better, thus moving code that would have been scattered throughout a user's code into an interface. For example, the standard *vector* is zero-based. Users who want ranges other than *0* to *size-1* must adjust their usage. For example:

```
void f()
{
    vector v<int>(10);         // range [0:9]

    // pretend v is in the range [1:10]:

    for (int i = 1; i<=10; i++) {
        v[i-1] = 7;       // remember to adjust index
        // ...
    }
}
```

A better way is to provide a *vector* with arbitrary bounds:

```
class Vector : public vector<int> {
      int lb;
public:
      Vector(int low, int high) : vector<int>(high-low+1) { lb=low; }

      int& operator[](int i) { return vector<int>::operator[](i-lb); }

      int low() { return lb; }
      int high() { return lb+size()-1; }
};
```

A *Vector* can be used like this:

```
void g()
{
    Vector v(1,10);             // range [1:10]

    for (int i = 1; i<=10; i++) {
        v[i] = 7;
        // ...
    }
}
```

This imposes no overhead compared to the previous example. Clearly, the *Vector* version is easier to read and write and is less error-prone.

Interface classes are usually rather small and (by definition) do rather little. However, they crop up wherever software written according to different traditions needs to cooperate because then there is a need to mediate between different conventions. For example, interface classes are often used to provide C++ interfaces to non-C++ code and to insulate application code from the details of libraries (to leave open the possibility of replacing the library with another).

Another important use of interface classes is to provide checked or restricted interfaces. For example, it is not uncommon to have integer variables that are supposed to have values in a given range only. This can be enforced (at run time) by a simple template:

```
template<int low, int high> class Range {
    int val;
public:
    class Error { }; // exception class

    Range(int i) { Assert<Error>(low<=i&&i<high); val = i; } // see §24.3.7.2
    Range operator=(int i) { return *this=Range(i); }

    operator int() { return val; }
    // ...
};

void f(Range<2,17>);
void g(Range<-10,10>);

void h(int x)
{
    Range<0,2001> i = x;       // might throw Range::Error
    int i1 = i;

    f(3);
    f(17);                     // throws Range::Error
    g(-7);
    g(100);                    // throws Range::Error
}
```

The *Range* template is easily extended to handle ranges of arbitrary scalar types (§25.10[7]).

An interface class that controls access to another class or adjusts its interface is sometimes called a *wrapper*.

25.7 Handle Classes

An abstract type provides an effective separation between an interface and its implementations. However, as used in §25.3 the connection between an interface provided by an abstract type and its implementation provided by a concrete type is permanent. For example, it is not possible to rebind an abstract iterator from one source – say, a set – to another – say, a stream – once the original source becomes exhausted.

Furthermore, unless one manipulates an object implementing an abstract class through pointers or references, the benefits of virtual functions are lost. User code may become dependent on details of the implementation classes because an abstract type cannot be allocated statically or on the stack (including being accepted as a by-value argument) without its size being known. Using pointers and references implies that the burden of memory management falls on the user.

Another limitation of the abstract class approach is that a class object is of fixed size. Classes, however, are used to represent concepts that require varying amounts of storage to implement them.

A popular technique for dealing with these issues is to separate what is used as a single object into two parts: a handle providing the user interface and a representation holding all or most of the object's state. The connection between the handle and the representation is typically a pointer in the handle. Often, handles have a bit more data than the simple representation pointer, but not much more. This implies that the layout of a handle is typically stable even when the representation changes and also that handles are small enough to move around relatively freely so that pointers and references need not be used by the user.

The *String* from §11.12 is a simple example of a handle. The handle provides an interface to, access control for, and memory management for the representation. In this case, both the handle and the representation are concrete types, but the representation class is often an abstract class.

Consider the abstract type *Set* from §25.3. How could one provide a handle for it, and what benefits and cost would that involve? Given a set class, one might simply define a handle by overloading the –> operator:

```
template<class T> class Set_handle {
    Set<T>* rep;
public:
    Set<T>* operator->() { return rep; }

    Set_handle(Set<T>* pp) : rep(pp) { }
};
```

This doesn't significantly affect the way *Set*s are used; one simply passes *Set_handle*s around instead of *Set*&s or *Set**s. For example:

```
void f(Set_handle<int> s)
{
    for (int* p = s->first(); p; p = s->next())
    {
        // ...
    }
}

void user()
{
    Set_handle<int> sl(new List_set<int>);
    Set_handle<int> v(new Vector_set<int>(100));

    f(sl);
    f(v);
}
```

Often, we want a handle to do more than just provide access. For example, if the *Set* class and the *Set_handle* class are designed together it is easy to do reference counting by including a use count in each *Set*. In general, we do not want to design a handle together with what it is a handle to, so we will have to store any information that needs to be shared by a handle in a separate object. In other words, we would like to have non-intrusive handles in addition to the intrusive ones. For example, here is a handle that removes an object when its last handle goes away:

```
template<class X> class Handle {
    X* rep;
    int* pcount;
public:
    X* operator->() { return rep; }

    Handle(X* pp) : rep(pp), pcount(new int(1)) { }
    Handle(const Handle& r) : rep(r.rep), pcount(r.pcount) { (*pcount)++; }

    Handle& operator=(const Handle& r)
    {
        if (rep == r.rep) return *this;
        if (--(*pcount) == 0) {
            delete rep;
            delete pcount;
        }
        rep = r.rep;
        pcount = r.pcount;
        (*pcount)++;
        return *this;
    }

    ~Handle() { if (--(*pcount) == 0) { delete rep; delete pcount; } }

    // ...
};
```

Such a handle can be passed around freely. For example:

```
void f1 (Handle<Set>) ;

Handle<Set> f2 ( )
{
    Handle<Set> h (new List_set<int>) ;
    // ...
    return  h ;
}

void  g ( )
{
    Handle<Set> hh = f2 ( ) ;
    f1 (hh) ;
    // ...
}
```

Here, the set created in *f2* ( ) will be deleted upon exit from *g* ( ) − unless *f1* ( ) held on to a copy; the programmer does not need to know.

Naturally, this convenience comes at a cost, but for many applications the cost of storing and maintaining the use count is acceptable.

Sometimes, it is useful to extract the representation pointer from a handle and use it directly. For example, this would be needed to pass an object to a function that does not know about handles. This works nicely provided the called function does not destroy the object passed to it or store a pointer to it for use after returning to its caller. An operation for rebinding a handle to a new representation can also be useful:

```
template<class X> class Handle {
    // ...

    X* get_rep ( ) { return  rep ; }

    void bind (X* pp)
    {
        if (pp != rep) {
            if (--*pcount == 0) {
                delete  rep ;
                *pcount = 1 ;                  // recycle pcount
            }
            else
                pcount = new int (1) ;      // new pcount
            rep = pp ;
        }
    }
} ;
```

Note that derivation of new classes from *Handle* isn't particularly useful. It is a concrete type without virtual functions. The idea is to have one handle class for a family of classes defined by a base class. Derivation from this base class can be a powerful technique. It applies to node classes as well as to abstract types.

As written, *Handle* doesn't deal with inheritance. To get a class that acts like a genuine use-counted pointer, *Handle* needs to be combined with *Ptr* from §13.6.3.1 (see §25.10[2]).

A handle that provides an interface that is close to identical to the class for which it is a handle is often called a *proxy*. This is particularly common for handles that refer to an object on a remote machine.

25.7.1 Operations in Handles

Overloading -> enables a handle to gain control and do some work on each access to an object. For example, one could collect statistics about the number of uses of the object accessed through a handle:

```
template <class T> class Xhandle {
    T* rep;
    int no_of_accesses;
public:
    T* operator->() { no_of_accesses++; return rep; }

    // ...
};
```

Handles for which work needs to be done both before *and* after access require more elaborate programming. For example, one might want a set with locking while an insertion or a removal is being done. Essentially, the representation class' interface needs to be replicated in the handle class:

```
template<class T> class Set_controller {
    Set<T>* rep;
    Lock lock;
    // ...
public:
    void insert(T* p) { Lock_ptr x(lock); rep->insert(p); }  // see §14.4.1
    void remove(T* p) { Lock_ptr x(lock); rep->remove(p); }

    int is_member(T* p) { return rep->is_member(p); }

    T get_first() { T* p = rep->first(); return p ? *p : T(); }
    T get_next() { T* p = rep->next(); return p ? *p : T(); }

    T first() { Lock_ptr x(lock); T tmp = *rep->first(); return tmp; }
    T next() { Lock_ptr x(lock); T tmp = *rep->next(); return tmp; }

    // ...
};
```

Providing these forwarding functions is tedious (and therefore somewhat error-prone), although it is neither difficult nor costly in run time.

Note that only some of the *Set* functions required locking. In my experience, it is typical that a class needing pre- and post-actions requires them for only some member functions. In the case of locking, locking on all operations − as is done for monitors in some systems − leads to excess locking and sometimes causes a noticeable decrease in concurrency.

An advantage of the elaborate definition of all operations on the handle over the overloading of
-> style of handles is that it is possible to derive from class *Set_controller*. Unfortunately, some
of the benefits of being a handle are compromised if data members are added in the derived class.
In particular, the amount of code shared (in the handled class) decreases compared to the amount of
code written in each handle.

25.8 Application Frameworks

Components built out of the kinds of classes described in §25.2–§25.7 support design and reuse of
code by supplying building blocks and ways of combining them; the application builder designs a
framework into which these common building blocks are fitted. An alternative, and sometimes
more ambitious, approach to the support of design and reuse is to provide code that establishes a
common framework into which the application builder fits application-specific code as building
blocks. Such an approach is often called an *application framework*. The classes establishing such
a framework often have such fat interfaces that they are hardly types in the traditional sense. They
approximate the ideal of being complete applications, except that they don't do anything. The specific actions are supplied by the application programmer.

As an example, consider a filter, that is, a program that reads an input stream, (maybe) performs
some actions based on that input, (maybe) produces an output stream, and (maybe) produces a final
result. A naive framework for such programs would provide a set of operations that an application
programmer might supply:

```
class  Filter {
public:
      class  Retry {
      public:
            virtual  const  char*  message () { return  0; }
      } ;

      virtual  void  start () { }
      virtual  int  read () = 0;
      virtual  void  write () { }
      virtual  void  compute () { }
      virtual  int  result () = 0;

      virtual  int  retry (Retry& m)  { cerr << m.message () << '\n'; return  2; }

      virtual  ~Filter () { }
} ;
```

Functions that a derived class must supply are declared pure virtual; other functions are simply
defined to do nothing.

The framework also provides a main loop and a rudimentary error-handling mechanism:

```
int main_loop (Filter* p)
{
    for(;;) {
        try {
            p->start();
            while (p->read()) {
                p->compute();
                p->write();
            }
            return p->result();
        }
        catch (Filter::Retry& m) {
            if (int i = p->retry(m)) return i;
        }
        catch ( ... ) {
            cerr << "Fatal filter error\n";
            return 1;
        }
    }
}
```

Finally, I could write my program like this:

```
class My_filter : public Filter {
    istream& is;
    ostream& os;
    int nchar;
public:
    int read() { char c; is.get(c); return is.good(); }
    void compute() { nchar++; }
    int result() { os << nchar << " characters read\n"; return 0; }

    My_filter(istream& ii, ostream& oo) : is(ii), os(oo), nchar(0) { }
};
```

and activate it like this:

```
int main()
{
    My_filter f(cin, cout);
    return main_loop(&f);
}
```

Naturally, for a framework to be of significant use, it must provide more structure and many more services than this simple example does. In particular, a framework is typically a hierarchy of node classes. Having the application programmer supply leaf classes in a deeply nested hierarchy allows commonality between applications and reuse of services provided by such a hierarchy. A framework will also be supported by a library that provides classes that are useful for the application programmer when specifying the action classes.

25.9 Advice

[1]   Make conscious decisions about how a class is to be used (both as a designer and as a user); §25.1.

[2]   Be aware of the tradeoffs involved among the different kinds of classes; §25.1.

[3]   Use concrete types to represent simple independent concepts; §25.2.

[4]   Use concrete types to represent concepts where close-to-optimal efficiency is essential; §25.2.

[5]   Don't derive from a concrete class; §25.2.

[6]   Use abstract classes to represent interfaces where the representation of objects might change; §25.3.

[7]   Use abstract classes to represent interfaces where different representations of objects need to coexist; §25.3.

[8]   Use abstract classes to represent new interfaces to existing types; §25.3.

[9]   Use node classes where similar concepts share significant implementation details; §25.4.

[10] Use node classes to incrementally augment an implementation; §25.4.

[11] Use Run-time Type Identification to obtain interfaces from an object; §25.4.1.

[12] Use classes to represent actions with associated state; §25.5.

[13] Use classes to represent actions that need to be stored, transmitted, or delayed; §25.5.

[14] Use interface classes to adapt a class for a new kind of use (without modifying the class); §25.6.

[15] Use interface classes to add checking; §25.6.1.

[16] Use handles to avoid direct use of pointers and references; §25.7.

[17] Use handles to manage shared representations; §25.7.

[18] Use an application framework where an application domain allows for the control structure to be predefined; §25.8.

25.10 Exercises

1. (*1) The *Io* template from §25.4.1 does not work for built-in types. Modify it so that it does.

2. (*1.5) The *Handle* template from §25.7 does not reflect inheritance relationships of the classes for which it is a handle. Modify it so that it does. That is, you should be able to assign a *Handle<Circle>* to a *Handle<Shape>* but not the other way around.

3. (*2.5) Given a *String* class, define another string class using it as the representation and providing its operations as virtual functions. Compare the performance of the two classes. Try to find a meaningful class that is best implemented by publicly deriving from the string with virtual functions.

4. (*4) Study two widely used libraries. Classify the library classes in terms of concrete types, abstract types, node classes, handle classes, and interface classes. Are abstract node classes and concrete node classes used? Is there a more appropriate classification for the classes in these libraries? Are fat interfaces used? What facilities – if any – are provided for run-time type information? What is the memory-management strategy?

5. (*2) Use the *Filter* framework (§25.8) to implement a program that removes adjacent duplicate words from an input stream but otherwise copies the input to output.

6. (*2) Use the *Filter* framework to implement a program that counts the frequency of words on

an input stream and produces a list of (word,count) pairs in frequency order as output.

7. (∗1.5) Write a *Range* template that takes both the range and the element type as template parameters.

8. (∗1) Write a *Range* template that takes the range as constructor arguments.

9. (∗2) Write a simple string class that performs no error checking. Write another class that checks access to the first. Discuss the pros and cons of separating basic function and checking for errors.

10. (∗2.5) Implement the object I/O system from §25.4.1 for a few types, including at least integers, strings, and a class hierarchy of your choice.

11. (∗2.5) Define a class *Storable* as an abstract base class with virtual functions *write_out* ( ) and *read_in* ( ). For simplicity, assume that a character string is sufficient to specify a permanent storage location. Use class *Storable* to provide a facility for writing objects of classes derived from *Storable* to disk, and for reading such objects from disk. Test it with a couple of classes of your own choice.

12. (∗4) Define a base class *Persistent* with operations *save* ( ) and *no_save* ( ) that control whether an object is written to permanent storage by a destructor. In addition to *save* ( ) and *no_save* ( ), what operations could *Persistent* usefully provide? Test class *Persistent* with a couple of classes of your own choice. Is *Persistent* a node class, a concrete type, or an abstract type? Why?

13. (∗3) Write a class *Stack* for which it is possible to change implementation at run time. Hint: "Every problem is solved by yet another indirection."

14. (∗3.5) Define a class *Oper* that holds an identifier of type *Id* (maybe a *string* or a C-style string) and an operation (a pointer to function or some function object). Define a class *Cat_object* that holds a list of *Oper*s and a *void**. Provide *Cat_object* with operations *add_oper* (*Oper*), which adds an *Oper* to the list; *remove_oper* (*Id*), which removes an *Oper* identified by *Id* from the list; and an *operator* ( ) (*Id*, *arg*), which invokes the *Oper* identified by *Id*. Implement a stack of *Cat*s by a *Cat_object*. Write a small program to exercise these classes.

15. (∗3) Define a template *Object* based on class *Cat_object*. Use *Object* to implement a stack of *String*s. Write a small program to exercise this template.

16. (∗2.5) Define a variant of class *Object* called *Class* that ensures that objects with identical operations share a list of operations. Write a small program to exercise this template.

17. (∗2) Define a *Stack* template that provides a conventional and type-safe interface to a stack implemented by the *Object* template. Compare this stack to the stack classes found in the previous exercises. Write a small program to exercise this template.

18. (∗3) Write a class for representing operations to be shipped to another computer to execute there. Test it either by actually sending commands to another machine or by writing commands to a file and then executing the commands read from the file.

19. (∗2) Write a class for composing operations represented as function objects. Given two function objects *f* and *g*, *Compose* (*f*, *g*) should make an object that can be invoked with an argument *x* suitable for *g* and return $f(g(x))$, provided the return value of *g* ( ) is an acceptable argument type for *f* ( ).

Appendices and Index

These Appendices provide the C++ grammar, a discussion of compatibility issues that arise between C++ and C and between Standard C++ and prestandard versions of C++, and a variety of language-technical details. The index is extensive and considered an integral part of the book.

Chapters

A Grammar
B Compatibility
C Technicalities
I Index

Appendix **A**

Grammar

There is no worse danger for a teacher
than to teach words instead of things.
– Marc Block

Introduction — keywords — lexical conventions — programs — expressions — statements — declarations — declarators — classes — derived classes — special member functions — overloading — templates — exception handling — preprocessing directives.

A.1 Introduction

This summary of C++ syntax is intended to be an aid to comprehension. It is not an exact statement of the language. In particular, the grammar described here accepts a superset of valid C++ constructs. Disambiguation rules (§A.5, §A.7) must be applied to distinguish expressions from declarations. Moreover, access control, ambiguity, and type rules must be used to weed out syntactically valid but meaningless constructs.

The C and C++ standard grammars express very minor distinctions syntactically rather than through constraints. That gives precision, but it doesn't always improve readability.

A.2 Keywords

New context-dependent keywords are introduced into a program by *typedef* (§4.9.7), namespace (§8.2), class (Chapter 10), enumeration (§4.8), and *template* (Chapter 13) declarations.

> *typedef-name:*
>   *identifier*

namespace-name:
    original-namespace-name
    namespace-alias

original-namespace-name:
    identifier

namespace-alias:
    identifier

class-name:
    identifier
    template-id

enum-name:
    identifier

template-name:
    identifier

Note that a *typedef-name* naming a class is also a *class-name.*

Unless an identifier is explicitly declared to name a type, it is assumed to name something that is not a type (see §C.13.5).

The C++ keywords are:

C++ Keywords					
and	*and_eq*	*asm*	*auto*	*bitand*	*bitor*
bool	*break*	*case*	*catch*	*char*	*class*
compl	*const*	*const_cast*	*continue*	*default*	*delete*
do	*double*	*dynamic_cast*	*else*	*enum*	*explicit*
export	*extern*	*false*	*float*	*for*	*friend*
goto	*if*	*inline*	*int*	*long*	*mutable*
namespace	*new*	*not*	*not_eq*	*operator*	*or*
or_eq	*private*	*protected*	*public*	*register*	*reinterpret_cast*
return	*short*	*signed*	*sizeof*	*static*	*static_cast*
struct	*switch*	*template*	*this*	*throw*	*true*
try	*typedef*	*typeid*	*typename*	*union*	*unsigned*
using	*virtual*	*void*	*volatile*	*wchar_t*	*while*
xor	*xor_eq*				

A.3 Lexical Conventions

The standard C and C++ grammars present lexical conventions as grammar productions. This adds precision but also makes for large grammars and doesn't always increase readability:

hex-quad:
    hexadecimal-digit hexadecimal-digit hexadecimal-digit hexadecimal-digit

universal-character-name:
>   \u *hex-quad*
>   \U *hex-quad hex-quad*

preprocessing-token:
>   *header-name*
>   *identifier*
>   *pp-number*
>   *character-literal*
>   *string-literal*
>   *preprocessing-op-or-punc*
>   *each non-white-space character that cannot be one of the above*

token:
>   *identifier*
>   *keyword*
>   *literal*
>   *operator*
>   *punctuator*

header-name:
>   *<h-char-sequence>*
>   *"q-char-sequence"*

h-char-sequence:
>   *h-char*
>   *h-char-sequence h-char*

h-char:
>   *any member of the source character set except new-line and >*

q-char-sequence:
>   *q-char*
>   *q-char-sequence q-char*

q-char:
>   *any member of the source character set except new-line and "*

pp-number:
>   *digit*
>   *. digit*
>   *pp-number digit*
>   *pp-number nondigit*
>   *pp-number* e *sign*
>   *pp-number* E *sign*
>   *pp-number .*

identifier:
>   *nondigit*
>   *identifier nondigit*
>   *identifier digit*

nondigit: one of
 universal-character-name
 _ a b c d e f g h i j k l m n o p q r s t u v w x y z
  A B C D E F G H I J K L M N O P Q R S T U V W X Y Z

digit: one of
 0 1 2 3 4 5 6 7 8 9

preprocessing-op-or-punc: one of

{	}	[	]	#	##	(	)	<:	:>	<%	%>	%:%:
%:	;	:	?	::	.	.*	+	–	*	/	%	^
&	|	~	!	=	<	>	+=	–=	*=	/=	%=	^=
&=	|=	<<=	>>=	<<	>>	==	!=	<=	>=	&&	||	++
––	,	–>	–>*	...	new	delete	and	and_eq		bitand		
bitor		compl		not	or	not_eq	xor	or_eq		xor_eq		

literal:
 integer-literal
 character-literal
 floating-literal
 string-literal
 boolean-literal

integer-literal:
 decimal-literal integer-suffix$_{opt}$
 octal-literal integer-suffix$_{opt}$
 hexadecimal-literal integer-suffix$_{opt}$

decimal-literal:
 nonzero-digit
 decimal-literal digit

octal-literal:
 0
 octal-literal octal-digit

hexadecimal-literal:
 0x *hexadecimal-digit*
 0X *hexadecimal-digit*
 hexadecimal-literal hexadecimal-digit

nonzero-digit: one of
 1 2 3 4 5 6 7 8 9

octal-digit: one of
 0 1 2 3 4 5 6 7

hexadecimal-digit: one of
 0 1 2 3 4 5 6 7 8 9
 a b c d e f
 A B C D E F

integer-suffix:
    unsigned-suffix long-suffix$_{opt}$
    long-suffix unsigned-suffix$_{opt}$

unsigned-suffix: one of
    u U

long-suffix: one of
    l L

character-literal:
    ' c-char-sequence '
    L*' c-char-sequence '*

c-char-sequence:
    c-char
    c-char-sequence c-char

c-char:
    any member of the source character set except the single-quote, backslash, or new-line character
    escape-sequence
    universal-character-name

escape-sequence:
    simple-escape-sequence
    octal-escape-sequence
    hexadecimal-escape-sequence

simple-escape-sequence: one of
    \' \" \? \\ \a \b \f \n \r \t \v

octal-escape-sequence:
    \ *octal-digit*
    \ *octal-digit octal-digit*
    \ *octal-digit octal-digit octal-digit*

hexadecimal-escape-sequence:
    \x *hexadecimal-digit*
    hexadecimal-escape-sequence hexadecimal-digit

floating-literal:
    fractional-constant exponent-part$_{opt}$ floating-suffix$_{opt}$
    digit-sequence exponent-part floating-suffix$_{opt}$

fractional-constant:
    digit-sequence$_{opt}$. digit-sequence
    digit-sequence .

exponent-part:
    e *sign$_{opt}$ digit-sequence*
    E *sign$_{opt}$ digit-sequence*

sign: one of
    + −

digit-sequence:
digit
digit-sequence digit

floating-suffix: one of
`f l F L`

string-literal:
`"`*s-char-sequence$_{opt}$*`"`
`L"`*s-char-sequence$_{opt}$*`"`

s-char-sequence:
s-char
s-char-sequence s-char

s-char:
any member of the source character set except double-quote, backslash , or new-line
escape-sequence
universal-character-name

boolean-literal:
`false`
`true`

A.4 Programs

A program is a collection of *translation-units* combined through linking (§9.4). A *translation-unit*, often called a *source file*, is a sequence of *declarations*:

translation-unit:
declaration-seq$_{opt}$

A.5 Expressions

Expressions are described in Chapter 6 and summarized in §6.2. The definition of *expression-list* is identical to that of *expression*. There are two rules to dinstinguish the function-argument comma separator from the comma (sequencing) operator (§6.2.2).

primary-expression:
literal
`this`
`::` *identifier*
`::` *operator-function-id*
`::` *qualified-id*
`(` *expression* `)`
id-expression

id-expression:
    unqualified-id
    qualified-id

unqualified-id:
    identifier
    operator-function-id
    conversion-function-id
    ~ *class-name*
    template-id

qualified-id:
    nested-name-specifier `template`$_{opt}$ *unqualified-id*

nested-name-specifier:
    class-or-namespace-name `::` *nested-name-specifier*$_{opt}$
    class-or-namespace-name `::` `template` *nested-name-specifier*

class-or-namespace-name:
    class-name
    namespace-name

postfix-expression:
    primary-expression
    postfix-expression [*expression*]
    postfix-expression (*expression-list*$_{opt}$)
    simple-type-specifier (*expression-list*$_{opt}$)
    `typename` `::`$_{opt}$ *nested-name-specifier identifier* (*expression-list*$_{opt}$)
    `typename` `::`$_{opt}$ *nested-name-specifier* `template`$_{opt}$ *template-id* (*expression-list*$_{opt}$)
    postfix-expression . `template`$_{opt}$ `::`$_{opt}$ *id-expression*
    postfix-expression -> `template`$_{opt}$ `::`$_{opt}$ *id-expression*
    postfix-expression . *pseudo-destructor-name*
    postfix-expression -> *pseudo-destructor-name*
    postfix-expression ++
    postfix-expression --
    `dynamic_cast` < *type-id* > (*expression*)
    `static_cast` < *type-id* > (*expression*)
    `reinterpret_cast` < *type-id* > (*expression*)
    `const_cast` < *type-id* > (*expression*)
    `typeid` (*expression*)
    `typeid` (*type-id*)

expression-list:
    assignment-expression
    expression-list , *assignment-expression*

pseudo-destructor-name:
    `::`$_{opt}$ *nested-name-specifier*$_{opt}$ *type-name* `::` ~ *type-name*
    `::`$_{opt}$ *nested-name-specifier* `template` *template-id* `::` ~ *type-name*
    `::`$_{opt}$ *nested-name-specifier*$_{opt}$ ~ *type-name*

unary-expression:
    postfix-expression
    `++` *cast-expression*
    `--` *cast-expression*
    unary-operator cast-expression
    `sizeof` *unary-expression*
    `sizeof` (*type-id*)
    new-expression
    delete-expression

unary-operator: one of
    `*`   `&`   `+`   `-`   `!`   `~`

new-expression:
    `::`$_{opt}$ `new` *new-placement*$_{opt}$ *new-type-id new-initializer*$_{opt}$
    `::`$_{opt}$ `new` *new-placement*$_{opt}$ (*type-id*) *new-initializer*$_{opt}$

new-placement:
    (*expression-list*)

new-type-id:
    type-specifier-seq new-declarator$_{opt}$

new-declarator:
    ptr-operator new-declarator$_{opt}$
    direct-new-declarator

direct-new-declarator:
    [*expression*]
    direct-new-declarator [*constant-expression*]

new-initializer:
    (*expression-list*$_{opt}$)

delete-expression:
    `::`$_{opt}$ `delete` *cast-expression*
    `::`$_{opt}$ `delete` [ ] *cast-expression*

cast-expression:
    unary-expression
    (*type-id*) *cast-expression*

pm-expression:
    cast-expression
    pm-expression `.*` *cast-expression*
    pm-expression `->*` *cast-expression*

multiplicative-expression:
    pm-expression
    multiplicative-expression `*` *pm-expression*
    multiplicative-expression `/` *pm-expression*
    multiplicative-expression `%` *pm-expression*

additive-expression:
    multiplicative-expression
    additive-expression + multiplicative-expression
    additive-expression – multiplicative-expression

shift-expression:
    additive-expression
    shift-expression << additive-expression
    shift-expression >> additive-expression

relational-expression:
    shift-expression
    relational-expression < shift-expression
    relational-expression > shift-expression
    relational-expression <= shift-expression
    relational-expression >= shift-expression

equality-expression:
    relational-expression
    equality-expression == relational-expression
    equality-expression != relational-expression

and-expression:
    equality-expression
    and-expression & equality-expression

exclusive-or-expression:
    and-expression
    exclusive-or-expression ^ and-expression

inclusive-or-expression:
    exclusive-or-expression
    inclusive-or-expression | exclusive-or-expression

logical-and-expression:
    inclusive-or-expression
    logical-and-expression && inclusive-or-expression

logical-or-expression:
    logical-and-expression
    logical-or-expression || logical-and-expression

conditional-expression:
    logical-or-expression
    logical-or-expression ? expression : assignment-expression

assignment-expression:
    conditional-expression
    logical-or-expression assignment-operator assignment-expression
    throw-expression

assignment-operator: one of
    = *= /= %= += -= >>= <<= &= ^= |=

expression:
    assignment-expression
    expression , assignment-expression

constant-expression:
    conditional-expression

Grammar ambiguities arise from the similarity between function style casts and declarations. For example:

int x;

void f( )
{
    char(x);   // conversion of x to char or declaration of a char called x?
}

All such ambiguities are resolved to declarations. That is, "if it could possibly be interpreted as a declaration, it is a declaration." For example:

T(a)->m;	*// expression statement*
T(a)++;	*// expression statement*
*T(*e)(int(3));*	*// declaration*
T(f)[4];	*// declaration*
T(a);	*// declaration*
T(a)=m;	*// declaration*
*T(*b)();*	*// declaration*
T(x),y,z=7;	*// declaration*

This disambiguation is purely syntactic. The only information used for a name is whether it is known to be a name of a type or a name of a template. If that cannot be determined, the name is assumed to name something that isn't a template or a type.

The construct *template unqualified-id* is used to state that the *unqualified-id* is the name of a template in a context in which that cannot be deduced (see §C.13.6).

A.6 Statements

See §6.3.

statement:
    labeled-statement
    expression-statement
    compound-statement
    selection-statement
    iteration-statement
    jump-statement
    declaration-statement
    try-block

labeled-statement:
  identifier : *statement*
  `case` *constant-expression* : *statement*
  `default` : *statement*

expression-statement:
  expression$_{opt}$;

compound-statement:
  { *statement-seq$_{opt}$* }

statement-seq:
  statement
  statement-seq statement

selection-statement:
  `if` (*condition*) *statement*
  `if` (*condition*) *statement* `else` *statement*
  `switch` (*condition*) *statement*

condition:
  expression
  type-specifier-seq declarator = *assignment-expression*

iteration-statement:
  `while` (*condition*) *statement*
  `do` *statement* `while` (*expression*) ;
  `for` (*for-init-statement condition$_{opt}$* ; *expression$_{opt}$*) *statement*

for-init-statement:
  expression-statement
  simple-declaration

jump-statement:
  `break` ;
  `continue` ;
  `return` *expression$_{opt}$* ;
  `goto` *identifier* ;

declaration-statement:
  block-declaration

A.7 Declarations

The structure of declarations is described in Chapter 4, enumerations in §4.8, pointers and arrays in Chapter 5, functions in Chapter 7, namespaces in §8.2, linkage directives in §9.2.4, and storage classes in §10.4.

declaration-seq:
  declaration
  declaration-seq declaration

declaration:
> *block-declaration*
> *function-definition*
> *template-declaration*
> *explicit-instantiation*
> *explicit-specialization*
> *linkage-specification*
> *namespace-definition*

block-declaration:
> *simple-declaration*
> *asm-definition*
> *namespace-alias-definition*
> *using-declaration*
> *using-directive*

simple-declaration:
> *decl-specifier-seq$_{opt}$ init-declarator-list$_{opt}$;*

decl-specifier:
> *storage-class-specifier*
> *type-specifier*
> *function-specifier*
> `friend`
> `typedef`

decl-specifier-seq:
> *decl-specifier-seq$_{opt}$ decl-specifier*

storage-class-specifier:
> `auto`
> `register`
> `static`
> `extern`
> `mutable`

function-specifier:
> `inline`
> `virtual`
> `explicit`

typedef-name:
> *identifier*

type-specifier:
> *simple-type-specifier*
> *class-specifier*
> *enum-specifier*
> *elaborated-type-specifier*
> *cv-qualifier*

simple-type-specifier:
    `::`$_{opt}$ *nested-name-specifier*$_{opt}$ *type-name*
    `::`$_{opt}$ *nested-name-specifier* `template`$_{opt}$ *template-id*
    char
    wchar_t
    bool
    short
    int
    long
    signed
    unsigned
    float
    double
    void

type-name:
    class-name
    enum-name
    typedef-name

elaborated-type-specifier:
    class-key `::`$_{opt}$ *nested-name-specifier*$_{opt}$ *identifier*
    `enum` `::`$_{opt}$ *nested-name-specifier*$_{opt}$ *identifier*
    `typename` `::`$_{opt}$ *nested-name-specifier* *identifier*
    `typename` `::`$_{opt}$ *nested-name-specifier* `template`$_{opt}$ *template-id*

enum-name:
    identifier

enum-specifier:
    `enum` *identifier*$_{opt}$ `{` *enumerator-list*$_{opt}$ `}`

enumerator-list:
    enumerator-definition
    enumerator-list `,` *enumerator-definition*

enumerator-definition:
    enumerator
    enumerator `=` *constant-expression*

enumerator:
    identifier

namespace-name:
    original-namespace-name
    namespace-alias

original-namespace-name:
    identifier

namespace-definition:
    named-namespace-definition
    unnamed-namespace-definition

named-namespace-definition:
    original-namespace-definition
    extension-namespace-definition

original-namespace-definition:
    `namespace` *identifier* `{` *namespace-body* `}`

extension-namespace-definition:
    `namespace` *original-namespace-name* `{` *namespace-body* `}`

unnamed-namespace-definition:
    `namespace` `{` *namespace-body* `}`

namespace-body:
    declaration-seq$_{opt}$

namespace-alias:
    identifier

namespace-alias-definition:
    `namespace` *identifier* `=` *qualified-namespace-specifier* `;`

qualified-namespace-specifier:
    `::`$_{opt}$ *nested-name-specifier$_{opt}$ namespace-name*

using-declaration:
    `using typename`$_{opt}$ `::`$_{opt}$ *nested-name-specifier unqualified-id* `;`
    `using ::` *unqualified-id* `;`

using-directive:
    `using  namespace ::`$_{opt}$ *nested-name-specifier$_{opt}$ namespace-name* `;`

asm-definition:
    `asm` `(` *string-literal* `)` `;`

linkage-specification:
    `extern` *string-literal* `{` *declaration-seq$_{opt}$* `}`
    `extern` *string-literal declaration*

The grammar allows for arbitrary nesting of declarations. However, some semantic restrictions apply. For example, nested functions (functions defined local to other functions) are not allowed.

The list of specifiers that starts a declaration cannot be empty (there is no "implicit *int*;" §B.2) and consists of the longest possible sequence of specifiers. For example:

typedef int I;
void f(unsigned I) { / ... */ }*

Here, *f*( ) takes an unnamed *unsigned int*.

An *asm* ( ) is an assembly code insert. Its meaning is implementation-defined, but the intent is for the string to be a piece of assembly code that will be inserted into the generated code at the place where it is specified.

Declaring a variable *register* is a hint to the compiler to optimize for frequent access; doing so is redundant with most modern compilers.

A.7.1 Declarators

See §4.9.1, Chapter 5 (pointers and arrays), §7.7 (pointers to functions), and §15.5 (pointers to members).

init-declarator-list:
     init-declarator
     init-declarator-list , *init-declarator*

init-declarator:
     declarator initializer$_{opt}$

declarator:
     direct-declarator
     ptr-operator declarator

direct-declarator:
     declarator-id
     direct-declarator (*parameter-declaration-clause*) *cv-qualifier-seq$_{opt}$ exception-specification$_{opt}$*
     direct-declarator [*constant-expression$_{opt}$*]
     (*declarator*)

ptr-operator:
     * *cv-qualifier-seq$_{opt}$*
     &
     : :$_{opt}$ *nested-name-specifier* * *cv-qualifier-seq$_{opt}$*

cv-qualifier-seq:
     cv-qualifier cv-qualifier-seq$_{opt}$

cv-qualifier:
     const
     volatile

declarator-id:
     : :$_{opt}$ *id-expression*
     : :$_{opt}$ *nested-name-specifier$_{opt}$ type-name*

type-id:
     type-specifier-seq abstract-declarator$_{opt}$

type-specifier-seq:
     type-specifier type-specifier-seq$_{opt}$

abstract-declarator:
     ptr-operator abstract-declarator$_{opt}$
     direct-abstract-declarator

direct-abstract-declarator:
     direct-abstract-declarator$_{opt}$ (*parameter-declaration-clause*) *cv-qualifier-seq$_{opt}$ exception-specification$_{opt}$*
     direct-abstract-declarator$_{opt}$ [*constant-expression$_{opt}$*]
     (*abstract-declarator*)

parameter-declaration-clause:
    parameter-declaration-list$_{opt}$ ... $_{opt}$
    parameter-declaration-list , ...

parameter-declaration-list:
    parameter-declaration
    parameter-declaration-list , *parameter-declaration*

parameter-declaration:
    decl-specifier-seq declarator
    decl-specifier-seq declarator = *assignment-expression*
    decl-specifier-seq abstract-declarator$_{opt}$
    decl-specifier-seq abstract-declarator$_{opt}$ = *assignment-expression*

function-definition:
    decl-specifier-seq$_{opt}$ declarator ctor-initializer$_{opt}$ function-body
    decl-specifier-seq$_{opt}$ declarator function-try-block

function-body:
    compound-statement

initializer:
    = *initializer-clause*
    (*expression-list*)

initializer-clause:
    assignment-expression
    { *initializer-list* , $_{opt}$ }
    { }

initializer-list:
    initializer-clause
    initializer-list , *initializer-clause*

A *volatile* specifier is a hint to a compiler that an object may change its value in ways not specified by the language so that aggressive optimizations must be avoided. For example, a real time clock might be declared:

    extern const volatile clock;

Two successive reads of *clock* might give different results.

A.8 Classes

See Chapter 10.

class-name:
    identifier
    template-id

class-specifier:
    class-head { *member-specification$_{opt}$* }

class-head:
    class-key identifier$_{opt}$ base-clause$_{opt}$
    class-key nested-name-specifier identifier base-clause$_{opt}$
    class-key nested-name-specifier `template` *template-id base-clause$_{opt}$*

class-key:
    `class`
    `struct`
    `union`

member-specification:
    member-declaration   member-specification$_{opt}$
    access-specifier   :   member-specification$_{opt}$

member-declaration:
    decl-specifier-seq$_{opt}$ member-declarator-list$_{opt}$;
    function-definition   ;$_{opt}$
    : :$_{opt}$ nested-name-specifier `template`$_{opt}$ *unqualified-id   ;*
    using-declaration
    template-declaration

member-declarator-list:
    member-declarator
    member-declarator-list   ,   member-declarator

member-declarator:
    declarator pure-specifier$_{opt}$
    declarator constant-initializer$_{opt}$
    identifier$_{opt}$:   constant-expression

pure-specifier:
    = 0

constant-initializer:
    = constant-expression

To preserve C compatibility, a class and a non-class of the same name can be declared in the same scope (§5.7). For example:

struct stat { / * ... * / } ;
int stat (char* name , struct stat* buf) ;

In this case, the plain name (*stat*) is the name of the non-class. The class must be referred to using a *class-key* prefix .

Constant expressions are defined in §C.5.

A.8.1 Derived Classes

See Chapter 12 and Chapter 15.

base-clause:
    :   base-specifier-list

base-specifier-list:
>   *base-specifier*
>   *base-specifier-list* , *base-specifier*

base-specifier:
>   : : *opt nested-name-specifier_opt class-name*
>   `virtual` *access-specifier_opt* : : *opt nested-name-specifier_opt class-name*
>   *access-specifier* `virtual`*_opt* : : *opt nested-name-specifier_opt class-name*

access-specifier:
>   `private`
>   `protected`
>   `public`

A.8.2 Special Member Functions

See §11.4 (conversion operators), §10.4.6 (class member initialization), and §12.2.2 (base initialization).

conversion-function-id:
>   `operator` *conversion-type-id*

conversion-type-id:
>   *type-specifier-seq conversion-declarator_opt*

conversion-declarator:
>   *ptr-operator conversion-declarator_opt*

ctor-initializer:
>   : *mem-initializer-list*

mem-initializer-list:
>   *mem-initializer*
>   *mem-initializer* , *mem-initializer-list*

mem-initializer:
>   *mem-initializer-id* (*expression-list_opt*)

mem-initializer-id:
>   : : *opt nested-name-specifier_opt class-name*
>   *identifier*

A.8.3 Overloading

See Chapter 11.

operator-function-id:
>   `operator` *operator*

operator: one of

```
    new    delete    new[]      delete[]
    +      -      *      /      %      ^      &      |      ~      !      =      <      >
    +=     -=     *=     /=     %=     ^=     &=     |=     <<     >>     >>=    <<=    ==
    !=     <=     >=     &&     ||     ++     --     ,      ->*    ->     ()     []
```

A.9 Templates

Templates are explained in Chapter 13 and §C.13.

template-declaration:
    export*opt* template < *template-parameter-list* > *declaration*

template-parameter-list:
    template-parameter
    template-parameter-list , *template-parameter*

template-parameter:
    type-parameter
    parameter-declaration

type-parameter:
    class *identifier_{opt}*
    class *identifier_{opt}* = *type-id*
    typename *identifier_{opt}*
    typename *identifier_{opt}* = *type-id*
    template < *template-parameter-list* > class *identifier_{opt}*
    template < *template-parameter-list* > class *identifier_{opt}* = *template-name*

template-id:
    template-name < *template-argument-list_{opt}* >

template-name:
    identifier

template-argument-list:
    template-argument
    template-argument-list , *template-argument*

template-argument:
    assignment-expression
    type-id
    template-name

explicit-instantiation:
    template *declaration*

explicit-specialization:
    template < > *declaration*

The explicit template argument specification opens up the possibility of an obscure syntactic ambiguity. Consider:

```
void h ( )
{
    f<1> (0);   // ambiguity: ((f)<1) > (0) or (f<1>)(0) ?
                 // resolution: f<1> is called with argument 0
}
```

The resolution is simple and effective: if *f* is a template name, *f<* is the beginning of a qualified template name and the subsequent tokens must be interpreted based on that; otherwise, < means less-than. Similarly, the first non-nested > terminates a template argument list. If a greater-than is needed, parentheses must be used:

```
f< a>b > (0);          // syntax error
f< (a>b) > (0);        // ok
```

A similar lexical ambiguity can occur when terminating >s get too close. For example:

```
list<vector<int>> lv1;      // syntax error: unexpected >> (right shift)
list< vector<int> > lv2;    // correct: list of vectors
```

Note the space between the two >s; >> is the right-shift operator. That can be a real nuisance.

A.10 Exception Handling

See §8.3 and Chapter 14.

try block:
> `try` *compound-statement handler-seq*

function-try-block:
> `try` *ctor-initializer*$_{opt}$ *function-body handler-seq*

handler-seq:
> *handler handler-seq*$_{opt}$

handler:
> `catch` (*exception-declaration*) *compound-statement*

exception-declaration:
> *type-specifier-seq declarator*
> *type-specifier-seq abstract-declarator*
> *type-specifier-seq*
> . . .

throw-expression:
> `throw` *assignment-expression*$_{opt}$

exception-specification:
> `throw` (*type-id-list*$_{opt}$)

type-id-list:
> *type-id*
> *type-id-list* , *type-id*

A.11 Preprocessing Directives

The preprocessor is a relatively unsophisticated macro processor that works primarily on lexical tokens rather than individual characters. In addition to the ability to define and use macros (§7.8), the preprocessor provides mechanisms for including text files and standard headers (§9.2.1) and conditional compilation based on macros (§9.3.3). For example:

```
#if OPT==4
#include "header4.h"
#elif 0<OPT
#include "someheader.h"
#else
#include<cstdlib>
#endif
```

All preprocessor directives start with a #, which must be the first non-whitespace character on its line.

preprocessing-file:
    group$_{opt}$

group:
    group-part
    group group-part

group-part:
    pp-tokens$_{opt}$ *new-line*
    if-section
    control-line

if-section:
    if-group elif-groups$_{opt}$ *else-group*$_{opt}$ *endif-line*

if-group:
    `# if` *constant-expression new-line group*$_{opt}$
    `# ifdef` *identifier new-line group*$_{opt}$
    `# ifndef` *identifier new-line group*$_{opt}$

elif-groups:
    elif-group
    elif-groups elif-group

elif-group:
    `# elif` *constant-expression new-line group*$_{opt}$

else-group:
    `# else` *new-line group*$_{opt}$

endif-line:
    `# endif` *new-line*

control-line:
>   # include *pp-tokens new-line*
>   # define *identifier replacement-list new-line*
>   # define *identifier lparen identifier-list_{opt}) replacement-list new-line*
>   # undef *identifier new-line*
>   # line *pp-tokens new-line*
>   # error *pp-tokens_{opt} new-line*
>   # pragma *pp-tokens_{opt} new-line*
>   # *new-line*

lparen:
>   *the left-parenthesis character without preceding white-space*

replacement-list:
>   *pp-tokens_{opt}*

pp-tokens:
>   *preprocessing-token*
>   *pp-tokens preprocessing-token*

new-line:
>   *the new-line character*

identifier-list:
>   *identifier*
>   *itentifier-list , identifier*

Appendix B

Compatibility

You go ahead and follow your customs,
and I'll follow mine.
– C. Napier

C/C++ compatibility — silent differences between C and C++ — C code that is not C++ — deprecated features — C++ code that is not C — coping with older C++ implementations — headers — the standard library — namespaces — allocation errors — templates — *for-statement* initializers — advice — exercises.

B.1 Introduction

This appendix discusses the incompatibilities between C and C++ and between Standard C++ and earlier versions of C++. The purpose is to document differences that can cause problems for the programmer and point to ways of dealing with such problems. Most compatibility problems surface when people try to upgrade a C program to a C++ program, to try port a C++ program from one pre-standard version of C++ to another, or try to compile C++ using modern features with an older compiler. The aim here is not to drown you in the details of every compatibility problem that ever surfaced in an implementation, but rather to list the most frequently occurring problems and present their standard solutions.

When you look at compatibility issues, a key question to consider is the range of implementations under which a program needs to work. For learning C++, it makes sense to use the most complete and helpful implementation. For delivering a product, a more conservative strategy might be in order to maximize the number of systems on which the product can run. In the past, this has been a reason (and sometimes just an excuse) to avoid C++ features deemed novel. However, implementations are converging, so the need for portability across platforms is less cause for extreme caution than it was a couple of years ago.

B.2 C/C++ Compatibility

With minor exceptions, C++ is a superset of C. Most differences stem from C++'s greater emphasis on type checking. Well-written C programs tend to be C++ programs as well. All differences between C++ and C can be diagnosed by a compiler.

B.2.1 "Silent" Differences

With a few exceptions, programs that are both C++ and C have the same meaning in both languages. Fortunately, these "silent differences" are rather obscure:

In C, the size of a character constant and of an enumeration equals *sizeof*(*int*). In C++, *sizeof*('*a*') equals *sizeof*(*char*), and a C++ implementation is allowed to choose whatever size is most appropriate for an enumeration (§4.8).

C++ provides the // comments; C does not (although many C implementations provide them as an extension). This difference can be used to construct programs that behave differently in the two languages. For example:

```
int f(int a, int b)
{
    return a //* pretty unlikely */ b
         ;      /* unrealistic: semicolon on separate line to avoid syntax error */
}
```

ISO C is being revised to allow // as in C++.

A structure name declared in an inner scope can hide the name of an object, function, enumerator, or type in an outer scope. For example:

```
int x[99];
void f()
{
    struct x { int a; };
    sizeof(x);  /* size of the array in C, size of the struct in C++ */
}
```

B.2.2 C Code That Is Not C++

The C/C++ incompatibilities that cause most real problems are not subtle. Most are easily caught by compilers. This section gives examples of C code that is not C++. Most are deemed poor style or even obsolete in modern C.

In C, most functions can be called without a previous declaration. For example:

```
main()      /* poor style C. Not C++ */
{
    double sq2 = sqrt(2);                          /* call undeclared function */
    printf("the square root of 2 is %g\n", sq2);   /* call undeclared function */
}
```

Complete and consistent use of function declarations (function prototypes) is generally recommended for C. Where that sensible advice is followed, and especially where C compilers provide options to enforce it, C code conforms to the C++ rule. Where undeclared functions are called, you have to know the functions and the rules for C pretty well to know whether you have made a mistake or introduced a portability problem. For example, the previous *main*() contains at least two errors as a C program.

In C, a function declared without specifying any argument types can take any number of arguments of any type at all. Such use is deemed obsolescent in Standard C, but it is not uncommon:

```
void f();   /* argument types not mentioned */

void g()
{
    f(2);      /* poor style C. Not C++ */
}
```

In C, functions can be defined using a syntax that optionally specifies argument types after the list of arguments:

```
void f(a,p,c) char *p; char c; { /* ... */ }   /* C. Not C++ */
```

Such definitions must be rewritten:

```
void f(int a, char* p, char c) { /* ... */ }
```

In C and in pre-standard versions of C++, the type specifier defaults to *int*. For example:

```
const a = 7;    /* In C, type int assumed. Not C++ */
```

ISO C is being revised to disallow "implicit *int*," just as in C++.

C allows the definition of *struct*s in return type and argument type declarations. For example:

```
struct S { int x,y; } f();        /* C. Not C++ */
void g(struct S { int x,y; } y);  /* C. Not C++ */
```

The C++ rules for defining types make such declarations useless, and they are not allowed.

In C, integers can be assigned to variables of enumeration type:

```
enum Direction { up, down };
Direction d = 1;            /* error: int assigned to Direction; ok in C */
```

C++ provides many more keywords than C does. If one of these appears as an identifier in a C program, that program must be modified to make a C++ program:

C++ Keywords That Are Not C Keywords					
and	*and_eq*	*asm*	*bitand*	*bitor*	*bool*
catch	*class*	*compl*	*const_cast*	*delete*	*dynamic_cast*
explicit	*export*	*false*	*friend*	*inline*	*mutable*
namespace	*new*	*not*	*not_eq*	*operator*	*or*
or_eq	*private*	*protected*	*public*	*reinterpret_cast*	*static_cast*
template	*this*	*throw*	*true*	*try*	*typeid*
typename	*using*	*virtual*	*wchar_t*	*xor*	*xor_eq*

In C, some of the C++ keywords are macros defined in standard headers:

C++ Keywords That Are C Macros					
and	*and_eq*	*bitand*	*bitor*	*compl*	*not*
not_eq	*or*	*or_eq*	*wchar_t*	*xor*	*xor_eq*

This implies that in C they can be tested using *#ifdef*, redefined, etc.

In C, a global data object may be declared several times in a single translation unit without using the *extern* specifier. As long as at most one such declaration provides an initializer, the object is considered defined only once. For example:

> *int i; int i;   /* defines or declares a single integer 'i'; not C++ */*

In C++, an entity must be defined exactly once; §9.2.3.

In C++, a class may not have the same name as a *typedef* declared to refer to a different type in the same scope; §5.7.

In C, a *void** may be used as the right-hand operand of an assignment to or initialization of a variable of any pointer type; in C++ it may not (§5.6). For example:

> *void f(int n)*
> *{*
> *   int* p = malloc (n*sizeof(int)); /* not C++. In C++, allocate using 'new' */*
> *}*

C allows jumps to bypass an initialization; C++ does not.

In C, a global *const* by default has external linkage; in C++ it does not and must be initialized, unless explicitly declared *extern* (§5.4).

In C, names of nested structures are placed in the same scope as the structure in which they are nested. For example:

> *struct S {*
> *   struct T { /* ... */ };*
> *   // ...*
> *};*
>
> *struct T x;   /* ok in C meaning 'S::T x;'. Not C++ */*

In C, an array can be initialized by an initializer that has more elements than the array requires. For example:

> *char v[5] = "Oscar";   /* ok in C, the terminating 0 is not used. Not C++ */*

B.2.3 Deprecated Features

By deprecating a feature, the standards committee expresses the wish that the feature would go away. However, the committee does not have a mandate to remove a heavily used feature − however redundant or dangerous it may be. Thus, a deprecation is a strong hint to the users to avoid the feature.

The keyword *static*, which usually means "statically allocated," can be used to indicate that a function or an object is local to a translation unit. For example:

```
// file1:
    static int glob;
// file2:
    static int glob;
```

This program genuinely has two integers called *glob*. Each *glob* is used exclusively by functions defined in its translation unit.

The use of *static* to indicate "local to translation unit" is deprecated in C++. Use unnamed namespaces instead (§8.2.5.1).

The implicit conversion of string literal to a (non-*const*) *char** is deprecated. Use named arrays of *char* or avoid assignment of string literals to *char**s (§5.2.2).

C-style casts should have been deprecated when the new-style casts were introduced. Programmers should seriously consider banning C-style casts from their own programs. Where explicit type conversion is necessary, *static_cast*, *reinterpret_cast*, *const_cast*, or a combination of these can do what a C-style cast can. The new-style casts should be preferred because they are more explicit and more visible (§6.2.7).

B.2.4 C++ Code That Is Not C

This section lists facilities offered by C++ but not by C. The features are sorted by purpose. However, many classifications are possible and most features serve multiple purposes, so this classification should not be taken too seriously.

- Features primarily for notational convenience:
  - [1] // comments (§2.3); being added to C
  - [2] Support for restricted character sets (§C.3.1)
  - [3] Support for extended character sets (§C.3.3); being added to C
  - [4] Non-constant initializers for objects in *static* storage (§9.4.1)
  - [5] *const* in constant expressions (§5.4, §C.5)
  - [6] Declarations as statements (§6.3.1)
  - [7] Declarations in *for-statement* initializers and conditions (§6.3.3, §6.3.2.1)
  - [8] Structure names need not be prefixed by *struct* (§5.7)
- Features primarily for strengthening the type system:
  - [1] Function argument type checking (§7.1); later added to C (§B.2.2)
  - [2] Type-safe linkage (§9.2, §9.2.3)
  - [3] Free store management using *new* and *delete* (§6.2.6, §10.4.5, §15.6)
  - [4] *const* (§5.4, §5.4.1); later added to C
  - [5] The Boolean type *bool* (§4.2)
  - [6] New cast syntax (§6.2.7)
- Facilities for user-defined types:
  - [1] Classes (Chapter 10)
  - [2] Member functions (§10.2.1) and member classes (§11.12)
  - [3] Constructors and destructors (§10.2.3, §10.4.1)
  - [4] Derived classes (Chapter 12, Chapter 15)
  - [5] *virtual* functions and abstract classes (§12.2.6, §12.3)

    [6] Public/protected/private access control (§10.2.2, §15.3, §C.11)
    [7] *friend*s (§11.5)
    [8] Pointers to members (§15.5, §C.12)
    [9] *static* members (§10.2.4)
    [10] *mutable* members (§10.2.7.2)
    [11] Operator overloading (Chapter 11)
    [12] References (§5.5)
 – Features primarily for program organization (in addition to classes):
    [1] Templates (Chapter 13, §C.13)
    [2] Inline functions (§7.1.1)
    [3] Default arguments (§7.5)
    [4] Function overloading (§7.4)
    [5] Namespaces (§8.2)
    [6] Explicit scope qualification (operator :: ; §4.9.4)
    [7] Exception handling (§8.3, Chapter 14)
    [8] Run-time Type Identification (§15.4)

The keywords added by C++ (§B.2.2) can be used to spot most C++-specific facilities. However, some facilities, such as function overloading and *const*s in constant expressions, are not identified by a keyword. In addition to the language features listed here, the C++ library (§16.1.2) is mostly C++ specific.

    The __*cplusplus* macro can be used to determine whether a program is being processed by a C or a C++ compiler (§9.2.4).

B.3 Coping with Older C++ Implementations

C++ has been in constant use since 1983 (§1.4). Since then, several versions have been defined and many separately developed implementations have emerged. The fundamental aim of the standards effort was to ensure that implementers and users would have a single definition of C++ to work from. Until that definition becomes pervasive in the C++ community, however, we have to deal with the fact that not every implementation provides every feature described in this book.

    It is unfortunately not uncommon for people to take their first serious look at C++ using a five-year-old implementation. The typical reason is that such implementations are widely available and free. Given a choice, no self-respecting professional would touch such an antique. For a novice, older implementations come with serious hidden costs. The lack of language features and library support means that the novice must struggle with problems that have been eliminated in newer implementations. Using a feature-poor older implementation also warps the novice's programming style and gives a biased view of what C++ is. The best subset of C++ to initially learn is *not* the set of low-level facilities (and not the common C and C++ subset; §1.2). In particular, I recommend relying on the standard library and on templates to ease learning and to get a good initial impression of what C++ programming can be.

    The first commercial release of C++ was in late 1985. The language was defined by the first edition of this book. At that point, C++ did not offer multiple inheritance, templates, run-time type information, exceptions, or namespaces. Today, I see no reason to use an implementation that doesn't provide at least some of these features. I added multiple inheritance, templates, and exceptions to the definition of C++ in 1989. However, early support for templates and exceptions was uneven and often poor. If you find problems with templates or exceptions in an older implementation, consider an immediate upgrade.

In general, it is wise to use an implementation that conforms to the standard wherever possible and to minimize the reliance on implementation-defined and undefined aspects of the language. Design as if the full language were available and then use whatever workarounds are needed. This leads to better organized and more maintainable programs than designing for the lowest-common-denominator subset of C++. Also, be careful to use implementation-specific language extensions only when absolutely necessary.

B.3.1 Headers

Traditionally, every header file had a *.h* suffix. Thus, C++ implementations provided headers such as *<map.h>* and *<iostream.h>*. For compatibility, most still do.

When the standards committee needed headers for redefined versions of standard libraries and for newly added library facilities, naming those headers became a problem. Using the old *.h* names would have caused compatibility problems. The solution was to drop the *.h* suffix in standard header names. The suffix is redundant anyway because the < > notation indicates that a standard header is being named.

Thus, the standard library provides non-suffixed headers, such as *<iostream>* and *<map>*. The declarations in those files are placed in namespace *std*. Older headers place their declarations in the global namespace and use a *.h* suffix. Consider:

```
#include<iostream>

int main()
{
    std::cout << "Hello, world!\n";
}
```

If this fails to compile on an implementation, try the more traditional version:

```
#include<iostream.h>

int main()
{
    cout << "Hello, world!\n";
}
```

Some of the most serious portability problems occur because of incompatible headers. The standard headers are only a minor contributor to this. Often, a program depends on a large number of headers that are not present on all systems, on a large number of declarations that don't appear in the same headers on all systems, and on declarations that appear to be standard (because they are found in headers with standard names) but are not part of any standard.

There are no fully-satisfactory approaches to dealing with portability in the face of inconsistent headers. A general idea is to avoid direct dependencies on inconsistent headers and localize the remaining dependencies. That is, we try to achieve portability through indirection and localization.

For example, if declarations that we need are provided in different headers in different systems, we may choose to #*include* an application specific header that in turn #*include*s the appropriate header(s) for each system. Similarly, if some functionality is provided in slightly different forms on different systems, we may choose to access that functionality through application-specific interface classes and functions.

B.3.2 The Standard Library

Naturally, pre-standard-C++ implementations may lack parts of the standard library. Most will have iostreams, non-templated *complex*, a different *string* class, and the C standard library. However, some may lack *map*, *list*, *valarray*, etc. In such cases, use the – typically proprietary – libraries available in a way that will allow conversion when your implementation gets upgraded to the standard. It is usually better to use a non-standard *string*, *list*, and *map* than to revert to C-style programming in the absence of these standard library classes. Also, good implementations of the STL part of the standard library (Chapter 16, Chapter 17, Chapter 18, Chapter 19) are available free for downloading.

Early implementations of the standard library were incomplete. For example, some had containers that didn't support allocators and others required allocators to be explicitly specified for each class. Similar problems occurred for other "policy arguments," such as comparison criteria. For example:

```
list<int> li ;                        // ok, but some implementations require an allocator
list<int, allocator<int> > li2 ;      // ok, but some implementations don't implement allocators

map<string, Record> m1 ;              // ok, but some implementations require a less-operation
map<string, Record, less<string> > m2 ;
```

Use whichever version an implementation accepts. Eventually, the implementations will accept all.

Early C++ implementations provided *istrstream* and *ostrstream* defined in *<strstream.h>* instead of *istringstream* and *ostringstream* defined in *<sstream>*. The *strstream*s operated directly on a *char*[ ] (see §21.10[26]).

The streams in pre-standard-C++ implementations were not parameterized. In particular, the templates with the *basic_* prefix are new in the standard, and the *basic_ios* class used to be called *ios*. Curiously enough, *iostate* used to be called *io_state*.

B.3.3 Namespaces

If your implementation does not support namespaces, use source files to express the logical structure of the program (Chapter 9). Similarly, use header files to express interfaces that you provide for implementations or that are shared with C.

In the absence of namespaces, use *static* to compensate for the lack of unnamed namespaces. Also use an identifying prefix to global names to distinguish your names from those of other parts of the code. For example:

```
// for use on pre-namespace implementations:

class bs_string { / * ... * / } ;    // Bjarne's string
typedef int bs_bool ;                // Bjarne's Boolean type
```

```
class joe_string;                         // Joe's string
enum joe_bool { joe_false, joe_true };    // Joe's bool
```

Be careful when choosing a prefix. Existing C and C++ libraries are littered with such prefixes.

B.3.4 Allocation Errors

In pre-exception-handling-C++, operator *new* returned *0* to indicate allocation failure. Standard C++'s *new* throws *bad_alloc* by default.

In general, it is best to convert to the standard. In this case, this means modify the code to catch *bad_alloc* rather than test for *0*. In either case, coping with memory exhaustion beyond giving an error message is hard on many systems.

However, when converting from testing *0* to catching *bad_alloc* is impractical, you can sometimes modify the program to revert to the pre-exception-handling behavior. If no *_new_handler* is installed, using the *nothrow* allocator will cause a *0* to be returned in case of allocation failure:

```
X* p1 = new X;            // throws bad_alloc if no memory
X* p2 = new(nothrow) X;   // returns 0 if no memory
```

B.3.5 Templates

The standard introduced new template features and clarified the rules for several existing ones.

If your implementation doesn't support partial specialization, use a separate name for the template that would otherwise have been a specialization. For example:

```
template<class T> class plist : private list<void*> {  // should have been list<T*>
    // ...
};
```

If your implementation doesn't support member templates, some techniques become infeasible. In particular, member templates allow the programmer to specify construction and conversion with a flexibility that cannot be matched without them (§13.6.2). Sometimes, providing a nonmember function that constructs an object is an alternative. Consider:

```
template<class T> class X {
    // ...
    template<class A> X(const A& a);
};
```

In the absence of member templates, we must restrict ourselves to specific types:

```
template<class T> class X {
    // ...
    X(const A1& a);
    X(const A2& a);
    // ...
};
```

Most early implementations generated definitions for all member functions defined within a template class when that template class was instantiated. This could lead to errors in unused member functions (§C.13.9.1). The solution is to place the definition of the member functions after the class declaration. For example, rather than

```
template<class T> class Container {
    // ...
public:
    void sort() { /* use < */ }        // in-class definition
};

class Glob { /* no < for Glob */ };

Container<Glob> cg; // some pre-standard implementations try to define Container<Glob>::sort()
```

use

```
template<class T> class Container {
    // ...
public:
    void sort();
};

template<class T> void Container<T>::sort() { /* use < */ }    // out-of-class definition

class Glob { /* no < for Glob */ };

Container<Glob> cg; // no problem as long as cg.sort() isn't called
```

Early implementations of C++ did not handle the use of members defined later in a class. For example:

```
template<class T> class Vector {
public:
    T& operator[](size_t i) { return v[i]; }  // v declared below
    // ...
private:
    T* v;                           // oops: not found!
    size_t sz;
};
```

In such cases, either sort the member declarations to avoid the problem or place the definition of the member function after the class declaration.

Some pre-standard-C++ implementations do not accept default arguments for templates (§13.4.1). In that case, every template parameter must be given an explicit argument. For example:

```
template<class Key, class T, class LT = less<T> > class map {
    // ...
};

map<string, int> m;                 // Oops: default template arguments not implemented
map< string, int, less<string> > m2;  // workaround: be explicit
```

B.3.6 For-Statement Initializers

Consider:

```
void f(vector<char>& v, int m)
{
    for (int i= 0; i<v.size() && i<=m; ++i) cout << v[i];

    if (i == m) {      // error: i referred to after end of for-statement
        // ...
    }
}
```

Such code used to work because in the original definition of C++, the scope of the controlled variable extended to the end of the scope in which the *for-statement* appears. If you find such code, simply declare the controlled variable before the *for-statement*:

```
void f2(vector<char>& v, int m)
{
    int i= 0;  // i needed after the loop
    for (; i<v.size() && i<=m; ++i) cout << v[i];

    if (i == m) {
        // ...
    }
}
```

B.4 Advice

[1] For learning C++, use the most up-to-date and complete implementation of Standard C++ that you can get access to; §B.3.

[2] The common subset of C and C++ is not the best initial subset of C++ to learn; §1.6, §B.3.

[3] For production code, remember that not every C++ implementation is completely up-to-date. Before using a major new feature in production code, try it out by writing small programs to test the standards conformance and performance of the implementations you plan to use; for example, see §8.5[6-7], §16.5[10], §B.5[7].

[4] Avoid deprecated features such as global *static*s; also avoid C-style casts; §6.2.7, §B.2.3.

[5] ''implicit *int*'' has been banned, so explicitly specify the type of every function, variable, *const*, etc.; §B.2.2.

[6] When converting a C program to C++, first make sure that function declarations (prototypes) and standard headers are used consistently; §B.2.2.

[7] When converting a C program to C++, rename variables that are C++ keywords; §B.2.2.

[8] When converting a C program to C++, cast the result of *malloc*() to the proper type or change all uses of *malloc*() to uses of *new*; §B.2.2.

[9] When converting from *malloc*() and *free*() to *new* and *delete*, consider using *vector*, *push_back*(), and *reserve*() instead of *realloc*(); §3.8, §16.3.5.

[10] When converting a C program to C++, remember that there are no implicit conversions from *int*s to enumerations; use explicit type conversion where necessary; §4.8.

[11] A facility defined in namespace *std* is defined in a header without a suffix (e.g. *std::cout* is declared in *<iostream>*). Older implementations have standard library facilities in the global namespace and declared in headers with a *.h* suffix (e.g. *::cout* declared in *<iostream.h>*); §9.2.2, §B.3.1.

[12] If older code tests the result of new against *0*, it must be modified to catch *bad_alloc* or to use *new(nothrow)*; §B.3.4.

[13] If your implementation doesn't support default template arguments, provide arguments explicitly; *typedef*s can often be used to avoid repetition of template arguments (similar to the way the typedef *string* saves you from saying *basic_string< char, char_traits<char>, allocator<char> >*); §B.3.5.

[14] Use *<string>* to get *std::string* (*<string.h>* holds the C-style string functions); §9.2.2, §B.3.1.

[15] For each standard C header *<X.h>* that places names in the global namespace, the header *<cX>* places the names in namespace *std*; §B.3.1.

[16] Many systems have a *"String.h"* header defining a string type. Note that such strings differ from the standard library *string*.

[17] Prefer standard facilities to non-standard ones; §20.1, §B.3, §C.2.

[18] Use *extern "C"* when declaring C functions; §9.2.4.

B.5 Exercises

1. (*2.5) Take a C program and convert it to a C++ program; list the kinds of non-C++ constructs used and determine if they are valid ANSI C constructs. First convert the program to strict ANSI C (adding prototypes, etc.), then to C++. Estimate the time it would take to convert a 100,000 line C program to C++.

2. (*2.5) Write a program to help convert C programs to C++ by renaming variables that are C++ keywords, replacing calls of *malloc()* by uses of *new*, etc. Hint: don't try to do a perfect job.

3. (*2) Replace all uses of *malloc()* in a C-style C++ program (maybe a recently converted C program) to uses of *new*. Hint: §B.4[8-9].

4. (*2.5) Minimize the use of macros, global variables, uninitialized variable, and casts in a C-style C++ program (maybe a recently converted C program).

5. (*3) Take a C++ program that is the result of a crude conversion from C and critique it as a C++ program considering locality of information, abstraction, readability, extensibility, and potential for reuse of parts. Make one significant change to the program based on that critique.

6. (*2) Take a small (say, 500 line) C++ program and convert it to C. Compare the original with the result for size and probable maintainability.

7. (*3) Write a small set of test programs to determine whether a C++ implementation has ''the latest'' standard features. For example, what is the scope of a variable defined in a *for-statement* initializer? (§B.3.6), are default template arguments supported? (§B.3.5), are member templates supported? (§13.6.2), and is argument-based lookup supported? (§8.2.6). Hint: §B.2.4.

8. (*2.5) Take a C++ program that use *<X.h>* headers and convert it to using *<X>* and *<cX>* headers. Minimize the use of *using-directive*s.

Appendix C

Technicalities

Deep in the fundamental
heart of mind and Universe,
there is a reason.
– Slartibartfast

What the standard promises — character sets — integer literals — constant expressions — promotions and conversions — multidimensional arrays — fields and unions — memory management — garbage collection — namespaces — access control — pointers to data members — templates — *static* members — *friends* — templates as template parameters — template argument deduction — *typename* and *template* qualification — instantiation — name binding — templates and namespaces — explicit instantiation — advice.

C.1 Introduction and Overview

This chapter presents technical details and examples that do not fit neatly into my presentation of the main C++ language features and their uses. The details presented here can be important when you are writing a program and essential when reading code written using them. However, I consider them technical details that should not be allowed to distract from the student's primary task of learning to use C++ well or the programmer's primary task of expressing ideas as clearly and as directly as possible in C++.

C.2 The Standard

Contrary to common belief, strictly adhering to the C++ language and library standard doesn't guarantee good code or even portable code. The standard doesn't say whether a piece of code is good or bad; it simply says what a programmer can and cannot rely on from an implementation. One can write perfectly awful standard-conforming programs, and most real-world programs rely on features not covered by the standard.

Many important things are deemed *implementation-defined* by the standard. This means that each implementation must provide a specific, well-defined behavior for a construct and that behavior must be documented. For example:

```
unsigned char c1 = 64;      // well-defined: a char has at least 8 bits and can always hold 64
unsigned char c2 = 1256;    // implementation-defined: truncation if a char has only 8 bits
```

The initialization of *c1* is well-defined because a *char* must be at least 8 bits. However, the behavior of the initialization of *c2* is implementation-defined because the number of bits in a *char* is implementation-defined. If the *char* has only 8 bits, the value *1256* will be truncated to *232* (§C.6.2.1). Most implementation-defined features relate to differences in the hardware used to run a program.

When writing real-world programs, it is usually necessary to rely on implementation-defined behavior. Such behavior is the price we pay for the ability to operate effectively on a large range of systems. For example, the language would have been much simpler if all characters had been 8 bits and all integers 32 bits. However, 16-bit and 32-bit character sets are not uncommon − nor are integers too large to fit in 32 bits. For example, many computers now have disks that hold more than *32G* bytes, so 48-bit or 64-bit integers can be useful for representing disk addresses.

To maximize portability, it is wise to be explicit about what implementation-defined features we rely on and to isolate the more subtle examples in clearly marked sections of a program. A typical example of this practice is to present all dependencies on hardware sizes in the form of constants and type definitions in some header file. To support such techniques, the standard library provides **numeric_limits** (§22.2).

Undefined behavior is nastier. A construct is deemed *undefined* by the standard if no reasonable behavior is required by an implementation. Typically, some obvious implementation technique will cause a program using an undefined feature to behave very badly. For example:

```
const int size = 4*1024;
char page[size];

void f()
{
    page[size+size] = 7; // undefined
}
```

Plausible outcomes of this code fragment include overwriting unrelated data and triggering a hardware error/exception. An implementation is not required to choose among plausible outcomes. Where powerful optimizers are used, the actual effects of undefined behavior can become quite unpredictable. If a set of plausible and easily implementable alternatives exist, a feature is deemed implementation-defined rather than undefined.

It is worth spending considerable time and effort to ensure that a program does not use something deemed undefined by the standard. In many cases, tools exist to help do this.

C.3 Character Sets

The examples in this book are written using the U.S. variant of the international 7-bit character set ISO 646-1983 called ASCII (ANSI3.4-1968). This can cause three problems for people who use C++ in an environment with a different character set:

> [1] ASCII contains punctuation characters and operator symbols – such as], {, and ! – that are not available in some character sets.
>
> [2] We need a notation for characters that do not have a convenient character representation (e.g., newline and ''the character with value 17''').
>
> [3] ASCII doesn't contain characters, such as – ζ , æ, and Π – that are used for writing languages other than English.

C.3.1 Restricted Character Sets

The ASCII special characters [,], {, }, |, and \ occupy character set positions designated as alphabetic by ISO. In most European national ISO-646 character sets, these positions are occupied by letters not found in the English alphabet. For example, the Danish national character set uses them for the vowels Æ, æ, Ø, ø, Å, and å. No significant amount of text can be written in Danish without them.

A set of trigraphs is provided to allow national characters to be expressed in a portable way using a truly standard minimal character set. This can be useful for interchange of programs, but it doesn't make it easier for people to read programs. Naturally, the long-term solution to this problem is for C++ programmers to get equipment that supports both their native language and C++ well. Unfortunately, this appears to be infeasible for some, and the introduction of new equipment can be a frustratingly slow process. To help programmers stuck with incomplete character sets, C++ provides alternatives:

Keywords		Digraphs		Trigraphs	
and	&&	<%	{	??=	#
and_eq	&=	%>	}	??(	[
bitand	&	<:	[	??<	{
bitor	|	:>	]	??/	\
compl	~	%:	#	??)	]
not	!	%:%:	##	??>	}
or	||			??'	^
or_eq	|=			??!	|
xor	^			??-	~
xor_eq	^=				
not_eq	!=				

Programs using the keywords and digraphs are far more readable than the equivalent programs written using trigraphs. However, if characters such as { are not available, trigraphs are necessary for putting ''missing'' characters into strings and character constants. For example, ´{´ becomes ´??<´.

Some people prefer the keywords such as *and* to their traditional operator notation.

C.3.2 Escape Characters

A few characters have standard names that use the backslash \ as an escape character:

Name	ASCII Name	C++ Name
newline	NL (LF)	\n
horizontal tab	HT	\t
vertical tab	VT	\v
backspace	BS	\b
carriage return	CR	\r
form feed	FF	\f
alert	BEL	\a
backslash	\	\\
question mark	?	\?
single quote	'	\'
double quote	"	\"
octal number	*ooo*	*ooo*
hex number	*hhh*	\x*hhh* ...

Despite their appearance, these are single characters.

It is possible to represent a character as a one-, two-, or three-digit octal number (\ followed by octal digits) or as a hexadecimal number (\x followed by hexadecimal digits). There is no limit to the number of hexadecimal digits in the sequence. A sequence of octal or hexadecimal digits is terminated by the first character that is not an octal digit or a hexadecimal digit, respectively. For example:

Octal	Hexadecimal	Decimal	ASCII
'\6'	'\x6'	6	ACK
'\60'	'\x30'	48	'0'
'\137'	'\x05f'	95	'_'

This makes it possible to represent every character in the machine's character set and, in particular, to embed such characters in character strings (see §5.2.2). Using any numeric notation for characters makes a program nonportable across machines with different character sets.

It is possible to enclose more than one character in a character literal, for example ´*ab*´. Such uses are archaic, implementation-dependent, and best avoided.

When embedding a numeric constant in a string using the octal notation, it is wise always to use three digits for the number. The notation is hard enough to read without having to worry about whether or not the character after a constant is a digit. For hexadecimal constants, use two digits. Consider these examples:

```
char v1[] = "a\xah\129";      // 6 chars: 'a' '\xa' 'h' '\12' '9' '\0'
char v2[] = "a\xah\127";      // 5 chars: 'a' '\xa' 'h' '\127' '\0'
char v3[] = "a\xad\127";      // 4 chars: 'a' '\xad' '\127' '\0'
char v4[] = "a\xad\0127";     // 5 chars: 'a' '\xad' '\012' '7' '\0'
```

C.3.3 Large Character Sets

A C++ program may be written and presented to the user in character sets that are much richer than the 127 character ASCII set. Where an implementation supports larger character sets, identifiers, comments, character constants, and strings may contain characters such as å, β, and Γ. However, to be portable the implementation must map these characters into an encoding using only characters available to every C++ user. In principle, this translation into the C++ basic source character set (the set used in this book) occurs before the compiler does any other processing. Therefore, it does not affect the semantics of the program.

The standard encoding of characters from large character sets into the smaller set supported directly by C++ is presented as sequences of four or eight hexadecimal digits:

> *universal-character-name:*
>   \U *X X X X X X X X*
>   \u *X X X X*

Here, *X* represents a hexadecimal digit. For example, \u*1e2b*. The shorter notation \u*XXXX* is equivalent to \U*0000XXXX*. A number of hexadecimal digits different from four or eight is a lexical error.

A programmer can use these character encodings directly. However, they are primarily meant as a way for an implementation that internally uses a small character set to handle characters from a large character set seen by the programmer.

If you rely on special environments to provide an extended character set for use in identifiers, the program becomes less portable. A program is hard to read unless you understand the natural language used for identifiers and comments. Consequently, for programs used internationally it is usually best to stick to English and ASCII.

C.3.4 Signed and Unsigned Characters

It is implementation-defined whether a plain *char* is considered signed or unsigned. This opens the possibility for some nasty surprises and implementation dependencies. For example:

```
char c = 255;    // 255 is "all ones," hexadecimal 0xFF
int i = c;
```

What will be the value of *i*? Unfortunately, the answer is undefined. On all implementations I know of, the answer depends on the meaning of the "all ones" *char* bit pattern when extended into an *int*. On a SGI Challenge machine, a *char* is unsigned, so the answer is *255*. On a Sun SPARC or an IBM PC, where a *char* is signed, the answer is *−1*. In this case, the compiler might warn about the conversion of the literal *255* to the *char* value *−1*. However, C++ does not offer a general mechanism for detecting this kind of problem. One solution is to avoid plain *char* and use the specific *char* types only. Unfortunately, some standard library functions, such as *strcmp* ( ), take plain *char*s only (§20.4.1).

A *char* must behave identically to either a **signed char** or an **unsigned char**. However, the three *char* types are distinct, so you can't mix pointers to different *char* types. For example:

```
void f(char c, signed char sc, unsigned char uc)
{
    char* pc = &uc;              // error: no pointer conversion
    signed char* psc = pc;       // error: no pointer conversion
    unsigned char* puc = pc;     // error: no pointer conversion
    psc = puc;                   // error: no pointer conversion
}
```

Variables of the three *char* types can be freely assigned to each other. However, assigning a too-large value to a signed *char* (§C.6.2.1) is still undefined. For example:

```
void f(char c, signed char sc, unsigned char uc)
{
    c = 255;     // implementation defined if plain chars are signed and have 8 bits

    c = sc;      // ok
    c = uc;      // implementation defined if plain chars are signed and if uc's value is too large
    sc = uc;     // implementation defined if uc's value is too large
    uc = sc;     // ok: conversion to unsigned
    sc = c;      // implementation defined if plain chars are unsigned and if c's value is too large
    uc = c;      // ok: conversion to unsigned
}
```

None of these potential problems occurs if you use plain *char* throughout.

C.4   Types of Integer Literals

In general, the type of an integer literal depends on its form, value, and suffix:
- If it is decimal and has no suffix, it has the first of these types in which its value can be represented: *int, long int, unsigned long int*.
- If it is octal or hexadecimal and has no suffix, it has the first of these types in which its value can be represented: *int, unsigned int, long int, unsigned long int*.
- If it is suffixed by *u* or *U*, its type is the first of these types in which its value can be represented: *unsigned int, unsigned long int*.
- If it is suffixed by *l* or *L*, its type is the first of these types in which its value can be represented: *long int, unsigned long int*.
- If it is suffixed by *ul, lu, uL, Lu, Ul, lU, UL*, or *LU*, its type is *unsigned long int*.

For example, *100000* is of type *int* on a machine with 32-bit *int*s but of type *long int* on a machine with 16-bit *int*s and 32-bit *long*s. Similarly, *0XA000* is of type *int* on a machine with 32-bit *int*s but of type *unsigned int* on a machine with 16-bit *int*s. These implementation dependencies can be avoided by using suffixes: *100000L* is of type *long int* on all machines and *0XA000U* is of type *unsigned int* on all machines.

C.5 Constant Expressions

In places such as array bounds (§5.2), case labels (§6.3.2), and initializers for enumerators (§4.8), C++ requires a *constant expression*. A constant expression evaluates to an integral or enumeration constant. Such an expression is composed of literals (§4.3.1, §4.4.1, §4.5.1), enumerators (§4.8), and *const*s initialized by constant expressions. In a template, an integer template parameter can also be used (§C.13.3). Floating literals (§4.5.1) can be used only if explicitly converted to an integral type. Functions, class objects, pointers, and references can be used as operands to the *sizeof* operator (§6.2) only.

Intuitively, constant expressions are simple expressions that can be evaluated by the compiler before the program is linked (§9.1) and starts to run.

C.6 Implicit Type Conversion

Integral and floating-point types (§4.1.1) can be mixed freely in assignments and expressions. Wherever possible, values are converted so as not to lose information. Unfortunately, value-destroying conversions are also performed implicitly. This section provides a description of conversion rules, conversion problems, and their resolution.

C.6.1 Promotions

The implicit conversions that preserve values are commonly referred to as *promotions*. Before an arithmetic operation is performed, *integral promotion* is used to create *int*s out of shorter integer types. Note that these promotions will *not* promote to *long* (unless the operand is a *wchar_t* or an enumeration that is already larger than an *int*). This reflects the original purpose of these promotions in C: to bring operands to the ''natural'' size for arithmetic operations.

The integral promotions are:

- A *char*, *signed char*, *unsigned char*, *short int*, or *unsigned short int* is converted to an *int* if *int* can represent all the values of the source type; otherwise, it is converted to an *unsigned int*.
- A *wchar_t* (§4.3) or an enumeration type (§4.8) is converted to the first of the following types that can represent all the values of its underlying type: *int*, *unsigned int*, *long*, or *unsigned long*.
- A bit-field (§C.8.1) is converted to an *int* if *int* can represent all the values of the bit-field; otherwise, it is converted to *unsigned int* if *unsigned int* can represent all the values of the bit-field. Otherwise, no integral promotion applies to it.
- A *bool* is converted to an *int*; *false* becomes *0* and *true* becomes *1*.

Promotions are used as part of the usual arithmetic conversions (§C.6.3).

C.6.2 Conversions

The fundamental types can be converted into each other in a bewildering number of ways. In my opinion, too many conversions are allowed. For example:

```
void f(double d)
{
    char c = d;      // beware: double-precision floating-point to char conversion
}
```

When writing code, you should always aim to avoid undefined behavior and conversions that quietly throw away information. A compiler can warn about many questionable conversions. Fortunately, many compilers actually do.

C.6.2.1 Integral Conversions

An integer can be converted to another integer type. An enumeration value can be converted to an integer type.

If the destination type is *unsigned*, the resulting value is simply as many bits from the source as will fit in the destination (high-order bits are thrown away if necessary). More precisely, the result is the least unsigned integer congruent to the source integer modulo 2 to the *n*th, where *n* is the number of bits used to represent the unsigned type. For example:

```
unsigned char uc = 1023;  // binary 1111111111: uc becomes binary 11111111; that is, 255
```

If the destination type is *signed*, the value is unchanged if it can be represented in the destination type; otherwise, the value is implementation-defined:

```
signed char sc = 1023;     // implementation-defined
```

Plausible results are *127* and *–1* (§C.3.4).

A Boolean or enumeration value can be implicitly converted to its integer equivalent (§4.2, §4.8).

C.6.2.2 Floating-Point Conversions

A floating-point value can be converted to another floating-point type. If the source value can be exactly represented in the destination type, the result is the original numeric value. If the source value is between two adjacent destination values, the result is one of those values. Otherwise, the behavior is undefined. For example:

```
float f = FLT_MAX;        // largest float value
double d = f;             // ok: d == f
float f2 = d;             // ok: f2 == f
double d3 = DBL_MAX;      // largest double value
float f3 = d3;            // undefined if FLT_MAX<DBL_MAX
```

C.6.2.3 Pointer and Reference Conversions

Any pointer to an object type can be implicitly converted to a *void** (§5.6). A pointer (reference) to a derived class can be implicitly converted to a pointer (reference) to an accessible and unambiguous base (§12.2). Note that a pointer to function or a pointer to member cannot be implicitly converted to a *void**.

A constant expression (§C.5) that evaluates to *0* can be implicitly converted to any pointer or pointer to member type (§5.1.1). For example:

```
int* p =
        !   !  !    !   !           !
        ! !  !   !    !   !           !
        !  ! !   !    !   !           !
        !    !   !!!!!!  !!!!!    !!!!1;
```

A *T** can be implicitly converted to a *const T** (§5.4.1). Similarly, a *T&* can be implicitly converted to a *const T&*.

C.6.2.4 Pointer-to-Member Conversions

Pointers and references to members can be implicitly converted as described in §15.5.1.

C.6.2.5 Boolean Conversions

Pointers, integral, and floating-point values can be implicitly converted to *bool* (§4.2). A nonzero value converts to *true*; a zero value converts to *false*. For example:

```
void f(int* p, int i)
{
    bool is_not_zero = p;      // true if p!=0
    bool b2 = i;               // true if i!=0
}
```

C.6.2.6 Floating-Integral Conversions

When a floating-point value is converted to an integer value, the fractional part is discarded. In other words, conversion from a floating-point type to an integer type truncates. For example, the value of *int* (*1.6*) is *1*. The behavior is undefined if the truncated value cannot be represented in the destination type. For example:

```
int i = 2.7;        // i becomes 2
char b = 2000.7;    // undefined for 8-bit chars: 2000 cannot be represented as an 8-bit char
```

Conversions from integer to floating types are as mathematically correct as the hardware allows. Loss of precision occurs if an integral value cannot be represented exactly as a value of the floating type. For example,

```
int i = float(1234567890);
```

left *i* with the value *1234567936* on a machine where both *int*s and *float*s are represented using 32 bits.

Clearly, it is best to avoid potentially value-destroying implicit conversions. In fact, compilers can detect and warn against some obviously dangerous conversions, such as floating to integral and *long int* to *char*. However, general compile-time detection is impractical, so the programmer must be careful. When ''being careful'' isn't enough, the programmer can insert explicit checks. For example:

```
class check_failed { };
char checked(int i)
{
    char c = i;                          // warning: not portable (§C.6.2.1)
    if (i != c) throw check_failed();
    return c;
}
void my_code(int i)
{
    char c = checked(i);
    // ...
}
```

To truncate in a way that is guaranteed to be portable requires the use of *numeric_limits* (§22.2).

C.6.3 Usual Arithmetic Conversions

These conversions are performed on the operands of a binary operator to bring them to a common type, which is then used as the type of the result:

[1] If either operand is of type *long double*, the other is converted to *long double*.
 – Otherwise, if either operand is *double*, the other is converted to *double*.
 – Otherwise, if either operand is *float*, the other is converted to *float*.
 – Otherwise, integral promotions (§C.6.1) are performed on both operands.

[2] Then, if either operand is *unsigned long*, the other is converted to *unsigned long*.
 – Otherwise, if one operand is a *long int* and the other is an *unsigned int*, then if a *long int* can represent all the values of an *unsigned int*, the *unsigned int* is converted to a *long int*; otherwise, both operands are converted to *unsigned long int*.
 – Otherwise, if either operand is *long*, the other is converted to *long*.
 – Otherwise, if either operand is *unsigned*, the other is converted to *unsigned*.
 – Otherwise, both operands are *int*.

C.7 Multidimensional Arrays

It is not uncommon to need a vector of vectors, a vector of vector of vectors, etc. The issue is how to represent these multidimensional vectors in C++. Here, I first show how to use the standard library *vector* class. Next, I present multidimensional arrays as they appear in C and C++ programs using only built-in facilities.

C.7.1 Vectors

The standard *vector* (§16.3) provides a very general solution:

```
vector< vector<int> > m(3, vector<int> (5));
```

This creates a vector of 3 vectors of 5 integers each. The 15 integer elements each have the default value *0*. We could assign new values the integer elements like this:

```
void init_m()
{
    for (int i = 0; i<m.size(); i++)
        for (int j = 0; j<m[i].size(); j++) m[i][j] = 10*i+j;
}
```

or graphically:

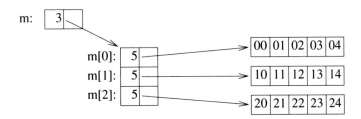

Each *vector* is implemented as a pointer to its elements plus the number of elements. The elements are typically held in an array. For illustration, I gave each *int* a value representing its coordinates.

Accessing an element is done by indexing twice. For example, *m*[*i*][*j*] is the *j*th element of the *i*th vector. We can print *m* like this:

```
void print_m()
{
    for (int i = 0; i<m.size(); i++) {
        for (int j = 0; j<m[i].size(); j++) cout << m[i][j] << '\t';
        cout << '\n';
    }
}
```

which gives:

```
0    1    2    3    4
10   11   12   13   14
20   21   22   23   24
```

Note that *m* is a vector of vectors rather than a simple multidimensional array. In particular, it is possible to resize (§16.3.8) an element. For example:

```
void reshape_m(int ns)
{
    for (int i = 0; i<m.size(); i++) m[i].resize(ns);
}
```

It is not necessary for the *vector<int>*s in the *vector< vector<int> >* to have the same size.

C.7.2 Arrays

The built-in arrays are a major source of errors – especially when they are used to build multidimensional arrays. For novices, they are also a major source of confusion. Wherever possible, use *vector*, *list*, *valarray*, *string*, etc.

Multidimensional arrays are represented as arrays of arrays; a 3-by-5 array is declared like this:

```
int ma[3][5];  // 3 arrays with 5 ints each
```

We can initialize *ma* like this:

```
void init_ma()
{
    for (int i = 0; i<3; i++)
        for (int j = 0; j<5; j++) ma[i][j] = 10*i+j;
}
```

or graphically:

ma: | 00 | 01 | 02 | 03 | 04 | 10 | 11 | 12 | 13 | 14 | 20 | 21 | 22 | 23 | 24 |

The array *ma* is simply 15 *ints* that we access as if it were 3 arrays of 5 *ints*. In particular, there is no single object in memory that is the matrix *ma* – only the elements are stored. The dimensions *3* and *5* exist in the compiler source only. When we write code, it is our job to remember them somehow and supply the dimensions where needed. For example, we might print *ma* like this:

```
void print_ma()
{
    for (int i = 0; i<3; i++) {
        for (int j = 0; j<5; j++) cout << ma[i][j] << '\t';
        cout << '\n';
    }
}
```

The comma notation used for array bounds in some languages cannot be used in C++ because the comma (,) is a sequencing operator (§6.2.2). Fortunately, most mistakes are caught by the compiler. For example:

```
int bad[3,5];            // error: comma not allowed in constant expression
int good[3][5];          // 3 arrays with 5 ints each
int ouch = good[1,4];    // error: int initialized by int* (good[1,4] means good[4], which is an int*)
int nice = good[1][4];
```

C.7.3 Passing Multidimensional Arrays

Consider defining a function to manipulate a two-dimensional matrix. If the dimensions are known at compile time, there is no problem:

```
void print_m35(int m[3][5])
{
    for (int i = 0; i<3; i++) {
        for (int j = 0; j<5; j++) cout << m[i][j] << '\t';
        cout << '\n';
    }
}
```

A matrix represented as a multidimensional array is passed as a pointer (rather than copied; §5.3). The first dimension of an array is irrelevant to the problem of finding the location of an element; it simply states how many elements (here *3*) of the appropriate type (here *int* [*5*]) are present. For example, look at the previous representation of *ma* and note that by our knowing only that the second dimension is *5*, we can locate *ma* [*i*] [*5*] for any *i*. The first dimension can therefore be passed as an argument:

```
void print_mi5 (int m[][5], int dim1)
{
    for (int i = 0; i<dim1; i++) {
        for (int j = 0; j<5; j++) cout << m[i][j] << '\t';
        cout << '\n';
    }
}
```

The difficult case is when both dimensions need to be passed. The "obvious solution" simply does not work:

```
void print_mij (int m[][], int dim1, int dim2) // doesn't behave as most people would think
{
    for (int i = 0; i<dim1; i++) {
        for (int j = 0; j<dim2; j++) cout << m[i][j] << '\t';    // surprise!
        cout << '\n';
    }
}
```

First, the argument declaration *m* [ ] [ ] is illegal because the second dimension of a multidimensional array must be known in order to find the location of an element. Second, the expression *m* [*i*] [*j*] is (correctly) interpreted as * (* (*m*+*i*) +*j*), although that is unlikely to be what the programmer intended. A correct solution is:

```
void print_mij (int* m, int dim1, int dim2)
{
    for (int i = 0; i<dim1; i++) {
        for (int j = 0; j<dim2; j++) cout << m[i*dim2+j] << '\t'; // obscure
        cout << '\n';
    }
}
```

The expression used for accessing the members in *print_mij* ( ) is equivalent to the one the compiler generates when it knows the last dimension.

To call this function, we pass a matrix as an ordinary pointer:

```
int main ()
{
    int v[3][5] = { {0,1,2,3,4}, {10,11,12,13,14}, {20,21,22,23,24} };

    print_m35 (v);
    print_mi5 (v,3);
    print_mij (&v[0][0],3,5);
}
```

Note the use of &v[0][0] for the last call; v[0] would do because it is equivalent, but v would be a type error. This kind of subtle and messy code is best hidden. If you must deal directly with multidimensional arrays, consider encapsulating the code relying on it. In that way, you might ease the task of the next programmer to touch the code. Providing a multidimensional array type with a proper subscripting operator saves most users from having to worry about the layout of the data in the array (§22.4.6).

The standard *vector* (§16.3) doesn't suffer from these problems.

C.8 Saving Space

When programming nontrivial applications, there often comes a time when you want more memory space than is available or affordable. There are two ways of squeezing more space out of what is available:

[1] Put more than one small object into a byte.

[2] Use the same space to hold different objects at different times.

The former can be achieved by using *fields*, and the latter by using *unions*. These constructs are described in the following sections. Many uses of fields and unions are pure optimizations, and these optimizations are often based on nonportable assumptions about memory layouts. Consequently, the programmer should think twice before using them. Often, a better approach is to change the way data is managed, for example, to rely more on dynamically allocated store (§6.2.6) and less on preallocated (static) storage.

C.8.1 Fields

It seems extravagant to use a whole byte (a *char* or a *bool*) to represent a binary variable – for example, an on/off switch – but a *char* is the smallest object that can be independently allocated and addressed in C++ (§5.1). It is possible, however, to bundle several such tiny variables together as *fields* in a *struct*. A member is defined to be a field by specifying the number of bits it is to occupy. Unnamed fields are allowed. They do not affect the meaning of the named fields, but they can be used to make the layout better in some machine-dependent way:

```
struct PPN {            // R6000 Physical Page Number
    unsigned int PFN : 22;    // Page Frame Number
    int : 3;                  // unused
    unsigned int CCA : 3;     // Cache Coherency Algorithm
    bool nonreachable : 1;
    bool dirty : 1;
    bool valid : 1;
    bool global : 1;
};
```

This example also illustrates the other main use of fields: to name parts of an externally imposed layout. A field must be of an integral or enumeration type (§4.1.1). It is not possible to take the address of a field. Apart from that, however, it can be used exactly like other variables. Note that a *bool* field really can be represented by a single bit. In an operating system kernel or in a debugger, the type *PPN* might be used like this:

```
void part_of_VM_system (PPN* p)
{
    // ...

    if (p->dirty) {  // contents changed
        // copy to disc
        p->dirty = 0;
    }

    // ...
}
```

Surprisingly, using fields to pack several variables into a single byte does not necessarily save space. It saves data space, but the size of the code needed to manipulate these variables increases on most machines. Programs have been known to shrink significantly when binary variables were converted from bit fields to characters! Furthermore, it is typically much faster to access a *char* or an *int* than to access a field. Fields are simply a convenient shorthand for using bitwise logical operators (§6.2.4) to extract information from and insert information into part of a word.

C.8.2 Unions

A *union* is a *struct* in which all members are allocated at the same address so that the *union* occupies only as much space as its largest member. Naturally, a *union* can hold a value for only one member at a time. For example, consider a symbol table entry that holds a name and a value:

```
enum Type { S, I };

struct Entry {
    char* name;
    Type t;
    char* s;    // use s if t==S
    int i;      // use i if t==I
};

void f(Entry* p)
{
    if (p->t == S) cout << p->s;
    // ...
}
```

The members *s* and *i* can never be used at the same time, so space is wasted. It can be easily recovered by specifying that both should be members of a *union*, like this:

```
union Value {
    char* s;
    int i;
};
```

The language doesn't keep track of which kind of value is held by a *union*, so the programmer must still do that:

```
struct Entry {
    char* name;
    Type t;
    Value v;  // use v.s if t==S; use v.i if t==I
};

void f(Entry* p)
{
    if (p->t == S) cout << p->v.s;
    // ...
}
```

Unfortunately, the introduction of the **union** forced us to rewrite code to say *v.s* instead of plain *s*. This can be avoided by using an *anonymous union*, which is a union that doesn't have a name and consequently doesn't define a type. Instead, it simply ensures that its members are allocated at the same address:

```
struct Entry {
    char* name;
    Type t;
    union {
        char* s;   // use s if t==S
        int i;     // use i if t==I
    };
};

void f(Entry* p)
{
    if (p->t == S) cout << p->s;
    // ...
}
```

This leaves all code using an *Entry* unchanged.

Using a **union** so that its value is always read using the member through which it was written is a pure optimization. However, it is not always easy to ensure that a **union** is used in this way only, and subtle errors can be introduced through misuse. To avoid errors, one can encapsulate a **union** so that the correspondence between a type field and access to the **union** members can be guaranteed (§10.6[20]).

Unions are sometimes misused for "type conversion." This misuse is practiced mainly by programmers trained in languages that do not have explicit type conversion facilities, where cheating is necessary. For example, the following "converts" an *int* to an *int** simply by assuming bitwise equivalence:

```
union Fudge {
    int i;
    int* p;
};
```

```
int* cheat (int i)
{
    Fudge a;
    a.i = i;
    return a.p;       // bad use
}
```

This is not really a conversion at all. On some machines, an *int* and an *int** do not occupy the same amount of space, while on others, no integer can have an odd address. Such use of a *union* is dangerous and nonportable, and there is an explicit and portable way of specifying type conversion (§6.2.7).

Unions are occasionally used deliberately to avoid type conversion. One might, for example, use a *Fudge* to find the representation of the pointer *0*:

```
int main ()
{
    Fudge foo;
    foo.p = 0;
    cout << "the integer value of the pointer 0 is " << foo.i << '\n';
}
```

C.8.3 Unions and Classes

Many nontrivial *union*s have some members that are much larger than the most frequently-used members. Because the size of a *union* is at least as large as its largest member, space is wasted. This waste can often be eliminated by using a set of derived classes instead of a *union*.

A class with a constructor, destructor, or copy operation cannot be the type of a *union* member (§10.4.12) because the compiler would not know which member to destroy.

C.9 Memory Management

There are three fundamental ways of using memory in C++:

Static memory, in which an object is allocated by the linker for the duration of the program. Global and namespace variables, *static* class members (§10.2.4), and *static* variables in functions (§7.1.2) are allocated in static memory. An object allocated in static memory is constructed once and persists to the end of the program. It always has the same address. Static objects can be a problem in programs using threads (shared-address space concurrency) because they are shared and require locking for proper access.

Automatic memory, in which function arguments and local variables are allocated. Each entry into a function or a block gets its own copy. This kind of memory is automatically created and destroyed; hence the name automatic memory. Automatic memory is also said ''to be on the stack.'' If you absolutely must be explicit about this, C++ provides the redundant keyword *auto*.

Free store, from which memory for objects is explicitly requested by the program and where a program can free memory again once it is done with it (using *new* and *delete*). When a program needs more free store, *new* requests it from the operating system. Typically, the free store (also called *dynamic memory* or *the heap*) grows throughout the lifetime of a program because no memory is ever returned to the operating system for use by other programs.

As far as the programmer is concerned, automatic and static storage are used in simple, obvious, and implicit ways. The interesting question is how to manage the free store. Allocation (using *new*) is simple, but unless we have a consistent policy for giving memory back to the free store manager, memory will fill up – especially for long-running programs.

The simplest strategy is to use automatic objects to manage corresponding objects in free store. Consequently, many containers are implemented as handles to elements stored in the free store (§25.7). For example, an automatic *String* (§11.12) manages a sequence of characters on the free store and automatically frees that memory when it itself goes out of scope. All of the standard containers (§16.3, Chapter 17, Chapter 20, §22.4) can be conveniently implemented in this way.

C.9.1 Automatic Garbage Collection

When this regular approach isn't sufficient, the programmer might use a memory manager that finds unreferenced objects and reclaims their memory in which to store new objects. This is usually called *automatic garbage collection*, or simply *garbage collection*. Naturally, such a memory manager is called a *garbage collector*.

The fundamental idea of garbage collection is that an object that is no longer referred to in a program will not be accessed again, so its memory can be safely reused for some new object. For example:

```
void f( )
{
    int* p = new int;
    p = 0;
    char* q = new char;
}
```

Here, the assignment *p=0* makes the *int* unreferenced so that its memory can be used for some other new object. Thus, the *char* might be allocated in the same memory as the *int* so that *q* holds the value that *p* originally had.

The standard does not require that an implementation supply a garbage collector, but garbage collectors are increasingly used for C++ in areas where their costs compare favorably to those of manual management of free store. When comparing costs, consider the run time, memory usage, reliability, portability, monetary cost of programming, monetary cost of a garbage collector, and predictability of performance.

C.9.1.1 Disguised Pointers

What should it mean for an object to be unreferenced? Consider:

```
void f( )
{
    int* p = new int;
    long i1 = reinterpret_cast<long> (p) &0xFFFF0000;
    long i2 = reinterpret_cast<long> (p) &0x0000FFFF;
    p = 0;
```

```
        // point #1: no pointer to the int exists here

        p = reinterpret_cast<int*> (i1 | i2);
        // now the int is referenced again
    }
```

Often, pointers stored as non-pointers in a program are called "disguised pointers." In particular, the pointer originally held in *p* is disguised in the integers *i1* and *i2*. However, a garbage collector need not be concerned about disguised pointers. If the garbage collector runs at point #*1*, the memory holding the *int* can be reclaimed. In fact, such programs are not guaranteed to work even if a garbage collector is not used because the use of *reinterpret_cast* to convert between integers and pointers is at best implementation-defined.

A *union* that can hold both pointers and non-pointers presents a garbage collector with a special problem. In general, it is not possible to know whether such a *union* contains a pointer. Consider:

```
union  U {        // union with both pointer and non-pointer members
      int* p;
      int  i;
};
void f(U  u,  U  u2,  U  u3)
{
      u.p = new  int;
      u2.i = 999999;
      u.i = 8;
      // ...
}
```

The safe assumption is that any value that appears in such a *union* is a pointer value. A clever garbage collector can do somewhat better. For example, it may notice that (for a given implementation) *int*s are not allocated with odd addresses and that no objects are allocated with an address as low as *8*. Noticing this will save the garbage collector from having to assume that objects containing locations *999999* and *8* are used by *f*( ).

C.9.1.2 Delete

If an implementation automatically collects garbage, the *delete* and *delete*[ ] operators are no longer needed to free memory for potential reuse. Thus, a user relying on a garbage collector could simply refrain from using these operators. However, in addition to freeing memory, *delete* and *delete*[ ] invoke destructors.

In the presence of a garbage collector,

```
    delete p;
```

invokes the destructor for the object pointed to by *p* (if any). However, reuse of the memory can be postponed until it is collected. Recycling lots of objects at once can help limit fragmentation (§C.9.1.4). It also renders harmless the otherwise serious mistake of deleting an object twice in the important case where the destructor simply deletes memory.

As always, access to an object after it has been deleted is undefined.

C.9.1.3 Destructors

When an object is about to be recycled by a garbage collector, two alternatives exist:

[1] Call the destructor (if any) for the object.

[2] Treat the object as raw memory (don't call its destructor).

By default, a garbage collector should choose option (2) because objects created using *new* and never *delete*d are never destroyed. Thus, one can see a garbage collector as a mechanism for simulating an infinite memory.

It is possible to design a garbage collector to invoke the destructors for objects that have been specifically "registered" with the collector. However, there is no standard way of "registering" objects. Note that it is always important to destroy objects in an order that ensures that the destructor for one object doesn't refer to an object that has been previously destroyed. Such ordering isn't easily achieved by a garbage collector without help from the programmer.

C.9.1.4 Memory Fragmentation

When a lot of objects of varying sizes are allocated and freed, the memory *fragments*. That is, much of memory is consumed by pieces of memory that are too small to use effectively. The reason is that a general allocator cannot always find a piece of memory of the exact right size for an object. Using a slightly larger piece means that a smaller fragment of memory remains. After running a program for a while with a naive allocator, it is not uncommon to find half the available memory taken up with fragments too small ever to get reused.

Several techniques exist for coping with fragmentation. The simplest is to request only larger chunks of memory from the allocator and use each such chunk for objects of the same size (§15.3, §19.4.2). Because most allocations and deallocations are of small objects of types such as tree nodes, links, etc., this technique can be very effective. An allocator can sometimes apply similar techniques automatically. In either case, fragmentation is further reduced if all of the larger "chunks" are of the same size (say, the size of a page) so that they themselves can be allocated and reallocated without fragmentation.

There are two main styles of garbage collectors:

[1] A *copying collector* moves objects in memory to compact fragmented space.

[2] A *conservative collector* allocates objects to minimize fragmentation.

From a C++ point of view, conservative collectors are preferable because it is very hard (probably impossible in real programs) to move an object and modify all pointers to it correctly. A conservative collector also allows C++ code fragments to coexist with code written in languages such as C. Traditionally, copying collectors have been favored by people using languages (such as Lisp and Smalltalk) that deal with objects only indirectly through unique pointers or references. However, modern conservative collectors seem to be at least as efficient as copying collectors for larger programs, in which the amount of copying and the interaction between the allocator and a paging system become important. For smaller programs, the ideal of simply never invoking the collector is often achievable – especially in C++, where many objects are naturally automatic.

C.10 Namespaces

This section presents minor points about namespaces that look like technicalities, yet frequently surface in discussions and in real code.

C.10.1 Convenience vs. Safety

A *using-declaration* adds a name to a local scope. A *using-directive* does not; it simply renders names accessible in the scope in which they were declared. For example:

```
namespace X {
    int i, j, k;
}

int k;

void f1 ( )
{
    int i = 0;
    using namespace X;     // make names from X accessible
    i++;                   // local i
    j++;                   // X::j
    k++;                   // error: X::k or global k ?
    ::k++;                 // the global k
    X::k++;                // X's k
}

void f2 ( )
{
    int i = 0;
    using X::i;     // error: i declared twice in f2()
    using X::j;
    using X::k;     // hides global k

    i++;
    j++;            // X::j
    k++;            // X::k
}
```

A locally declared name (declared either by an ordinary declaration or by a *using-declaration*) hides nonlocal declarations of the same name, and any illegal overloadings of the name are detected at the point of declaration.

Note the ambiguity error for k++ in $f1$ ( ). Global names are not given preference over names from namespaces made accessible in the global scope. This provides significant protection against accidental name clashes, and − importantly − ensures that there are no advantages to be gained from polluting the global namespace.

When libraries declaring *many* names are made accessible through *using-directives*, it is a significant advantage that clashes of unused names are not considered errors.

The global scope is just another namespace. The global namespace is odd only in that you don't have to mention its name in an explicit qualification. That is, ::k means "look for k in the global namespace and in namespaces mentioned in *using−directives* in the global namespace," whereas $X::k$ means "the k declared in namespace X and namespaces mentioned in *using-directives* in X" (§8.2.8).

I hope to see a radical decrease in the use of global names in new programs using namespaces compared to traditional C and C++ programs. The rules for namespaces were specifically crafted to give no advantages to a "lazy" user of global names over someone who takes care not to pollute the global scope.

C.10.2 Nesting of Namespaces

One obvious use of namespaces is to wrap a complete set of declarations and definitions in a separate namespace:

```
namespace X {
    // all my declarations
}
```

The list of declarations will, in general, contain namespaces. Thus, nested namespaces are allowed. This is allowed for practical reasons, as well as for the simple reason that constructs ought to nest unless there is a strong reason for them not to. For example:

```
void h();

namespace X {
    void g();
    // ...
    namespace Y {
        void f();
        void ff();
        // ...
    }
}
```

The usual scope and qualification rules apply:

```
void X::Y::ff()
{
    f(); g(); h();
}

void X::g()
{
    f();         // error: no f() in X
    Y::f();      // ok
}

void h()
{
    f();            // error: no global f()
    Y::f();         // error: no global Y
    X::f();         // error: no f() in X
    X::Y::f();      // ok
}
```

C.10.3 Namespaces and Classes

A namespace is a named scope. A class is a type defined by a named scope that describes how objects of that type can be created and used. Thus, a namespace is a simpler concept than a class and ideally a class would be defined as a namespace with a few extra facilities included. This is almost the case. A namespace is open (§8.2.9.3), but a class is closed. This difference stems from the observation that a class needs to define the layout of an object and that is best done in one place. Furthermore, *using-declarations* and *using-directives* can be applied to classes only in a very restricted way (§15.2.2).

Namespaces are preferred over classes when all that is needed is encapsulation of names. In this case, the class apparatus for type checking and for creating objects is not needed; the simpler namespace concept suffices.

C.11 Access Control

This section presents a few technical examples illustrating access control to supplement those presented in §15.3.

C.11.1 Access to Members

Consider:

```
class X {
// private by default:
        int priv;
protected:
        int prot;
public:
        int publ;
        void m();
};
```

The member *X::m()* has unrestricted access:

```
void X::m()
{
    priv = 1;   // ok
    prot = 2;   // ok
    publ = 3;   // ok
}
```

A member of a derived class has access to public and protected members (§15.3):

```
class Y : public X {
    void mderived();
};
```

```
void  Y::mderived()
{
      priv = 1;   // error: priv is private
      prot = 2;   // ok: prot is protected and mderived() is a member of the derived class Y
      publ = 3;   // ok: publ is public
}
```

A global function can access only the public members:

```
void  f(Y* p)
{
      p->priv = 1;    // error: priv is private
      p->prot = 2;    // error: prot is protected and f() is not a friend or a member of X or Y
      p->publ = 3;    // ok: publ is public
}
```

C.11.2 Access to Base Classes

Like a member, a base class can be declared *private*, *protected*, or *public*. Consider:

```
class  X {
public:
      int  a;
      // ...
};

class  Y1 : public  X { };
class  Y2 : protected  X { };
class  Y3 : private  X { };
```

Because *X* is a public base of *Y1*, any function can (implicitly) convert a *Y1** to an *X** where needed just as it can access the public members of class *X*. For example:

```
void  f(Y1* py1, Y2* py2, Y3* py3)
{
      X* px = py1;    // ok: X is a public base class of Y1
      py1->a = 7;     // ok

      px = py2;       // error: X is a protected base of Y2
      py2->a = 7;     // error

      px = py3;       // error: X is a private base of Y3
      py3->a = 7;     // error
}
```

Consider:

```
class  Y2 : protected  X { };
class  Z2 : public  Y2 { void  f(Y1*, Y2*, Y3*); };
```

Because *X* is a protected base of *Y2*, only members and friends of *Y2* and members and friends of *Y2*'s derived classes (e.g., *Z2*) can (implicitly) convert a *Y2** to an *X** where needed, just as they can access the public and protected members of class *X*. For example:

```
void Z2::f(Y1* py1, Y2* py2, Y3* py3)
{
    X* px = py1;    // ok: X is a public base class of Y1
    py1->a = 7;     // ok

    px = py2;       // ok: X is a protected base of Y2, and Z2 is derived from Y2
    py2->a = 7;     // ok

    px = py3;       // error: X is a private base of Y3
    py3->a = 7;     // error
}
```

Consider finally:

```
class Y3 : private X { void f(Y1*, Y2*, Y3*); };
```

Because *X* is a private base of *Y3*, only members and friends of *Y3* can (implicitly) convert a *Y3** to an *X** where needed, just as they can access the public and protected members of class *X*. For example:

```
void Y3::f(Y1* py1, Y2* py2, Y3* py3)
{
    X* px = py1;    // ok: X is a public base class of Y1
    py1->a = 7;     // ok

    px = py2;       // error: X is a protected base of Y2
    py2->a = 7;     // error

    px = py3;       // ok: X is a private base of Y3, and Y3::f() is a member of Y3
    py3->a = 7;     // ok
}
```

C.11.3 Access to Member Class

The members of a member class have no special access to members of an enclosing class. Similarly members of an enclosing class have no special access to members of a nested class; the usual access rules (§10.2.2) shall be obeyed. For example:

```
class Outer {
    typedef int T;
    int i;
public:
    int i2;
    static int s;

    class Inner {
        int x;
        T y; // error: Outer::T is private
    public:
        void f(Outer* p, int v);
    };
```

```
        int g (Inner* p);
};

void Outer::Inner::f(Outer* p, int v)
{
    p->i = v;          // error: Outer::i is private
    p->i2 = v;         // ok: Outer::i2 is public
}

int Outer::g (Inner* p)
{
    p->f(this, 2);     // ok: Inner::f() is public
    return p->x;       // error: Inner::x is private
}
```

However, it is often useful to grant a member class access to its enclosing class. This can be done by making the member a *friend*. For example:

```
class Outer {
    typedef int T;
    int i;
public:
    class Inner;               // forward declaration of member class
    friend class Inner;        // grant access to Outer::Inner

    class Inner {
        int x;
        T y;          // ok: Inner is a friend
    public:
        void f(Outer* p, int v);
    };
};

void Outer::Inner::f(Outer* p, int v)
{
    p->i = v;  // ok: Inner is a friend
}
```

C.11.4 Friendship

Friendship is neither inherited nor transitive. For example:

```
class A {
    friend class B;
    int a;
};

class B {
    friend class C;
};
```

```
class C {
    void f(A* p)
    {
        p->a++;   // error: C is not a friend of A, despite being a friend of a friend of A
    }
};
class D : public B {
    void f(A* p)
    {
        p->a++;   // error: D is not a friend of A, despite being derived from a friend of A
    }
};
```

C.12 Pointers to Data Members

Naturally, the notion of pointer to member (§15.5) applies to data members and to member functions with arguments and return types. For example:

```
struct C {
    const char* val;
    int i;
    void print(int x) { cout << val << x << '\n'; }
    int f1(int);
    void f2();
    C(const char* v) { val = v; }
};

typedef void (C::*PMFI)(int);       // pointer to member function of C taking an int
typedef const char* C::*PM;         // pointer to char* data member of C

void f(C& z1, C& z2)
{
    C* p = &z2;
    PMFI pf = &C::print;
    PM pm = &C::val;

    z1.print(1);
    (z1.*pf)(2);
    z1.*pm = "nv1 ";
    p->*pm = "nv2 ";
    z2.print(3);
    (p->*pf)(4);

    pf = &C::f1;      // error: return type mismatch
    pf = &C::f2;      // error: argument type mismatch
    pm = &C::i;       // error: type mismatch
    pm = pf;          // error: type mismatch
}
```

The type of a pointer to function is checked just like any other type.

C.13 Templates

A class template specifies how a class can be generated given a suitable set of template arguments. Similarly, a function template specifies how a function can be generated given a suitable set of template arguments. Thus, a template can be used to generate types and executable code. With this expressive power comes some complexity. Most of this complexity relates to the variety of contexts involved in the definition and use of templates.

C.13.1 Static Members

A class template can have *static* members. Each class generated from the template has its own copy of the static members. Static members must be separately defined and can be specialized. For example:

```
template<class T> class X {
     // ...
     static T def_val;
     static T* new_X(T a = def_val);
};

template<class T> T X<T>::def_val(0,0);
template<class T> T* X<T>::new_X(T a) { /* ... */ }

template<> int X<int>::def_val<int> = 0;
template<> int* X<int>::new_X<int>(int i) { /* ... */ }
```

If you want to share an object or function among all members of every class generated from a template, you can place it in a non-templatized base class. For example:

```
struct B {
     static B* nil;    // to be used as common null pointer for every class derived from B
};

template<class T> class X : public B {
     // ...
};

B* B::nil = 0;
```

C.13.2 Friends

Like other classes, a template class can have friends. Consider the *Matrix* and *Vector* example from §11.5. Typically, both *Matrix* and *Vector* will be templates:

```
template<class T> class Matrix;

template<class T> class Vector {
     T v[4];
public:
     friend Vector operator*<>(const Matrix<T>&, const Vector&);
     // ...
};
```

```
template<class T> class Matrix {
    Vector<T> v[4];
public:
    friend Vector<T> operator*<>(const Matrix&, const Vector<T>&);
    // ...
};
```

The `<>` after the name of the friend function is needed to make clear that the friend is a template function. Without the `<>`, a non-template function would be assumed. The multiplication operator can then be defined to access data from *Vector* and *Matrix* directly :

```
template<class T> Vector<T> operator* (const Matrix<T>& m, const Vector<T>& v)
{
    // ... use m.v[i] and v.v[i] for direct access to elements ...
}
```

Friends do not affect the scope in which the template class is defined, nor do they affect the scope in which the template is used. Instead, friend functions and operators are found using a lookup based on their argument types (§11.2.4, §11.5.1). Like a member function, a friend function is instantiated (§C.13.9.1) only if it is called.

C.13.3 Templates as Template Parameters

Sometimes it is useful to pass templates – rather than classes or objects – as template arguments. For example:

```
template<class T, template<class> class C> class Xrefd {
    C<T> mems;
    C<T*> refs;
    // ...
};

Xrefd<Entry, vector> x1;      // store cross references for Entries in a vector

Xrefd<Record, set> x2;        // store cross references for Records in a set
```

To use a template as a template parameter, you specify its required arguments. The template parameters of the template parameter need to be known in order to use the template parameter. The point of using a template as a template parameter is usually that we want to instantiate it with a variety of argument types (such as *T* and *T** in the previous example). That is, we want to express the member declarations of a template in terms of another template, but we want that other template to be a parameter so that it can be specified by users.

The common case in which a template needs a container to hold elements of its own argument type is often better handled by passing the container type (§13.6, §17.3.1).

Only class templates can be template arguments.

C.13.4 Deducing Function Template Arguments

A compiler can deduce a type template argument, *T* or *TT*, and a non-type template argument, *I*, from a template function argument with a type composed of the following constructs:

T	*const T*	*volatile T*
T*	*T&*	*T*[*constant_expression*]
type[*I*]	*class_template_name<T>*	*class_template_name<I>*
TT<T>	*T<I>*	*T<>*
T type::*	*T T*::*	*type T*::*
T (***) (*args*)	*type* (*T*::*) (*args*)	*T* (*type*::*) (*args*)
type (*type*::*) (*args_TI*)	*T* (*T*::*) (*args_TI*)	*type* (*T*::*) (*args_TI*)
T (*type*::*) (*args_TI*)	*type* (***) (*args_TI*)	

Here, *args_TI* is a parameter list from which a *T* or an *I* can be determined by recursive application of these rules and *args* is a parameter list that does not allow deduction. If not all parameters can be deduced in this way, a call is ambiguous. For example:

```
template<class T, class U> void f(const T*, U(*)(U));

int g(int);

void h(const char* p)
{
    f(p,g);    // T is char, U is int
    f(p,h);    // error: can't deduce U
}
```

Looking at the arguments of the first call of *f*(), we easily deduce the template arguments. Looking at the second call of *f*(), we see that *h*() doesn't match the pattern *U*(***)(*U*) because *h*()'s argument and return types differ.

If a template parameter can be deduced from more than one function argument, the same type must be the result of each deduction. Otherwise, the call is an error. For example:

```
template<class T> void f(T i, T* p);

void g(int i)
{
    f(i,&i);            // ok
    f(i,"Remember!");   // error, ambiguous: T is int or T is const char?
}
```

C.13.5 Typename and Template

To make generic programming easier and more general, the standard library containers provide a set of standard functions and types (§16.3.1). For example:

```
template<class T> class vector {
public:
    typedef T* iterator;
```

```
        iterator begin ( ) ;
        iterator end ( ) ;

        // ...
};
template<class T> class list {
        class link { / * ... * / } ;
public :
        typedef link* iterator;

        iterator begin ( ) ;
        iterator end ( ) ;

        // ...
};
```

This tempts us to write:

```
template<class C> void f(C& v)
{
        C::iterator i = v.begin ( ) ; // syntax error
        // ...
}
```

Unfortunately, the compiler isn't psychic, so it doesn't know that $C::iterator$ is the name of a type. In some cases, a clever compiler would be able to guess whether a name was intended as a type name or as the name of something that is not a type (such as a function or a template), but in general that is not possible. Consider an example stripped of clues as to its meaning:

```
int y;
template<class T> void g (T& v)
{
        T::x(y); // function call or variable declaration?
}
```

Is $T::x$ a function called with y as its argument? Or, did we intend to declare a local variable y with the type $T::x$ perversely using redundant parentheses? We could imagine a context in which $X::x(y)$ was a function call and $Y::x(y)$ was a declaration.

The resolution is simple: unless otherwise stated, an identifier is assumed to refer to something that is not a type or a template. If we want to state that something should be treated as a type, we can do so using the *typename* keyword:

```
template<class C> void h (C& v)
{
        typename C::iterator i = v.begin ( ) ;
        // ...
}
```

The *typename* keyword can be placed in front of a qualified name to state that the entity named is a type. In this, it resembles *struct* and *class*.

The *typename* keyword is required whenever a type name depends on a template parameter.

For example:

```
template<class T>
void k(vector<T>& v)
{
      vector<T>::iterator i = v.begin();             // syntax error: "typename" missing
      typename vector<T>::iterator i = v.begin();    // ok
      // ...
}
```

In this case, compiler might be able to determine that *iterator* was the name of a type in every instantiation of *vector*, but the compiler is not required to. Doing so would be a nonstandard and nonportable language extension. The only contexts where a compiler assumes that a name that depends on a template argument is a type name is in a few cases where only type names are allowed by the grammar. For example, in a *base-specifier* (§A.8.1).

The *typename* keyword can also be used as an alternative to *class* in template declarations:

```
template<typename T> void f(T);
```

Being an indifferent typist and always short of screen space, I prefer the shorter:

```
template<class T> void f(T);
```

C.13.6 Template as a Qualifier

The need for the *typename* qualifier arises because we can refer both to members that are types and to members that are non-types. Similarly, the need to distinguish the name of a template member from other member names can arise. Consider a possible interface to a general memory manager:

```
class Memory { // some Allocator
public:
      template<class T> T* get_new();
      template<class T> void release(T&);
      // ...
};

template<class Allocator> void f(Allocator& m)
{
      int* p1 = m.get_new<int>();             // syntax error: int after less-than operator
      int* p2 = m.template get_new<int>();    // explicit qualification
      // ...
      m.release(p1); // template argument deduced: no explicit qualification needed
      m.release(p2);
}
```

Explicit qualification of *get_new*() is necessary because its template parameter cannot be deduced. In this case, the *template* prefix must be used to inform the compiler (and the human reader) that *get_new* is a member template so that explicit qualification with the desired type of element is possible. Without the qualification with *template*, we would get a syntax error because the < would be assumed to be a less-than operator. The need for qualification with *template* is rare because most template parameters are deduced.

C.13.7 Instantiation

Given a template definition and a use of that template, it is the implementation's job to generate correct code. From a class template and a set of template arguments, the compiler needs to generate the definition of a class and the definitions of those of its member functions that were used. From a template function, a function needs to be generated. This process is commonly called *template instantiation.*

The generated classes and functions are called *specializations.* When there is a need to distinguish between generated specializations and specializations explicitly written by the programmer (§13.5), these are referred to as *generated specializations* and *explicit specializations,* respectively. An explicit specialization is sometimes referred to as a *user-defined specialization,* or simply a *user specialization.*

To use templates in nontrivial programs, a programmer must understand how names used in a template definition are bound to declarations and how source code can be organized (§13.7).

By default, the compiler generates classes and functions from the templates used in accordance with the name-binding rules (§C.13.8). That is, a programmer need not state explicitly which versions of which templates must be generated. This is important because it is not easy for a programmer to know exactly which versions of a template are needed. Often, templates that the programmer hasn't even heard of are used in the implementation of libraries, and sometimes templates that the programmer does know of are used with unknown template argument types. In general, the set of generated functions needed can be known only by recursive examination of the templates used in application code libraries. Computers are better suited than humans for doing such analysis.

However, it is sometimes important for a programmer to be able to state specifically where code should be generated from a template (§C.13.10). By doing so, the programmer gains detailed control over the context of the instantiation. In most compilation environments, this also implies control over exactly when that instantiation is done. In particular, explicit instantiation can be used to force compilation errors to occur at predictable times rather than occurring whenever an implementation determines the need to generate a specialization. A perfectly predictable build process is essential to some users.

C.13.8 Name Binding

It is important to define template functions so that they have as few dependencies as possible on nonlocal information. The reason is that a template will be used to generate functions and classes based on unknown types and in unknown contexts. Every subtle context dependency is likely to surface as a debugging problem for some programmer – and that programmer is unlikely to want to know the implementation details of the template. The general rule of avoiding global names as far as possible should be taken especially seriously in template code. Thus, we try to make template definitions as self-contained as possible and to supply much of what would otherwise have been global context in the form of template parameters (e.g., traits; §13.4, §20.2.1).

However, some nonlocal names must be used. In particular, it is more common to write a set of cooperating template functions than to write just one self-contained function. Sometimes, such functions can be class members, but not always. Sometimes, nonlocal functions are the best choice. Typical examples of that are *sort* ( )'s calls to *swap* ( ) and *less* ( ) (§13.5.2). The standard library algorithms provide a large-scale example (Chapter 18).

Operations with conventional names and semantics, such as +, *, [ ], and *sort* ( ), are another source of nonlocal name use in a template definition. Consider:

```
#include<vector>

bool  tracing;

// ...

template<class  T>  T  sum (std::vector<T>& v)
{
    T  t = 0;
    if (tracing) cerr << "sum(" << &v << ")\n";
    for (int  i = 0; i<v.size(); i++) t = t + v[i];
    return  t;
}

// ...

#include<quad.h>

void  f(std::vector<Quad>& v)
{
    Quad  c = sum(v);
}
```

The innocent-looking template function *sum* ( ) depends on the + operator. In this example, + is defined in *<quad.h>*:

```
Quad  operator+(Quad, Quad);
```

Importantly, nothing related to complex numbers is in scope when *sum* ( ) is defined and the writer of *sum* ( ) cannot be assumed to know about class **Quad**. In particular, the + may be defined later than *sum* ( ) in the program text, and even later in time.

The process of finding the declaration for each name explicitly or implicitly used in a template is called *name binding*. The general problem with template name binding is that three contexts are involved in a template instantiation and they cannot be cleanly separated:

[1] The context of the template definition

[2] The context of the argument type declaration

[3] The context of the use of the template

C.13.8.1 Dependent Names

When defining a function template, we want to assure that enough context is available for the template definition to make sense in terms of its actual arguments without picking up ''accidental'' stuff from the environment of a point of use. To help with this, the language separates names used in a template definition into two categories:

[1] Names that depend on a template argument. Such names are bound at some point of instantiation (§C.13.8.3). In the *sum* ( ) example, the definition of + can be found in the instantiation context because it takes operands of the template argument type.

[2] Names that don't depend on a template argument. Such names are bound at the point of definition of the template (§C.13.8.2). In the *sum*( ) example, the template *vector* is defined in the standard header *<vector>* and the Boolean *tracing* is in scope when the definition of *sum*( ) is encountered by the compiler.

The simplest definition of ''*N* depends on a template parameter *T*'' would be ''*N* is a member of *T*.'' Unfortunately, this doesn't quite suffice; addition of *Quad*s (§C.13.8) is a counter-example. Consequently, a function call is said to *depend on* a template argument if and only if one of these conditions hold:

[1] The type of the actual argument depends on a template parameter *T* according to the type deduction rules (§13.3.1). For example, $f(T(1))$, $f(t)$, $f(g(t))$, and $f(\&t)$, assuming that *t* is a *T*.

[2] The function called has a formal parameter that depends on *T* according to the type deduction rules (§13.3.1). For example, $f(T)$, $f(list<T>\&)$, and $f(const\ T^*)$.

Basically, the name of a function called is dependent if it is obviously dependent by looking at its arguments or at its formal parameters.

A call that by coincidence has an argument that matches an actual template parameter type is not dependent. For example:

```
template<class T> T f(T a)
{
    return g(1);    // error: no g() in scope and g(1) doesn't depend on T
}

int g(int);

int z = f(2);
```

It doesn't matter that for the call $f(2)$, *T* happens to be *int* and $g()$'s argument just happens to be an *int*. Had $g(1)$ been considered dependent, its meaning would have been most subtle and mysterious to the reader of the template definition. If a programmer wants $g(int)$ to be called, $g(int)$'s declaration should be placed before the definition of $f()$ so that $g(int)$ is in scope when $f()$ is analyzed. This is exactly the same rule as for non-template function definitions.

In addition to function names, the name of a variable, type, *const*, etc., can be dependent if its type depends on a template parameter. For example:

```
template<class T> void fct(const T& a)
{
    typename T::Memtype p = a.p;    // p and Memtype depend on T
    cout << a.i << ' ' << p->j;    // i and j depend on T
}
```

C.13.8.2 Point of Definition Binding

When the compiler sees a template definition, it determines which names are dependent (§C.13.8.1). If a name is dependent, looking for its declaration must be postponed until instantiation time (§C.13.8.3).

Names that do not depend on a template argument must be in scope (§4.9.4) at the point of definition. For example:

```
int x;

template<class T> T f(T a)
{
      x++;        // ok
      y++;        // error: no y in scope, and y doesn't depend on T
      return a;
}

int y;

int z = f(2);
```

If a declaration is found, that declaration is used even if a ''better'' declaration might be found later. For example:

```
void g(double);

template<class T> class X : public T {
public:
      void f() { g(2); }   // call g(double);
      // ...
};

void g(int);

class Z { };

void h(X<Z> x)
{
      x.f();
}
```

When a definition for *X<Z>::f()* is generated, *g(int)* is not considered because it is declared after *X*. It doesn't matter that *X* is not used until after the declaration of *g(int)*. Also, a call that isn't dependent cannot be hijacked in a base class:

```
class Y { public: void g(int); };

void h(X<Y> x)
{
      x.f();
}
```

Again, *X<Y>::f()* will call *g(double)*. If the programmer had wanted the *g()* from the base class *T* to be called, the definition of *f()* should have said so:

```
template<class T> class XX : public T {
      void f() { T::g(2); }     // calls T::g()
      // ...
};
```

This is, of course, an application of the rule of thumb that a template definition should be as self-contained as possible (§C.13.8).

C.13.8.3 Point of Instantiation Binding

Each use of a template for a given set of template arguments defines a point of instantiation. That point is in the nearest global or namespace scope enclosing its use, just before the declaration that contains that use. For example:

```
template<class T> void f(T a) { g(a); }

void g(int);

void h()
{
    extern g(double);
    f(2);
}
```

Here, the point of instantiation for $f<int>()$ is just before $h()$, so the $g()$ called in $f()$ is the global $g(int)$ rather than the local $g(double)$. The definition of "instantiation point" implies that a template parameter can never be bound to a local name or a class member. For example:

```
void f()
{
    struct X { /* ... */ };      // local structure
    vector<X> v;                 // error: cannot use local structure as template parameter
    // ...
}
```

Nor can an unqualified name used in a template ever be bound to a local name. Finally, even if a template is first used within a class, unqualified names used in the template will not be bound to members of that class. Ignoring local names is essential to prevent a lot of nasty macro-like behavior. For example:

```
template<class T> void sort(vector<T>& v)
{
    sort(v.begin(), v.end());     // use standard library sort() (without explicitly saying std::)
}

class Container {
    vector<int> v;   // elements
public:
    void sort()      // sort elements
    {
        ::sort(v);   // sort(vector<int>&) which calls std::sort() rather than Container::sort()
    }
    // ...
};
```

Had $sort(vector<T>\&)$ called $sort()$ using the $std::sort()$ notation, the result would have been the same and the code would have been clearer.

If the point of instantiation for a template defined in a namespace is in another namespace, names from both namespaces are available for name binding. As always, overload resolution is used to choose between names from different namespaces (§8.2.9.2).

Note that a template used several times with the same set of template arguments has several points of instantiation. If the bindings of independent names differ, the program is illegal. However, this is a difficult error for an implementation to detect, especially if the points of instantiation are in different translation units. It is best to avoid subtleties in name binding by minimizing the use of nonlocal names in templates and by using header files to keep use contexts consistent.

C.13.8.4 Templates and Namespaces

When a function is called, its declaration can be found even if it is not in scope, provided it is declared in the same namespace as one of its arguments (§8.2.6). This is very important for functions called in template definitions because it is the mechanism by which dependent functions are found during instantiation.

A template specialization may be generated at any point of instantiation (§C.13.8.3), any point subsequent to that in a translation unit, or in a translation unit specifically created for generating specializations. This reflects three obvious strategies an implementation can use for generating specializations:

[1] Generate a specialization the first time a call is seen.

[2] At the end of a translation unit, generate all specializations needed for that translation unit.

[3] Once every translation unit of a program has been seen, generate all specializations needed for the program.

All three strategies have strengths and weaknesses, and combinations of these strategies are also possible.

In any case, the binding of independent names is done at a point of template definition. The binding of dependent names is done by looking at

[1] the names in scope at the point where the template is defined, plus

[2] the names in the namespace of an argument of a dependent call (global functions are considered in the namespace of built-in types).

For example:

```
namespace N {
    class A { / * ... * / } ;

    char f(A);
}

char f(int);

template<class T> char g(T t) { return f(t); }

char c = g(N::A());          // causes N::f(N::A) to be called
```

Here, $f(t)$ is clearly dependent, so we can't bind f to $f(N::A)$ or $f(int)$ at the point of definition. To generate a specialization for $g<N::A>(N::A)$, the implementation looks in namespace N for functions called $f()$ and finds $N::f(N::A)$.

A program is illegal if it is possible to construct two different meanings by choosing different points of instantiation or different contents of namespaces at different possible contexts for generating the specialization. For example:

```
namespace N {
    class A { /* ... */ };

    char f(A, int);
}

template<class T, class T2> char g(T t, T2 t2) { return f(t, t2); }

char c = g(N::A(), 'a');       // error (alternative resolutions of f(t) possible)

namespace N {                  // add to namespace N (§8.2.9.3)
    void f(A, char);
}
```

We could generate the specialization at the point of instantiation and get $f(N::A, int)$ called. Alternatively, we could wait and generate the specialization at the end of the translation unit and get $f(N::A, char)$ called. Consequently, the call $g(N::A(), 'a')$ is an error.

It is sloppy programming to call an overloaded function in between two of its declarations. Looking at a large program, a programmer would have no reason to suspect a problem. In this particular case, a compiler could catch the ambiguity. However, similar problems can occur in separate translation units, and then detection becomes much harder. An implementation is not obliged to catch problems of this kind.

Most problems with alternative resolutions of function calls involve built-in types. Consequently, most remedies rely on more-careful use of arguments of built-in types.

As usual, use of global functions can make matters worse. The global namespace is considered the namespace associated with built-in types, so global functions can be used to resolve dependent calls that take built-in types. For example:

```
int f(int);

template<class T> T g(T t) { return f(t); }

char c = g('a');      // error: alternative resolutions of f(t) are possible

char f(char);
```

We could generate the specialization $g<char>(char)$ at the point of instantiation and get $f(int)$ called. Alternatively, we could wait and generate the specialization at the end of the translation unit and get $f(char)$ called. Consequently, the call $g('a')$ is an error.

C.13.9 When Is a Specialization Needed?

It is necessary to generate a specialization of a class template only if the class' definition is needed. In particular, to declare a pointer to some class, the actual definition of a class is not needed. For example:

```
class X;
X* p;       // ok: no definition of X needed
X a;        // error: definition of X needed
```

When defining template classes, this distinction can be crucial. A template class is *not* instantiated unless its definition is actually needed. For example:

```
template<class T> class Link {
      Link* suc;  // ok: no definition of Link needed (yet)
      // ...
};

Link<int>* pl;   // no instantiation of Link<int> needed

Link<int> lnk;   // now we need to instantiate Link<int>
```

The point of instantiation is where a definition is first needed.

C.13.9.1 Template Function Instantiation

An implementation instantiates a template function only if that function has been used. In particular, instantiation of a class template does not imply the instantiation of all of its members or even of all of the members defined in the template class declaration. This allows the programmer an important degree of flexibility when defining a template class. Consider:

```
template<class T> class List {
      // ...
      void sort();
};

class Glob { /* no comparison operators */ };

void f(List<Glob>& lb, List<string>& ls)
{
      ls.sort();
      // use operations on lb, but not lb.sort()
}
```

Here, *List<string>::sort()* is instantiated, but *List<Glob>::sort()* isn't. This both reduces the amount of code generated and saves us from having to redesign the program. Had *List<Glob>::sort()* been generated, we would have had to either add the operations needed by *List::sort()* to *Glob*, redefine *sort()* so that it wasn't a member of *List*, or use some other container for *Glob*s.

C.13.10 Explicit Instantiation

An explicit instantiation request is a declaration of a specialization prefixed by the keyword *template* (not followed by <):

```
template class vector<int>;                     // class
template int& vector<int>::operator[](int);     // member
template int convert<int,double>(double);       // function
```

A template declaration starts with *template<*, whereas plain *template* starts an instantiation request. Note that *template* prefixes a complete declaration; just stating a name is not sufficient:

```
template vector<int>::operator[];    // syntax error
template convert<int,double>;        // syntax error
```

As in template function calls, the template arguments that can be deduced from the function arguments can be omitted (§13.3.1). For example:

```
template  int  convert<int, double> (double) ;       // ok (redundant)
template  int  convert<int> (double) ;                // ok
```

When a class template is explicitly instantiated, every member function is also instantiated.

Note that an explicit instantiation can be used as a constraints check (§13.6.2). For example:

```
template<class  T> class  Calls_foo {
    void  constraints (T  t) { foo (t) ; }       // call from every constructor
    // ...
} ;

template  class  Calls_foo<int> ;                        // error: foo(int) undefined
template  Calls_foo<Shape*> : : constraints () ;         // error: foo(Shape*) undefined
```

The link-time and recompilation efficiency impact of instantiation requests can be significant. I have seen examples in which bundling most template instantiations into a single compilation unit cut the compile time from a number of hours to the equivalent number of minutes.

It is an error to have two definitions for the same specialization. It does not matter if such multiple specializations are user-defined (§13.5), implicitly generated (§C.13.7), or explicitly requested. However, a compiler is not required to diagnose multiple instantiations in separate compilation units. This allows a smart implementation to ignore redundant instantiations and thereby avoid problems related to composition of programs from libraries using explicit instantiation (§C.13.7). However, implementations are not required to be smart. Users of ''less smart'' implementations must avoid multiple instantiations. However, the worst that will happen if they don't is that their program won't load; there will be no silent changes of meaning.

The language does not require that a user request explicit instantiation. Explicit instantiation is an optional mechanism for optimization and manual control of the compile-and-link process (§C.13.7).

C.14 Advice

[1] Focus on software development rather than technicalities; §C.1.
[2] Adherence to the standard does not guarantee portability; §C.2.
[3] Avoid undefined behavior (including proprietary extensions); §C.2.
[4] Localize implementation-defined behavior; §C.2.
[5] Use keywords and digraphs to represent programs on systems where {, }, [,], |, or ! are missing and trigraphs if \ is missing; §C.3.1.
[6] To ease communication, use the ANSI characters to represent programs; §C.3.3.
[7] Prefer symbolic escape characters to numeric representation of characters; §C.3.2.
[8] Do not rely on signedness or unsignedness of *char*; §C.3.4.
[9] If in doubt about the type of an integer literal, use a suffix; §C.4.
[10] Avoid value-destroying implicit conversions; §C.6.
[11] Prefer *vector* over array; §C.7.
[12] Avoid *unions*; §C.8.2.

[13] Use fields to represent externally-imposed layouts; §C.8.1.

[14] Be aware of the tradeoffs between different styles of memory management; §C.9.

[15] Don't pollute the global namespace; §C.10.1.

[16] Where a scope (module) rather than a type is needed, prefer a *namespace* over a *class*; §C.10.3.

[17] Remember to define *static* class template members; §C.13.1.

[18] Use *typename* to disambiguate type members of a template parameter; §C.13.5.

[19] Where explicit qualification by template arguments is necessary, use *template* to disambiguate template class members; §C.13.6.

[20] Write template definitions with minimal dependence on their instantiation context; §C.13.8.

[21] If template instantiation takes too long, consider explicit instantiation; §C.13.10.

[22] If the order of compilation needs to be perfectly predictable, consider explicit instantiation; §C.13.10.

Locales

When in Rome,
do as the Romans do.
– proverb

Handling cultural differences — class *locale* — named locales — constructing locales — copying and comparing locales — the *global* ( ) and *classic* ( ) locales — comparing strings — class *facet* — accessing facets in a locale — a simple user-defined facet — standard facets — string comparison — numeric I/O — money I/O — date and time I/O — low-level time operations — a *Date* class — character classification — character code conversion — message catalogs — advice — exercises.

D.1 Handling Cultural Differences

A *locale* is an object that represents a set of cultural preferences, such as how strings are compared, the way numbers appear as human-readable output, and the way characters are represented in external storage. The notion of a locale is extensible so that a programmer can add new *facet*s to a *locale* representing locale-specific entities not directly supported by the standard library, such as postal codes (zip codes) and phone numbers. The primary use of *locale*s in the standard library is to control the appearance of information put to an *ostream* and the format accepted by an *istream*.

Section §21.7 describes how to change *locale* for a stream; this appendix describes how a *locale* is constructed out of *facet*s and explains the mechanisms through which a *locale* affects its stream. This appendix also describes how *facet*s are defined, lists the standard *facet*s that define specific properties of a stream, and presents techniques for implementing and using *locale*s and *facet*s. The standard library facilities for representing data and time are discussed as part of the presentation of date I/O.

The discussion of locales and facets is organized like this:

§D.1 introduces the basic ideas for representing cultural differences using locales.
§D.2 presents the *locale* class.
§D.3 presents the *facet* class.
§D.4 gives an overview of the standard *facet*s and presents details of each:

§D.4.1 String comparison
§D.4.2 Input and output of numeric values
§D.4.3 Input and output of monetary values
§D.4.4 Input and output of dates and time
§D.4.5 Character classification
§D.4.6 Character code conversions
§D.4.7 Message catalogs

The notion of a locale is not primarily a C++ notion. Most operating systems and application environments have a notion of locale. Such a notion is – in principle – shared among all programs on a system, independently of which programming language they are written in. Thus, the C++ standard library notion of a locale can be seen as a standard and portable way for C++ programs to access information that has very different representations on different systems. Among other things, a C++ *locale* is a common interface to system information that is represented in incompatible ways on different systems.

D.1.1 Programming Cultural Differences

Consider writing a program that needs to be used in several countries. Writing a program in a style that allows that is often called "internationalization" (emphasizing the use of a program in many countries) or "localization" (emphasizing the adaptation of a program to local conditions). Many of the entities that a program manipulates will conventionally be displayed differently in those countries. We can handle this by writing our I/O routines to take this into account. For example:

```
void print_date(const Date& d)  // print in the appropriate format
{
    switch(where_am_I) {        // user-defined style indicator
    case DK:            // e.g., 7. marts 1999
        cout << d.day() << ". " << dk_month[d.month()] << " " << d.year();
        break;
    case UK:            // e.g., 7/3/1999
        cout << d.day() << " / " << d.month() << " / " << d.year();
        break;
    case US:            // e.g., 3/7/1999
        cout << d.month() << "/" << d.day() << "/" << d.year();
        break;
    // ...
    }
}
```

This style of code does the job. However, it's rather ugly, and we have to use this style consistently to ensure that all output is properly adjusted to local conventions. Worse, if we want to add a new way of writing a date, we must modify the code. We could imagine handling this problem by creating a class hierarchy (§12.2.4). However, the information in a *Date* is independent of the way we want to look at it. Consequently, we don't want a hierarchy of *Date* types: for example, *US_date*, *UK_date*, and *JP_date*. Instead, we want a variety of ways of displaying *Date*s: for example, US-style output, UK-style output, and Japanese-style output; see §D.4.4.5.

Other problems arise with the "let the user write I/O functions that take care of cultural differences" approach:

[1] An application programmer cannot easily, portably, and efficiently change the appearance of built-in types without the help of the standard library.

[2] Finding every I/O operation (and every operation that prepares data for I/O in a locale-sensitive manner) in a large program is not always feasible.

[3] Sometimes, we cannot rewrite a program to take care of a new convention – and even if we could, we'd prefer a solution that didn't involve a rewrite.

[4] Having each user design and implement a solution to the problems of different cultural convention is wasteful.

[5] Different programmers will handle low-level cultural preferences in different ways, so programs dealing with the same information will differ for non-fundamental reasons. Thus, programmers maintaining code from a number of sources will have to learn a variety of programming conventions. This is tedious and error prone.

Consequently, the standard library provides an extensible way of handling cultural conventions. The iostreams library (§21.7) relies on this framework to handle both built-in and user-defined types. For example, consider a simple loop copying *(Date, double)* pairs that might represent a series of measurements or a set of transactions:

```
void cpy (istream& is, ostream& os)    // copy (Date,double) stream
{
    Date d;
    double volume;

    while (is >> d >> volume) os << d << ' ' << volume << '\n';
}
```

Naturally, a real program would do something with the records, and ideally also be a bit more careful about error handling.

How would we make this program read a file that conformed to French conventions (where comma is the character used to represent the decimal point in a floating-point number; for example, *12,5* means twelve and a half) and write it according to American conventions? We can define *locale*s and I/O operations so that *cpy* ( ) can be used to convert between conventions:

```
void f (istream& fin, ostream& fout, istream& fin2, ostream& fout2)
{
    fin . imbue (locale ("en_US"));         // American English
    fout . imbue (locale ("fr"));           // French
    cpy (fin, fout);                        // read American English, write French

    fin2 . imbue (locale ("fr"));           // French
    fout2 . imbue (locale ("en_US"));       // American English
    cpy (fin2, fout2);                      // read French, write American English
}
```

Given streams,

```
Apr 12, 1999   1000.3
Apr 13, 1999   345.45
Apr 14, 1999   9688.321
   . . .

3 juillet 1950   10,3
3 juillet 1951   134,45
3 juillet 1952   67,9
   . . .
```

this program would produce:

```
12 avril 1999 1000,3
13 avril 1999 345,45
14 avril 1999 9688,321
   . . .

July 3, 1950 10.3
July 3, 1951 134.45
July 3, 1952 67.9
   . . .
```

Much of the rest of this appendix is devoted to describing the mechanisms that make this possible and explaining how to use them. Please note that most programmers will have little reason to deal with the details of *locale*s. Many programmers will never explicitly manipulate a *locale*, and most who do will just retrieve a standard locale and imbue a stream with it (§21.7). However, the mechanisms provided to compose those *locale*s and to make them trivial to use constitute a little programming language of their own.

If a program or a system is successful, it will be used by people with needs and preferences that the original designers and programmers didn't anticipate. Most successful programs will be run in countries where (natural) languages and character sets differ from those familiar to the original designers and programmers. Wide use of a program is a sign of success, so designing and programming for portability across linguistic and cultural borders is to prepare for success.

The concept of localization (internationalization) is simple. However, practical constraints make the design and implementation of *locale* quite intricate:

[1] A *locale* encapsulates cultural conventions, such as the appearance of a date. Such conventions vary in many subtle and unsystematic ways. These conventions have nothing to do with programming languages, so a programming language cannot standardize them.

[2] The concept of a *locale* must be extensible, because it is not possible to enumerate every cultural convention that is important to every C++ user.

[3] A *locale* is used in I/O operations from which people demand run-time efficiency.

[4] A *locale* must be invisible to the majority of programmers who want to benefit from stream I/O ''doing the right thing'' without having to know exactly what that is or how it is achieved.

[5] A *locale* must be available to designers of facilities that deal with cultural-sensitive information beyond the scope of the stream I/O library.

Designing a program doing I/O requires a choice between controlling formatting through ''ordinary code'' and the use of *locale*s. The former (traditional) approach is feasible where we can ensure that every input operation can be easily converted from one convention to another. However, if the appearance of built-in types needs to vary, if different character sets are needed, or if we need to choose among an extensible set of I/O conventions, the *locale* mechanism begins to look attractive.

A *locale* is composed of *facet*s that control individual aspects, such as the character used for punctuation in the output of a floating-point value (*decimal_point* ( ) ; §D.4.2) and the format used to read a monetary value (*moneypunct*; §D.4.3). A *facet* is an object of a class derived from class *locale* :: *facet* (§D.3). We can think of a *locale* as a container of *facet*s (§D.2, §D.3.1).

D.2 The *locale* Class

The *locale* class and its associated facilities are presented in *<locale>*:

```
class std::locale {
public:
        class facet;                // type used to represent aspects of a locale; §D.3
        class id;                   // type used to identify a locale; §D.3
        typedef int category;       // type used to group/categorize facets

        static const category       // the actual values are implementation defined
                none = 0,
                collate = 1,
                ctype = 1<<1,
                monetary = 1<<2,
                numeric = 1<<3,
                time = 1<<4,
                messages = 1<<5,
                all = collate | ctype | monetary | numeric | time | messages;

        locale() throw();                   // copy of global locale (§D.2.1)
        locale(const locale& x) throw();    // copy of x
        explicit locale(const char* p);     // copy of locale named p (§D.2.1)

        ~locale() throw();

        locale(const locale& x, const char* p, category c);    // copy of x plus facets from p's c
        locale(const locale& x, const locale& y, category c);  // copy of x plus facets from y's c

        template <class Facet> locale(const locale& x, Facet* f);  // copy of x plus facet f
        template <class Facet> locale combine(const locale& x);    // copy of *this plus Facet from x

        const locale& operator=(const locale& x) throw();

        bool operator==(const locale&) const;    // compare locales
        bool operator!=(const locale&) const;

        string name() const;                     // name of this locale (§D.2.1)

        template <class Ch, class Tr, class A>   // compare strings using this locale
        bool operator()(const basic_string<Ch,Tr,A>&, const basic_string<Ch,Tr,A>&) const;
```

```
        static locale global (const locale&);        // set global locale and return old global locale
        static const locale& classic ();             // get "classic" C-style locale
    private:
        // representation
    };
```

A *locale* can be thought of as an interface to a *map<id, facet*>*; that is, something that allows us to use a *locale::id* to find a corresponding object of a class derived from *locale::facet*. A real implementation of *locale* is an efficient variant of this idea. The layout will be something like this:

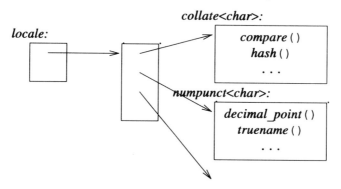

Here, *collate<char>* and *numpunct<char>* are standard library facets (§D.4). As all facets, they are derived from *locale::facet*.

A *locale* is meant to be copied freely and cheaply. Consequently, a *locale* is almost certainly implemented as a handle to the specialized *map<id, facet*>* that constitutes the main part of its implementation. The *facets* must be quickly accessible in a *locale*. Consequently, the specialized *map<id, facet*>* will be optimized to provide array-like fast access. The *facets* of a *locale* are accessed by using the *use_facet<Facet>* (*loc*) notation; see §D.3.1.

The standard library provides a rich set of *facets*. To help the programmer manipulate *facets* in logical groups, the standard *facets* are grouped into categories, such as *numeric* and *collate* (§D.4).

A programmer can replace *facets* from existing categories (§D.4, §D.4.2.1). However, it is not possible to add new categories; there is no way for a programmer to define a new category. The notion of "category" applies to standard library facets only, and it is not extensible. Thus, a facet need not belong to any category, and many user-defined facets do not.

By far the dominant use of *locales* is implicitly, in stream I/O. Each *istream* and *ostream* has its own *locale*. The *locale* of a stream is by default the global *locale* (§D.2.1) at the time of the stream's creation. The *locale* of a stream can be set by the *imbue* () operation and we can extract a copy of a stream's *locale* using *getloc* () (§21.6.3).

D.2.1 Named Locales

A *locale* is constructed from another *locale* and from *facets*. The simplest way of making a locale is to copy an existing one. For example:

```
locale  loc0 ;                              // copy of the current global locale (§D.2.3)

locale  loc1 = locale ( ) ;                 // copy of the current global locale (§D.2.3)
locale  loc2 ( " " ) ;                      // copy of "the user's preferred locale"

locale  loc3 ( " C " ) ;                    // copy of the "C" locale
locale  loc4 = locale : : classic ( ) ;    // copy of the "C" locale

locale  loc5 ( " POSIX " ) ;               // copy of the implementation-defined "POSIX" locale
```

The meaning of *locale* (" *C* ") is defined by the standard to be the "classic" C locale; this is the locale that has been used throughout this book. Other *locale* names are implementation defined.

The *locale* (" ") is deemed to be the "the user's preferred locale." This locale is set by extralinguistic means in a program's execution environment.

Most operating systems have ways of setting a locale for a program. Often, a locale suitable to the person using a system is chosen when that person first encounters a system. For example, I would expect a person who configures a system to use Argentine Spanish as its default setting will find *locale* (" ") to mean *locale* (" *es_AR* ") . A quick check on one of my systems revealed 51 locales with mnemonic names, such as *POSIX*, *de*, *en_UK*, *en_US*, *es*, *es_AR*, *fr*, *sv*, *da*, *pl*, and *iso_8859_1*. POSIX recommends a format of a lowercase language name, optionally followed by an uppercase country name, optionally followed by an encoding specifier; for example, *jp_JP* . *jit*. However, these names are not standardized across platforms. On another system, among many other locale names, I found *g*, *uk*, *us*, *s*, *fr*, *sw*, and *da*. The C++ standard does not define the meaning of a *locale* for a given country or language, though there may be platform-specific standards. Consequently, to use named *locale*s on a given system, a programmer must refer to system documentation and experiment.

It is generally a good idea to avoid embedding *locale* name strings in the program text. Mentioning a file name or a system constant in the program text limits the portability of a program and often forces a programmer who wants to adapt a program to a new environment to find and change such values. Mentioning a locale name string has similar unpleasent consequences. Instead, locales can be picked up from the program's execution environment (for example, using *locale* (" ")), or the program can request an expert user to specify alternative locales by entering a string. For example:

```
void  user_set_locale (const  string& question_string)
{
     cout << question_string ;     // e.g., "If you want to use a different locale, please enter its name"
     string  s ;
     cin >> s ;
     locale : : global (locale (s . c_str ( ) ) ) ;   // set global locale as specified by user
}
```

It is usually better to let a non-expert user pick from a list of alternatives. A routine for doing this would need to know where and how a system kept its locales.

If the string argument doesn't refer to a defined *locale*, the constructor throws the *runtime_error* exception (§14.10). For example:

```
void set_loc (locale& loc, const char* name)
try
{
    loc = locale (name);
}
catch (runtime_error) {
    cerr << "locale \"" << name << "\" isn´t defined\n";
    // ...
}
```

If a *locale* has a name string, *name()* will return it. If not, *name()* will return *string("*")*. A name string is primarily a way to refer to a *locale* stored in the execution environment. Secondarily, a name string can be used as a debugging aid. For example:

```
void print_locale_names (const locale& my_loc)
{
    cout << "name of current global locale: " << locale().name() << "\n";
    cout << "name of classic C locale: " << locale::classic().name() << "\n";
    cout << "name of ``user´s preferred locale´´: " << locale("").name() << "\n";
    cout << "name of my locale: " << my_loc.name() << "\n";
}
```

Locales with identical name strings different from the default *string("*")* compare equal. However, == or != provide more direct ways of comparing locales.

The copy of a *locale* with a name string gets the same name as that *locale* (if it has one), so many *locale*s can have the same name string. That's logical because *locale*s are immutable, so all of these objects define the same set of cultural conventions.

A call *locale(loc, "Foo", cat)* makes a locale that is like *loc* except that it takes the facets from the category *cat* of *locale("Foo")*. The resulting locale has a name string if and only if *loc* has one. The standard doesn't specify exactly which name string the new locale gets, but it is supposed to be different from *loc*'s. One obvious implementation would be to compose the new string out of *loc*'s name string and *"Foo"*. For example, if *loc*'s name string is *en_UK*, the new locale may have *"en_UK:Foo"* as its name string.

The name strings for a newly created *locale* can be summarized like this:

Locale	Name String
locale("Foo")	"Foo"
locale(loc)	*loc.name()*
locale(loc,"Foo",cat)	New name string if *loc* has a name string; otherwise, *string("*")*
locale(loc,loc2,cat)	New name string if *loc* and *loc2* have strings; otherwise, *string("*")*
locale(loc,Facet)	*string("*")*
loc.combine(loc2)	*string("*")*

There are no facilities for a programmer to specify a C-style string as a name for a newly created *locale* in a program. Name strings are either defined in the program's execution environment or created as combinations of such names by *locale* constructors.

D.2.1.1 Constructing New Locales

A new locale is made by taking an existing *locale* and adding or replacing *facet*s. Typically, a new *locale* is a minor variation on an existing one. For example:

```
void f(const locale& loc, const My_money_io* mio)   // My_money_io defined in §D.4.3.1
{
        locale loc1(locale("POSIX"), loc, locale::monetary);      // use monetary facets from loc
        locale loc2 = locale(locale::classic(), mio);             // classic plus mio
        // ...
}
```

Here, *loc1* is a copy of the *POSIX* locale modified to use *loc*'s monetary facets (§D.4.3). Similarly, *loc2* is a copy of the *C* locale modified to use a *My_money_io* (§D.4.3.1). If a *Facet** argument (here, *My_money_io*) is *0*, the resulting *locale* is simply a copy of the *locale* argument.

When using

```
locale(const locale& x, Facet* f);
```

the *f* argument must identify a specific facet type. A plain *facet** is not sufficient. For example:

```
void g(const locale::facet* mio1, const My_money_io* mio2)
{
        locale loc3 = locale(locale::classic(), mio1);   // error: type of facet not known
        locale loc4 = locale(locale::classic(), mio2);   // ok: type of facet known
        // ...
}
```

The reason is that the *locale* uses the type of the *Facet** argument to determine the type of the facet at compile time. Specifically, the implementation of *locale* uses a facet's identifying type, *facet::id* (§D.3), to find that facet in the locale (§D.3.1).

Note that the

```
template <class Facet> locale(const locale& x, Facet* f);
```

constructor is the only mechanism offered within the language for the programmer to supply a *facet* to be used through a *locale*. Other *locale*s are supplied by implementers as named locales (§D.2.1). These named locales can be retrieved from the program's execution environment. A programmer who understands the implementation-specific mechanism used for that might be able to add new *locale*s that way (§D.6[11,12]).

The set of constructors for *locale* is designed so that the type of every *facet* is known either from type deduction (of the *Facet* template parameter) or because it came from another *locale* (that knew its type). Specifying a *category* argument specifies the type of *facet*s indirectly, because the *locale* knows the type of the *facet*s in the categories. This implies that the *locale* class can (and does) keep track of the types of *facet* types so that it can manipulate them with minimal overhead.

The *locale::id* member type is used by *locale* to identify *facet* types (§D.3).

It is sometimes useful to construct a *locale* that is a copy of another except for a *facet* copied from yet another *locale*. The *combine*() template member function does that. For example:

```
void f(const locale& loc, const locale& loc2)
{
      locale loc3 = loc.combine< My_money_io >(loc2);
      // ...
}
```

The resulting *loc3* behaves like *loc* except that it uses a copy of *My_money_io* (§D.4.3.1) from *loc2* to format monetary I/O. If *loc2* doesn't have a *My_money_io* to give to the new *locale*, *com-bine* ( ) will throw a *runtime_error* (§14.10). The result of *combine* ( ) has no name string.

D.2.2 Copying and Comparing Locales

A *locale* can be copied by initialization and by assignment. For example:

```
void swap (locale& x, locale& y)          // just like std::swap()
{
      locale temp = x;
      x = y;
      y = temp;
}
```

The copy of a *locale* compares equal to the original, but the copy is an independent and separate object. For example:

```
void f(locale* my_locale)
{
      locale loc = locale::classic();   // "C" locale

      if (loc != locale::classic()) {
            cerr << "implementation error: send bug report to vendor\n";
            exit(1);
      }

      if (&loc != &locale::classic()) cout << "no surprise: addresses differ\n";

      locale loc2 = locale(loc, my_locale, locale::numeric);

      if (loc == loc2) {
            cout << "my numeric facets are the same as classic()´s numeric facets\n";
            // ...
      }

      // ...
}
```

If *my_locale* has a numeric punctuation facet, *my_numpunct<char>*, that is different from *classic* ( )'s standard *numpunct<char>*, the resulting *locale*s can be represented like this:

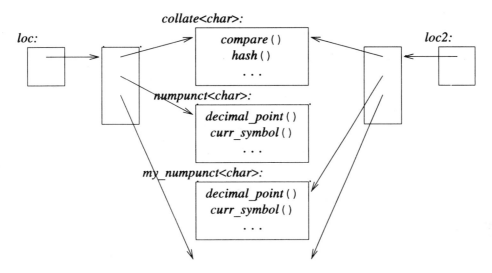

There is no way of modifying a *locale*. Instead, the *locale* operations provide ways of making new *locales* from existing ones. The fact that a *locale* is immutable after it has been created is essential for run-time efficiency. This allows someone using a *locale* to call virtual functions of a *facet* and to cache the values returned. For example, an *istream* can know what character is used to represent the decimal point and how *true* is represented, without calling *decimal_point*() each time it reads a number and *truename*() each time it reads to a *bool* (§D.4.2). Only a call of *imbue*() for the stream (§21.6.3) can cause such calls to return a different value.

D.2.3 The *global()* and the *classic()* Locales

The notion of a current locale for a program is provided by *locale*(), which yields a copy of the current locale, and *locale::global*(*x*), which sets the current locale to *x*. The current locale is commonly referred to as the ''global locale,'' reflecting its probable implementation as a global (or *static*) object.

The global locale is implicitly used when a stream is initialized. That is, every new stream is imbued (§21.1, §21.6.3) with a copy of *locale*(). Initially, the global locale is the standard C locale, *locale::classic*().

The *locale::global*() static member function allows a programmer to specify a locale to be used as the global locale. A copy of the previous global locale is returned by *global*(). This allows a user to restore the global locale. For example:

```
void f(const locale& my_loc)
{
    ifstream fin1(some_name);                      // fin1 is imbued with the global locale
    locale& old_global = locale::global(my_loc);   // set new global locale
    ifstream fin2(some_other_name);                // fin2 is imbued with my_loc
    // ...
    locale::global(old_global);                    // restore old global locale
}
```

If a locale *x* has a name string, *locale*::*global*(*x*) also sets the C global locale. This implies that if a C++ program calls a locale-sensitive function from the C standard library, the treatment of locale will be consistent throughout a mixed C and C++ program.

If a locale *x* does not have a name string, it is undefined whether *locale*::*global*(*x*) affects the C global locale. This implies that a C++ program cannot reliably and portably set the C locale to a locale that wasn't retrieved from the execution environment. There is no standard way for a C program to set the C++ global locale (except by calling a C++ function to do so). In a mixed C and C++ program, having the C global locale differ from *global*() is error prone.

Setting the global locale does not affect existing I/O streams; those still use the locales that they were imbued with before the global locale was reset. For example, *fin1* is unaffected by the manipulation of the global locale that caused *fin2* to be imbued with *my_loc*.

Changing the global locale suffers the same problems as all other techniques relying on changing global data: It is essentially impossible to know what is affected by a change. It is therefore best to reduce use of *global*() to a minimum and to localize those changes in a few sections of code that obey a simple strategy for the changes. The ability to imbue (§21.6.3) individual streams with specific *locale*s makes that easier. However, too many explicit uses of *locale*s and *facet*s scattered throughout a program will also become a maintenance problem.

D.2.4 Comparing Strings

Comparing two strings according to a *locale* is possibly the most common *explicit* use of a *locale*. Consequently, this operation is provided directly by *locale* so that users don't have to build their own comparison function from the *collate* facet (§D.4.1). To be directly useful as a predicate (§18.4.2), this comparison function is defined as *locale*'s *operator*()(). For example:

```
void f(vector<string>& v, const locale& my_locale)
{
        sort(v.begin(),v.end());                    // sort using the global locale
        // ...
        sort(v.begin(),v.end(),my_locale);          // sort according to the rules of my_locale
        // ...
}
```

By default, the standard library *sort*() uses < for the numerical value of the implementation character set to determine collation order (§18.7, §18.6.3.1).

Note that *locale*s compare *basic_string*s rather then C-style strings.

D.3 Facets

A *facet* is an object of a class derived from *locale*'s member class *facet*:

```
class std::locale::facet {
protected:
        explicit facet(size_t r = 0);        // "r==0": the locale controls the lifetime of this facet
        virtual ~facet();                    // note: protected destructor
```

```
private:
        facet(const facet&);              // not defined
        void operator=(const facet&);     // not defined

        // representation
};
```

The copy operations are *private* and are left undefined to prevent copying (§11.2.2).

The *facet* class is designed to be a base class and has no public functions. Its constructor is *protected* to prevent the creation of "plain *facet*" objects, and its destructor is virtual to ensure proper destruction of derived-class objects.

A *facet* is intended to be managed through pointers by *locale*s. A *0* argument to the *facet* constructor means that *locale* should delete the *facet* when the last reference to it goes away. Conversely, a nonzero constructor argument ensures that *locale* never deletes the *facet*. A nonzero argument is meant for the rare case in which the lifetime of a facet is controlled directly by the programmer rather than indirectly through a locale. For example, we could try to create objects of the standard facet type *collate_byname<char>* (§D.4.1.1) like this:

```
void f(const string& s1, const string& s2)
{
        // normal case: (default) argument 0 means that locale is responsible for deletion:
        collate<char>* p = new collate_byname<char>("pl");
        locale loc(locale(), p);

        // rare case: argument 1 means that user is responsible for deletion:
        collate<char>* q = new collate_byname<char>("ge", 1);

        collate_byname<char> bug1("sw");        // error: cannot destroy local variable
        collate_byname<char> bug2("no", 1);     // error: cannot destroy local variable

        // ...

        // q cannot be deleted: collate_byname<char>'s destructor is protected
        // no delete p; locale manages deletion of *p
}
```

That is, standard facets are useful when managed by locales, as base classes, and only rarely in other ways.

A *_byname*() facet is a facet from a named locale in the the execution environment (§D.2.1).

For a *facet* to be found in a *locale* by *has_facet*() and *use_facet*() (§D.3.1), each kind of facet must have an *id*:

```
class std::locale::id {
public:
        id();
private:
        id(const id&);                  // not defined
        void operator=(const id&);      // not defined

        // representation
};
```

The copy operations are declared private and are left undefined to prevent copying (§11.2.2).

The intended use of *id* is for the user to define a *static* member of type *id* of each class supplying a new *facet* interface (for example, see §D.4.1). The *locale* mechanisms use *id*s to identify facets (§D.2, §D.3.1). In the obvious implementation of a *locale*, an *id* is used as an index into a vector of pointers to facets, thereby implementing an efficient *map<id, facet*>*.

Data used to define a (derived) *facet* is defined in the derived class rather than in the base class *facet* itself. This implies that the programmer defining a *facet* has full control over the data and that arbitrary amounts of data can be used to implement the concept represented by a *facet*.

Note that all member functions of a user-defined *facet* should be *const* members. Generally, a facet is intended to be immutable (§D.2.2).

D.3.1 Accessing Facets in a Locale

The facets of a *locale* are accessed through the template function *use_facet*, and we can inquire whether a *locale* has a specific *facet*, using the template function *has_facet*:

```
template <class Facet> bool has_facet(const locale&) throw();
template <class Facet> const Facet& use_facet(const locale&);   // may throw bad_cast
```

Think of these template functions as doing a lookup in their *locale* argument for their template parameter *Facet*. Alternatively, think of *use_facet* as a kind of explicit type conversion (cast) of a *locale* to a specific *facet*. This is feasible because a *locale* can have only one *facet* of a given type. For example:

```
void f(const locale& my_locale)
{
        char c = use_facet< numpunct<char> >(my_locale).decimal_point() // use standard facet
        // ...

        if (has_facet<Encrypt>(my_locale)) {       // does my_locale contain an Encrypt facet?
                const Encrypt& f = use_facet<Encrypt>(my_locale);   // retrieve Encrypt facet
                const Crypto c = f.get_crypto();                    // use Encrypt facet
                // ...
        }
        // ...
}
```

Note that *use_facet* returns a reference to a *const* facet, so we cannot assign the result of *use_facet* to a non-*const*. This makes sense because a facet is meant to be immutable and to have only *const* members.

If we try *use_facet<X>(loc)* and *loc* doesn't have an *X* facet, *use_facet()* throws *bad_cast* (§14.10). The standard *facet*s are guaranteed to be available for all locales (§D.4), so we don't need to use *has_facet* for standard facets. For standard facets, *use_facet* will not throw *bad_cast*.

How might *use_facet* and *has_facet* be implemented? Remember that we can think of a *locale* as a *map<id, facet*>* (§D.2). Given a *facet* type as the *Facet* template argument, the implementation of *has_facet* or *use_facet* can refer to *Facet::id* and use that to find the corresponding facet. A very naive implementation of *has_facet* and *use_facet* might look like this:

```
// pseudoimplementation: imagine that a locale has a map<id,facet*> called facet_map

template <class Facet> bool has_facet(const locale& loc) throw()
{
    const locale::facet* f = loc.facet_map[Facet::id];
    return f ? true : false;
}

template <class Facet> const Facet& use_facet(const locale& loc)
{
    const locale::facet* f = loc.facet_map[Facet::id];
    if (f) return static_cast<const Facet&>(*f);
    throw bad_cast();
}
```

Another way of looking at the *facet::id* mechanism is as an implementation of a form of compile-time polymorphism. A *dynamic_cast* can be used to get very similar results to what *use_facet* produces. However, the specialized *use_facet* can be implemented more efficiently than the more general *dynamic_cast*.

An *id* really identifies an interface and a behavior rather than a class. That is, if two facet classes have exactly the same interface and implement the same semantics (as far as a *locale* is concerned), they should be identified by the same *id*. For example, *collate<char>* and *collate_byname<char>* are interchangeable in a *locale*, so both are identified by *collate<char>::id* (§D.4.1).

If we define a *facet* with a new interface – such as *Encrypt* in *f()* – we must define a corresponding *id* to identify it (see §D.3.2 and §D.4.1).

D.3.2 A Simple User-Defined Facet

The standard library provides standard facets for the most critical areas of cultural differences, such as character sets and I/O of numbers. To examine the facet mechanism in isolation from the complexities of widely used types and the efficiency concerns that accompany them, let me first present a *facet* for a trivial user-defined type:

```
enum Season { spring, summer, fall, winter };
```

This was just about the simplest user-defined type I could think of. The style of I/O outlined here can be used with little variation for most simple user-defined types.

```
class Season_io : public locale::facet {
public:
    Season_io(int i = 0) : locale::facet(i) { }

    ~Season_io() { }      // to make it possible to destroy Season_io objects (§D.3)

    virtual const string& to_str(Season x) const = 0;            // string representation of x

    // place Season corresponding to s in x:
    virtual bool from_str(const string& s, Season& x) const = 0;
```

```
        static  locale::id  id;  // facet identifier object (§D.2, §D.3, §D.3.1)
};

locale::id  Season_io::id;  // define the identifier object
```

For simplicity, this *facet* is limited to representations using *char*.

The *Season_io* class provides a general and abstract interface for all *Season_io* facets. To define the I/O representation of a *Season* for a particular locale, we derive a class from *Season_io*, defining *to_str()* and *from_str()* appropriately.

Output of a *Season* is easy. If the stream has a *Season_io* facet, we can use that to convert the value into a string. If not, we can output the *int* value of the *Season*:

```
ostream& operator<<(ostream& s, Season x)
{
        const locale& loc = s.getloc();  // extract the stream's locale (§21.7.1)
        if (has_facet<Season_io>(loc)) return s << use_facet<Season_io>(loc).to_str(x);
        return s << int(x);
}
```

Note that this << operator is implemented by invoking << for other types. This way, we benefit from the simplicity of using << compared to accessing the *ostream*'s stream buffers directly, from the locale sensitivity of those << operators, and from the error handling provided for those << operators. Standard *facet*s tend to operate directly on stream buffers (§D.4.2.2, §D.4.2.3) for maximum efficiency and flexibility, but for many simple user-defined types, there is no need to drop to the *streambuf* level of abstraction.

As is typical, input is a bit more complicated than output:

```
istream& operator>>(istream& s, Season& x)
{
        const locale& loc = s.getloc();          // extract the stream's locale (§21.7.1)

        if (has_facet<Season_io>(loc)) {      // read alphabetic representation
                const Season_io& f = use_facet<Season_io>(loc);
                string buf;
                if (!(s>>buf && f.from_str(buf,x))) s.setstate(ios_base::failbit);
                return s;
        }

        int i;                // read numeric representation
        s >> i;
        x = Season(i);
        return s;
}
```

The error handling is simple and follows the error-handling style for built-in types. That is, if the input string didn't represent a *Season* in the chosen locale, the stream is put into the *failure* state. If exceptions are enabled, this implies that an *ios_base::failure* exception is thrown (§21.3.6).

Here is a trivial test program:

```
int main ( )        // trivial test
{
     Season x;

     // Use default locale (no Season_io facet) implies integer I/O:
     cin >> x;
     cout << x << endl;

     locale loc (locale ( ), new US_season_io);
     cout.imbue (loc);       // Use locale with Season_io facet
     cin.imbue (loc);        // Use locale with Season_io facet

     cin >> x;
     cout << x << endl;
}
```

Given the input

```
2
summer
```

this program responded:

```
2
summer
```

To get this, we must define *US_season_io* to do define the string representation of the seasons and override the *Season_io* functions that convert between string representations and the enumerators:

```
class US_season_io : public Season_io {
     static const string seasons[];
public:
     const string& to_str (Season) const;
     bool from_str (const string&, Season&) const;

     // note: no US_season_io::id
};

const string US_season_io::seasons[] = { "spring", "summer", "fall", "winter" };

const string& US_season_io::to_str (Season x) const
{
     if (x<spring || winter<x) {
          static const string ss = "no-such-season";
          return ss;
     }
     return seasons[x];
}
```

```
bool US_season_io::from_str(const string& s, Season& x) const
{
    const string* beg = &seasons[spring];
    const string* end = &seasons[winter]+1;
    const string* p = find(beg,end,s);    // §3.8.1, §18.5.2
    if (p==end) return false;
    x = Season(p-beg);
    return true;
}
```

Note that because *US_season_io* is simply an implementation of the *Season_io* interface, I did not define an *id* for *US_season_io*. In fact, if we want *US_season_io* to be used as a *Season_io*, we must not give *US_season_io* its own *id*. Operations on *locales*, such as *has_facet* (§D.3.1), rely on facets implementing the same concepts being identified by the same *id* (§D.3).

The only interesting implementation question was what to do if asked to output an invalid *Season*. Naturally, that shouldn't happen. However, it is not uncommon to find an invalid value for a simple user-defined types, so it is realistic to take that possibility into account. I could have thrown an exception, but when dealing with simple output intended for humans to read, it is often helpful to produce an "out of range" representation for an out-of-range value. Note that for input, the error-handling policy is left to the >> operator, whereas for output, the facet function *to_str*() implements an error-handling policy. This was done to illustrate the design alternatives. In a "production design," the *facet* functions would either implement error handling for both input and output or just report errors for >> and << to handle.

This *Season_io* design relied on derived classes to supply the locale-specific strings. An alternative design would have *Season_io* itself retrieve those strings from a locale-specific repository (see §D.4.7). The possibility of having a single *Season_io* class to which the season strings are passed as constructor arguments is left as an exercise (§D.6[2]).

D.3.3 Uses of Locales and Facets

The primary use of *locales* is within the standard library is in I/O streams. However, the *locale* mechanism is a general and extensible mechanism for representing culture-sensitive information. The *messages* facet (§D.4.7) is an example of a facet that has nothing to do with I/O streams. Extensions to the iostreams library and even I/O facilities that are not based on streams might take advantage of locales. Also, a user may use *locales* as a convenient way of organizing arbitrary culture-sensitive information.

Because of the generality of the *locale*/*facet* mechanism, the possibilities for user-defined *facets* are unlimited. Plausible candidates for representation as *facets* are dates, time zones, phone numbers, social security numbers (personal identification numbers), product codes, temperatures, general (unit,value) pairs, postal codes (zip codes), clothe sizes, and ISBN numbers.

As with every other powerful mechanism, *facets* should be used with care. That something can be represented as a *facet* doesn't mean that it is best represented that way. The key issues to consider when selecting a representation for cultural dependencies are – as ever – how the various decisions affect the difficulty of writing code, the ease of reading the resulting code, the maintainability of the resulting program, and the efficiency in time and space of the resulting I/O operations.

D.4 Standard Facets

In *<locale>*, the standard library provides these *facet*s for the *classic* ( ) locale:

Standard Facets (in the *classic()* locale)			
	Category	**Purpose**	**Facets**
§D.4.1	*collate*	String comparison	*collate<Ch>*
§D.4.2	*numeric*	Numeric I/O	*numpunct<Ch>* *num_get<Ch>* *num_put<Ch>*
§D.4.3	*monetary*	Money I/O	*moneypunct<Ch>* *moneypunct<Ch,true>* *money_get<Ch>* *money_put<Ch>*
§D.4.4	*time*	Time I/O	*time_get<Ch>* *time_put<Ch>*
§D.4.5	*ctype*	Character classification	*ctype<Ch>* *codecvt<Ch,char,mbstate_t>*
§D.4.7	*messages*	Message retrieval	*messages<Ch>*

In this table, *Ch* is as shorthand for *char* or *wchar_t*. A user who needs standard I/O to deal with another character type *X* must provide suitable versions of facets for *X*. For example, *codecvt<X,char,mbstate_t>* (§D.4.6) might be needed to control conversions between *X* and *char*. The *mbstate_t* type is used to represent the shift states of a multibyte character representation (§D.4.6); *mbstate_t* is defined in *<cwchar>* and *<wchar.h>*. The equivalent to *mbstate_t* for an arbitrary character type *X* is *char_traits<X>::state_type*.

In addition, the standard library provides these *facet*s in *<locale>*:

Standard Facets			
	Category	**Purpose**	**Facets**
§D.4.1	*collate*	String comparison	*collate_byname<Ch>*
§D.4.2	*numeric*	Numeric I/O	*numpunct_byname<Ch>* *num_get<C,In>* *num_put<C,Out>*
§D.4.3	*monetary*	Money I/O	*moneypunct_byname<Ch,International>* *money_get<C,In>* *money_put<C,Out>*
§D.4.4	*time*	Time I/O	*time_put_byname<Ch,Out>*
§D.4.5	*ctype*	Character classification	*ctype_byname<Ch>*
§D.4.7	*messages*	Message retrieval	*messages_byname<Ch>*

When instantiating a facet from this table, *Ch* can be *char* or *wchar_t*; *C* can be any character type (§20.1). *International* can be *true* or *false*; *true* means that a four-character "international" representation of a currency symbol is used (§D.4.3.1). The *mbstate_t* type is used to represent the shift states of a multibyte character representation (§D.4.6); *mbstate_t* is defined in *<cwchar>* and *<wchar.h>*.

In and *Out* are input iterators and output iterators, respectively (§19.1, §19.2.1). Providing the *_put* and *_get* facets with these template arguments allows a programmer to provide facets that access nonstandard buffers (§D.4.2.2). Buffers associated with iostreams are stream buffers, so the iterators provided for those are *ostreambuf_iterator*s (§19.2.6.1, §D.4.2.2). Consequently, the function *failed*() (§19.2.6.1) is available for error handling.

An *F_byname* facet is derived from the facet *F*. *F_byname* provides the identical interface to *F*, except that it adds a constructor taking a string argument naming a *locale* (see §D.4.1). The *F_byname*(*name*) provides the appropriate semantics for *F* defined in *locale*(*name*). The idea is to pick a version of a standard facet from a named *locale* (§D.2.1) in the program's execution environment. For example:

```
void f(vector<string>& v, const locale& loc)
{
    locale dl(loc,new collate_byname<char>("da"));   // use Danish string comparison
    locale dk(dl,new ctype_byname<char>("da"));       // use Danish character classification
    sort(v.begin(),v.end(),dk);
    // ...
}
```

This new *dk* locale will use Danish-style strings but will retain the default conventions for numbers. Note that because *facet*'s second argument is by default *0*, the *locale* manages the lifetime of a *facet* created using operator *new* (§D.3).

Like the *locale* constructors that take string arguments, the *_byname* constructors access the program's execution environment. This implies that they are very slow compared to constructors that do not need to consult the environment. It is almost always faster to construct a locale and then to access its facets than it is to use *_byname* facets in many places in a program. Thus, reading a facet from the environment once and then using the copy in main memory repeatedly is usually a good idea. For example:

```
locale dk("da");      // read the Danish locale (incl. all of its facets) once
                      // then use the dk locale and its facets as needed

void f(vector<string>& v, const locale& loc)
{
    const collate<char>& col = use_facet< collate<char> >(dk);
    const collate<char>& ctyp = use_facet< ctype<char> >(dk);

    locale dl(loc,col);   // use Danish string comparison
    locale d2(dl,ctyp);   // use Danish character classification and Danish string comparison

    sort(v.begin(),v.end(),d2);
    // ...
}
```

The notion of categories gives a simpler way of manipulating standard facets in locales. For example, given the *dk* locale, we can construct a *locale* that reads and compares strings according to the rules of Danish (that give three extra vowels compared to English) but that retains the syntax of numbers used in C++:

> *locale dk_us (locale :: classic ( ) , dk , collate | ctype) ;*   // *Danish letters, American numbers*

The presentations of individual standard *facet*s contains more examples of *facet* use. In particular, the discussion of *collate* (§D.4.1) brings out many of the common structural aspects of *facet*s.

Note that the standard *facet*s often depend on each other. For example, *num_put* depends on *numpunct*. Only if you have a detailed knowledge of individual *facet*s can you successfully mix and match facets or add new versions of the standard facets. In other words, beyond the simple operations mentioned in §21.7, the *locale* mechanisms are not meant to be directly used by novices.

The design of an individual facet is often messy. The reason is partially that facets have to reflect messy cultural conventions outside the control of the library designer, and partially that the C++ standard library facilities have to remain largely compatible with what is offered by the C standard library and various platform-specific standards. For example, POSIX provides locale facilities that it would be unwise for a library designer to ignore.

On the other hand, the framework provided by locales and facets is very general and flexible. A facet can be designed to hold any data, and the facet's operations can provide any desired operation based on that data. If the behavior of a new facet isn't overconstrained by convention, its design can be simple and clean (§D.3.2).

D.4.1 String Comparison

The standard *collate* facet provides ways of comparing arrays of characters of type *Ch*:

```
template <class Ch>
class std :: collate : public locale :: facet {
public :
        typedef Ch char_type ;
        typedef basic_string<Ch> string_type ;

        explicit collate (size_t r = 0) ;

        int compare (const Ch* b, const Ch* e, const Ch* b2, const Ch* e2) const
            { return do_compare (b, e, b2, e2) ; }

        long hash (const Ch* b, const Ch* e) const { return do_hash (b, e) ; }
        string_type transform (const Ch* b, const Ch* e) const { return do_transform (b, e) ; }

        static locale :: id id ;  // facet identifier object (§D.2, §D.3, §D.3.1)

protected :
        ~collate ( ) ;       // note: protected destructor

        virtual int do_compare (const Ch* b, const Ch* e, const Ch* b2, const Ch* e2) const ;
        virtual string_type do_transform (const Ch* b, const Ch* e) const ;
        virtual long do_hash (const Ch* b, const Ch* e) const ;
} ;
```

Like all facets, *collate* is publically derived from *facet* and provides a constructor that takes an argument that tells whether class *locale* controls the lifetime of the facet (§D.3).

Note that the destructor is protected. The *collate* facet isn't meant to be used directly. Rather, it is intended as a base class for all (derived) collation classes and for *locale* to manage (§D.3). Application programmers, implementation providers, and library vendors will write the string comparison facets to be used through the interface provided by *collate*.

The *compare* () function does the basic string comparison according to the rules defined for a particular *collate*; it returns *1* if the first string is lexicographically greater than the second, *0* if the strings are identical, and *– 1* if the second string is greater than the first. For example:

```
void f(const string& s1, const string& s2, collate<char>& cmp)
{
    const char* cs1 = s1.data();    // because compare() operates on char[]s
    const char* cs2 = s2.data();
    switch (cmp.compare(cs1,cs1+s1.size(),cs2,cs2+s2.size())) {
    case 0:          // identical strings according to cmp
        // ...
        break;
    case –1:         // s1 < s2
        // ...
        break;
    case 1:          // s1 > s2
        // ...
        break;
    }
}
```

Note that the *collate* member functions compare arrays of *Ch* rather than *basic_string*s or zero-terminated C-style strings. In particular, a *Ch* with the numeric value *0* is treated as an ordinary character rather than as a terminator. Also, *compare* () differs from *strcmp* (), returning exactly the values *– 1*, *0*, and *1* rather than simply *0* and (arbitrary) negative and positive values (§20.4.1).

The standard library *string* is not *locale* sensitive. That is, it compares strings according to the rules of the implementation's character set (§C.2). Furthermore, the standard *string* does not provide a direct way of specifying comparison criteria (Chapter 20). To do a *locale*-sensitive comparison, we can use a *collate*'s *compare* (). Notationally, it can be more convenient to use *collate*'s *compare* () indirectly through a *locale*'s *operator* () (§D.2.4). For example:

```
void f(const string& s1, const string& s2, const char* n)
{
    bool b = s1 == s2;               // compare using implementation's character set values

    const char* cs1 = s1.data();    // because compare() operates on char[]s
    const char* cs2 = s2.data();

    typedef collate<char> Col;

    const Col& glob = use_facet<Col>(locale());          // from the current global locale
    int i0 = glob.compare(cs1,cs1+s1.size(),cs2,cs2+s2.size());

    const Col& my_coll = use_facet<Col>(locale(""));     // from my preferred locale
    int i1 = my_coll.compare(cs1,cs1+s1.size(),cs2,cs2+s2.size());
```

```
        const Col& coll = use_facet<Col> (locale (n));              // from locale named n
        int i2 = coll.compare (cs1, cs1+s1.size(), cs2, cs2+s2.size());

        int i3 = locale() (s1, s2);              // compare using the current global locale
        int i4 = locale("") (s1, s2);            // compare using my preferred locale
        int i5 = locale(n) (s1, s2);             // compare using the locale named n

        // ...
}
```

Here, *i0*==*i3*, *i1*==*i4*, and *i2*==*i5*. It is not difficult to imagine cases in which *i2*, *i3*, and *i4* differ. Consider this sequence of words from a German dictionary:

  Dialekt, Diät, dich, dichten, Dichtung

According to convention, nouns (only) are capitalized, but the ordering is not case sensitive.
  A case-sensitive German sort would place all words starting with *D* before *d*:

  Dialekt, Diät, Dichtung, dich, dichten

The *ä* (umlaut *a*) is treated as "a kind of *a*," so it comes before *c*. However, in most common character sets, the numeric value of *ä* is larger than the numeric value of *c*. Consequently, *int* (*'c'*) <*int* (*'ä'*), and the simple default sort based on numeric values gives:

  Dialekt, Dichtung, Diät, dich, dichten

Writing a compare function that orders this sequence correctly according to the dictionary is an interesting exercise (§D.6[3]).
  The *hash* () function calculates a hash value (§17.6.2.3). Obviously, this can be useful for building hash tables.
  The *transform* () function produces a string that, when compared to other strings, gives the same result as would a comparison to the argument string. The purpose of *transform* () is to allow optimization of code in which one string is compared to many others. This is useful when implementing a search for one or more strings among a set of strings.
  The public *compare* (), *hash* (), and *transform* () functions are implemented by calls to the public virtual functions *do_compare* (), *do_hash* (), and *do_transform* (), respectively. These "*do_* functions" can be overridden in derived classes. This two-function strategy allows the library implementer who writes the non-virtual functions to provide some common functionality for all calls independently of what the user-supplied *do_* function might do.
  The use of virtual functions preserves the polymorphic nature of the *facet* but could be costly. To avoid excess function calls, a *locale* can determine the exact *facet* used and cache any values it might need for efficient execution (§D.2.2).
  The static member *id* of type *locale*::*id* is used to identify a *facet* (§D.3). The standard functions *has_facet* and *use_facet* depend on the correspondence between *id*s and *facet*s (§D.3.1). Two *facet*s providing exactly the same interface and semantics to *locale* should have the same *id*. For example, *collate<char>* and *collate_byname<char>* (§D.4.1.1) have the same *id*. Conversely, two *facet*s performing different functions (as far as *locale* is concerned) must have different *id*s. For example, *numpunct<char>* and *num_put<char>* have different *id*s (§D.4.2).

D.4.1.1 Named Collate

A *collate_byname* is a facet that provides a version of *collate* for a particular locale named by a constructor string argument:

```
template <class Ch>
class std::collate_byname : public collate<Ch> {
public:
        typedef basic_string<Ch> string_type;

        explicit collate_byname(const char*, size_t r = 0);    // construct from named locale

        // note: no id and no new functions

protected:
        ~collate_byname();    // note: protected destructor

        // override collate<Ch>'s virtual functions:

        int do_compare(const Ch* b, const Ch* e, const Ch* b2, const Ch* e2) const;
        string_type do_transform(const Ch* b, const Ch* e) const;
        long do_hash(const Ch* b, const Ch* e) const;
};
```

Thus, a *collate_byname* can be used to pick out a *collate* from a locale named in the program's execution environment (§D.4). One obvious way of storing facets in an execution environment would be as data in a file. A less flexible alternative would be to represent a facet as program text and data in a *_byname* facet.

The *collate_byname<char>* class is an example of a *facet* that doesn't have its own *id* (§D.3). In a *locale*, *collate_byname<Ch>* is interchangeable with *collate<Ch>*. A *collate* and a *collate_byname* for the same locale differ only in the extra constructor offered by the *collate_byname* and in the semantics provided by the *collate_byname*.

Note that the *_byname* destructor is *protected*. This implies that you cannot have a *_byname* facet as a local variable. For example:

```
void f()
{
    collate_byname<char> my_coll("");    // error: cannot destroy my_coll
    // ...
}
```

This reflects the view that using locales and facets is something that is best done at a fairly high level in a program to affect large bodies of code. An example is setting the global locale (§D.2.3) or imbuing a stream (§21.6.3, §D.1). If necessary, we could derive a class with a public destructor from a *_byname* class and create local variables of that class.

D.4.2 Numeric Input and Output

Numeric output is done by a *num_put* facet writing into a stream buffer (§21.6.4). Conversely, numeric input is done by a *num_get* facet reading from a stream buffer. The format used by *num_put* and *num_get* is defined by a ''numerical punctuation'' facet, *numpunct*.

D.4.2.1 Numeric Punctuation

The *numpunct* facet defines the I/O format of built-in types, such as *bool*, *int*, and *double*:

```
template <class Ch>
class std::numpunct : public locale::facet {
public:
      typedef Ch char_type;
      typedef basic_string<Ch> string_type;

      explicit numpunct(size_t r = 0);

      Ch decimal_point() const;         // '.' in classic()
      Ch thousands_sep() const;         // ',' in classic()
      string grouping() const;          // "" in classic(), meaning no grouping

      string_type truename() const;     // "true" in classic()
      string_type falsename() const;    // "false" in classic()

      static locale::id id;  // facet identifier object (§D.2, §D.3, §D.3.1)
protected:
      ~numpunct();

      // virtual ''do_'' functions for public functions (see §D.4.1)
};
```

The characters of the string returned by *grouping*() are read as a sequence of small integer values. Each number specifies a number of digits for a group. Character 0 specifies the rightmost group (the least-significant digits), character 1 the group to the left of that, etc. Thus, "\004\002\003" describes a number, such as $123-45-6789$ (provided you use ´ $-$ ´ as the separation character). If necessary, the last number in a grouping pattern is used repeatedly, so "\003" is equivalent to "\003\003\003". As the name of the separation character, *thousands_sep*(), indicates, the most common use of grouping is to make large integers more readable. The *grouping*() and *thousands_sep*() functions define a format for both input and output of integers. They are not used for standard floating-point number I/O. Thus, we can not get 1234567.89 printed as $1,234,567.89$ simply by defining *grouping*() and *thousands_sep*().

We can define a new punctuation style by deriving from *numpunct*. For example, I could define facet *My_punct* to write integer values using spaces to group the digits by threes and floating-point values, using a European-style comma as the ''decimal point:''

```
class My_punct : public std::numpunct<char> {
public:
      typedef char char_type;
      typedef string string_type;

      explicit My_punct(size_t r = 0) : numpunct<char>(r) { }

protected:
      char do_decimal_point() const { return ','; }    // comma
      char do_thousands_sep() const { return ' '; }    // space
      string do_grouping() const { return "\003"; }    // 3-digit groups
};
```

```
void f()
{
    cout << "style A: " << 12345678 << " *** "<< 1234567.8 << '\n';

    locale loc(locale(), new My_punct);
    cout.imbue(loc);
    cout << "style B: " << 12345678 << " *** "<< 1234567.8 << '\n';
}
```

This produced:

```
style A: 12345678 *** 1234567.8
style B: 12 345 678 *** 1234567,8
```

Note that *imbue*() stores a copy of its argument in its stream. Consequently, a stream can rely on an imbued locale even after the original copy of that locale has been destroyed. If an iostream has its *boolalpha* flag set (§21.2.2, §21.4.1), the strings returned by *truename*() and *falsename*() are used to represent *true* and *false*, respectively; otherwise, *1* and *0* are used.

A *_byname* version (§D.4, §D.4.1) of *numpunct* is provided:

```
template <class Ch>
class std::numpunct_byname : public numpunct<Ch> { /* ... */ };
```

D.4.2.2 Numeric Output

When writing to a stream buffer (§21.6.4), an *ostream* relies on the *num_put* facet:

```
template <class Ch, class Out = ostreambuf_iterator<Ch> >
class std::num_put : public locale::facet {
public:
    typedef Ch char_type;
    typedef Out iter_type;

    explicit num_put(size_t r = 0);

    // put value "v" to buffer position "b" in stream "s":
    Out put(Out b, ios_base& s, Ch fill, bool v) const;
    Out put(Out b, ios_base& s, Ch fill, long v) const;
    Out put(Out b, ios_base& s, Ch fill, unsigned long v) const;
    Out put(Out b, ios_base& s, Ch fill, double v) const;
    Out put(Out b, ios_base& s, Ch fill, long double v) const;
    Out put(Out b, ios_base& s, Ch fill, const void* v) const;

    static locale::id id; // facet identifier object (§D.2, §D.3, §D.3.1)

protected:
    ~num_put();

    // virtual ``do_'' functions for public functions (see §D.4.1)
};
```

The output iterator (§19.1, §19.2.1) argument, *Out*, identifies where in an *ostream*'s stream buffer (§21.6.4) *put*() places characters representing the numeric value on output. The value of *put*() is that iterator positioned one past the last character position written.

Note that the default specialization of *num_put* (the one where the iterator used to access characters is of type *ostreambuf_iterator<Ch>*) is part of the standard locales (§D.4). If you want to use another specialization, you'll have to make it yourself. For example:

```
template<class Ch>
class String_numput : public std::num_put<Ch, typename basic_string<Ch>::iterator> {
public:
    String_numput() : num_put<Ch, typename basic_string<Ch>::iterator>(1) { }
};

void f(int i, string& s, int pos)        // format i into s starting at pos
{
    String_numput<char> f;
    ios_base& xxx = cout;                 // use cout's formatting rules
    f.put(s.begin()+pos, xxx, ' ', i);    // format i into s
}
```

The *ios_base* argument is used to get information about formatting state and locale. For example, if padding is needed, the *fill* character is used as required by the *ios_base* argument. Typically, the stream buffer written to through *b* is the buffer associated with an *ostream* for which *s* is the base. Note that an *ios_base* is not a simple object to construct. In particular, it controls many aspects of formatting that must be consistent to achieve acceptable output. Consequently, *ios_base* has no public constructor (§21.3.3).

A *put()* function also uses its *ios_base* argument to get the stream's *locale()*. That *locale* is used to determine punctuation (§D.4.2.1), the alphabetic representation of Booleans, and the conversion to *Ch*. For example, assuming that *s* is *put()*'s *ios_base* argument, we might find code like this in a *put()* function:

```
const locale& loc = s.getloc();
// ...
wchar_t w = use_facet< ctype<char> >(loc).widen(c);        // char to Ch conversion
// ...
string pnt = use_facet< numpunct<char> >(loc).decimal_point();    // default: '.'
// ...
string flse = use_facet< numpunct<char> >(loc).falsename();       // default: "false"
```

A standard facet, such as *num_put<char>*, is typically used implicitly through a standard I/O stream function. Consequently, most programmers need not know about it. However, the use of such facets by standard library functions is interesting because they show how I/O streams work and how facets can be used. As ever, the standard library provides examples of interesting programming techniques.

Using *num_put*, the implementer of *ostream* might write:

```
template<class Ch, class Tr>
ostream& std::basic_ostream<Ch, Tr>::operator<<(double d)
{
    sentry guard(*this);        // see §21.3.8
    if (!guard) return *this;
```

```
    try {
        if (use_facet< num_put<Ch> > (getloc()) .put (*this, *this, fill(), d) .failed())
            setstate (badbit);
    }
    catch (...) {
        handle_ioexception (*this);
    }
    return *this;
}
```

A lot is going on here. The sentry ensures that all prefix and suffix operations are performed (§21.3.8). We get the *ostream*'s *locale* by calling its member function *getloc*() (§21.7). We extract *num_put* from that *locale* using *use_facet* (§D.3.1). That done, we call the appropriate *put*() function to do the real work. An *ostreambuf_iterator* can be constructed from an *ostream* (§19.2.6), and an *ostream* can be implicitly converted to its base class *ios_base* (§21.2.1), so the two first arguments to *put*() are easily supplied.

A call of *put*() returns its output iterator argument. This output iterator is obtained from a *basic_ostream*, so it is an *ostreambuf_iterator*. Consequently, *failed*() (§19.2.6.1) is available to test for failure and to allow us to set the stream state appropriately.

I did not use *has_facet*, because the standard facets (§D.4) are guaranteed to be present in every locale. If that guarantee is violated, *bad_cast* is thrown (§D.3.1).

The *put*() function calls the virtual *do_put*(). Consequently, user-defined code may be executed, and *operator<<*() must be prepared to handle an exception thrown by the overriding *do_put*(). Also, *num_put* may not exist for some character types, so *use_facet*() might throw *std::bad_cast* (§D.3.1). The behavior of a << for a built-in type, such as *double*, is defined by the C++ standard. Consequently, the question is not what *handle_ioexception*() should do but rather how it should do what the standard prescribes. If *badbit* is set in this *ostream*'s exception state (§21.3.6), the exception is simply rethrown. Otherwise, an exception is handled by setting the stream state and continuing. In either case, *badbit* must be set in the stream state (§21.3.3):

```
template<class Ch, class Tr>
void handle_ioexception (std::basic_ostream<Ch, Tr>& s)     // called from catch clause
{
    if (s.exceptions() &ios_base::badbit) {
        try { s.setstate (ios_base::badbit); } catch (...) { }
        throw;       // rethrow
    }
    s.setstate (ios_base::badbit);      // might throw basic_ios::failure
}
```

The *try-block* is needed because *setstate*() might throw *basic_ios::failure* (§21.3.3, §21.3.6). However, if *badbit* is set in the exception state, *operator<<*() must rethrow the exception that caused *handle_ioexception*() to be called (rather than simply throwing *basic_ios::failure*).

The << for a built-in type, such as *double*, must be implemented by writing directly to a stream buffer. When writing a << for a user-defined type, we can often avoid the resulting complexity by expressing the output of the user-defined type in terms of output of existing types (§D.3.2).

D.4.2.3 Numeric Input

When reading from a stream buffer (§21.6.4), an *istream* relies on the *num_get* facet:

```
template <class Ch, class In = istreambuf_iterator<Ch> >
class std::num_get : public locale::facet {
public:
    typedef Ch char_type;
    typedef In iter_type;

    explicit num_get(size_t r = 0);

    // read [b:e) into v, using formatting rules from s, reporting errors by setting r:
    In get(In b, In e, ios_base& s, ios_base::iostate& r, bool& v) const;
    In get(In b, In e, ios_base& s, ios_base::iostate& r, long& v) const;
    In get(In b, In e, ios_base& s, ios_base::iostate& r, unsigned short& v) const;
    In get(In b, In e, ios_base& s, ios_base::iostate& r, unsigned int& v) const;
    In get(In b, In e, ios_base& s, ios_base::iostate& r, unsigned long& v) const;
    In get(In b, In e, ios_base& s, ios_base::iostate& r, float& v) const;
    In get(In b, In e, ios_base& s, ios_base::iostate& r, double& v) const;
    In get(In b, In e, ios_base& s, ios_base::iostate& r, long double& v) const;
    In get(In b, In e, ios_base& s, ios_base::iostate& r, void*& v) const;

    static locale::id id;   // facet identifier object (§D.2, §D.3, §D.3.1)

protected:
    ~num_get();

    // virtual "do_" functions for public functions (see §D.4.1)
};
```

Basically, *num_get* is organized like *num_put* (§D.4.2.2). Since it reads rather than writes, *get*() needs a pair of input iterators, and the argument designating the target of the read is a reference. The *iostate* variable *r* is set to reflect the state of the stream. If a value of the desired type could not be read, *failbit* is set in *r*; if the end of input was reached, *eofbit* is set in *r*. An input operator will use *r* to determine how to set the state of its stream. If no error was encountered, the value read is assigned though *v*; otherwise, *v* is left unchanged.

The implementer of *istream* might write:

```
template<class Ch, class Tr>
istream& std::basic_istream<Ch,Tr>::operator>>(double& d)
{
    sentry guard(*this);        // see §21.3.8
    if (!guard) {
        setstate(failbit);
        return *this;
    }

    iostate state = 0;      // good
    istreambuf_iterator<Ch> eos;
    double dd;
```

```
        try {
            use_facet< num_get<Ch> > (getloc()) .get (*this, eos, state, dd);
        }
        catch ( ... ) {
            handle_ioexception (*this);        // see §D.4.2.2
            return *this;
        }
        if (state==0 || state==eofbit) d = dd; // set value only if get() succeeded
        setstate (state);
        return *this;
    }
```

Exceptions enabled for the *istream* will be thrown by *setstate* ( ) in case of error (§21.3.6).

By defining a *numpunct*, such as *my_numpunct* from §D.4.2, we can read using nonstandard punctuation. For example:

```
    void f()
    {
        cout << "style A: "
        int i1;
        double d1;
        cin >> i1 >> d1;              // read using standard "12345678" format

        locale loc (locale::classic(), new My_punct);
        cin.imbue (loc);
        cout << "style B: "
        int i2;
        double d2;
        cin >> i1 >> d2;             // read using the "12 345 678" format
    }
```

If we want to read really unusual numeric formats, we have to override *do_get* ( ). For example, we might define a *num_get* that read Roman numerals, such as *XXI* and *MM* (§D.6[15]).

D.4.3 Input and Output of Monetary Values

The formatting of monetary amounts is technically similar to the formatting of ''plain'' numbers (§D.4.2). However, the presentation of monetary amounts is even more sensitive to cultural differences. For example, a negative amount (a loss, a debit), such as *– 1.25*, should in some contexts be presented as a (positive) number in parentheses: (*1.25*). Similarly, color is in some contexts used to ease the recognition of negative amounts.

There is no standard ''money type.'' Instead, the money facets are meant to be used explicitly for numeric values that the programmer knows to represent monetary amounts. For example:

```
    class Money { // simple type to hold a monetary amount
        long int amount;
    public:
        Money (long int i) : amount (i) { }
        operator long int() const { return amount; }
    };
```

```
// ...
void f(long int i)
{
    cout << "value= " << i << " amount= " << Money(i) << endl;
}
```

The task of the monetary facets is to make it reasonably easy to write an output operator for *Money* so that the amount is printed according to local convention (see §D.4.3.2). The output would vary depending on *cout*'s locale. Possible outputs are:

```
value= 1234567 amount= $12345.67
value= 1234567 amount= 12345,67 DKr
value= -1234567 amount= $-12345.67
value= -1234567 amount= -$12345.67
value= -1234567 amount= (CHF12345,67)
```

For money, accuracy to the smallest currency unit is usually considered essential. Consequently, I adopted the common convention of having the integer value represent the number of cents (pence, øre, fils, cents, etc.) rather than the number of dollars (pounds, kroner, dinar, euro, etc.). This convention is supported by *money_punct*'s *frac_digits*() function (§D.4.3.1). Similarly, the appearance of the ''decimal point'' is defined by *decimal_point*().

The facets *money_get* and *money_put* provide functions that perform I/O based on the format defined by the *money_base* facet.

A simple *Money* type can be used simply to control I/O formats or to hold monetary values. In the former case, we cast values of (other) types used to hold monetary amounts to *Money* before writing, and we read into *Money* variables before converting them to other types. It is less error prone to consistently hold monetary amounts in a *Money* type; that way, we cannot forget to cast a value to *Money* before writing it, and we don't get input errors by trying to read monetary values in locale-insensitive ways. However, it may be infeasible to introduce a *Money* type into a system that wasn't designed for that. In such cases, applying *Money* conversions (casts) to read and write operations is necessary.

D.4.3.1 Money Punctuation

The facet controlling the presentation of monetary amounts, *moneypunct*, naturally resembles the facet for controlling plain numbers, *numpunct* (§D.4.2.1):

```
class std::money_base {
public:
    enum part { none, space, symbol, sign, value };      // parts of value layout
    struct pattern { char field[4]; };                   // layout specification
};
```

```
template <class Ch, bool International = false>
class std::moneypunct : public locale::facet, public money_base {
public:
      typedef Ch char_type;
      typedef basic_string<Ch> string_type;

      explicit moneypunct(size_t r = 0);

      Ch decimal_point() const;          // '.' in classic()
      Ch thousands_sep() const;          // ',' in classic()
      string grouping() const;           // "" in classic(), meaning "no grouping"

      string_type curr_symbol() const;   // "$" in classic()
      string_type positive_sign() const; // "" in classic()
      string_type negative_sign() const; // "-" in classic()

      int frac_digits() const;           // number of digits after the decimal point; 2 in classic()
      pattern pos_format() const;        // { symbol, sign, none, value } in classic()
      pattern neg_format() const;        // { symbol, sign, none, value } in classic()

      static const bool intl = International;    // use international monetary formats

      static locale::id id; // facet identifier object (§D.2, §D.3, §D.3.1)
protected:
      ~moneypunct();

      // virtual ''do_'' functions for public functions (see §D.4.1)
};
```

The facilities offered by *moneypunct* are intended primarily for use by implementers of *money_put* and *money_get* facets (§D.4.3.2, §D.4.3.3).

The *decimal_point()*, *thousands_sep()*, and *grouping()* members behave as their equivalents in *numpunct*.

The *curr_symbol()*, *positive_sign()*, and *negative_sign()* members return the string to be used to represent the currency symbol (for example, $, ¥, *FrF*, *DKr*), the plus sign, and the minus sign, respectively. If the *International* template argument was *true*, the *intl* member will also be *true*, and ''international'' representations of the currency symbols will be used. Such an ''international'' representation is a four-character string. For example:

```
"USD "
"DKr "
"EUR "
```

Usually, the last character is a space. The three-letter currency identifier is defined by the ISO-4217 standard. When *International* is *false*, a ''local'' currency symbol, such as $, £, and ¥, can be used.

A *pattern* returned by *pos_format()* or *neg_format()* is four *parts* defining the sequence in which the numeric value, the currency symbol, the sign symbol, and whitespace occur. Most common formats are trivially represented using this simple notion of a pattern. For example:

```
+$ 123.45       // { sign, symbol, space, value } where positive_sign() returns "+"
$+123.45        // { symbol, sign, value, none } where positive_sign() returns "+"
$123.45         // { symbol, sign, value, none } where positive_sign() returns ""
$123.45-        // { symbol, value, sign, none }
-123.45 DKr     // { sign, value, space, symbol }
($123.45)       // { sign, symbol, value, none } where negative_sign() returns "()"
(123.45DKr)     // { sign, value, symbol, none } where negative_sign() returns "()"
```

Representing a negative number using parentheses is achieved by having *negative_sign* () return a string containing the two characters (). The first character of a sign string is placed where *sign* is found in the pattern, and the rest of the sign string is placed after all other parts of the pattern. The most common use of this facility is to represent the financial community's convention of using parentheses for negative amounts, but other uses are possible. For example:

```
-$123.45           // { sign, symbol, value, none } where negative_sign() returns "-"
*$123.45 silly     // { sign, symbol, value, none } where negative_sign() returns "* silly"
```

The values *sign*, *value*, and *symbol* must each appear exactly once in a pattern. The remaining value can be either *space* or *none*. Where *space* appears, at least one and possibly more whitespace characters may appear in the representation. Where *none* appears, except at the end of a pattern, zero or more whitespace characters may appear in the representation.

Note that these strict rules ban some apparently reasonable patterns:

```
pattern pat = { sign, value, none, none };      // error: no symbol
```

The *frac_digits* () function indicates where the *decimal_point* () is placed. Often, monetary amounts are represented in the smallest currency unit (§D.4.3). This unit is typically one hundredth of the major unit (for example, a ¢ is one hundredth of a $), so *frac_digits* () is often 2.

Here is a simple format defined as a facet:

```
class My_money_io : public moneypunct<char, true> {
public:
    explicit My_money_io (size_t r = 0) : moneypunct<char, true> (r) { }

    Ch do_decimal_point () const { return "."; }
    Ch do_thousands_sep () const { return ","; }
    string do_grouping () const { return "\003\003\003"; }

    string_type do_curr_symbol () const { return "USD "; }
    string_type do_positive_sign () const { return ""; }
    string_type do_negative_sign () const { return "()"; }

    int do_frac_digits () const { return 2; }     // two digits after decimal point

    pattern do_pos_format () const
    {
        static pattern pat = { sign, symbol, value, none };
        return pat;
    }
```

```
    pattern do_neg_format() const
    {
        static pattern pat = { sign, symbol, value, none };
        return pat;
    }
};
```

This facet is used in the *Money* input and output operations defined in §D.4.3.2 and §D.4.3.3.
    A *_byname* version (§D.4, §D.4.1) of *moneypunct* is provided:

```
template <class Ch, bool Intl = false>
class std::moneypunct_byname : public moneypunct<Ch, Intl> { /* ... */ };
```

D.4.3.2 Money Output

The *money_put* facet writes monetary amounts according to the format specified by *moneypunct*.
Specifically, *money_put* provides *put*() functions that place a suitably formatted character representation into the stream buffer of a stream:

```
template <class Ch, class Out = ostreambuf_iterator<Ch> >
class std::money_put : public std::locale::facet {
public:
        typedef Ch char_type;
        typedef Out iter_type;
        typedef basic_string<Ch> string_type;

        explicit money_put(size_t r = 0);

        // put value "v" into buffer position "b":
        Out put(Out b, bool intl, ios_base& s, Ch fill, long double v) const;
        Out put(Out b, bool intl, ios_base& s, Ch fill, const string_type& v) const;

        static locale::id id;   // facet identifier object (§D.2, §D.3, §D.3.1)

protected:
        ~money_put();

        // virtual "do_" functions for public functions (see §D.4.1)
};
```

The *b*, *s*, *fill*, and *v* arguments are used as for *num_put*'s *put*() functions (§D.4.2.2). The *intl*
argument indicates whether a standard four-character "international" currency symbol or a
"local" symbol is used (§D.4.3.1).
    Given *money_put*, we can define an output operator for *Money* (§D.4.3):

```
ostream& operator<<(ostream& s, Money m)
{
        ostream::sentry guard(s);           // see §21.3.8
        if (!guard) return s;
```

```
    try {
        const money_put<char>& f = use_facet< money_put<char> > (s.getloc());
        if (m==static_cast<long double>(m)) {  // m can be represented as a long double
            if (f.put(s,true,s,s.fill(),m).failed()) s.setstate(ios_base::badbit);
        }
        else {
            ostringstream v;
            v << m;          // convert to string representation
            if (f.put(s,true,s,s.fill(),v.str()).failed()) s.setstate(ios_base::badbit);
        }
    }
    catch (...) {
        handle_ioexception(s);      // see §D.4.2.2
    }
    return s;
}
```

If a *long double* doesn't have sufficient precision to represent the monetary value exactly, I convert the value to its string representation and output that using the *put* ( ) that takes a *string*.

D.4.3.3 Money Input

The *money_get* facet reads monetary amounts according to the format specified by *moneypunct*. Specifically, *money_get* provides *get* ( ) functions that extract a suitably formatted character representation from the stream buffer of a stream:

```
template <class Ch, class In = istreambuf_iterator<Ch> >
class std::money_get : public std::locale::facet {
public:
    typedef Ch char_type;
    typedef In iter_type;
    typedef basic_string<Ch> string_type;

    explicit money_get(size_t r = 0);

    // read [b:e) into v, using formatting rules from s, reporting errors by setting r:
    In get(In b, In e, bool intl, ios_base& s, ios_base::iostate& r, long double& v) const;
    In get(In b, In e, bool intl, ios_base& s, ios_base::iostate& r, string_type& v) const;

    static locale::id id;  // facet identifier object (§D.2, §D.3, §D.3.1)
protected:
    ~money_get();

    // virtual "do_" functions for public functions (see §D.4.1)
};
```

The *b, e, s, fill*, and *v* arguments are used as for *num_get*'s *get* ( ) functions (§D.4.2.3). The *intl* argument indicates whether a standard four-character "international" currency symbol or a "local" symbol is used (§D.4.3.1).

A well-defined pair of *money_get* and *money_put* facets will provide output in a form that can be read back in without errors or loss of information. For example:

```
int main()
{
    Money m;
    while (cin>>m) cout << m << "\n";
}
```

The output of this simple program should be acceptable as its input. Furthermore, the output produced by a second run given the output from a first run should be identical to its input.

A plausible input operator for *Money* would be:

```
istream& operator>>(istream& s, Money& m)
{
    istream::sentry guard(s);          // see §21.3.8
    if (!guard) {
        s.setstate(ios_base::failbit);
        return s;
    }

    ios_base::iostate state = 0;       // good
    istreambuf_iterator<char> eos;
    double dd;
    try {
        const money_get<char> &f = use_facet< money_get<char> >(s.getloc());
        f.get(s, eos, true, state, dd);
    }
    catch (...) {
        handle_ioexception(s);         // see §D.4.2.2
        return s;
    }
    if (state==0 || state==ios_base::eofbit) m = dd;      // set value only if get() succeeded
    s.setstate(state);
    return s;
}
```

D.4.4 Date and Time Input and Output

Unfortunately, the C++ standard library does not provide a proper *date* type. However, from the C standard library, it inherits low-level facilities for dealing with dates and time intervals. These C facilities are the basis for C++'s facilities for dealing with time in a system-independent manner.

The following sections demonstrate how the presentation of date and time-of-day information can be made *locale* sensitive. In addition, they provide an example of how a user-defined type (*Date*) can fit into the framework provided by *iostream* (Chapter 21) and *locale* (§D.2). The implementation of *Date* shows techniques that are useful for dealing with time if you don't have a *Date* type available.

D.4.4.1 Clocks and Timers

At the lowest level, most systems have a fine-grained timer. The standard library provides a function *clock* ( ) that returns an implementation-defined arithmetic type *clock_t*. The result of *clock* ( ) can be calibrated by using the ***CLOCKS_PER_SEC*** macro. If you don't have access to a reliable timing utility, you might measure a loop like this:

```
int main (int argc, char* argv [ ])      // §6.1.7
{
    int n = atoi (argv [1]);             // §20.4.1

    clock_t t1 = clock ();
    if (t1 == clock_t (-1)) {            // clock_t(-1) means "clock() didn't work"
        cerr << "sorry, no clock\n";
        exit (1);
    }

    for (int i = 0; i<n; i++) do_something (); // timing loop

    clock_t t2 = clock ();
    if (t2 == clock_t (-1)) {
        cerr << "sorry, clock overflow\n";
        exit (2);
    }
    cout << "do_something () " << n << " times took "
        << double (t2-t1) / CLOCKS_PER_SEC << " seconds"
        << " (measurement granularity: " << CLOCKS_PER_SEC << " of a second)\n";
}
```

The explicit conversion *double* (*t2-t1*) before dividing is necessary because *clock_t* might be an integer. Exactly when the *clock* ( ) starts running is implementation defined; *clock* ( ) is meant to measure time intervals within a single run of a program. For values *t1* and *t2* returned by *clock* ( ), *double* (*t2-t1*) */CLOCKS_PER_SEC* is the system's best approximation of the time in seconds between the two calls.

If *clock* ( ) isn't provided for a processor or if a time interval was too long to measure, *clock* ( ) returns *clock_t* (*-1*).

The *clock* ( ) function is meant to measure intervals from a fraction of a second to a few seconds. For example, if *clock_t* is a 32-bit signed *int* and ***CLOCKS_PER_SEC*** is 1,000,000 , we can use *clock* ( ) to measure from 0 to just over 2,000 seconds (about half an hour) in microseconds.

Please note that getting meaningful measurements of a program can be tricky. Other programs running on a machine may severely affect the time used by a run, cache and pipelining effects are difficult to predict, and algorithms may have surprising dependencies on data. If you try to time something, make several runs and reject the results as flawed if the run times vary significantly.

To cope with longer time intervals and with calendar time, the standard library provides *time_t* for representing a point in time and a structure *tm* for separating a point in time into its conventional parts:

```
typedef implementation_defined time_t;        // implementation-defined arithmetic type (§4.1.1)
                                               // capable of representing a period of time,
                                               // often, a 32-bit integer

struct tm {
    int tm_sec;        // second of minute [0,61]; 60 and 61 to represent leap seconds
    int tm_min;        // minute of hour [0,59]
    int tm_hour;       // hour of day [0,23]
    int tm_mday;       // day of month [1,31]
    int tm_mon;        // month of year [0,11]; 0 means January (note: not [1:12])
    int tm_year;       // year since 1900; 0 means year 1900, and 102 means 2002
    int tm_wday;       // days since Sunday [0,6]; 0 means Sunday
    int tm_yday;       // days since January 1 [0,365]; 0 means January 1
    int tm_isdst;      // hours of daylight savings time
};
```

Note that the standard guarantees only that *tm* has the *int* members mentioned here. The standard does not guarantee that the members appear in this order or that there are no other fields.

The *time_t* and *tm* types and the basic facilities for using them are presented in *<ctime>* and *<time.h>*. For example::

```
clock_t clock();                               // number of clock ticks since the start of the program

time_t time(time_t* pt);                       // current calendar time
double difftime(time_t t2, time_t t1);         // t2–t1 in seconds

tm* localtime(const time_t* pt);               // local time for the *pt
tm* gmtime(const time_t* pt);                  // Grenwich Mean Time (GMT) tm for *pt, or 0
                                               // (officially called Coordinated Universal Time, UTC)

time_t mktime(tm* ptm);                        // time_t for *ptm, or time_t(-1)

char* asctime(const tm* ptm);                  // C-style string representation for *ptm
                                               // for example, "Sun Sep 16 01:03:52 1973\n"
char* ctime(const time_t* t) { return asctime(localtime(t)); }
```

Beware: both *localtime*() and *gmtime*() return a *tm** to a statically allocated object; a subsequent call of that function will change the value of that object. Either use such a return value immediately, or copy the *tm* into storage that you control. Similarly, *asctime*() returns a pointer to a statically allocated character array.

A *tm* can represent dates in a range of at least tens of thousands of years (about [-32000,32000] for a minimally sized *int*). However, *time_t* is most often a (signed) 32-bit *long int*. Counting seconds, this makes *time_t* capable of representing a range just over 68 years on each side of a base year. This base year is most commonly 1970, with the exact base time being 0:00 of January 1 GMT (UTC). If *time_t* is a 32-bit signed integer, we'll run out of "time" in 2038 unless we upgrade *time_t* to a larger integer type, as is already done on some systems.

The *time_t* mechanism is meant primarily for representing "near current time." Thus, we should not expect *time_t* to be able to represent dates outside the [1902,2038] range. Worse, not all implementations of the functions dealing with time handle negative values in the same way. For portability, a value that needs to be represented as both a *tm* and a *time_t* should be in the

[1970,2038] range. People who want to represent dates outside the 1970 to 2038 time frame must devise some additional mechanism to do so.

One consequence of this is that *mktime* () can fail. If the argument for *mktime* () cannot be represented as a *time_t*, the error indicator *time_t* (*-1*) is returned.

If we have a long-running program, we might time it like this:

```
int main (int argc, char* argv[])      // §6.1.7
{
      time_t t1 = time (0);
      do_a_lot (argc, argv);
      time_t t2 = time (0);
      double d = difftime (t2, t1);
      cout << "do_a_lot() took" << d << " seconds\n";
}
```

If the argument to *time* () is not *0*, the resulting time is also assigned to the *time_t* pointed to. If the calendar time is not available (say, on a specialized processor), the value *time_t* (*-1*) is returned. We could cautiously try to find today's date like this:

```
int main ()
{
      time_t t;

      if (time (&t) == time_t (-1)) {      // time_t(-1) means ''time() didn't work''
            cerr << "Bad time\n";
            exit (1);
      }

      tm* gt = gmtime (&t);
      cout << gt->tm_mon+1 << ´/´ << gt->tm_mday << ´/´ << 1900+gt->tm_year << endl;
}
```

D.4.4.2 A Date Class

As mentioned in §10.3, it is unlikely that a single *Date* type can serve all purposes. The uses of date information dictate a variety of representations, and calendar information before the 19th century is very dependent on historical vagaries. However, as an example, we could define a *Date* type along the lines from §10.3, using *time_t* as the implementation:

```
class Date {
public:
      enum Month { jan=1, feb, mar, apr, may, jun, jul, aug, sep, oct, nov, dec };

      class Bad_date { };

      Date (int dd, Month mm, int yy);
      Date ();

      friend ostream& operator<< (ostream& s, const Date& d);
```

```
        // ...
private:
        time_t  d;    // standard date and time representation
};

Date::Date(int dd, Month mm, int yy)
{
        tm  x = { 0 };
        if (dd<0 || 31<dd) throw Bad_date();      // oversimplified: see §10.3.1
        x.tm_mday = dd;
        if (mm<jan || dec<mm) throw Bad_date();
        x.tm_mon = mm-1;            // tm_mon is zero based
        x.tm_year = yy-1900;        // tm_year is 1900 based
        d = mktime(&x);
}

Date::Date()
{
        d = time(0);      // default Date: today
        if (d == time_t(-1)) throw Bad_date();
}
```

The task here is to define locale-sensitive implementations for *Date* << and >>.

D.4.4.3 Date and Time Output

Like *num_put* (§D.4.2), *time_put* provides *put*() functions for writing to buffers through iterators:

```
template <class Ch, class Out = ostreambuf_iterator<Ch> >
class std::time_put : public locale::facet {
public:
        typedef Ch char_type;
        typedef Out iter_type;

        explicit time_put(size_t r = 0);

        // put t into s's stream buffer through b, using format fmt:
        Out put(Out b, ios_base& s, Ch fill, const tm* t,
                                       const Ch* fmt_b, const Ch* fmt_e) const;

        Out put(Out b, ios_base& s, Ch fill, const tm* t, char fmt, char mod = 0) const
              { return do_put(b,s,fill,t,fmt,mod); }

        static locale::id id;  // facet identifier object (§D.2, §D.3, §D.3.1)

protected:
        ~time_put();

        virtual Out do_put(Out, ios_base&, Ch, const tm*, char, char) const;
};
```

A call *put*(*b*,*s*,*fill*,*t*,*fmt_b*,*fmt_e*) places the date information from *t* into *s*'s stream buffer through *b*. The *fill* character is used where needed for padding. The output format is specified by a *printf*()-like format string [*fmt_b*,*fmt_e*). The *printf*-like (§21.8) format is used to produce an actual output and may contain the following special-purpose format specifiers:

%a	abbreviated weekday name (e.g., Sat)
%A	full weekday name (e.g., Saturday)
%b	abbreviated month name (e.g., Feb)
%B	full month name (e.g., February)
%c	date and time (e.g., Sat Feb 06 21:46:05 1999)
%d	day of month [01,31] (e.g., 06)
%H	24-hour clock hour [00,23] (e.g., 21)
%I	12-hour clock hour [01,12] (e.g., 09)
%j	day of year [001,366] (e.g., 037)
%m	month of year [01,12] (e.g., 02)
%M	minute of hour [00,59] (e.g., 48)
%p	a.m./p.m. indicator for 12-hour clock (e.g., PM)
%S	second of minute [00,61] (e.g., 40)
%U	week of year [00,53] starting with Sunday (e.g., 05); the first Sunday starts week 1
%w	day of week [0,6]; 0 means Sunday (e.g., 6)
%W	week of year [00,53] starting with Monday (e.g., 05); the first Monday starts week 1
%x	date (e.g., 02/06/99)
%X	time (e.g., 21:48:40)
%y	year without century [00,99] (e.g., 99)
%Y	year (e.g., 1999)
%Z	time zone indicator (e.g., EST) if the time zone is known

This long list of very specialized formatting rules could be used as an argument for the use of extensible I/O systems. However, as with most specialized notations, it is adequate for its task and often even convenient.

In addition to these formatting directives, most implementations support "modifiers," such as an integer specifying a field width (§21.8), *%10X*. Modifiers for the time-and-date formats are not part of the C++ standard, but some platform standards, such as POSIX, require them. Consequently, modifiers can be difficult to avoid even if their use isn't perfectly portable.

The *sprintf*-like (§21.8) function *strftime* () from *<ctime>* or *<time.h>* produces output using the time and date format directives:

> *size_t strftime (char* s, size_t max, const char* format, const tm* tmp);*

This function places a maximum of ***max*** characters from **tmp* and the *format* into **s* according the *format*. For example:

```
int main ( )
{
    char buf[20];   // sloppy: no protection against buffer overflow
    time_t t = time (0);
    strftime (buf, 20, "%A\n", localtime (&t) );
    cout << buf;
}
```

On a Wednesday, this will print *Wednesday* in the default *classic* ( ) locale (§D.2.3) and *onsdag* in a Danish locale.

Characters that are not part of a format specified, such as the newline in the example, are simply copied into the first argument (*s*).

When *put* ( ) identifies a format character *f* (and optional modifier character *m*), it calls the virtual *do_put* ( ) to do the actual formatting: *do_put* (*b*, *s*, *fill*, *t*, *f*, *m*).

A call *put* (*b*, *s*, *fill*, *t*, *f*, *m*) is a simplified form of *put* ( ), where a format character (*f*) and a modifier character (*m*) are explicitly provided. Thus,

```
const char fmt[] = "%10X";
put (b, s, fill, t, fmt, fmt+sizeof(fmt));
```

can be abbreviated to

```
put (b, s, fill, t, 'X', 10);
```

If a format contains multibyte characters, it must both begin and end in the default state (§D.4.6).

We can use *put* ( ) to implement a *locale*-sensitive output operator for *Date*:

```
ostream& operator<< (ostream& s, const Date& d)
{
        ostream::sentry guard(s);              // see §21.3.8
        if (!guard) return s;

        tm* tmp = localtime(&d.d);
        try {
                if (use_facet< time_put<char> >(s.getloc()).put(s,s,s.fill(),tmp,'x').failed())
                        s.setstate(ios_base::failbit);
        }
        catch (...) {
                handle_ioexception(s);         // see §D.4.2.2
        }
        return s;
}
```

Since there is no standard *Date* type, there is no default layout for date I/O. Here, I specified the %*x* format by passing the character ´*x*´ as the format character. Because the %*x* format is the default for *get_time* ( ) (§D.4.4.4), that is probably as close to a standard as one can get. See §D.4.4.5 for an example of how to use alternative formats.

D.4.4.4 Date and Time Input

As ever, input is trickier than output. When we write code to output a value, we often have a choice among different formats. In addition, when we write input code, we must deal with errors and sometimes the possibility of several alternative formats.

The *time_get* facet implements input of time and date. The idea is that *time_get* of a *locale* can read the times and dates produced by the *locale*'s *time_put*. However, there are no standard *date* and *time* classes, so a programmer can use a locale to produce output according to a variety of formats. For example, the following representations could all be produced by using a single output statement, using *time_put* (§D.4.4.5) from different locales:

January 15th 1999
Thursday 15th January 1999
15 Jan 1999AD
Thurs 15/1/99

The C++ standard encourages implementers of *time_get* to accept dates and time formats as specified by POSIX and other standards. The problem is that it is difficult to standardize the intent to read dates and times in whatever format is conventional in a given culture. It is wise to experiment to see what a given locale provides (§D.6[8]). If a format isn't accepted, a programmer can provide a suitable alternative *time_get* facet.

The standard time input *facet*, *time_get*, is derived from *time_base*:

```
class std::time_base {
public:
    enum dateorder {
        no_order,    // no order, possibly more elements (such as day of week)
        dmy,         // day before month before year
        mdy,         // month before day before year
        ymd,         // year before month before day
        ydm          // year before day before month
    };
};
```

An implementer can use this enumeration to simplify the parsing on date formats.

Like *num_get*, *time_get* accesses its buffer through a pair of input iterators:

```
template <class Ch, class In = istreambuf_iterator<Ch> >
class time_get : public locale::facet, public time_base {
public:
    typedef Ch char_type;
    typedef In iter_type;

    explicit time_get(size_t r = 0);

    dateorder date_order() const { return do_date_order(); }

    // read [b,e) into d, using formatting rules from s, reporting errors by setting r:
    In get_time(In b, In e, ios_base& s, ios_base::iostate& r, tm* d) const;
    In get_date(In b, In e, ios_base& s, ios_base::iostate& r, tm* d) const;
    In get_year(In b, In e, ios_base& s, ios_base::iostate& r, tm* d) const;

    In get_weekday(In b, In e, ios_base& s, ios_base::iostate& r, tm* d) const;
    In get_monthname(In b, In e, ios_base& s, ios_base::iostate& r, tm* d) const;

    static locale::id id;    // facet identifier object (§D.2, §D.3, §D.3.1)

protected:
    ~time_get();

    // virtual "do_" functions for public functions (see §D.4.1)
};
```

The *get_time*() function calls *do_get_time*(). The default *get_time*() reads time as produced by the *locale*'s *time_put* ( ), using the %*X* format (§D.4.4). Similarly, the *get_date* ( ) function calls *do_get_date* ( ). The default reads time as produced by the *locale*'s *time_put* ( ), using the %*x* format (§D.4.4).

Thus, the simplest input operator for *Date*s is something like this:

```
istream& operator>> (istream& s, Date& d)
{
    istream::sentry guard(s);        // see §21.3.8
    if (!guard) return s;

    ios_base::iostate res = 0;
    tm x = { 0 };
    istreambuf_iterator<char, char_traits<char> > end;
    try {
        use_facet< time_get<char> >(s.getloc()).get_date(s,end,s,res,&x);
    }
    catch (...) {
        handle_ioexception(s);        // see §D.4.2.2
        return s;
    }
    d = Date(x.tm_mday, Date::Month(x.tm_mon+1), x.tm_year+1900);
    return s;
}
```

The call *get_date* (*s*, *end*, *s*, *res*, &*x*) relies on two implicit conversions from *istream*: As the first argument *s* is used to construct an *istreambuf_iterator*. As third argument, *s* is converted to the *istream* base class *ios_base*.

This input operator will work correctly for dates in the range that can be represented by *time_t*. A trivial test case would be:

```
int main()
try {
    Date today;
    cout << today << endl;            // write using %x format
    Date d(12, Date::may, 1998);

    cout << d << endl;
    Date dd;
    while (cin >> dd) cout << dd << endl;        // read dates produced by %x format
}
catch (Date::Bad_date) {
    cout << "exit: bad date caught\n";
}
```

A *_byname* version (§D.4, §D.4.1) of *put_time* is also provided:

```
template <class Ch, class Out = ostreambuf_iterator<Ch> >
class std::time_put_byname : public time_put<Ch,Out> { /* ... */ };
```

D.4.4.5 A More Flexible Date Class

If you tried to use the *Date* class from §D.4.4.2 with the I/O from §D.4.4.3 and §D.4.4.4, you'd soon find it restrictive:

[1] It can handle only dates that can be represented by a *time_t*; that typically means in the [1970,2038] range.

[2] It accepts dates only in the standard format – whatever that might be.

[3] Its reporting of input errors is unacceptable.

[4] It supports only streams of *char* – not streams of arbitrary character types.

A more interesting and more useful input operator would accept a wider range of dates, recognize a few common formats, and reliably report errors in a useful form. To do this, we must depart from the *time_t* representation:

```
class Date {
public:
    enum Month { jan=1, feb, mar, apr, may, jun, jul, aug, sep, oct, nov, dec };

    struct Bad_date {
        const char* why;
        Bad_date(const char* p) : why(p) { }
    };

    Date(int dd, Month mm, int yy, int day_of_week = 0);
    Date();

    void make_tm(tm* t) const;        // place tm representation of Date in *t
    time_t make_time_t() const;       // return time_t representation of Date

    int year() const { return y; }
    Month month() const { return m; }
    int day() const { return d; }

    // ...
private:
    char d;
    Month m;
    int y;
};
```

For simplicity, I reverted to the (d, m, y) representation (§10.2).

The constructor might be defined like this:

```
Date::Date(int dd, Month mm, int yy, int day_of_week)
    :d(dd), m(mm), y(yy)
{
    if (d==0 && m==Month(0) && y==0) return;    // Date(0,0,0) is the "null date"
    if (mm<jan || dec<mm) throw Bad_date("bad month");
```

```
if (dd<1 || 31<dd)    // oversimplified; see §10.3.1
    throw Bad_date("bad day of month");
if (day_of_week && day_in_week(yy,mm,dd)!=day_of_week)
    throw Bad_date("bad day of week");
}

Date::Date() :d(0), m(0), y(0) { } // a "null date"
```

The *day_in_week*() calculation is nontrivial and immaterial to the *locale* mechanisms, so I have left it out. If you need one, your system will have one somewhere.

Comparison operations are always useful for types such as *Date*:

```
bool operator==(const Date& x, const Date& y)
{
    return x.year()==y.year() && x.month()==y.month() && x.day()==y.day();
}

bool operator!=(const Date& x, const Date& y)
{
    return !(x==y);
}
```

Having departed from the standard *tm* and *time_t* formats, we need conversion functions to cooperate with software that expects those types:

```
void Date::make_tm(tm* p) const      // put date into *p
{
    tm x = { 0 };
    *p = x;
    p->tm_year = y-1900;
    p->tm_mday = d;
    p->tm_mon = m-1;
}

time_t Date::make_time_t() const
{
    if (y<1970 || 2038<y)       // oversimplified
        throw Bad_date("date out of range for time_t");
    tm x;
    make_tm(&x);
    return mktime(&x);
}
```

D.4.4.6 Specifying a *Date* Format

C++ doesn't define a standard output format for dates (%x is as close we get; §D.4.4.3). However, even if a standard format existed, we would probably want to be able to use alternatives. This could be done by providing a ''default format'' and a way of changing it. For example:

```
class Date_format {
      static char fmt[];            // default format
      const char* curr;             // current format
      const char* curr_end;
public:
      Date_format() :curr(fmt), curr_end(fmt+strlen(fmt)) { }

      const char* begin() const { return curr; }
      const char* end() const { return curr_end; }

      void set(const char* p, const char* q) { curr=p; curr_end=q; }
      void set(const char* p) { curr=p; curr_end=curr+strlen(p); }

      static const char* default_fmt() { return fmt; }
};

const char Date_format<char>::fmt[] = "%A, %B %d, %Y";   // e.g., Friday, February 5, 1999

Date_format date_fmt;
```

To be able to use that *strftime*() format (§D.4.4.3), I have refrained from parameterizing the *Date_format* class on the character type used. This implies that this solution allows only date notations for which the format can be expressed as a *char*[]. I also used a global format object (*date_fmt*) to provide a default *Date* format. Since the value of *date_fmt* can be changed, this provides a crude way of controlling *Date* formatting, similar to the way *global*() (§D.2.3) can be used to control formatting.

A more general solution is to add *Date_in* and *Date_out* facets to control reading and writing from a stream. That approach is presented in §D.4.4.7.

Given *Date_format*, *Date::operator<<*() can be written like this:

```
template<class Ch, class Tr>
basic_ostream<Ch,Tr>& operator<<(basic_ostream<Ch,Tr>& s, const Date& d)
// write according to user-specified format
{
      typename basic_ostream<Ch,Tr>::sentry guard(s);   // see _io.sentry
      if (!guard) return s;

      tm t;
      d.make_tm(&t);
      try {
            const time_put<Ch>& f = use_facet< time_put<Ch> >(s.getloc());
            if (f.put(s,s,s.fill(),&t,date_fmt.begin(),date_fmt.end()).failed())
                  s.setstate(ios_base::failbit);
      }
      catch (...) {
            handle_ioexception(s);      // see §D.4.2.2
      }
      return s;
}
```

I could have used *has_facet* to verify that *s*'s locale had a *time_put<Ch>* facet. However, here it seemed simpler to handle that problem by catching any exception thrown by *use_facet*.

Here is a simple test program that controls the output format through *date_fmt*:

```
int main()
try {

    while (cin >> dd && dd != Date()) cout << dd << endl;      // write using default date_fmt

    date_fmt.set("%Y/%m/%d");

    while (cin >> dd && dd != Date()) cout << dd << endl;      // write using "%Y/%m/%d"
}
catch (Date::Bad_date e) {
    cout << "bad date caught: " << e.why << endl;
}
```

D.4.4.7 A *Date* Input Facet

As ever, input is a bit more difficult than output. However, because the interface to low-level input is fixed by *get_date*() and because the *operator>>*() defined for *Date* in §D.4.4.4 didn't directly access the representation of a *Date*, we could use that *operator>>*() unchanged. Here is a templatized version to match the *operator<<*():

```
template<class Ch, class Tr>
istream<Ch,Tr>& operator>>(istream<Ch,Tr>& s, Date& d)
{
    typename istream<Ch,Tr>::sentry guard(s);
    if (!guard) return s;

    ios_base::iostate res = 0;
    tm x = { 0 };
    istreambuf_iterator<Ch,Tr> end;
    try {
        use_facet< time_get<Ch> >(s.getloc()).get_date(s,end,s,res,&x);
    }
    catch (...) {
        handle_ioexception(s);      // see §D.4.2.2
        return s;
    }
    if (res == ios_base::badbit)
        s.setstate(res);
    else
        d = Date(x.tm_mday,Date::Month(x.tm_mon+1),x.tm_year+1900,x.tm_wday);
    return s;
}
```

This *Date* input operator calls *get_date*() from the *istream*'s *time_get* facet (§D.4.4.4). Therefore, we can provide a different and more flexible form of input by defining a new facet derived from *time_get*:

```
template<class Ch, class In = istreambuf_iterator<Ch> >
class Date_in : public std::time_get<Ch,In> {
public:
      Date_in(size_t r = 0)  : std::time_get<Ch>(r)  { }
protected:
      In do_get_date(In b, In e, ios_base& s, ios_base::iostate& r, tm* tmp) const;
private:
      enum Vtype { novalue, unknown, dayofweek, month } ;
      In getval(In b, In e, ios_base& s, ios_base::iostate& r, int* v, Vtype* res) const;
};
```

The *getval*() needs to read a year, a month, a day of the month, and optionally a day of the week and compose the result into a *tm*.

The names of the months and the names of the days of the week are locale specific. Consequently, we can't mention them directly in our input function. Instead, we recognize months and days by calling the functions that *time_get* provides for that: *get_monthname*() and *get_weekday*() (§D.4.4.4).

The year, the day of the month, and possibly the month are represented as integers. Unfortunately, a number does not indicate whether it denotes a day or a month, or whatever. For example, 7 could denote July, day 7 of a month, or even the year 2007. The real purpose of *time_get*'s *date_order*() is to resolve such ambiguities.

The strategy of *Date_in* is to read values, classify them, and then use *date_order*() to see whether (or how) the values entered make sense. The private *getval*() function does the actual reading from the stream buffer and the initial classification:

```
template<class Ch, class In>
In Date_in<Ch,In>::getval(In b, In e,
                          ios_base& s, ios_base::iostate& r, int* v, Vtype* res) const
      // read part of Date: number, day_of_week, or month. Skip whitespace and punctuation.
{
      const ctype<Ch>& ct = use_facet< ctype<Ch> >(s.getloc());  // ctype is defined in §D.4.5
      Ch c;

      *res = novalue;  // no value found

      for (;;) { // skip whitespace and punctuation
            if (b == e) return e;
            c = *b;
            if (!(ct.is(ctype_base::space,c) || ct.is(ctype_base::punct,c))) break;
            ++b;
      }

      if (ct.is(ctype_base::digit,c)) {    //  read integer without regard for numpunct
            int i = 0;
            do {  // turn digit from arbitrary character set into decimal value:
                  static char const digits[] = "0123456789";
                  i = i*10 + find(digits,digits+10,ct.narrow(c,' '))-digits;
                  c = *++b;
            } while (ct.is(ctype_base::digit,c));
```

```
            *v = i;
            *res = unknown;        // an integer, but we don't know what it represents
            return b;
    }

    if (ct.is(ctype_base::alpha,c)) {    // look for name of month or day of week
        basic_string<Ch> str;
        while (ct.is(ctype_base::alpha,c)) {        // read characters into string
            str += c;
            if (++b == e) break;
            c = *b;
        }

        tm t;
        basic_stringstream<Ch> ss(str);
        typedef istreambuf_iterator<Ch> SI;    // iterator type for ss' buffer
        get_monthname(ss.rdbuf(),SI(),s,r,&t); // read from in-memory stream buffer
        if (((r&(ios_base::badbit|ios_base::failbit))==0) {
            *v= t.tm_mon;
            *res = month;
            r = 0;
            return b;
        }

        r = 0;        // clear state before trying to read a second time
        get_weekday(ss.rdbuf(),SI(),s,r,&t);     // read from in-memory stream buffer
        if (((r&ios_base::badbit)==0) {
            *v = t.tm_wday;
            *res = dayofweek;
            r = 0;
            return b;
        }
    }
    r |= ios_base::failbit;
    return b;
}
```

The tricky part here is to distinguish months from weekdays. We read through input iterators, so we cannot read [b, e] twice, looking first for a month and then for a day. On the other hand, we cannot look at one character at a time and decide, because only *get_monthname*() and *get_weekday*() know which character sequences make up the names of the months and the names of the days of the week in a given locale. The solution I chose was to read strings of alphabetic characters into a *string*, make a *stringstream* from that string, and then repeatedly read from that stream's *streambuf*.

The error recording uses the state bits, such as *ios_base::badbit*, directly. This is necessary because the more convenient functions for manipulating stream state, such as *clear*() and *setstate*(), are defined in *basic_ios* rather than in its base *ios_base* (§21.3.3). If necessary, the >> operator then uses the error results reported by *get_date*() to reset the state of the input stream.

Given *getval*(), we can read values first and then try to see whether they make sense later. The *dateorder*() can be crucial:

```
template<class Ch, class In>
In Date_in<Ch,In>::do_get_date(In b, In e, ios_base& s, ios_base::iostate& r, tm* tmp) const
// optional day of week followed by ymd, dmy, mdy, or ydm
{
        int val[3];                       // for day, month, and year values in some order
        Vtype res[3] = { novalue };       // for value classifications

        for (int i=0; b!=e && i<3; ++i) { // read day, month, and year
            b = getval(b,e,s,r,&val[i],&res[i]);
            if (r) return b;              // oops: error
            if (res[i]==novalue) {        // couldn't complete date
                r |= ios_base::badbit;
                return b;
            }
            if (res[i]==dayofweek) {
                tmp->tm_wday = val[i];
                --i; // oops: not a day, month, or year
            }
        }

        time_base::dateorder order = dateorder();    // now try to make sense of the values read

        if (res[0] == month) {            // mdy or error
            // ...
        }
        else if (res[1] == month) {       // dmy or ymd or error
            tmp->tm_mon = val[1];
            switch (order) {
            case dmy:
                tmp->tm_mday = val[0];
                tmp->tm_year = val[2];
                break;
            case ymd:
                tmp->tm_year = val[0];
                tmp->tm_mday = val[1];
                break;
            default:
                r |= ios_base::badbit;
                return b;
            }
        }
        else if (res[2] == month) {       // ydm or error
            // ...
        }
        else {                            // rely on dateorder or error
            // ...
        }

        tmp->tm_year -= 1900;    // adjust base year to suit tm convention
        return b;
}
```

I have omitted bits of code that do not add to the understanding of locales, dates, or the handling of input. Writing better and more general date input functions are left as exercises (§D.6[9-10]).

Here is a simple test program:

```
int main()
try {
    cin.imbue(loc(locale(), new Date_in));   // read Dates using Date_in

    while (cin >> dd && dd != Date()) cout << dd << endl;
}
catch (Date::Bad_date e) {
    cout << "bad date caught: " << e.why << endl;
}
```

Note that *do_get_date*() will accept meaningless dates, such as

Thursday October 7, 1998

and

1999/Feb/31

The checks for consistency of the year, month, day, and optional day of the week are done in *Date*'s constructor. It is the *Date* class' job to know what constitutes a correct date, and it is not necessary for *Date_in* to share that knowledge.

It would be possible to have *getval*() or *do_get_date*() guess about the meaning of numeric values. For example,

12 May 1922

is clearly not the day 1922 of year 12. That is, we could "guess" that a numeric value that couldn't be a day of the specified month must be a year. Such "guessing" can be useful in specific constrained context. However, it in not a good idea in more general contexts. For example,

12 May 15

could be a date in the year 12, 15, 1912, 1915, 2012, or 2015. Sometimes, a better approach is to augment the notation with clues that disambiguate years and days. For example, *1st* and *15th* are clearly days of a month. Similarly, *751BC* and *1453AD* are explicitly identified as years.

D.4.5 Character Classification

When reading characters from input, it is often necessary to classify them to make sense of what is being read. For example, to read a number, an input routine needs to know which letters are digits. Similarly, §6.1.2 showed a use of standard character classification functions for parsing input.

Naturally, classification of characters depends on the alphabet used. Consequently, a facet *ctype* is provided to represent character classification in a locale.

The character classes as described by an enumeration called *mask*:

```
class std::ctype_base {
public:
      enum mask {                       // the actual values are implementation defined
            space = 1,                  // whitespace (in "C" locale: ' ', '\n', '\t', ...)
            print = 1<<1,               // printing characters
            cntrl = 1<<2,               // control characters
            upper = 1<<3,               // uppercase characters
            lower = 1<<4,               // lowercase characters
            alpha = 1<<5,               // alphabetic characters
            digit = 1<<6,               // decimal digits
            punct = 1<<7,               // punctuation characters
            xdigit = 1<<8,              // hexadecimal digits
            alnum=alpha|digit,          // alphanumeric characters
            graph=alnum|punct
      };
};
```

This *mask* doesn't depend on a particular character type. Consequently, this enumeration is placed in a (non-template) base class.

Clearly, *mask* reflects the traditional C and C++ classification (§20.4.1). However, for different character sets, different character values fall into different classes. For example, for the ASCII character set, the integer value *125* represents the character ´}´, which is a punctuation character (*punct*). However, in the Danish national character set, *125* represents the vowel ´å´, which in a Danish locale must be classified as an *alpha*.

The classification is called a "mask" because the traditional efficient implementation of character classification for small character sets is a table in which each entry holds bits representing the classification. For example:

```
table['a'] == lower|alpha|xdigit
table['1'] == digit
table[' '] == space
```

Given that implementation, *table*[*c*]&*m* is nonzero if the character *c* is an *m* and *0* otherwise.

The *ctype* facet is defined like this:

```
template <class Ch>
class std::ctype : public locale::facet, public ctype_base {
public:
      typedef Ch char_type;
      explicit ctype(size_t r = 0);

      bool is(mask m, Ch c) const; // is "c" an "m"?

      // place classification for each Ch in [b:e) into v:
      const Ch* is(const Ch* b, const Ch* e, mask* v) const;

      const Ch* scan_is(mask m, const Ch* b, const Ch* e) const;    // find an m
      const Ch* scan_not(mask m, const Ch* b, const Ch* e) const; // find a non-m
```

```
Ch  toupper (Ch  c)  const;
const  Ch*  toupper (Ch*  b,  const  Ch*  e)  const;  // convert [b:e)
Ch  tolower (Ch  c)  const;
const  Ch*  tolower (Ch*  b,  const  Ch*  e)  const;

Ch  widen (char  c)  const;
const  char*  widen (const  char*  b,  const  char*  e,  Ch*  b2)  const;
char  narrow (Ch  c,  char  def)  const;
const  Ch*  narrow (const  Ch*  b,  const  Ch*  e,  char  def,  char*  b2)  const;

static  locale::id  id;  // facet identifier object (§D.2, §D.3, §D.3.1)
protected:
    ~ctype ();

    // virtual "do_" functions for public functions (see §D.4.1)
};
```

A call *is* (*m*, *c*) tests whether the character *c* belongs to the classification *m*. For example:

```
int  count_spaces (const  string& s,  const  locale& loc)
{
    const  ctype<char>& ct = use_facet< ctype<char> > (loc);
    int  i = 0;
    for (string::const_iterator  p = s.begin ();  p != s.end ();  ++p)
        if (ct.is (ctype_base::space, *p)) ++i;    // whitespace as defined by ct
    return  i;
}
```

Note that it is also possible to use *is* ( ) to check whether a character belongs to one of a number of classifications. For example:

```
ct.is (ctype_base::space | ctype_base::punct, c);  // is c whitespace or punctuation in ct?
```

A call *is* (*b*, *e*, *v*) determines the classification of each character in [*b*, *e*) and places it in the corresponding position in the array *v*.

A call *scan_is* (*m*, *b*, *e*) returns a pointer to the first character in [*b*, *e*) that is an *m*. If no character is classified as an *m*, *e* is returned. As ever for standard facets, the public member function is implemented by a call to its "*do_*" virtual function. A simple implementation might be:

```
template <class  Ch>
const  Ch*  std::ctype<Ch>::do_scan_is (mask  m,  const  Ch*  b,  const  Ch*  e)  const
{
    while (b!=e && !is (m, *b)) ++b;
    return  b;
}
```

A call *scan_not* (*m*, *b*, *e*) returns a pointer to the first character in [*b*, *e*) that is not an *m*. If all characters are classified as *m*, *e* is returned.

A call *toupper* (*c*) returns the uppercase version of *c* if such a version exists in the character set used and *c* itself otherwise.

A call *toupper* (*b*, *e*) converts each character in the range [*b*, *e*) to uppercase and returns *e*. A simple implementation might be:

```
template <class Ch>
const Ch* std::ctype<Ch>::to_upper(Ch* b, const Ch* e)
{
    for (; b!=e; ++b) *b = toupper(*b);
    return e;
}
```

The *tolower*() functions are similar to *toupper*() except that they convert to lowercase.

A call *widen*(*c*) transforms the character *c* into its corresponding *Ch* value. If *Ch*'s character set provides several characters corresponding to *c*, the standard specifies that "the simplest reasonable transformation" be used. For example,

> *wcout* << *use_facet*< *ctype*<*wchar_t*> > (*wcout*.*getloc*()).*widen*('e');

will output a reasonable equivalent to the character *e* in *wcout*'s locale.

Translation between unrelated character representations, such as ASCII and EBCDIC, can also be done by using *widen*(). For example, assume that an *ebcdic* locale exists:

> *char EBCDIC_e* = *use_facet*< *ctype*<*char*> > (*ebcdic*).*widen*('e');

A call *widen*(*b*, *e*, *v*) takes each character in the range [*b*, *e*) and places a widened version in the corresponding position in the array *v*.

A call *narrow*(*ch*, *def*) produces a *char* value corresponding to the character *ch* from the *Ch* type. Again, "the simplest reasonable transformation" is to be used. If no such corresponding *char* exist, *def* is returned.

A call *narrow*(*b*, *e*, *def*, *v*) takes each character in the range [*b*, *e*) and places a narrowed version in the corresponding position in the array *v*.

The general idea is that *narrow*() converts from a larger character set to a smaller one and that *widen*() performs the inverse operation. For a character *c* from the smaller character set, we expect:

> *c* == *narrow*(*widen*(*c*), 0) // not guaranteed

This is true provided that the character represented by *c* has only one representation in "the smaller character set." However, that is not guaranteed. If the characters represented by a *char* are not a subset of those represented by the larger character set (*Ch*), we should expect anomalies and potential problems with code treating characters generically.

Similarly, for a character *ch* from the larger character set, we might expect:

> *widen*(*narrow*(*ch*, *def*)) == *ch* || *widen*(*narrow*(*ch*, *def*)) == *widen*(*def*) // not guaranteed

However, even though this is often the case, it cannot be guaranteed for a character that is represented by several values in the larger character set but only once in the smaller character set. For example, a digit, such as 7, often has several separate representations in a large character set. The reason for that is typically that a large character set has several conventional character sets as subsets and that the characters from the smaller sets are replicated for ease of conversion.

For every character in the basic source character set (§C.3.3), it is guaranteed that

> *widen*(*narrow*(*ch_lit*, 0)) == *ch_lit*

For example:

> *widen* (*narrow* (´*x*´)) == ´*x*´

The *narrow* ( ) and *widen* ( ) functions respect character classifications wherever possible. For example, if *is* (*alpha, c*) , then *is* (*alpha, narrow* (*c, ´a´*)) and *is* (*alpha, widen* (*c*)) wherever *alpha* is a valid mask for the locale used.

A major reason for using a *ctype* facet in general and for using *narrow* ( ) and *widen* ( ) functions in particular is to be able to write code that does I/O and string manipulation for any character set; that is, to make such code generic with respect to character sets. This implies that *iostream* implementations depend critically on these facilities. By relying on *<iostream>* and *<string>*, a user can avoid most direct uses of the *ctype* facet.

A *_byname* version (§D.4, §D.4.1) of *ctype* is provided:

> *template <class Ch> class std* : : *ctype_byname* : *public ctype<Ch>* { / * ... * / } ;

D.4.5.1 Convenience Interfaces

The most common use of the *ctype* facet is to inquire whether a character belongs to a given classification. Consequently, a set of functions is provided for that:

```
template <class Ch> bool isspace (Ch c, const locale& loc);
template <class Ch> bool isprint (Ch c, const locale& loc);
template <class Ch> bool iscntrl (Ch c, const locale& loc);
template <class Ch> bool isupper (Ch c, const locale& loc);
template <class Ch> bool islower (Ch c, const locale& loc);
template <class Ch> bool isalpha (Ch c, const locale& loc);
template <class Ch> bool isdigit (Ch c, const locale& loc);
template <class Ch> bool ispunct (Ch c, const locale& loc);
template <class Ch> bool isxdigit (Ch c, const locale& loc);
template <class Ch> bool isalnum (Ch c, const locale& loc);
template <class Ch> bool isgraph (Ch c, const locale& loc);
```

These functions are trivially implemented by using *use_facet*. For example:

```
template <class Ch>
inline bool isspace (Ch c, const locale& loc)
{
        return use_facet< ctype<Ch> > (loc) . is (space, c);
}
```

The one-argument versions of these functions, presented in §20.4.2, are simply these functions for the current C global locale (not the global C++ locale, *locale* ( )). Except for the rare cases in which the C global locale and the C++ global locale differ (§D.2.3), we can think of a one-argument version as the two-argument version applied to *locale* ( ) . For example:

```
inline int isspace (int i)
{
        return isspace (i, locale ( ));      // almost
}
```

D.4.6 Character Code Conversion

Sometimes, the representation of characters stored in a file differs from the desired representation of those same characters in main memory. For example, Japanese characters are often stored in files in which indicators (''shifts'') tell to which of the four common character sets (kanji, katakana, hiragana, and romaji) a given sequence of characters belongs. This is a bit unwieldy because the meaning of each byte depends on its ''shift state,'' but it can save memory because only a kanji requires more than one byte for its representation. In main memory, these characters are easier to manipulate when represented in a multi-byte character set where every character has the same size. Such characters (for example, Unicode characters) are typically placed in wide characters (*wchar_t*; §4.3). Consequently, the *codecvt* facet provides a mechanism for converting characters from one representation to another as they are read or written. For example:

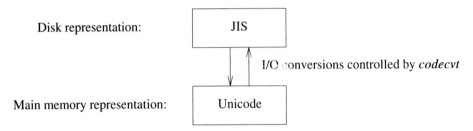

Disk representation: JIS

                    I/O conversions controlled by *codecvt*

Main memory representation: Unicode

This code-conversion mechanism is general enough to provide arbitrary conversions of character representations. It allows us to write a program to use a suitable internal character representation (stored in *char*, *wchar_t*, or whatever) and to then accept a variety of input character stream representations by adjusting the locale used by iostreams. The alternative would be to modify the program itself or to convert input and output files from/to a variety of formats.

The *codecvt* facet provides conversion between different character sets when a character is moved between a stream buffer and external storage:

```
class std::codecvt_base {
public:
    enum result { ok, partial, error, noconv };      // result indicators
};

template <class I, class E, class State>
class std::codecvt : public locale::facet, public codecvt_base {
public:
    typedef I intern_type;
    typedef E extern_type;
    typedef State state_type;

    explicit codecvt(size_t r = 0);

    result in(State&, const E* from, const E* from_end, const E*& from_next, // read
              I* to, I* to_end, I*& to_next) const;
```

```
        result  out (State&, const I* from, const I* from_end, const I*& from_next, // write
                    E* to, E* to_end, E*& to_next) const;

        result  unshift (State&, E* to, E* to_end, E*& to_next) const;  // end character sequence

        int  encoding () const throw ();            // characterize basic encoding properties
        bool  always_noconv () const throw ();      // can we do I/O without code translation?

        int  length (const State&, const E* from, const E* from_end, size_t max) const;
        int  max_length () const throw ();          // maximum possible length()

        static  locale::id  id;  // facet identifier object (§D.2, §D.3, §D.3.1)
    protected:
        ~codecvt ();

        // virtual "do_" functions for public functions (see §D.4.1)
    };
```

A *codecvt* facet is used by *basic_filebuf* (§21.5) to read or write characters. A *basic_filebuf*
obtains this facet from the stream's locale (§21.7.1).

The *State* template argument is the type used to hold the shift state of the stream being converted. *State* can also be used to identify different conversions by specifying a specialization. The
latter is useful because characters of a variety of character encodings (character sets) can be stored
in objects of the same type. For example:

```
    class JISstate { /* .. */ };

    p = new  codecvt<wchar_t, char, mbstate_t>;     // standard char to wide char
    q = new  codecvt<wchar_t, char, JISstate>;      // JIS to wide char
```

Without the different *State* arguments, there would be no way for the facet to know which encoding
to assume for the stream of *char*s. The *mbstate_t* type from *<cwchar>* or *<wchar.h>* identifies
the system's standard conversion between *char* and *wchar_t*.

A new *codecvt* can be also created as a derived class and identified by name. For example:

```
    class JIScvt : public codecvt<wchar_t, char, mbstate_t> { /* ... */ };
```

A call *in* (*s, from, from_end, from_next, to, to_end, to_next*) reads each character in the range
[*from, from_end*) and tries to convert it. If a character is converted, *in*() writes its converted
form to the corresponding position in the [*to, to_end*) range; if not, *in*() stops at that point.
Upon return, *in*() stores the position one-beyond-the-last character read in *from_next* and the position one-beyond-the-last character written in *to_next*. The *result* value returned by *in*() indicates
how much work was done:

  ok: all characters in the [*from, from_end*) range converted
  partial: not all characters in the [*from, from_end*) range were converted
  error: *out*() encountered a character it couldn't convert
  noconv: no conversion was needed

Note that a *partial* conversion is not necessarily an error. Possibly more characters have to be read
before a multibyte character is complete and can be written, or maybe the output buffer has to be
emptied to make room for more characters.

The *s* argument of type *State* indicates the state of the input character sequence at the start of the call of *in* ( ) . This is significant when the external character representation uses shift states. Note that *s* is a (non-*const*) reference argument: At the end of the call, *s* holds the state of shift state of the input sequence. This allows a programmer to deal with *partial* conversions and to convert a long sequence using several calls to *in* ( ) .

A call *out* (*s* , *from* , *from_end* , *from_next* , *to* , *to_end* , *to_next*) converts [*from* , *from_end*) from the internal to the external representation in the same way the *in* ( ) converts from the external to the internal representation.

A character stream must start and end in a "neutral" (unshifted) state. Typically, that state is *State* ( ) . A call *unshift* (*s* , *to* , *to_end* , *to_next*) looks at *s* and places characters in [*to* , *to_end*) as needed to bring a sequence of characters back to that unshifted state. The result of *unshift* ( ) and the use of *to_next* are done just like *out* ( ) .

A call *length* (*s* , *from* , *from_end* , *max*) returns the number of characters that *in* ( ) could convert from [*from* , *from_end*) .

A call *encoding* ( ) returns

–1   if the encoding of the external character set uses state (for example, uses shift and unshift character sequences)

0   if the encoding uses varying number of bytes to represent individual characters (for example, a character representation might use a bit in a byte to indicate whether one or two bytes are used to represents that character)

n   if every character of the external character representation is *n* bytes

A call *always_noconv* ( ) returns *true* if no conversion is required between the internal and the external character sets and *false* otherwise. Clearly, *always_no_conv* ( ) ==*true* opens the possibility for the implementation to provide the maximally efficient implementation that simply doesn't invoke the conversion functions.

A call *max_length* ( ) returns the maximum value that *length* ( ) can return for a valid set of arguments.

The simplest code conversion that I can think of is one that converts input to uppercase. Thus, this is about as simple as a *codecvt* can be and still perform a service:

```
class  Cvt_to_upper : public  codecvt<char , char , mbstate_t> {       // convert to uppercase

    explicit  Cvt_to_upper (size_t  r = 0) : codecvt (r) { }

protected :
    // read external representation write internal representation:
    result  do_in (State& s , const char* from , const char* from_end , const char*& from_next ,
                char* to , char* to_end , char*& to_next) const ;

    // read internal representation write external representation:
    result  do_out (State& s , const char* from , const char* from_end , const char*& from_next ,
                char* to , char* to_end , char*& to_next) const
    {
        return  codecvt<char , char , mbstate_t> ::do_out
            (s , from , from_end , from_next , to , to_end , to_next) ;
    }
}
```

```
        result  do_unshift (State&, E* to, E* to_end, E*& to_next) const { return ok; }

        int  do_encoding () const throw () { return 1; }
        bool  do_always_noconv () const  throw () { return false; }

        int  do_length (const State&, const E* from, const E* from_end, size_t max) const;
        int  do_max_length () const  throw ();          // maximum possible length()
};
```

```
codecvt<char, char, mbstate_t> :: result
Cvt_to_upper :: do_in (State& s, const char* from, const char* from_end,
                        const char*& from_next, char* to, char* to_end, char*& to_next) const
{
        // ... §D.6[16] ...
}
int  main ()         // trivial test
{
        locale  ulocale (locale (), new  Cvt_to_upper);

        cin . imbue (ulocale);

        while  (cin>>ch) cout << ch;
}
```

A _byname_ version (§D.4, §D.4.1) of *codecvt* is provided:

```
template <class I, class E, class State>
class std :: codecvt_byname : public codecvt<I, E, State> { /* ... */ };
```


D.4.7 Messages

Naturally, most end users prefer to use their native language to interact with a program. However, we cannot provide a standard mechanism for expressing *locale*-specific general interactions. Instead, the library provides a simple mechanism for keeping a *locale*-specific set of strings from which a programmer can compose simple messages. In essence, *messages* implements a trivial read-only database:

```
class std :: messages_base {
public :
        typedef int catalog;  // catalog identifier type
};

template <class Ch>
class std :: messages : public locale :: facet, public messages_base {
public :
        typedef Ch char_type;
        typedef basic_string<Ch> string_type;

        explicit messages (size_t  r = 0);
```

```
        catalog open(const basic_string<char>& fn, const locale&) const;
        string_type get(catalog c, int set, int msgid, const string_type& d) const;
        void close(catalog c) const;

        static locale::id id;  // facet identifier object (§D.2, §D.3, §D.3.1)
protected:
        ~messages();

        // virtual "do_" functions for public functions (see §D.4.1)
};
```

A call *open*(*s*, *loc*) opens a "catalog" of messages called *s* for the locale *loc*. A catalog is a set of strings organized in an implementation-specific way and accessed through the *messages*::*get*() function. A negative value is returned if no catalog named *s* can be opened. A catalog must be opened before the first use of *get*().

A call *close*(*cat*) closes the catalog identified by *cat* and frees all resources associated with that catalog.

A call *get*(*cat*, *set*, *id*, "*foo*") looks for a message identified by (*set*, *id*) in the catalog *cat*. If a string is found, *get*() returns that string; otherwise, *get*() returns the default string (here, *string*("*foo*")).

Here is an example of a *messages* facet for an implementation in which a message catalog is a vector of sets of "messages" and a "message" is a string:

```
struct Set {
        vector<string> msgs;
};

struct Cat {
        vector<Set> sets;
};

class My_messages : public messages<char> {
        vector<Cat>& catalogs;
public:
        explicit My_messages(size_t = 0) : catalogs(*new vector<Cat>) { }

        catalog do_open(const string& s, const locale& loc) const;      // open catalog s
        string do_get(catalog c, int s, int m, const string&) const;    // get message (s,m) in c
        void do_close(catalog c) const
        {
                if (catalogs.size() <=cat) catalogs.erase(catalogs.begin()+cat);
        }

        ~My_messages() { delete &catalogs; }
};
```

All *messages*' member functions are *const*, so the catalog data structure (the *vector<Set>*) is stored outside the facet.

A message is selected by specifying a catalog, a set within that catalog, and a message string within that set. A string is supplied as an argument, to be used as a default result in case no message is found in the catalog:

```
string My_messages::do_get(catalog cat, int set, int msg, const string& def) const
{
    if (catalogs.size()<=cat) return def;
    Cat& c = catalogs[cat];
    if (c.sets.size()<=set) return def;
    Set& s = c.sets[set];
    if (s.msgs.size()<=msg) return def;
    return s.msgs[msg];
}
```

Opening a catalog involves reading a textual representation from disk into a *Cat* structure. Here, I chose a representation that is trivial to read. A set is delimited by <<< and >>>, and each message is a line of text:

```
messages<char>::catalog My_messages::do_open(const string& n, const locale& loc) const
{
    string nn = n + locale().name();
    ifstream f(nn.c_str());
    if (!f) return -1;

    catalogs.push_back(Cat());          // make in-core catalog
    Cat& c = catalogs.back();
    string s;
    while (f>>s && s=="<<<") {           // read Set
        c.sets.push_back(Set());
        Set& ss = c.sets.back();
        while (getline(f,s) && s != ">>>") ss.msgs.push_back(s);      // read message
    }
    return catalogs.size()-1;
}
```

Here is a trivial use:

```
int main()
{
    if (!has_facet< My_messages >(locale())) {
        cerr << "no messages facet found in " << locale().name() << '\n';
        exit(1);
    }

    const messages<char>& m = use_facet< My_messages >(locale());
    extern string message_directory;       // where I keep my messages
    int cat = m.open(message_directory,locale());
    if (cat<0) {
        cerr << "no catalog found\n";
        exit(1);
    }

    cout << m.get(cat,0,0,"Missed again!") << endl;
    cout << m.get(cat,1,2,"Missed again!") << endl;
```

```
        cout << m.get(cat, 1, 3, "Missed again!") << endl;
        cout << m.get(cat, 3, 0, "Missed again!") << endl;
}
```

If the catalog is

```
<<<
hello
goodbye
>>>
<<<
yes
no
maybe
>>>
```

this program prints

hello
maybe
Missed again!
Missed again!

D.4.7.1 Using Messages from Other Facets

In addition to being a repository for *locale*-dependent strings used to communicate with users, messages can be used to hold strings for other facets. For example, the *Season_io* facet (§D.3.2) could have been written like this:

```
class Season_io : public locale::facet {
    const messages<char>& m;           // message directory
    int cat;                           // message catalog
public:
    class Missing_messages { };

    Season_io(int i = 0)
        : locale::facet(i),
          m(use_facet<Season_messages>(locale())),
          cat(m.open(message_directory, locale()))
    { if (cat<0) throw Missing_messages(); }

    ~Season_io() { }      // to make it possible to destroy Season_io objects (§D.3)

    const string& to_str(Season x) const;              // string representation of x

    bool from_str(const string& s, Season& x) const;   // place Season corresponding to s in x

    static locale::id id; // facet identifier object (§D.2, §D.3, §D.3.1)
};

locale::id Season_io::id; // define the identifier object
```

```
const string& Season_io::to_str(Season x) const
{
    return m->get(cat, x, "no-such-season");
}

bool Season_io::from_str(const string& s, Season& x) const
{
    for (int i = Season::spring; i<=Season::winter; i++)
        if (m->get(cat, i, "no-such-season") == s) {
            x = Season(i);
            return true;
        }
    return false;
}
```

This *messages*-based solution differs from the original solution (§D.3.2) in that the implementer of a set of *Season* strings for a new locale needs to be able to add them to a *messages* directory. This is easy for someone adding a new locale to an execution environment. However, since *messages* provides only a read-only interface, adding a new set of season names may be beyond the scope of an application programmer.

A *_byname* version (§D.4, §D.4.1) of *messages* is provided:

```
template <class Ch>
class std::messages_byname : public messages<Ch> { /* ... */ };
```

D.5 Advice

[1] Expect that every nontrivial program or system that interacts directly with people will be used in several different countries; §D.1.

[2] Don't assume that everyone uses the same character set as you do; §D.4.1.

[3] Prefer using *locale*s to writing ad hoc code for culture-sensitive I/O; §D.1.

[4] Avoid embedding locale name strings in program text; §D.2.1.

[5] Minimize the use of global format information; §D.2.3, §D.4.4.7.

[6] Prefer locale-sensitive string comparisons and sorts; §D.2.4, §D.4.1.

[7] Make *facet*s immutable; §D.2.2, §D.3.

[8] Keep changes of *locale* to a few places in a program; §D.2.3.

[9] Let *locale* handle the lifetime of *facet*s; §D.3.

[10] When writing locale-sensitive I/O functions, remember to handle exceptions from user-supplied (overriding) functions; §D.4.2.2.

[11] Use a simple *Money* type to hold monetary values; §D.4.3.

[12] Use simple user-defined types to hold values that require locale-sensitive I/O (rather than casting to and from values of built-in types); §D.4.3.

[13] Don't believe timing figures until you have a good idea of all factors involved; §D.4.4.1.

[14] Be aware of the limitations of *time_t*; §D.4.4.1, §D.4.4.5.

[15] Use a date-input routine that accepts a range of input formats; §D.4.4.5.

[16] Prefer the character classification functions in which the locale is explicit; §D.4.5, §D.4.5.1.

D.6 Exercises

1. (*2.5) Define a *Season_io* (§D.3.2) for a language other than American English.
2. (*2) Define a *Season_io* (§D.3.2) class that takes a set of name strings as a constructor argument so that *Season* names for different locales can be represented as objects of this class.
3. (*3) Write a *collate<char>::compare* ( ) that gives dictionary order. Preferably, do this for a language, such as German or French, that has more letters in its alphabet than English does.
4. (*2) Write a program that reads and writes *bool*s as numbers, as English words, and as words in another language of your choice.
5. (*2.5) Define a *Time* type for representing time of day. Define a *Date_and_time* type by using *Time* and a *Date* type. Discuss the pros and cons of this approach compared to the *Date* from (§D.4.4). Implement *locale*-sensitive I/O for *Time* and *Date_and_time*.
6. (*2.5) Design and implement a postal code (zip code) facet. Implement it for for at least two countries with dissimilar conventions for writing addresses. For example: *NJ 07932* and *CB21QA* .
7. (*2.5) Design and implement a phone number facet. Implement it for at least two countries with dissimilar conventions for writing phone numbers. For example, (*973*) *360–8000* and *1223 343000*.
8. (*2.5) Experiment to find out what input and output formats your implementation uses for data information.
9. (*2.5) Define a *get_time* ( ) that "guesses" about the meaning of ambiguous dates, such as 12 May 1995, but still rejects all or almost all mistakes. Be precise about what "guesses" are accepted, and discuss the likelihood of a mistake.
10. (*2) Define a *get_time* ( ) that accepts a greater variety of input format than the one in §D.4.4.5.
11. (*2) Make a list of the locales supported on your system.
12. (*2.5) Figure out where named locales are stored on your system. If you have access to the part of the system where locales are stored, make a new named locale. Be very careful not to break existing locales.
13. (*2) Compare the two *Season_io* implementations (§D.3.2 and §D.4.7.1).
14. (*2) Write and test a *Date_out* facet that writes *Date*s using a format supplied as a constructor argument. Discuss the pros and cons of this approach compared to the global data format provided by *date_fmt* (§D.4.4.6).
15. (*2.5) Implement I/O of Roman numerals (such as *XI* and *MDCLII*).
16. (*2.5) Implement and test *Cvt_to_upper* (§D.4.6).
17. (*2.5) Use *clock* ( ) to determine average cost of (1) a function call, (2) a virtual function call, (3) reading a *char*, (4) reading a 1-digit *int*, (5) reading a 5-digit *int*, (6) reading a 5-digit *double*, (7) a 1-character *string*, (8) a 5-character *string* , and (9) a 40-character *string*.
18. (*6.5) Learn another natural language.

Standard-Library Exception Safety

Everything will work just as you expect it to,
unless your expectations are incorrect.
– Hyman Rosen

Exception safety — exception-safe implementation techniques — representing resources — assignment — *push_back* ( ) — constructors and invariants — standard container guarantees — insertion and removal of elements — guarantees and tradeoffs — *swap* ( ) — initialization and iterators — references to elements — predicates — *strings*, streams, algorithms, *valarray*, and *complex* — the C standard library — implications for library users — advice — exercises.

E.1 Introduction

Standard-library functions often invoke operations that a user supplies as function or template arguments. Naturally, some of these user-supplied operations will occasionally throw exceptions. Other functions, such as allocator functions, can also throw exceptions. Consider:

```
void f(vector<X>& v, const X& g)
{
    v[2] = g;                       // X's assignment might throw an exception
    v.push_back(g);                 // vector<X>'s allocator might throw an exception
    sort(v.begin(),v.end());        // X's less-than operation might throw an exception
    vector<X> u = v;                // X's copy constructor might throw an exception
    // ...

    // u destroyed here: we must ensure that X's destructor can work correctly
}
```

What happens if the assignment throws an exception while trying to copy *g*? Will *v* be left with an invalid element? What happens if the constructor that *v.push_back*() uses to copy *g* throws *std::bad_alloc*? Has the number of elements changed? Has an invalid element been added to the container? What happens if *X*'s less-than operator throws an exception during the sort? Have the elements been partially sorted? Could an element have been removed from the container by the sorting algorithm and not put back?

Finding the complete list of possible exceptions in this example is left as an exercise (§E.8[1]). Explaining how this example is well behaved for every well-defined type *X* – even an *X* that throws exceptions – is part of the aim of this appendix. Naturally, a major part of this explanation involves giving meaning and effective terminology to the notions of ''well behaved'' and ''well defined'' in the context of exceptions.

The purpose of this appendix is to

[1] identify how a user can design types that meet the standard library's requirements,
[2] state the guarantees offered by the standard library,
[3] state the standard-library requirements on user-supplied code,
[4] demonstrate effective techniques for crafting exception-safe and efficient containers, and
[5] present a few general rules for exception-safe programming.

The discussion of exception safety necessarily focuses on worst-case behavior. That is, where could an exception cause the most problems? How does the standard library protect itself and its users from potential problems? And, how can users help prevent problems? Please don't let this discussion of exception-handling techniques distract from the central fact that throwing an exception is the best method for reporting an error (§14.1, §14.9). The discussion of concepts, techniques, and standard-library guarantees is organized like this:

§E.2 discusses the notion of exception safety.
§E.3 presents techniques for implementing efficient exception-safe containers and operations.
§E.4 outlines the guarantees offered for standard-library containers and their operations.
§E.5 summarizes exception-safety issues for the non-container parts of the standard library.
§E.6 reviews exception safety from the point of view of a standard-library user.

As ever, the standard library provides examples of the kinds of concerns that must be addressed in demanding applications. The techniques used to provide exception safety for the standard library can be applied to a wide range of problems.

E.2 Exception Safety

An operation on an object is said to be *exception safe* if that operation leaves the object in a valid state when the operation is terminated by throwing an exception. This valid state could be an error state requiring cleanup, but it must be well defined so that reasonable error-handling code can be written for the object. For example, an exception handler might destroy the object, repair the object, repeat a variant of the operation, just carry on, etc.

In other words, the object will have an invariant (§24.3.7.1), its constructors will establish that invariant, all further operations maintain that invariant even if an exception is thrown, and its destructor will do final cleanup. An operation should take care that the invariant is maintained before throwing an exception, so that the object is in a valid state. However, it is quite possible for that valid state to be one that doesn't suit the application. For example, a string may have been left as the empty string or a container may have been left unsorted. Thus, "repair" means giving an object a value that is more appropriate/desirable for the application than the one it was left with after an operation failed. In the context of the standard library, the most interesting objects are containers.

Here, we consider under which conditions operations on standard-library containers can be considered exception safe. There can be only two conceptually really simple strategies:

[1] "*No guarantees*:" If an exception is thrown, any container being manipulated is possibly corrupted.

[2] "*Strong guarantee*:" If an exception is thrown, any container being manipulated remains in the state in which it was before the standard-library operation started.

Unfortunately, both answers are too simple for real use. Alternative [1] is unacceptable because it implies that after an exception is thrown from a container operation, the container cannot be accessed; it can't even be destroyed without fear of run-time errors. Alternative [2] is unacceptable because it imposes the cost of roll-back semantics on every individual standard-library operation.

To resolve this dilemma, the C++ standard library provides a set of exception-safety guarantees that share the burden of producing correct programs between implementers of the standard library and users of the standard library:

[3a] "*Basic guarantee* for all operations:" The basic invariants of the standard library are maintained, and no resources, such as memory, are leaked.

[3b] "*Strong guarantee* for key operations:" In addition to providing the basic guarantee, either the operation succeeds, or has no effects. This guarantee is provided for key library operations, such as *push_back* ( ), single-element *insert* ( ) on a *list*, and *uninitialized_copy* ( ) (§E.3.1, §E.4.1).

[3c] "*Nothrow guarantee* for some operations:" In addition to providing the basic guarantee, some operations are guaranteed not to throw an exception This guarantee is provided for a few simple operations, such as *swap* ( ) and *pop_back* ( ) (§E.4.1).

Both the basic guarantee and the strong guarantee are provided on the condition that user-supplied operations (such as assignments and *swap* ( ) functions) do not leave container elements in invalid states, that user-supplied operations do not leak resources, and that destructors do not throw exceptions. For example, consider these "handle-like" (§25.7) classes:

```
template<class T> class Safe {
    T* p;        // p points to a T allocated using new
public:
    Safe() :p(new T) { }
    ~Safe() { delete p; }
    Safe& operator=(const Safe& a) { *p = *a.p; return *this; }
    // ...
};

template<class T> class Unsafe {        // sloppy and dangerous code
    T* p;        // p points to a T
public:
    Unsafe(T* pp) :p(pp) { }
    ~Unsafe() { if (!p->destructible()) throw E(); delete p; }
```

```
    Unsafe& operator=(const Unsafe& a)
    {
        p->~T();              // destroy old value (§10.4.11)
        new(p) T(a.p);        // construct copy of a.p in *p (§10.4.11)
        return *this;
    }
    // ...
};

void f(vector< Safe<Some_type> >&vg, vector< Unsafe<Some_type> >&vb)
{
    vg.at(1) = Safe<Some_type>();
    vb.at(1) = Unsafe<Some_type>(new Some_type);
    // ...
}
```

In this example, construction of a *Safe* succeeds only if a *T* is successfully constructed. The construction of a *T* can fail because allocation might fail (and throw *std::bad_alloc*) and because *T*'s constructor might throw an exception. However, in every successfully constructed *Safe*, *p* will point to a successfully constructed *T*; if a constructor fails, no *T* object (or *Safe* object) is created. Similarly, *T*'s assignment operator may throw an exception, causing *Safe*'s assignment operator to implicitly re-throw that exception. However, that is no problem as long as *T*'s assignment operator always leaves its operands in a good state. Therefore, *Safe* is well behaved, and consequently every standard-library operation on a *Safe* will have a reasonable and well-defined result.

On the other hand, *Unsafe*() is carelessly written (or rather, it is carefully written to demonstrate undesirable behavior). The construction of an *Unsafe* will not fail. Instead, the operations on *Unsafe*, such as assignment and destruction, are left to deal with a variety of potential problems. The assignment operator may fail by throwing an exception from *T*'s copy constructor. This would leave a *T* in an undefined state because the old value of **p* was destroyed and no new value replaced it. In general, the results of that are unpredictable. *Unsafe*'s destructor contains an ill-conceived attempt to protect against undesirable destruction. However, throwing an exception during exception handling will cause a call of *terminate*() (§14.7), and the standard library requires that a destructor return normally after destroying an object. The standard library does not – and cannot – make any guarantees when a user supplies objects this badly behaved.

From the point of view of exception handling, *Safe* and *Unsafe* differ in that *Safe* uses its constructor to establish an invariant (§24.3.7.1) that allows its operations to be implemented simply and safely. If that invariant cannot be established, an exception is thrown before an invalid object is constructed. *Unsafe*, on the other hand, muddles along without a meaningful invariant, and the individual operations throw exceptions without an overall error-handling strategy. Naturally, this results in violations of the standard library's (reasonable) assumptions about the behavior of types. For example, *Unsafe* can leave invalid elements in a container after throwing an exception from *T::operator=*() and may throw an exception from its destructor.

Note that the standard-library guarantees relative to ill-behaved user-supplied operations are analogous to the language guarantees relative to violations of the basic type system. If a basic operation is not used according to its specification, the resulting behavior is undefined. For example, if you throw an exception from a destructor for a *vector* element, you have no more reason to hope for a reasonable result than if you dereference a pointer initialized to a random number:

```
class Bomb {
public:
    // ...
    ~Bomb() { throw Trouble(); };
};

vector<Bomb> b(10);                              // leads to undefined behavior

void f()
{
    int* p = reinterpret_cast<int*>(rand());    // leads to undefined behavior
    *p = 7;
}
```

Stated positively: If you obey the basic rules of the language and the standard library, the library will behave well even when you throw exceptions.

In addition to achieving pure exception safety, we usually prefer to avoid resource leaks. That is, an operation that throws an exception should not only leave its operands in well-defined states but also ensure that every resource that it acquired is (eventually) released. For example, at the point where an exception is thrown, all memory allocated must be either deallocated or owned by some object, which in turn must ensure that the memory is properly deallocated.

The standard-library guarantees the absence of resource leaks provided that user-supplied operations called by the library also avoid resource leaks. Consider:

```
void leak(bool abort)
{
    vector<int> v(10);                              // no leak
    vector<int>* p = new vector<int>(10);          // potential memory leak
    auto_ptr< vector<int> > q(new vector<int>(10)); // no leak (§14.4.2)

    if (abort) throw Up();
    // ...
    delete p;
}
```

Upon throwing the exception, the *vector* called *v* and the *vector* held by *q* will be correctly destroyed so that their resources are released. The *vector* pointed to by *p* is not guarded against exceptions and will not be destroyed. To make this piece of code safe, we must either explicitly delete *p* before throwing the exception or make sure it is owned by an object – such as an *auto_ptr* (§14.4.2) – that will properly destroy it if an exception is thrown.

Note that the language rules for partial construction and destruction ensure that exceptions thrown while constructing sub-objects and members will be handled correctly without special attention from standard-library code (§14.4.1). This rule is an essential underpinning for all techniques dealing with exceptions.

Also, remember that memory isn't the only kind of resource that can leak. Opened files, locks, network connections, and threads are examples of system resources that a function may have to release or hand over to an object before throwing an exception.

E.3 Exception-Safe Implementation Techniques

As usual, the standard library provides examples of problems that occur in many other contexts and of solutions that apply widely. The basic tools available for writing exception-safe code are

[1] the *try-block* (§8.3.1), and
[2] the support for the "resource acquisition is initialization" technique (§14.4).
The general principles to follow are to
[3] never let go of a piece of information before we can store its replacement, and
[4] always leave objects in valid states when throwing or re-throwing an exception.
That way, we can always back out of an error situation. The practical difficulty in following these principles is that innocent-looking operations (such as <, =, and *sort* ( )) might throw exceptions. Knowing what to look for in an application takes experience.

When you are writing a library, the ideal is to aim at the strong exception-safety guarantee (§E.2) and always to provide the basic guarantee. When writing a specific program, there may be less concern for exception safety. For example, if I write a simple data analysis program for my own use, I'm usually quite willing to have the program terminate in the unlikely event of virtual memory exhaustion. However, correctness and basic exception safety are closely related.

The techniques for providing basic exception safety, such as defining and checking invariants (§24.3.7.1), are similar to the techniques that are useful to get a program small and correct. It follows that the overhead of providing basic exception safety (the basic guarantee; §E.2) – or even the strong guarantee – can be minimal or even insignificant; see §E.8[17].

Here, I will consider an implementation of the standard container *vector* (§16.3) to see what it takes to achieve that ideal and where we might prefer to settle for more conditional safety.

E.3.1 A Simple Vector

A typical implementation of *vector* (§16.3) will consist of a handle holding pointers to the first element, one-past-the-last element, and one-past-the-last allocated space (§17.1.3) (or the equivalent information represented as a pointer plus offsets):

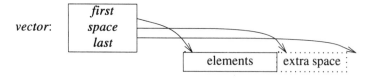

Here is a declaration of *vector* simplified to present only what is needed to discuss exception safety and avoidance of resource leaks:

```
template<class T, class A = allocator<T> > class vector {
public:
        T* v;        // start of allocation
        T* space;    // end of element sequence, start of space allocated for possible expansion
        T* last;     // end of allocated space
        A alloc;     // allocator
```

```
        explicit vector (size_type n, const T& val = T ( ), const A& = A ( ) ) ;

        vector (const vector& a ) ;              // copy constructor
        vector& operator= (const vector& a ) ;  // copy assignment

        ~vector ( ) ;

        size_type size ( ) const { return space-v ; }
        size_type capacity ( ) const { return last-v ; }

        void push_back (const T& ) ;

        // ...
    } ;
```

Consider first a naive implementation of a constructor:

```
    template<class T, class A>
    vector<T,A>::vector (size_type n, const T& val, const A& a)  // warning: naive implementation
        : alloc (a)                                              // copy the allocator
    {
        v = alloc . allocate (n) ;                                      // get memory for elements (§19.4.1)
        space = last = v+n ;
        for (T* p = v ; p !=last ; ++p) a . construct (p, val) ;        // construct copy of val in *p (§19.4.1)
    }
```

There are three sources of exceptions here:
   [1] *allocate* ( ) throws an exception indicating that no memory is available;
   [2] the allocator's copy constructor throws an exception;
   [3] the copy constructor for the element type *T* throws an exception because it can't copy *val*.
In all cases, no object is created, so *vector*'s destructor is not called (§14.4.1).
   When *allocate* ( ) fails, the *throw* will exit before any resources are acquired, so all is well.
   When *T*'s copy constructor fails, we have acquired some memory that must be freed to avoid memory leaks. A more difficult problem is that the copy constructor for *T* might throw an exception after correctly constructing a few elements but before constructing them all.
   To handle this problem, we could keep track of which elements have been constructed and destroy those (and only those) in case of an error:

```
    template<class T, class A>
    vector<T,A>::vector (size_type n, const T& val, const A& a)     // elaborate implementation
        : alloc (a)                 // copy the allocator
    {
        v = alloc . allocate (n) ;   // get memory for elements

        iterator p ;

        try {
            iterator end = v+n ;
            for (p=v ; p !=end ; ++p) alloc . construct (p, val) ;    // construct element (§19.4.1)
            last = space = p ;
        }
```

```
        catch ( ... ) {
               for (iterator  q = v;  q!=p;  ++q)  alloc.destroy(q);      // destroy constructed elements
               alloc.deallocate(v,n);                // free memory
               throw;                                // re-throw
        }
}
```

The overhead here is the overhead of the *try-block*. In a good C++ implementation, this overhead is negligible compared to the cost of allocating memory and initializing elements. For implementations where entering a *try-block* incurs a cost, it may be worthwhile to add a test *if(n)* before the *try* and handle the empty vector case separately.

The main part of this constructor is an exception-safe implementation of *uninitialized_fill()* :

```
template<class For, class T>
void uninitialized_fill(For beg, For end, const T& x)
{
        For p;
        try {
               for (p=beg; p!=end; ++p)
                       new (static_cast<void*>(&*p)) T(x);        // construct copy of x in *p (§10.4.11)
        }
        catch ( ... ) {  // destroy constructed elements and rethrow:
               for (For q = beg; q!=p; ++q) (&*q)->~T();  // (§10.4.11)
               throw;
        }
}
```

The curious construct &*p takes care of iterators that are not pointers. In that case, we need to take the address of the element obtained by dereference to get a pointer. The explicit cast to *void** ensures that the standard library placement function is used (§19.4.5), and not some user-defined *operator new()* for *T**s. This code is operating at a rather low level where writing truly general code can be difficult.

Fortunately, we don't have to reimplement *uninitialized_fill()*, because the standard library provides the desired strong guarantee for it (§E.2). It is often essential to have initialization operations that either complete successfully, having initialized every element, or fail leaving no constructed elements behind. Consequently, the standard-library algorithms *uninitialized_fill()*, *uninitialized_fill_n()*, and *uninitialized_copy()* (§19.4.4) are guaranteed to have this strong exception-safety property (§E.4.4).

Note that the *uninitialized_fill()* algorithm does not protect against exceptions thrown by element destructors or iterator operations (§E.4.4). Doing so would be prohibitively expensive (see §E.8[16-17]).

The *uninitialized_fill()* algorithm can be applied to many kinds of sequences. Consequently, it takes a forward iterator (§19.2.1) and cannot guarantee to destroy elements in the reverse order of their construction.

Using *uninitialized_fill()*, we can write:

```
template<class T, class A>
vector<T,A>::vector(size_type n, const T& val, const A& a)       // messy implementation
    : alloc(a)                              // copy the allocator
{
    v = alloc.allocate(n);                  // get memory for elements
    try {
        uninitialized_fill(v,v+n,val);      // copy elements
        space = last = v+n;
    }
    catch (...) {
        alloc.deallocate(v,n);              // free memory
        throw;                              // re-throw
    }
}
```

However, I wouldn't call that pretty code. The next section will demonstrate how it can be made much simpler.

Note that the constructor re-throws a caught exception. The intent is to make *vector* transparent to exceptions so that the user can determine the exact cause of a problem. All standard-library containers have this property. Exception transparency is often the best policy for templates and other "thin" layers of software. This is in contrast to major parts of a system ("modules") that generally need to take responsibility for all exceptions thrown. That is, the implementer of such a module must be able to list every exception that the module can throw. Achieving this may involve grouping exceptions (§14.2), mapping exceptions from lower-level routines into the module's own exceptions (§14.6.3), or exception specification (§14.6).

E.3.2 Representing Memory Explicitly

Experience revealed that writing correct exception-safe code using explicit *try-block*s is more difficult than most people expect. In fact, it is unnecessarily difficult because there is an alternative: The "resource acquisition is initialization" technique (§14.4) can be used to reduce the amount of code needing to be written and to make the code more stylized. In this case, the key resource required by the *vector* is memory to hold its elements. By providing an auxiliary class to represent the notion of memory used by a *vector*, we can simplify the code and decrease the chance of accidentally forgetting to release it:

```
template<class T, class A = allocator<T> >
struct vector_base {
    A alloc;    // allocator
    T* v;       // start of allocation
    T* space;   // end of element sequence, start of space allocated for possible expansion
    T* last;    // end of allocated space

    vector_base(const A& a, typename A::size_type n)
            : alloc(a), v(a.allocate(n)), space(v+n), last(v+n) { }
    ~vector_base() { alloc.deallocate(v, last-v); }
};
```

As long as *v* and *last* are correct, *vector_base* can be destroyed. Class *vector_base* deals with memory for a type *T*, not objects of type *T*. Consequently, a user of *vector_base* must destroy all constructed objects in a *vector_base* before the *vector_base* itself is destroyed.

Naturally, *vector_base* itself is written so that if an exception is thrown (by the allocator's copy constructor or **allocate** ( ) function) no *vector_base* object is created and no memory is leaked.

Given *vector_base*, *vector* can be defined like this:

```
template<class T, class A = allocator<T> >
class vector : private vector_base<T,A> {
    void destroy_elements() { for (T* p = v; p!=space; ++p) p->~T(); }  // §10.4.11
public:
    explicit vector(size_type n, const T& val = T(), const A& = A());

    vector(const vector& a);              // copy constructor
    vector& operator=(const vector& a);   // copy assignment

    ~vector() { destroy_elements(); }

    size_type size() const { return space-v; }
    size_type capacity() const { return last-v; }

    void push_back(const T&);

    // ...
};
```

The *vector* destructor explicitly invokes the *T* destructor for every element. This implies that if an element destructor throws an exception, the *vector* destruction fails. This can be a disaster if it happens during stack unwinding caused by an exception and **terminate** ( ) is called (§14.7). In the case of normal destruction, throwing an exception from a destructor typically leads to resource leaks and unpredictable behavior of code relying on reasonable behavior of objects. There is no really good way to protect against exceptions thrown from destructors, so the library makes no guarantees if an element destructor throws (§E.4).

Now the constructor can be simply defined:

```
template<class T, class A>
vector<T,A>::vector(size_type n, const T& val, const A& a)
    : vector_base(a,n)           // allocate space for n elements
{
    uninitialized_fill(v, v+n, val);    // copy elements
}
```

The copy constructor differs by using *uninitialized_copy* ( ) instead of *uninitialized_fill* ( ) :

```
template<class T, class A>
vector<T,A>::vector(const vector<T,A>& a)
    : vector_base(a, a.size())
{
    uninitialized_copy(a.begin(), a.end(), v);
}
```

Note that this style of constructor relies on the fundamental language rule that when an exception is thrown from a constructor, sub-objects (such as bases) that have already been completely constructed will be properly destroyed (§14.4.1). The *uninitialized_fill*() algorithm and its cousins (§E.4.4) provide the equivalent guarantee for partially constructed sequences.

E.3.3 Assignment

As usual, assignment differs from construction in that an old value must be taken care of. Consider a straightforward implementation:

```
template<class T, class A>
vector<T,A>& vector<T,A>::operator=(const vector& a)    // offers the strong guarantee (§E.2)
{
        vector_base<T,A> b(alloc,a.size());             // get memory
        uninitialized_copy(a.begin(),a.end(),b.v);      // copy elements
        destroy_elements();
        alloc.deallocate(v,last-v);                     // free old memory
        vector_base::operator=(b);                      // install new representation
        b.v = 0;                                        // prevent deallocation
        return *this;
}
```

This assignment is nice and exception safe. However, it repeats a lot of code from constructors and destructors. To avoid this, we could write:

```
template<class T, class A>
vector<T,A>& vector<T,A>::operator=(const vector& a)    // offers the strong guarantee (§E.2)
{
        vector temp(a);                                 // copy a
        swap< vector_base<T,A> >(*this,temp);           // swap representations
        return *this;
}
```

The old elements are destroyed by *temp*'s destructor, and the memory used to hold them is deallocated by *temp*'s *vector_base*'s destructor.

The performance of the two versions ought to be equivalent. Essentially, they are just two different ways of specifying the same set of operations. However, the second implementation is shorter and doesn't replicate code from related *vector* functions, so writing the assignment that way ought to be less error prone and lead to simpler maintenance.

Note the absence of the traditional test for self-assignment (§10.4.4):

```
        if (this == &a) return *this;
```

These assignment implementations work by first constructing a copy and then swapping representations. This obviously handles self-assignment correctly. I decided that the efficiency gained from the test in the rare case of self-assignment was more than offset by its cost in the common case where a different *vector* is assigned.

In either case, two potentially significant optimizations are missing:

[1] If the capacity of the vector assigned to is large enough to hold the assigned vector, we don't need to allocate new memory.

[2] An element assignment may be more efficient than an element destruction followed by an element construction.

Implementing these optimizations, we get:

```
template<class T, class A>
vector<T,A>& vector<T,A>::operator=(const vector& a)    // optimized, basic guarantee (§E.2)
{
        if (capacity() < a.size()) {     // allocate new vector representation:
                vector temp(a);                          // copy a
                swap< vector_base<T,A> >(*this,temp);    // swap representations
                return *this;
        }

        if (this == &a) return *this;     // protect against self assignment (§10.4.4)

                                          // assign to old elements:
        size_type sz = size();
        size_type asz = a.size();
        alloc = a.get_allocator();                       // copy the allocator
        if (asz<=sz) {
                copy(a.begin(),a.begin()+asz,v);
                for (T* p = v+asz; p!=space; ++p) p->~T();    // destroy surplus elements (§10.4.11)
        }
        else {
                copy(a.begin(),a.begin()+sz,v);
                uninitialized_copy(a.begin()+sz,a.end(),space);    // construct extra elements
        }
        space = v+asz;
        return *this;
}
```

These optimizations are not free. The *copy*() algorithm (§18.6.1) does *not* offer the strong exception-safety guarantee. It does not guarantee that it will leave its target unchanged if an exception is thrown during copying. Thus, if $T::operator=$() throws an exception during *copy*(), the *vector* being assigned to need not be a copy of the vector being assigned, and it need not be unchanged. For example, the first five elements might be copies of elements of the assigned vector and the rest unchanged. It is also plausible that an element – the element that was being copied when $T::operator=$() threw an exception – ends up with a value that is neither the old value nor a copy of the corresponding element in the vector being assigned. However, if $T::operator=$() leaves its operands in a valid state if it throws an exception, the *vector* is still in a valid state – even if it wasn't the state we would have preferred.

Here, I have copied the allocator using an assignment. It is actually not required that every allocator support assignment (§19.4.3); see also §E.8[9].

The standard-library *vector* assignment offers the weaker exception-safety property of this last implementation – and its potential performance advantages. That is, *vector* assignment provides the basic guarantee, so it meets most people's idea of exception safety. However, it does not provide the strong guarantee (§E.2). If you need an assignment that leaves the *vector* unchanged if an exception is thrown, you must either use a library implementation that provides the strong guarantee or provide your own assignment operation. For example:

```
template<class T, class A>
void safe_assign(vector<T,A>& a, const vector<T,A>& b) // "obvious" a = b
{
    vector<T,A> temp(a.get_allocator());
    temp.reserve(b.size());
    for (typename vector<T,A>::iterator p = b.begin(); p!=b.end(); ++p)
        temp.push_back(*p);
    swap(a,temp);
}
```

If there is insufficient memory for *temp* to be created with room for *b.size*() elements, *std::bad_alloc* is thrown before any changes are made to *a*. Similarly, if *push_back*() fails for any reason, *a* will remain untouched because we apply *push_back*() to *temp* rather than to *a*. In that case, any elements of *temp* created by *push_back*() will be destroyed before the exception that caused the failure is re-thrown.

Swap does not copy *vector* elements. It simply swaps the data members of a *vector*; that is, it swaps *vector_base*s. Consequently, it does not throw exceptions even if operations on the elements might (§E.4.3). Consequently, *safe_assign*() does not do spurious copies of elements and is reasonably efficient.

As is often the case, there are alternatives to the obvious implementation. We can let the library perform the copy into the temporary for us:

```
template<class T, class A>
void safe_assign(vector<T,A>& a, const vector<T,A>& b) // simple a = b
{
    vector<T,A> temp(b);     // copy the elements of b into a temporary
    swap(a,temp);
}
```

Indeed, we could simply use call-by-value (§7.2):

```
template<class T, class A>
void safe_assign(vector<T,A>& a, vector<T,A> b)    // simple a = b (note: b is passed by value)
{
    swap(a,b);
}
```

The last two variants of *safe_assign*() don't copy the *vector*'s allocator. This is a permitted optimization; see §19.4.3.

E.3.4 *push_back()*

From an exception-safety point of view, *push_back*() is similar to the assignment in that we must take care that the *vector* remains unchanged if we fail to add a new element:

```
template< class T, class A>
void vector<T,A>::push_back(const T& x)
{
        if (space == last) {    // no more free space; relocate:
                vector_base b(alloc, size() ?2*size() :2); // double the allocation
                uninitialized_copy(v, space, b.v);
                new(b.space) T(x);                          // place a copy of x in *b.space (§10.4.11)
                ++b.space;
                destroy_elements();
                swap<vector_base<T,A> >(b, *this);          // swap representations
                return;
        }
        new(space) T(x);                                    // place a copy of x in *space (§10.4.11)
        ++space;
}
```

Naturally, the copy constructor used to initialize *space* might throw an exception. If that happens, the value of the *vector* remains unchanged, with *space* left unincremented. In that case, the *vector* elements are not reallocated so that iterators referring to them are not invalidated. Thus, this implementation implements the strong guarantee that an exception thrown by an allocator or even a user-supplied copy constructor leaves the *vector* unchanged. The standard library offers that guarantee for *push_back*() (§E.4.1).

Note the absence of a *try-block* (except for the one hidden in *uninitialized_copy*()). The update was done by carefully ordering the operations so that if an exception is thrown, the *vector* remains unchanged.

The approach of gaining exception safety through ordering and the "resource acquisition is initialization" technique (§14.4) tends to be more elegant and more efficient than explicitly handling errors using *try-blocks*. More problems with exception safety arise from a programmer ordering code in unfortunate ways than from lack of specific exception-handling code. The basic rule of ordering is not to destroy information before its replacement has been constructed and can be assigned without the possibility of an exception.

Exceptions introduce possibilities for surprises in the form of unexpected control flows. For a piece of code with a simple local control flow, such as the *operator*=(), *safe_assign*(), and *push_back*() examples, the opportunities for surprises are limited. It is relatively simple to look at such code and ask oneself "can this line of code throw an exception, and what happens if it does?" For large functions with complicated control structures, such as complicated conditional statements and nested loops, this can be hard. Adding *try-blocks* increases this local control structure complexity and can therefore be a source of confusion and errors (§14.4). I conjecture that the effectiveness of the ordering approach and the "resource acquisition is initialization" approach compared to more extensive use of *try-blocks* stems from the simplification of the local control flow. Simple, stylized code is easier to understand and easier to get right.

Note that the *vector* implementation is presented as an example of the problems that exceptions can pose and of techniques for addressing those problems. The standard does not require an implementation to be exactly like the one presented here. What the standard does guarantee is the subject of §E.4.

E.3.5 Constructors and Invariants

From the point of view of exception safety, other *vector* operations are either equivalent to the ones already examined (because they acquire and release resources in similar ways) or trivial (because they don't perform operations that require cleverness to maintain valid states). However, for most classes, such "trivial" functions constitute the majority of code. The difficulty of writing such functions depends critically on the environment that a constructor established for them to operate in. Said differently, the complexity of "ordinary member functions" depends critically on choosing a good class invariant (§24.3.7.1). By examining the "trivial" *vector* functions, it is possible to gain insight into the interesting question of what makes a good invariant for a class and how constructors should be written to establish such invariants.

Operations such as *vector* subscripting (§16.3.3) are easy to write because they can rely on the invariant established by the constructors and maintained by all functions that acquire or release resources. In particular, a subscript operator can rely on *v* referring to an array of elements:

```
template< class  T,  class  A>
T& vector<T,A>::operator[] (size_type  i)
{
      return  v[i];
}
```

It is important and fundamental to have constructors acquire resources and establish a simple invariant. To see why, consider an alternative definition of *vector_base*:

```
template<class  T,  class  A = allocator<T> >        // clumsy use of constructor
class  vector_base {
public:
      A  alloc;    // allocator
      T*  v;       // start of allocation
      T*  space;   // end of element sequence, start of space allocated for possible expansion
      T*  last;    // end of allocated space

      vector_base (const  A& a,  typename  A::size_type  n)  : alloc(a),  v(0),  space(0),  last(0)
      {
            v = alloc.allocate(n);
            space = last = v+n;
      }

      ~vector_base() { if (v) alloc.deallocate(v,last-v); }
};
```

Here, I construct a *vector_base* in two stages: First, I establish a "safe state" where *v*, *space*, and *last* are set to *0*. Only after that has been done do I try to allocate memory. This is done out of misplaced fear that if an exception happens during element allocation, a partially constructed object could be left behind. This fear is misplaced because a partially constructed object cannot be "left behind" and later accessed. The rules for static objects, automatic objects, member objects, and elements of the standard-library containers prevent that. However, it could/can happen in pre-standard libraries that used/use placement new (§10.4.11) to construct objects in containers designed without concern for exception safety. Old habits can be hard to break.

Note that this attempt to write safer code complicates the invariant for the class: It is no longer guaranteed that *v* points to allocated memory. Now *v* might be *0*. This has one immediate cost. The standard-library requirements for allocators do not guarantee that we can safely deallocate a pointer with the value *0* (§19.4.1). In this, allocators differ from *delete* (§6.2.6). Consequently, I had to add a test in the destructor. Also, each element is first initialized and then assigned. The cost of doing that extra work can be significant for element types for which assignment is nontrivial, such as *string* and *list*.

This two-stage construct is not an uncommon style. Sometimes, it is even made explicit by having the constructor do only some "simple and safe" initialization to put the object into a destructible state. The real construction is left to an *init* ( ) function that the user must explicitly call. For example:

```
template<class T>    // archaic (pre-standard, pre-exception) style
class vector_base {
public :
        T* v;        // start of allocation
        T* space;  // end of element sequence, start of space allocated for possible expansion
        T* last;     // end of allocated space

        vector_base ( ) : v (0), space (0), last (0) { }
        ~vector_base ( ) { free (v); }

        bool  init (size_t  n)    // return true if initialization succeeded
        {
                if (v = (T*) malloc (sizeof(T) *n) ) {
                        uninitialized_fill (v, v+n, T ( ) );
                        space = last = v+n;
                        return  true;
                }
                return  false;
        }
};
```

The perceived value of this style is
[1] The constructor can't throw an exception, and the success of an initialization using *init* ( ) can be tested by "usual" (that is, non-exception) means.
[2] There exists a trivial valid state. In case of a serious problem, an operation can give an object that state.
[3] The acquisition of resources is delayed until a fully initialized object is actually needed.
The following subsections examine these points and shows why this two-stage construction technique doesn't deliver its expected benefits. It can also be a source of problems.

E.3.5.1 Using *init()* Functions

The first point (using an *init* ( ) function in preference to a constructor) is bogus. Using constructors and exception handling is a more general and systematic way of dealing with resource acquisition and initialization errors (§14.1, §14.4). This style is a relic of pre-exception C++.

Carefully written code using the two styles are roughly equivalent. Consider:

```
int f1 (int n)
{
    vector<X> v;
    // ...
    if (v.init(n)) {
        // use v as vector of n elements
    }
    else {
        // handle_problem
    }
}
```

and

```
int f2 (int n)
try {
    vector v<X> v(n);
    // ...
    // use v as vector of n elements
}
catch ( . . . ) {
    // handle problem
}
```

However, having a separate *init()* function is an opportunity to

[1] forget to call *init()* (§10.2.3),

[2] forget to test on the success of *init()*,

[3] forget that *init()* might throw an exception, and

[4] use the object before calling *init()*.

The definition of *vector<T> :: init()* illustrates [3].

In a good C++ implementation, *f2()* will be marginally faster than *f1()* because it avoids the test in the common case.

E.3.5.2 Relying on a Default Valid State

The second point (having an easy-to-construct ''default'' valid state) is correct in general, but in the case of *vector*, it is achieved at an unnecessary cost. It is now possible to have a *vector_base* with *v==0*, so the *vector* implementation must protect against that possibility throughout. For example:

```
template< class T>
T& vector<T> :: operator[] (size_t i)
{
    if (v) return v[i];
    // handle error
}
```

Leaving the possibility of *v==0* open makes the cost of non-range-checked subscripting equivalent to range-checked access:

```
template< class T>
T& vector<T>::at(size_t i)
{
    if (i<v.size()) return v[i];
    throw out_of_range("vector index");
}
```

What fundamentally happened here was that I complicated the basic invariant for *vector_base* by introducing the possibility of *v==0*. In consequence, the basic invariant for *vector* was similarly complicated. The end result of this is that all code in *vector* and *vector_base* must be more complicated to cope. This is a source of potential errors, maintenance problems, and run-time overhead. Note that conditional statements can be surprisingly costly on modern machine architectures. Where efficiency matters, it can be crucial to implement a key operation, such as vector subscripting, without conditional statements.

Interestingly, the original definition of *vector_base* already did have an easy-to-construct valid state. No *vector_base* object could exist unless the initial allocation succeeded. Consequently, the implementer of *vector* could write an "emergency exit" function like this:

```
template< class T, class A>
void vector<T,A>::emergency_exit()
{
    space = v;              // set the size of *this to 0
    throw Total_failure();
}
```

This is a bit drastic because it fails to call element destructors and to deallocate the space for elements held by the *vector_base*. That is, it fails to provide the basic guarantee (§E.2). If we are willing to trust the values of *v* and *space* and the element destructors, we can avoid potential resource leaks:

```
template< class T, class A>
void vector<T,A>::emergency_exit()
{
    destroy_elements();     // clean up
    throw Total_failure();
}
```

Please note that the standard *vector* is such a clean design that it minimizes the problems caused by two-phase construction. The *init*() function is roughly equivalent to *resize*(), and in most places the possibility of *v==0* is already covered by *size*()*==0* tests. The negative effects described for two-phase construction become more marked when we consider application classes that acquire significant resources, such as network connections and files. Such classes are rarely part of a framework that guides their use and their implementation in the way the standard-library requirements guide the definition and use of *vector*. The problems also tend to increase as the mapping between the application concepts and the resources required to implement them becomes more complex. Few classes map as directly onto system resources as does *vector*.

The idea of having a "safe state" is in principle a good one. If we can't put an object into a valid state without fear of throwing an exception before completing that operation, we do indeed have a problem. However, this "safe state" should be one that is a natural part of the semantics of the class rather than an implementation artifact that complicates the class invariant.

E.3.5.3 Delaying resource acquisition

Like the second point (§E.3.5.2), the third (to delay acquisition until a resource is needed) misapplies a good idea in a way that imposes cost without yielding benefits. In many cases, notably in containers such as *vector*, the best way of delaying resource acquisition is for the programmer to delay the creation of objects until they are needed. Consider a naive use of *vector*:

```
void f(int n)
{
    vector<X> v(n);        // make n default objects of type X
    // ...
    v[3] = X(99);          // real "initialization" of v[3]
    // ...
}
```

Constructing an *X* only to assign a new value to it later is wasteful – especially if an *X* assignment is expensive. Therefore, two-phase construction of *X* can seem attractive. For example, the type *X* may itself be a *vector*, so we might consider two-phase construction of *vector* to optimize creation of empty *vector*s. However, creating default (empty) vectors is already efficient, so complicating the implementation with a special case for the empty vector seems futile. More generally, the best solution to spurious initialization is rarely to remove complicated initialization from the element constructors. Instead, a user can create elements only when needed. For example:

```
void f2(int n)
{
    vector<X> v;           // make empty vector
    // ...
    v.push_back(X(99));    // construct element when needed
    // ...
}
```

To sum up: the two-phase construction approach leads to more complicated invariants and typically to less elegant, more error-prone, and harder-to-maintain code. Consequently, the language-supported "constructor approach" should be preferred to the "*init*()-function approach" whenever feasible. That is, resources should be acquired in constructors whenever delayed resource acquisition isn't mandated by the inherent semantics of a class.

E.4 Standard Container Guarantees

If a library operation itself throws an exception, it can – and does – make sure that the objects on which it operates are left in a well-defined state. For example, *at*() throwing *out_of_range* for a *vector* (§16.3.3) is not a problem with exception safety for the *vector*. The writer of *at*() has no problem making sure that a *vector* is in a well-defined state before throwing. The problems – for library implementers, for library users, and for people trying to understand code – come when a user-supplied function throws an exception.

The standard-library containers offer the basic guarantee (§E.2): The basic invariants of the library are maintained, and no resources are leaked as long as user code behaves as required. That is, user-supplied operations should not leave container elements in invalid states or throw exceptions from destructors. By ''operations,'' I mean operations used by the standard-library implementation, such as constructors, assignments, destructors, and operations on iterators (§E.4.4).

It is relatively easy for the programmer to ensure that such operations meet the library's expectations. In fact, much naively written code conforms to the library's requirements. The following types clearly meet the standard library's requirements for container element types:

[1] built-in types – including pointers,

[2] types without user-defined operations,

[3] classes with operations that neither throw exceptions nor leave operands in invalid states,

[4] classes with destructors that don't throw exceptions and for which it is simple to verify that operations used by the standard library (such as constructors, assignments, <, ==, and *swap* ( )) don't leave operands in invalid states.

In each case, we must also make sure that no resource is leaked. For example:

```
void f(Circle* pc, Triangle* pt, vector<Shape*>& v2)
{
    vector<Shape*> v(10);              // either create vector or throw bad_alloc
    v[3] = pc;                         // no exception thrown
    v.insert(v.begin()+4,pt);         // either insert pt or no effect on v
    v2.erase(v2.begin()+3);           // either erase v2[3] or no effect on v2
    v2 = v;                            // copy v or no effect on v2
    // ...
}
```

When $f()$ exits, v will be properly destroyed, and $v2$ will be in a valid state. This fragment does not indicate who is responsible for deleting pc and pt. If $f()$ is responsible, it can either catch exceptions and do the required deletion, or assign the pointers to local *auto_ptr*s.

The more interesting question is: When do the library operations offer the strong guarantee that an operation either succeeds or has no effect on its operands? For example:

```
void f(vector<X>& vx)
{
    vx.insert(vx.begin()+4,X(7));     // add element
}
```

In general, X's operations and *vector<X>*'s allocator can throw an exception. What can we say about the elements of vx when $f()$ exits because of an exception? The basic guarantee ensures that no resources have been leaked and that vx has a set of valid elements. However, exactly what elements? Is vx unchanged? Could a default X have been added? Could an element have been removed because that was the only way for *insert* ( ) to recover while maintaining the basic guarantee? Sometimes, it is not enough to know that a container is in a good state; we also want to know exactly what state that is. After catching an exception, we typically want to know that the elements are exactly those we intended, or we will have to start error recovery.

E.4.1 Insertion and Removal of Elements

Inserting an element into a container and removing one are obvious examples of operations that might leave a container in an unpredictable state if an exception is thrown. The reason is that insertions and deletions invoke many operations that may throw exceptions:

[1] A new value is copied into a container.
[2] An element deleted from (erased from) a container must be destroyed.
[3] Sometimes, memory must be allocated to hold a new element.
[4] Sometimes, *vector* and *deque* elements must be copied to new locations.
[5] Associative containers call comparison functions for elements.
[6] Many insertions and deletions involve iterator operations.

Each of these cases can cause an exception to be thrown.

If a destructor throws an exception, no guarantees are made (§E.2). Making guarantees in this case would be prohibitively expensive. However, the library can and does protect itself – and its users – from exceptions thrown by other user-supplied operations.

When manipulating a linked data structure, such as a *list* or a *map*, elements can be added and removed without affecting other elements in the container. This is not the case for a container implemented using contiguous allocation of elements, such as a *vector* or a *deque*. There, elements sometimes need to be moved to new locations.

In addition to the basic guarantee, the standard library offers the strong guarantee for a few operations that insert or remove elements. Because containers implemented as linked data structures behave differently from containers with contiguous allocation of elements, the standard provides slightly different guarantees for different kinds of containers:

[1] Guarantees for *vector* (§16.3) and *deque* (§17.2.3):
  – If an exception is thrown by a *push_back* ( ) or a *push_front* ( ), that function has no effect.
  – Unless thrown by the copy constructor or the assignment operator of the element type, if an exception is thrown by an *insert* ( ), that function has no effect.
  – Unless thrown by the copy constructor or the assignment operator of the element type, no *erase* ( ) throws an exception.
  – No *pop_back* ( ) or *pop_front* ( ) throws an exception.

[2] Guarantees for *list* (§17.2.2):
  – If an exception is thrown by a *push_back* ( ) or a *push_front* ( ), that function has no effect.
  – If an exception is thrown by an *insert* ( ), that function has no effect.
  – No *erase* ( ), *pop_back* ( ), *pop_front* ( ), *splice* ( ), or *reverse* ( ) throws an exception.
  – Unless thrown by a predicate or a comparison function, the *list* member functions *remove* ( ), *remove_if* ( ), *unique* ( ), *sort* ( ), and *merge* ( ) do not throw exceptions.

[3] Guarantees for associative containers (§17.4):
  – If an exception is thrown by an *insert* ( ) while inserting a single element, that function has no effect.
  – No *erase* ( ) throws an exception.

Note that where the strong guarantee is provided for an operation on a container, all iterators, pointers to elements, and references to elements remain valid if an exception is thrown.

These rules can be summarized in a table:

Container-Operation Guarantees				
	vector	**deque**	**list**	**map**
clear()	nothrow *(copy)*	nothrow *(copy)*	nothrow	nothrow
erase()	nothrow *(copy)*	nothrow *(copy)*	nothrow	nothrow
1-element insert()	strong *(copy)*	strong *(copy)*	strong	strong
N-element insert()	strong *(copy)*	strong *(copy)*	strong	basic
merge()	—	—	nothrow *(comparison)*	—
push_back()	strong	strong	strong	—
push_front()	—	strong	strong	—
pop_back()	nothrow	nothrow	nothrow	—
pop_front()	—	nothrow	nothrow	—
remove()	—	—	nothrow *(comparison)*	—
remove_if()	—	—	nothrow *(predicate)*	—
reverse()	—	—	nothrow	—
splice()	—	—	nothrow	—
swap()	nothrow	nothrow	nothrow	nothrow *(copy-of-comparison)*
unique()	—	—	nothrow *(comparison)*	—

In this table:

> **basic**   means that the operation provides only the basic guarantee (§E.2)
> **strong**   means that the operation provides the strong guarantee (§E.2)
> **nothrow** means that the operation does not throw an exception (§E.2)
> —   means that the operation is not provided as a member of this container

Where a guarantee requires that some user-supplied operations not throw exceptions, those operations are indicated in parentheses under the guarantee. These requirements are precisely stated in the text preceding the table.

The *swap* () functions differ from the other functions mentioned by not being members. The guarantee for *clear* () is derived from that offered by *erase* () (§16.3.6). This table lists guarantees offered in addition to the basic guarantee. Consequently this table does not list operations, such as *reverse* () and *unique* () for *vector*, that are provided only as algoritms for all sequences without additional guarantees.

The ''almost container'' *basic_string* (§17.5, §20.3) offers the basic guarantee for all operations (§E.5.1). The standard also guarantees that *basic_string*'s *erase* () and *swap* () don't throw, and offers the strong guarantee for *basic_string*'s *insert* () and *push_back* ().

In addition to ensuring that a container iₔ unchanged, an operation providing the strong guarantee also leaves all iterators, pointers, and references valid. For example:

```
void  update (map<string, X>& m , map<string, X>::iterator  current)
{
      X  x;
      string  s;
      while  (cin>>s>>x)
      try {
            current = m.insert (current, make_pair (s, x));
      }
      catch ( . . . ) {
            // here current still denotes the current element
      }
}
```

E.4.2 Guarantees and Tradeoffs

The patchwork of additional guarantees reflects implementation realities. Programmers prefer the strong guarantee with as few conditions as possible, but they also tend to insist that each individual standard-library operation be optimally efficient. Both concerns are reasonable, but for many operations, it is not possible to satisfy both simultaneously. To give a better idea of the tradeoffs involved, I'll examine ways of adding of single and multiple elements to *list*s, *vector*s, and *map*s.

Consider adding a single element to a *list* or a *vector*. As ever, *push_back* () provides the simplest way of doing that:

```
void  f (list<X>& lst , vector<X>& vec , const  X& x)
{
      try {
            lst.push_back (x);             // add to list
      }
      catch ( . . . ) {
            // lst is unchanged
            return;
      }
```

```
try {
    vec.push_back(x);              // add to vector
}
catch (...) {
    // vec is unchanged
    return;
}

// lst and vec each have a new element with the value x
}
```

Providing the strong guarantee in these cases is simple and cheap. It is also very useful because it provides a completely exception-safe way of adding elements. However, *push_back*() isn't defined for associative containers – a *map* has no *back*(). After all, the last element of an associative container is defined by the order relation rather than by position.

The guarantees for *insert*() are a bit more complicated. The reason is that sometimes *insert*() has to place an element in "the middle" of a container. This is no problem for a linked data structure, such as *list* or *map*. However, if there is free reserved space in a *vector*, the obvious implementation of *vector<X>::insert*() copies the elements after the insertion point to make room. This is optimally efficient, but there is no simple way of restoring a *vector* if *X*'s copy assignment or copy constructor throws an exception (see §E.8[10-11]). Consequently, *vector* provides a guarantee that is conditional upon element copy operations not throwing exceptions. However, *list* and *map* don't need such a condition; they can simply link in new elements after doing any necessary copying.

As an example, assume that *X*'s copy assignment and copy constructor throw *X::cannot_copy* if they cannot successfully create a copy:

```
void f(list<X>& lst, vector<X>& vec, map<string,X>& m, const X& x, const string& s)
{
    try {
        lst.insert(lst.begin(),x);       // add to list
    }
    catch (...) {
        // lst is unchanged
        return;
    }

    try {
        vec.insert(vec.begin(),x);       // add to vector
    }
    catch (X::cannot_copy) {
        // oops: vec may or may not have a new element
        return;
    }
    catch (...) {
        // vec is unchanged
        return;
    }
```

```
try {
    m.insert(make_pair(s,x));        // add to map
}
catch ( ... ) {
    // m is unchanged
    return;
}

// lst and vec each have a new element with the value x
// m has an element with the value (s,x)
}
```

If *X::cannot_copy* is caught, a new element may or may not have been inserted into *vec*. If a new element was inserted, it will be an object in a valid state, but it is unspecified exactly what the value is. It is possible that after *X::cannot_copy*, some element will have been ''mysteriously'' duplicated (see §E.8[11]). Alternatively, *insert()* may be implemented so that it deletes some ''trailing'' elements to be certain that no invalid elements are left in a container.

Unfortunately, providing the strong guarantee for *vector*'s *insert()* without the caveat about exceptions thrown by copy operations is not feasible. The cost of completely protecting against an exception while moving elements in a *vector* would be significant compared to simply providing the basic guarantee in that case.

Element types with copy operations that can throw exceptions are not uncommon. Examples from the standard library itself are *vector<string>*, *vector< vector<double> >*, and *map<string, int>*.

The *list* and *vector* containers provide the same guarantees for *insert()* of single and multiple elements. The reason is simply that for *vector* and *list*, the same implementation strategies apply to both single-element and multiple-element *insert()*. However, *map* provides the strong guarantee for single-element *insert()*, but only the basic guarantee for multiple-element *insert()*. A single-element *insert()* for *map* that provides the strong guarantee is easily implemented. However, the obvious strategy for implementing multiple-element *insert()* for a *map* is to insert the new elements one after another, and it is not easy to provide the strong guarantee for that. The problem with this is that there is no simple way of backing out of previous successful insertions if the insertion of an element fails.

If we want an insertion function that provides the strong guarantee that either every element was successfully added or the operation had no effect, we can build it by constructing a new container and then *swap()*:

```
template<class C, class Iter>
void safe_insert(C& c, typename C::const_iterator i, Iter begin, Iter end)
{
    C tmp(c.begin(),i);                        // copy leading elements to temporary
    copy(begin,end,inserter(tmp,tmp.end()));   // copy new elements
    copy(i,c.end(),inserter(tmp,tmp.end()));   // copy trailing elements
    swap(c,tmp);
}
```

As ever, this code may misbehave if the element destructor throws an exception. However, if an element copy operation throws an exception, the argument container is unchanged.

E.4.3 Swap

Like copy constructors and assignments, *swap*( ) operations are essential to many standard algorithms and are often supplied by users. For example, *sort*( ) and *stable_sort*( ) typically reorder elements, using *swap*( ). Thus, if a *swap*( ) function throws an exception while exchanging values from a container, the container could be left with unchanged elements or a duplicate element rather than a pair of swapped elements.

Consider the obvious definition of the standard-library *swap*( ) function (§18.6.8):

```
template<class T> void swap (T& a, T& b)
{
    T tmp = a;
    a = b;
    b = tmp;
}
```

Clearly, *swap*( ) doesn't throw an exception unless the element type's copy constructor or copy assignment does.

With one minor exception for associative containers, standard container *swap*( ) functions are guaranteed not to throw exceptions. Basically, containers are swapped by exchanging the data structures that act as handles for the elements (§13.5, §17.1.3). Since the elements themselves are not moved, element constructors and assignments are not invoked, so they don't get an opportunity to throw an exception. In addition, the standard guarantees that no standard-library *swap*( ) function invalidates any references, pointers, or iterators referring to the elements of the containers being swapped. This leaves only one potential source of exceptions: The comparison object in an associative container is copied as part of the handle. The only possible exception from a *swap*( ) of standard containers is the copy constructor and assignment of the container's comparison object (§17.1.4.1). Fortunately, comparison objects usually have trivial copy operations that do not have opportunities to throw exceptions.

A user-supplied *swap*( ) should be written to provide the same guarantees. This is relatively simple to do as long as one remembers to swap types represented as handles by swapping their handles, rather than slowly and elaborately copying the information referred to by the handles (§13.5, §16.3.9, §17.1.3).

E.4.4 Initialization and Iterators

Allocation of memory for elements and the initialization of such memory are fundamental parts of every container implementation (§E.3). Consequently, the standard algorithms for constructing objects in uninitialized memory – *uninitialized_fill*( ), *uninitialized_fill_n*( ), and *uninitialized_copy*( ) (§19.4.4) – are guaranteed to leave no constructed objects behind if they throw an exception. They provide the strong guarantee (§E.2). This sometimes involves destroying elements, so the requirement that destructors not throw exceptions is essential to these algorithms; see §E.8[14]. In addition, the iterators supplied as arguments to these algorithms are required to be well behaved. That is, they must be valid iterators, refer to valid sequences, and iterator operations (such as ++ and != and *) on a valid iterator are not allowed to throw exceptions.

Iterators are examples of objects that are copied freely by standard algorithms and operations on standard containers. Thus, copy constructors and copy assignments of iterators should not throw exceptions. In particular, the standard guarantees that no copy constructor or assignment operator of an iterator returned from a standard container throws an exception. For example, an iterator returned by *vector<T>*::*begin* ( ) can be copied without fear of exceptions.

Note that ++ and -- on an iterator can throw exceptions. For example, an *istreambuf_iterator* (§19.2.6) could reasonably throw an exception to indicate an input error, and a range-checked iterator could throw an exception to indicate an attempt to move outside its valid range (§19.3). However, they cannot throw exceptions when moving an iterator from one element of a sequence to another, without violating the definition of ++ and -- on an iterator. Thus, *uninitialized_fill* ( ), *uninitialized_fill_n* ( ), and *uninitialized_copy* ( ) assume that ++ and -- on their iterator arguments will not throw; if they do throw, either those "iterators" weren't iterators according to the standard, or the "sequence" specified by them wasn't a sequence. Again, the standard containers do not protect the user from the user's own undefined behavior (§E.2).

E.4.5 References to Elements

When a reference, a pointer, or an iterator to an element of a container is handed to some code, that code can corrupt the container by corrupting the element. For example:

```
void f(const X& x)
{
    list<X> lst;
    lst.push_back(x);
    list<X>::iterator i = lst.begin();
    *i = x;      // copy x into list
    // ...
}
```

If *x* is corrupted, *list*'s destructor may not be able to properly destroy *lst*. For example:

```
struct X {
    int* p;

    X() { p = new int; }
    ~X() { delete p; }
    // ...
};

void malicious()
{
    X x;
    x.p = reinterpret_cast<int*>(7);      // corrupt x
    f(x);                                  // time bomb
}
```

When the execution reaches the end on *f* ( ), the *list<X>* destructor is called, and that will in turn invoke *X*'s destructor for the corrupted value. The effect of executing *delete p* when *p* isn't *0* and doesn't point to an *X* is undefined and could be an immediate crash. Alternatively, it might leave the free store corrupted in a way that causes difficult-to-track problems much later on in an apparently unrelated part of a program.

This possibility of corruption should not stop people from manipulating container elements through references and iterators; it is often the simplest and most efficient way of doing things. However, it is wise to take extra care with such references into containers. When the integrity of a container is crucial, it might be worthwhile to offer safer alternatives to less experienced users. For example, we might provide an operation that checks the validity of a new element before copying it into an important container. Naturally, such checking can only be done with knowledge of the application types.

In general, if an element of a container is corrupted, subsequent operations on the container can fail in nasty ways. This is not particular to containers. Any object left in a bad state can cause subsequent failure.

E.4.6 Predicates

Many standard algorithms and many operations on standard containers rely on predicates that can be supplied by users. In particular, all associative containers depend on predicates for both lookup and insertion.

A predicate used by a standard container operation may throw an exception. In that case, every standard-library operation provides the basic guarantee, and some operations, such as *insert* ( ) of a single element, provide the strong guarantee (§E.4.1). If a predicate throws an exception from an operation on a container, the resulting set of elements in the container may not be exactly what the user wanted, but it will be a set of valid elements. For example, if == throws an exception when invoked from *list* : : *unique* ( ) (§17.2.2.3), the user cannot assume that no duplicates are in the list. All the user can safely assume is that every element on the list is valid (see §E.5.3).

Fortunately, predicates rarely do anything that might throw an exception. However, user-defined <, ==, and ! = predicates must be taken into account when considering exception safety.

The comparison object of an associative container is copied as part of a *swap* ( ) (§E.4.3). Consequently, it is a good idea to ensure that the copy operations of predicates that might be used as comparison objects do not throw exceptions.

E.5 The Rest of the Standard Library

The crucial issue in exception safety is to maintain the consistency of objects; that is, we must maintain the basic invariants for individual objects and the consistency of collections of objects. In the context of the standard library, the objects for which it is the most difficult to provide exception safety are the containers. From the point of view of exception safety, the rest of the standard library is less interesting. However, note that from the perspective of exception safety, a built-in array is a container that might be corrupted by an unsafe operation.

In general, standard-library functions throw only the exceptions that they are specified to throw, plus any thrown by user-supplied operations that they may call. In addition, any function that (directly or indirectly) allocates memory can throw an exception to indicate memory exhaustion (typically, *std* : : *bad_alloc*).

E.5.1 Strings

The operations on *string*s can throw a variety of exceptions. However, *basic_string* manipulates its characters through the functions provided by *char_traits* (§20.2), and these functions are not allowed to throw exceptions. That is, the *char_traits* supplied by the standard library do not throw exceptions, and no guarantees are made if an operation of a user-defined *char_traits* throws an exception. In particular, note that a type used as the element (character) type for a *basic_string* is not allowed to have a user-defined copy constructor or a user-defined copy assignment. This removes a significant potential source of exception throws.

A *basic_string* is very much like a standard container (§17.5, §20.3). In fact, its elements constitute a sequence that can be accessed using *basic_string<Ch,Tr,A>::iterator*s and *basic_string<Ch,Tr,A>::const_iterator*s. Consequently, a string implementation offers the basic guarantee (§E.2), and the guarantees for *erase*(), *insert*(), *push_back*() and *swap*() (§E.4.1) apply to *basic_string*s. For example, *basic_string<Ch,Tr,A>::push_back*() offers the strong guarantee.

E.5.2 Streams

If required to do so, iostream functions throw exceptions to signal state changes (§21.3.6). The semantics of this are well defined and pose no exception-safety problems. If a user-defined *operator<<*() or *operator>>*() throws an exception, it may appear to the user as if the iostream library threw an exception. However, such an exception will not affect the stream state (§21.3.3). Further operations on the stream may not find the expected data – because the previous operation threw an exception instead of completing normally – but the stream itself is uncorrupted. As ever after an I/O problem, a *clear*() may be needed before doing further reads/writes (§21.3.3, §21.3.5).

Like *basic_string*, the *iostream*s rely on *char_traits* to manipulate characters (§20.2.1, §E.5.1). Thus, an implementation can assume that operations on characters do not throw exceptions, and no guarantees are made if the user violates that assumption.

To allow for crucial optimizations, *locale*s (§D.2) and *facet*s (§D.3) are assumed not to throw exceptions. If they do, a stream using them could be corrupted. However, the most likely exception, a *std::bad_cast* from a *use_facet* (§D.3.1), can occur only in user-supplied code outside the standard stream implementation. At worst, this will produce incomplete output or cause a read to fail rather than corrupt the *ostream* (or *istream*) itself.

E.5.3 Algorithms

Aside from *uninitialized_copy*(), *uninitialized_fill*(), and *uninitialized_fill_n*() (§E.4.4), the standard offers only the basic guarantee (§E.2) for algorithms. That is, provided that user-supplied objects are well behaved, the algorithms will maintain all standard-library invariants and leak no resources. To avoid undefined behavior, user-supplied operations should always leave their operands in valid states, and destructors should not throw exceptions.

The algorithms themselves do not throw exceptions. Instead, they report errors and failures through their return values. For example, search algorithms generally return the end of a sequence to indicate "not found" (§18.2). Thus, exceptions thrown from a standard algorithm must originate from a user-supplied operation. That is, the exception must come from an operation on an element – such as a predicate (§18.4), an assignment, or a *swap* ( ) – or from an allocator (§19.4).

If such an operation throws an exception, the algorithm terminates immediately, and it is up to the functions that invoked the algorithm to handle the exception. For some algorithms, it is possible for an exception to occur at a point where the container is not in a state that the user would consider good. For example, some sorting algorithms temporarily copy elements into a buffer and later put them back into the container. Such a *sort* ( ) might copy elements out of the container (planning to write them back in proper order later), overwrite them, and then throw an exception. From a user's point of view, the container was corrupted. However, all elements are in a valid state, so recovery should be reasonably straightforward.

Note that the standard algorithms access sequences through iterators. That is, the standard algorithms never operate on containers directly, only on elements in a container. The fact that a standard algorithm never directly adds or removes elements from a container simplifies the analysis of the impact of exceptions. Similarly, if a data structure is accessed only through iterators, pointers, and references to *const* (for example, through a *const Rec**), it is usually trivial to verify that an exception has no undesired effects.

E.5.4 Valarray and Complex

The numeric functions do not explicitly throw exceptions (Chapter 22). However, *valarray* needs to allocate memory and thus might throw *std* : : *bad_alloc*. Furthermore, *valarray* or *complex* may be given an element type (scalar type) that throws exceptions. As ever, the standard library provides the basic guarantee (§E.2), but no specific guarantees are made about the effects of a computation terminated by an exception.

Like *basic_string* (§E.5.1), *valarray* and *complex* are allowed to assume that their template argument type does not have user-defined copy operations so that they can be bitwise copied. Typically, these standard-library numeric types are optimized for speed, assuming that their element type (scalar type) does not throw exceptions.

E.5.5 The C Standard Library

A standard-library operation without an exception specification may throw exceptions in an implementation-defined manner. However, functions from the standard C library do not throw exceptions unless they take a function argument that does. After all, these functions are shared with C, and C doesn't have exceptions. An implementation may declare a standard C function with an empty *exception-specification*, *throw* ( ), to help the compiler generate better code.

Functions such as *qsort* ( ) and *bsearch* ( ) (§18.11) take a pointer to function as argument. They can therefore throw an exception if their arguments can. The basic guarantee (§E.2) covers these functions.

E.6 Implications for Library Users

One way to look at exception safety in the context of the standard library is that we have no problems unless we create them for ourselves: The library will function correctly as long as user-supplied operations meet the standard library's basic requirements (§E.2). In particular, no exception thrown by a standard container operation will cause memory leaks from containers or leave a container in an invalid state. Thus, the problem for the library user becomes: How can I define my types so that they don't cause undefined behavior or leak resources?

The basic rules are:

[1] When updating an object, don't destroy its old representation before a new representation is completely constructed and can replace the old one without risk of exceptions. For example, see the implementations of *vector::operator=*( ), *safe_assign*( ), and *vector::push_back*( ) in §E.3.

[2] Before throwing an exception, release every resource acquired that is not owned by some (other) object.

    [2a] The ''resource acquisition is initialization'' technique (§14.4) and the language rule that partially constructed objects are destroyed to the extent that they were constructed (§14.4.1) can be most helpful here. For example, see *leak*( ) in §E.2.

    [2b] The *uninitialized_copy*( ) algorithm and its cousins provide automatic release of resources in case of failure to complete construction of a set of objects (§E.4.4).

[3] Before throwing an exception, make sure that every operand is in a valid state. That is, leave each object in a state that allows it to be accessed and destroyed without causing undefined behavior or an exception to be thrown from a destructor. For example, see *vector*'s assignment in §E.3.2.

    [3a] Note that constructors are special in that when an exception is thrown from a constructor, no object is left behind to be destroyed later. This implies that we don't have to establish an invariant and that we must be sure to release all resources acquired during a failed construction before throwing an exception.

    [3b] Note that destructors are special in that an exception thrown from a destructor almost certainly leads to violation of invariants and/or calls to *terminate*( ).

In practice, it can be surprisingly difficult to follow these rules. The primary reason is that exceptions can be thrown from places where people don't expect them. A good example is *std::bad_alloc*. Every function that directly or indirectly uses *new* or an *allocator* to acquire memory can throw *bad_alloc*. In some programs, we can solve this particular problem by not running out of memory. However, for programs that are meant to run for a long time or to accept arbitrary amounts of input, we must expect to handle various failures to acquire resources. Thus, we must assume every function capable of throwing an exception until we have proved otherwise.

One simple way to try to avoid surprises is to use containers of elements that do not throw exceptions (such as containers of pointers and containers of simple concrete types) or linked containers (such as *list*) that provide the strong guarantee (§E.4). Another, complementary, approach is to rely primarily on operations, such as *push_back*( ), that offer the strong guarantee that an operation either succeeds or has no effect (§E.2). However, these approaches are by themselves insufficient to avoid resource leaks and can lead to an ad hoc, overly restrictive, and pessimistic approach to error handling and recovery. For example, a *vector<T*>* is trivially exception safe if operations on *T* don't throw exceptions. However, unless the objects pointed to are deleted somewhere, an exception from the *vector* will lead to a resource leak. Thus, introducing a *Handle* class to deal with deallocation (§25.7) and using *vector*<Handle<T> > rather than the plain *vector<T*>* will probably improve the resilience of the code.

When writing new code, it is possible to take a more systematic approach and make sure that every resource is represented by a class with an invariant that provides the basic guarantee (§E.2). Given that, it becomes feasible to identify the critical objects in an application and provide roll-back semantics (that is, the strong guarantee – possibly under some specific conditions) for operations on such objects.

Most applications contain data structures and code that are not written with exception safety in mind. Where necessary, such code can be fitted into an exception-safe framework by either verifying that it doesn't throw exception (as was the case for the C standard library; §E.5.5) or through the use of interface classes for which the exception behavior and resource management can be precisely specified.

When designing types intended for use in an exception-safe environment, we must pay special attention to the operations used by the standard library: constructors, destructors, assignments, comparisons, swap functions, functions used as predicates, and operations on iterators. This is best done by defining a class invariant that can be simply established by all constructors. Sometimes, we must design our class invariants so that we can put an object into a state where it can be destroyed even when an operation suffers a failure at an ''inconvenient'' point. Ideally, that state isn't an artifact defined simply to aid exception handling, but a state that follows naturally from the semantics of the type (§E.3.5).

When considering exception safety, the emphasis should be on defining valid states for objects (invariants) and on proper release of resources. It is therefore important to represent resources directly as classes. The *vector_base* (§E.3.2) is a simple example of this. The constructors for such resource classes acquire lower-level resources (such as the raw memory for *vector_base*) and establish invariants (such as the proper initialization of the pointers of a *vector_base*). The destructors of such classes implicitly free lower-level resources. The rules for partial construction (§14.4.1) and the ''resource acquisition is initialization'' technique (§14.4) support this way of handling resources.

A well-written constructor establishes the class invariant for an object (§24.3.7.1). That is, the constructor gives the object a value that allows subsequent operations to be written simply and to complete successfully. This implies that a constructor often needs to acquire resources. If that cannot be done, the constructor can throw an exception so that we can deal with that problem before an object is created. This approach is directly supported by the language and the standard library (§E.3.5).

The requirement to release resources and to place operands in valid states before throwing an exception means that the burden of exception handling is shared among the function throwing, the functions on the call chain to the handler, and the handler. Throwing an exception does not make handling an error ''somebody else's problem.'' It is the obligation of functions throwing or passing along an exception to release resources that they own and to put operands in consistent states. Unless they do that, an exception handler can do little more than try to terminate gracefully.

E.7 Advice

[1] Be clear about what degree of exception safety you want; §E.2.

[2] Exception safety should be part of an overall strategy for fault tolerance; §E.2.

[3] Provide the basic guarantee for all classes. That is, maintain an invariant, and don't leak resources; §E.2, §E.3.2, §E.4.

[4] Where possible and affordable, provide the strong guarantee that an operation either succeeds or leaves all operands unchanged; §E.2, §E.3.

[5] Don't throw an exception from a destructor; §E.2, §E.3.2, §E.4.

[6] Don't throw an exception from an iterator navigating a valid sequence; §E.4.1, §E.4.4.

[7] Exception safety involves careful examination of individual operations; §E.3.

[8] Design templates to be transparent to exceptions; §E.3.1.

[9] Prefer the constructor approach to resource requisition to using *init* ( ) functions; §E.3.5.

[10] Define an invariant for a class to make it clear what is a valid state; §E.2, §E.6.

[11] Make sure that an object can always be put into a valid state without fear of an exception being thrown; §E.3.2, §E.6.

[12] Keep invariants simple; §E.3.5.

[13] Leave all operands in valid states before throwing an exception; §E.2, §E.6.

[14] Avoid resource leaks; §E.2, §E.3.1, §E.6.

[15] Represent resources directly; §E.3.2, §E.6.

[16] Remember that *swap* ( ) can sometimes be an alternative to copying elements; §E.3.3.

[17] Where possible, rely on ordering of operations rather than on explicit use of *try-blocks*; §E.3.4.

[18] Don't destroy ''old'' information until its replacement has been safely produced; §E.3.3, §E.6.

[19] Rely on the ''resource acquisition is initialization'' technique; §E.3, §E.3.2, §E.6.

[20] Make sure that comparison operations for associative containers can be copied; §E.3.3.

[21] Identify critical data structures and provide them with operations that provide the strong guarantee; §E.6

E.8 Exercises

1. (∗1) List all exceptions that could possibly be thrown from *f* ( ) in §E.1.

2. (∗1) Answer the questions after the example in §E.1.

3. (∗1) Define a class *Tester* that occasionally throws exceptions from basic operations, such as copy constructors. Use *Tester* to test your standard-library containers.

4. (∗1) Find the error in the ''messy'' version of *vector*'s constructor (§E.3.1), and write a program to get it to crash. Hint: First implement *vector*'s destructor.

5. (∗2) Implement a simple list providing the basic guarantee. Be very specific about what the list requires of its users to provide the guarantee.

6. (∗3) Implement a simple list providing the strong guarantee. Carefully test this list. Give an argument why people should believe it to be safe.

7. (∗2.5) Reimplement *String* from §11.12 to be as safe as a standard container.

8. (∗2) Compare the run time of the various versions of *vector*'s assignment and

safe_assign ( ) (§E.3.3).

9. (∗1.5) Copy an allocator without using an assignment operator (as needed to improve *operator*= ( ) in §E.3.3).

10. (∗2) Add single-element and multiple-element *erase* ( ) and *insert* ( ) that provide the basic guarantee to *vector* (§E.3.2).

11. (∗2) Add single-element and multiple-element *erase* ( ) and *insert* ( ) that provide the strong guarantee to *vector* (§E.3.2). Compare the cost and complexity of these solutions to the solutions to exercise 10.

12. (∗2) Write a *safe_insert* ( ) (§E.4.2) that inserts elements into the existing *vector* (rather than copying to a temporary). What constraints do you have to impose on operations?

13. (∗2) Write a *safe_insert* ( ) (§E.4.2) that inserts elements into the existing *map* (rather than copying to a temporary). What constraints do you have to impose on operations?

14. (∗2.5) Compare the size, complexity, and performance of the *safe_insert* ( ) functions from exercises 12 and 13 to the *safe_insert* ( ) from §E.4.2.

15. (∗2.5) Write a better (simpler and faster) *safe_insert* ( ) for associative containers only. Use traits to write a *safe_insert* ( ) that automatically selects the optimal *safe_insert* ( ) for a container. Hint: §19.2.3.

16. (∗2.5) Try to rewrite *uninitialized_fill* ( ) (§19.4.4, §E.3.1) to handle destructors that throw exceptions. Is that possible? If so, at what cost? If not, why not?

17. (∗2.5) Try to rewrite *uninitialized_fill* ( ) (§19.4.4, §E.3.1) to handle iterators that throw exceptions for ++ and −−. Is that possible? If so, at what cost? If not, why not?

18. (∗3) Take a container from a library different from the standard library. Examine its documentation to see what exception-safety guarantees it provides. Do some tests to see how resilient it is against exceptions thrown by memory allocation and user-supplied code. Compare it to a corresponding standard-library container.

19. (∗3) Try to optimize the *vector* from §E.3 by disregarding the possibility of exceptions. For example, remove all *try-block*s. Compare the performance against the version from §E.3 and against a standard-library *vector* implementation. Also, compare the size and the complexity of the source code of these different *vector*s.

20. (∗1) Define invariants for *vector* (§E.3) with and without the possibility of *v==0* (§E.3.5) .

21. (∗2.5) Read the source of an implementation of *vector*. What guarantees are implemented for assignment, multi-element *insert* ( ) , and *resize* ( ) ?

22. (∗3) Write a version of *hash_map* (§17.6) that is as safe as a standard container.

I

Index

Knowledge is of two kinds.
We know a subject ourselves,
or we know where
we can find information on it.
– Samuel Johnson

`## ` 162
`** ` 263
`-1 ` 831
`<> ` 855
16-bit character 580
8-bit `char` 580
`'`
    and `[]` 838
    operator 123
    predefined 264
    prohibiting 264
`!`
    `basic_ios` 616
    `logical_not` 516
    `valarray` 664
`!=`
    `bitset` 494
    `complex` 680
    generated 468
    iterator 551
    not equal operator 24
    `not_equal_to` 516
    `string` 591
    `valarray` 667
`#` preprocessing directive 813
`$` character 81

`%`
    format character 652
    modulus 517
    modulus operator 24
    `valarray` 667
`%:` digraph 829
`%:%:` digraph 829
`%=, valarray` 664
`%>` digraph 829
`&`
    `bitset` 495
    bitwise and operator 124
    predefined 264
    prohibiting 264
    reference 97
    `valarray` 667
`&&`
    logical and operator 123
    `logical_and` 516
    `valarray` 667
`&=`
    of `bitset` 494
    `valarray` 664
`'`, character literal 73
`()` and initializer 84
`*`

and [], -> and 290
`complex` 680
`iterator` 551
`multiplies` 517
`multiply` operator 24
`valarray` 667
`*/` end of comment 27
`*=`
    `complex` 679
    `valarray` 664
`+`
    `complex` 680
    `iterator` 551
    `plus` 517
    plus operator 24
    `string` 593
    user-defined operator 265, 281
    `valarray` 667
`++`
    increment operator 125
    `iterator` 551
    user-defined operator 264, 291
`+=`
    `advance()` and 551
    `complex` 679
    `iterator` 551
    operator 109
    `string` 592
    user-defined operator 264, 268, 281
    `valarray` 664
`-`
    `complex` 680
    `distance()` and 551, 554
    `iterator` 551
    `minus` 517
    minus operator 24
    `negate` 517
    `valarray` 664, 667
`--`
    decrement operator 125
    `iterator` 551
    user-defined operator 291
`-=`
    `complex` 679
    `iterator` 551
    operator 109
    `valarray` 664
`->`
    and `*` and [] 290
    `iterator` 551
    member access operator 102
    user-defined operator 289
`->*`
    operator 853
    pointer to member 418
`.`

floating-point 74
    member access operator 101
`.*`
    operator 853
    pointer to member 418
`...`, ellipsis 154
`/`
    `complex` 680
    divide operator 24
    `divides` 517
    `valarray` 667
`/*`
    comment 161
    start of comment 27
`//`
    comment 10
    difference from C 816
`/=`
    `complex` 679
    `valarray` 664
`:`
    arithmetic-if `?` 134
    bit field 840
    derived class 303
    label 132
`::`
    and `virtual` function, operator 312
    explicit qualification 847
    namespace and 169
    operator 305
    scope resolution operator 82, 228
`::*`, pointer to member 418
`:>` digraph 829
`;`, semicolon 79, 101, 132
`<`
    comparison 467
    `iterator` 551
    `less` 516
    less than operator 24
    `string` 591
    template syntax 811
    `valarray` 667
    `vector` 457
`<%` digraph 829
`<:` digraph 829
`<<`
    `bitset` 494–495
    `char` 610
    `complex` 612, 680
    example, `Season` 884, 931
    exception and 896
    for output why 607
    inserter 608
    `money_put` and 902
    `num_put` and 895
    `ostream` 609

output 46
output operator 607
pointer to function 631
precedence 608
put to 607
streambuf 642
string 598
time_put and 915
valarray 667
virtual 612
<<=
    of bitset 494
    valarray 664
<=
    generated 468
    iterator 551
    less than or equal operator 24
    less_equal 516
    string 591
    valarray 667
<>, template 341, 344
=
    generated 284
    inheritance and 307
    map 484
    predefined 264
    prohibiting 264
    string 587
    user-defined operator 281
    valarray 663
    vector 447
==
    bitset 494
    complex 680
    equal operator 24
    equal_to 516
    equality without 468
    iterator 551
    string 591
    user-defined 534
    valarray 667
    vector 457
>
    and >> 812
    generated 468
    greater 516
    greater than operator 24
    iterator 551
    string 591
    valarray 667
>=
    generated 468
    greater than or equal operator 24
    greater_equal 516
    iterator 551
    string 591

valarray 667
>>
    > and 812
    bitset 494–495
    char 615
    complex 621, 680
    example, Season 884, 931
    extractor 608
    get from 607
    input cin 50, 112
    istream 614
    money_get and 904
    num_get and 897
    pointer to function 632
    string 598
    time_get and 912, 916
    valarray 667
>>=
    of bitset 494
    valarray 664
? :, arithmetic-if 134
?:, operator 134
[ ]
    , and 838
    -> and * and 290
    and insert() 488
    bitset 494
    design of 295
    iterator 551
    map 482
    of vector 445
    on string 584
    valarray 663
\
    backslash 830
    escape character 73, 830
\', single quote 830
^
    bitset 495
    bitwise exclusive or operator 124
    valarray 667
^=
    of bitset 494
    valarray 664
_ character 81
|
    bitset 495
    bitwise or operator 124
    valarray 667
|=
    of bitset 494
    valarray 664
||
    logical or operator 123
    logical_or 516
    valarray 667

~
    and destructor 243
    `bitset` 494
    bitwise complement operator 124
    `valarray` 664
0
    constant-expression 835
    `false` and 71
    null pointer 835
    `string` and 587
    zero null 88
−1 and `size_t` 448
1, `true` and 71

A

Aarhus 536
`abort()` 218, 380
`abs()` 660–661, 680
    `valarray` 667
abstract
    and concrete type 771
    `class` 708
    class 313
    class and design 318
    class, class hierarchy and 324
    iterator 435
    node `class` 774
    type 34, 767, 769
abstraction
    classes and 733
    data 30
    late 437
    levels of 733
access 278
    checked 445
    control 225, 402
    control and base class 405
    control and multiple-inheritance 406
    control, cast and 414
    control, run-time 785
    control, *using-declaration* and 407
    element 445
    operator, design of 295
    to base 850
    to `facet` 882
    to member 849
    to member `class` 851
    unchecked 445
`accumulate()` 682
`acos()`, `valarray` 667
acquisition
    constructor and resource 950, 966
    delayed resource 953
    resource 364
action 776

Ada 10, 725
adapter
    container 469
    member function 520
    pointer to function 521
    sequence 469
add element to sequence 529
adding
    facet to `locale` 877
    to container 555
    to sequence 555
    to standard library 434
address of element 454
addressing, unit of 88
`adjacent_difference()` 684
`adjacent_find()` 525
`adjustfield` 626, 630
adoption of C++, gradual 718
`advance()` and += 551
aggregate
    array 101
    `struct` 101
aims
    and means 694
    design 700
Algol68 10
algorithm 56
    C-style function and 522
    and exception 963
    and member function 520
    and polymorphic object 63
    and polymorphism 520
    and sequence 508
    and `string` 584
    container and 507
    conventions 508
    design 510
    exception and 566
    generalized numeric 682
    generic 41
    modifying sequence 529
    nonmodifying sequence 523
    on array 544
    return value 508
    summary 509
`<algorithm>` 432, 509
algorithms, standard library 64
alias
    namespace 178
    re-open, namespace 185
alignment 102
all, `catch` 362
allocate array 128
`allocate()` 567
allocation
    C-style 577

and deallocation 127
 static 843
 unit of 88
allocator 567
 Pool_alloc 572
 copy of 941
 general 573
 nothrow 823
 use of 568
 user-defined 570
allocator, default 567
allocator_type 443, 480
alternative
 design 710
 error handling 192, 355
 implementation 320
 interface 173
 return 357
 to macro 161
always_noconv(), codecvt 927
ambiguity
 dynamic_cast and 412
 resolution, multiple-inheritance 391
ambiguous
 date 920
 type conversion 276
ambition 693
analogy
 bridge 724
 car factory 698
 plug 728
 proof by 692
 units 728
analysis
 design and 696
 error 711
 experimentation and 710
 method, choosing an 696
 stage 697
and
 keyword 829
 operator &, bitwise 124
 operator &&, logical 123
and_eq keyword 829
Annemarie 92
anomaly, constructor and destructor 245
anonymous union 841
ANSI
 C 13
 C++ 11
any() 494
app append to file 639
append to file, app 639
append(), string 592
application
 framework 731, 786

operator 287
apply(), valarray 664
architecture 696
arg() 680
argc, main() argv 117
argument
 array 147
 command line 117
 deducing template 335, 856
 default 153
 dependency on template 861
 explicit template 335
 function template 335
 passing, function 145, 283
 reference 98
 template 331
 type check, function 145
 type conversion, function 145
 type, difference from C 817
 types, virtual function 310
 undeclared 154
 value, example of default 227
 variable number of 154
argv argc, main() 117
arithmetic
 conversions, usual 122, 836
 function object 517
 mixed-mode 268
 operator 24
 pointer 88, 93, 125
 type 70
 vector 65, 662
arithmetic-if ? : 134
array 26, 88
 aggregate 101
 algorithm on 544
 allocate 128
 argument 147
 array of 837
 as container 496
 assignment 92
 associative 286, 480
 by string, initialization of 89
 deallocate 128
 delete 250
 element, constructor for 250
 element object 244
 exception and 962
 initializer 89
 initializer, difference from C 818
 layout 669
 multidimensional 668, 677, 836
 new and 423
 numeric 662
 of array 837
 of objects 250

passing multidimensional 839
pointer and 91, 147
string and 589
valarray and 663
valarray and vector and 662
ASCII 580, 829
    character set 73, 601
asctime() 906
asin() 660
    valarray 667
asm assembler 806
assembler 8, 11
    asm 806
Assert() 750
assert() 750
<assert.h> 432
assertion checking 750
assign()
    char_traits 581
    string 588
    vector 447
assignment
    and initialization 283
    and template, copy 348
    array 92
    copy 246, 283
    derived 307
    function call and 99
    inheritance and 307
    map 484
    of class object 245
    of istream 609
    of ostream 609
    operator 110, 268
    string 587
    to self 246, 945
    valarray 663
Assoc example 286
associative
    array 286, 480
    array – see map
    container 480
    container and exception 955
    container, sequence and 461
associativity of operator 121
asynchronous event 357
at() 53
    on string 585
    on vector 445
    out_of_range and 385
atan() 660
    valarray 667
atan2() 660
    valarray 667
ate 639
atexit()

and destructor 218
and exception 382
atof() 600
atoi() 589, 600
atol() 600
AT&T Bell Laboratories 11
auto 843
automatic
    garbage collection 247, 844
    memory 843
    memory management 844
    object 244
auto_ptr 367

B

\b, backspace 830
back() 446
    of queue 476
back_inserter() 57, 555
back_insert_iterator 555
backslash \ 830
backspace \b 830
bad() 616
bad_alloc 129
    and new 384
    exception 576, 965
    missing 823
badbit 617
bad_cast 410, 882
    and dynamic_cast 384
bad_exception 378, 384
bad_typeid and typeid() 384
balance 695
base
    access to 850
    and derived class 39, 737
    class 303
    class, access control and 405
    class, initialization of 306
    class, override from virtual 401
    class, private 743
    class, private member of 305
    class, protected 743
    class, replicated 394
    class, universal 438
    class, virtual 396
    member or 740
    override private 738
    private 405, 742
    protected 319, 405
base() 565
based container 438
basefield 626–627
Basic 725
basic guarantee 937

basic_filebuf, class 648
basic_ifstream 638
basic_ios 608, 616, 622, 629
   ! 616
   format state 606
   stream state 606
basic_iostream 637
   formatting 606
basic_istream 613
basic_istringstream 640
basic_ofstream 638
basic_ostream 608–609
basic_ostringstream 640
basic_streambuf 645
   buffering 606
basic_string 582
   begin() 584
   const_iterator 583
   const_pointer 583
   const_reference 583
   const_reverse_iterator 583
   difference_type 583
   end() 584
   iterator 583
   member type 582
   pointer 583
   rbegin() 584
   reference 583
   rend() 584
   reverse_iterator 583
   size_type 583
   traits_type 583
   value_type 583
basic_stringstream 640
BCPL 10
before() 415
beg, seekdir and
begin() 54, 481
   basic_string 584
   iterator 444
behavior, undefined 828
Bell Laboratories, AT&T 11
Bi 511
bibliography, design 719
bidirectional iterator 550
bidirectional_iterator_tag 553
big-O notation 464
binary
   mode, binary 639
   operator, user-defined 263
   search 540, 546
binary binary mode 639
binary_function 515
binary_negate 518
   not2() and 522
binary_search() 540

bind1st() 518, 520
bind2nd() 518–519
binder1st 518, 520
binder2nd 518–519
binding
   name 860
   strength, operator 121, 607
BinOp 511
BinPred 511
bit
   field 125
   field : 840
   field, bitset and 492
   pattern 73
   position 492
   reference to 492
   vector 124
bitand keyword 829
bitor keyword 829
bits
   in char 658
   in float 658
   in int 658
<bitset> 431
bitset 492
   != 494
   & 495
   &= of 494
   << 494–495
   <<= of 494
   == 494
   >> 494–495
   >>= of 494
   [] 494
   ^ 495
   ^= of 494
   and bit field 492
   and enum 492
   and set 492
   and vector<bool> 492
   constructor 493
   flip() 494
   input 495
   operation 494
   output 495
   reset() 494
   set() 494
   | 495
   |= of 494
   ~ 494
bitset(), invalid_argument and 385
bitwise
   and operator & 124
   complement operator ~ 124
   exclusive or operator ^ 124
   logical operators 124

or operator | 124
blackboard as design tool 703
BLAS 668
Blixen, Karen 2
Bomb example 939
bool 71
    conversion to 835
    input of 615
    output of 611
    vector of 458
boolalpha 611, 625
boolalpha() 634
break 109, 116
    case and 134
    statement 116
bridge analogy 724
bsearch() 546
    and exception 964
buffer
    memory 575
    ostream and 642
    position in 642
Buffer 331, 335
    example 738
buffering 642
    I/O 645
    basic_streambuf 606
built-in
    feature vs technique 43
    type 70
    type, constructor for 131
    type, input of 614
    type, output of 609
    type, user-defined operator and 265
_byname facet 888
byte 76

C

C
    //, difference from 816
    ANSI 13
    and C++ 7, 14, 199
    and C++ compatibility 13, 816
    and C++ global locale 924
    and C++, learning 7
    and C++ locale 880
    and C++, mixing 719
    and exception 383
    argument type, difference from 817
    array initializer, difference from 818
    declaration and definition, difference from 818
    difference from 816
    enum, difference from 817
    function and exception 382, 964
    function call, difference from 816

function definition, difference from 817
initialization and goto, difference from 818
input and output 651
int implicit, difference from 817
jump past initialization, difference from 818
linkage to 205
locale 875
macro, difference from 818
programmer 14
scope, difference from 816
sizeof, difference from 816
standard library 599
struct name, difference from 818
struct scope, difference from 818
void* assignment, difference from 818
with Classes 10, 686
%c format 653
.c file 202
cache example 232
calculator example 107, 165, 190, 208
call
    by reference 98, 146, 282
    by value 146
    function 145
    of destructor, explicit 256
    operator 287
callback, stream 650
callC() example 384
call_from_C() example 384
calloc() 577
capacity
    of vector, decrease 457
    of vector, increase 456
capacity(), vector 455
car factory analogy 698
Car example 772
card, CRC 703
c_array 496
carriage return \r 830
CASE 711, 725, 730
case and break 134
case-sensitive comparison 591
<cassert> 432
cast
    C-style 131
    and access control 414
    cross 408
    deprecated C-style 819
    down 408
    up 408
casting away const 414
catalog, message 928
catch all 362
catch 186, 361
    all 362
    by reference 360

by value 359
every exception 54
catch(...) 54
category
　facet 887–888
　iterator 553
category, locale 873
<cctype> 432, 601
ceil() 660
cerr 609
　and clog 624
　initialization 637
<cerrno> 432
<cfloat> 433, 660
C++ 21
　ANSI 11
　C and 7, 14, 199
　ISO 11
　compatibility, C and 13, 816
　design of 7, 10
　feature summary 819
　functional decomposition and 726
　gradual adoption of 718
　gradual approach to learning 7
　introducing 718
　large program and 9
　learning 6, 718, 820
　learning C and 7
　library, first 686
　locale, C and 880
　meaning 10
　misuse of 725
　mixing C and 719
　procedural programming and 725
　programmer 14
　pronounciation 10
　properties of 724
　standardization 11
　style subscript 674
　teaching and 12
　use of 12
change 700
　incremental 684
　response to 698
　size of sequence 529
changing
　interface 774
　locale 880
char 73, 76
　8-bit 580
　<< 610
　>> 615
　bits in 658
　character type 71
　get() 620
　input of 615, 618

output of 610
　signed 831
　unsigned 831
char*, specialization and 344
character 580
　$ 81
　%, format 652
　16-bit 580
　\, escape 73, 830
　_ 81
　buffer, streambuf and 642
　classification 920
　classification, convenient 924
　classification, wide 601
　code conversion 925
　encoding, multibyte 925
　in name 81
　literal ' 73
　mask 920
　name, universal 831
　national 829
　representation, converting 925
　set 829
　set, ASCII 73, 601
　set, large 831
　set, restricted 829
　special 830
　string 432
　thousands_sep() separator 893
　traits 580
　type 580
　type char 71
　value of 580
CHAR_BIT 660
char_traits 580
　assign() 581
　char_type 580
　compare() 581
　copy() 581
　eof() 581
　eq() 581
　eq_int_type() 581
　find() 581
　get_state() 581
　int_type() 581
　length() 581
　lt() 581
　move() 581
　not_eof() 581
　off_type 581
　pos_type 581
　state_type 581
　to_char_type() 581
　to_int_type() 581
char_traits<char> 580
char_traits<wchar_t> 581

`char_type` 608
    `char_traits` 580
check, range 445, 561
checked
    access 445
    iterator 561
    pointer 291
Checked example 565
`Checked_iter` example 561
checking
    assertion 750
    for wild pointer 722
    invariant 749
    missing 823
    of *exception-specification* 376
    range 275, 781
choosing
    a design method 696
    an analysis method 696
`cin` 614
    >>, input 50, 112
    `cout` and 624
    initialization 637
    value of 276
circle and ellipse 703
class
    :, derived 303
    abstract 313
    and design, abstract 318
    and type 724
    base 303
    `basic_filebuf` 648
    concept and 301
    constructor for derived 306
    conversion of pointer to 304
    derived 15
    destructor for derived 306
    forward reference to 278
    `friend` 279
    function 776
    handle 782
    hierarchy 15, 307, 734
    hierarchy and abstract class 324
    hierarchy and `template` 345
    hierarchy design 314
    hierarchy, reorganization of 707
    initialization of base 306
    interface 778
    member, constructor for 247
    member of derived 304
    member, private 225
    member, public 225
    node 772
    object, assignment of 245
    operations, set of 237
    override from `virtual` base 401

    pointer to 304
    `private` base 743
    `private` member of base 305
    `protected` base 743
    storage 244
    use of 725
`class` 16, 32
    abstract 708
    abstract node 774
    access to member 851
    and concept 223
    base and derived 39, 737
    concrete 236, 241, 766
    concrete node 774
    declaration 225
    definition 225
    `facet` 880
    free-standing 732
    function-like 514
    helper 293
    hierarchy 38, 389
    hierarchy navigation 411
    kind of 765
    lattice 389
    leaf 774
    `locale` 873
    member 293
    `namespace` and 849
    nested 293
    not a 705
    random number 685
    `string` 292
    `struct` and 234
    `template` and 348
    `typename` and 858
    `union` and 843
    universal base 438
    user-defined type 224
classes
    and abstraction 733
    and concepts 732
    and real-world 734
    design and 732
    finding the 702, 734
    stream 637
    use of 733
classic C `locale` 875
`classic()` `locale` 649, 879
classification 703
    character 920
    convenient character 924
cleanup, initialization and 364
clear goal 698
`clear()` 616
    and exception 956
    `failure` and 385

map 487
vector 452
<climits> 433, 660
<clocale> 433, 650
clock and timer 905
Clock example 398
clock() 905
CLOCKS_PER_SEC 905
clock_t 905
clog 609
  cerr and 624
  initialization 637
clone 424
clone() 426
close() 639
  messages 929
closing
  of file 638
  of stream 639
closure 676
cloud example 700
Clu 10
Club_eq 516
<cmath> 434, 660
Cmp 339, 511
Cobol 725
code
  bloat, curbing 342
  exception-safe 943
  uniformity of 767
codecvt
  always_noconv() 927
  encoding() 927
  facet 925
  in() 926
  length() 927
  max_length() 927
  out() 927
  unshift() 927
codecvt_base result 925
coders and designers 695
coercion 267
collaboration, design 708
collate
  compare() 889–890
  do_compare() 889
  do_hash() 889
  do_transform() 889
  facet 889
  hash() 889, 891
  transform() 889, 891
collate_byname 892
collating
  order 891
  sequence 338
collector,

conservative 846
  copying 846
combine() 877
comma and subscripting 838
command line argument 117
comment 138
  */ end of 27
  /* 161
  /* start of 27
  // 10
common
  code and constructor 624
  code and destructor 624
commonality 301
communication 694–695, 717
compare()
  char_traits 581
  collate 889–890
  string 590
comparison
  < 467
  case-sensitive 591
  default 467
  equality and 457
  in map 484
  locale used for string 880
  operator, operator 24
  requirement 467
  string 590
  string 889
  user-supplied 467
compatibility, C and C++ 13, 816
compilation
  separate 27, 198
  template separate 351
  unit of 197
compile time, header and 211
compile-time polymorphism 347
compl keyword 829
complement operator ~, bitwise 124
complete encapsulation 283
complex 64, 267
  != 680
  * 680
  *= 679
  + 680
  += 679
  - 680
  -= 679
  / 680
  /= 679
  << 612, 680
  == 680
  >> 621, 680
  and complex<> 680
  and exception 964

conversion 681
cos() 680
cosh() 680
expr() 680
input 680
log() 680
log10() 680
mathematical functions 680
operations 679
output 680
pow() 680
sin() 680
sinh() 680
sqrt() 680
tanh() 680
complex<>, complex and 680
complexity divide and conquer 693
component 701, 755
    standard 698, 714
composite operator 268
composition, namespace 179, 181
compositor 677
computation, numerical 64
concatenation, string 592–593
concept 15
    and class 301
    class and 223
    independent 327
    locale 869
concepts, classes and 732
concrete
    class 236, 241, 766
    class, derive from 780
    node class 774
    type 33, 236, 766–767
    type, abstract and 771
    type and derivation 768
    type, problems with 37
    type, reuse of 241, 768
condition 753
    declaration in 135
    exception safety 937
conditional expression 134
conj() 680
connection between input and output 623
const 94
    C-style string and 90
    and linkage 199
    and overloading 600
    casting away 414
    function, inspector 706
    iterator 443, 508
    member 249
    member function 229
    physical and logical 231
    pointer 96

pointer to 96
constant
    enumerator as in-class 249
    expression 833
    in-class definition of 249
    member 249
    time 464
constant-expression 0 835
const_cast 131, 232, 414
const_iterator 54, 443, 480
    basic_string 583
const_mem_fun1_ref_t 518, 521
const_mem_fun1_t 518, 521
const_mem_fun_ref_t 518, 521
const_mem_fun_t 518, 521
const_pointer 443
    basic_string 583
const_reference 443, 480
    basic_string 583
const_reverse_iterator 443, 480
    basic_string 583
construct, two-stage 949
construct() 567
construction
    and destruction 244
    and destruction, order of 414
    order of 248, 252
    partial 366, 939
    valarray 662
constructor 32–33, 226, 706
    and C-style initialization 270
    and conversion 272
    and destructor 242, 246–247
    and destructor anomaly 245
    and initializer list 270
    and invariant 949
    and resource acquisition 950, 966
    and template, copy 348
    and type conversion 269, 275
    and union 257
    and virtual base 397
    bitset 493
    common code and 624
    copy 246, 283
    default 243
    default copy 271
    exception and 366–367, 371
    explicit 284
    for array element 250
    for built-in type 131
    for class member 247
    for derived class 306
    for free store object 246
    for global variable 252
    for local variable 245
    generated 284

inheritance and 307
init() and 953
locale 877
map 484
pointer to 424
protected 881
string 585
vector 447
virtual 323, 424
container 40, 52
    STL 441
    Simula-style 438
    Smalltalk-style 438
    adapter 469
    adding to 555
    and algorithm 507
    and exception 953, 955
    and iterator 435, 444
    and polymorphism 520
    array as 496
    associative 480
    based 438
    design 434, 441
    guarantee 953
    implementation of 465
    input into 451
    intrusive 438
    iterator 464
    kind of 461
    memory management 455, 567
    operation on 464
    optimal 435
    representation of 465
    sequence and 512
    standard library 56, 442
    string as 491
    summary 464
    user-defined 497
    valarray as 492
containers, list of 431
containment 738
    and inheritance 740
context
    of template definition 860
    of template instantiation 860
continue 116
    statement 116
contravariance 420
control, format 625
controlled statement 136
convenience
    and orthogonality 431
    vs. safety 847
convenient character classification 924
conventions
    algorithm 508

lexical 794
national 649
conversion 706
    ambiguous type 276
    character code 925
    complex 681
    constructor and 272
    constructor and type 269, 275
    explicit type 130, 284
    floating-point 834
    implicit type 76, 275–276, 281, 284, 833
    integer 834
    of pointer to class 304
    of string, implicit 590
    operator, type 275
    pointer 834
    signed unsigned integer 834
    string 589
    to bool 835
    to floating-point 835
    to integer type 835
    to integral 835
    undefined enum 77
    user-defined 347
    user-defined pointer 349
    user-defined type 267, 281
conversions 747
    usual arithmetic 122, 836
converting character representation 925
cookbook method 692
copy 229, 245, 271
    assignment 246, 283
    assignment and template 348
    constructor 246, 283
    constructor and template 348
    constructor, default 271
    delayed 295
    elimination of 675
    generated 284
    istream 609
    memberwise 283
    of allocator 941
    of exception 362
    ostream 609
    requirement 466
copy() 42, 529, 589
    char_traits 581
_copy suffix 533
copy_backward() 529
copyfmt() 627
    copyfmt_event 651
copyfmt_event, copyfmt() 651
copy_if() not standard 530
copy-on-write 295
cos() 660
    complex 680

valarray 667
cosh() 660
    complex 680
    valarray 667
cost of exception 381
count() 57, 494, 526
    in map 485
count_if() 62, 526
counting, reference 783
coupling, efficiency and 768
cout 609
    and cin 624
    initialization 637
    output 46
covariant return type 424
Cowboy example 778
__cplusplus 206
CRC card 703
create dependency 745
creation
    localization of object 322
    object 242
criteria
    sorting 534
    standard library 430
cross cast 408
<csetjmp> 433
cshift() 664
<csignal> 433
<cstdarg> 433
<cstdio> 202, 432
<cstdlib> 219, 432, 434, 546, 577, 600, 661
c_str() 589
<cstring> 432, 577, 599
C-style
    allocation 577
    cast 131
    cast, deprecated 819
    error handling 661
    function and algorithm 522
    initialization, constructor and 270
    string and const 90
    string, string and 579, 589
<ctime> 431, 433, 906
ctype
    facet 921
    is() 922
    narrow() 923
    scan_is() 922
    scan_not() 922
    tolower() 923
    toupper() 922
    widen() 923
ctype_base 920
<ctype.h> 432, 601
cultural preference, locale 869

cur, seekdir and
curbing code bloat 342
currency
    symbol, international 900
    symbol, local 900
    symbol, standard 900
curr_symbol(), moneypunct 900
Currying 520
Cvt_to_upper example 927
<cwchar> 432, 887
<cwctype> 432, 601
cycle, development 698

D

%d format 652
Darwin, Charles 690
data
    abstraction 30
    abstraction vs inheritance 727
    member, pointer to 853
    per-object 573
    per-type 573
data() 589
date
    ambiguous 920
    format %x 909
    format of 649
    input of 910
    output of 908
    range 906
Date example 236, 907, 913
Date_format example 914
Date_in example 916
dateorder 911
date_order() 917
DBL_MINEXP 660
deallocate array 128
deallocate() 567
deallocation, allocation and 127
debugging 226
dec 626–627, 634
decimal 73
    output 626
decimal_point() 893
    moneypunct 900
decision, delaying 706
declaration 23, 78–79
    and definition, difference from C 818
    and definition, namespace member 167
    class 225
    friend 279
    function 143
    in condition 135
    in for statement 137
    of member class, forward 293

point of 82
declaration 803
declarations, keeping consistent 201
declarator operator 80
declarator 807
decomposition, functional 725
decrease capacity of `vector` 457
decrement
    increment and 291
    operator `--` 125
deducing `template` argument 335, 856
default
    `allocator` 567
    argument 153
    argument value, example of 227
    comparison 467
    constructor 243
    copy constructor 271
    initializer 83
    `locale` 879
    `template` argument 340, 824
    value 239
    value, supplying 500
`default` 109
`#define` 160
definition 78
    class 225
    context of `template` 860
    difference from C declaration and 818
    function 144
    in-class 235
    `namespace` member declaration and 167
    of constant, in-class 249
    of `virtual` function 310
    point of 861
    using-directive and 180
degrees of exception safety 940
delayed
    copy 295
    resource acquisition 953
delaying decision 706
delegation 290
delete
    element from sequence 529, 534
    from `hash_map` 501
`delete`
    and garbage collection 845
    array 250
    `delete[]` and 250
    operator 127
    size and 421
`delete()`, operator 129, 576
`delete[]` 128
    and `delete` 250
`delete[]()`, operator 423, 576
`delete_ptr()` example 531

`denorm_min()` 659
dependency 15, 702, 706, 724
    create 745
    hardware 828
    inheritance 737
    minimize 173
    on `template` argument 861
    parameterization and 707
    use 745
dependent name 857, 861
deprecated
    C-style cast 819
    feature 818
    non-`const` string literal 819
    `static` 818
`<deque>` 431
deque
    and exception 955
    double-ended queue 474
derivation, concrete type and 768
derive
    from concrete class 780
    without `virtual` 780
derived
    and `friend` 852
    assignment 307
    class 15
    class : 303
    class, base and 39, 737
    class, constructor for 306
    class, destructor for 306
    class, member of 304
    exception 359
design 696
    I/O 605
    abstract class and 318
    aims 700
    algorithm 510
    alternative 710
    and analysis 696
    and classes 732
    and language 724
    and language, gap between 725
    and programming 692
    bibliography 719
    class hierarchy 314
    collaboration 708
    container 434, 441
    criteria, `locale` 872
    error 711
    for testing 712
    how to start a 708
    hybrid 718
    inheritance and 707
    integrity of 716
    language and programming language 730

method 694
method, choosing a 696
object-oriented 692, 726
of C++ 7, 10
of [] 295
of access operator 295
reuse 709
stability of 708
stage 697
standard library 429–430
steps 701
string 579
template in 757
tool, blackboard as 703
tool, presentation as 704
tool, tutorial as 708
tools 711
unit of 755
designers, coders and 695
destroy() 567
destruction
construction and 244
order of construction and 414
destructor 33, 283
and garbage collection 846
and union 257
anomaly, constructor and 245
atexit() and 218
common code and 624
constructor and 242, 246–247
exception and 366, 373
exception safety and 937
explicit call of 256
for derived class 306
virtual 319
˜ and 243
development
cycle 698
process 696
software 692
stage 697
diagnostics 432
diamond-shaped inheritance 399
dictionary 480
– see map
difference
from C 816
from C // 816
from C argument type 817
from C array initializer 818
from C declaration and definition 818
from C enum 817
from C function call 816
from C function definition 817
from C initialization and goto 818
from C int implicit 817

from C jump past initialization 818
from C macro 818
from C scope 816
from C sizeof 816
from C struct name 818
from C struct scope 818
from C void* assignment 818
difference_type 443, 480, 552
basic_string 583
digits 658
digits10 659
digraph
%: 829
%:%: 829
%> 829
:> 829
<% 829
<: 829
direct manipulation 730
directed acyclic graph 308
direction
of seek, seekdir
of seekg()
of seekp()
directive
preprocessing 813
template instantiation 866
discrimination of exception 188
disguised pointer 844
dispatch, double 326
distance() and - 551, 554
distribution
exponential 685
uniform 685
div() 661
divide
and conquer, complexity 693
operator / 24
divides / 517
div_t 661
do statement 114, 137
do_compare(), collate 889
documentation 714–715
do_hash(), collate 889
do_it() example 777
domain error 661
dominance 401
dot product 684
do_transform(), collate 889
double
dispatch 326
quote 830
double 74
long 74
output 626
double-ended queue deque 474

doubly-linked `list` 470
down cast 408
`draw_all()` example 520
Duff's device 141
duplicate key 480, 490
dynamic
 memory 127, 576, 843
 store 34
 type checking 727
 type checking, misuse of 439
`dynamic_cast` 407–408
 and ambiguity 412
 and polymorphism 409
 and `static_cast` 413
 `bad_cast` and 384
 implementation of 409
 to reference 410
 use of 774

E

`%e` format 652
`eatwhite()` 620
`eback()` 645
EDOM 661
efficiency 8, 713
 and coupling 768
 and generality 431
 of operation 464
`egptr()` 645
element
 access 445
 access, `list` 472
 access, map 482
 address of 454
 constructor for array 250
 first 446
 from sequence, delete 529, 534
 last 446
 object, array 244
 requirements for 466
 to sequence, add 529
`#elif` 813
`eliminate_duplicates()` example 534
elimination
 of copy 675
 of programmers 730
 of temporary 675
ellipse, circle and 703
ellipsis ... 154
`#else` 813
`else` 134
emphasis, examples and 5
`Employee` example 302
empty `string` 585
`empty()` 455, 489

`string` 598
encapsulation 754
 complete 283
`encoding()`, `codecvt` 927
end, `seekdir` and
`end()` 54, 481
 `basic_string` 584
 iterator 444
`#endif` 162
`endl` 634
 and `std` 632
`ends` 634
engineering, viewgraph 704
`enum` 76
 and integer 77
 `bitset` and 492
 conversion, undefined 77
 difference from C 817
 member 249
 `sizeof` 78
 user-defined operator and 265
enumeration 76
 `switch` on 77
enumerator 76
 as in-class constant 249
EOF 620, 653
`eof()` 616
 `char_traits` 581
`eofbit` 617
`epptr()` 645
`epsilon()` 659
`eq()`, `char_traits` 581
`eq_int_type()`, `char_traits` 581
equal operator `==` 24
`equal()` 527
equality
 and comparison 457
 `hash_map` 497
 without `==` 468
`equal_range()` 540
 in map 485
`equal_to ==` 516
equivalence, type 104
`Erand` 685
ERANGE 601, 661
`erase()`
 and exception 955
 in `string` 595
 map 487
 `vector` 452
`errno` 383, 601, 661
`<errno.h>` 432
error
 analysis 711
 design 711
 domain 661

exception and 355, 374, 622
    handling 566
    handling 115, 186, 383
    handling, C-style 661
    handling alternative 192, 355
    handling, multilevel 383
    linkage 199
    loop and 523
    range 661
    recovery 566, 966
    reporting 186
    run-time 29, 355
    sequence 512
    state 936
    string 586
#error 813
escape character \ 73, 830
essential operators 283
evaluation
    lazy 707
    order of 122
    short-circuit 123, 134
event
    asynchronous 357
    driven simulation 326
event 651
event_callback 651
example
    (bad), Shape 417
    Assoc 286
    Bomb 939
    Buffer 738
    Car 772
    Checked 565
    Checked_iter 561
    Clock 398
    Cowboy 778
    Cvt_to_upper 927
    Date 236, 907, 913
    Date_format 914
    Date_in 916
    Employee 302
    Expr 424
    Extract_officers 524
    Filter 786
    Form 635
    Hello, world! 46
    Io_obj 774
    Ival_box 315, 407
    Lock_ptr 366
    Math_container 346
    Matrix 282
    Money 898
    My_messages 929
    My_money_io 901
    My_punct 893
    Object 417
    Plane 729
    Pool 570
    Range 781
    Rational 747
    Saab 728
    Safe 937
    Season 883
    Season << 884, 931
    Season >> 884, 931
    Set 769
    Set_controller 785
    Shape 774
    Slice_iter 670
    Stack 27
    Storable 396
    String 328
    String_numput 895
    Substring 596
    Table 243
    Tiny 275
    Unsafe 937
    Vector 341, 780
    Vehicle 734
    Window 398
    cache 232
    calculator 107, 165, 190, 208
    callC() 384
    call_from_C() 384
    cloud 700
    delete_ptr() 531
    do_it() 777
    draw_all() 520
    eliminate_duplicates() 534
    identity() 531
    iocopy() 617
    iosbase::Init 639
    iseq() 513
    member template 349
    of default argument value 227
    of input 114
    of operator overloading 292
    of reference 292
    of user-defined memory management 292
    of virtual function 646
    oseq() 556
    scrollbar 743
    sort() 158, 334
    update() 957
examples and emphasis 5
exception 29, 186, 355, 357
    C and 383
    C function and 382, 964
    I/O 622
    I/O stream and 963
    algorithm and 963

and << 896
and algorithm 566
and array 962
and constructor 366–367, 371
and destructor 366, 373
and error 355, 374, 622
and function 375
and interface 375
and invariant 949
and main() 54
and member 366, 939
and member initialization 373
and multiple inheritance 360
and new 367, 369
and recursive function 374
and sub-object 366, 939
and undefined behavior 938
associative container and 955
atexit() and 382
bad_alloc 576, 965
bsearch() and 964
catch every 54
clear() and 956
complex and 964
container and 953, 955
copy of 362
cost of 381
deque and 955
derived 359
discrimination of 188
erase() and 955
goto and 137
grouping 358
guarantee 937
guarantee summary 956
handler 812
handling 966
initialization and 960
insert() and 955
invariant and 936
iostream and 963
istream and 963
iterator and 961
list and 955
map and 955
mapping 378
new and 576
ostream and 963
pointer and 961
pop_back() and 955
pop_front() and 955
predicate and 962
push_back() and 955
push_front() and 955
qsort() and 382, 964
reference and 961

remove() and 955
remove_if() and 955
rules for library 965
runtime_error 875
safety 936
safety and destructor 937
safety condition 937
safety, degrees of 940
safety, techniques for 940
sort() and 955
splice() and 955
standard 384
standard library and 935, 962
string and 963
swap() and 956, 960
transparency 943
type of 379
uncaught 380
unexpected 377
uninitialized_copy() and 960, 963
uninitialized_fill() and 960, 963
uninitialized_fill_n() and 960, 963
unique() and 955
valarray and 964
vector and 955
<exception> 379–380, 384–385, 433
exception hierarchy 385
exceptions() 622, 896
exception-safe code 943
exception-specification 375
  checking of 376
exclusive or operator ^, bitwise 124
exhaustion
  free store 129
  memory 965
  resource 369
exit() 116, 218
exp(), valarray 667
experimentation and analysis 710
explicit
  call of destructor 256
  qualification :: 847
  template argument 335
  template instantiation 866
  type conversion 130, 284
explicit constructor 284
exponent, size of 659
exponential distribution 685
exponentiation, vector 667
export 205, 351
Expr example 424
expr() 660
  complex 680
expression
  conditional 134
  constant 833

full 254
expression 798
extended type information 416
extensibility 700
extensible I/O 605
extern 205
extern 198
external linkage 199
Extract_officers example 524
extractor, >> 608

F

%f format 652
\f, formfeed 830
fabs() 660
facet
    Season_io, user-defined 883
    _byname 888
    access to 882
    category 887–888
    class 880
    codecvt 925
    collate 889
    ctype 921
    identifier id 881
    lifetime of 881
    locale and 869, 874
    messages 928
    money_get 903
    money_put 902
    moneypunct 899
    num_get 897
    num_put 894
    numpunct 893
    put() iterator 894
    standard 887
    time_get 911
    time_put 908
    to locale, adding 877
    use of 882
    user-defined 886
facilities, standard library 66, 429
factory 323
fail() 616
failbit 617
failed() 896
failure 709, 716
    output 896
failure and clear() 385
false and 0 71
falsename() 894
fat interface 439, 761
fault tolerance 383
feature
    deprecated 818

summary, C++ 819
vs technique, built-in 43
features, portability and 815
feedback 695, 698
field
    :, bit 840
    bit 125
    output 629–630
    type of 75
fields, order of 75
file
    .c 202
    .h 201
    and stream 637
    closing of 638
    header 27, 201
    input from 637
    mode of 639
    opening of 638
    output to 637
    position in 642
    source 197
filebuf 649
fill() 537, 629
fill_n() 537
Filter example 786
finally 362
find() 57, 525
    char_traits 581
    in map 485
    in string 594
find_end() 528
find_first_not_of() in string 594
find_first_of() 525
    in string 594
find_if() 62, 525
finding the classes 702, 734
find_last() 444
find_last_of() in string 594
fine-grained timer 905
firewall 383
first
    C++ library 686
    element 446
first-time switch 253, 640
fixed 626, 628
fixed() 634
flag manipulation 626
flags() 626
flexibility 700
flip() bitset 494
float 74
    bits in 658
    output 626
float_denorm_style 659
floatfield 626, 628

`<float.h>` 433
floating-point
    . 74
    conversion 834
    conversion to 835
    literal 74
    output 626, 628
    promotion 833
    type 74
`float_round_style` 659
`floor()` 660
`FLT_RADIX` 660
`flush` 634
`flush()` 631, 642
flushing of output 626
`fmod()` 660
For 511
for
    statement 26, 136
    statement, declaration in 137
`for(;;)` 109
`for_each()` 62, 523
Form example 635
formal
    method 711
    model 730
format
    `%G` 653
    `%X` 652
    `%X`, time 909
    `%c` 653
    `%d` 652
    `%e` 652
    `%f` 652
    `%g` 653
    `%i` 652
    `%n` 653
    `%o` 652
    `%p` 653
    `%s` 653
    `%u` 653
    `%x` 652
    `%x`, date 909
    character `%` 652
    control 625
    information, `locale` 606
    modifier, POSIX 909
    number 893
    object 635
    of date 649
    of integer 649
    of monetary amount 898–899
    state 625
    state, `basic_ios` 606
    state, `ios_base` 606
    string 652

formatted output 625
formatting
    `basic_iostream` 606
    in core 641
formfeed \f 830
for-statement initializer 825
Fortran
    style subscript 674
    vector 668
forward
    and output iterator 554
    declaration of member class 293
    iterator 550
    reference to class 278
forwarding function 778, 780
`forward_iterator_tag` 553
foundation operator 706
`frac_digits()`
    monetary 901
    money_punct 899
fragmentation, memory 846
framework, application 731, 786
free
    store 34, 127, 421, 576, 843
    store exhaustion 129
    store object 244
    store object, constructor for 246
`free()` 577
free-standing
    class 732
    function 732
`frexp()` 660
`friend` 16, 278, 852
    and member 265, 280
    class 279
    declaration 279
    derived and 852
    function 279
    of `friend` 852
    `template` and 854
front operation 472
`front()` 446, 472
    of queue 476
`front_inserter()` 555
`front_insert_iterator` 555
`<fstream>` 432, 638
`fstream` 638
full expression 254
function
    adapter, pointer to 521
    and algorithm, C-style 522
    and exception, C 382, 964
    argument passing 145, 283
    argument type check 145
    argument type conversion 145
    argument types, `virtual` 310

body, *try-block* as 54, 373
call 145
call and assignment 99
call, difference from C 816
class 776
const member 229
declaration 143
definition 144
definition, difference from C 817
definition of virtual 310
definition, old-style 817
example of virtual 646
exception and 375
forwarding 778, 780
free-standing 732
friend 279
get() 759
helper 273
higher-order 518
implementation of virtual 36
init() 226, 950
inline 144
inline member 235
inspector const 706
member 224, 238
name, overloaded 149
nested 806
object 287, 514, 776
object, arithmetic 517
only, instantiate used 866
operator :: and virtual 312
pointer to 156
pointer to member 418
pure virtual 313
set() 759
specialization 344
static member 228, 278
template 334
template argument 335
template overloading 336
type of overriding 424
value return 148
value return 283
virtual 310, 390, 706
virtual 15
virtual output 612
virtual template 348
functional
    decomposition 725
    decomposition and C++ 726
<functional> 431, 516–519, 521
function-like class 514
functions, list of operator 262
functor 514
fundamental
    sequence 469

type 23, 70

G

%G format 653
%g format 653
game 685
gap between design and language 725
garbage
    collection, automatic 247, 844
    collection, delete and 845
    collection, destructor and 846
    collector 128, 130
gargantuanism 713
gbump() 645
gcount() 618
general allocator 573
generality
    efficiency and 431
    of sequence 512
    of solution 701
generalized
    numeric algorithm 682
    slice 677
general-purpose programming-language 21
generate() 537
generated
    != 468
    <= 468
    = 284
    > 468
    >= 468
    constructor 284
    copy 284
    specialization 859
generate_n() 537
generator
    random number 537
    type 348
generic
    algorithm 41
    programming 40, 757–758
    programming, template and 327
get
    area 645
    from, >> 607
    position, tellp() 642
get() 618, 643
    char 620
    function 759
    messages 929
    money_get 903
    num_get 897
get_allocator() 457
    from string 598
getchar() 653

get_date() 911
getline() 51, 618
        into string 598
getloc() 646, 650
get_monthname() 911, 917
get_state(), char_traits 581
get_temporary_buffer() 575
get_time() 911
        time_get 911
get_weekday() 911, 917
get_year() 911
global 16
        initialization of 217
        locale, C and C++ 924
        namespace 847
        object 244, 252, 640
        scope 82, 847
        variable 200, 228
        variable, constructor for 252
        variable, use of 111
global() locale 649, 879
gmtime() 906
goal, clear 698
good() 616
goodbit 617
goto
        and exception 137
        and initializer 137
        difference from C initialization and 818
        nonlocal 357
        statement 137
gptr() 645
gradual
        adoption of C++ 718
        approach to learning C++ 7
grammar 793
graph, directed acyclic 308
greater
        than operator > 24
        than or equal operator >= 24
greater > 516
greater_equal >= 516
grouping, exception 358
grouping() 893
        moneypunct 900
growing system 711
gslice 677
gslice_array 677
guarantee
        and tradeoff 957
        basic 937
        container 953
        exception 937
        nothrow 937
        standard 827
        strong 937

summary, exception 956

H

.h
        file 201
        header 821
hack, struct 809
half-open sequence 512
handle
        class 782
        intrusive 783
handle_ioexception() 896
handler, exception 812
handling
        error 566
        exception 966
hardware 75
        dependency 828
has-a 741
has_denorm 659
has_denorm_loss 659
has_facet() 882
hash
        function 502
        function, hash_map 497
        table 497
hash(), collate 889, 891
hashing 502
hash_map 497
        delete from 501
        equality 497
        hash function 497
        lookup 500
        representation 498
        resize() 502
has_infinity 659
has_quiet_NaN 659
has_signaling_NaN 659
header 117, 201
        .h 821
        and compile time 211
        file 27, 201
        standard library 202, 431
heap 34, 543, 576
        and priority_queue 543
        memory 843
        store 127
heap, priority_queue and 479
Hello, world! example 46
helper
        class 293
        function 273
        function and namespace 240
hex 626–627, 634
hexadecimal 73

output 626
hiding
    information 27
    name 82
hierarchy 732
    class 38, 389
    class 15, 307, 734
    design, class 314
    exception 385
    interface 708
    navigation, class 411
    object 739, 748
    reorganization of class 707
    stream 637
    traditional 315
higher-order function 518
high-level language 7
Histogram 455
horizontal tab \t 830
how to start a design 708
human activity, programming as a 693
hybrid design 718

I

%i format 652
id, facet identifier 881
ideas, real-world as source of 734
identifier 81
    id, facet 881
    meaning of 857
identity() example 531
IEC-559, is_iec559 659
#if 813
if
    statement 133
    switch and 134
_if suffix 525
#ifdef 162
#ifndef 216
ifstream 638
ignore() 618
imag() 679–680
imbue() 644, 647, 650, 880
    imbue_event 651
    iostream locale 871
imbue_event, imbue() 651
immutable, locale is 879
implementation
    alternative 320
    and interface 317
    dependency type of integer literal 832
    inheritance 400, 743
    interface and 224, 314, 399, 758, 771
    iterator 59
    of I/O 606

of RTTI 409
of container 465
of dynamic_cast 409
of virtual function 36
pre-standard 820
priority_queue 478
stack 475–476
stage 697
implementation-defined 827
implicit
    conversion of string 590
    type conversion 76, 275–276, 281, 284, 833
implicit_cast 335
in core formatting 641
In 511
in open for reading 639
in(), codecvt 926
in_avail() 644, 646
in-class
    constant, enumerator as 249
    definition 235
    definition of constant 249
    initializer 249
#include guard 216
include directory, standard 201
#include 27, 117, 183, 201
includes() 542
inclusion, template 350
increase
    capacity of vector 456
    size of vector 455
increment
    and decrement 291
    operator ++ 125
incremental change 684
indentation 138
independent concept 327
index 454
indirect_array 679
indirection 290
individual 716
inertia, organizational 713
infinity() 659
information hiding 27
inheritance 39, 303, 307, 703
    and = 307
    and assignment 307
    and constructor 307
    and design 707
    and template 349
    containment and 740
    data abstraction vs 727
    dependency 737
    diamond-shaped 399
    implementation 400, 743
    interface 400, 743

multiple 308, 390, 735
  template and 347
  using multiple 399
  using-declaration and 392
  using-directive and 392
init()
  and constructor 953
  function 226, 950
initial locale 879
initialization 79, 83, 226, 244
  and cleanup 364
  and exception 960
  and goto, difference from C 818
  assignment and 283
  cerr 637
  cin 637
  clog 637
  constructor and C-style 270
  cout 637
  difference from C jump past 818
  library 640
  main() and 217
  member 248
  of array by string 89
  of base class 306
  of global 217
  of reference 98
  of structure 102
  order of member 247
  reference member 244, 250
  resource acquisition is 366
  run-time 217
initializer
  () and 84
  array 89
  default 83
  for-statement 825
  goto and 137
  in-class 249
  list, constructor and 270
  member 247
initiative 695
inline
  and linkage 199
  function 144
  member function 235
inner product 684
inner_product() 683
innovation 717
inplace_merge() 541
input
  and output 432, 605
  and output, C 651
  and output, connection between 623
  bitset 495
  cin >> 50, 112

complex 680
  example of 114
  from file 637
  into container 451
  into vector 451
  iterator 550
  manipulator 632
  of bool 615
  of built-in type 614
  of char 615, 618
  of date 910
  of monetary amount 903
  of numeric value 897
  of pointer 615
  of time 910
  of user-defined type 621
  sequence 513
  string 598
  unbuffered 642
  unformatted 618
  valarray 668
  width() of 616
input_iterator_tag 553
insert() 55
  [] and 488
  and exception 955
  list 958
  map 487, 958
  multiple-element 959
  string 592
  vector 452, 958
inserter, << 608
inserter() 555
insertion, overwriting vs 555
insert_iterator 555
inspector const function 706
inspiration 734
instantiate used function only 866
instantiation
  context of template 860
  directive, template 866
  explicit template 866
  multiple 867
  point of 863
  template 859
int 73, 76
  bits in 658
  implicit, difference from C 817
  largest 658
  output bits of 495
  smallest 658
integer
  conversion 834
  conversion, signed unsigned 834
  enum and 77
  format of 649

literal 73, 76
literal, implementation dependency type of 832
literal, type of 832
output 627
type 70, 73
type, conversion to 835
integral
    conversion to 835
    promotion 833
    type 70
integration 728
integrity of design 716
interface
    alternative 173
    and implementation 224, 314, 399, 758, 771
    changing 774
    class 778
    exception and 375
    fat 439, 761
    hierarchy 708
    implementation and 317
    inheritance 400, 743
    module and 165
    multiple 172
    public and protected 645
    specifying 707
internal
    linkage 199
    structure 694
internal 625, 630
internal() 634
international currency symbol 900
internationalization, approaches to 870
INT_MAX 660
introducing C++ 718
intrusive
    container 438
    handle 783
int_type 608
int_type(), char_traits 581
invalid iterator 454, 501, 550
invalid_argument and bitset() 385
invariant 748
    and exception 936
    and simplicity 949
    checking 749
    constructor and 949
    exception and 949
    simple 951
I/O 47, 50
    buffering 645
    design 605
    exception 622
    extensible 605
    implementation of 606
    iterator and 60

object 774
    sentry 624
    stream and exception 963
    system, organization of 606
    type safe 607
    unbuffered 647
    wide character 608
iocopy() example 617
<iomanip> 432, 633
Io_obj example 774
<ios> 432, 608
ios 625, 822
ios_base 626, 628–629, 650
    format state 606
iosbase::Init example 639
<iosfwd> 432, 607
iostate 617, 822
io_state 822
<iostream> 46, 432, 609, 614
    <istream> and 613
    <ostream> and 608
iostream 637
    and exception 963
    locale and 886
    locale, imbue() 871
    locale in 874
    sentry 624
is(), ctype 922
is-a 741
isalnum() 601
    and locale 924
isalpha() 113, 601
    and locale 924
is_bounded 659
iscntrl() 601
    and locale 924
isdigit() 601, 917
    and locale 924
Iseq 513
iseq() example 513
is_exact 659
isgraph() 601
    and locale 924
is_iec559 IEC-559 659
is_integer 658
islower() 601
    and locale 924
is_modulo 659
ISO C++ 11
ISO-14882 11
ISO-4217 900
ISO-646 829
isprint() 601
    and locale 924
ispunct() and locale 924
is_signed 658

isspace and locale 924
isspace() 601, 615
    whitespace 114
is_specialized 658
<istream> 432
    and <iostream> 613
istream 614, 643
    >> 614
    and exception 963
    and iterator 559
    assignment of 609
    copy 609
istreambuf_iterator 559
istream_iterator 60, 559
istringstream 641
istrstream 641, 656
isupper() 601
    and locale 924
isxdigit() 601
    and locale 924
iterator 57, 549
    != 551
    * 551
    + 551
    ++ 551
    += 551
    - 551
    -- 551
    -= 551
    -> 551
    < 551
    <= 551
    == 551
    > 551
    >= 551
    STL 441
    [] 551
    abstract 435
    and I/O 60
    and exception 961
    and sequence 550
    begin() 444
    bidirectional 550
    category 553
    checked 561
    const 443, 508
    container 464
    container and 435, 444
    end() 444
    facet put() 894
    forward 550
    forward and output 554
    implementation 59
    input 550
    invalid 454, 501, 550
    istream and 559

map 481
naming convention 511
operation 551
ostream and 558
ostreambuf 560
output 550
random-access 550
rbegin() 444
read through 551
rend() 444
resize() and 501
reverse 443, 557
stream 558
streambuf 559
string 584
user-defined 561
valarray 670
valid 550
write through 551
<iterator> 432
iterator 54, 443, 480
    basic_string 583
iterator_category 552
iterator_traits 552
iter_swap() 538
itoa() 155
Itor 435
Ival_box example 315, 407
Ival_slider 399
iword() 650

J

JIS 925
jump past initialization, difference from C 818

K

keeping consistent declarations 201
Kernighan and Ritchie 654
key
    and value 55, 480
    duplicate 480, 490
    unique 480
key_comp() 485
key_compare 480, 485
key_type 480
keyword 793–794
    and 829
    and_eq 829
    bitand 829
    bitor 829
    compl 829
    not 829
    not_eq 829

or 829
    or_eq 829
    xor 829
    xor_eq 829
kind
    of class 765
    of container 461
    of object 244
Knuth Donald 713

L

L', wide-character literal 73
label
    : 132
    scope of 137
labs() 661
lack of modularity 309
language
    and library 45
    design and 724
    gap between design and 725
    high-level 7
    low-level 8
    people and machines 9
    programming 15
    programming styles technique 6
    support 433–434
large
    character set 831
    program 211–212
    program and C++ 9
largest int 658
last element 446
last-time switch 640
late abstraction 437
Latin-1 580
lattice, class 389
layout, array 669
lazy evaluation 707
ldexp() 660
ldiv() 661
ldiv_t 661
leaf class 774
leak
    memory 939, 965
    resource 939, 965
learning
    C and C++ 7
  ꞌ C++ 6, 718, 820
    C++, gradual approach to 7
left 625, 630
left() 634
legacy 708
length of valarray 664, 679
length()

char_traits 581
    codecvt 927
    of string 598
    string 586
less
    than operator < 24
    than or equal operator <= 24
less 515
    < 516
less_equal <= 516
less_than 519
levels of abstraction 733
lexical conventions 794
lexicographical_compare() of sequence 544
libraries, standard 700
library 15, 701, 714, 755
    C standard 599
    algorithms, standard 64
    and exception, standard 935, 962
    container, standard 56, 442
    exception rules for 965
    facilities, standard 66, 429
    first C++ 686
    initialization 640
    language and 45
    non-standard 45
    standard 45, 182
    standard – see standard library
lifetime
    of facet 881
    of locale 894
    of object 84
    of temporary 254
limits, numeric 658
<limits> 433, 658
<limits.h> 433, 660
line, read 618
#line 813
linear time 464
Link 394
linkage
    and namespace 207
    and pointer to function 207
    const and 199
    error 199
    external 199
    inline and 199
    internal 199
    to C 205
    type-safe 198
linker 198
Liskov substitution 743
Lisp 725
list
    of containers 431
    of operator functions 262

operation 452
`<list>` 431
List 435
list 54
    and exception 955
    doubly-linked 470
    element access 472
    insert() 958
    merge() algorithm and 541
    merge() stable 470
    push_back() 957
    remove() 472
    remove_if() 472
    reverse() 472
    sort() stable 470
    unique() 472
literal
    ', character 73
    L', wide-character 73
    floating-point 74
    implementation dependency type of integer 832
    integer 73, 76
    of user-defined type 273
    string 294
    string 46, 90
    type of integer 832
loader 198
local
    currency symbol 900
    fix 697
    scope 82
    static 145
    static store 251
    variable, constructor for 245
`<locale>` 433, 649, 887
locale 649
    C 875
    C and C++ 880
    C and C++ global 924
    POSIX 649
    adding facet to 877
    and facet 869, 874
    and iostream 886
    category 873
    changing 880
    class 873
    classic C 875
    classic() 649, 879
    concept 869
    constructor 877
    cultural preference 869
    default 879
    design criteria 872
    format information 606
    global() 649, 879
    imbue() iostream 871

    in iostream 874
    initial 879
    is immutable 879
    isalnum() and 924
    isalpha() and 924
    iscntrl() and 924
    isdigit() and 924
    isgraph() and 924
    islower() and 924
    isprint() and 924
    ispunct() and 924
    isspace and 924
    isupper() and 924
    isxdigit() and 924
    lifetime of 894
    modify 879
    name 874–875
    name string 876
    preferred 875
    setting 880
    string 890
    used for string comparison 880
locale() 649
`<locale.h>` 433, 650
locale-sensitive message 928
locality 212
localization of object creation 322
localtime() 906
locking 366, 785
Lock_ptr example 366
log() 660
    complex 680
    valarray 667
log10() 660
    complex 680
    valarray 667
logarithmic time 464
logical
    and operator && 123
    const, physical and 231
    operators, bitwise 124
    or operator || 123
    structure of program 198
logical_and && 516
logical_not 515
    ! 516
logical_or || 516
long namespace name 178
long 73
    double 74
longer term 699
lookup
    hash_map 500
    namespace name 177, 265
loop
    and error 523

merging 675
   statement 116
lower_bound() 540
   in map 485
low-level language 8
lt(), char_traits 581
lvalue 84, 264, 281
lying 705

M

Machiavelli, Niccolò 222
machines, language people and 9
macro 160, 813
   alternative to 161
   difference from C 818
   template and 863
main() 46, 116, 218
   and initialization 217
   argv argc 117
   exception and 54
maintenance 212
   software 712
make_heap() 543
make_pair() 482
malloc() 577
management 713
   memory 843
manipulator
   and scope 632
   and std 632
   input 632
   output 631
   standard 633
   user-defined 635
   with argument 633
mantissa, size of 659
manual overload resolution 151
map 480
<map> 431
map 55, 480
   = 484
   [] 482
   and exception 955
   assignment 484
   clear() 487
   comparison in 484
   constructor 484
   count() in 485
   element access 482
   equal_range() in 485
   erase() 487
   find() in 485
   insert() 487, 958
   iterator 481
   lower_bound() in 485
   member type 480
   modify a 487
   subscripting 482
   upper_bound() in 485
   use of 774
mapped type, value 55
mapped_type 480
mapping exception 378
Marian 79
mask, character 920
masks_array 678
Math_container example 346
mathematical
   functions, complex 680
   functions, standard 660
   functions, valarray 667
   functions, vector 667
   model 711
<math.h> 434, 660
Matrix 672, 854
   example 282
max() 544, 658
   valarray 664
max_element() of sequence 544
max_exponent 659
max_exponent10 659
max_length(), codecvt 927
max_size() 455, 489
   of string 598
mbstate_t 887
meaning
   C++ 10
   for operator, predefined 264
   of identifier 857
means, aims and 694
measurement, productivity 716
member
   ->*, pointer to 418
   .*, pointer to 418
   ::*, pointer to 418
   access operator -> 102
   access operator . 101
   access to 849
   and nonmember operators 267
   class 293
   class, access to 851
   class, forward declaration of 293
   const 249
   constant 249
   constructor for class 247
   enum 249
   exception and 366, 939
   friend and 265, 280
   function 224, 238
   function adapter 520
   function, algorithm and 520

function, `const` 229
function, `inline` 235
function, pointer to 418
function, `static` 228, 278
initialization 248
initialization, exception and 373
initialization, order of 247
initialization, reference 244, 250
initializer 247
    object 244
    object, `union` 244
    of base class, private 305
    of derived class 304
    of `template`, `static` 854
    or base 740
    or pointer 738
    pointer to data 853
    private class 225
    `protected` 404–405
    public class 225
    reference 740
    `static` 228, 421
    `template` 330
    `template` example 349
    `template`, missing 823
    type, `basic_string` 582
    type, `map` 480
    type, `vector` 442
    `union` 257, 843
member-declaration 808
memberwise copy 283
`memchr()` 577
`memcmp()` 577
`memcpy()` 577
`mem_fun()` 63, 518, 521
`mem_fun1_ref_t` 518, 521
`mem_fun1_t` 518, 521
`mem_fun_ref()` 518, 521
`mem_fun_ref_t` 518, 521
`mem_fun_t` 518, 520–521
`memmove()` 577
memory
    automatic 843
    buffer 575
    dynamic 127, 576, 843
    exhaustion 965
    fragmentation 846
    heap 843
    leak 939, 965
    management 843
    management, automatic 844
    management, container 455, 567
    management, example of user-defined 292
    representing 943
    stack 843
    static 843

    uninitialized 574
`<memory>` 431, 574
`memset()` 577
`merge()` 541
    algorithm and `list` 541
    stable, `list` 470
message
    catalog 928
    `locale`-sensitive 928
    queue 477
messages
    `close()` 929
    facet 928
    `get()` 929
    `open()` 929
`messages_base` 928
method 310
    choosing a design 696
    choosing an analysis 696
    cookbook 692
    design 694
    formal 711
`min()` 544, 658
    `valarray` 664
`min_element()` of sequence 544
`min_exponent` 659
`min_exponent10` 659
minimalism 706
minimize dependency 173
minus operator − 24
minus − 517
`mismatch()` 516, 527
missing
    `bad_alloc` 823
    checking 823
    member `template` 823
    namespace 822
    specialization partial 823
    standard library 822
misuse
    of C++ 725
    of RTTI 417, 439
    of dynamic type checking 439
mixed-mode arithmetic 268
mixin 402
mixing C and C++ 719
`mktime()` 906
ML 10
mode of file 639
model 708
    formal 730
    mathematical 711
    waterfall 697
`modf()` 660
modifier 706
    POSIX format 909

modify
    a map 487
    locale 879
modifying sequence algorithm 529
modular programming 26
modularity 312
    lack of 309
module
    and interface 165
    and type 30
modulus operator % 24
modulus % 517
monetary
    amount, format of 898–899
    amount, input of 903
    amount, output of 902
    amount, punctuation of 899
monetary frac_digits() 901
Money example 898
money_base 899
money_get
    and >> 904
    facet 903
    get() 903
moneypunct
    curr_symbol() 900
    decimal_point() 900
    facet 899
    grouping() 900
    neg_format() 900
    negative_sign() 900
    pattern 900
    pos_format() 900
    positive_sign() 900
    thousands_sep() 900
money_punct frac_digits() 899
money_put
    and << 902
    facet 902
    put() 902
moron 713, 717
move(), char_traits 581
multibyte character encoding 925
multidimensional
    array 668, 677, 836
    array, passing 839
multilevel error handling 383
multimap 490
multi-method 326
multiple
    inheritance 308, 390, 735
    inheritance, exception and 360
    inheritance, use of 776
    inheritance, using 399
    instantiation 867
    interface 172

multiple-element insert() 959
multiple-inheritance
    access control and 406
    ambiguity resolution 391
multiplies * 517
multiply operator * 24
multiset 491
mutable 232
mutual reference 278
My_messages example 929
My_money_io example 901
My_punct example 893

N

%n format 653
\n, newline 830
name 81
    binding 860
    binding, template 859
    character in 81
    clash 176
    dependent 857, 861
    hiding 82
    locale 874–875
    long namespace 178
    lookup, namespace 177, 265
    namespace qualified 169
    short namespace 178
    string, locale 876
names, reserved 81
namespace
    nested 848
    transition to 182
namespace 27, 167, 847
    alias 178
    alias re-open 185
    and :: 169
    and class 849
    and overloading 183
    composition 179, 181
    global 847
    helper function and 240
    is open 184
    linkage and 207
    member declaration and definition 167
    missing 822
    name, long 178
    name lookup 177, 265
    name, short 178
    operators and 265
    purpose of 180
    qualified name 169
    re-open 185
    rel_ops 468
    selection from 180

std 46
unnamed 177, 200
using 183
naming convention, iterator 511
narrow() 644, 917
    ctype 923
n-ary operators 675
national
    character 829
    conventions 649
natural operation 767
NDEBUG 750
negate - 517
negative_sign(), moneypunct 900
neg_format(), moneypunct 900
nested
    class 293
    function 806
    namespace 848
nesting 756
<new> 384, 433, 576
new
    and array 423
    and exception 576
    bad_alloc and 384
    exception and 367, 369
    operator 127
    placement 255
    size and 421
new()
    operator 129, 576
    placement 576
new[](), operator 423, 576
new_handler 129, 576
_new_handler 370
newline \n 830
next_permutation() 545
Nicholas 49
noboolalpha() 634
Nocase 467
node
    class 772
    class, abstract 774
    class, concrete 774
non-C++ program 217
non-const string literal, deprecated 819
none() 494
nonlocal goto 357
nonmember operators, member and 267
nonmodifying sequence algorithm 523
non-standard library 45
non-type template parameter 331
norm() 680
noshowbase() 634
noshowpoint() 634
noshowpos() 634

noskipws() 634
not
    a class 705
    equal operator != 24
not keyword 829
not1() 518
    and unary_negate 522
not2() 518
    and binary_negate 522
notation, value of 261
not_eof(), char_traits 581
not_eq keyword 829
not_equal_to != 516
nothrow guarantee 937
nothrow 576
    allocator 823
nouppercase() 634
npos 586
nth_element() 540
null
    0 zero 88
    pointer 0 835
NULL 88, 433
number
    format 893
    punctuation 893
    size of 75
numeric
    algorithm, generalized 682
    array 662
    limits 658
    value, input of 897
    value, output of 894
<numeric> 434, 682
numerical computation 64
numeric_limits 658
num_get
    and >> 897
    facet 897
    get() 897
numpunct facet 893
num_put
    and << 895
    facet 894
    put() 894

O

O notation 464
%o format 652
object 32, 84
    I/O 774
    array element 244
    automatic 244
    constructor for free store 246
    creation 242

creation, localization of 322
format 635
free store 244
function 287, 514, 776
global 244, 252, 640
hierarchy 739, 748
kind of 244
lifetime of 84
member 244
placement of 255
real-world 732
state of 748
static 244
temporary 244, 254
union member 244
variably-sized 243
Object 438
example 417
object-oriented
design 692, 726
programming 37–38, 301
pure 732
objects, array of 250
oct 626–627
oct() 634
octal 73
output 626
ODR the one-definition-rule 203
offset, pointer to member and 419
off_type 608, 643
char_traits 581
ofstream 638
old-style function definition 817
one right way 693
one-beyond-last 512
one-definition-rule, ODR the 203
Op 511
open
for reading, in 639
for writing, out 639
namespace is 184
open(), messages 929
opening of file 638
openmode 639
operation
bitset 494
efficiency of 464
front 472
iterator 551
list 452
natural 767
on container 464
operations
complex 679
on references 97
on structure 102

selecting 705
set of class 237
valarray 664, 667
vector 664, 667
operator
, 123
!=, not equal 24
%, modulus 24
&, bitwise and 124
&&, logical and 123
*, multiply 24
+, plus 24
+, user-defined 265, 281
++, increment 125
++, user-defined 264, 291
+= 109
+=, user-defined 264, 268, 281
-, minus 24
--, decrement 125
--, user-defined 291
-= 109
->, member access 102
->, user-defined 289
->* 853
., member access 101
.* 853
/, divide 24
:: 305
:: and virtual function 312
::, scope resolution 82, 228
<, less than 24
<<, output 607
<=, less than or equal 24
=, user-defined 281
==, equal 24
>, greater than 24
>=, greater than or equal 24
?: 134
^, bitwise exclusive or 124
and built-in type, user-defined 265
and enum, user-defined 265
application 287
arithmetic 24
assignment 110, 268
associativity of 121
binding strength 121, 607
call 287
comparison operator 24
composite 268
declarator 80
delete 127
design of access 295
foundation 706
new 127
operator comparison 24
overloaded 241

overloading, example of 292
    precedence 121
    predefined meaning for 264
    stack 450
    summary 119
    ternary 636
    type conversion 275
    user-defined 263
    user-defined binary 263
    user-defined unary 263
    |, bitwise or 124
    ||, logical or 123
    ~, bitwise complement 124
operator
    delete() 129, 576
    delete[]() 423, 576
    functions, list of 262
    new() 129, 576
    new[]() 423, 576
    void*() 616
operator() 287
operator=, vector 946
operator[] 286
operator 810
operators
    and namespace 265
    bitwise logical 124
    essential 283
    member and nonmember 267
    n-ary 675
optimal container 435
optimization 675
or
    keyword 829
    operator |, bitwise 124
    operator ||, logical 123
order 467
    collating 891
    of construction 248, 252
    of construction and destruction 414
    of evaluation 122
    of fields 75
    of member initialization 247
    of specialization 343
    string 891
or_eq keyword 829
organization
    of I/O system 606
    standard library 431
organizational inertia 713
orthogonality, convenience and 431
oseq() example 556
<ostream> 432
    and <iostream> 608
ostream 608, 642
    << 609
    and buffer 642
    and exception 963
    and iterator 558
    and streambuf 642
    assignment of 609
    copy 609
    put() 609
    template and 608
    write() 609
ostreambuf iterator 560
ostreambuf_iterator 560
ostream_iterator 60, 558
ostringstream 641
ostrstream 641, 656
Out 511
out open for writing 639
out(), codecvt 927
out_of_range 53, 446
    and at() 385
    string 586
output 47
    << 46
    C input and 651
    bits of int 495
    bitset 495
    complex 680
    connection between input and 623
    cout 46
    decimal 626
    double 626
    failure 896
    field 629–630
    float 626
    floating-point 626, 628
    flushing of 626
    formatted 625
    function, virtual 612
    hexadecimal 626
    input and 432, 605
    integer 627
    iterator 550
    manipulator 631
    octal 626
    of bool 611
    of built-in type 609
    of char 610
    of date 908
    of monetary amount 902
    of numeric value 894
    of pointer 611
    of time 908
    of user-defined type 612
    operator << 607
    padding 625
    sequence 556
    string 598

to file 637
unbuffered 642
valarray 668
why, << for 607
output_iterator_tag 553
overflow, stack 476
overflow() 648
overflow_error and to_ulong() 385
overhead 8
overlapping sequences 529
overload
    resolution 149
    resolution, manual 151
    return type and 151
    scope and 151
overloaded
    function name 149
    operator 241
overloading
    const and 600
    example of operator 292
    function template 336
    namespace and 183
override 313, 395
    from virtual base class 401
    private base 738
overriding function, type of 424
overwriting vs insertion 555

P

%p format 653
padding 630
    output 625
pair 482
paradigm, programming 22
parameter
    non-type template 331
    template 331
parameterization
    and dependency 707
    policy 757
    template 707
parametric polymorphism 347
parentheses, uses of 123
parser, recursive decent 108
partial
    construction 366, 939
    sort 539
    specialization 342
partial_sort() 539
partial_sort_copy() 539
partial_sum() 684
partition 542
partition() 542
partitioning of program 208, 211

passing multidimensional array 839
pattern 709
    specialization 342
pattern, moneypunct 900
pbackfail() 648
pbase() 645
pbump() 645
peek() 643
people and machines, language 9
perfection 43
permutation 545
per-object data 573
per-type data 573
phone_book example 52
physical
    and logical const 231
    structure of program 198
placement
    new 255
    new() 576
    of object 255
Plane example 729
plug analogy 728
plus operator + 24
plus + 517
point
    of declaration 82
    of definition 861
    of instantiation 863
pointer 26, 87
    0, null 835
    and array 91, 147
    and exception 961
    arithmetic 88, 93, 125
    checked 291
    checking for wild 722
    const 96
    conversion 834
    conversion, user-defined 349
    disguised 844
    input of 615
    member or 738
    output of 611
    semantics 294
    size of 75
    smart 289, 291
    to class 304
    to class, conversion of 304
    to const 96
    to constructor 424
    to data member 853
    to function 156
    to function, << 631
    to function, >> 632
    to function adapter 521
    to function, linkage and 207

to member ->* 418
to member .* 418
to member ::* 418
to member and offset 419
to member function 418
to void 100
type 569
pointer 443, 552, 567
    basic_string 583
pointers and union 845
pointer_to_binary_function 521
pointer_to_unary_function 518, 521
polar() 680
policy parameterization 757
polymorphic 35
    object, algorithm and 63
polymorphism 158, 312
    algorithm and 520
    compile-time 347
    container and 520
    dynamic_cast and 409
    parametric 347
    run-time 347
    see virtual function
Pool example 570
Pool_alloc allocator 572
pop()
    of priority_queue 478
    of queue 476
    of stack 475
pop_back() 450
    and exception 955
pop_front() 472
    and exception 955
pop_heap() 543
portability 9, 700, 828
    and features 815
pos_format(), moneypunct 900
position
    bit 492
    in buffer 642
    in file 642
positive_sign(), moneypunct 900
POSIX
    format modifier 909
    locale 649
postcondition 753
pos_type 608, 643
    char_traits 581
pow() 660
    complex 680
    valarray 667
pptr() 645
#pragma 813
precedence
    << 608

operator 121
precision() 628
precondition 753
Pred 511
predefined
    , 264
    & 264
    = 264
    meaning for operator 264
predicate 61, 63, 515
    and exception 962
    standard library 516
    user-defined 516
preferred locale 875
prefix code 624
preprocessing directive, # 813
presentation as design tool 704
pre-standard implementation 820
prev_permutation() 545
printf() 651
priority queue 478
priority_queue
    and heap 479
    heap and 543
    implementation 478
    pop() of 478
    push() of 478
    top() of 478
private
    class member 225
    member of base class 305
private 402
    base 405, 742
    base class 743
    base, override 738
    public protected 849–850
private: 234
problems
    of scale 715
    with concrete type 37
procedural
    programming 23
    programming and C++ 725
process, development 696
product
    dot 684
    inner 684
productivity measurement 716
program 46, 798
    and C++, large 9
    large 211–212
    logical structure of 198
    non-C++ 217
    partitioning of 208, 211
    physical structure of 198
    size of 8

start 217
structure of 8
termination 218
timing a 905
programmed-in relationship 746
programmer
    C 14
    C++ 14
programmers, elimination of 730
programming 16
    and C++, procedural 725
    as a human activity 693
    design and 692
    generic 40, 757–758
    language 15
    language, design language and 730
    modular 26
    object-oriented 37–38, 301
    paradigm 22
    procedural 23
    purpose of 694
    style 22
    styles technique language 6
    template and generic 327
programming-language, general-purpose 21
prohibiting
    , 264
    & 264
    = 264
promotion
    floating-point 833
    integral 833
    standard 833
pronounciation, C++ 10
proof by analogy 692
properties of C++ 724
protected 402
    base 319, 405
    base class 743
    constructor 881
    interface, public and 645
    member 404–405
    private, public 849–850
protection 226
    unit of 754
prototypes 710
proxy 785
Ptr 349
ptrdiff_t 122, 433
ptr_fun() 518, 521
pubimbue() 646
public class member 225
public 402
    and protected interface 645
    protected private 849–850
public: 225, 234

pubseekoff()
pubseekpos()
pubsetbuf() 646
pubsync() 646
punctuation
    number 893
    of monetary amount 899
pure
    object-oriented 732
    virtual function 313
purpose
    of namespace 180
    of programming 694
push()
    of priority_queue 478
    of queue 476
    of stack 475
pushback(), vector 947
push_back() 55, 450
    and exception 955
    and realloc() 451
    list 957
    vector 957
push_front() 55, 472
    and exception 955
push_heap() 543
put
    area 645
    to, << 607
put()
    iterator, facet 894
    money_put 902
    num_put 894
    ostream 609
    time_put 908
putback() 643
pword() 650

Q

qsort() 158, 546
    and exception 382, 964
quadratic time 464
qualification ::, explicit 847
qualified name, namespace 169
qualifier, template as 858
quality 717
queue
    deque, double-ended 474
    priority 478
<queue> 431
queue
    back() of 476
    front() of 476
    message 477
    pop() of 476

push() of 476
quiet_NaN() 659
quote
        \ ', single 830
        double 830
quotient 661

R

\r, carriage return 830
Ran 511
rand(), random number 685
Randint 685
RAND_MAX 685
random
        number 538
        number class 685
        number generator 537
        number rand() 685
random-access iterator 550
random_access_iterator_tag 553
random_shuffle() 537
range
        check 445, 561
        check of string 584
        check, valarray 664
        checking 275, 781
        checking Vec 53, 405
        date 906
        error 661
        sequence and 512
Range example 781
Rational example 747
raw storage 574
raw_storage_iterator 575
rbegin() 481
        basic_string 584
        iterator 444
rdbuf() 644
rdstate() 616
rdstr() 640
read
        line 618
        through iterator 551
read() 618
readsome() 643
real() 679–680
realloc() 577
        push_back() and 451
real-world
        as source of ideas 734
        classes and 734
        object 732
rebind 567
        use of 569
recovery, error 566, 966

recursion 148
recursive
        decent parser 108
        function, exception and 374
reduce 683
reduction 683
redundancy 712
reference
        & 97
        and exception 961
        argument 98
        call by 98, 146, 282
        catch by 360
        count 292
        counting 783
        dynamic_cast to 410
        example of 292
        initialization of 98
        member 740
        member initialization 244, 250
        mutual 278
        return by 148
        return by 283
        to class, forward 278
reference 443, 480, 552, 567
        basic_string 583
        to bit 492
references, operations on 97
register 806
register_callback() 651
reinterpret_cast 130, 256
relationship, programmed-in 746
relationships between templates 348
relaxation of return type 424
release, resource 364
reliability 383
rel_ops, namespace 468
remainder 661
remove() 536
        and exception 955
        list 472
remove_copy_if() 536
remove_if() 536
        and exception 955
        list 472
renaming virtual function 778
rend() 481
        basic_string 584
        iterator 444
re-open
        namespace 185
        namespace alias 185
reorganization of class hierarchy 707
replace() 535
        in string 595
replace_copy() 535

replace_copy_if() 535
replace_if() 535
replicated base class 394
representation
    converting character 925
    hash_map 498
    of container 465
representing memory 943
requirement
    comparison 467
    copy 466
requirements for element 466
reserve(), vector 455
reserved names 81
reset() bitset 494
resetiosflags() 634
resize() 52
    and iterator 501
    hash_map 502
    of string 598
    valarray 664, 666
    vector 455
resource
    acquisition 364
    acquisition, constructor and 950, 966
    acquisition, delayed 953
    acquisition is initialization 366
    exhaustion 369
    leak 939, 965
    release 364
response to change 698
responsibility 700, 706
restricted character set 829
restriction 9
result
    of sizeof 122
    type 122
result, codecvt_base 925
resumption 370
re-throw 362, 379
return
    \r, carriage 830
    by reference 283
    function value 283
    type and overload 151
    type, covariant 424
    type of virtual 424
    type, relaxation of 424
    value, algorithm 508
    value type check 148
    value type conversion 148
return
    alternative 357
    by reference 148
    by value 148
    function value 148

    of void expression 148
return; 148
return_temporary_buffer() 575
reuse 714
    design 709
    of concrete type 241, 768
reverse iterator 443, 557
reverse() 537
    list 472
reverse_copy() 537
reverse_iterator 443, 480, 557
    basic_string 583
reward 713
rfind() in string 594
right 625, 630
right() 634
Ritchie, Kernighan and 654
roll-back 937, 966
rotate() 537
rotate_copy() 537
round_error() 659
RTTI 407
    implementation of 409
    misuse of 417, 439
    use of 417
rule of two 741
rules for library, exception 965
run-time
    access control 785
    error 29, 355
    initialization 217
    polymorphism 347
    support 8
    type identification 407
    type information 407, 774
runtime_error exception 875

S

%s format 653
Saab example 728
Safe example 937
safe_assign() 946
safety
    and destructor, exception 937
    condition, exception 937
    convenience vs. 847
    exception 936
Satellite 390
saving space 840
sbumpc() 646
scale 212, 692
    problems of 715
scaling 665
scan_is(), ctype 922
scan_not(), ctype 922

scientific 626, 628
scientific() 634
scope 278
    and overload 151
    difference from C 816
    global 82, 847
    local 82
    manipulator and 632
    of label 137
    resolution operator :: 82, 228
scrollbar example 743
search, binary 540, 546
search() 528
search_n() 528
Season
    << example 884, 931
    >> example 884, 931
    example 883
Season_io, user-defined facet 883
seekdir
    and beg 643
    and cur 643
    and end 643
    direction of seek
seekg()
    direction of 643
seekoff()
seekp()
    direction of 643
    set position 642
seekpos()
selecting operations 705
selection from namespace 180
self, assignment to 246, 945
self-reference this 230
semantics
    pointer 294
    value 294
semicolon ; 79, 101, 132
sentry
    I/O 624
    iostream 624
separate
    compilation 27, 198
    compilation, template 351
separation of concerns 694
separator character, thousands_sep() 893
sequence 41, 469
    adapter 469
    add element to 529
    adding to 555
    algorithm and 508
    algorithm, modifying 529
    algorithm, nonmodifying 523
    and associative container 461
    and container 512

    and range 512
    change size of 529
    delete element from 529, 534
    error 512
    fundamental 469
    generality of 512
    half-open 512
    input 513
    iterator and 550
    lexicographical_compare() of 544
    max_element() of 544
    min_element() of 544
    output 556
    set operation on 542
    sorted 539
    string 579
sequences, overlapping 529
set 124
    of class operations 237
    operation on sequence 542
    position, seekp()
<set> 431
Set example 769
set 491
    bitset and 492
    of Shape* 348
set()
    bitset 494
    function 759
setbase() 634
setbuf() 647
Set_controller example 785
set_difference() 543
setf() 626, 630
setfill() 634
setg() 645
set_intersection() 542
setiosflags() 634
<setjmp.h> 433
set_new_handler() 129, 576
setp() 645
setprecision() 633–634
setstate() 616
set_symmetric_difference() 543
set_terminate() 380
setting locale 880
set_unexpected() 379
set_union() 542
setw() 634
sgetc() 646
sgetn() 646
Shakespeare 709
Shape
    example 774
    example 37
    example (bad) 417

Shape*, set of 348
shift state 925
shift() 664
short namespace name 178
short 73
short-circuit evaluation 123, 134
showbase 626, 628
showbase() 634
showmanyc() 648
showpoint 626
showpoint() 634
showpos 626
showpos() 634
shuffle 538
sign extension 831
signal 357
<signal.h> 157, 433
signaling_NaN() 659
signed
    char 831
    type 73
    unsigned integer conversion 834
simple invariant 951
simplicity, invariant and 949
Simula 10, 38
Simula-style container 438
simulation 685, 711
    event driven 326
sin() 660
    complex 680
    valarray 667
single quote \' 830
sinh() 660
    complex 680
    valarray 667
size
    and delete 421
    and new 421
    of exponent 659
    of mantissa 659
    of number 75
    of pointer 75
    of program 8
    of sequence, change 529
    of string 147
    of structure 102
    of vector, increase 455
size() 455, 489, 494
    of string 598
    string 586
    valarray 664
sizeof 75
    difference from C 816
    enum 78
    result of 122
size_t 122, 433

-1 and 448
size_type 443, 480
    basic_string 583
skipws 625
skipws() 634
slice, generalized 677
slice 664, 668
slice_array 671
Slice_iter example 670
slicing 307
smallest int 658
Smalltalk 725
    style 417
Smalltalk-style container 438
smanip 633
smart pointer 289, 291
snextc() 646
software
    development 692
    maintenance 712
solution, generality of 701
sort 546
    partial 539
    stable 539
sort() 56, 539
    and exception 955
    example 158, 334
    stable, list 470
sorted sequence 539
sort_heap() 543
sorting 338
    criteria 534
source
    code, template 350
    file 197
    of ideas, real-world as 734
space, saving 840
special character 830
specialization 859
    and char* 344
    and void* 341
    function 344
    generated 859
    order of 343
    partial 342
    partial, missing 823
    pattern 342
    template 341
    use of 865
    user 859
specialized, more 343
specifying interface 707
splice() 470
    and exception 955
sputbackc() 646
sputc() 646

sputn() 646
sqrt() 660
    complex 680
    valarray 667
srand() 685
<sstream> 119, 432, 640
stability of design 708
stable
    list merge() 470
    list sort() 470
    sort 539
stable_partition() 542
stable_sort() 539
stack
    memory 843
    operator 450
<stack> 431
Stack example 27
stack
    implementation 475–476
    overflow 476
    pop() of 475
    push() of 475
    top() of 475
    underflow 476
stage
    analysis 697
    design 697
    development 697
    implementation 697
standard
    component 698, 714
    currency symbol 900
    exception 384
    facet 887
    guarantee 827
    include directory 201
    libraries 700
    library 45, 182
    library, C 599
    library, adding to 434
    library algorithms 64
    library and exception 935, 962
    library container 56, 442
    library criteria 430
    library design 429–430
    library facilities 66, 429
    library header 202, 431
    library, missing 822
    library organization 431
    library predicate 516
    manipulator 633
    mathematical functions 660
    promotion 833
standardization, C++ 11
start, program 217

starting from scratch 708
state
    error 936
    format 625
    machine 730
    of object 748
    stream 616
    valid 936
statement
    break 116
    continue 116
    controlled 136
    do 114, 137
    for 26, 136
    goto 137
    if 133
    loop 116
    summary 132
    switch 25, 133
    while 136
statement 802
state_type, char_traits 581
static
    allocation 843
    memory 843
    type checking 727
static
    anachronism 200
    deprecated 818
    local 145
    member 228, 421
    member function 228, 278
    member of template 854
    object 244
    store, local 251
static_cast 130, 159
    dynamic_cast and 413
std
    manipulator and 632
    namespace 46
std:: 46
<stdarg.h> 155, 433
<stddef> 433
<stddef.h> 433
<stdexcept> 385, 432
<stdio.h> 182, 202, 432
<stdlib.h> 432, 434, 546, 577, 600, 661
steps, design 701
STL 66
    container 441
    iterator 441
Storable example 396
storage
    class 244
    raw 574
store

dynamic 34
free 34, 127, 421, 576, 843
heap 127
local static 251
str() 640
strcat() 599
strchr() 599
strcmp() 599
strcpy() 599
strcspn() 599
stream 432
    and exception, I/O 963
    callback 650
    classes 637
    closing of 639
    file and 637
    hierarchy 637
    iterator 558
    state 616
    state, basic_ios 606
    string 640–641
<streambuf> 432
streambuf 646–647, 649
    << 642
    and character buffer 642
    iterator 559
    ostream and 642
streamoff 609
streamsize 609
strftime() 909
stride() 668
string
    and const, C-style 90
    character 432
    comparison 889
    comparison, locale used for 880
    format 652
    initialization of array by 89
    literal 46, 90
    literal, deprecated non-const 819
    locale name 876
    order 891
    size of 147
<string> 48, 432, 580, 598
String example 328
string 48, 582
    != 591
    + 593
    += 592
    < 591
    << 598
    <= 591
    = 587
    == 591
    > 591
    >= 591

    >> 598
    [] on 584
    algorithm and 584
    and 0 587
    and C-style string 579, 589
    and array 589
    and exception 963
    append() 592
    as container 491
    assign() 588
    assignment 587
    at() on 585
    class 292
    compare() 590
    comparison 590
    concatenation 592–593
    constructor 585
    conversion 589
    design 579
    empty 585
    empty() 598
    erase() in 595
    error 586
    find() in 594
    find_first_not_of() in 594
    find_first_of() in 594
    find_last_of() in 594
    get_allocator() from 598
    getline() into 598
    implicit conversion of 590
    input 598
    insert() 592
    iterator 584
    length() 586
    length() of 598
    literal 294
    locale 890
    max_size() of 598
    of user-defined type 583
    out_of_range 586
    output 598
    range check of 584
    replace() in 595
    resize() of 598
    rfind() in 594
    sequence 579
    size() 586
    size() of 598
    stream 640–641
    subscripting of 584
    substr() of 596
    swap() 599
    unsigned 583
stringbuf 649
<string.h> 432, 577, 599
String_numput example 895

stringstream 641
strlen() 599
strncat() 599
strncmp() 599
strncpy() 599
strong guarantee 937
strpbrk() 599
strrchr() 599
strstr() 599
<strstream.h> 656
struct
    aggregate 101
    and class 234
    hack 809
    name, difference from C 818
    scope, difference from C 818
structure 101
    initialization of 102
    internal 694
    of program 8
    operations on 102
    size of 102
style, programming 22
subarray 663, 668, 671, 677–679
subclass 303
    superclass and 39
sub-object, exception and 366, 939
subrange 781
subscript
    C++ style 674
    Fortran style 674
subscripting 445, 454
    comma and 838
    map 482
    of string 584
    user-defined 286
    valarray 663
substitution, Liskov 743
substr() of string 596
substring 596
Substring example 596
subtype 730, 742–743
successful large system 709
suffix
    _copy 533
    _if 525
    code 624
Sum 514
sum(), valarray 664
summary
    algorithm 509
    container 464
    exception guarantee 956
    syntax 793
sungetc() 646
superclass 303

and subclass 39
supplying default value 500
support 714
    run-time 8
swap() 344, 457–458, 489, 538, 945
    and exception 956, 960
    string 599
swap_ranges() 538
switch
    first-time 253, 640
    last-time 640
    on type 417
switch 109
    and if 134
    on enumeration 77
    statement 25, 133
sync() 643, 647
sync_with_stdio() 651
synonym, see typedef
syntax
    <, template 811
    summary 793
system
    growing 711
    successful large 709
    working 709

T

\t, horizontal tab 830
tab
    \t, horizontal 830
    \v, vertical 830
Table example 243
tan(), valarray 667
tanh() 660
    complex 680
    valarray 667
Task 394
taxonomy 703
teaching and C++ 12
technique
    built-in feature vs 43
    language, programming styles 6
techniques for exception safety 940
tellg() 643
tellp() get position 642
template, use of 776
template 16, 40, 328, 854
    <> 341, 344
    and class 348
    and friend 854
    and generic programming 327
    and inheritance 347
    and macro 863
    and ostream 608

argument 331
argument, deducing 335, 856
argument, default 340, 824
argument, dependency on 861
argument, explicit 335
argument, function 335
as qualifier 858
as `template` parameter 855
class hierarchy and 345
copy assignment and 348
copy constructor and 348
definition, context of 860
example, member 349
function 334
function, `virtual` 348
in design 757
inclusion 350
inheritance and 349
instantiation 859
instantiation, context of 860
instantiation directive 866
instantiation, explicit 866
member 330
missing member 823
name binding 859
overloading, function 336
parameter 331
parameter, non-type 331
parameter, `template` as 855
parameterization 707
separate compilation 351
source code 350
specialization 341
`static` member of 854
syntax < 811
template-declaration 811
templates, relationships between 348
temporary 98
    elimination of 675
    lifetime of 254
    object 244, 254
    variable 244, 254
term, longer 699
`terminate()` 380
`terminate_handler` 380
termination 370
    program 218
ternary operator 636
`test()` 494
testing 712
    design for 712
`this` 278
    self-reference 230
`thousands_sep()`
    `moneypunct` 900
    separator character 893

`throw` 186, 362, 379
`tie()` 623
time
    constant 464
    format `%X` 909
    input of 910
    linear 464
    logarithmic 464
    output of 908
    quadratic 464
    representation `time_t` 905
    representation `tm` 905
`time()` 907
`time_base` 911
`time_get`
    and >> 912, 916
    facet 911
    `get_time()` 911
`<time.h>` 431, 433, 906
`time_put`
    and << 915
    facet 908
    `put()` 908
timer
    clock and 905
    fine-grained 905
`time_t`, time representation 905
timing a program 905
Tiny example 275
`tinyness_before` 659
`tm`, time representation 905
`to_char_type()`, `char_traits` 581
`to_int_type()`, `char_traits` 581
`tolower()`, `ctype` 923
tools, design 711
`top()`
    of `priority_queue` 478
    of `stack` 475
`to_ulong()` 494
    `overflow_error` and 385
`toupper()` 591
    `ctype` 922
tradeoff, guarantee and 957
traditional hierarchy 315
traits, character 580
`traits_type` 608
    `basic_string` 583
`transform()` 530
    `collate` 889, 891
transition 717–718
    and *using-directive* 183
    to namespace 182
translation unit 197
transparency, exception 943
traps 659
traversal 61

tree 307
trigraphs 829
true and 1 71
truename() 894
trunc truncate file 639
truncate file, trunc 639
truncation 835
try 187
try-block 187, 812, 943
    as function body 54, 373
tutorial as design tool 708
two, rule of 741
two-stage construct 949
type 23, 69
    abstract 34, 767, 769
    abstract and concrete 771
    arithmetic 70
    built-in 70
    char, character 71
    character 580
    check, function argument 145
    check, return value 148
    checking, dynamic 727
    checking, misuse of dynamic 439
    checking, static 727
    class and 724
    class user-defined 224
    concrete 33, 236, 766–767
    constructor for built-in 131
    conversion, ambiguous 276
    conversion, constructor and 269, 275
    conversion, explicit 130, 284
    conversion, function argument 145
    conversion, implicit 76, 275–276, 281, 284, 833
    conversion operator 275
    conversion, return value 148
    conversion, unions and 842
    conversion, user-defined 267, 281
    covariant return 424
    equivalence 104
    floating-point 74
    fundamental 23, 70
    generator 348
    identification, run-time 407
    information, extended 416
    information, run-time 407, 774
    input of built-in 614
    input of user-defined 621
    integer 70, 73
    integral 70
    literal of user-defined 273
    module and 30
    of exception 379
    of field 75
    of integer literal 832
    of integer literal, implementation dependency 832

    of overriding function 424
    of virtual, return 424
    output of built-in 609
    output of user-defined 612
    pointer 569
    problems with concrete 37
    relaxation of return 424
    result 122
    reuse of concrete 241, 768
    safe I/O 607
    signed 73
    string of user-defined 583
    switch on 417
    unsigned 73
    user-defined 32, 70
    user-defined operator and built-in 265
typedef 84
type-field 308
typeid() 414
    bad_typeid and 384
<typeinfo> 384, 415, 433
type_info 414
typename 443, 856
    and class 858
type-safe linkage 198

U

%u format 653
uflow() 648
unary operator, user-defined 263
unary_function 515
unary_negate 518
    not1() and 522
unbuffered
    I/O 647
    input 642
    output 642
uncaught exception 380
uncaught_exception() 374
unchecked access 445
undeclared argument 154
#undef 162
undefined
    behavior 828
    behavior, exception and 938
    enum conversion 77
underflow, stack 476
underflow() 648
unexpected exception 377
unexpected() 375
unexpected_handler 379
unformatted input 618
unget() 643
Unicode 580, 925
uniform distribution 685

uniformity of code 767
uninitialized memory 574
uninitialized_copy() 574
    and exception 960, 963
uninitialized_fill() 574, 942
    and exception 960, 963
uninitialized_fill_n() 574
    and exception 960, 963
union 841
    and class 843
    anonymous 841
    constructor and 257
    destructor and 257
    member 257, 843
    member object 244
    pointers and 845
    unnamed 841
unions and type conversion 842
unique key 480
unique() 532
    and exception 955
    list 472
unique_copy() 56, 532
unit
    of addressing 88
    of allocation 88
    of compilation 197
    of design 755
    of protection 754
    translation 197
unitbuf 626
units analogy 728
universal
    base class 438
    character name 831
UNIX 8, 13
unnamed
    namespace 177, 200
    union 841
Unsafe example 937
unsetf() 626
unshift(), codecvt 927
unsigned
    char 831
    integer conversion, signed 834
    string 583
    type 73
up cast 408
update() example 957
upper_bound() 540
    in map 485
uppercase 626
uppercase() 634
Urand 685
use
    case 704

count 292
dependency 745
of C++ 12
of RTTI 417
of allocator 568
of class 725
of classes 733
of dynamic_cast 774
of facet 882
of global variable 111
of map 774
of multiple inheritance 776
of rebind 569
of specialization 865
of template 776
used function only, instantiate 866
use_facet() 882
user specialization 859
user-defined
    == 534
    allocator 570
    binary operator 263
    container 497
    conversion 347
    facet 886
    facet Season_io 883
    iterator 561
    manipulator 635
    memory management, example of 292
    operator 263
    operator + 265, 281
    operator ++ 264, 291
    operator += 264, 268, 281
    operator -- 291
    operator -> 289
    operator = 281
    operator and built-in type 265
    operator and enum 265
    pointer conversion 349
    predicate 516
    subscripting 286
    type 32, 70
    type, class 224
    type conversion 267, 281
    type, input of 621
    type, literal of 273
    type, output of 612
    type, string of 583
    unary operator 263
user-supplied comparison 467
uses of parentheses 123
using multiple inheritance 399
using
    namespace 183
    namespace, using vs. 847
    vs. using namespace 847

using-declaration 169, 180
    and access control 407
    and inheritance 392
    vs. *using-directive* 847
using-directive 171
    and definition 180
    and inheritance 392
    transition and 183
    using-declaration vs. 847
usual arithmetic conversions 122, 836
utilities 431
`<utility>` 431, 468

V

`\v`, vertical tab 830
`va_arg()` 155
`<valarray>` 434, 662
valarray 65, 662
    `!` 664
    `!=` 667
    `%` 667
    `%=` 664
    `&` 667
    `&&` 667
    `&=` 664
    `*` 667
    `*=` 664
    `+` 667
    `+=` 664
    `-` 664, 667
    `-=` 664
    `/` 667
    `/=` 664
    `<` 667
    `<<` 667
    `<<=` 664
    `<=` 667
    `=` 663
    `==` 667
    `>` 667
    `>=` 667
    `>>` 667
    `>>=` 664
    `[]` 663
    `^` 667
    `^=` 664
    `abs()` 667
    `acos()` 667
    and array 663
    and exception 964
    and `vector` and array 662
    `apply()` 664
    as container 492
    `asin()` 667
    assignment 663

    `atan()` 667
    `atan2()` 667
    construction 662
    `cos()` 667
    `cosh()` 667
    `exp()` 667
    input 668
    iterator 670
    length of 664, 679
    `log()` 667
    `log10()` 667
    mathematical functions 667
    `max()` 664
    `min()` 664
    operations 664, 667
    output 668
    `pow()` 667
    range check 664
    `resize()` 664, 666
    `sin()` 667
    `sinh()` 667
    `size()` 664
    `sqrt()` 667
    subscripting 663
    `sum()` 664
    `tan()` 667
    `tanh()` 667
    `|` 667
    `|=` 664
    `||` 667
    `~` 664
valid
    iterator 550
    state 936
value
    call by 146
    `catch` by 359
    default 239
    key and 55, 480
    mapped type 55
    of character 580
    of `cin` 276
    of notation 261
    `return` by 148
    `return`, function 148
    return, function 283
    semantics 294
`value_comp()` 485
`value_compare` 485
`value_type` 443, 480, 552
    `basic_string` 583
variable
    constructor for global 252
    constructor for local 245
    global 200, 228
    number of argument 154

temporary 244, 254
variably-sized object 243
Vec, range checking 53, 405
vector
    Fortran 668
    arithmetic 65, 662
    bit 124
    exponentiation 667
    mathematical functions 667
    operations 664, 667
<vector> 431
Vector 435, 854
    example 341, 780
vector 52, 442, 469
    < 457
    = 447
    == 457
    [] of 445
    and array, valarray and 662
    and exception 955
    assign() 447
    at() on 445
    capacity() 455
    clear()
    constructor 447
    decrease capacity of 457
    erase() 452
    increase capacity of 456
    increase size of 455
    input into 451
    insert() 452, 958
    member type 442
    of bool 458
    of vector 836
    operator= 946
    push_back() 957
    pushback() 947
    reserve() 455
    resize() 455
    vector of 836
vector_base 943
vector<bool> 458
    bitset and 492
Vehicle example 734
vertical tab \v 830
viewgraph engineering 704
virtual
    function 15
    function, renaming 778
virtual 34
    << 612
    base class 396
    base class, override from 401
    base, constructor and 397
    constructor 323, 424
    derive without 780

destructor 319
    function 310, 390, 706
    function argument types 310
    function, definition of 310
    function, example of 646
    function, implementation of 36
    function, operator :: and 312
    function, pure 313
    output function 612
    return type of 424
    template function 348
vision 698
void 76
    expression, return of 148
    pointer to 100
void*
    assignment, difference from C 818
    specialization and 341
void*(), operator 616
volatile 808

W

waterfall model 697
wcerr 609
<wchar.h> 432, 887
wchar_t 72–73, 925
wcin 614
    wcout and 624
wclog 609
wcout 609
    and wcin 624
<wctype.h> 601
wfilebuf 649
wfstream 638
while statement 136
whitespace 614–615
    isspace() 114
wide
    character I/O 608
    character classification 601
wide-character literal L' 73
widen() 644
    ctype 923
width() 629
    of input 616
wifstream 638
wild pointer, checking for 722
Window example 398
wiostream 637
wistream 614
wistringstream 641
wofstream 638
word 76
working system 709
wostream 608

wostringstream 641
wrapper 781
write through iterator 551
write(), ostream 609
ws 634
wstreambuf 649
wstring 582
wstringbuf 649
wstringstream 641
<wtype.h> 432

X

%X
        format 652
        time format 909
%x
        date format 909
        format 652
X3J16 11
xalloc() 650
xgetn() 648
xor keyword 829
xor_eq keyword 829
xputn() 648

Y

Year 285

Z

zero null, 0 88